LAND USE

CASES AND MATERIALS

Seventh Edition

■ ■ ■

David L. Callies
Benjamin A. Kudo Professor of Law
William S. Richardson School of Law
University of Hawaii at Manoa

Robert H. Freilich
Professor of Law Emeritus
University of Missouri-Kansas City School of Law

Shelley Ross Saxer
Vice Dean and Laure Sudreau-Rippe
Endowed Professor of Law
Pepperdine University School of Law

AMERICAN CASEBOOK SERIES®

American Casebook Series is a trademark registered in the U.S. Patent and Trademark Office.

ISBN: 978-1-63459-687-9

Dedicated

To:

Laurie
DLC

Carole
RHF

Jennifer, Robyn, Randi, & Jonalyn
SRS

PREFACE TO THE SEVENTH EDITION

This book addresses the public and private decisions by which we determine the policies and law as to whether, when, and how to use land. Multiple parties play a role in this process, and their interests often conflict with the felt needs of society. Development that benefits private landowners and provides housing may impair neighborhood character and other public needs, including the preservation of open space, the prevention of sprawl, and revitalization of existing areas. Accommodating growth and protecting personal freedom without permitting illegitimate discrimination and preventing environmental degradation are weighty challenges.

A note on editing practices. We have deleted footnotes from cases without notation, but footnotes that have been retained carry their original numbers. We place ellipses where major or extensive omissions occur, but minor omissions have not been noted so as to make the reading flow easily.

Professor Callies wishes to thank his research assistants Lauren Corcoran, Jacob Garner, Christina Lizzi, Travis Moon, Derek Simon, Tina Tsuchiyama, and Ian Wesley-Smith of the William S. Richardson School of Law for their assistance, and his Faculty Support Specialist Dana Lum for assembling and monitoring all the moving parts.

Professor Freilich wishes to thank Neil Popowitz of Freilich & Popowitz for his major research assistance for the sections of the book relating to smart growth, new urbanism, green development and renewable energy. As always to my wife Carole, whose understanding and forbearance has enabled this casebook to be completed.

Professor Saxer thanks Dean Deanell Reece Taha of Pepperdine University School of Law for providing support for her work. She also wishes to thank her research assistant, Calvin Marshall, for his editing work and her husband, Gary, for his patience.

DAVID L. CALLIES
ROBERT H. FREILICH
SHELLEY ROSS SAXER

March 1, 2017

SUMMARY OF CONTENTS

TABLE OF CONTENTS

TABLE OF CASES

The principal cases are in bold type.

LAND USE
CASES AND MATERIALS

Seventh Edition

CHAPTER 1

SETTING THE STAGE

■ ■ ■

A. INTRODUCTION AND HISTORICAL OVERVIEW

Land use law deals with the way in which society enacts and implements governmental plans in order to regulate the use and reuse of land. Through planning, state and local legislative bodies determine goals, objectives, policies and strategies (GOPS) with respect to land use and development. Regulations, ordinances, and development approvals then implement that planning. In the 21st Century GOPS increasingly seek to improve the quality of life through: (1) containing urban sprawl through growth management, (2) providing sustainable and walkable transit oriented and traditional neighborhood mixed use development; to reduce traffic congestion, greenhouse gas emissions and global warming; (3) addressing the need to provide affordable housing for low and moderate income families, the disabled, aged and homeless; (4) protecting the environment, (5) preserving open space, agricultural and natural resources lands; and (6) redeveloping and infilling existing cities and first ring suburbs.

Land use planning and regulation constitutes the land development process affecting the property and constitutional rights of developers, owners, and neighbors. While regulations may increase land values by establishing orderly development and reducing the external impacts (fiscal and environmental) that accompany development, they may also diminish the value of regulated land or impose disproportionate fees on development.

20th Century suburban zoning encouraged the segregation of uses, leading to dependence on automobile use, creating excessive greenhouse gas emissions from geometrically increasing vehicle miles traveled, discouraging mass transit and, often in the name of aesthetics and fiscal considerations, excluding low income families and racial and ethnic minorities. Exclusionary practices still occur and when they do, resort to fair housing laws and constitutional protections is available. Where sign regulation discourages free speech, where single family zoning definitions impose unreasonable limitations on families and non-traditional living arrangements, where religious uses of land are interfered with or granted privileged status, and where land values are destroyed or physically taken, the First, Fifth, and Fourteenth Amendments to the constitution, through

1

section 1983 of the Civil Rights Act, and equivalent state constitutional remedies are available to provide relief.

Regulation (sticks) does not occupy the entire field. Where there is a need to attract development to distressed areas, to encourage affordable housing and introduce new concepts of renewable energy, reduction in global warming, protecting the environment and providing mixed use walkable density, tax and regulatory incentives (carrots) may play a larger role than regulation. While positive benefits flow from planning and regulation, negative environmental consequences often accompany poorly considered land use decisions. Permitted development may cause the loss of prime agricultural land or harm environmentally sensitive land. Endangered species habitat may be destroyed, infrastructure needs generated by new development may be postponed and global warming may be accelerated by uncontrolled development.

Regulation of land use today is extensive, but it is not new. While comprehensive land use controls did not develop in the United States until the 1920s, their roots go back to early English law. Shortly after the Norman Conquest in 1066, courts began to deal with land use disputes through the common law of nuisance. During this nation's first century, abundance of land coupled with a largely agrarian economy and a strong belief in private property rights all combined to confine most land use disputes to those involving common law nuisance. As we discuss below in part B of this chapter, the shortcomings of nuisance law to satisfactorily control land use in an urbanizing society led to the increased use of government regulatory power. Alfred Bettman* wrote in the Harvard Law Review in 1923:

> Though, as we have seen, zoning, and, in truth, all property regulation has the same fundamental basis as the law against nuisances, no greater fallacy could exist than that zoning is restricted to or is identical with nuisance regulation. On the contrary, the need for zoning arises from the utter inadequacy of the law of nuisances to cope with the problems of municipal growth.

The Constitutionality of Zoning, 37 HARV.L.REV. 834, 841 (1923).

Land use controls can be traced back in our Anglo-American heritage to Elizabethan England where, in order to arrest urban congestion and untrammeled growth, Parliament enacted the following:**

---

* Alfred Bettman, a Cincinnati lawyer, filed an influential amicus brief in the 1926 case of *Village of Euclid v. Ambler Realty Co.* where the U.S. Supreme Court upheld the constitutionality of zoning as an exercise of the police power. He also played a major role in the drafting of the model Standard Zoning Enabling Act (1926). *See* Seymour Toll, *Zoned American* 236–38 (1969). *Euclid* is set out in Chapter 2.

** The purpose clause of the statute reads as follows—and is frighteningly modern:

> After the end of this session of Parliament, no person shall within this realm of England make, build, or erect, or cause to be made, built or erected, any manner of cottage for habitation or dwelling, nor convert or ordain any building or housing made or hereafter to be made, to be used as a cottage for habitation or dwelling, unless the same person do assign and lay to the same cottage or building four acres of ground at the least * * * being his or her freehold [and] inheritance lying near to the said cottage, so long as the same cottage shall be inhabited.

31 Eliz. I C. 7 (Statutes at Large, Vol. 6 at 409 et seq.)

A hundred years or so later, royal proclamations were issued against overcrowding and the building of houses in and around London. According to 4 W.S. Holdsworth, *A History of English Law*, 304 (1924) such proclamations were issued in 1604, 1605, 1607, 1608, 1611, 1615, 1618, 1619, 1620, 1622, 1625, and 1630. One such proclamation in 1620 established both building height and window size. Holdsworth, *id.* at 132–3. After the great fire of 1666, Parliament's Act for the Rebuilding of London divided all housing into four classes with separate regulations for each, replete with bulk and yard requirements forbidding, among other things, jetties and seats from extending beyond the dwelling foundations. 19 Ch. II C. 3 paragraphs XIII–XV.

The colonies also controlled land use, going well beyond ordinances to abate common law nuisances. Some of these took the form of building laws. *See* Mass. Laws (1672) 269. Others appear to be forerunners of current aesthetic-based design regulations, such as the following from Pennsylvania:

The Queen's Majesty perceiving the state of the City of London (being anciently termed her chamber) and the suburbs and confines thereof to increase daily, by access of people to inhabit the same, in such ample sort, as thereby many inconveniences are seen already, but many greater of necessity like to follow, being such as her Majesty cannot neglect to remedy, having the principal care, under Almighty God to foresee aforehand, to have her people in such a city and confines not only well governed by ordinary justice, to serve God and obey her Majesty, (which by reason of such multitudes lately increased can hardly be done without device of more new jurisdictions and offices for that purpose) but to be also provided of substantiation of victual, food and other like necessaries for man's life, upon reasonable prices, without no city can long continue.—And finally, to the preservation of her people in health by God's goodness, the same is perceived to be in better estate universally than hath been in man's memory; yet where there are such great multitude of people brought to inhabit in small rooms, whereof a great part are seen very poor, yea, such as must live of begging, only worse means, and they heaped up together, and in a sort smothered with many families of children and servants in one house or small tenement; it must needs follow, if one plague or popular sickness should, by God's permission, enter amongst these multitudes, that the same would not only spread itself, and invade the whole city and confines, but that a great mortality would ensue the same, where her Majesties personal preserve is many times required: besides (by) the great confluence of people from all parts of the realm, by reason of the ordinary terms of justice there holden, the infection would be also dispensed through all other parts of the realm, to the manifest detriment of the whole body thereof. * * *

(from Steen Eiler Rasmussen, *London: The Unique City. London: Jonathan Cape*, 1937, at 67–8.)

Every owner or inhabitant of any and every house in Philadelphia,
Newcastle and Chester shall plant one or more tree or trees, viz.,
pines, nonbearing mulberries, water poplars, lime or other shady
and wholesome trees before the door of his, her or their house and
houses, not exceeding eight feet from the front of the house, and
preserving the same, to the end that the said town may be well
shaded from the violence of the sun in the heat of summer and
thereby be rendered more healthy.

2 Pa.Stat. § 66, Ch. 53.

See, John F. Hart, *Colonial Land Use Law and Its Significance for Modern
Takings Doctrine*, 109 HARV.L.REV. 1252 (1996); Eric Freyfogle, *Land Use
and the Study of Early American History*, 94 YALE L.J. 717 (1985); Fred
Bosselman, David L. Callies and John Banta, *The Taking Issue: An
Analysis of the Constitutional Limits of Land Use Control*, Chaps. 5 and 6
(1973).

Some trace the history of land use controls, especially through zoning,
to continental Europe, and in particular Germany in the 19th century.
Thomas H. Logan, *The Americanization of German Zoning*, 42
J.AM.INST.PLANNERS 377 (1966). Still, others stress the use of restrictive
covenants running with the land as an early private regulation of land use
in the United States. Edward Ziegler, 1 *Rathkopf's, The Law of Zoning and
Planning*, § 1.01(1) (2016).

It was through zoning that land use controls came into their own
in the United States. The first quarter of the twentieth century
was a critical period. Land use restrictions on building heights
were upheld by the United States Supreme Court in *Welch v.
Swasey*, 214 U.S. 91, 29 (1909). New York enacted the first
comprehensive zoning ordinance in 1916, though more
rudimentary forms appeared in both Boston and Los Angeles at
least ten years earlier. *See* Julian C. Juergensmeyer and Thomas
E. Roberts, *Land Use Planning and Development Regulation Law*
§ 3.4 (3d ed.2016); J. F. Garner and David L. Callies, *Planning
Law in England and Wales and in the United States*, 1 ANGLO-
AMERICAN L.REV. 292, 304–305 (1972). The New York City zoning
ordinance (New York Building Zone Resolution), divided New
York City into use, area and height districts. It was upheld by the
New York Court of Appeals in *Lincoln Trust Co. v. Williams Bldg.
Corp.*, 128 N.E. 209 (N.Y.1920). [As described more fully in
Chapter 2,] it was *Village of Euclid v. Ambler Realty Co.*, 272 U.S.
365 (1926), upholding the constitutionality of zoning under the
police power, coupled with the Standard Zoning Enabling Act of
1926, which gave land use controls their true impetus in the
United States.

1922 witnessed judicial creation of a new constitutional limitation on land use controls exercised via the police power: the theory that a land use regulation, if too onerous, constituted a taking of property without compensation contrary to the Fifth Amendment to the federal constitution. *Pennsylvania Coal Co. v. Mahon*, 260 U.S. 393 (1922) (Holmes J.)

B. COMMON LAW NUISANCE

Though increasingly overshadowed by zoning and planning controls, the common law doctrine of nuisance merits study for several reasons. As we shall see in Chapter 2, the United States Supreme Court used nuisance law as an analogy in upholding the constitutionality of zoning in the Euclid case. Nuisance law is sometimes referred to as "judicial zoning," available when legislative controls are absent. *See* Beuscher and Morrison, *Judicial Zoning Through Recent Nuisance Cases*, 1955 WIS.L.REV. 440. Despite zoning and planning becoming ever increasingly widespread in the 20th and 21st centuries, nuisance law is not inconsequential, especially in rural and congested urban areas, and to combat environmental pollution. Further, as we shall see in Chapter 3, the law of nuisance is important in defining the meaning of property for purposes of deciding when property is taken by the state under the Fifth Amendment. *See Lucas v. South Carolina Coastal Council*, 505 U.S. 1003 (1992), discussed in Chapter 3, and Carlos A. Ball, *The Curious Intersection of Nuisance and Takings Law*, 86 B.U.L.REV. 819 (2006). Finally, understanding nuisance law helps one appreciate the differences between legislative controls and judicial common law. The former were enacted in part because the latter was perceived as inadequate to deal with the lack of planning and governmental regulation necessary to resolve the array of land use problems that communities experienced as the population grew and the pressures to develop land increased. Nuisance law, however, affords a significant supplemental tool lacking in zoning and other legislative controls, **because nuisance law is retroactively applicable to existing buildings and land uses while zoning and building codes are prospective only**. We will explore vested and nonconforming uses in Chapter 2.

1. CATEGORIES OF COMMON LAW NUISANCE

Nuisances, whether public or private can be per se (in law) or per accidens (in fact). A nuisance per se, is conduct that creates a conclusive presumption of nuisance as a matter of law (the sale of illegal drugs) while a nuisance per accidens is otherwise lawful conduct that is wrongful because of the particular circumstances of the case. Halfway houses might be nuisances per accidens in residential areas, but they are not nuisances per se. *See Smith v. Gill*, 310 So.2d 214, 219 (Ala.1975). An activity that is licensed or permitted by statute cannot be a public nuisance. *See North Carolina, ex rel. Cooper v. Tennessee Valley Auth.*, 615 F.3d 291 (4th

Cir.2010) (emissions from electric power plant not a public nuisance where plant was acting in accord with federal permit).

A private nuisance involves an invasion of the interest in the enjoyment of private land while a public nuisance involves an interference with the rights of the public. Frequently, both are, and could be, involved in the same case. Air pollution that results from a landowner's industrial operation, if shown to injure a considerable number of people, would be a public nuisance, while simultaneously a private nuisance to an immediate neighbor. Crack and other drug house operations are usually dealt with as both public and private nuisances, *see Keshbro v. City of Miami*, 801 So.2d 864 (Fla.2001).

Both private and public nuisances are abatable by either an injunction in equity or a damages at law suit. Thus a plaintiff may in the same suit seek damages for past activity and an injunction to enjoin future activity, or the suit may be for both past and future damages if the nuisance is permanent. Under the common law, even if the harm to the defendant is far greater than the damage to the plaintiff, injunctive relief will always be granted once the court determines that the defendant's conduct amounts to either a private or public nuisance.

Neighbor to neighbor disputes are examples of actions that are, at best, private nuisances. See, for example, the saga of the neighbors who erected toilet seats, one nailed to a tree and the other displayed from a pole, each directed toward the other's property. *Wernke v. Halas*, 600 N.E.2d 117 (Ind.App.1992) (though tasteless and an aesthetic affront, a toilet seat was held not to be a nuisance). What about neighbors who have large outdoor open fires in their backyard for religious ceremonial purposes? Private or public nuisance? Both? *See Castillo v. Pacheco*, 58 Cal.Rptr.3d 305 (Cal.App.2007).

Some activities may be only public nuisances. While the court found the planting of trees and posting of signs that blocked the public's view of a competitor's business not to be a private nuisance, it found them to be a public nuisance since the trees and signs were a traffic hazard. *See 44 Plaza, Inc. v. Gray-Pac Land Co.*, 845 S.W.2d 576 (Mo.App.1992).

Courts can deny both injunctive and damage relief if it is shown that the plaintiffs were "coming to the nuisance" (similar to contributory negligence). *See Bove v. Donner-Hanna Coke Corp.*, 236 App.Div. 37 (N.Y.App.1932) *infra*. For most courts, a zoning classification supporting the use claimed to be a nuisance is a rebuttable presumption of suitability of use in the area. One important current application of common law public nuisance is to obtain a judicial injunction against violations of zoning or other municipal ordinances, which carry a rebuttable presumption of being public nuisances. The following case is illustrative of that usage.

2.   PUBLIC NUISANCE

CITY OF MONTEREY V. CARRNSHIMBA

California Court of Appeal, 2013.
215 Cal.App.4th 1068.

MARQUEZ, J.

In December 2009, Jhonrico Carrnshimba, operating a nonprofit corporation, My Caregiver Cooperative, Inc. (collectively, appellants), opened a collective to dispense medical marijuana (Dispensary; Dispensaries) in the City of Monterey (City or Monterey). Before incorporation of MyCaregiver, Carrnshimba applied for a business license. Shortly afterward, City personnel learned that appellants were dispensing medical marijuana. The City's Assistant City Manager advised Carrnshimba that he had failed to disclose his intention to operate a Dispensary in the City; the operation of a Dispensary was not a permitted use under the City Code; the use was therefore prohibited; his business license application was denied; and he was to immediately cease and desist operating the Dispensary business. Eight days later (January 19, 2010), the City passed an ordinance declaring a moratorium temporarily prohibiting the operation of any Dispensaries within the City.

On February 8, 2010, the City brought an action against appellants to abate a public nuisance. After obtaining a preliminary injunction prohibiting appellants from dispensing medical marijuana, the City successfully moved for summary judgment. The court thereafter entered a judgment that included a permanent injunction prohibiting appellants from operating a Dispensary as long as there was a citywide moratorium prohibiting such an operation.

Appellants assert that the City ordinance creating a moratorium prohibiting businesses from dispensing medical marijuana, adopted after appellants had commenced their operation, could not be applied retroactively against them. They also challenge the City's positions below that their business operation was a public nuisance.

We conclude that the controversy is moot because the permanent injunction entered against appellants expired, and appellants vacated the Monterey property where they operated the Dispensary. But because this case involves issues that are important and of continuing public interest, we will exercise our discretion to consider the merits of the appeal. We decide that the use of property in the City as a Dispensary was an impermissible use under the pre-moratorium City Code and appellants' operation of a Dispensary therefore constituted a public nuisance per se. We hold further that because appellants acquired no vested right to operate their illegal Dispensary, the trial court properly found that appellants' continued post-moratorium operation of its Dispensary was a public nuisance per se. Accordingly, we will affirm the judgment.

A city is constitutionally authorized to "make and enforce within its limits all local, police, sanitary, and other ordinances and regulations not in conflict with general laws." (Cal.Const., art. XI, § 7.) It may by legislative declaration state what activities or conditions may constitute a nuisance. (Gov.Code, § 38771; *see also Amusing Sandwich, Inc. v. City of Palm Springs* (1985) 165 Cal.App.3d 1116, 1129.) Thus, a city council may, by ordinance, declare what it deems to constitute a public nuisance. (*Flahive v. City of Dana Point* (1999) 72 Cal.App.4th 241, 244.)

An act or condition legislatively declared to be a public nuisance is " 'a nuisance per se against which an injunction may issue without allegation or proof of irreparable injury.' " (*Outdoor Media, supra,* 13 Cal.App.4th at p. 1076.) "[T]o rephrase the rule, to be considered a nuisance per se the object, substance, activity or circumstance at issue must be expressly declared to be a nuisance by its very existence by some applicable law." (*Beck Development Co. v. Southern Pacific Transportation Co.* (1996) 44 Cal.App.4th 1160, 1207.) Thus, the only issues for the court's resolution in a nuisance per se proceeding are whether the statutory violation occurred and whether the statute is constitutional. (*City of Bakersfield v. Miller* (1966) 64 Cal.2d 93, 100, 410 P.2d 393; *see also City of Costa Mesa v. Soffer* (1992) 11 Cal.App.4th 378, 382–383.)

Monterey asserted that appellants' use of the premises constituted a nuisance per se because the operation of a Dispensary was not a permitted use under the City Code as it existed before the Dispensary moratorium was adopted. Although the court below did not decide this question, we will address it here because we deem it both dispositive and to be an issue related to the ground upon which the court based its ruling (i.e., that appellants' operation was in violation of the Dispensary moratorium).

The trial court based its order granting summary judgment on the finding that appellants' operation of a Dispensary violated the City's moratorium, as embodied in Ordinance numbers 3441 and 3445, and that appellants' use of the premises therefore constituted a nuisance per se. Appellants challenge this conclusion, arguing that the court improperly applied the moratorium retroactively to their operation of a Dispensary. While we have concluded that summary judgment was proper on another ground—i.e., that appellants' Dispensary was not a permitted use under the pre-moratorium City Code—we nonetheless conclude that, because appellants' use of the premises was unlawful at the time the moratorium went into effect, the trial court's basis for granting summary judgment was likewise proper.

As a final contention, appellants assert that the City Code, as applied here by Monterey, was "unreasonable, arbitrary and therefore discriminatory." They argue in a most cursory fashion that "[g]iven the broad use classifications set forth in the City Code, and the stated purposes and activities of My Caregiver that easily fit the classifications, . . . the City is discriminating against a lawful organization for no valid reason."

Appellants fail to develop their "discriminatory as-applied" argument beyond the very general statement quoted above.

Our high court has noted that " '[i]t is well settled that a municipality may divide land into districts and prescribe regulations governing the uses permitted therein, and that zoning ordinances, when reasonable in object and not arbitrary in operation, constitute a justifiable exercise of police power.' [Citations.]" (*Hernandez v. City of Hanford* (2007) 41 Cal.4th 279, 296, 159 P.3d 33; *see also Wilkins v. San Bernardino* (1946) 29 Cal.2d 332, 337, 175 P.2d 542.) The City Code here set forth 50 commercial use classifications potentially available for property located in a C-2 District. The mere fact that a Dispensary was not included as one of those specified use classifications does not render the City Code discriminatory. Nor does the fact that the Deputy City Manager made the determination that a Dispensary was not within any of those specified use classifications mean that the City Code was discriminatory as applied to appellants. Thus, the central premise underlying appellants' challenge—that their Dispensary operation was a use of property "that easily fit the [specified commercial use] classifications"—is insupportable. We therefore reject appellants' claim that the City Code, as applied to their use of the premises, was "unreasonable, arbitrary and therefore discriminatory."

NOTES

1. *Federal and State Law Governing Marijuana Distribution Centers.*

Both federal and California laws prohibit the general use, possession, cultivation, transportation, and furnishing of marijuana. However, California statutes, the Compassionate Use Act of 1996 (CUA; Health & Safety Code, § 11362.5,1 added by initiative, Prop. 15, as approved by voters, Gen. Elec. (Nov. 5, 1996)) and the more recent Medical Marijuana Program (MMP; § 11362.7 et seq., have removed certain state law obstacles from the ability of qualified patients to obtain and use marijuana for legitimate medical purposes. Among other things, these statutes exempt the "collective or cooperative cultivation]" of medical marijuana by qualified patients and their designated caregivers from prosecution or abatement under specified state criminal and nuisance laws that would otherwise prohibit those activities. (§ 11362.775.)

2. *Federal and State Preemption of Local Ordinances.*

In City of Monterey above, the plaintiffs did not raise the issue of state and federal preemption of the City's marijuana moratorium or the proscription of marijuana use by the zoning ordinance. However, in a parallel case, *City of Riverside v. Inland Empire Patients Health and Wellness Center, Inc.*, 300 P.3d 494 (Cal.2013), the California Supreme Court expressly held that neither the federal or state statutes preempted the City's use of home rule power to adopt a local ban on facilities that distribute medical marijuana:

"The issue in this case is whether California's medical marijuana statutes preempt a local ban on facilities that distribute medical marijuana. We conclude they do not.

The California Constitution recognizes the authority of cities and counties to make and enforce, within their borders, "all local, police, sanitary, and other ordinances and regulations not in conflict with general laws." (Cal.Const., art. XI, § 7.) This inherent local police power includes broad authority to determine, for purposes of the public health, safety, and welfare, the appropriate uses of land within a local jurisdiction's borders, and preemption by state law is not lightly presumed.

In the exercise of its inherent land use power, the City of Riverside (City) has declared, by zoning ordinances, that a "[m]edical marijuana dispensary"—"[a] facility where marijuana is made available for medical purposes in accordance with" the CUA (Riverside Municipal Code (RMC), § 19.910.140)2—is a prohibited use of land within the city and may be abated as a public nuisance. (RMC, §§ 1.01.110E, 6.15.020Q, 19.150.020 & table 19.150.020 A.) The City's ordinance also bans, and declares a nuisance, any use that is prohibited by federal or state law. (RMC, §§ 1.01.110E, 6.15.020Q, 9.150.020.)

Invoking these provisions, the City brought a nuisance action against a facility operated by defendants. The trial court issued a preliminary injunction against the distribution of marijuana from the facility. The Court of Appeal affirmed the injunctive order. Challenging the injunction, defendants urge, as they did below, that the City's total ban on facilities that cultivate and distribute medical marijuana in compliance with the CUA and the MMP is invalid. Defendants insist the local ban is in conflict with, and thus preempted by, those state statutes.

As we will explain, we disagree. We have consistently maintained that the CUA and the MMP are but incremental steps toward freer access to medical marijuana, and the scope of these statutes is limited and circumscribed. They merely declare that the conduct they describe cannot lead to arrest or conviction, or be abated as a nuisance, as violations of enumerated provisions of the Health and Safety Code. Nothing in the CUA or the MMP expressly or impliedly limits the inherent authority of a local jurisdiction, by its own ordinances, to regulate the use of its land, including the authority to provide that facilities for the distribution of medical marijuana will not be permitted to operate within its borders. We must therefore reject defendants' preemption argument, and must affirm the judgment of the Court of Appeal."

Similarly, in *Merrick v. Diageo Americas Supply, Inc.*, 805 F.3d 685 (6th Cir.2015), the Court held that the Clean Air Act did not preempt local legislation:

> "The legislative history of the Clean Air Act also indicates that it was not Congress's purpose to preempt state common law nuisance claims like those of the plaintiffs. For instance, the Report of the Senate Committee on Public Works explained that the citizen suit provision of the Clean Air Act "would specifically preserve any rights or remedies under any other law. Thus, if damages could be shown, other remedies would remain available. Compliance with standards under this Act would not be a defense to a common law nuisance action for pollution damages. S.Rep. No. 91–1196, at 38 (1970)."

As drone usage becomes more pervasive, issues of federal preemption of state and local attempts to control potential nuisance impacts may be raised by regulations of the Federal Aviation Administration (FAA). If you were advising state and local officials about rising concerns regarding the use of drones, what are some of the potential legal issues you might consider in addition to federal preemption of local zoning? *See* Troy A. Rule, *Drone Zoning*, 94 N.C.L.REV. (2016); Wendie L. Kellington and Michael Berger, *Why Land Use Lawyers Care About the Law of Unmanned Systems*, Vol. 37 Zoning and Planning Law Report No. 6 (June 2014); *National League of Cities, What Cities Need to Know About Unmanned Aerial Vehicles (UAVs)* (2016).

3. FEDERAL COMMON LAW OF NUISANCE

Is there a federal common law of nuisance since *Erie R. Co. v. Tompkins*, 304 U.S. 64, 78 (1938) famously announced: "There is no federal general common law"? seemingly abolishing it in connection with actions in federal district courts sitting in diversity of jurisdiction cases? See the surprising decision of the U.S. Supreme Court relating to an injunction suit brought under the federal common law of nuisance to abate power plant greenhouse gas emissions in the absence of EPA action.

AMERICAN ELECTRIC POWER COMPANY, INC. V. CONNECTICUT

Supreme Court of the United States, 2011.
131 S.Ct. 2527, 180 L.Ed.2d 435.

JUSTICE GINSBURG delivered the Opinion of the Court.

In December of 2009, the EPA concluded that greenhouse gas emissions from motor vehicles "cause, or contribute to, air pollution which may reasonably be anticipated to endanger the public. Responding to our decision in *Massachusetts v. EPA*, 549 U.S 497 (2007) (that EPA failed to undertake regulations of greenhouse gas emissions as directed to by the Clean Air Act), EPA undertook greenhouse gas regulation. The agency observed that "atmospheric greenhouse gas concentrations are now at elevated and essentially unprecedented levels," almost entirely "due to anthropogenic emissions; mean global temperatures, the agency continued, demonstrate an "unambiguous warming trend over the last 100 years," and particularly "over the past 30 years," Acknowledging that not all scientists agreed on the causes and consequences of the rise in global temperature, EPA concluded that "compelling" evidence supported the "attribution of observed climate change to anthropogenic" emissions of greenhouse gases."

Consequent dangers of greenhouse gas emissions, EPA determined, included increases in heat-related deaths; coastal inundation and erosion caused by melting icecaps and rising sea levels; more frequent and intense hurricanes, floods, and other "extreme weather events" that cause death and destroy infrastructure; drought due to reductions in mountain snowpack and shifting precipitation patterns; destruction of ecosystems supporting animals and plants; and potentially "significant disruptions" of food production.

EPA began phasing in requirements that new or modified "[m]ajor [greenhouse gas] emitting facilities" use the "best available control technology," 75 Fed.Reg. 31520–31521. Finally, EPA commenced a rulemaking process under § 111 of the Act, 42 U.S.C. § 7411, to set limits on greenhouse gas emissions from new, modified, and existing fossil-fuel fired power plants. Pursuant to a settlement finalized in March 2011, EPA has committed to issuing a proposed rule by July 2011 and a final rule by May 2012. See Reply Brief for Tennessee Valley Authority at 18.

The lawsuits we consider here began well before EPA initiated the efforts to regulate greenhouse gases just described. In July 2004, two groups of plaintiffs filed separate complaints in the Southern District of New York against the same five major electric power companies. The first group of plaintiffs included eight States and New York City, the second joined three nonprofit land trusts; both groups are respondents here. The defendants are four private companies and the Tennessee Valley Authority, a federally owned corporation that operates fossil-fuel fired power plants in several States. According to the complaints, the defendants "are the five largest emitters of carbon dioxide in the United States." Their collective annual emissions of 650 million tons constitute 25 percent of emissions from the domestic electric power sector, 10 percent of emissions from all domestic human activities and 2.5 percent of all anthropogenic emissions worldwide.

By contributing to global warming, the plaintiffs asserted, the defendants' carbon-dioxide emissions created a "substantial and unreasonable interference with public rights," in violation of the federal common law of interstate nuisance, or, in the alternative, of state tort law. The States and New York City alleged that public lands, infrastructure, and health were at risk from climate change. The trusts urged that climate change would destroy habitats for animals and rare species of trees and plants on land the trusts owned and conserved. All plaintiffs sought injunctive relief requiring each defendant "to cap its carbon dioxide emissions and then reduce them by a specified percentage each year for at least a decade."

The federal District Court dismissed both suits as presenting non-justiciable political questions, citing *Baker v. Carr*, 369 U.S. 186 (1962), but the Second Circuit reversed, 582 F.3d 309 (2009). On the threshold questions, the Court of Appeals held that the suits were not barred by the political question doctrine and that the plaintiffs had adequately alleged Article III standing.

Turning to the merits, the Second Circuit held that all plaintiffs had stated a claim under the "federal common law of nuisance." For this determination, the court relied dominantly on a series of this Court's decisions holding that States may maintain suits to abate air and water pollution produced by other States or by out-of-state industry. *See, e.g., Illinois v. Milwaukee*, 406 U.S. 91, 93 (1972) (Milwaukee I) (recognizing the right of Illinois to sue in federal district court to abate the discharge of sewage into Lake Michigan).

The Court of Appeals further determined that the Clean Air Act did not "displace" federal common law. In *Milwaukee v. Illinois*, 451 U.S. 304, 316–319, 1981) (Milwaukee II), this Court held that Congress had displaced the federal common law right of action recognized in Milwaukee I by adopting amendments to the Clean Water Act, 33 U.S.C. § 1251 et seq. That legislation installed an all-encompassing regulatory program, supervised by an expert administrative agency, to deal comprehensively with interstate water pollution. The legislation itself prohibited the discharge of pollutants into the waters of the United States without a permit from a proper permitting authority. Milwaukee II, 451 U.S., at 310–311 (citing 33 U.S.C. § 1311).

At the time of the Second Circuit's decision, by contrast, EPA had not yet promulgated any rule regulating greenhouse gases, a fact the court thought dispositive. 582 F.3d, at 379–381. "Until EPA completes the rulemaking process," the court reasoned, "we cannot speculate as to whether the hypothetical regulation of greenhouse gases under the Clean Air Act would in fact 'speak directly' to the 'particular issue' raised here by Plaintiffs." *Id.*, at 380.

"In the wake of Erie, however, a keener understanding developed. Erie le[ft] to the states what ought be left to them, and thus required "federal courts [to] follow state decisions on matters of substantive law appropriately cognizable by the states. Erie also sparked the emergence of a federal decisional law in areas of national concern." The "new" federal common law addresses "subjects within national legislative power where Congress has so directed" or where the basic scheme of the Constitution so demands. Environmental protection is undoubtedly an area "within national legislative power," one in which federal courts may fill in "statutory interstices," and, if necessary, even "fashion federal law." As the Court stated in Milwaukee I: "When we deal with air and water in their ambient or interstate aspects, there is a federal common law." 406 U.S., at 103.

Decisions of this Court predating Erie, but compatible with the distinction emerging from that decision between "general common law" and "specialized federal common law," have approved federal common law suits brought by one State to abate pollution emanating from another State. *See, e.g., Missouri v. Illinois*, 180 U.S. 208, 241–243 (1901) (permitting suit by Missouri to enjoin Chicago from discharging untreated sewage into interstate waters); *New Jersey v. City of New York*, 283 U.S. 473, 477, 481–483 (1931) (ordering New York City to stop dumping garbage off New Jersey coast); *Georgia v. Tennessee Copper Co.*, 240 U.S. 650 (1916) (ordering private copper companies to curtail sulfur-dioxide discharges in Tennessee that caused harm in Georgia). *See also Milwaukee I*, 406 U.S., at 107 (post-Erie decision upholding federal common law suit by Illinois to abate sewage discharges into Lake Michigan). The plaintiffs contend that their right to maintain this suit follows inexorably from that line of decisions.

The plaintiffs also sought relief under state law, in particular, the law of each State where the defendants operate power plants. The Second Circuit did not reach the state law claims because it held that federal common law governed. 582 F.3d, at 392; *see International Paper Co. v. Ouellette*, 479 U.S. 481, 488 (1987) (if a case "should be resolved by reference to federal common law [,] . . . state common law [is] preempted"). In light of our holding that the Clean Air Act displaces federal common law, the availability vel non of a state lawsuit depends, inter alia, on the preemptive effect of the federal Act. *Id., Paper Co.* at 489, 491, 497, (holding that the Clean Water Act does not preclude aggrieved individuals from bringing a "nuisance claim pursuant to the law of the source State"). None of the parties have briefed preemption or otherwise addressed the availability of a claim under state nuisance law. We therefore leave the matter open for consideration on remand.

For the reasons stated, we reverse the judgment of the Second Circuit and remand the case for further proceedings consistent with this opinion. It is so ordered.

NOTES

1. Once you learn from the American Electric Power case that a federal common law of nuisance still lives after *Erie*, you must determine how you can use substantive common law nuisance in either federal or state court.

2. The Court suggests that the plaintiffs pursued the wrong remedy: "EPA may not decline to regulate carbon-dioxide emissions from power plants if refusal to act would be 'arbitrary, capricious, an abuse of discretion, or

otherwise not in accordance with law'. If the plaintiffs in this case are dissatisfied with the outcome of EPA's forthcoming rulemaking, their recourse under federal law is to seek Court of Appeals review, and, ultimately, to petition for certiorari in this Court [citing to *Massachusetts v. EPA*, 549 U.S. 497 (2007)]."

Since this litigation started in 2004, well before the EPA had ever started rule making for stationary utility greenhouse gas emissions under the Clean Air Act, why didn't the plaintiffs pursue the alternative *Massachusetts v. EPA* remedy in this case. Surely the lapse of 7 years from 2004 to 2011 was more than sufficient for the EPA to adopt a final rule in this area. The reason, of course, was that the Court did not announce the rule that an aggrieved party could compel the EPA to adopt a rule where Congress had mandated that greenhouse gas emissions be regulated, until *Massachusetts v. EPA* was decided in 2007. Should the plaintiffs have amended their complaint to plead the alternative remedy at that point? Apparently so, because the Court holds that "the critical point is that Congress delegated to EPA the decision whether and how to regulate carbon-dioxide emissions from power plants; the delegation is what displaces federal common law. Indeed, were EPA to decline to regulate carbon-dioxide emissions altogether at the conclusion of its ongoing § 7411 rulemaking, the federal courts would have no warrant to employ the federal common law of nuisance to upset the agency's expert determination."

3. The Supreme Court implies that a suit alleging federal common law of nuisance can be used only if Congress has completely abdicated legislation in the particular field, i.e. global warming. That dictum appears to be contradictory to other dicta in the case, since the Supreme Court stated that federal courts can only exercise federal common law when "the new federal common law addresses "subjects within national legislative power where Congress has so directed" or where the basic scheme of the Constitution so demands. Yet, the Court states that "environmental protection is undoubtedly an area within national legislative power," one in which federal courts may fill in "statutory interstices," and, if necessary, even "fashion federal law." As the Court stated in *Milwaukee I*: "When we deal with air and water in their ambient or interstate aspects, there is a federal common law." *Illinois v. City of Milwaukee*, 406 U.S. 91, 103 (1972). Since EPA had not acted on adopting greenhouse gas emission standards for stationary utility power plants, why wasn't the plaintiffs' nuisance suit "filling in the statutory interstices"?

4. Subsequent to Massachussetts v. EPA, several other federal court decisions have refused to contemplate federal common law nuisance relief with respect to water pollution and greenhouse gas emissions:

- *Haynes v. Blue Ridge Paper Products, Inc.*, 2010 WL 3075738 (W.D.N.C. Aug. 5, 2010) (Property owners' federal common law private nuisance claim against paper manufacturer, arising out of manufacturer's pollution of river with waste and chemicals, was preempted by the Federal Water Pollution Control Act (FWPCA). Regardless of language in "citizen suit" provision of the FWPCA, the Supreme Court had previously held that the FWPCA entirely preempted the federal common law of nuisance for water pollution, including claims by private citizens).

- *Native Village of Kivalina v. Exxon Mobil Corp.*, 663 F.Supp.2d 863 (N.D.Cal.2009), *aff'd*, 696 F.3d 849 (9th Cir.2012) (Claim brought by Alaskan village for federal common law nuisance against oil, energy, and utility companies based on emission of greenhouse gases that contributed to erosion of Arctic sea ice due to global warming presented "lack of judicially discoverable and manageable standards that would guide court in rendering decision that was" principled, rational, and based on reasoned distinctions, *see Vieth v. Jubelirer*, 541 U.S. 267, 278 (2004), and thus, was subject to dismissal under political question doctrine; court would have to weigh energy-producing alternatives that were available in past, safety considerations, and impact of different alternatives on consumers and business at every level, then weigh benefits derived from those choices against risk that increasing greenhouse gases would in turn increase risk of flooding along coast, and global warming resulted from common pollutants from innumerable sources, mixed together in atmosphere, that could not be geographically circumscribed).

- *People of the State of California v. General Motors*, 2007 WL 2726871 (N.D.Cal.2007) (dismissing an action brought by the State of California seeking damages against various automakers for creating, and contributing to, an alleged public nuisance of facilitating global warming, for "lack of judicially discoverable and manageable standards that would guide the court in rendering a decision that was principled, rational, and based on reasoned distinctions," and thus, was subject to dismissal under political question doctrine).

4. STATE COMMON LAW AND STATUTORY GLOBAL WARMING NUISANCE

The other remedy that the U.S. Supreme Court in *American Electric* requested the 2nd Circuit to reconsider on remand is the availability of state common law global warming nuisance claims. Note the Supreme Court's language:

> The plaintiffs also sought relief under state law, in particular, the law of each State where the defendants operate power plants. The Second Circuit did not reach the state law claims because it held that federal common law governed. 582 F.3d, at 392; *see International Paper Co. v. Ouellette*, 479 U.S. 481, 488 (1987) (if a case "should be resolved by reference to federal common law [,] . . . state common law [is] preempted"). In light of our holding that the Clean Air Act displaces federal common law, the availability of a state lawsuit depends, inter alia, on the preemptive effect of the

federal Act. 479 U.S. at 489, 491, 497 (holding that the Clean Water Act does not preclude aggrieved individuals from bringing a "nuisance claim pursuant to the law of the source State"). None of the parties have briefed preemption or otherwise addressed the availability of a claim under state nuisance law. We therefore leave the matter open for consideration on remand.

BRUCE MERRICK V. DIAGEO AMERICAN SUPPLY, INC.

U.S. Court of Appeals for the Sixth Circuit, 2015.
805 F.3d 685.

This interlocutory appeal concerns whether the federal Clean Air Act preempts common law claims brought against an emitter based on the law of the state in which the emitter operates. The Clean Air Act's text makes clear that the Act does not preempt such claims. This conclusion is further supported by the Act's structure and history, together with relevant Supreme Court precedents.

The plaintiffs in this case—owners, lessors, and renters of nearby properties affected by whiskey fungus—complained to the air pollution control district about the proliferation of whiskey fungus on their properties. In response, the district undertook an investigation that resulted in the issuance of a Notice of Violation letter to Diageo on September 7, 2012. In the letter, the district stated that, between June 2011 and May 2012, it received 27 complaints from residents living near the facilities of a "black, sooty substance covering everything exposed to the outdoors." The district found that Diageo had violated District Regulation 1.09 because:

> "Diageo caused and allowed the emission of an air pollutant which crossed its property line causing an injury and nuisance to nearby neighborhoods and the public. Diageo's warehouse emissions present a current and continuing threat to [the] public, endangering the comfort and repose of its neighbors. Diageo's warehouse emissions cause damage to nearby property and have the natural tendency to continue causing damage".

In addition to complaining to the air pollution control district, plaintiffs filed a class action complaint in federal district court, seeking compensatory and punitive damages from Diageo for negligence, nuisance, and trespass, and an injunction requiring Diageo to abate its ethanol emissions by implementing certain control technologies at the facilities. Diageo moved to dismiss the complaint on two grounds. First, Diageo argued that it had no duty to curb ethanol emissions from its Louisville facilities. In support of this contention, Diageo relied on EPA decisions, agency actions from other jurisdictions, and its own permits. Second, in a notice of supplemental authority, Diageo argued that plaintiffs' claims were preempted by the Clean Air Act.

The states' rights savings clause of the Clean Air Act expressly preserves the state common law standards on which plaintiffs sue. The clause saves from preemption "the right of any State or political subdivision thereof to adopt or enforce (1) any standard or limitation respecting emissions of air pollutants or (2) any requirement respecting control or abatement of air pollution," except that the "State or political subdivision may not adopt or enforce any emission standard or limitation" that is "less stringent" than a standard or limitation under an applicable implementation plan or specified federal statute. 42 U.S.C. § 7416. State courts are arms of the "State," and the common law standards they adopt are "requirement[s] respecting control or abatement of air pollution." *Id.* Thus, the states' rights savings clause makes clear that states retain the right to "adopt or enforce" common law standards that apply to emissions. A federal statute does not preempt state law if Congress did not intend the statute to do so, and "the best evidence of" Congress's intent "is the statutory text adopted by both Houses of Congress and submitted to the President." *W. Va. Univ. Hosps., Inc. v. Casey*, 499 U.S. 83, 98 (1991).

The phrase "any requirement," as used in the states' rights savings clause, clearly encompasses common law standards. As a four-Justice plurality of the Supreme Court has reasoned with respect to preempting language in a different statute, "[t]he phrase '[n]o requirement or prohibition' sweeps broadly and suggests no distinction between positive enactments and common law; to the contrary, those words easily encompass obligations that take the form of common law rules." *Cipollone v. Liggett Grp., Inc.*, 505 U.S. 504, 521, 112 S.Ct. 2608, 120 L.Ed.2d 407 (1992) (plurality opinion State common law standards therefore qualify as "requirements" for purposes of the Clean Air Act states' rights savings clause.

It is also plain that state courts are parts of the "State" for purposes of the states' rights savings clause. The states' rights savings clause implies that "State" refers to something that can "adopt or enforce . . . requirement[s]." State courts "adopt" state law "requirements" by making and modifying the common law, and state courts are the branch of state government most often tasked with "enforcing" state law "requirements." Indeed, the Supreme Court has interpreted the word "State" in the Clean Water Act states' rights savings clause, 33 U.S.C. § 1370(1)—which is materially indistinguishable from the Clean Air Act states' rights savings clause, *see Bell*, 734 F.3d at 195—to cover state courts and the common law rules they shape. *See Int'l Paper Co. v. Ouellette*, 479 U.S. 481, 497–98, 107 S.Ct. 805, 93 L.Ed.2d 883 (1987). The Court's interpretation of the word "State" in the Clean Water Act states' rights savings clause strongly indicates that the same word in the Clean Air Act states' rights saving clause, 42 U.S.C. § 7416, includes state courts. State common law standards are thus "requirements" adopted by "States," such that the

Clean Air Act states' rights savings clause preserves them against preemption.

We acknowledge the concern that a comprehensive federal scheme imposes substantial costs on industries, and that some suggest it is unduly burdensome for such industries to remain subject, in addition, to the requirements and remedies of state common law. Such a concern must however be directed to Congress. There is no basis in the Clean Air Act on which to hold that the source state common law claims of plaintiffs are preempted.

The order of the district court is affirmed.

NOTES

1. *See, Piedmont Envtl. Council v. Federal Energy Regulatory Commission (FERC)*, 558 F.3d 304 (4th Cir.2009) (approving the power of states to regulate the siting of electrical transmission lines):

"Section 216(b)(1)(C)(i) of the Federal Power Act grants FERC the authority to issue permits for the construction or modification of electric transmission facilities in national interest corridors when a state commission has "withheld approval for more than 1 year after the filing of an application." 16 U.S.C. § 824p (b)(1)(C)(i). The petitioners challenge FERC's broad interpretation of this jurisdiction-granting provision.

FERC interprets § 216(b)(1)(C)(i)'s phrase "withheld approval for more than 1 year after the filing of a permit application" to include a state's outright denial of an application within one year. We conclude that FERC's interpretation is contrary to the plain meaning of the statute. Simply put, the statute does not give FERC permitting authority when a state has affirmatively denied a permit application within the one-year deadline".

2. *See also, Comer v. Murphy Oil USA*, 585 F.3d 855 (5th Cir.2009), refusing to grant defendant's Federal Rule 12(b)(6) motion to dismiss a state nuisance complaint brought under the diversity of citizenship jurisdiction of the federal courts.

5. PRIVATE NUISANCE

(a) Injunctive Relief or Damages

Note the following early greenhouse gas emission private nuisance case in which the court failed to follow its own common law rule that injunctive relief is mandatory in nuisance cases, by denying injunctive relief and ordering that damages be paid in lieu.

Boomer v. Atlantic Cement Company, Inc.

Court of Appeals of New York, 1970.
26 N.Y.2d 219, 309 N.Y.S.2d 312, 257 N.E.2d 870.

Defendant operates a large cement plant near Albany. These are actions for injunction and damages by neighboring land owners alleging injury to property from dirt, smoke and vibration emanating from the plant. A nuisance has been found after trial, temporary damages have been allowed; but an injunction has been denied.

Defendant operates a large cement plant near Albany. These are actions for injunction and damages by neighboring land owners alleging injury to property from dirt, smoke and vibration emanating from the plant. A nuisance has been found after trial, temporary damages have been allowed; but an injunction has been denied.

The public concern with air pollution arising from many sources in industry and in transportation is currently accorded ever wider recognition accompanied by a growing sense of responsibility in State and Federal Governments to control it. Cement plants are obvious sources of air pollution in the neighborhoods where they operate.

Effective control of air pollution is a problem presently far from solution even with the full public and financial powers of government. In large measure adequate technical procedures are yet to be developed and some that appear possible may be economically impracticable.

It seems apparent that the amelioration of air pollution will depend on technical research in great depth; on a carefully balanced consideration of the economic impact of close regulation; and of the actual effect on public health. It is likely to require massive public expenditure and to demand more than any local community can accomplish and to depend on regional and interstate controls.

A court should not try to do this on its own as a by-product of private litigation and it seems manifest that the judicial establishment is neither equipped in the limited nature of any judgment it can pronounce nor prepared to lay down and implement an effective policy for the elimination of air pollution. This is an area beyond the circumference of one private lawsuit. It is a direct responsibility for government and should not thus be undertaken as an incident to solving a dispute between property owners and a single cement plant—one of many—in the Hudson River valley.

The ground for the denial of injunction, notwithstanding the finding both that there is a nuisance and that plaintiffs have been damaged substantially, is the large disparity in economic consequences of the nuisance and of the injunction. This theory cannot, however, be sustained without overruling a doctrine which has been consistently reaffirmed in several leading cases in this court and which has never been disavowed here, namely that where a nuisance has been found and where there has been any substantial damage shown by the party complaining an injunction will be granted.

The rule in New York has been that such a nuisance will be enjoined although marked disparity be shown in economic consequence between the effect of the injunction and the effect of the nuisance. *Whalen v. Union Bag & Paper Co.*, 101 N.E. 805 (N.Y.1913).

The problem of disparity in economic consequence was sharply in focus in Whalen. A pulp mill entailing an investment of more than a million dollars polluted a stream in which plaintiff, who owned a farm, was 'a lower riparian owner'. The economic loss to plaintiff from this pollution was small. This court, reversing the Appellate Division, reinstated the injunction granted by the Special Term against the argument of the mill owner that in view of 'the slight advantage to plaintiff and the great loss that will be inflicted on defendant' an injunction should not be granted (p. 2, 101 N.E. p. 805). 'Such a balancing of injuries cannot be justified by the circumstances of this case', Judge Werner noted (p. 4, 101 N.E. p. 805). He continued: 'Although the damage to the plaintiff may be slight as compared with the defendant's expense of abating the condition, that is not a good reason for refusing an injunction' (p. 5, 101 N.E. p. 806).

The present cases and the remedy here proposed are in a number of other respects rather similar to *Northern Indiana Public Service Co. v. W. J. & M. S. Vesey*, 210 Ind. 338, 200 N.E. 620 decided by the Supreme Court of Indiana. The gases, odors, ammonia and smoke from the Northern Indiana company's gas plant damaged the nearby Vesey greenhouse operation. An injunction and damages were sought, but an injunction was denied and the relief granted was limited to permanent damages 'present, past, and future' (p. 371, 200 N.E. 620).

Denial of injunction was grounded on a public interest in the operation of the gas plant and on the court's conclusion 'that less injury would be occasioned by requiring the appellant (Public Service) to pay the appellee (Vesey) all damages suffered by it * * * than by enjoining the operation of the gas plant; and that the maintenance and operation of the gas plant should not be enjoined' (p. 349, 200 N.E. p. 625).

The orders should be reversed, without costs, and the cases remitted to Supreme Court, Albany County to grant an injunction which shall be vacated upon payment by defendant of such amounts of permanent damage to the respective plaintiffs as shall for this purpose be determined by the court.

NOTES

1. In Boomer, the court found that a cement plant was a nuisance but refused to follow its long standing mandatory injunction rule and awarded

permanent damages to the neighbors in lieu of injunctive relief. In the eyes of the court, the plant was a major employer and taxpayer and, using the balancing approach, supplanted the rights of the plant's neighbors to be free from a nuisance. Is the award of damages in lieu of an injunction the equivalent of a compensable judicial taking of property without a proper public purpose (i.e. allowing a private party to acquire an easement to pollute by paying for it)? Are saving jobs and protecting the tax base valid public purposes? See the dissent in Boomer which characterized the granting of damages for an illegal purpose (public nuisance) an inverse condemnation, and *infra* Chapter 6 with respect to the question as to whether economic development, standing alone, constitutes a valid public purpose to support condemnation.

2.   What would a court do with the conflict between agricultural uses and invading suburban residential? In 1949, a farmer started a hog farm in a rural community. His business prospered and the number of hogs increased. The farm was operated in compliance with state law (there was no negligence), but it smelled horribly nonetheless. Over the years development had spread toward the farm, and in 1960, a small subdivision was built nearby. The farmer's new neighbors, bothered by the strong odors, wanted the hog farm shut down. In *Pendoley v. Ferreira*, 187 N.E.2d 142 (Mass.1963), on which the facts are based, the court held the farmer was conducting a nuisance and ordered him to liquidate his business. Shouldn't the court have denied the nuisance since the residential development was "coming to the nuisance." Would Boomer compensatory damages be applicable if the loss to the farmer was greater than the depreciation of the suburban lots?

3.   In response to sprawling development and the consequent loss of valuable farmland, in the 1970s and early 1980s, many state legislatures passed "right-to-farm" statutes that immunized farm operations from being declared nuisances. In authorizing a property owner to conduct a nuisance, a right-to-farm statute deprives neighbors of the right to be free from nuisance. Is that an unconstitutional deprivation of a property right? For contrary views, compare *Bormann v. Board of Supervisors in and for Kossuth County*, 584 N.W.2d 309 (Iowa 1998), *cert. denied* 525 U.S. 1172 (1999) (finding a taking of the residential property); and *Moon v. North Idaho Farmers Ass'n*, 96 P.3d 637 (Idaho 2004), *cert. denied* 543 U.S. 1146 (2005) (finding no constitutional violation). *See* Terence J. Centner, *Governments and Unconstitutional Takings: When Do Right-To-Farm Laws Go Too Far?*, 33 B.C.ENVTL.AFF.L.REV. 87 (2006).

Concentrated animal feeding operations (CAFOs) densely pack thousands of hogs, cattle or chickens into small areas, producing odors and air and groundwater pollution on a scale vastly larger than the impact of the small family farm in the Pendoley case discussed above. A later Iowa case found that these CAFO "factory farms" should not be treated as agricultural uses under right-to-farm laws, but as non-agricultural commercial industrial uses where the exemption did not apply and the adjacent property owners had the right to bring a nuisance suit. *Harms v. City of Sibley*, 695 N.W.2d 43 (Iowa App.2004). CAFOs are discussed in Chapter 9C. *See also* J.B. Ruhl, *Farms, Their*

Environmental Harms, and Environmental Law, 27 ECOLOGY L.Q. 263 (2000); Terence J. Centner, *Nuisances from Animal Feeding Operations: Reconciling Agricultural Production and Neighboring Property Rights*, 11 DRAKE J.AGRIC.L. 5 (2006). What about a sugar refinery? Is it an agricultural use? If the right-to-farm statute bars a nuisance claim, what other common law theory might landowners use?

(b) Aesthetic, Emotional and Psychological Injuries

RANKIN v. FPL ENERGY, LLC
Court of Appeals of Texas, 2008.
266 S.W.3d 506.

Several individuals and one corporation (Plaintiffs) filed suit against FPL Energy, LLC; FPL Energy Horse Hollow Wind, LP; FPL Energy Horse Hollow Wind, LP, LLC; FPL Energy Horse Hollow Wind GP, LLC; FPL Energy Callahan Wind Group, LLC; and FPL Energy Callahan, LP (FPL). Plaintiffs sought injunctive relief and asserted public and private nuisance claims relating to the construction and operation of the Horse Hollow Wind Farm in southwest Taylor County. FPL filed a motion for partial summary judgment directed at Plaintiffs' nuisance claims, and the trial court granted it in part dismissing Plaintiffs' claims to the extent they were based on the wind farm's visual impact. Plaintiffs' remaining private nuisance claim proceeded to trial. The jury found against Plaintiffs, and the trial court entered a take-nothing judgment.

FPL asked the trial court to dismiss Plaintiffs' public and private nuisance claims contending that Plaintiffs could not assert a nuisance claim based upon the wind farm's aesthetical impact and that Plaintiffs' deposition testimony precluded their remaining nuisance claims. The trial court granted the motion in part and dismissed "Plaintiffs' claims of public and private nuisance asserted in whole or in part on the basis of any alleged aesthetic impact of [FPL's] activities." The trial court later included an instruction in the jury charge that excluded their consideration of the wind farm's aesthetic impact.

Texas law defines "nuisance" as "a condition that substantially interferes with the use and enjoyment of land by causing unreasonable discomfort or annoyance to persons of ordinary sensibilities." *See Schneider Nat'l Carriers, Inc. v. Bates*, 147 S.W.3d 264, 269 (Tex.2004). Nuisance claims are frequently described as a "non-trespassory invasion of another's interest in the use and enjoyment of land." *See GTE Mobilnet of S. Tex. Ltd. Partnership v. Pascouet*, 61 S.W.3d 599, 615 (Tex.App.2001). But despite this exclusionary description, in some instances an action can be both a trespass and a nuisance. *See Allen v. Virginia Hill Water Supply Corp.*, 609 S.W.2d 633, 636 (Tex.App.1980) (continuing encroachment upon the land of an adjoining owner by either erecting or maintaining a building without any right to do so is a trespass and a private nuisance).

In practice, successful nuisance actions typically involve an invasion of a plaintiff's property by light, sound, odor, or foreign substance. For example, in Pascouet, floodlights that illuminated the plaintiffs' backyard all night and noisy air conditioners that interfered with normal conversation in the backyard, that could be heard indoors, and that interrupted plaintiffs' sleep constituted a nuisance. In Bates, the court noted that foul odors, dust, noise, and bright lights could create a nuisance. A cotton gin's operations were a nuisance because of its loud noises and bright lights that could be seen and heard on plaintiff's property and because of the dust, lint, and cotton burrs that would be carried there.

Texas courts have not found a nuisance merely because of aesthetical-based complaints. Plaintiffs advance several arguments why this case law does not preclude their private nuisance action. First, they argue that aesthetics may be considered as one of the *conditions* that creates a nuisance. Plaintiffs concede that, if their only complaint is subjectively not liking the wind turbines' appearance, no nuisance action exists. But, they contend that the jury was entitled to consider the wind farm's visual impact in connection with other testimony such as: the turbines' blinking lights, the shadow flicker affect they create early in the morning and late at night, and their operational noises to determine if it was a nuisance. Second, they note that nuisance law is dynamic and fact-specific; therefore, they contend that older case holdings should not be blindly followed without considering intervening societal changes. Third, nuisance claims should be viewed through the prism of a person of ordinary sensibilities and case law involving unreasonable plaintiffs asserting subjective complaints should be considered accordingly.

FPL responds that the trial court ruled correctly because no Texas court has ever recognized a nuisance claim based upon aesthetical complaints and notes that, in fact, numerous courts have specifically rejected the premises behind such a claim. FPL argues that sound public policy supports such a rule because notions of beauty or unsightliness are necessarily subjective in nature and that giving someone an aesthetic veto over a neighbor's use of his land would be a recipe for legal chaos. Finally, FPL argues that the wind farm does not prevent any of the plaintiffs from using their property but at most involves an emotional reaction to the sight of the wind turbines and contends that an emotional reaction alone is insufficient to sustain a nuisance claim.

When FPL moved for summary judgment, Plaintiffs presented affidavits from the plaintiffs to establish that the wind farm was a nuisance. They express a consistent theme: the presence of numerous 400-foot-tall wind turbines has permanently and significantly diminished the area's scenic beauty and, with it, the enjoyment of their property. Some Plaintiffs, such as Linda L. Brasher, took issue with the characterization of her complaint as just aesthetics. She acknowledged not liking the turbines' looks but contended that they had a larger impact than mere appearance. Brasher stated that she and her husband had purchased their land to build a home and to have a place "for strength, for rest, for hope, for joy, for security—for release." They had plans for building and operating a small bed and breakfast but cancelled those plans in response to the wind farm. Brasher characterized the presence of the wind farm as "the death of hope."

Plaintiffs' summary judgment evidence makes clear that, if the wind farm is a nuisance, it is because Plaintiffs' emotional response to the loss of their view due to the presence of numerous wind turbines substantially interferes with the use and enjoyment of their property. The question, then, is whether Plaintiffs' emotional response is sufficient to establish a cause of action. One Texas court has held that an emotional response to a defendant's lawful activity is insufficient. *Maranatha Temple, Inc. v. Enterprise Products Co.*, 893 S.W.2d 92, 96, 99, 100 (Tex.App.1994), involved a suit brought by a church against the owners and operators of companies involved in an underground hydrocarbon storage facility. The church's claims included a nuisance action. The trial court granted summary judgment against the church. The question before the Houston First Court was whether a nuisance action could exist when the only claimed injury was an emotional reaction to the defendants' operations. The court found that a nuisance could occur in one of three ways: (1) by the encroachment of a physically damaging substance; (2) by the encroachment of a sensory damaging substance; and (3) by the emotional harm to a person from the deprivation of the enjoyment of his or her property, such as by fear, apprehension, offense, or loss of peace of mind. The court noted that nuisance claims are subdivided into nuisance per se and nuisance in fact. Because the operation of the storage facility—just like FPL's wind farm— was lawful, it could not constitute a nuisance per se. This last factor was critical. The court recognized that no case or other authority specifically gives a nuisance-in-fact cause of action based on fear, apprehension, or other emotional reaction resulting from the lawful operation of industry and affirmed the summary judgment.

Plaintiffs do not contend that FPL's operations are unlawful but minimize this factor by arguing that even a lawful business can be considered a nuisance if it is abnormal and out of place in its surroundings. Plaintiffs are correct that several Texas courts have recited this general principle; but, in each of the cases cited by Plaintiffs, the nuisance resulted from an invasion of the plaintiff's property by flooding, flies, or odors. We cannot, therefore, agree with Plaintiffs that merely characterizing the wind farm as abnormal and out of place in its surroundings allows a nuisance claim based on an emotional reaction to the sight of FPL's wind turbines.

We do not minimize the impact of FPL's wind farm by characterizing it as an emotional reaction. Unobstructed sunsets, panoramic landscapes, and starlit skies have inspired countless artists and authors and have brought great pleasure to those fortunate enough to live in scenic rural settings. The loss of this view has undoubtedly impacted Plaintiffs. A landowner's view, however, is largely defined by what his neighbors are utilizing their property for. Texas case law recognizes few restrictions on the lawful use of property. If Plaintiffs have the right to bring a nuisance action because a neighbor's lawful activity substantially interferes with their view, they have, in effect, the right to zone the surrounding property. Conversely, we realize that Plaintiffs produced evidence that the wind farm will harm neighboring property values and that it has restricted the uses they can make of their property. FPL's development, therefore, could be characterized as a condemnation without the obligation to pay damages.

Texas case law has balanced these conflicting interests by limiting a nuisance action when the challenged activity is lawful to instances in which the activity results in some invasion of the plaintiff's property and by not allowing recovery for emotional reaction alone. Altering this balance by recognizing a new cause of action for aesthetical impact causing an emotional injury is beyond the purview of an intermediate appellate court. Alternatively, allowing Plaintiffs to include aesthetics as a condition in connection with other forms of interference is a distinction without a difference. Aesthetical impact either is or is not a substantial interference with the use and enjoyment of land. If a jury can consider aesthetics as a condition, then it can find nuisance because of aesthetics. Because Texas law does not provide a nuisance action for aesthetical impact, the trial court did not err by granting FPL's motion for partial summary judgment and by instructing the jury to exclude from its consideration the aesthetical impact of the wind farm. Issue One is overruled.

We reverse the judgment of the trial court in part and remand the cause for determination of the allocation of taxable costs. We affirm the judgment of the trial court in all other respects.

NOTES

1.   Reluctant to make what they perceive would be subjective judgments, courts generally find aesthetic, emotional and psychological objections to a neighboring land uses not actionable. When four 300-foot high office towers were approved by Arlington County on the Virginia side of the Potomac River across from Washington, D.C., the federal government sued on nuisance grounds. It claimed that the towers would visually interfere with the green backdrop that L'Enfant, the French architect who planned the city, intended the monuments to have. The court, following the common law rule, refused to recognize aesthetic injury as a nuisance. *See United States v. County Bd. of Arlington County*, 487 F.Supp. 137 (E.D.Va.1979); *City of Newport News v. Hertzler*, 221 S.E.2d 146 (Va.1976) (portable toilets facing plaintiff's house from a city park, "while undoubtedly offending the aesthetic sensibilities," did not constitute a nuisance).

Plaintiffs may be able to avoid dismissal by alleging a physical harm. In *Burch v. Nedpower Mount Storm, LLC*, 647 S.E.2d 879 (W.Va.2007), the court found complaints of the unsightliness of a neighboring wind farm would not support a nuisance claim. However, the additional complaints of noise led the court to find that the plaintiffs stated a private nuisance claim. In addition to noise and vibrations, some contend that the unattractive strobe light effects from wind farms may also cause headaches and create anxiety. *See* Stephen Harland Butler, *Headwinds to a Clean Energy Future: Nuisance Suits Against Wind Energy Projects in the United States*, 97 CAL.L.REV. 1337 (2009). See Chapter 8 for a detailed examination of the expanding role of federal and state common law nuisance to deal with solar and wind power and reduce global warming greenhouse gas emissions.

2. Judicial unease with judging "beauty" may be misplaced or, at least, overstated. Some courts allow an aesthetic-based claim where a diminution in value can be shown. *See Foley v. Harris*, 286 S.E.2d 186 (Va.1982), where neighbors complained about wrecked cars kept on defendant's lot. While the complaint was based on the unsightliness of the defendant's lot, the evidence showed that a prospective purchaser of one of the plaintiff's houses lost interest when he saw the cars. An objective measure of loss demonstrates that the plaintiff's complaints are those of a "normal person in the community." *Id.*; compare *Cavallo v. Star Enter.*, 100 F.3d 1150 (4th Cir.1996) (nuisance claims dismissed where plaintiff was highly susceptible to petroleum vapors); with *Adkins v. Thomas Solvent Co.*, 487 N.W.2d 715 (Mich.1992) (an unfounded fear of loss of value insufficient).

3. Objections to funeral parlors in residential neighborhoods might be taken to be aesthetically-based, but many courts, finding them to inflict a psychological injury, have found them to be nuisances. *See e.g., Powell v. Taylor*, 263 S.W.2d 906 (Ark.1954). How about nude sunbathing? *See Mark v. State Dept. of Fish & Wildlife*, 84 P.3d 155 (Or.App.2004) and John Copeland Nagle, *Moral Nuisances*, 50 EMORY L.J. 265 (2001).

Some urge courts to be more receptive to aesthetic and psychological injuries. *See* John Copeland Nagle, *Cell Phone Towers as Visual Pollution*, 23 NOTRE DAME J.L.ETHICS & PUB.POL'Y 537 (2009); Robert D. Dodson, *Rethinking Private Nuisance Law: Recognizing Aesthetic Nuisances in the New Millennium*, 10 S.C.ENVTL.L.J. 1 (2002). Numerous courts are more receptive. *See Rattigan v. Wile*, 841 N.E.2d 680 (Mass.2006); *Tarlton v. Kaufman*, 199 P.3d 263 (Mont.2008); *Hay v. Stevens*, 530 P.2d 37 (Or.1975); *See also Loughhend v. 1717 Bissonnet LLC*, No. 2013–26 slip opinion (Tex.D.Ct.2014); Michael Lewyn, *Yes to Infill, No to Nuisance*, 42 FORDHAM UNIV.L.J. 841 (2015).

6. SUNLIGHT AND SOLAR ENERGY NUISANCE LITIGATION

PRAH V. MARETTI
Supreme Court of Wisconsin, 1982.
321 N.W.2d 182.

This appeal from a judgment of the circuit court for Waukesha county, Max Raskin, circuit judge, was certified to this court by the court of appeals, as presenting an issue of first impression, namely, whether an owner of a solar-heated residence states a claim upon which relief can be granted when he asserts that his neighbor's proposed construction of a residence (which conforms to existing deed restrictions and local ordinances) interferes with his access to an unobstructed path for sunlight across the neighbor's property. This case thus involves a conflict between one landowner (Glenn Prah, the plaintiff) interested in unobstructed access to sunlight across adjoining property as a natural source of energy and an adjoining landowner (Richard D. Maretti, the defendant) interested in the development of his land.

The circuit court concluded that the plaintiff presented no claim upon which relief could be granted and granted summary judgment for the defendant. We reverse the judgment of the circuit court and remand the cause to the circuit court for further proceedings.

According to the complaint, the plaintiff is the owner of a residence which was constructed during the years 1978–1979. The complaint alleges that the residence has a solar system which includes collectors on the roof to supply energy for heat and hot water and that after the plaintiff built his solar-heated house, the defendant purchased the lot adjacent to and immediately to the south of the plaintiff's lot and commenced planning construction of a home. The complaint further states that when the plaintiff learned of defendant's plans to build the house he advised the defendant that if the house were built at the proposed location, defendant's house would substantially and adversely affect the integrity of plaintiff's solar system and could cause plaintiff other damage. Nevertheless, the defendant began construction. The complaint further alleges that the plaintiff is entitled to "unrestricted use of the sun and its solar power" and demands judgment for injunctive relief and damages.

Although the defendant's obstruction of the plaintiff's access to sunlight appears to fall within the Restatement's broad concept of a private nuisance as a non-trespassory invasion of another's interest in the private use and enjoyment of land, the defendant asserts that he has a right to develop his property in compliance with statutes, ordinances and private covenants without regard to the effect of such development upon the plaintiff's access to sunlight. In essence, the defendant is asking this court to hold that the private nuisance doctrine is not applicable in the instant case and that his right to develop his land is a right which is per se superior to his neighbor's interest in access to sunlight.

The defendant is not completely correct in asserting that the common law did not protect a landowner's access to sunlight across adjoining property. At English common law a landowner could acquire a right to receive sunlight across adjoining land by both express agreement and under the judge-made doctrine of "ancient lights." Under the doctrine of ancient lights if the landowner had received sunlight across adjoining property for a specified period of time, the landowner was entitled to continue to receive unobstructed access to sunlight across the adjoining property. Under the doctrine the landowner acquired a negative prescriptive easement and could prevent the adjoining landowner from obstructing access to light.

Although American courts have not been as receptive to protecting a landowner's access to sunlight as the English courts, American courts have afforded some protection to a landowner's interest in access to sunlight. American courts honor express easements to sunlight. American courts initially enforced the English common law doctrine of ancient lights, but later every state which considered the doctrine repudiated it as inconsistent with the needs of a developing country. Indeed, for just that reason this court concluded that an easement to light and air over adjacent property could not be created or acquired by prescription and has been unwilling to recognize such an easement by implication.

Many jurisdictions in this country have protected a landowner from malicious obstruction of access to light (the spite fence cases) under the common law private nuisance doctrine. If an activity is motivated by malice it lacks utility and the harm it causes others outweighs any social values. VI-A Law of Property sec. 28.28, p. 79 (1954). This court was reluctant to protect a landowner's interest in sunlight even against a spite fence, only to be overruled by the legislature. Shortly after this court upheld a landowner's right to erect a useless and unsightly sixteen-foot spite fence four feet from his neighbor's windows,), the legislature enacted a law specifically defining a spite fence as an actionable private nuisance. Thus a landowner's interest in sunlight has been protected in this country by common law private nuisance law at least in the narrow context of the modern American rule invalidating spite fences. *See, e.g., Sundowner, Inc. v. King*, 95 Idaho 367, 509 P.2d 785 (1973); Restatement (Second) of Torts, sec. 829 (1977).

This court's reluctance in the nineteenth and early part of the twentieth century to provide broader protection for a landowner's access to sunlight was premised on three policy considerations. First, the right of landowners to use their property as they wished, as long as they did not cause physical damage to a neighbor, was jealously guarded.

First, society has increasingly regulated the use of land by the landowner for the general welfare. *Euclid v. Ambler Realty Co.*, 272 U.S. 365, 47 S.Ct. 114, 71 L.Ed. 303 (1926); *Just v. Marinette*, 56 Wis.2d 7, 201 N.W.2d 761 (1972). Second, sunlight was valued only for aesthetic enjoyment or as illumination. Since artificial light could be used for illumination, loss of sunlight was at most a personal annoyance which was given little, if any, weight by society. Third, society had a significant interest in not restricting or impeding land development.). This court repeatedly emphasized that in the growth period of the nineteenth and early twentieth centuries change is to be expected and is essential to property and that recognition of a right to sunlight would hinder property development. The court expressed this concept as follows:

> "As the city grows, large grounds appurtenant to residences must be cut up to supply more residences. . . . The cistern, the outhouse, the cesspool, and the private drain must disappear in deference to the public waterworks and sewer; the terrace and the garden, to the need for more complete occupancy. . . . Strict limitation [on the recognition of easements of light and air over adjacent premises is] in accord with the popular conception upon which real estate has been and is daily being conveyed in Wisconsin and to be essential to easy and rapid development at least of our municipalities."

Considering these three policies, this court concluded that in the absence of an express agreement granting access to sunlight, a landowner's obstruction of another's access to sunlight was not actionable. These three policies are no longer fully accepted or applicable. They reflect factual circumstances and social priorities that are now obsolete.

Courts should not implement obsolete policies that have lost their vigor over the course of the years. The law of private nuisance is better suited to resolve landowners' disputes about property development in the 1980's than is a rigid rule which does not recognize a landowner's interest in access to sunlight. As we said in *Ballstadt v. Pagel*, 202 Wis. 484, 489, 232 N.W. 862 (1930), "What is regarded in law as constituting a nuisance in modern times would no doubt have been tolerated without question in former times." We read *State v. Deetz*, 66 Wis.2d 1, 224 N.W.2d 407 (1974), as an endorsement of the application of common law nuisance to situations involving the conflicting interests of landowners and as rejecting per se exclusions to the nuisance law reasonable use doctrine.

Private nuisance law, the law traditionally used to adjudicate conflicts between private landowners, has the flexibility to protect both a landowner's right of access to sunlight and another landowner's right to develop land. Private nuisance law is better suited to regulate access to sunlight in modern society and is more in harmony with legislative policy and the prior decisions of this court than is an inflexible doctrine of non-recognition of any interest in access to sunlight across adjoining land.

We therefore hold that private nuisance law, that is, the reasonable use doctrine as set forth in the Restatement, is applicable to the instant case.

NOTES

1.   How can you explain the different results reached in the Texas and Wisconsin courts? Would Texas agree that the blocking of sunlight for renewable energy is not an "aesthetic" issue but one dealing with physical impacts?

2.   Many states enacted inadequate solar easement statutes, which define solar easements but only provide a voluntary contractual structure for their creation and protection and preempt the use of private nuisance litigation to protect solar energy systems. Usually, the statute itself does not create private rights. Rather, it provides a framework for future implementation, either by private bargaining for conveyances or by state or local legislation. One example is the Illinois Comprehensive Solar Energy Act of 1977, Ill Compiled Stat Ch. 30, §§ 725/1 to 725/8.2. *See O'Neill v. Brown*, 609 N.E.2d 835 (Ill.App.1993) (Solar Energy Act, which defines "solar sky-space easement," but illogically does not create such easement to protect solar access to greenhouse from neighbor's addition of second story to house).

3.   These early laws have been substantially amended to provide public and private nuisance remedies protecting landowners' solar roof systems from neighboring properties erecting buildings and landscaping that block the sunlight from reaching the solar system. *See* James C. Smith & Jacqueline P. Hand, *Common Law Property Rights*, § 5:5 Rights to Prevent Development of Adjacent Airspace (West 2015):

> "A number of states, have passed statutes that facilitate the development of solar energy systems by limiting the ability of local governments to use their zoning powers to exclude them. *E.g.*, Cal. Gov. Code § 65850.5(c) ("A city or county may not deny an application for a use permit to install a solar energy system unless it makes written findings based upon substantial evidence in the record that the proposed installation would have a specific, adverse impact upon the public health or safety, and there is no feasible method to satisfactorily mitigate or avoid the specific, adverse impact"); Fla.Stat. § 163.04(2) ("A deed restriction, covenant, declaration, or similar binding agreement may not prohibit or have the effect of prohibiting solar collectors, clotheslines, or other energy devices based on renewable resources from being installed on buildings erected on the lots or parcels covered by the deed restriction, covenant, declaration, or binding agreement"); Wis.Stat. § 66.0401(1) ("No county, city, town, or village may place any restriction, either directly or in effect, on the installation or use of a solar energy system

. . . or a wind energy system . . . unless the restriction satisfies one of the following conditions: (a) Serves to preserve or protect the public health or safety, (b) Does not significantly increase the cost of the system or significantly decrease its efficiency [or] (c) Allows for an alternative system of comparable cost and efficiency"). *See State ex rel. Numrich v. City of Mequon Bd. of Zoning Appeals*, 626 N.W.2d 366 (Wis.App.2001) (applicant for conditional use permit from local government does not have to satisfy criteria for issuance of permit under § 66.0403 that restricts neighbors from interfering with operation of system). Similarly, some states have statutes that override covenants and other private restrictions. *E.g.*, Ariz.Rev.Stat. § 33–439(A); Col.Rev.Stat. § 38–30–168(1)(a); Fla.Stat. § 163.04(2) ("A deed restriction, covenant, declaration, or similar binding agreement may not prohibit or have the effect of prohibiting solar collectors, clotheslines, or other energy devices based on renewable resources from being installed on buildings erected on the lots or parcels covered by the deed restriction, covenant, declaration, or binding agreement"); Nev.Rev.Stat. § 111.239 ("Any covenant, restriction or condition contained in a deed, contract or other legal instrument which affects the transfer or sale of, or any other interest in, real property and which prohibits or unreasonably restricts or has the effect of prohibiting or unreasonably restricting the owner of the property from using a system for obtaining solar energy on his property is void and unenforceable")".

4.   California has gone further and adopted a Solar Rights Act that prevents adjoining property owners from erecting structures or growing trees that block adjoining solar systems. *See* Cal. Civil Code § 801.5 (2015). Solar easement and solar energy system:

(a) The right of receiving sunlight as specified in subdivision 18 of Section 801 shall be referred to as a solar easement. "Solar easement" means the right of receiving sunlight across real property of another for any solar energy system.

(b) As used in this section, "solar energy system" means either of the following:

(1) Any solar collector or other solar energy device whose primary purpose is to provide for the collection, storage, and distribution of solar energy for space heating, cooling, electricity or water heating.

(2) Any structural design feature of a building, whose primary purpose is to provide for the collection, storage, and distribution of solar energy for electricity, space heating or cooling, or for water heating.

(c) Any instrument creating a solar easement shall include, at a minimum, all of the following:

(1)   A description of the dimensions of the easement expressed in measurable terms, such as vertical or horizontal angles measured in degrees, or the hours of the day on specified dates during which direct sunlight to a specified surface of a solar collector, device, or structural design feature may not be obstructed, or a combination of these descriptions.

(2)   The restrictions placed upon vegetation, structures, and other objects that would impair or obstruct the passage of sunlight through the easement.

(3)   The terms or conditions, if any, under which the easement may be revised or terminated.

7.   SHORTCOMINGS OF NUISANCE LAW

Nuisance law has proved inadequate to deal with the problems brought by a growing population and increased land development. For landowners wishing to develop their land, the law leaves them in a state of uncertainty. Nuisance law determinations with their second guessing, after-the-fact, determinations about the appropriateness of a use are not easily predictable. For neighbors, the reach of nuisance law traditionally has been limited to fairly nasty activities. There are exceptions of course, such as the treatment of funeral parlors noted above, but, aesthetic concerns are generally not protected.

Nuisance law does not reach cumulative harms created by multiple defendants where the harm cannot be equitably apportioned. In *Bove v. Donner-Hanna Coke Co.*, 236 App.Div. 37 (N.Y.App.1932) the plaintiff's case failed in part due to her inability to prove that the defendant was the cause of her harm. Nuisance law does not concern itself with the fact that the air may have been badly polluted in the vicinity of plaintiff's land as a result of numerous polluters.

As recognized in this Chapter's historical overview, legislative regulation of land use developed alongside, rather than grew out of, the common law of nuisance. As Chief Justice Rehnquist has noted, "zoning regulations existed as far back as colonial Boston, . . . thus, . . . zoning and permit regimes are a longstanding feature of state property law and part of a landowner's reasonable investment-backed expectations." *Tahoe-Sierra Preservation Council, Inc. v. Tahoe Regional Planning Agency*, 535 U.S. 302 (2002) (dissenting opinion).

In part due to shortcomings of the judicially created common law of nuisance, the late nineteenth and early twentieth centuries witnessed a surge in legislative activity to regulate specific problems such as overcrowding, fire prevention, and safety.

Nevertheless, in defining takings liability, *Lucas v. South Carolina Coastal Council*, 505 U.S. 1003 (1992), set out in Chapter 3, the Court determined that nuisance law a critical factor in deciding whether a state statute regulating land use to prevent serious coastal shore erosion must compensate a property owner who is deprived of all economically viable use and value of her land. The Supreme Court held that a landowner has no constitutionally protected property right when its activities constitute a public nuisance under principles of previously established state common or statutory law. For further resurrection of public nuisance in global warming lawsuits, see Chapter 8, *infra*.

As we gain new insight into the effects of human conduct on the environment, the capacity of nuisance law to change to meet current societal problems becomes critically important. A century ago filling wetlands, typically denominated swamps, was considered a beneficial action. Today we know that filling wetlands results in increased flooding, depletes groundwater, and destroys fish spawning grounds. See the historic trend setting case of *Just v. Marinette County*, 201 N.W.2d 761 (Wis.1972). *See* John A. Humbach, *Evolving Thresholds of Nuisance and the Takings Clause*, 18 COL.J.ENVTL.L. 1 (1993) and 1 Edward H. Ziegler, Jr., Rathkopf, *The Law of Zoning and Planning* § 7.01 et seq. (2015).

C. PRIVATE LAND USE CONTROLS: COVENANTS, CONDITIONS AND RESTRICTIONS (CC&Rs)

Prior to the twentieth century and the advent of zoning, privately created restrictions, along with nuisance law, were used to control land use. Today, while overshadowed by zoning, private covenants, known to the trade as CC&Rs, continue to be used primarily to control use in gated subdivisions, planned communities and condominiums.

The development of the doctrines of negative easements, real covenants and equitable servitudes over centuries is well-known to law students studying these incorporeal heritaditaments in first year Property courses. At early common law, covenants running with the land relating to land use faced unfriendly law courts, which constructed significant hurdles, particularly complicated rules of horizontal and vertical privity of estate, touch and concern to the land, and restrictive intent requirements to the enforceability of covenants against subsequent owners of the restricted land. Without the ability to hold subsequent owners to covenants entered into by their grantors, effective covenant protected communities were not feasible. The Court of Chancery in *Tulk v. Moxhay*, 41 Eng.Rep. 1143 (Ch. 1848), removed this major drawback by holding that covenants were enforceable in equity without privity of estate. With this holding, land developers, who gradually began using covenants in the latter half of the nineteenth century to create large scale residential communities, could do so with a reasonable expectation that their common plan scheme would be effective.

Professor Korngold describes the growing use of covenants in residential land development in the early twentieth century:

> A new breed of subdividers, sometimes known as 'community builders,' began developing large tracts of land into complete residential communities. These communities were typically developed in stages, with the subdivider dividing the land into lots and installing utilities, streets, and other communal facilities section by section. These lots were then marketed to individual buyers for the construction of homes. The first phase of community building, which reached maturity in the 1920s, created residential subdivisions for expensive homes to be occupied by the wealthy. By the time of the Great Depression, luxury subdivisions had been built across the country. These large-scale developers sought to produce high-quality developments with beautifully designed environments and fine homes harmonious with each other and their surroundings. The community builders believed that maintaining high standards would not only achieve their vision of beauty but would also bring far more profits than the practice of speculative lot selling. * * * Early twentieth-century developers imposed restrictive covenants on the lots containing racial and religious exclusions, building and use restrictions, architectural and design controls, housing standards, lot size rules, landscaping guidelines, and other minimum lot and building size standards designed to accomplish their goals.

Gerald Korngold, *The Emergence of Private Land Use Controls in Large-Scale Subdivisions: The Companion Story to* Village of Euclid v. Ambler Realty Co., 51 CASE W.RES.L.REV. 617, 623 (2001).[1]

The reception of covenants in the courts remained cool. Intoning the canon that the law favors the free use of land, courts, consistent with the attitude of the mid-millennium English judges, interpreted such provisions narrowly. In some states, the attitude persists. *See Schurenberg v. Butler County Bd. of Elections*, 605 N.E.2d 1330, 1332 (Ohio App.1992) ("This court is well aware of the law's general aversion toward efforts to restrict land use."). However, today, even in states where the courts construe covenants strictly, carefully drafted documents can assure buyers that the restrictions will be enforceable even if they are not recorded in the deeds of lots emanating from the subdivision. There is an inherent incompatibility between the policy favoring free use of land and the policy favoring freedom of contract. People who buy within privately regulated communities expressly agree to such limits or buy with record notice of preexisting restrictions. There is strong public interest in protecting the expectations of the neighbors who seek to enforce the restrictions, and little equity in

---

[1]   © Gerald Korngold. Used with permission.

favor of those who bought with or without notice of the restrictions. *See Green v. Lawrence*, 877 A.2d 1079 (Me.2005).

These CC&Rs are often recorded only with the subdivision plat map and are not recorded or even mentioned in deeds emanating from the subdivider so that the restrictions do not appear in the purchaser's chain of title. Nevertheless, they become binding as equitable servitudes, dispensing with the elements required for covenants running with the land. *Citizens for Covenant Compliance v. Anderson*, 906 P.2d 1314 (Cal.1996) ("A declaration, establishing a common plan for ownership in a subdivision, containing restrictions upon use and recorded solely with the subdivision map before execution of contract of sale, which describes property, and states that it is binding on all purchasers and successors, binds subsequent purchasers who, have constructive notice of the declaration, and are deemed agreed to be bound by the common plan, and the restrictions are not unenforceable merely because they are not additionally cited in the deed or other document at the time of sale, and (2) this rule will be applied retroactively.")

Reciprocity of benefits and burdens accompany homebuyers' acceptance of restrictive covenants: one who purchases a home in a covenant-protected community is not free to do as she wishes, but neither are her neighbors. On the benefit side, residential covenants are intended to provide homeowners with pleasant and aesthetically attractive communities. They provide stability to home prices. Numbers attest to the popularity of covenant-protected communities. In 1960, there were 50,000 homeowner associations. Today, there are over 300,000. It is estimated that in 1970 2.1 million people lived in such communities. By 2010, the number had grown to 62 million, approximately 20% of the country's population. Community Associations Institute, http://www.caionline.org/ info/research/Pages/default.aspx.

Along with the benefits that covenant-protected communities provide, there are many downside burdens. In theory, people who buy homes in such communities do so voluntarily. Yet, the reality is that buyers' choices are limited due to the ubiquitous presence of covenants limiting free use of their land in urban condominiums and suburban residential neighborhoods, so that buyers' freedom of choice is restricted.

In these restricted communities, covenants impose landscaping requirements, regulate not just house size but also house color, limit the type of roof and fencing, and whether the flying of flags or posting of signs is permitted. The more extreme may regulate, the permissibility and, if permitted, the design of one's doghouse and birdhouse, the permissibility of screen doors, and bans on open garage doors. They may also prevent use of solar collectors on roofs. Once property owners move into the subdivision, they often chafe at the excessive bundle of restrictions and unbridled discretion exercised by small cliques against individual home owners, which have taken over the association governance and may act with personal motives unduly hindering personal freedom. Paula A. Franzese, *Privatization and Its Discontents: Common Interest Communities and the Rise of Government for "The Nice,"* 37 URBAN LAWYER 335, 336–37 (2005).

Over the past several decades, concern has been raised about the intrusive nature of some covenants and the fact that they are enforced by property owners' associations whose powers resemble those of local governments. *See* Gregory Alexander, *Freedom, Coercion, and the Law of Servitudes*, 73 CORNELL L.REV. 883 (1988); Clayton P. Gillette, *Courts, Covenants, and Communities*, 61 U.CHIC.L.REV. 1375 (1994); Paula A. Franzese, *Does It Take a Village? Privatization, Patterns of Restrictiveness and the Demise of Community*, 47 VILL.L.REV. 553 (2002).

Troubling is the exclusionary nature of covenant-protected communities. Racial restrictions, common in the first half of the twentieth century, led to the segregated communities that persist today. After the Supreme Court declared race-based zoning unconstitutional in *Buchanan v. Warley*, 245 U.S. 60 (1917), the use of racial covenants increased in the North and West as African-Americans migrated from the South. Korngold, *supra* at 640. From its creation in 1934 until 1947, the Federal Housing Administration aided in the establishment of segregated communities by strongly encouraging the use of racial restrictions in FHA guaranteed homeownership insurance programs. *See* Robert F. Drinan, S.J., *Untying the White Noose*, 94 YALE L.J. 435, 437 (1993). By the time the Supreme Court held judicial enforcement of race-based covenants unconstitutional in *Shelley v. Kraemer,* 334 U.S. 1 (1948), white enclaves dominated suburban America.

The rise of gated communities raised exclusivity to new heights. Residents of such communities, often protected by guards, gain a sense of security and insulation from the "outside world." While the freedom of choice we enjoy enables those who can afford to live in such communities to do so, some raise concerns over the harm done to the social fabric by the substantial degree of separateness created by these isolated enclaves. Complaints are also made about the private use of public resources. *See Citizens Against Gated Enclaves v. Whitley Heights Civic Ass'n*, 28 Cal.Rptr.2d 451 (Cal.App.1994) (homeowners' association could not erect gates restricting use of public streets); *see generally* David L. Callies, Paula A. Franzese, Heidi Kai Guth, *Ramapo Looking Forward: Gated Communities, Covenants, and Concerns*, 35 URBAN LAWYER 177 (2003); David L. Callies, *Common Interest Communities: An Introduction*, 37 URBAN LAWYER 325 (2005) (stressing the problems arising from community association "private governments" with articulate minorities controlling the quality of life and freedoms of the majority lot owners).

"Many homeowners' associations exercise powers and provide services traditionally associated with municipal or local governments and have taken on other characteristics of governmental entities. Residents often become confused as to what entity governs their property when the line between government and homeowners' association becomes blurred. Case law has recognized that homeowners' associations operate as quasi-governmental entities.

A significant reason homeowners' associations have become "mini-governments" is the pressure on local governments to privatize services and lessen the burden on taxpayers. Local governments do this by "transferring" the power to provide these services to private organizations, such as homeowners' associations. Homeowners' associations take over many municipal functions "for those who can pay the price" such as for "pay-as-you-go utilities," which have been called "the most significant privatization of local government responsibilities in recent times." This has been called a "fundamental shift" in power to private governments.

The issue concerning private governments is "at what point does the [private] community become public enough so that it should be held accountable for its actions as would any governmental entity?" "By any standard, these associations clearly strain the distinction between public and private," and have been considered "privately owned and operated shadow governments that can control immense residential areas."

Monique C.M. Leahy, *Homeowner Association as Quasi-Governmental Entity*, 76 AM.JUR.3D PROOF OF FACTS 89 (2011).

In some states, protesting homeowners are protected from defamation retaliatory slander and libel lawsuits filed by developers by anti-SLAPP (Strategic Litigation Against Public Participation) statutes. *See, e.g.,* Cal. Code of Civil Proc. § 425.16 (b) (1): "A cause of action against a person arising from any act of that person's right of petition or free speech under the United States or California constitutions in connection with a public issue shall be subject to a special motion to strike." *Damon v. Ocean Hills Journalism Club*, 102 Cal.Rptr.2d 205 (Cal.App.2000) (criticism of a community association property manager expressed in a community newsletter and at board meetings by homeowner's association members and directors is protected by the anti-SLAPP statute as the association is a quasi-governmental entity, thus the comments are being made in a public forum concerning matters of public interest); *see also Ruiz v. Harbor View Community Ass'n*, 37 Cal.Rptr.3d 133 (Cal.App.2005).

Many of the problems with, and concerns raised about, restrictions in common interest communities also exist with similar exclusionary policies exhibited in zoning and other public controls. Do you agree with the author below, that the protections afforded by nuisance law and the availability of private covenants render zoning unnecessary? Robert C. Ellickson, *Alternatives to Zoning: Covenants, Nuisance Rules, and Fines as Land Use Controls*, 40 U.CHI.L.REV. 681 (1973).

D. PLANNING AS THE CRITICAL TOOL FOR FRAMING STATUTORY LAND USE CONTROLS

1. THE STANDARD CITY PLANNING ENABLING ACT (1928)

AN ACT to provide for city and regional planning; the creation, organization, and powers of planning commissions; the regulation of subdivision of land and the acquisition of right to keep planned streets free from buildings; and providing penalties for violation of this act.

Sec. 6. General Powers and Duties.

It shall be the function and duty of the planning commission to make and adopt a master plan for the physical development of the municipality, including any areas outside of its boundaries which, in the commission's judgment, bear relation to the planning of such municipality. Such plan, with the accompanying maps, plats, charts, and descriptive matter shall show the commission's recommendations for the development of said territory, including among other things, the general location, character, and extent of streets, viaducts, subways, bridges, waterways, water fronts, boulevards, parkways, playgrounds, squares, parks, aviation fields and other public ways, grounds and open spaces, the general location of public buildings and other public property, and the general location and extent of public utilities and terminals, whether publicly or privately owned or operated, for water, light, sanitation, transportation, communication, power, and other purposes; also the removal, relocation, widening, narrowing, vacating, abandonment, change of use or extension of any of the foregoing ways, grounds, open spaces, buildings, property, utilities, or terminals; as well as a zoning plan for the control of the height, area, bulk, location, and use of buildings and premises.

Sec. 7. Purposes in View.

In the preparation of such plan the commission shall make careful and comprehensive surveys and studies of present conditions and future growth of the municipality and with due regard to its relation to neighboring territory. **The plan shall be made with the general purpose of guiding and accomplishing a coordinated, adjusted, and harmonious development of the municipality** and its environs which will, in accordance with present and future needs, best promote health, safety, morals, order, convenience, prosperity, and general welfare, 41 as well as efficiency and economy in the process of development; including, among other things, adequate provision for traffic, the promotion of safety from fire and other dangers, adequate provision for light and air, the promotion of the healthful and convenient distribution of population, the promotion of good civic design and arrangement, wise and efficient expenditure of public funds and the adequate provision of public utilities and other public requirements.

2. THE STANDARD ZONING ENABLING ACT (1926)

Sec. 3.   Purposes in View.

Such Regulations shall be made in accordance with a comprehensive plan and designed to lessen congestion in the streets; to secure safety from fire, panic, and other dangers; to promote health and the general welfare; to provide adequate light and air; to prevent overcrowding of land; to avoid undue concentration of population; to facilitate the adequate provision of transportation, water, sewage, schools, parks, and other public requirements. (emphasis supplied)

The SCPEA, did not use the words "comprehensive plan," although it did use the terms "city plan" and "master plan." The question then arose as to whether the "comprehensive plan" in the SZEA was equivalent to the "master" or "city" plan of the Standard City Planning Enabling Act. This definitional problem, along with the fact that most local governments did not prepare plans, when they did undertake zoning and other forms of land use regulation, created much difficulty in interpreting the "in accordance with a comprehensive plan" language. Alternatively, if there was a plan, it was not seen as binding on land use regulations or decisions thereunder. Thus, the zoning ordinance became the principal focus of local governments and the courts in land use cases. In effect, the zoning ordinance and its accompanying map *became* the "comprehensive plan," which was always "in accordance" with itself."

Times are changing. The Standard State Zoning Enabling Act and Standard City Planning Enabling Act, both products of the 1920s, are outdated. While zoning and planning were created in part because of the unpredictability of nuisance law, many regard planning and zoning as they have developed under the standard acts as suffering severe defects. In addition to changes by individual states, such as the Florida and California acts referred to in section 3 *infra*, there have been national efforts to modernize the enabling acts. After a twelve-year effort financed by the Ford Foundation, the American Law Institute released the Model Land Development Code (MLDC) in 1976. The MLDC integrates zoning and subdivision regulations and streamlines the development approval process.

The primary focus of the MLDC with regard to local governments, however, was development, not planning. Its major achievement to date has been the acceptance by Florida of the "developments of regional impact" and "areas of state concern". That has led to a broader role for state oversight of local government planning and regulation, accompanied by state and regional planning in the Florida. *See* Robert M. Rhodes, *Florida Growth Management, Past, Present and Future*, 9 FLA.COASTAL L.REV. 107 (2007); Thomas G. Pelham, *The Florida Experience: Creating a State, Regional and Local Comprehensive Planning Process*, 102, 107, 109 and 110, in Peter Buchsbaum and Larry Smith, eds., *State and Regional Comprehensive Planning: Implementing New Methods for Growth Management* (1993). However, in 2011, under the pressure of property rights organizations, the Governor and state legislature adopted amendments to the "State and Local Government Land Use Planning Act," to rescind state oversight of local government planning, regulation and development approval.

The American Planning Association "Growing Smart" Project is a further effort to modernize the standard planning and zoning enabling acts of the 1920s. Its Growing Smart Legislative Guidebook: Model Statutes for Planning and the Management of Change (2002) contains various model statutes and provides commentary with legislative alternatives and suggestions for implementation. The guidebook offers state legislatures the following fundamental choices:

(1) planning as an advisory function; (2) planning as an activity to be encouraged through incentives; (3) planning as a mandatory activity necessary in order to exercise regulatory and related powers; and (4) mandated state-regional-local planning that is integrated both vertically and horizontally.

The Association also has published drafts of model smart growth codes covering such topics as mixed-use, town centers, affordable housing, density bonuses, unified development permit review process, transferable development rights, cluster development, and pedestrian overlay districts. http://www.planning.org/growingsmart/.

3. THE COMPREHENSIVE, MASTER OR GENERAL PLAN

Through its Local Government Comprehensive Planning and Land Development Regulation Act, Florida requires the adoption of a city or county comprehensive plan before zoning can be enacted, with the following mandatory elements: capital improvements program, future land use, traffic circulation, sewer and solid waste, conservation, recreation, open space, housing, and coastal management (where applicable). The plan must also provide for intergovernmental coordination with the plans of adjacent governmental units and the state. Fla.St.Ann. § 163.3177.

California requires that each planning agency prepare and each county and city legislative body adopt "a comprehensive long-term general plan." West's Ann. Cal. Gov't Code § 65300. In fairly detailed fashion the statute defines what that means:

> The general plan shall consist of a statement of development policies and shall include a diagram or diagrams and text setting forth objectives, principles, standards, and plan proposals. The plan shall include the following elements:
>
> (a) A land use element which designates the proposed general distribution and general location and extent of the uses of the land for housing, business, industry, open space, including agriculture, natural resources, recreation, and enjoyment of scenic beauty, education, public buildings and grounds, solid and liquid waste disposal facilities, and other categories of public and private uses of land. * * *
>
> (b) A circulation element consisting of the general location and extent of existing and proposed major thoroughfares, transportation routes, terminals, and other local public utilities and facilities, all correlated with the land use element of the plan.
>
> (c) A housing element.
>
> (d) A conservation element for the conservation, development, and utilization of natural resources including water and its hydraulic force, forests, soils, rivers and other waters, harbors, fisheries, wildlife, minerals, and other natural resources. * * *
>
> (e) An open-space element.
>
> (f) A noise element which shall identify and appraise noise problems in the community.
>
> (g) A safety element for the protection of the community from any unreasonable risks associated with the effects of seismically induced surface rupture, dam failure; slope instability leading to mudslides and landslides; subsidence and other geologic hazards known to the legislative body; flooding; and wild land and urban fires.

West's Ann. Cal. Gov't Code § 65302. Other optional elements may also be included. California calls its "comprehensive long term plan" a "general" plan. The word "general" implies a plan for the entire jurisdiction, rather than for an area or neighborhood. For a novel take on the role of plans and planning, *see* Nicole Stelle Garnett, *Planning as a Public Use?* 36 ECOLOGY LAW Q. 443 (2007).

4. THE SPECIFIC PLAN

The specific plan is a planning document adopted concurrently with an application for discretionary development approval that might consist of a rezoning of the property, a development agreement between the government and the applicant establishing their mutual obligations and rights, or a more complex type of development approval that contains mixed uses or planned unit development (PUD) patterns such as shopping centers, office campuses or industrial parks. The specific plan incorporates the zoning for the property, and the detailed performance standards, feasible environmental mitigation and the processing steps, that cannot adequately be worded in an ordinance or on a map. *See Azalea Lakes Partnership v. Parish of St. Tammany*, 859 So.2d 57 (La.2003) (a specific plan is used principally as a device for providing specific, definitive and identifiable standards needed to uphold the validity of a Planned Unit Development approval or development agreement).

Indeed, discretionary approvals will be set aside where they are not based on specific, identifiable and definite standards set forth in the enabling act, zoning or subdivision ordinance. *See Azzarito v. Planning and Zoning Commission of Eltington Township*, 830 A.2d 827 (Conn.App.2007). It has long been settled that civil statutes can be tested for vagueness under the due process clause. *Kaur v. New York State Urban Development Corporation*, 933 N.E.2d 721 (N.Y.2010) (due process requires that a statute be sufficiently definite "so that individuals of ordinary intelligence are not forced to guess at the meaning of statutory terms"). *See also* Cal.Gov't Code § 65867.5. "A development agreement shall not be approved unless the legislative body finds that the provisions of the proposed agreement are consistent with the general plan and any applicable *specific plan*." Without the definitive standards of the specific plan, the agreement or PUD will be found to be void for indefiniteness. The excerpt from the following case, set out as a principal case *infra* Chapter 2.G., is instructive in that regard:

SANTA MARGARITA AREA RESIDENTS TOGETHER V. COUNTY OF SAN LUIS OBISPO

Court of Appeals of California, 2000.
84 Cal.App.4th 221, 100 Cal.Rptr.2d 740.

In general, the [Development] Agreement freezes zoning on the Project property in return for the developer's commitment to submit *a specific plan* for construction *in compliance with County land use requirements.*

Specifically, the Agreement provides that Santa Margarita Limited will file a comprehensive application for approval of the Project, *including a specific plan,* a vesting tentative map, and an environmental impact report. The *specific plan* must incorporate *the standards* set forth in the Salinas River Area Plan. The application must state that Santa Margarita

Limited will commit itself to develop the Project in its entirety and to engage in all necessary environmental review. The Agreement also provides that Santa Margarita Limited will dedicate land for a public swimming pool, sewer treatment plant, and cemetery expansion.

In return for these commitments, the County agrees to process, review, and approve or disapprove the *specific plan*, and to apply the zoning and other land use regulations set forth in the specific plan without change for up to five years during the review and approval period. The Agreement is entered into under the authority of the Development Agreement Statute and satisfies its technical requirements. Cal.Gov't Code § 65867.5 provides: "A Development Agreement is a legislative act that shall not be approved unless the legislative body finds that the provisions of the proposed development agreement are consistent with the general plan and *any specific plan.*" *See also* Hawaii Rev.Stat. § 46–124, "... are consistent with the general plan and *applicable [specific] development plan*".

5.   AREA OR NEIGHBORHOOD PLANS

In most states, comprehensive plan statutes allow for the creation of sub-planning areas and a host of other types of plans needed to flesh out uniquely detailed policies and programs that can be covered only sparingly in the general plan. We cover many of these types of plans in this casebook. In Chapter 7 we will discuss Hawaii's requirements that each county be divided into four distinct sub-areas: urban; transitional; natural resource and conservation; and agricultural areas. Each of these sub-areas requires that a sub-general "area" plan be developed. Maryland requires sub-area plans for the delineation of smart priority growth areas for the 11 counties of the state. Within cities neighborhood plans are extremely valuable in delineating the unique character of different geographical, historical and ethnic communities. Blighted areas will require redevelopment area plans. Airports and ports require plans to control and protect adjacent neighborhoods. Other types of Area Plans include Neighborhood, Regional, Local Coastal, Habitat Conservation, Floodplain, Annexation, Capital Improvement, Redevelopment, Large Facility, Utility, Sewer, Water, Drainage and Historic District Plans.

Monterey County, California, for example, has the Central Salinas Valley Sub-Area Plan, a comprehensive long range plan designed to guide the area's unique agricultural, resource, environmental protection and preservation character, while limiting growth that would destroy these valuable lands and resources. While the General Plan sets forth the framework for overall county development, the day-to-day actions of the unique areas of the County truly shape the community. Thus, the manner in which the General Plan is implemented is the real test of the worth of its goals, objectives, and policies. The major role of detail and implementation falls into eight area plans. Because each area plan is a subunit of the General Plan, all sub-area plans are automatically incorporated into the General Plan.

Some of the more important implementation measures for the County that are fully fleshed out in the eight area plans include more detailed land use maps, capable of being incorporated into the zoning ordinance, specific subdivision regulation for conservation areas, unique sub-area capital improvements programming, delineation of urban service boundaries, preparation of specific plans, and project review under the California Environmental Quality Act. The Salinas Valley Area plan concentrates on techniques unique to the area including: preservation of agricultural and environmentally sensitive lands through mandatory cluster development; transfers of development rights to urban areas; establishing exclusive agricultural districts that exclude road, sewer and water extensions; special bond issues for acquiring habitat corridors and recreational trails; and authorization of solar and wind renewable energy farms and renewable energy transmission lines.

The unique goals, objectives and policies laid out in the area plan are as follows:

1. Agriculture will remain the leading industry in the Central Salinas Valley;

2. The preservation of viable agricultural land shall implement the statements expressed in the Monterey County General Plan and shall constitute the guiding principles used to develop the Area Plan;

3. The growth rate in the Central Salinas Valley Planning Area will follow historically low growth patterns;

4. Residential, commercial, and industrial growth will be kept out of the agricultural, open space, and environmentally sensitive lands in the Salinas Valley, and shall be concentrated within the Valley's four incorporated cities;

5. The cities of King, Greenfield, Soledad, and Gonzales will moderately expand their jurisdictional boundaries and their spheres of influence;

6. County, state, and federal budget limitations will restrain the future provision of public services and facilities throughout the Valley; * * *

9. Scenic and open space protection in the Central Salinas Valley are valued resources.

6. REGULATING PLANS (FORM BASED CODES)

As you will see in Chapter 2, "New Urbanism and Form Based Codes" are an increasingly viable alternative to the current planning and zoning system that has dominated land use controls for the past 80 years. Typical comprehensive and area plans include a "Land Use Element" which sets out general land use categories on a very large scale map. Specific land uses are not shown for individual parcels or lots. Zoning then interprets the land uses shown on the land use map by creating zoning district maps and text that define uses permitted for all properties in the zoning district. These districts are constructed to segregate uses into single categories. Thus there will be an R1 district for single family detached residences, an R2 district for attached townhomes or duplexes; an R3 for apartment houses or condominiums; a CN for neighborhood retail commercial; a CR for regional shopping centers; an O for office and an IL for light industry. Each district will also have area restrictions for front yard, side yard, minimum lot size, maximum floor area and height. The structure segregates all uses and doesn't allow for mixed use developments and neighborhoods that are architecturally designed to meet the existing character of the community. To fill that gap new urbanism and form based codes are based on architectural design, interconnected streets, rear parking, build to street, apartments over stores, front porches, pedestrian rather than automobile orientation, jobs-housing balance and a mix of residential, office, cultural, governmental, commercial and recreational uses. A "regulating plan" is used to carry out objectives.

A regulating plan is comparable to an area plan or a specific plan, falling more in the planning category than the regulatory category. A regulating plan has characteristics similar to a detailed development plan and/or preliminary subdivision plat. The only difference is that creation of the regulating plan usually precedes development, whereas the development or plat is part of the approval process. Preparing a regulating plan usually involves a public process that starts with the identification of an overall vision for the area being planned and moves through a series of refinements until it reaches the level of plan detail required by the community. In addition to the regulating plan images, there are specific rules for the design of blocks and alleys, a hierarchy of building envelope standards, streetscape requirements, parking requirements, and instructions for the distribution of retail uses. These rules are drafted in a similar manner and with similar language to conventional zoning and subdivision regulations.

The Columbia Pike Special Revitalization District Form-Based Code provides an example of a regulating plan. After Columbia Pike, once considered the "Main Street" of South Arlington, Virginia, began experiencing disinvestment and blight, the city and community undertook a neo-traditional planning process. In 2003, the city created and adopted a form-based code. The Regulating Plan for the Columbia Pike code provides images of the various streets and building types within the redevelopment area and identifies appropriate building and parking requirements.

E. CONSISTENCY WITH COMPREHENSIVE PLANNING

As we have seen in Section C, the term "comprehensive planning" encompasses a wide range of planning documents contained within city and county "Comprehensive, Master or General" ("Comprehensive") Plans, including: required and optional plan elements; interim strategies preceding future plan and code amendments; demographic and infrastructure studies and land use analyses; and specific and neighborhood plans. Yet none of these comprehensive plan documents are self-implementing. All require legislative codes and zoning regulations to carry out the goals, objectives, policies and standards contained within the comprehensive plan. The principal tool to carry out planning is the zoning ordinance. Other critical legislation includes, but is not limited to: subdivision and environmental regulations; annexation and sphere of influence regulations; capital improvement programs and public improvement and assessment district bonding and financing ordinances to implement infrastructure and service needs; dedication, impact fee, excise tax and assessment ordinances; official maps to protect future acquisition areas; building and housing codes; sustainability, renewable energy and green development codes.

A major issue confronting the courts over the past 85 years since uniform state adoption of the model Standard Zoning Enabling Act (1926) and the Standard Planning Enabling Act (1928) has been whether an adopted comprehensive plan is binding upon subsequent implementing land use legislation or administrative approval of development permits and subdivisions. The Standard Zoning Enabling Act provides that zoning be "in accord with a comprehensive plan," § 3, but the Act does not define "plan." When the issue arose as to what type of planning had to be done in order to meet the "in accord with" requirement, numerous courts, including the U.S. Supreme Court decision in *Village of Euclid v. Ambler Realty Co.*, 272 U.S. 365 (1926) rejected the idea that a planning document or planning process was required at all, and the zoning ordinance itself, so long as reasonable, could stand as the comprehensive plan. Note that in *Euclid*, *infra*, Chapter 2, the court stated "On November 13, 1922, an ordinance was adopted by the village council, establishing a comprehensive zoning *plan*". This sentence, referred to by over 50 years of state zoning decisions, eviscerated the requirement of the SZEA that "zoning be in accordance with a comprehensive plan." This omission led to an early failure by the state courts to understand the relationship between planning and zoning. Yet this relationship is critical to appreciating the legal and political difficulties communities face as they attempt to control their land use environment.

1. UNITARY VIEW (MAJORITY RULE)

BRIAR MEADOWS DEVELOPMENT, INC. v. SOUTH CENTRE TOWNSHIP BOARD OF SUPERVISORS

Commonwealth Court of Pennsylvania, 2010.
2 A.3d 1303.

On July 13, 2007, Briar filed a curative amendment application with the South Centre Township Board of Supervisors (Board). Briar sought to rezone certain property in South Centre Township (Township) from Agricultural to Commercial/Industrial. Briar holds an option on two tracts of land in the Township. The properties are bounded to the north by Interstate 80 and to the east by an adjoining property owner and the Interstate 80 exit ramp. To the south, the property is bordered by property owned by Laura Baker (Baker) and State Route 11, and to the west by State Route 1003/Lows Road. The properties consist of one 33.89 acre parcel which is located entirely within the Agricultural Zoning district, and one 91.5 acre parcel which is located in both the Agricultural and Commercial Districts. Only 21% of the total site is located within the Commercial district. After a hearing, the Board issued a decision denying the curative amendment application.

Section 303(c) of the MPC, 53 P.S. § 10303(c) states:

> Notwithstanding any other provision of this act, no action by the governing body of a municipality shall be invalid nor shall the same be subject to challenge or appeal on the basis that such action is inconsistent with, or fails to comply with, the provision of the comprehensive plan.

The Board responds that Briar filed its challenge on the basis that the Ordinance, which zones a certain part of the property Agricultural, is inconsistent with and fails to comply with the comprehensive plan. Based on the language contained in 53 P.S. § 10303(c), such a challenge may not be brought. We agree. In *CACO Three, Inc. v. Board of Supervisors of Huntington Township*, 845 A.2d 991 (Pa.Cmwlth.), petition for allowance of appeal denied, 580 Pa. 707, 860 A.2d 491 (2004), this court addressed the status of a comprehensive plan in reviewing a lower court's disapproval of a preliminary land development plan. This court stated that while a comprehensive plan is a useful tool for guiding growth and development, it is by its nature, an abstract recommendation as to land utilization. Inconsistency with a comprehensive plan is not a proper basis for denying a land development plan. Similarly, it cannot be a basis for a substantive challenge to a zoning ordinance. Here, Briar filed its challenge on the basis that the Ordinance, which zones some of the property Agricultural, is inconsistent with and fails to comply with the comprehensive plan. As acknowledged by Briar, however, 53 P.S. § 10303(c) does not authorize such a challenge.

NOTES

1.   The Standard City Planning Enabling Act published in 1928, two years after the SZEA, defines a master plan and directs its development. The planning act is set out at 8 Zoning and Land Use Controls § 53.01A (Rohan and Kelly eds. 2015). While zoning in accordance with a comprehensive plan was an early presupposition for zoning, the requirement was virtually destroyed by a majority of states holding that comprehensive plans (even where none in fact existed) could be found solely in the zoning ordinance itself. *Kozesnik v. Township of Montgomery*, 131 A.2d 1 (N.J.1957); Charles M. Haar, *"In Accordance with a Comprehensive Plan,"* 68 HARV.L.REV. 1154 (1955). While not all courts were so forthright, the oft-quoted language of Justice Weintraub in Kozesnik is typical of the view of planning as optional that prevailed in zoning's early post World War II years:

> "No doubt good housekeeping would be served if a zoning ordinance followed and implemented a master plan * * * but the history of the subject dictated another course. * * * A plan may be readily revealed in an end-product—here a zoning ordinance—and no more is required by statute. * * * "

131 A.2d 1, 7–8 (N.J.1957).

Thus, whatever significance the "in accord with" requirement should have had was rendered superfluous with the interpretation that the comprehensive plan could be contained solely within the zoning ordinance itself, so long as the zoning ordinance comprised a comprehensive scheme. *Nestle Waters v. Town of Fryeburg*, 967 A.2d 702 (Me.2009); *Iowa Coal Mining Co. v. Monroe County*, 494 N.W.2d 664, 669 (Iowa 1993) (declaring that "the planning necessary to implement a comprehensive zoning scheme need not be reduced to writing; it may be found in the ordinance itself"). Furthermore, even when comprehensive plans were adopted, they were often seen as advisory, non-binding guides. *Barrie v. Kitsap County*, 613 P.2d 1148 (Wash.1980); *Saenger v. Planning Comm'n of Berks County*, 308 A.2d 175 (Pa.Cmwlth.1973); *City of Jacksonville v. City of Sherwood*, 289 S.W.3d 90 (Ark.2008) (annexation element of plan not legally binding and the real authority lies with the zoning ordinance). In some states unincorporated areas (counties and townships) are required to conform their zoning to a comprehensive plan, but home rule cities are not. *See State ex rel. Phillips Supply Co. v. Cincinnati*, 985 N.E.2d 257 (Ohio App.2012) ("The Queensgate Businesses also argue that because the zoning is not in accordance with a comprehensive zoning plan, it constitutes spot zoning. They rely upon this court's decision in *Monsanto Co. v. Bd. of Elections of Hamilton Cty.*, 1st Dist. Nos. C–950735 and C–950748, 1996 WL 577848 (Oct. 9, 1996). But *Monsanto* is distinguishable because it involved a township. Townships lack home rule authority and are required under R.C. 519.02 to adopt zoning regulations in accordance with a comprehensive plan. There is no similar requirement for municipalities. *See Columbia Oldsmobile v. Montgomery,* 564 N.E.2d 455 (1990) ("there is no statutory requirement that cities * * * enact a comprehensive community plan pursuant to its power to zone under R.C. 713.06 et seq.")

2.   In a number of states where conventional judicial views on consistency have prevailed, the state legislature has intervened. The Washington courts, for example, prior to 1991, held that building permits, issued in violation of a county comprehensive plan, were valid on the ground that the plan was only advisory, *see Toandos Peninsula Ass'n v. Jefferson County*, 648 P.2d 448 (Wash.App.1982), and rezoning not in accordance with a county comprehensive plan is not necessarily arbitrary and capricious. *See, Pease Hill Community Group v. County of Spokane*, 816 P.2d 37, 42 (Wash.App.1991). Since 1991, however, the more populous and growing counties and cities in Washington are now required to develop a comprehensive plan by statute, and development approvals must be consistent with the plan. Wash.Ann. §§ 36.70A.040 and 36.70A.120.

2.   PLANNING AS A FACTOR RULE

UDELL V. HAAS
Court of Appeals of New York, 1968.
21 N.Y.2d 463, 288 N.Y.S.2d 888, 235 N.E.2d 897.

[The facts have been consolidated and shortened by the editors: The background of the dispute is this: The Village of Lake Success is a small, suburban community in the extreme westerly portion of Nassau County. It has a rather irregular shape, but generally is bounded on the south by the Northern State Parkway and on the north and east by the Town of North Hempstead. To the west lies its giant neighbor, the City of New York.

The village is approximately two square miles in size. Running through it in a generally north-south direction is the main artery of the village, Lakeville Road. That street intersects with Northern Boulevard, a major east-west thoroughfare in this section of Long Island.

Prior to the 1960 rezoning in question, almost the entire area north of Northern Boulevard (a small neck) was zoned for business. For a distance of some 400 feet south of Northern Boulevard, the area was zoned Business "A" which permitted retailing and similar uses as well as laboratories and office and public buildings. North of Northern Boulevard the land was zoned Business "B" where essentially the only nonresidential use allowed was neighborhood retailing.

The parcel of land in question consists of approximately two and one-half acres, covering all of the area formerly zoned Business "A" on the east side of Lakeville Road. Twenty-four feet of the southern end of the east parcel extend into the former Business "B" zone.

When appellant assembled this east parcel in 1951, the only use being made of this property was in the northerly portion facing Northern Boulevard. It was then being operated as a restaurant. In 1951, plaintiff acquired two and one-half acres of vacant lots on the west side of Lakeville Road

The zoning amendment, ordinance No. 60, rezoned the entire east and west parcels, into a Residence "C" category. Permitted uses in the new classification include public and religious buildings and residences with minimum lot area set at 13,000 square feet and minimum frontage of 100 feet on Lakeville Road.

The trial court held the rezoning with respect to the west parcel unconstitutional as being confiscatory, but sustained the ordinance insofar as it affected the east parcel. The decision with respect to the west parcel rested on three grounds. First, there was the size and shape of the plot; second, the topography of the land, which sloped down some 15 feet from Lakeville Road to University Place; and third, the existing neighboring uses. After a careful evaluation of the evidence, the trial court concluded that "residential zoning precludes use for any purpose to which it is reasonably adaptable." It also held the rezoning to be discriminatory.

With respect to the east parcel, however, a contrary conclusion was reached as to the validity of the ordinance. In essence, the court held that since the appellant also owned contiguous lots fronting on Summer Avenue in the Town of North Hempstead, residential use was practical for the east parcel since the residences could face Summer Avenue. In addition, it found residential zoning would not be inconsistent with the character of the neighborhood and that a nursery school located on the south side of the east parcel was not incompatible with residential use. The problem raised by the commerce of Northern Boulevard could be remedied by appropriate fencing.

On the landowner's appeal, the Appellate Division affirmed. Justice Hopkins, dissenting, stated in a brief opinion that he could see no justification for treating the two properties differently and that the "same considerations that prompted the declaration of the invalidity of the ordinance exist on the one side of Lakeville Road as on the other" (27 A.D.2d 750, 751, 279 N.Y.S.2d 701).]

We hold that ordinance No. 60 is invalid with respect to the east parcel as well as the west parcel. We have concluded that the rezoning was discriminatory and that it was not done "in accordance with [the] comprehensive plan" of the Village of Lake Success (Village Law, § 177). In our view, sound zoning principles were not followed in this case, and the root cause of this failure was a misunderstanding of the nature of zoning, and, even more importantly, of its relationship to the statutory requirement that it be "in accordance with a comprehensive plan."

Zoning is not just an expansion of the common law of nuisance. It seeks to achieve much more than the removal of obnoxious gases and unsightly uses. Underlying the entire concept of zoning is the assumption that zoning can be a vital tool for maintaining a civilized form of existence only if we employ the insights and the learning of the philosopher, the city planner, the economist, the sociologist, the public health expert and all the other professions concerned with urban problems.

This fundamental conception of zoning has been present from its inception. The almost universal statutory requirement that zoning conform to a "well-considered plan" or "comprehensive plan" is a reflection of that view. (See Standard State Zoning Enabling Act, U.S. Dept. of Commerce [1926].) The thought behind the requirement is that consideration must be given to the needs of the community as a whole. In exercising their zoning powers, the local authorities must act for the benefit of the community as a whole following a calm and deliberate consideration of the alternatives, and not because of the whims of either an articulate minority or even majority of the community. Thus, the mandate of the Village Law (§ 177) is not a mere technicality which serves only as an obstacle course for public officials to overcome in carrying out their duties. Rather, the comprehensive plan is the essence of zoning. Without it, there can be no rational allocation of land use. It is the insurance that the public welfare is being served and that zoning does not become nothing more than just a Gallup poll.

Moreover, the "comprehensive plan" protects the landowner from arbitrary restrictions on the use of his property which can result from the pressures which outraged voters can bring to bear on public officials. "With the heavy presumption of constitutional validity that attaches to legislation purportedly under the police power, and the difficulty in judicially applying a 'reasonableness' standard, there is danger that zoning, considered as a self-contained activity rather than as a means to a broader end, may tyrannize individual property owners. Exercise of the legislative power to zone should be governed by rules and standards as clearly defined as possible, so that it cannot operate in an arbitrary and discriminatory fashion, and will actually be directed to the health, safety, welfare and morals of the community. The more clarity and specificity required will effectively enable the courts to review the regulation, declaring it ultra vires if it is not in reality 'in accordance with a comprehensive plan.' " (Haar, *In Accordance with a Comprehensive Plan,* 68 HARV.L.REV. 1154, 1157–1158.)

As Professor Haar points out, zoning may easily degenerate into a talismanic word, like the "police power," to excuse all sorts of arbitrary infringements on the property rights of the landowner. To assure that this does not happen, our courts must require local zoning authorities to pay more than mock obeisance to the statutory mandate that zoning be "in accordance with a comprehensive plan". There must be some showing that the change does not conflict with the community's basic scheme for land use.

One of the key factors used by our courts in determining whether the statutory requirement has been met is whether forethought has been given to the community's land use problems. (*See* 68 HARV.L.REV. 1154, 1171; Note, *Comprehensive Plan Requirement in Zoning*, 12 SYRACUSE L.REV. 342, 344–345.)

Where a community, after a careful and deliberate review of "the present and reasonably foreseeable needs of the community," adopts a general developmental policy for the community as a whole and amends its zoning law in accordance with that plan, courts can have some confidence that the public interest is being served. Where, however, local officials adopt a zoning amendment to deal with various problems that have arisen, but give no consideration to alternatives which might minimize the adverse effects of a change on particular landowners, and then call in the experts to justify the steps already taken in contemplation of anticipated litigation, closer judicial scrutiny is required to determine whether the amendment conforms to the comprehensive plan.

The role of these experts must be more than that of giving rationalizations for actions previously decided upon or already carried out. In recent years, many experts on land use problems have expressed the pessimistic view that the task of bringing about a rational allocation of land use in an ever more urbanized America will prove impossible. But of one thing, we may all be certain. The difficulties involved in developing rational schemes of land use controls become insuperable when zoning or changes in zoning are followed rather than preceded by study and consideration.

By this statement, we do not mean to imply that the courts should examine the motives of local officials. What we do mean is that the courts must satisfy themselves that the rezoning meets the statutory requirement that zoning be "in accordance with [the] comprehensive plan" of the community.

Exactly what constitutes a "comprehensive plan" has never been made clear. Professor Haar in his article discusses most of the meanings which courts have given the term. In the conclusion of his article he notes (68 HARV.L.REV. 1173): "As we have seen, the courts have taken a number of rather different approaches in testing zoning measures for consonance with the enabling act mandate of 'accordance with a comprehensive plan.' None of the meanings suggested—broad geographical coverage, 'policy' of the planning or zoning commission, the zoning ordinance itself, the rational basis underlying the ordinance—do extreme violence to the statutory wording. But all of them share a common defect: they emphasize the question whether the zoning ordinance is a comprehensive plan, not whether it is in accordance with a comprehensive plan. Thus construed, the enabling act demands little more than that zoning be 'reasonable,' and impartial in treatment, to satisfy the constitutional conditions for exercise of the state's police power."

No New York case has defined the term "comprehensive plan". Nor have our courts equated the term with any particular document. We have found the "comprehensive plan" by examining all relevant evidence. As the trial court noted, generally New York cases "have analyzed the ordinance * * * in terms of consistency and rationality". While these elements are important, the "comprehensive plan" requires that the rezoning should not conflict with the fundamental land use policies and development plans of the community. These policies may be garnered from any available source, most especially the master plan of the community, if any has been adopted, the zoning law itself and the zoning map.

In the case at bar, the search for the village's "comprehensive plan" is relatively easy. It may be found both in the village's zoning ordinance and in its zoning map.

In 1925 the Village of Lake Success adopted its first zoning ordinance. At least since 1938, appellant's [east] parcel has been placed in a business use district. Over the years, various amendments were passed, none of them, however, affecting appellant's property. If anything, the changes tended to reinforce the conclusion that the community had decided that the neck of land was most appropriately fitted for business use because of its proximity to Northern Boulevard. Thus, in the early 1950s the west side of University Place near Northern Boulevard was rezoned for business use.

When appellants acquired the parcel, it had been zoned for business use for some 12 or 13 years and so it remained for the next 8 or 9 years.

In 1958 the village undertook to set forth expressly the essential development goals of the community. It did so in the form of an amendment to the zoning ordinance and entitled the statement a "developmental policy". According to the statement, Lake Success was and was to remain a suburban community of low density, one-family residential development. Other uses were to be permitted only to the extent that they were related to residential use, e.g., schools, churches and community institutions, or as they might contribute to the strengthening of the tax base of the community.

If one examines the zoning map of the village as it stood prior to June, 1960, this policy is carried out almost perfectly. Only a small portion of the community's land was zoned for business use. It is important to note that almost, if not, every piece of property in the nonresidential category was located on the periphery of the community, usually adjacent to lands in neighboring communities with similar nonresidential use. Consistent with this "developmental policy," a portion of the northeast section of the community had previously been rezoned for commercial use.

Thus, as matters stood on the morning of June 21, 1960, the village had a zoning plan with stated community goals and a zoning map which consistently carried out these policies.

On June 21, 1960 Fred Rudinger, an associate of the appellant, appeared at the village's offices with a preliminary sketch for the development of the vacant west parcel with a bowling alley and a supermarket or discount house. That same evening, the village planning board recommended a change in zoning from business to residential use.

The minutes of that meeting indicate that, following a discussion of the severe traffic problem which had developed on Lakeville Road, a proposed amendment to the zoning map was recommended to the village trustees. A month or so later, this proposal became, in slightly modified form, ordinance No. 60.

Only after adopting this recommendation did the planning board vote to ask the board of trustees to retain a planning expert to review the village's master plan. On July 5, 1960 the trustees retained Mr. Hugh Pomeroy to make just such an investigation. Later that same day, the planning board and the trustees met in joint session, and it was agreed that a required public hearing should be held promptly. On July 27, 1960 ordinance No. 60 became law following the holding of a public hearing two days earlier.

This history of ordinance No. 60 must immediately raise doubts whether this race to the statute books was in accord with sound zoning principles or was a subversion of them for the process by which a zoning revision is carried out is important in determining the validity of the particular action taken. The village argues that there was no longer any need for shopping facilities in the area. Assuming that to be so, this does not explain why consideration was only given to zoning the area as "Residence C". A fair respect for the community's need for taxables, as set forth in its "developmental policy," required that some thought be given to other possible land use controls.

A more substantial justification for the rezoning was the serious traffic conditions on Lakeville Road. However, at the trial, the village's own expert, Mr. Frederick P. Clark, who was retained by the village after Mr. Pomeroy's death, admitted that business use of the east parcel would create less of a traffic problem than business use of the west parcel would. The reason for this was that access to the east parcel could be restricted to Northern Boulevard, while access to the west parcel would probably have to be from Lakeville Road.

The point here is not only that the expert's argument does not support the village's position, but that his testimony also conflicted sharply with the community's "developmental policy" and his own earlier recommendations for modifications of that policy, which he had made in 1962 when he drafted a proposed "Comprehensive Zoning Plan" for the community.

In that report, Mr. Clark had recommended the rezoning of various perimeter areas in the community for commercial and light manufacturing use to take account of property developments outside the community and to strengthen the tax base. For example, he suggested that the entire area of the community south of the Northern State Parkway be rezoned for commercial or light manufacturing. On cross-examination, Mr. Clark admitted that the east parcel was in a perimeter area. The fair implication, therefore, is that commercial use of this property would conform with his recommendations for land use control. * * *

Aside from this testimony, examining the zoning map, one would find it difficult to locate a more fitting area to use for commercial purposes than this isolated neck near Northern Boulevard of which the subject parcel is part.

It is not disputed that the village officials faced a traffic problem in the Northern Boulevard-Lakeville Road area. Nevertheless, we can come to no other conclusion that the rezoning was not "accomplished in a proper, careful and reasonable manner". Ordinance No. 60 not only did not conform to the village's general "developmental policy," but it was also inconsistent with what had been the fundamental rationale of the village's zoning law and map. The amendment was not the result of a deliberate change in community policy and was enacted without sufficient forethought or planning. The particular conditions existing in the area did not support the radical change, which ordinance No. 60 embodied.

More than 60% of the value, of appellant's property, or $260,000, was wiped out because, to use the words of the village's first expert, "in his discussions he had found it is the feeling of the Village that it does not want extensive business in that area". (Emphasis supplied.)

These vague desires of a segment of the public were not a proper reason to interfere with the appellant's right to use his property in a manner which for some 20 odd years was considered perfectly proper. If there is to be any justification for this interference with appellant's use of his property, it must be found in the needs and goals of the community as articulated in a rational statement of land use control policies known as the "comprehensive plan". We find that appellant has demonstrated that ordinance No. 60 did not conform to the established "comprehensive plan" of the village. Hence, ordinance No. 60 must be held to be ultra vires as not meeting the requirement of section 177 of the Village Law that zoning be "in accordance with a comprehensive plan."

NOTES

1. The court says the "root cause" of the problem was the town's misunderstanding of the relationship between planning and zoning. How so?

2. Would the town have won if it had not adopted the 1958 policy, and simply rezoned the land? In other words, would it have been "better off," in the narrow, short-term sense of winning the case, to have done less or no planning at all?

3.   In *Dunes West Golf Club, LLC v. Town of Mount Pleasant*, 737 S.E.2d 601 (S.Car.2013) the court found that an open space ordinance limiting golf courses to recreational uses was consistent with comprehensive planning for preservation of open space. As a result, to "more effectively control the process of converting golf course property to other uses" and to "balance the interests of golf course property owners and golf course community residents with respect to such conversion of use," the Town's planning commission proposed implementing a new zoning district—namely, the Conservation Recreation Open Space ("CRO") district. *See* Town of Mt. Pleasant, S.C., Code § 156.333 (2006) after completing an amendment to the comprehensive plan. The CRO zoning designation permits only recreation and conservation uses and prohibits residential development. The court rejected a golf course applicant's constitutional argument of denial of substantive due process finding that the open space planning basis for the ordinance was not arbitrary or capricious.

4.   A secondary and important rationale for the planning factor approach is to analyze whether the granting of a discretionary permit is consistent with the comprehensive plan. In *Wastewater One, LLC v. Floyd County Bd. of Zoning Appeals*, 947 N.E.2d 1040 (Ind.App.2011) the court held that that the provision of the zoning ordinance at issue conferred "upon the BZA a significant amount of discretion" in that it requires an applicant to prove:

a.   The proposed use will not be injurious to the public health, safety, comfort, morals, convenience or general welfare of the community;

b.   The proposed use will not injure or adversely affect the use or value of other property in the immediate area in a substantially adverse manner; and

c.   The approval of the conditional use will not contradict the goals and objectives of the Floyd County Comprehensive Plan.

3.   PLANNING MANDATE RULE

In recent years, however, courts and state legislatures increasingly mandate that planning must be done prior to, and apart from, the enactment of zoning regulations. California and Florida, for example, require that each planning agency prepare and each legislative body adopt a long term comprehensive (Fla.), general (Cal.) plan to which zoning and other land use regulations must be consistent with. *See* West's Ann. Cal. Govt. Code § 65300. Not only has planning become mandatory in many states, but even in states that do not require a separate comprehensive plan apart from the zoning ordinance itself, a comprehensive plan, once adopted, is no longer simply an advisory tool. It becomes binding law. *See Mayhew v. Town of Sunnyvale*, 774 S.W.2d 284, 294 (Tex.App.1989).

The return of the comprehensive plan from its moribund status in zoning's early years, to its "constitutional" status today provides it with a measure of importance significantly greater than that originally envisioned by the early proponents of zoning. *See* Edward J. Sullivan and Jennifer Bragar, *Recent Developments in Planning*, 46 URB.LAW. 685, 686 (2015) citing Charles M. Haar, *The Master Plan: An Impermanent Constitution*, 20 LAW & CONTEMP.PROBS. 353, 364 (1955) and Daniel R. Mandelker, *The Role of the Local Comprehensive Plan in Land Use Regulation*, 74 MICH.L.REV. 899, 904 (1976).

The mandatory legal status of the comprehensive plan is set out in Fla.St.Ann. § 163.3194:

(1)(a) After a comprehensive plan, or element or portion thereof, has been adopted in conformity with this act, all development undertaken by, and all actions taken in regard to development orders by, governmental agencies in regard to land covered by such plan or element shall be consistent with such plan or element as adopted.

(b) All land development regulations enacted or amended shall be consistent with the adopted comprehensive plan, or element or portion thereof, and any land development regulations existing at the time of adoption which are not consistent with the adopted comprehensive plan, or element or portion thereof, shall be amended so as to be consistent. * * *

(3)(a)(b) A development order (development approval) or land development regulation shall be consistent with the comprehensive plan if the land uses, densities or intensities, capacity or size, timing and other aspects of development permitted by such order or regulation are compatible with and further the objectives, policies, land uses, and densities or intensities in the comprehensive plan and if it meets all other criteria enumerated by the local government.

(4)(a) A court, in reviewing local governmental action or development regulations under this act, may consider, among other things, the reasonableness of the comprehensive plan, or element or elements thereof, relating to the issue justifiably raised or the appropriateness and completeness of the comprehensive plan, or element or elements thereof, in relation to the governmental action or development regulation under consideration. The court may consider the relationship of the comprehensive plan, or element or elements thereof, to the governmental action taken or the development regulation involved in litigation, but private property shall not be taken without due process of law and the payment of just compensation.

How is this consistency requirement carried out? Does the court weigh the wisdom of the plan provisions? How much discretion does the court grant to the county or city adopting the comprehensive plan in determining whether the implementing zoning or development approval is consistent with its own plan? See, a finding of fact related to a local governing body's determination that a project is consistent with a general plan is not supported by substantial evidence, and thus is an abuse of discretion, if, based on the evidence before the local governing body, a reasonable person could not have reached the same conclusion. *Sierra Club v. Cty. of Fresno* (226 Cal.App.4th 704)) review granted and opinion superseded on other grounds, sub nom. *Sierra Club v. County of Fresno*, 334 P.3d 686 (Cal.2014). See the following Florida case:

NASSAU COUNTY V. WILLIS

Supreme Court of Florida, 2010.
41 So.3d 270.

This action concerns the development of a privately-owned 207-acre site known as Crane Island located in Nassau County, Florida. In June 1993, Nassau County and the Florida Department of Community Affairs (the Department) entered into a stipulated settlement agreement approving and amending Nassau County's Comprehensive Plan (the Comprehensive Plan). The Comprehensive Plan contains a future land use element which sets forth several polices, goals, and objectives concerning the treatment and development of wetlands in Nassau County.

A critical part of the Comprehensive Plan is the Future Land Use Map in which each parcel of property is given a land use designation. That designation determines the density at which the property may be developed. The Comprehensive Plan, as amended per the settlement agreement, provides:

> Conservation lands placed under the Limited Development Overlay may not be developed at a density greater than 1 residential dwelling unit per five acres with all permitted development clustered on the upland portion of the site or on that portion of the site which will be least environmentally impacted by construction/development.

> If there is indication that wetland is present on a proposed development site, the developer shall be required to request a wetland determination from the St. Johns River Water Management District Areas of Nassau County designated as "Conservation" land use to be included under a Limited Development Overlay, include all areas shown as wetlands on the Future Land Use Map series. * * *

In 2006, the owners and prospective developers of Crane Island submitted a proposal to change Crane Island's land use designation from wetlands to Planned Unit Development. The proposal included 169 residential units, up to 50 townhomes, 90 boat slips, boat basin, "lock" system, and marina. This process required an application for a formal determination and wetlands delineation. The Water Management District determined that 71.58 acres of the Crane Island site were actually *uplands,* not wetlands.

Upon submission of the Planned Unit Development application in 2006, county planning staff evaluated its consistency with the Comprehensive Plan. The county planning director concluded that Policy 1.09.03 allowed development of the uplands portion of Crane Island. After a public hearing, Nassau County's Planning and Zoning Board recommended approving Policy 1.09.03 and allowing development of the uplands portion of Crane Island. The County categorized the uplands area as *low-density residential,* which permits two units per acre, rather than one unit per five acres in jurisdictional wetlands. Following an additional public hearing, the Board of County Commissioners issued Ordinance 2006–08 approving the densities requested in the Planned Unit Development application.

Plaintiffs (opposing adjoining land owners) vigorously argue that deference should not be given to a local government's interpretation of its comprehensive plan. *See Dixon v. City of Jacksonville,* 774 So.2d 763, 764– 65 (Fla.App.2000). Interpretation of the Comprehensive Plan is reviewed *de novo. Id.* at 765 (explaining "[i]t is well established that the construction of statutes, ordinances, contracts, or other written instruments is a question of law that is reviewable *de novo,* unless their meaning is ambiguous."); *cf. B.B. McCormick & Sons, Inc. v. City of Jacksonville,* 559 So.2d 252, 257 (Fla.App.1990) (applying deferential standard, instead of strict scrutiny, where consistency with comprehensive plan was "heavily dependent upon interpretation of the terms of the plan").

Policy 1.09.03 of the Comprehensive Plan is direct, clear, and simple: "Those land areas determined by the Board of County Commissioners with the advice of the St. Johns River Water Management District that are determined not to be jurisdictional wetlands will be allowed to be developed at the least intense adjacent land use densities and intensities." It is undisputed that the Water Management District designated the relevant property as uplands, not wetlands. Whether Policy 1.09.03 is a wise provision, or whether the Department now thinks the policy gives Nassau County too much latitude, are issues not before us.

Neither Nassau County nor the Intervenors have any power to force the Water Management District to make a particular decision regarding the ecological status of the relevant property. It is not alleged that the County acted without the advice of the Water Management District; the County simply adopted the Water Management District's findings. The County's action is consistent with the Comprehensive Plan, because Policy 1.09.03 precisely provides that wetlands may be redefined after the County receives advice from the Water Management District.

Plaintiffs argued below, and the trial court found, that Nassau County's utilization of Policy 1.09.03 leads to an "absurd result" because its application significantly changes the land use designation of 71.58 acres from wetlands to uplands. Witnesses from the Department provided similar testimony. But the plain language of the Comprehensive Plan's provision provides for this expected result. It is legally irrelevant that Nassau County unsuccessfully attempted to amend the Comprehensive Plan under other provisions of state law to reach the same result, perhaps due to objections by the Department. While some of the Department's employees now think the County's interpretation of Policy 1.09.03 is unlawful, the Department and Nassau County negotiated the approval of the Comprehensive Plan, which included Policy 1.09.03.

Courts should exercise great caution before deviating from the plain text of a constitution, statute, or legislative document to purportedly avoid reaching what a court considers an "absurd result." When inappropriately utilized, the absurdity doctrine allows courts to substitute their judgment of how legislation *should* read, rather than how it *does* read, in violation of the separation of powers.

Plaintiffs acknowledge that a "local comprehensive land use plan is a statutorily mandated legislative plan to control and direct the use and development of property within a county or municipality. The plan is likened to a constitution for all future development with the governmental boundary." *Machado v. Musgrove,* 519 So.2d 629, 631 (Fla.App.1987). The Comprehensive Plan provides that the County can make wetlands designation changes based on the advice of a disinterested scientific decision of a governmental body charged with delineating jurisdictional wetlands. Nassau County did just that here.

We disagree with the trial court's ruling on consistency. The trial court's order quashing Nassau County Ordinance 2006–08 is reversed and remanded with directions to reinstate the ordinance and Nassau County's action approving the Crane Island Planned Unit Development pursuant to Policy 1.09.03 of the Comprehensive Plan.

NOTES

1.   The legislative standard applicable to consistency, means "exact compliance" when the language of the comprehensive plan is not ambiguous or open to interpretation. Section 163.3177(6)(a) requires "a future land use plan element designating proposed future general distribution, location, and extent of the uses of land * * * categories of land use shall be shown on a land use map * * * [and] [e]ach land use category shall be defined in terms of the types of uses included and specific standards for the density or intensity of use." For background on the Florida law, *see* Thomas G. Pelham, William L. Hyde, and Robert P. Banks, *Managing Florida's Growth: Toward an Integrated State,*

Regional, and Local Comprehensive Planning Process, 13 FLA.ST.U.L.REV. 515 (1985).

2.   Arizona requires that "all zoning be consistent with the adopted general and specific plans of the municipality." Ariz.Rev.Stat. § 9–462.01(F). The statute, unlike the Florida statute, does not define consistency. In *Haines v. City of Phoenix*, 727 P.2d 339, 343 (Ariz.App.1986), the court defined consistency as meaning "basic harmony." As to the standard of review, the court rejected both strict scrutiny and rational basis review. Instead, it said its review would consist of "viewing the record that was before the city council and determining if, from that evidence, the council could have decided that despite the deviation from the letter of the plan there was consistency."

3.   Similar to the Nassau County case above, reviewing courts in California afford great deference to the "unique competence" and "ability" of local government to interpret and apply the general plan policies they have authored, to development approvals. *See San Francisco Tomorrow v. City and County of San Francisco*, 175 Cal.Rptr.3d 300 (Cal.App.2014) ("The Legislature has required every county and city to adopt 'a comprehensive, long-term general plan for the physical development of the county or city. . . .' (Gov. Code, § 65300.) A general plan provides a "charter for future development" and sets forth a city or county's fundamental policy decisions about such development." Citing *Friends of Lagoon Valley v. City of Vacaville*, 65 Cal.Rptr.3d 251 (Cal.App.2007) (in a case challenging a city's zoning and planning development approval, the city's conclusion that a particular project is consistent with the relevant general plan carries a strong presumption of regularity that can be overcome only by a showing of arbitrary and capricious abuse of discretion). West's Ann. Cal. Gov. Code § 65300; West's Ann. Cal. C.C.P. § 1094.5(b). Nevertheless, courts will override a determination of consistency, where no reasonable person could have reached the same conclusion upon the relevant evidence.

4.   Zoning that is created by the city initiative petition process rather than originating with the legislative body must also be consistent with the plan. *Building Industry Association v. City of Oceanside*, 33 Cal.Rptr.2d 137 (Cal.App.1994) (a zoning initiative establishing a numerical residential cap conflicted with the housing goals of the general plan housing element). Similarly, zoning established within a specific or area plan must be consistent with the comprehensive plan. *Napa Citizens for Honest Government v. County of Napa*, 110 Cal.Rptr.2d 579 (Cal.App.2001) (even though the specific plan did not directly conflict with the general plan, it was determined to be incompatible with, and failed to advance certain goals and policies of the general plan).

5.   Consistency is not limited to development approvals tied to zoning. Land use decisions also require consistency between subdivision regulations and approvals and the comprehensive or general plan for the community. See the following cases: *Save Centennial Valley Assn. v. Schultz*, 284 N.W.2d 452 (S.D.1979) (approval of a subdivision in an agricultural area consistent with residential zoning was ruled void because the planning commission in approving it disregarded the clear intent of the comprehensive plan to preserve

the agricultural area); *Board of County Commissioners v. Conder*, 927 P.2d 1339 (Colo.1996) (subdivision can be denied based upon plan inconsistency provided plan is legally adopted by legislative body or compliance with the comprehensive plan is required in the subdivision ordinance).

The old view still enforced by a few courts requires only consistency of the subdivision approval with zoning ordinance requirements. *See Board of Supervisors of Augusta County v. Countryside Inv. Co.*, 522 S.E.2d 610 (Va.1999) (subdivision denial "if the proposed subdivision is not conducive to the rural environment" is unauthorized if in conflict with the county's minimum lot size zoning requirements); *Urrutia v. Blaine County*, 2 P.3d 738 (Idaho 2000). The new view of consistency authorizes denial of a subdivision solely because applications do not comport with a strict reading of the comprehensive plan. The proposed use must also comply with the comprehensive plan. *Madison River R.V. Ltd. v. Town of Ennis*, 994 P.2d 1098 (Mont.2000) (not improper for Town Council to deny preliminary plat based on conflict with town's comprehensive plan even though proposed use was permitted by the underlying zoning district). *Lake City Corp. v. City of Mequon*, 544 N.W.2d 60 (Wis.App.1996) (planning commission has the authority to curtail development below that permitted in the zoning envelope at subdivision approval if not consistent with the comprehensive plan); *see also Board of County Commissioners of Cecil County v. Gaster*, 401 A.2d 666 (Md.1979); *Coffey v. Maryland National Capital Park and Planning Commission*, 441 A.2d 1041 (Md.1982).

6.   Consistency with the comprehensive plan is also required for environmental review. County's climate action plan failed to comply with mitigation measure adopted in county's general plan update's program environmental impact report (EIR) requiring a climate action plan to include detailed greenhouse gas (GHG) emissions reduction targets and deadlines and to achieve comprehensive and enforceable GHG emissions reduction by 2020 in compliance with the Governor's Executive Order establishing targets for reducing GHG emissions, where many of the mitigation measures set forth in the general plan's mitigation monitoring and reporting program (MMRP) were not currently funded, the climate action plan failed to assess the likelihood that the GHG reduction measures it discussed would be implemented, the automobile driving reductions needed to achieve the Executive Order's targets were not met, the climate action plan did not include an analysis of the county's own operations, and the deadlines in the climate action plan were no more detailed than the deadlines that had already been set forth in the in the general plan mitigation monitoring and reporting program and the Governor's Executive Order. *Sierra Club v. County of San Diego*, 180 Cal.Rptr.3d 154 (Cal.App.2014), review denied (Mar. 11, 2015). For a critical view of comprehensive planning, *see* Michael Lewyn, *The (Somewhat) False Hope of Comprehensive Planning*, 37 U.HAW.L.R. 39 (2015).

7.   Other states have provided that zoning, development approvals and other land development regulations, must be consistent with, and implement

adopted local comprehensive plans. *See* Rohan & Kelly, *Zoning and Land Use Controls*, § 53C.08 (2015) citing to the following examples:

- Del.Code tit. 9 §§ 2653, 2656 provides that the land use map in a comprehensive plan has "the force of law" and "no development shall be permitted except in conformity with the land use map . . . and with land development regulations enacted to implement the other elements of the adopted comprehensive plan."

- Neb.Rev.Stat. § 23–114.03 provides that zoning regulations must be preceded by the adoption of a comprehensive development plan and must be consistent with that plan.

- Ore.Rev.Stat. § 197.010(1): ("In order to ensure the highest possible level of livability in Oregon, it is necessary to provide for properly prepared and coordinated comprehensive plans for cities and counties, regional areas and the state as a whole. Comprehensive plans shall be prepared to insure that all [land use regulations and development approvals] shall be consistent with the adopted plan."

- Wis.Stat. § 236.01 requires that all programs or actions of a local government that affect land use must be consistent with the local comprehensive plan, including annexation and cooperative boundary agreements as well as zoning and subdivision regulation.

8.   What happens to "grandfathered" existing zoning classifications when a new plan is adopted which contemplates a different use for the land? In *Nuuanu Neighborhood Ass'n v. Department of Land Utilization*, 630 P.2d 107, 110 (Haw.1981), the owner of land in a residential zone sought subdivision approval. Neighbors sought to enjoin the proposed subdivision claiming that the city's 1964 General Plan, which designated the land as Preservation, prevailed over the pre-existing residential zone classification. The court was not impressed with the neighbors' argument and pointed to the 1964 General Plan that provided:

Such zoning regulations as are currently in force and effect will continue in force and effect until such time as they are superseded by appropriate legislative action consonant with the guides established by the General Plan.

9.   Internal consistency within the plan arises when the plan's goals, objectives and policies appear to conflict with each other. Not surprisingly, courts have not been terribly receptive to so-called "precedence" priorities in the plan itself. Thus, a California court held an ordinance passed in accordance with one element of a plan but not in accordance with another was void due to inconsistency within the plan, despite a provision which declared one plan provision to take precedence over the other in the event of conflict. *See Sierra Club v. Kern County Bd. of Supervisors*, 179 Cal.Rptr. 261 (Cal.App.1981).

10. In 2002, the American Planning Association released its Growing Smart Legislative Guidebook. The Guidebook recommended the following provisions be adopted relating to consistency with the comprehensive plan:

8–104 Consistency of Land Development Regulations with Local Comprehensive Plan

"(1) Land development regulations and any amendments thereto, including amendments to the zoning map, and land-use actions shall be consistent with the local comprehensive plan, provided that in the event the land development regulations become inconsistent with the local comprehensive plan by reason of amendment to the plan or adoption of a new plan, the regulations shall be amended within [6] months of the date of amendment or adoption so that they are consistent with the local comprehensive plan as amended.

(a) Except as provided in paragraph (1) above, any land development regulations or amendments thereto and any land-use actions that are not consistent with the local comprehensive plan shall be voidable to the extent of the inconsistency.

(b) Any land development regulations or amendments thereto shall be void [6] months from the date on which a local comprehensive plan is required to be adopted, if a comprehensive plan must be adopted pursuant to Section [7–201] but no comprehensive plan has been adopted.

(c) In determining whether the regulations, amendment, or action satisfies the requirements of subparagraph (a) above, the local planning agency may take into account any relevant guidelines contained in the local comprehensive plan." (emphasis supplied).[2]

After reading the cases and materials in this chapter, do you find the Smart Growth Guidebook § 8–104 addressing the problem of consistency with planning helpful? What about: (1) consistency with regional and state plans, federal acts and programs; (2) internal consistency within the comprehensive plan itself; and (3) consistency of specific, area or neighborhood plans with the comprehensive plan.

---

[2] Reprinted with permission. Copyright 2002 by the American Planning Association.

CHAPTER 2

ZONING: CLASSIC TO CONTEMPORARY

■ ■ ■

A. LOCAL ZONING: THE CLASSICS

Zoning reached puberty in company with the Stutz Bearcat and the speakeasy. F. Scott Fitzgerald and the Lindy Hop were products of the same generation. Of all these phenomena of the twenties, only local zoning has remained viable a generation [or several] later.

Richard F. Babcock, *The Zoning Game* 3 (1966).*

While zoning is still with us, a host of land use control techniques, many at the state and federal levels, have come into prominence in the years since Babcock penned these words. Still, many, if not most, important land use decisions continue to be made at the local level, and the majority of these involve the local zoning ordinance.

Many regard land use planning as quintessentially local. Whether it is wise to vest so much power locally is a subject of never-ending debate. As you will see in the cases that follow, communities often plan and zone from a parochial perspective, failing or refusing to consider the extralocal effects of their actions. Generally, state legislatures and courts have not questioned this (except for a growing number of regional general welfare cases and legislation involving affordable housing and environmental impacts), and for the most part applaud the virtues of local autonomy. There is, however, a downside. As Professor Briffault argues:

> [T]he virtues of enhancing local autonomy tend to be greatly exaggerated. Localism reflects territorial economic and social inequalities and reinforces them with political power. Its benefits accrue primarily to a minority of affluent localities, to the detriment of other communities and to the system of local government as a whole. Moreover, localism is primarily centered on the affirmation of private values. Localist ideology and local political action tend not to build up public life, but rather contribute to the pervasive privatism that is the hallmark of contemporary American politics. Localism may be more of an

---

*   Richard Babcock, often referred to as the 'dean of American planning lawyers,' wrote many influential books and articles in the land use field.

obstacle to achieving social justice and the development of public life than a prescription for their attainment.

Richard Briffault, *Our Localism: Part I—The Structure of Local Government Law*, 90 COLUM.L.REV. 1 (1990). *See also* Part II of the Briffault article at 90 COLUM.L.REV. 346 (1990).

Professor Reynolds suggests that we have a "rather schizophrenic love affair with localism." Laurie Reynolds, *Local Governments and Regional Governance*, 39 URB.LAW. 483 (2007). While an overwhelming majority lives in municipalities with fewer than 50,000 people, most of these smaller municipalities lie within large urbanized metropolitan areas. The former may provide a sense of "small town," while the latter provides jobs, health care, cultural amenities, and other opportunities the truly small town lacks. Many think that the myriad problems generated by localism that Briffault only hints at above likely will never be solved by *general purpose* regional governments, which, by and large, are unpopular and do not work well.

Over the years, solutions to regional problems often have been met by the formation of regional special purpose districts. These districts, which often overlap multiple local governments and other special districts, typically are formed to provide such services as water, transit, waste disposal, and education. They may have a degree of regulatory authority, as well taxing and borrowing authority. According to Professor Reynolds, proliferating regional special districts have not only failed to cure regional ills but have added to the problem. *See also* Janice Griffith, *Regional Governance Reconsidered*, 21 J.L. & POL. 505 (2005).

The reality today is that while we have a few general regional governments, some state supervised controls, and an array of regional special districts, it is local government that retains control over land use in most states.

This chapter focuses upon the basic elements of the local zoning ordinance, the classic cases dealing with its constitutionality, and a few of the new twists which have been added to the basic framework established in the 1920s. As you read the following cases, look for evidence of a plan and note particularly the early identification of zoning with the protection of neighborhoods—albeit primarily the property values therein—and the almost immediate abandonment of any pretensions of direct relationship with health and safety. Keep these factors in mind when wrestling with the takings issue and the reach of the police power that so concerned Justice Holmes in *Pennsylvania Coal v. Mahon*, referred to in Chapter 1 and set out in Chapter 3.

1. THE CLASSIC CASES

The ten-year period from 1916 to 1926, when American cities began comprehensive zoning, was one of legal turmoil. New York City adopted the first comprehensive zoning law in 1916 and a number of cities followed suit. While numerous state courts upheld the constitutionality of zoning, *see Lincoln Trust Co. v. Williams Bldg. Corp.*, 128 N.E. 209 (N.Y.1920), others rejected it. The Maryland Court of Appeals did so, observing that the zoning ordinance "at a stroke arrests that process of natural evolution and growth, and substitutes for it an artificial and arbitrary plan of segregation." *Goldman v. Crowther*, 128 A. 50, 53 (Md.1925). Concerns over the legitimacy of zoning through the police power led some communities to enact zoning through the power of eminent domain by paying compensation. *See* Julian C. Juergensmeyer and Thomas E. Roberts, *Land Use Planning and Development Regulation Law* § 3.28 (2nd ed.2012). More generally, *see* J. Berry Cullingworth, *The Political Culture of Planning: American Land Use Planning in Comparative Perspective*, Ch. 2 (1993) and *Zoning and the American Dream: Promises Still to Keep* (Charles M. Haar and Jerold S. Kayden eds.1989). In the case that follows, the Supreme Court upheld the constitutionality of zoning.

VILLAGE OF EUCLID, OHIO V. AMBLER REALTY CO.

Supreme Court of the United States, 1926.
272 U.S. 365, 47 S.Ct. 114, 71 L.Ed. 303.

MR. JUSTICE SUTHERLAND delivered the opinion of the Court.

The village of Euclid is an Ohio municipal corporation. It adjoins and practically is a suburb of the city of Cleveland. Its estimated population is between 5,000 and 10,000, and its area from 12 to 14 square miles, the greater part of which is farm lands or unimproved acreage. It lies, roughly, in the form of a parallelogram measuring approximately 3½ miles each way. East and west it is traversed by three principal highways: Euclid avenue, through the southerly border, St. Clair avenue, through the central portion, and Lake Shore boulevard, through the northerly border, in close proximity to the shore of Lake Erie. The Nickel Plate Railroad lies from 1,500 to 1,800 feet north of Euclid avenue, and the Lake Shore Railroad 1,600 feet farther to the north. The three highways and the two railroads are substantially parallel.

Appellee is the owner of a tract of land containing 68 acres, situated in the westerly end of the village, abutting on Euclid avenue to the south and the Nickel Plate Railroad to the north. Adjoining this tract, both on the east and on the west, there have been laid out restricted residential plats upon which residences have been erected.

On November 13, 1922, an ordinance was adopted by the village council, establishing a comprehensive zoning plan.

* * *

The entire area of the village is divided by the ordinance into six classes of use districts, denominated U-1 to U-6, inclusive; three classes of height districts, denominated H-1 to H-3, inclusive; and four classes of area districts, denominated A-1 to A-4, inclusive. The use districts are classified in respect of the buildings which may be erected within their respective limits, as follows: U-1 is restricted to single family dwellings, public parks, water towers and reservoirs, suburban and interurban electric railway passenger stations and rights of way, and farming, noncommercial greenhouse nurseries, and truck gardening; U-2 is extended to include two-family dwellings; U-3 is further extended to include apartment houses, hotels, churches, schools, public libraries, museums, private clubs, community center buildings, hospitals, sanitariums, public playgrounds, and recreation buildings, and a city hall and courthouse; U-4 is further extended to include banks, offices, studios, telephone exchanges, fire and police stations, restaurants, theaters and moving picture shows, retail stores and shops, sales offices, sample rooms, wholesale stores for hardware, drugs, and groceries, stations for gasoline and oil (not exceeding 1,000 gallons storage) and for ice delivery, skating rinks and dance halls, electric substations, job and newspaper printing, public garages for motor vehicles, stables and wagon sheds (not exceeding five horses, wagons or motor trucks), and distributing stations for central store and commercial enterprises; U-5 is further extended to include billboards and advertising signs (if permitted), warehouses, ice and ice cream manufacturing and cold storage plants, bottling works, milk bottling and central distribution stations, laundries, carpet cleaning, dry cleaning, and dyeing establishments, blacksmith, horseshoeing, wagon and motor vehicle repair shops, freight stations, street car barns, stables and wagon sheds (for more than five horses, wagons or motor trucks), and wholesale produce markets and salesrooms; U-6 is further extended to include plants for sewage disposal and for producing gas, garbage and refuse incineration, scrap iron, junk, scrap paper, and rag storage, aviation fields, cemeteries, crematories, penal and correctional institutions, insane and feeble-minded institutions, storage of oil and gasoline (not to exceed 25,000 gallons), and manufacturing and industrial operations of any kind other than, and any public utility not included in, a class U-1, U-2, U-3, U-4, or U-5 use. There is a seventh class of uses which is prohibited altogether.

Class U-1 is the only district in which buildings are restricted to those enumerated. In the other classes the uses are cumulative—that is to say, uses in class U-2 include those enumerated in the preceding class U-1; class U-3 includes uses enumerated in the preceding classes, U-2 and U-1; and so on. In addition to the enumerated uses, the ordinance provides for accessory uses; that is, for uses customarily incident to the principal use, such as private garages. * * *

The height districts are classified as follows: In class H-1, buildings are limited to a height of 2½ stories, or 35 feet; in class H-2, to 4 stories, or 50 feet; in class H-3, to 80 feet. To all of these, certain exceptions are made, as in the case of church spires, water tanks, etc.

The classification of area districts is: In A-1 districts, dwellings or apartment houses to accommodate more than one family must have at least 5,000 square feet for interior lots and at least 4,000 square feet for corner lots; in A-2 districts, the area must be at least 2,500 square feet for interior lots, and 2,000 square feet for corner lots; in A-3 districts, the limits are 1,250 and 1,000 square feet, respectively; in A-4 districts, the limits are 900 and 700 square feet, respectively. The ordinance contains, in great variety and detail, provisions in respect of width of lots, front, side, and rear yards, and other matters, including restrictions and regulations as to the use of billboards, signboards, and advertising signs.

* * *

Appellee's tract of land comes under U-2, U-3 and U-6. The first strip of 620 feet immediately north of Euclid avenue falls in class U-2, the next 130 feet to the north, in U-3, and the remainder in U-6.

* * *

Annexed to the ordinance, and made a part of it, is a zone map, showing the location and limits of the various use, height, and area districts, from which it appears that the three classes overlap one another; that is to say, for example, both U-5 and U-6 use districts are in A-4 area districts, but the former is in H-2 and the latter in H-3 height districts.

* * *

The lands lying between the two railroads for the entire length of the village area and extending some distance on either side to the north and south, having an average width of about 1,600 feet, are left open, with slight exceptions, for industrial and all other uses. This includes the larger part of appellee's tract. Approximately one-sixth of the area of the entire village is included in U-5 and U-6 use districts. That part of the village lying south of Euclid avenue is principally in U-1 districts. The lands lying north of Euclid avenue and bordering on the long strip just described are included in U-1, U-2, U-3, and U-4 districts, principally in U-2.

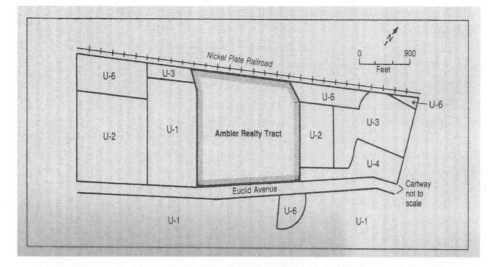

The enforcement of the ordinance is intrusted to the inspector of buildings, under rules and regulations of the board of zoning appeals. Meetings of the board are public, and minutes of its proceedings are kept. It is authorized to adopt rules and regulations to carry into effect provisions of the ordinance. Decisions of the inspector of buildings may be appealed to the board by any person claiming to be adversely affected by any such decision. The board is given power in specific cases of practical difficulty or unnecessary hardship to interpret the ordinance in harmony with its general purpose and intent, so that the public health, safety and general welfare may be secure and substantial justice done. Penalties are prescribed for violations.

* * *

The ordinance is assailed on the grounds that it is in derogation of section 1 of the Fourteenth Amendment to the federal Constitution in that it deprives appellee of liberty and property without due process of law and denies it the equal protection of the law, and that it offends against certain provisions of the Constitution of the state of Ohio. The prayer of the bill is for an injunction restraining the enforcement of the ordinance and all attempts to impose or maintain as to appellee's property any of the restrictions, limitations or conditions. The court below held the ordinance to be unconstitutional and void, and enjoined its enforcement. * * * The bill alleges that the tract of land in question is vacant and has been held for years for the purpose of selling and developing it for industrial uses, for which it is especially adapted, being immediately in the path of progressive industrial development; that for such uses it has a market value of about $10,000 per acre, but if the use be limited to residential purposes the market value is not in excess of $2,500 per acre; that the first 200 feet of the parcel back from Euclid avenue, if unrestricted in respect of use, has a value of $150 per front foot, but if limited to residential uses, and ordinary mercantile business be excluded therefrom, its value is not in excess of $50 per front foot.

It is specifically averred that the ordinance attempts to restrict and control the lawful uses of appellee's land, so as to confiscate and destroy a great part of its value; that it is being enforced in accordance with its terms; that prospective buyers of land for industrial, commercial, and residential uses in the metropolitan district of Cleveland are deterred from buying any part of this land because of the existence of the ordinance and the necessity thereby entailed of conducting burdensome and expensive litigation in order to vindicate the right to use the land for lawful and legitimate purposes; that the ordinance constitutes a cloud upon the land, reduces and destroys its value, and has the effect of diverting the normal industrial, commercial, and residential development thereof to other and less favorable locations.

The record goes no farther than to show, as the lower court found, that the normal and reasonably to be expected use and development of that part of appellee's land adjoining Euclid avenue is for general trade and commercial purposes, particularly retail stores and like establishments, and that the normal and reasonably to be expected use and development of the residue of the land is for industrial and trade purposes. Whatever injury is inflicted by the mere existence and threatened enforcement of the ordinance is due to restrictions in respect of these and similar uses, to which perhaps should be added—if not included in the foregoing— restrictions in respect of apartment houses.

* * *

A motion was made in the court below to dismiss the bill on the ground that, because complainant (appellee) had made no effort to obtain a building permit or apply to the zoning board of appeals for relief, as it might have done under the terms of the ordinance, the suit was premature. The motion was properly overruled. The effect of the allegations of the bill is that the ordinance of its own force operates greatly to reduce the value of appellee's lands and destroy their marketability for industrial, commercial and residential uses, and the attack is directed, not against any specific provision or provisions, but against the ordinance as an entirety. Assuming the premises, the existence and maintenance of the ordinance in effect constitutes a present invasion of appellee's property rights and a threat to continue it.

It is not necessary to set forth the provisions of the Ohio Constitution which are thought to be infringed. The question is the same under both Constitutions, namely, as stated by appellee: Is the ordinance invalid, in that it violates the constitutional protection "to the right of property in the appellee by attempted regulations under the guise of the police power, which are unreasonable and confiscatory"?

Building zone laws are of modern origin. They began in this country about 25 years ago. Until recent years, urban life was comparatively simple; but, with the great increase and concentration of population, problems have developed, and constantly are developing, which require, and will continue to require, additional restrictions in respect of the use and occupation of private lands in urban communities. Regulations, the wisdom, necessity, and validity of which, as applied to existing conditions, are so apparent that they are now uniformly sustained, a century ago, or even half a century ago, probably would have been rejected as arbitrary and oppressive. Such regulations are sustained, under the complex conditions of our day, for reasons analogous to those which justify traffic regulations, which, before the advent of automobiles and rapid transit street railways, would have been condemned as fatally arbitrary and unreasonable. And in this there is no inconsistency, for, while the meaning of constitutional guaranties never varies, the scope of their application must expand or contract to meet the new and different conditions which are constantly coming within the field of their operation. In a changing world it is impossible that it should be otherwise. But although a degree of elasticity is thus imparted, not to the *meaning,* but to the *application* of constitutional principles, statutes and ordinances, which, after giving due weight to the new conditions, are found clearly not to conform to the Constitution, of course, must fall.

The ordinance now under review, and all similar laws and regulations, must find their justification in some aspect of the police power, asserted for the public welfare. The line which in this field separates the legitimate from the illegitimate assumption of power is not capable of precise delimitation. It varies with circumstances and conditions. A regulatory zoning ordinance, which would be clearly valid as applied to the great cities, might be clearly invalid as applied to rural communities. In solving doubts, the maxim "sic utere tuo ut alienum non laedas," which lies at the foundation of so much of the common law of nuisances, ordinarily will furnish a fairly helpful clew. And the law of nuisances, likewise, may be consulted, not for the purpose of controlling, but for the helpful aid of its analogies in the process of ascertaining the scope of, the power. Thus the question whether the power exists to forbid the erection of a building of a particular kind or for a particular use, like the question whether a particular thing is a nuisance, is to be determined, not by an abstract consideration of the building or of the thing considered apart, but by considering it in connection with the circumstances and the locality. *Sturgis v. Bridgeman*, L.R. 11 Ch. 852, 865. A nuisance may be merely a right thing in the wrong place, like a pig in the parlor instead of the barnyard. If the validity of the legislative classification for zoning purposes be fairly debatable, the legislative judgment must be allowed to control.

There is no serious difference of opinion in respect of the validity of laws and regulations fixing the height of buildings within reasonable limits, the character of materials and methods of construction, and the adjoining area which must be left open, in order to minimize the danger of fire or collapse, the evils of overcrowding and the like, and excluding from residential sections offensive trades, industries and structures likely to create nuisances.

Here, however, the exclusion is in general terms of all industrial establishments, and it may thereby happen that not only offensive or dangerous industries will be excluded, but those which are neither offensive nor dangerous will share the same fate. But this is no more than happens in respect of many practice-forbidding laws which this court has upheld, although drawn in general terms so as to include individual cases that may turn out to be innocuous in themselves. The inclusion of a reasonable margin, to insure effective enforcement, will not put upon a law, otherwise valid, the stamp of invalidity. Such laws may also find their justification in the fact that, in some fields, the bad fades into the good by such insensible degrees that the two are not capable of being readily distinguished and separated in terms of legislation. In the light of these considerations, we are not prepared to say that the end in view was not sufficient to justify the general rule of the ordinance, although some industries of an innocent character might fall within the proscribed class. It cannot be said that the ordinance in this respect "passes the bounds of reason and assumes the character of a merely arbitrary fiat." Moreover, the restrictive provisions of the ordinance in this particular may be sustained upon the principles applicable to the broader exclusion from residential districts of all business and trade structures, presently to be discussed.

It is said that the village of Euclid is a mere suburb of the city of Cleveland; that the industrial development of that city has now reached and in some degree extended into the village, and in the obvious course of things will soon absorb the entire area for industrial enterprises; that the effect of the ordinance is to divert this natural development elsewhere, with the consequent loss of increased values to the owners of the lands within the village borders. But the village, though physically a suburb of Cleveland, is politically a separate municipality, with powers of its own and authority to govern itself as it sees fit, within the limits of the organic law of its creation and the state and federal Constitutions. Its governing authorities, presumably representing a majority of its inhabitants and voicing their will, have determined, not that industrial development shall cease at its boundaries, but that the course of such development shall proceed within definitely fixed lines. If it be a proper exercise of the police power to relegate industrial establishments to localities separated from residential sections, it is not easy to find a sufficient reason for denying the power because the effect of its exercise is to divert an industrial flow from the course which it would follow, to the injury of the residential public, if left alone, to another course where such injury will be obviated. It is not meant by this, however, to exclude the possibility of cases where the general public interest would so far outweigh the interest of the municipality that the municipality would not be allowed to stand in the way.

We find no difficulty in sustaining restrictions of the kind thus far reviewed. The serious question in the case arises over the provisions of the ordinance excluding from residential districts apartment houses, business houses, retail stores and shops, and other like establishments. This question involves the validity of what is really the crux of the more recent zoning legislation, namely, the creation and maintenance of residential districts, from which business and trade of every sort, including hotels and apartment houses, are excluded. Upon that question this court has not thus far spoken. The decisions of the state courts are numerous and conflicting; but those which broadly sustain the power greatly outnumber those which deny it altogether or narrowly limit it, and it is very apparent that there is a constantly increasing tendency in the direction of the broader view.

As evidence of the decided trend toward the broader view, it is significant that in some instances the state courts in later decisions have reversed their former decisions holding the other way.

The decisions * * * agree that the exclusion of buildings devoted to business, trade, etc., from residential districts, bears a rational relation to the health and safety of the community. Some of the grounds for this conclusion are promotion of the health and security from injury of children and others by separating dwelling houses from territory devoted to trade and industry; suppression and prevention of disorder; facilitating the extinguishment of fires, and the enforcement of street traffic regulations and other general welfare ordinances; aiding the health and safety of the community, by excluding from residential areas the confusion and danger of fire, contagion, and disorder, which in greater or less degree attach to the location of stores, shops, and factories. Another ground is that the construction and repair of streets may be rendered easier and less expensive, by confining the greater part of the heavy traffic to the streets where business is carried on.

* * *

The matter of zoning has received much attention at the hands of commissions and experts, and the results of their investigations have been set forth in comprehensive reports. These reports, which bear every evidence of painstaking consideration, concur in the view that the segregation of residential, business and industrial buildings will make it easier to provide fire apparatus suitable for the character and intensity of the development in each section; that it will increase the safety and security of home life, greatly tend to prevent street accidents, especially to children, by reducing the traffic and resulting confusion in residential sections, decrease noise and other conditions which produce or intensify nervous disorders, preserve a more favorable environment in which to rear children, etc. With particular reference to apartment houses, it is pointed out that the development of detached house sections is greatly retarded by the coming of apartment houses, which has sometimes resulted in destroying the entire section for private house purposes; that in such sections very often the apartment house is a mere parasite, constructed in order to take advantage of the open spaces and attractive surroundings created by the residential character of the district. Moreover, the coming of one apartment house is followed by others, interfering by their height and bulk with the free circulation of air and monopolizing the rays of the sun which otherwise would fall upon the smaller homes, and bringing, as their necessary accompaniments, the disturbing noises incident to increased traffic and business, and the occupation, by means of moving and parked automobiles, of larger portions of the streets, thus detracting from their safety and depriving children of the privilege of quiet and open spaces for play, enjoyed by those in more favored localities—until, finally, the residential character of the neighborhood and its desirability as a place of detached residences are utterly destroyed. Under these circumstances, apartment houses, which in a different environment would be not only entirely unobjectionable but highly desirable, come very near to being nuisances.

If these reasons, thus summarized, do not demonstrate the wisdom or sound policy in all respects of those restrictions which we have indicated as pertinent to the inquiry, at least, the reasons are sufficiently cogent to preclude us from saying, as it must be said before the ordinance can be declared unconstitutional, that such provisions are clearly arbitrary and unreasonable, having no substantial relation to the public health, safety, morals, or general welfare.

It is true that when, if ever, the provisions set forth in the ordinance in tedious and minute detail, come to be concretely applied to particular premises, including those of the appellee, or to particular conditions, or to be considered in connection with specific complaints, some of them, or even many of them, may be found to be clearly arbitrary and unreasonable. But where the equitable remedy of injunction is sought, as it is here, not upon the ground of a present infringement or denial of a specific right, or of a particular injury in process of actual execution, but upon the broad ground that the mere existence and threatened enforcement of the ordinance, by materially and adversely affecting values and curtailing the opportunities of the market, constitute a present and irreparable injury, the court will not scrutinize its provisions, sentence by sentence, to ascertain by a process of piecemeal dissection whether there may be, here and there, provisions of a minor character, or relating to matters of administration, or not shown to contribute to the injury complained of, which, if attacked separately, might not withstand the test of constitutionality. In respect of such provisions, of which specific complaint is not made, it cannot be said that the landowner has suffered or is threatened with an injury which entitles him to challenge their constitutionality. * * * The gravamen of the complaint is that a portion of the land of the appellee cannot be sold for certain enumerated uses because of the general and broad restraints of the ordinance. What would be the effect of a restraint imposed by one or more of the innumerable provisions of the ordinance, considered apart, upon the value or marketability of the lands, is neither disclosed by the bill nor by the evidence, and we are afforded no basis, apart from mere speculation, upon which to rest a conclusion that it or they would have any appreciable effect upon those matters. Under these circumstances, therefore, it is enough for us to determine, as we do, that the ordinance in its general scope and dominant features, so far as its provisions are here involved, is a valid exercise of authority, leaving other provisions to be dealt with as cases arise directly involving them.

And this is in accordance with the traditional policy of this court. In the realm of constitutional law, especially, this court has perceived the embarrassment which is likely to result from an attempt to formulate rules or decide questions beyond the necessities of the immediate issue. It has preferred to follow the method of a gradual approach to the general by a systematically guarded application and extension of constitutional principles to particular cases as they arise, rather than by out of hand attempts to establish general rules to which future cases must be fitted. This process applies with peculiar force to the solution of questions arising under the due process clause of the Constitution as applied to the exercise of the flexible powers of police, with which we are here concerned.

Decree reversed.

MR. JUSTICE VAN DEVANTER, MR. JUSTICE MCREYNOLDS, and MR. JUSTICE BUTLER dissent.

NECTOW V. CITY OF CAMBRIDGE
Supreme Court of the United States, 1928.
277 U.S. 183, 48 S.Ct. 447, 72 L.Ed. 842.

SUTHERLAND, JUSTICE.

A zoning ordinance of the city of Cambridge divides the city into three kinds of districts, residential, business, and unrestricted. Each of these districts is subclassified in respect of the kind of buildings which may be erected. The ordinance is an elaborate one, and of the same general character as that considered by this court in Euclid v. Ambler Co. In its general scope it is conceded to be constitutional within that decision. The land of plaintiff in error was put in district R-3, in which are permitted only dwellings, hotels, clubs, churches, schools, philanthropic institutions, greenhouses and gardening, with customary incidental accessories. The attack upon the ordinance is that, as specifically applied to plaintiff in

error, it deprived him of his property without due process of law in
contravention of the Fourteenth Amendment.

argues

The suit was for a mandatory injunction directing the city and its
inspector of buildings to pass upon an application of the plaintiff in error
for a permit to erect any lawful buildings upon a tract of land without
regard to the provisions of the ordinance including such tract within a
residential district. The case was referred to a master to make and report
findings of fact. After a view of the premises and the surrounding territory,
and a hearing, the master made and reported his findings. The case came
on to be heard by a justice of the court, who, after confirming the master's
report, reported the case for the determination of the full court. Upon
consideration, that court sustained the ordinance as applied to plaintiff in
error, and dismissed the bill.

A condensed statement of facts, taken from the master's report, is all
that is necessary. When the zoning ordinance was enacted, plaintiff in error
was and still is the owner of a tract of land containing 140,000 square feet,
of which the locus here in question is a part. The locus contains about
29,000 square feet, with a frontage on Brookline street, lying west, of
304.75 feet, on Henry street, lying north, of 100 feet, on the other land of
the plaintiff in error, lying east, of 264 feet, and on land of the Ford Motor
Company, lying southerly, of 75 feet. The territory lying east and south is
unrestricted. The lands beyond Henry street to the north and beyond
Brookline street to the west are within a restricted residential district. The
effect of the zoning is to separate from the west end of plaintiff in error's
tract a strip 100 feet in width. The Ford Motor Company has a large auto
assembling factory south of the locus; and a soap factory and the tracks of
the Boston & Albany Railroad lie near. Opposite the locus, on Brookline
street, and included in the same district, there are some residences; and
opposite the locus, on Henry street, and in the same district, are other
residences. The locus is now vacant, although it was once occupied by a
mansion house. Before the passage of the ordinance in question, plaintiff
in error had outstanding a contract for the sale of the greater part of his
entire tract of land for the sum of $63,000. Because of the zoning
restrictions, the purchaser refused to comply with the contract. Under the
ordinance, business and industry of all sorts are excluded from the locus,
while the remainder of the tract is unrestricted. It further appears that
provision has been made for widening Brookline street, the effect of which,
if carried out, will be to reduce the depth of the locus to 65 feet.

* * *

It is made pretty clear that because of the industrial and railroad
purposes to which the immediately adjoining lands to the south and east
have been devoted and for which they are zoned, the locus is of
comparatively little value for the limited uses permitted by the ordinance.

PLATE 15

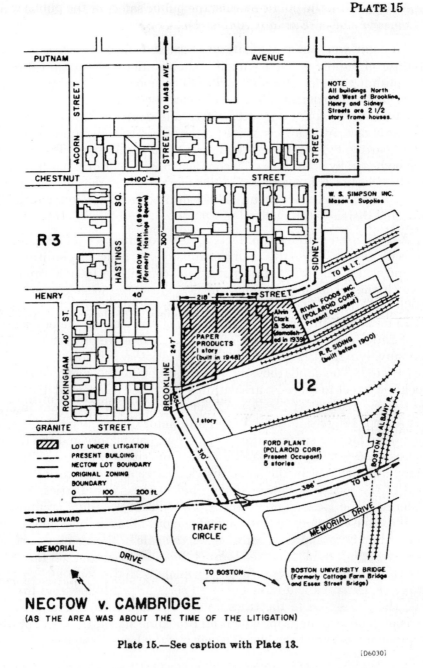

NECTOW v. CAMBRIDGE
(AS THE AREA WAS ABOUT THE TIME OF THE LITIGATION)

Plate 15.—See caption with Plate 13.

[D6030]

We quite agree with the opinion expressed below that a court should not set aside the determination of public officers in such a matter unless it is clear that their action "has no foundation in reason and is a mere arbitrary or irrational exercise of power having no substantial relation to the public health, the public morals, the public safety or the public welfare in its proper sense." *Euclid v. Ambler Co.*, 47 S.Ct. 114.

An inspection of a plat of the city upon which the zoning districts are outlined, taken in connection with the master's findings, shows with reasonable certainty that the inclusion of the locus in question is not indispensable to the general plan. The boundary line of the residential district before reaching the locus runs for some distance along the streets, and to exclude the locus from the residential district requires only that such line shall be continued 100 feet further along Henry street and thence south along Brookline street. There does not appear to be any reason why this should not be done. Nevertheless, if that were all, we should not be warranted in substituting our judgment for that of the zoning authorities primarily charged with the duty and responsibility of determining the question. *Zahn v. Board of Public Works*, 274 U.S. 325, 328, 47 S.Ct. 594, 71 L. Ed. 1074, and cases cited. But that is not all. The governmental power to interfere by zoning regulations with the general rights of the land owner by restricting the character of his use, is not unlimited, and, other questions aside, such restriction cannot be imposed if it does not bear a substantial relation to the public health, safety, morals, or general welfare. *Euclid v. Ambler Co., supra*, p. 69 (47 S.Ct. 114). Here, the express finding of the master * * * , is that the health, safety, convenience, and general welfare of the inhabitants of the part of the city affected will not be promoted by the disposition made by the ordinance of the locus in question. This finding of the master, after a hearing and an inspection of the entire area affected, supported, as we think it is, by other findings of fact, is determinative of the case. That the invasion of the property of plaintiff in error was serious and highly injurious is clearly established; and, since a necessary basis for the support of that invasion is wanting, the action of the zoning authorities comes within the ban of the Fourteenth Amendment and cannot be sustained.

Judgment reversed.

NOTES

1.   Examine the uses permitted on appellee's land in *Euclid* in each of the three use districts in which it is classified. How similar are these to adjacent uses? To other nearby uses? Under the *Nectow* decision, which of these, if any, could be construed to be unconstitutional classifications as applied?

2.   Note that the Supreme Court decided both *Euclid* and *Nectow* under 5th and 14th amendment substantive due process analysis rather than the takings analysis of Justice Holmes in *Pennsylvania Coal*. As we will see in Chapter 3, this treatment subsequently resulted in the rejection of substantive due process claims from all takings litigation. *See Lingle v. Chevron, U.S.A., Inc., infra* Chapter 3.

3.   What is the *Euclid* Court's purpose in bringing the law of nuisance into its analysis? Nuisance law has been widely interpreted as the foundation of zoning. Do you agree?

4.   Note that appellee attacks the Village of Euclid's zoning ordinance in its "entirety." What does this mean? Would the 75% diminution in value suffered by the appellee have mattered if it had been an as applied challenge? A few years before *Euclid*, the Court upheld a regulation prohibiting the manufacture of bricks in a developing residential area when the diminution in value was 92.5%! *See Hadacheck v. Sebastian*, 239 U.S. 394 (1915). We will examine the significance of the degree of loss of value in more detail in Chapter 3.

5.   The *Euclid* case was decided in favor of zoning upon rehearing. The Court reportedly was prepared to hold zoning unconstitutional, but was persuaded upon rehearing to change its mind. Much has been written on the history of the case and much continues to be. *See, e.g., Symposium on the Seventy-Fifth Anniversary of* Village of Euclid v. Ambler Realty Co.*, 51 CASE W.RES.L.REV. 593–719 (2001); Garrett Power, *Advocates at Cross-Purposes: The Briefs of Zoning in the Supreme Court*, 1997 J.SUP.CT.HIST., Vol. II at 79; Michael Allan Wolf, *"Compelled by Conscientious Duty:"* Village of Euclid v. Ambler Realty Co. *As Romance*, 1997 J.SUP.CT.HIST., Vol. II at 88 and David L. Callies, Village of Euclid v. Ambler Realty Co. *in Property Stories* (G. Korngold and A. P. Morriss, eds. 2004). Does it surprise you that the Court in 1926, the days of *Lochnerian* analysis, found zoning valid? Note the plea of the landowner in *Euclid* that if left alone "in the obvious course of things [industrial development] will soon absorb the entire area."

6.   Both *Euclid* and *Nectow* are rightly concerned with the character not only of the subject property, but with the surrounding area as well. Is the City of Cambridge really unreasonable to include the subject parcel in a residential zone? On balance, would the parcel more appropriately fit in a commercial zone? Note the test for reversal which the Court imposes on itself. Is the Court then justified in interfering? After all, lines must be drawn somewhere.

7.   What plans did the Village of Euclid and the City of Cambridge have? How much attention did the Court pay to the towns' plans?

8.   After holding zoning facially or generally constitutional on the one hand (*Euclid*), but susceptible of being unconstitutionally applied on the other (*Nectow*), the Supreme Court abandoned the area of land use controls for half-a-century. This left to the state courts the task of sorting out what aspects of zoning, subdivision and other public land use controls were legal, when, and why. Unfortunately, when the Supreme Court decided to jump back into the land use control forum in the 1970s, it virtually ignored the common law of zoning that had evolved in these state courts in many areas.

9.   Did the *Euclid* Court majority principally rely on the law of nuisance to be the constitutional foundation of zoning? Nuisance law has not subsequently been interpreted by the courts as the principle foundation of zoning. Despite the insistence of the early proponents of zoning that its

purposes centered on planning and health/safety issues, *see, e.g.,* Bettman, *Constitutionality of Zoning*, 37 HARV.L.R. 834 (1923–1924), it is difficult to read *Euclid* and other contemporary state court opinions without concluding that the primary purpose of zoning was neither nuisance nor planning, but was to preserve single-family residential neighborhoods from the incursion not only of commercial and industrial uses but also apartment uses. *See* Martha A. Lees, *Preserving Property Values? Preserving Proper Homes? Preserving Privilege? The Pre-*Euclid *Debate Over Zoning for Exclusively Private Residential Areas,* 1916–1926, 56 U.PITT.L.REV. 367 (1994). There is of course the parasite language of the *Euclid* court inveighing directly against such uses and their effect on light and air and increased traffic. But for sheer rhetoric of social engineering and property rights protectionism, it is hard to beat the language of the California Supreme Court in *Miller v. Board of Public Works,* 234 P. 381 (Cal.1925), which the Supreme Court cites in its *Euclid* opinion. While the California court in *Miller* labors mightily to disclaim bias ("We do not wish to unduly emphasize the single family residence as a means of perpetuating the home life of a people." 234 P. at 387), it nevertheless says:

> In addition to all that has been said in support of the constitutionality of residential zoning as part of a comprehensive plan, we think it may be safely and sensibly said that justification for residential zoning may, in the last analysis, be rested upon the protection of the civic and social values of the American home. The establishment of such districts is for the general welfare because it tends to promote and perpetuate the American home. It is axiomatic that the welfare, and indeed the very existence, of a nation depends upon the character and caliber of its citizenry. The character and quality of manhood and womanhood are in a large measure the result of home environment. The home and its intrinsic influences are the very foundation of good citizenship and any factor contributing to the establishment of homes and the fostering of home life doubtless tends to the enhancement, not only of community life, but of the life of the nation as a whole.

> The establishment of single family residence districts offers inducements, not only to the wealthy, but to those of moderate means to own their own homes. With ownership comes stability, the welding together of family ties, and better attention to the rearing of children. With ownership comes increased interest in the promotion of public agencies, such as church and school, which have for their purpose a desired development of the moral and mental make-up of the citizenry of the country. With ownership of one's home comes recognition of the individual's responsibility for his share in the safeguarding of the welfare of the community and increased pride in personal achievement which must come from personal participation in projects looking toward community betterment.

234 P. at 386–387. *See also* Nadav Shoked, *The Reinvention of Ownership: The Embrace of Residential Zoning and the Modern Populist Reading of Property,* 28 YALE J. ON REG. 91, 92 (2011) (With zoning, "[t]he entitlements associated

with a property right in land became mostly concerned with assuring the homeowner's security—protecting her from intrusions and changes in the residential environment.")

10. Is the anti multi-family housing view of *Euclid* and *Miller* out-of-date? Proposed multi-family housing projects still provoke objection from single-family uses nearby. Is the objection an aesthetic one, based on the physical structure? Or is the objection to "the kind of people" likely to occupy the units?

2.   INTERGOVERNMENTAL CONFLICTS

Isolationism and Regionalism: The effectiveness of a local zoning ordinance is undercut by the inability of a city to isolate itself from regional needs and to act free from concern as to what other governmental units with overlapping jurisdiction might do. By and large, it is a good thing to subordinate local government needs to regional and state needs. As we point out in the introduction to this chapter, serious problems arise from municipal parochialism. The *Euclid* Court also makes the very important observation that a city does not operate in a vacuum, pointing out that regional considerations might affect what a city is able to do regarding land within its own borders.

Localism is a powerful force. Many communities resist any hint that prisons, waste disposal sites, homeless shelters, half-way homes for violent offenders, electric substations, or airports might be located nearby. No small town will welcome these LULUs (locally undesirable land uses) as they are known. Yet, it is obvious that we need these types of facilities. To prevent local governments from interfering with regional needs, state agencies and other local governmental units that administer these facilities need, in many cases, to be exempt from local zoning.

At the same time, the immunity from zoning conferred on other governmental units may wreak havoc with legitimate local planning. Is partial preemption the answer? Might a city or county be obligated to accept a state prison yet be able to regulate the location and site plan requirements or to exclude it from residential zones? Where one entity preempts the other, there should be a mandate for cooperation and coordination. Note the following judicial approach for resolving conflicts between adjacent municipalities each exercising zoning and planning controls. *Borough of Cresskill v. Borough of Dumont*, 104 A.2d 441 (N.J.1954):

> [S]ignificant disputes arise when one municipality's land use policies pose a threat to an adjacent municipality. For many decades, land use law in New Jersey, in cases and statutes, has recognized that each municipality must, in framing its land use plans and ordinances, give consideration to impact on the surrounding area.

The appellant spells out from the language of these constitutional and statutory provisions that the responsibility of a municipality for zoning halts at the municipal boundary lines without regard to the effect of its zoning ordinances on adjoining and nearby land outside the municipality. . . . At the very least Dumont owes a duty to hear any residents and taxpayers of adjoining municipalities who may be adversely affected by proposed zoning changes and to give as much consideration to their rights as they would to those of residents and taxpayers of Dumont. To do less would be to make a fetish out of invisible municipal boundary lines and a mockery of the principles of zoning. There is no merit to the defendant's contention.

The views set forth in *Duffcon Concrete Products, Inc. v. Borough of Cresskill*, 1 N.J. 509, 513, 64 A.2d 347 (1949) apply here with equal force.

What may be the most appropriate use of any particular property depends not only on all the conditions, physical, economic and social, prevailing within the municipality and its needs, present and reasonably prospective, but also on the nature of the entire region in which the municipality is located and the use to which the land in that region has been or may be put most advantageously. The effective development of a region should not and cannot be made to depend upon the adventitious location of municipal boundaries, often prescribed decades or even centuries ago, and based in many instances on considerations of geography, of commerce, or of politics that are no longer significant with respect to zoning. The direction of growth of residential areas on the one hand and of industrial concentration on the other refuses to be governed by such artificial lines. Changes in methods of transportation as well as in living conditions have served only to accentuate the unreality in dealing with zoning problems on the basis of the territorial limits of a municipality, improved highways and new transportation facilities have made possible the concentration of industry at places best suited to its development to a degree not contemplated in the earlier stages of zoning. The same forces make practicable the presently existing and currently developing suburban and rural sections given over solely to residential purposes and local retail business services coextensive with the needs of the community. The resulting advantages enure alike to industry and residential properties and, at the same time, advance the general welfare of the entire region.

Ultimately these pathfinding New Jersey decisions on regional impact have led to the emerging doctrine of regional general welfare across the nation for ensuring that each municipality accept its fair share of affordable housing within the region, evaluate and mitigate regional environmental impacts from development, and accommodate regional mixed use high density walkable growth centers. *See Britton v. Town of Chester*, 595 A.2d 492 (N.H.1991); *John Boothroyd v. Zoning Bd. of Appeals of Amherst*, 868 N.E.2d 83 (Mass.2007); *Southern Burlington County N.A.A.C.P. v. Twp. of Mount Laurel*, 456 A.2d 390 (N.J.1983) (fair share of regional affordable housing); *City of Del Mar v. City of San Diego*, 133 Cal.App.3d 401 (1982) (regional mixed use high density new town); and *S.A.V.E. v. City of Bothell*, 576 P.2d 401 (Wash.1978) (regional environmental impacts). *See also* Shelley Ross Saxer, *Local Autonomy or Regionalism?: Sharing the Benefits and Burdens of Suburban Commercial Development*, 30 IND.L.REV. 659 (1997).

Conflicts also arise between two governmental units, only one of which has zoning authority. To name but a few, the actions of state departments of transportation, correction, public utilities, public schools, airports, and sewage or waste control boards may be at odds with the local zoning code. When there is conflict, which prevails?

Charter Twp. of Northville v. Northville Public Schools, 666 N.W.2d 213, 218 (2003), illustrates the problem. Before beginning construction of a new high school, the school board met with township officials to discuss the effect the zoning code would have on its plans. The meeting did not go well. The school board did not want to do what the planning officials said would be required so it proceeded to build in violation of the code. The township sought an injunction.

Mich.Comp. Laws § 380.1263(3) provided:

> * * * The superintendent of public instruction has sole and exclusive jurisdiction over the review and approval of plans and specifications for the construction, reconstruction, or remodeling of school buildings used for instructional or noninstructional school purposes and of site plans for those school buildings.

The court found the school board exempt from the zoning code. The statute was unambiguous, said the court. The superintendent had the "sole and exclusive jurisdiction" over construction and site plans of schools. This may make sense as a matter of statutory construction, but is it good policy? Note that the record showed that the superintendent's office had no standards for site design and, in fact, did not review site plans for land-use matters.

How far did the immunity extend? Did it apply to construction only? What does the term "site plan" mean? A concurring justice said "there is no reason to presume the state superintendent's review power over local school districts is necessarily limited to activities contained within the site itself." 666 N.W.2d at 221. "No reason?" Do you suppose this was what the legislature intended?

The dissenting justice who read the statute narrowly posed some difficult questions. He asked whether sewage and drainage pipes that extend beyond the "site itself" and into the surrounding community affect the site plan. [Do roads and paths, environmental regulations, and] noise regulations that have a general effect on the community 'affect' the site plan? 666 N.W.2d at 229–230. Is there a way to give a school board freedom in site planning while still accommodating important planning interests and infrastructure needs of the community? *See, e.g.,* Chad D. Emerson, *Smart Growth and Schools: Legal Hurdles and Legal Solutions for Community-Scale Schools*, 37 MCGEORGE L.REV. 363 (2006).

The potential conflicts with other governmental units whose actions within a city or ownership of land within a city are many. State legislatures ought to, and sometimes do, anticipate the problem. In North Carolina, for example, a statute provides that "[a]ll of the provisions of the code relating to [zoning by cities] are hereby made applicable to the erection, construction, and use of buildings and land by the State of North Carolina and its political subdivisions." N.C. Gen.Stat. § 160A–392. Kentucky goes the other way: "Nothing in this [zoning] chapter shall impair the sovereignty of the Commonwealth of Kentucky over its political subdivisions. Any proposal affecting land use by any department, commission, board, authority, agency, or instrumentality of state government shall not require approval of the local planning unit." Ky.Rev.Stat.Ann. § 100.361(2) (West), applied in *Hopkinsville-Christian County Planning Comm'n v. Christian County Bd. of Educ.*, 903 S.W.2d 531 (Ky.App.1995) (statute conferred immunity on school board). All too often, however, state legislatures fail to provide for resolution of potential conflicts, leaving it to the courts to sort it out. Yet, this task of divining state legislative intent has been difficult and the tests employed have yielded unpredictable results.

Judicial Approaches to Immunity: Courts have used several tests to decide when immunity attaches, yet none has proven satisfactory. While acknowledging the task is to determine legislative intent, the tests many courts have used are ill-suited for this purpose. Early tests used include the superior sovereign test and the eminent domain test. While easy to apply, these mechanical tests have long since been rejected by the courts for failing to take into account the purposes of the delegated zoning power. *See City of Ames v. Story County*, 392 N.W.2d 145 (Iowa 1986).

The test used most often in zoning's early years was the governmental-proprietary distinction drawn from tort law. The test's source indicates one difficulty in its application. A governmental activity for purposes of determining municipal tort liability ought not necessarily be considered a governmental activity for purposes of determining immunity from zoning regulations. Courts, however, are not always careful to avoid mixing precedent. Moreover, no unanimity exists as to what is a governmental function even in the zoning context. *See, e.g., City of Scottsdale v. Municipal Court of City of Tempe*, 90 Ariz. 393, 368 P.2d 637 (1962) (sewage plant held to be a governmental function, thus immune) and *Jefferson County v. Birmingham*, 256 Ala. 436, 55 So.2d 196 (1951) (sewage plant held to be a proprietary function, so that the city's residential zoning bound the county).

A balancing of interests test is used by a number of courts today. The test balances the nature and scope of the instrumentality seeking immunity, the kind of function involved and the public interest it serves, and the effect local land use regulation would have upon the enterprise concerned and the impact upon legitimate local interests. *See Native Village of Eklutna v. Alaska R.R. Corp.*, 87 P.3d 41 (Alaska 2004). This approach, too, has been strongly criticized. Not only does the test put the court in the position of making value judgments typically within the province of the legislature, it has shown itself to be highly unpredictable in result. *Macon Ass'n for Retarded Citizens v. Macon-Bibb County Planning & Zoning Comm'n*, 314 S.E.2d 218, 223 (Ga.1984) ("We reject the balancing-of-interests test, because it * * * is too nebulous and judicially unmanageable."). *See also* Laurie Reynolds, *The Judicial Role in Intergovernmental Land Use Disputes: The Case Against Balancing*, 71 MINN.L.REV. 611 (1987).

A better approach is to avoid obfuscating the question of intent with the mechanical and unworkable tests noted above. The answer to intent will most often not be obvious and not be highly predictable, but courts have rules of statutory construction that they are accustomed to applying and which can be used in this context as well as in any other. A number of courts do this by beginning with a presumption that an exemption is unwarranted unless there is a clear expression of intent by the legislature. *See Macon Ass'n for Retarded Citizens v. Macon-Bibb County Planning & Zoning Comm'n*, 314 S.E.2d 218, 223 (Ga.1984) ("We find the better rule to be that property owned by a nonprofit corporation is not immune from local zoning regulations, even if the corporation is performing services which are governmental in nature, at least in the absence of a clear expression of intent by the legislature that such immunity be extended."). *See also Byrne v. State*, 624 N.W.2d 906 (Mich.2001); *City of Malibu v. Santa Monica Mountains Conservancy*, 119 Cal.Rptr.2d 777 (Cal.App.2002); *City of Everett v. Snohomish County*, 772 P.2d 992 (Wash.App.1989); *Kee v. Pennsylvania Turnpike Comm'n*, 722 A.2d 1123 (Pa.Cmwlth.1998).

Professor Reynolds, stressing the importance of intergovernmental cooperation, suggests a rule that requires the intruding governmental unit to participate in good faith in all relevant local proceedings. *See* Reynolds, *supra. See also* Gary D. Taylor and Mark A. Wyckoff, *Intergovernmental Zoning Conflicts Over Public Facilities Siting: A Model Framework for Standard State Acts*, URB.LAW. 653 (2009).

Conflict with Federal Law: Federal law is, of course, supreme, *New York SMSA Ltd. P'ship v. Town of Clarkstown*, 612 F.3d 97 (2d Cir.2010), but where there is a conflict the question of whether Congress intended to preempt local law must still be confronted. Congress may express its intent. An important example in the land use area is the Telecommunications Act of 1996, 47 U.S.C. § 332, which partially preempts local control over cellular towers. See discussion *infra* Ch. 2.B for more detail. However, in many cases, as with local v. state conflicts, federal v. state or local conflicts often call upon the courts to determine whether preemption should be implied.

Where Congress recognizes the need for a cooperative effort with local authorities, it may direct federal agencies to consult with local authorities. Federal urban land use policy, for example, requires that agencies cooperate with local authorities by directing that actions taken "shall be consistent with zoning and land use practices and with the planning and development objectives of local governments and planning agencies." Intergovernmental Cooperation Act, 40 U.S.C.A. § 901.

Fed must comply w/ state

The statute was applied in *Smith v. County of Santa Barbara*, 251 Cal.Rptr. 1 (Cal.App.1988). A developer built an office building based on his agreement with the United States Forest Service that the Service would lease the building once completed. The developer unsuccessfully sought an exemption from local zoning and building codes based on federal preemption. After construction, the Forest Service leased the building. The developer then brought suit seeking a refund for building fees he had paid and damages from the regulatory interference by the county during the construction process. The court held that federal law did not preempt local law for several reasons. While the Forest Service imposed building specifications on the developer, it denied that building project was itself a federal project and it had required the developer to comply with local law in their agreement. Finally, the actions by the Forest Service complied with the congressional desire set out above in 40 U.S.C.A. § 901 for federal agencies to cooperate with local government.

3. AUTHORITY TO ZONE

Herbert Hoover as Secretary of Commerce under the Harding administration, with the United States Department of Commerce issued the Standard State Zoning Enabling Act (SZEA) in draft form in 1922, giving zoning a boost during the turbulent period preceding *Euclid*. By the time the final version of the SZEA was released in 1926, 43 states had enacted it. By the early 1920s, over 22 million people lived in some 200 zoned municipalities—40 percent of the urban population of the United States. Alfred Bettman, *Constitutionality of Zoning*, 37 HARV.L.REV. 834, 834–35 (1924).

A STANDARD STATE ZONING ENABLING ACT UNDER WHICH MUNICIPALITIES MAY ADOPT ZONING REGULATIONS

(Recommended by the U.S. Department of Commerce, 1926).

Section 1.   Grant of Power.—For the purpose of promoting health, safety, morals, or the general welfare of the community, the legislative body of cities and incorporated villages is hereby empowered to regulate and restrict the height, number of stories, and size of buildings and other structures, the percentage of lot that may be occupied, the size of yards, courts, and other open spaces, the density of population, and the location and use of buildings, structures, and land for trade, industry, residence or other purposes.

Sec. 2.   Districts.—For any or all of said purposes the local legislative body may divide the municipality into districts of such number, shape, and area as may be deemed best suited to carry out the purposes of this act; and within such districts it may regulate and restrict the erection, construction, reconstruction, alteration, repair, or use of buildings, structures, or land. All such regulations shall be uniform for each class or kind of buildings throughout each district, but the regulations in one district may differ from those in other districts.

Sec. 3.   Purposes in View.—Such regulations shall be made in accordance with a comprehensive plan and designed to lessen congestion in the streets; to secure safety from fire, panic, and other dangers; to promote health and the general welfare; to provide adequate light and air; to prevent the overcrowding of land; to avoid undue concentration of population; to facilitate the adequate provision of transportation, water, sewerage, schools, parks, and other public requirements. Such regulations shall be made with reasonable consideration, among other things, to the character of the district and its peculiar suitability for particular uses, and with a view to conserving the value of buildings and encouraging the most appropriate use of land throughout such municipality.

Sec. 4.   Method of Procedure.—The legislative body of such municipality shall provide for the manner in which such regulations and restrictions and the boundaries of such districts shall be determined, established, and enforced, and from time to time amended, supplemented, or changed. However, no such regulation, restriction, or boundary shall become effective until after a public hearing in relation thereto, at which parties in interest and citizens shall have an opportunity to be heard. At least 15 days' notice of the time and place of such hearing shall be published in an official paper, or a paper of general circulation, in such municipality.

Sec. 5.   Changes.—Such regulations, restrictions, and boundaries may from time to time be amended, supplemented, changed, modified, or repealed. In case, however, of a protest against such change, signed by the owners of 20 per cent or more either of the area of the lots included in such proposed change, or of those immediately adjacent in the rear thereof extending _____ feet therefrom, or of those directly opposite thereto extending _____ feet from the street frontage of such opposite lots, such amendment shall not become effective except by the favorable vote of three-fourths of all the members of the legislative body of such municipality. The provisions of the previous section relative to public hearings and official notice shall apply equally to all changes or amendments.

Sec. 6. Zoning Commission.—In order to avail itself of the powers conferred by this act, such legislative body shall appoint a commission, to be known as the zoning commission, to recommend the boundaries of the various original districts and appropriate regulations to be enforced therein. Such commission shall make a preliminary report and hold public hearings thereon before submitting its final report, and such legislative body shall not hold its public hearings or take action, until it has received the final report of such commission. Where a city plan commission already exists, it may be appointed as the zoning commission.

Sec. 7. Board of Adjustment.—Such local legislative body may provide for the appointment of a board of adjustment, and in the regulations and restrictions adopted pursuant to the authority of this act may provide that the said board of adjustment may, in appropriate cases and subject to appropriate conditions and safeguards, make special exceptions to the terms of the ordinance in harmony with its general purpose and intent and in accordance with general or specific rules therein contained.

The board of adjustment shall consist of five members, each to be appointed for a term of three years and removable for cause by the appointing authority upon written charges and after public hearing. Vacancies shall be filled for the unexpired term of any member whose term becomes vacant.

The board shall adopt rules in accordance with the provisions of any ordinance adopted pursuant to this act. Meetings of the board shall be held at the call of the chairman and at such other times as the board may determine. Such chairman, or in his absence the acting chairman, may administer oaths and compel the attendance of witnesses. All meetings of the board shall be open to the public. The board shall keep minutes of its proceedings, showing the vote of each member upon each question, or, if absent or failing to vote, indicating such fact, and shall keep records of its examinations and other official actions, all of which shall be immediately filed in the office of the board and shall be a public record.

Appeals to the board of adjustment may be taken by any person aggrieved or by any officer, department, board, or bureau of the municipality affected by any decision of the administrative officer. Such appeal shall be taken within a reasonable time, as provided by the rules of the board, by filing with the officer from whom the appeal is taken and with the board of adjustment a notice of appeal specifying the grounds thereof. The officer from whom the appeal is taken shall forthwith transmit to the board all the papers constituting the record upon which the action appealed from was taken.

An appeal stays all proceedings in furtherance of the action appealed from, unless the officer from whom the appeal is taken certifies to the board of adjustment after the notice of appeal shall have been filed with him that by reason of facts stated in the certificate a stay would, in his opinion, cause imminent peril to life or property. In such case proceedings shall not be stayed otherwise than by a restraining order which may be granted by the board of adjustment or by a court of record on application on notice to the officer from whom the appeal is taken and on due cause shown.

The board of adjustment shall fix a reasonable time for the hearing of the appeal, give public notice thereof, as well as due notice to the parties in interest, and decide the same within a reasonable time. Upon the hearing any party may appear in person or by agent or by attorney.

The board of adjustment shall have the following powers:

1.   To hear and decide appeals where it is alleged there is error in any order, requirement, decision, or determination made by an administrative official in the enforcement of this act or of any ordinance adopted pursuant thereto.

2.   To hear and decide special exceptions to the terms of the ordinance upon which such board is required to pass under such ordinance.

3.   To authorize upon appeal in specific cases such variance from the terms of the ordinance as will not be contrary to the public interest, where, owing to special conditions, a literal enforcement of the provisions of the ordinance will result in unnecessary hardship, and so that the spirit of the ordinance shall be observed and substantial justice done.

In exercising the above-mentioned powers such board may, in conformity with the provisions of this act, reverse or affirm, wholly or partly, or may modify the order, requirement, decision, or determination appealed from and may make such order, requirement, decision, or determination as ought to be made, and to that end shall have all the powers of the officer from whom the appeal is taken.

The concurring vote of four members of the board shall be necessary to reverse any order, requirement, decision, or determination of any such administrative official, or to decide in favor of the applicant on any matter upon which it is required to pass under any such ordinance, or to effect any variation in such ordinance.

Any person or persons, jointly or severally, aggrieved by any decision of the board of adjustment, or any taxpayer, or any officer, department, board, or bureau of the municipality, may present to a court of record a petition, duly verified, setting forth that such decision is illegal, in whole or in part, specifying the grounds of the illegality. Such petition shall be presented to the court within 30 days after the filing of the decision in the office of the board.

* * *

Sec. 8. Enforcement and Remedies.—The local legislative body may provide by ordinance for the enforcement of this act and of any ordinance or regulation made thereunder. A violation of this act or of such ordinance or regulation is hereby declared to be a misdemeanor, and such local legislative body may provide for the punishment thereof by fine or imprisonment or both. It is also empowered to provide civil penalties for such violation.

In case any building or structure is erected, constructed, reconstructed, altered, repaired, converted, or maintained, or any building, structure, or land is used in violation of this act or of any ordinance or other regulation made under authority conferred hereby, the proper local authorities of the municipality, in addition to other remedies, may institute any appropriate action or proceedings to prevent such unlawful erection, construction, reconstruction, alteration, repair, conversion, maintenance, or use, to restrain, correct, or abate such violation, to prevent the occupancy of said building, structure, or land, or to prevent any illegal act, conduct, business, or use in or about such premises.

* * *

NOTES

1.   The Standard State Zoning Enabling Act ("SZEA") and Standard City Planning Enabling Act ("SPEA"), both products of the 1920s, are outdated. While zoning and planning were created in part because of the unpredictability of nuisance law, many regard planning and zoning as they have developed under the standard acts as suffering the same defect. In addition to changes by individual states, such as the California act referred to in Chapter 1 D 3, there have been national efforts to modernize the enabling acts. After a twelve year effort financed by the Ford Foundation, the American Law Institute released the Model Land Development Code (MLDC) in 1976. The MLDC integrates zoning and subdivision regulations and streamlines the development permission process. The primary focus of the MLDC, however, is development, not planning. The act received limited acceptance only in the state of Florida. *See* Juergensmeyer and Roberts, *Land Use Planning and Development Regulation Law* § 3.24 (3rd ed.2012).

2.   Home rule authority exists in a number of states. In California, for example, the state constitution grants police power authority directly to

counties and cities for matters of mixed local and state control. Cal.Const., art. XI, § 7. Municipalities and counties in California may choose to become a "charter city" instead of a "general law" city by a local vote. Charter cities are allowed under the home rule provisions in California's state constitution and give voters greater local control to determine how their city government is organized and, with respect to municipal affairs, enact legislation different than that adopted by the state. http://www.cacities.org/Resources/Charter-Cities. While this concept might seem mundane and unnecessary because in home rule states local governments have broad, but not unlimited, power to zone, the City of Bell took advantage of "charter city" self-governance by putting the Charter adoption on a special election ballot in 2005. *Id.* Only one percent of the municipal population voted to adopt the Charter and subsequently the city with a population of 40,000 people "was paying its city manager almost $800,000.00, its police chief, around $475,000.00, with most of its City Council pulling down about $100,000.00 each." http://www. frontporchrepublic.com/2010/08/the-city-of-bell-and-the-problem-of-local-control/. This "corruption scandal [ ] resulted in multiple convictions over excessive salaries paid to officials and a 12-year sentence [ ] for a former city administrator." http://www.abajournal.com/news/article/city_of_bell_sues_its_former_bond_counsel_says_law_firm_didnt_sound_alarm/.   Following   the scandal, the City of Bell retained its Charter status, but in 2015 the voters amended the Charter to subject itself to compensation and reimbursement regulations set at the State level for "general law" cities and amended other provisions to protect against corruption. http://www.cityofbell.org/home/showdocument?id=7537 (see 2015 amendments beginning with Section 502).

Home rule authority is granted by statute in some states. Where home rule authority exists, local ordinances cannot conflict with state law. For example, the Colorado Supreme Court rejected, as a home rule measure, an affordable housing mitigation ordinance that addressed a matter of mixed local and statewide concern. *See Town of Telluride v. Lot Thirty-Four Venture, L.L.C.*, 3 P.3d 30 (Colo.2000). In some states, home rule authority does not confer zoning power. *See* Juergensmeyer and Roberts, *Land Use Planning and Development Regulation Law*, § 3.9 (3rd ed.2012).

3.   As noted in Chapter 1, the "Growing Smart" Project of the American Planning Association aims to modernize the standard planning and zoning enabling acts of the 1920s. See Ch. 1.D.2, note 3.

4.   In 2008, a joint task force of the State and Local Government and Administrative Law and Regulatory Practice Sections of the American Bar Association has issued a "Model Statute on Local Land Use Process." www.americanbar.org/content/dam/aba/migrated/2011_build/administrative_law/hod_final_resolution.authcheckdam.pdf.

B. TRADITIONAL ZONING: USES, FLEXIBILITY, AND DESIGN

1. PURPOSES OF ZONING

Early on, promoters pressed zoning as necessary for health and safety. Recall the *Euclid* Court repeatedly referred to dangers from traffic, fire, contagion, safety and security as justifications for zoning. Then, there is also the Court's health-related parasite reference to apartments. Health and safety, of course, made zoning an easier sell to the Court as zoning got its start. There was little doubt though that the preservation of property values loomed high on the purposes list of zoning reformers. Indeed as we point out in Note 8 following *Euclid*, the California Supreme Court a year before *Euclid* enthusiastically described zoning in terms of social engineering and property rights protectionism.

Section 1 of the SZEA broadly grants municipalities the power to zone "for the purpose of promoting health, safety, morals, or the general welfare of the community." While this grant on its face might be viewed as a delegation of the state's full police power to local government, courts generally do not read it that way. Section 1's grant necessarily limits zoning to police power goals, or in the words of the New York Court of Appeals, it provides the "constitutional predicate" for zoning. *Golden v. Planning Bd. of Town of Ramapo*, 285 N.E.2d 291, 334 N.Y.S.2d 138, 145 (1972), appeal dismissed 409 U.S. 1003 (1972). Section 3 enumerates the "purposes in view." It provides:

> Such regulations shall be made in accordance with a comprehensive plan and designed to lessen congestion in the streets; to secure safety from fire, panic, and other dangers; to promote health and the general welfare; to provide adequate light and air; to prevent the overcrowding of land; to avoid undue concentration of population; to facilitate the adequate provision of transportation, water, sewerage, schools, parks, and other public requirements. Such regulations shall be made with reasonable consideration, among other things, to the character of the district and its peculiar suitability for particular uses, and with a view to conserving the value of buildings and encouraging the most appropriate use of land throughout such municipality.

Many states retain the SZEA's language. *See* N.Y. Town Law § 263. Those that do not list purposes similar to the SZEA. *See, e.g.,* N.M.Stat.Ann. § 3–21–1 (West). As needs change, zoning's purposes may change. In 2003 New York, for example, added that zoning may be used "to make provision for, so far as conditions may permit, the accommodation of solar energy systems and equipment and access to sunlight necessary therefor [and] to facilitate the practice of forestry; . . . " N.Y. Town Law § 263.

Most zoning code provisions fall easily within the express allowable purposes. Where they do not, courts may find the purpose implied. In 1969, the Town of Ramapo, New York enacted the nation's first comprehensive growth management plan, which tied development approval with the availability of public services and infrastructure. Though lacking a precise basis in the enabling act, the New York Court Appeals held the power to implement the plan necessarily implied from various provisions of Section 3. *Golden v. Planning Bd. of Town of Ramapo, supra.*

There are, of course, exceptions. After the Village of Hempstead, New York rezoned land from residential to light manufacturing, neighbors picketed city hall, held demonstrations and threatened an economic boycott. In the face of this opposition, the village rezoned the land for residential use. In *DeSena v. Gulde*, 265 N.Y.S.2d 239, 246 (App.Div.1965), the court held the rezoning invalid as an act "alien to the legitimate objects of zoning." Regulating competition has often been held as ultra vires. We will discuss this in more detail *infra*, Section C 2. Many successful ultra vires challenges involve procedure. *See Buckhorn Ventures, LLC v. Forsyth County*, 585 S.E.2d 229 (Ga.App.2003) (settlement agreement void as ultra vires because it forever bound future commissioners from changing zoning of property). An ordinance may be sustained under another source of power. *See, e.g., T.J.R. Holding Co., Inc. v. Alachua County*, 617 So.2d 798 (Fla.App.1993) (ordinance prohibiting nudity in bars held to be a general ordinance and not a zoning ordinance so county was not required to provide notice and hearing prior to adoption).

2.   USE DISTRICTS AND AREA REQUIREMENTS

The structure of a standard zoning ordinance has changed little since its inception. A zoning ordinance consists of two parts: text and map. On the map the various use districts are delineated, usually in three general categories: residential, commercial and industrial. We will discuss modern variations and additions later in the chapter. This division of the entire land area under the jurisdiction of the local government in accordance with some type of comprehensive plan is the essence of zoning and the major way of effecting land use changes via the amendment process discussed below. The text is then divided into essentially four parts: zoning district standards (usually grouped by district as in the principal cases), provisions for change (amendments, variances, and conditional uses), nonconformities, and definitions. *See* John Garner and David L. Callies, *Planning Law in England and Wales and in the United States*, 1 ANGLO-AMER.L.REV. 292, 304–315 (1973). Today, the zoning code is likely to be a part of a Unified Development Ordinance (UDO), which is a collection of all land use regulations within the jurisdiction, including subdivision regulations, environmental ordinances, and sign controls.

The process for creating a zoning ordinance *ab initio* is similarly stated in most state enabling statutes. So is the requirement of § 7 of the SZEA that, once a local government opts to exercise the zoning power, it must create an administrative process for dealing with special "hardship" cases justifying the varying of the zoning ordinance requirements in particular and unique cases. This power is critical to avoid constitutional challenges to the application of zoning ordinances in many cases. We will return to this "variance" situation later in this chapter. Many local governments derive substantial governmental authority not only from state municipal codes but also from home-rule provisions in state constitutions. David J. Barron, *Reclaiming Home Rule*, 116 HARV.L.REV. 2255 (2003).

Early zoning ordinances were relatively simple. They told a property owner what he might do with his property. Development was, in the language of zoning, "as of right." Over the years codes became increasingly complex and considerable discretion was vested in the permit granting authorities. Consider as you read the following materials on zoning and other land use controls whether we have moved from the right to use land subject to needful regulations for the health, safety and welfare of the people to a system of public land use management where the use of land, especially its "development," is a privilege available from the government only upon application and at its discretion. For an example of such a system, see the British Town and Country Planning Act 1990, at sections 55 and 57:

> In this Act, except where the context otherwise requires, "development," subject to the following provisions of this section, means the carrying out of building, engineering, mining or other operations in, on, over or under land, or the making of any material change in the use of any buildings or other land. * * * Subject to the provisions of this section, planning permission is required for the carrying out of any development of land.

http://www.legislation.gov.uk/ukpga/1990/8/contents.

On the British system, *see* Malcolm Grant, *Urban Planning Law* (1982); Desmond Heap, *An Outline of Planning Law* (11th ed.1996); Victor Moore, *A Practical Approach to Planning Law* (3d ed.1992); and J. Barry Cullingworth and Vincent Nadin, *Town and Country Planning in the UK* (14th ed.2006). *See also* Shelley Ross Saxer, *Planning Gain, Exactions, and Impact Fees: A Comparative Study of Planning Law in England, Wales, and the United States*, 32 URB.LAW. 21 (2000).

The most important parts of any zoning ordinance are the zoning map and the applicable zoning district regulations. Typically, a zoning ordinance text incorporates by reference a map of the municipality upon which the boundaries of the various districts described in the ordinance text are drawn. Rezonings by map amendment are common.

The map is usually required to be kept in the offices of the city clerk, planning department or some such office for the public. Some ordinances require that it be available for sale as well. The map may also be available in book form, with each page representing a small part of the city, with a grid key or guide at the front. Today, however, access is available online. Typical of this format is the zoning ordinance of the City of Chicago:

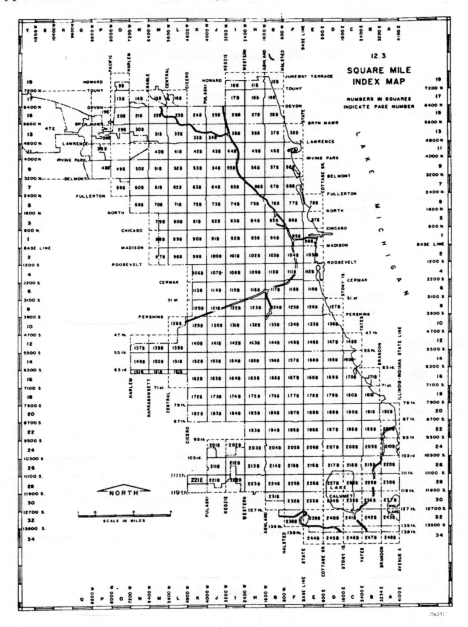

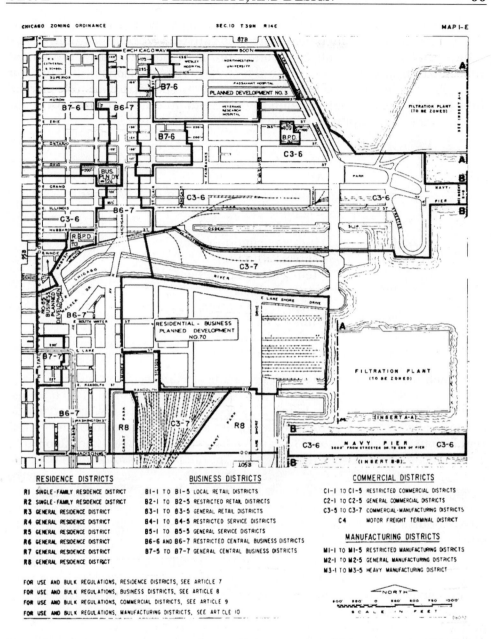

For the current map, go to https://gisapps.cityofchicago.org/zoning/view frame.htm.

The zoning district regulations are generally found toward the beginning of the text of a zoning ordinance. As the *Euclid* case demonstrates, the early ordinances were "cumulative" in nature: starting usually with the single family zone, each successive, more-intensely used zone would include as permitted uses all those listed in all the preceding zones, so that the heavy industrial zone—typically at the bottom of the zoning "pyramid," would permit just about anything. Many ordinances still reflect this early Euclidean format. In the modern zoning ordinance, classifications are more refined, and many districts are noncumulative. For example, residences are rarely permitted in industrial or commercial zones. Although it is not unusual to find 30 to 40 different districts in the text of a zoning ordinance, a basic list might look like this:

District	Permitted Uses
R-1	Single-family residence
R-2	All R-1 and duplex
R-3	Duplex and multiple-family dwellings
C-1	Neighborhood business
C-2	Central commercial
C-3	Highway commercial
I-1	Light manufacturing
I-2	Medium manufacturing
I-3	Heavy industry
O & R	Office and research
P	Public uses and universities
O	Parks and open space
A	Agriculture

Each district as described in the zoning ordinance text will contain a list of permitted uses, together with permitted accessory uses (garage, carport, home occupations), temporary uses (fruit stands, construction sheds), parking and loading requirements and limits, and so-called "bulk" regulations: height, side-front-rear yards, lot coverage, and floor/area ratios. Most also list special exceptions, special or conditional uses that are permitted in that district with administrative permission from the Board of Adjustment, which may include conditions applicable to such uses. For example, a convenience store or delicatessen in a residential zone might have conditions on hours of operation, off street parking, and special outdoor lighting standards.

When drawn on the zoning map, Euclidean zoning theory follows a use-intensity pattern. Low density residential uses do not abut industrial or intensive commercial development. In theory, the most intense of the "higher" uses abut the least intense of the "lower"[1] uses so as to form a buffer between the most intense of the lower and the least intense of the higher. Thus, for example, a zone permitting townhouses or apartment buildings might separate a single-family zone from a commercial zone.

---

[1]   Under Euclidean zoning, the "highest" use is not the equivalent of the common appraisal phrase, "the highest and best use of land." The former refers to the community's value of the use as determined by its elected officials in zoning land. The latter means the use that will confer the highest market value on the land. In fact, land zoned for single-family use (the "highest" use) generally will have a lower dollar value than it would have if zoned for more intensive "lower" uses (e.g., commercial or industrial).

Often a major arterial street or a natural feature such as a river or stream serves the same "buffering" purpose.

Increasingly, cities link their Geographic Information System (GIS) to their zoning code. Try to locate the corner of Henry St. and Brookline St. involved in the Nectow v. City of Cambridge case, *supra*. http:// www2.cambridgema.gov/cdd/cp/zng/zord/index.html#maps. *See generally* Rutherford H. Platt, *Land Use and Society: Geography, Law, and Public Policy* (Rev.ed.2004); J. Barry Cullingworth, *The Political Culture of Planning: American Land Use Planning in Comparative Perspective*, Ch. 3 (1993).

For city and county codes plus much more online, go to State and Local Government Law on the Net: http://www.statelocalgov.net/index.cfm. The Library of Congress also has links to state and local government law resources: http://www.loc.gov/rr/news/stategov/stategov.html.

Compatibility of uses in zoning districts has been a major issue since *Euclid*.

PIERRO V. BAXENDALE
Supreme Court of New Jersey, 1955.
20 N.J. 17, 118 A.2d 401.

JACOBS, J.

In 1939 Palisades Park adopted a zoning ordinance which divided the borough into residential, business and industrial districts. District AA was generally restricted to one-and two-family dwellings and District A to one-and two-family dwellings and apartment houses. Hotels and motels were not expressly permitted in Districts AA and A although "boarding and rooming houses" (and other limited uses not pertinent here) were expressly permitted. The ordinance defined a boarding house as "any dwelling in which more than six persons not related to the owner or occupant by blood or marriage are lodged and boarded for compensation"; it defined a rooming house as "any dwelling where furnished rooms are rented to more than six persons for compensation, provided however, the lodging of relatives, by blood or marriage, of the owner or occupant of such dwelling shall not come within these terms."

The plaintiffs are the owners of land located within residential District A. On May 19, 1954 they applied to the building inspector of the borough for a permit to erect a 27-unit motel on their land but the application was denied; no administrative appeal from the denial was taken by the plaintiffs nor did they ever seek a variance under N.J.S.A. 40:55–39. On May 25, 1954 the borough adopted a supplemental zoning ordinance which expressly prohibited the construction within Palisades Park of "motels, motor courts, motor lodges, motor hotels, tourist camps, tourist courts, and structures of a similar character intended for a similar use." On May 28,

1954 the plaintiffs filed a complaint in the Law Division seeking a judgment directing the issuance of a permit to them in accordance with their application to the building inspector and setting aside the supplemental ordinance.

* * *

[T]he parties in open court entered into a short stipulation on which the judgment ultimately entered must rest. The stipulation set forth that the Borough of Palisades Park is approximately a mile square and is located about a mile and a half south (west) of the George Washington Bridge; it is a residential community composed principally of one-family homes and "is zoned percentagewise as follows: 80 percent for residential purposes, 9 percent for business purposes, 3 percent for light industry, and 8 percent for heavy industry, which area lies solely west of the Northern Railroad tracks"; there are no motels in Palisades Park but there are motels in the Borough of Fort Lee (which lies immediately to the north(east) thereof) and in other nearby communities; the plaintiffs' property is located on Temple Terrace in a residential area "and on the same block, or immediately adjacent to the property, there is a two-family house with considerable shrub area immediately adjacent to it," and "on the opposite side of Temple Terrace there is a large ranch type house presently being built"; "both sides of (nearby) Sunset Place have been built up with one-family residences, many of them within the last 4 or 5 years"; and "another large ranch type home is being built on East Edsal Boulevard near the property in question." In answer to an interrogatory submitted by the plaintiffs, the Borough of Palisades Park stated that it had issued 19 tavern licenses and 12 licenses for the sale of alcoholic beverages for off-premises consumption; apparently all of these establishments are in the business district.

After considering the arguments and briefs of counsel the trial judge expressed the view that "a motel is a rooming house" and that there is no "fair and reasonable discrimination between a motel as a rooming house and some other type of rooming house"; he therefore concluded that the supplementary ordinance was invalid and that the plaintiffs were entitled to a building permit for the erection of a motel on their property in residential District A, provided its manner of construction was in conformity with the borough's building requirements:

* * *

The plaintiffs do not attack the validity of the 1939 ordinance which placed their property in a residential zone. And in the absence of an affirmative showing of unreasonableness they admittedly could not attack the right of the borough to exclude all private business operations, including boarding and rooming houses, hotels, motels and tourist camps, from the residential zones within the borough. They do, however, deny the borough's right to permit boarding and rooming houses in residential zones

and at the same time exclude motels therefrom; as we view the terms of
the 1939 ordinance the borough contemplated the exclusion of hotels,
motels and similar businesses from the residential zones without,
nevertheless, curbing the right of dwelling house owners or occupants to
use their premises for boarding and rooming house purposes. If this
classification by the borough has no reasonable basis then it must fall as
the plaintiffs contend; if, on the other hand, it has reasonable basis then it
may be permitted to stand and serve to exclude the operation of a motel in
a residential zone as proposed by the plaintiffs.

[L]egislative bodies may make such classifications as they deem
necessary and as long as their classifications are based upon reasonable
grounds "so as not to be arbitrary or capricious" they will not be upset by
the courts.

[W]e recently upheld a zoning ordinance which permitted public and
parochial elementary and high schools, but prohibited colleges and other
schools of higher learning, in residential areas. In the course of his opinion,
Justice Burling set forth grounds for differentiating schools for the
education of community children from institutions of higher learning and
quoted approvingly from the Euclid case where Justice Sutherland
pointedly remarked that " 'if the validity of the legislative classification for
zoning purposes be fairly debatable, the legislative judgment must be
allowed to control.' "

Motels have some but by no means all of the aspects of hotels. It is true
that motels and hotels both furnish overnight lodging to transient guests
but they differ generally in their structural design and location, in the
services they render and the uses to which they are put, and in the extent
of control or supervision readily available to their operators. However,
passing the differences between motels and hotels, it seems clear to us that
motels may without difficulty be differentiated from boarding and rooming
houses. Motels are business institutions which cater to members of the
general public and by and large are obliged to serve them indiscriminately.
As such business institutions they possess, in substantial degree, the
attributes which have led to the exclusion of businesses generally from
residential zones. On the other hand, boarding and rooming houses may
select guests with care and are admittedly "less public in character." They
are located in buildings which have the outward appearances of private
dwelling houses and their commercial features and incidents are
insignificant when compared to those of motels.

The officials of Palisades Park viewed boarding and rooming houses as
being consistent with residential areas and motels as being inconsistent
therewith; it seems clear to us that their views may not be said to be wholly
without reasonable basis and that the lower court's conclusion to the
contrary was erroneous. It must always be remembered that the duty of
selecting particular uses which are congruous in residential zones was

vested by the Legislature in the municipal officials rather than in the courts. Once the selections were made and duly embodied in the comprehensive zoning ordinance of 1939 they became presumptively valid and they are not to be nullified except upon an affirmative showing that the action taken by the municipal officials was unreasonable, arbitrary or capricious. No such showing was made in the instant matter and, consequently, the plaintiffs were not legally entitled to the building permit which they requested for the construction of a motel in a residential zone.

agency deference

The judgment entered in the lower court not only directed the issuance of the building permit but also set aside the supplemental ordinance enacted on May 25, 1954. In support of this action the plaintiffs have advanced the far-reaching contention that no municipality in the State has power to exclude motels from all zoning districts within its territorial limits, and that the supplemental ordinance must, therefore, be deemed void on its face. They cite cases where the courts disapproved municipal zoning ordinances which sought to exclude particular types of residences such as three-family houses and particular types of businesses such as gasoline stations. However, those cases were decided before the adoption of our Constitution of 1947 and the many broad statutory provisions and judicial determinations thereunder which must now serve as our guides. In *Duffcon Concrete Products v. Borough of Cresskill,* this court sustained a zoning ordinance which excluded heavy industry from all districts in the borough; in *Lionshead Lake, Inc. v. Township of Wayne*, an ordinance which prohibited the construction of very small houses (containing less than 768 square feet for a one-story dwelling) anywhere in the township was sustained by this court; and in *Guaclides v. Borough of Englewood Cliffs*, the Appellate Division sustained a zoning restriction which excluded apartment houses from substantially the entire borough. In *Fischer v. Township of Bedminster*, we sustained a five-acre zoning requirement and rested our holding on the primary ground that there was 'ample justification for the ordinance in preserving the character of the community, maintaining the value of property therein and devoting the land throughout the township for its most appropriate use.'

case references

In *State ex rel. Saveland Park Holding Corp. v. Wieland*, 69 N.W.2d 217 (Wis.1955), *cert. denied* 350 U.S. 841 (1955), the court quoted approvingly from the opinion of Justice Douglas in *Berman v. Parker*, 348 U.S. 26, 33 (1954) where the Supreme Court said:

> The concept of the public welfare is broad and inclusive. The values it represents are spiritual as well as physical, aesthetic as well as monetary. It is within the power of the legislature to determine that the community should be beautiful as well as healthy, spacious as well as clean, well-balanced as well as carefully patrolled. In the present case, the Congress and its authorized agencies have made determinations that take into

Great Breadth in what goals can be

account a wide variety of values. It is not for us to reappraise them. If those who govern the District of Columbia decide that the Nation's capital should be beautiful as well as sanitary, there is nothing in the Fifth Amendment that stands in the way.

In our own State the general welfare concept has received similarly broad definition.

The environmental characteristics of many of our beautiful residential communities are such that the establishment and operation of motels therein would be highly incongruous and would seriously impair existing property values. We know of no sound reason why such communities may not, as part of their comprehensive zoning, reasonably exclude such enterprises. On the other hand, there are many communities which are so constituted and located that they could not properly advance any sound objections to motels within their borders; although such communities may not entirely exclude them, they may reasonably confine them to compatible districts. In the instant matter the parties have not given us any oral testimony with respect to the characteristics of Palisades Park and its surrounding territory, nor have they suggested that we take judicial notice thereof. They have told us in their short stipulation that the borough is mostly residential with part of its territory zoned for business and industrial purposes, but we know little or nothing about the nature of its residences or the nature of its businesses and industries or the need for additional motel facilities in the general area. The burden of the attack by the plaintiffs has not been directed against the supplemental ordinance in its particular application to the evidence before the lower court; instead their contention has consistently been that the supplemental ordinance is void on its face and should therefore be stricken without more, and that they are entitled to construct and operate their proposed motel within an area which has long been zoned for residential purposes. This contention has been rejected by us in both of its aspects. And, in any event, we do not feel free to say on the inadequate record before us and at the behest of objectors whose property is in a residential zone, that the borough's general restriction against motels is wholly invalid in the light of its own and surrounding characteristics.

[handwritten margin note: limited record— justify why motels needed]

Reversed.

HEHER, J. (dissenting).

By the supplement to the zoning ordinance adopted May 25, 1954, "motels, motor courts, motor lodges, motor hotels, tourist camps, tourist courts, and structures of a similar character intended for a similar use, by whatever name the same may be called, whether one or more stories in height," are forbidden within the borough.

But this community-wide interdiction evinces, I would suggest, a basic misconception of the philosophy of zoning and the constitutional and

Acting beyond one's legal pwr & authority

statutory zoning process. The supplement is *ultra vires* the local municipal corporation.

* * *

The essence of zoning, we have so often said, is territorial division according to the character of the lands and structures and their peculiar suitability for particular uses, and uniformity of use within the division. Due process demands that the exercise of the power shall not be unreasonable, arbitrary or capricious, and the means selected for the fulfillment of the policy shall bear a real and substantial relation to that end. There must be a rational relation between the regulation and the service of the common welfare in an area within the reach of the police power. Restraints upon property cannot be exorbitant or unduly discriminatory. A police regulation that goes beyond the public need is not effective to curtail the rights of person or of private property made the subject of constitutional guaranties. Arbitrary or unreasonable restraints may not be put upon the exercise of the basic right of private property.

Thus, the genius of the constitutional and statutory zoning process is the regulation of land and buildings by districts according to the nature and extent of their use; and the particular regulation is not in that category. The fields of regulation authorized in state enabling acts are usually height, area, and use of buildings, use of land, and density of population. It is fundamental that zoning is not based on the doctrine of common-law nuisance. Zoning regulations and common-law nuisances involve different legal principles.

And it is generally recognized that in the nature of the business and the accommodations furnished, there is no substantial difference between motels or bungalow courts and hotels or multiple dwellings. Zoning ordinances permitting the operation of hotels or multiple dwellings in certain areas have been held to apply with equal force to the maintenance of motels or bungalow courts.

It cannot be that motels are beyond effective regulation. They are now in general use throughout the country, providing in many areas reasonably priced, comfortable living facilities on a par with hotel service, in keeping with the highest standards of conduct—in many cases serving a distinct public need. The fact that there are occasional operational faults and lapses does not justify the complete suppression of the use as a public nuisance, or otherwise a peremptory requirement in the essential public interest; there is no showing here that such is the case. If and when the need arises, the police power may be exerted to supply the remedy.

[H]ere we have, by the supplement to the ordinance, not a regulation, but rather a prohibition of the motel use throughout the community, in a residence zone by express provision open to multiple-family dwellings, group houses, garden-type apartments, and boarding and rooming houses, and in the business and industrial zones as well; and so, I submit, the rule of the supplement is utterly unreasonable, arbitrary and discriminatory, at odds with the constitutional and statutory zoning policy and violative of the basic standards of due process and equal protection. See Professor Haar's penetrating analysis of the principles determinative of the issue of discrimination, *In Accordance with a Comprehensive Plan*, 68 HARVARD L.REV. 1154 (1955). Even motels of more than one story are banned. There is in all this no distinction of substance reasonably related to any of the constitutional and statutory considerations to be served by zoning; the classification is illusive and unreal.

I would affirm the judgment.

NOTES: USE CLASSIFICATIONS

1. One of the thorniest problems in the drafting of use district regulations is illustrated in the *Pierro* case: how to differentiate between included and excluded uses. Bear in mind, as Judge Craig ably warns in *Amcare 2 Partners v. Zoning Hearing Bd.*, 609 A.2d 887, 891 (Pa.Cmwlth.1992), that "[i]n construing a zoning ordinance, the permissive widest use of land is the rule and not the exception, unless specifically restrained in the valid and reasonable exercise of the police power." In *Pierro*, the court struggles with the types of guest accommodations, which may have different land use characteristics. One troubling tendency of courts when determining whether a use is permitted is to look to decisions defining the term in a non-zoning context. For example, a court permitted an ice-making plant to remain in a business district from which manufacturing was prohibited by finding the plant was not a manufacturing use. To reach this conclusion, the court referred to opinions from other states involving tax issues, which had nothing to do with proper zoning considerations. *Atkinson v. City of Pierre*, 706 N.W.2d 791 (S.D.2005). Did the *Pierro* court make this mistake?

In other contexts, courts have struggled with different types of group homes for the disabled and halfway houses for prison parolees. *See* Louise C. Malkin, Comment, *Troubles at the Doorstep: The Fair Housing Act of 1988 and Group Homes for Recovering Substance Abusers*, 144 U.PA.L.REV. 759 (1995); Lester D. Steinman, *The Effect of Land-Use Restrictions on the Establishment of Community Residences for the Disabled: A National Study*, 19 URB.LAW. 1 (1987). The Fair Housing Amendments Act of 1988 significantly limits local government's ability to zone out the disabled. *See infra* Ch. 5.

2. The *Pierro* majority emphasizes the general welfare leg of the police power, as it endorses the goals of neighborhood appearance and aesthetics. The court treats rather cavalierly the potentially exclusionary and discriminatory effects of its decision. A desire to maintain quiet neighborhoods often leads to ordinances that define "single family" to exclude persons who are unrelated or do not constitute a single housekeeping unit. These ordinances are frequently litigated on both constitutional and statutory grounds. After a rowdy weekend celebration by students at a local college, a town amended its ordinance to

Looking outside zoning considerations

allow only single family housekeeping units that were "stable and permanent." In *Borough of Glassboro v. Vallorosi*, 568 A.2d 888 (N.J.1990), ten college students convinced the court that they were such a family. The *Glassboro* court suggested, similar to the *Pierro* dissent, that if behavior by college students (or persons in motels as in *Pierro*) is offensive, there are less onerous means of dealing with them than exclusion. In Chapter 5, we will see how the U.S. Supreme Court deals with the definition of family in the constitutional context in *Village of Belle Terre v. Boraas*, 416 U.S. 1 (1974).

3.   It is common to put some land in an agricultural use zone. Limiting property to agricultural uses depresses the land's market value, making the ordinance susceptible to attack as being arbitrary and unduly onerous. The suspicion sometimes exists that the professed desire to preserve agricultural land is a sham to create public open space at the farmer's expense. The chances for successful defense of an agricultural district are much improved if the government, in adopting the restriction, considered factors such as soil type, the need for agricultural production, and resources like groundwater. *See Boundary Drive Assocs. v. Shrewsbury Township*, 491 A.2d 86 (Pa.1985); Mark W. Cordes, *Agricultural Zoning: Impacts and Future Directions*, 22 N.Ill.U.L.Rev. 419 (2002). For a more detailed discussion of agricultural land preservation issues and techniques, see Chapter 9.

4.   In *Pierro* and several cases below, the local government has an ordinance that *may* ban the proposed uses, but just to be sure it enacts an amendment leaving no doubt. In other cases, the government may face a permit application for an allowed use, and then promptly enact an ordinance to bar the use. Is it fair to subject the developer to such new laws? We deal the question of vested rights *infra* Ch. 2.F.

HERNANDEZ V. CITY OF HANFORD

Supreme Court of California, 2007.
41 Cal.4th 279, 159 P.3d 33, 59 Cal.Rptr.3d 442.

GEORGE, C.J.

This case involves a constitutional challenge to a zoning ordinance enacted by the City of Hanford in 2003. In order to protect the economic viability of Hanford's downtown commercial district—a prominent feature of which is a large number of regionally well-regarded retail furniture stores—the challenged ordinance generally prohibits the sale of furniture in another commercial district in Hanford (currently designated the Planned Commercial or PC district) that contains a large shopping mall in which several department stores as well as other retail stores are located. At the same time, the ordinance creates a limited exception to the general prohibition on the sale of furniture in the PC district, permitting large department stores (those with 50,000 or more square feet of floor space) located within that district to sell furniture within a specifically prescribed area (occupying no more than 2,500 square feet of floor space) within the department store.

The owners of a "stand-alone" home furnishings and mattress store located within the PC district, who wished to sell bedroom furniture along with mattresses and home accessories (such as lamps and carpets) in their store, brought this action contesting the validity of the foregoing provisions of the zoning ordinance. The trial court rejected the constitutional challenge, but the Court of Appeal disagreed with the trial court's determination. The Court of Appeal concluded that although the ordinance's general prohibition of the sale of furniture in the PC district was reasonably related to a legitimate governmental interest—the preservation of the economic viability of the downtown commercial district—the ordinance's exception permitting limited furniture sales only by large department stores in the PC district violated equal protection principles by drawing an unwarranted distinction between large department stores and other retail stores located within the PC district. The appellate court reasoned that "when all retailers limit the furniture display space in compliance with the ordinance to the permitted 2,500 square feet, the difference in total floor space between the retailers is largely irrelevant. Thus, the disparate treatment of these similarly situated retailers based on square footage is not rationally related to the purpose behind the ordinance and is unconstitutional as a violation of equal protection." We granted the city's petition for review to consider the validity of the Court of Appeal's determination that the ordinance is unconstitutional.

For the reasons discussed below, we conclude that the Court of Appeal erred in finding the ordinance unconstitutional. As we shall explain, the appellate court's analysis fails adequately to take into account the *two* legitimate purposes underlying the ordinance in question: (a) the objective of protecting and preserving the economic viability of the city's downtown commercial district by generally prohibiting within the PC district a particular retail activity—the sale of furniture—that is a prominent feature of the downtown commercial district, *and* (b) the objective of attracting to, and retaining within, the city's PC district the type of large department stores (which typically carry furniture) that the city views as essential to the economic viability of the PC district. Restricting the ordinance's limited exception for the sale of furniture within the PC district to sales by large department stores—and only such stores—is rationally related to the second of these legislative purposes served by the ordinance. Accordingly, we conclude that the decision rendered by the Court of Appeal, invalidating the zoning ordinance here at issue, must be reversed.

In 1989, the City of Hanford amended its general plan to provide for a new commercial district in the vicinity of 12th Avenue and Lacey Boulevard. This new district originally was designated the Regional Commercial district but later was renamed the Planned Commercial or PC district. The district encompassed several hundred acres of land and was intended to accommodate the location of malls, large "big box" stores, and other retail uses.

At trial, Jim Beath, the city's community development director, testified regarding the background of the city's adoption of the new district in 1989. * * * Beath explained that when the city was considering the creation of the new district in 1989, it was concerned that the extent of anticipated commercial development in the proposed district might well have a negative effect on the city's downtown commercial district. In light of that concern, the city council appointed the Retail Strategy Development Committee (the Committee) "made up of people from the mall area as well as the downtown district and other citizens." The Committee was asked to propose land use rules for the new district that would "provide for the large box and other kinds of retail use that the City . . . had grown to need and yet still make sure that [the new district] didn't have a negative impact on the downtown district."

The Committee ultimately recommended that certain designated uses generally not be permitted in the new district, and Beath testified that those uses "were ones that were already established in the downtown district that they didn't want to see removed from the downtown district and relocate[d] out at the planned commercial district, and those were car dealerships, banks, professional offices, and furniture stores." In establishing the new district, the city council limited the uses that were to be permitted in that district in line with the Committee's recommendations.

Accordingly, as relevant here, the 1989 ordinance included department stores and the sale of home furnishings within the list of permitted uses within the new district, but did not include furniture stores or the sale of furniture as a permitted use. The 1989 ordinance, however, did not specifically define "department store" or "home furnishings," and did not explicitly state whether department stores located within the new district would or would not be permitted to sell furniture.

In the fall of 2002, more than a decade after establishment of the PC district, plaintiffs Adrian and Tracy Hernandez leased space in a building located in the PC district with the intent to establish a new business at that location to be called Country Hutch Home Furnishings and Mattress Gallery (hereafter Country Hutch Home Furnishings). For more than 10 years preceding the time they proposed to start this new business, plaintiffs had owned and operated a retail furniture store, the Country Hutch, that was located in the city's downtown commercial district. In planning for the new store, plaintiffs intended to sell mattresses, home accessories, and some bedroom furniture at their new location in the PC district.

From November 2002 to January 2003, plaintiffs continued with their plans to open and operate the Country Hutch Home Furnishings store in the PC district, and in February 2003 the city issued a certificate of occupancy to plaintiffs stating that the building in question could be used to sell "home furnishing accessories," but also specifying that this term excluded "all types of furniture."

After receiving the certificate of occupancy, plaintiffs opened the Country Hutch Home Furnishings store. Soon thereafter a city inspector, citing plaintiffs for violating the zoning ordinance by offering furniture for sale in their new store, instructed them to remove all of the furniture from the store. Plaintiffs thereafter sent a letter to the members of the Hanford City Council, complaining that the zoning code was being applied in a discriminatory fashion because numerous department stores in the PC district were selling furniture and had not been cited by the city, while plaintiffs were cited for engaging in the same conduct.

On March 4, 2003, one week after receiving plaintiffs' letter, the city council held a "study session" to consider the issues raised by plaintiffs' letter. Plaintiffs, as well as representatives of the downtown furniture stores and representatives of the PC district department stores, attended and participated in the study session. * * * At the session, Beath informed the city council that he believed it was advisable to consider revising the applicable zoning ordinance to clarify whether, and to what extent, furniture could be sold in the PC district, either by department stores or other retail stores. * * * A representative of the mall maintained that the type of furniture currently sold in the existing department stores in the PC district differed from the furniture sold in the downtown furniture stores and should remain locally available through the department stores. At the conclusion of the session, the council instructed the city staff to draft a proposed revision of the ordinance to clarify its application * * * .

Ultimately, on July 15, 2003, the city council adopted the amendment to the city zoning provisions relating to the sale of furniture in the PC district that is challenged in this case, Hanford Ordinance 03–03 (Ordinance No. 03–03).

Accordingly, the ordinance in question generally prohibits the sale of furniture in the PC district, but at the same time creates a limited exception permitting a large department store within the PC district to display and sell furniture within a single location in the store measuring no more than 2,500 square feet.

Shortly after the ordinance was enacted, plaintiffs filed the present action against the city, challenging the validity of the ordinance on a number of grounds. Plaintiffs' complaint contended that the ordinance was invalid (1) because it was enacted for the primary purpose of regulating economic competition, and (2) because it violated the equal protection clauses of the federal and state Constitutions. After a bench trial, the trial court rejected plaintiffs' contentions and upheld the validity of the ordinance. * * * On appeal, the Court of Appeal reversed the trial court's decision. * * * We granted the city's petition for review.

Before reaching the equal protection issue upon which the Court of Appeal based its decision, we turn first to the more general (and more sweeping) contention that plaintiffs raised below and upon which they continue to rely in this court—that the zoning ordinance at issue is invalid because the "primary purpose" of the ordinance's general prohibition of the sale of furniture in the PC district assertedly was to "regulat[e] economic competition." Although neither the trial court nor the Court of Appeal found the ordinance invalid on this basis, as we shall see, plaintiffs' claim that the city exceeded its authority under the police power by enacting a zoning ordinance that regulates or restricts economic competition apparently is based upon some ambiguous and at least potentially misleading language that appears in a number of zoning decisions of the Courts of Appeal. As we shall explain, despite some arguably ambiguous language the decisions in these cases plainly do not support plaintiffs' challenge to the validity of the zoning ordinance here at issue, and we shall attempt to clarify the language in question to avoid possible confusion in the future.

As stated in *Metromedia, Inc. v. City of Pasadena*, 30 Cal.Rptr. 731 (Cal.App.1963): 'Today, economic and aesthetic considerations together constitute the nearly inseparable warp and woof of the fabric upon which the modern city must design its future.' Taking cognizance of this concept we perceive that planning and zoning ordinances traditionally seek to maintain property values, protect tax revenues, provide neighborhood social and economic stability, attract business and industry and encourage conditions which make a community a pleasant place to live and work. Whether these be classified as 'planning considerations' or 'economic considerations,' we hold that so long as the primary purpose of the zoning ordinance is not to regulate economic competition, but to subserve a valid objective pursuant to a city's police powers, such ordinance is not invalid even though it might have an indirect impact on economic competition."

As one leading zoning treatise accurately observes: "[A]ll zoning has some impact on competition. The simple division of the community into districts has an inherent and profound effect on the real estate market, because some land is withdrawn from the commercial market and placed in the residential market. . . . Some competitive impact results from nearly every provision of the original zoning ordinance, and from each amendment. Accordingly, competitive impact alone cannot invalidate a zoning ordinance. A zoning ordinance which serves some established purpose of zoning is not necessarily invalid simply because it has the additional effect of limiting competition." (1 Anderson's American Law of Zoning (4th ed.1996) § 7.28, p. 807; *see, e.g., Boone v. Redevelopment Agency of San Jose* (9th Cir.1988) 841 F.2d 886, 890 ["The power to zone and rezone . . . by its very nature encompasses the power to exclude competition"].)

Second, we believe that the additional statement in the quoted passage—that "so long as the primary purpose of the zoning ordinance is not to regulate economic competition, but to subserve a valid objective pursuant to [the] city's police powers, such ordinance is not invalid even though it might have an indirect impact on economic competition" also is ambiguous and at least potentially misleading. That language could be interpreted to suggest that a zoning ordinance is valid *only* when the ordinance has merely an "indirect impact" on economic competition, and *never* when the regulation of economic competition is a direct and intended effect of the ordinance, even in instances in which a zoning ordinance uses the regulation of competition simply as a means or tool to achieve an authorized and valid *public* purpose—such as the preservation of an existing downtown commercial district—rather than to serve an impermissible *private* anticompetitive purpose or interest—such as securing a financial advantage or monopoly position for the benefit of a favored business or individual or imposing a disadvantage on an unpopular business or individual. As so interpreted, the language would be inaccurate.

The more recent case of *Wal-Mart Stores, Inc. v. City of Turlock* (2006) 138 Cal.App.4th 273, 41 Cal.Rptr.3d 420 *(Wal-Mart)* provides another apt example. In *Wal-Mart,* the City of Turlock enacted a zoning ordinance that, while permitting the operation of traditional "big box" discount stores in a designated district, prohibited the development, anywhere in the city, of so-called discount superstores—defined generally as large discount stores that include a full-service grocery department. In explaining the rationale underlying the restriction on discount superstores, the ordinance set forth a series of facts or findings, stating in part that (1) " 'the Turlock General Plan . . . establishes locational requirements for [regional and neighborhood] retail centers; encouraging a number of neighborhood centers equally dispersed throughout the city while encouraging a concentration of regional shopping centers along the Highway 99/Countryside Drive corridor' " (2) the city's " 'General Plan policies promote and encourage vital neighborhood commercial districts that are evenly distributed throughout the city so that residents are able to meet their basic daily shopping needs at neighborhood shopping centers' " (3) " 'discount superstores compete directly with existing grocery stores that anchor neighborhood-serving commercial centers' " (4) " 'the establishment of discount superstores in Turlock is likely to negatively impact the vitality and economic viability of the city's neighborhood commercial centers by drawing sales away from traditional supermarkets located in these centers' " and (5) " 'smaller stores within a neighborhood center rely upon the foot traffic generated by the grocery store for their existence and in neighborhood centers where the grocery store closes, vacancy rates typically increase and deterioration takes place in the remaining center.'"

Wal-Mart filed an action challenging the validity of the ordinance on a variety of grounds, including the contention that the ordinance exceeded the city's police powers because it was "designed to suppress economic competition, and is not reasonably related to the public welfare." In rejecting this argument, the Court of Appeal in *Wal-Mart* stated: "With respect to Wal-Mart's claim of anticompetitive purpose, we agree with the trial court that, while the Ordinance likely will have an anticompetitive effect in the grocery business in [the City of Turlock], that incidental effect does not render arbitrary an ordinance that was enacted for a valid purpose. While zoning ordinances may not legitimately be used to control economic competition, they may be used to address the urban/suburban decay that can be its effect." The appellate court in *Wal-Mart* concluded: "In summary, the police power empowers cities to control and organize development within their boundaries as a means of serving the general welfare. [The City of Turlock] legitimately chose to organize the development within its boundaries using neighborhood shopping centers dispersed throughout the city. The Ordinance is reasonably related to protecting that development choice."

* * *

Our court has not previously had occasion to address the question whether a municipality, in order to protect or preserve the economic viability of its downtown business district or neighborhood shopping areas, may enact a zoning ordinance that regulates or controls competition by placing limits on potentially competing commercial activities or development in other areas of the municipality. As the circumstances underlying the decisions in *Ensign Bickford, supra,* 68 Cal.App.3d 467, 137 Cal.Rptr. 304, and *Wal-Mart, supra,* 138 Cal.App.4th 273, 41 Cal.Rptr.3d 420, demonstrate, even when the regulation of economic competition reasonably can be viewed as a direct and intended effect of a zoning ordinance or action, so long as the primary purpose of the ordinance or action—that is, its principal and ultimate objective—is not the impermissible *private* anticompetitive goal of protecting or disadvantaging a particular favored or disfavored business or individual, but instead is the advancement of a legitimate *public* purpose—such as the preservation of a municipality's downtown business district for the benefit of the municipality as a whole—the ordinance reasonably relates to the general welfare of the municipality and constitutes a legitimate exercise of the municipality's police power. * * *

In the present case, it is clear that the zoning ordinance's general prohibition on the sale of furniture in the PC district—although concededly intended, at least in part, to regulate competition—was adopted to promote the legitimate public purpose of preserving the economic viability of the

Hanford downtown business district, rather than to serve any impermissible private anticompetitive purpose. Furthermore, as in *Ensign Bickford,* here the zoning ordinance's restrictions are aimed at regulating "*where,* within the city," a particular type of business generally may be located, a very traditional zoning objective. Under these circumstances, we agree with the lower courts' conclusion that the zoning ordinance cannot be found invalid as an improper limitation on competition.

* * *

The zoning ordinance at issue in the present case does not involve suspect classifications or touch upon fundamental interests and thus, as the Court of Appeal recognized and as all parties agree, the applicable standard under which plaintiffs' equal protection challenge properly must be evaluated is the rational relationship or rational basis standard. As noted above, in finding the exception set forth in the ordinance invalid under the rational relationship test, the Court of Appeal reasoned that "with the blanket 2,500-square-foot restrictions on furniture in the PC zone, the small retailer poses the same potential threat, if any, to the downtown merchants as the larger store. Thus, limiting the furniture sales exception to stores with more than 50,000 square feet is arbitrary. A rational relationship between the size classification and the goal of protecting downtown simply does not exist."

We disagree with the Court of Appeal's determination that the ordinance violates the equal protection clause. The Court of Appeal's conclusion effectively rests on the premise that there was only a single purpose underlying the challenged ordinance—the protection of furniture stores located in the downtown business district from potential competition by retail establishments conducting business within the PC district. Because the Court of Appeal was of the view that the disparate treatment in the ordinance's exception of large department stores and other stores was not rationally related to *that* purpose, the appellate court concluded the exception was invalid.

Both the terms and legislative history of the measure at issue disclose, however, that the ordinance was intended to serve *multiple* purposes: to protect the economic health and viability of the city's downtown furniture stores, but to do so in a manner that did not threaten or detract from the city's ability to attract and retain large department stores in the PC district. Past cases establish that the equal protection clause does not preclude a governmental entity from adopting a legislative measure that is aimed at achieving multiple objectives, even when such objectives in some respects may be in tension or conflict.

The United States Supreme Court's decision in *Fitzgerald v. Racing Assn. of Central Iowa,* 539 U.S. 103 (2003) (*Fitzgerald*) demonstrates this point. [In *Fitzgerald,* racetrack owners challenged on equal protection grounds an Iowa statute that taxed racetrack revenue at 36% while taxing riverboat gambling at 20%. Eds.] In holding that the challenged statute did not violate equal protection principles, the United States Supreme Court explained in *Fitzgerald* that the Iowa Supreme Court could not deny "that the Iowa law, like most laws, might predominantly serve one general objective, say, helping the racetracks, while containing subsidiary provisions that seek to achieve other desirable (perhaps even contrary) ends as well, thereby producing a law that balances objectives but still serves the general objective when seen as a whole."

Like the Iowa statute at issue in *Fitzgerald,* the Hanford ordinance challenged here was intended to serve multiple purposes. The city desired to protect the economic viability of its downtown business district, but at the same time it did not wish to diminish the financial benefits of the PC district for the large department stores that it wanted to attract and maintain in that district.

In sum, the Court of Appeal erred in invalidating the ordinance at issue. The judgment of the Court of Appeal is reversed.

NOTES

1.   Traditionally, courts frowned on what they called "fiscal zoning." While acknowledging that the mere act of districting has an effect on competition, regulation of competition was often said to be an improper purpose of zoning. The *Hernandez* decision's approval of fiscal planning and zoning is reflective of modern decisions approving the use of fiscal impact analyses for a variety of land use decisions:

   (a)   Rezonings: *Bell v. Planning & Zoning Com'n of City of Bridgeport*, 1997 WL 133447 (Conn.Super.1997); *Guest v. Board of Supervisors of King George County*, 42 Va.Cir. 348 (1997);

   (b)   Tax Increment Finance for Redevelopment: *Torres v. City of Yorba Linda*, 17 Cal.Rptr.2d 400 (Cal.App.1992);

   (c)   Zoning Initiatives: *In re Advisory Opinion*, 644 So.2d 486 (Fla.1994);

   (d)   Administrative Regulations: *In re Dep't of Health*, 681 A.2d 484 (Md.1996);

   (e)   Public Facility Siting: *West Chester Area School District v. Collegium Charter School*, 760 A.2d 452 (Pa.Cmwlth.2000); and

   (f)   Urban Service Area Boundaries: *Theobald v. Board of County Comm'rs*, 644 P.2d 942 (Colo.1982).

Hernandez shows how far we have come from the traditional view against fiscal zoning, but does it also show that we have gone too far in allowing economic planning? Is that an appropriate role for government?

When the City of Pensacola amended its zoning ordinance to allow new types of dry cleaners using particular solvents, it delayed the effective date of the ordinance to give existing businesses a chance to adjust to the new competition. Deeming the purpose improper, the court invalidated the portion of the ordinance that delayed the effective date of the new zoning. *See Wyatt v. City of Pensacola*, 196 So.2d 777 (Fla.App.1967). Would the California court that decided *Hernandez* permit this?

2.   Communities interested in maintaining a unique or special local character have a difficult task in the age of chain stores, whether they are restaurants, grocery stores, clothing stores, or building supply stores. These "formula businesses," have common signage and exterior appearances, and consequently towns look more and more the same. Yearning to maintain a degree of distinctiveness, communities may adopt "anti-formula business" ordinances. The anti-formula retail ordinance of Islamorada, Florida covered (until it was declared unconstitutional, see below) "a retail sales establishment . . . required by contractual or other arrangement to maintain any of the following: standardized array of services or merchandise, trademark, logo, service mark, symbol, decor, architecture, layout, uniform, or similar standardized feature." Ord. § 30–1264. Such a business could be "approved only as a major conditional use and must have met the following criteria: (1) Shall not have a street level business frontage of greater than 50 linear feet; and (2) Shall not exceed 2,000 square feet of floor area." Ord. 02–02, § 1.6.4.4 (2002). Does the Standard State Zoning Enabling Act confer authority on cities to do this? *See*, Patricia E. Salkin, *Municipal Regulation of Formula Businesses: Creating and Protecting Communities*, 58 CASE W.RES.L.REV. 1251 (2008).

If authorized by enabling legislation, are such ordinances constitutional? The sale of a locally owned "tropical department store" for use as a Walgreen Drug Store failed when the parties learned that the ordinance precluded a Walgreen's. *See Island Silver & Spice, Inc. v. Islamorada, Village of Islands*, 542 F.3d 844 (11th Cir.2008). The court held that the ordinance violated the dormant commerce clause. While the ordinance did not discriminate on its face against out-of-state businesses, it had that practical effect since national retail chain stores could not operate within the strict size constraints imposed by the ordinance. The town failed to justify its ordinance under the strict scrutiny applied. The court said that preserving a small town community is a legitimate purpose, but found that the village had not demonstrated that it had any small town character to preserve. Even if the town had a small town character to preserve, the ordinance also failed to achieve the goal since, in part, the town wanted "small scale uses" but the ordinance did not ban small formula businesses. *See* John M. Baker and Mehmet K. Konar-Steenberg, *"Drawn from Local Knowledge . . . and Conformed to Local Wants": Zoning and Incremental Reform of Dormant Commerce Clause Doctrine*, 38 LOY.U.CHI.L.J. 1 (2006).

3.   How things change! As note 2 following *Pierro* highlights, the 1950s roadside strip motel of small cubicles is likely worthy of historic landmarking these days. In the retail arena, changes are equally striking: from downtown department stores to retail strips, to open (then enclosed) shopping malls, to big boxes, then power centers (1,000,000 sq. ft.). A big box store typically

contains 100,000 square feet of floor area. As Stanley Abrams points out, that is more retail space than small and modest size towns have and is equal to the size of many suburban shopping malls. Abrams, *The Big Box Store: Regulating and Controlling Godzilla, ALI-ABA, CA*, 34 ALI-ABA 1103 (1995).

4. Big boxes are, for some, "singularly unattractive [in] appearance." *Abrams, supra* note 3. There are other reasons why some object to them. Often located on the fringe of town, they may reflect sprawl development, with its attendant cost increases in municipal infrastructure, road congestion, and loss of open space. Big boxes also may cause a disruption in the local economy, presenting problems for competitors, including downtown retailers, enclosed shopping malls, and small, local businesses. *See* George Lefcoe, *The Regulation of Superstores: The Legality of Zoning Ordinances Emerging from the Skirmishes Between Wal-Mart and the United Food and Commercial Workers Union*, 58 ARK.L.REV. 833 (2006). Finally, there is the problem of "dark stores." Big boxes keep getting bigger. As Target, Costco, or any other big box retailer builds a new superstore, it vacates its existing store. Only infrequently reused, these vacated stores become eyesores and invite vandalism.

5. When a new business seeks to break into a local market, its prospective competitor may participate in, and perhaps lead, the movement to block the development. Does such anti-competitive conduct violate federal antitrust laws that prohibit conspiracies in restraint of trade? In *City of Columbia v. Omni Outdoor Advertising, Inc.*, 499 U.S. 365 (1991), an outdoor advertising company tried to break into the local market of Columbia, South Carolina. In part as a result of local opposition, the city enacted a restrictive billboard measure that had the effect of banning most new billboards and allowing most existing ones to continue in place. Much of the opposition allegedly came from a local company that controlled 95% of the billboard business in town. The outside company brought suit against the city and the competitor alleging their conduct constituted a conspiracy in restraint of trade under the Sherman Act. The city argued that it was immune from liability under the state action doctrine of *Parker v. Brown*, 317 U.S. 341 (1943), which shields states from liability for anti-competitive actions. The Court in *Omni* agreed, holding that municipalities acquire derivative immunity from the state's delegation of zoning power.

The *Noerr-Pennington* doctrine saved the *Omni* hometown competitor from liability for malicious prosecution. *See Eastern R.R. Presidents Conference v. Noerr Motor Freight, Inc.*, 365 U.S. 127 (1961) and *United Mine Workers v. Pennington*, 381 U.S. 657 (1965). *Noerr-Pennington* prevents a person from being penalized for exercising the First Amendment right to petition the government. Thus, private parties can urge the government to enact anti-competitive laws, which are to their economic benefit, without fear of antitrust liability. Should government actors be protected under *Noerr-Pennington*? *See Manistee Town Center v. City of Glendale*, 227 F.3d 1090 (9th Cir.2000). See also discussion of SLAPP and anti-SLAPP litigation, *infra* Ch. 2.D, note 8.

Antitrust liability, which may carry treble damages, is something cities want to avoid. *Omni* helps them do that. There is also the Local Government

Antitrust Act of 1984, 15 U.S.C.A. §§ 34–36, which forbids antitrust damage claims against local governments and their officials: "no damages, interest on damages, costs or attorney's fees may be recovered under Section 4, 4A, or 4C of the Clayton Act * * * from any local government, or official or employee thereof acting in an official capacity." Both the plain language of the Section and the legislative history of the Act make clear that a local government is absolutely immune from antitrust damage claims even though the local government may have acted beyond its authority or in bad faith. *See* Juergensmeyer and Roberts, *Land Use Planning and Development Regulation Law* § 10.21 (3rd ed.2012).

COMMENT: FEDERAL LAND USE CONTROLS

The federal government's role in land use planning, negligible for most of our history, has dramatically increased over the past 40 years. Major laws enacted during that time include the Fair Housing Act, 42 U.S.C.A. § 3601, the Surface Mining Control and Reclamation Act, 30 U.S.C.A. § 1201, the Clean Water Act, 33 U.S.C.A. § 1251, particularly § 404 wetlands controls, the Clean Air Act, 42 U.S.C.A. § 7401, and the Endangered Species Act, 16 U.S.C.A. § 1531. These acts contain direct regulations of private land use activities based in whole or in part on the commerce clause. The Clean Water Act and the Endangered Species Act are covered *infra* Ch. 9. For broader coverage, *see* Linda A. Malone, *Environmental Regulation of Land Use* (2006).

Another area of congressional activity is telecommunications. Federal legislation promoting telecommunications facilities partially preempts local control. A common thorn in the sides, or eyes, of neighbors is the 100- to 400-foot tower built for antennas to transmit and receive signals for cellular telephone use. As many cases attest, prospective neighbors think the tower will be an eyesore, diminishing their quality of life and their property values. They may also fear the tower will be a health hazard due to radioactive emissions. In trying to keep the tower out of their neighborhood, the neighbors may discover federal law limits their ability to influence local boards. The Telecommunications Act of 1996 partially preempts local authority to regulate cellular towers by providing that local authorities may not unreasonably discriminate among providers of functionally equivalent services, may not act in such a way that it has the effect of totally prohibiting such services, and may not consider the environmental effects of radio frequency emissions if the facility complies with federal regulations concerning such emissions. The Act also provides for expedited judicial review of adverse state or local government agency rulings. *See* 47 U.S.C.A. § 332. Substantial evidence must support a local denial of service. Robert B. Foster & Mitchell A. Carrel, *Tell Me What You Really Think: Judicial Review of Land Use Decisions on Cellular Telecommunications Facilities Under the Telecommunications Act of 1996*, 37 URB.LAW. 551 (2005). The lower federal courts vary widely in their application of the act's provisions. *See* Juergensmeyer and Roberts, *Land Use Planning and Development Regulation Law* § 4.25 (3rd ed.2012). State law may also affect local authority if the tower is considered a "public utility" since most states totally or partially preempt public utilities from local control. Id.

While the constitutionality of these and other such acts was once assumed in light of the Supreme Court's traditional deference to congressional determinations that interstate commerce was affected, recent cases eliminate that facile assumption. The Court has shown a renewed interest in scrutinizing federal commerce clause-based intervention into state and local affairs. *See United States v. Morrison*, 529 U.S. 598 (2000) (striking the federal Violence Against Women Act) and *United States v. Lopez*, 514 U.S. 549 (1995) (striking down the Gun Free School Zones Act). In the land use context, the Court has observed that the regulation of land use is " 'a function traditionally performed by local governments.' " *Solid Waste Agency of Northern Cook County v. United States Army Corps of Engineers*, 531 U.S. 159 (2001) (finding agency rule exceeded the authority granted to regulate wetlands and noting that such a ruling enabled the Court to avoid addressing a "significant" commerce clause issue).

COMMENT: DORMANT COMMERCE CLAUSE

The commerce clause, in addition to constituting a source of federal power to control land use, is also a negative restraint on the ability of state and local governments to control land use. The doctrine serves to protect against economic protectionism. *United Haulers Ass'n, Inc. v. Oneida-Herkimer Solid Waste Management Authority*, 550 U.S. 330 (2007). A state statute or local ordinance which "regulates even-handedly to effectuate a legitimate local public interest, and its effects on interstate commerce are only incidental, * * * will be upheld unless the burden imposed on such commerce is clearly excessive in relation to the putative local benefits." *Pike v. Bruce Church, Inc.*, 397 U.S. 137, 142 (1970).

Zoning laws have typically survived dormant commerce clause challenges. For example, an ordinance that imposed restrictions on manufactured homes, dealing with such matters as roof pitch, roof strength, utility hookups, and appearance, was asserted to violate the dormant commerce clause. The Eleventh Circuit rejected the claim, holding that an aesthetic-based requirement that housing have a defined roof pitch applied equally to in-state and out-of-state manufacturers and the burden on interstate commerce was negligible. *Georgia Manufactured Housing Association v. Spalding County*, 148 F.3d 1304 (11th Cir.1998). *See also Texas Manufactured Housing Ass'n, Inc. v. City of Nederland*, 101 F.3d 1095 (5th Cir.1996), *cert. denied,* 521 U.S. 1112 (1997) (ordinance limiting mobile homes to trailer parks did not violate commerce clause).

Limits on the size of big box stores and restrictions on formula businesses raise a dormant commerce clause issue. In *Island Silver & Spice, Inc. v. Islamorada, Village of Islands*, discussed *supra* note 2, the court held an ordinance that had the effect of excluding national retail chain stores discriminated against interstate commerce. The town's goal to remain unique free from formula businesses was held illegitimate. *See* John M. Baker and Mehmet K. Konar-Steenberg, *"Drawn from Local Knowledge . . . and Conformed to Local Wants": Zoning and Incremental Reform of Dormant*

Commerce Clause Doctrine, 38 LOY.U.CHI.L.J. 1 (2006), arguing that the dormant commerce clause should be discarded, freeing states and local government to preserve local character. *See* Brannon P. Denning and Rachel M. Lary, *Retail Store Size-Capping Ordinances and the Dormant Commerce Clause Doctrine*, 37 URB.LAW. 907, 955 (2005); Justin Shoemaker, *Note, The Smalling of America?: Growth Management Statutes and the Dormant Commerce Clause*, 48 DUKE L.J. 891 (1999).

3. ACCESSORY USES AND HOME OCCUPATIONS

Ordinances generally allow accessory activities that are necessary or convenient to principal, permitted uses. Edward Bassett noted that "from time immemorial," people had used parts of their homes for office and other non-residential purposes, and that from their inception, zoning codes acknowledged this tradition. Edward Bassett, *Zoning 100* (2d ed.1940).* Had the early Euclidean codes been highly restrictive in defining residential use, zoning might not have not taken hold as it did. In addition to what people had come to expect to be able to do at home, considerations of personal liberty require concessions about what one can do at home. Accessory uses are also allowed for non-residential uses.

DAPURIFICACAO V. ZONING BD. OF ADJUSTMENT OF TP. OF UNION

Superior Court of New Jersey, 2005.
377 N.J.Super. 436, 873 A.2d 582.

C.S. FISHER, J.A.D.

This appeal requires that we consider whether the housing of racing pigeons on residential property constitutes an accessory use. Like the trial court, we answer this question in the negative and affirm.

In 1981, plaintiff Manuel DaPurificacao purchased a single-family home, on a 50 by 140 foot lot, located in a residential zone in Union Township. Soon thereafter, plaintiff applied for and was granted a permit to do work on his home. At that time, plaintiff also built a shed to house the sixty-five pigeons he then owned. He did not seek a permit to construct this shed nor was his intention to construct this shed included within the description of work for which plaintiff had been given a permit.

In 1984, plaintiff applied for a variance to convert his single-family home into a two-family home with a garage. The application was granted on the condition that the construction "strictly confirm" to the specifications in his application and the plans that had been approved. Neither the application nor the approved plans made any mention of the construction of a pigeon coop or that the coop was present on the property.

---

* Bassett has been described as the "father of zoning." Seymour Toll, *Zoned American* 143 (1969).

In 1988, plaintiff added a structure to the top of his garage in order to house his pigeons. He took this action without obtaining either a permit or a variance.

In 1999 plaintiff was issued summonses that triggered the present disputes about his pigeon coop. The first summons cited plaintiff for maintaining a structure that exceeded the height requirements for accessory uses in a residential zone, contrary to Ordinance 170–5. Another summons cited plaintiff for maintaining an impermissible accessory structure on his residential property, contrary to Ordinance 170–51. By that time, the coop referred to in these summonses was housing eighty-five pigeons.

Before any proceedings occurred with regard to these summonses, plaintiff applied to the board of adjustment for a determination that his pigeon coop constituted a permitted accessory use. That application was denied by way of a March 22, 2000 resolution. On June 5, 2000, plaintiff filed a complaint in lieu of prerogative writs seeking, among other things, a reversal of the board's denial of his application, permission to file an application for a height variance, and a determination that the ordinances were unconstitutional.

Plaintiff thereafter moved for a stay of any municipal proceedings regarding the summonses and for an amendment of his pleadings to join Union Township as a party. These motions were granted.

When the matter eventually came before the trial judge for a consideration of the merits, an oral decision was rendered on October 3, 2001. In that decision the trial judge presented his reasons for affirming the board's decision that the pigeon coop was not a permitted accessory use in a residential zone. The judge also lifted the stay so that the municipal proceedings could go forward.

In the proceedings that followed in municipal court on March 5, and April 2, 2002, plaintiff acknowledged his violation of Ordinance 170–5 (the height summons) and, after a trial, was found to have maintained a structure that constituted a non-confirming use in violation of Ordinance 170–51. Fines were assessed but held in abeyance pending plaintiff's appeal to the Law Division.

Plaintiff appealed the municipal adjudications to the Law Division on April 12, 2002. An order entered on June 7, 2002 consolidated this municipal appeal with the constitutional issues that remained undecided in the prerogative writ action.

On January 17, 2003, the trial judge ruled on the merits of the matter by rejecting plaintiff's constitutional arguments, reaffirming the board's determination that the plaintiff's housing of his pigeons on his residential property did not constitute a legitimate accessory use, and affirming the municipal court conviction.

We commence our consideration of plaintiff's argument by recognizing that a literal interpretation of the ordinances in question demonstrates that the maintenance of a pigeon coop was not an expressly permitted accessory use.

Ordinance 170–5 defines an accessory use as "[a] use naturally and normally incident and subordinate to the principal use of a structure or lot." Ordinance 170–51, which lists those accessory use *permitted* in a residential zone, must also be read in conjunction with 170–23, which lists those uses that are *prohibited* anywhere in the township. To close any loophole with regard to those things that did not appear in either list—such as pigeon coops—Ordinance 170–23 states that "[a]ll uses not expressly permitted by this chapter are prohibited." The plain meaning of these provisions, in this context, is readily apparent. Pigeon coops are not expressly permitted.

Of course, whether an unmentioned use may be a permissible accessory use is not determinable solely by resort to a listing of those things which are authorized and those things which are prohibited. We must also consider, as did the trial judge, whether the circumstances permit a determination that the use in question is an *implied* accessory use. *See State v. P.T. & L. Construction Co.*, 77 N.J. 20, 25–26, 389 A.2d 448 (1978); *Tanis v. Tp. of Hampton*, 306 N.J.Super. 588, 601, 704 A.2d 62 (App.Div.1977); *Shim v. Washington Tp. Planning Bd.*, 298 N.J.Super. 395, 400–03, 689 A.2d 804 (App.Div.1997). Accordingly, despite the fact that the express terms of the ordinances, standing alone, exclude pigeon coops as accessory uses, the particular factual circumstances must be examined to determine whether it may be implied that a pigeon coop is an accessory use.

As observed, Ordinance 170–5 defines accessory uses as those "naturally and normally incident and subordinate to the principal use." In *Charlie Brown of Chatham v. Bd. of Adjust. of Chatham Tp.*, 202 N.J.Super. 312, 324, 495 A.2d 119 (App.Div.1985) we held that "incidental" in this context incorporates two concepts—the use must be subordinate or minor in significance when compared to the primary use of the property and the use in question must bear a reasonable relationship to the primary use. In determining whether plaintiff's pigeon coop is an implied accessory use, its presence must bear a close resemblance and obvious relation to the main use to which the premises are put—here, a residence. It must also be a customary use in such a zone. As explained by the Supreme Court in *P.T. v. L.*, "[g]enerally, a use which is so necessary or commonly to be expected that it cannot be supposed that the ordinance was intended to prevent it will be found to be a customary use." 77 N.J. at 27, 389 A.2d 448.

Here, there is no obvious or close relationship between a residence and a pigeon coop, nor is it customary for homeowners in Union Township to have pigeon coops. The factual record indicates that at the times relevant to this case there were 52,000 residents of Union Township, but only one other pigeon coop, which had been closed down by the time of the hearing before the board. Thus, there is no merit to the argument that it is customary for Union Township residents to maintain pigeon coops. Accordingly, we conclude that the ordinances do not on their face permit a pigeon coop to be considered an accessory use nor should a pigeon coop be deemed an implied accessory use.

We also reject plaintiff's constitutional arguments. Whether an ordinance is unconstitutionally vague cannot be decided in a vacuum but must be made in light of its context and with a firm understanding of its purpose. *State v. Cameron*, 100 N.J. 586, 591, 498 A.2d 1217 (1985). In stressing the importance of context, we likewise recognize that the constitutional standard that plaintiff seeks to invoke must not be mechanically implied. *Ibid.* Thus, it is well understood that not all ordinances need attain the same level of definitional clarity, nor can it be expected that an ordinance will expressly provide for all possible lawful uses. *Tanis, supra,* 306 N.J.Super. at 602, 704 A.2d 62. The ordinances in question utilize traditional terms in defining what constitutes an accessory use in a residential zone and further amplify upon their underlying intentions by providing specific examples of what is and is not permitted. The ordinances also indicate, in clear language, that all uses not enumerated are prohibited. There is no vagueness in these ordinances. Nor do these ordinances become vague because the law deems that they must have more "play in their joints" and because the law permits a finding that a particular use, not expressly dealt with in an ordinance, may be found by implication to be a legitimate accessory use. This implied accessory doctrine simply permits a determination of whether a use, perhaps not contemplated at the time of an ordinance's enactment, should be authorized regardless of the brightlines drawn by the ordinance, and hardly creates a basis from which it could be argued that the ordinance is impermissibly vague. *See State v. Russo*, 328 N.J.Super. 181, 191–92, 745 A.2d 540 (App.Div.), *certif. denied*, 165 N.J. 134, 751 A.2d 1210 (2000). We thus find no substance in plaintiff's argument that the ordinances either on their face or as applied to his pigeon coop are unconstitutionally vague.

After having carefully reviewed the record, we conclude that plaintiff's remaining arguments are without sufficient merit to warrant discussion in a written opinion. *R.* 2:11–3(e)(1)(E).

NOTES

1.   As courts have observed, there are diametrically opposed approaches to permissible accessory uses: "if it isn't listed as permitted in the ordinance, you can't do it" vs. "if it isn't listed as prohibited, go right ahead." *See Graf v. Zoning Bd. of Appeals of the Twn. of Killingworth*, 894 A.2d 285 (2006). Which do you prefer? The ordinance at issue in *DaPurificacao* appears to incorporate both approaches. According to the court, the ordinance enumerates both

permitted and prohibited uses, and then closes "any loophole" with respect to uses not listed by stating that "[a]ll uses not expressly permitted by this chapter are prohibited." According to the court, however, the inquiry does not end there. Do you see why?

The court in *DaPurificacao* also rejected the landowner's argument that the accessory use ordinances were unconstitutionally vague and therefore void. Do you agree with the court? For an example of a court finding an accessory use ordinance unconstitutionally vague, *see Mayor & Bd. of Alderman, City of Clinton v. Welch*, 888 So.2d 416 (Miss.2004), where a family built a tree house in their front yard costing over $5000. Upon complaint by a neighbor, the city sought to bring the tree house down as an illegal accessory building. The city had a messy ordinance prohibiting accessory buildings and uses in one section and defining "accessory structures and uses" in another. The court found that "[a]ccording to the ordinance an 'accessory structure' can be either a 'detached structure' or a 'use.' We are then told there is no definition of 'detached structure,' but there is a definition of 'structure' which is 'anything constructed or erected, the use of which requires a fixed location on the ground, or attached to something having a fixed location on the ground.' We find the application of this definition to Section 401.05 of the City's Ordinance to be unconstitutionally vague." 888 So.2d at 435. A dissenting judge opined that "[a] common sense reading of those definitions would clearly inform the reader of what is prohibited under the ordinance. The definition of structure is 'anything constructed or erected, the use of which requires a fixed location on the ground, or attached to something having a fixed location on the ground.' Any person would be able to determine that a tree house falls within this definition and would not have guess at its meaning." 888 So.2d at 435.

2. The "incidental" and "customary" requirements are common, but not necessarily sound. They both look backwards, requiring proof of past use. Under the *DaPurificacao* standard that a use "be a customary use in such a zone," new uses can never gain legal status. Upholding a board's finding that a wind turbine was a valid accessory use in a residential zone, a court said that the customary requirement for an accessory use structure "should [not] be construed so as to prevent the implementation of new technologies in residential districts." *Hamby v. Bd. of Zoning Appeals of Area Plan Comm'n of Warrick Cnty.*, 932 N.E.2d 1251, 1255 (Ind.App.2010). The court was not clear on how "customary" should be defined, but rather found that the objecting neighbors had the burden of proof and failed to prove that wind turbines were uncommon. Maintaining a stable for horses on a residential lot was once customary. Presumably it has lost that status. Does the requirement confer non-conforming use status on uses that were once, but are no longer, customary?

If the goal of the legislation is to allow greater personal freedom of use while avoiding an adverse impact on neighbors, the customary requirement does not achieve its goal. New uses might be inoffensive and customary ones may have become offensive over time with changing tastes. The requirement also operates in a discriminatory manner. In one case, a court denied a barber the right to have a part-time shop in his home because it found that cutting hair in the home was not customary. Sewing and cooking would be fine, said the court, but not barbering. *Gold v. Zoning Bd. of Adj.*, 143 A.2d 59, 60 (Pa.1958). The court did not bother asking whether the barber had more client traffic than seamstresses and chefs.

A court applying a deferential standard of review will not find the customary requirement to violate the due process or equal protection clauses. *See* Thomas E. Roberts, *The Regulation of Home Occupations Under Zoning Ordinances: Some Constitutional Considerations*, 56 TEMP.L.Q. 49 (1983). Yet, there are better ways to measure compatibility, such as performance standards and specific limitations on outside employees, sales of goods, and limitations on hours to receive clients. For a comprehensive discussion of home occupations and recent zoning code solutions, *see* Patricia E. Salkin, *Zoning for Home Occupations: Modernizing Zoning Codes to Accommodate Growth in Home-Based Businesses*, 35 REAL ESTATE L.J. 181 (2006).

3.   Had the court ruled in DaPurificacao's favor, the town might have amended its ordinances to make it clear that pigeon coops were prohibited. Then, the town could have forced him to comply with the new law. Or, would he have a right to continue his pre-existing use?

4.   The predominant accessory use is the home occupation. Ordinances vary in what qualifies as a home occupation, but they often allow such uses as sewing and clothing alterations, childcare, teaching of music, and part-time offices for doctors, lawyers, and real estate agents. Many home occupation ordinances are elitist, allowing only for offices of "professionals," and often expressly recognize doctors, lawyers and clergy as "professionals." Courts sometimes require others who want to claim status as professionals, such as real estate or insurance agents, musicians, or artists, to prove that they have specialized training, follow a code of ethics, and render a public service. After all, that is a common dictionary definition of "professional." Something is wrong here, isn't it? *See* Thomas E. Roberts, *The Regulation of Home Occupations Under Zoning Ordinances: Some Constitutional Considerations*, 56 TEMP.L.Q. 49 (1983); Nicole Stelle Garnett, *On Castles and Commerce: Zoning Law and the Home-Business Dilemma*, 42 WM. & MARY L.REV. 1191 (2001).

5.   Accessory living units provide one source of affordable housing, particularly for university students. Those units may be created by the subdivision of existing single-family homes or they may be separate structures. Often not welcomed by neighbors, cities may limit occupancy to persons related to the owners of the principal unit by blood, marriage, or adoption. *See Anderson v. Provo City Corp.*, 108 P.3d 701 (Utah 2005) (sustaining occupancy limits); *but see Coalition Advocating Legal Housing Options v. City of Santa Monica*, 105 Cal.Rptr.2d 802 (Cal.App.2001) (requirement that second housing unit in single-family district be occupied only by relatives or caregivers violated state constitution's right of privacy). For an argument against rental restrictions, *see* Ngai Pindell, *Home Sweet Home? The Efficacy of Rental*

Restrictions to Promote Neighborhood Stability, 29 ST. LOUIS U.PUB.L.REV. 41 (2009).

6. What animals fall within the definition of "household pets?" A pig on a small, residential lot? Yes, said Hawaii's Intermediate Court of Appeals in *Foster Village Community Ass'n v. Hess*, 667 P.2d 850 (Haw.App.1983), but, no, said an Illinois court in *Village of Glenview v. Ramaker*, 668 N.E.2d 106 (Ill.App.1996). How would you react if your neighbors announced plans to use their land to provide a safe haven for endangered gorillas? Or a tiger? *See Board of Commissioners of Roane Cnty. v. Parker*, 88 S.W.3d 916 (Tenn.App.2002). Can a town ban "exotic animals"? *See Rhoads v. City of Battle Ground*, 63 P.3d 142 (Wash.App.2002) (ordinance prohibiting possession of exotic animals did not violate the owners' equal protection or due process rights); *see also Greater Chicago Combine and Center, Inc. v. City of Chicago*, 431 F.3d 1065 (7th Cir.2005) (ban on keeping pigeons in residential areas constitutional).

RICHARD M. RUDOLPH AND MARGARET E. RUDOLPH, APPELLANTS V. THE ZONING HEARING BOARD OF CAMBRIA TOWNSHIP, TOWNSHIP OF CAMBRIA, AND MATT R. NIEBAUER

Commonwealth Court of Pennsylvania, 2003.
839 A.2d 475.

Opinion by JUDGE COHN.

In this appeal, we must decide whether, under a vested rights theory, a commercial landscaping business can operate in a residential zone by virtue of a building permit issued to build a "pole building," and whether or not a landscaping business can qualify as a "home occupation."

The property in question is located in an R-2 residential district and is part of a cluster of approximately 30 homes that lie about a mile outside the downtown section of the Township. In 1997, Beverly Niebauer owned the property, the east end of which contained a house and a modular home, and the west end of which was vacant.

In 1997 Mrs. Niebauer's son, Todd Niebauer, applied for a permit to construct a pole building, measuring 40' x 56' x 12', on the west end of the property. The application for the building permit contained a section entitled "Proposed use," which had two columns: one with the heading "RESIDENTIAL" and the other with the heading "NONRESIDENTIAL." Each column contained a list of several uses relating to residential and nonresidential development, respectively. Each column also included a line entitled "Other Specify," followed by space for writing in an answer. Todd Niebauer checked the "Other Specify" block under the *residential* column of his application and, in the space provided, wrote "Pole Bldg–Landscaping Business." Todd Niebauer did not check the "Other Specify" block under the non-residential column. The zoning officer indicated that he understood the application to mean that the Niebauers would be using the pole building to store vehicles.

Commercial enterprises are not permitted in this district. Home occupants are permitted, but the owner must first obtain from the Township a certificate authorizing the home occupation. Pole buildings are also permitted in R-2 districts.

In conformance with the zoning ordinance, the Township granted a building permit to Mrs. Beverly Niebauer, then the record owner of the property, to build the pole building. The permit did not indicate that the building could be used for a landscaping business, nor for any business but, instead, merely provided that it could be used for "storage." The pole building was constructed in accordance with the permit.

Several months later, in May 1998, Mrs. Niebauer filed a subdivision plan to split the lot into two parcels, one measuring .875 acres (Lot No. 1) containing the two houses, the other measuring 2.875 acres (Lot No. 2) containing only the pole building. The subdivision plan was granted. Shortly thereafter, Mrs. Niebauer conveyed her interest in Lot No. 2 to her sons, Todd Niebauer and Matt Niebauer, but retained her interest in Lot No. 1.

Matt Niebauer utilized the pole building on Lot No. 2 for his landscaping business, by storing equipment and supplies in it. Although the actual landscaping work was conducted off site, the company employees would meet on the property at the start of each day before departing for the day's worksite. While assembled on the property, the employees would typically load equipment and supplies necessary for the day's work onto trucks that were stored on-site. The loaded trucks would leave early in the morning and return at the end of each day, at which time they would be unloaded.

Over the course of time, the landscaping business expanded in size. Matt Niebauer hired five employees to assist with the work. None of these employees were family members. As the business grew, the need for materials grew with it, and the business began receiving regular deliveries of landscaping materials several times each month by tractor trailer. Many of these materials, which included stacks of brick pavers, numerous plants, and mounds of mulch and manure, were stored in plain view on the open grounds surrounding the pole building.

The appellants in this case, the Rudolphs, live in the property adjacent to Lot No. 2. On a daily basis, the Rudolphs heard a variety of noises coming from Lot No. 2, including the sounds of the mechanical equipment used to load and unload the materials onto trucks in preparation for the day's landscaping work. In addition to the business-associated noises, the Rudolphs also had to contend with a number of business-related smells emanating from the fertilizer and organic material stored on site.

In May 2002, the Township issued an enforcement notice against Matt Niebauer and Todd Niebauer, as owners of Lot No. 2, for operating a commercial enterprise within the R-2 district, "namely, a landscaping type business . . . involving the storage of equipment and other bulk items, i.e. manure, etc., on the premises." (Enforcement Notice, pg. 1). Matt Niebauer, as the operator of the landscaping business, challenged the enforcement notice.

The home occupation argument is premised on Matt Niebauer's appeal from the enforcement notice. In his response to the enforcement notice that gave rise to this appeal, he argued that: "Use of real estate as set forth in No. 6 above is a permitted use in an R2 district due to the fact it will qualify as a home occupation pursuant to Section 315, et seq., and Section 801.15 [of the local zoning ordinance]". (Appeal Notice of Matt R. Niebauer and Todd Niebauer, No. 10). At the hearing conducted pursuant to these appeal documents, Matt Niebauer's counsel confirmed that the home occupation theory formed the basis of the appeal.

We conclude that the operation of the landscaping business does not comply with the Township zoning ordinance for engaging in a home occupation. The zoning ordinance places very clear limitations on conducting a home occupation, and requires that the home occupation "be carried on wholly within the principal or accessory structures," (Cambria Township Zoning Ordinance, Section 315.2), that the occupation be conducted "by a member of the family residing in the dwelling unit with not more than one employee who is not part of the family," (*id.*, Section 315.1), that "[o]bjectionable noise, vibration, smoke, dust, odors, heat or glare shall not be produced," (*id.*, Section 315.4), and that a "zoning certificate shall be required" (*id.*, Section 315.6). None of these requirements were met.

First, there is no home on this parcel. The property, Lot No. 2, contains many things: a dump truck, a skid mover, many potted plants, hundreds of masonry stones and bricks and even a fourteen foot tall mound of manure. It does not, however, contain a home, and has not contained one for several years. We see no basis to expand a home occupation where the property has no home. Matt Niebauer's belated attempt to remedy this deficiency by obtaining ownership of residential Lot No. 1, and merging it with pole building Lot No. 2, does not bring this operation within the ambit of a home occupation. Second, Matt Niebauer acknowledges hiring up to five non-family members to assist with the occupation, which is in conflict with the home occupation requirement that no more than one employee can be from outside the owner's family. Third, significant noise is produced on a daily basis. Full-size tractor trailers come onto the property within 100 feet of the neighbor's bedroom window and substantial quantities of materials, some malodorous, are delivered and stored on site. The zoning ordinance does not classify such an operation as a home occupation. Fourth, Matt

Niebauer did not obtain a home occupancy zoning certificate as required by the ordinance.

In summary, we do not find that the 1997 application for a building permit authorized the operation of a landscaping business or home occupation on the property. On this basis we reverse the order of the common pleas court.

4. HEIGHT AND BULK CONTROLS

In addition to regulating uses, comprehensive Euclidean zoning controls building height and bulk by establishing setbacks, minimum lot size, lot coverage limitations, and permissible floor area ratios. Early Supreme Court decisions upheld both types of controls. *See Welch v. Swasey*, 214 U.S. 91 (1909) (height controls) and *Gorieb v. Fox*, 274 U.S. 603 (1927) (setbacks).

Concerns with building height and bulk played a significant role in stimulating the adoption of zoning. The skyscraper and the tenement house were the culprits. In the building boom that New York City experienced in the late nineteenth and early twentieth centuries, massive buildings occupying the entirety of their building lot spread throughout Manhattan. When a skyscraper went up, owners and occupants of neighboring buildings often found their natural light and air blocked. Rental income of neighboring owners fell, as their buildings now sat in the shadow of the new skyscraper. City real estate tax revenues also dropped as assessed values fell, and the streets became dark and unattractive to shoppers. These problems led to the appointment of the New York City Advisory Commission on the Height of Buildings, which recommended that regulating building height alone was insufficient and that setbacks of the upper stories of buildings in a pyramid-like style was needed. *See* Seymour Toll, *Zoned American* 46–73 (1969).

In 1961, New York City changed direction and adopted a system of incentive zoning that granted bonuses allowing larger buildings. As developers moved quickly to take advantage of these bonuses, owners of low-rise brownstones on the Upper East Side complained of loss of sunshine and views caused by their new high-rise neighbors. Such concerns led the city to rethink its policies and limit again building height and bulk. *See* Georgette C. Poindexter, *Light, Air, or Manhattanization?: Communal Aesthetics in Zoning Central City Real Estate Development*, 78 B.U.L.REV. 445 (1998); McKinley, *Zoning Changes Reduce Size of East Side Projects*, New York Times, Feb. 10, 1994, Section B, p. 3.

Concern with tall and bulky buildings persists across the country. In the latter part of the 20th century, such major cities as Seattle, San Francisco, and Philadelphia, tightened restrictions on building height and bulk due to concerns over losses of view, sunlight, and air.

RUMSON ESTATES, INC. V. MAYOR & COUNCIL OF THE BOROUGH OF FAIR HAVEN

Supreme Court of New Jersey, 2003.
177 N.J. 338, 828 A.2d 317.

LONG, J.

Two basic issues are presented by these appeals.[1] The first is whether a municipality may enact a zoning ordinance that alters the definitions in the Municipal Land Use Law (MLUL). *N.J.S.A.* 40:55D–1 to –136. The second is whether zoning regulations may make provision for different conditions within a zone without violating the uniformity principle of *N.J.S.A.* 40:55D–62a. We hold that, with a narrow exception, the MLUL does not preclude a municipality from adopting a zoning ordinance that defines terms differently from the definitions in the MLUL. We also hold that the notion of uniformity does not prohibit classifications within a district so long as they are reasonable and so long as all similarly situated property receives the same treatment.

Fair Haven is a fully developed municipality of approximately one square mile. Its population of 6,000 is basically dispersed among single lot construction and small subdivisions. In 1999, as part of a comprehensive revision of its Development Regulations, Fair Haven changed the zoning of the William Street block from R-7.5 (requiring sixty feet of frontage and a minimum lot area of 7,500 square feet) to R-5 (requiring fifty feet of frontage and a minimum lot area of 5,000 square feet). It included a maximum floor area ratio of .40. Such a ratio essentially limits habitable floor area to a percentage of the total lot. The ordinance also capped the floor area at 2,200 square feet for all single-family dwellings in the district. Under the ordinance, the smaller of the floor area ratio or the cap applies.

Plaintiff, Rumson Estates, Inc., is the owner of an approximately 27,000 square foot parcel of property in Fair Haven that it proposed to subdivide into three lots of fairly equal size. Each lot was to have fifty feet of frontage, a depth of 181.5 feet and a total area of 9,066.4 square feet. Applying the floor area ratio only, plaintiff would have been able to build a house of approximately 3,600 square feet on each lot. However, the cap limited plaintiff to 2,200 square feet.

* * *

What is at issue in this case is the regulation of the intensity of land use. *See Rumson Estates, supra,* 350 N.J.Super. at 331, 795 A.2d 290 (indicating that phrase "intensity of land use" refers to size of structures on property). In that connection, *N.J.S.A.* 40:55D–65 provides that: A zoning ordinance may:

---

[1] [The court consolidated two cases. We have omitted the companion case, which involves a steep slope ordinance to prevent landslides. Eds.]

b.   Regulate the bulk, height, number of stories, orientation, and size of buildings and the other structures; the percentage of lot or development area that may be occupied by structures; lot sizes and dimensions; and for these purposes may specify floor area ratios and other ratios and regulatory techniques governing the intensity of land use and the provision of adequate light and air, including, but not limited to the potential for utilization of renewable energy resources.

Among the definitions set forth in *N.J.S.A.* 40:55D–3 to –7 are several that are in play in that statute. "Density" is "the permitted number of dwelling units per gross area of land to be developed." "Floor area ratio" is "the sum of the area of all floors of buildings or structures compared to the total area of the site." * * * When those definitions are read together, it is clear that floor area ratio under the MLUL expresses a pure mathematical relationship between the size of buildings and the total land area. According to plaintiffs, any variation from that definition is invalid under *Manalapan Builders*. It is that notion that will be tested in this case.

In *Manalapan Builders, supra,* the Appellate Division was faced with an ordinance that specifically included a floor area ratio but provided that the mathematical calculation would be undertaken only after the lot size was reduced by certain specified environmental land features. Among the features excluded from the calculation were rights-of-way; floodways; wetlands; steep slopes; stream corridors; hydric soils; and buffer zones.

[The intermediate appellate court in *Manalapan,* cited above, invalidated the ordinance and here the Supreme Court discusses that opinion, with which it disagrees. Eds.]

* * *

Turning to this case, if the MLUL had provided that the exclusive method available to a municipality for controlling intensity of residential land use was floor area ratio and had defined that term, both the method and the definition would be binding. In fact, *N.J.S.A.* 40:55D–65b does just the opposite and specifically provides authority for municipalities to use any number of methods to control the intensity of residential use. Included along with floor area ratios are "other ratios and regulatory techniques." Floor area ratio is defined in *N.J.S.A.* 40:55D–4 but other ratios and regulatory techniques are not so defined. The lack of definitions of the latter terms reflects the reality that they encompass a large number of possibilities and that the Legislature intended to empower municipalities to address creatively the subject of the intensity of land use without definitional restriction. There is nothing in the statutory scheme to suggest that the Legislature wished to preclude or otherwise limit the use of other ratios or regulatory techniques either alone or in conjunction with floor area ratio. Indeed, the very notion of "other ratios" seems specifically to encompass a ratio that is *not* simply "the sum of all areas of all floors of buildings or structures compared to the total area of the site." *N.J.S.A.* 40:55D–4.

That is where we think the court in *Manalapan Builders* went astray. Plainly the environmental set-asides in that case did not strictly conform with the MLUL definition of lot to the extent that the total "unit" was reduced by environmental factors. It follows that that reduction altered the floor area ratio which was not based on the "total area" of the site. However, as we have indicated, that did not render the ordinance invalid. As the plaintiffs in *Manalapan Builders* argued, the set-aside was "another formula" authorized by the statute.

* * *

In sum, a municipality may enact a zoning ordinance that alters the non-mandatory definitions in the MLUL. Likewise, in regulating the intensity of land use, a municipality may adopt not only a floor area ratio based on the relationship between the lot and buildings, but any other ratio or regulatory technique that advances a goal of the MLUL and conforms with the other legal principles to which we have adverted. To the extent that *Manalapan Builders* reached a different conclusion it is disapproved.

We turn next to plaintiffs' uniformity argument. * * * That uniformity of process is not at issue in this case. * * * What is at issue is *N.J.S.A.* 40:55D–62a, which provides in relevant part:

> The zoning ordinance shall be drawn with reasonable consideration to the character of each district and its peculiar suitability for particular uses and to encourage the most appropriate use of land. *The regulations in the zoning ordinance shall be uniform throughout each district for each class or kind of buildings or other structures or uses of land,* including planned unit development, planned unit residential development and residential cluster, but the regulations in one district may differ from those in other districts. [(Emphasis added).]

That statute dates back to our original zoning law, which was enacted in 1928 and was modeled on the Standard State Zoning Enabling Act published by the United States Department of Commerce in 1924. Both Acts contained a uniformity section.

Legal commentators note that there were two sources underpinning the uniformity provision. The first was extra-legal. During the early debates over zoning, "while the subject was in the balance," the assurance to "potentially hostile landowners that all property which was similarly situated would be treated alike" was critical. * * *

The other basis for the uniformity requirement was, and continues to be, the constitutional guarantees of due process and equal protection that guard against the arbitrary and unreasonable exercise of the police power. * * *

Plaintiffs broadly misinterpret that uniformity principle to mean that there can be no differences in the regulation of property within a zone. More particularly, plaintiffs in *Rumson Estates* contend that because the cap only has an effect on the larger lots in the zone, it renders the ordinance non-uniform. * * *

In fact, nearly thirty-five years ago, in commenting on an identical uniformity provision in the prior zoning statute, this Court clearly established that uniformity "does not prohibit classifications within a district so long as they are reasonable." *Quinton v. Edison Park Dev. Corp.*, 59 N.J. 571, 580, 285 A.2d 5 (1971) (interpreting uniformity requirement to allow distinctions among uses within given zone so long as distinctions are not arbitrary and unduly discriminatory). * * *

In short, plaintiffs are wrong in their crabbed interpretation of *N.J.S.A.* 40:55D–62a. Uniformity is not absolute and rational regulations based on different conditions within a zone are permissible so long as similarly situated property is treated the same. Reasonableness of classification is the key. "Constitutional uniformity and equality requires that classification be founded in real and not feigned differences having to do with the purpose for which the classes are formed."

Applying the standards to which we have referred, we turn now to the zoning ordinances in question. Like the Appellate Division, we hold that plaintiffs did not overcome the presumption of validity that attached to the ordinances.

The cap in the Fair Haven ordinance overrides the floor area ratio in situations in which lots are oversized and would otherwise result in the building of huge houses in a zone, which basically is fully established, with much more modest residences. Fair Haven advanced two rationales for the cap. The first was the proportionality of new construction to other houses in the zone and the second, the diversification of housing stock by the building of smaller, more affordable homes. The Appellate Division placed its imprimatur on those goals as do we.

N.J.S.A. 40:55D–2(i) specifically underscores the promotion of a desirable visual environment through the use of creative zoning techniques as an end point of the MLUL. That visual component comes into play, where, as here, zoning is enacted after certain areas of a municipality substantially are built up. In such locations, zoning should generally reflect existing conditions. Yet, as commentators have observed,

> [o]ne of the phenomena of the late 20th Century and early 21st Century has been the construction of what have been referred to as 'monster homes', *i.e.,* homes built to a scale completely out of keeping with the homes in the surrounding area. . . . These

homes, in addition to impinging on the light, air and open space, *N.J.S.A.* 40:55D–2c, of their neighbors particularly in already dense zones also create an adverse visual environment.

[Cox, *New Jersey Zoning,* § 34–7.5 at 735.] *See also* Paul J. Weinberg, 24 ZONING & PLAN. L. REP. 17 (2001) (commenting that " 'monster houses' are . . . failing to match the fabric of the neighborhood" (citations omitted)). It is that disconnection that was a legitimate focus of Fair Haven's disproportionality rationale.

Regarding the diversification of housing stock, Fair Haven maintains that it is attempting to achieve a laudable goal that, in other contexts, we generally have recognized. *See, e.g., Oakwood at Madison, Inc. v. Township of Madison,* 72 N.J. 481, 548, 371 A.2d 1192 (1977) (adopting notion that general welfare encompasses recognition of local and regional housing needs). Fair Haven underscores the need to build smaller, more affordable houses, observing that many municipal workers cannot afford to live in town. The municipality chose to confront that problem by initiating the cap. Whether that is the most efficient methodology may be debatable. But that is a decision for the municipality rather than for us. *Pierro v. Baxendale,* 20 N.J. 17, 26, 118 A.2d 401 (1955). Once the decision was made to cap the size of houses in the R-2 zone it became "presumptively valid and . . . [is] not to be nullified except upon an affirmative showing that the action taken . . . was unreasonable, arbitrary or capricious." We cannot say that that showing was made in this case.

The judgments of the Appellate Division are affirmed.

NOTES

1. Authority to enact height and bulk controls is not usually challenged, and when it is the results usually are in accord with *Rumson Estates.* The Standard Zoning Enabling Act confers express power to regulate the size of buildings, the percentage of lot that may be covered, and density. Bulk controls serve a number of purposes that fall within Standard Act, including the preservation of light and air, the preservation of view for traffic safety, and access for firefighting. They also protect an aesthetically pleasing building scale and relationship between structures, as in *Rumson Estates. See supra,* Chapter 2B on aesthetics for more discussion of this issue. Some controls are more specific in purpose. Denver, for example, has a height limitation in certain zones to preserve mountain views from several city parks. *Landmark Land Co. v. City and County of Denver,* 728 P.2d 1281 (Colo.1986) (upholding act as legitimate effort to promote aesthetics).

2. Shortly after World War II, when residential development moved rapidly into suburban areas across the country, a New Jersey builder chose a sparsely developed suburban community outside Trenton to begin construction of modest homes ranging in size from 484 to 676 square feet. The town reacted to these "doll houses" with an ordinance requiring single story houses to have

at least 768 square feet, two story houses with an attached garage, 1000 square feet, and two story houses without an attached garage, 1200 square feet. Noting that the town lay within the path of development the court found the town acted with commendable vigilance to bar these small, and notably, affordable houses. *Lionshead Lake, Inc. v. Wayne Township*, 89 A.2d 693 (N.J.1952). Later, the same court reversed itself and invalidated an 1100 minimum square foot requirement. *Home Builders League v. Township of Berlin*, 405 A.2d 381 (N.J.1979). We explore these "exclusionary zoning" practices and their implications for affordable housing in Chapter 5A.

Rumson Estates deals with the other extreme. "Monster houses" or "McMansions" boasting 5,000 square feet and up have become common. Believing that these houses have an adverse impact on the supply of affordable housing and are also aesthetically dissonant in some areas, a number of communities, like those in *Rumson Estates*, have started to limit house size. For pros and cons on the big house syndrome, *see* Robert E. Lang and Karen A. Danielsen, *Monster Houses? Yes! They Make Good Infill—and They Make Good Economic Sense, and Mark L. Hinshaw, Monster Houses? No! A Commendable Example of Smart Growth? I Don't Think So, 68 Planning,* pp. 24–27 (May 2002). For a nice summary of relatively recent trends and issues, *see* Nancy Kubasek, *MegaMansions: A New Source of Conflict Between Environmentalists and Developers*, 35 Real Estate L.J. 173 (2006). Monster homes are discussed *infra* Ch. 5.A.

3. Courts examining a decision on calculating bulk requirements employ a statutory interpretation analysis of the relevant local ordinance. Local zoning ordinances often define lot depth, width, and setback, explaining how to calculate such values. *See, e.g.,* Medina Muni. C. §§ 20.23.010–.080; S.F. Muni. C. § 270. In *Kaplan v. City of Linwood*, 252 N.J.Super. 538, 542, 600 A.2d 180, 183 (N.J.Super.1991), the appellate court was asked to decide whether the planning Board should have included an area of the lot in question that lay in a conservation zone in their calculation of lot size for bulk controls. In reversing the board's decision to limit the calculations to the dwelling zone, the court examined the relevant definitional section of the City's planning code:

> In the instant case, an examination of § 57–18(A), in light of the definitions set forth in the ordinance, shows that the board's decision to limit the calculations to the land located only within the dwelling zone cannot be supported. To arrive at such a conclusion would render the definitional sections of the ordinance meaningless. Both lot width and lot depth are defined as distances between lot lines. Setbacks are measured from property lines. Rear yard is measured to the rear property line. There is no language in the ordinance which would limit between lot or property lines. The board in making its determination made no attempt to reconcile the definitions with the language of § 57–18(A). Without engaging in such a process, the board's decision was arbitrary. Definitions are contained in an ordinance to provide guidance and consistency in ordinance interpretation. An ordinance should not be read in a manner which

would render a portion thereof meaningless. Construction of a legislative enactment which would render any part thereof meaningless. Construction of a legislative enactment which would render any part thereof superfluous is disfavored. *Pepper v. Princeton Univ. Bd. of Trustees*, 77 N.J. 55, 389 A.2d 465 (1978).

Kaplan, 252 N.J. Super. at 542–43, 600 A.2d at 183 (footnote added).

The Supreme Court of New Hampshire similarly examined the definition section of a local zoning ordinance to decide whether setbacks are included in the calculation of lot size for bulk controls. *See Doyle v. Town of Gilmanton*, 155 N.H. 733, 736, 927 A.2d 1211, 1214 (2007). In this case, the land owner wished to include the setback area in the total calculation of his land for compliance with bulk controls relating to minimum lot size. However, the zoning board argued that setbacks do not factor into minimum lot size because they cannot be built upon. Examining the town's zoning ordinance, the court ruled that setback areas cannot be included in the calculation for minimum lot size: The ordinance defines a setback as that area between the property line and a line running parallel to it, which "shall contain no structures." *Gilmanton Zoning Ordinance* art. XVI. The ordinance defines structure as: "*Anything* constructed or erected with a fixed location on the ground or attached to something having a fixed location on the ground." *Id.* (emphasis added). Logically, therefore, because a setback cannot be in an area where a building or other structure is placed, it cannot be part of a "building site" as defined in the regulations. Because setbacks are excluded from the definition of "building site," we conclude, as did the board and the superior court, that the area covered by setback should not be included when calculating whether a proposed building site meets the minimum building site size requirement.

Doyle, 155 N.H. at 736, 927 A.2d at 1214.

The Court of Appeals of New York also referred to the zoning ordinance's definition section in ruling that cellar spaces are expressly excluded from Floor Area Ration ("FAR") calculations under New York City's Zoning Ordinance. *Raritan Dev. Corp. v. Silva*, 91 N.Y.2d 98, 103, 689 N.E.2d 1373, 1375 (1997). In overturning the decision of the Board of Standards and Appeals of the City of New York ("BSA") to include cellar space in the FAR calculations because cellars were being used as living spaces, the court pointed to explicit language in the zoning ordinance: The statutory language could not be clearer. As noted above, a cellar is defined within the Zoning Resolution in terms of its physical location in a building. "Floor area" includes dwelling spaces when not specifically excluded and "cellar space," without qualification, is expressly excluded from FAR calculations. Thus, FAR calculations should not include cellars regardless of the intended use of the space.

BSA's interpretation conflicts with the plain statutory language and may not be sustained.

Silva, 91 N.Y.2d at 103, 689 N.E.2d at 1375.

Some courts have also given more deference to zoning boards' decisions regarding calculations, providing they are reasonable in light of the definitions in the zoning ordinance. In *Moore v. Noyes*, No. 10 MISC 434088CWT, 2010 WL 5423714, at *4 (Mass. Land. Ct. Dec. 22, 2010), the Massachusetts Land Court examined the definition section of the zoning regulation in question to determine whether the zoning board's calculation of the building height in question was reasonable: § 97–11.D of the [zoning ordinance] clearly states that the height of the building shall be measured from the mean level of the established grade at the building to the mean height of the highest roof. This definition is somewhat uncertain; therefore, deference should be given to the board in its interpretation of it, *so long as it is reasonable*. The Defendants claim the established grade at the building was calculated using the average of the grades at ground level in each of the four corners of the existing structure.

To determine the mean height of the highest roof, Defendants contend the cupola or lookout" is less than 70 square feet, is not habitable, and is not intended for continued occupancy. The Building Inspector, in his affidavit, further claims that the Town, for purposes of calculating roof height, ignores such spaces. As a result, the mean roof height was taken as the *average* of the highest point of the cupola and the eave height. When these two figures are calculated, the building height is 34′–10″. Plaintiffs provide an alternative to calculating the building height, but it need not be considered. As long as the building height calculation accepted by the Board and restricted in the Special Permit was concluded reasonably, the Board's interpretation will suffice. Considering all the evidence and the definitions provided in the by-laws, this court concludes the building height as determined by the Board of 34′10″ is reasonable and was properly calculated.

4.   As with any exercise of the police power, bulk controls may be unreasonable as applied. Minimum lot size requirements, for example, protect light and view and regulate density. However, when they allow only large lot development (e.g., one unit per four acres), they may run afoul of judicial limitations on exclusionary zoning. See Chapter 5.

5.   The key bulk control, as dealt with in *Rumson Estates,* is the floor-area ratio (FAR), or the ratio which the floor area within the building bears to the lot area of the zoning lot containing the building. A FAR ordinance designates a floor-area ratio for a particular zone. If the ratio is 1:1, a one story building can cover the entire buildable area of the lot, a two-story building can cover half the buildable area, a four-story building can cover one-fourth of the buildable area and so on. In commercial office areas in large cities the floor-

area ratio may be 10:1, which allows a twenty-story building on half the buildable area of the lot. FAR may be used with maximum height limits and other bulk controls, so that in a 10:1 area, it may not be possible to build a 20-story building on 1/20th of the buildable area of a lot or to eliminate yards entirely and build a 10-story building up to all lot lines. *See* Juergensmeyer and Roberts, *Land Use Planning and Development Regulation Law* § 4.14 (3rd ed.2012).

6.   Height and bulk controls, as opposed to use, are in the forefront of major code changes being made across the country under the rubric of form-based zoning. Deemphasizing the segregation of land uses under Euclidean codes, form-based zoning is most concerned with the building envelope and its fit with its neighbors. See discussion *infra* Ch. 2 J.

5.   CONDITIONAL USES

Under many zoning ordinances, some uses may be required to obtain a conditional use permit. The label varies, and such permits are often called special permits, special uses or, using the language of the SZEA, special exceptions.* The conditional or special use process deals with uses that by their nature are difficult to fit within a particular use zone where they can operate by right. The purpose is explained in the Portland, Oregon ordinance:

> Certain uses are conditional uses instead of being allowed outright, although they may have beneficial effects and serve important public interests. They are subject to the conditional use regulations because they may, but do not necessarily, have significant adverse effects on the environment, overburden public services, change the desired character of an area, or create major nuisances. A review of these uses is necessary due to the potential individual or cumulative impacts they may have on the surrounding area or neighborhood. The conditional use review provides an opportunity to allow the use when there are minimal impacts, to allow the use but impose mitigation measures to address identified concerns, or to deny the use if the concerns cannot be resolved.

Portland Zoning Ord. § 33.815.010. In Portland, conditional uses include group homes, community service facilities, parks, schools, medical centers, religious institutions, daycare, agriculture, aviation and surface passenger terminals, mining, radio frequency transmission facilities, railroad lines, and utility corridors. Do you see how these uses fit the purpose clause? When a use is listed as special or conditional, specified criteria must be met before a permit is issued. What kinds of requirements or conditions would you place on the various uses listed above from the Portland ordinance?

---

*   These terms are used interchangeably by courts and commentators. The SZEA uses the term "special exception." See SZEA § 7. We will use the label "conditional uses."

PEOPLE'S COUNSEL FOR BALTIMORE COUNTY V. LOYOLA COLLEGE IN MARYLAND

Court of Appeals of Maryland, 2008.
406 Md. 54, 956 A.2d 166.[2]

HARRELL, JUDGE.

The legacy in Maryland land use law of *Schultz v. Pritts,* 291 Md. 1, 432 A.2d 1319 (1981), has been beneficial and well-applied for the most part over the ensuing years. The synthesis of earlier cases threaded through its reasoning supplies a lucid explanation of the legislative calculus for why some land uses, at the time of original adoption or later amendment of the text of a zoning ordinance, are placed in the blessed category of permitted uses in a zone or zones while other uses in the same zone or zones receive a more measured imprimatur of presumptive compatibility as allowed only with the grant of a special exception or conditional use. *Schultz* also iterated how special exception uses are useful zoning tools for fleshing out the grand design of land use planning, as well as postulated an analytical paradigm for how individual special exception applications are to be evaluated. In carrying-out the latter goal, however, some of the language of Judge Davidson's opinion for the Court in *Schultz* occasionally has been mis-perceived by subsequent appellate courts and frequently misunderstood by some attorneys, planners, governmental authorities, and other citizens. We aim in the present case for greater clarity in explaining the proper evaluative framework for discrete special exception/conditional use applications and dispelling any lingering mis-understandings of what the Court truly intended when it filed the opinion in *Schultz* twenty-seven years ago.

Facts and Procedural History

In October 2001, Loyola College in Maryland ("Loyola") contracted to purchase a fifty-three acre parcel (the Property) in northern Baltimore County for the purpose of constructing several buildings to be used for weekend spiritual retreats. The Property is located in the R.C.2 (Resource Conservation) zone. According to the Baltimore County Zoning Regulations (BCZR) § 1A01.1(B), the purpose of the Resource Conservation zone is "to foster conditions favorable to a continued agricultural use of the productive agricultural areas of Baltimore County by preventing incompatible forms and degrees of urban uses." Among the permitted uses allowed as of right in the R.C.2 zone are "one-family detached" dwellings, "agricultural operations," "open space," and "public schools." BCZR § 1A01.2. BCZR § 1A01.2(C) allows "churches or other buildings for religious worship," "camps, including day camps," and "schools, including but not limited to private preparatory schools, colleges, business and trade schools,

---

[2]   [Heavily edited without notation. Eds.]

conservatories or other fine arts schools" as special exceptions in the R.C.2 zone.

In early 2004, Loyola submitted to Baltimore County a plan to develop the Property into a Retreat Center. The plan proposed development of just over ten of the fifty-three acres of the Property, leaving the balance in an "as is" state. Loyola concurrently filed a petition for special exception for the Retreat Center as a school or college, church, or camp.[3] The Baltimore County Zoning Commissioner/Hearing Officer, in April 2004, conducted a three-day hearing on the development plan and special exception petition. The hearing officer issued an opinion and order on 10 June 2004 approving the development plan and granting the special exception. A group of citizens acting individually and collectively as Citizens Against Loyola Multi-use Center ("Citizens") appealed to the Baltimore County Board of Appeals (Board of Appeals). The Board of Appeals held a *de novo* hearing regarding the special exception and an appeal on the record regarding the development plan. The combined hearing continued over a total of six days between 15 September 2004 and 4 January 2005.

Both sides presented voluminous evidence regarding the effect that the proposed special exception use would have on the surrounding neighborhood. Because Petitioners narrowed the legal issue before this Court in their Petition for Certiorari, we shall summarize only the relevant evidence presented at the hearing. Loyola produced evidence, which the Board of Appeals credited, that the impacts of the proposed use on agriculture would be minimal. Loyola pointed out that the proposed Retreat Center would occupy only 10.18 acres of land, less than twenty percent of the Property. The remainder of the Property would be used for agriculture or open space. Robert Sheelsey, an environmental consultant and licensed sanitarian, testified for Loyola that the Property is located "right on the fringe" of the agricultural zone and within the Interstate 83 corridor. Based on this evidence, the Board of Appeals concluded that the Retreat Center "will not harm agricultural activity in the vicinity." Loyola presented evidence that the outdoor lighting at the Retreat Center would be "dark skies compliant." Two additional experts testified on behalf of Loyola that the Retreat Center would not be detrimental to the neighborhood because "it was a very low intensity use" of the Property.

Substantial testimony at the hearing concerned the onsite septic system and water usage of the Retreat Center. Sheelsey testified that there are proper soils for septic discharge in the proposed septic field. He further explained that the discharge from the septic system would undergo "biological/biochemical pretreatment" prior to discharge, making the discharge "most likely 99% clear and treated." The proposed septic discharge system would contain a "flow equalization" mechanism to

---

[3] [Ct's fn 1] Petitioners here concede that the proposed Retreat Center falls within the special exception regulatory scheme as a "college," thus requiring a special exception.

account for the nature of the use of the Retreat Center (heavy use for a few days followed by no use at all for the remainder of the week). Regarding water usage, Thomas Mills, an expert geologist, testified for Loyola that the "supply of groundwater was more than adequate" for the Retreat Center, even under drought scenarios, and that the Retreat Center's water usage would not affect neighboring wells.

There was controversy over [whether] the "thermal impacts" from proposed stormwater ponds would warm a local trout stream, impairing the ability of the trout to reproduce. Professor Edward J. Bouwer of Johns Hopkins University and Charles Gougeon of the Maryland Department of Natural Resources testified as to their belief that the run-off from the stormwater ponds would warm the tributary. Loyola countered with the testimony of an ecologist, Joseph Berg, Jr. Berg testified that the tributary would not be a sustainable habitat for trout in any event. In addition, he testified that any impact from rain run-off would be minimal. In its written opinion, the Board of Appeals stated that it "was not persuaded by the testimony of Professor Bouwer or Mr. Gougeon. . . ."

The parties also disputed the impact of nitrogen and phosphorous discharges from the septic system. The Board found that Loyola met its burden regarding the nitrogen and phosphorous impacts.

Petitioners described Stablersville Road, the main ingress/egress public road for the Retreat Center, as being a narrow country road with no shoulder and steep banks on both sides. It was claimed to be impossible for traffic to pass safely around slow-moving farm vehicles that used the road to move from property to property. [Loyola responded that it] will take to minimize the traffic impact from the Retreat Center. The Board of Appeals found his testimony to be credible and noted that "Loyola has made a concerted effort to keep traffic to and from the site to a bare minimum."

Citizens also presented certain evidence that the Board of Appeals chose not to consider. Citizens argued that the standard established in *Schultz* for special exception applicants required Loyola to show that there are no other locations within the R.C.2 zone in Baltimore County where the proposed use would have less of an adverse effect than on the local neighborhood of the Property. The Board of Appeals dismissed this argument, noting:

> We disagree with [Petitioners'] argument that [the *Schultz*] standard should be interpreted to mean that, as long as there are other locations in the zone in which certain adverse effects would be less adverse, the use should be denied in the subject location. The standard is very clear that only the general vicinity of the subject property is to be taken into account. Therefore, the fact that there are wider roads in other areas of the R.C.2 zone, or other areas of the zone without Class 3 trout streams, are beside the point. The Board must examine each criterion of BCZR Section

502.1 and determine whether the impacts in the subject location are above and beyond those inherent to the use-in this case, a college facility-itself.

Accordingly, the Board ignored evidence presented by Petitioners that there were other areas in the R.C.2 zone in Baltimore County that would be less adversely affected by the proposed use than the area surrounding the Property. Paul Solomon testified to that effect on behalf of Petitioners. Solomon identified four other areas within the R.C.2 zone where the proposed use could be located "without the impact on the subject area."[4] Solomon argued that the proposed use would have the least amount of adverse impact in areas where farms are smaller in size, and therefore less productive, and where there already were existing intrusions or developments within the adjacent farming community. [Two others supported the plaintiffs.]

Loyola, by contrast, presented no evidence regarding how its Retreat Center proposal would operate at other sites in Baltimore County in the R.C.2 zone. Thus, Solomon's [and the others] testimonies largely were uncontradicted by the applicant for the special exception and ignored by the Board.

The Board of Appeals held public deliberations on 24 March 2005. On 21 June 2005, the Board, in a written opinion, affirmed the conclusions of the hearing officer with regard to the development plan and granted Loyola's petition for a special exception as a "college."

Citizens timely filed, in the Circuit Court for Baltimore County, a Petition for Judicial Review of the Board of Appeals's decision. People's Counsel filed a Petition for Judicial Review as well. The Circuit Court remanded the case to the Board of Appeals for further action. Specifically, the Circuit Court held that the "appropriate geographic scope of inquiry is a broad, comprehensive, zone-wide analysis." Thus, the Circuit Court concluded that the Board "did err as a matter of law and misapplied the special exception standards of *Schultz* in restricting its geographic scope of inquiry." Loyola appealed to the Court of Special Appeals. In an unreported opinion, the intermediate appellate court vacated the Circuit Court's judgment and remanded the case with instructions to affirm the decision of the Board of Appeals. We granted the Petition for Writ of Certiorari filed by Citizens and People's Counsel. Although the Petition presents three questions for our review, all three questions share a common legal theme. Thus, the sole legal issue in this case properly may be distilled into a sole question presented:

> Does *Schultz v. Pritts,* 291 Md. 1, 432 A.2d 1319 (1981), require that, before a special exception may be granted, an applicant must

---

4   [Ct's fn 12] None of these areas could be described fairly as belonging to the same "neighborhood" as the Property. Each alternative site suggested by Solomon appears to be at least nine miles away from the Property.

adduce evidence of, and the zoning body must consider, a comparison of the potential adverse effects of the proposed use at the proposed location to the potential adverse effects of the proposed use at other, similarly-zoned locations throughout the jurisdiction?

We conclude that *Schultz* imposes no such requirement. Thus, we affirm the judgment of the Court of Special Appeals.

Standard of Review

There is some dispute mounted in the present case as to the appropriate standard of review to be afforded the Board of Appeals's legal conclusions. Loyola argues that the Board of Appeals's legal analysis is to be afforded some deference. To support this proposition, Loyola relies on *Marzullo v. Kahl,* 366 Md. 158, 172, 783 A.2d 169, 177 (2001), where we stated that "[e]ven with regard to some legal issues, a degree of deference should often be accorded the position of the administrative agency. Thus, an administrative agency's interpretation and application of the statute which the agency administers should ordinarily be given considerable weight by reviewing courts." This argument is without merit. By its own terms, the deference "often . . . accorded" an agency's interpretation extends only to the application of the statutes or regulations that the agency administers. The controversy before us concerns the proper application and analysis of caselaw, specifically *Schultz v. Pritts* and its progeny. This is a purely legal issue uniquely within the ken of a reviewing court. "Generally, a decision of an administrative agency, including a local zoning board, is owed no deference when its conclusions are based upon an error of law." Thus, the Board of Appeals's legal conclusions, if erroneous, are entitled to no deference.

Standards Governing Special Exceptions

As noted earlier, § 502.1 of the BCZR provides:

> Before any special exception may be granted, it must appear that the use for which the special exception is requested will not:
>
>> A.   Be detrimental to the health, safety or general welfare of the locality involved;
>>
>> B.   Tend to create congestion in roads, streets or alleys therein;
>>
>> C.   Create a potential hazard from fire, panic or other danger;
>>
>> D.   Tend to overcrowd land and cause undue concentration of population;

E. Interfere with adequate provisions for schools, parks, water, sewerage, transportation or other public requirements, conveniences or improvements;

F. Interfere with adequate light and air;

G. Be inconsistent with the purposes of the property's zoning classification nor in any other way inconsistent with the spirit and intent of these Zoning Regulations;

H. Be inconsistent with the impermeable surface and vegetative retention provisions of these Zoning Regulations; nor

I. Be detrimental to the environmental and natural resources of the site and vicinity including forests, streams, wetlands, aquifers and floodplains in an R.C.2, R.C.4, R.C.5 or R.C.7 Zone.

Within each individual factor, including the general factor in § 502.1(A) of the BCZR, lurks another test, the *Schultz v. Pritts* standard. In *Mossburg v. Montgomery County,* 107 Md.App. 1, 21, 666 A.2d 1253, 1263 (1995) (the court noted that the test announced in *Schultz* essentially adds language to statutory factors to be considered in evaluating proposed special exceptions). In this respect, the *Schultz* analytical paradigm is not a second, separate test (in addition to the statutory requirements) that an applicant must meet in order to qualify for the grant of a special exception. Rather, the *Schultz* explication speaks to two different contexts, one by which a legislative body decides to classify a particular use as requiring the grant of a special exception before it may be established in a given zone, and a second one by which individual applications for special exceptions are to be evaluated by the zoning body delegated with responsibility to consider and act on those applications in accordance with criteria promulgated in the zoning ordinance.

In The Beginning . . .

In *Village of Euclid, Ohio v. Ambler Realty Co.,* the U.S. Supreme Court upheld Euclid's (a suburb of Cleveland) comprehensive zoning ordinance against a challenge brought by a local landowner. Forever named Euclidean zoning, the type of zoning regulations enacted by Euclid represented a "fairly static and rigid form of zoning." *Mayor & Council of Rockville v. Rylyns Enterprises, Inc.,* 372 Md. 514, 534, 814 A.2d 469, 480 (2002) *(Rylyns).* "Euclidian zoning is designed to achieve stability in land use planning and zoning and to be a comparatively inflexible, self-executing mechanism which, once in place, allows for little modification beyond self-contained procedures for predetermined exceptions or variances." *Rylyns,* 372 Md. at 534, 814 A.2d at 481.

As a charter county, Maryland Code Article 25A authorizes Baltimore County to enact local laws for the protection and promotion of public safety, health, morals, and welfare, relating to zoning and planning.

The zoning device at the heart of the present case, the special exception, introduces some flexibility to a "fairly static and rigid" Euclidean zoning scheme. The special exception adds flexibility to a comprehensive legislative zoning scheme by serving as a "middle ground" between permitted uses and prohibited uses in a particular zone. Permitted and prohibited uses serve as binary, polar opposites in a zoning scheme. A permitted use in a given zone is permitted as of right within the zone, without regard to any potential or actual adverse effect that the use will have on neighboring properties. A special exception, by contrast, is merely deemed *prima facie* compatible in a given zone. The special exception requires a case-by-case evaluation by an administrative zoning body or officer according to legislatively-defined standards. That case-by-case evaluation is what enables special exception uses to achieve some flexibility in an otherwise semi-rigid comprehensive legislative zoning scheme.

History of the Special Exception in Maryland

[I]n *Gowl v. Atlantic Richfield Co.,* 27 Md.App. 410, 341 A.2d 832 (1975), the Court of Special Appeals purported to inject a new twist to the standards for evaluating special exceptions. *Gowl* held that, in deciding whether to grant a special exception, the zoning body should compare the adverse effects of a proposed special exception use to the adverse effects of permitted uses allowed in the zone at the site proposed for the special exception. For example, the potential for adverse effect of a proposed use on traffic congestion at a critical intersection in the neighborhood was to be compared to the effect on traffic congestion of permitted uses within the zone.

In 1981, we decided *Schultz v. Pritts,* a case all parties to this litigation acknowledge as a bellwether case regarding special exceptions in Maryland. In *Schultz,* Robert and Ann Pritts petitioned for a special exception to operate a funeral home in an area zoned for single-family residential homes in Carroll County. The Carroll County Board of Zoning Appeals denied the special exception. On judicial review, the Circuit Court for Carroll County remanded the case to the Board of Zoning Appeals on due process grounds unrelated to the special exception standard. The Court of Special Appeals dismissed an appeal and cross-appeal as premature. Thus, the proper evaluative standard to be applied in special exception cases was not considered until the case reached us. The Court of Appeals issued a writ of certiorari to consider all issues raised in the case.

The Prittses argued that the Board of Zoning Appeals erred because it declined to apply the *Gowl* standard in evaluating their application for the special exception. Specifically, they contended that their proposed use, a funeral home, would generate less traffic than several permitted uses allowed in the zone in which the subject property was placed. Thus, they contended, the Board of Zoning Appeals should have approved the special exception to operate a funeral home.

In finding no merit in the Prittses' argument, the Court unequivocally rejected the *Gowl* standard. The Court began its analysis by reviewing the proper standard to be applied by a zoning body in reviewing an application for a special exception.

> This Court has frequently expressed the applicable standards for judicial review of the grant or denial of a special exception use. The special exception use is a part of the comprehensive zoning plan sharing the presumption that, as such, it is in the interest of the general welfare, and therefore, valid. The special exception use is a valid zoning mechanism that delegates to an administrative board a limited authority to allow enumerated uses which the legislature has determined to be permissible absent any fact or circumstance negating the presumption. The duties given the Board are to judge whether the neighboring properties in the general neighborhood would be adversely affected and whether the use in the particular case is in harmony with the general purpose and intent of the plan.

> Whereas, the applicant has the burden of adducing testimony which will show that his use meets the prescribed standards and requirements, he does not have the burden of establishing affirmatively that his proposed use would be a benefit to the community. If he shows to the satisfaction of the Board that the proposed use would be conducted without real detriment to the neighborhood and would not actually adversely affect the public interest, he has met his burden. The extent of any harm or disturbance to the neighboring area and uses is, of course, material. If the evidence makes the question of harm or disturbance or the question of the disruption of the harmony of the comprehensive plan of zoning fairly debatable, the matter is one for the Board to decide. But if there is no probative evidence of harm or disturbance in light of the nature of the zone involved or of factors causing disharmony to the operation of the comprehensive plan, a denial of an application for a special exception use is arbitrary, capricious, and illegal. These standards dictate that if a requested special exception use is properly determined to have an adverse effect upon neighboring properties in the general area, it must be denied.

Schultz, 291 Md. at 11–12, 432 A.2d at 1325.

Schultz has been cited in over 100 reported Maryland appellate decisions. Both sides in this litigation have sifted through this vast body of law and highlighted particular applications of parts of the relevant language in *Schultz* that, they contend, support their respective positions.

Evaluation of a special exception application is not an equation to be balanced with formulaic precision. *See Sharp,* 98 Md.App. at 73, 632 A.2d at 256 (rejecting "appellants' interpretation of the holding of *Schultz* as if it were the atomic chart of elements from which a formula for divining inherent and peculiar adverse effects could be derived"). That lack of a precise rubric is reflected in the standard of judicial review applied to zoning decisions. Courts are to defer to the conclusions of the zoning body where the "evidence makes the question of harm or disturbance or the question of the disruption of the harmony of the comprehensive plan of zoning *fairly debatable." Schultz.*

It is clear in examining the plain language of *Schultz,* and the cases upon which *Schultz* relies, that the *Schultz* analytical overlay for applications for individual special exceptions is focused entirely on the neighborhood involved in each case. The requirement for such an analysis focused on the local neighborhood is apparent in the often-quoted *Schultz* holding:

> We now hold that the appropriate standard to be used in determining whether a requested special exception use would have an adverse effect and, therefore, should be denied is whether there are facts and circumstances that show that the particular use proposed at the particular location proposed would have any adverse effects above and beyond those inherently associated with such a special exception use irrespective of its location within the zone.

Schultz, 291 Md. at 22–23, 432 A.2d at 1331.

The *Schultz* standard requires an analysis of the effects of a proposed use "irrespective of its location within the zone." Petitioners' argument urges the opposite result. Petitioners contend that *Schultz* requires an applicant for a special exception to compare, and concomitantly the zoning body to consider, the adverse effects of the proposed use at the proposed location to, at least, a reasonable selection or representative sampling of other sites within the same zone throughout the district or jurisdiction, *taking into account* the particular characteristics of the areas surrounding those other test sites. The *Schultz* standard requires no such evidentiary burden be shouldered by an applicant nor analysis undertaken by the zoning decision-maker.

Schultz speaks pointedly to an individual case analysis focused on the particular locality involved around the proposed site. *See Schultz,* 291 Md. at 15, 432 A.2d at 1327 ("These cases establish that a special exception use has an adverse effect and must be denied when it is determined from the facts and circumstances that the grant of the requested special exception use would result in *an adverse effect upon adjoining and surrounding properties* unique and different from the adverse effect that would otherwise result from the development of such a special exception use located anywhere within the zone." (emphasis added)); *Schultz,* 291 Md. at 11, 432 A.2d at 1324 ("The duties given the Board are to judge whether *the neighboring properties in the general neighborhood would be adversely affected* and whether the use in the particular case is in harmony with the general purpose and intent of the plan." (emphasis added)).

The local legislature, when it determines to adopt or amend the text of a zoning ordinance with regard to designating various uses as allowed only by special exception in various zones, considers in a generic sense that certain adverse effects, at least in type, potentially associated with (inherent to, if you will) these uses are likely to occur wherever in the particular zone they may be located. In that sense, the local legislature puts on its "Sorting Hat"[5] and separates permitted uses, special exceptions, and all other uses. That is why the uses are designated special exception uses, not permitted uses. The inherent effects notwithstanding, the legislative determination necessarily is that the uses conceptually are compatible in the particular zone with otherwise permitted uses and with surrounding zones and uses already in place, provided that, at a given location, adduced evidence does not convince the body to whom the power to grant or deny individual applications is given that actual incompatibility would occur. With this understanding of the legislative process (the "presumptive finding") in mind, the otherwise problematic language in *Schultz* makes perfect sense. The language is a backwards-looking reference to the legislative "presumptive finding" in the first instance made when the particular use was made a special exception use in the zoning ordinance. It is not a part of the required analysis to be made in the review process for each special exception application. It is a point of reference explication only.

Judgment of The Court of Special Appeals Affirmed; Petitioners to Divide the Costs Equally. MURPHY, J. concurs and files opinion [omitted].

NOTES

1.   The Standard State Zoning Enabling Act allows the legislative body to delegate power to an administrative body by establishing a board of adjustment. Section 7 of the Act provides that the board of adjustment: "[m]ay, in appropriate cases and subject to appropriate conditions and safeguards, make special exceptions to the terms of the ordinance in harmony with its

---

[5]   [Ct's fn 33] In the HARRY POTTER series of books, the "Sorting Hat" is a magical artifact that is used to determine in which house (Gryffindor, Hufflepuff, Ravenclaw or Slytherin) first-year students at Hogwarts School of Wizardry and Witchcraft are to be assigned. After being placed on a student's head, the Sorting Hat measures the inherent qualities of the student and assigns him or her to the appropriate house. J.K. ROWLING, HARRY POTTER AND THE SORCERER'S STONE (1998).

general purpose and intent and in accordance with general or specific rules therein contained." Most jurisdictions use the term "conditional use" or "special use." It is necessary to check the local zoning code to see what term is used and what it means.

2.   The conditional use process was adopted to provide flexibility to overcome the rigidity of the traditional Euclidean zoning scheme. Flexibility can only be achieved if the board administering the process has discretion to determine whether to grant a permit. Yet, the discretion must be guided by standards to assure that the legislative intent is followed. Many courts tolerate fairly vague standards since predicting all types of problems that may arise is difficult, if not impossible, but as one court has said, the standards "may not be so general or tautological as to allow unchecked discretion." *Tandem Holding Corp. v. Bd. of Zoning Appeals of the Town of Hempstead*, 402 N.Y.S.2d 388, 389, 373 N.E.2d 282 (1977). If an ordinance simply provides that the board of adjustment shall find that the granting of the conditional use permit "will not adversely affect the public interest," a court may find that the legislative body has abdicated the ultimate question of public interest that the legislature is to decide for itself. *Jackson v. Guilford County Bd. of Adjustment*, 166 S.E.2d 78 (N.C.1969). In contrast, an ordinance that requires the board to find that the use "will not adversely affect the value of adjacent property" is more likely to be upheld. Do you see why?

Section 502.1 (A) of the Baltimore County ordinance provides that the use will not be "detrimental to the health, safety or general welfare of the locality involved." This vague standard is accompanied by eight other, more specific standards. If part (A) were the only measure or if the board were to find all criteria met except for the first, would a court uphold the denial?

In *Kosalka v. Town of Georgetown*, 752 A.2d 183 (Me.2000), the Maine supreme court found that requiring the board to determine that a proposed development will "conserve natural beauty" was an unconstitutional delegation of legislative authority. As the court observed:

all development, to some extent, destroys or impairs "natural beauty." If the provision means that all natural beauty must be conserved, then all development must be banned. Because the provision cannot reasonably be interpreted to ban all development, the question becomes: How much destruction is okay? Or, put another way; how much conservation is required? On this question, however, the [ordinance] is silent. Neither developers nor the [board] are given any guidance on how to interpret the "conserve natural beauty" requirement. Instead, developers are left guessing at how much conservation is necessary, and the [board] is free to grant or deny permits as it sees fit.

752 A.2d at 187.

3.   Occasionally, a city may dispense with permitted uses of right and attempt to handle all development by the conditional use process. This resembles the British system where "planning permission is required for the

carrying out of any development of land." British Town and Country Planning Act 1990, § 57. Generally, however, this has been met with disapproval by American courts who have viewed the process as the "antithesis of zoning." *Rockhill v. Township of Chesterfield*, 128 A.2d 473, 479 (N.J.1957). Is there something inherently wrong about controlling land use on a case by case basis? *See, e.g., Town of Rhine v. Bizzell*, 751 N.W.2d 780 (Wis.2008). If the concern is with the degree of deference the ordinance confers, that can be overcome by well-crafted standards.

4.   In *Loyola College*, the court uses the Harry Potter books' "sorting hat" (see court's footnote 33) as an analogy to stress the legislative choice to create a category of uses that are conceptually compatible with uses permitted of right. The power granted to the administrative board is limited to deciding whether a listed conceptually compatible use will in fact be compatible with surrounding uses at a particular location. The board is not free to reject the "presumptive finding" of compatibility. In *City of Chicago Heights v. Living Word Outreach Full Gospel Church and Ministries, Inc.*, 749 N.E.2d 916 (Ill.2001), a church acquired a building located in a business district in which churches were listed as a special use. The church was required to satisfy the city that its use would not be "injurious to other property in the immediate vicinity" nor be "unreasonably detrimental to the public interest." The city council, acting in an administrative capacity, denied the permit because it determined that religious use of the land would frustrate the city's plan to develop the area as a strong commercial corridor. The state supreme court reversed, finding that the city's rationale for denying the permit was the equivalent of a declaration that churches were per se incompatible uses in the district, and thus contrary to the ordinance recognizing churches as permissible special uses. The court ordered the city to issue the permit.

5.   Traditionally conditional use permit applications are heard by an administrative board or hearing officer. In many cities, however, the legislative body retains the power to issue conditional use permits for certain uses, typically those that have community-wide impact. Some courts reject this practice, interpreting the Standard Zoning Enabling Act (the board "may" grant special use permits) to vest the power to issue special use permits exclusively in the Board of Adjustment. *See Holland v. City Council of Decorah*, 662 N.W.2d 681 (Iowa 2003).

6.   When an unsuccessful permit applicant challenges the standards for obtaining a conditional use permit as "too subjective" to sufficiently guide the board, what happens if the court agrees? What is the remedy? If the conditional use ordinance is found invalid by the court, doesn't that mean that the city now lacks a conditional use procedure and the landowner is left with the underlying zoning district? If so, the plaintiff-applicant has won the battle but lost the war. His proposed use is no longer even conceptually compatible.

7.   Conditional uses often involve uses that are unpopular in residential districts such as residential care facilities and halfway houses. By relegating these to conditional use status, the authorities can control their location in residential districts. The discretionary nature of such permits makes it difficult

to attack the refusal of local authorities to grant such permits in the event of successful local opposition to a particular facility at a particular location. The Fair Housing Act, however, may limit such municipal denials. See discussion in Ch. 5.D.

In *Cleburne v. Cleburne Living Center, Inc.*, 473 U.S. 432 (1985), the Supreme Court faced an ordinance that subjected group homes for the mentally-retarded to a conditional use permit process, but allowed such uses as fraternities, multi-family use, hospitals, sanitariums, and nursing homes to operate by right. Finding no rational basis to treat group homes more harshly than these similar, permitted uses, the Court invalidated the ordinance on equal protection grounds. *Cleburne* is set out in Ch. 5.D.2.

8.   In addition to the legislative criteria that must be met, the board typically can add "appropriate conditions and safeguards" to a permit. SZEA, § 7. Assume you are a neighbor of property for which a conditional use permit is being sought for a half-way house for parolees. What conditions would you suggest be imposed? What about an airport? A school?

9.   An applicant who can establish that the proposed use is permitted of right does not have to jump through the discretionary conditional use administrative hoop. Consider the following problem: Assume there is a proposed residential care facility for disabled persons. The zoning ordinance allows of right "single family residential dwellings" and allows, as conditional uses, "institutions for medical care." Which applies?

Operators of group homes for the disabled have tried to avoid the public hearing that is part of the conditional use process. They claim the hearing stigmatizes the disabled and compels them to endure the public hostility of the home's future neighbors. Resort to the Fair Housing Act has been unsuccessful. *See, e.g., United States v. Village of Palatine*, 37 F.3d 1230 (7th Cir.1994) (noting that towns have a legitimate interest in conducting nondiscriminatory, public hearings). The statutory, constitutional, and policy issues raised by the regulation of group homes are dealt with in Chapter 5.D.

6.   CONTRACT AND CONDITIONAL ZONING

If a municipality foresees problems or identifies needs, it can use the techniques addressed above in Sections 2 and 3. It may deal with predictable problem uses by listing them as special or conditional uses and may deal with predictable community needs by establishing floating zones. At times, however, rezoning applications bring to light unanticipated problems or opportunities. A general rezoning request is an all or nothing proposition. When a city is asked to grant a general rezoning without limiting conditions, all permitted uses in the zoning classification will be available to the landowner. This may not be desirable, but the municipality must decide whether to grant the request or deny it. Or, perhaps make a deal.

It is black-letter law that government cannot "bargain away the police power." However, it is rare for a city council to fail to exhibit an abiding interest in precisely what a developer proposes to construct on the subject property. The developer's proposal often leads to differences of opinion concerning everything from use, intensity, design, and impacts on the city's infrastructure. Then the bargaining begins. When a deal is reached and the ordinance passed, a suit claiming the action to be illegal contract zoning may follow.

Judicial condemnation of contract zoning is common, but it is not always clear what is meant by the label. In contrast to "contract zoning," many courts uphold what they label "conditional use zoning." *See* Juergensmeyer and Roberts, *Land Use Planning and Development Regulation Law* §§ 4.17 and 5.11 (3rd ed.2012). As the following case shows, labeling and defining impermissible and permissible actions in cases with deal making aspects is an imprecise undertaking.

Consider whether, when employed, these techniques make it impossible for the average citizen, landowner, or prospective developer, to determine the permissible uses for a parcel by looking at the official zoning map. If not, is there a better way for cities to handle situations that present problems planners have not anticipated?

DURAND V. IDC BELLINGHAM, LLC

Supreme Judicial Court of Massachusetts, 2003.
440 Mass. 45, 793 N.E.2d 359.

CORDY, J.

The essential facts of this case are undisputed. In 1993, the town began to examine ways to increase its property tax base. An economic development task force was appointed by the town's board of selectmen (board) to study the issue. The task force prepared a report recommending that development of industrial land in the town be a priority. The report identified a parcel on the corner of Depot Street and Box Pond Road (locus), which abutted land that was already zoned for industrial use, as a candidate for rezoning from agricultural and suburban use to industrial use. Subsequently, at the town's May, 1995, town meeting, a zoning article proposing the rezoning of the locus and an adjacent parcel for industrial use fell eight votes short of the required two-thirds majority.

In 1997, IDC, which owned a power plant in the town, began discussions with town officials about the possibility of rezoning the locus so that a second plant might ultimately be built on it. These discussions included the subject of what public benefits and financial inducements IDC might offer the town with regard to the proposed plant. The town administrator told IDC officials that the town was facing an $8 million shortfall in its plans to construct a much needed new high school. Shortly thereafter, the president of IDC publicly announced that IDC would make an $8 million gift to the town if IDC (1) decided to build the plant; (2) obtained the financing and permits necessary to build the plant; and (3) operated the plant successfully for one year. The offer was made to generate support for the plant and became common knowledge in the town.

While the genesis of the offer was the need for a new high school, IDC made it clear that the town could use the money for any municipal purpose. The town's high school building committee, the town's finance committee, the town's master plan steering committee, and certain town officials voiced strong support for the plant and the zoning change required for its construction on the locus. Some committee members engaged in a campaign to get voters to the town meeting at which the rezoning was to be considered.

On May 28, 1997, the town held its open town meeting and a zoning article calling for the rezoning of the locus was introduced. IDC made a presentation of its proposed use of the locus for a second power plant and reiterated its offer of an $8 million gift to the town if the plant was built and became operational. The planning board and finance committee both recommended passage of the zoning article. There was some discussion of the zoning aspects of the proposal, as well as discussion regarding the offered gift. Residents for and against the proposal to build a plant on the site spoke, and IDC responded to their comments. The zoning article passed by more than the necessary two-thirds vote of the town meeting.

Between May, 1997, and January, 2001, IDC spent approximately $7 million to develop the locus for a power plant. At some point in the summer of 1998, the board learned that IDC was proposing to increase the size of the plant beyond what it had presented to the town meeting in 1997. Consequently, the board wrote a letter to the energy facilities siting board withdrawing its support for the plant. Shortly thereafter, representatives of IDC and the board met to negotiate a compromise. The outcome of those negotiations was an agreement by IDC to reduce the size of the plant and, in April, 1999, the execution of an "Agreement for Water/Wastewater Services" between IDC and the town. The agreement provided in part that:

> "IDC shall provide funds ($8,000,000.00) to the Town for its various capital expenditures, municipal projects and municipal improvements. . . . This Agreement is intended to memorialize, without duplicating the $8,000,000 commitment IDC and its affiliates previously made to the Town in connection with the Plant."

IDC submitted a request for five special permits to the town's zoning board of appeals on May 5, 2000, and the special permits were granted on January 2, 2001. On January 23, 2001, the plaintiffs, [filed suit seeking a] declaratory judgment, * * * that the rezoning of the locus on May 28, 1997, was void because it constituted illegal "contract" or "spot" zoning. . . . The defendants filed an answer alleging several affirmative defenses, including statute of limitations and laches. *delayed claim (equitable solution)*

The defendants moved for summary judgment * * * arguing that the zoning amendment constituted neither "contract" nor "spot" zoning and reasserting their affirmative defense of laches. * * * The judge denied summary judgment to the defendants and, on his own motion, granted *what*. summary judgment to the plaintiffs.

In his decision, the judge discussed whether "contract zoning" existed as a "separate ground for invalidating a zoning ordinance." Assuming that it did, the judge found that "contract zoning" had not occurred here, at least within the meaning he ascribed to that term. He then found that "there would be little doubt that the 1997 rezoning was valid" if the $8 million gift offer had not been made, and proceeded to discuss its implications. He viewed the offer of the gift as an "extraneous consideration," because it was not defended as being in mitigation of the impacts of the project, and therefore concluded that it was "offensive to public policy." He ultimately concluded that the fact that the offer was made was sufficient, without the necessity of finding that voting town meeting members were influenced by it, to nullify the rezoning vote, citing *Sylvania Elec. Prods. Inc. v. Newton*, 344 Mass. 428, 434, 183 N.E.2d 118 (1962) (stating that developer's consideration to town did not nullify zoning vote because it was not "extraneous consideration" unconnected to project). The defendants appealed and this court transferred the cases on its own motion. Because we conclude that the voluntary offer of public benefits beyond what might *Holding* be necessary to mitigate the development of a parcel of land does not, standing alone, invalidate a legislative act of the town meeting, we reverse.

2.   *Discussion.* Prior to the passage of art. 89 of the Amendments to the Massachusetts Constitution (the "Home Rule Amendment") in 1966, the power of a municipality to enact or amend zoning bylaws was a power derived exclusively from the "supreme" power of the Legislature in zoning matters, and a municipality had only such authority as the Legislature saw fit to delegate specifically to it. The Home Rule Amendment granted cities and towns "independent municipal powers which they did not previously inherently possess" to adopt, amend, or repeal local ordinances or bylaws "for the protection of the public health, safety and general welfare." The zoning power was one of the "independent municipal powers" granted to cities and towns by the Home Rule Amendment, enabling them to enact zoning ordinances or bylaws as an exercise of their "independent police powers" to control "land usages in an orderly, efficient, and safe manner to promote the public welfare," as long as their enactments were "not inconsistent with the Constitution or laws enacted by the Legislature."

The enactment of a zoning bylaw by the voters at town meeting is not only the exercise of an independent police power; it is also a legislative act, carrying a strong presumption of validity. It will not normally be undone unless the plaintiff can demonstrate "by a preponderance of the evidence that the zoning regulation is arbitrary and unreasonable, or substantially unrelated to the public health, safety . . . or general welfare." If the reasonableness of a zoning bylaw is even "fairly debatable, the judgment of the local legislative body responsible for the enactment must be sustained." Such an analysis is not affected by consideration of the various possible motives that may have inspired legislative action. * * * *Simon v. Needham*, 311 Mass. 560, 566, 42 N.E.2d 516 (1942) ("action of the voters is not to be invalidated simply because someone presented a reason that was unsound or insufficient in law to support the conclusion for which it was urged"). * * *

It is within this framework that the court reviews the validity of the town's enactment of the article rezoning the locus. We determine first whether its enactment violated State law or any constitutional limitation (the plaintiffs have made no constitutional claim), and second whether it was an arbitrary or unreasonable exercise of police power having no substantial relationship to the public health, safety, or general welfare. The plaintiffs bear a heavy burden on both counts, and to sustain that burden "must prove facts which compel a conclusion that the question [of the validity of the ordinance] is not even fairly debatable."

An agreement between a property owner and a municipality to rezone a parcel of land may cause the municipality to violate the process mandated by § 5. Such an instance of "contract zoning," as we will refer to it, involving a promise by a municipality to rezone a property either before the vote to rezone has been taken or before the required § 5 process has been undertaken, evades the dictates of G.L. c. 40A, and may render the subsequent rezoning invalid. The Land Court judge correctly concluded that no such advance agreement existed in this case. IDC pledged that if the town were to rezone the locus for industrial use (and if other events occurred), IDC would pay the town $8 million. At no time before the May 28, 1997, town meeting were the voters of town meeting bound to approve the zoning change. Because the town followed the procedures dictated by § 5, the rezoning was not invalid on statutory grounds.

In his decision, the Land Court judge also noted this court's suggestion in *Sylvania Elec. Prods. Inc. v. Newton*, 344 Mass. 428, 183 N.E.2d 118 (1962), that "contract zoning" encompasses the express conditioning of rezoning on a developer's promises to restrict the use of his land and provide benefits to the town. While the judge proceeded to find that "[w]e do not have that here," we note that zoning law and practice have changed since the Sylvania case was decided in 1962, and labels such as "contract zoning" may not be helpful or determinative in resolving the validity of a zoning enactment. Courts and commentators have given different meanings to the term "contract zoning," and those meanings have changed over time. More importantly, the legal context in which zoning actions are evaluated has also changed. The Sylvania court was concerned with the use by municipalities of the device of contract to restrict or condition the use of land in a manner beyond the authority then delegated to them by the Legislature and embodied in zoning enabling laws. The municipal power of zoning is, however, no longer a matter of delegated State legislative power. The practice of conditioning otherwise valid zoning enactments on agreements reached between municipalities and landowners that include limitations on the use of their land or other forms of mitigation for the adverse impacts of its development is a commonly accepted tool of modern land use planning, *see* 4 A.H. Rathkopf & D.A. Rathkopf, *Zoning and Planning* § 44.12 (2001) (noting general approval of practice as "valuable planning tool"), constrained, of course, by constitutional limitations not at issue here.

Validity of the bylaw as exercise of legislative police power. The judge found that absent the $8 million offer, the rezoning was substantively valid. We take that to mean that it was neither arbitrary nor unreasonable, and was substantially related to the public health, safety, or general welfare of the town. In other words, its adoption served a valid public purpose. The record fully supports this conclusion. The locus abutted land zoned for industrial use; a town-appointed task force (preceding and completely unrelated to the power plant development proposal) had recommended its rezoning after studying the town's tax base and the need for economic development; and a previous rezoning attempt based on that recommendation had just barely failed to get the necessary two-thirds majority at the 1995 town meeting.

In sum, the enactment of the bylaw rezoning the locus was not violative of State law or constitutional provisions, and met the substantive requirements of a valid exercise of legislative police power. Nevertheless, the judge set it aside because he concluded that the $8 million offer was an "extraneous consideration," that is, an offer not "tied to the impacts of the project" and therefore "offensive to public policy." We must decide whether such a consideration, voluntarily offered as part of a campaign in support of a development project, constitutes an independent ground on which to set aside a legislative act, regardless of its otherwise valid nature. If it is, we must decide further whether the mere existence of an "extraneous consideration" invalidates the legislative act as a matter of law, regardless whether it is proved to have actually influenced the votes of the legislative body. Because we conclude that a voluntary offer of public benefits is not, standing alone, an adequate ground on which to set aside an otherwise valid legislative act, we do not reach the second question.

The judge's conclusion that an "extraneous consideration" invalidates a zoning ordinance is based on a remark of this court in *Sylvania Elec. Prods. Inc. v. Newton*, 344 Mass. 428, 434, 183 N.E.2d 118 (1962), that a developer's voluntary promise of benefits did not include an "extraneous consideration . . . which could impeach the enacting vote as a decision solely in respect of rezoning the locus." The opinion cites no supporting authority for the proposition that the presence of an "extraneous consideration" at the time of the vote on a zoning amendment would invalidate the vote, but the language has since been given added life in two cases decided by the Appeals Court, *see McLean Hosp. Corp. v. Town of Belmont*, 56 Mass.App.Ct. 540, 546–547, 778 N.E.2d 1016 (2002) (noting that "extraneous consideration" is ground on which to challenge zoning enactment); *Rando v. North Attleborough*, 44 Mass.App.Ct. 603, 608–609, 692 N.E.2d 544 (1998) (no "extraneous consideration" where voluntary promise of payment by developer reasonably intended to meet public needs arising from project). Both cases cite the Sylvania language, but neither invalidated the zoning ordinance in issue.

In general, there is no reason to invalidate a legislative act on the basis of an "extraneous consideration," because we defer to legislative findings and choices without regard to motive. We see no reason to make an exception for legislative acts that are in the nature of zoning enactments, and find no persuasive authority for the proposition that an otherwise valid zoning enactment is invalid if it is in any way prompted or encouraged by a public benefit voluntarily offered. We conclude that the proper focus of review of a zoning enactment is whether it violates State law or constitutional provisions, is arbitrary or unreasonable, or is substantially unrelated to the public health, safety, or general welfare. In the absence of any infirmity other than the existence of a voluntary offer to make a gift to the town at some time in the future when the power plant became operational, we conclude that the judge erred in holding the zoning ordinance invalid and granting summary judgment to the plaintiffs.

SPINA, J. (concurring in part and dissenting in part, with whom IRELAND and COWIN, JJ., join).

I concur with the result the court reaches, but I disagree with the reasoning of the decision.

* * * The vote of a town meeting, valid on its face, may be invalid if it can be shown that the dominant motives or reasons for the action were unlawful. *See Sylvania Elec. Prods. Inc. v. City of Newton*, 344 Mass. 428, 433–434, 183 N.E.2d 118 (1962) ("significant inducement . . . [if] extraneous . . . could impeach the enacting vote as a decision solely in respect of rezoning the locus"). The motives and reasons of a town meeting, unlike the motives and reasons of members of the Legislature, may be the proper subject of inquiry.

* * * There is no dispute here that the zoning change is valid on its face, but the issue that must be addressed is whether the town meeting entered into an unlawful agreement that called for it to relinquish its zoning power. In my view, there is no material fact in dispute, and the facts show that the town meeting improperly agreed to exercise its power to

rezone land in exchange for a promise to pay money. The exercise of that power to approve the requested zoning change was a condition precedent to the promise of IDC Bellingham, LLC (IDC Bellingham), to pay money under its agreement with the town of Bellingham (town). *See Massachusetts Mun. Wholesale Elec. Co. v. Town of Danvers*, 411 Mass. 39, 45, 577 N.E.2d 283 (1991).

* * *

It was a sale of the police power because there is nothing in the record to legitimize the $8 million offer as "intended to mitigate the impact of the development upon the town," or as "reasonably intended to meet public needs arising out of the proposed development." *Rando v. North Attleborough*, 44 Mass.App.Ct. 603, 609, 692 N.E.2d 544 (1998). * * * See, e.g., *Middlesex & Boston St. Ry. v. Aldermen of Newton*, 371 Mass. 849, 853–859, 359 N.E.2d 1279 (1977) (city could not condition special permit for garden apartments on developer's leasing five apartments to town's low income housing program).

NOTES

1. The court observes that the voters were "not bound to approve the zoning change" and adds that it is "difficult to imagine how there could be an agreement in advance of the vote to approve such an action." What is the court's point? In the end, does this finding justify the conclusion drawn? Is it fair to say, as commentators have, that *Durand* is "a decision remarkable for the court's willingness to sanction an overt trade of zoning for cash?" Daniel J. Curtin, Jr. and Jonathan D. Witten, *Windfalls, Wipeouts, Givings, and Takings in Dramatic Redevelopment Projects: Bargaining for Better Zoning on Density, Views, and Public Access*, 32 B.C.ENVTL.AFF.L.REV. 325, 337 (2005).

2. How would a court adopting the *Fasano* approach decide this case?

3. The court characterizes the $8 million as a "voluntary gift." Despite the redundancy (a gift, by definition, is a voluntary transfer), does the offer being "voluntary" fit the facts of the case? Who came up with the idea? A contract requires consideration, the antithesis of a gift. Consideration was present, but was there an agreement? Was it enforceable by the parties? Should common law gift and contract doctrines be used to rule on the validity of a rezoning?

4. The *Durand* court quotes its decision in *Simon v. Needham* for the proposition that "action of the voters is not to be invalidated simply because someone presented a reason that was unsound or insufficient in law to support the conclusion for which it was urged." Here, it wasn't just "someone" who may have been influenced by the $8 million offer but likely most of those voting in favor. Voter actions at town meetings or at the polls when voting on zoning initiatives and referenda aren't immune from review, are they? The dissent suggests that the motives of voters at a town meeting are properly examined even when the motives of the legislature are not.

5. "Community benefits agreements" (CBAs) involve direct negotiations between the developer and representatives of affected neighborhoods, as well as environmental or preservation groups. To mollify potential adversaries and buy support, the developer may scale down a project or offer benefits to the community. In 2005, the developer of a mixed-use project to be built adjacent to the new downtown baseball stadium in San Diego entered into a CBA, promising, among other things, to use environmentally-friendly design standards and construction practices, to offer living wages for employees of service contractors at the project, to put up $1.5 million for job training of local residents, $100,000 to fund a gentrification study of the impact of downtown development on surrounding communities; and $50,000 for arts, youth, and culture services in the surrounding communities. *See* http://www. forworkingfamilies.org; http://www.piconetwork.org/news-media/news/2005/a-0130.

Though such agreements are not new, they have reappeared in recent years as more far-reaching than their predecessors. Some examples: a hospital in New Haven, Connecticut promised to create an outreach program for children with asthma, a developer in Brooklyn promised to make half of the rental units affordable for low-and moderate-income families, and a retail project in the Bronx promised to bar Wal-Mart as a tenant. How do these deals affect the public planning process? Since they are private negotiations between private parties, does it matter? If such a deal were done by the government, the benefits would have to relate to the project's impact in some fashion. Not so with a CBA. The groups, self-appointed to represent the community, may secure benefits that serve a narrow interest, raising the issue of what part of the "community" actually benefits. *See* Edward W. DeBargieri, *Do Community Benefit Agreements Benefit Communities?*, 37 Cardozo L.Rev. 1973 (2016). City planning officials might, or might not, be aware of or involved in the negotiations. In the best scenario, the agreement will be incorporated into the city's formal approval. *See* Terry Pristin, *In Major Projects, Agreeing Not to Disagree*, New York Times, June 14, 2006, discussing New York City's less than favorable reaction to some CBAs. If the city is not a party, can it enforce the agreement? On what theory might it do so? *See State ex rel. Zupancic v. Schimenz*, 174 N.W.2d 533 (Wis.1970). Is the promise of the neighborhood group to support the project enforceable? Neighborhood groups may pop up at any time that were not part of the deal and they, or individuals, may contest the project. Then what? *See generally*, Steven P. Frank, *Yes in My Backyard: Developers, Government and Communities Working Together Through Development Agreements and Community Benefit Agreements*, 42 Ind.L.Rev. 227 (2009); Nathan Markey, *Atlantic Yards Community Benefit Agreement: A Case Study of Organizing Community Support for Development*, 27 Pace Envtl.L.Rev. 377 (2010).

6. What about a court-sanctioned agreement? A city, when sued by a disappointed permit applicant, may agree to settle the case out of fear of liability and the cost of defense. The court's decree may effectively grant the permit that the city previously denied. For example, in *BPG Real Estate Inv'rs-Straw Party II, L.P. v. Bd. of Sup'rs of Newtown Twp.*, 990 A.2d 140, 148

(Pa.Commw.Ct.2010), an appellate court held that settlement agreements were permissible tools for settling land use disputes, even when such agreements departed from existing zoning regulations. The Court did, however, hold that the trial court exceeded its authority by allowing the settlement agreement to reach lands not included in the original land use application. One problem with court-sanctioned settlements is that it cuts the public out of the process since there is no public hearing on such a settlement agreement. *See, e.g., League of Residential Neighborhood Advocates v. City of Los Angeles*, 498 F.3d 1052 (9th Cir.2007). See also comment on consent decrees, *infra* Ch. 5.C.

[handwritten: problem w/ court involvement]

7.   If a court does find that local government has engaged in illegal contract zoning, what should the proper remedy be? Should the court leave the land use agreement in place while striking the illegal conditions, or nullify the entire agreement and return the parties to their original positions? *See Cederberg v. City of Rockford*, 291 N.E.2d 249, 252 (Ill.App.1972), holding that a land use decision was void because the government relied on the conditions imposed on the applicant in adopting the ordinance. *But see Sprint Spectrum L.P. v. Borough of Ringwood Zoning Bd. of Adjustment*, 898 A.2d 1054 (N.J.Super.2005), upholding a rezoning based on the finding that invalid conditions were severable.

[handwritten: severability!]

COMMENT: BONUS AND INCENTIVE ZONING

Bonus or incentive zoning is a sophisticated form of barter, designed to achieve both developer profit and municipal amenity. A community, through its zoning ordinance, offers economic incentives to developers by relaxing various zoning restrictions in exchange for the development of, or monetary contributions for, desired projects or amenities within projects. It is most frequently used in urban areas, particularly in downtowns, for the purpose of encouraging attractive buildings with facilities that the public can use.

Numerous cities have enacted comprehensive ordinances detailing the trades they are willing to make in exchange for such amenities as a theater, off-street parking, a public plaza, child care facilities, or access to rapid transit. Each amenity the developer agrees to provide allows the developer a certain density increase. The normal undesirability of the increased density is offset by an increase in public amenities. The illustration below of Seattle's Washington Mutual Tower illustrates how, with bonuses received for donations to city housing and transit projects and the creation of a public plaza, atrium, terrace, and the building of a public escalator so that pedestrians could avoid walking up the city's hills under their own power, the developer acquired the rights to construct 28 additional stories over the 27 stories allowed of right.

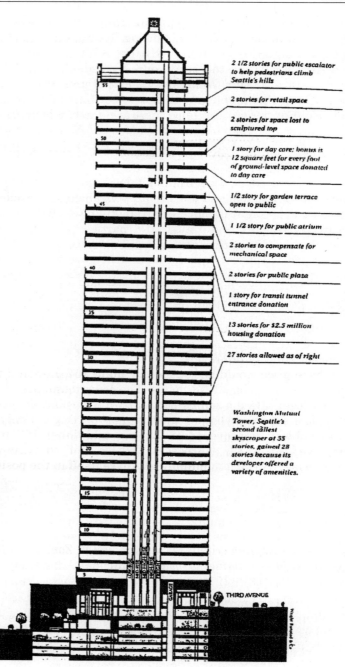

2 1/2 stories for public escalator to help pedestrians climb Seattle's hills

2 stories for retail space

2 stories for space lost to sculptured top

1 story for day care; bonus is 12 square feet for every foot of ground-level space donated to day care

1/2 story for garden terrace open to public

1 1/2 story for public atrium

2 stories to compensate for mechanical space

2 stories for public plaza

1 story for transit tunnel entrance donation

13 stories for $2.5 million housing donation

27 stories allowed as of right

Washington Mutual Tower, Seattle's second tallest skyscraper at 55 stories, gained 28 stories because its developer offered a variety of amenities.

Diagram reprinted with permission of Wright Runstead & Company, Seattle, Washington, as it appeared in Colwell, Child Care Grows Up, Planning, p. 12 (APA May, 1989).

The granting of such incentives raises a number of questions. Is the bonus granted an asset the city owns that it can sell? Are the amenities gained by the city (theaters, plazas, park areas) worth the light and air "taken" by additional height of the structure, or increased traffic spawned by higher density? Is it fair to impose these "servitudes" on the neighbors who bear the burdens of the gains? Is it too intrusive to allow a building more than twice the size permitted of right, as was done in the case of the Seattle tower noted above? See Judith Wegner's discussion of ways in which "new coinage might be minted" by local government. Judith Welch Wegner, *Utopian Visions: Cooperation without Conflicts in Public/Private Ventures*, 31 SANTA CLARA L.REV. 313 (1991). *See also* M. Filler, *High Rise, Part II, Art in America*, Oct. 1984, p. 168.

The most common incentive offered is increased floor area ratio (FAR). See discussion of FAR, *supra* section B.4 of this chapter. How does the city derive the additional floor area that it allocates to the developer? If the city seeks an amenity, it may simply create the floor area *ex nihilo* and bestow it upon the developer as a so-called "zoning bonus." The amount of the bonus is calculated to equal or slightly to exceed in value the cost that the developer incurs in providing the amenity. John J. Costonis, *The Chicago Plan: Incentive Zoning and the Preservation of Urban Landmarks*, 85 HARV.L.REV. 574, 576 (1972).

Incentive zoning has encountered some legal problems. In *Municipal Art Society of New York v. City of New York*, 522 N.Y.S.2d 800 (Sup.Ct.1987), Boston Properties contracted to purchase the New York Coliseum from the city for redevelopment, and the sale included an incentive zoning clause which allowed a maximum 20% increase in the floor area ratio (FAR) in exchange for adjacent subway improvements. A provision also stated that the $455 million purchase price would be reduced by up to $57 million if the developer did not receive the promised FAR bonus. The court found that the contract amounted to an illegal sale of a zoning bonus. "[I]n return for the grant by the CPC of the 20% floor area ratio bonus, the City is obtaining not only $35 to $40 million of local subway improvements, but an additional $57 million in cash to be employed for other purposes. This is not contemplated by the Zoning Resolution. [G]overnment may not place itself in the position of reaping a cash premium because one of its agencies bestows a zoning benefit upon a developer. Zoning benefits are not cash items." The city might have avoided this pitfall by earmarking the additional $57 million for adjacent subway station improvements.

Jerold Kayden criticizes this decision in *Zoning for Dollars: New Rules for an Old Game? Comments on the* Municipal Art Society *and* Nollan *Cases*, 39 J.URB. & CONTEMP.L. 3, 13, 25 (1991):

Justice Lehner's misunderstanding of the city's multifaceted role in this transaction fatally taints his legal conclusion. His analysis founders precisely on its failure to apprehend the crucial distinction between a "pure" incentive zoning transaction and the elaborate public-private interactions factually presented by the Coliseum deal. In the former, the city acts strictly as a regulator, while in the latter, the city acts first as a land seller, and then as a regulator. [J]ustice Lehner's opinion bears witness to the formidable complication posed by the "two hat" problem: the conflict of interest in the public sector's identity as both land seller and land regulator.

* * *

> [W]hen the $57 million is correctly understood as part of the
> incentive's value to the landowner, and thus as legitimately
> retainable by the city in its capacity as a land seller, the $57 million
> becomes equivalent to ordinary revenue generated by public land
> sales. As such, the money would face no geographical or other
> earmarking restriction and could fund city-wide municipal budgetary
> activities such as police, fire, and sanitation, without contravening
> zoning or other laws governing city conduct.

For additional discussion of incentive zoning on a nation-wide scale, *see* Robert
A. Johnston et al., *Selling Zoning: Do Density Bonus Incentives for Moderate-
Cost Housing Work?*, 36 J.URB. & CONTEMP.L. 45 (1989).

Density bonuses are commonly used to encourage construction of
affordable housing. See discussion *infra*, Ch. 5.B.

7.   OVERLAY AND FLOATING ZONES

The failure of the typical Euclidean zoning district and classification
scheme to address numerous development control issues led to a search for
more precise and more flexible techniques to control the use of land.
Overlay zones, floating zones and mixed-use planned unit developments
are inter-related techniques used to achieve that goal. Like the conditional
use process seen in the preceding section, they are devices used to inject
flexibility into the land development process. Though none are new, dating
back to at least the 1950s, they are frequently used today.

Overlay Zones: As the name indicates, such a zone overlies established use
districts. By imposing its own restrictions on land use within the zone, it
subjects landowners to two sets of regulations. Generally, an overlay zone's
boundary does not coincide with any existing use district, but spreads itself
over two or more use districts without regard to their boundaries.

Historic districts, which are often overlay zones, illustrate the zone's
purposes and mechanics. In the 1970s, Raleigh, North Carolina identified
a neighborhood near downtown, which contained a number of Victorian
houses. To preserve the area from deteriorating, the city created an historic
district overlay zone that covered portions of a residential zone and an
office zone. Property owners were restricted in the changes they could
make to their homes. New development was also required to avoid
incongruity with the area's historic aspects. A portion of the office zone was
included so as to buffer the residential area. *See A-S-P Associates v. City of
Raleigh*, 258 S.E.2d 444 (N.C.1979). The case is a principle case *infra* Ch.
6 where we cover historic district and landmarking controls.

Cities make extensive use of overlay zones. Portland, Oregon, for
example, has thirteen overlay zones, including two environmental overlay
zones: an Environmental Protection Zone and an Environmental

Conservation Zone. The protection zone "provides the highest level of protection to the most important resources and functional values. These resources and functional values are identified and assigned value in the inventory and economic, social, environmental, and energy analysis for each specific study area. Development will be approved in the environmental protection zone only in rare and unusual circumstances." Code of City of Portland, Oregon, § 33.430.01. The conservation zone "conserves important resources and functional values in areas where the resources and functional values can be protected while allowing environmentally sensitive urban development." Id., § 33.430.017.

The City and County of Honolulu uses Special Design and Historic, Scenic and Cultural overlay districts in its Comprehensive Zoning Code to drastically reduce building heights in order to preserve views of particular importance from its downtown toward both mountains and ocean. *See Life of the Land, Inc. v. City Council*, 606 P.2d 866 (Haw.1980), for a thorough discussion—but an odd result—in the application of these overlays.

Another common use of overlay zones is to show natural site limitations that may inhibit or prohibit the use of land as otherwise zoned. Thus, land zoned for single-family residences may be undevelopable because of overlaying zones showing it to be on a steep slope, to contain unsuitable soil, or to be in a flood hazard area. Carroll County, Maryland, has a Mineral Resource Overlay Zone in which land uses that are otherwise permitted in the underlying zone are prohibited if they would preclude recovery of certain minerals. Carroll County Code, § 14.1. *Summerwind Cottage, LLC v. Town of Scarborough*, is an example where the court upheld the constitutionality of a shoreland overlay district. 61 A.3d 698, 704 (Me.2013). The property owners bought the lot before the zoning ordinances were in place and sought to acquire a variance to build a retirement cottage on the property. *Id.* at 700. The variance was granted but neighboring landowners appealed, arguing that the shoreland zoning map's classification of the lot as within the buildable Shoreland Overlay District was "merely illustrative" of the boundary locations. *Id.* at 703. The court held that the town's shoreland zoning map was part of the shoreland zoning ordinance because it was the result of the legislative process by the town council and was thus entitled to deference by the zoning board of appeals and the court, even though the ordinance stated that the map was "merely illustrative" of boundary locations. *Id.* at 702.

Overlay zones may run afoul of the Standard Zoning Enabling Act's requirement that "[a]ll such regulations shall be uniform for each class or kind of buildings throughout each district * * * ." After all, if the height limitation in the commercial zone is 100 feet and in the overlay portion of the commercial zone the height limit is 40 feet, the regulations are not uniform. *See Jachimek v. Superior Court in and for County of Maricopa*,

819 P.2d 487 (Ariz.1991). Other courts interpret the uniformity requirement more loosely. *See A-S-P Associates*, discussed above.

Floating Zones: Not all land use districts found in the text of a zoning ordinance are initially drawn on the official zoning map. Some are purposely held back to "float" until an "appropriate" development for which such zoning was formulated comes along. Thereafter—once "mapped"—the zone no longer floats. *See Campion v. Bd. of Aldermen of City of New Haven*, 278 Conn. 500, 899 A.2d 542 (2006). Floating zones often are used to deal with community needs that have a significant community impact such as industrial parks or affordable housing. Two rezonings occur. A zone is initially created as a text amendment providing for certain uses if specified criteria are met. Then, at a later date, typically upon the application of a landowner for a map amendment, a specific tract is rezoned for the prior unmapped use. The neighbors who wind up with an industrial park or mobile home park next door may not be pleased. Then, particularly if the parcel is small and the abutting districts significantly inconsistent, the frequently heard cry of spot zoning will be raised. Spot zoning is covered *infra*, Ch. 2.C.1.

The floating zone closely resembles the conditional use permit. Recall the *Loyola College* court compared a floating zone with a conditional use. Like conditional use permits, floating zones enable a city to achieve flexibility that would be impossible under a pure Euclidean zoning scheme. The adoption of a floating zone is a legislative act as is the listing of conditional uses. The second step in the floating zone process, the rezoning of a specific parcel, is nominally legislative, but, like the administrative board that issues a conditional use permit, it is reviewed as a quasi-judicial decision by many courts. See *infra*, Ch. 2.C.2.

Some courts balked when floating zones were first introduced. With Euclidean zoning as its frame of reference, the Pennsylvania supreme court one court declared a floating zone to be the "antithesis of zoning * * * [since actual land use] await[s] solicitation by individual landowners." *Eves v. Zoning Bd. of Adjustment of Lower Gwynedd Twp.*, 164 A.2d 7, 11 (Pa.1960) (invalidating rezoning of a 103 acre tract from single family to light industrial for a sewage treatment plant). In contrast, in another early case, the New York Court of Appeals lauded the approach as "the first step in a reasoned plan of rezoning, * * * [which ought not be condemned] merely because the board employed two steps to accomplish what may be, and usually is, done in one * * * ." *Rodgers v. Village of Tarrytown*, 96 N.E.2d 731, 735–36 (N.Y.1951) (upholding the rezoning of a 10 acre tract from single-family to multi-family housing for garden apartments).

Mixed-Use Planned Unit Development: The basics of the technique are contained in the name: the precise planning of a development, usually composed of mixed-uses, as a "unit" on one parcel of land. An appropriate local governmental agency is presented by a landowner with a preliminary concept plan and a subsequent development plan. This is different from a traditional rezoning which grants district-wide uses without detail. A planned unit development, or PUD, works either legislatively as a floating zone or administratively through a special or conditional use. In either case, the local government exercises more precise control than would otherwise be theoretically possible when acting upon a request for a map or text amendment. See discussion *infra* this chapter, section G.

Brunswick Smart Growth, Inc. v. Town Bd. of Town of Brunswick supports this statement. 51 A.D.3d 1119, 856 N.Y.S.2d 308 (3d Dep't 2008). The New York Court of Appeals noted that the "floating zone is the common and preferred method for creating planned development districts." *Id.* at 1120, 310. Moreover, the court outlined the two-step legislative process, "the initial ordinance outlines procedures for a planned development district without setting boundaries, and the second legislative act amends the zoning ordinance and/or map to place an approved district" and held that the action was rightly dismissed because the petitioner commenced the proceeding before the second legislative step was taken by the town. *Id.* at 1121, 310.

Buffer Zones: The zoning "pyramid" so popular after *Euclid* decrees that incompatible zoning uses should be separated one from the other, if not by natural features (rivers and streams) or surface infrastructure (highways) then perhaps by intervening medium intensity zones. Is this a valid purpose for classifying someone's property in a way objectionable (and economically detrimental) to the owner? The answer is given in *Evanston Best & Co., Inc. v. Goodman*, 16 N.E.2d 131 (Ill.1938):

> The city of Evanston adopted a comprehensive zoning ordinance in 1921 which divided the city into five districts. "B residential districts" were created between "commercial" and "A residential districts," wherein quasi-commercial and multiple-occupancy structures might be erected. By means of this device, a so-called buffer area has been established to prevent an impact between the intensity of the use to which commercial areas are put with the quiet and cleanliness which are essential to property devoted to higher type residential uses. While the existence of such an area is not necessary, its creation cannot be said to be an unreasonable exercise of the police power.

> Petitioner emphasizes the fact that its property would be more valuable if zoned for commercial purposes, but this fact exists in every case where the intensity with which property may be used is restricted by zoning laws. * * * Petitioner was well aware of the restrictions upon the use of the property in this district when it purchased the lot in question and the evidence it has produced in this case raises questions which, at most, are

debatable. In such cases, the decision of the zoning authorities is controlling.

16 N.E.2d at 132.

In *Arlington Heights v. Metropolitan Housing Dev. Corp.*, 429 U.S. 252 (1977), a multi-family zone classification was sought by a group hoping to build low-income housing in an all-white Chicago suburb. According to the Village's apartment policy (formally adopted), that classification was primarily to serve as a buffer between commercial and single family residential uses. As the subject parcel adjoined no such commercial or industrial districts, the Village refused to grant the rezoning request. The Court held the Village's exclusionary actions not violative of the federal constitution. A silver lining in the decision was the uncharacteristic approval for planning policy that the Court adopted in relying on the Village's plan. *Arlington Heights* is discussed in the context of exclusionary zoning in Chapter 5. *See also* David L. Callies and Clifford L. Weaver, *The Arlington Heights Case: The Exclusion of Exclusionary Zoning Challenges*, 2 REAL ESTATE ISSUES 37 (1978).

Zoning land for multi-family use because it is to buffer single-family land from industrial uses may mean the land is useless for the purpose zoned. What challenge might then be made?

Performance Zoning: Performance or impact zoning establishes criteria to measure a land use's spillover effects onto neighbors. In theory, it is an alternative to use zoning, but in practice, it serves as a supplement to, rather than a substitute for, use zoning. In *DeCoals, Inc. v. Bd. of Zoning Appeals*, 284 S.E.2d 856 (W.Va.1981), the city's zoning ordinance used performance standards for industrially zoned property. The ordinance required:

> A. An Industrial Use is one which requires both buildings and open area for manufacturing, fabrication, processing, extraction, heavy repairing, dismantling, storage or disposal of equipment, raw materials, manufactured products or wastes, and provided the use conforms to the following performance standards: * * *

> > (3) *Dust.* No dust of any kind produced by the industrial operations shall be permitted to escape beyond the limits of the property being used. * * *

> > (8) *Noise and Sound.* A maximum of 70 decibels at the property line is permitted. Noise is required to be muffled so as not to become objectionable due to intermittance [sic], beat frequency or shrillness. Sound may equal but not exceed street traffic noise in the vicinity during a normal day shift work period.

284 S.E.2d at 858. The court upheld these industrial performance standards against a substantive due process challenge. In *Easy Way of Lee County, Inc. v. Lee County*, 674 So.2d 863 (Fla.App.1996), however, the court invalidated a noise standard of "plainly audible" on vagueness grounds. *See also Anderson v. City of Issaquah*, where the court struck down requirements that a development be "harmonious" and "compatible in its surroundings because such standards did not give meaningful direction and that it was necessary to define aesthetic requirements with specific, workable guidelines so as to avoid "determinations based on whim, caprice, or subjective considerations." 70 Wash.App. 64, 851 P.2d 744, 754 (Div. 1 1993).

Performance zoning, its past and future, is discussed in Alan C. Weinstein, *Performance Zoning: A Silver Anniversary Evaluation*, 21 ZONING AND PLANNING LAW REPORT 53 (July–Aug. 1998). In addition, *see* Chris Duersken, *Modern Industrial Performance Standards: Key Implementation and Legal Issues*, 18 ZONING AND PLANNING LAW REPORT 33 (May 1995); Lane Kendig, *Performance Zoning* (1980); and Frederick W. Acker, *Note, Performance Zoning*, 67 NOTRE DAME L.REV. 363 (1991).

8. PLANNED UNIT DEVELOPMENT

The failure of the typical Euclidean zoning district and classification scheme to address numerous development control issues led in the late 1950s to a search for more precise and flexible techniques to control the use of land. One of the most popular of those techniques is planned development (PD), or planned unit development (PUD). The basics of the technique are contained in the name: the precise planning of a development—as a "unit" on one parcel of land. An appropriate local governmental agency is presented by a landowner with a preliminary concept plan and a subsequent detailed site plan. This differs from traditional rezoning which authorizes all of the uses within the zoning district district-wide common uses without detailed. A PUD works as a flexible but detailed zoning device, either: (1) legislatively by rezoning to a "floating zone," a zone that is created in the text of the zoning ordinance but is not mapped on any land until an applicant requests that it "float down" on his or her land; or, (2) administratively through a special or conditional use. In either case, the local government exercises more precise control than would otherwise be theoretically possible when acting upon a request for a map or text amendment where, recall, the only pertinent question on land use is whether the LIST of uses permitted in the new district would be appropriate, NOT whether just the particular use the landowner proposes would be so appropriate—see previous sections on conditional zoning and special permit uses for other mechanisms to restrict the landowner's choice upon rezoning to a certain use or uses only).

Contrary to popular notions about the genesis of the PUD, the concept of such flexibility in exchange for tighter controls on the development process first emerged, not in the 1950s when it began to become popular, but in the 1920s prior to the Euclid decision. The power of local planning boards or commissions to approve mixed residential/commercial subdivisions which would take precedence over underlying local zoning was part of the model planning enabling law prepared by the Committee on the Regional Plan of New York in 1925, and enacted into law by the New York legislature in 1926. *See* Jan Z. Krasnowiecki, Richard F. Babcock, and David N. McBride, *Legal Aspects of Planned Unit Residential Development With Suggested Legislation*, Urban Land Institute Technical Bulletin No. 52, Part I, The Legal Aspects 11 (1965).

Among the critical questions and legal issues associated with PUD are: (a) is it an authorized technique absent specific enabling legislation? (b) If the zoning ordinance places the authority to approve a PUD with the planning commission or the governing board under a special or conditional use permit (in lieu of a legislative floating zone), are there sufficient defined and unambiguous standards and conditions as to design, uses, and improvements to avoid an arbitrary or capricious delegation, or being voided because of vagueness? *See Anderson v. Village of Issaquah*, 851 P.2d 744 (Wash.App.1993); (c) what procedures are generally employed in making it effective? (d) at what point in that process does the landowner have a vested right, taking into account that large-scale developments which will be built over a long period of time, such as transit oriented developments nodes and major phased traditional neighborhood mixed-use developments; (e) does approval of the concept site plan and phase I development plan vest all of the phases from subsequent rezoning without an accompanying development agreement? *See National Parks and Conservation Ass'n v. County of Riverside*, 50 Cal.Rptr.2d 339 (Cal.App.1996) (finding that the legislative purpose and objectives behind the California Development Agreement statute "was to encourage multiphase developments by reducing the risk of subsequent regulatory changes").

PLANNED UNIT DEVELOPMENT: A CHALLENGE TO ESTABLISHED THEORY AND PRACTICE OF LAND USE CONTROL

Jan Z. Krasnowiecki, 114 U.Penn.L.Rev. 47, 47–48 (1965).*

We have, I believe, become convinced that existing zoning, subdivision and other development controls have failed to encourage, and in fact have directly discouraged, a more imaginative product, particularly in new residential development. The existing controls, it is often noted, tend to focus on the individual lot, a focus which makes sense where development

---

* © University of Pennsylvania Law Review. Excerpt reprinted with permission.

occurs on an individual lot basis but which offers the residential developer nothing better than a "cookie cutter" with which to create a community. Current subdivision controls, for example, assume that the entire site (excepting streets and drainage rights of way) will be distributed in lots for the individual enjoyment of each home. In fact, however, the lots are frequently used in common by the children and sometimes even by the adults. It may be appropriate to ask why we do not allow the developer to borrow a part of each lot and assemble some areas for common use and recreation from the start.

There is much to be gained by a fresh approach. By recognizing the need for common recreation, the homes can be designed and sited for greater privacy and the home owner need not be put to the choice between suffering daily invasion or becoming an outcast. The ability to use a portion of the entire site as common open space will give the developer "play" in the siting of his homes so that if he is forced to use one design he can cluster them around cul-de-sacs instead of stringing them out like matchboxes in a row. If we abandon the idea that the automobile must have access to the lot and allow the developer to use interior lots, walkways and common parking facilities, a whole range of interesting site planning possibilities would become available. From here, why not escape the matchbox effect entirely by encouraging the developer to use a combination of different housing types? By adding new urbanist mixed uses the local government can use planned development to achieve green and sustainable communities. *See* Daniel R. Mandelker, *Designing Planned Communities* (Universe Books, 2010).

These are some of the ideas associated with the current movement in favor of "cluster" and "planned unit" residential development. They are not new ideas. Contrary to popular belief, the draftsmen of the original model enabling legislation did not overlook the project approach to residential development.

Consider the following model PUD statute.

Planned Unit Development Statute

§ 24–67–101. Short title

This article shall be known and may be cited as the "Planned Unit Development Act of _____".

§ 24–67–102. Legislative declaration

(1) In order that the public health, safety, integrity, and general welfare may be furthered in an era of increasing urbanization and of growing demand for housing of all types and design, the powers set forth in this article are granted to all counties and municipalities for the following purposes:

(a) To provide for necessary commercial, recreational, and educational facilities conveniently located to such housing;

(b) To provide for well-located, clean, safe, and pleasant industrial sites involving a minimum of strain on transportation facilities;

(c) To ensure that the provisions of the zoning laws which direct the uniform treatment of dwelling type, bulk, density, and open space within each zoning district will not be applied to the improvement of land by other than lot-by-lot development in a manner which would distort the objectives of the zoning laws;

(d) To encourage innovations in residential, commercial, and industrial development and renewal so that the growing demands of the population may be met by greater variety in type, design, and layout of buildings and by the conservation and more efficient use of open space ancillary to said buildings;

(e) To encourage a more efficient use of land and of public services, or private services in lieu thereof, and to reflect changes in the technology of land development so that resulting economies may enure to the benefit of those who need homes;

(f) To lessen the burden of traffic on streets and highways;

(g) To encourage the building of new towns incorporating the best features of modern design;

(h) To conserve the value of the land;

(i) To provide a procedure which can relate the type, design, and layout of residential, commercial, and industrial development to the particular site, thereby encouraging preservation of the site's natural characteristics; and

(j) To encourage integrated planning in order to achieve the above purposes.

§ 24–67–105. Standards and conditions for planned unit development

(1) Every resolution or ordinance adopted pursuant to the provisions of this article shall set forth the standards and conditions by which a proposed planned unit development shall be evaluated, which shall be consistent with the provisions of this section. No planned unit development may be approved by a county or municipality without the written consent of the landowner whose properties are included within the planned unit development.

(2) Such resolution or ordinance shall set forth the uses permitted in a planned unit development and the minimum number of units or acres which may constitute a planned unit development.

(3) Such resolution or ordinance may establish the sequence of development among the various types of uses.

(4) Such resolution or ordinance shall establish standards governing the density or intensity of land use, or methods for determining such density or intensity, in a planned unit development.

(5) Such resolution or ordinance shall specify information which shall be submitted with the planned unit development application to ensure full evaluation of the application, and the board designated pursuant to section 24–67–104(1)(c) may require such additional relevant information as it may deem necessary.

(6)(a) Such resolution . . . may provide standards for inclusion of common open space.

(b) The ordinance or resolution may require that the landowner provide for and establish an organization for the ownership and maintenance of any common open space or that other adequate arrangements for the ownership and maintenance thereof be made.

(7) Design, construction, and other requirements applicable to a planned unit development may be different from or modifications of the requirements otherwise applicable by reason of any zoning or subdivision regulation, resolution, or ordinance of the county or municipality. Subdivision regulations applicable to planned unit developments may differ from those otherwise applicable.

NOTES

1. Is the above enabling legislation necessary or could the authority to approve PUDs be implied from the Standard Zoning Enabling Act? *Cheney v. Village 2 at New Hope*, 241 A.2d 81 (Pa.1968) (authority implied); *but see Schride Associates v. Wall Twp.*, 464 A.2d 1189 (N.J.App.1983) (PUD authorized only if it complies with state enabling act). *See Giger v. City of Omaha*, 442 N.W.2d 182 (Neb.1989), where the court found implied authority based on the grant of home rule powers for a city to enter into a conditional rezoning coupled with a development agreement that contained a PUD.

2. PUDs do not necessarily consist of a wide variety of uses. Often, what is allowed within a PUD may be dictated by what is allowed as a principal or special use in a particular zoning ordinance, i.e., "all uses allowed in the commercial zone are allowed in this PUD." Where a community wishes to adopt "New Urbanism" traditional neighborhood development (discussed below in section I) a PUD may consist of a group of businesses, retail and offices, or a mixed group of single and multi-family housing, or mixed non-residential and residential use. In cities with Euclidean zoning a PUD is used to provide a variety of residential arrangements within a given area (such as apartments,

condominiums, and single-family dwellings). Such developments are commonly referred to as "planned residential developments," or PRDs.

EVANS V. TETON COUNTY

Supreme Court of Idaho, 2003.
139 Idaho 71, 73 P.3d 84.

KIDWELL, JUSTICE.

Richard Evans and Matthew Finnegan (appellants) appeal the Teton County Board of County Commissioners' (Board of Commissioners) decision to approve Teton Springs, L.L.C.'s (Teton Springs) final plat of phase 1 of the Teton Springs subdivision, request for a zone change from A-2.5 to R-1, and application for a Planned Unit Development (PUD). The Board of Commissioners' decision is affirmed.

I.   Facts and Procedure

Teton Springs, a Wyoming limited liability company, proposed to convert 780 acres of mostly undeveloped farmland and wetland in southern Teton County into a PUD consisting of a golf course and residential resort. The PUD is adjacent to the Targhee National Forest in southern Teton County Upon completion, the proposed development will include an 18-hole golf course, clubhouse, pro shop, maintenance buildings, fishing ponds, equestrian facility, 100-room hotel, 50 overnight units, health club and tennis facility, swimming pool, restaurant, conference rooms, nordic ski facility, storage facilities, helicopter pad, parking lots, 18 two to three acre ranch estates, 100 three-quarters to one acre golf estates, 170 one-third to one-half acre golf homes, 180 five thousand square foot residential lots, and 100 overnight cabin lots from one thousand to twenty-five hundred square feet.

Of the 780 acres upon which the PUD will be built, the respondents Rammel own 460 acres, the Hastings own 160 acres, the Kearsleys own 80 acres, and the Wingers own 80 acres. Approximately 140 of the 780 acres are located within the "Area of City Impact," an unincorporated area of Teton County neighboring the city of Victor. In addition to the national forest to the south, the acreage surrounding the PUD supports a mix of agricultural, residential, and commercial uses. There are some pre-existing subdivisions to the north of the PUD. The appellants live on two-and-one-half acre residential lots near the PUD.

On August 2, 1999, Teton Springs filed an application for approval of the PUD. Teton Springs also requested a zone change from A-2.5 to R-1. On September 1, 1999, the Teton County Planning and Zoning Commission (Zoning Commission) held a public hearing to consider the application. Following the hearing, the Zoning Commission recommended approval of the concept plan for the PUD and zone change. On October 25, 1999, the Board of Commissioners conducted a public hearing to consider the Teton

Springs PUD and proposed zone change. At the conclusion of the hearing, the Board of Commissioners approved the concept plan of the PUD conditionally upon resolution of issues regarding natural stream flows, the development's impact on the city of Victor, traffic flow, impact on county services, sewer system capacity, and density. The Board of Commissioners decided to wait to consider the zoning change when it considered Teton Springs' final plat.

After the October hearing, the Zoning Commission obtained comments regarding the PUD application from the Idaho Department of Water Resources, the U.S. Environmental Protection Agency, the Idaho Department of Environmental Quality, the U.S. Fish and Wildlife Service, the Idaho Fish and Game Department, the District 7 Health Department, and various other county and local agencies. On May 3, 2000, the Zoning Commission held another public hearing to consider the Teton Springs PUD application and the proposed zone change. At the hearing's conclusion, the Zoning Commission recommended accepting the PUD application and granting the zone change. On May 9, 2000, the Zoning Commission issued Findings of Fact and Conclusions in support of its decision.

On June 12, 2000, the Board of Commissioners and the city of Victor held a joint public hearing to consider the Teton Springs PUD and request for a zone change. At the conclusion of this hearing, the Board of Commissioners and the city of Victor approved the PUD and granted the zone change. The Board of Commissioners also adopted the Findings of Fact and Conclusions issued by the Zoning Commission.

On July 7, 2000, the appellants filed a Petition for Judicial Review of Teton Springs' application for approval of a PUD and zone change. The appellants alleged the Board of Commissioners violated Teton County Zoning Ordinance (Zoning Ordinance), Teton County Subdivision Ordinance (Subdivision Ordinance), and the Teton County Comprehensive Plan (Comprehensive Plan) by approving the PUD and granting a zone change. As a result, the appellants alleged they would suffer substantial injury. On September 25, 2001, the district court issued a decision affirming the Board of Commissioners' approval of Teton Springs' application for a PUD and zone change. The appellants timely filed this appeal.

II. Standard of Review

This Court must affirm the Board of Commissioners unless it determines the Board of Commissioners' findings, inferences, conclusions, or decisions: (1) violated the constitution or statutory provisions; (2) exceeded its statutory authority; (3) were made upon unlawful procedure; (4) were not supported by substantial evidence on the record; or (5) were arbitrary, capricious, or an abuse of discretion. There is a strong

standard for court

presumption that the actions of the Board of Commissioners, where it has interpreted and applied its own zoning ordinances, are valid.

The Board of Commissioners Did Not Violate The Teton County Zoning And Subdivision Ordinance Or Comprehensive Plan When It Approved Teton Spring's Application For A PUD.

1.   The Subdivision Ordinance's two percent limitation on developed acreage that can be used for incidental purposes does not apply to the Teton Springs PUD.

The Subdivision Ordinance allows all PUDs to contain "incidental components" inconsistent with the underlying land use zones as long as: (1) the uses are incidental and necessary to the primary purpose of the PUD; and (2) no more than two percent of the developed acreage within the PUD is devoted to incidental use. The appellants argue the PUD violates the Subdivision Ordinance's two percent limitation on land developed for uses incompatible with the underlying zoning because the PUD's proposed commercial uses are incidental, not primary uses. As a result, the appellants claim that many of the uses proposed by Teton Springs are prohibited in a residential zone.

The Subdivision Ordinance permits three types of PUDs, including RCI PUDs. The Subdivision Ordinance defines an RCI PUD as one where "[p]roperty located in residential, commercial, and industrial zones may be developed pursuant to an approved" residential, commercial, or industrial (RCI) PUD. In terms of the permitted uses in an R-1 zone, the Subdivision Ordinance states, "[p]roperty located within an R-1 . . . zone may be developed pursuant to an approved 'Residential, Commercial or Industrial PUD' (referred to as an 'RCI PUD')." Under the Subdivision Ordinance, all PUD's may be used for primarily residential developments, but only an RCI PUD may be used for primarily commercial or industrial developments. Under the Zoning Restrictions and Land Use Table found in the Zoning Ordinance, an RCI PUD is a permitted use in R-1 zones as long as the use is permitted as outlined in the PUD Process of the Zoning Ordinance.

The Teton Springs PUD is an RCI PUD. The Zoning Ordinance unambiguously permits use of an RCI PUD in an R-1 Zone as long as the use is permitted as outlined in the PUD process. The Subdivision Ordinance unambiguously allows development of property located within an R-1 zone pursuant to an approved RCI PUD. The Subdivision Ordinance also unambiguously allows commercial or industrial development in an approved RCI PUD. Based on the plain meaning of the Zoning and Subdivision Ordinance, the two percent incidental use limitation of § 1–7–5 of the Subdivision Ordinance does not apply to an approved RCI PUD built in an R-1 zone as long as the use is permitted as outlined in the PUD process.

2.   The density of the Teton Springs PUD is not impermissible.

The appellants claim the PUD violates the Comprehensive Plan because the density of development is too high and many of the lots are smaller than allowed. Under the Subdivision Ordinance, "A PUD application may depart from applicable height, setback and lot size restrictions when . . . approved by the Board." T.C.S.O. § 1–7–3. "Any departures from the height, setback, and lot size . . . [required by] the Zoning Ordinance must be recorded and justified as not compromising the health, safety and general welfare of the county."

The Subdivision Ordinance also states that "[t]he protection of open space is a central feature of all PUD's." "In the case of an RCI PUD, a minimum of fifty percent (50%) of the land within the gross acreage of the PUD shall be dedicated to open space." "Open spaces may take a variety of forms, including . . . a golf course."

The Subdivision Ordinance also expects that in a well-planned PUD, the housing units will be clustered in higher density groups allowing for open space. However, the Subdivision Ordinance does not provide a formula for clustering because a prescribed method for clustering would be counterproductive given the uniqueness of each development. Rather, the Board of Commissioners is instructed to decide on projects based on how intelligently the project uses the existing land within the PUD. The Subdivision Ordinance limits the base density of an RCI PUD, on that portion of the property that is not open space, to a maximum of one unit per one-half acre. Nonetheless, the Subdivision Ordinance allows the Board of Commissioners to approve a greater or lesser density, provided it determines the public health, safety, and welfare service of the county will not be negatively impacted.

Based on the provisions of the Subdivision Ordinance and the Board of Commissioners' unique position in interpreting and applying its own zoning laws, the Teton Springs PUD does not violate the density requirements of Teton County's zoning laws. The PUD departs from the allowed lot size restrictions, but under the Subdivision Ordinance the Board of Commissioners has flexibility to approve such departures as long as it finds the departure does not compromise the health, safety and general welfare of the county. The Board of Commissioners specifically found no such compromise, as discussed above.

3.   Approval of the Teton Springs PUD application is not dependent upon compliance with the policies of the Teton County Comprehensive Plan.

The appellants assert that the Teton Springs PUD violates several important policies of the Comprehensive Plan. The respondents counter that the Comprehensive Plan is not a zoning ordinance that regulates project compliance.

While the Board of Commissioners may not disregard the Comprehensive Plan, it is not a zoning ordinance by which a development project's compliance is measured. Rather, the Comprehensive Plan provides guidance to the local agency charged with making zoning decisions. The appellants may or may not be correct in their concern that the Teton Springs PUD will adversely affect the present lifestyle and alter the character of the area in violation of the policies of the Comprehensive Plan, that point was heavily debated during the approval process. Similarly, the fear of the "Jacksonization" of the Teton Valley, as the billionaires force the millionaires over Teton Pass into Driggs and Victor, may be well founded. However, regardless of the wisdom, or lack thereof, in approving Teton Springs' PUD application, the Comprehensive Plan does not provide a legal basis for this Court to reverse the Board of Commissioners' decision to approve the application.

I.C. § 67–6535 governs the issuance of findings of fact or conclusions of law relevant to a local land use agency's approval or denial of a land use application. Approval or denial of a land use application must be in writing explaining the relevant criteria and standards, the relevant contested facts, and the rationale for the decision based on the applicable provisions of the comprehensive plan and relevant ordinances. There is no requirement that both the Commission and Board make written findings and conclusions, only that they are made. The Board of Commissioners did not err by adopting the written findings of fact and conclusions issued by the Zoning Commission.

The Board of Commissioners concluded the zone change satisfied the Comprehensive Plan based on the material submitted by the developer, engineer, and Staff Reports. The Board of Commissioners also concluded the zone change will preserve compatibility with the surrounding zoning districts and secure public health, safety, and general welfare based on the approval process as a whole.

While the Board of Commissioners would be better served by more specifically and extensively articulating its findings of fact and conclusions, the required information can be found in the record produced during the application process. This is in accord with I.C. § 67–6535(c), which requires a reviewing court to consider the whole process, and T.C.S.O. § 1–7–13(J), which does not require written findings where the public documents or records of the public meetings are already contained in the record. Therefore, we conclude the record, when viewed in its entirety, contains sufficient findings of fact to support the Board of Commissioners' decision.

NOTES

1.   For plat and aerial views of the Teton Springs PUD, go to http://www.tetonsprings.com/club/scripts/section/section.asp?NS=RE.

2.   The choice of local government agency to approve the PUD is critical, and has been the subject of considerable comment, both early and late in the development of the PUD (see ULI Tech. Bulletin No. 52, at 19–37, cited in the introduction to this section). If a whole new mini-community is created, should the decision be left to an administrative agency like a planning commission as a conditional or special use? If so, under what circumstances and according to how detailed a set of standards within a required site plan? Too many standards and restrictions will destroy the utility of the concept. On the other hand, too few will run the risk of an unconstitutional delegation of legislative authority. *See, City of Miami v. Save Brickell Avenue*, 426 So.2d 1100 (Fla.1983). If the legislative body reserves the special or conditional use permit to itself, as in the Teton Springs case, it will still be treated as "quasi-judicial," subject to procedural due process, and a requirement that there be substantial evidence to support the development approval as complying with the standards established in the state enabling act and the zoning ordinance. *See Teton Springs*, 139 Idaho 71, 74, 80, 73 P.3d 84, 87, 93. Only if the approval of a PUD is treated as a legislative floating zone (see note 4 below) will the approving legislative body be limited to quasi-judicial review.

3.   When a legislative body, as in Teton Springs case, decides to enact standards for consideration within the PUD application process, those standards must thereafter be used. If an application is approved without considering the standards, or if the standards are ambiguous, the reviewing court will overturn the PUD approval. In *Peters v. Spearfish ETJ Planning Comm'n*, 567 N.W.2d 880, 884–85 (S.D.1997), a group of individuals protesting a PUD alleged that the PUD section of the zoning ordinance which "provided that overall population densities do not exceed the densities of specific residential districts" was ambiguous, and therefore the planning commission and city council exceeded their authority by approving the developer's PUD. The South Dakota Supreme Court agreed, finding that the ordinance was not specific as to whether population density was governed by residential population densities or agricultural population densities since the term "residential districts" was ambiguous in the Spearfish city ordinance. Depending on the interpretation of the term, population density might range from one dwelling per 7,500 square feet to one dwelling per forty acres.

4.   PUDs may also be treated as a legislative spin-off of the floating zone. If what is permitted is spelled out in the concept plan, to what extent can the appropriate local agency refuse to approve a subsequent development plan because it does not like the layout and design of the proposed structures? *See generally* Frank F. Turner and Terry D. Morgan, *Planned Development Zoning: A Texas Perspective, Ch. 5, Inst. Planning, Zoning, and Eminent Domain* (1992), and David L. Callies, *Vested Rights*, § 52D.03[3], 8 Zoning and Land Use Controls (Rohan and Kelly eds. 2011). If the developer seeks to change the final development plan, the courts require approval of the legislative body and the planning commission after public hearings if the change is "major" or "substantial." *See Makowski v. City of Naperville*, 617 N.E.2d 1251 (Ill.App.1993) (discussing what constitutes major change). In *Cherokee County v. Martin*, 559 S.E.2d 138 (Ga.App.2002), a change from assisted living

facilities to apartments was held not to be a major change since both were forms of multi-family use.

5.   Where the PUD process is quasi-judicial, requiring a special or conditional use permit, under the usual rule governing quasi-judicial proceedings, a decision of the planning commission or legislative body will be sustained as not arbitrary or capricious if the proposed PUD fails to meet only one of the numerous objective standards set out in the ordinance. *See Robal Associates, Inc. v. Bd. of Supervisors of Charlestown Twp.*, 999 A.2d 630 (Pa.Cmwlth.2010). What advantages or disadvantages can you see in permitting a PUD as a special or conditional use, rather than rezoning to a floating zoning district? To the developer? To the neighborhood community association?

6.   The traditional American subdivision of single houses on separate, and frequently large, lots has advantages and disadvantages. For some, an advantage is privacy and for others a disadvantage is aesthetic. It works, according to one court, "so long as no one cares that the overall appearance of the municipality resembles the design achieved by using a cookie cutter on a sheet of dough." *Cheney v. Village 2 at New Hope*, 241 A.2d 81, 83 (Pa.1968). One of the advantages of the PUD is the preservation of open space achieved by clustering units on part of the tract, leaving open areas that would otherwise be developed. In addition to the aesthetic appeal of the open space, clustering is environmentally friendly as sensitive lands (hillsides, wetlands) that might otherwise be built upon will be saved. For the developer, savings result because infrastructure costs will be lower since streets, driveways, water and sewer lines can be run over shorter distances. If the PUD has mixed uses and walkability, it will reduce greenhouse gas emissions that lead to aggravation of global warming. *See* Chapter 8, *supra*.

7.   Who owns the open space set aside in a PUD? Some form of common tenancy ownership scheme that includes the owners of the units of the clustered housing might be established, or the land might be dedicated to either a homeowners association or to the local government. What happens if subsequent housing shortages lead to an effort to rezone the open space to allow its development? New Hampshire requires creation of "a conservation restriction * * * , which shall run with the land, and shall be enforceable by the municipality, or by the owner of any property which would be specifically damaged by the violation of such restriction, regardless of whether any deed or other instrument conveying such restrictions has been executed or recorded." New Hampshire Rev.Stat.Ann. 674:21–a. Charitable deductions are available for dedication of permanent conservation easements or grants in fee simple where the land is used for conserving environmentally sensitive, open space or agricultural land. *See* Internal Revenue Code, 26 U.S.C. § 170(h).

8.   *Density*. Assume that a PUD is being designed on a 100-acre tract of land, forty acres of which lie within environmentally sensitive areas that are unsuitable for development. Under a net density calculation, if one unit per acre were allowed, the developer would only be allowed to develop sixty units because the environmentally sensitive lands are netted out of the land. Under

a gross density calculation, however, the developer would still be allowed to build one hundred units on the remaining sixty acres because the entire tract is considered despite the fact that forty acres are undevelopable. In the situation above, where 40 acres are determined by a planning commission to be undevelopable because of environmental sensitivity, should this be viewed as a 100% loss of use of the forty acres, or a forty percent loss of use of the 100 acres? For a similar dilemma in takings cases, should a regulation requiring that 90% of the land be set aside for open space be deemed a restriction of 100% of 90% (a taking) or 90% of 100% (not a taking)? See Chapter 3 on regulatory takings.

9.   *Open Space.* Since one of the purposes of the PUD is to preserve open space, some cities offer the incentive of calculating density based on gross density. *See* City of Grand Junction, Colorado, Comprehensive plan (2009). Such a calculation might amount to a violation of the density requirements of the comprehensive plan. When the PUD zone ordinance is created, if a density requirement in the PUD is different from that of the overall requirements of the comprehensive plan, the comprehensive plan will either have to be amended, or the PUD approval will be invalidated. *Madison River R.V. Ltd. v. Town of Ennis*, 994 P.2d 1098 (Mont.2000) (Town Council properly denied development approval based on conflict with town's comprehensive plan even though proposed use was permitted by the underlying zoning district). *See generally* Kenneth Young, *Anderson's American Law of Zoning*, § 24:19 (5th ed.2011). Suppose a developer has 100 acres in an area zoned for one house per acre. Its preference is to cluster 100 units on 30% of the tract and leave 70% for open space, but the zoning ordinance only allows traditional lot development? Can the developer demand the right to cluster? Since overall density is not increased, what justification or policy does the state have in precluding the cluster?

10.   *Judicial Review.* In *Hensler v. City of Glendale*, 876 P.2d 1043 (Cal.1994), plaintiff brought suit for inverse condemnation, claiming that a PUD subdivision ordinance precluded development of 40% of his property which was reserved for open space. The allowable "cluster" did not make up for the original 400-plus units sought but allowed only 300. The developer proceeded with buildout and then brought suit for an injunction and declaratory judgment to declare the open space dedication to be a Fifth Amendment taking. The California Supreme Court held that the developer could not proceed with the injunction or declaratory judgment suit but had to raise the taking issue at the planning commission and then bring a writ of administrative mandamus within a 90 day statute of limitations period for writ proceedings. California and most other states have short statutes of limitations for judicial writ (certiorari or administrative mandamus) review of subdivisions which the developer in Hensler failed to use. For a thorough examination and analysis of PUDs, *see* Daniel Mandelker, *Planned Unit Developments* (APA 2011).

C. ZONING ADMINISTRATION

With a zoning ordinance in place, the focus of the process is typically directed toward efforts to obtain, or to prevent someone from obtaining, development permission. Under early theory, permits were to issue as of right as a landowner asked to build one of the various specific permitted uses of the district in which the land was located. Often, however, development pressures suggested a use of the land in a manner that was not permitted. Or, a city confronted with a request for a permit for a use that was expressly allowed, decided that granting the permit would not serve the public interest. For one participant or another, the code did not match present needs or desires. Applications to change became the norm. As Richard Babcock famously wrote, the name of the zoning game is change. Richard F. Babcock, *The Zoning Game: Municipal Practices and Policies* (1966).

The materials that follow deal with these changes, whether they occur as the result of a comprehensive rezoning amendment, changed conditions in a particular neighborhood, or the desires of a particular landowner-developer. For the one seeking change, the first question is what avenue to follow: a map or text amendment, a conditional use permit, or a variance, collectively what the late Professor Donald Hagman called the "zoning forms of action." For the neighbors, the question often is how to prevent the change from being made, and for the government, the questions include whether the request is in accord with the plan, how to accommodate the request for change while protecting the neighbors from undue harm, and assessing the project's infrastructure impact. *See* Juergensmeyer and Roberts, *Land Use Planning and Development Regulation Law* § 5.1 (3rd ed.2012).

Throughout this section, note the rationale for effecting the change in the way sought and what public/private results flow from the particular means used in each case. Here in particular, process is important. Moreover, the changing of uses, by whatever means, is increasingly cumbersome and frequently criticized. More than thirty years ago, commentators complained of a "permit explosion." Fred Bosselman, Duane A. Feurer and Charles L. Siemon, *The Permit Explosion* (1976). Yet today, more permits are required, and the need for multiple permits from various authorities adds more time to the process. Development of right is often a fiction. Recent efforts to implement form-based zoning (see discussion *infra* Ch. 2.J.) are prompted in part by a desire to allow more development of right. Yet, the desire for public input to development proposals causes some to resist automatic approval out of the public eye. Tension between these goals persists.

As you study the cases that follow, be alert to whether it is the legislative body or an administrative agency that is asked to make the change or grant the permit. Regardless of the name of the acting body, is the nature of the act taken legislative or administrative? Legislative actions generally are accorded a presumption of validity and receive limited judicial review. Administrative or quasi-judicial actions, in contrast, are subject to more intensive judicial review. How do you tell the difference? One court put it this way: "Ordinances laying down general policies without regard to a specific piece of property are usually an exercise of legislative authority * * * [while] a determination whether the permissible use of a specific piece of property should be changed is usually an exercise of judicial authority and its propriety is subject to an altogether different [and more strenuous] test." *Fasano v. Board of County Comm'rs of Washington County*, 507 P.2d 23, 26 (Or.1973).

For a thorough and exceptionally lucid description of the rezoning process in the context of land development and its multiple permit stages generally, *see* Witold Rybczynski, *Last Harvest: How a Cornfield Became New Daleville* (2007).

1.   SPOT ZONING AND UNIFORMITY

We begin with the most common, yet the most radical of the changes, the zoning amendment. In theory, it is a legislative act for the good of the community, regardless of the advantages or disadvantages to the owner and neighbors of the property affected by the amendment. As you read the case that follows, ask yourself whether the court's analysis and holding are consistent with this theory.

Two enabling act mandates that are often tested in the amendment process are Section 2 of the SZEA, which provides in part that "[a]ll such regulations shall be uniform for each class or kind of buildings throughout each district, but the regulations in one district may differ from those in other districts," and Section 3, which provides that "regulations shall be made in accordance with a comprehensive plan * * * ."

PLAINS GRAINS LIMITED PARTNERSHIP v. BOARD OF COUNTY COMMISSIONERS OF CASCADE COUNTY

Supreme Court of Montana, 2010.
357 Mont. 61, 238 P.3d 332.

JUSTICE BRIAN MORRIS.

Plains Grains Limited Partnership (Plains Grains) appeals from an order of the Eighth Judicial District Court, Cascade County, granting summary judgment to the Board of Commissioners of Cascade County (County) and Southern Montana Electric (SME) and denying Plains Grains' spot zoning claim. We reverse. We review the following issues on appeal:

Did Cascade County's adoption of a new county-wide zoning regulation in 2009 render moot Plains Grains' spot zoning claim? Did Plains Grains' failure to seek a stay or injunction to prevent the sale or development of the land render moot its spot zoning claim? Did the rezoning of 668 acres of land from Agricultural to Heavy Industrial constitute impermissible spot zoning?

Duane and Mary E. Urquhart and Scott and Linda Urquhart (Urquharts) sought a zone change from Agricultural (A-2) to Heavy Industrial (I-2) for 668 acres of land in the northeast portion of Cascade County. The Urquharts submitted their rezoning application on October 30, 2007, to allow for the construction and operation of SME's proposed coal-fired power plant, known as the Highwood Generating Station (HGS). SME changed its proposal for the HGS to a natural gas fired plant following the Department of Environmental Quality's revocation of SME's air quality permit. The Urquharts and SME participated jointly in the preparation of the application for rezoning. The Urquharts had agreed to sell the property to SME before the County approved the rezone.

The Urquharts' rezone application claimed that "the requested zoning to heavy industrial use is a prerequisite to the planned construction and operation of an electric generating station." The Cascade County Planning Department adopted and made public its initial Staff Report on November 19, 2007. The Staff Report described the surrounding land uses as agricultural for more than twenty acres in every direction. Approximately 200 acres of the land fell within the boundaries of the Lewis and Clark Great Falls Portage National Historic Landmark. The Staff Report cited the Urquharts' attempt to "take advantage of the Tax Increment Financing mechanisms provided in state statutes" as the primary reason that the Urquharts had requested rezoning.

The Staff Report acknowledged that the construction and operation of the HGS would be "out of character with the existing agricultural land uses in the vicinity of the proposed rezoning." The Staff Report noted, however, that construction and operation of the HGS would not necessarily be "out of character with the land uses *allowed* under the existing A-2 zoning district." (Emphasis added). The Staff Report based this conclusion on the fact that the A-2 zone permitted electrical generation facilities through the special use permit process. As a result, the Staff Report determined that "the rezoning is not necessary to accommodate the HGS facility, as such a use is permissible with a special use permit." The Staff Report further noted that the actual construction of any structures or development of the property would require a zoning location-conformance permit.

SME submitted a letter on January 9, 2008, in response to the Staff Report and the Planning Board's report to the Commissioners. SME's letter contained eleven proposed "conditions" that were intended to address the Planning Board's comments. The SME letter contained, in pertinent part, an agreement by SME that "as a condition of rezoning to heavy industrial use, such use shall be solely for purposes of an electrical power plant."

Plains Grains claims to have been unaware of the SME letter until the Commission's public hearing on the proposed rezone on January 15, 2008. SME submitted an array of documentation at the public hearing, including a traffic impact study, a baseline noise study, a report on the health impacts of coal-fired power plants, a property appraisal report, and a landscape plan. The County adopted a resolution of intent on January 31, 2008, to rezone the Urquharts' property.

The resolution of intent incorporated by reference the eleven conditions offered in SME's letter. The County published notice of the resolution on four dates over the course of two weeks in February of 2008. The Commissioners met on March 11, 2008, to consider Final Resolution 08–22 to rezone the Urquharts' property from A-2 to I-2. The Commissioners adopted the Planning Board's report as their findings on the proposed rezone. More than 1900 citizens submitted comments on the proposed rezone. The Commission approved the motion to rezone.

Plains Grains filed a complaint on April 10, 2008. Plains Grains requested that the court set aside the County's approval of the rezone and requested that the court issue a writ of mandate, a writ of review before this Court, and a declaratory judgment. Plains Grains claimed first that the adoption of the zone change constituted "conditional zoning" and violated the Zoning Enabling Act and statutory and constitutional public notice and participation requirements. Plains Grains also alleged that the zone change constituted impermissible spot zoning. SME and the Urquharts intervened on May 1, 2008. The County and SME responded to Plains Grains complaint with motions for summary judgment that the sale of the property by the Urquharts to SME on August 25, 2008, had rendered moot both issues. The District Court issued its order on November 28, 2008.

The District Court denied Plains Grains' motion for summary judgment and its application for writs of mandate and review. The court found first that the eleven allegedly improper conditions constituted merely an adoption of the Planning Board's suggestions and findings. The court rejected Plains Grains' public participation claims after it determined that the County had satisfied the notice and public participation requirements of both the Montana constitution and statutory provisions. Finally, the District Court denied Plains Grains' spot zoning claim on the basis that the rezone did not satisfy the three-part test for impermissible spot zoning articulated by this Court in *Little v. Board of County Comm'rs*, 193 Mont. 334, 346, 631 P.2d 1282, 1289 (1981).

The District Court issued its final order and judgment on May 27, 2009. The court denied summary judgment to Plains Grains on all claims and granted the County summary judgment on the merits. Plains Grains filed its notice of appeal with this Court on June 1, 2009. Plains Grains raised on appeal its conditional zoning, spot zoning, and public participation claims.

Did the rezoning of 668 acres of land from Agricultural to Heavy Industrial constitute impermissible spot zoning?

Plains Grains claims that the rezoning of 668 acres of land from agricultural to heavy industrial constitutes impermissible spot zoning. The County and SME counter that the construction of the HGS did not require rezoning. The District Court determined that Plains Grains could not satisfy the *Little* test based on its determination that SME could construct the HGS through the special use permit process without obtaining a zone change. The District Court acknowledged that important indicators of spot zoning were present. The District Court placed greater weight, however, on two internal planning staff reports that concluded that the HGS would have been allowed within the existing Agricultural zoning district with a special use permit. As a result, the District Court determined that conversion from agricultural to industrial use would not constitute a significantly different use from those prevailing in the area.

Plains Grains argues that the District Court incorrectly conflated activities allowed "as of right" in a given zone with those allowed only under a special use permit. Plains Grains argues that a fundamental difference exists between the administrative procedures involved in obtaining a special use permit and the quasi-legislative process required for a zone change. A party must seek a special use permit from the Board of Adjustment, an administrative body appointed by the county commission, an elected body. The county commission itself must approve a zone change.

We need not determine definitively whether SME could have obtained a special use permit to build the generating station. The District Court's determination that the HGS would have been allowed under a special use permit implies that the issuance of a special use permit constitutes a ministerial act over which the board exercises no discretion. *Beasley v. Flathead County Bd. of Adjustments,* 350 Mont. 171, 205 P.3d 812 (2009). The Board of Adjustment exercises considerable discretion, however, with respect to whether to grant a special use permit. For instance, a property owner in *Beasley* sought a writ of mandate to compel the Board of Adjustment to grant the transfer of a conditional use permit (CUP) obtained by the previous owners. The CUP would have allowed the property owner to operate a gravel pit. We denied the request on the grounds that a writ of mandate cannot be used to compel a discretionary act.

SME likely would face more than a mere ministerial act in seeking to obtain a special use permit to construct the HGS. Section 8 of the Cascade County Zoning Regulations provide that a "special use is a use for which conformance to additional standards will be required and shall be deemed to be a permitted use in its respective district." Section 8 enumerates the procedural requirements to obtain a special use permit. These requirements include the submission of a site plan, public notice, and a hearing process.

The Board may not issue a special use permit unless it first makes five required findings. These findings include that the proposed development will not "materially endanger" the public health, safety, or welfare; that the development will not harm surrounding property values unless it is deemed to be a public necessity; and that the development will be "in harmony" with the area in which it is to be located. The petitioner bears the burden of presenting sufficient evidence to allow the board to make each of the required findings. Nothing in the CCZR compels the Board to issue a special use permit once it makes the required findings. This fact suggests that the granting of a special use permit is a discretionary act.

SME cited the rezone as a "prerequisite" to building the HGS in its petition for rezoning. SME arguably had two procedural paths open to it. Both paths required public notice, a hearing, and a comprehensive application process. SME opted for rezoning because it wished simultaneously to create a tax increment financing district to help finance the HGS. [Editors' note: see Chapter 6 for a complete discussion of tax increment financing ("TIF")]. The rezone became truly a "prerequisite" to building the HGS once SME elected to proceed down the quasi-legislative path of a rezone application. The District Court improperly concluded that the availability of the special use permit option rendered unnecessary SME's zone change request even though SME elected to pursue rezoning rather than seeking to obtain a special use permit. The fact that SME arguably could have pursued a special use permit does not undermine Plains Grains' spot zoning claim.

We turn then to the merits of Plains Grains' spot zoning claim. Whether impermissible spot zoning has occurred presents a fact-specific inquiry that will vary from one case to the next. The presence of three conditions generally will indicate, however, that a given situation constitutes spot zoning, regardless of variations in factual scenarios.

The first prong of the three-part *Little* test examines whether the requested use would differ significantly from the prevailing land uses in the area. The second prong explores whether the area requested for the rezone would be "rather small" in terms of the number of landowners benefitted by the requested zone change. Finally, the third prong analyzes whether the requested zone change would be in the nature of "special legislation" designed to benefit one or a few landowners at the expense of the surrounding landowners or the public. A court must analyze the second and third prongs of the *Little* test in concert. *Boland v. City of Great Falls*, 275 Mont. 128, 134, 910 P.2d 890, 894 (1996). The number of landowners benefitted by the zone change speaks directly to the issue of whether the requested change constitutes special legislation in favor of one or a small number of landowners.

We first must determine "whether the requested use differs from the prevailing use in the area." *North 93 Neighbors, Inc. v. Bd. of County Comm'rs,* 332 Mont. 327, 137 P.3d 557 (2006)(citing *Little,* 193 Mont. at 346, 631 P.2d at 1289). The District Court acknowledged that there "unquestionably" would be a change from the current agricultural use to the proposed heavy industrial use represented by the HGS. The County cites *North 93 Neighbors* for the proposition that a court applying the first prong of the *Little* test may look to the land uses allowed under current zoning rather than the prevailing uses in the area. We analyzed the land uses allowed by current zoning in *North 93 Neighbors* only *after* we thoroughly had considered the existing uses in the area. Our conclusion that the prevailing uses were not significantly different from the proposed use was based on our consideration of both the prevailing uses *and* the uses allowed by current zoning. Thus a court may consider the existing zoning in addition to prevailing uses. Nothing in *North 93 Neighbors* directs a court to consider what uses would be available under existing zoning in lieu of prevailing uses, as the County suggests.

We further distinguish *North 93 Neighbors* from the instant facts in that the proposed rezone in that case would have constituted merely an extension of existing zoning. We observed in *North 93 Neighbors* that "[e]xtending a preexisting zone classification to include a larger area does not constitute spot zoning." By contrast, the proposed rezone to facilitate construction of the HGS would create an island of heavy industrial zoning within a large area zoned for agricultural use.

Finally, the County's reliance on *North 93 Neighbors* fails because existing zoning adjacent to the proposed rezone in that case allowed for commercial use as of right. Here, as Plains Grains points out, SME's proposed use would be allowed-if at all-only by the granting of a special use permit. The District Court applied the wrong test in rejecting the first prong of the *Little* spot zoning analysis. The District Court concluded that the requested use of the 668 acres for the proposed rezone would differ significantly from surrounding uses. SME does not challenge seriously this conclusion. Plains Grains has established the first prong of the *Little* test.

The second prong of the spot zoning test looks at whether the size of the parcel to be rezoned would be "relatively small." Consideration of the actual size of the parcel comprises only one element of this inquiry, but nonetheless constitutes a relevant factor. This Court determined in *Greater Yellowstone Coalition, Inc. v. Bd. of Comm'rs,* 305 Mont. 232, 25 P.3d 168 (2001), that the County had engaged in impermissible spot zoning of a 323 acre parcel that comprised "a mere 2% of the District's 13,280 acres." *Greater Yellowstone Coalition.* The 668 acres at issue in this case comprise a similarly small percentage of the land zoned for agriculture in Cascade County. The District Court acknowledged that Plains Grains "appears to have a compelling argument" with regard to the relatively small size of the area to be rezoned.

The number of landowners affected by the proposed rezone must be analyzed in concert with the third factor-whether the proposed zone change constitutes "special legislation." The number of landowners affected relates directly to whether the zoning constitutes special legislation designed to benefit one person. This inquiry should focus on the benefits of the proposed rezone to surrounding landowners, not the benefits-financial or otherwise-that would accrue from the proposed development. The Urquharts' application for rezoning acknowledged that grain farming and cattle ranching constituted the predominant surrounding land uses. The Staff Report likewise confirms that agricultural production dominates the surrounding land uses.

The District Court found that "one landowner (be it viewed as either SME, the current deed holder, or the Urquharts, the applicants) will benefit at the expense of others." The court recognized that these costs constituted "not merely the location of a power plant in the 'Back 40' but the power lines, rail spurs, and other industrial detritus of a large, power generating facility." The court acknowledged that the impacts of this special legislation would be "imposed on some landowners by way of eminent domain." We agree. No discernible benefit for the rezone would accrue to the neighboring farmers and ranchers. The benefits of the rezone inure solely to the owners of the 668 acres, first the Urquharts and now SME.

The District Court based its determination that no spot zoning had occurred on its conclusion that the zone change "was in name only" and did not change the uses allowed under the existing Cascade County regulations. Our application of the *Little* factors reveals, however, that the rezoning of the HGS property constituted spot zoning. The requested heavy industrial use differs significantly from the current agricultural uses that dominate the surrounding area. The area to be rezoned is relatively small-both in absolute size and in terms of landowners affected. The proposed rezone smacks of "special legislation" in that the benefits would accrue to a single landowner to the detriment of the surrounding farmers and ranchers.

NOTES

1. Generally, a zoning amendment that a court finds to be illegal spot zoning "is not invalid per se merely because only a single parcel is involved or benefited; the real test for spot zoning is whether the change is other than part of a well-considered and comprehensive plan calculated to serve the general welfare of the community." *Collard v. Village of Flower Hill*, 52 N.Y.2d 594, 600–01, 421 N.E.2d 818, 821 (1981). "The vice of spot zoning lies in the fact that it singles out for special treatment a lot or a small area in a way that does

not further such a plan." *Bartram v. Zoning Commission of City of Bridgeport*, 68 A.2d 308 (Conn.1949). Is this true in Montana?

Occasionally, the phrase "spot zoning" is used to state the conclusion that an illegal rezoning has occurred, but most courts are careful to do as the *Plains Grains* court did and speak of *impermissible* or illegal spot zoning. The court included a map of the area, which, according to the plaintiff, revealed a "black island of Industrial land surrounded by a sea of green Agricultural land." See the map in color in the opinion online at Westlaw Next. Just as the mere fact that a single parcel is benefited does not constitute illegal zoning, according to the authorities cited above, the mere appearance of the rezoned land as a spot on the map does not necessarily mean the rezoning is invalid.

2.   The *Plains Grains* court's third prong asks whether the rezoning is in "the nature of 'special legislation' designed to benefit one or a few landowners at the expense of the surrounding landowners *or the public*." The court concludes that "no discernible benefit for the rezone would accrue to the neighboring farmers and ranchers" and that "the benefits of the rezone inure solely to the owners of the 668 acres." What about the public in general? In most states, the bottom line in a spot zoning challenge is whether the general welfare is advanced by the rezoning. *See, e.g., Thomas v. Bd. of Supervisors of Panola County*, 45 So.3d 1173 (Miss.2010) ("Evidence was sufficient to establish . . . that there was a public need for recycling facility/junkyard, such that the rezoning of landowner's property from agricultural to industrial and the granting of a special exception to operate a junkyard was justified and did not constitute spot zoning.").

Since "the public" appears as a listed consideration in the court's third prong, why didn't the county argue that the local economy needed the jobs and that the county needed the tax revenue that SME would bring? Perhaps that would be deemed illegal as fiscal zoning. *See Hernandez, supra*. What about the county's need for electricity? Might not the harm to the few landowners in the vicinity of the plant be outweighed by the overall gain to the county? What was Cascade County's plan?

3.   The court notes that the Urquharts needed a rezoning in order to take advantage of a tax increment financing mechanism. A TIF constitutes a major subsidy to develop within a blighted redevelopment district. The property taxes collected from the new development above the existing tax collections are used to pay for infrastructure for the project, enhancing the development's profitability to the detriment of the school district and county by diverting taxes that would have been paid to those governmental entities. Established by state law, TIF incentives clearly advance the public purpose of redeveloping blighted land. *See W.R. Grace & Co.-Conn. v. Cambridge City Council*, 779 N.E.2d 141, 152 (Mass.App.2002); D. Callies and A. Gowder (eds.) *Tax Increment Financing* (2010).

4.   In a general rezoning, land within the zone can be used for a number of different uses, which often number a dozen or more. In such a case, a city council should not concern itself with the rezoning proponent's intended use

but should determine whether all of the uses that will be permitted of right will be appropriate to the area. For example, in *Cherokee County v. Martin*, 559 S.E.2d 138 (Ga.App.2002), the county zoned land for a planned unit development "on the understanding" that the owner would build assisted living facilities for the elderly. After the county rezoned the land to multi-family uses, the developer found the market for apartments was better than the market for assisted living facilities, and proceeded to build apartments. Unhappy with this turn of events, the county sought to enjoin the developer. Since both uses were multi-family uses, the court refused. The "understanding" did not bind the landowner. The ordinance in *Plains Grains* rezoned the land to heavy industrial use provided that use of the land would be limited to electrical power plant. This "conditional zoning" precludes the owner from choosing to put the property to any other use of right. In some states conditional zoning may be found to be illegal contract zoning. See discussion *infra* at Ch. 2.D.4.

5.   The commissioners received more than 1900 comments. Do you suppose most opposed the rezoning? Might those in the county who did not own land in the vicinity of the land object? Why might they favor the rezoning? In general, consider the effect of public participation. Opponents, the neighbors, often outnumber a single proponent, the petitioning landowner. They pack the meeting room attempting to sway the vote, and are often successful as the number of opponents, who are also voters, outweigh the merits of their argument. Would this be grounds for a legal challenge by the landowner? Recall *Udell v. Haas*, 235 N.E.2d 897 (N.Y.1968), in Chapter 1, *supra*, that zoning is not a Gallup poll and a rezoning of land to frustrate a proposed development project application must be supported by a comprehensive plan policy.

6.   Pushed to its adversarial limits, "the zoning game" can have high costs. As neighbors use the administrative, legislative, and judicial system to delay or prevent development proposals, developers increasingly turn to the SLAPP suit (strategic lawsuit against public participation) to deter citizen action and deplete citizen resources. Such suits typically claim that negative comments about the development proposal or the developer constitute tortious interference with business relations or are defamatory. When Berkeley, California neighbors resisted zoning permission for a group home for the disabled by speaking out at public meetings, HUD sued them, alleging violations of the Fair Housing Act. *See White v. Lee*, 227 F.3d 1214 (9th Cir.2000). HUD lost. The First Amendment concerns that these suits raise has led to the adoption in several states of statutes designed to lead to early dismissal of unworthy suits. The California anti-slapp suit statute, for example, provides that "a cause of action against a person arising from any act of that person in furtherance of the person's right of petition or free speech under the United States or California Constitution in connection with a public issue shall be subject to a special motion to strike, unless the court determines that the plaintiff has established that there is a probability that the plaintiff will prevail on the claim". Cal.Civ.Proc. § 425.16(b)(1). *See* Juergensmeyer and Roberts, *Land Use Planning and Development Regulation Law* § 5.2A (3rd ed.2012). Neighbors who are sued may "SLAPP-back" with an abuse of process

or malicious prosecution suit against the developer. *See* Frederick M. Rowe and Leo M. Romero, *Resolving Land-Use Disputes by Intimidation: SLAPP Suits in New Mexico*, 32 N.M.L.REV. 217 (2002).

Mediation can reduce the costs of zoning. While the mandatory public hearing process properly prevents purely private negotiated settlements, mediation nonetheless can serve to assist the public officials in responding to the request for development permission and create better understanding among all the interested groups. *See* Cory R. Gangle, Comment, *Is There a Middle Ground? One Approach to Resolution of Land Use Disputes in the Northwest*, 64 MONT.L.REV. 493 (2003); Shelley Ross Saxer, *Local Autonomy or Regionalism?: Sharing the Benefits and Burdens of Suburban Commercial Development*, 30 IND.L.REV. 659 (1997) (proposing that mediation be used to resolve disputes between municipalities over benefits and burdens of development).

COMMENT: UNIFORMITY

Section 2 of the SZEA provides in part that "[a]ll such regulations shall be uniform for each class or kind of buildings throughout each district, but the regulations in one district may differ from those in other districts." This is in effect a statutory equal protection command that like uses be treated the same. *Anderson House, LLC v. Mayor & City Council of Rockville*, 402 Md. 689, 939 A.2d 116, 133 (2008). Zoning that singles out one lot for "different treatment from that accorded to similar surrounding land indistinguishable from it in character, all for the economic benefit of the owner of that lot, * * * constitutes a denial of equal protection under the law guaranteed by the State and Federal Constitutions, and violates the 'uniformity' requirement of the state enabling act." *Rando v. Town of N. Attleborough*, 692 N.E.2d 544, 546 (Mass.App.1998).

But must there be identical treatment of all land within the district or is there some leeway given to accommodate these flexibility devices? If so, the use of such flexibility tools as conditional zoning, overlay zones, and development agreements, where often one landowner within a district is treated differently than others, are in trouble.

Generally, courts hold that uniformly applicable regulations that might produce different results on land within a district do not violate the uniformity requirement. The requirement of "[u]niformity is not absolute and rational regulations based on different conditions within a zone are permissible so long as similarly situated property is treated the same." *Rumson Estates, Inc. v. Mayor & Council of Borough of Fair Haven*, 828 A.2d 317, 329–30 (N.J.2003).

Conditional rezoning may run afoul of the uniformity clause. In *Decker v. Coleman*, 169 S.E.2d 487, 489 (N.C.App.1969), defendants petitioned to have their property zoned for "roadside business." The council granted the rezoning subject to the condition that the owners maintain a 50-foot buffer zone adjacent to the residential area. Defendants then began clearing the area within the buffer zone. When neighbors complained, the court held the condition, which did not apply to other land zoned "roadside business," violated the uniformity clause. *But see Collard v. Incorporated Village of Flower Hill*, 421 N.E.2d 818, 821 (N.Y.1981), reasoning that since the landowner consents to additional restrictions that will limit use of the land beyond the limitations, there is no benefit conferred which discriminates against others within the district. In *J-Marion Co. v. County of Sacramento*, 142 Cal.Rptr. 723, 726 (Cal.App.1977), defendant's predecessors in title sought an upzoning to a commercial zone and neighbors objected. To mollify them, the then owner requested the city to condition the rezoning to prohibit the sale of alcohol. The new owner sought to be relieved of the condition on the basis that it violated the uniformity clause. The court rejected the argument holding that "only use conditions unilaterally imposed by the legislative body as a condition and not consented to or acquiesced in by the owner or possessor come within the ambit of [the uniformity clause]."

In *Neighbors in Support of Appropriate Land Use v. County of Tuolumne*, 68 Cal.Rptr.3d 882 (Cal.App.2007), the Petersons wanted to operate a business hosting weddings and similar events on land they owned in an agricultural zone. Unfortunately, such commercial use was not allowed with or without a conditional use permit. Jumping the gun, they sought permission based on a proposed amendment that would allow "lawn parties, weddings, or similar outdoor activities" as conditional uses. The Board of Supervisors rejected the proposed amendments and the Petersons' application was rejected. The planning staff, however, thought it found a way to give the Petersons what they wanted. It recommended the county enter into a development agreement which would contain the power to issue a conditional use permit for hosting weddings. The Board of Supervisors agreed and approved a development agreement granting the Petersons a conditional use permit to do what the code prohibited. The agreement was subject to a condition subsequent. It "acknowledged that its purpose was to stand in for amendments to the zoning ordinance that would allow the uses in question [and] that it would terminate when 'commercial events such as lawn parties, weddings or similar activities are made conditional uses in the AE-37 zone.' " Id., 68 Cal.Rptr.3d at 885.

The court held the county violated the uniformity requirement. Generally, it said, limitations "*imposed upon land* by consensual agreement [do not violate the uniformity clause, but] *limitations lifted from land* by agreement between the owner and [a city are another matter]." In the former case, the owner or a successor in interest cannot complain of restrictions he voluntarily agreed but in the latter case the "complaining parties-the neighbors-never agreed to a use violative of the use limitations in the zone." Id., 68 Cal.Rptr.3d at 893. Conditional zoning is discussed in more detail *infra*, Section C 4 this chapter.

Overlay zoning may raise uniformity objections. The City of Phoenix created a bizarrely, but perhaps accurately, named "inebriate district" as an overlay in a large commercially zoned area where certain otherwise allowable uses (establishments selling alcohol, pawn shops, blood banks, second hand stores, and missions) were required to get special permits. The city denied a permit to operate a pawn shop in the "inebriate" zone and the owner challenged the law on uniformity grounds. The court held that the city could not create an overlay in which use permits were required for certain uses that were not required for the same uses in the same underlying zone elsewhere within the city. *Jachimek v. Superior Court*, 819 P.2d 487 (Ariz.1991). *But see A-S-P Associates v. City of Raleigh*, 258 S.E.2d 444 (N.C.1979), where the court found an historic overlay that subjected some commercially zoned property to restrictions not applied to other commercially zoned land did not violate the uniformity clause. The court took the position that the uniformity clause did not prohibit overlay districts even though they imposed additional regulations on some property. After all, said the court, the overlay did "not destroy the uniformity of the regulations applicable to the underlying use-district." 258 S.E.2d at 458–59.

2.   ZONING: LEGISLATIVE OR QUASI-JUDICIAL

Most state courts treat, or purport to treat, all zoning amendments, whether general or site-specific, as legislative acts and accord them a presumption of validity. *Board of Sup'rs of Rockingham County v. Stickley*, 556 S.E.2d 748 (Va.2002); *Cabana v. Kenai Peninsula Borough*, 21 P.3d 833 (Alaska 2001). The same is true of a denial of a request to rezone. *Mehlhorn v. Pima County*, 194 Ariz. 140, 978 P.2d 117 (Ariz.App.1998); *Petersen v. Riverton City*, 243 P.3d 1261 (Utah 2010). The fairly debatable test from *Euclid* is most often used and overcoming the presumption of validity is a heavy burden to carry.

Highly deferential review tends to confer virtually unrestrained power on local legislative bodies. Some courts, sensing this and willing to set aside deference to local land use authorities, have found ways to scrutinize zoning decisions without necessarily saying so. For example, it has been observed that the presumption of validity has an evanescent quality in North Carolina and vanishes without comment when the courts are suspicious of wrongdoing. Michael B. Brough, *Flexibility without Arbitrariness in the Zoning System: Observations on North Carolina Special Exception and Zoning Amendment Cases*, 53 N.C.L.REV. 925, 945 (1975). As we have seen, in spot zoning cases some courts review zoning decisions more closely than is usual, particularly those involving relatively small parcels. A few apply a "change or mistake" rule, which eliminates the deference and reverses the burden of proof. *Albuquerque Commons Partnership v. City Council of City of Albuquerque*, 184 P.3d 411 (N.M.2008).

In contrast to this deference, think back to our discussion of conditional uses and the *Loyola College* case. There we pointed out that zoning boards of adjustment charged with ruling on variances and conditional use permit applications act in a quasi-judicial capacity. They adjudicate the rights of applicants by applying legislative policy. For example if the city council has listed colleges as a conditional use in a residential zone if certain conditions are met, the board must examine the proposed site plan to decide whether it is a proper case to allow such a use.

No presumption of validity attached to such quasi-judicial decisions. They are subject to close judicial scrutiny.

Over the last several decades, some courts have come to openly acknowledge that many nominally legislative actions are in fact quasi-judicial. This has major consequences in how the zoning game is conducted.

FASANO V. BOARD OF COUNTY COMMISSIONERS OF WASHINGTON COUNTY

Supreme Court of Oregon, 1973.
264 Or. 574, 507 P.2d 23.

HOWELL, JUSTICE.

The plaintiffs, homeowners in Washington County, unsuccessfully opposed a zone change before the Board of County Commissioners of Washington County. Plaintiffs applied for and received a writ of review of the action of the commissioners allowing the change. The trial court found in favor of plaintiffs, disallowed the zone change, and reversed the commissioners' order. The Court of Appeals affirmed, and this court granted review.

The defendants are the Board of County Commissioners and A.G.S. Development Company. A.G.S., the owner of 32 acres which had been zoned R-7 (Single Family Residential), applied for a zone change to P-R (Planned Residential), which allows for the construction of a mobile home park. The change failed to receive a majority vote of the Planning Commission. The Board of County Commissioners approved the change and found, among other matters, that the change allows for "increased densities and different types of housing to meet the needs of urbanization over that allowed by the existing zoning."

The trial court, relying on its interpretation of Roseta v. County of Washington, reversed the order of the commissioners because the commissioners had not shown any change in the character of the neighborhood which would justify the rezoning. The Court of Appeals affirmed for the same reason, but added the additional ground that the defendants failed to show that the change was consistent with the comprehensive plan for Washington County.

According to the briefs, the comprehensive plan of development for Washington County was adopted in 1959 and included classifications in the county for residential, neighborhood commercial, retail commercial, general commercial, industrial park and light industry, general and heavy industry, and agricultural areas.

The land in question, which was designated "residential" by the comprehensive plan, was zoned R-7, Single Family Residential.

Subsequent to the time the comprehensive plan was adopted, Washington County established a Planned Residential (P-R) zoning classification in 1963. The P-R classification was adopted by ordinance and provided that a planned residential unit development could be established and should include open space for utilities, access, and recreation; should not be less than 10 acres in size; and should be located in or adjacent to a residential zone. The P-R zone adopted by the 1963 ordinance is of the type known as a "floating zone," so-called because the ordinance creates a zone classification authorized for future use but not placed on the zoning map until its use at a particular location is approved by the governing body. The R-7 classification for the 32 acres continued until April 1970 when the classification was changed to P-R to permit the defendant A.G.S. to construct the mobile home park on the 32 acres involved.

The defendants argue that (1) the action of the county commissioners approving the change is presumptively valid, requiring plaintiffs to show that the commissioners acted arbitrarily in approving the zone change; (2) it was not necessary to show a change of conditions in the area before a zone change could be accomplished; and (3) the change from R-7 to P-R was in accordance with the Washington county comprehensive plan.

We granted review in this case to consider the questions—by what standards does a county commission exercise its authority in zoning matters; who has the burden of meeting those standards when a request for change of zone is made; and what is the scope of court review of such actions?

Any meaningful decision as to the proper scope of judicial review of a zoning decision must start with a characterization of the nature of that decision. The majority of jurisdictions state that a zoning ordinance is a legislative act and is thereby entitled to presumptive validity. This court made such a characterization of zoning decisions in *Smith v. County of Washington*, 241 Or. 380, 406 P.2d 545 (1965):

> Inasmuch as ORS 215.110 specifically grants to the governing board of the county the power to amend zoning ordinances, a challenged amendment is a legislative act and is clothed with a presumption in its favor. *Jehovah's Witnesses v. Mullen et al.*, 214 Or. 281, 292, 330 P.2d 5, 74 A.L.R.2d 347 (1958), appeal dismissed and *cert. denied*, 359 U.S. 436 (1959). 241 Or. at 383, 406 P.2d at 547.

However, in *Smith* an exception to the presumption was found and the zoning held invalid. Furthermore, the case cited by the *Smith* court, *Jehovah's Witnesses v. Mullen et al., supra*, at least at one point viewed the contested zoning in that case as an administrative as opposed to legislative act.

At this juncture we feel we would be ignoring reality to rigidly view all zoning decisions by local governing bodies as legislative acts to be accorded a full presumption of validity and shielded from less than constitutional scrutiny by the theory of separation of powers. Local and small decision groups are simply not the equivalent in all respects of state and national legislatures. There is a growing judicial recognition of this fact of life:

> It is not a part of the legislative function to grant permits, make special exceptions, or decide particular cases. Such activities are not legislative but administrative, quasi-judicial, or judicial in character. To place them in the hands of legislative bodies, whose acts as such are not judicially reviewable, is to open the door completely to arbitrary government. *Ward v. Village of Skokie*, 26 Ill.2d 415, 186 N.E.2d 529, 533 (1962) (Klingbiel, J., specially concurring).

The Supreme Court of Washington, in reviewing a rezoning decision, recently stated:

> Whatever descriptive characterization may be otherwise attached to the role or function of the planning commission in zoning procedures, e.g., advisory, recommendatory, investigatory, administrative or legislative, it is manifest * * * that it is a public agency, * * * a principle [sic] and statutory duty of which is to conduct public hearings in specified planning and zoning matters, enter findings of fact—often on the basis of disputed facts—and make recommendations with reasons assigned thereto. Certainly, in its role as a hearing and fact-finding tribunal, the planning commission's function more nearly than not partakes of the nature of an administrative, quasi-judicial proceeding, * * *. *Chrobuck v. Snohomish County*, 78 Wash.2d 858, 480 P.2d 489, 495–496 (1971).

Ordinances laying down general policies without regard to a specific piece of property are usually an exercise of legislative authority, are subject to limited review, and may only be attacked upon constitutional grounds for an arbitrary abuse of authority. On the other hand, a determination whether the permissible use of a specific piece of property should be changed is usually an exercise of judicial authority and its propriety is subject to an altogether different test. An illustration of an exercise of legislative authority is the passage of the ordinance by the Washington County Commission in 1963 which provided for the formation of a planned residential classification to be located in or adjacent to any residential zone. An exercise of judicial authority is the county commissioners' determination in this particular matter to change the classification of A.G.S. Development Company's specific piece of property. The distinction is stated, as follows, in Comment, *Zoning Amendments—The Product of Judicial or Quasi-Judicial Action*, 33 OHIO ST.L.J. 130 (1972):

* * * Basically, this test involves the determination of whether action produces a general rule or policy which is applicable to an open class of individuals, interest, or situations, or whether it entails the application of a general rule or policy to specific individuals, interests, or situations. If the former determination is satisfied, there is legislative action; if the latter determination is satisfied, the action is judicial. 33 OHIO ST.L.J. at 137.

We reject the proposition that judicial review of the county commissioners' determination to change the zoning of the particular property in question is limited to a determination whether the change was arbitrary and capricious.

In order to establish a standard of review, it is necessary to delineate certain basic principles relating to land use regulation.

The basic instrument for county or municipal land use planning is the "comprehensive plan." Haar, *In Accordance with a Comprehensive Plan*, 68 HARV.L.REV. 1154 (1955). The plan has been described as a general plan to control and direct the use and development of property in a municipality.

In Oregon the county planning commission is required by ORS 215.050 to adopt a comprehensive plan for the use of some or all of the land in the county. Under ORS 215.110(1), after the comprehensive plan has been adopted, the planning commission recommends to the governing body of the county the ordinances necessary to "carry out" the comprehensive plan. The purpose of the zoning ordinances, both under our statute and the general law of land use regulation, is to "carry out" or implement the comprehensive plan. 1 Anderson, *American Law of Zoning*, § 1.12 (1968). Although we are aware of the analytical distinction between zoning and planning, it is clear that under our statutes the plan adopted by the planning commission and the zoning ordinances enacted by the county governing body are closely related; both are intended to be parts of a single integrated procedure for land use control. The plan embodies policy determinations and guiding principles; the zoning ordinances provide the detailed means of giving effect to those principles.

ORS 215.050 states county planning commissions "shall adopt and may from time to time revise a comprehensive plan." In a hearing of the Senate Committee on Local Government, the proponents of ORS 215.050 described its purpose as follows:

* * * The intent here is to require a basic document, geared into population, land use, and economic forecasts, which should be the basis of any zoning or other regulations to be adopted by the county. * * *

In addition, ORS 215.055 provides:

> 215.055 Standards for plan. (1) The plan and all legislation and regulations authorized by ORS 215.010 to 215.233 shall be designed to promote the public health, safety and general welfare and shall be based on the following considerations, among others: The various characteristics of the various areas in the county, the suitability of the areas for particular land uses and improvements, the land uses and improvements in the areas, trends in land improvement, density of development, property values, the needs of economic enterprises in the future development of the areas, needed access to particular sites in the areas, natural resources of the county and prospective needs for development thereof, and the public need for healthful, safe, aesthetic surroundings and conditions.

We believe that the state legislature has conditioned the county's power to zone upon the prerequisite that the zoning attempt to further the general welfare of the community through consciousness, in a prospective sense, of the factors mentioned above. In other words, except as noted later in this opinion, it must be proved that the change is in conformance with the comprehensive plan.

In proving that the change is in conformance with the comprehensive plan in this case, the proof, at a minimum, should show (1) there is a public need for a change of the kind in question, and (2) that need will be best served by changing the classification of the particular piece of property in question as compared with other available property.

* * *

Because the action of the commission in this instance is an exercise of judicial authority, the burden of proof should be placed, as is usual in judicial proceedings, upon the one seeking change. The more drastic the change, the greater will be the burden of showing that it is in conformance with the comprehensive plan as implemented by the ordinance, that there is a public need for the kind of change in question, and that the need is best met by the proposal under consideration. As the degree of change increases, the burden of showing that the potential impact upon the area in question was carefully considered and weighed will also increase. If other areas have previously been designated for the particular type of development, it must be shown why it is necessary to introduce it into an area not previously contemplated and why the property owners there should bear the burden of the departure.[3]

---

[3] For example, if an area is designated by the plan as generally appropriate for residential development, the plan may also indicate that some high-density residential development within the area is to be anticipated, without specifying the exact location at which that development is to take place. The comprehensive plan might provide that its goal for residential development is to

Although we have said that zoning changes may be justified without a showing of a mistake in the original plan or ordinance, or of changes in the physical characteristics of an affected area, any of these factors which are present in a particular case would, of course, be relevant. Their importance would depend upon the nature of the precise change under consideration.

By treating the exercise of authority by the commission in this case as the exercise of judicial rather than of legislative authority and thus enlarging the scope of review on appeal, and by placing the burden of the above level of proof upon the one seeking change, we may lay the court open to criticism by legal scholars who think it desirable that planning authorities be vested with the ability to adjust more freely to changed conditions. However, having weighed the dangers of making desirable change more difficult against the dangers of the almost irresistible pressures that can be asserted by private economic interests on local government, we believe that the latter dangers are more to be feared.

What we have said above is necessarily general, as the approach we adopt contains no absolute standards or mechanical tests. We believe, however, that it is adequate to provide meaningful guidance for local governments making zoning decisions and for trial courts called upon to review them. With future cases in mind, it is appropriate to add some brief remarks on questions of procedure. Parties at the hearing before the county governing body are entitled to an opportunity to be heard, to an opportunity to present and rebut evidence, to a tribunal which is impartial in the matter—i.e., having had no pre-hearing or ex parte contacts concerning the question at issue—and to a record made and adequate findings executed.

When we apply the standards we have adopted to the present case, we find that the burden was not sustained before the commission. The record

---

assure that residential areas are healthful, pleasant and safe places in which to live. The plan might also list the following policies which, among others, are to be pursued in achieving that goal:

1. High-density residential areas should be located close to the urban core area.

2. Residential neighborhoods should be protected from any land use activity involving an excessive level of noise, pollution or traffic volume.

3. High trip-generating multiple family units should have ready access to arterial or collector streets.

4. A variety of living areas and housing types should be provided appropriate to the needs of the special and general groups they are to serve.

5. Residential development at urban densities should be within planned sewer and water service areas and where other utilities can be adequately provided.

Under such a hypothetical plan, property originally zoned for single family dwellings might later be rezoned for duplexes, for garden apartments, or for high-rise apartment buildings. Each of these changes could be shown to be consistent with the plan. Although in addition we would require a showing that the county governing body found a bona fide need for a zone change in order to accommodate new high-density development which at least balanced the disruption shown by the challengers, that requirement would be met in most instances by a record which disclosed that the governing body had considered the facts relevant to this question and exercised its judgment in good faith. However, these changes, while all could be shown to be consistent with the plan, could be expected to have differing impacts on the surrounding area, depending on the nature of that area. As the potential impact on the area in question increases, so will the necessity to show a justification.

now before us is insufficient to ascertain whether there was a justifiable basis for the decision. The only evidence in the record, that of the staff report of the Washington County Planning Department, is too conclusory and superficial to support the zoning change. It merely states:

> The staff finds that the requested use does conform to the residential designation of the Plan of Development. It further finds that the proposed use reflects the urbanization of the County and the necessity to provide increased densities and different types of housing to meet the needs of urbanization over that allowed by the existing zoning. * * *

Such generalizations and conclusions, without any statement of the facts on which they are based, are insufficient to justify a change of use. Moreover, no portions of the comprehensive plan of Washington County are before us, and we feel it would be improper for us to take judicial notice of the plan without at least some reference to its specifics by counsel.

As there has not been an adequate showing that the change was in accord with the plan, or that the factors listed in ORS 215.055 were given proper consideration, the judgment is affirmed.

BOARD OF COUNTY COMMISSIONERS OF BREVARD COUNTY v. SNYDER

Supreme Court of Florida, 1993.
627 So.2d 469.

GRIMES, JUSTICE.

Jack and Gail Snyder owned a one-half acre parcel of property on Merritt Island in the unincorporated area of Brevard County. The property is zoned GU (general use) which allows construction of a single-family residence. The Snyders filed an application to rezone their property to the RU-2-15 zoning classification which allows the construction of fifteen units per acre. The area is designated for residential use under the 1988 Brevard County Comprehensive Plan Future Land Use Map. Twenty-nine zoning classifications are considered potentially consistent with this land use designation, including both the GU and the RU-2-15 classifications.

After the application for rezoning was filed, the Brevard County Planning and Zoning staff reviewed the application and completed the county's standard "rezoning review worksheet." The worksheet indicated that the proposed multifamily use of the Snyders' property was consistent with all aspects of the comprehensive plan except for the fact that it was located in the one-hundred-year flood plain in which a maximum of only two units per acre was permitted. For this reason, the staff recommended that the request be denied.

At the planning and zoning board meeting, the county planning and zoning director indicated that when the property was developed the land elevation would be raised to the point where the one-hundred-year-flood plain restriction would no longer be applicable. Thus, the director stated that the staff no longer opposed the application. The planning and zoning board voted to approve the Snyders' rezoning request.

When the matter came before the board of county commissioners, Snyder stated that he intended to build only five or six units on the property. However, a number of citizens spoke in opposition to the rezoning request. Their primary concern was the increase in traffic which would be caused by the development. Ultimately, the commission voted to deny the rezoning request without stating a reason for the denial.

The Snyders filed a petition for certiorari in the circuit court. Three circuit judges, sitting en banc, reviewed the petition and denied it by a two-to-one decision. The Snyders then filed a petition for certiorari in the Fifth District Court of Appeal.

The district court of appeal acknowledged that zoning decisions have traditionally been considered legislative in nature. Therefore, courts were required to uphold them if they could be justified as being "fairly debatable." Drawing heavily on *Fasano v. Board of County Commissioners*, 264 Or. 574, 507 P.2d 23 (1973), however, the court concluded that, unlike initial zoning enactments and comprehensive rezonings or rezonings affecting a large portion of the public, a rezoning action which entails the application of a general rule or policy to specific individuals, interests, or activities is quasi-judicial in nature. Under the latter circumstances, the court reasoned that a stricter standard of judicial review of the rezoning decision was required. The court went on to hold:

> Since a property owner's right to own and use his property is constitutionally protected, review of any governmental action denying or abridging that right is subject to close judicial scrutiny. Effective judicial review, constitutional due process and other essential requirements of law, all necessitate that the governmental agency (by whatever name it may be characterized) applying legislated land use restrictions to particular parcels of privately owned lands, must state reasons for action that denies the owner the use of his land and must make findings of fact and a record of its proceedings, sufficient for judicial review of: the legal sufficiency of the evidence to support the findings of fact made, the legal sufficiency of the findings of fact supporting the reasons given and the legal adequacy, under applicable law (i.e., under general comprehensive zoning ordinances, applicable state and case law and state and federal constitutional provisions) of the reasons given for the result of the action taken.

> The initial burden is upon the landowner to demonstrate that his petition or application for use of privately owned lands, (rezoning, special exception, conditional use permit, variance, site plan

approval, etc.) complies with the reasonable procedural requirements of the ordinance and that the use sought is consistent with the applicable comprehensive zoning plan. Upon such a showing the landowner is presumptively entitled to use his property in the manner he seeks unless the opposing governmental agency asserts and proves by clear and convincing evidence that a specifically stated public necessity requires a specified, more restrictive, use. After such a showing the burden shifts to the landowner to assert and prove that such specified more restrictive land use constitutes a taking of his property for public use for which he is entitled to compensation under the taking provisions of the state or federal constitutions.

Snyder v. Board of County Commissioners, 595 So.2d at 81 (footnotes omitted).

Applying these principles to the facts of the case, the court found (1) that the Snyders' petition for rezoning was consistent with the comprehensive plan; (2) that there was no assertion or evidence that a more restrictive zoning classification was necessary to protect the health, safety, morals, or welfare of the general public; and (3) that the denial of the requested zoning classification without reasons supported by facts was, as a matter of law, arbitrary and unreasonable. The court granted the petition for certiorari.

Before this Court, the county contends that the standard of review for the county's denial of the Snyders' rezoning application is whether or not the decision was fairly debatable. The county further argues that the opinion below eliminates a local government's ability to operate in a legislative context and impairs its ability to respond to public comment. The county refers to *Jennings v. Dade County*, 589 So.2d 1337 (Fla.3d DCA 1991), review denied, 598 So.2d 75 (Fla.1992), for the proposition that if its rezoning decision is quasi-judicial, the commissioners will be prohibited from obtaining community input by way of ex parte communications from its citizens. In addition, the county suggests that the requirement to make findings in support of its rezoning decision will place an insurmountable burden on the zoning authorities. The county also asserts that the salutary purpose of the comprehensive plan to provide controlled growth will be thwarted by the court's ruling that the maximum use permitted by the plan must be approved once the rezoning application is determined to be consistent with it.

The Snyders respond that the decision below should be upheld in all of its major premises. They argue that the rationale for the early decisions that rezonings are legislative in nature has been changed by the enactment of the Growth Management Act. Thus, in order to ensure that local governments follow the principles enunciated in their comprehensive plans, it is necessary for the courts to exercise stricter scrutiny than would be provided under the fairly debatable rule. The Snyders contend that their rezoning application was consistent with the comprehensive plan. Because there are no findings of fact or reasons given for the denial by the board of county commissioners, there is no basis upon which the denial could be upheld. Various amici curiae have also submitted briefs in support of their several positions.

Historically, local governments have exercised the zoning power pursuant to a broad delegation of state legislative power subject only to constitutional limitations. Both federal and state courts adopted a highly deferential standard of judicial review early in the history of local zoning. In *Village of Euclid v. Ambler Realty Co.*, 272 U.S. 365 (1926), the United States Supreme Court held that "[i]f the validity of the legislative classification for zoning purposes be fairly debatable, the legislative judgment must be allowed to control." 272 U.S. at 388. This Court expressly adopted the fairly debatable principle in *City of Miami Beach v. Ocean & Inland Co..*, 147 Fla. 480, 3 So.2d 364 (1941).

Inhibited only by the loose judicial scrutiny afforded by the fairly debatable rule, local zoning systems developed in a markedly inconsistent manner. Many land use experts and practitioners have been critical of the local zoning system. Richard Babcock deplored the effect of "neighborhoodism" and rank political influence on the local decision-making process. Richard F. Babcock, *The Zoning Game* (1966). Mandelker and Tarlock recently stated that "zoning decisions are too often ad hoc, sloppy and self-serving decisions with well-defined adverse consequences without off-setting benefits." Daniel R. Mandelker and A. Dan Tarlock, *Shifting the Presumption of Constitutionality in Land-Use Law*, 24 URBAN LAWYER 1, 2 (1992).

Professor Charles Haar, a leading proponent of zoning reform, was an early advocate of requiring that local land use regulation be consistent with a legally binding comprehensive plan which would serve long range goals, counteract local pressures for preferential treatment, and provide courts with a meaningful standard of review. Charles M. Harr, "*In Accordance With A Comprehensive Plan*," 68 HARV.L.REV. 1154 (1955). In 1975, the American Law Institute adopted the Model Land Development Code, which provided for procedural and planning reforms at the local level and increased state participation in land use decision-making for developments of regional impact and areas of critical state concern.

Reacting to the increasing calls for reform, numerous states have adopted legislation to change the local land use decision-making process. As one of the leaders of this national reform, Florida adopted the Local Government Comprehensive Planning Act of 1975. Ch. 75–257, Laws of Fla. This law was substantially strengthened in 1985 by the Growth Management Act. Ch. 85–55, Laws of Fla.

Pursuant to the Growth Management Act, each county and municipality is required to prepare a comprehensive plan for approval by the Department of Community Affairs. The adopted local plan must include "principles, guidelines, and standards for the orderly and balanced future economic, social, physical, environmental, and fiscal development" of the local government's jurisdictional area. Section 163.3177(1), Fla.Stat. (1991). At the minimum, the local plan must include elements covering future land use; capital improvements generally; sanitary sewer, solid waste, drainage, potable water, and natural ground water aquifer protection specifically; conservation; recreation and open space; housing; traffic circulation; intergovernmental coordination; coastal management (for local government in the coastal zone); and mass transit (for local jurisdictions with 50,000 or more people). Id., Section 163.3177(6).

Of special relevance to local rezoning actions, the future land use plan element of the local plan must contain a future land use map and goals accompanied by measurable objectives to guide future land use decisions. This plan element must designate the "proposed future general distribution, location, and extent of the uses of land" for various purposes. Id., Section 163.3177(6)(a). It must include standards to be utilized in the control and distribution of densities and intensities of development. In addition, the future land use plan must be based on adequate data and analysis concerning the local jurisdiction, including the projected population, the amount of land needed to accommodate the estimated population, the availability of public services and facilities, and the character of undeveloped land. *Id.*, Section 163.3177(6)(a).

The local plan must be implemented through the adoption of land development regulations that are consistent with the plan. *Id.* Section 163.3202. In addition, all development, both public and private, and all development orders approved by local governments must be consistent with the adopted local plan. *Id.*, Section 163.3194(1)(a). Section 163.3194(3), Florida Statutes (1991), explains consistency as follows:

(a) A development order or land development regulation shall be consistent with the comprehensive plan if the land uses, densities or intensities, and other aspects of development permitted by such order or regulation are compatible with and further the objectives, policies, land uses, and densities or intensities in the comprehensive plan and if it meets all other criteria enumerated by the local government.

Section 163.3164, Florida Statutes (1991), reads in pertinent part:

(6) "Development order" means any order granting, denying, or granting with conditions an application for a development permit.

(7) "Development permit" includes any building permit, zoning permit, subdivision approval, rezoning, certification, special

exception, variance, or any other official action of local government having the effect of permitting the development of land.

Because an order granting or denying rezoning constitutes a development order and development orders must be consistent with the comprehensive plan, it is clear that orders on rezoning applications must be consistent with the comprehensive plan.

The first issue we must decide is whether the Board's action on Snyder's rezoning application was legislative or quasi-judicial. A board's legislative action is subject to attack in circuit court. However, in deference to the policy-making function of a board when acting in a legislative capacity, its actions will be sustained as long as they are fairly debatable. On the other hand, the rulings of a board acting in its quasi-judicial capacity are subject to review by certiorari and will be upheld only if they are supported by substantial competent evidence.

Enactments of original zoning ordinances have always been considered legislative. In *Schauer v. City of Miami Beach*, this Court held that the passage of an amending zoning ordinance was the exercise of a legislative function. 112 So.2d at 839. However, the amendment in that case was comprehensive in nature in that it effected a change in the zoning of a large area so as to permit it to be used as locations for multiple family buildings and hotels.

It is the character of the hearing that determines whether or not board action is legislative or quasi-judicial. Generally speaking, legislative action results in the formulation of a general rule of policy, whereas judicial action results in the application of a general rule of policy. Carl J. Peckingpaugh, Jr., Comment, *Burden of Proof in Land Use Regulations: A Unified Approach and Application to Florida*, 8 FLA.ST.U.L.REV. 499, 504 (1980). In *West Flagler Amusement Co. v. State Racing Commission*, 122 Fla. 222, 225, 165 So. 64, 65 (1935), we explained:

> A judicial or quasi-judicial act determines the rules of law applicable, and the rights affected by them, in relation to past transactions. On the other hand, a quasi-legislative or administrative order prescribes what the rule or requirement of administratively determined duty shall be with respect to transactions to be executed in the future, in order that same shall be considered lawful. But even so, quasi-legislative and quasi-executive orders, after they have already been entered, may have a quasi-judicial attribute if capable of being arrived at and provided by law to be declared by the administrative agency only after express statutory notice, hearing and consideration of evidence to be adduced as a basis for the making thereof.

Applying this criterion, it is evident that comprehensive rezonings affecting a large portion of the public are legislative in nature. However, we agree with the court below when it said:

> [R]ezoning actions which have an impact on a limited number of persons or property owners, on identifiable parties and interests, where the decision is contingent on a fact or facts arrived at from distinct alternatives presented at a hearing, and where the decision can be functionally viewed as policy application, rather than policy setting, are in the nature of . . . quasi-judicial action. . . .

when they are quasi-judicial

Application not Formation

Snyder, 595 So.2d at 78. Therefore, the board's action on Snyder's application was in the nature of a quasi-judicial proceeding and properly reviewable by petition for certiorari.

We also agree with the court below that the review is subject to strict scrutiny. In practical effect, the review by strict scrutiny in zoning cases appears to be the same as that given in the review of other quasi-judicial decisions. *See Lee County v. Sunbelt Equities, II, Ltd. Partnership*, 619 So.2d 996 (Fla.2d DCA 1993) (The term "strict scrutiny" arises from the necessity of strict compliance with comprehensive plan.). This term as used in the review of land use decisions must be distinguished from the type of strict scrutiny review afforded in some constitutional cases.

* * *

At this point, we depart from the rationale of the court below. In the first place, the opinion overlooks the premise that the comprehensive plan is intended to provide for the future use of land, which contemplates a gradual and ordered growth. *See City of Jacksonville Beach*, 461 So.2d at 163, in which the following statement from *Marracci v. City of Scappoose*, 552 P.2d 552, 553 (Or.Ct.App.1976), was approved:

> [A] comprehensive plan only establishes a long-range maximum limit on the possible intensity of land use; a plan does not simultaneously establish an immediate minimum limit on the possible intensity of land use. The present use of land may, by zoning ordinance, continue to be more limited than the future use contemplated by the comprehensive plan.

Even where a denial of a zoning application would be inconsistent with the plan, the local government should have the discretion to decide that the maximum development density should not be allowed provided the governmental body approves some development that is consistent with the plan and the government's decision is supported by substantial, competent evidence.

Further, we cannot accept the proposition that once the landowner demonstrates that the proposed use is consistent with the comprehensive plan, he is presumptively entitled to this use unless the opposing governmental agency proves by clear and convincing evidence that specifically stated public necessity requires a more restricted use. We do not believe that a property owner is necessarily entitled to relief by proving consistency when the board action is also consistent with the plan. As noted in *Lee County v. Sunbelt Equities II, Limited Partnership*:

> [A]bsent the assertion of some enforceable property right, an application for rezoning appeals at least in part to local officials' discretion to accept or reject the applicant's argument that change is desirable. The right of judicial review does not ipso facto ease the burden on a party seeking to overturn a decision made by a local government, and certainly does not confer any property-based right upon the owner where none previously existed.

* * *

Moreover, when it is the zoning classification that is challenged, the comprehensive plan is relevant only when the suggested use is inconsistent with that plan. Where any of several zoning classifications is consistent with the plan, the applicant seeking a change from one to the other is not entitled to judicial relief absent proof the status quo is no longer reasonable. It is not enough simply to be "consistent"; the proposed change cannot be inconsistent, and will be subject to the "strict scrutiny" of *Machado* to insure this does not happen.

This raises a question of whether the Growth Management Act provides any comfort to the landowner when the denial of the rezoning request is consistent with the comprehensive plan. It could be argued that the only recourse is to pursue the traditional remedy of attempting to prove that the denial of the application was arbitrary, discriminatory, or unreasonable. Yet, the fact that a proposed use is consistent with the plan means that the planners contemplated that that use would be acceptable at some point in the future. We do not believe the Growth Management Act was intended to preclude development but only to insure that it proceed in an orderly manner.

Upon consideration, we hold that a landowner seeking to rezone property has the burden of proving that the proposal is consistent with the comprehensive plan and complies with all procedural requirements of the zoning ordinance. At this point, the burden shifts to the governmental board to demonstrate that maintaining the existing zoning classification with respect to the property accomplishes a legitimate public purpose. In effect, the landowners' traditional remedies will be subsumed within this rule, and the board will now have the burden of showing that the refusal to rezone the property is not arbitrary, discriminatory, or unreasonable. If the board carries its burden, the application should be denied.

While they may be useful, the board will not be required to make findings of fact. However, in order to sustain the board's action, upon review by certiorari in the circuit court it must be shown that there was competent substantial evidence presented to the board to support its ruling.

* * *

Based on the foregoing, we quash the decision below and disapprove *City of Jacksonville Beach v. Grubbs* and *Palm Beach County v. Tinnerman*, to the extent they are inconsistent with this opinion. However, in the posture of this case, we are reluctant to preclude the Snyders from any avenue of relief. Because of the possibility that conditions have changed during the extended lapse of time since their original application was filed, we believe that justice would be best served by permitting them to file a new application for rezoning of the property. The application will be without prejudice of the result reached by this decision and will allow the process to begin anew according to the procedure outlined in our opinion.

It is so ordered.

NOTES

1. The treatment of site specific rezonings in *Fasano* and *Snyder* as quasi-judicial has met mixed reactions. *See, e.g., Cabana v. Kenai Peninsula Borough*, 21 P.3d 833 (Alaska 2001) (rejecting the approach). The California court in *Arnel Development Co. v. City of Costa Mesa*, 620 P.2d 565 (Cal.1980), rejected the quasi-judicial view of *Fasano*, noting that the classification of rezonings as legislative "enjoys the obvious advantage of economy." 620 P.2d at 572. Whether a rezoning is quasi-judicial depends on why the question is asked. *See Margolis v. District Court*, 638 P.2d 297 (Colo.1981) (rezoning is legislative for purpose of availability of the referendum, but quasi-judicial for purpose of standard of judicial review). *See* Juergensmeyer and Roberts, *Land Use Planning and Development Regulation Law* § 5.9 (2012).

Quasi-judicial decisions, while subjected to greater scrutiny than legislative decisions, are not reviewed de novo. In most jurisdictions, review is regulated by a state administrative procedure act that calls for courts to defer to findings of administrative bodies and uphold decisions supported by substantial evidence. Thus, courts may speak of according a presumption of validity to administrative decisions. *See, e.g., Whitted v. Canyon County Board of Commissioners*, 44 P.3d 1173, 1176 (Idaho 2002). This presumption, however, is easier to overcome than the one that attaches to legislative decisions.

2. *Snyder* categorizes zoning actions as legislative, quasi-legislative, quasi-judicial and administrative. Can you tell from the opinion what these mean? In the zoning context quasi-legislative most often refers to non-elected planning commissions and, on occasion, to boards of adjustment, when a court

is exploring whether an action taken more closely resembles legislation or adjudication. If the court decides the decision involved a weighing of interests and the adoption of a general policy, the action by the nominally administrative body will be labeled quasi-legislative and conferred with the presumption of validity. If found to be adjudicatory, the action will be labeled quasi-judicial and the court will scrutinize the decision. On occasion, a rezoning decision by the elected body of the jurisdiction will be labeled quasi-legislative without explanation as to why the action is simply not declared legislative. *Plains Grains* in the prior section on spot zoning is such a case. The court calls the rezoning quasi-legislative but it accords it a presumption of validity. Courts often use "legislative" and "quasi-legislative" in the same case, indeed the same paragraph, to mean the same thing. *See 431 Fifth Ave. Corp. v. City of New York*, 55 N.Y.S.2d 203, 212 (NY.Sup.Ct.1945) (delegation of zoning power to planning commission was "quasi-legislative or wholly legislative").

3.   Should the functional analysis employed by the Florida Supreme Court in *Snyder* also apply also to comprehensive plans when amended to apply to a specific parcel?

4.   In contrast to *Fasano*, the Florida court in *Snyder* left the procedures to be followed vague. It did not require findings, but only said there must be substantial evidence to support the ruling. *See* Thomas G. Pelham, *Quasi-Judicial Rezonings: A Commentary on the Snyder Decision and the Consistency Requirement*, 9 J. LAND USE & ENVTL.L. 16 (1994).

5.   Federalist Paper No. 10 is the philosophical basis for decisions like *Fasano* and *Snyder*. As Professor Carol Rose has said:

> [James Madison's] celebrated *The Federalist* No. 10 merits study here, for it suggests why a local elected government should not always be seen as a legislature. * * * Madison's essay begins with the argument that the chief obstacle to fairness in a legislative body is "faction": the tendency of one interest group to impose its will at the expense of others. The antidote to faction, Madison says, lies in a constituency of sufficient size and variety. *The Federalist* No. 10 argued that the great advantage of the "extended republic" was that it would contain such a variety of interests that no one faction could tyrannize the others. Where the constituency is large, action is possible only through persuasion and coalitions of interest groups. Through a pattern of shifting alliances and vote trading, every interest can obtain at least partial satisfaction in the legislature of the "extended republic." * * * Because of these factors, then, the courts can safely trust the larger legislature to make fair and careful decisions under most circumstances, and can give broad leeway to those decisions. But this justification of large legislatures' decisions contains an implicit criticism of small-scale government.

Carol M. Rose, *Planning and Dealing: Piecemeal Land Controls as Problem of Local Legitimacy*, 71 CAL.L.REV. 837, 854–56 (1983) (citations omitted).

6. Due process demands a hearing when quasi-judicial decisions are to be made. But what about decisions by the zoning administrator or other officials within the planning department? As one court explains:

> Administrative decisions are routine, nondiscretionary zoning ordinance implementation matters carried out by the staff, including issuance of permits for permitted uses. In general, the zoning administrator is a purely administrative or ministerial agent following the literal provisions of the ordinance. The zoning administrator may well engage in some fact finding, as in making an initial determination as to whether a nonconforming use was in existence at the time a zoning ordinance was adopted. But, in such instances, this involves determining objective facts that do not involve an element of discretion.

County of Lancaster, S.C. v. Mecklenburg County, 334 N.C. 496, 434 S.E.2d 604, 612 (1993). In this case, the code authorized the zoning enforcement officer to issue landfill permits as "uses by right subject to special requirements." The court held that the permit issuing decision was an administrative zoning decision rather than a quasi-judicial decision since the "special requirements" allowed only objective determinations (e.g., determining yard requirements, screening, hours of operation, access, and notification of adjoining property owners, and reclamation requirements), and did not require an evidentiary hearing.

A hearing is not always held when an administrator denies a permit application for a claimed permitted use, but typically the decision can be appealed to a board of adjustment where a hearing will be held. Must the board review the matter de novo or may it defer to findings of the administrator which were made without a hearing? The West Virginia Supreme Court found "no basis for the circuit court's conclusion that the Board is required on an appeal to reconsider each and every aspect of the decisions reached by the zoning administrator and is expressly prohibited from deferring to any determination made by the zoning administrator." *Jefferson Utilities, Inc. v. Jefferson County Bd. of Zoning Appeals*, 218 W.Va. 436, 437, 624 S.E.2d 873, 874 (2005).

7. Beyond determining the need for a hearing, other consequences follow a determination that a decision of a zoning administrator is administrative or quasi-judicial. Immunity may be conferred under state law if a planning director's action is taken in a discretionary capacity. *Biser v. Deibel*, 128 Md.App. 670, 739 A.2d 948 (Md.App.1999). Issuance of a writ of mandamus is improper only if the act is discretionary. No writ of mandamus may issue against a zoning administrator who has the discretion to deny a permit on the ground that the act for which the permit is sought might soon be rendered illegal. *West Coast Advertising Co. v. City & County of San Francisco*, 64 Cal.Rptr. 94, 96 (Cal.App.1967). Also, no writ of mandamus will issue where a zoning administrator has discretion to determine whether a proposed use is a permitted use. *Ancient Art Tattoo Studio, Ltd. v. City of Virginia Beach*, 263

Va. 593, 598, 561 S.E.2d 690, 692–93 (2002) (discretion to decide whether a tattoo parlor was a "personal service establishment").

What about ex parte contracts? The reality is that parties interested in city council decisions will make ex parte contact without a moment's thought as to whether the contact is proper. After all, one is speaking to an elected official. In one case, the head of a downtown business association contacted a city council member in an attempt to dissuade her from attempting to change a proposed downtown development plan and to suggest that she try to get four others to vote in the way the downtown association preferred. The court observed that "[s]uch contacts and influence are common and appropriate in the normal legislative functioning of a city council. However, when a council sits in a quasi-judicial capacity, as it must to effect a downzoning, its members must be insulated from such contact." *Albuquerque Commons Partnership v. City Council of City of Albuquerque*, 144 N.M. 99, 110, 184 P.3d 411, 422 (2008). The failure of a council to act as it should can be expensive. *See Albuquerque Commons Partnership v. City Council of City of Albuquerque*, 248 P.3d 856 (N.Mex.2011) (jury verdict awarding $8.3 million in damages to developer for violation of due process arising from rezoning affecting developer's property upheld).

3. INITIATIVE AND REFERENDUM

The framers of the Constitution and institutions existing at the time the United States was formed rejected direct democracy as a form of government. Direct democracy survived primarily as a method for adopting constitutions and their amendments. In the later part of the nineteenth century, direct democracy resurfaced in the form of the initiative and referendum as part of the progressive movement's struggle against legislative abuse. States used initiatives and referenda, however, primarily for laws and policies concerning the general welfare, and not to initiate or repeal specific decisions applicable to specific individuals or property. Even the use of the initiative and referendum to decide more narrow issues has tended to avoid targeting specific people or property. Although the effects of such votes often have threatened a relatively small group, initiatives in particular give rise to the sort of majoritarian tyranny that some of our founding fathers sought vigorously to avoid.

While there are points to be made in favor of direct democracy, on balance it is difficult to make a consistent case for the use of initiative or referendum to plan land use or rezone land. As noted above, initiative and referendum have been used primarily to make policies which affect the population of a particular jurisdiction generally, not to overturn a specific implementation of such policies. For example, both initiatives and referenda in the progressive era were used to decide whether particular states or counties would continue to permit the sale of alcoholic beverages, but not whether a particular distillery or brewery should remain open or closed. By analogy, popular voting on whether to undertake zoning or planning would be a proper policy issue, but how that policy is implemented by placing a particular parcel in a particular zone would not.

Nevertheless, in some states the electorate can use initiative and referendum powers to carry out or veto zoning changes. The predominant use of what has become known as ballot box zoning is to prevent growth that the legislative body would otherwise allow. In the typical initiative scenario, a developer announces an intent to develop land presently zoned for an intensive use. Local citizens, realizing their vulnerability to this unwanted development, place an initiative on the ballot to downzone the land before the developer acquires a vested right. The referendum, in contrast, is reactive. Citizens who disagree with an approved upzoning must petition to place the issue on the ballot, hoping to rescind the rezoning at the polls. Usually, the referendum process is permissive, but some communities hold a mandatory referendum on all rezonings.

The use of these powers is controversial, and their validity differs around the country based on state constitutional and statutory provisions. While some applaud ballot box zoning as the essence of direct democracy, others worry that its use may serve to mask illegitimate exclusionary zoning, may render planning efforts superfluous, and may undermine the due process rights of property owners who are subjected to the fancy of voters. The pros and cons are presented in Robert H. Freilich and Derek B. Guemmer, *Removing Artificial Barriers to Public Participation in Land Use Policy: Effective Zoning and Planning by Initiative and Referendum*, 21 URB.LAW. 511 (1989) (generally taking the favorable view); David L. Callies, Nancy C. Neuffer, and Carlito P. Caliboso, *Ballot Box Zoning in Hawaii: Initiative, Referendum and the Law*, 39 J.URB.CONTEM.L. 53 (1991) (an unfavorable view). *See* Daniel P. Selmi, *Reconsidering the Use of Direct Democracy in Making Land Use Decisions*, 19 UCLA J.ENVTL.L. & POL'Y 293 (2002); Aaron J. Reber and Karin Mika, *Democratic Excess in the Use of Zoning Referenda*, 29 URB.LAW. 277 (1997).

CITY OF EASTLAKE V. FOREST CITY ENTERPRISES, INC.

Supreme Court of the United States, 1976.
426 U.S. 668, 96 S.Ct. 2358, 49 L.Ed.2d 132.

MR. CHIEF JUSTICE BURGER delivered the opinion of the Court.

The question in this case is whether a city charter provision requiring proposed land use changes to be ratified by 55% of the votes cast violates the due process rights of a landowner who applies for a zoning change.

The city of Eastlake, Ohio, a suburb of Cleveland, has a comprehensive zoning plan codified in a municipal ordinance. Respondent, a real estate developer, acquired an eight-acre parcel of real estate in Eastlake zoned for "light industrial" uses at the time of purchase.

In May 1971, respondent applied to the City Planning Commission for a zoning change to permit construction of a multi-family, high-rise apartment building. The Planning Commission recommended the proposed change to the City Council, which under Eastlake's procedures could either accept or reject the Planning Commission's recommendation. Meanwhile, by popular vote, the voters of Eastlake amended the city charter to require that any changes in land use agreed to by the Council be approved by a 55% vote in a referendum. The City Council approved the Planning Commission's recommendation for reclassification of respondent's property to permit the proposed project. Respondent then applied to the Planning Commission for "parking and yard" approval for the proposed building. The Commission rejected the application, on the ground that the City Council's rezoning action had not yet been submitted to the voters for ratification. [In the May 1972 election the ordinance rezoning appellant's property failed to obtain the requisite 55 percent of the votes cast. 324 N.E.2d at 742.]

* * *

The conclusion that Eastlake's procedure violates federal constitutional guarantees rests upon the proposition that a zoning referendum involves a delegation of legislative power. A referendum cannot, however, be characterized as a delegation of power. Under our constitutional assumptions, all power derives from the people, who can delegate it to representative instruments which they create. See, e.g., The Federalist No. 39 (v. Madison). In establishing legislative bodies, the people can reserve to themselves power to deal directly with matters which might otherwise be assigned to the legislature.

The reservation of such power is the basis for the town meeting, a tradition which continues to this day in some States as both a practical and symbolic part of our democratic processes. The referendum, similarly, is a means for direct political participation, allowing the people the final decision, amounting to a veto power, over enactments of representative bodies. The practice is designed to "give citizens a voice on questions of public policy." James v. Valtierra.

In framing a state constitution, the people of Ohio specifically reserved the power of referendum to the people of each municipality within the State.

> The initiative and referendum powers are hereby reserved to the people of each municipality on all questions which such municipalities may now or hereafter be authorized by law to control by legislative action * * * . Ohio Const., Art. II, § 1f.

To be subject to Ohio's referendum procedure, the question must be one within the scope of legislative power. The Ohio Supreme Court expressly found that the City Council's action in rezoning respondent's

eight acres from light industrial to high-density residential use was
legislative in nature. Distinguishing between administrative and
legislative acts, the court separated the power to zone or rezone, by passage
or amendment of a zoning ordinance, from the power to grant relief from
unnecessary hardship. The former function was found to be legislative in
nature.

The Ohio Supreme Court further concluded that the amendment to the
city charter constituted a "delegation" of power violative of federal
constitutional guarantees because the voters were given no standards to
guide their decision. Under Eastlake's procedure, the Ohio Supreme Court
reasoned, no mechanism existed, nor indeed could exist, to assure that the
voters would act rationally in passing upon a proposed zoning change. This
meant that "appropriate legislative action [would] be made dependent
upon the potentially arbitrary and unreasonable whims of the voting
public." The potential for arbitrariness in the process, the court concluded,
violated due process.

Courts have frequently held in other contexts that a congressional
delegation of power to a regulatory entity must be accompanied by
discernible standards, so that the delegatee's action can be measured for
its fidelity to the legislative will. Assuming, *arguendo*, their relevance to
state governmental functions, these cases involved a delegation of power
by the legislature to regulatory bodies, which are not directly responsible
to the people; this doctrine is inapplicable where, as here, rather than
dealing with a delegation of power, we deal with a power reserved by the
people to themselves.

In basing its claim on federal due process requirements, respondent
also invokes Euclid v. Ambler Realty Co., but it does not rely on the direct
teaching of that case. Under *Euclid*, a property owner can challenge a
zoning restriction if the measure is "clearly arbitrary and unreasonable,
having no substantial relation to the public health, safety, morals, or
general welfare." If the substantive result of the referendum is arbitrary
and capricious, bearing no relation to the police power, then the fact that
the voters of Eastlake wish it so would not save the restriction. As this
Court held in invalidating a charter amendment enacted by referendum:

> The sovereignty of the people is itself subject to those
> constitutional limitations which have been duly adopted and
> remain unrepealed. Hunter v. Erickson.

But no challenge of the sort contemplated in Euclid v. Ambler Realty
is before us. The Ohio Supreme Court did not hold, and respondent does
not argue, that the present zoning classification under Eastlake's
comprehensive ordinance violates the principles established in Euclid v.
Ambler Realty. If respondent considers the referendum result itself to be
unreasonable, the zoning restriction is open to challenge in state court,
where the scope of the state remedy available to respondent would be

determined as a matter of state law, as well as under Fourteenth Amendment standards. That being so, nothing more is required by the Constitution.

Nothing in our cases is inconsistent with this conclusion. Two decisions of this Court were relied on by the Ohio Supreme Court in invalidating Eastlake's procedure. The thread common to both decisions is the delegation of legislative power, originally given by the people to a legislative body, and in turn delegated by the legislature to a *narrow segment* of the community, not to the people at large. In Eubank v. Richmond, the Court invalidated a city ordinance which conferred the power to establish building setback lines upon the owners of two-thirds of the property abutting any street. Similarly, in Washington ex rel. Seattle Title Trust Co. v. Roberge, the Court struck down an ordinance which permitted the establishment of philanthropic homes for the aged in residential areas, but only upon the written consent of the owners of two-thirds of the property within 400 feet of the proposed facility.

Neither *Eubank* nor *Roberge* involved a referendum procedure such as we have in this case; the standardless delegation of power to a limited group of property owners condemned by the Court in *Eubank* and *Roberge* is not to be equated with decision-making by the people through the referendum process. The Court of Appeals for the Ninth Circuit put it this way:

> A referendum, however, is far more than an expression of ambiguously founded neighborhood preference. It is the city itself legislating through its voters—an exercise by the voters of their traditional right through direct legislation to override the views of their elected representatives as to what serves the public interest. *Southern Alameda Spanish Speaking Organization v. Union City, California*, 424 F.2d 291, 294 (1970).

Our decision in James v. Valtierra, upholding California's mandatory referendum requirement, confirms this view. Mr. Justice Black, speaking for the Court in that case, said:

> This procedure ensures that *all the people* of a community will have a voice in a decision which may lead to large expenditures of local governmental funds for increased public services * * * . 402 U.S., at 143 (emphasis added).

Mr. Justice Black went on to say that a referendum procedure, such as the one at issue here, is a classic demonstration of "devotion to democracy * * * ." Id., at 141. As a basic instrument of democratic government, the referendum process does not, in itself, violate the Due Process Clause of the Fourteenth Amendment when applied to a rezoning ordinance. Since the rezoning decision in this case was properly reserved to the People of Eastlake under the Ohio Constitution, the Ohio Supreme Court erred in holding invalid, on federal constitutional grounds, the charter amendment permitting the voters to decide whether the zoned use of respondent's property could be altered.

* * *

MR. JUSTICE POWELL, dissenting.

There can be no doubt as to the propriety and legality of submitting generally applicable legislative questions, including zoning provisions, to a popular referendum. But here the only issue concerned the status of a single small parcel owned by a single "person." This procedure, affording no realistic opportunity for the affected person to be heard, even by the electorate, is fundamentally unfair. The "spot" referendum technique appears to open disquieting opportunities for local government bodies to bypass normal protective procedures for resolving issues affecting individual rights.

MR. JUSTICE STEVENS, with whom MR. JUSTICE BRENNAN joins, dissenting.

Although this Court has decided only a handful of zoning cases, literally thousands of zoning disputes have been resolved by state courts. Those courts have repeatedly identified the obvious difference between the adoption of a comprehensive citywide plan by legislative action and the decision of particular issues involving specific uses of specific parcels. In the former situation there is generally great deference to the judgment of the legislature; in the latter situation state courts have not hesitated to correct manifest injustice.

The distinction was plainly drawn by the Supreme Court of Oregon:

Ordinances laying down general policies without regard to a specific piece of property are usually an exercise of legislative authority, are subject to limited review, and may only be attacked upon constitutional grounds for an arbitrary abuse of authority. On the other hand, a determination whether the permissible use of a specific piece of property should be changed is usually an exercise of judicial authority and its propriety is subject to an altogether different test. *Fasano v. Board of County Comm'rs.*

As the Justices of the Ohio Supreme Court recognized, we are concerned with the fairness of a provision for determining the right to make a particular use of a particular parcel of land. In such cases, the state courts have frequently described the capricious character of a decision supported by majority sentiment rather than reference to articulable standards. Moreover, they have limited statutory referendum procedures to apply only to approvals of comprehensive zoning ordinances as opposed to amendments affecting specific parcels. This conclusion has been supported by characterizing particular amendments as "administrative" and revision of an entire plan as "legislative."

In this case the Ohio Supreme Court characterized the Council's approval of respondent's proposal as "legislative." I think many state courts would have characterized it as "administrative." The courts thus may well differ in their selection of the label to apply to this action, but I find substantial agreement among state tribunals on the proposition that requiring a citywide referendum for approval of a particular proposal like this is manifestly unreasonable. Surely that is my view.

The essence of fair procedure is that the interested parties be given a reasonable opportunity to have their dispute resolved on the merits by reference to articulable rules. If a dispute involves only the conflicting rights of private litigants, it is elementary that the decision-maker must be impartial and qualified to understand and to apply the controlling rules.

I have no doubt about the validity of the initiative or the referendum as an appropriate method of deciding questions of community policy. I think it is equally clear that the popular vote is not an acceptable method of adjudicating the rights of individual litigants. The problem presented by this case is unique, because it may involve a three-sided controversy, in which there is at least potential conflict between the rights of the property owner and the rights of his neighbors, and also potential conflict with the public interest in preserving the city's basic zoning plan. If the latter aspect of the controversy were predominant, the referendum would be an acceptable procedure. On the other hand, when the record indicates without contradiction that there is no threat to the general public interest in preserving the city's plan—as it does in this case, since respondent's proposal was approved by both the Planning Commission and the City Council and there has been no allegation that the use of this eight-acre parcel for apartments rather than light industry would adversely affect the community or raise any policy issue of citywide concern—I think the case should be treated as one in which it is essential that the private property owner be given a fair opportunity to have his claim determined on its merits.

I therefore conclude that the Ohio Supreme Court correctly held that Art. VIII, § 3, of the Eastlake charter violates the Due Process Clause of the Fourteenth Amendment, and that its judgment should be affirmed.

CITY OF CUYAHOGA FALLS v. BUCKEYE COMMUNITY HOPE FOUNDATION

Supreme Court of the United States, 2003.
538 U.S. 188, 123 S.Ct. 1389, 155 L.Ed.2d 349.

JUSTICE O'CONNOR delivered the opinion of the Court.

In 1995, the city of Cuyahoga Falls, Ohio (hereinafter City), submitted to voters a facially neutral referendum petition that called for the repeal of a municipal housing ordinance authorizing construction of a low-income housing complex. The United States Court of Appeals for the Sixth Circuit found genuine issues of material fact with regard to whether the City violated the Equal Protection Clause, the Due Process Clause, and the Fair Housing Act, 82 Stat. 81, as amended, 42 U.S.C. § 3601 *et seq.,* by placing the petition on the ballot. We granted certiorari to determine whether the Sixth Circuit erred in ruling that respondents' suit against the City could proceed to trial.

I

A

In June 1995, respondents Buckeye Community Hope Foundation, a nonprofit corporation dedicated to developing affordable housing through the use of low-income tax credits, and others (hereinafter Buckeye or respondents), purchased land zoned for apartments in Cuyahoga Falls, Ohio. In February 1996, Buckeye submitted a site plan for Pleasant Meadows, a multifamily, low-income housing complex, to the city planning commission. Residents of Cuyahoga Falls immediately expressed opposition to the proposal. After respondents agreed to various conditions, including that it build an earthen wall surrounded by a fence on one side of the complex, the commission unanimously approved the site plan and submitted it to the city council for final authorization.

As the final approval process unfolded, public opposition to the plan resurfaced and eventually coalesced into a referendum petition drive. See Cuyahoga Falls City Charter, Art. 9, § 2 (hereinafter City Charter) (giving voters "the power to approve or reject at the polls any ordinance or resolution passed by the Council" within 30 days of the ordinance's passage). At city council meetings and independent gatherings, some of which the mayor attended to express his personal opposition to the site plan, citizens of Cuyahoga Falls voiced various concerns: that the development would cause crime and drug activity to escalate, that families with children would move in, and that the complex would attract a population similar to the one on Prange Drive, the City's only African-American neighborhood. *See, e.g.,* 263 F.3d, at 636–637. Nevertheless, because the plan met all municipal zoning requirements, the city council approved the project on April 1, 1996, through City Ordinance No. 48–1996.

On April 29, a group of citizens filed a formal petition with the City requesting that the ordinance be repealed or submitted to a popular vote. Pursuant to the City Charter, which provides that an ordinance challenged by a petition "shall [not] go into effect until approved by a majority" of voters, the filing stayed the implementation of the site plan. Art. 9, § 2, App. 15. On April 30, respondents sought an injunction against the petition in state court, arguing that the Ohio Constitution does not authorize popular referendums on administrative matters. On May 31, the Court of Common Pleas denied the injunction. *Buckeye Community Hope Foundation v. Cuyahoga Falls,* Civ. No. 96–05–1701 (Summit County). A month later, respondents nonetheless requested building permits from the City in order to begin construction. On June 26, the city engineer rejected the request after being advised by the city law director that the permits "could not be issued because the site plan ordinance 'does not take effect' due to the petitions." 263 F.3d, at 633.

In November 1996, the voters of Cuyahoga Falls passed the referendum, thus repealing Ordinance No. 48–1996. In a joint stipulation, however, the parties agreed that the results of the election would not be certified until the litigation over the referendum was resolved. In July 1998, the Ohio Supreme Court, having initially concluded that the referendum was proper, reversed itself and declared the referendum unconstitutional. *Buckeye Community Hope Foundation v. Cuyahoga Falls,* 82 Ohio St.3d 539, 697 N.E.2d 181 (1998) (holding that the Ohio State Constitution authorizes referendums only in relation to legislative acts, not administrative acts, such as the site-plan ordinance). The City subsequently issued the building permits, and Buckeye commenced construction of Pleasant Meadows.

B

In July 1996, with the state-court litigation still pending, respondents filed suit in federal court against the City and several city officials, seeking an injunction ordering the City to issue the building permits, as well as declaratory and monetary relief. Buckeye alleged that "in allowing a site plan approval ordinance to be submitted to the electors of Cuyahoga Falls through a referendum and in rejecting [its] application for building permits," the City and its officials violated the Equal Protection and Due Process Clauses of the Fourteenth Amendment, as well as the Fair Housing Act, 42 U.S.C. § 3601. In June 1997, the District Court dismissed the case against the mayor in his individual capacity but denied the City's motion for summary judgment on the equal protection and due process claims, concluding that genuine issues of material fact existed as to both claims. After the Ohio Supreme Court declared the referendum invalid in 1998, thus reducing respondents' action to a claim for damages for the delay in construction, the City and its officials again moved for summary judgment. On November 19, 1999, the District Court granted the motion on all counts.

The Court of Appeals for the Sixth Circuit reversed. As to respondents' equal protection claim, the court concluded that they had produced sufficient evidence to go to trial on the allegation that the City, by allowing the referendum petition to stay the implementation of the site plan, gave effect to the racial bias reflected in the public's opposition to the project. The court then held that even if respondents failed to prove intentional discrimination, they stated a valid claim under the Fair Housing Act on the theory that the City's actions had a disparate impact based on race and family status. Finally, the court concluded that a genuine issue of material fact existed as to whether the City, by denying respondents the benefit of the lawfully approved site plan, engaged in arbitrary and irrational government conduct in violation of substantive due process. We granted certiorari, and now reverse the constitutional holdings and vacate the Fair Housing Act holding.

II

Respondents allege that by submitting the petition to the voters and refusing to issue building permits while the petition was pending, the City and its officials violated the Equal Protection Clause. Petitioners claim that the Sixth Circuit went astray by ascribing the motivations of a handful of citizens supportive of the referendum to the City. We agree with petitioners that respondents have failed to present sufficient evidence of an equal protection violation to survive summary judgment.

We have made clear that "[p]roof of racially discriminatory intent or purpose is required" to show a violation of the Equal Protection Clause. In deciding the equal protection question, the Sixth Circuit erred in relying on cases in which we have subjected enacted, discretionary measures to equal protection scrutiny and treated decisionmakers' statements as evidence of such intent. * * * Because respondents claim injury from the referendum petitioning *process* and not from the referendum itself—which never went into effect—these cases are inapposite. Ultimately, neither of the official acts respondents challenge reflects the intent required to support equal protection liability.

First, in submitting the referendum petition to the voters, the City acted pursuant to the requirements of its charter, which sets out a facially neutral petitioning procedure. By placing the referendum on the ballot, the City did not enact the referendum and therefore cannot be said to have given effect to voters' allegedly discriminatory motives for supporting the petition. Similarly, the city engineer, in refusing to issue the building permits while the referendum was still pending, performed a nondiscretionary, ministerial act. He acted in response to the city law director's instruction that the building permits "could not . . . issue" because the City Charter prohibited a challenged site-plan ordinance from going into effect until "approved by a majority of those voting thereon," * * * . Respondents point to no evidence suggesting that these official acts were themselves motivated by racial animus. Respondents do not, for example, offer evidence that the City followed the obligations set forth in its charter *because of* the referendum's discriminatory purpose, or that city officials would have selectively refused to follow standard charter procedures in a different case.

Instead, to establish discriminatory intent, respondents and the Sixth Circuit both rely heavily on evidence of allegedly discriminatory voter sentiment. But statements made by private individuals in the course of a citizen-driven petition drive, while sometimes relevant to equal protection analysis do not, in and of themselves, constitute state action for the purposes of the Fourteenth Amendment. Moreover, respondents put forth no evidence that the "private motives [that] triggered" the referendum drive "can fairly be attributable to the State."

In fact, by adhering to charter procedures, city officials enabled public debate on the referendum to take place, thus advancing significant First Amendment interests. In assessing the referendum as a "basic instrument of democratic government," *Eastlake v. Forest City Enterprises, Inc.,* 426 U.S. 668, 679 (1976), we have observed that "[p]rovisions for referendums demonstrate devotion to democracy, not to bias, discrimination, or prejudice," *James v. Valtierra,* 402 U.S. 137, 141 (1971). And our well established First Amendment admonition that "government may not prohibit the expression of an idea simply because society finds the idea itself offensive or disagreeable," dovetails with the notion that all citizens, regardless of the content of their ideas, have the right to petition their government. Cf. *Meyer v. Grant,* 486 U.S. 414, 421–422 (1988) (describing the circulation of an initiative petition as " 'core political speech' "). Again, statements made by decisionmakers or referendum sponsors during deliberation over a referendum may constitute relevant evidence of discriminatory intent in a challenge to an ultimately enacted initiative. *See, e.g., Washington v. Seattle School Dist. No. 1,* 458 U.S. 457, 471 (1982) (considering statements of initiative sponsors in subjecting enacted referendum to equal protection scrutiny). But respondents do not challenge an enacted referendum.

* * *

III

In evaluating respondents' substantive due process claim, the Sixth Circuit found, as a threshold matter, that respondents had a legitimate claim of entitlement to the building permits, and therefore a property interest in those permits, in light of the city council's approval of the site plan. The court then held that respondents had presented sufficient evidence to survive summary judgment on their claim that the City engaged in arbitrary conduct by denying respondents the benefit of the plan. Both in their complaint and before this Court, respondents contend that the City violated substantive due process, not only for the reason articulated by the Sixth Circuit, but also on the grounds that the City's submission of an administrative land-use determination to the charter's referendum procedures constituted *per se* arbitrary conduct We find no merit in either claim.

We need not decide whether respondents possessed a property interest in the building permits, because the city engineer's refusal to issue the permits while the petition was pending in no sense constituted egregious or arbitrary government conduct. *See County of Sacramento v. Lewis,* 523 U.S. 833, 846 (1998) (noting that in our evaluations of "abusive executive action," we have held that "only the most egregious official conduct can be said to be 'arbitrary in the constitutional sense' "). In light of the charter's provision that "[n]o such ordinance [challenged by a petition] shall go into effect until approved by a majority of those voting thereon," the law director's instruction to the engineer to not issue the permits represented an eminently rational directive. Indeed, the site plan, by law, could not be implemented until the voters passed on the referendum.

Respondents' second theory of liability has no basis in our precedent. As a matter of federal constitutional law, we have rejected the distinction that respondents ask us to draw, and that the Ohio Supreme Court drew as a matter of state law, between legislative and administrative referendums. In *Eastlake v. Forest City Enterprises, Inc.,* 426 U.S., at 672, 675, we made clear that because all power stems from the people, "[a] referendum cannot . . . be characterized as a delegation of power," unlawful unless accompanied by "discernible standards." The people retain the power to govern through referendum " 'with respect to any matter, legislative or administrative, within the realm of local affairs.' " *Id.,* at 674, n. 9. Though the "substantive result" of a referendum may be invalid if it is "arbitrary and capricious," *Eastlake v. Forest City Enterprises, supra,* at 676, respondents do not challenge the referendum itself. The subjection of the site-plan ordinance to the City's referendum process, regardless of whether that ordinance reflected an administrative or legislative decision, did not constitute *per se* arbitrary government conduct in violation of due process.

IV

For the reasons detailed above, we reverse the Sixth Circuit's judgment with regard to respondents' equal protection and substantive due process claims. The Sixth Circuit also held that respondents' disparate impact claim under the Fair Housing Act could proceed to trial, but respondents have now abandoned the claim. We therefore vacate the Sixth Circuit's disparate impact holding and remand with instructions to dismiss, with prejudice, the relevant portion of the complaint.

It is so ordered.

JUSTICE SCALIA, with whom JUSTICE THOMAS joins, concurring. [omitted]

NOTES

1.   Note the callous disregard which the Supreme Court accorded planning in *Eastlake*. Despite considerable evidence presented to the Court of the importance of comprehensive planning and its irrelevance if submitted to popular referendum, the Court upheld the referendum process in part because it somehow reminded the majority of the New England town meeting. As you will note in Chapter 5 C on exclusionary zoning, one of the few bright spots in the U.S. Supreme Court's decision in *Village of Arlington Heights v. Metropolitan Housing Development Corp.*, 429 U.S. 252 (1977), was its support for the planning process. The Court viewed it as indicative of the reasonableness of the Village of Arlington Heights' use of its multi-family zone primarily as a buffer zone rather than as the free-standing zone sought by MHDC to construct a low-and moderate-income housing development.

2.   In *Buckeye*, for the second time in a quarter of a century, the U.S. Supreme Court reverses the Ohio Supreme Court in a ballot box zoning case, unanimously finding nothing procedurally irregular from a constitutional perspective in subjecting administrative acts to a popular vote. Even Justice Stevens abandons his opposition to the use of referenda for all but legislative issues which he argued so effectively in his *Eastlake* dissent, observing that: "[I]t would be absurd to use a referendum to decide whether a gasoline station could be operated on a particular corner in the City of Cleveland." 426 U.S. at 694. So also it is absurd to use a referendum to decide whether a site plan for a low-income housing project should be approved for a particular site in the City of Cuyahoga Falls.

3.   Is *Buckeye's* statement in Part III of the opinion that voters can decide "any matter legislative or administrative within the realm of local affairs," an extension of *Eastlake*? If so, was it intentional or accidental? The *Eastlake* Court accepted the Ohio court's characterization of the referendum as legislative, and proceeded, with one exception, to speak of referenda being available for "matters which otherwise might be assigned to the legislature," that " 'give citizens a voice on questions of public policy' " and where the "question must be one within the scope of legislative power." Out of sync with those statements referring to policy issues, in footnote 9, the *Eastlake* Court cited a treatise for the proposition that "the people retain the power to govern through referendum with respect to any matter, legislative *or administrative*, within the realm of local affairs." 426 U.S. at 674, n. 9 [internal quotation marks omitted and emphasis added].

The *Buckeye* opinion's statement in Part III relies on Eastlake's footnote 9 for a matter of enormous importance. Should that footnote's inclusion of "administrative" matters take precedence over the *Eastlake* text's emphasis on legislative matters? Would it have mattered if the Court had updated its research? In an edition subsequent to *Eastlake*, the treatise authors who are cited in footnote 9, changed their minds, and now say if the act is administrative it is not referendable. *See* E. McQuillin, *The Law of Municipal Corporations* § 25.246 at 275 (Rev.ed.1994).

4.   Consider which land use decisions are legislative—and so subject to referendum—or quasi-judicial, and not subject to referendum. Should it depend upon whether a plan is detailed as opposed to general? As Justice Stevens also noted in his *Eastlake* dissent, the ballot box should be reserved for policy issues, not for the implementation of policy. Courts in virtually every state which has considered the matter recognize the legislative-administrative distinction, uniformly permitting initiative or referendum on the former, but not the latter. For example, in *Hanson v. City of Granite Falls*, 529 N.W.2d 485 (Minn.App.1995), a case with facts similar to *Buckeye*, the court examined a referendum that overturned the City's approval of an airport site plan. According to the court, the "resolution [approving the site plan] is not an act laying down a permanent . . . law. It simply approves a layout plan for the proposed airport, and is more in the nature of an administrative act relating to the daily administration of municipal affairs." 529 N.W. 2d at 488. In *Heitman v. City of Mauston Common Council*, 595 N.W.2d 450 (Wis.App.1999), Heitman and others opposed the construction of a treatment facility for sexually violent offenders. The court held that the proposed initiative was invalid "because the zoning enabling act has established procedures and standards for zoning and Heitman may not modify them by zoning through the initiative process." 595 N.W. 2d at 457. ("referendum powers reserved to the people are very broad, but are limited to legislation."); *DeVita v. County of Napa*, 889 P.2d 1019 (Cal.1995) ("These and other cases led to the formulation of a general dichotomy between a governing body's legislative acts, which are subject to . . . referendum, and its administrative or executive acts, which are not."). For commentary on and criticism of the *Buckeye* decision, *see* 55 Land Use Law and Zoning Digest 3–14 (July 2003).

The South Dakota Supreme Court confirmed its restriction of referenda to legislative actions which it set out in *Kirschenman* cited above in *Bechen v. Moody County Board of Commissioners*, 703 N.W.2d 662 (S.D.2005). Emphasizing that its language in that case was not meant to broaden the availability of referendum beyond legislative acts, the court held that a county commission (a legislative body) sitting as a board of adjustment is acting administratively and so such actions are not subject to referendum. The Utah Supreme Court holds that all rezonings are legislative acts and hence subject to a referendum, implying that administrative acts are not. *Mouty v. The Sandy City Recorder*, 122 P.3d 521 (Utah 2005).

5.   A majority of states disallow zoning by initiative, but a fairly even split exists with respect to zoning by referendum. Most of those disallowing voter action find the absence of notice and hearing required by zoning enabling legislation to be fatal. Some courts that allow such action reason that the affected landowner obtains the equivalent of a public hearing through the debate that ensues with the campaign. It is, however, doubtful that there is anything resembling a campaign for the typical initiative or referendum or a specific parcel. If the zoning problem does not involve a community wide issue,

it is likely that there will be little debate and that the only ones who will vote will be those living near the parcel in issue. *See* Juergensmeyer and Roberts, *Land Use Planning and Development Regulation Law* § 5.5 (3rd ed.2012).

The concern over notice and hearing explains why courts treat initiatives less favorably than referenda. Arizona, for example, prohibits zoning by initiative because of the absence of notice and a hearing, but allows zoning by referendum on the theory that the zoning process that precedes the referendum provides notice and a hearing, *see Transamerica Title Ins. Co. v. City of Tucson*, 757 P.2d 1055 (Ariz.1988); and *Queen Creek Land and Cattle Corp. v. Yavapai County Bd. of Supervisors*, 501 P.2d 391 (Ariz.1972), even if the zoning is consistent with a general plan, *Fritz v. City of Kingman*, 957 P.2d 337 (Ariz.1998). If a state constitutional provision reserves the initiative and the referendum to the people, it will trump a statutory mandate regarding notice and hearing.

COMMENT: NEIGHBORHOOD CONSENT ORDINANCES*

Several United States Supreme Court cases deal with neighborhood consent ordinances. In a 1912 decision, *Eubank v. City of Richmond*, 226 U.S. 137 (1912), the Court reviewed an ordinance that required the municipality to establish a setback line if two-thirds of the property owners abutting a street requested it. A property owner of a lot who wished to build a house 11 feet from the street was prevented from doing so when his neighbors, by petition, established the setback at 14 feet. The Court held the delegation to violate the due process clause since it contained no standards, allowing the neighbors to act capriciously in their own interests. Three years later, in *Thomas Cusack Co. v. City of Chicago*, 242 U.S. 526 (1917), the Court reviewed an ordinance that prohibited signs on public streets where more than half of the buildings were used for residential purposes unless the applicant obtained the consent of a majority of the owners of property on the street. The Court upheld this ordinance. It reasoned that since the ordinance prohibited signs, the owner wishing to put up a sign only stood to gain by being able to seek consent. *Eubank* was distinguished because the restriction was imposed by the property owners. In *Cusack*, they simply waived an existing restriction. *Eubank* was also distinguished by *Gorieb v. Fox*, 274 U.S. 603 (1927). In *Gorieb*, the ordinance established a setback line for new houses based on the average distance from the street of the other houses on the block. The application was automatic, did not depend on consent, and was not an improper delegation. The city merely based its decision on the rational ground that a setback should be established based on de facto setbacks in the area.

Finally, in *State of Washington ex rel. Seattle Title Trust Co. v. Roberge*, 278 U.S. 116 (1928), the ordinance provided that a home for the elderly poor could be built in an area only if neighbors consented. Despite the similarity between the ordinances in *Cusack* and *Roberge*, the *Roberge* Court considered the signs in *Cusack* and the home for the elderly of *Roberge* to be

---

    *   This comment on consent ordinances, slightly modified, is taken from Juergensmeyer and Roberts, *Land Use Planning and Development Regulation Law* § 5.4 (3rd ed.2012) with permission.

distinguishable. Signs were viewed as nuisances, justifying greater control by property owners. Homes for the elderly, in contrast, had not been determined to be inimical to other uses, and the Court thus invalidated the delegation.

Many courts take these cases to establish the rule that granting neighbors the power to impose control violates due process, but granting them the power to waive an existing limitation does not. The cases have, however, "posed a long-standing puzzle to legal theorists," and many are critical of the rule derived from them. Some courts also find it troubling. As the Supreme Court of Illinois said, the distinction "between 'creating' and 'waiving' a restriction" is too subtle and in any event, each "leave[s] the ultimate determination of * * * the public welfare in the discretion of individuals rather than the city." *Drovers Trust & Sav. Bank v. City of Chicago*, 165 N.E.2d 314, 315 (Ill.1960).

In sum, the impulse to delegate decision-making power to the neighbors is understandable, though not necessarily commendable. It allows those most directly affected to decide the matter. This may be appropriate if the spillover effects of the use are limited to the neighbors who have the delegated power. However, the benefits of granting or denying the proposed use may spread beyond the confines of the neighborhood. Since the legislators have stepped out of the picture to avoid making what might be an unpopular decision, no one may be guarding the public interest. A delegation to neighbors also has the potential of subjecting proponents of change to their neighbors' arbitrary whims, and raises due process concerns. For critical comment on the process, *see* Aaron J. Reber and Karin Mika, *Democratic Excess in the Use of Zoning Referenda*, 29 URB.LAW. 277 (1997); Nicolas M. Kublicki, *Land Use by, for, and of the People: Problems with the Application of Initiatives and Referenda to the Zoning Process*, 19 PEPP.L.REV. 99 (1991).

D. VARIANCES

Among the troublesome issues confronting drafters of zoning ordinances were the potential hardships caused to individual property owners by the literal application of the zoning ordinance to particular pieces of property. The problem is addressed by the variance (sometimes also called a variation or a special exception). Variances may alter the use to which property may be put (e.g., commercial use in a residential zone), or grant area or bulk concessions (e.g., modify setback lines or height requirements). In the case that follows, note the type of variance sought.

The Standard Zoning Enabling Act provides for the creation of a local zoning board of adjustment to, among other things, "authorize upon appeal in specific cases such variance from the terms of the ordinance as will not be contrary to the public interest, where, owing to special conditions, a literal enforcement of the provisions of the ordinance will result in unnecessary hardship, and so that the spirit of the ordinance shall be observed and substantial justice done." § 7. While arguably hedged in by a host of administrative restrictions, the variance is one of the most important and commonly used (and some would say abused) techniques for changing the land use regulations which apply to particular parcels.

SURFRIDER FOUNDATION V. ZONING BD. OF APPEALS

Supreme Court of Hawai'i, 2015.
136 Hawai'i 95, 358 P.3d 664.

Opinion of the Court by POLLACK, J.

In 1976, the Honolulu City Council established the Waikiki Special Design district in response "to the paid development of the 1960s and 1970s, and the changes produced by that development." The City Council found that "[t]o the world, Waikiki is a recognized symbol of Hawai'i [ ] and the allure of Waikiki continues, serving as the anchor for the state's tourist industry." The Council concluded that while "Waikiki needs to maintain its place as one of the world's premier resorts in an international market [ ], the sense of place that makes Waikiki unique needs to be retained and enhanced." Accordingly, the City Council development specific requirements and design controls "to guide carefully Waikiki's future and protect its unique Hawaiian identity."

Among the provisions enacted to protect Waikiki's Hawaiian identity is a limitation on development next to the shoreline. The Council established a coastal height setback requirement because of the "need to step back tall buildings from the shoreline to maximize public safety and the sense of open space and public enjoyment associated with coastal resources." The Council also provided for a variance process when compliance with the Land Use Ordinance would result in unnecessary buildup.

In this case, we are called upon to determine whether a variance granted for a proposed 26-story hotel and residential tower that permitted a 74 percent encroachment into the coastal height setback along the Waikiki shoreline was properly used.

Kyo-ya Hotels & Resorts LP (Kyo-ya) is the fee-simple owner of the Moana Surfrider hotel complex, which contains three hotel buildings—the Surfrider Tower, the Banyan Wong, and the Diamond Head Tower (DHT)—on a combined zoning lot located on Kalakaua Avenue along the Waikiki shoreline. In 2010, Kyo-ya submitted a land use permit to redevelop the existing 8-story DHT with a 26-story, 282 foot hotel and residential tower (the Project). Due to the Project's size, location, and design, the Project required several permits and approvals, including a variance to allow the Project to encroach into the Coastal Height Setback.

On March 19, 2010, Kyo-ya submitted variance application No. 2010/VAR–9 (variance application) to the Department of Planning and Permitting requesting that the Project be allowed to encroach into the Coastal Height Setback. As proposed, the Project would encroach about 40

feet into the 100-foot coastal setback at the building's ewa corner and about
60 feet at the Diamond Head corner. Additionally, a significant portion of
the building up to the 16th floor would encroach into the 1:1 height setback
measured from the certified shoreline, and "from the 17th floor, the entire
building encroaches into the coastal height setback." In total, "about 74.3
percent of the building encroaches into the Coastal Height Setback";
"Conversely, only 28.7 percent of the building complies with the coastal
height setback."

In its variance application, Kyo-ya maintained that although the
Project was "unable to comply with the strict requirements of [the Coastal
Height Setback]," the Project satisfied the three requirements for issuance
of a variance.

Kyo-ya argued it would be deprived of the reasonable use of its land if
the LUO was strictly applied because the ordinance would "reduce the
buildable portion of the property to roughly 11,283 square feet, or
approximately 33% of the whole lot area." If the LUO "were strictly
followed," Kyo-ya contended that it "would not even be able to rebuild the
existing [DHT]."

Kyo-ya maintained that the State of Hawai'i entered into an
agreement in 1965 with the owners of certain beach front parcels under
which the State committee to expand the beach an "[p]rotect and preserve
all existing beach" in a designated area (1965 Beach Agreement). Although
the contemplated beach expansion was never completed, Kyo-ya asserted
that had "the beach been constructed by the State" pursuant to the 1965
Beach Agreement, "it is likely that the beach fronting the [DHT] site would
be approximately 180 feet wider than it is today" and the shoreline would
have been recertified to reflect the increased width. Additionally, if the
beach had been extended, Kyo-ya submitted that "almost no portion of the
[Project] would encroach into the coastal height setback."

[handwritten margin note: if the beach extension would have happened]

Kyo-ya contended that the reasonableness of the neighborhood zoning
was not drawn into question by its variance request because it was "forced"
to apply for a variance due to unique circumstance, rather than as a result
of general conditions in the neighborhood. For example, the Project site "is
bounded on the Ewa side by the historic Banyan Wing," which is listed on
the National and State Register of Historic Places. Kyo-ya argued that it
had foregone considerable financial gain by choosing not to redevelop the
Banyan Wing and that "[i]f Kyo-ya chose to redevelop this portion of the
complex, it could develop a hotel or residential tower that meets all LUO,
WED and [Planned Development-Resort (PD-R)] requirements."

Additionally, Kyo-ya contended the Project site "is among the
narrowest parcels of land along Waikiki Beach" that is subject to the
Coastal Height Setback." The narrowness of the Project site "is
exacerbated," Kyo-ya argued, "by the absence of the substantial beach
which was to have been built by the State per the 1965 Beach Agreement"

in addition to the presence of the historic Banyan Wing. Kyo-ya further argued that the parcel's "unique size and shape" caused the impact of the Coastal Height Setback to be "greater than on any other parcel along Waikiki Beach."

With respect to the third requirement, Kyo-ya submitted that the variance "will not alter the essential character of the locality nor be contrary to the intent and purpose of the zoning code." Kyo-ya characterized Waikiki as "a densely developed, urbanized area, filled with large hotels, condominiums, and mixed-use projects which push (and in many cases exceed) the limits of permitted heights, densities, and other zoning and building regulations." Kyo-ya argued that many of the "existing hotels along Waikiki Beach already encroach into the coastal height setback" and that allowing the Project to similarly encroach would not alter the essential character of Waikiki. Kyo-ya contended the Project's "mauka-makai orientation, increased public open space, improved beach access and addition of surfboard racks should go a long way toward restoring the character of Waikiki."

Additionally, Kyo-ya asserted the Project was consistent with WSD objectives to "[p]rovide for the ability to renovate and redevelop existing structures which might otherwise experience deterioration" and allow for "creative development capable of substantially contributing to rejuvenation and revitalization of the [WSD]." Kyo-ya maintained that the Project was consistent with the WSD objective to "improve where possible mauka views . . . and a visual relationship with the ocean" and the objective to "[p]rovide people-oriented, interactive, landscaped open spaces to offset the high-density urban ambience."

objective

Finally, Kyo-ya argued that the impact of the encroachment into the Coastal Height Setback would be mitigated by the State of Hawai'i's planned Waikiki Beach Maintenance Project (Beach Maintenance Project) that is "expected to add roughly forty-feet (40') of dry beach to the beach fronting the [DHT]."

The Director held a public hearing on Kyo-ya's variance application and subsequently issued Findings of Fact, Conclusions of Law, and Decision and Order (Director's Decision or Decision) granting "Partial Approval" of Kyo-ya's variance application.

In his Decision, the Director described the variance application as a request to allow the Project to encroach approximately 74 percent into the Coastal Height Setback. The Director noted that in addition to the variance request from the Coastal Height Setback, the Project required additional approvals and permits, including a Planned Development-Resort (PD-R) Permit.

After analyzing the variance test's three requirements, the Director made the following Conclusions of Law:

1) There is evidence that the Applicant would be deprived of a reasonable use of the land or building if the provisions of the zoning code were strictly applied.

2) The request of the applicant is due to unique circumstances and not to general neighborhood conditions, and it does not question the reasonableness of the neighborhood zoning.

3) The request will not alter the essential character of the neighborhood nor be contrary to the intent and purpose of the zoning ordinance.

Accordingly, the Director granted partial approval of Kyo-ya's variance application to allow the Project to encroach approximately 74 percent into the Coastal Height Setback. The Director's partial approval was conditioned on, inter alia, submission of revised plans "which show the [Project] shall comply with the 1–1 (45-degree angle) coastal height setback as measured from . . . the approximate beach width intended in the [1965 Beach Agreement]."

Surfrider Foundation, Hawai'i's Thousand Friends, Ka Iwi Coalition, and KAHEA—The Hawaiian Environmental Alliance (collectively, Surfrider) filed a petition (Petition) to the Zoning Board of Appeals (ZBA) challenging the Director's findings and conclusion that Kyo-ya's request for a variance from the Coastal Height Setback met the requirements for issuance of a variance as set forth by the City Charter. In its position statement, Surfrider argued that the Director's conclusion that the Project satisfied the three requirements of RCCH § 6–1517 was based on erroneous finding of material facts.

Surfrider maintained that Kyo-ya did not meet the first requirement for issuance of a variance because "the record indicates that [Kyo-ya] would not be deprived of reasonable use of the property if the variance is denied." Surfrider contended that the "property is already occupied by a non-confirming, 8-story hotel building that can be fully renovated without the need for a variance under the [LUO]," that Kyo-ya was not entitled to achieve all of the applicable maximum development standards in the LUO, and that the 1968 Beach Agreement had not been realized.

Surfrider argued that Kyo-ya failed to meet the second requirement because the property is not particularly unique and is typical of the general conditions of ocean-front property in that part of Waikiki." Thus, Surfrider maintained that the reasonableness of the neighborhood zoning is in fact drawn into question by the variance request.

Surfrider argued the third requirement was also not met because "the request, if approved, will alter the essential character of the locality and is contrary to the intent and purpose of the zoning code." Surfrider pointed out that the Director's finding "did not even address whether the project is contrary to the intent and purpose of the WSD, whose objectives center on maintaining Waikiki's unique Hawaiian identity and reducing the apparent height of buildings."

The ZBA issued its Finding of Fact, Conclusions of Law, and Decision and Order (ZBA Order) on February 14, 2013. The ZBA found Surfrider "offered insufficient competent, reliable and probative evidence to establish that the Director's Decision was clearly erroneous" or that any material fact relied upon by the Director was clearly erroneous. The ZBA also found that Surfrider "offered no competent, reliable and probative evidence" to demonstrate the following:

> 103. That the 1965 Beach Agreement . . . was without legal effect, had terminated by its terms, or had been terminated by the parties or operation of law, [or] that the Director was precluded from considering, or in error for considering, the 1965 Beach Agreement to aid in his determination of what would be reasonable limits to the extent of variance.

Accordingly, the ZBA denied Surfrider's appeal of the Director's Decision. Surfrider timely filed a notice of appeal to the Circuit Court of the First Circuit (circuit court) from the ZBA Order.

Kyo-ya and Friends of Labor argued in their respective answering briefs that none of the alleged erroneous facts Surfrider identified were actually erroneous or materials to the Director's Decision. Kyo-ya asserted that contrary to Surfrider's contention, the ZBA's findings of fact were "more than adequate" to support its conclusion.

Kyo-ya also contended that Surfrider "misconstrue[d] the Director's Decision," which "did not grant a variance that is 'conditioned upon compliance with a hypothetical certified shoreline.'" Kyo-ya further argued that Surfrider's interpretation of case law as requiring the applicant to prove that it "would have been denied 'any reasonable use' but for" the variance is misleading, would eliminate the Director's discretion, and "would bring an end to land use in Hawai'i as it has been practiced since statehood."

After a hearing on Surfrider's appeal, the circuit court entered its Findings of Fact, Conclusions of Law, and Decision and Order Affirming the Decision and Order of the ZBA (circuit court's Order). The circuit court concluded that Surfrider "failed to satisfy [its] burden to demonstrate that the Director's action in partially approving the [Zoning] Variance Application was based on any erroneous findings of material fact."

Surfrider filed a notice of appeal from the circuit court's Order affirming the ZBA Order.

In its opening brief, Surfrider reiterates that is was Kyo-ya's burden to prove that its project satisfies all three requirements of the variance test and that the Director's decision "plainly indicate[s] that neither [Kyo-ya] nor the Director met [their] burden. Surfrider again points out that the 1965 Beach Agreement "does not provide a legal basis for a variance" from the LUO "which requires building setbacks to be measured from the current certified shoreline." Surfrider asks that this court reverse the circuit court's Order and the Director's Decision and deny Kyo-ya's variance application.

Kyo-ya responds that the Director did not rely on the 1965 Beach Agreement to justify the variance, but rather looked to the agreement after the Director determined "a variance was warranted" to determine the extent of the variance to grant. In any event, Kyo-ya argues that "even if Surfrider could somehow show that consideration of the 1965 Beach Agreement was improper, this would not be sufficient to reverse the ZBA." With respect to finding deprivation of "reasonable use," Kyo-ya argues "this was not a situation where Kyo-ya was simply trying to make a 'greater profit'; instead, the Director found that the variance was '*necessary* to maintain economic viability.' " Kyo-ya additionally reasserts arguments that it previously made in prior proceedings.

To satisfy the first variance requirement, the record must show that "the applicant would be deprived of the reasonable use of such land or building if the provisions of the zoning code were strictly applicable." RCCCH § 6–1517. "Reasonable use," within the meaning of the charter, "is not necessarily the use most desired by the property owner"; rather, to be deprived of the reasonable use of its property, the property owner must establish an inability to make reasonable use of its lands or building without the variance. *Korean Buddhist*, 87 Hawai'i at 234–5, 953 P.2d at 1332–33 (applicant failed to show that it could not make reasonable use of the land or its hall without the requested variance); *McPherson*, 67 Haw. at 605–06, 699 P.2d at 28 (finding the applicant had not established deprivation of reasonable use because the record was "devoid of any evidence that the applicant could not make reasonable use of the land or buildings in conformity with the [zoning code] or her pre-existing nonconforming use"); *see also* RCCCH § 6–1517 n.30 ("[W]ithin the meaning of the charter, "reasonable use" "is not the use most desired by the property owner; [the] property owner must show inability to make any reasonable use of his land without the variance.").

In this case, the Director concluded "[t]here is evidence that [Kyo-ya] would be deprived of a reasonable use of the land or building if the [Coastal Height Setback] was strictly applied" for the following reasons: the Project is necessary to maintain economic viability; the zoning code would reduce the buildable area of the DHT lot; if not allowed the variance, Kyo-ya would not be able to develop in accordance with the PD–R permit; the 1965 Beach Agreement would have resulted in a significantly different buildable area on the site; and the current beach replenishment project will extend the beach width by a minimum of 40 feet and the certified shoreline will likely reflect the beach expansion.

Surfrider challenges both the Director's ultimate conclusion that Kyo-ya satisfied this requirement of the variance text, as well as several of the underlying findings the Director based his conclusion upon. Surfrider specifically contends that the Director erroneously found that Kyo-ya would be denied reasonable use of land based on the 1965 Beach Agreement and that the Project "is necessary to maintain economic viability." Each of the Director's reasons for concluding that "there is evidence" that Kyo-ya would be deprived of the reasonable use of the land is addressed below.

The second requirement of the City Charter's variance test requires a showing that "the request of the applicant is due to unique circumstances and not the general conditions in the neighborhood, so that the reasonableness of the neighboring zoning is not drawn into question." RCCCH § 6–1517. The City Charter provides the meaning for unique circumstances: unique circumstances "has to do with *whether specific attributes of the parcel* are present that justify the request for a variance." RCCCH § 6–1517 n.30 (emphasis added)(citing *Korean Buddhist*, 87 Hawai'i 217, 953 P.2d 1315). Thus, an owner's unusual plans for a parcel do not, in themselves, constitute "unique circumstances." *McPherson*, 67 Haw. at 606, 699 P.2d at 28.

In his Decision, the Director concluded that Kyo-ya's variance application was based upon unique circumstances and not general neighborhood conditions and that the variance would not draw into question the reasonableness of the neighborhood zoning. In support of his conclusion, the Director made the following relevant findings: (1) the Project site is one of the narrowest along the shoreline in the area with an average lot depth of about 182 feet; (2) compared with the DHT tower and Surfrider Tower, the Banyan Wing generates the least amount of revenue per room; (3) the Project site is subject to the 100-foot coastal setback and an average 20-foot front yard setback along Kalakaua Avenue, thereby reducing the buildable area by an average of 120 feet; (4) the shoreline along the site is subject to drastic change by artificial means compared with natural beaches that cannot be altered; and (5) the Beach Maintenance Project may extend the beach by roughly 40 feet and thus reduce the Project's encroachments by 40 feet.

To satisfy the third requirement for granting a variance, the record must show that "the *request*, if approved, will not alter the essential character of the neighborhood nor be contrary to the intent and purpose of the zoning ordinance." RCCCH § 6–1517 (emphasis added). Thus, in this case, the pivotal determination is whether the 74.3 percent encroachment into the Coastal Height Setback would alter the essential character of the neighborhood or be contrary to the intent and purpose of the zoning ordinance. *See Korean Buddhist*, 87 Hawai'i at 234–35, 953 P.2d at 1332–

33 (court considered whether the increased height of the temple hall, not the temple hall itself, would alter the essential character of the neighborhood). Notably, in contrast to the first two requirements of the variance test requiring affirmative findings of deprivation of the reasonable use of the property and unique circumstances of the property, the third requirement necessitates factual findings that the variance will *not* alter the neighborhood's essential character and will *not* be contrary to the intent and purpose of the variance test.

Surfrider argues that the Director erroneously found that the Project, rather than the variance, would not alter the essential character of the neighborhood and would not be contrary to the intent and purpose of the zoning ordinance. Surfrider additionally argues that the Director did not address whether or not the 74.3 percent encroachment itself "might be contrary to the intent and purpose of the WSD." In response, the Appellees argue that the Director properly considered the intent of the zoning code, as well as the essential character of the neighborhood, and correctly concluded that the variance would be consistent with both.

Finally, even if consideration of the Project, rather than the effects of granting the variance application, were the correct measure for issuance of a variance, the Director's summary finding as to the three WSD objectives were clearly insufficient to support a conclusion that a 74 percent encroachment is not contrary to the intent and purpose of the Coastal Height Setback and the WSD. This is particularly true when the magnitude of the variance is significant. "[I]t is self-evident that the greater the disparity between the variance granted and the ordinance's restriction, the more compelling and specific the proofs must be that the grant of the variance" will not be contrary to the intent and purpose of the zoning ordinance. *N. Bergen Action Grp.*, 585 A.2d at 944.

As further explained by the Supreme Court of New Jersey,

> an impingement of the zoning restrictions may be of varying degrees [;][t]he less of an impact, the more likely the restriction is not that vital to valid public interest. Conversely, *where the change sought is substantial, the applicant will have to demonstrate more convincingly that the variance will not be contrary to the public good* and general welfare expressed in the ordinance.

Chirichello v. Zoning Bd. of Adjustment of Monmouth Beach, 78 M.J. 544, 397 A.2d 646 (1979) (emphasis added); *cf. McPherson*, 67 Haw. at 606, 699 P.2d at 29 (holding that the requisite evidence that must be adduced to satisfy the variance requirements involves proof of a rather narrow and somewhat technical set of facts).

In this case, because of the great disparity of Kyo-ya's request from the ordinance's restriction–an encroachment of 74.3 percent into the Coastal

Height Setback–"the more compelling and specific the proofs must be that the grant of the variance" will not be contrary to the intent and purpose of the zoning ordinance. Thus, the findings set forth in the Director's Decision are markedly inadequate in light of the magnitude of the requested encroachment into the Coastal Height Setback. Further, the lack of specificity in the Director's findings does not allow this court to conduct a meaningful review of the Director's Decision regarding this aspect of the third requirement of the variance test. *See also Gougeon v. Bd. of Adjustment of Stone Harbor*, 52 N.J. 212, 245 A.2d 7, 10 (1968) ("Supporting and explanatory facts and factual findings for the conclusions must be set forth. Unless such facts and findings are recited, a reviewing court cannot determine whether the Board acted properly and within the limits of its authority.")

In summary, in concluding that the Project was consistent with the intent and purpose of the ordinance, the Director erred for several reasons. First, the Director did not make findings demonstrating that the *variance request*—a 74 percent encroachment into the Coastal Height Setback—was not contrary to the intent and purpose of the WSD and the Coastal Height Setback, and instead the Director relied entirely on the Project's compliance with portions of three of fourteen WSD objectives. Secondly, the Director did not evaluate the impacts implicated by the variance request in relation to the purpose of the zoning ordinance. Third, the Director's analysis did not expressly take into consideration the *extent* of the variance requested, and thus his abbreviated findings were insufficient to conclude that a 74 percent encroachment into the Coastal Height Setback was not contrary to the intent and purpose of the zoning ordinance.

Accordingly, the Director's finding that the Project is consistent with "several important WSD objectives" misapprehended applicable law, and the Director's conclusion that a 74 percent encroachment into the Coastal Height Setback was not contrary to the intent and purpose of the zoning ordinance was not supported by findings that "specify the particular evidence which supports the granting of the variance" RCCCH § 6–1517. Consequently, the third requirement of the variance test was not satisfied.

In order for the Director to grant a variance request, the applicant must satisfy each requirement of the variance test. Here, none of the requirements were met. Accordingly, the circuit court's judgment, the ZBA Order, and the Director's Decision are reversed. *See Town v. Land Use Comm'n*, 55 Haw. 538, 550, 524 P.2d 84, 92 (1974).

Opinion Concurring in the Judgment by RECKTENWALD, C.J.

Respectfully, I concur in the judgment because the Director clearly erred in concluding that Kyo-ya would be deprived of the reasonable use of the property. I agree with the majority that the Director inappropriately relied on the 1965 Beach Agreement, and that the record did not support the Director's conclusion that a variance was necessary to maintain economic viability. Majority Opinion at 110–11, 113–15, 358 P.3d at 679–80, 682–84. In regard to the latter issue, I assume arguendo that the variance could be granted even if Kyo-ya would not otherwise have been deprived of *all* reasonable use of the property. Nevertheless, the evidence in the record on that point is inadequate.

The Director also considered the comparative undesirability of an alternative design that would not require a variance, which the Director characterized as a "monolithic wall." While I believe that this could be a legitimate consideration in evaluating the proposed variance, nevertheless the Director's decision cannot be affirmed in light of the errors cited above, particularly given the substantial extent of the variance approved by the Director. Majority Opinion at 100, 358 P.3d at 669. Because those errors require reversal, I would not reach the second or third variance requirements of RCCCH § 6–1517.

NOTES

1. Note the court's concern for an adequate record in *Surfrider*. Why do you suppose it is so critical here? Does the distinction the court draws between legislative and administrative actions offer a clue?

2. The *Surfrider* court appears to favor the proposed development on the subject property, yet it denies the variance. Why? If you represented the property owner, what would you ask the authorities to do?

3. The Standard Zoning Enabling Act's provision on variances is more general than the New Jersey statute cited in *Surfrider*. It provides that a variance should be granted "as will not be contrary to the public interest, where, owing to special conditions, a literal enforcement of the provisions of the ordinance will result in unnecessary hardship, and so that the spirit of the ordinance shall be observed and substantial justice done."

The leading case of *Otto v. Steinhilber*, 24 N.E.2d 851, 853 (N.Y.1939), interpreted language similar to the SZEA's as requiring the applicant to show:

> (1) the land in question cannot yield a reasonable return if used only for a purpose allowed in that zone; (2) that the plight of the owner is due to unique circumstances and not to the general conditions in the neighborhood which may reflect the unreasonableness of the zoning ordinance itself; and (3) that the use to be authorized by the variance will not alter the essential character of the locality.

Absent from the *Otto* criteria is the Standard Act's provision that authorizes a variance where the zoning "will result in unnecessary hardship." Some courts use the unnecessary hardship language to describe the overall showing of the elements that the applicant must make. For other courts, it specifically embodies the first element noted above and requires a showing that the applicant can make no reasonable return from the property as zoned. As with any delegation of legislative authority, standards must be sufficiently clear to guide the administrative decisionmaking and prevent the exercise of uncontrolled discretion. Most courts have found the "unnecessary hardship" standard to meet this test. *See* Juergensmeyer and Roberts, *Land Use Planning and Development Regulation Law* § 5.16 (3rd ed.2012).

The "unique" requirement is best typified by topographical difficulties, like those in *Surfrider*. What else might satisfy the requirement? If all, or most, surrounding property is devoted to commercial use, does an applicant with residentially zoned land meet the unique test? It may make a difference whether the commercial uses that the applicant points to are in a commercial zone. If they are, and the applicant's lot is a border lot, a variance is unlikely. Do you see why?

The "no reasonable return" showing is difficult to make. Is it justifiable to be so demanding? If an applicant can show that granting a variance would not adversely affect the public or harm the neighbors and that the property is unique, shouldn't a variance be granted? After all, if no one could be hurt, the present zoning, and therefore the hardship, is unnecessary. *See, e.g., Simplex Technologies, Inc. v. Town of Newington*, 766 A.2d 713 (N.H.2001).

4.   An applicant is entitled only to that degree of variance that will relieve the particular hardship. For example, if a homeowner can show that side yard requirements leave only eight feet in which to construct a garage and she needs nine, she should, at the most, get a variance of one foot.

5.   *Area and Dimensional Variances:* In many states variances are authorized where either "practical difficulties or unnecessary hardships" are shown. The disjunctive "or" has been used to establish a less stringent test for area variances where only practical difficulties must be established. *See Village of Bronxville v. Francis*, 150 N.Y.S.2d 906 (App.Div.1956), affirmed, 135 N.E.2d 724 (N.Y.1956); *City and Borough of Juneau v. Thibodeau*, 595 P.2d 626, 634 (Alaska 1979). Where "practical difficulties" are not further defined by statute, some courts use the following criteria:

> (1)   how substantial the variation is in relation to the requirement,
> (2)   the effect, if the variance is allowed, of the increased population density thus produced on available governmental facilities (fire, water, garbage and the like), (3) whether a substantial change will be produced in the character of the neighborhood or a substantial detriment to adjoining properties created, (4) whether the difficulty can be obviated by some method, feasible for the applicant to pursue, other than a variance, and (5) whether in view of the manner in which the difficulty arose and considering all of the above factors the interests of justice will be served by allowing the variance.

Wachsberger v. Michalis, 191 N.Y.S.2d 621, 624 (N.Y.Sup.1959). New York codified an area variance balancing formula in 1992 that is substantially similar to the above judicial test and eliminated "practical difficulties" from the formulation. *See* McKinney's N.Y. Village Law § 7–712–b3(b). In *Sasso v. Osgood*, 657 N.E.2d 254 (N.Y.1995), the Court of Appeals held that the new statute governing area variances requires the Zoning Board to engage in a balancing test, weighing the benefit to the applicant against the detriment to health, safety and welfare of the neighborhood or community if an area variance is granted, and the applicant need not show "practical difficulties."

Some states have gone in the other direction and have increased the difficulty of obtaining an area variance. In 1998, the Wisconsin Supreme Court reversed its long standing rule applying a lesser standard to area variances and applied the strict unnecessary hardship rule to all variances. *State v. Kenosha County Bd. of Adj.*, 577 N.W.2d 813 (Wis.1998). Three years later, the court reversed itself again going back to a lesser standard. Why do you suppose it did that?

6.   It is well established that variances are not to be granted for personal hardships, but rather for hardships generated by the land. Thus, parents who wanted a variance from setbacks to build a deck in their backyard for their child to play failed to meet the unnecessary hardship standard. *See Larsen v. Zoning Bd. of Adj. of Pittsburgh*, 672 A.2d 286, 290 (Pa.1996). The rule, however, may need to bend when the Fair Housing Act or the Americans with Disabilities Act is invoked. See the notes following the *Edmonds* case in Ch. 5.D. For example, a disabled person who wants to build a special ramp in her front yard to have access to her house may seek a variance from front yard setbacks. Since federal law requires cities to make "reasonable accommodations" for the disabled, must the variance be granted? Normally variances run with the land to new owners. If granted, will this variance also run or will it expire when the protected person no longer lives in the house? *See* Juergensmeyer and Roberts, *Land Use Planning and Development Regulation Law* § 5.17B (3rd ed.2012).

7.   What about variances to cure alleged hardships "after the fact?" In *Board of Adjustment v. McBride*, 676 S.W.2d 705 (Tex.App.1984), a landowner who had spent $75,000 on construction of a home that was 80 percent complete was told to stop because he was in violation of the zoning ordinance's 25-foot setback requirement. He then sought a variance. The court noted that compliance with the setback restrictions would adversely affect the structural integrity of the house, would cost at least $4,200, would render the house unsightly, and would serve no useful function. The court ordered the variance granted in view of uncontested findings showing hardship and evidence that the variance would not adversely affect the public interest. The landowner in *McBride* might be described as lucky, since self-created hardships normally are not grounds for a variance. *See Korean Buddhist Dae Won Sa Temple of Hawaii v. Sullivan*, 953 P.2d 1315 (Haw.1998), where a Buddhist Temple was constructed nine feet higher than the building permit allowed. Upon discovery of the violation, the Temple sought a variance to maintain the illegal structure. The request was denied and the roof was lowered.

8.   By express or implied authority, conditions can be attached to variances. They must relate to the land and be reasonable. Conditions on fencing and lighting are common. What about limiting the number of employees allowed to work on site? What about limiting employees to persons who are related to the owner? New Jersey courts have approved variances issued on the condition that if the neighbors offer to buy the property at its fair

market value, the variance will not issue. Why? Does this make sense? *Davis Enterprises v. Karpf*, 523 A.2d 137 (N.J.1987).

E. NONCONFORMITIES

The initial application of a zoning ordinance to an established community may result in some existing structures and uses no longer permitted in the new use districts in which they find themselves. The same potential for creating nonconformities exists upon a rezoning amendment, or in changing the list of permitted or special uses in an existing district.

To qualify for nonconformity status, a use or structure must have been legally commenced or used *ab initio*. A related problem arises for developments that are in the permitting process or are partially constructed when zoning changes occur. Vested rights rules, which grew directly from the law of nonconformities, cover this problem and are dealt with in Section F.

Some state zoning enabling acts provide expressly for such "nonconformities," prohibiting local governments from immediate elimination of nonconforming uses and buildings. *See, e.g.,* N.H.Stat. § 674:16. Even where not mandated by state law, most zoning ordinances permit nonconforming uses to continue. In the absence of such state restraints, can a local government immediately terminate nonconformities? In 1927 Los Angeles prohibited sanitariums from residential areas. Unlike most zoning ordinances, it did not have an exemption to protect sanitariums already established. An astonished state Supreme Court invalidated it, stating:

> The exercise of power in this instance is, on the whole, far more drastic than in those in which a mere right to engage in a particular business is restricted. We are asked to uphold a municipal ordinance which destroys valuable businesses, built up over a period of years. * * * The approval of such a doctrine would be a blow to rights in private property such as this court has never before witnessed. Only a paramount and compelling public necessity could sanction so extraordinary an interference with useful business.

Jones v. City of Los Angeles, 295 P. 14, 19 (Cal.1930).

Los Angeles' next effort to partially eliminate nonconformities, as the following case demonstrates, met with judicial success.

CITY OF LOS ANGELES V. GAGE

District Court of Appeal, Second District, Division 3, California, 1954.
127 Cal.App.2d 442, 274 P.2d 34.

VALLÉE, JUSTICE.

This appeal involves the constitutionality of the provisions of a zoning ordinance which require that certain nonconforming existing uses shall be discontinued within five years after its passage, as they apply to defendants' property.

Plaintiff brought this suit for an injunction to command defendants to discontinue their use of certain property for the conduct of a plumbing business and to remove various materials therefrom, and to restrain them from using the property for any purpose not permitted by the comprehensive zoning plan provisions of the Los Angeles Municipal Code. * * *

In 1930 Gage acquired adjoining lots 220 and 221 located on Cochran Avenue in Los Angeles. He constructed a two-family residential building on lot 221 and rented the upper half solely for residential purposes. He established a wholesale and retail plumbing supply business on the property. He used a room in the lower half of the residential building on lot 221 as the office for the conduct of the business, and the rest of the lower half for residential purposes for himself and his family; he used a garage on lot 221 for the storage of plumbing supplies and materials; and he constructed and used racks, bins, and stalls for the storage of such supplies and materials on lot 220. Later Gage incorporated the defendant company. The realty and the assets of the plumbing business were transferred to the company. The case is presented as though the property had been owned continuously from 1930 to date by the same defendant. The use of lots 220 and 221 begun in 1930, has been substantially the same at all times since.

In 1930 the two lots and other property facing on Cochran Avenue in their vicinity were classified in "C" zone by the zoning ordinance then in effect. Under this classification the use to which Gage put the property was permitted. Shortly after Gage acquired lots 220 and 221, they were classified in "C-3" zone and the use to which he put the property was expressly permitted. In 1936 the city council of the city passed Ordinance 77,000 which contained a comprehensive zoning plan for the city. Ordinance 77,000 re-enacted the prior ordinances with respect to the use of lots 220 and 221. In 1941 the city council passed Ordinance 85,015 by the terms of which the use of a residential building for the conduct of an office in connection with the plumbing supply business was permitted. Ordinance 85,015 prohibited the open storage of materials in zone "C-3" but permitted such uses as had been established to continue as nonconforming uses. The use to which lots 220 and 221 was put by defendants was a nonconforming use that might be continued. In 1946 the city council passed Ordinance 90,500. This ordinance reclassified lots 220 and 221 and other property fronting on Cochran Avenue in their vicinity from zone "C-3" to zone "R-4" (Multiple dwelling zone). Use of lots 220 and 221 for the conduct of a plumbing business was not permitted in zone "R-4." At the time Ordinance 90,500 was passed, and at all times since, the Los Angeles Municipal Code (§ 12.23 B & C) provided: "(a) The nonconforming use of a conforming building or structure may be continued, except that in the 'R' Zones any nonconforming commercial or industrial use of a residential building or residential accessory building shall be discontinued within five (5) years from June 1, 1946, or five (5) years from the date the use becomes nonconforming, whichever date is later. * * *

Prior to the passage of Ordinance 90,500, about 50% of the city had been zoned. It was the first ordinance which "attempted to zone the entire corporate limits of the city." Prior to its passage, several thousand exceptions and variances, were granted from restrictive provisions of prior ordinances, some of which permitted commercial use of property zoned for residential use, "and in some cases permitted the use of land for particular purposes like or similar to use of subject property which otherwise would have been prohibited." Under Ordinance 90,500, the uses permitted by these exceptions and variances that did not carry a time limit may be continued indefinitely.

The business conducted by Gage on the property has produced a gross revenue varying between $125,000 and $350,000 a year. If he is required to abandon the use of the property for his business, he will be put to the following expenses: (1) The value of a suitable site for the conduct of its business would be about $10,000; which would be offset by the value of $7,500 of the lot now used. (2) The cost incident to removing of supplies to another location and construction of the necessary racks, sheds, bins and stalls which would be about $2,500. (3) The cost necessary to expend to advertise a new location. (4) The risk of a gain or a loss of business while moving, and the cost necessary to reestablish the business at a new location, the amount of which is uncertain.

The court found: the business conducted by Gage has a substantial value; he could not, either prior to June 1, 1951, or at any time thereafter or in the future, remove the business without substantial loss or expense; the value of Gage's property has not been increased or stabilized by the passage of Ordinance 90,500, nor will observance or enforcement of the ordinance increase the value of the property; the use of the property for the purpose that it has been used continuously since 1930 will not adversely and detrimentally effect [sic] the use or value of other property in the neighborhood thereof; the use to which the property has been put by Gage has not been unsanitary, unsightly, noisy, or otherwise incompatible with the legal uses of adjoining property; Gage has not, nor will he in the future, operate to disturb the peace and quiet of the residents of the neighborhood as long as the property is operated substantially as it was operated at the date of the filing of the complaint; the use to which the property has been put does not interfere with the lawful and reasonable use of the streets and alleys in the vicinity by the residents in the neighborhood or others entitled thereto.

The court concluded: Gage became vested with the right to use the property for the purpose that it was used; insofar as the Los Angeles Municipal Code purports to require the abandonment of the use of the building on lot 221 as an office for the plumbing and plumbing supply business or the use of lot 220 for the open storage of plumbing supplies in the manner that it has been and is being used by Gage, it is void and of no legal effect; Ordinance 90,500 is void insofar as it affects Gage's use of the property in that it deprives him of a vested right to use the property for the purpose it has been used continuously since 1930 and deprives him of property without due process of law. Judgment was that plaintiff take nothing. Plaintiff appeals.

Plaintiff contends that the mandatory discontinuance of a nonconforming use after a fixed period is a reasonable exercise of the police power, and that on the agreed facts the Los Angeles ordinance is a valid exercise of such power as applied to Gage's property. Gage does not question the validity of the ordinance as a whole, but he contends it may not be constitutionally applied to require the removal of his existing business. He asserts that under *Jones v. City of Los Angeles*, the decision of the trial court was correct.

* * *

A nonconforming use is a lawful use existing on the effective date of the zoning restriction and continuing since that time in nonconformance to the ordinance. A provision permitting the continuance of a nonconforming use is ordinarily included in zoning ordinances because of the hardship and doubtful constitutionality of compelling the immediate discontinuance of nonconforming uses. It is generally held that a zoning ordinance may not operate to immediately suppress or remove from a particular district an otherwise lawful business or use already established therein.

No case seems to have been decided in this state squarely involving the precise question presented in the case at bar. Until recently zoning ordinances have made no provision for any systematic and comprehensive elimination of the nonconforming use. The expectation seems to have been that existing nonconforming uses would be of little consequence and that they would eventually disappear. The contrary appears to be the case. It is said that the fundamental problem facing zoning is the inability to eliminate the nonconforming use. The general purpose of present-day zoning ordinances is to eventually end all nonconforming uses. There is a growing tendency to guard against the indefinite continuance of nonconforming uses by providing for their liquidation within a prescribed period. It is said, "The only positive method of getting rid of non-conforming uses yet devised is to amortize a non-conforming building. That is, to determine the normal useful remaining life of the building and prohibit the owner from maintaining it after the expiration of that time." Crolly and Norton, *Termination of Nonconforming Uses*, 62 ZONING BULLETIN 1, Regional Plan Assn., June 1952.

Amortization of nonconforming uses has been expressly authorized by recent amendments to zoning enabling laws in a number of states. Ordinances providing for amortization of nonconforming uses have been passed in a number of large cities. The length of time given the owner to eliminate his nonconforming use or building varies with the city and with the type of structure.

* * *

The theory in zoning is that each district is an appropriate area for the location of the uses which the zone plan permits in that area, and that the existence or entrance of other uses will tend to impair the development and stability of the area for the appropriate uses. The public welfare must be considered from the standpoint of the objective of zoning and of all the property within any particular use district. It was not and is not contemplated that preexisting nonconforming uses are to be perpetual. The presence of any nonconforming use endangers the benefits to be derived from a comprehensive zoning plan. Having the undoubted power to establish residential districts, the legislative body has the power to make such classification really effective by adopting such reasonable regulations as would be conducive to the welfare, health, and safety of those desiring to live in such district and enjoy the benefits thereof. There would be no object in creating a residential district unless there were to be secured to those dwelling therein the advantages which are ordinarily considered the benefits of such residence. It would seem to be the logical and reasonable method of approach to place a time limit upon the continuance of existing nonconforming uses, commensurate with the investment involved and based on the nature of the use; and in cases of nonconforming structures, on their character, age, and other relevant factors.

Exercise of the police power frequently impairs rights in property because the exercise of those rights is detrimental to the public interest. Every zoning ordinance effects some impairment of vested rights either by restricting prospective uses or by prohibiting the continuation of existing uses, because it affects property already owned by individuals at the time of its enactment. In essence there is no distinction between requiring the discontinuance of a nonconforming use within a reasonable period and provisions which deny the right to add to or extend buildings devoted to an existing nonconforming use, which deny the right to resume a nonconforming use after a period of nonuse, which deny the right to extend or enlarge an existing nonconforming use, which deny the right to substitute new buildings for those devoted to an existing nonconforming use—all of which have been held to be valid exercises of the police power.

The distinction between an ordinance restricting future uses and one requiring the termination of present uses within a reasonable period of time is merely one of degree, and constitutionality depends on the relative importance to be given to the public gain and to the private loss. Zoning as it affects every piece of property is to some extent retroactive in that it applies to property already owned at the time of the effective date of the ordinance. The elimination of existing uses within a reasonable time does not amount to a taking of property nor does it necessarily restrict the use of property so that it cannot be used for any reasonable purpose. Use of a reasonable amortization scheme provides an equitable means of reconciliation of the conflicting interests in satisfaction of due process requirements. As a method of eliminating existing nonconforming uses it allows the owner of the nonconforming use, by affording an opportunity to make new plans, at least partially to offset any loss he might suffer. The loss he suffers, if any is spread out over a period of years, and he enjoys a monopolistic position by virtue of the zoning ordinance as long as he remains. If the amortization period is reasonable the loss to the owner may be small when compared with the benefit to the public. Nonconforming uses will eventually be eliminated. A legislative body may well conclude that the beneficial effect on the community of the eventual elimination of all nonconforming uses by a reasonable amortization plan more than offsets individual losses.

The ordinance in question provides, according to a graduated periodic schedule, for the gradual and ultimate elimination of all commercial and industrial uses in residential zones. These provisions require the discontinuance of nonconforming uses of land within a five-year period, and the discontinuance of nonconforming commercial and industrial uses of residential buildings in the "R" zones within the same five-year period. These provisions are the only ones pertinent to the decision in this case. However, it may be noted that other provisions of the ordinance require the discontinuance of nonconforming billboards and, in residential zones, the discontinuance of nonconforming buildings and of nonconforming uses of nonconforming buildings, within specified periods running from 20 to 40 years according to the type of building construction.

We have no doubt that Ordinance 90,500, in compelling the discontinuance of the use of defendants' property for a wholesale and retail plumbing and plumbing supply business, and for the open storage of plumbing supplies within five years after its passage, is a valid exercise of the police power. Lots 220 and 221 are several blocks from a business center and it appears that they are not within any reasonable or logical extension of such a center. The ordinance does not prevent the operation of defendants' business; it merely restricts its location. Discontinuance of the nonconforming use requires only that Gage move his plumbing business to property that is zoned for it. Such property can be found within a half mile of Gage's property. The cost of moving is $5,000, or less than 1% of Gage's minimum gross business for five years, or less than half of 1% of the mean of his gross business for five years. He has had eight years within which to move. The property is usable for residential purpose. Since 1930 lot 221 has been used for residential purposes. All of the land within 500 feet of Gage's property is now improved and used for such purposes. Lot 220, now unimproved, can be improved for the same purposes.

We think it apparent that none of the agreed facts and none of the ultimate facts found by the court justify the conclusion that Ordinance 90,500, as applied to Gage's property, is clearly arbitrary or unreasonable, or has no substantial relation to the public's health, safety, morals, or general welfare, or that it is an unconstitutional impairment of his property rights.

It is enough for us to determine and we determine only that Ordinance 90,500 of the city of Los Angeles, insofar as it required the discontinuance of Gage's wholesale and retail plumbing business on lots 220 and 221 within five years from the date of its passage, is a constitutional exercise of the police power.

NOTES

1.   An activity can be enjoined by a court if found to be a private nuisance in a suit initiated by neighbors, but it is easier on the neighbors if the town council simply legislates offensive operations out of business. Los Angeles did that when it banned existing brickyards from residential areas. Both the state and federal supreme courts upheld that ordinance when challenged by a brickyard owner whose property dropped in value from $800,000 to $60,000. *See Hadacheck v. Sebastian*, 239 U.S. 394 (1915), set out in Ch. 1. The extent of a state's power to immediately terminate uses, and whether it matters that the use is a nuisance, will be considered further in Chapter 3 when we deal with constitutional limitations.

2.   The *Gage* court stops considerably short of endorsing the immediate termination of such uses as Gage's, holding only that five years was enough in this case. In upholding this delayed termination of Gage's plumbing business, the court is swayed by the economic (and monopolistic) success of the use and the relatively low costs of relocating it. But does it pick and choose its facts too selectively? Should it have deferred to the trial court's findings? Note that the court all but characterizes the business as nuisance-like, despite evidence that the business is apparently conducted quietly and without demonstrable adverse land use consequences for the neighboring properties.

3.   The *Gage* court distinguishes between nonconforming uses and nonconforming structures, noting that the fact that the building presently in use as a plumbing business is usable as a conforming house in the residence

district is one of the factors it considered in deciding the case. Presumably, the sanitariums in the *Jones* case (mentioned in *Gage* and in this section's headnote) were not residential-like structures. If they were "halfway houses" for those with histories of drug abuse, mental illness or alcoholism, would the *Gage* technique work?

4.   Five years was reasonable in *Gage*. What about other uses, like sanitariums? Should a use be treated differently from a structure for purposes of determining a proper termination period? If so, why? What special problems can you foresee in terminating a structure? *See City of La Mesa v. Tweed and Gambrell Planing Mill*, 304 P.2d 803 (Cal.App.1956) (five years insufficient for building with remaining economic life of 20 years).

5.   What considerations go into deciding the reasonableness of the amortization period?

6.   Most Courts uphold the use of amortization periods, *see Baird v. City of Melissa*, 170 S.W.3d 921 (Tex.App.2005) (ordinances requiring termination of nonconforming uses under reasonable conditions are within the scope of municipal police power) and *National Advertising Co. v. City of Raleigh*, 947 F.2d 1158, 1164, n. 6 (4th Cir.1991) (collecting cases), and limit their review to the reasonableness of specific clauses in as applied challenges. *See Board of Zoning Appeals, Bloomington v. Leisz*, 702 N.E.2d 1026 (Ind.1998). Pennsylvania Courts, however, invalidate amortization provisions on their face based on a provision in the state constitution. *See PA Northwestern Distributors, Inc. v. Zoning Hearing Board*, 584 A.2d 1372 (Pa.1991) (finding ordinance with 90-day amortization period for adult book stores a facial taking under the state constitution). Factors to be considered in determining "reasonableness" include: nature of the business; improvements to the subject property; character of the neighborhood; and detriment caused to the property owner. *See Suffolk Asphalt Supply, Inc. v. Board of Trustees of the Village of Westhampton Beach*, 872 N.Y.S.2d 516, 518 (App.Div.2009).

7.   Signs, from enormous billboards to small flashing temporary ones, are the targets of many amortization ordinances. How much time do signs get? *See Art Neon Co. v. City and County of Denver*, 488 F.2d 118, 122–23 (10th Cir.1973) (amortization period of five years valid for nonconforming signs; mere thirty days valid for flashing, blinking, fluctuating, animated, or portable signs). Federal law inhibits the use of amortization on certain federally funded highways by threatening withdrawal of federal money. *See* note 11 below. A number of states have enacted legislation effectively eliminating amortization of signs by requiring compensation be paid before sign removal. *See, e.g.,* Md. Code, Local Gov't § 1–1305; Miss. Code. § 49–23–17. The outdoor advertising industry heavily lobbies state legislatures to ban amortization. *See, e.g.,* N.C. Gen. Stat. § 160A–199 (banning amortization of outdoor signs).

8.   Amortization and other regulations of signs have produced numerous challenges on First as well as Fifth Amendment grounds. *See, e.g., Eller Media Co. v. City of Houston*, 101 S.W.3d 668 (Tex.App.2003) (no First or Fifth Amendment violation). One problem in a Fifth Amendment takings challenge

involves determining the appropriate unit of property to measure the loss. With respect to a sign company facing a ban on signs in parts of a town, does it make a difference if you look at each individual sign as the property taken, lump together all signs in the town, or look to all signs the company has in the regional or national market? *See Naegele Outdoor Advertising, Inc. v. City of Durham*, 803 F.Supp. 1068 (M.D.N.C.1992) (using regional market and finding no takings). We will look at these issues in more detail in Chapter 3.

Assume a sign amortization ordinance was adopted on January 1, 2016, declaring billboards illegal and granting the owners five years to remove them. Assume also that the statute of limitations to challenge an ordinance is 90 days. If a billboard company wants or wanted to challenge the ordinance, did it need to file before April 1, 2016 or does it have until December 31, 2020? See *infra*, Ch. 2.L.3.

9.   Amortization is not the only limitation nonconforming uses face. Most ordinances provide that nonconforming structures may not be repaired or enlarged so as to extend their "lives." Ordinances may allow conversion to another use, but not if it is deemed more harmful or intense. In *Triangle Fraternity v. City of Norman, ex rel. Norman Bd. of Adj.*, 63 P.3d 1 (Okla.2002), a change from use of a house as retired women's boarding house to a fraternity house was permitted, but in *Perkins v. Madison County Livestock & Fair Association*, 613 N.W.2d 264 (Iowa 2000), converting nonconforming rodeo arena to an auto racetrack was deemed impermissible expansion. In Pennsylvania, the "natural expansion" of a nonconforming use is constitutionally protected. *See Sweeney v. Zoning Hearing Bd.*, 626 A.2d 1147 (Pa.1993). What about replacing a 675 sq. ft. house with a 3600 sq. ft. house on a non-conforming lot? *See Bjorklund v. Zoning Bd. of Appeals of Norwell*, 450 Mass. 357, 878 N.E.2d 915, 919 (2008).

Most ordinances also provide that nonconforming structures which are partially destroyed by fire—usually 50 percent or more—may not be reconstructed except according to the then-existing zoning regulations. *See City of Emporia Bd. of Zoning Appeals v. Mangum*, 556 S.E.2d 779 (Va.2002). What are the rights of homeowners who have had houses destroyed by fire or flood on lots which now have but a fraction of the minimum area now required for a single-family house in that zone?

Finally, a nonconforming use that has been discontinued cannot be recommenced. This may require an assessment of intent to abandon, and a temporary cessation is likely not fatal. *See Hartley v. City of Colorado Springs*, 764 P.2d 1216 (Colo.1988) (no showing of intent required). *See also* Eric J. Strauss and Mary M. Giese, *Elimination of Nonconformities: The Case of Voluntary Discontinuance*, 25 URB.LAW. 159 (1993).

10.   There are a host of administrative problems involved in terminating nonconformities according to useful life, value and other standards over time. Someone must first find, then keep track of each nonconformity, as well as make some determination of value and useful life.

11. The Federal Highway Beautification Act of 1965, 23 U.S.C.A. §§ 131–35 mandated that states either make provision for the control and removal of outdoor advertising signs erected within 660 feet of interstate or primary highway rights-of-way or forfeit federal highway funds. In 1977, the Federal Highway Administration relaxed rules on clearing vegetation in the public right of way to improve visibility. Congress also has lessened the Act's effectiveness by amendment. In 1978, Congress amended the act to require compensation for removed billboards. The act provides:

(g) Just compensation shall be paid upon the removal of any outdoor advertising sign, display, or device lawfully erected under State law and not permitted under subsection (c) of this section, whether or not removed pursuant to or because of this section. The Federal share of such compensation shall be 75 per centum. Such compensation shall be paid for the following:

(A) The taking from the owner of such sign, display, or device of all right, title, leasehold, and interest in such sign, display or device; and

(B) The taking from the owner of the real property on which the sign, display, or device is located, of the right to erect and maintain such signs, displays, and devices thereon.

(k) Subject to compliance with subsection (g) of this section for the payment of just compensation, nothing in this section shall prohibit a State from establishing standards imposing stricter limitations with respect to signs, displays, and devices on the Federal-aid highway systems than those established under this section.

On the basis of these provisions, billboard owners protested the removal of nonconforming signs under a zoning ordinance banning billboards throughout the town of Southampton, New York, arguing that under the federal act compensation must be paid. In *Suffolk Outdoor Advert. Co. v. Town of Southampton*, 60 N.Y.2d 70 (1983), the New York Court of Appeals held that the federal act did not preempt the town's power to require removal of billboards without compensation. The federal act is a taxing and spending measure, and as such does not prohibit removal without compensation through amortization. Although it may cause withholding of federal funds from a state failing to pay compensation, states are free to permit municipalities to provide for uncompensated removal of billboards. Five years after *Suffolk*, however, the New York legislature passed amendments requiring compensation for the removal of billboards covered by the Highway Beautification Act. *See* N.Y. High. Law § 88; *Town of Macedon v. Hsarman*, 844 N.Y.S.2d 825, 831 (Sup.Ct.2007) (noting that *Suffolk* was legislatively overruled by the 1989 amendments to N.Y. High. Law § 88).

For jurisdictions unwilling to amortize signs as non-conforming uses or to wait out the amortization period, the problem in removing them is coming up with the money to compensate. The Intermodal Surface Transportation Infrastructure Act of 1991 made funds available for the first time since 1982, but a 1992 amendment gave states the option of using the funds for other transportation purposes, 23 U.S.C.A. § 131(n). Unsurprisingly, nonconforming billboards have not disappeared. In 1995, for example, only 503 were removed. The Transportation Equity Act for the 21st Century (TEA-21), enacted in 1998, set aside $3.7 billion for "transportation enhancement" programs, which include billboard removal among a host of other programs. However, based on past experience, little of that money will be spent on billboard removal. Should it be? Are there more pressing needs? Should the federal statutory compensation requirement be repealed?

Removal of the federal ban would not help local governments in states like Virginia, Va. Code § 33.2–1217 (E) and North Carolina, which ban amortization. N.C.Gen.Stat. § 153A–143 (d) provides:

> No county may enact or amend an ordinance of general applicability to require the removal of any nonconforming, lawfully erected off-premises outdoor advertising sign without the payment of monetary compensation to the owners of the off-premises outdoor advertising, * * * .

F. VESTED RIGHTS

Despite the sustained effort of regulators to do away with nonconformities (see the preceding section), they persist, and such status affords a property owner significant protection. However, as zoning controls change over time, and often in response to a specific development proposal, it is critical to know whether, and if so when, developments in the permitting process or projects partially constructed are subject to new regulations.

One of the most vexing problems in comprehensively amending a zoning ordinance is the public notice it provides the private landowner contemplating development. Public discussion proposing a zoning classification from a use permitting reasonably intensive development (multiple family residential or commercial, for example) to something like single-family or agricultural classifications, or the reduction of permitted uses in existing zone classifications, is likely to result in a "race" by the landowner to commence the still-permitted, more intense development—or to change position sufficiently to acquire vested rights to proceed in the face of any subsequently enacted amendment making such development illegal. This is particularly true if the amendment process is prolonged by multiple hearings and/or required comprehensive plan changes in advance of the zoning amendment. It is for these reasons that many local governments attempt to preserve the status quo pending such amendments by means of moratoria and other interim land use controls in order to prevent the comprehensive amendments from being rendered ineffective through the grandfathering in of a host of new nonconformities. Interim planning controls and moratoria, and their relationship to the vested rights issue are considered in Chapter 7.

Specific development proposals often trigger rezoning petitions. Once neighbors learn that a big box superstore is planned next door or a nearby parcel of open land is about to be developed and that existing zoning permits the proposed uses, they may petition the city to downzone the land. Then, the race is on.

The point at which a developer-landowner has proceeded sufficiently far enough with a project so that the right to proceed is "vested" is a land management problem of vast proportions. For an analysis of the theories upon which courts have rested decisions for and against vested rights generally, together with a discussion of the range of governmental actions held to vest landowner rights, *see* David L. Callies, Daniel J. Curtin, Jr., and Julie A. Tappendorf, *Bargaining for Development: A Handbook on Development Agreements, Annexation Agreements, Land Development Conditions, Vested Rights, and the Provision of Public Services* (2003). *See also* Kupchack, Kugle & Thomas, *Arrow of Time: Vested Rights, Zoning Estoppel and Development Agreements*, 27 U.HAW.L.REV. 17 (2004); Charles L. Siemon, Wendy U. Larsen and Douglas R. Porter, *Vested Rights: Balancing Public and Private Development Expectations* (1982).

GALLUP WESTSIDE DEVELOPMENT, LLC V. CITY OF GALLUP, A MUNICIPAL CORPORATION

Court of Appeals of New Mexico, 2003.
135 N.M. 30, 84 P.3d 78, certiorari denied January 9, 2004.

CASTILLO, JUDGE.

In spite of its long history and abundant record, this case has but one determinative question: Does Gallup Westside Development. LLC, (Westside) have vested rights in the development of Unit 3 of the Mentmore East subdivision, thus precluding the City of Gallup (City) from making any changes to the terms of an expired Assessment Procedure Agreement (APA) pertaining to Unit 3 of the subdivision? This case began in 1997, when the City approved a letter agreement (1997 Letter Agreement) amending and extending the APA. After a number of intervening events, the City's decision was appealed to the district court. Acting in its appellate capacity, the district court issued an order reversing the City's decision and issued a writ of mandamus requiring the City to comply with the terms of the original APA without amendment. The City contends that the district court erred when (1) it substituted its judgment for that of the Planning and Zoning Commission (PZC) and City, (2) it issued the writ, and (3) it made findings of fact and conclusions of law. We hold that Westside has no vested rights. Accordingly, we quash the writ of mandamus issued in the district court and reverse its final order.

I. BACKGROUND

In 1975, final plats for Phase 1 development of a subdivision known as Mentmore East were submitted to and approved by the City, conditioned upon the developers' making certain infrastructure improvements. Phase 1 development was divided into Units 1, 2, and 3, each platted separately, with Unit4 added later. The original developers, predecessors-in-interest to Westside, executed an APA for Units 1, 2, and 3 with the City and a separate APA for Unit 4.

The APA sets forth procedures by which required improvements are to be installed, restricts the sale of any lot prior to the completion of infrastructure improvements, and provides that plat approval is on the express condition that developers comply with conditions in the APA; it also allows for the City to vacate the plats if conditions are not met. Additionally, the APA provides that developers can make infrastructure improvements "only after approval of the plans and specifications for such improvements by the public works director of the city of Gallup, such plans and specifications to be in accordance with any plans and specifications then in use by the city of Gallup." Paragraph 6 of the APA states that the agreement is to remain in effect for twenty years from the date of its March 10, 1975, execution, or until March 10, 1995. The APA was recorded in 1975. Development proceeded on Units 1, 2, and 4.

The development of Unit 3 is the subject of this appeal. Unit 3 was originally platted with 135 single-family residences and a separate 12.85-acre parcel. In 1980, Unit 3 was split into separate ownership. In 1981, all of Unit 3, including the 12.85-acre parcel was rezoned to allow development of a mobile home subdivision. Title to the 135 lots passed to Westside when it was formed in 1996; the district court, in 1999, quieted title to the 12.85-acre parcel in the name of Hadden [84 P.3d 81] Construction Co., Inc. (HCI). The owner of HCI is the sole owner of Westside.

Although initial grading of roads in Unit 3 was done in the 1970s and some electric utilities were installed in platted easements in the rear of Unit 3 lots abutting Unit 4, it was not until 1996, when Westside requested it, that anyone requested a site development review in order to develop Unit 3. The parties agree that by then, the APA had expired. Rather than vacate the original plat, City staff recommended to the PZC that the APA be extended and amended to bring the development in line with the then current building standards and practices.

At its May 14, 1997, meeting, the PZC agreed with the City staff's recommendation and approved the 1997 Letter Agreement extending and amending the APA. While Westside did not oppose the extension of the APA's effective date, it strongly opposed other provisions of the 1997 Letter Agreement, including the relocation of utilities to the front of lots, the retention of a minimum of 3.5 acres by the City for a park, and certain

[handwritten margin note: Wanted APA extended]

drainage and sidewalk requirements. Westside did not execute the 1997 Letter Agreement, nor did it appeal the PZC's approval.

One year later, Westside renewed its application for site development review and proposed its own version of a letter agreement. The PZC voted to deny Westside's version of a letter agreement, thereby reaffirming its approval of the 1997 Letter Agreement. Westside appealed to the City Council (hereafter referred to as City). On August 25, 1998, the City, after a public hearing, voted to affirm the decision of the PZC. Westside then appealed to the district court. Because technical problems with the tape recorder prevented the district court from reviewing the complete record of the hearing by the City, the district court remanded the case to the City for a de novo hearing on Westside's application.

The rehearing held on December 14, 1999, lasted three hours. Prior to the rehearing, Westside had submitted to the City more than 760 Pages of record with a total of seventy-eight exhibits, including maps, plans, and plats. The City heard testimony from Westside, a former City engineer, the City planner, and thirteen citizens. Once again, the City affirmed the PZC's approval of the 1997 Letter Agreement]

[handwritten: City Denovo hearing]

II.   DISCUSSION

A.   FINAL ORDER REVERSING THE CITY'S DECISION

2.   VESTED RIGHTS

In reversing the City's decision, the district court concluded that Developers "acquired vested rights in the approved subdivision." Vested rights protect a developer from retroactive application of newly adopted regulations. *Brazos Land Inc. v. Bd. of County Comm'rs,* 115 N.M. 168, 170, 848 P.2d 1095, 1097 (Ct.App.1993). Developers argue that their vested rights protect them from having to comply with regulations adopted after the City gave the subdivision final plat approval in 1975. Therefore, they contend, their vested rights justify the district court's determination that the 1975 APA must be extended without amendments.

We view the question of vested rights as determinative in this case. There is a two-pronged test for vested rights in New Mexico: First, there must be approval by a regulatory body; second, there must be a substantial change in position in reliance thereon. *Brazos Land, Inc.,* 115 N.M. at 170, 848 P.2d at 1097: *In re Sundance Mountain Ranches, Inc.,* 107 N.M. 192, 194, 754 P.2d 1211, 1213 (Ct.App.1988). We conclude that Developers failed to meet either prong of the test.

[handwritten: 2 prong test]

The City did give final plat approval to the subdivision. Nevertheless, the first prong of the vested rights test is not met as long as revocation of that approval remains a possibility. *Parker v. Bd. of County Comm'rs,* 93 N.M. 641, 644, 603 P.2d 1098, 1101 (1979) ("We cannot equate the approved subdivision plat in this case with vested property rights, as the approval

Rights were conditional And revocable

was conditioned upon performance by the subdivider."); *cf. In re Sundance Mountain Ranches, Inc.,* 107 N.M. at 194–95, 754 P.2d at 1213–14 (stating that rights vested in a subdivider after compliance with statutory prerequisites and a determination by the board of county commissioners that compliance actually occurred). Here, the final approval of the subdivision plat in 1975 was expressly conditioned on compliance with the terms of the APA. Because the City was able to vacate the plat if conditions were not met, Developers did not have vested rights in the property. We acknowledge that Developers on appeal argue approval of the plat was not conditional. Paragraph 3 of the APA specifically states that plat approval is on the expressed condition, that [Developers] shall fulfill and comply with each and every condition contained within this agreement. It is expressly agreed that upon the failure of [Developers] to fulfill and comply with each and every provision of this agreement, the plat hereby approved will be vacated.

Given this express conditional language of the APA, we reject Developers' argument.

The language in paragraph 6 of the APA further supports this conclusion. Pursuant to paragraph 6, the APA expired by its own terms on March 10, 1995. The district court, however, construed the agreement in such a way as to exclude paragraph 6. In interpreting a written contract, each part must be given meaning and significance according to its importance to the contract as a whole. *Bank of N.M. v. Shaler,* 102 N.M. 78, 79, 691 P.2d 465, 466 (1984); *Nearburg v. Yates Petroleum Corp.,* 1997–NMCA–069, ¶ 28, 123 N.M. 526, 943 P.2d 560; 13 Eugene McQuillin, *The Law of Municipal Corporations* § 37.130, at 346–48 (3d ed.1997). Public improvement contracts are "construed with reference to the ordinance authorizing the improvement." *McQuillin, supra,* at 347.

According to the pertinent subdivision regulations that are part of the record, a developer must provide assurances for the installation of public improvements by one of three methods: (1) installation prior to final plat approval, (2) posting bond and installing the improvements within one year after final plat approval, or (3) completing an approved assessment procedure. Gallup, N.M., Ordinance, Subdivision Regulations, § IX (3) (1975). Here, the third method was chosen. The first two methods require action before or within one year. It is reasonable to construe the third method to at least require performance under the approved assessment procedure within a reasonable time; and in the present case, twenty years, and no more, is undoubtedly a reasonable time. *W. Commerce Bank v. Gillespie,* 108 N.M. 535, 538, 775 P.2d 737, 740 (1989) (holding that where no time for performance is specified, law implies a reasonable time for performance). The district court's interpretation renders paragraph 6 irrelevant and meaningless. This Court declines to adopt such a construction of the APA. *Brooks v. Tanner,* 101 N.M. 203, 206, 680 P.2d

343, 346 (1984) (refusing to adopt a proposed construction that would render meaningless an important contractual phrase).

Even if the first prong had been met, the second prong of the test requires a substantial change in position in reliance on the approval. Developers contend that had they known the 135 lots could not be developed without the imposition of further requirements or that the City would expect a park, the price they paid for the land would have been considerably less. Among the district court's findings were that Developers "substantially relied on the approved plats and paid higher prices for their parts of Unit 3 than they would have if the plats had not been approved." We do not agree with the district court that the purchase price, in this case, resulted in substantial reliance. *Purchase Price ≠ Sub. reliance*

Our review of the record discloses no evidence that Developers expended money other than the purchase price in reliance on plat approval. The purchase of land, by itself, does not confer vested rights upon the purchaser. *N. Ga. Mountain Crisis Network. Inc.* v. *City of Blue Ridge*, 248 Ga.App. 450, 546 S.E.2d 850, 853 (2001). Nor does the record show that Developers incurred extensive contractual obligations pursuant to the purchase or otherwise substantially changed their position in reliance on plat approval. *See Brazos Land, Inc.,* 115 N.M. at 170, 848 P.2d at 1097 (concluding vested rights did not exist where developer showed no change in position); 8 Eugene McQuillin, *The Law of Municipal Corporations* § 25.157, at 575–80 (3d ed.2000) (discussing and compiling case law on how substantial reliance on a permit protects permittee from subsequent zoning laws). In this case, the APA expired in 1995; title to the 135 lots transferred to Westside in 1996; and the 12.85-acre parcel was not quieted in HCI's name until 1999. From this timetable, it is clear that at the time of purchase, Developers were or should have been aware of the conditional language in the APA and its expiration date. Developers argue that they changed their position by paying an excess purchase price and donating a park. We see no substantial evidence in the record that ties such asserted actions to any government assurances to support reasonable, actual reliance or change in position. *See Brazos Land, Inc.,* 115 N.M. at 170, 848 P.2d at 1097 (holding no finding of substantial reliance or change in position); *see also Debold* v. *Township of Monroe,* 110 N.J.Super. 287, 265 A.2d 399, 403–04 (Ch.Div.1970) (rejecting factually and legally that the developer's excess purchase price estopped municipality from applying later zoning).

Developers appear to rely on some statements made by City staff in briefing memos to elected officials in arguing their vested rights position. Although this issue is not separately briefed and no authority is cited for it, Developers appear to contend that those statements establish that they in fact have vested rights. We disagree. Developers' argument is akin to applying estoppel against a government or applying a theory of judicial admissions. Yet, estoppel against a government is exceedingly difficult to prove. *See Lopez* v. *State,* 1996–NMSC–071, ¶¶ 18, 20, 122 N.M. 611, 930 P.2d 146. There is no suggestion that the elements were proved here. Similarly, the theory of judicial admissions contains its own requirements, including that admission be that of a party and not be an opinion. *See Lebeck* v. *Lebeck,* 118 N.M. 367, 372, 881 P.2d 727, 732 (Ct.App.1994). The memo by staff was accompanied by a supporting letter containing a caveat that a court may ultimately disagree. We conclude that the evidence presented to the City supports the conclusion that Developers do not have vested rights in Unit 3 and are therefore not entitled under a vested rights theory to have the APA extended as originally written.

Because, as we have determined, Developers did not have vested rights in development of Unit 3, the district court acted improperly in ordering the City to approve an extension of the APA without amendment. Accordingly, there is no basis for the writ of mandamus; hence, we need not and do not address the City's points on appeal regarding the trial courts exceeding its writ of mandamus authority.

We quash the writ of mandamus and reverse the district court's final order. Finally, we affirm the City's authority to offer to extend the APA on terms other than the original terms of the agreement.

NOTES

1.   The *Lake Bluff* court notes that "in order for a developer's rights to vest, the developer must submit an application for a building permit which conforms to the zoning or building code requirements in effect at the time of the application." *Lake Bluff,* 197 Wis.2d at 177. But what about large projects in multi-permit jurisdictions? *See* Grayson P. Hanes and J. Randall Minchew, *On Vested Rights to Land Use and Development,* 46 WASH. & LEE L.REV. 373, 405 (1989).

2.   The California Supreme Court has suggested that special or conditional use permits might be treated differently in a vested rights analysis. *See Avco Community Developers, Inc. v. South Coast Regional Commission,* 17 Cal.3d 785 (1976). Why would this be so?

3.   Wisconsin follows the early vesting rule: a developer's rights vest when the developer applies for a building permit which complies with the applicable regulations. Other jurisdictions, including California, follow the late vesting rule, which specifies that a developer's rights have not vested until a valid building permit has been issued. Under this approach, a developer may be required to put at risk large sums of money without being assured of protection from subsequent changes in legal requirements. Further, the permit must be lawfully granted, a fact which may not be capable of discernment except through legal proceedings. In *Russian Hill Improvement Ass'n v. Board of Permit Appeals,* 423 P.2d 824 (Cal.1967), a zoning ordinance change, which was passed while an appeal from the permit bureau's issuance of building

permit was still pending, superseded the actions of the permit board because the permit was "not lawfully granted" until all administrative action had been completed.

4. *Final discretionary approval.* As we saw earlier, *supra* Section C.3, most states allow zoning by referendum. At what point in the permit processing stage is a development project immune from revocation by referendum? The issue arose in *County of Kauai v. Pacific Standard Life Insurance Co.*, 653 P.2d 766 (Haw.1982). In February, 1979, at the behest of a developer seeking to build a large resort, the County of Kauai, Hawaii, rezoned land from open space and agricultural use to resort use. A month later, a citizen organization, the Committee to Save Nukolii (the name of the site that was the subject of the development proposal and the name by which the case is known) started a drive to repeal the rezoning by referendum. In December, 1979, the developer applied for a permit and in January, 1980, the county certified the referendum petition and placed the issue on the November, 1980 general election ballot. Nonetheless, the county, advised by counsel that the certification of the petition did not suspend the rezoning, proceeded with the permitting process, issuing a building permit for a 350-room hotel on November 3, 1980. On November 4, the voters approved the referendum repealing the rezoning on which the permit issued the day before was based.

The state supreme court rejected the developer's claim that the permits it had obtained and the expenditures it had made ($159,798) conferred on it a vested right.

> Despite a plethora of case law on the subject of zoning estoppel, few courts have applied the theory in the unique context of zoning referenda. "[T]he critical questions become: (1) What reliance is 'good faith'; (2) what sums are 'substantial'; (3) what constitutes 'assurance' by officials; and (4) when does a developer have a right to rely on such assurances?" Callies, *Land Use: Herein of Vested Rights, Plans, and the Relationship of Planning and Controls*, 2 U.HAWAII L.REV. 167, 174 (1979). Because the logical analytical progression begins with the last two questions, we shall consider these together first.

> Final discretionary action constitutes official assurance for zoning estoppel purposes. This rule acknowledges the incremental nature of the modern development process and strikes the appropriate balance between competing private and public interests. It preserves government control over development until the government's own process for making land use decisions leaves nothing to discretion.

> Certification of a petition triggers the referendum mechanism. Until that point, the complicated modern permit system controls development. Zoning estoppel analysis therefore must focus on the status of government approval for any proposed project at the time the referendum mechanism is activated.

If a developer obtains final discretionary action for a project under the permit system while the referendum mechanism remains dormant, then . . . the common law of zoning estoppel will recognize that action as official assurance on which a developer has a right to rely. The law looks to the conduct of the parties in light of the operative procedures for advancing development. Certification of a referendum does not intervene retroactively into the permit system.

If a developer has not received final discretionary action under the permit system before the referendum mechanism is operative, then the estoppel analysis will recognize that timely intervention of the referendum procedure has made discretionary approval or disapproval of underlying zoning an integral part of the development process as applied to that project. Any administrative or council approvals given after certification and before a referendum vote have no estoppel effect.

We hold, as a matter of law that any approvals or permits for a proposed development issued after certification of a referendum to repeal a zoning ordinance affecting the project site but before termination of the referendum procedure do not constitute official assurance on which the developer has a right to rely. Because the government had not taken final discretionary action authorizing the Developers' project before the referendum was certified, the County is not estopped from enforcing prior zoning that prohibits resort development at Nukolii and resulted from the referendum.

653 P.2d at 774–776 (ellipsis not shown).

Some courts reject Hawaii's strict application of the final discretionary approval. "In Oregon, a state with a lenient version of the rule, the last discretionary approval may occur prior to a final approval involving discretion so long as the approval is based on a sufficiently defined proposal. In *Milcrest Corp. v. Clackamas County*, [650 P.2d 963, 966–67 (Or.App.1982)], a developer obtained a vested right to develop a 440-acre nonconforming planned unit development based on preliminary subdivision plat approval, even though a revised proposal including an additional 220 acres was later approved." Brad K. Schwartz, *Development Agreements: Contracting for Vested Rights*, 28 B.C.ENVTL.AFF.L.REV. 719, 724 (2001).

Should a landowner proceed if an appeal is taken challenging a permit? *See Powell v. Calvert County*, 795 A.2d 96, 101 (Md.App.2002) ("until all necessary approvals, including all final court approvals, are obtained, nothing can vest or even begin to vest"). While waiting for the appeal time to run its course may place a serious strain on the economic viability of a project, a developer who proceeds during appeal does so at risk, as courts can, and do, order buildings razed." Juergensmeyer and Roberts, *supra*, § 5.28 B.

5.   The court in Lake Bluff and subsequent courts in the same string of litigation addressed both the common law doctrine of vested rights and the equitable doctrine of estoppel. In a vested rights analysis, the focus is on

whether the landowner has the right to proceed notwithstanding a change in regulations. When determining whether an estoppel is appropriate, the focus is on the municipality's conduct and the degree and nature of the landowner's reliance on that conduct. The former is a legal right of a landowner, notwithstanding what the landowner knew or should have known. The latter is an equitable right, and since "clean hands" are required, what the landowner knew is often critical. Which theory one pursues can therefore have critical consequences for how the case is ultimately proved. However, whether the decision is that the landowner has a vested right or that the municipality is estopped from using new regulations to prohibit the development, the outcome is often the same: the landowner can proceed with the planned use and development of his land assured of protection from changing legal requirements.

How is an estoppel claim different from a vested rights claim? In the *Nukolii* decision, *supra* note 4, the Hawaii Supreme Court says they are the same. In this respect the court follows both a line of Hawaii cases, and an early analysis of the vested rights and estoppel doctrines as applied to land use controls, which conclude that they are largely the same on the ground that the result is usually the same under either. Do you agree? *See* David L. Callies, *Land Use: Herein of Vested Rights, Plans and the Relationship of Planning and Control*, 2 U.HAW.L.REV. 167 (1979). What differences in pleading and proof can you think of that might substantially affect the result in the *Nukolii* case? *See* David G. Heeter, *Zoning Estoppel: Application of the Principles of Equitable Estoppel and Vested Rights to Zoning Disputes*, 1971 URB.LAW.ANN. 63.

A long time lapse does not, standing alone, give rise to an estoppel. *See In re Appeal of Crawford*, 531 A.2d 865 (Pa.Cmwlth.1987), where business use of residentially zoned land for 20 years did not give rise to estoppel. The government knew of the violation, but had not engaged in the necessary "active acquiescence." What is "active acquiescence?" It may be the erroneous issuance of a permit or a zoning official erroneously interpreting the code. *Id.* at 868; *Jones v. City of Aurora*, 772 P.2d 645 (Colo.App.1988) (equitable award of damages). If one builds in reliance on an improperly issued permit, where estoppel is not justified, the consequences may be harsh. *See Parkview Associates v. City of New York*, 519 N.E.2d 1372 (N.Y.1988), where the mistaken issuance of a permit led to the court ordered demolition of the top 12 floors of a 31 story building. How do you dismantle a building in crowded Manhattan? *See Cutting a Building Down to Size, Very Carefully*, N.Y. Times, October 1, 1992, p. 3B.

6.   The test to determine whether a governmental entity should be estopped from enforcing the regulation and thereby vest the right of development has been commonly stated as follows:

The doctrine [of equitable estoppel] will preclude a municipality from changing its regulations as they apply to a particular parcel of land when a property owner in good faith, upon some act or omission of the government, has made such a substantial change in position or has incurred such extensive obligations and expenses that it would be highly inequitable and unjust to destroy the right he acquired.

Florida Companies v. Orange County, 411 So.2d 1008, 1010 (Fla.App.1982).

This test may be broken down into four prongs, all of which must be established by the developer in order for an estoppel to issue: governmental action, substantial expenditures, good faith, and a balancing of public and private interests. The same factors *may* be used in vested rights analysis as well. The following notes explore these factors:

a. *Governmental action which apparently authorizes a particular course of action by the developer.* Existing zoning is not an act that creates a vested right or a right of reliance. *Town of Stephens City v. Russell*, 399 S.E.2d 814 (Va.1991). In California, there must be "a valid building permit, or its functional equivalent." *Hermosa Beach Stop Oil Coalition v. City of Hermosa Beach*, 103 Cal.Rptr.2d 447, 460 (Cal.App.2001). Where the county approved a traffic study, sanitary sewer line plan, drainage plan, and the subdivision map and the state issued a stormwater permit, the issuance of the building permit was ministerial. *Wal-Mart Stores, Inc. v. County of Clark*, 125 F.Supp.2d 420 (D.Nev.1999). Some jurisdictions equate the issuance of a special permit or approval of a site plan with the issuance of a building permit. *Board of Supervisors v. Medical Structures, Inc.*, 192 S.E.2d 799, 801 (Va.1972) ("The site plan has virtually replaced the building permit as the most vital document in the development process.")

b. *Substantial expenditures in pursuing the approved development plan.* The courts have not settled on any one method of determining whether reliance by the developer was substantial. In order to be considered by the court, the expenditure must be made in good faith in reliance on the government's action. Therefore, the mere purchase of land is rarely sufficient to create a vested right. *See, e.g., Sautto v. Edenboro Apartments, Inc.*, 174 A.2d 497 (N.J.Super.1961) ("cost of land to a property owner should not ordinarily or invariably be regarded as a factor of reliance to prevent subsequent zoning upgrading beneficial to the community"). Money spent for architectural plans, engineering, economic feasibility studies, and planning in order to prepare and submit an application for approval are often not considered to be reliance expenditures because they are not made in reliance on a governmental act. *See, e.g., Snake River Venture v. Board of County Com'rs, Teton County*, 616 P.2d 744 (Wyo.1980) (The developer had no vested rights even though he had expended $56,000 for a development plan and planning, environmental and economic feasibility studies prior to initial approval). Contra: *Town of Largo v. Imperial Homes Corp.*, 309 So.2d 571 (Fla.App.1975) (preliminary expenses were considered reliance expenditures) and *Allen v. City and County of Honolulu*, 571 P.2d 328 (Haw.1977). Other pre-approval expenditures which the courts frequently discount as reliance expenditures include contract obligations, carrying costs, and maintenance expenses. Post application expenses are now often seen as being made in reliance on governmental action. However, some states apply a strict test which requires a substantial change in the land itself with associated expenses before vested rights are found. *See*

County Council v. District Land Corp., 337 A.2d 712 (Md.1975) (no vested rights because no substantial construction had begun even though developer spent over $1 million on development studies).

A second factor the court must evaluate is whether the reliance expenditures were substantial. No single method of analysis has been established for evaluating substantiality. Some courts will look at the expenditures to date in proportion to the estimated total project cost. *Western Land Equities, Inc. v. City of Logan*, 617 P.2d 388 (Utah 1980). Where that percentage is very high or very low, the courts have an easy decision. It is the broad middle range is much more troublesome. Other courts look simply at the total dollar amount on a case by case method. *See American National Bank & Trust Co. v. City of Chicago*, 311 N.E.2d 325 (Ill.App.1974).

c. *The reliance on a governmental act must have been in good faith*, at least when the landowner's theory is equitable estoppel. In theory, good faith ought not be necessary under a pure vested rights rule, but courts, notwithstanding theory, require good faith. David L. Callies, Daniel J. Curtin, Jr., and Julie A. Tappendorf, *Bargaining for Development: A Handbook on Development Agreements, Annexation Agreements, Land Development Conditions, Vested Rights, and the Provision of Public Services* 132 (2003). According to Siemon, Larsen, and Porter, the issue of good faith becomes significant under five general circumstances:

(1) when a landowner acts at a time when a new regulation or ordinance is pending or under consideration;

(2) when the landowner acts after an amendment has been adopted but is not yet effective;

(3) when the landowner or developer has misled the governmental authority;

(4) when the landowner acts with knowledge that he is relying on an invalid permit; and

(5) when the landowner makes expenditures while the "act" upon which he is relying is being contested in the courts.

Charles L. Siemon, Wendy U. Larsen, and Douglas R. Porter, *Vested Rights: Balancing Public and Private Development Expectations* 30 (1982).

The point at which the courts find a developer acted in bad faith disqualifies any expenditures from consideration in the substantial reliance point of analysis. But what is good faith reliance? According to the Hawaii Supreme Court in *Nukolii*, "in considering whether a developer's expenditures were made in good faith, we employ an objective standard that reflects 'reasonableness according to the practices of the development industry.'" 653 P.2d at 777. The court is most likely to find good faith by the developer under the first circumstance. *See Miller v. Dassler*, 155 N.Y.S.2d 975, 979 (Sup.Ct.1956) (a landowner is entitled to believe, in good faith, that not every proposed ordinance or regulation before a governmental body will be adopted). *But see Boron Oil Co. v. Kimple*, 284 A.2d 744 (Pa.1971) (permit properly denied because a new zoning ordinance was pending at the time of application). Many courts state that good faith means "without knowledge," and where it is clear that the developer has proceeded despite knowledge of a proposed zoning change, they are not willing to find good faith. *See Von Bokel v. City of Breese*, 427 N.E.2d 322 (Ill.App.1981).

In the remaining four circumstances, good faith reliance is much less likely to be found by the courts. *City of Coral Gables v. Puiggros*, 376 So.2d 281, 284 (Fla.App.1979) (developer cannot claim to have acted in good faith when he concealed facts or misled the governmental body); *Kirk v. Village of Hillcrest*, 304 N.E.2d 452 (Ill.App.1973) (when developer knows that permit was invalid, there can be no valid claim of detrimental reliance in good faith); and *Pascale v. Board of Zoning Appeals*, 136 A.2d 377 (Conn.1962).

Municipalities, like developers, must act in good faith. Governmental action taken in response to a particular development proposal occurs frequently. So long as a court finds that protection of the general welfare motivated the new law and that the time delay was reasonable, the court will apply the law even where permit issuance triggered its passage. *Home Depot U.S.A., Inc. v. Village of Rockville Centre*, 743 N.Y.S.2d 541 (App.Div.2002) (moratorium on building permit approvals not in bad faith, and village did not unduly delay processing of application to allow time for new amendments, unfavorable to applicant, to become effective). Most instances of governmental bad faith are encountered where authorities drag their feet and mislead or otherwise hinder an applicant in the permitting process. If a permit is willfully withheld by deceptive conduct, a new intervening law will not apply. *Figgie Int'l v. Town of Huntington*, 610 N.Y.S.2d 563 (App.Div.1994). *See Mission Springs, Inc. v. City of Spokane*, 954 P.2d 250 (Washington 1998). Generally, estoppel will be found only where the facts reveal: (1) a false representation of a material fact; (2) that the party asserting the estoppel did not know or could not discover the truth; (3) the false representation was made with the intent that it be relied upon; and (4) the person to whom the false representation was made, relied and acted upon the representation to its prejudice. In such a case, an action for damages may lie. *See Twin Falls Clinic and Hospital Bldg. Corp v. Hamill*, 644 P.2d 341, 344 (Idaho 1982).

Under the doctrine of quasi-estoppel, where the government changes its legal position during the processing of an application for development approval, there is no need to show detrimental reliance. *Atwood v. Smith*, 138 P.3d 310 (Idaho 2006). *See also C & G, Inc. v. Canyon Highway District No. 4*, 75 P.3d 194, 198 (Idaho 2003) ("quasi-estoppel applies when (1) the offending party took a different position than its original position, and (2) either the offending party gained an advantage or caused a disadvantage to the other party"). The California Court of Appeals upheld a mediation settlement agreement which fixed the issues to be considered at a subsequent county public hearing on a discretionary approval against the arguments of neighboring interveners that the County had bargained away its police power or proscribed the statutory hearing process. *Santa Margarita Area Residents Together v. County of San Luis Obispo*, 100 Cal.Rptr.2d 740 (Cal.App.2000).

d. *Balancing of the public and the private interests:* A fundamental fairness analysis has been adopted by a few courts. Illinois has employed such a test by looking at the gain to the public as compared to the hardship of the property owner. The following factors are considered:

(1) existing uses and zoning of nearby properties;

(2) extent to which the desired nonconformity will diminish property values;

(3) extent to which destruction of plaintiff's property value promotes the public health, safety, morals, or general welfare;

(4) relative gain to the public compared to hardship imposed on property owner;

(5) suitability of the property for zoned purposes;

(6) length of time the property has been vacant under present zoning.

See Smith v. City of Macomb, 352 N.E.2d 697 (Ill.App.1976) and *Nott v. Wolff*, 163 N.E.2d 809 (Ill.1960). Utah follows the early vesting "pending ordinance rule," but tempers it by using a balancing of interest test. *See Western Land Equities, Inc. v. City of Logan*, 617 P.2d 388 (Utah 1980) (applicant entitled to approval if his proposal meets zoning requirements in effect at time of application, absent a compelling, countervailing public interest).

7. The *Nukolii* case, *supra* note 4, raises an issue concerning the virtually unanimously held view that there is no vested right to a zoning classification. Should the rule be applied when the classification is both (1) recent and (2) changed at the behest of a landowner? Recall that zoning is in theory a legislative act. *See, e.g., Board of County Comm'rs v. Lutz*, 314 So.2d 815 (Fla.App.1975); *Jones v. United States Steel Credit Corp.*, 382 So.2d 48 (Fla.App.1979). But what if it is characterized as quasi-judicial, as when the change is at a landowner's request, and the owner has presented a *specific project,* as in *Nukolii?* The *Nukolii* decision has been subject to considerable criticism based upon its novel use of the "last discretionary permit" theory as applied to the referendum process. *See* David L. Callies, *Comment on* County of Kaua'i v. Pacific Standard Life Insurance Co., 35 LAND USE LAW AND ZONING DIGEST I, p.11; Benjamin A. Kudo, Nukolii*: Private Development Rights and the Public Interest*, 16 URB.LAW. 279 (1984). As stated, when is a landowner entitled to rely on existing land use development permissions? What if the next general election on a certified petition for rezoning is a year or two away? Can the developer force the county to call the special election provided for in the *Nukolii* case? What if the county responds that it can't afford it? Can the developer pay for it? Must the county then hold the special election? In fact, another referendum petition was certified and a second election held in 1984 on Kauai which had the effect of returning the county zoning to a district permitting the development as originally contemplated. It was challenged on equal protection grounds because the developer-landowner paid for it. In

Soules v. Kauaians for Nukolii Campaign Committee, 849 F.2d 1176 (9th Cir.1988), the court found that laches barred the claim.

8.   There is also increasing judicial recognition that developers who proceed on multi-phased projects based upon existing zoning may be entitled to rely on such zoning on either a vested rights or estoppel theory. See, for example, *Maryland Reclamation Ass'n v. Harford County*, 994 A.2d 842, 875 (Md.2010):

> We have not explicitly adopted the doctrine of zoning estoppel, but we recognize that as zoning and permitting processes become more complex, the need for such a doctrine grows. Today, land use is much more highly regulated than it was fifty years ago-environmental concerns abound, and vehicular traffic demands seem to mushroom every year. Thus, a property owner who seeks to build or develop may well incur sizable expenses for experts in engineering, various environmental fields, traffic flow, archeology, etc., before putting a spade into the ground. With increasing public appreciation for open space and environmental protection causing apprehension about new construction, the likelihood a developing landowner will face serious opposition is high.

> But we also cannot ignore a local government's responsibility to its residents, and thus Maryland courts should not apply the doctrine casually. As open space disappears, and scientific knowledge about the adverse environmental impact from people's use of land grows, local governments struggle to balance the legitimate interests and rights of landowners wishing to develop against equally legitimate environmental and community concerns. Due to the delicacy of this balancing act, and the overriding need to protect the public, local government cannot always chart a steady course through the Scylla and Charybdis of these disparate interests. Land developers must understand that, to a limited extent, the local government will meander, and before they incur significant expense without final permitting, they must carefully assess the risk that the government will shift course. On the other hand, there may be situations in which the developer's good faith reliance on government action in the pre-construction stage is so extensive and expensive that zoning estoppel is an appropriate doctrine to apply.

9.   The *Nukolii* facts illustrate once again the difficulties associated with development in a multi-permit jurisdiction which applies a version of the "building permit" vested rights rule. The "final discretionary permit" rule can be difficult to apply. It is especially difficult to apply to the phased development that usually characterizes planned development of a large tract. We will reconsider this problem when we study planned unit developments in section H of this Chapter. If one considers the time period that elapses during which the landowner seeks the various required permits, and the fact that the composition of local agencies may change after every election, the risk is considerable if no rights vest until the entire process is completed, unless tight

approval deadlines are available and rigorously adhered to. *See* Fred Bosselman, Duane A. Feurer and Charles L. Siemon, *The Permit Explosion* (1976); Michael M. Schultz, *Vested Property Rights in Colorado: The Legislature Rushes in Where . . .* , 66 DEN.L.REV. 31, 43 (1988) (discussing staged projects).

10. If the risk imposed by the majority late vesting rights rule, *see* note 3, is deemed too great or unfair, one option is to use vesting rules that are more developer-protective. In some states legislation grants developers immunity from subsequent zoning changes after approval of plans. Under the Pennsylvania statute:

> When an application for approval of a plat, whether preliminary or final, has been approved without conditions or approved by the applicant's acceptance of conditions, no subsequent change or amendment in the zoning, subdivision or other governing ordinance or plan shall be applied to affect adversely the right of the applicant to commence and to complete any aspect of the approved development in accordance with the terms of such approval within five years from such approval.

Pa.Stat.Ann. tit. 53, § 10508(4)(ii). In *Board of Comm'rs v. Toll Brothers, Inc.*, 607 A.2d 824 (Pa.Cmwlth.1992), the court held that an increase in water and sewer connection fees was an "other governing ordinance" under the terms of the above act from which the developer was exempt. The North Carolina act provides two years of protection after the approval of a site specific development plan but subjects such plans to newly adopted "overlay zoning which imposes additional requirements but does not affect the allowable type or intensity or use, or ordinances or regulations which are general in nature and are applicable to all property * * * ." N.C.Gen.Stat. § 160A–385.1(e)(2). For similar legislation, *see* West's Colo.Rev.St.Ann. § 24–68–101 and 103 and Mass.Gen.L.Ann. 40A, § 6 (eight years).

Courts in several states have created similar vesting rules to the Wisconsin courts. These rules are more protective than the majority rule; generally, these provide that rights vest at the time the developer applies for a permit. *See, e.g., Union Oil Co. v. City of Worthington*, 405 N.E.2d 277 (Ohio 1980) and *Mercer Enterprises v. City of Bremerton*, 611 P.2d 1237 (Wash.1980). The courts may require that the application be in conformity with the zoning law in effect at the time of the application. *See Lake Bluff.* If a proposed change is pending at the time the application is filed, a vested right may not be acquired. *See Sherman v. Reavis*, 257 S.E.2d 735 (S.C.1979).

Another response to the instability associated with the majority vested rights rules may be the adoption of a development agreement law. For a summary and analysis of such statutes, *see* J. Spencer Hall, *State Vested Rights Statutes: Developing Certainty and Equity and Protecting the Public Interest*, 40 URB.LAW. 451 (2008).

G. DEVELOPMENT AGREEMENTS AND COMMUNITY BENEFIT AGREEMENTS

Decisions vesting development rights late in the process, like the *Avco* case from California and the *Nukolii* case from Hawaii, together with the need for greater public facilities than can be legally exacted from the development community through impact fees and exactions, has led developers and government to seek common ground upon which both needs (vested rights and additional public facilities) could be negotiated. What resulted was the development agreement. *See* David L. Callies, Daniel J. Curtin, Jr., and Julie A. Tappendorf, *Bargaining for Development: A Handbook on Development Agreements, Annexation Agreements, Land Development Conditions, Vested Rights, and the Provision of Public Services* (2003). The development agreement is provided for by statute in at least fourteen states,* and is particularly prolific in rapidly developing, multi-permit jurisdictions like California. *See* Daniel J. Curtin and Scott A. Edelstein, *Development Agreement Practice in California and Other States*, 22 STETSON L.R. 761 (1993). The Community Benefit Agreement (CBA) has little effect on vested rights, but, like the Development Agreement, is a contractual mechanism for obtaining community benefits not legally available through land development conditions. The CBA is generally a part of an urban redevelopment package.

California Development Agreements Statute

§ 65864. Legislative Findings and Declarations

The Legislature finds and declares that:

(a) The lack of certainty in the approval of development projects can result in a waste of resources, escalate the cost of housing and other development to the consumer, and discourage investment in and commitment to comprehensive planning which would make maximum efficient utilization of resources at the least economic cost to the public.

(b) Assurance to the applicant for a development project that upon approval of the project, the applicant may proceed with the project in accordance with existing policies, rules and regulations, and subject to conditions of approval, will strengthen the public planning process, encourage private participation in comprehensive planning, and reduce the economic costs of development.

(c) The lack of public facilities, including, but not limited to, streets, sewerage, transportation, drinking water, school, and utility facilities, is a serious impediment to the development of new housing. Whenever possible, applicants and local governments may include provisions in

---

*   Arizona, California, Colorado, Florida, Hawaii, Idaho, Louisiana, Maine, Maryland, Nevada, New Jersey, Oregon, Virginia, and Washington.

agreements whereby applicants are reimbursed over time for financing public facilities.

§ 65865. Authorizations, Procedures, and Requirements; Recovery of Costs

(a) Any city, county, or city and county, may enter into a development agreement with any person having a legal or equitable interest in real property for the development of the property as provided in this article.

(b) Any city may enter into a development agreement with any person having a legal or equitable interest in real property in unincorporated territory within that city's sphere of influence for the development of the property as provided in this article. However, the agreement shall not become operative unless annexation proceedings annexing the property to the city are completed within the period of time specified by the agreement. If the annexation is not completed within the time specified in the agreement or any extension of the agreement, the agreement is null and void.

(c) Every city, county, or city and county, shall, upon request of an applicant, by resolution or ordinance, establish procedures and requirements for the consideration of development agreements upon application by, or on behalf of, the property owner or other person having a legal or equitable interest in the property.

(d) A city, county, or city and county may recover from applicants the direct costs associated with adopting a resolution or ordinance to establish procedures and requirements for the consideration of development agreements.

§ 65865.1 Periodic Review; Termination or Modification of Agreement

Procedures established pursuant to Section 65865 shall include provisions requiring periodic review at least every 12 months, at which time the applicant, or successor in interest thereto, shall be required to demonstrate good faith compliance with the terms of the agreement. If, as a result of such periodic review, the local agency finds and determines, on the basis of substantial evidence, that the applicant or successor in interest thereto has not complied in good faith with terms or conditions of the agreement, the local agency may terminate or modify the agreement.

§ 65865.2 Contents

A development agreement shall specify the duration of the agreement, the permitted uses of the property, the density or intensity of use, the maximum height and size of proposed buildings, and provisions for reservation or dedication of land for public purposes. The development agreement may include conditions, terms, restrictions, and requirements for subsequent discretionary actions, provided that such conditions, terms, restrictions, and requirements for subsequent discretionary actions shall not prevent development of the land for the uses and to the density or intensity of development set forth in the agreement. The agreement may provide that construction shall be commenced within a specified time and that the project or any phase thereof be completed within a specified time.

The agreement may also include terms and conditions relating to applicant financing of necessary public facilities and subsequent reimbursement over time.

§ 65865.4   Enforcement

Unless amended or canceled pursuant to Section 65868, or modified or suspended pursuant to Section 65869.5, and except as otherwise provided in subdivision (b) of Section 65865.3, a development agreement shall be enforceable by any party thereto notwithstanding any change in any applicable general or specific plan, zoning, subdivision, or building regulation adopted by the city, county, or city and county entering the agreement, which alters or amends the rules, regulations, or policies specified in Section 65866.

§ 65866.   Rules, Regulations and Official Policies

Unless otherwise provided by the development agreement, rules, regulations, and official policies governing permitted uses of the land, governing density, and governing design, improvement, and construction standards and specifications, applicable to development of the property subject to a development agreement, shall be those rules, regulations, and official policies in force at the time of execution of the agreement. A development agreement shall not prevent a city, county, or city and county, in subsequent actions applicable to the property, from applying new rules, regulations, and policies which do not conflict with those rules, regulations, and policies applicable to the property as set forth herein, nor shall a development agreement prevent a city, county, or city and county from denying or conditionally approving any subsequent development project application on the basis of such existing or new rules, regulations, and policies.

§ 65867.   Public Hearing; Notice of Intention to Consider Adoption

A public hearing on an application for a development agreement shall be held by the planning agency and by the legislative body. Notice of intention to consider adoption of a development agreement shall be given as provided in Section 65090 and 65091 in addition to any other notice required by law for other actions to be considered concurrently with the development agreement.

§ 65867.5   Approval by Ordinance; Referendum

A development agreement is a legislative act which shall be approved by ordinance and is subject to referendum. A development agreement shall not be approved unless the legislative body finds that the provisions of the agreement are consistent with the general plan and any applicable specific plan.

§ 65868. Amendment or Cancellation; Notice of Intent

A development agreement may be amended, or canceled in whole or in part, by mutual consent of the parties to the agreement or their successors in interest. Notice of intention to amend or cancel any portion of the agreement shall be given in the manner provided by Section 65867. An amendment to an agreement shall be subject to the provisions of Section 65867.5.

§ 65869.5 Modification or Suspension to Comply With State or Federal Laws or Regulations

In the event that state or federal laws or regulations, enacted after a development agreement has been entered into, prevent or preclude compliance with one or more provisions of the development agreement, such provisions of the agreement shall be modified or suspended as may be necessary to comply with such state or federal laws or regulations.

SANTA MARGARITA AREA RESIDENTS TOGETHER V. COUNTY OF SAN LUIS OBISPO

California Court of Appeal, 2000.
84 Cal.App.4th 221, 100 Cal.Rptr.2d 740.

PERREN, J.

Santa Margarita Area Residents Together, an association; Kenneth Haggard; and Otto Schmidt appeal the judgment denying their petition for writ of mandate to set aside a development agreement between defendant and real party in interest Santa Margarita Limited. To develop its property, Santa Margarita Limited needs to be certain that the law governing local development will not change during the development process. Relying on the development agreement statute, the landowner and County agreed to a development plan. Appellants contend that the agreement is invalid under the statute because it covers the planning stage of a real estate development before buildings or other structures have been designed or approved. Appellants also contend that, under these circumstances, the zoning "freeze" in the agreement unconstitutionally contracts away the County's police power. We conclude that this agreement, which assigns rights and obligations to both government and developer concerning the planning of a large real estate project, complies with the statute and does not contract away the County's police power. We affirm.

The Santa Margarita Ranch (Ranch) consists of approximately 13,800 acres of real property in San Luis Obispo County. The owner of the Ranch, Santa Margarita Limited, has long desired to develop the Ranch. Santa

Margarita Area Advisory Council, a community organization, has opposed the development. After Santa Margarita Limited sued the County to facilitate development by increasing the number of legal parcels in the Ranch, Santa Margarita Limited, the County, and representatives of the Santa Margarita Area Advisory Council agreed to mediate their differences over long-range development of the Ranch. The mediation achieved a consensus among most of the participants, including representatives from the Santa Margarita Area Advisory Council. A mediation report reflecting the consensus recommended approval of a project which would include 550 housing units and non-residential improvements in an 1,800 acre area, devote at least 8,400 acres to permanent open space easements, and place a minimum of 3,600 acres under 40-year Williamson Act contracts for preservation of agricultural land.[2] The report also recommended use of a development agreement to guarantee that the 550 residential units would be "subject to applicable laws and regulations."

Shortly after the mediation, the County began preparing a development agreement with Santa Margarita Limited for the specific planning of a project which would include the improvements and other land uses specified in the mediation report and which also designated a golf course, guest lodge, equestrian center, bikeways, and parklands as non-residential improvements (Project). At the same time, the County amended part of its general plan, the Salinas River Area Plan, to describe the Project and establish certain criteria for its ultimate implementation. After lengthy negotiations and a public hearing, the County enacted an ordinance authorizing it to enter into the development agreement (Agreement). The next day, the chairperson of the County's Board of Supervisors signed the Agreement.

Santa Margarita Agreement

In general, the Agreement freezes zoning on the Project property in return for the developer's commitment to submit a specific plan for construction in compliance with County land use requirements. Contingencies and further approvals remain, but the Agreement commits the County and Santa Margarita Limited to the Project, including its public improvements and amenities.

Specifically, the Agreement provides that Santa Margarita Limited will file a comprehensive application for approval of the Project, including a specific plan, a vesting tentative map, and an environmental impact report. The specific plan must incorporate the standards set forth in the Salinas River Area Plan. The application must state that Santa Margarita Limited will commit itself to develop the Project in its entirety and to engage in all necessary environmental review. The Agreement also

---

[2] The Williamson Act, section 51200 et seq., permits local governments to enter into contracts limiting the use of land to agricultural purposes in return for preferential tax treatment.

provides that Santa Margarita Limited will dedicate land for a public swimming pool, sewer treatment plant, and cemetery expansion.

In return for these commitments, the County agrees to process, review, and approve or disapprove the specific plan, and to apply its current zoning and other land use regulations to the plan without change for up to five years during the review and approval period. The Agreement is entered into under the authority of the Development Agreement Statute and satisfies its technical requirements.

The Agreement does not give Santa Margarita Limited a right to construct the Project or impose upon it an obligation to do so. Rather, the Agreement contemplates a second development agreement pertaining to the actual construction of the Project, and requires that the County and Santa Margarita Limited "will make a good faith effort to negotiate a Subsequent Development Agreement that shall, if agreed upon, provide [Santa Margarita Limited] with a vested right to the benefits and burdens of the Project." It provides that the parties "ultimately seek to secure . . . an enforceable arrangement" allowing construction, but neither party "obligates itself to benefit or burden the Project Site with the above-described Project until such time as a Final EIR is certified, the Specific Plan application is favorably acted upon by the County, [and] the Subsequent Development Agreement . . . becomes binding on the parties. . . ."

The development agreement statute permits a city or county to "enter into a development agreement" with any property owner "for the development of the property." (§ 65865, subd. (a).) In essence, the statute allows a city or county to freeze zoning and other land use regulation applicable to specified property to guarantee that a developer will not be affected by changes in the standards for government approval during the period of development. (*City of West Hollywood v. Beverly Towers, Inc.* (1991) 52 Cal.3d 1184, 1193, fn. 6, 278 Cal.Rptr. 375, 805 P.2d 329; *Citizens for Responsible Government v. City of Albany*, 66 Cal.Rptr.2d 102 (1997)) In the words of the statute, "[u]nless otherwise provided by the development agreement, rules, regulations, and official policies governing permitted uses of the land, governing density, and governing design, improvement, and construction standards and specifications, applicable to development of the property subject to a development agreement, shall be those rules, regulations, and official policies in force at the time of execution of the agreement." (§ 65866.)

The statute declares that "lack of certainty in the approval of development projects can result in a waste of resources, escalate the cost of housing and other development to the consumer, and discourage investment in and commitment to comprehensive planning which would make maximum efficient utilization of resources at the least economic cost to the public." (§ 65864, subd. (a).) The statute reflects the Legislature's conclusion that giving "[a]ssurance to the applicant for a development project that upon approval of the project, the applicant may proceed with the project in accordance with existing policies, rules and regulations, and subject to conditions of approval, will strengthen the public planning process, encourage private participation in comprehensive planning, and reduce the economic costs of development." (§ 65864, subd. (b).) Particulars of the statute include requirements that a development agreement may be approved only after a public hearing (§ 65867) and must be consistent with the general plan and any specific plan (§ 65867.5), a provision permitting annual review by the governmental entity and termination for noncompliance (§ 65865.1), and a statement that the agreement is subject to referendum (§ 65867.5). The statute also specifies certain provisions which may or must be included in a development agreement. (§ 65865.2.)

In reviewing the Agreement and ordinance approving the Agreement, we must consider two standards of review. A development agreement is a legislative act (§ 65867.5) and the County's Board of Supervisors has the discretion to determine what legislation is necessary and appropriate. A reviewing court will not set aside a legislative act unless it is arbitrary, capricious, or unlawful. On the other hand, courts independently decide purely legal issues such as statutory interpretation. We review the Agreement to determine if it enlarges or impairs the terms of the authorizing statute without deference to the County. Based on these standards, we conclude that the Agreement complies with the development agreement statute, and that the County's exercise of its legislative power to enter into the Agreement was not arbitrary or capricious.

Appellants contend that the Agreement is invalid under the statute because the statute permits a development agreement only after a project has been approved for actual construction. Appellants claim that, without a fully-designed and approved project, the Agreement is essentially a unilateral County agreement to freeze zoning without obtaining any public benefits in return.

Appellants interpret the statute and the Agreement too narrowly. The statute is best served through a liberal construction which encompasses agreements that substantially comply with its specific terms and conditions and achieve its essential objectives. To interpret the statute and Agreement in any other manner would unduly restrict the County from working with a private landowner to plan and develop facilities which support public needs.

Moreover, the statement of legislative purpose in section 65864 encourages the creation of rights and obligations early in a project in order to promote public and private participation during planning, especially when the scope of a project requires a lengthy process of obtaining regulatory approvals. The statute recognizes that comprehensive planning is important in controlling the economic and environmental costs of development. It should be construed to allow development agreements as soon as the government and developer are required to make significant financial and personnel commitments to a project.

The Agreement conforms to this construction of the statute. Because it focuses on the planning stage of the Project, the Agreement meets, rather than evades, the purpose of the statute. The Agreement maximizes the public's role in the final development and control over the inclusion of public facilities and benefits in the project. It also permits the County to monitor the planning of the Project to effectively assure compliance with existing County land use regulations.

Additionally, environmental review is advanced by considering environmental issues at the earliest feasible time. The Agreement makes environmental review an integral part of the planning process, thus avoiding the sort of "post hoc rationalizations to support action already taken" which might occur if environmental review were deferred until later.

Appellants contend that the County does not approve an actual development project in the Agreement. We disagree. The Agreement establishes the scope of the Project and precise parameters for future construction as well as a procedure to process Project approvals. It also provides for a variety of improvements for public use which may not have been offered by the developer without corresponding commitments by the County as outlined in the Agreement.

The Agreement must be construed as an approval of the Project because it commits the parties to a definite course of action aimed at assuring construction of the Project, provided certain contingencies are met. While further agreement and discretionary approvals are necessary, every approval or denial permitted by the Agreement is designed to advance the project in accordance with the standards for Ranch development adopted by the County in the Salinas River Area Plan. As shown by the record, the County and the participants in the mediation which preceded the Agreement intend the Agreement to play a critical role in facilitating the completion of a large-scale real estate development. There is nothing in the Development Agreement Statute inconsistent with this type of development agreement.

The development agreement statute was enacted after *Avco Community Developers, Inc. v. South Coast Regional Com.* (1976) 17 Cal.3d 785, 132 Cal.Rptr. 386, 553 P.2d 546. In Avco, a new land use requirement was enacted after pre-building permit construction work had been done on a project. The Supreme Court held that a developer has no vested right to complete a project before building permits are issued. In so ruling, the court stated that any change in the rule that a developer has no vested rights in existing zoning must come from the Legislature.

The Legislature accepted the Supreme Court's invitation and responded with a statute permitting local governments to freeze zoning early in the development process and before the issuance of building permits. Indeed, appellants concede that development agreements are permitted before the issuance of building permits, just not too much before. Appellants seek to limit the statute to situations which roughly correspond to the facts in Avco.

The statute does not support this position. The statute is limited to actual projects, but does not require deferral of development agreements until construction is ready to begin or require any particular stage of project approval as a prerequisite. In fact, by permitting conditional development agreements when property is subject to future annexation, section 65865, subdivision (b) expressly permits local government to freeze zoning and other land use regulation before a project is finalized.

This specific provision supports the general conclusion that the development agreement statute permits local government to make commitments to developers at the time the developer makes a substantial investment in a project. Here, that time had certainly arrived when the Agreement was executed.

Appellants cite no legal authority, and we have found none, which limits the statute to development agreements which create "vested rights" to complete construction of a project according to completed plans. In fact, the scant authority dealing with development agreements is to the contrary and focuses on the broad purpose of the statute to provide assurances to developers as soon as project commitments must be made.

Moreover, the statute expressly contemplates "discretionary approvals" after the execution of a development agreement (§ 65865.2) and includes a provision concerning annual review and termination. Under section 65865.1, a landowner is "required to demonstrate good faith compliance with the terms of the agreement" at the time of each annual review. "If, as a result of such periodic review, the local agency finds and determines, on the basis of substantial evidence, that the applicant or successor in interest thereto has not complied in good faith with terms or conditions of the agreement, the local agency may terminate or modify the agreement." Contrary to claims by appellants, these provisions are not so narrow as to restrict the scope of the statute to situations where all planning and design work has been completed and approved.

Appellants also contend that the Agreement is invalid under the statute because it does not include all of the provisions required by section 65865.2. Again, we disagree. Section 65865.2 states that a development agreement "shall specify the duration of the agreement, the permitted uses of the property, the density or intensity of use, the maximum height and size of proposed buildings, and provisions for reservation or dedication of land for public purposes." The Agreement substantially complies with the requirements of this section.

The Agreement specifies its duration, the permitted uses of the Ranch and the density or intensity of use, and provides for reservation or dedication of land for public purposes.

The Agreement fails to mention the maximum height and size of proposed buildings. But, as Santa Margarita Limited points out, the Agreement is subject to the existing County land use ordinances which limit the height and size of buildings in two ways. First, they explicitly limit building height in general. Second, they limit the total size of buildings by requiring setbacks from lot lines.

The Salinas River Area Plan also sets a maximum building height for the Ranch and, by specifying the total number of residential units, the Agreement creates a frame of reference for building size. Moreover, both the Agreement and the statute contemplate annual review with final approval vested in the County. What remains static are the rules under which the approval will be sought.

Finally, the Agreement was approved by an ordinance duly enacted by the County Board of Supervisors and we defer to that body in matters pertaining to the merits, usefulness and public advantages of the Agreement. One of the purposes of development agreements is to obtain benefits for the public, and the record shows that the County believed that an agreement was required as an incentive to the developer to engage in the comprehensive planning desired by the County, and also as an incentive to expand the public facilities and benefits included in the Project.

The Agreement also represents the resolution of a protracted dispute and balances the interests of all concerned parties. Santa Margarita Limited sought a more comprehensive agreement but, according to a planning commission staff report, the County decided to "lock-in" the Salinas River Area Plan standards while deferring construction approval. The record reveals that the County's decision resulted from careful assessment of the importance of the Ranch to the region.

The record also reveals that the Agreement resulted from a mediation by parties interested in the future of the Ranch. The mediation did not result in unanimity but produced an agreement among most participants, including representatives of the public. As such, the mediation and Agreement reflect an inclusive and open governmental process.

As well as arguing that the Agreement does too little to satisfy the statute, appellants argue that it does too much to avoid constitutional infirmity. Appellants contend that the freeze on Ranch zoning before a project that is ready for construction constitutes the contracting away of the County's zoning authority and, therefore, a surrender of the right to exercise its police power in the future. We disagree. If anything, case law concerning a municipality's "surrender" of its regulatory authority supports the conclusion that the Agreement, as well as the development agreement statute, satisfy all constitutional mandates concerning a city or county's exercise of its regulatory authority.

It is established that a city or county may not contract away its right to exercise police power in the future (*Avco Community Developers, Inc. v. South Coast Regional Com., supra*, 17 Cal.3d at p. 800, 132 Cal.Rptr. 386, 553 P.2d 546) and that the power to enact, modify, and amend zoning and other land use regulations constitutes a part of a county's police power. Therefore, the development agreement statute must be construed in a manner that does not permit the County to surrender its police power in the name of planning efficiency.

The Agreement in this case presents no such constitutional infirmity. Land use regulation is an established function of local government and the County has authority to enter into contracts to carry out this function. A contract which "appears to have been fair, just, and reasonable at the time of its execution, and prompted by the necessities of the situation or in its nature advantageous to the municipality at the time it was entered into, is neither void nor voidable merely because some of its executory features may extend beyond the terms of office of the members" of the legislative body which entered into the contract.

A governmental entity does not contract away its police power unless the contract amounts to the "surrender" or "abnegation" of a proper governmental function. (*Morrison Homes Corp. v. City of Pleasanton* (1976) 58 Cal.App.3d 724, 734, 130 Cal.Rptr. 196.) The zoning freeze in the Agreement is not such a surrender or abnegation. The Project must be developed in accordance with the County's general plan (§ 65867.5), and the Agreement does not permit construction until the County has approved detailed building plans. The Agreement retains the County's discretionary authority in the future and, in any event, the zoning freeze is for five years. It is not of unlimited duration.

The County concluded that the zoning freeze in the Agreement advances the public interest by preserving future options. This type of action by the County is more accurately described as a legitimate exercise of governmental police power in the public interest than as a surrender of police power to a special interest. [*Morrison Homes, supra*.]

Seventy-five years ago, the Supreme Court stated that the "police power, as such, is not confined within the narrow circumspection of precedents, resting upon past conditions which do not cover and control present-day conditions obviously calling for revised regulations to promote the health, safety, morals, or general welfare of the public. That is to say, as a commonwealth develops politically, economically, and socially, the police power likewise develops, within reason, to meet the changed and changing conditions." (*Miller v. Board of Public Works* (1925) 195 Cal. 477, 484, 234 P. 381.) If anything, the court's statement in Miller resonates more clearly today than when it was first made, and provides a framework for the analysis of this case. Here, the development agreement statute and the constitutional mandate requiring the County to retain its regulatory power intersect to permit the contemporary approach to land use regulation reflected in the Agreement.

It is true that local government may not surrender its regulatory power through ad hoc commitments. It may, however, act in partnership with private enterprise, as authorized by the development agreement statute and the Agreement. The Agreement addresses recurring land use issues without limiting the County's regulatory discretion. Through the Agreement, the County tailors the exercise of its legislative power to the complex issues involved in regulating a major real estate project in the public interest. By requiring expeditious Project planning and preserving future options, the Agreement enhances the County's power to regulate land use to achieve its Salinas River Area Plan and other land use goals.

The judgment is affirmed. Costs on appeal are awarded to Santa Margarita Limited.

NOTES

1.   The most often-expressed concern about the validity of the development agreement is the "bargaining away of the police power" by the local government. Are you satisfied with the court's treatment of this issue? *See* David L. Callies, Daniel J. Curtin, Jr., and Julie A. Tappendorf, *Bargaining for Development: A Handbook on Development Agreements, Annexation Agreements, Land Development Conditions, Vested Rights, and the Provision of Public Services* (2003); Judith W. Wegner, *Moving Toward the Bargaining Table: Contract Zoning, Development Agreements, and the Theoretical Foundations of Government Land Use Deals*, 65 N.C.L.REV. 957 (1987); Janice Griffith, *Local Government Contracts: Escaping From the Governmental/Proprietary Maze*, 75 IOWA L.REV. 277 (1990).

Mel Martinez, on behalf of the Board of County Commissioners of Orange County, Florida, of which he was Chairman, entered into a "Developer's Agreement" with developer Morgran. The County promised to adopt an amendment to its plan and to "support and expeditiously process" the rezoning application in exchange for Morgran's promise to donate 50 acres to the County for use as a park once the rezoning was accomplished. When it came time to vote on the rezoning, Chairman Martinez issued what the court labeled an "edict" that the county reject any rezoning where schools were overcrowded. That apparently was the case, since the board denied the rezoning request. When Morgran reminded the board of the agreement, it disavowed the contract as a void effort to engage in contract zoning. The court agreed with the county. Though aware that Florida has a development agreements statute, the court also noted that it viewed contract in zoning with more hostility than many courts. The court reasoned:

> Florida law permits local governments to impose "conditions, terms and restrictions" as part of these agreements, where necessary for the public health, safety or welfare of its citizens. § 163.3227(1)(h), Fla. Stat. (1999). The problem in this case lies with Orange County's obligation to "support" Morgran's request for rezoning, as part of that development agreement. If the Board of County Commissioners has already contracted to "support" Morgran's request for rezoning, it has invalidly contracted away its discretionary legislative power as the final decisionmaking authority.

Morgran Co., Inc. v. Orange County, 818 So.2d 640, 643 (Fla.App.2002). Do you agree with the court? Would the California court that decided the *SMART* case agree? For a summary of the arguments favoring development agreements even if zoning is "bargained-for," *see* Shelby D. Green, *Development Agreements: Bargained-For Zoning that is Neither Illegal Contract nor Conditional Zoning*, 33 CAP.U.L.REV. 383 (2004).

2.   California Courts muddled their common law somewhat in a later Court of Appeals decision. In *Trancas Property Owners Ass'n v. City of Malibu*, 41 Cal.Rptr.3d 200 (Cal.App.2006), the city entered into a development agreement with a developer, granting approval for a "downsized" development and freezing zoning regulations for the property in question, in exchange for dedication of the property. A property owner association sued, challenging the agreement. The agreement, reached in closed meetings in violation of state open meetings law, was invalidated as "impermissibly attempt[ing] to abrogate the city's zoning authority and provisions." The *SMART* case was distinguished as having followed procedures ignored here, in particular that public hearings be held, that the agreement conform to the general and any specific plans, for omitting a provision providing for annual review and termination for noncompliance, and a statement that the agreement is subject to referendum. More consistent with *SMART* is *Glendale I Mall Associates v. City of Glendale*, 2005 WL 3214845 (Cal.App.2005), where the City of Glendale entered into a development agreement for a commercial and residential development in downtown Glendale. The owner of a neighboring mall attacked the form of the agreement. Relying on the *SMART* case in support of the proposition that the agreement did not alter, supplement, or repeal any zoning regulation, the court upheld the agreement as a "freeze" on regulations.

3.   The California statute permits enforcement of a development agreement by any party thereto, notwithstanding any change in applicable plans, zoning, subdivision or building regulation adopted by a city or county as a party. Is it accurate to say that a landowner has a vested right to proceed with a development after the execution of a development agreement? At least one state Supreme Court suggests not. *Sprenger, Grubb & Assocs., Inc. v. City of Hailey*, 903 P.2d 741 (Idaho 1995). What about a new class of legal regulations, like impact fees or growth controls? *See Pardee Construction Co. v. City of Camarillo*, 690 P.2d 701 (Cal.1984). What about subsequent state

and federal regulations? As a landowner proposing the multi-stage development of a large project involving hundreds of acres, what state and federal agencies would you like to include? The advisability, if not the outright need, to bind state agencies which have land use regulatory authority like Hawaii's Land Use Commission is clear from current litigation in both state and federal court over the authority of the LUC to "revert" a landowner's Urban District classification (the only one which permits high-density residential and commercial development) to an Agricultural District classification (which permits neither). The result is the elimination of all county land use "entitlements" including zoning, subdivision and coastal zone management permits and the rendering of a number of already-constructed affordable housing units all nonconforming. *See Bridge Aina Le'a LLC v. State of Hawaii Land Use Comm'n*, Civ. No. 11–1–1145–06 KKS, Complaint filed June 7, 2011, Circuit Court of the First Circuit, State of Hawaii. Available at www.inversecondemnation.com. *See also* Andrew Gomes, *Aina Le'a Suit Seeks Damages. Reversal of Ruling, Honolulu Star-Advertiser*, 8/2/11, at B-5. Think about this in connection with statewide land use controls and federal environmental regulations that affect the use of land. How does this work? Can an agency that executes a development agreement bind the state? The federal government?

4. What if a local government fails to establish the procedures contemplated by § 65865 of the California act? Can the local government enter into a development agreement simply based on the general statutory authorization? If it does, it still must follow the uniformity clause of the zoning enabling act. *See Neighbors in Support of Appropriate Land Use v. County of Tuolumne*, 68 Cal.Rptr.3d 882 (2007) (development agreement cannot allow a use prohibited by the zoning code). For a thoughtful review of the need for appropriate legislative language to support the use of the development agreement, *see* Michael B. Keny, Jr., *Forming A Tie That Binds: Development Agreements in Georgia and the Need for Legislative Clarity*, 30 ENVT'L L. & POLICY J. 1 (2006).

5. What if a development is found to be hazardous to the environment three years after the execution of a development agreement which has 10 years to run? Hawaii's statute provides that the laws and regulations in effect at the time of execution and frozen during the duration of the agreement can be unilaterally modified by local government if it finds that the development results in conditions perilous to the health and safety of the residents of the subdivision or immediate community. Haw.Rev.Stat. § 46–127. Does this suffice?

6. Can—or should—a development agreement be the subject of a popular initiative or referendum? What kind of act is it in California? Is a negotiated development agreement applicable to a single parcel a legislative act or an administrative act?

7. A development agreement was the backdrop for a California appellate court's holding that a substantial fee for affordable housing levied on a market-priced residential subdivision failed for lack of a comprehensive

study that demonstrates that the market rate housing generates the need for affordable housing. *See* Chapter 4 *infra*. For further analysis of affordable housing requirements in development agreements, *see* Ngai Pindell, *Developing Las Vegas: Creating Inclusionary Affordable Housing Requirements in Development Agreements*, 42 WAKE FOREST L.REV. 419 (2007).

Community Benefits Agreements

"A community benefit agreement (CBA) is a private contract negotiated between a prospective developer and community representative." D. Callies, Cecily Talbot Barclay and Julie Tappendorf, *Development By Agreement* (2012) at 61. *See also* P. Salkin and A. Lavine, *Understanding Community Benefit Agreements*, 26 UCLA J.ENV.L. & POL'Y 291 (2008) at 318. This basic definition incorporates the limitations, problems and opportunities inherent in the CBA. It starts with development agreements and community agreements the landowner-developer applies to, and the purpose is to provide community benefits not otherwise available through land development conditions imposed within the policy power. First, the CBA differs from Development Agreements and Association Agreements in two important ways: (1) government is separate, not a part of; and (2) besides the landowner-developer, the potential other contractual party is a vaguely-defined community or community group.

Second, the CBA was born out of a need to solve vested rights problems for the landowner-developer and the problem of illegal erecting of public facilities for local government, but rather as a means for providing meaningful public participation of informal community organization, or groups who might otherwise lodge formal complaints to a proposed development. E.W. De Barbieri, *"Do Community Development Agreements Benefit Communities?,"* 37 CARDOZO L.REV. 1773 (2016) at 3; Callies, et al., *supra*, at 62.

Applicants first used in 2001 in Los Angeles in negotiations surrounding Staples Center, there were more than 25 CBA's in place, mostly in urban development centers in New York, Chicago, Seattle, Milwaukee, Miami, Charleston, Minneapolis, Pittsburgh, and Atlanta. Callies, et al., at 62–63; De Barbieri, *supra*, pp. 4–5. The consensus is that CBA's provide community coalitions with the opportunity to engage in meaningful and enforced negotiations for community benefits, in so-called public development projects like stadiums and university expansion. While many such benefits can also be secured in the DA/PXA/PUD process, the benefit of direct and enforceable community participation is usually substantially reduced; the parties under these three techniques are usually limited to the landowner-developer and local government.

Third, enforceability is an issue at two levels. While the DA, PXA and PUD is usually authorized by statute, and while the parties mutually exchange benefits and burdens, there is no conciliation provided by the community group for the developer-provider benefits. Simply forgetting to formally object or sue is probably insufficient. There is so far no reported case approving CBA's. Callies, *supra*, at 63–4. *See generally* V. Been, *Community Benefit Agreements*, 77 U.CHI.L.REV. 5 (2010) and C. Fazio and J. Wallace, *"Legal and Policy Issues Related to Community Benefit Agreements,"* 21 FORDHAM ENVT'L L.REV. 543 (2010).

The CBA should be distinguished from other public-private agreements like Concession Agreements often associated with public-private partnerships (PPA's). *See* G. Hammel, *"Public-Private Partnerships: The United States Experience, Lessons and Best Practices,"* and G. Gilheot, *"Concession Agreements: Critical Provisions that Require Higher Levels of Consideration"* at the ACREL Papers, Spring 2015, ALI/CLE 2015, pp. 71–119.

H. AESTHETIC CONTROLS

Early on, advocates pressed zoning as necessary for public health and safety. Recall that the *Euclid* court repeatedly referred to dangers from traffic, fire, contagion, safety, and security as justification for upholding the zoning power. Although health and safety made an easier sell to the court, there was little doubt that the preservation of property values loomed high on the purposes list of zoning reformers.

As zoning has spread across the nation, courts have been forced to grapple with justifications for zoning that are more baldly premised on the protection of property values. Perhaps more controversial are zoning ordinances that are clearly designed to promote aesthetics.

REID V. ARCHITECTURAL BOARD OF REVIEW OF CITY OF CLEVELAND HEIGHTS

Court of Appeals of Ohio, 1963.
119 Ohio App. 67, 192 N.E.2d 74.

KOVACHY, PRESIDING JUDGE.

Donna S. Reid, plaintiff appellant, hereinafter designated applicant, applied to the Building Commissioner of the City of Cleveland Heights for a permit to build a residence on a lot owned by her and her husband on North Park Boulevard in Cleveland Heights. As required by ordinance, the plans and specifications were referred to the Architectural Board of Review, which Board, after due consideration, made the following order:

> This plan is for a single-story building and is submitted for a site in a multi-story residential neighborhood. The Board disapproves this project for the reason that it does not maintain the high character of community development in that it does not conform to the character of the houses in the area.

Upon appeal to the Court of Common Pleas, that court rendered a judgment in favor of the Board, holding (1) that the Codified Ordinances were constitutional enactments under the police power of the City; (2) that the Board had the power and authority to render the decision appealed from; (3) that the Board did not abuse its discretion; and (4) that due process was accorded applicant.

The Board is composed of three architects registered and authorized to practice architecture under Ohio laws with ten years of general practice as such.

Section 137.05 of the Codified Ordinances of the City of Cleveland Heights, titled "Purpose" reads as follows:

> The purposes of the Architectural Board of Review are to protect property on which buildings are constructed or altered, to maintain the high character of community development, and to protect real estate within this City from impairment or destruction of value, by regulating according to proper architectural principles the design, use of materials, finished grade lines and orientation of all new buildings, hereafter erected, and the moving, alteration, improvement, repair, adding to or razing in whole or in part of all existing buildings, and said Board shall exercise its powers and perform its duties for the accomplishment of said purposes only.

This ordinance is intended to:

1.   protect property,

2.   maintain high character of community development,

3.   protect real estate from impairment or destruction of value, and the Board's powers are restricted "for the accomplishment of said purposes only."

These objectives are sought to be accomplished by regulating:

1.   design,

2.   use of material,

3.   finished grade lines,

4.   orientation (new buildings).

* * *

The City of Cleveland Heights is a suburb of the City of Cleveland and was organized to provide suitable and comfortable home surroundings for residents employed in Cleveland and its environs. It has no industry or railroads within its confines and is a well-regulated and carefully groomed community, primarily residential in character. An ordinance designed to protect values and to maintain "a high character of community development" is in the public interest and contributes to the general welfare. Moreover, the employment of highly trained personages such as architects for the purpose of applying their knowledge and experience in helping to maintain the high standards of the community is laudable and salutary and serves the public good.

We determine and hold that Ordinance 137.05 is a constitutional exercise of the police power by the City Council and is, therefore, valid.

Section 137.05, as outlined above, sets out criteria and standards for the Board to follow in passing upon an application for the building of a new home which are definite as to the objective to be attained—to protect property, to maintain high character of community development, to protect real estate from impairment and destruction of value; specific as to matters to be considered and regulated—design, use of material, finished grade lines, orientation; instructive as to the method by which the matters specified are to be adjudged—"proper architectural principles" and informative as to the bounds within which it is to exercise these powers— "for the accomplishment of said purposes only."

When borne in mind that the members of the Board are highly trained experts in the field of architecture, the instruction that they resolve these questions on "proper architectural principles" is profoundly reasonable since such expression has reference to the basic knowledge on which their profession is founded.

It is our view, therefore, that Section 137.05 contains all the criteria and standards reasonably necessary for the Board to carry on the duties conferred upon it. * * *

We have read the bill of exceptions filed in this case carefully. It discloses that North Park Boulevard is in a district zoned for Class 1A residences not to exceed thirty-five feet in height or two and one-half stories, whichever is lesser, and which are required to cover not less than fifteen thousand square feet of lot space. This district extends through a park area with buildings on the north side and trees, ravines, and bushes hundreds of feet wide on its south side. The buildings on this Boulevard are, in the main, dignified, stately and conventional structures, two and one-half stories high.

The house designed for the applicant, as described by applicant, is a flat-roofed complex of twenty modules, each of which is ten feet high, twelve feet square and arranged in a loosely formed "U" which winds its way through a grove of trees. About sixty per cent of the wall area of the house is glass and opens on an enclosed garden; the rest of the walls are of cement panels. A garage of the same modular construction stands off from the house, and these two structures, with their associated garden walls, trellises and courts, form a series of interior and exterior spaces, all under a canopy of trees and baffled from the street by a garden wall.

A wall ten feet high is part of the front structure of the house and garage and extends all around the garden area. It has no windows. Since the wall is of the same height as the structure of the house, no part of the house can be seen from the street. From all appearances, it is just a high wall with no indication of what is behind it. Not only does the house fail to conform in any manner with the other buildings but presents no identification that it is a structure for people to live in.

The Board, as well as the architect for the applicant, concede that this structure would be a very interesting home placed in a different environment. It is obvious that placed on North Parks Boulevard, it would not only be out of keeping with and a radical departure from the structures now standing but would be most detrimental to the further development of the area since there are two vacant lots immediately to the west and a third vacant lot on the street bordering the westernmost lot.

Esthetics was a consideration that played a part in the ruling of the Board, but there were many other factors that influenced its decision. The structure designed is a single-story home in a multi-story neighborhood; it does not conform to general character of other houses; it would affect adjacent homes and three vacant lots; it is of such a radical concept that any design not conforming to the general character of the neighborhood would have to be thereafter approved; when viewed from the street, it could indicate a commercial building; it does not conform to standards of the neighborhood; it does not preserve high character of neighborhood; it does not preserve property values; it would be detrimental to neighborhood on the lot where proposed and it would be detrimental to the future development of the neighborhood.

16 C.J.S. Constitutional Law § 195, Esthetic Conditions, p. 939, states:

"The concept of the public welfare is broad and inclusive. The values it represents are spiritual as well as physical, esthetic as well as monetary. It is within the power of the legislature to determine that the community should be beautiful as well as healthy, spacious as well as clean, well-balanced as well as carefully patrolled. [Editors' Note: the preceding language of this C.J.S. cite is taken directly from Berman v. Parker—see note 1 after the case.] Nevertheless, it is held that esthetic conditions alone are insufficient to support the invocation of the police power, although if a regulation finds a reasonable justification in serving a generally recognized ground for the exercise of that power, the fact that esthetic considerations play a part in its adoption does not affect its validity."

It is our determination and we hold that the record in this case discloses ample evidence to support the judgment of the trial court that the Board did not abuse its discretion in its decision in this matter.

* * *

CORRIGAN, JUDGE (dissenting).

It should be borne in mind that there is an important principle of eclecticism in architecture which implies freedom on the part of the architect or client or both to choose among the styles of the past and present that which seems to them most appropriate.

Should the appellant be required to sacrifice her choice of architectural plan for her property under the official municipal juggernaut of conformity in this case? Should her aesthetic sensibilities in connection with her selection of design for her proposed home be stifled because of the apparent belief in this community of the group as a source of creativity? Is she to sublimate herself in this group and suffer the frustration of individual creative aspirations? Is her artistic spirit to be imprisoned by the apparent beneficence of community life in Cleveland Heights? This member of the court thinks not under the record in this case and the pertinent legal principles applicable thereto.

NOTES

1. For years courts debated whether aesthetic considerations constituted a legitimate basis for the exercise of the police power. Today all state courts have addressed the issue. A survey reveals that twenty-three courts allow regulation based on aesthetics alone and the others allow such regulation if combined with other factors such as tourism, historic preservation, traffic safety, or "community character." Kenneth Pearlman, Elizabeth Linville, Andrea Phillips, and Erin Prosser, *Beyond the Eye of the Beholder Once Again: A New Review of Aesthetic Regulation*, 38 URB.LAW. 1119 (2006) (state by state analysis). *See also* Meg Stevenson, *Aesthetic Regulations: A History*, 35 REAL EST.L.J. 519 (2007). Where does the *Reid* case stand on the question of whether aesthetics alone can justify a police power regulation? The court lists numerous "other factors" that warrant examination. If not aesthetic considerations, what are they?

What do we mean when we speak of "aesthetics"? John Costonis suggests that the aesthetics of the law not be treated as the aesthetics of the museum. It is, he says, not taste or beauty that legal aesthetics deals or ought to deal with, but stability and protection for that which we have come to expect. John J. Costonis, Icons and Aliens: Law, Aesthetics, and Environmental Change (1989). Does this thesis conform to the rationale of the *Reid* court?

2. The constitutionality of architectural preservation schemes often depends upon the process used to evaluate the merits of the proposed structure and the finality of the decision. Are you satisfied with the fact that "highly trained personages such as architects," as the *Reid* court puts it, are entrusted with the decision of whether the applicant gets to build the kind of house she wants? Does the ordinance adequately guide their decisionmaking and limit their discretion? For some courts, standards directing a board to determine

whether a proposed house is "inappropriate" or "incompatible" with surrounding property are unconstitutionally vague. *See Anderson v. City of Issaquah*, 851 P.2d 744 (Wash.App.1993) (ordinance, which required that buildings be "harmonious," "interesting," and "compatible," and where one commissioner denied approval in part because the suggested "Tahoe blue may be too dark," found unconstitutionally vague); *Rolling Pines Ltd. Partnership v. City of Little Rock*, 40 S.W.3d 828 (Ark.App.2001) (compatibility standard not unconstitutionally vague to determine whether to allow manufactured homes in "residential" subdivision). Would it be better to have a standard that "no permit shall issue if the proposed structure will be so incompatible so as to cause substantial depreciation in the value of surrounding property?" *See State ex rel. Saveland Park Holding Corp. v. Wieland*, 69 N.W.2d 217 (Wis.1955).

3.   "Many local governments are discovering the desirability of architectural controls in the wake of the "McMansion" trend, in which homeowners build oversized houses that intrude, both visually and physically, on surrounding properties." *See* Julian Conrad Juergensmeyer & Thomas E. Roberts, *Land Use Planning and Development Regulation Law* § 12:3 (3d ed.). Architectural controls are also crucial to the successful implementation of "New Urbanism" designs. See discussion *infra* Ch. 2, Section 1.

4.   Aesthetics is a major, although not inclusive, motivator of tree and view protection ordinances. Denver, for example, has a height limitation in certain zones to preserve the view of the mountains from several city parks. *See Landmark Land Co. v. City and County of Denver*, 728 P.2d 1281 (Colo.1986)(upholding acts as legitimate effort to promote aesthetics). *See also Echevarrieta v. City of Rancho Palos Verdes*, 103 Cal.Rptr.2d 165 (Cal.App.2001). DeKalb County, Georgia, has tree preservation ordinances that protects trees of certain sizes from being cut without permission of the county arborist and requires a certain density of trees per acre of residential land. *Greater Atlanta Homebuilders Ass'n v. DeKalb County*, 588 S.E.2d 694 (Ga.2003)(upholding tree preservation ordinance against facial takings claim and finding due process claim unripe). *See also Zimmerman v. Wabaunsee County*, 218 P.3d 400 (Kan.2009)(county-wide prohibition on commercial wind farms based on aesthetic concerns and protection of rural character of county was reasonable land use regulation).

5.   Since the turn of the century, courts have upheld prohibitions of billboards and other signs. Since earlier cases refused to concede that aesthetic regulation was justified, other grounds for regulating signs were used, ranging from public safety to traffic safety. Perhaps the most bizarre were attempts to justify such regulations on moral grounds because of sexual crimes and behavior that might take place behind billboards. *See Thomas Cusack Co. v. City of Chicago*, 242 U.S. 526 (1917); *St. Louis Gunning Advertising Co. v. St. Louis*, 137 S.W. 929, 942 (Mo.1911); and *Murphy, Inc. v. Town of Westport*, 40 A.2d 177, 178 (Conn.1944), in which the court said:

> In the earlier cases, courts apparently did not realize as clearly as they do now, as the result of facts found upon various trials, that billboards may be a source of danger to travelers upon highways

through insecure construction, that accumulations of debris behind and around them may increase fire hazards and produce unsanitary conditions, that they may obstruct the view of operators of automobiles on the highway and may distract their attention from their driving, that behind them nuisances and immoral acts are often committed, and that they may serve as places of concealment for the criminal.

Apart from the traffic safety rationale, the reasons offered in the Connecticut case ring rather hollow. In *Hawaii v. Diamond Motors, Inc.*, 429 P.2d 825 (Haw.1967), an ordinance prohibited signs exceeding 75 square feet in area and 16 feet in height in industrial districts. When challenged by the owner of an offending sign on the ground that the ordinance was based solely on aesthetics, the city argued that aesthetic considerations were really a means to promote the general welfare, especially the tourist trade. The state supreme court, not thinking it necessary to be tied to the city's cautious approach, adopted what it called "a more modern and forthright position." 429 P.2d at 827:

> We accept beauty as a proper community objective, attainable through the use of the police power. We are mindful of the reasoning of most courts that have upheld the validity of ordinances regulating outdoor advertising and of the need felt by them to find some basis in economics, health, safety, or even morality. *See Thomas Cusack Co. v. City of Chicago*, 242 U.S. 526 (1917). We do not feel so constrained.

> Hawaii's constitution provides:

>> The State shall have power to conserve and develop its natural beauty, objects and places of historic or cultural interest, sightliness and physical good order, and for that purpose private property shall be subject to reasonable regulation. (Article VIII, Section 5.)

> Appellants argue that this constitutional provision has no application to this case because the offending sign is located in an industrial area. We do not agree. The natural beauty of the Hawaiian Islands is not confined to mountain areas and beaches. The term "sightliness and physical good order" does not refer only to junk yards, slaughter houses, sanitation, cleanliness, or incongruous business activities in residential areas, as appellants argue. [429 P.2d at 827–28.]

For a different view on the positive and negative values that flow from billboards, *see* The Outdoor Advertising Association of America, http://www.oaaa.org and Scenic America, http://scenic.org. *See generally* David Burnett, Note: *Judging the Aesthetics of Billboards*, 23 J.L. & POL. 171 (2007).

The more difficult aspect of sign regulation today is the First Amendment, which we cover in Chapter 3.

6.   "Have citizens come to have unrealistic expectations of zoning? In today's climate one anticipates that neighbors will object to any project. These

neighbors are often described by developers with several pejorative acronyms. First, there is the well-known NIMBY (Not in My Back Yard) syndrome, followed by the increasingly prevalent CAVE people (Citizens Against Virtually Everything) and the BANANA (Build Absolutely Nothing Anywhere Near Anything) mindset."

7.   Architectural controls are often imposed by private covenant. The increasingly intrusive nature of private covenants is of concern to those who see a resemblance between the power of homeowners' associations and local governments, and worry over whether residents may be subject to arbitrary controls. *See* David L. Callies, Paula A. Franzese, and Heidi Kai Guth, Ramapo *Looking Forward: Gated Communities, Covenants, and Concerns*, 35 URB.LAW. 177 (2003); Clayton P. Gillette, *Courts, Covenants, and Communities*, 61 U.CHIC.L.REV. 1375 (1994). Common law rules against undue restraints on alienation and against enforcement of contracts deemed violative of public policy can be used by courts to review the reasonableness of covenants. In *Rhue v. Cheyenne Homes, Inc.*, 449 P.2d 361 (Colo.1969), the court upheld a board's rejection of a proposed Spanish-style house in a neighborhood of ranch style and split-level style homes as a reasonable application of an architectural compatibility standard. In so holding, the court mentioned the due process clause as the source of its requirement that covenants be reasonable. But, how can that be? The lack of state action precludes application of the federal due process clause, and similar clauses in most state constitutions, to private covenants. One exception is New Jersey, where the free speech guarantee in the state constitution is applied against private parties under a balancing test crafted by the state supreme court. In *Committee for a Better Twin Rivers v. Twin Rivers Homeowners' Association*, 929 A.2d 1060 (N.J.2007), the court held that a homeowners' association did not violate the free speech rights of its members when it banned posting political signs in their yards. Also, the right of privacy guarantee of the California constitution applies to private conduct. *Nahrstedt v. Lakeside Village Condominium Ass'n.*, 33 Cal.Rptr.2d 63, 878 P.2d 1275 (1994). *See* Lisa J. Chadderdon, *No Political Speech Allowed: Common Interest Developments, Homeowners Associations, and Restrictions on Free Speech*, 21 J.LAND USE & ENVTL.L. 233 (2006). Shelley Ross Saxer, *Judicial State Action;* Shelley v. Kraemer, *State Action, and Judicial Takings (Symposium)*, 21 WIDENER L.J. 847 (2012). For other issues regarding gated communities, including their effect on social disintegration, *see* Chapter 4, *infra*.

8.   Aesthetics is a major, though not exclusive, motivator of tree and view protection ordinances. Denver, for example, has a height limitation in certain zones to preserve the view of the mountains from several city parks. *See Landmark Land Co. v. City and County of Denver*, 728 P.2d 1281 (Colo.1986) (upholding act as legitimate effort to promote aesthetics). *See also Echevarrieta v. City of Rancho Palos Verdes*, 103 Cal.Rptr.2d 165 (Cal.App.2001), *cert. denied*, 534 U.S. 950 (2001). DeKalb County, Georgia, has a tree preservation ordinance that protects trees of certain sizes from being cut without permission of the county arborist and requires a certain density of trees per acre of residential land. *Greater Atlanta Homebuilders Ass'n v.*

DeKalb County, 588 S.E.2d 694 (Ga.2003) (upholding tree preservation ordinance against facial takings claim and finding due process claim unripe). *See also Zimmerman v. Wabaunsee County*, 218 P.3d 400 (Kan.2009) (county-wide prohibition on commercial wind farms based on aesthetic concerns and protection of rural character of county was reasonable land use regulation).

I. HISTORIC PRESERVATION: DISTRICTS AND LANDMARKS

[T]he historical and cultural foundations of the Nation should be preserved as a living part of our community life and development in order to give a sense of orientation to the American people.

16 U.S.C.A. § 470(2)

How did protection of cultural values come to be viewed as a proper public concern in a modern world centered on the liberty and autonomy of the individual? *See* Joseph Sax, *Heritage Preservation as a Public Duty: The Abbé Grégoire and the Origins of an Idea*, 88 MICH.L.REV. 1142 (1990).

Assuming there is a consensus that the preservation of historic areas, buildings, and artifacts, is a proper and desirable public goal, the questions we address here are, first, how that goal is achieved, and, second, whether it should be the owners of the property or taxpayers who bear the often high associated costs. The use of the police power to require a private property owner to maintain a historic building (whether a landmark or as part of a historic district) is a fairly draconian measure to accomplish what is surely a secondary general welfare goal. After all, not all police power goals are equal, are they? It is only somewhat more defensible to forbid alteration or demolition of such structures, yet the cases are legion in support of such police power regulations—provided the owner is left with some economic use, and provided the designation process is done equitably. *See* David L. Callies, *Historic Preservation Law in the United States*, 32 ENVTL.L.RPTR. 10348 (2002).

Local preservation ordinances first appeared in the 1930s in Charleston, South Carolina and New Orleans, Louisiana. The preservation movement subsequently spread throughout the country at local, state, and federal levels. Every state and more than 2300 municipalities now have laws dealing with historic preservation. *See Zoning and Land Use Controls* § 7.01[1] (P. Rohan and E. Kelly, eds. 2015); National Trust for Historic Preservation, A Citizen's Guide to Protecting Historic Places, http://www.preservationnation.org/issues/smart-growth/ (follow link after the "Smart Growth Toolkit" heading).

"In modern times, historic preservation efforts generally involve either the designation of landmarks, of the creation of entire historic districts. The leading historic landmarks case is *Penn Central Transportation Co. v. City of New York*, 438 U.S. 104 (1978), in which the Supreme Court considered "whether a city may, as part of a comprehensive program to preserve historic landmarks and historic districts, place restrictions on the development of individual historic landmarks—in addition to those imposed by applicable zoning ordinances—without effecting a "taking" requiring the payment of "just compensation." Id.

The New York historic preservation law at issue targeted specific structures with historic, cultural or architectural significance. Significantly, New York sought to protect these urban landmarks not by acquiring the properties, but by "involving public entities in land-use decisions affecting th[e] properties and providing services, standards, controls, and incentives [to] encourage preservation by private owners[.]" Id. The law tasked an 11-member Commission, assisted by technical staff, with identifying significant "landmarks" and "historic districts," and created a process by which such sites could ultimately be designated as historic. Upon designation, the property owner's rights concerning use of the landmark site were drastically restricted. Among other things, the law imposed a duty on the owner to keep exterior features of the building in good repair, and required the owner to secure the Commission's advanced approval before the exterior could be altered or improved. According to the court, these restrictions on the owner's control of the parcel were counteracted by an economic benefit: the right to transfer "development rights" to other nearby parcels. In summary, from a landowner's perspective, "[a]ctivities ranging from replacing windows to total demolition would now be subject to the control of governmental third parties." See Designating Penn Central Transportation Co. v. New York City, A Landmark of Constitutional Jurisprudence, National Trust Forum, Spring 2003, SJ053 ALI-ABA 775, 778.

The Supreme Court ultimately upheld the constitutionality of the New York Landmark Preservation Law by applying a "partial takings" analysis that we will examine in detail in Chapter 3 Section C. Significantly, Penn Central definitively upheld the practice of designating individual parcels and structures for historic preservation. In doing so, the court sanctioned preservation laws that financially burden specific individual landowners without providing the reciprocity of benefit and burden that have historically justified the zoning power.

The following case deals with the second type of historic preservation: historic districting.

A-S-P ASSOCIATES V. CITY OF RALEIGH

Supreme Court of North Carolina, 1979.
298 N.C. 207, 258 S.E.2d 444.

Plaintiff brought this action seeking a declaratory judgment that two ordinances adopted on 3 June 1975 by the City of Raleigh are invalid both on constitutional and statutory grounds. The two ordinances (hereinafter referred to collectively as the Oakwood Ordinance) amended the City's zoning ordinance to create a 98 acre, overlay historic district in the City's Oakwood neighborhood (hereinafter referred to as the Historic District), established the Raleigh Historic District Commission (hereinafter referred to as the Historic District Commission), adopted architectural guidelines and design standards to be applied by the Historic District Commission in its administration of the Oakwood Ordinance, and provided civil and criminal penalties for failure to comply with the Oakwood Ordinance. See Code of the City of Raleigh §§ 24–57 through 57.8 (1959).

The Ordinance was adopted pursuant to G.S. §§ 160A–395 through 399, which authorize municipalities to designate historic districts and to require that after the designation of a historic district any property owner within it who desires to erect, alter, restore, or move the exterior portion of any building or other structure first obtain a certificate of appropriateness from a historic district commission. A historic district commission's action is limited by G.S. § 160A–397 to "preventing the construction, reconstruction, alteration, restoration, or moving of buildings, structures, appurtenant fixtures, or outdoor advertising signs in the historic district which would be incongruous with the historic aspects of the district." who defines

In May of 1974, the Division of Archives and History of the North Carolina Department of Cultural Resources nominated Raleigh's Oakwood neighborhood for inclusion on the United States Department of Interior's National Register of Historic Places. In the required statement of significance, the Division's Survey and Planning Unit observed:

Oakwood, a twenty-block area representing the only intact nineteenth century neighborhood remaining in Raleigh, is composed predominantly of Victorian houses built between the Civil War and 1914. Its depressed economic state during most of the twentieth century preserved the neighborhood until 1971, when individuals began its revitalization. The great variety of Victorian architectural styles represented by the houses reflects the primarily middle-class tastes of the business and political leaders of Raleigh for whom they were built, as well as the skill of local architects and builders. Oakwood is a valuable physical document of Southern suburban life during the last quarter of the nineteenth century.

On 25 June 1974, the Oakwood neighborhood was placed on the National Register.

At the request of The Society for the Preservation of Historic Oakwood, the Planning Department of the City of Raleigh conducted a study of the Oakwood neighborhood in 1974. Those conducting the study found that a high rate of absentee ownership existed in the neighborhood, that banks were reticent to lend money in the Oakwood area as a result of its unstable property values, that significant private efforts to preserve the historic aspects of the neighborhood had been undertaken, and that the neighborhood was at a transition point with an uncertain future. The

Choice during Econ. Trial

recommendation of the study was that the City take affirmative action in one of two ways: (1) Plan and zone the neighborhood for high density residential and commercial development, which would result in the loss of most aspects of the historic significance of the neighborhood, or (2) maintain the neighborhood as medium density residential with an emphasis on preserving its historic aspects.

In January of 1975, the Planning Department submitted to the City Council a Proposal for the Designation of Oakwood as an Historic District. A proposed ordinance was submitted to the State Division of Archives and History for review, and recommended changes were made. On 10 April 1975, a joint public hearing was held before the Raleigh City Council and Planning Commission at which both proponents and opponents of the ordinance presented their views. On 3 June 1975 the City Council adopted the Oakwood Ordinance.

The Historic District thus created is an overlay zoning district. All zoning regulations in the area in effect prior to passage of the Oakwood Ordinance remain in effect. Compliance with the Oakwood Ordinance is required in addition to compliance with the preexisting, underlying zoning regulations. Most of the area covered by the Historic District is zoned residential. A relatively small portion of the area covered by it is zoned as office and institutional. Associates own a vacant lot, located within the Historic District at 210 North Person Street. The lot is within the office and institutional zoning district.

* * *

Associates' first contentions are that the Oakwood Ordinance deprives them of their property without due process of law in contravention of the Fourteenth Amendment to the United States Constitution, and that it deprives them of their property otherwise than by the law of the land in contravention of Article I, Section 19, of the North Carolina Constitution. The terms "law of the land" and "due process of law" are synonymous. *Horton v. Gulledge*, 277 N.C. 353, 177 S.E.2d 885 (1970); *State v. Ballance*, 229 N.C. 764, 51 S.E.2d 731 (1949).

Associates' claim is premised on a line of cases in which this Court has indicated that a statute or ordinance based purely on aesthetic considerations, without any real or substantial relation to the public health, safety or morals, or the general welfare, deprives individuals of due process of law.

Associates contend that the Oakwood Ordinance falls within the scope of such impermissible exercise of the police power because it focuses entirely on the exterior appearance of structures within the Historic District. Associates further contend that even if the Ordinance is a valid exercise of the police power insofar as it is applied to historic structures, it is invalid when applied to new construction on property such as Associates' vacant lot.   *New lots/ Structures*

* * *

Legislative exercise of the police power to regulate private property in the interest of historic preservation has met with increasing acceptance by the courts of other jurisdictions. * * * *See* Comment, *Historic Preservation Cases: A Collection*, 12 WAKE FOREST L.REV. 227 (1976). Historic district legislation similar to the provisions of G.S. §§ 160A–395 through 399 has now been enacted by at least thirty-nine states. Beckwith, *Developments in the Law of Historic Preservation and a Reflection on Liberty*, 12 WAKE FOREST L.REV. 93, 95 n. 18 (1976); Wilson and Winkler, *The Response of State Legislation to Historic Preservation*, 36 LAW AND CONTEMP. PROB., 329 (1971). More than 500 cities and towns have passed local landmark or historic district ordinances. National Trust for Historic Preservation, Historic Preservation and the Law, Part IV, ch. 5, p. 3 (1978). More than 500 cities and towns have passed local landmark or historic district ordinances.

Trend

In *Maher v. City of New Orleans*, [516 F.2d 1051 (5th Cir.1975)], plaintiff challenged an ordinance that regulates the preservation and maintenance of buildings in the historic Vieux Carré section of that City. In rejecting plaintiff's contention that the architectural controls imposed by the ordinance were not within the parameters of police power regulation, the Court observed: "[p]roper state purposes may encompass not only the goal of abating undesirable conditions, but of fostering ends the community deems worthy. * * * Nor need the values advanced be solely economic or directed at health and safety in their narrowest senses. The police power inhering in the lawmaker is more generous, comprehending subtler and ephemeral* societal interests." *Id.* at 1060.

* * *

The preservation of historically significant residential and commercial districts protects and promotes the general welfare in distinct yet intricately related ways. It provides a visual, educational medium by which an understanding of our country's historic and cultural heritage may be imparted to present and future generations. That understanding provides in turn a unique and valuable perspective on the social, cultural, and economic mores of past generations of Americans, which remain operative to varying degrees today. Historic preservation moreover serves as a stimulus to protection and promotion of the general welfare in related, more tangible respects. It can stimulate revitalization of deteriorating residential and commercial districts in urban areas, thus contributing to their economic and social stability. It tends to foster architectural creativity by preserving physical examples of outstanding architectural techniques of the past. It also has the potential, documented in numerous instances, e.g., in the Vieux Carré section of New Orleans, of generating

Benefits to Society

substantial tourism revenues. Although it is also recognized that historic preservation legislation, particularly historic district ordinances, may adversely affect the welfare of certain segments of society and infringe on individual liberty, the wisdom of such legislation is "fairly debatable," precluding substitution of our judgment for that of the General Assembly.

Comprehensive regulation of the "construction, reconstruction, alteration, restoration, or moving of buildings, structures, appurtenant fixtures, or outdoor advertising signs in the historic district which would be incongruous with the historic aspects of the district" is the only feasible manner in which the historic aspects of an entire district can be maintained. Associates' contention that the provisions in the Oakwood Ordinance requiring issuance of a certificate of appropriateness for new construction is unreasonable, particularly when applied to Associates' plans to construct an office building on its now vacant lot, is without merit. It is widely recognized that preservation of the historic aspects of a district requires more than simply the preservation of those buildings of historical and architectural significance within the district. In rejecting a similar challenge, the District Court in *Maher v. City of New Orleans* observed: "just as important is the preservation and protection of the setting or scene in which [structures of architectural and historical significance] are situated." This "tout ensemble" doctrine, as it is now often termed, is an integral and reasonable part of effective historic district preservation.

Most important, however, is the fact that Associates and other property owners similarly situated are not prohibited by the Oakwood Ordinance from erecting new structures. They are only required to construct them in a manner that will not result in a structure incongruous with the historic aspects of the Historic District. Property owners within the Historic District may, by virtue of this requirement, be unable to develop their property for its most profitable use or at the cost they would prefer. But the mere fact that an ordinance results in the depreciation of the value of an individual's property or restricts to a certain degree the right to develop it as he deems appropriate is not sufficient reason to render the ordinance invalid. The test of reasonableness necessarily involves a balancing of the diminution in value of an individual's property and the corresponding gain to the public.

* * *

Associates contend that adequate standards have not been established in this instance. * * * The delegation of legislative power to municipal governing bodies is not in this instance, however, an unlimited delegation. G.S. § 160A–396 provides that before a city or county may designate one or more historic districts it must establish a historic district commission. G.S. § 160A–396 further limits the delegation of power by specifying that, "[a] majority of the members of such a commission shall have demonstrated special interest, experience, or education in history or architecture * * * ."

G.S. § 160A–397 imposes another limitation by specifying the method by which a historic district ordinance adopted by a city or county is to be enforced:

> From and after the designation of a historic district, no exterior portion of any building or other structure (including stone walls, fences, light fixtures, steps and pavement, or other appurtenant features) nor above-ground utility structure nor any type of outdoor advertising sign shall be erected, altered, restored, or moved within such district until after an application for a certificate of appropriateness as to exterior architectural features has been submitted to and approved by the historic district commission.

G.S. § 160A–397 then establishes the standard by which a historic district commission is to be bound in its administration of a historic district by approving or disapproving applications for Certificates of Appropriateness:

> The commission shall not consider interior arrangement and shall take no action under this section except for the purpose of preventing the construction, reconstruction, alteration, restoration, or moving of buildings, structures, appurtenant fixtures, or outdoor advertising signs in the historic district *which would be incongruous with the historic aspects of the district.* (Emphasis added.)

[handwritten margin note: limitations on authority]

A historic district ordinance is to be administered by a historic district commission, the composition of which is specified by the General Assembly, in accordance with the standard of "incongruity" set directly by the General Assembly in G.S. § 160A–397.

The Oakwood Ordinance itself reflects this statutory mixture of delegated legislative and administrative powers. The Ordinance first establishes the Historic District and its boundaries. Section 24–57.4 of the Code of the City of Raleigh establishes the Raleigh Historic District Commission to enforce the Ordinance; Section 24–57.1 authorizes the Historic District Commission to require applications for a Certificate of Appropriateness for any proposed activities within the Historic District which are covered by the specific provisions of G.S. § 160A–397, quoted *supra*; Section 24–57.3 adopts the standard set forth in G.S. § 160A–397 of preventing those activities specified in G.S. § 160A–397 "which would be incongruous with the historic aspects of the district" as the limitation on the discretion conferred on the Historic District Commission.

Section 24–57.5 incorporates by reference "architectural guidelines and design standards," which are set forth in a January 1975 report prepared by Raleigh's Planning Department entitled A Proposal for the Designation of Oakwood as an Historic District. The Historic District

[handwritten margin note: set std. in advance]

Commission is directed to apply the incorporated guidelines and standards in its consideration of applications for Certificates of Appropriateness.

It is on these "architectural guidelines and design standards" that Associates mistakenly focus their contention that power to administer the Oakwood Ordinance has been delegated to the Historic District Commission without adequate standards. Associates contend the architectural guidelines and design standards "vest the Commission with the untrammeled authority to compel individual property owners in the Historic District to comply with whatever arbitrary or subjective views the members of the Commission might have as to how property in the district should be maintained or developed."

From the foregoing analysis of the enabling statutes and the Oakwood Ordinance itself, however, it is manifestly clear that it is not the guidelines and standards incorporated into the Oakwood Ordinance which must meet the legal test of sufficiency, but rather it is the standard set forth in G.S. § 160A–397 and in the Ordinance itself, which limits the discretion of the Historic District Commission to preventing only those of certain specified activities, "which would be incongruous with the historic aspects of the district." Although we cannot ignore in our consideration the guidelines and standards incorporated into the Oakwood Ordinance, if the general standard of "incongruity" is legally sufficient to withstand a delegation challenge, the incorporated guidelines and standards, which give varying degrees of specificity to that general standard are sufficient a fortiori.

* * *

Although the neighborhood encompassed by the Historic District is to a considerable extent an architectural mélange, that heterogeneity of architectural style is not such as to render the standard of "incongruity" meaningless. The predominant architectural style found in the area is Victorian, the characteristics of which are readily identifiable. City of Raleigh, Planning Department, A Proposal to Designate Oakwood as a Historic District, p. 1 (1975); N.C. Department of Cultural Resources, National Register Nomination Form, Oakwood Historic District (1974). In his deposition, Raleigh's Planning Director, A.C. Hall, Jr., testified:

> [T]he remaining part of Oakwood, yes, has been developed since that time, with varying types of architecture, filling in the holes, so to speak, in the neighborhood, but still this is in my opinion and my recollection, this is the only and the best example, and has a majority of worthwhile Victorian or Victorian Era structures in it, in the neighborhood that we have.

The characteristics of other architectural styles of historical interest found in the Historic District are equally distinctive and objectively ascertainable. City of Raleigh Planning Dept., *supra*, pp. 16–17. The architectural guidelines and design standards incorporated into the

[handwritten marginal note: General observable trend of the neighborhood]

Oakwood Ordinance (described in note 4, *supra*) provide an analysis of the structural elements of the different styles and provide additional support for our conclusion that the contextual standard of "incongruity" is a sufficient limitation on the Historic District Commission's discretion.

It will be remembered that G.S. § 160A–396 requires that a majority of the members of a historic district commission shall have demonstrated special interest, experience, or education in history or architecture. There is no evidence that Raleigh's Historic District Commission is not so constituted. To achieve the ultimate purposes of historic district preservation, it is a practical necessity that a substantial degree of discretionary authority guided by policies and goals set by the legislature, be delegated to such an administrative body possessing the expertise to adapt the legislative policies and goals to varying, particular circumstances.

It is therefore sufficient that a general, yet meaningful, contextual standard has been set forth to limit the discretion of the Historic District Commission. Strikingly similar standards for administration of historic district ordinances have long been approved by courts of other jurisdictions.

The procedural safeguards provided will serve as an additional check on potential abuse of the Historic District Commission's discretion. Provisions for appeal to the Board of Adjustment from an adverse decision of the Historic District Commission will afford an affected property owner the opportunity to offer expert evidence, cross-examine witnesses, inspect documents, and offer rebuttal evidence. Similar protection is afforded to a property owner by the right to appeal from a decision of the Board of Adjustment to the Superior Court of Wake County.

The decision of the Court of Appeals is reversed, and the entry of summary judgment by the superior court in favor of defendant City on all claims raised by Associates' complaint is affirmed.

Reversed and remanded.

Views of the Historic Oakwood Neighborhood at issue in A-S-P Associates v. City of Raleigh

Photographs provided by, and used with the permission of, the N.C. Dept. of Cultural Resources (Photo #1 by Randall Page, 1974, Photo #2 by David Black, 1988).

The photograph below pictures the N.C. Beer Wholesalers building that sits on the formerly vacant lot at 210 N. Person St. at issue in ASP.

The building received a certificate of appropriateness from the City and was built in 1985.

NOTES

1.   Examine the photographs of Oakwood reproduced above. Do the photos make the "incongruity" standard meaningful? The third photograph shows what was ultimately built on the lot. Consider what happened in *Maher v. City of New Orleans*, 371 F.Supp. 653 (E.D.La.1974), *aff'd* 516 F.2d 1051 (5th Cir.1975), *cert. denied* 426 U.S. 905 (1976), relied on by the A-S-P court for the "tout ensemble" doctrine. Maher wanted to tear down a Victorian cottage in the French Quarter and replace it with a Spanish style building more in keeping with the style of other buildings in the Quarter. Upholding the commission's disapproval of Maher's request, the court noted that "[s]ome architects thought that the existing juxtaposition of the cottage with its immediate neighbors created an aesthetically pleasing scene, itself worthy of preservation." *Id.* at 664. *See Estate of Tippett v. City of Miami*, 645 So.2d 533, 537 (Fla.App.1994), for a list of decisions that have rejected vagueness challenges to historic preservation ordinances.

Under the Raleigh ordinance, could one replace the original, non-insulated wood-frame windows with vinyl insulated glass windows? What about in the chillier northeast? *See* Tad Heuer, Note, *Living History: How Homeowners in a New Local Historic District Negotiate Their Legal Obligations*, 116 YALE L.J. 768 (2007) (an empirical study of how owner-occupiers reacted to a new historic district in New Haven, Connecticut).

2.   If you owned a house in an area like Oakwood that was being considered for historic districting, would you support or oppose the proposal? How would you react to a proposed historic districting if you were a renter rather than a wealthy New Haven landowner? In fact, a study of the Oakwood area in 1985 demonstrated the effects of historic districting. The district had, in the words of a resident, "arrived," and was "very small-towny in a positive" sense. One realtor bought a house in 1979 for $17,500, converted it into a single family home from what she called "several crummy apartments," and sold it a year later for $54,000. In 1983, the same house sold for $71,000. Raleigh News and Observer, May 5, 1985, at 1-F. What do you suppose happened to the people that lived in the "crummy" apartments?

In fact, much of the criticism levied at redevelopment schemes—that they result in the eviction of the poor who are predominantly racial and ethnic minorities—can also be applied to historic preservation schemes. The true effect of historic districting is, however, hardly a settled matter. David B. Fein, Note, *Historic Districts: Preserving City Neighborhoods for the Privileged*, 60 N.Y.U.L.REV. 64 (1985) (focusing on the injustice in displacement) and Richard F. Babcock and David L. Callies, *Ecology and Housing: Virtues in Conflict, in Modernizing Urban Land Policy* 205 (Clawson ed.1973). *But see* J. Peter Byrne, *Two Cheers for Gentrification*, 46 HOW.L.J. 405 (2003) (conceding the loss of affordable housing, but arguing that the benefits that flow from neighborhood revitalization may offset the loss and ultimately lead to the creation of more affordable housing); Ryan Howell, Note, *Throw the "Bums" Out? A Discussion of the Effects of Historic Preservation Statutes on Low-Income Households Through the Process of Urban Gentrification in Old Neighborhoods*, 11 J.GENDER RACE & JUST. 541 (2008) (arguing historic preservation is an "ideal vehicle to cure the social evils of gentrification."); Geoff Wagner, *Virtue and Vice: A Reassessment of Gentrification*, 7 J.L.SOCIETY 271 (2006) (criticizing the common arguments both for and against gentrification).

3.   As to the procedural issues, there are generous opportunities for objection and appeal in the ordinances in *Penn Central* (*see* case *supra* Ch. 3) and A-S-P both at the designation and the prohibition stages. Note the use of expert panels and detailed standards for designation and regulation. *See* footnote 8 in *Penn Central*. The A-S-P court observes, these "procedural safeguards * * * serve as an additional check on potential abuse of the Historic District Commission's discretion." 258 S.E.2d at 455. Perhaps, but are they constitutionally required? *See* David E. Hollowell, Note, *Historic Zoning in North Carolina:* A-S-P Associates v. City of Raleigh, 16 WAKE FOREST L.REV. 495 (1980). On the other hand, are they constitutionally sound? If you were the owner seeking a certificate of appropriateness, would you be comfortable with "expert panels"?

4.   *The Federal Role*. Note the references in the A-S-P case to the registration of the property on the U.S. Dep't of Interior's National Register of Historic Places. In 1949 Congress created the National Trust for Historic Preservation as a federally chartered, non-profit corporation to administer historic sites donated to the government and facilitate public participation in

[handwritten margin note: Cost to the poor of historic districting]

preservation. *See* 54 U.S.C.A. § 312102. *See Landmarks Preservation Council v. City of Chicago*, 531 N.E.2d 9 (Ill.1988) (conferring standing on the Trust to challenge the decertification of a historic landmark even though it was not a national landmark). The National Historic Preservation Act of 1966 (NHPA), 54 U.S.C.A § 312101 et. seq., created a system, for listing historic properties (the National Register of Historic Places), imposed an obligation on federal agencies, including federally funded or licensed undertakings, to consider the impact of their actions on listed or eligible sites. Those engaged in covered federal activities are required to consult with the Advisory Council on Historic Preservation. *See, e.g., National Min. Ass'n v. Fowler*, 324 F.3d 752 (D.C.Cir.2003) (Advisory Council exceeded its statutory authority by defining federal undertakings to include those that are subject to state or local regulation administered pursuant to a delegation or approval by a federal agency). In *Pye v. United States Army Corps of Engineers*, 269 F.3d 459 (4th Cir.2001), the court found that neighboring landowners, trying to protect an African-American cemetery and other historic sites from the consequences of a federal agency's grant of a permit to fill wetlands, had standing to challenge the agency's compliance with NHPA.

The historical review process, known as Section 106 review, under NHPA is similar to the environmental review dictated by the National Environmental Policy Act (NEPA). *See, e.g., Coliseum Square Ass'n, Inc. v. Jackson*, 465 F.3d 215 (5th Cir.2006), *cert. denied*, 522 U.S. 810 (2007) (finding HUD's funding of a housing development revitalization project did not violate § 106 of NHPA or NEPA). The NHPA process is advisory only, but it has the potential for the same delay of federal action that will adversely affect historic properties as NEPA does for actions affecting the environment. *Friends of the Atglen-Susquehanna Trail, Inc. v. Surface Transp. Bd.*, 252 F.3d 246 (3d Cir.2001) (Board abused its discretion when it unilaterally terminated NHPA process). For an example in which an ancient rock carving (a petroglyph) effectively delayed for years a major federal highway project in part due to noncompliance with NHPA, *see Stop H-3 Ass'n v. Coleman*, 533 F.2d 434 (9th Cir.1976). The listing function thus performed and supervised by the National Trust for Historic Preservation is potent protection against precipitous federal governmental activities that affect adversely a historic site or structure. Listing does not affect private or state activities. *See* David L. Callies, *Historic Preservation Law in the United States*, 32 ENVTL.L.RPTR. 10348, 10353 (2002); Andrea C. Ferster, *Recent Developments in Case Law Interpreting the National Historic Preservation Act, 1990 to the Present*, SM056 ALI-ABA 305 (2007).

5.   *Landmarks*. Recall that the Supreme Court upheld the landmark designation of Grand Central against a takings claim in the Penn Central case. Numerous courts have followed suit. *See District Intown Properties Ltd. Partnership v. District of Columbia*, 198 F.3d 874 (D.C.Cir.1999), *cert. denied*, 531 U.S. 812 (2000); *International College of Surgeons v. City of Chicago*, 153 F.3d 356 (7th Cir.1998) (no taking under state constitution); *State ex rel. BSW Development Group v. City of Dayton*, 699 N.E.2d 1271 (Ohio 1998); *United Artists Theater Circuit, Inc. v. City of Philadelphia*, 635 A.2d 612 (Pa.1993) and

Teachers Insurance and Annuity Ass'n of America v. City of New York, 185 A.D.2d 207, 586 N.Y.S.2d 262 (1992).

Most would agree that the designation of property as landmarks is constitutionally more suspect than the creation of historic districts, Penn Central notwithstanding. The latter create the reciprocity of benefit and burden that helps justify zoning. Landmarking is harder, but not impossible (see the majority opinion in Penn Central), to fit within the reciprocity principle. While the Court rejected the takings claim in Penn Central, there remains the question of whether it is fair to place the financial burden on the owner of the landmark. After all, the property, or a negative easement in the property, could be acquired by eminent domain, and the public, the predominant beneficiary, could bear the cost by paying just compensation. *See generally* David L. Callies, *Historic Preservation in the United States*, 32 ENVTL L.RPTR. 10348, 10351 (2002).

6.   First Amendment problems may arise in several contexts when historic preservation is involved. *See* Stephan R. Miller, *Historic Signs, Commercial Speech, and the Limits of Preservation*, 25 J.LAND USE & ENVTL.LAW 227 (2010) (exploring whether regulations requiring the preservation of historical signs constitutes compelled commercial speech under the First Amendment). A more familiar example involves the landmarking of religious structures. Decisions such as that involving St. Bartholomew's Church in New York, discussed in Chapter 3 G.4 sparked passage of the Religious Freedom Restoration Act in 1993. The Supreme Court held the act unconstitutional in *City of Boerne v. Flores*, 521 U.S. 507 (1997), itself a case involving the landmarking of a religious building. *See* Elizabeth C. Williamson, City of Boerne v. Flores and the Religious Freedom Restoration Act*: The Delicate Balance Between Religious Freedom and Historic Preservation*, 13 J.LAND USE & ENVTL.L. 107 (1997); Alan C. Weinstein, *The Myth of Ministry vs. Mortar: A Legal and Policy Analysis of Landmark Designation of Religious Institutions,* 65 TEMP.L.R. 91 (1992).

The Religious Land Use and Institutionalized Persons Act (RLUIPA), expressly covers landmarking of religious buildings. 42 U.S.C.A. § 2000cc–5(5). *See* Julia H. Miller, *Regulating Historic Religious Properties Under RLUIPA* (NHTP Preservation Law Reporter Educational Materials, 2007), ALI-ABA, SM056 ALI-ABA 817. *See also* discussion of RLUIPA, *supra* Ch. 3.G.4.

Religious property may qualify for National Register designation based on the historical importance of its architecture. *See* 36 C.F.R. § 60.4 (2016). In 1992, reversing long standing federal policy, Congress amended the National Historic Preservation Act to authorize grants to religious properties listed on the National Register, "provided that the purpose of the grant is secular, does not promote religion, and seeks to protect those qualities that are historically significant." 54 U.S.C.A. 302 905 (2014). Does this violate the establishment clause?

7.   Can government use its eminent domain power to acquire religious property? After state courts held the City of San Diego violated the state

constitution by displaying a cross in its Mt. Soledad Park, the federal government stepped in and took the property by eminent domain in order to preserve the cross. That action has been challenged. *See Jewish War Veterans of the U.S. of America, Inc. v. Gates*, 506 F.Supp.2d 30 (D.D.C.2007). *See also* Jason Marques, Note, *To Bear a Cross: The Establishment Clause, Historic Preservation, and Eminent Domain Intersect at the Mt. Soledad Veterans Memorial*, 59 FLA.L.REV. 829 (2007).

In 1994, the California legislature exempted religious properties from historic preservation laws. *See* West's Cal. Govt. Code § 25373. The stimulus for the act was the announced intention of the Catholic Archdiocese of San Francisco to cut costs by closing nine churches. When opponents of the closings sought to have the churches designated as landmarks, the church persuaded the legislature to come to its aid with an amendment to the state historic preservation statute exempting religious properties from designation. Does such an exemption violate the establishment clause? *See supra* Ch. 3.G.4. *See* Felipe M. Nuñez and Eric Sidman, *California's Statutory Exemption for Religious Properties from Landmark Ordinances: A Constitutional and Policy Analysis*, 12 J.L. & RELIGION 271 (1995–1996). The California court upheld the exemption. *East Bay Asian Local Development Corp. v. State of California*, 13 P.3d 1122 (Cal.2000), *cert. denied* 532 U.S. 1008 (2001).

8. In *Society of Jesus of New England v. Boston Landmarks Commission*, 564 N.E.2d 571 (Mass.1990), the court struck down the designation of the interior of a church on state constitutional grounds. The "configuration of the church interior is so freighted with religious meaning that it must be considered part and parcel of the Jesuits' religious worship." *Id.* at 573. What about interiors of commercial buildings? Should it matter whether such interiors are primarily public—like a railway station, or primarily private—like a corporate headquarters building? Under such a distinction, how would an office building with a highly public lobby fare? New York City landmarked the Seagram Building, its interior lobby, and the interior space occupied by the Four Seasons restaurant. The designation was upheld. *Teachers Insurance and Annuity Ass'n of America v. City of New York*, 623 N.E.2d 526 (N.Y.1993). For full treatment of these and other issues, *see* John J. Costonis, *Icons and Aliens: Law, Aesthetics and Environmental Change* (1989); William J. Murtagh, *Keeping Time: The History and Theory of Preservation in America* (1988).

9. Historic preservation includes cultural artifacts and activities as well. The Hawaii State Constitution provides:

> The State shall have the power to conserve and develop objects and places of historic or cultural interest, and provide for public sightliness and physical good order. For these purposes private property shall be subject to reasonable regulation. [Art. IX, section 7.]

See also Aluli v. Brown, 437 F.Supp. 602 (D.Haw.1977), in which the court ordered the Navy to prepare a new EIS under NEPA before recommencing target practice bombardment of the Hawaiian Island of Kahoolawe after the discovery of additional archeological sites, in part to effectuate the purpose of NHPA. The federal Archeological Resources Protection Act of 1979, 16 U.S.C.A. §§ 470aa–470ll, limits removal of such resources from public or Indian lands.

10.   Tax law plays an important role in historic preservation. Before 1976, the laws indirectly encouraged the destruction of historic structures since demolition costs could be written off. Tax incentives were created in 1976, and revised in 1981, in the form of rehabilitation investment credits. As a consequence, significant amounts of money were put into historic properties between 1976 and 1986. The Tax Reform Act of 1986, however, limited the availability of the tax credit and the amounts that could be invested were reduced. The results of the 1986 act led to diminished use of the rehabilitation credit. *See* Bradford J. White & Lee Keatinge, *Historic Preservation and Architectural Control Law*, 24 URB.LAW. 865, 866 (1992) and Richard Roddewig, *Recent Developments in Land Use, Planning, and Zoning Law*, 22 URB.LAW. 719, 750 (1990). For a review of the past and present tax aspects of historic preservation and a suggestion for ways to create better incentives, *see* Carolyn Ells Cheverine & Charlotte Hayes, *Rehabilitation Tax Credit: Does It Still Provide Incentives?*, 10 VA.TAX REV. 167 (1990). For help from overseas, *see* Mariah Fogleman, *A Capital Tax System to Preserve America's Heritage: A Proposal Based on the British National Heritage Capital Tax System*, 23 VAND.J.TRANSNAT'L L. 1 (1990).

Tax deductions are available for the donation of preservation easements. *See* Richard J. Roddewig, *Outline: Conservation and Historic Preservation Easements: An Appraiser's Primer on Tax Rules and Valuation Issues*, SL053 ALI-ABA 13 (Nov. 2005). *See generally* Richard Roddewig, *Preservation Law and Economics, A Handbook on Historic Preservation Law* 427 (C. Duerksen). *See* in *Texas Department of Housing and Community Affairs*, 135 S.Ct. 2507, 192 L.Ed.2d 514:

> "These unlawful practices include zoning laws and other housing restrictions that function unfairly to exclude minorities from certain neighborhoods without any sufficient justification. Suits targeting such practices reside at the heartland of disparate-impact liability. *See, e.g., Huntington*, 488 U.S., at 16–18, 109 S.Ct. 276 (invalidating zoning law preventing construction of multifamily rental units); *Black Jack*, 508 F.2d, at 1182–1188 (invalidating ordinance prohibiting construction of new multifamily dwellings); *Greater New Orleans Fair Housing Action Center v. St. Bernard Parish*, 641 F.Supp.2d 563, 569, 577–578 (E.D.La.2009) (invalidating post-Hurricane Katrina ordinance restricting the rental of housing units to only " 'blood relative[s]' " in an area of the city that was 88.3% white and 7.6% black); *see also* Tr. of Oral Arg. 52–53 (discussing these cases). The availability of disparate-impact liability, furthermore, has allowed private developers to vindicate the FHA's objectives and to protect their property rights by stopping

municipalities from enforcing arbitrary and, in practice, discriminatory ordinances barring the construction of certain types of housing units. *See, e.g., Huntington, supra,* at 18, 109 S.Ct. 276. Recognition of disparate-impact liability under the FHA also plays a role in uncovering discriminatory intent: It permits plaintiffs to counteract unconscious prejudices and disguised animus that escape easy classification as disparate treatment. In this way disparate-impact liability may prevent segregated housing patterns that might otherwise result from covert and illicit stereotyping.

11. When regulation, tax incentives, and tax abatement prove insufficient or ineffective, there is the option of acquiring the historic property through eminent domain. In *United States v. Gettysburg Electric Railway Co.,* 160 U.S. 668 (1896), the Court held the use of the power of eminent domain to buy the battlefield to be a public use. Acquisition of the fee is not always required; agreements and easements have sometimes sufficed. Public-private ventures may also be used. Singer Ani DiFranco and her company, Righteous Babe Records, acquired an abandoned historic church that was scheduled for demolition in DiFranco's hometown of Buffalo, N.Y. The city and county provided $5.8 million in inducements to enable the purchase and restoration. *See* Buffalo Business First, June 11, 2003.

12. There is also the option for the City to sue the developer who demolishes an historic building for damages. The following case is instructive.

CITY OF DALLAS v. TCI WEST END, INC.

Supreme Court of Texas, 2015.
463 S.W.3d 53.

The City of Dallas contends that TCI West End, Inc. (TCI) demolished a building located in a historic overlay district in violation of a city ordinance. *See* Dallas City Ordinance No. 21391, as amended by Ordinance No. 22158, § 7.1 (requiring building owner, prior to demolishing or altering building located in historic overlay district, to apply for determination as to whether structure is "contributing structure" subject to strict demolition requirements); *see also id.* at § 4 (incorporating chapter 51A of the Dallas City Code); Dallas, Tex. City Code § 51A–4.501(a)–(p) (regulating historic overlay districts). Among other claims, the City sued TCI for civil penalties under section 54.017 of the Texas Local Government Code, as authorized by section 54.012 of the code. *See* TEX. LOC. GOV'T CODE § 54.012 (listing types of ordinances municipality can enforce by civil action), .017 (authorizing civil penalties for ordinance violations). Following a jury verdict in the City's favor, the trial court rendered judgment awarding the City $750,000 in civil penalties.

The court of appeals reversed, holding that sections 54.012 and 54.017 apply only to health and safety ordinances, not "general zoning ordinances regulating the use of land." 407 S.W.3d at 301. On rehearing, one justice dissented on both counts, explaining that (1) sections 54.012 and 54.017 do not contain the health-and-safety limitation imposed by the court and (2) sufficient evidence supported the jury's finding that TCI had actual notice of the ordinance provision before demolishing the building. *Id.* at 302–05.

Although other issues have been raised on appeal, the threshold issue is whether sections 54.012(3) and 54.017 are limited to enforcement of "health and safety" zoning ordinances. This matter present questions of law that we review de novo. *City of Rockwall v. Hughes*, 246 S.W.3d 621, 625 (Tex.2008).

The court of appeals determined that all the provisions in subchapter B, including sections 54.012(3) and 54.017, "relate only" to health and safety matters and thus do not apply to general zoning ordinances regulating the use of land. 407 S.W.3d at 301. The court further held that the City's historic-district regulation does not qualify for enforcement as a health-and-safety ordinance under subchapter B because its stated purpose is to "protect buildings of historical, cultural, and architectural significance" in the historic overlay district. *Id.* (citing Dallas City Ordinance No. 21391, as amended by Ordinance No. 22158). As a result, the court concluded that the ordinance can only be enforced under chapter 211 of the local government code, *id.* which governs municipal zoning and has a stated purpose of "promoting the public health, safety, morals, or general welfare and protecting and preserving places and areas of historical, cultural, or architectural importance and significance," TEX. LOC. GOV'T CODE § 211.001.

To support this construction of subchapter B, the court of appeals cited a Texas Attorney General opinion limiting the statute's application to health and safety matters because (1) it is entitled "Municipal Health and Safety Ordinances" and (2) section 54.012 specifically refers to those types of matters in some of its subsections. *Id.* (citing Tex. Att'y Gen. Op. No. GA–0267 (2004)). The court also cited *Hollingsworth v. City of Dallas*, 931 S.W.2d 699 (Tex.App.—Dallas 1996, writ denied), in which the court had previously resolved an apparent conflict between the injunctive-relief provisions in chapters 54 and 211 as they pertain to general zoning ordinances regulating the use of land. In Hollingsworth, a property owner had argued that the City of Dallas could not obtain injunctive relief for a zoning-ordinance violation without complying with section 54.106, which authorizes injunctive relief only on "a showing of substantial danger of injury or an adverse health impact to any person or to the property of any person other than the defendant." *Id.* at 702; TEX. LOC. GOV'T CODE § 54.016. Section 211.012(c)'s injunctive-relief remedy includes no similar requirement. TEX. LOC. GOV'T CODE § 211.012(c). The court resolved the conflict in favor of section 211.012's application because it specifically applies to ordinances regulating the use of land and section 54.016 does not. 931 S.W.2d at 703 (construing statutes to avoid creating a conflict and determining that "the Legislature intended section 211.012 to apply to ordinances regulating the use of land and intended section 54.016 to apply to other types of ordinances not at issue").

We hold that the court of appeals' interpretation of section 54.012(3) as incorporating a health-and-safety limitation is contrary to the plain and unambiguous language in the statute and would render meaningless and redundant language in that section expressly circumscribing other categories of ordinances enforceable under subchapter B.

Section 54.012(3) expressly authorizes municipalities, such as the City, to enforce ordinances "for zoning that provides for the use of land or classifies a parcel of land according to the municipality's district classification scheme." TEX. LOC. GOV'T CODE § 54.012(3). Section 54.012(3)'s language plainly encompasses the zoning ordinance at issue in this case, and neither the words "health" and "safety" nor analogous limitations are included anywhere therein. In comparison, at least three other subsections of section 54.012 expressly limit the types of ordinances that may be enforced to those involving health or safety matters or use comparable terminology. *See id.* § 54.012(1) (pertaining to ordinances "for the preservation of public safety, relating to [building construction]"), .012(2) (referring to ordinances "relating to the preservation of public health or to the fire safety of a building or other structure or improvement"), .012(6) (applying to ordinances "relating to dangerously damaged or deteriorated structures or improvements").

Accordingly, we reverse the portion of the court of appeals' judgment concluding that chapter 54, subchapter B does not authorize the City's enforcement action against TCI and remand the cause to that court for further proceedings consistent with this opinion.

NOTE: TRANSFERABLE DEVELOPMENT RIGHTS

Historic landmark designations may significantly limit development options, giving rise to takings claims based on loss of economically viable use. The same is true of programs for the preservation of farmland and environmentally sensitive lands, such as wetlands, forests, and open space. *See* Chapter 9 *infra*. In order to mitigate the economic impact of such regulations, communities may use transferable development rights programs (TDRs), such as the one described in the Penn Central case in Chapter 3.

Historically, development rights, including their use, severance, and transfer, go back to the law pertaining to air rights. Development rights depend on both police power regulation and the law of eminent domain, especially in the land banking permutation. In modern times, the concept of independent and valuable rights to develop land at some distance above the surface is well established. A good example is the separation and sale of air rights above the Illinois Central Railroad tracks in Chicago, where investors have bought such rights in order the develop hotels and offices. If air rights are separable for the purposes of ownership, it is a simple logical extension to allow them to be moved for use elsewhere in a jurisdiction, Julian Conrad Juergensmeyer, James C. Nicholas, and Brian D. Leebrick, *Transferable Development Rights and Alternatives After Suitum*, 30 URB.LAW. 441, 444–448 (1997).

TRANSFERABLE DEVELOPMENT RIGHTS AND ALTERNATIVES AFTER SUITUM

Julian Conrad Juergensmeyer, James C. Nicholas, and Brian D. Leebrick
30 Urb.Law. 441, 444–48 (1997).

Due to inherent differences in the condition or location of land, Euclidean zoning and related regulatory means frequently result in uneven impacts on landowners. Landowners in areas where higher intensity development is encouraged economically benefit, while landowners in areas where land is protected from development are hurt. A fairer system would allow all landowners to benefit from the area's development, and require all benefitted landowners to pay the costs associated with the preservation and protection of sensitive land. TDR programs offer this alternative by separating the need to preserve a particular parcel of land and any rights that a landowner may have to develop that land. The promise of the TDR is that it will provide a means to economically benefit owners of sensitive land by a means other than development of that land.

* * *

Simply put, TDR programs separate the development potential of a parcel from the land itself and create a market where that development potential can be sold. Planning agencies then identify areas they wish to protect and other areas which are suitable for development. An effective TDR program will have delineated sending and receiving zones. Since the need to protect sensitive land is often the impetus for TDR schemes, identifying the land from which development potential will be sent, the sending zones, is relatively simple. Local governments especially, often have a difficult time politically and practically identifying receiving zones that will then have denser development than would otherwise be allowed.

Sending zones, as the name suggests, are simply zones or areas that will export development potential. The sending areas should be identified as areas for limited development within the context of a comprehensive plan. The plan could designate an area for limited development for any number of reasons: habitat preservation, wetland protection, erosion control, protection of historic resources, and agricultural land retention.

Once an owner of land in a sending zone has recorded the necessary covenants and received her TDRs, she no longer has the right to develop the land in the manner or manners restricted by the general regulations, or by any additional restrictions that may be contained in the covenants. Generally, sending area property owners are required to record a covenant running with the land permanently removing certain development rights. * * *

In order to achieve fairness, the TDRs must have a meaningful economic value. To make sure a market is created, there must be a balance between sending and receiving zones. If there are too many TDRs on the market, the price falls and the fairness of the TDR scheme is questioned. Additionally, if receiving area property owners need not acquire TDRs in order to attain their desired level of developmental intensity, then there will be no demand for those rights and their economic value will be zero. Ideally, each owner of restricted land would get enough TDRs to mitigate the development value loss, and the value of the use of those TDRs in the receiving areas will deliver that value to sending area property owners.

Receiving zones are regions set aside by the regulating jurisdiction to accept development potential from restricted land elsewhere in the jurisdiction. To maintain a market for the TDRs from the sending zone, receiving zones must be growing areas with a market demand for increased density. In a free market, the value of the TDRs will be set near the marginal value of that increased density. However, if landowners in receiving zones can increase density through variances or rezoning, those administrative procedures are, in effect, competing with TDRs. If it is less costly or less time consuming to go through the administrative process for a rezoning, the TDR market will flounder. Local governments instituting TDR programs should be careful not to cannibalize the TDR program by providing administrative alternatives to the market. Additionally, if receiving areas are already "overzoned," marginal increases in land development intensity will have no economic value, and TDRs will also have no economic value.

There are economic benefits associated with [protecting environmentally sensitive lands and historically significant properties]. By requiring landowners of nonsensitive land to buy development rights from the owners of sensitive land, the government is forcing developers to "internalize" the costs associated with land development. The standard approach to development regulation permits private landowners that are benefitted from environmental amenities not to consider the social costs of destroying environmental or similar benefits enjoyed by a community. If places are made for bald eagles, the community is better for it. If those places are lost, the community, as well as the bald eagles, are worse for it. TDRs create a greater social efficiency by forcing the developers that benefit from land preservation to recognize costs associated with such preservation.

NOTE: TDRs IN THE SUPREME COURT

In *Penn Central*, discussed earlier in this section, the railroad's airspace lessee was unable to build the 50 to 55 story tower atop Grand Central Station. The railroad, however, had transferable development rights that it could use on property that it owned in the vicinity of the station. After losing its takings clam, the railroad did use some of its development rights elsewhere. *See* Linda J. Bozung and M. Randall McRoberts, *Land Use, Planning and Zoning in 1987: A National Survey*, 19 URB.LAW. 899, 948 (1987).

Suitum v. Tahoe Regional Planning Agency, 520 U.S. 725 (1997), is a later TDR case. Bernadine Suitum owned a lot in Incline Village, Nevada, an area that falls within the jurisdiction of the Tahoe Regional Planning Authority (TRPA). Land development permission under TRPA is obtained pursuant to an Individual Parcel Evaluation System (IPES). When Suitum applied for an IPES score, TRPA assigned her lot a zero since the lot was found to lie within a Stream Environment Zone, which drains into Lake Tahoe. While the zero score prohibited her from building on her lot, under a transferable development rights program, she was able to transfer 183 square feet of development rights (one percent of her 18,300 square foot lot) to other parcels within the same hydrologic zone. Rather than applying for her TDRs, Suitum filed suit claiming that the inability to build on her lot constituted a taking under the Fifth Amendment.

The Ninth Circuit found her claim unripe under Williamson County (see discussion *supra* Chapter 3). Likening the TDR program to traditional variance relief, the court of appeals found that Suitum should first pursue her rights under the program. Finding that a TDR was a "use" of property for the purposes of a takings challenge, the court said it could not assess the economic impact of the TRPA regulatory scheme on Suitum until she applied for relief.

The Supreme Court reversed the Ninth Circuit and held that the final decision ripeness rule of Williamson County deals solely with rights to use of a claimant's land. There was agreement that TRPA had definitively determined that no building could be constructed on Suitum's lot, and that made the case ripe. While the majority left open the role that TDRs play in deciding whether a taking has occurred, Justice Scalia, in concurring, makes clear that he (and Justices O'Connor and Thomas) think TDRs are irrelevant to the question of whether a taking has occurred. His reasoning:

> TDRs, of course, have nothing to do with the use or development of the land to which they are (by regulatory decree) "attached." The right to use and develop one's own land is quite distinct from the right to confer upon someone else an increased power to use and develop his land. The latter is valuable, to be sure, but it is a new right conferred upon the landowner in exchange for the taking, rather than a reduction of the taking. In essence, the TDR permits the landowner whose right to use and develop his property has been restricted or extinguished to extract money from others. Just as a cash payment from the government would not relate to whether the regulation "goes too far" (i.e., restricts use of the land so severely as to constitute a taking), but rather to whether there has been adequate compensation for the taking; and just as a chit or coupon from the government, redeemable by and hence marketable to third parties, would relate not to the question of taking but to the question of compensation; so also the marketable TDR, a peculiar type of chit which enables a third party not to get cash from the government but to use his land in ways the government would otherwise not

permit, relates not to taking but to compensation. It has no bearing upon whether there has been a "final decision" concerning the extent to which the plaintiff's land use has been constrained.

Putting TDRs on the taking rather than the just compensation side of the equation (as the Ninth Circuit did below) is a clever, albeit transparent, device that seeks to take advantage of a peculiarity of our takings clause jurisprudence: Whereas once there is a taking, the Constitution requires just (i.e., full) compensation, * * * , a regulatory taking generally does not occur so long as the land retains substantial (albeit not its full) value, *see, e.g.,* Penn Central. If money that the government-regulator gives to the landowner can be counted on the question of whether there is a taking (causing the courts to say that the land retains substantial value, and has thus not been taken), rather than on the question of whether the compensation for the taking is adequate, the government can get away with paying much less. That is all that is going on here.

* * *

I do not mean to suggest that there is anything undesirable or devious about TDRs themselves. To the contrary, TDRs can serve a commendable purpose in mitigating the economic loss suffered by an individual whose property use is restricted, and property value diminished, but not so substantially as to produce a compensable taking. They may also form a proper part, or indeed the entirety, of the full compensation accorded a landowner when his property is taken". [117 S.Ct. at 1672.]

Regarding TDRs, other articles of interest include John J. Costonis, *The Chicago Plan: Incentive Zoning and The Preservation of Urban Landmarks*, 85 HARV.L.REV. 574 (1972); John J. Costonis, *Development Rights Transfer: An Exploratory Essay*, 83 YALE L.J. 75 (1973); Note, *The Unconstitutionality of TDR*, 84 YALE L.J. 1101 (1975); and David L. Callies, Commonwealth v. Rosso*: Land Banking and the Expanded Concept of Public Use*, 2 MICH.J.L.REF. 199 (1969). Generally, *see* Juergensmeyer and Roberts, *Land Use Planning and Development Regulation Law* § 9.9 (2nd ed.2015). For a planning perspective on TDRs, *see From Landmarks to Landscapes: A Review of Current Practices in the Transfer of Development Rights*, 63 J.AM.PLAN.ASS'N 365 (June 1997), 1997 WL 11458032.

For an article from a real estate marketing aspect, *see* Martin A. Schwartz, *It's Up in the Air: Air Rights in Modern Development*, 89 FLORIDA BAR JOURNAL 42 (2015):

Although the Miami 21 Zoning Code imposes height limits for buildings in the Miami Modern Biscayne Boulevard historic district, the code allows for TDRs. The TDRs enable owners of historic property to sell to developers whose projects are located in specifically designated, high-density zoning areas of Miami, the development rights that they are unable to utilize because of historic designation. In such transactions, the property in the high-density zone obtains a development bonus in the form of greater height or density rights. The revenue from such transfers for the contributing site, which can amount to millions of dollars, can then be used for renovations of the historic property.

As an example, developer Avra Jain sold 440,000 square feet of Vagabond Motel's historic development rights for $3 million in 2014 to developers who were able to enlarge the size of their condominium projects in Coconut Grove, Edgewater, and Brickell. She also sold the Royal Motel's 142,868 square feet of air rights to a developer for a 57-story Brickell project. Jain commented that the ability to raise money through a TDR sale "is key to the restoration of the deteriorated boulevard motels, whose small size and big renovation needs would otherwise make the job financially unfeasible." TDRs also appeal to condominium developers because they have been able to purchase them for $7–9 per square foot, considerably cheaper than the cost of buying additional development capacity through the city's Miami 21 bonus' program, which also permits builders to purchase the right to add volume to their projects at about $17 per square foot.

On TDRs generally, *see* Arthur C. Nelson, Rick Pruetz, and Doug Woodruff, *The TDR Handbook: Designing and Implementing Transfer of Development Rights Programs* (2011). The authors present a series of case studies on TDRs and PDRs (purchase of development rights) in the following areas: farmland preservation, environmental protection, rural character, historic preservation, and urban design and revitalization. The book explores the designing of TDR and PDR programs, sending and receiving areas, analyzing the economics of programs and legal issues. Historic preservation case studies include San Francisco, Denver, and New York.

For a TDR program that is not tied to preservation of historic buildings, *see* Matt A. Charan, *As a New High Society Climbs in Manhattan, It's a Race to the Top*, New York Times, December 22, 2015 at A-1 (As recently as two years ago, only five towers in New York City topped 1,000 feet. Now there are that many "supertall" towers in the works on from 53rd to 60th Streets alone. The list is staggering: (1) 220 Central Park South (59th Street) at 950 feet; (2) One 57th Street, 1005 feet; (3) 36 Central Park South (59th Street), 1,000 feet; (4) 53 West 53rd Street, 1050 feet; (5) 432 Park Avenue (57th Street), 1,396 feet; (6) 520 Park Avenue at 60th Street, 780 feet; (7) 111 57th Street, 1,428 feet; and (8) Central Park Tower, 217 W. 57th Street, 1,550 feet; and there These buildings, which are super thin and have very few units, some of which have sold for over $100 million dollars, utilize the sale of air rights from nearby underutilized sites, and are not restricted to TDRs from historic sites. This area of the city has no restriction on height. These slender cloud-busters result from the confluence of super strong concrete and new wind testing. The 432 Park building is only 93 feet square and is 15 times as tall as it is wide.

J. NEW URBANISM

1. INTRODUCTION

The move toward diversity in use and innovation in design, which began with PUDs in the 1960s, evolved in the 1990s, continuing today into an even more creative mode with the onset of "New Urbanism," particularly TND. Today, "new urbanism" offers a far greater range of alternative development use and patterns than that delivered by the conventional cookie cutter subdivision or a typical PUD that does little more than save open space by clustering. New Urbanism achieves this by invigorating building design and community planning with lessons from the past.

New Urbanism consists of three primary patterns of development, each of which differ substantially from Euclidean zoning: (1) traditional neighborhood development; (2) transit oriented development (TOD); and (3) freestanding mixed use centers. The critical focal point of this section will be on the development of mixed use walkable communities, known as "traditional neighborhood development." This first, and primary, goal of new urbanism is to build pedestrian-friendly communities with diverse land uses that enable residents to walk to shopping, recreation, schools, libraries, government offices, parks, trails and work. New Urbanist architects and planners point to compact European cities as a model. Today's younger adult population, as well as ethnic, gender and racial minorities, share the vision of narrow tree-lined streets with sidewalks, and a mix of store front shops, offices, theaters, and moderate to higher density residential development serving the neighborhood's recreational social and economic need, and improving the quality of life by adding front porches that permit community interaction, granting diversified free time, reducing the mental and physical strain arising from commuting and mandatory auto trips for every urban activity.

The principles of new urbanism are most cogently illustrated by their application at the neighborhood level. The following list of principles is distilled from more extensive discussion appearing in Daniel Kennon Slone, Doris Sussman Goldstein, and W. Andrew Gowder, *A Legal Guide to Urban and Sustainable Development for Planners* (Wiley 2008):

- Compact Development. This hinges on well-designed, appropriate density, and efficiency in land use.

- Mixture of Uses and Housing Types. Vertical and horizontal mix of uses and a wide selection of housing options cre activity within the building and area at different times of day, creating a vibrant and safe environment.

- Human Scale. The concept of "walkability" includes a fo on the pedestrian experience, usually done through interconnected network of streets, sidewalks, and transit options, as well as building and public space placement.

The TOD segment of new urbanism is designed to build mixed use centers at station stops on transit corridors. We will discuss TODs in Chapter 7, "Smart Growth," focusing on city, county, regional and state controls of urban sprawl by creating three major forms of priority growth areas featuring non-sprawl development patterns: (a) infill featuring TND; (b) transportation corridor centers featuring TODs; and (c) freestanding suburban mixed use centers.

Smart growth and new urbanism, working together with green development and renewable energy (see Chapter 8) are also designed to limit the length and number of vehicle trips in order to reduce greenhouse gas emissions and global warming. Once Smart Growth principles are in place, new urbanism determines the use, type, design and community character of development that will occur within the different smart growth priority development areas.

2.   TRADITIONAL NEIGHBORHOOD DEVELOPMENT (TND)

New urbanism began as a movement by individual design practitioners, largely architects, responding in their own ways to what they considered a decline in quality of life and loss of community. In promoting their alternative to sprawl, these practitioners found in Euclidean zoning a convenient villain. Indeed, many of them initially operated under the misconception that zoning itself was an institutional cause of sprawl because of the predilection of suburban governments to segregate residential development on large lots (an extremely narrow view of a very complex issue). Other vocal practitioners espoused the view that unless zoning and custom were modified, communities would continue to sacrifice their quality of life for unsustainable standards of living. This quality of life, they argued, could best be restored by looking to pre-World War II models of development, using the design of the public realm as a springboard. This is likely the atmosphere in which the earlier term associated with what is now known as new urbanism—Traditional Neighborhood Development, or TND—found its foothold.

There is nothing new about attempts to ameliorate the anti-cultural and social aspects of sprawl by returning to urban neighborhood and pre-auto-age small town development patterns that were widely used before World War II. Simply put: "Without too much overstatement, if you think of your favorite neighborhood or your favorite place to spend a long weekend, you will probably have a good image of what a Traditional Neighborhood Development should look like." What is new is the realization of new urbanists that eliminating sprawl requires both building more compact mixed use walkable traditional communities, and, just as important, locating such communities within and adjacent to existing neighborhoods and cities with adequate public facilities and services in order to reduce the regional fiscal, global warming, air pollution, and transportation congestion impacts of sprawl. *See* Robert H. Freilich, *From Sprawl to Smart Growth*, Chapter 6, New Urbanism, Form Based Codes and LEED for Neighborhood Development pp. 171–175 (American Bar Association, 2010):[6]

Contrary to Euclidean zoning's segregation of uses, there are a number of legal issues facing the successful implementation of New Urbanist development that are similar to those facing PUDs. The first is whether the state enabling legislation, or the zoning ordinance, permits a mix of business and residence within a single zoning district. States may have to amend the zoning enabling statutes to encourage such mixed use development, perhaps as a part of an overall smart growth and sustainability package of legislation.

The second hurdle facing mixed use new urbanism development within a conventional zoning district, even if the TND use is permitted, is the need to obtain variances for architectural design, density, area, side, front and rear yards, height, parking, and front porches encroaching on the front yard. Such variances are both difficult to obtain or take so much time, cost and loss of investment return that they defy the will of even the most patient of developers. Section J will deal with the rise of "form based codes" which replace the proscriptive nature of Euclidean zoning with positive requirements for architecture, design, community facilities, interconnectivity of streets, creating build to lines, and replacing front setbacks.

According to New Urban News, a new urbanist trade publication, the ordinance adopted in 1991 by Dade County, Florida, developed by the town planning firm of Duany Plater-Zyberk & Company (DPZ), is recognized as the first and, at the time, most widely disseminated "TND Code." In designing a substantial number of privately owned communities, DPZ's work in proposing and implementing the "codes" (actually private covenants) for these communities drove the form and content of many of the earlier adopted ordinances.

Since then, cities throughout the United States have included in their land use regulations provisions to promote this type of development. Generally, these types of regulations have been of two varieties: (1) some municipalities have rewritten portions of or entire ordinances to incorporate new urbanist principles; and (2) some have enacted special districts for this purpose. Presumably, the emergence of these two

---

approaches is attributed to the political culture of the particular municipality adopting the ordinance. Notwithstanding the dictates of a comprehensive plan that requires the implementation of new urbanist principles, a standoff can ensue between those who would implement the principles on the ground, making new urbanism the "default setting" for all the development in that district, and those who advocate allowing applicants to propose landing a flexible floating or planned district zone.

Several characteristics emerge when one examines the range of regulating approaches to achieve the new urbanism. In whatever form, these land development regulations reflect the principles described above and typically contain provisions for

- vertical and horizontal mixed use;
- a mix of housing types;
- compact design;
- pedestrian orientation;
- the design of all types of formal open space, including streets; and
- an emphasis on design aspects.

The 21st Century Land Development Code takes this a step further and integrates these principles into growth management tiers, corridors, transit centers, and infill and establishes zoning districts to eliminate Euclidian restraints. This approach to regulation can help to halt sprawl by reducing vehicle miles traveled and by concentrating growth in compact patterns, again with a preference to existing built-up areas. See traditional neighborhood development standards found in Robert H. Freilich and S. Mark White, *21st Century Land Development Code*, § 2.6 at p.50 (American Planning Association, 2008).

Until recently, ordinances incorporating new urbanist development standards tended to be overly prescriptive, especially those that attempted to emulate private covenant-enforced codes. A number of the striking features of these older ordinances were to legislatively mandate the following specific details: a specific percentage in the mix of uses and building types; a maximum size of lots; "build-to" lines (as opposed to minimum setbacks); the proportions and relationships between building facades; street widths; and, in some cases, an attempt to regulate architectural details and materials. This approach to regulation stands in stark contrast with conventional, more proscriptive, zoning ordinances. Recent attempts to reach a more acceptable middle ground of new urbanist-influenced land development regulations have led to the form-based code movement.

The following case discusses a number of the legal hurdles that a new urbanist mixed use or traditional neighborhood development has to contend with, albeit successfully in the case below.

PINECREST HOMEOWNERS ASSOCIATION V. GLEN A. CLONINGER & ASSOCIATES

Supreme Court of Washington, En Banc, 2004.
151 Wash.2d 279, 87 P.3d 1176.

OWENS, J.

The Spokane City Council (City Council) determined that the rezone application of developer Glen A. Cloninger Associates (Cloninger) could be processed prior to the drafting and enactment of a specific zoning ordinance called for in an immediately effective amendment of the Spokane City Comprehensive Plan. The superior court upheld the City Council's land use decision, but the Court of Appeals then reversed it, prompting Cloninger's petition for review. We reverse the Court of Appeals and affirm, as the superior court did, the City Council's decision.

Cloninger's property is located on the northeast corner of Napa Street and 29th Avenue in the Lincoln Heights area of Spokane. In 1991, the property was rezoned from multifamily to RO-1L (Limited Residential Office), permitting Cloninger to develop the parcel as an office park. In May 1992, the City Council passed a resolution allowing restaurants in office parks of five acres or more on sites covered by the Lincoln Heights Neighborhood Specific Plan, a part of the Spokane City Comprehensive Plan. Because building a restaurant on the site also required a rezone to RO-L (Limited Residential Office). Cloninger applied for the rezone, which was granted on April 8, 1993. Cloninger built the restaurant (on the southeast corner of the site) but deferred development of the office park.

In October 1996, Cloninger applied for an amendment to Land Use Policy 6 of the Lincoln Heights Neighborhood Specific Plan to permit office developments of at least five acres to qualify for mixed use development-that is, development that combines residential, office, and retail uses. Cloninger's proposed development involved a lower level of retail with a second level of office space and, above that, multifamily housing. The City Council passed Resolution 98–69 on September 21, 1998, approving the amendment. Land Use Policy 6 was amended to read as follows:

POLICY 6: Allow low-rise office use along 29th Avenue, as designated on the Land Use Plan Map, subject to the following criteria:

a) Developments should extend generally no more than one block in depth from 29th Avenue.

b) The minimum site area for office development should be two acres.

c)   Building height should be limited to 30 feet.

d)   Access to developments should be from existing curb cuts on 29th Avenue, not from streets serving residential areas.

e)   If a site is not separated from a single family residential area by a street, then increased building and parking setbacks and landscaping should be provided.

f)   Rezone proposals should be processed under the P.U.D. [planned unit development] provisions of the zoning code and provide transitions between significantly different residential uses.

g)   Allow high density residential office on the Land Use Plan map, providing that restaurants be developed in conjunction with [a] P.U.D. of five acres or more.

h)   Allow large developments (five acres or more) to qualify for the "Design" zone designation in accordance with the provisions of SMC 11.19.2405.A, which allows mixed use developments that include specific land uses. Proposals that qualify for the mixed use designation and incorporate mixed uses in a comprehensive site development should demonstrate compliance with the following concepts:

   1.   To enable sustainable development of integrated, mixed use communities, containing a variety of housing types arranged around an activity center (neighborhood, district, corridor); that provide a pleasant living, shopping, and working environment; that provide a sense of community; and that provide a balance of compatible retail, office, residential, recreational and public uses.

   2.   To enable a land use pattern that will reduce dependence on automobile use, especially drive-alone vehicle use during morning and evening commute hours.

   3.   To enable the design of new development in a manner that will ensure the safe and efficient movement of goods and people.

   4.   To provide direct, convenient pedestrian, bicycle and vehicular access between residences and nearby activity centers, in order to facilitate pedestrian and bicycle travel and reduce the number and length of automobile trips.

   5.   To discourage automobile dominated businesses, which are characterized by drive-in and drive-through facilities that allow people to remain in their vehicles while

receiving products or services, and uses that traditionally require large amounts of off-street parking.

6. To provide sufficient housing density to enable cost-effective extension of utilities, services, and streets; facilitate frequent transit service; and help sustain neighborhood businesses.

7. To enable many of the community's residents to live within one-fourth (1/4) mile of a grocery store and transit stop.

8. To ensure that activity centers are arranged, scaled and designed to be compatible with surrounding land uses.

9. To ensure that buildings and other development components are arranged, designed and oriented to facilitate pedestrian access and access for transit.

10. To allow innovative site and building designs while providing for design harmony and continuity (e.g., coordinated architectural styles, street trees, lighting, signage and benches).

11. To ensure adequate light, air, privacy and readily accessible open space for each dwelling unit in order to maintain public health, safety and welfare.

12. To provide for appropriately located community open spaces for informal social activity, recreation and aesthetic enhancement of the development.

13. To provide mixed use development with a character that is less physically and visually intrusive than traditional commercial centers, districts and strips.

14. To insure the mixed use development does not undermine the buffer concept described in subsection e of this policy.

Cloninger applied for a rezone from RO-L to RO-1D, a revision of his existing PUD, and a special permit to allow B1 uses per SMC 11.19.249. On July 26, 2000, the city design review committee voted 7–0 with one abstention to recommend approval of the PUD amendment and special permit, subject to Cloninger's "more fully addressing" concepts 4, 9, 11, and 12 listed in the Lincoln Heights Neighborhood Specific Plan, Land Use Policy 6. h). On October 31 and November 2, 2000, the city hearing examiner conducted a public hearing on Cloninger's application. One day before the hearing, the planning department gave Cloninger its staff report, recommending that the application be denied, because it was premature to zone the property to mixed use where the City had yet to adopt mixed use design standards to govern Cloninger's request for a special use permit under RO-1D for mixed use. On December 11, 2000, the hearing examiner denied the application "subject to the development of appropriate zoning regulations and design review criteria." On January 16, 2001, the hearing examiner denied Cloninger's request for reconsideration. Cloninger appealed the decision to the City Council, and on March 26, 2001, the City Council held a hearing on the appeal. On April 2, 2001, the City Council reversed and remanded the hearing examiner's decision. The City Council instructed the hearing examiner to process the application "in such a way as to accomplish permitting of the mixed use land use as a rezone to RO-ID, and . . . to do so with reference to the provisions of the Lincoln Heights Neighborhood Specific Plan.

On April 20, 2001, the Pinecrest Homeowners Association, the Rockwood Neighborhood Council, and various homeowners (hereafter "Pinecrest") filed a petition in Spokane County Superior Court under the Land Use Petition Act (LUPA), chapter 36.70C RCW, seeking reversal of the City Council decision. On November 14, 2001, Spokane County Superior Court Judge Michael E. Donohue affirmed the City Council decision "in all respects."

The hearing examiner approved the rezone to RO-1D on August 9, 2002, and Cloninger was thereafter issued a building permit for the parking lot. On February 13, 2003, Division Three of the Court of Appeals reversed the superior court's decision. *Pinecrest Homeowners Ass'n v. Glen A. Cloninger & Assocs.*, 62 P.3d 938 (Wash.App.2003). The Court of Appeals held that the rezone to RO-1D was properly denied by the Hearing Examiner. We granted Cloninger's petition for review.

ISSUE

Has Pinecrest shown that the City Council misinterpreted the Spokane Municipal Code (SMC) when it allowed Cloninger's land use application to be processed under the similar design zone designation of RO-1D and in accordance with the immediately effective amendment of the Lincoln Heights Neighborhood Specific Plan?

As a reason for warranting the hearing examiner's second action upon Cloninger's application, the City Council asserted that Resolution 98–69, which amended the Lincoln Heights Neighborhood Specific Plan and changed the land use map to designate the area subject to the amendment, "required the Hearing Examiner to process a rezone which would accomplish the fulfillment of the purposes of the amended plan." The City Council had clearly expressed its intention to make the amended specific plan immediately effective, not contingent on the later enactment of the new zoning category and design review criteria. The City Council reasoned further that, because specific plans " 'amend and become part of the comprehensive plan' " and because "land use codes 'shall be consistent with and implement the comprehensive plan,' " the city's zoning code had to "be consistent with and implement" Resolution 98–69's amendment of the

Lincoln Heights Neighborhood Specific Plan. The City Council thus concluded that Cloninger's site "ha[d] been zoned for mixed-use."

Accordingly, the City Council's order directed the hearing examiner to process Cloninger's application as a rezone to RO-1D (allowing a mixed use special permit, to ensure that the mixed-use proposed by the applicant demonstrates compliance with the concepts set forth in the Lincoln Heights Neighborhood Specific Plan, Policy 6, h), and the Land Use Map (of the Specific Plan) to which such Policy applies."

Pinecrest advanced no persuasive arguments that the City Council decision was based on an erroneous interpretation of its municipal code or Washington case law. First, Pinecrest contends that, because "[t]he RO-1D zone is permitted in areas designated only for 'High Density Residential/Low Rise Office' on the adopted Comprehensive Plan" and because "Cloninger's property is designated Medium Density Residential/Office," the RO-1D zone cannot be used to process Cloninger's application. . . . Second, Pinecrest turned to Washington case law to attack the City Council's view that, pending the drafting and enactment of the newly prescribed mixed use zoning ordinances, the Lincoln Heights Neighborhood Specific Plan could serve as a basis for considering Cloninger's rezone application and special permit. Pinecrest argued that this court has "rejected the argument that a Comprehensive Plan [of which the Lincoln Heights [Neighborhood] Specific Plan is an element] can be used to make specific land use decisions." citing *Citizens for Mount Vernon v. City of Mount Vernon*, 947 P.2d 1208 (Wash.1997). . . . Rather, as the Spokane planning director and City Council determined, SMC 11.19.320 allowed processing of the rezone application by reference to the similar RO-1D zoning category, which allowed high density mixed use. *See* SMC 11.19.249. Moreover, in the present case, the circumstance is not a conflict between an existing explicit zoning restriction and the city's comprehensive plan; instead, the problem is a time lag between an immediately effective, targeted amendment of the plan and the drafting and enactment of the zoning ordinance referenced in that amendment.

Pinecrest also maintains that *Anderson v. City of Issaquah*, 851 P.2d 744 (Wash.App.1993), supports its contention that the adoption of mixed use regulations must precede any action on Cloninger's rezone application. At issue in Anderson was a section of the Issaquah Municipal Code setting forth the aesthetic standards governing building design. The criteria amounted to little more than the general requirement that buildings-in their colors, components, materials, and proportions-must be harmonious with the natural environment and neighboring structures. The Anderson decision chronicled the repeated efforts of one developer to intuit and satisfy the shifting personal demands of members of the development commission. (The developer was told, for example, to drive up and down Gilman Boulevard to look for good and bad building facades, and one commissioner actually read into the meeting minutes his own notes, entitled "'My General Observation From Driving Up and Down Gilman Boulevard'" *id.* at 70, 851 P. 2d 744. Pinecrest likens the 14 design concepts in the amended Lincoln Heights Specific Neighborhood Plan to the Issaquah ordinance's statement of aesthetic standards; in Pinecrest's view, the amended plan is too vague to guide the city's consideration of Cloninger's rezone request. But that comparison is not convincing. The aesthetic standards in Anderson were much more general than the design criteria at issue here. Also the 14 concepts in paragraph h) are considered along with the requirements set forth in the seven preceding paragraphs in Land Use Policy 6.

Additionally, whereas in Anderson it was the ordinance itself that suffered from excessive vagueness, in the present case Pinecrest has not claimed that the RO-1D zoning ordinance was too vague to serve as the basis for Cloninger's rezone application. While the ordinance in Anderson set up an extremely vague building review process, the City Council decision in the present case authorized a process that relied on a sufficiently detailed zoning ordinance (SMC 11.19.249) in concert with a considerable number of design review concepts (in Land Use Policy 6, as amended by Resolution 98–69).

* * *

CONCLUSION

We conclude that Pinecrest has not met its burden under RCW 36.70C.130(1)(b) of showing that the City Council decision was an erroneous interpretation of the law. Consequently, pursuant to RCW 36.70C.140, we affirm the land use decision of the City Council, thereby reversing the Court of Appeals and upholding the decision of the superior court.

NOTES

1.   *Anderson v. City of Issaquah*, 851 P.2d 744 (Wash.App.1993), cited in the main opinion, has also been carefully distinguished by other subsequent cases. *See Connor v. City of Seattle*, 223 P.3d 1201 (Wash.App.2009) (approving historic preservation regulations that require that new additions, exterior alterations, or related new construction shall be differentiated from the old and shall be compatible with the massing, size, scale, and architectural features to protect the historic integrity of the property and its environment).

2.   As a land development theory, new urbanism has captured and solidified the imagination of the development and planning community to a degree perhaps not even anticipated by its originators. In doing so during a time of growth and prosperity, it has moved from largely a fringe design theory to an established success with a strong minority of development projects. Indeed, in many parts of the country, it has become the preferred method for land development.

The primary thrust of the theory is to move away from Euclidean zoning's hierarchy of separated use districts with their fixed front, rear, and side yard requirements. New urbanists strive to create mixed use walkable communities in the style of traditional neighborhoods, while integrating design, open space, transit systems, and public places to create a higher quality of life. In the early days of new urbanism, practitioners emphasized building these communities to replace the architectural ugliness and loneliness of typical suburban fringe development. Only since the late 1990s have they recognized that new urbanism complements the growth management and sustainable green development movements by locating projects in infill areas and existing neighborhoods, thus reducing sprawl, vehicle miles traveled, and carbon emissions.

There is a critical need for new types of flexible and planned district land development regulation to enable new urbanist forms of development to fully become established. While interest in this form of compact sustainable development remains strong, the mortgage and lending crisis has negatively affected the number of new urbanist development projects and created hesitancy in local government planning and implementation, which will likely slow the pace of the movement's growth.

New urbanism began as a movement by individual design practitioners, largely architects, responding in their own ways to what they considered a decline in quality of life and loss of community. In promoting their alternative to sprawl, these practitioners found in Euclidean zoning a convenient villain. Indeed, many of them initially operated under the misconception that zoning itself was an institutional cause of sprawl because of the predilection of suburban governments to segregate residential development on large lots (an extremely narrow view of a very complex issue). Other vocal practitioners espoused the view that unless zoning and custom were modified, communities would continue to sacrifice their quality of life for unsustainable standards of living. This quality of life, they argued, could best be restored by looking to pre-World War II models of development, using the design of the public realm as a springboard. This is likely the atmosphere in which the earlier term associated with what is now known as new urbanism—Traditional Neighborhood Development, or TND—found its foothold.

As frustration grew among the practitioners who were trying to fit the "round peg" of their vision into the "square hole" of existing institutionalized development practices, several prominent practitioners discovered that they had much in common. In 1993, Andres Duany and Elizabeth Plater-Zyberk of Florida, and Peter Calthorpe, Daniel Solomon, Elizabeth Moule, and Stephanos Polyzoides of California created a new organization, the Congress for the New Urbanism. The Congress, increasingly a multidisciplinary group, has met every year since then and established a growing network of state and regional chapters.

3.   FORM BASED CODES

FROM SPRAWL TO SMART GROWTH, CHAPTER 6, NEW URBANISM, FORM BASED CODES AND LEED FOR NEW DEVELOPMENT

Robert H. Freilich, Robert J. Sitkowski and Seth D. Mennillo
pp. 175–186 (ABA 2010)[7] (freely edited)

In contrast to conventional land development regulations, which are oriented to regulating use rather than the form of development, form-based codes are designed to place the ultimate physical form [primarily new urbanism] in a superior position to the use to which individual property can be put.

(a) Form-based codes typically look different from conventional zoning regulations because they tend to be more graphically intense, but perhaps their most unique attribute is the recommended process by which they are initially developed. The goal of form-based codes is to be prescriptive rather than proscriptive. Put simply, [t]he [Euclidean zoning] setback line is proscriptive, specifying prohibitions. The build-to line of new urbanism and traditional neighborhood development is prescriptive, prescribing what is expected. These regulations are inherently place-specific, so a great deal of planning and public participation, often undertaken through a citizen "charrette" planning process (the evaluation and amendment of mounted alternative design and architectural drawings), typically occurs well before the regulations are drafted. Some architects have developed their own "codes," but these are basically not capable of being integrated into the zoning ordinance, but rather resemble private covenants, conditions and restrictions (CC&Rs) that are placed in deeds and subdivision plats. The SmartCode, a comprehensive model form-based code promulgated by the new urbanist pioneering architectural firm of Duany, Plater-Zyberk, is based on a physical organizing system described as "The Transect"—a continuum of high to low density from the urban core to the rural environment. The SmartCode is increasingly being proposed in various forms, from Gulf Coast communities to the City of Miami. SmartCode Version 9.2 is available online at http://www.smartcode central.com/; for an annotated version with sample plans and additional resources, *see* Andrés Duany, William Wright & Sandy Sorlien, *SmartCode Version 9 and Manual* (2008). *See also* Andrés Duany & Emily Talen, *Making the Good Easy: The Smart Code Alternative*, 29 FORDHAM URB.L.J. 1445 (2002); Chad D. Emerson, *The SmartCode Solution to Sprawl* (2007).

(b) Regulating Plan. The key element in a Form Based Code is the "regulating plan." The regulating plan is akin to the "specific plan," that we reviewed in Chapter 1D.4, being more detailed than a zoning map that typically shows streets and public open spaces and designates the specific locations where the various building form standards will apply. It also contains the standards that will be crucial to the validity of the Code against void and indefinite challenges. Most regulating plans look quite different from traditional zoning maps and are presented in many different formats. A regulating plan is an essential tool for translating a traditional neighborhood vision into legal place-specific development regulations that are capable of shaping the form of a new zoning district, whether constituting a mapped base district, floating or overlay mixed use or planned unit development district, or a special or conditional use within a base zoning district.

(c) Public Space/Street Standards. These regulations present in a graphic form the widths and dimensions of streets, sidewalks, paths, street trees and furniture, and other standards applicable to the public realm. This term is a central organizing principle in the form-based code because it ties together the policy objective of putting into place walkable, interconnected aspects of a neighborhood with the standards to govern how streets, lots, and buildings fit together, with regard to those parts of the urban fabric that are held in common such as plazas, squares, parks, thoroughfares and civic buildings. Street and sidewalk standards should be included in the zoning regulations and in the subdivision regulations in those jurisdictions that have a bifurcated zoning/subdivision scheme The "Urban" or "Building Form" standards are commonly presented in a graphic form with supporting text covering bulk, height, coverage, and use standards.

(d) Administration and Definitions. A definitions section is critical because many of the architectural and design terms of form based codes could be held to be vague and indefinite without accompanying definitions which are generally not found in conventional zoning or subdivision regulations. Since another of the goals of a form-based code is to promote predictability in process and effect—allowing development applications that meet all requirements to be approved administratively rather than through multiple public hearing processes, a clearly defined application and project review process should be included. Form-based codes are packed with specific instructions, details, and unique graphics and illustrations, the majority of which are geared toward the design of physical space. In *City of Mobile v. Weinacker*, 720 So.2d 953 (Ala.App.1998), the court held that without definitions of terms such as "modern materials" and "modern architectural design," an aesthetic ordinance lacked "ascertainable criteria, requirements, or guidelines for approval" and was therefore impermissibly vague, indefinite and ambiguous. Given the effort of new urbanists to distance form-based codes from conventional regulations, the definition section can be very important to a community making the switch from conventional zoning to form-based codes. Elizabeth Garvin & Dawn Jourdan, 23 J. LAND USE & ENVT'L LAW 395, 410 (2008).

For visual examples of how conventional v. form-based codes work, *see* Introduction to Form-Based Coding, Development Code, City of Raleigh, NC (Feb. 4, 2010) http://www.raleighnc.gov/content/PlanCurrent/ Documents/DevelopmentPlansReview/NewRaleighCode/NRC_Form-Based_Coding_Presentation.pdf.

4.   LEGAL CHALLENGES TO NEW URBANISM

(a) Authority to Enact

(1) *General Authority:* Since many of the enabling statutes around the country are rooted, to one degree or another, in the 1926 Standard State Zoning Enabling Act (SZEA), it is worth examining the provisions of the SZEA to see whether they support a form-based approach. Not surprisingly, they likely do. The "Grant of Power" provisions in the SZEA anticipate that local government can explicitly consider form of development (i.e., coverage, setbacks, height, number of stories, density, and location of structures). It also authorizes regulation by use of structures and land, and describes use in the broadest terms of commercial, residential, and industrial. The list does not preclude the consideration of form in local land regulation. Likewise, the "Purposes in View" provisions of the SZEA do not appear to limit regulation to the use of land. In fact, one additional item in the SZEA's list of purposes places a fine point on this issue: "Such regulations shall be made with reasonable consideration, among other things, to the character of the district and its peculiar suitability for particular uses, and with a view to conserving the value of buildings and encouraging the most appropriate use of land throughout such municipality." This provision seems to strike a balance between the use of land and the form of development (i.e., the character of the district). Contrary to conventional belief, then, the SZEA cannot be considered to be exclusively use-based; indeed, it does not arguably reveal a preference for use over form. Accordingly, there should be sufficient support for a form-based approach in SZEA-influenced states. Elizabeth Garvin & Dawn Jourdan, *Through the Looking Glass: Analyzing the Potential Legal Challenges to Form-Based Codes*, 23 J.LAND USE & ENVT'L LAW 395, 410 (2008).

(2) *Specific Statutory Authority:* California's Government Code authorizes a General Plan's land use element and the zoning ordinances that implement the land use element's provisions, to express community intentions regarding urban form and design:

> The text and diagrams in the land use element that address the location and extent of land uses, and the zoning ordinances that

> implement these provisions, may also express community
> intentions regarding urban form and design. These expressions
> may differentiate neighborhoods, districts, and corridors, provide
> for a mixture of land uses and housing types within each, and
> provide specific measures for regulating relationships between
> buildings, and between buildings and outdoor public areas,
> including streets.

Cal.Gov't. Code § 65302.4.

Other states have also explicitly authorized the adoption of form-based codes. Four other states, aside from California, are Florida, Pennsylvania, Wisconsin, and Connecticut, but activity in over three dozen states indicates that change, at least in terms of authority, is on the way. Pennsylvania and Wisconsin expressly provide that local governments have authority to promulgate "traditional neighborhood" regulations as part of their zoning powers. The Connecticut legislature has enacted a wide-ranging community character statute, the "Village Districts Act," that may be used to support the adoption of new urbanist influenced land development regulations. An example of progressive enabling legislation is Florida, perhaps the leading state in terms of the number of completed new urbanist projects. There is a provision in a section of the Florida Growth Management Act related to land development regulations that provides: "[t]his section shall be construed to encourage the use of innovative land development regulations which include provisions such as transfer of development rights, incentive and inclusionary zoning, planned-unit development, impact fees, and performance zoning." *See* Fla.Stat. § 163.3202. In much the same way, the Rhode Island legislature provides a rather exhaustive list of "general purposes of zoning ordinances" which, inter alia, includes "the need to shape and balance urban and rural development," "the use of innovative development regulations and techniques," and "promoting a high level of quality and design in the development of private and public facilities." *See* Elizabeth Garvin & Dawn Jourdan, 23 J.LAND USE & ENVT'L LAW 395, 411 (2008).

(b) First Amendment

Given the demands of some proponents for design specificity in architectural regulations, there is another potential problem. Highly detailed standards were not much of an administrative problem in early form based codes since they were overwhelmingly enforced as private CC&Rs. But the same standards, if contained in a duly-adopted set of governmental regulations, may rise to the level of a prior restraint on expressive activity, in derogation of the First Amendment. One way to avoid such problems is to ensure that the form-based code regulations constitute a broad tool to shape public space, infill neighborhoods, reduce greenhouse gases and global warming and to control sprawl impacts rather than as a "mere" architectural design regulation, predicated on the government's duty to promote and maintain an environmentally healthy and safe public realm. *See* Janet Haws, *Architecture as Art, Not in My Neocolonial Neighborhood, A Case for Providing First Amendment Protection to Expressive Residential Architecture*, 2005 B.Y.U.L.Rev. 1625.

(c) Substantive Due Process: Vague and Indefinite Standards

The cases reported earlier in this Chapter on new urbanism and planned unit developments are fully applicable to form based codes. A recent Washington Court of Appeals case relating to neighborhood historic preservation is almost prescient as to how a form based code will be judicially treated with respect to special location, siting, identifiable physical features and quality and uniqueness of the neighborhood.

> Conner next contends the ordinance is unconstitutionally vague as applied in this case. We begin with the presumption that the ordinance is constitutional. Conner has the burden of establishing its vagueness. The ordinance provides that [new construction] shall be "compatible with the massing, size, scale, and architectural features to protect the historic integrity of the property and its environment." The features and characteristics to be protected here are the "prominence of spatial location, contrasts of siting, age, or scale which make the house an easily identifiable visual feature of its neighborhood or the city and contributes to the distinctive quality or identity of such neighborhood or the city. Similarly here, the standards derive meaning from the unique conditions and characteristics of the subject to which they are applied. There is no constitutional impediment to such regulations.
>
> Conner's argument, in its essence, is that the ordinance is impermissibly vague because it does not tell him exactly what he can do with his property. This is not the test. The question is whether Conner can ascertain the requirements for an acceptable project. The ordinance contains both contextual standards and a process for clarification and guidance as to individual sites. From these, a landowner can ascertain what changes may be made. The constitution requires no more.

Connor v. City of Seattle, 223 P.3d 1201, 1207–08 (Wash.App.2009).

(d) Procedural Due Process

Where the form based code mixed use traditional neighborhood development regulating plan is confined primarily to one property, the courts applying the *Fasano* rule may require the form based code to be adopted at a quasi-judicial hearing with full procedural due process rights given to the land owner to cross-examine witnesses and given the opportunity to present evidence both oral and documentary. The failure of the City of Albuquerque to hold a quasi-judicial hearing (in lieu of the legislative hearing the city held) with respect to adopting a new mixed use neighborhood plan, in which more than 2/3 of the property affected belonged to the plaintiff, was held to be a denial of procedural due process and was disastrous to the city. The property owner was awarded over $8 million dollars in damages plus interest and attorney's fees. *See Albuquerque Commons Partnership v. City of Albuquerque*, 184 P.3d 411 (N.M.2008).

CHAPTER 3

CONSTITUTIONAL AND JURISPRUDENTIAL LIMITS ON LAND USE CONTROLS

■ ■ ■

A. INTRODUCTION

Land use ordinances, as we know them today, were originally enacted early in the twentieth century. They were upheld by the Supreme Court partly as an extension of the well-recognized governmental police power to abate nuisances. *See, e.g., Hadacheck v. Sebastian*, 239 U.S. 394 (1915). As early as 1894, the Supreme Court began to set the bounds and limitations of the police power. In *Lawton v. Steele*, 152 U.S. 133, 137 (1894), the Court held that for an exercise of the police power to be valid it must employ a reasonable means to a lawful end, and not be "unduly oppressive upon individuals." Some thirty years later, the Court in *Village of Euclid v. Ambler Realty Co.*, 272 U.S. 365 (1926) upheld a zoning ordinance against a challenge that the mere enactment of the ordinance was *on its face* unconstitutional. Two years later in *Nectow v. City of Cambridge*, 277 U.S. 183 (1928), the Court set limitations and guidelines on the constitutionality of zoning ordinances *as applied* to a particular property. Thereafter, the Supreme Court did not decide a single zoning case until 1974, leaving the shaping of land use law to the states for over forty critical years. During this period, state supreme courts expanded traditional police power in response to America's urban problems to include such areas as aesthetics, elimination of blight, historic preservation, growth management, environmental protection, sustainability and flexible planning techniques.

In 1974, the Court broke its self-imposed silence in *Village of Belle Terre v. Boraas*, 416 U.S. 1 (1974), by upholding single family zoning restrictions against equal protection challenges (the exclusion of group student housing). This, however, was only a prelude to numerous decisions delineating the federal constitutional limits on land use controls. Since its reentry into the field, the Court has reaffirmed the reach and scope of the police power in such areas as slum clearance, preservation of community character, historic preservation, regulation of sexually-oriented businesses, open space preservation and environmental protection. *See, e.g.*, George P. Smith and David M. Steenburg, *Environmental Hedonism, or Securing the Environment through the Common Law*, 40 WM & MARY ENVTL L. & POL'Y REV. 65 (2015).

Though the Court has endorsed the ability of state and local government to solve problems through the use of a flexible police power, it has also increased federal constitutional protections of private property. Justice Brennan's prophetic rhetorical question in his dissenting opinion in *San Diego Gas & Electric Co. v. City of San Diego*, 450 U.S. 621 (1981), that "after all if a policeman must know the Constitution then why not a planner," hearkened back to Justice Holmes' dictum that when this "seemingly absolute protection [afforded property] is found to be qualified by the police power, the natural tendency of human nature is to extend the qualification more and more until at last private property disappears. But that cannot be accomplished in this way under the Constitution of the United States." *Pennsylvania Coal Co. v. Mahon*, 260 U.S. 393, 415 (1922). The Court showed less than traditional deference to governmental exercises of power in a number of decisions in the late 1980s and early 1990s, strengthening the protection afforded property under the Fifth Amendment, and in one instance equating it with First and Fourth Amendment rights of freedom of press, assembly, religion and speech, and from unreasonable search and seizure. *See Dolan v. City of Tigard*, 512 U.S. 374 (1994). For recent discussion of private property protection, *see generally* Michael M. Berger, *Property, Democracy and the Constitution*, 5 BRIGHAM-KANNER PROPERTY RIGHTS JOURNAL 45 (2016) and Christopher Serkin, *Private Takings: The State's Affirmative Duty to Protect Property*, 113 MICH.L.REV. 345 (2014).

Rights other than those of property are also affected by land use controls. The guarantee of equal protection limits government regulation from irrational classifications and has the most force when ordinances affect the rights of suspect classes or the exercise of fundamental rights of some in ways different from others. Race-based zoning certainly falls in this category, but even non-suspect classes and non-fundamental rights may receive meaningful judicial scrutiny. *See infra* Chapter 5.D.1. First Amendment protections of free speech and religion also curtail the power of government to regulate land use. The First Amendment is especially relevant concerning ordinances that regulate signs, sexually-oriented businesses, and religious uses. Over the past three decades or so, the Supreme Court has dealt with all these issues.

The commerce clause, in addition to constituting a source of federal power to control land use, is also a negative restraint on the ability of state and local governments to control land use. The doctrine serves to guard against economic protectionism. *United Haulers Ass'n, Inc. v. Oneida-Herkimer Solid Waste Management Authority*, 550 U.S. 330 (2007). A state statute or local ordinance which "regulates even-handedly to effectuate a legitimate local public interest, and its effects on interstate commerce are only incidental, * * * will be upheld unless the burden imposed on such commerce is clearly excessive in relation to the putative local benefits."

Pike v. Bruce Church, Inc., 397 U.S. 137, 142 (1970). It is discussed *supra*, Chapter 2.B., page 120.

In areas where the United States Supreme Court has limited federal constitutional protection, state courts have turned to state constitutional provisions to protect persons from intrusive land use regulations. *See First Covenant Church of Seattle v. City of Seattle*, 840 P.2d 174 (Wash.1992) (state constitution's counterpart to the federal constitution's First Amendment invalidated historic landmark designation of church); *State v. Baker*, 405 A.2d 368 (N.J.1979) (state constitution's counterpart to the Fourteenth Amendment's due process clause invalidated zoning ordinance that prohibited more than four unrelated persons from sharing single family housing); *County of Wayne v. Hathcock*, 684 N.W.2d 765 (Mich.2004) (condemnation of parcels of land for business and technology park not a public use under state constitution); *City of Norwood v. Horney*, 853 N.E.2d 1115 (Ohio 2006) (public economic benefit, standing alone, does not meet the public use requirement of state constitution). These last two cases are discussed *infra* Chapter 6, note 3, following the *Kaur v. New York State Urban Development Corp.* case.

B. FIFTH AMENDMENT TAKING

1. INTRODUCTION

" * * * nor shall *private property* be *taken* for *public use*, without *just compensation.*"

Fifth Amendment, United States Constitution (*emphasis added*).

Property rights, and in particular rights in land, have always been fundamental to and part of the preservation of liberty and personal freedom in the United States. For a summary of the 13th and 14th century roots of our present constitutional principles and the treatment of property rights through the late 1980s, *see* Norman Karlin, *Back to the Future: From Nollan to Lochner*, 17 SW.U.L.REV. 627, 637–38 (1988): "To the framers [of the Constitution] identifying property with freedom meant that if you could own property you were free. Ownership of property was protected." *See also* Bernard H. Siegan, *Constitutional Protection of Property and Economic Rights*, 29 SAN DIEGO L.REV. 161 (1992) and Phillip A. Talmadge, *The Myth of Property Absolutism and Modern Government: The Interaction of Police Power and Property Rights*, 75 WASH.L.REV. 857 (2000).

This "guarantee in the Fifth Amendment" was designed to bar Government from forcing some people alone to bear public burdens which, in all fairness and justice, should be borne by the public as a whole." *Armstrong v. United States*, 364 U.S. 40, 49 (1960). It "prevents the public from loading upon one individual more than his just share of the burdens of government, and says that when he surrenders to the public something more and different from that which is exacted from other members of the public, a full and just equivalent shall be returned to him." *Monongahela Navigation Co. v. United States*, 148 U.S. 312, 325 (1893).

Many questions confront the courts in interpreting the Fifth Amendment. How is the private property at issue defined? Who defines it? What constitutes public use? Is physical use by the public required or is a public purpose sufficient? Is every physical invasion by the public a taking or can some be excused by public need? Is a regulation that diminishes the value of pro a taking? If so, how much diminution is necessary? What is just compensation? Who may bring litigation on takings and in which courts?

We begin our study by discussing how we identify the private property interest allegedly being impacted by the challenged government action.

2. PRIVATE PROPERTY

Inherent in the analysis of constitutional issues involving land use is the recognition of a property interest.

The term "property" as used in the Taking Clause includes the entire "group of rights inhering in the citizen's [ownership]." * * * It is not used in the "vulgar and untechnical sense of the physical thing with respect to which the citizen exercises rights recognized by law. [Instead, it] [denotes] the group of rights inhering in the citizen's relation to the physical thing, as the right to possess, use and dispose of it. . . . The constitutional provision is addressed to every sort of interest the citizen may possess." * * *

PruneYard Shopping Ctr. v. Robins, 447 U.S. 74, 83, n.6 (1980).

Today, courts commonly recognize numerous landowner interests as property within the meaning of the Fifth Amendment. Property has been held to include riparian rights, easements, covenants, franchises, leasehold interests, and trade secrets. *See* Thomas W. Merrill, *The Landscape of Constitutional Property*, 86 VA.L.REV. 885 (2000); Alexandra George, *The Difficulty of Defining "Property,"* 25 OXFORD J.LEGAL STUD. 793 (2005). Thus, in addition to the loss of restrictive covenant benefits, interference with riparian rights, easements, and lateral support, may lead to a claim for compensation. *See Leigh v. Village of Los Lunas*, 108 P.3d 525 (N.M.Ct.App.2004) (the destruction of the benefit of a restrictive covenant requires compensation), and *Daniels v. Area Plan Comm'n of Allen County*, 306 F.3d 445 (7th Cir.2002) (restrictive covenant a separable property interest from the unencumbered land under Indiana law for purposes of takings claim). The search for the property interest may vary with the constitutional right asserted. See discussion in Section C of this Chapter regarding due process claims.

Many courts recognize an implied negative easement to light, air, and view from the property over the public street it abuts. Since American jurisdictions have universally rejected the English doctrine of ancient lights, it is anomalous that many do so in the eminent domain context. In contrast to a right to *view from the property,* there is no right to be *seen from the street. See, e.g., Regency Outdoor Advert., Inc. v. City of Los Angeles*, 139 P.3d 119 (Cal.2006). *See also* Juergensmeyer and Roberts, Land Use Planning and Development Regulation Law § 16.3B (3rd ed.2012). What law controls in deciding what constitutes property? The Court has often said that "[p]roperty interests * * * are not created by the Constitution. Rather, they are created and their dimensions are defined by existing rules or understandings that stem from an independent source such as state law * * * ." *Board of Regents of State College v. Roth*, 408 U.S. 564, 577 (1972). "Though the meaning of 'property' as used in * * * the Fifth Amendment is a federal question, it will *normally* obtain its content by reference to local law." *U.S. ex rel. Tennessee Valley Auth. v. Powelson*, 319 U.S. 266, 279 (1943). Yet, when dissatisfied with a state definition of property that afforded what it saw as inadequate protection to the individual, the Court overrode that limiting definition and noted that "a State, by ipse dixit, may not transform private property into public property without compensation." *Webb's Fabulous Pharmacies, Inc. v. Beckwith*, 449 U.S. 155, 164 (1980). On the other hand, when dissatisfied with a state definition that defined property in a manner that unduly hampered state regulatory powers, the Court refused to use the state definition. *Keystone Bituminous Coal Ass'n v. DeBenedictis*, 480 U.S. 470, 500 (1987). *See also Lucas, infra* n.18.

Once it has been determined what constitutes a private property interest subject to the Takings Clause, we must decide "what is the *property* being taken" in a particular action? When the government directly condemns private property, it will identify the property interest it wishes to take. However, in an inverse condemnation action based upon indirect physical invasions or regulatory restraints, it may be necessary to determine how much of a landowner's overall property interest is being unconstitutionally impacted. This issue has been referred to as the denominator or "whole parcel" issue when we determine what relevant physical portion of a landowner's property is being taken. The "conceptual severance" issue may also come into play when considering a regulation that impacts one stick, but not all sticks, in a property owner's bundle of rights.

The "parcel as a whole" doctrine: The "whole parcel" approach to the denominator issue "seems to indicate that the more property a person owns, the less likely he or she is to be compensated for a partial regulatory loss." *See* John E. Fee, *The Takings Clause as a Comparative Right*, 76 S.CAL.L.REV. 1003, 1006 (2003). Courts tend to use a broad approach in determining the denominator, by considering a variety of factors in determining the appropriate unit. These may include "unity and contiguity of ownership, the dates of acquisition, the extent to which the proposed parcel has been treated as a single unit, the extent to which the regulated holding benefits the unregulated holdings, the timing of transfers, if any, in light of the developing regulatory environment, the owner's investment backed-expectations, and the landowner's plans for development." *Machipongo Land and Coal Co., Inc. v. Commonwealth*, 799 A.2d 751, 768 (Pa.2002). *See also Brace v. United States*, 72 Fed.Cl. 337 (Fed.Cl.2006), *aff'd* 250 Fed.Appx. 359 (Fed.Cir.2007). The Massachusetts courts use a rebuttable presumption that contiguous, commonly-owned property is the appropriate unit. *See Giovanella v. Conservation Comm'n of Ashland*, 857 N.E.2d 451 (Mass.2006).

The approach taken to the denominator issue by the U.S. Supreme Court has been mixed. Beginning as early as the *Pennsylvania Coal v. Mahon*, 260 U.S. 393 (1922) decision, the Court distinguished the subsurface coal ownership of mined coal as separate from the pillars of coal that the regulation required to remain in place to protect surface rights from subsidence. The Court viewed the pillars of coal as the denominator such that the legislation went "too far" and resulted in a regulatory taking of the pillars of coal. Subsequently, in *Keystone Bituminous Coal Ass'n v. DeBenedictis*, 480 U.S. 470 (1987) the Court, in reviewing very similar legislation protecting surface rights, held that in viewing the subsurface coal rights "as a whole" the regulatory impact on the small portion of the subsurface coal required to support the surface did not "go too far" and was not a taking.

The Court first articulated the parcel as a whole doctrine in *Penn Central Transportation Co. v. New York City*, 438 U.S. 104 (1978) where the denominator was based on the landowner's properties on the same city tax block and the Court refused to sever air rights from surface rights in evaluating restrictions on building above the historic Grand Central Terminal. The parcel as a whole doctrine was unanimously supported by the Court in *Concrete Pipe and Prods. Inc. v. Construction Laborers Pension Trust*, 508 U.S. 602, 644 (1993) to reject a takings challenge against federal legislation that held employers liable for withdrawing from pension plans. However, in *Palazzolo v. Rhode Island*, 533 U.S. 606, 631 (2001), the Court raised some doubts about the whole parcel rule in a case where the owner of a 74-lot coastal subdivision was unable to develop a majority of the lots due to a state wetland protection regulation, but some upland lots were arguably still developable. Then the majority of the Court in *Tahoe-Sierra Preservation Council, Inc. v. Tahoe Regional Planning Agency*, 535 U.S. 302 (2002) once again embraced the rule when it refused to separate the present use moratoria restriction from the future use available after the moratoria were lifted. For further discussion of the "parcel as a whole" doctrine see Steven J. Eagle, *The Parcel and Then Some: Unity of Ownership and the Parcel as a Whole*, 36 VT.L.REV. 549 (2012). The Court will consider the "parcel as a whole" rule again in *Murr v. Wisconsin*, 2016 WL 205943, *cert. granted,* Jan. 15, 2016, as applied to development restrictions on two parcels owned by one family.

Strategic behavior is one concern in defining what constitutes the denominator in a taking challenge. In *Regency Outdoor Advertising, Inc. v. City of Los Angeles*, 139 P.3d 119 (Cal.2006), the court noted that "[t]hrough its lease agreements Regency [Outdoor Advertising] has acquired a property interest acutely sensitive to impairments to visibility. But as a general matter, 'we do not believe that a property owner, confronted with an imminent property regulation, can nullify . . . a legitimate exercise of the police power by leasing narrow parcels or interests in his property so that the regulation could be characterized as a taking only because of its disproportionate effect on the narrow parcel or interest leased,' " *quoting Adams Outdoor Advertising v. City of East Lansing*, 614 N.W.2d 634 (Mich.2000), *cert. denied* 532 U.S. 920 (2001) (lease that grants or retains a small portion of property does not create separate unit to serve as denominator). When a landowner transferred one of his parcels during litigation, the city alleged he was engaged in such strategic behavior. *See City of Coeur D'Alene v. Simpson*, 136 P.3d 310, 322 (Idaho 2006). The court found that even if the transfer had been done for the purpose of creating a more favorable unit against which the court would measure his loss, it would not matter if the owner of both parcels never intended to develop them as a unit.

For other applications of the "whole parcel" rule, *see Seiber v. State ex rel. Bd. of Forestry*, 149 P.3d 1243 (Or.Ct.App.), *cert. denied*, 552 U.S. 1061 (2007) (state wildlife regulation, temporarily preventing landowners from harvesting timber from 40 acres of a 200-acre parcel that were identified as nesting site for spotted owls, did not effect a taking under the "whole parcel" rule); *Coast Range Conifers, LLC v. State ex rel. Oregon State Board of Forestry*, 117 P.3d 990 (Or.2005) (40-acre tract used as denominator rather than the 9 acres which could not be logged to protect bald eagle habitat); *Byrd v. City of Hartsville*, 620 S.E.2d 76, 80 (S.C.2005).

3. PUBLIC USE

The Fifth Amendment to the U.S. Constitution provides, in part, that private property can be taken for a "public use" upon payment of just compensation. State constitutions have similar provisions. Although early state court decisions required actual use by the public in order to satisfy the constitutional requirement, later decisions often found it satisfied if the condemnation resulted in some "public benefit." Federal courts adopted this more expansive view early on. *See Mount Vernon-Woodberry Cotton Duck Co. v. Alabama Interstate Power Co.*, 240 U.S. 30 (1916), where Justice Holmes rejected the "use by the public" test, and *United States ex rel. TVA v. Welch,* 327 U.S. 546 (1946), in which the Court expressed deference to legislative declarations of public use.

The *Kelo* case, located in Chapter 6, addressed "whether a city's decision to take property for the purpose of economic development satisfies the 'public use' requirement of the Fifth Amendment." The Court noted that the concept of "public use" has been broadly defined in previous cases and explained how its two prior decisions, *Berman v. Parker* and *Hawaii Housing Authority v. Midkiff,* compelled its affirmation of the Supreme Court of Connecticut's decision that "the City's proposed condemnations are for a 'public use' within the meaning of the Fifth Amendment to the Federal Constitution."

In *Berman v. Parker,* 348 U.S. 26 (1954), this Court upheld a redevelopment plan targeting a blighted area of Washington, D. C., in which most of the housing for the area's 5,000 inhabitants was beyond repair. Under the plan, the area would be condemned and part of it utilized for the construction of streets, schools, and other public facilities. The remainder of the land would be leased or sold to private parties for the purpose of redevelopment, including the construction of low-cost housing.

The owner of a department store located in the area challenged the condemnation, pointing out that his store was not itself blighted and arguing that the creation of a "better balanced, more attractive community" was not a valid public use. Writing for a unanimous Court, Justice Douglas refused to evaluate this claim in isolation, deferring instead to the legislative and agency judgment that the area "must be planned as a whole" for the plan to be successful. The Court explained that "community redevelopment programs need not, by force of the Constitution, be on a piecemeal basis—lot by lot, building by building." The public use underlying the taking was unequivocally affirmed:

> "We do not sit to determine whether a particular housing project is or is not desirable. The concept of the public welfare is broad and inclusive * * * The values it represents are spiritual as well as physical, aesthetic as well as monetary. It is within the power of the legislature to determine that the community should be beautiful as well as healthy, spacious as well as clean, well-balanced as well as carefully patrolled. In the present case, the Congress and its authorized agencies have made determinations that take into account a wide variety of values. It is not for us to reappraise them. If those who govern the District of Columbia decide that the Nation's Capital should be beautiful as well as sanitary, there is nothing in the Fifth Amendment that stands in the way." *Id.,* at 33, 75 S.Ct. 98.

In *Hawaii Housing Authority v. Midkiff*, 467 U.S. 229 (1984), the Court considered a Hawaii statute whereby fee title was taken from lessors and transferred to lessees (for just compensation) in order to reduce the concentration of land ownership. We unanimously upheld the statute and rejected the Ninth Circuit's view that it was "a naked attempt on the part of the state of Hawaii to take the property of A and transfer it to B solely for B's private use and benefit." Reaffirming *Berman's* deferential approach to legislative judgments in this field, we concluded that the State's purpose of eliminating the "social and economic evils of a land oligopoly" qualified as a valid public use. 467 U.S., at 241–242. Our opinion also rejected the contention that the mere fact that the State immediately transferred the properties to private individuals upon condemnation somehow diminished the public character of the taking. "[I]t is only the taking's purpose, and not its mechanics," we explained, that matters in determining public use.

Kelo v. City of New London, 545 U.S. 469, 480–82 (2005).

KELO V. CITY OF NEW LONDON

Supreme Court of the United States, 2005.
545 U.S. 469, 125 S.Ct. 2655, 162 L.Ed.2d 439.

[Read *Kelo*, *infra* page 712]

NOTES

1.   Is the Court's holding that "economic revitalization" is a public purpose (which the Court determines is the equivalent of "public use" in its eminent domain jurisprudence) a change from the public use test applied in *Berman v. Parker* and *Hawaii Housing Authority v. Midkiff*? What factors persuaded the majority to reiterate and perhaps extend its reasoning beyond these two earlier cases? For discussions of these factors, *see* Gideon Kanner, *We Don't Have to Follow Any Stinkin' Planning—Sorry About That, Justice Stevens*, 39 URB. LAW. 529 (2007); and, Nicole Stelle Garnett, *Planning as Public Use?*, 34 ECOL.L.Q. 443 (2007), taking the position that the holding in *Kelo* changed very little indeed.

For photos of Ms. Kelo's house and the land covered by the city's project, see Duke Law, Voices of American Law, http://www.law.duke.edu/voices/kelo. See also Jeff Benedict, *Little Pink House: A True Story of Defiance and Courage* (2009).

2.   What is the basis for permitting states to devise a stricter definition of public use, according to the majority in *Kelo*? For discussion of that basis and the odd bedfellows it made, see David L. Callies, Kelo v. City of New London: *Of Planning, Federalism and a Switch in Time*, 28 U.HAW.L.REV. 327 (2006); Peter W. Salsich, Jr., *Privatization and Democratization—Reflections*

on the Power of Eminent Domain, 50 ST. LOUIS U.L.J. 751 (2006). States have indeed reacted in the ten years following the decision. Forty-four states either amended their constitutions or enacted legislation, often by ballot measures, to address concerns expressed by Justice O'Connor's dissent.

For a summary of the status of public use/public purpose decisions in all 50 states, see "*A State by State Survey of Public Use Standards*," the appendix to Eminent Domain: A Handbook of Condemnation Law (W. Scheiderich, C. Fraser and D. Callies, eds. ABA Press, 2011) written by Hawaii attorneys Calvert Chipchase, Christian Adams and Kamaile Nichols. For two articles on California's and New York's resistance to so-called "*Kelo*" reform, see Robert H. Freilich and Seth D. Mennillo: (1) *The Kelo Revolution Ends in California, California Real Estate Journal* (2006); and (2) Kelo v. City of New London: *How Does the Supreme Court Decision Affect New York Law on Condemnation for Economic Development and Municipal Revitalization?* New York Zoning Law and Practice Report (2005).

State courts have also gotten into the act. *See, e.g., City of Norwood v. Horney*, 853 N.E.2d 1115 (Ohio 2006) (public economic benefit, standing alone, does not meet the public use requirement of state constitution). *But see Kaur v. New York State Urban Development Corp.*, 933 N.E.2d 721 (N.Y.2010) (upholding massive economic development project in Harlem adjacent to Columbia University's upper west side campus); and *Hoffman Family, LLC v. City of Alexandria*, 634 S.E.2d 722 (Va.2006) (taking land for the relocation of a city storm water culvert to permit adjacent private development to proceed held to be for a public use). For analysis of this response, see David L. Callies, *Current Critical Issues in Real Estate Law: Public Use and Public Purpose After* Kelo v. City of New London (LexisNexis 2008).

3.   No one would contest that plaintiffs' land could have been taken if New London were to use the land for a park, a library, or a parking garage. Would Ms. Kelo and the others have been less offended if their land was to be used as a city parking lot? Is the taking of a home worse than that of a business? See John Fee, *Eminent Domain and the Sanctity of Home*, 81 NOTRE DAME L.REV. 783 (2006). Dwight Merriam, a leading author and land use attorney in Connecticut who has closely followed and written about *Kelo*, notes that according to the City of New London's redevelopment plan, the land upon which Kelo's "little pink house" actually sits was designated for a public road. Shouldn't this have rendered any discussion of the extent of public use beyond public purpose superfluous if not irrelevant? Is any public use more obviously and unquestionably public than a public road? See, however, the following note and the discussion of Hawaii's *Coupe* litigation over just such a road.

4.   What's left of the Fifth Amendment's public use clause? Is there ever a situation in which the use of eminent domain will fall afoul of it? See David L. Callies, *Current Critical Issues in Real Estate Law: Public Use and Public Purpose after* Kelo v. City of New London (LexisNexis 2008). See also David L. Callies and Christina N. Wakayama, *Public Use/Public Purpose After* Kelo v. City of New London: *What's Happened Since*, 2007 Institute for Planning Zoning and Eminent Domain, Ch. 1. In a strange interpretation of Justice

Kennedy's concurring opinion, particularly that part referring to "pretextual" public purposes, a three-justice majority of the Hawaii Supreme Court found that the exercise of eminent domain for a public road (a 6-mile bypass road to relieve an overcrowded two-lane principle arterial road) could amount to a pretextual public use, apparently because the road was constructed by a private developer in accordance with the terms of a development agreement, and the road passed through part of the developer's residential project. *C&J Coupe Family Limited Partnership v. County of Hawaii*, 198 P.3d 615 (Haw.2008). The astonished Chief Justice, writing for the two-justice dissent, observed that a public road was a classic public use, let alone public purpose. On remand to the trial court to take more evidence, the trial court and ultimately the Supreme Court agreed that this public road was indeed a sufficient public use.

4. TAKEN

Historically, only direct condemnations under the eminent domain power were regarded as compensable under the Fifth Amendment's takings clause, applicable to the states through the Fourteenth Amendment. The law gradually evolved to require compensation for different types of government conduct causing indirect physical invasion or a non-trespassory invasion such as a regulatory measure that imposes economic loss or deprives a property owner of a legally actionable right, such as the right to enforce a covenant, the right to use an easement, or the right to bring a nuisance claim. These indirect physical invasions or non-trespassory invasions, while not asserted under the eminent domain power, may nevertheless subject the government to just compensation liability as an inverse condemnation challenge. Courts are more likely to find a taking and award compensation when there has been a physical invasion or the loss of a legally actionable right than when economic harm is imposed by a regulation limiting the use of land. Whether the reluctance to find a taking for economic loss produces the fairness and justice demanded by the Fifth Amendment is much debated. *See generally Taking Sides on Takings Issues: Public and Private Perspectives* (T. Roberts, ed.2002) and John E. Fee, *The Takings Clause as a Comparative Right*, 76 S.CAL.L.REV. 1003 (2003).

Government action by physical invasion of property or regulatory action affecting property rights may result in a Fifth Amendment taking. The former may arise, for example, when a government dams a river, flooding upstream property, or, by statute, authorizes an invasion of property by a third party. The latter, a "constructive" as opposed to physical taking, may occur when a regulation deprives property of all economically viable use or imposes a significant economic harm, upsetting the owner's reasonable investment-backed expectations. These "tests share a common touchstone," the Court says, which is "to identify regulatory actions that are functionally equivalent to a direct appropriation of or ouster from private property." Lingle v. Chevron U.S.A. Inc., 544 U.S. 528, 529 (2005).

These types of takings claims are litigated by way of inverse condemnation actions. They differ from cases of direct condemnation under the power of eminent domain, where the government initiates condemnation proceedings. Direct eminent proceedings establish that the taking is for a public use or purpose and assess just compensation to be paid to the owner. In contrast, when a government dams a river, flooding upstream property, or zones land for open space so that no economically viable use can be made of it, and makes no offer of compensation, nor brings a direct condemnation proceeding, the owner has the burden of initiating an inverse condemnation action against the government. As the Court explained in *United States v. Clarke*, 445 U.S. 253 (1980):

> There are important legal and practical differences between an inverse condemnation suit and a condemnation proceeding. Although a landowner's action to recover just compensation for a taking by physical intrusion has come to be referred to as "inverse" or "reverse" condemnation, the simple terms "condemn" and "condemnation" are not commonly used to describe such an action. Rather, a "condemnation" proceeding is commonly understood to be an action brought *by* a condemning authority such as the Government in the exercise of its power of eminent domain. * * *

> A landowner is entitled to bring such an action as a result of "the self-executing character of the constitutional provision with respect to compensation. * * * " See 6 P. Nichols, Eminent Domain § 25.41 (3d rev.ed.1972). A condemnation proceeding, by contrast, typically involves an action by the condemnor to effect a taking and acquire title. The phrase "inverse condemnation," as a common understanding of that phrase would suggest, simply describes an action that is the "inverse" or "reverse" of a condemnation proceeding. * * *

> Likewise, the choice of the condemning authority to take property by physical invasion rather than by a formal condemnation action may also have important monetary consequences. The value of property taken by a governmental body is to be ascertained as of the date of taking. *United States v. Miller*, 317 U.S. 369, 374 (1943). In a condemnation proceeding, the taking generally occurs sometime during the course of the proceeding, and thus compensation is based on a relatively current valuation of the land. When a taking occurs by physical invasion, on the other hand, the usual rule is that the time of the invasion constitutes the act of taking, and "[i]t is that event which gives rise to the claim for compensation and fixes the date as of

which the land is to be valued. * * * " *United States v. Dow*, 357 U.S. 17, 22 (1958). 445 U.S. at 255–58.

The case that follows generally is viewed as the origin of the regulatory takings doctrine, the principle that a police power regulation can, if excessive, be declared by a court to be a Fifth Amendment taking. There is much debate over the historical underpinnings of *Pennsylvania Coal. See* James W. Ely, Jr., *The Fuller Court and Takings Jurisprudence*, 1996 J.SUP.CT.HIST. vol. II at 120 and Robert Brauneis, *The Foundation of Our "Regulatory Takings" Jurisprudence: The Myth and Meaning of Justice Holmes's Opinion in* Pennsylvania Coal Co. v. Mahon, 106 YALE L.J. 613 (1996).

Regardless of the doctrine's provenance, as you will soon discover, courts have had difficulty articulating a functional test to determine when regulatory measures constitute takings. *See* David L. Callies, *Regulatory Takings and the Supreme Court: How Perspectives on Property Rights Have Changed from* Penn Central *to* Dolan*, and What State and Federal Courts Are Doing About It*, 28 STETSON L.REV. 523 (1999); Symposium, *Litigating Takings*, 34 ECOLOGY L.REV. 291 (2007). Like the courts, commentators, spanning decades, have struggled to understand the law of regulatory takings. For many, takings law is, or at least has been, at best, extraordinarily complex, and, at worst, hopelessly muddled.

> Regulatory takings law combines the worst of two worlds— constitutional law's arid generalities and property law's substantive difficulties. To hear the Supreme Court tell it, this confusion is the best we can expect. In *Penn Central Transportation Co. v. New York City*, the leading regulatory takings case of our time, the Supreme Court complained that regulatory takings law "has proved to be a problem of considerable difficulty." "[Q]uite simply," the Court confessed, it 'has been unable to develop any set formula for determining regulatory takings cases.'

Eric R. Claeys, *Takings, Regulations, and Natural Property Rights*, 88 CORNELL L.REV. 1549, 1553 (2003). *See also* John E. Fee, *The Takings Clause as a Comparative Right*, 76 S.CAL.L.REV. 1003, 1006–1007, 1066 (2003) ("jurisprudential mess").

PENNSYLVANIA COAL CO. V. MAHON

Supreme Court of the United States, 1922.
260 U.S. 393, 43 S.Ct. 158, 67 L.Ed. 322.

MR. JUSTICE HOLMES delivered the opinion of the Court.

This is a bill in equity brought by the defendants in error to prevent the Pennsylvania Coal Company from mining under their property in such way as to remove the supports and cause a subsidence of the surface and of their house. The bill sets out a deed executed by the Coal Company in 1878, under which the plaintiffs claim. The deed conveys the surface but in express terms reserves the right to remove all the coal under the same and the grantee takes the premises with the risk and waives all claim for damages that may arise from mining out the coal. But the plaintiffs say that whatever may have been the Coal Company's rights, they were taken away by an Act of Pennsylvania, approved May 27, 1921 (P.L.1198), commonly known there as the Kohler Act. The Court of Common Pleas found that if not restrained the defendant would cause the damage to prevent which the bill was brought but denied an injunction, holding that the statute if applied to this case would be unconstitutional. On appeal the Supreme Court of the State agreed that the defendant had contract and property rights protected by the Constitution of the United States, but held that the statute was a legitimate exercise of the police power and directed a decree for the plaintiffs. A writ of error was granted bringing the case to this Court.

The statute forbids the mining of anthracite coal in such way as to cause the subsidence of, among other things, any structure used as a human habitation, with certain exceptions, including among them land where the surface is owned by the owner of the underlying coal and is distant more than one hundred and fifty feet from any improved property belonging to any other person. As applied to this case the statute is admitted to destroy previously existing rights of property and contract. The question is whether the police power can be stretched so far.

Government hardly could go on if to some extent values incident to property could not be diminished without paying for every such change in the general law. As long recognized some values are enjoyed under an implied limitation and must yield to the police power. But obviously the implied limitation must have its limits or the contract and due process clauses are gone. One fact for consideration in determining such limits is the extent of the diminution. When it reaches a certain magnitude, in most if not in all cases there must be an exercise of eminent domain and compensation to sustain the act. So the question depends upon the particular facts. The greatest weight is given to the judgment of the legislature but it always is open to interested parties to contend that the legislature has gone beyond its constitutional power.

This is the case of a single private house. No doubt there is a public interest even in this, as there is in every purchase and sale and in all that happens within the commonwealth. Some existing rights may be modified even in such a case. *Rideout v. Knox*, 148 Mass. 368, 19 N.E. 390, 2 L.R.A. 81, 12 Am.St.Rep. 560. But usually in ordinary private affairs the public interest does not warrant much of this kind of interference. A source of damage to such a house is not a public nuisance even if similar damage is inflicted on others in different places. The damage is not common or public.

Wesson v. Washburn Iron Co., 13 Allen (Mass.) 95, 103, 90 Am.Dec. 181. The extent of the public interest is shown by the statute to be limited, since the statute ordinarily does not apply to land when the surface is owned by the owner of the coal. Furthermore, it is not justified as a protection of personal safety. That could be provided for by notice. Indeed the very foundation of this bill is that the defendant gave timely notice of its intent to mine under the house. On the other hand the extent of the taking is great. It purports to abolish what is recognized in Pennsylvania as an estate in land—a very valuable estate—and what is declared by the Court below to be a contract hitherto binding the plaintiffs. If we were called upon to deal with the plaintiffs' position alone we should think it clear that the statute does not disclose a public interest sufficient to warrant so extensive a destruction of the defendant's constitutionally protected rights.

But the case has been treated as one in which the general validity of the act should be discussed. The Attorney General of the State, the City of Scranton and the representatives of other extensive interests were allowed to take part in the argument below and have submitted their contentions here. It seems, therefore, to be our duty to go farther in the statement of our opinion, in order that it may be known at once, and that further suits should not be brought in vain.

It is our opinion that the act cannot be sustained as an exercise of the police power, so far as it affects the mining of coal under streets or cities in places where the right to mine such coal has been reserved. * * * What makes the right to mine coal valuable is that it can be exercised with profit. To make it commercially impracticable to mine certain coal has very nearly the same effect for constitutional purposes as appropriating or destroying it. This we think that we are warranted in assuming that the statute does.

It is true that in *Plymouth Coal Co. v. Pennsylvania*, 232 U.S. 531, it was held competent for the legislature to require a pillar of coal to be left along the line of adjoining property, that with the pillar on the other side of the line would be a barrier sufficient for the safety of the employees of either mine in case the other should be abandoned and allowed to fill with water. But that was a requirement for the safety of employees invited into the mine, and secured an average reciprocity of advantage that has been recognized as a justification of various laws.

The rights of the public in a street purchased or laid out by eminent domain are those that it has paid for. If in any case its representatives have been so short sighted as to acquire only surface rights without the right of support we see no more authority for supplying the latter without compensation than there was for taking the right of way in the first place and refusing to pay for it because the public wanted it very much. The protection of private property in the Fifth Amendment presupposes that it is wanted for public use, but provides that it shall not be taken for such use without compensation. A similar assumption is made in the decisions upon the Fourteenth Amendment. When this seemingly absolute protection is found to be qualified by the police power, the natural tendency of human nature is to extend the qualification more and more until at last private property disappears. But that cannot be accomplished in this way under the Constitution of the United States.

The general rule at least is that while property may be regulated to a certain extent, if regulation goes too far it will be recognized as a taking. * * *

We are in danger of forgetting that a strong public desire to improve the public condition is not enough to warrant achieving the desire by a shorter cut than the constitutional way of paying for the change. As we already have said this is a question of degree—and therefore cannot be disposed of by general propositions. But we regard this as going beyond any of the cases decided by this Court.

* * *

We assume, of course, that the statute was passed upon the conviction that an exigency existed that would warrant it, and we assume that an exigency exists that would warrant the exercise of eminent domain. But the question at bottom is upon whom the loss of the changes desired should fall. So far as private persons or communities have seen fit to take the risk of acquiring only surface rights, we cannot see that the fact that their risk has become a danger warrants the giving to them greater rights than they bought.

Decree reversed.

MR. JUSTICE BRANDEIS dissenting.

* * *

The restriction here in question is merely the prohibition of a noxious use. The property so restricted remains in the possession of its owner. The state does not appropriate it or make any use of it. The state merely prevents the owner from making a use which interferes with paramount rights of the public. Whenever the use prohibited ceases to be noxious-as it may because of further change in local or social conditions-the restriction will have to be removed and the owner will again be free to enjoy his property as heretofore.

The restriction upon the use of this property cannot, of course, be lawfully imposed, unless its purpose is to protect the public. But the purpose of a restriction does not cease to be public, because incidentally some private persons may thereby receive gratuitously valuable special benefits. Thus, owners of low buildings may obtain, through statutory restrictions upon the height of neighboring structures, benefits equivalent to an easement of light and air. * * * Furthermore, a restriction, though imposed for a public purpose, will not be lawful, unless the restriction is an appropriate means to the public end. But to keep coal in place is surely an appropriate means of preventing subsidence of the surface; and ordinarily it is the only available means. Restriction upon use does not become inappropriate as a means, merely because it deprives the owner of the only use to which the property can then be profitably put. The liquor and the oleomargarine cases settled that. *Mugler v. Kansas*; *Powell v. Pennsylvania. See also Hadacheck v. Los Angeles.* * * *

It is said that one fact for consideration in determining whether the limits of the police power have been exceeded is the extent of the resulting diminution in value, and that here the restriction destroys existing rights of property and contract. But values are relative. If we are to consider the value of the coal kept in place by the restriction, we should compare it with the value of all other parts of the land. That is, with the value not of the coal alone, but with the value of the whole property. The rights of an owner as against the public are not increased by dividing the interests in his property into surface and subsoil. The sum of the rights in the parts can not be greater than the rights in the whole. The estate of an owner in land is grandiloquently described as extending ab orco usque ad coelum. But I suppose no one would contend that by selling his interest above 100 feet from the surface he could prevent the state from limiting, by the police power, the height of structures in a city. And why should a sale of underground rights bar the state's power? For aught that appears the value of the coal kept in place by the restriction may be negligible as compared with the value of the whole property, or even as compared with that part of it which is represented by the coal remaining in place and which may be extracted despite the statute.

NOTES

1.   The prevailing context of land use in nineteenth century America—an abundance of available land and the relatively minor nuisance impact of industrialization in its embryonic stages—created little need for the extensive reliance on zoning regulation that is characteristic of state and local government today. In *Mugler v. Kansas*, 123 U.S. 623 (1887), the petitioner claimed that state prohibition of the manufacture and sale of intoxicating liquor deprived his brewery of most of its value, and thus was a taking of property without due process requiring compensation. "This interpretation of the fourteenth amendment is inadmissible," said the Court. *Id.* at 664. The Court took the stance that a regulation, if reasonably related to a valid public purpose, could never constitute a taking. *Pennsylvania Coal's* recognition of a regulation going "too far" and becoming a taking changed that. *See* Fred Bosselman, David L. Callies, and John Banta, *The Taking Issue* (1973), Ch. 8, entitled "Pennsylvania Coal v. Mahon: *Holmes Rewrites the Constitution*," and Robert Meltz, Dwight Merriam and Richard Frank, *The Takings Issue*, Ch. 1 (1999). For the view that *Pennsylvania Coal* was not a regulatory takings case at all, see Robert Brauneis, *The Foundation of Our "Regulatory Takings"*

Jurisprudence: The Myth and Meaning of Justice Holmes's Opinion in Pennsylvania Coal Co. v. Mahon, 106 YALE L.J. 613 (1996).

For decades it was the position of some courts and commentators that the "takings" language of Justice Holmes in *Pennsylvania Coal* was merely symbolic, at least in the sense that the remedy for a regulatory taking was not the mandated just compensation of the Fifth Amendment, but invalidation of the ordinance. In 1987, the Court rejected that view. *See First English Evangelical Lutheran Church v. County of Los Angeles*, 482 U.S. 304 (1987).

2.   While the regulatory takings theory of *Pennsylvania Coal* and its "too far" test persists, the application of the test to coal subsidence legislation was dramatically altered in *Keystone Bituminous Coal Ass'n v. DeBenedictis*, 480 U.S. 470 (1987). In a 5–4 decision, the Court upheld a Pennsylvania anti-subsidence statute that was strikingly similar to the Kohler Act that fell in *Pennsylvania Coal*. While the *Keystone* Court adhered to *Pennsylvania Coal*'s regulatory takings theory, it rejected the argument that the coal that had to be left in place in a specific mine to prevent subsidence was the unit of property against which to measure the impact of the ordinance. Rather, the Court suggested examination of the "entirety" of the property (the entire mining operation including all of the subsurface area below the subsidence level) constitutes the base against which the loss is measured to determine whether all or substantially all use and value of the property was lost. The following cases address that and other issues raised by *Pennsylvania Coal*, like how far is "too far."

(a) Physical Invasions

The right to exclude is one of "the most essential sticks in the bundle of rights that are commonly characterized as property * * *" and is "universally held to be a fundamental element of the property right." *Kaiser Aetna v. United States*, 444 U.S. 164, 176, 179–80 (1979). Professor Richard Epstein in his book *Takings: Private Property and Power of Eminent Domain* (1985) describes "[t]he notion of exclusive possession" as "implicit in the basic conception of private property." (at 63) It was also recognized in the American Law Institute's Restatement of the Law of Property in 1936:

> A possessory interest in land exists in a person who has (a) a physical relation to the land of a kind which gives a certain degree of physical control over the land, and an intent so to exercise *such control as to exclude* other members of society in general from any present occupation of the land. (emphasis added)

The United States Supreme Court has cited this section with approval in several cases discussing physical takings of property.

LORETTO V. TELEPROMPTER MANHATTAN CATV CORP.

Supreme Court of the United States, 1982.
458 U.S. 419, 102 S.Ct. 3164, 73 L.Ed.2d 868.

JUSTICE MARSHALL.

This case presents the question whether a minor but permanent physical occupation of an owner's property authorized by government constitutes a "taking" of property for which just compensation is due under the Fifth and Fourteenth Amendments of the Constitution. New York law provides that a landlord must permit a cable television company to install its cable facilities upon his property. In this case, the cable installation occupied portions of appellant's roof and the side of her building. The New York Court of Appeals ruled that this appropriation does not amount to a taking. 53 N.Y.2d 124, 440 N.Y.S.2d 843, 423 N.E.2d 320 (1981). Because we conclude that such a physical occupation of property is a taking, we reverse.

I

Appellant Jean Loretto purchased a five-story apartment building located at 303 West 105th Street, New York City, in 1971. The previous owner had granted appellees Teleprompter Corp. and Teleprompter Manhattan CATV (collectively Teleprompter) permission to install a cable on the building and the exclusive privilege of furnishing cable television (CATV) services to the tenants. The New York Court of Appeals described the installation as follows:

"On June 1, 1970 Teleprompter installed a cable slightly less than one-half inch in diameter and of approximately 30 feet in length along the length of the building about 18 inches above the roof top, and directional taps, approximately 4 inches by 4 inches by 4 inches, on the front and rear of the roof. By June 8, 1970 the cable had been extended another 4 to 6 feet and cable had been run from the directional taps to the adjoining building at 305 West 105th Street." Teleprompter also installed two large silver boxes along the roof cables. The cables are attached by screws or nails penetrating the masonry at approximately two-foot intervals, and other equipment is installed by bolts.

Initially, Teleprompter's roof cables did not service appellant's building. They were part of what could be described as a cable "highway" circumnavigating the city block, with service cables periodically dropped over the front or back of a building in which a tenant desired service. Crucial to such a network is the use of so-called "crossovers"—cable lines extending from one building to another in order to reach a new group of tenants. Two years after appellant purchased the building, Teleprompter connected a "noncrossover" line—i.e., one that provided CATV service to appellant's own tenants—by dropping a line to the first floor down the front of appellant's building.

Prior to 1973, Teleprompter routinely obtained authorization for its installations from property owners along the cable's route, compensating the owners at the standard rate of 5% of the gross revenues that Teleprompter realized from the particular property. To facilitate tenant access to CATV, New York enacted § 828 of the Executive Law, which provides that a landlord may not "interfere with the installation of cable television facilities upon his property or premises," and may not demand payment from any tenant for permitting CATV, or demand payment from any CATV company "in excess of any amount which the [State Commission on Cable Television] shall, by regulation, determine to be reasonable." The landlord may, however, require the CATV company or the tenant to bear the cost of installation and to indemnify for any damage caused by the installation. Pursuant to § 828(1)(b), the State Commission has ruled that a one-time $1 payment is the normal fee to which a landlord is entitled. The Commission ruled that this nominal fee, which the Commission concluded was equivalent to what the landlord would receive if the property were condemned pursuant to New York's Transportation Corporations Law, satisfied constitutional requirements "in the absence of a special showing of greater damages attributable to the taking."

Appellant did not discover the existence of the cable until after she had purchased the building. She brought a class action against Teleprompter in 1976 on behalf of all owners of real property in the State on which Teleprompter has placed CATV components, alleging that Teleprompter's installation was a trespass and, insofar as it relied on § 828, a taking without just compensation. She requested damages and injunctive relief. * * *

II

The Court of Appeals determined that § 828 serves the legitimate public purpose of "rapid development of and maximum penetration by a means of communication which has important educational and community aspects," 423 N.E.2d, at 329, and thus is within the State's police power. We have no reason to question that determination. It is a separate question, however, whether an otherwise valid regulation so frustrates property rights that compensation must be paid.

* * *

In *Penn Central Transportation Co. v. New York City*, 438 U.S. 104 (1978), the Court surveyed some of the general principles governing the Takings Clause. The Court noted that no "set formula" existed to determine, in all cases, whether compensation is constitutionally due for a government restriction of property. Ordinarily, the Court must engage in "essentially ad hoc, factual inquiries." Id., at 124. But the inquiry is not standardless. The economic impact of the regulation, especially the degree of interference with investment-backed expectations, is of particular significance. "So, too, is the character of the governmental action. A 'taking' may more readily be found when the interference with property can be characterized as a physical invasion by government, * * * than when interference arises from some public program adjusting the benefits and burdens of economic life to promote the common good."

As *Penn Central* affirms, the Court has often upheld substantial regulation of an owner's use of his own property where deemed necessary to promote the public interest. At the same time, we have long considered a physical intrusion by government to be a property restriction of an unusually serious character for purposes of the Takings Clause. Our cases further establish that when the physical intrusion reaches the extreme form of a permanent physical occupation, a taking has occurred. In such a case, "the character of the government action" not only is an important factor in resolving whether the action works a taking but is determinative.

When faced with a constitutional challenge to a permanent physical occupation of real property, this Court has invariably found a taking. As early as 1871, in *Pumpelly v. Green Bay Company*, 13 Wall. (80 U.S.) 166, 20 L.Ed. 557 (1871), this Court held that the defendant's construction, pursuant to state authority, of a dam which permanently flooded plaintiff's property constituted a taking. A unanimous Court stated, without qualification, that "where real estate is actually invaded by superinduced additions of water, earth, sand, or other material, or by having any artificial structure placed on it, so as to effectually destroy or impair its usefulness, it is a taking, within the meaning of the Constitution."

Since these early cases, this Court has consistently distinguished between flooding cases involving a permanent physical occupation and cases involving a more temporary invasion, or government action outside the owner's property that causes consequential damages within. A taking has always been found only in the former situation.

* * *

More recent cases confirm the distinction between a permanent physical occupation, a physical invasion short of an occupation, and a regulation that merely restricts the use of property. In *United States v. Causby*, 328 U.S. 256 (1946), the Court ruled that frequent flights immediately above a land owner's property constituted a taking. * * * The Court concluded that the damages to the respondents "were not merely consequential. They were the product of a direct invasion of respondents' domain." Id., at 265–266. *See also Griggs v. Allegheny County*, 369 U.S. 84 (1962).

* * *

Although this Court's most recent cases have not addressed the precise issue before us, they have emphasized that physical invasion cases are special and have not repudiated the rule that any permanent physical occupation is a taking. The cases state or imply that a physical invasion is subject to a balancing process, but they do not suggest that a permanent physical occupation would ever be exempt from the Takings Clause.

Penn Central Transportation Co. v. New York City, as noted above, contains one of the most complete discussions of the Takings Clause. The Court explained that resolving whether public action works a taking is ordinarily an ad hoc inquiry in which several factors are particularly significant—the economic impact of the regulation, the extent to which it interferes with investment-backed expectations, and the character of the governmental action. The opinion does not repudiate the rule that a permanent physical occupation is a government action of such a unique character that it is a taking without regard to other factors that a court might ordinarily examine.

In *Kaiser Aetna v. United States*, 444 U.S. 164 (1979), the Court held that the government's imposition of a navigational servitude requiring public access to a pond was a taking where the land owner had reasonably relied on government consent in connecting the pond to navigable water. The Court emphasized that the servitude took the land owner's right to exclude, "one of the most essential sticks in the bundle of rights that are commonly characterized as property." * * * Although the easement of passage, not being a permanent occupation of land, was not considered a taking *per se*, Kaiser Aetna reemphasizes that a physical invasion is a government intrusion of an unusually serious character.

In short, when the "character of the governmental action," *Penn Central*, 438 U.S. at 124, is a permanent physical occupation of property, our cases uniformly have found a taking to the extent of the occupation, without regard to whether the action achieves an important public benefit or has only minimal economic impact on the owner.

The historical rule that a permanent physical occupation of another's property is a taking has more than tradition to commend it. Such an appropriation is perhaps the most serious form of invasion of an owner's property interests. To borrow a metaphor, *cf. Andrus v. Allard*, 444 U.S., at 65–66, 100 S.Ct., at 326–327, the government does not simply take a single "strand" from the "bundle" of property rights: it chops through the bundle, taking a slice of every strand.

Property rights in a physical thing have been described as the rights "to possess, use and dispose of it." *United States v. General Motors Corp.*, 323 U.S. 373, 378 (1945). To the extent that the government permanently occupies physical property, it effectively destroys each of these rights. First, the owner has no right to possess the occupied space himself, and also has no power to exclude the occupier from possession and use of the space. The power to exclude has traditionally been considered one of the most treasured strands in an owner's bundle of property rights.[12] *See Kaiser Aetna*, 444 U.S., at 179–180; see also Restatement of Property § 7 (1936). Second, the permanent physical occupation of property forever denies the owner any power to control the use of the property; he not only cannot exclude others, but can make no non-possessory use of the property. Although deprivation of the right to use and obtain a profit from property is not, in every case, independently sufficient to establish a taking, *see Andrus v. Allard*, 444 U.S., at 66, it is clearly relevant. Finally, even though the owner may retain the bare legal right to dispose of the occupied space by transfer or sale, the permanent occupation of that space by a stranger will ordinarily empty the right of any value, since the purchaser will also be unable to make any use of the property.

* * *

Finally, whether a permanent physical occupation has occurred presents relatively few problems of proof. The placement of a fixed structure on land or real property is an obvious fact that will rarely be subject to dispute. Once the fact of occupation is shown, of course, a court should consider the *extent* of the occupation as one relevant factor in determining the compensation due. For that reason, moreover, there is less need to consider the extent of the occupation in determining whether there is a taking in the first instance.

Teleprompter's cable installation on appellant's building constitutes a taking under the traditional test. The installation involved a direct physical attachment of plates, boxes, wires, bolts and screws to the building, completely occupying space immediately above and upon the roof and along the building's exterior wall.

In light of our analysis, we find no constitutional difference between a crossover and a noncrossover installation. The portions of the installation necessary for both crossovers and noncrossovers permanently appropriate appellant's property. Accordingly, each type of installation is a taking.

* * *

Our holding today is very narrow. We affirm the traditional rule that a permanent physical occupation of property is a taking. In such a case, the property owner entertains an historically-rooted expectation of

---

[12] The permanence and absolute exclusivity of a physical occupation distinguish it from temporary limitations on the right to exclude. Not every physical *invasion* is a taking. As *PruneYard Shopping Center, Kaiser Aetna* and the intermittent flooding cases reveal, such temporary limitations are subject to a more complex balancing process to determine whether they are a taking. The rationale is evident: they do not absolutely dispossess the owner of his rights to use, and exclude others from, his property.

The dissent objects that the distinction between a permanent physical occupation and a temporary invasion will not always be clear. This objection is overstated, and in any event is irrelevant to the critical point that a permanent physical occupation *is* unquestionably a taking. In the antitrust area, similarly, this Court has not declined to apply a *per se* rule simply because a court must, at the boundary of the rule, apply the rule of reason and engage in a more complex balancing analysis.

compensation, and the character of the invasion is qualitatively more intrusive than perhaps any other category of property regulation. We do not, however, question the equally substantial authority upholding a State's broad power to impose appropriate restrictions upon an owner's *use* of his property.

Furthermore, our conclusion that § 828 works a taking of a portion of appellant's property does not presuppose that the fee which many landlords had obtained from Teleprompter prior to the law's enactment is a proper measure of the value of the property taken. The issue of the amount of compensation that is due, on which we express no opinion, is a matter for the state courts to consider on remand.

The judgment of the New York Court of Appeals is reversed and the case is remanded for further proceedings not inconsistent with this opinion.

It is so ordered.

JUSTICE BLACKMUN, with whom JUSTICE BRENNAN and JUSTICE WHITE join, dissenting (omitted).

NOTES

1. Physical invasions sufficient to support an action for inverse condemnation have been found in a variety of circumstances, some permanent, like *Loretto*, and some temporary. *See, e.g., Kaiser Aetna v. United States,* 444 U.S. 164 (1979), cited in *Loretto* as an example of a temporary invasion, finding a taking where the owners of a private lagoon made it accessible to navigable waters and were then forced to allow the public to use the lagoon. In the pre-*Loretto* case of *United States v. Causby,* 328 U.S. 256 (1946), frequent overflights of land adjoining a municipal airport leased to the federal government had rendered plaintiff's land unusable as a chicken farm. The Court noted:

> If, by reason of the frequency and altitude of the flights, respondents could not use this land for any purpose, their loss would be complete. It would be as complete as if the United States had entered upon the surface of the land and taken exclusive possession of it. * * * We would not doubt that, if the United States erected an elevated railway over respondents' land at the precise altitude where its planes now fly, there would be a partial taking, even though none of the supports of the structure rested on the land. The reason is that there would be an intrusion so immediate and direct as to subtract from the owner's full enjoyment of the property and to limit his exploitation of it. *Id.* at 261, 264–65.

In *McCarran Intern. Airport v. Sisolak,* 137 P.3d 1110 (Nev.2006), *cert. denied,* 549 U.S. 1206 (2007), the Nevada supreme court found that an ordinance imposing a height restriction on buildings near a public airport was a permanent avigation easement constituting a taking under *Loretto. See also Judlo, Inc. v. Vons Cos.,* 259 Cal.Rptr. 624 (Cal.App.1989) (holding that an injunction issued pursuant to a state constitutional clause protecting freedom of speech, which required a store owner to permit a newspaper publisher to place a news rack in front of the store, was a permanent physical occupation amounting to a taking).

2.   In *Yee v. City of Escondido*, 503 U.S. 519 (1992), the Court rejected an effort to expand *Loretto*'s physical takings rule. In *Yee*, mobile home park owners complained that the combined effect of a local rent control ordinance and state landlord tenant laws effected a physical taking because tenants had a "right to occupy the land indefinitely at a sub-market rent." 503 U.S. at 527. Rejecting the argument, the Court found that state law may have made it time consuming and difficult for the owners to terminate the leases and use their land for other purposes, but on its face the law did not permanently deprive the owners of the right to terminate the leases. Since "[p]etitioners' tenants were invited by petitioners, not forced upon them by the government," 503 U.S. at 528, the "required acquiescence" needed to invoke *Loretto* did not exist.

3.   In *Horne v. Department of Agriculture*, 135 S.Ct. 2419 (2015) the Court confirmed that *Loretto*'s physical takings rule also applies to personal property. In a challenge to federal legislation requiring raisin producers to reserve a certain percentage of their crop in order to regulate prices under the Raisin Marketing Order, the Court distinguished between the confiscation of real or personal property and the regulation of such property. The Court noted that direct appropriations of real property and personal property must be treated alike under the Fifth Amendment. *Id.* at 2427–28. See Shelley Ross Saxer, *When Local Government Misbehaves*, 2016 UTAH L.REV. 105, 121.

4.   The Hawaii Supreme Court has declared that native Hawaiians, who make up 20% of the state's population, may enter any "undeveloped" private property to undertake traditional and customary subsistence, cultural, and religious activities. *Pele Defense Fund v. Paty*, 837 P.2d 1247 (Haw.1992). The court then held in *Public Access Shoreline Hawaii v. Hawaii County Planning Commission*, 903 P.2d 1246 (Haw.1995), that such "traditional and customary" rights-here access over a hotel development site-may be exercised on partially developed land as well, and that "Western concepts" of property rights "may not be applicable in Hawaii."[1] Is this the type of physical invasion that the U.S. Supreme Court—and the Fifth Amendment—prohibit without compensation? Who defines property?

5.   Does it matter why the invasion occurs? *Loretto* suggests that it does not since it rejected the argument that the use of the building for rental purposes justified the intrusion. Suppose a municipality requires a residential developer to provide land for a public school made necessary to meet the demands of the new residents brought in by the developer. It is a permanent physical occupation, but is it a taking? *See Nollan v. California Coastal*

---

[1]   In State v. Hanapi, 970 P.2d 485 (1998), the Hawaii Supreme Court clarified its PASH decision by holding that a residential lot with a house on it was always "developed" and so not subject to native Hawaiian traditional and customary rights. In *Hanapi*, the lot was several acres with only one house, raising a presumption that the Court will permit such exercise only on land which is substantially open space.

Comm'n, 483 U.S. 825 (1987), where the Court conceded, for the sake of argument, that a permanent physical occupation might be justified as a condition for issuing a land use permit. Where the state can demonstrate that the physical exaction placed on the owner is substantially in response to the perceived adverse impact that the community will suffer from the landowner's development, there is no taking. This concession is critical in enabling government to finance infrastructure via the police power. *Nollan* is set out in full in Chapter 4.H. in the material on infrastructure financing.

6.   What if a flood control dam operation impacts private property by the government's act of releasing water that floods the private land? The Court in *Pumpelly v. Green Bay Co.*, 80 U.S. 166 (1871) first held that flooding caused by government action can constitute a taking. The Court then ruled in *United States v. Cress*, 243 U.S. 316, 318 (1917) that seasonal flooding could constitute a taking. Most recently, in *Arkansas Game and Fish Comm'n v. U.S.*, 133 S.Ct. 511, 522 (2012), the Court held "that government-induced flooding temporary in duration gains no automatic exemption from Takings Clause inspection."

7.   When one suffers harm from nuisance-like activity by the government without a physical invasion, there may be no taking. In *Batten v. United States*, 306 F.2d 580 (10th Cir.1962), *cert. denied*, 371 U.S. 955 (1963), the court refused to find a taking where the damage suffered from airport noise was much like that in *Causby*, discussed in Note 1 after *Loretto*, except that there were no overflights. All the noise, vibration, and smoke entered horizontally from a neighboring air force base rather than from above. The case has been criticized, see Richard A. Epstein, *Takings: Private Property and the Power of Eminent Domain* 50 (1985); but, the case represents the " 'great weight' of federal authority." *Branning v. United States*, 654 F.2d 88 (Ct.Cl.1981). Right to farm statutes prohibit a neighbor's private nuisance action against a farmer. Courts differ on whether this is a taking of a neighbor's property under the Fifth Amendment. See the 1998 Iowa decision in *Bormann* and the 2004 Idaho decision in *Moon*, discussed in Note 3. after *Boomer v. Atlantic Cement Co., Inc.* in Chapter 1. As to whether a government's land use constitutes a nuisance and may be a taking, see Carlos A. Ball, *The Curious Intersection of Nuisance and Takings Law*, 86 B.U.L.REV. 819 (2006).

(b) Denial of All Economically Beneficial Use

In *Loretto*, the Court confirmed that a permanent physical occupation of real property is a *"per se"* taking not subject to further inquiry under the factors identified in the *Penn Central* case (discussed in subsection (c) below). In *Horne*, the Court also confirmed that a permanent physical occupation of personal property requiring farmers to turn over raisins to the government based on a federal Raisin Marketing Order constitutes a *"per se"* taking under the Fifth Amendment.

In the case below, the Court identified another *"per se"* taking rule in situations where the government action results in a "denial of all economically viable use." However, note that there are potential exceptions to this *"per se"* rule as identified by Justice Scalia in the *Lucas* opinion below.

LUCAS V. SOUTH CAROLINA COASTAL COUNCIL
Supreme Court of the United States, 1992.
505 U.S. 1003, 112 S.Ct. 2886, 120 L.Ed.2d 798.

JUSTICE SCALIA delivered the opinion of the Court.

In 1986, petitioner David H. Lucas paid $975,000 for two residential lots on the Isle of Palms in Charleston County, South Carolina, on which he intended to build single-family homes. In 1988, however, the South Carolina Legislature enacted the Beachfront Management Act, S.C.Code § 48–39–250 *et seq.* (Supp.1990) (Act), which had the direct effect of barring petitioner from erecting any permanent habitable structures on his two parcels. See § 48–39–290(A). A state trial court found that this prohibition rendered Lucas's parcels "valueless." This case requires us to decide whether the Act's dramatic effect on the economic value of Lucas's lots accomplished a taking of private property under the Fifth and Fourteenth Amendments requiring the payment of "just compensation."

[I–A]

South Carolina's expressed interest in intensively managing development activities in the so-called "coastal zone" dates from 1977 when, in the aftermath of Congress's passage of the federal Coastal Zone Management Act of 1972, 86 Stat. 1280, as amended, 16 U.S.C. § 1451 *et seq.*, the legislature enacted a Coastal Zone Management Act of its own. See S.C.Code § 48–39–10 *et seq.* (1987). In its original form, the South Carolina Act required owners of coastal zone land that qualified as a "critical area" (defined in the legislation to include beaches and immediately adjacent sand dunes, § 48–39–10(J)) to obtain a permit from the newly created South Carolina Coastal Council (respondent here) prior to committing the land to a "use other than the use the critical area was devoted to on [September 28, 1977]." § 48–39–130(A).

In the late 1970's, Lucas and others began extensive residential development of the Isle of Palms, a barrier island situated eastward of the City of Charleston. Toward the close of the development cycle for one residential subdivision known as "Beachwood East," Lucas in 1986 purchased the two lots at issue in this litigation for his own account. No portion of the lots, which were located approximately 300 feet from the beach, qualified as a "critical area" under the 1977 Act; accordingly, at the time Lucas acquired these parcels, he was not legally obliged to obtain a permit from the Council in advance of any development activity. His intention with respect to the lots was to do what the owners of the immediately adjacent parcels had already done: erect single-family residences. He commissioned architectural drawings for this purpose.

The Beachfront Management Act brought Lucas's plans to an abrupt end. Under that 1988 legislation, the Council was directed to establish a "baseline" connecting the landward-most "point[s] of erosion * * * during the past forty years" in the region of the Isle of Palms that includes Lucas's lots. § 48–39–280(A)(2) (Supp.1988). In action not challenged here, the Council fixed this baseline landward of Lucas's parcels. That was significant, for under the Act construction of occupiable improvements[2] was flatly prohibited seaward of a line drawn 20 feet landward of, and parallel to, the baseline, § 48–39–290(A) (Supp.1988). The Act provided no exceptions.

B

Lucas promptly filed suit in the South Carolina Court of Common Pleas, contending that the Beachfront Management Act's construction bar effected a taking of his property without just compensation. Lucas did not take issue with the validity of the Act as a lawful exercise of South Carolina's police power, but contended that the Act's complete extinguishment of his property's value entitled him to compensation regardless of whether the legislature had acted in furtherance of legitimate police power objectives. Following a bench trial, the court agreed. Among its factual determinations was the finding that "at the time Lucas purchased the two lots, both were zoned for single-family residential construction and * * * there were no restrictions imposed upon such use of the property by either the State of South Carolina, the County of Charleston, or the Town of the Isle of Palms." The trial court further found that the Beachfront Management Act decreed a permanent ban on construction insofar as Lucas's lots were concerned, and that this prohibition "deprive[d] Lucas of any reasonable economic use of the lots, * * * eliminated the unrestricted right of use, and render[ed] them valueless." The court thus concluded that Lucas's properties had been "taken" by operation of the Act, and it ordered respondent to pay "just compensation" in the amount of $1,232,387.50.

The Supreme Court of South Carolina reversed. It found dispositive what it described as Lucas's concession "that the Beachfront Management Act [was] properly and validly designed to preserve * * * South Carolina's beaches." Failing an attack on the validity of the statute as such, the court believed itself bound to accept the "uncontested * * * findings" of the South Carolina legislature that new construction in the coastal zone—such as petitioner intended—threatened this public resource. The Court ruled that when a regulation respecting the use of property is designed "to prevent serious public harm," no compensation is owing under the Takings Clause regardless of the regulation's effect on the property value.

---

[2] The Act did allow the construction of certain nonhabitable improvements, e.g., "wooden walkways no larger in width than six feet," and "small wooden decks no larger than one hundred forty-four square feet." §§ 48–39–290(A)(1) and (2) (Supp.1988).

* * *

[III–A]

Prior to Justice Holmes' exposition in *Pennsylvania Coal Co. v. Mahon* it was generally thought that the Takings Clause reached only a "direct appropriation" of property, or the functional equivalent of a "practical ouster of [the owner's] possession." Justice Holmes recognized in *Mahon*, however, that if the protection against physical appropriations of private property was to be meaningfully enforced, the government's power to redefine the range of interests included in the ownership of property was necessarily constrained by constitutional limits. If, instead, the uses of private property were subject to unbridled, uncompensated qualification under the police power, "the natural tendency of human nature [would be] to extend the qualification more and more until at last private property disappear[ed]." These considerations gave birth in that case to the oft-cited maxim that, "while property may be regulated to a certain extent, if regulation goes too far it will be recognized as a taking."

Nevertheless, our decision in *Mahon* offered little insight into when, and under what circumstances, a given regulation would be seen as going "too far" for purposes of the Fifth Amendment. In 70-odd years of succeeding "regulatory takings" jurisprudence, we have generally eschewed any " 'set formula' " for determining how far is too far, preferring to "engag[e] in * * * essentially ad hoc, factual inquiries," *Penn Central Transportation Co. v. New York City*, 438 U.S. 104, 124 (1978) * * * . We have, however, described at least two discrete categories of regulatory action as compensable without case-specific inquiry into the public interest advanced in support of the restraint. The first encompasses regulations that compel the property owner to suffer a physical "invasion" of his property. In general (at least with regard to permanent invasions), no matter how minute the intrusion, and no matter how weighty the public purpose behind it, we have required compensation. For example, in *Loretto v. Teleprompter Manhattan CATV Corp.* we determined that New York's law requiring landlords to allow television cable companies to emplace cable facilities in their apartment buildings constituted a taking, even though the facilities occupied at most only 1½ cubic feet of the landlords' property. * * *

The second situation in which we have found categorical treatment appropriate is where regulation denies all economically beneficial or productive use of land. * * * As we have said on numerous occasions, the Fifth Amendment is violated when land-use regulation "does not substantially advance legitimate state interests or denies an owner economically viable use of his land." *Agins, supra*, 447 U.S., at 260 (citations omitted) (emphasis added).[7]

We have never set forth the justification for this rule. Perhaps it is simply, as Justice Brennan suggested, that total deprivation of beneficial use is, from the landowner's point of view, the equivalent of a physical appropriation. *See San Diego Gas & Electric Co. v. San Diego*, 450 U.S., at 652, 101 S.Ct., at 1304 (BRENNAN, J., dissenting). "[F]or what is the land but the profits thereof[?]" 1 E. Coke, Institutes ch. 1, § 1 (1st Am. ed.1812). Surely, at least, in the extraordinary circumstance when *no* productive or economically beneficial use of land is permitted, it is less realistic to indulge our usual assumption that the legislature is simply "adjusting the benefits and burdens of economic life," * * * in a manner that secures an "average reciprocity of advantage" to everyone concerned. * * * And the *functional* basis for permitting the government, by regulation, to affect property values without compensation—that "Government hardly could go on if to some extent values incident to property could not be diminished without paying for every such change in the general law,"—does not apply to the relatively rare situations where the government has deprived a landowner of all economically beneficial uses.

* * *

We think, in short, that there are good reasons for our frequently expressed belief that when the owner of real property has been called upon to sacrifice *all* economically beneficial uses in the name of the common good, that is, to leave his property economically idle, he has suffered a taking.[8]

---

[7] Regrettably, the rhetorical force of our "deprivation of all economically feasible use" rule is greater than its precision, since the rule does not make clear the "property interest" against which the loss of value is to be measured. When, for example, a regulation requires a developer to leave 90% of a rural tract in its natural state, it is unclear whether we would analyze the situation as one in which the owner has been deprived of all economically beneficial use of the burdened portion of the tract, or as one in which the owner has suffered a mere diminution in value of the tract as a whole. (For an extreme—and, we think, unsupportable—view of the relevant calculus, see Penn Central Transportation Co. v. New York City, 42 N.Y.2d 324, 333–334, 397 N.Y.S.2d 914, 920, 366 N.E.2d 1271, 1276–1277 (1977), aff'd, 438 U.S. 104 (1978), where the state court examined the diminution in a particular parcel's value produced by a municipal ordinance in light of total value of the taking claimant's other holdings in the vicinity.) Unsurprisingly, this uncertainty regarding the composition of the denominator in our "deprivation" fraction has produced inconsistent pronouncements by the Court

[8] Justice Stevens criticizes the "deprivation of all economically beneficial use" rule as "wholly arbitrary", in that "[the] landowner whose property is diminished in value 95% recovers nothing," while the landowner who suffers a complete elimination of value "recovers the land's full value." This analysis errs in its assumption that the landowner whose deprivation is one step short of complete is not entitled to compensation. Such an owner might not be able to claim the benefit of our categorical formulation, but, as we have acknowledged time and again, "[t]he economic impact of the regulation on the claimant and . . . the extent to which the regulation has interfered with distinct investment-backed expectations" are keenly relevant to takings analysis generally. *Penn Central Transportation Co. v. New York City*, 438 U.S. 104, 124 (1978). It is true that in at least some cases the landowner with 95% loss will get nothing, while the landowner with total loss will recover in full. But that occasional result is no more strange than the gross disparity between the landowner whose premises are taken for a highway (who recovers in full) and the [off-site]

B

The trial court found Lucas's two beachfront lots to have been rendered valueless by respondent's enforcement of the coastal-zone construction ban. Under Lucas's theory of the case, which rested upon our "no economically viable use" statements, that finding entitled him to compensation. Lucas believed it unnecessary to take issue with either the purposes behind the Beachfront Management Act, or the means chosen by the South Carolina Legislature to effectuate those purposes. The South Carolina Supreme Court, however, thought otherwise. In its view, the Beachfront Management Act was no ordinary enactment, but involved an exercise of South Carolina's "police powers" to mitigate the harm to the public interest that petitioner's use of his land might occasion. By neglecting to dispute the findings enumerated in the Act or otherwise to challenge the legislature's purposes, petitioner "concede[d] that the beach/dune area of South Carolina's shores is an extremely valuable public resource; that the erection of new construction, *inter alia*, contributes to the erosion and destruction of this public resource; and that discouraging new construction in close proximity to the beach/dune area is necessary to prevent a great public harm." In the court's view, these concessions brought petitioner's challenge within a long line of this Court's cases sustaining against Due Process and Takings Clause challenges the State's use of its "police powers" to enjoin a property owner from activities akin to public nuisances. *See Mugler v. Kansas*, 123 U.S. 623 (1887) (law prohibiting manufacture of alcoholic beverages); *Hadacheck v. Sebastian*, 239 U.S. 394 (1915) (law barring operation of brick mill in residential area); *Miller v. Schoene*, 276 U.S. 272 (1928) (order to destroy diseased cedar trees to prevent infection of nearby orchards); *Goldblatt v. Hempstead*, 369 U.S. 590 (1962) (law effectively preventing continued operation of quarry in residential area).

It is correct that many of our prior opinions have suggested that "harmful or noxious uses" of property may be proscribed by government regulation without the requirement of compensation. For a number of reasons, however, we think the South Carolina Supreme Court was too quick to conclude that that principle decides the present case. The "harmful or noxious uses" principle was the Court's early attempt to describe in theoretical terms why government may, consistent with the Takings Clause, affect property values by regulation without incurring an obligation to compensate—a reality we nowadays acknowledge explicitly

---

landowner whose property is reduced to 5% of its former value by the highway (who recovers nothing). Takings law is full of these "all-or-nothing" situations. Justice Stevens similarly misinterprets our focus on "developmental" uses of property (the uses proscribed by the Beachfront Management Act) as betraying an "assumption that the only uses of property cognizable under the Constitution are *developmental* uses." *Post*, at 2919, n. 3. We make no such assumption. Though our prior takings cases evince an abiding concern for the productive use of, and economic investment in, land, there are plainly a number of noneconomic interests in land whose impairment will invite exceedingly close scrutiny under the Takings Clause. *See, e.g., Loretto v. Teleprompter Manhattan CATV Corp.*, 458 U.S. 419, 436 (1982) (interest in excluding strangers from one's land).

with respect to the full scope of the State's police power. *See, e.g., Penn Central Transportation Co.*, 438 U.S., at 125 (where State "reasonably conclude[s] that 'the health, safety, morals, or general welfare' would be promoted by prohibiting particular contemplated uses of land," compensation need not accompany prohibition); see also *Nollan v. California Coastal Commission*, 483 U.S., at 834–835 ("Our cases have not elaborated on the standards for determining what constitutes a 'legitimate state interest[,]' [but] [t]hey have made clear . . . that a broad range of governmental purposes and regulations satisfy these requirements"). We made this very point in *Penn Central Transportation Co.*, where, in the course of sustaining New York City's landmarks preservation program against a takings challenge, we rejected the petitioner's suggestion that *Mugler* and the cases following it were premised on, and thus limited by, some objective conception of "noxiousness":

> "[T]he uses in issue in *Hadacheck, Miller, and Goldblatt* were perfectly lawful in themselves. They involved no 'blameworthiness, . . . moral wrongdoing or conscious act of dangerous risk-taking which induce[d society] to shift the cost to a pa[rt]icular individual.' Sax, *Takings and the Police Power*, 74 YALE L.J. 36, 50 (1964). These cases are better understood as resting not on any supposed 'noxious' quality of the prohibited uses but rather on the ground that the restrictions were reasonably related to the implementation of a policy—not unlike historic preservation—expected to produce a widespread public benefit and applicable to all similarly situated property." 438 U.S., at 133–134, n. 30.

"Harmful or noxious use" analysis was, in other words, simply the progenitor of our more contemporary statements that "land-use regulation does not effect a taking if it 'substantially advance[s] legitimate state interests'. . . ." *Nollan, supra*, 483 U.S., at 834 (quoting *Agins v. Tiburon*, 447 U.S., at 260). * * *

The transition from our early focus on control of "noxious" uses to our contemporary understanding of the broad realm within which government may regulate without compensation was an easy one, since the distinction between "harm-preventing" and "benefit-conferring" regulation is often in the eye of the beholder. It is quite possible, for example, to describe in *either* fashion the ecological, economic, and aesthetic concerns that inspired the South Carolina legislature in the present case. One could say that imposing a servitude on Lucas's land is necessary in order to prevent his use of it from "harming" South Carolina's ecological resources; or, instead, in order to achieve the "benefits" of an ecological preserve. * * * Whether Lucas's construction of single-family residences on his parcels should be described as bringing "harm" to South Carolina's adjacent ecological resources thus depends principally upon whether the describer believes that the State's use interest in nurturing those resources is so important that *any* competing adjacent use must yield.[12]

When it is understood that "prevention of harmful use" was merely our early formulation of the police power justification necessary to sustain (without compensation) *any* regulatory diminution in value; and that the distinction between regulation that "prevents harmful use" and that which "confers benefits" is difficult, if not impossible, to discern on an objective, value-free basis; it becomes self-evident that noxious-use logic cannot serve as a touchstone to distinguish regulatory "takings"—which require compensation—from regulatory deprivations that do not require compensation. A *fortiori* the legislature's recitation of a noxious-use justification cannot be the basis for departing from our categorical rule that total regulatory takings must be compensated. If it were, departure would virtually always be allowed. The South Carolina Supreme Court's approach would essentially nullify *Mahon's* affirmation of limits to the noncompensable exercise of the police power. Our cases provide no support for this: None of them that employed the logic of "harmful use" prevention to sustain a regulation involved an allegation that the regulation wholly eliminated the value of the claimant's land. See *Keystone Bituminous Coal Assn.*, 480 U.S., at 513–514 (REHNQUIST, C.J., dissenting).

Where the State seeks to sustain regulation that deprives land of all economically beneficial use, we think it may resist compensation only if the logically antecedent inquiry into the nature of the owner's estate shows that the proscribed use interests were not part of his title to begin with. This accords, we think, with our "takings" jurisprudence, which has traditionally been guided by the understandings of our citizens regarding the content of, and the State's power over, the "bundle of rights" that they acquire when they obtain title to property. It seems to us that the property owner necessarily expects the uses of his property to be restricted, from time to time, by various measures newly enacted by the State in legitimate exercise of its police powers; "[a]s long recognized, some values are enjoyed under an implied limitation and must yield to the police power." And in the case of personal property, by reason of the State's traditionally high degree of control over commercial dealings, he ought to be aware of the possibility that new regulation might even render his property economically worthless (at least if the property's only economically productive use is sale or manufacture for sale), *see Andrus v. Allard,* 444 U.S. 51 (1979) (prohibition on sale of eagle feathers). In the case of land, however, we think the notion pressed by the Council that title is somehow held subject to the "implied limitation" that the State may subsequently eliminate all economically

---

[12] In Justice BLACKMUN's view, even with respect to regulations that deprive an owner of all developmental or economically beneficial land uses, the test for required compensation is whether the legislature has recited a harm-preventing justification for its action. Since such a justification can be formulated in practically every case, this amounts to a test of whether the legislature has a stupid staff. We think the Takings Clause requires courts to do more than insist upon artful harm-preventing characterizations.

valuable use is inconsistent with the historical compact recorded in the Takings Clause that has become part of our constitutional culture.

Where "permanent physical occupation" of land is concerned, we have refused to allow the government to decree it anew (without compensation), no matter how weighty the asserted "public interests" involved, *Loretto v. Teleprompter Manhattan CATV Corp.*—though we assuredly would permit the government to assert a permanent easement that was a pre-existing limitation upon the landowner's title. *Compare Scranton v. Wheeler,* 179 U.S. 141, 163 (1900) (interests of "riparian owner in the submerged lands . . . bordering on a public navigable water" held subject to Government's navigational servitude), *with Kaiser Aetna v. United States,* 444 U.S., at 178–180 (imposition of navigational servitude on marina created and rendered navigable at private expense held to constitute a taking). We believe similar treatment must be accorded confiscatory regulations, i.e., regulations that prohibit all economically beneficial use of land: Any limitation so severe cannot be newly legislated or decreed (without compensation), but must inhere in the title itself, in the restrictions that background principles of the State's law of property and nuisance already place upon land ownership. A law or decree with such an effect must, in other words, do no more than duplicate the result that could have been achieved in the courts—by adjacent landowners (or other uniquely affected persons) under the State's law of private nuisance, or by the State under its complementary power to abate nuisances that affect the public generally, or otherwise.

On this analysis, the owner of a lake bed, for example, would not be entitled to compensation when he is denied the requisite permit to engage in a landfilling operation that would have the effect of flooding others' land. Nor the corporate owner of a nuclear generating plant, when it is directed to remove all improvements from its land upon discovery that the plant sits astride an earthquake fault. Such regulatory action may well have the effect of eliminating the land's only economically productive use, but it does not proscribe a productive use that was previously permissible under relevant property and nuisance principles. The use of these properties for what are now expressly prohibited purposes was always unlawful, and (subject to other constitutional limitations) it was open to the State at any point to make the implication of those background principles of nuisance and property law explicit. See Frank I. Michelman, *Property, Utility, and Fairness, Comments on the Ethical Foundations of "Just Compensation" Law,* 80 HARV.L.REV. 1165, 1239–41 (1967). In light of our traditional resort to "existing rules or understandings that stem from an independent source such as state law" to define the range of interests that qualify for protection as "property" under the Fifth (and Fourteenth) amendments, *Board of Regents of State Colleges v. Roth,* 408 U.S. 564, 577 (1972), * * * this recognition that the Takings Clause does not require compensation when an owner is barred from putting land to a use that is proscribed by those "existing rules or understandings" is surely unexceptional. When, however, a regulation that declares "off-limits" all economically productive or beneficial uses of land goes beyond what the relevant background principles would dictate, compensation must be paid to sustain it.

The "total taking" inquiry we require today will ordinarily entail (as the application of state nuisance law ordinarily entails) analysis of, among other things, the degree of harm to public lands and resources, or adjacent private property, posed by the claimant's proposed activities, see, e.g., Restatement (Second) of Torts §§ 826, 827, the social value of the claimant's activities and their suitability to the locality in question, *see, e.g.,* id., §§ 828(a) and (b), 831, and the relative ease with which the alleged harm can be avoided through measures taken by the claimant and the government (or adjacent private landowners) alike, *see, e.g.,* id., §§ 827(e), 828(c), 830. The fact that a particular use has long been engaged in by similarly situated owners ordinarily imports a lack of any common-law prohibition (though changed circumstances or new knowledge may make what was previously permissible no longer so, see Restatement (Second) of Torts, *supra*, § 827, comment *g*. So also does the fact that other landowners, similarly situated, are permitted to continue the use denied to the claimant).

It seems unlikely that common-law principles would have prevented the erection of any habitable or productive improvements on petitioner's land; they rarely support prohibition of the "essential use" of land, *Curtin v. Benson,* 222 U.S. 78, 86 (1911). The question, however, is one of state law to be dealt with on remand. We emphasize that to win its case South Carolina must do more than proffer the legislature's declaration that the uses Lucas desires are inconsistent with the public interest, or the conclusory assertion that they violate a common-law maxim such as sic utere tuo ut alienum non laedas. As we have said, a "State, by ipse dixit, may not transform private property into public property without compensation. . . ." *Webb's Fabulous Pharmacies, Inc. v. Beckwith,* 449 U.S. 155, 164 (1980). Instead, as it would be required to do if it sought to restrain Lucas in a common-law action for public nuisance, South Carolina must identify background principles of nuisance and property law that prohibit the uses he now intends in the circumstances in which the property is presently found. Only on this showing can the State fairly claim that, in proscribing all such beneficial uses, the Beachfront Management Act is taking nothing.[18]

---

[18] JUSTICE BLACKMUN decries our reliance on background nuisance principles at least in part because he believes those principles to be as manipulable as we find the "harm prevention"/"benefit conferral" dichotomy. There is no doubt some leeway in a court's interpretation of what existing state law permits—but not remotely as much, we think, as in a legislative crafting of the reasons for its confiscatory regulation. We stress that an affirmative decree eliminating all economically beneficial uses may be defended only if an *objectively reasonable application* of relevant precedents would exclude those beneficial uses in the circumstances in which the land is presently found.

* * *

The judgment is reversed and the cause remanded for proceedings not inconsistent with this opinion.

So ordered.

JUSTICE KENNEDY, concurring in the judgment.

* * *

The South Carolina Court of Common Pleas found that petitioner's real property has been rendered valueless by the State's regulation. The finding appears to presume that the property has no significant market value or resale potential. This is a curious finding, and I share the reservations of some of my colleagues about a finding that a beach front lot loses all value because of a development restriction. * * *

* * *

In my view, reasonable expectations must be understood in light of the whole of our legal tradition. The common law of nuisance is too narrow a confine for the exercise of regulatory power in a complex and interdependent society. *Goldblatt v. Hempstead,* 369 U.S. 590, 593 (1962). The State should not be prevented from enacting new regulatory initiatives in response to changing conditions, and courts must consider all reasonable expectations whatever their source. The Takings Clause does not require a static body of state property law; it protects private expectations to ensure private investment. I agree with the Court that nuisance prevention accords with the most common expectations of property owners who face regulation, but I do not believe this can be the sole source of state authority to impose severe restrictions. Coastal property may present such unique concerns for a fragile land system that the State can go further in regulating its development and use than the common law of nuisance might otherwise permit.

JUSTICE BLACKMUN, dissenting.

Today the Court launches a missile to kill a mouse.

The State of South Carolina prohibited petitioner Lucas from building a permanent structure on his property from 1988 to 1990. Relying on an unreviewed (and implausible) state trial court finding that this restriction left Lucas' property valueless, this Court granted review to determine whether compensation must be paid in cases where the State prohibits all economic use of real estate. According to the Court, such an occasion never has arisen in any of our prior cases, and the Court imagines that it will arise "relatively rarely" or only in "extraordinary circumstances." Almost certainly it did not happen in this case.

* * *

Until today, the Court explicitly had rejected the contention that the government's power to act without paying compensation turns on whether the prohibited activity is a common law nuisance. The brewery closed in *Mugler* itself was not a common law nuisance, and the Court specifically stated that it was the role of the legislature to determine what measures would be appropriate for the protection of public health and safety. *See* 123 U.S. at 661. In upholding the state action in *Miller,* the Court found it unnecessary to "weigh with nicety the question whether the infected cedars constitute a nuisance according to common law; or whether they may be so declared by statute." 276 U.S. at 280. *See also* Goldblatt, 369 U.S. at 593; Hadacheck, 239 U.S. at 411. Instead the Court has relied in the past, as the South Carolina Court has done here, on legislative judgments of what constitutes a harm.

* * *

JUSTICE STEVENS, dissenting.

Today the Court restricts one judge-made rule and expands another. In my opinion it errs on both counts. Proper application of the doctrine of judicial restraint would avoid the premature adjudication of an important constitutional question. Proper respect for our precedents would avoid an illogical expansion of the concept of "regulatory takings."

* * *

In short, the Court's new rule is unsupported by prior decisions, arbitrary and unsound in practice, and theoretically unjustified. In my opinion, a categorical rule as important as the one established by the Court today should be supported by more history or more reasons than has yet been provided.

The Nuisance Exception

Like many bright-line rules, the categorical rule established in this case is only "categorical" for a page or two in the U.S. Reports. No sooner does the Court state that "total regulatory takings must be compensated," than it quickly establishes an exception to that rule.

The exception provides that a regulation that renders property valueless is not a taking if it prohibits uses of property that were not "previously permissible under relevant property and nuisance principles." The Court thus rejects the basic holding in *Mugler v. Kansas,* 123 U.S. 623 (1887). There we held that a state-wide statute that prohibited the owner of a brewery from making alcoholic beverages did not effect a taking, even though the use of the property had been perfectly lawful and caused no public harm before the statute was enacted. We squarely rejected the rule the Court adopts today:

* * *

Accordingly, I respectfully dissent.

Statement of JUSTICE SOUTER.

I would dismiss the writ of certiorari in this case as having been granted improvidently. After briefing and argument it is abundantly clear that an unreviewable assumption on which this case comes to us is both questionable as a conclusion of Fifth Amendment law and sufficient to frustrate the Court's ability to render certain the legal premises on which its holding rests. * * *

NOTES

1.   South Carolina's wisdom in preventing the development of the last two undeveloped lots in the Isle of Palms subdivision, if not the public purpose of the beachfront preservation statute itself, was seriously undermined when the State of South Carolina, after paying Lucas $1.5 million in compensation, proceeded to sell the two lots to a developer for the construction of residences—the very proposed use which generated the lawsuit in the first place. Lucas was given the two lots as compensation for his executive management of the lots in the Isle of Palms subdivision. Why didn't the court consider that there was no substantial loss of the two lots compared to the totality of the 20-lot subdivision? This is similar to the scenario in *Keystone Bituminous Coal Ass'n. v. DeBenedictis*, 480 U.S. 470 (1987), where the restriction on mining only pertained to the land immediately below the surface compared to the thousands of feet of total depth of the mine.

Hurricane Hugo hit South Carolina in 1989, a year after passage of the Beachfront Management Act. Hugo destroyed one house on the Isle of Palms and the majority of the 19 other homes were damaged. Hugo's damage only exemplifies what many know: construction on the beach is risky business. Over the past several decades, as the coastline has shifted and the waterline moved, Lucas's two lots likewise have changed. At one time, they were under the surf, and at another time they were covered by a shallow pool of water. If it is so risky, why build there? Why would a bank finance such construction? According to one study, private mortgages and insurance are not available for development within 1000 feet of the beachfront. Insurance is only available because it is federally subsidized. *See* John R. Nolan, *Footprints in the Shifting Sands of the Isle of Palms: A Practical Analysis of Regulatory Takings Cases*, 8 J.LAND USE & ENVTL.LAW 1, 10, n.58 (1992). There are periodic proposals to eliminate this insurance subsidy. See discussion of federal disaster relief in Chapter 9.

2.   The categorical or per se rule established by the Court in *Lucas* applies only to so-called "total takings," where the landowner is deprived of all economically beneficial use of the totality of the land. The Court specifically leaves for another day clarification of its partial takings jurisprudence (footnote 7) leaving us with *Penn Central Transportation Co. v. City of New York*, 438 U.S. 104 (1978), to deal with such takings. *Penn Central* (the next principal case in this chapter) decided that " '[t]aking' jurisprudence does not

divide a single parcel into discrete segments and attempt to determine whether rights in a particular segment have been entirely abrogated. In deciding whether a particular governmental action has effected a taking, this Court focuses rather both on the character of the action and on the nature and extent of the interference with rights in the parcel as a whole."

3.   A debate has ensued over whether the *per se* regulatory takings test is a deprivation of all economically viable or beneficial *use*, or a deprivation of all *value*. The *Lucas* Court uses both terms though it focuses more on use. In *Tahoe-Sierra Preservation Council, Inc. v. Tahoe Regional Planning Agency*, 535 U.S. 302 (2002), the majority read the *per se* test as requiring an "obliteration of value" as well as use. For discussions of the use v. value debate, see Douglas T. Kendall, *Defining the* Lucas *Box:* Palazzolo, Tahoe *and the Use/Value Debate*, Ch. 18 and James Burling, *Can the Existence of Value in Property Avert a Regulatory Taking When Economically Beneficial Use Has Been Destroyed?* Ch. 19, in *Taking Sides on Takings Issues Public and Private Perspectives* (T. Roberts ed.2002).

4.   What are we to make of "background principles" of state property law? Certainly more than a statute or a few cases, or the majority's discussion and holding would seem insufficient and the application of its categorical or *per se* rule would be marginalized to the point of irrelevance. See David L. Callies and J. David Breemer, *Selected Legal and Policy Trends in Takings Law: Background Principles, Custom and Public Trust "Exceptions" and the (Mis)use of Investment-Backed Expectations*, 36 VAL.U.L.REV. 339 (2002).

Among the possible examples of "background principles" is the doctrine of public trust.[2] *In R.W. Docks & Slips v. Wisconsin*, 628 N.W.2d 781 (Wis. 2001), *cert. denied,* 534 U.S. 1041 (2001), the court extended the public trust doctrine to a weedbed (which became a bird sanctuary) created by the property owner in the course of land development. *See also McQueen v. South Carolina Coastal Council*, 580 S.E.2d 116 (S.C.2003), *cert. denied,* 540 U.S. 982 (2003), and *Esplanade Properties v. City of Seattle*, 307 F.3d 978 (9th Cir.2002), *cert. denied,* 539 U.S. 926 (2003), both holding that the public trust doctrine is a background principle of a state's law of property within the exception to the *Lucas per se* rule. There are limitations to the extent of the public trust doctrine. In *Purdie v. Attorney General*, 732 A.2d 442 (N.H.1999), the state effected an unconstitutional taking of private property without just compensation by extending public trust rights to the high water mark. The end result appears to be that private land affected with a public trust moves about if the coastal landscape changes gradually, but not if it changes avulsively. *See Stop the Beach Renourishment, Inc. v. Florida Depart. of Environmental Protection*, 560 U.S. 702 (2010).

---

[2]   The public trust doctrine "is founded upon the necessity of preserving to the public the use of navigable waters from private interruption and encroachment." *Illinois Central R. Co. v. Illinois*, 146 U.S. 387, 436 (1892). With variation among jurisdictions, the trust doctrine protects the public rights to fishing, commerce, and recreational water uses. *See generally* Alexandra B. Klass, *Modern Public Trust Principles: Recognizing Rights and Integrating Standards*, 82 NOTRE DAME L.REV. 699 (2006).

5.   The law of custom has also emerged as a background principle exception to the *Lucas per se* rule. In *Stevens v. City of Cannon Beach*, 854 P.2d 449 (Or.1993), *cert. denied*, 510 U.S. 1207 (1994), the court specifically held that a judicially previously-established customary right of all of Oregon's citizens to use the dry sand area of the state's beaches was a background principle of the state's law of property, defeating a *per se* takings claim by owners of lots made undevelopable by the exercise of that customary right. In a stinging dissent from the denial of the landowner's petition for a writ of certiorari in *Stevens*, Justice Scalia declared it was an "understatement that this case raise[d] a serious Fifth Amendment takings issue." 114 S.Ct. at 1335. For an extended discussion of customary law criteria, see David L. Callies, *Custom and Public Trust: Background Principles of State Property Law?* 30 ENVTL L.REP. 10003 (2000); David J. Bederman, *The Curious Resurrection of Custom: Beach Access and Judicial Takings*, 96 COL.L.REV. 1375 (1996) and Paul Sullivan, *Customary Revolutions: The Law of Custom and the Conflict of Traditions in Hawaii*, 20 U.HAW.L.REV. 99 (1998).

6.   What about statutes? Recall that *Lucas* arose under a South Carolina coastal protection statute, raising at least a presumption that statutes that effect the land cannot at the same time constitute background principles of law. Nevertheless, in *Sanderson v. Town of Candia*, 787 A.2d 167 (N.H.2001) the court held that a "positive law" (a statute) could be construed as a background principle if it were passed prior to the landowner's acquisition of the subject parcel. For a comprehensive summary of categories beyond public trust and custom, see Michael C. Blumm & Lucas Ritchie, Lucas's *Unlikely Legacy: The Rise of Background Principles as Categorical Takings Defenses*, 29 HARV.ENVTL.L.REV. 321 (2005).

7.   There is, of course, a considerable body of law on nuisance. As for the nuisance exception, *see Osceola County v. Best Diversified, Inc.*, 936 So.2d 55 (Fla.App.2006), where a takings claim based on a landfill permit denial failed because the landfill constituted a nuisance. In *M & J Coal Co. v. United States*, 47 F.3d 1148 (Fed.Cir.1995), the court held prohibition of mining was not a taking even though the company had a mining permit, because, under the circumstances of the case, mining would constitute a nuisance and therefore no property right was lost. *See also Mutschler v. City of Phoenix*, 129 P.3d 71 (Ariz.App.2006) (club featuring live sex acts was a nuisance and therefore no taking occurred when it was shut down).

(c)   Partial Deprivations of Economic Use

Although many Supreme Court observers had anticipated that the *Lucas* decision would either overrule or severely diminish the importance of the Court's prior regulatory takings decision in *Penn Central Transportation Co. v. New York City* (below), *Lucas* instead established a two-pronged analytical structure for regulatory takings. One prong involves factual situations that trigger a so-called *per se* takings test. The other prong involves balancing various factors that were set forth in the *Penn Central* decision. To date, the Supreme Court has determined that two factual circumstances constitute a regulatory taking *per se*. In *Loretto*, the Court held that a regulation that authorizes permanent physical invasion of property, no matter how minimal, constitutes a *per se* taking. *Lucas* directs that "where a regulation denies all economically beneficial or productive use of land," and common law principles would not have prevented the regulated use, a *per se* taking will be found. Any alleged regulatory takings with factual circumstances that fall outside these two *per se* categories must be analyzed by weighing and balancing the *Penn Central* factors, using an ad hoc factual inquiry as to: (1) the economic impact of the regulation on the claimant; (2) the extent to which the regulation has interfered with the claimant's distinct investment-backed expectations; and (3) the character of the governmental action.

PENN CENTRAL TRANSPORTATION COMPANY V. CITY OF NEW YORK

Supreme Court of the United States, 1978.
438 U.S. 104, 98 S.Ct. 2646, 57 L.Ed.2d 631.

MR. JUSTICE BRENNAN delivered the opinion of the Court.

The question presented is whether a city may, as part of a comprehensive program to preserve historic landmarks and historic districts, place restrictions on the development of individual historic landmarks—in addition to those imposed by applicable zoning ordinances—without effecting a "taking" requiring the payment of "just compensation." Specifically, we must decide whether the application of New York City's Landmarks Preservation Law to the parcel of land occupied by Grand Central Terminal has "taken" its owners' property in violation of the Fifth and Fourteenth Amendments.

[I—A]

Over the past 50 years, all 50 States and over 500 municipalities have enacted laws to encourage or require the preservation of buildings and areas with historic or aesthetic importance.[1] These nationwide legislative efforts have been precipitated by two concerns. The first is recognition that, in recent years, large numbers of historic structures, landmarks, and areas have been destroyed[2] without adequate consideration of either the values

---

[1] *See* National Trust for Historic Preservation, A Guide to State Historic Preservation Programs (1976); National Trust for Historic Preservation, Directory of Landmark and Historic District Commissions (1976). In addition to these state and municipal legislative efforts, Congress has determined that "the historical and cultural foundations of the Nation should be preserved as a living part of our community life and development in order to give a sense of orientation to the American people," National Historic Preservation Act of 1966, 80 Stat. 915, 16 U.S.C. § 470(b) (1976 ed.).

[2] Over one-half of the buildings listed in the Historic American Buildings Survey, begun by the Federal Government in 1933, have been destroyed. *See* Costonis, *The Chicago Plan: Incentive Zoning and the Preservation of Urban Landmarks*, 85 HARV.L.REV. 574, 574 n. 1 (1972), citing Huxtable, *Bank's Building Plan Sets Off Debate on "Progress,"* N.Y. Times, Jan. 17, 1971, section 8, p. 1, col. 2.

represented therein or the possibility of preserving the destroyed properties for use in economically productive ways. The second is a widely shared belief that structures with special historic, cultural, or architectural significance enhance the quality of life for all. Not only do these buildings and their workmanship represent the lessons of the past and embody precious features of our heritage, they serve as examples of quality for today. "[H]istoric conservation is but one aspect of the much larger problem, basically an environmental one, of enhancing—or perhaps developing for the first time—the quality of life for people."

New York City, responding to similar concerns and acting pursuant to a New York State enabling Act,[5] adopted its Landmarks Preservation Law in 1965. The city acted from the conviction that "the standing of [New York City] as a world-wide tourist center and world capital of business, culture and government" would be threatened if legislation were not enacted to protect historic landmarks and neighborhoods from precipitate decisions to destroy or fundamentally alter their character. The city believed that comprehensive measures to safeguard desirable features of the existing urban fabric would benefit its citizens in a variety of ways: e.g., fostering "civic pride in the beauty and noble accomplishments of the past"; protecting and enhancing "the city's attractions to tourists and visitors"; "support[ing] and stimul[ating] business and industry"; "strengthen[ing] the economy of the city"; and promoting "the use of historic districts, landmarks, interior landmarks and scenic landmarks for the education, pleasure and welfare of the people of the city."

The New York City law is typical of many urban landmark laws in that its primary method of achieving its goals is not by acquisitions of historic properties,[6] but rather by involving public entities in land-use decisions affecting these properties and providing services, standards, controls, and incentives that will encourage preservation by private owners and users. While the law does place special restrictions on landmark properties as a necessary feature to the attainment of its larger objectives, the major theme of the law is to ensure the owners of any such properties both a "reasonable return" on their investments and maximum latitude to use their parcels for purposes not inconsistent with the preservation goals.

The operation of the law can be briefly summarized. The primary responsibility for administering the law is vested in the Landmarks

---

[5] *See* N.Y.Gen.Mun.Law § 96–a (McKinney 1977). It declares that it is the public policy of the State of New York to preserve structures and areas with special historical or aesthetic interest or value and authorizes local governments to impose reasonable restrictions to perpetuate such structures and areas.

[6] The consensus is that widespread public ownership of historic properties in urban settings is neither feasible nor wise. Public ownership reduces the tax base, burdens the public budget with costs of acquisitions and maintenance, and results in the preservation of public buildings as museums and similar facilities, rather than as economically productive features of the urban scene. *See* Wilson & Winkler, *The Response of State Legislation to Historic Preservation*, 36 LAW & CONTEMP.PROB. 329, 330–331, 339–340 (1971).

Preservation Commission (Commission), a broad based, 11-member agency[8] assisted by a technical staff. The Commission first performs the function, critical to any landmark preservation effort, of identifying properties and areas that have "a special character or special historical or aesthetic interest or value as part of the development, heritage or cultural characteristics of the city, state or nation." If the Commission determines, after giving all interested parties an opportunity to be heard, that a building or area satisfies the ordinance's criteria, it will designate a building to be a "landmark,"[9] situated on a particular "landmark site,"[10] or will designate an area to be a "historic district."[11] After the Commission makes a designation, New York City's Board of Estimate, after considering the relationship of the designated property "to the master plan, the zoning resolution, projected public improvements and any plans for the renewal of the area involved," may modify or disapprove the designation, and the owner may seek judicial review of the final designation decision. Thus far, 31 historic districts and over 400 individual landmarks have been finally designated, and the process is a continuing one.

Final designation as a landmark results in restrictions upon the property owner's options concerning use of the landmark site. First, the law imposes a duty upon the owner to keep the exterior features of the building "in good repair" to assure that the law's objectives not be defeated by the landmark's falling into a state of irremediable disrepair. Second, the Commission must approve in advance any proposal to alter the exterior architectural features of the landmark or to construct any exterior improvement on the landmark site, thus ensuring that decisions concerning construction on the landmark site are made with due consideration of both the public interest in the maintenance of the structure and the landowner's interest in use of the property.

---

[8] The ordinance creating the Commission requires that it include at least three architects, one historian qualified in the field, one city planner or landscape architect, one realtor, and at least one resident of each of the city's five boroughs. N.Y.C. Charter § 534 (1976). In addition to the ordinance's requirements concerning the composition of the Commission, there is, according to a former chairman, a "prudent tradition" that the Commission include one or two lawyers, preferably with experience in municipal government, and several laymen with no specialized qualifications other than concern for the good of the city.

[9] " 'Landmark.' Any improvement, any part of which is thirty years old or older, which has a special character or special historical or aesthetic interest or value as part of the development, heritage or cultural characteristics of the city, state or nation and which has been designated as a landmark pursuant to the provisions of this chapter." § 207–1.0(n).

[10] " 'Landmark site.' An improvement parcel or part thereof on which is situated a landmark and any abutting improvement parcel or part thereof used as and constituting part of the premises on which the landmark is situated, and which has been designated as a landmark site pursuant to the provisions of this chapter." § 207.–1.0(o).

[11] " 'Historic district.' Any area which: (1) contains improvements which: (a) have a special character or special historical or aesthetic interest or value; and (b) represent one or more periods or styles of architecture typical of one or more eras in the history of the city; and (c) cause such area, by reason of such factors, to constitute a distinct section of the city; and (2) has been designated as a historic district pursuant to the provisions of this chapter." § 207–1.0(h). The Act also provides for the designation of a "scenic landmark," see § 207–1.0(w), and an "interior landmark." See § 207–1.0(m).

In the event an owner wishes to alter a landmark site, three separate procedures are available through which administrative approval may be obtained. First, the owner may apply to the Commission for a "certificate of no effect on protected architectural features": that is, for an order approving the improvement or alteration on the ground that it will not change or affect any architectural feature of the landmark and will be in harmony therewith. Denial of the certificate is subject to judicial review.

Second, the owner may apply to the Commission for a certificate of "appropriateness." Such certificates will be granted if the Commission concludes—focusing upon aesthetic, historical, and architectural values— that the proposed construction on the landmark site would not unduly hinder the protection, enhancement, perpetuation, and use of the landmark. Again, denial of the certificate is subject to judicial review. Moreover, the owner who is denied either a certificate of no exterior effect or a certificate of appropriateness may submit an alternative or modified plan for approval. The final procedure—seeking a certificate of appropriateness on the ground of "insufficient return,"—provides special mechanisms, which vary depending on whether or not the landmark enjoys a tax exemption,[13] to ensure that designation does not cause economic hardship.

Although the designation of a landmark and landmark site restricts the owner's control over the parcel, designation also enhances the economic position of the landmark owner in one significant respect. Under New York City's zoning laws, owners of real property who have not developed their property to the full extent permitted by the applicable zoning laws are allowed to transfer development rights to contiguous parcels on the same city block. A 1968 ordinance gave the owners of landmark sites additional opportunities to transfer development rights to other parcels. Subject to a restriction that the floor area of the transferee lot may not be increased by more than 20% above its authorized level, the ordinance permitted transfers from a landmark parcel to property across the street or across a street intersection. * * * The class of recipient lots was expanded to include lots "across a street and opposite to another lot or lots which except for the intervention of streets or street intersections f[or]m a series extending to the lot occupied by the landmark building[, provided that] all lots [are] in the same ownership." In addition, the 1969 amendment permits, in highly commercialized areas like midtown Manhattan, the transfer of all unused development rights to a single parcel. Ibid.

---

[13]   If the owner of a non-tax-exempt parcel has been denied certificates of appropriateness for a proposed alteration and shows that he is not earning a reasonable return on the property in its present state, the Commission and other city agencies must assume the burden of developing a plan that will enable the landmark owner to earn a reasonable return on the landmark site. . . . If he accepts the plan, he proceeds to operate the property pursuant to the plan. If he rejects the plan, the Commission may recommend that the city proceed by eminent domain to acquire a protective interest in the landmark. . . .

B

This case involves the application of New York City's Landmarks Preservation Law to Grand Central Terminal (Terminal). The Terminal, which is owned by the Penn Central Transportation Co. and its affiliates (Penn Central), is one of New York City's most famous buildings. Opened in 1913, it is regarded not only as providing an ingenious engineering solution to the problems presented by urban railroad stations, but also as a magnificent example of the French beaux-arts style.

* * *

On August 2, 1967, following a public hearing, the Commission designated the Terminal a "landmark" and designated the "city tax block" it occupies a "landmark site." The Board of Estimate confirmed this action on September 21, 1967. Although appellant Penn Central had opposed the designation before the Commission, it did not seek judicial review of the final designation decision.

On January 22, 1968, appellant Penn Central, to increase its income, entered into a renewable 50-year lease and sublease agreement with appellant UGP Properties, Inc. (UGP), a wholly owned subsidiary of Union General Properties, Ltd., a United Kingdom corporation. Under the terms of the agreement, UGP was to construct a multistory office building above the Terminal. UGP promised to pay Penn Central $1 million annually during construction and at least $3 million annually thereafter. The rentals would be offset in part by a loss of some $700,000 to $1 million in net rentals presently received from concessionaires displaced by the new building.

Appellants UGP and Penn Central then applied to the Commission for permission to construct an office building atop the Terminal. Two separate plans, both designed by architect Marcel Breuer and both apparently satisfying the terms of the applicable zoning ordinance, were submitted to the Commission for approval. The first, Breuer I, provided for the construction of a 55-story office building, to be cantilevered above the existing facade and to rest on the roof of the Terminal. The second, Breuer II Revised, called for tearing down a portion of the Terminal that included the 42d Street facade, stripping off some of the remaining features of the Terminal's facade, and constructing a 53-story office building. The Commission denied a certificate of no exterior effect on September 20, 1968. Appellants then applied for a certificate of "appropriateness" as to both proposals. After four days of hearings at which over 80 witnesses testified, the Commission denied this application as to both proposals.

The Commission's reasons for rejecting certificates respecting Breuer II Revised are summarized in the following statement: "To protect a Landmark, one does not tear it down. To perpetuate its architectural features, one does not strip them off." Breuer I, which would have preserved the existing vertical facades of the present structure, received more sympathetic consideration. The Commission first focused on the effect that the proposed tower would have on one desirable feature created by the present structure and its surroundings: the dramatic view of the Terminal from Park Avenue South. Although appellants had contended that the Pan-American Building had already destroyed the silhouette of the south facade and that one additional tower could do no further damage and might even provide a better background for the facade, the Commission disagreed, stating that it found the majestic approach from the south to be still unique in the city and that a 55-story tower atop the Terminal would be far more detrimental to its south facade than the Pan-American Building 375 feet away. Moreover, the Commission found that from closer vantage points the Pan Am Building and the other towers were largely cut off from view, which would not be the case of the mass on top of the Terminal planned under Breuer I. In conclusion, the Commission stated:

> [We have] no fixed rule against making additions to designated buildings—it all depends on how they are done * * * . But to balance a 55-story office tower above a flamboyant Beaux-Arts facade seems nothing more than an aesthetic joke. Quite simply, the tower would overwhelm the Terminal by its sheer mass. The "addition" would be four times as high as the existing structure and would reduce the Landmark itself to the status of a curiosity.
>
> Landmarks cannot be divorced from their settings—particularly when the setting is a dramatic and integral part of the original concept. The Terminal, in its setting, is a great example of urban design. Such examples are not so plentiful in New York City that we can afford to lose any of the few we have. And we must preserve them in a meaningful way—with alterations and additions of such character, scale, materials and mass as will protect, enhance and perpetuate the original design rather than overwhelm it. Id., at 2251.

Appellants did not seek judicial review of the denial of either certificate. Because the Terminal site enjoyed a tax exemption, remained suitable for its present and future uses, and was not the subject of a contract of sale, there were no further administrative remedies available to appellants as to the Breuer I and Breuer II Revised plans. *See* n. 13, *supra*. Further, appellants did not avail themselves of the opportunity to develop and submit other plans for the Commission's consideration and approval. Instead, appellants filed suit in New York Supreme Court, Trial Term, claiming, *inter alia,* that the application of the Landmarks Preservation Law had "taken" their property without just compensation in violation of the Fifth and Fourteenth Amendments and arbitrarily deprived them of their property without due process of law in violation of the Fourteenth Amendment. * * * The trial court granted the injunctive and declaratory relief, but severed the question of damages for a "temporary taking."

Appellees appealed, and the New York Supreme Court, Appellate Division, reversed. The Appellate Division held that the restrictions on the development of the Terminal site were necessary to promote the legitimate public purpose of protecting landmarks and therefore that appellants could sustain their constitutional claims only by proof that the regulation deprived them of all reasonable beneficial use of the property. The Appellate Division held that the evidence appellants introduced at trial—"Statements of Revenues and Costs," purporting to show a net operating loss for the years 1969 and 1971, which were prepared for the instant litigation—had not satisfied their burden. * * * The Appellate Division concluded that all appellants had succeeded in showing was that they had been deprived of the property's most profitable use, and that this showing did not establish that appellants had been unconstitutionally deprived of their property.

The New York Court of Appeals affirmed. That court summarily rejected any claim that the Landmarks Law had "taken" property without "just compensation," indicating that there could be no "taking" since the law had not transferred control of the property to the city, but only restricted appellants' exploitation of it. In that circumstance, the Court of Appeals held that appellants' attack on the law could prevail only if the law deprived appellants of their property in violation of the Due Process Clause of the Fourteenth Amendment. Whether or not there was a denial of substantive due process turned on whether the restrictions deprived Penn Central of a "reasonable return" on the "privately created and privately managed ingredient" of the Terminal. The Court of Appeals concluded that the Landmarks Law had not effected a denial of due process because: (1) the landmark regulation permitted the same use as had been made of the Terminal for more than half a century; (2) the appellants had failed to show that they could not earn a reasonable return on their investment in the Terminal itself; (3) even if the Terminal proper could never operate at a reasonable profit some of the income from Penn Central's extensive real estate holdings in the area, which include hotels and office buildings, must realistically be imputed to the Terminal; and (4) the development rights above the Terminal, which had been made transferable to numerous sites in the vicinity of the Terminal, one or two of which were suitable for the construction of office buildings, were valuable to appellants and provided "significant, perhaps 'fair,' compensation for the loss of rights above the terminal itself."

Observing that its affirmance was "[o]n the present record," and that its analysis had not been fully developed by counsel at any level of the New York judicial system, the Court of Appeals directed that counsel "should be entitled to present * * * any additional submissions which, in the light of [the court's] opinion, may usefully develop further the factors discussed." Appellants chose not to avail themselves of this opportunity and filed a notice of appeal in this Court. We noted probable jurisdiction. We affirm.

II

The issues presented by appellants are (1) whether the restrictions imposed by New York City's law upon appellants' exploitation of the Terminal site effect a "taking" of appellants' property for a public use within the meaning of the Fifth Amendment, which of course is made applicable to the States through the Fourteenth Amendment, and, (2), if so, whether the transferable development rights afforded appellants constitute "just compensation" within the meaning of the Fifth Amendment. We need only address the question whether a "taking" has occurred.

Before considering appellants' specific contentions, it will be useful to review the factors that have shaped the jurisprudence of the Fifth Amendment injunction "nor shall private property be taken for public use, without just compensation." The question of what constitutes a "taking" for purposes of the Fifth Amendment has proved to be a problem of considerable difficulty. While this Court has recognized that the "Fifth Amendment's guarantee * * * [is] designed to bar Government from forcing some people alone to bear public burdens which, in all fairness and justice, should be borne by the public as a whole," this Court, quite simply, has been unable to develop any "set formula" for determining when "justice and fairness" require that economic injuries caused by public action be compensated by the government, rather than remain disproportionately concentrated on a few persons. Indeed, we have frequently observed that whether a particular restriction will be rendered invalid by the government's failure to pay for any losses proximately caused by it depends largely "upon the particular circumstances [in that] case."

In engaging in these essentially ad hoc, factual inquiries, the Court's decisions have identified several factors that have particular significance. The economic impact of the regulation on the claimant and, particularly, the extent to which the regulation has interfered with distinct investment-backed expectations are, of course, relevant considerations. So, too, is the character of the governmental action. A "taking" may more readily be found when the interference with property can be characterized as a physical invasion by government than when interference arises from some public program adjusting the benefits and burdens of economic life to promote the common good.

"Government hardly could go on if to some extent values incident to property could not be diminished without paying for every such change in the general law," and this Court has accordingly recognized, in a wide variety of contexts, that government may execute laws or programs that adversely affect recognized economic values. Exercises of the taxing power are one obvious example. A second are the decisions in which this Court has dismissed "taking" challenges on the ground that, while the challenged government action caused economic harm, it did not interfere with interests that were sufficiently bound up with the reasonable expectations of the claimant to constitute "property" for Fifth Amendment purposes.

More importantly for the present case, in instances in which a state tribunal reasonably concluded that "the health, safety, morals, or general welfare" would be promoted by prohibiting particular contemplated uses of land, this Court has upheld land-use regulations that destroyed or adversely affected recognized real property interests.

Zoning laws generally do not affect existing uses of real property, but "taking" challenges have also been held to be without merit in a wide variety of situations when the challenged governmental actions prohibited a beneficial use to which individual parcels had previously been devoted and thus caused substantial individualized harm. [The Court discusses *Hadacheck v. Sebastian*, 239 U.S. 394 (1915) (law barring manufacture of brick in residential area), *Miller v. Schoene*, 276 U.S. 272 (1928) (order to destroy diseased cedar trees to prevent infection of nearby orchards) and *Goldblatt v. Hempstead*, 369 U.S. 590 (1962) (law prohibiting operation of quarry in residential area). Eds.]

Pennsylvania Coal Co. v. Mahon, 260 U.S. 393 (1922), is the leading case for the proposition that a state statute that substantially furthers important public policies may so frustrate distinct investment-backed expectations as to amount to a "taking."

Finally, government actions that may be characterized as acquisitions of resources to permit or facilitate uniquely public functions have often been held to constitute "takings." *United States v. Causby*, 328 U.S. 256 (1946).

B

In contending that the New York City law has "taken" their property in violation of the Fifth and Fourteenth Amendments, appellants make a series of arguments, which, while tailored to the facts of this case, essentially urge that any substantial restriction imposed pursuant to a landmark law must be accompanied by just compensation if it is to be constitutional.

* * *

They first observe that the airspace above the Terminal is a valuable property interest, citing *United States v. Causby, supra*. They urge that the Landmarks Law has deprived them of any gainful use of their "air rights" above the Terminal and that, irrespective of the value of the remainder of their parcel, the city has "taken" their right to this superadjacent airspace, thus entitling them to "just compensation" measured by the fair market value of these air rights.

Apart from our own disagreement with appellants' characterization of the effect of the New York City law, the submission that appellants may establish a "taking" simply by showing that they have been denied the ability to exploit a property interest that they heretofore had believed was available for development is quite simply untenable. Were this the rule, this Court would have erred not only in upholding laws restricting the development of air rights, but also in approving those prohibiting both the subjacent, development of particular parcels. "Taking" jurisprudence does not divide a single parcel into discrete segments and attempt to determine whether rights in a particular segment have been entirely abrogated. In deciding whether a particular governmental action has effected a taking, this Court focuses rather both on the character of the action and on the nature and extent of the interference with rights in the parcel as a whole— here, the city tax block designated as the "landmark site."

Secondly, appellants, focusing on the character and impact of the New York City law, argue that New York City's regulation of individual landmarks is fundamentally different from zoning or from historic-district legislation because the controls imposed by New York City's law apply only to individuals who own selected properties.

* * *

It is true, as appellants emphasize, that both historic-district legislation and zoning laws regulate all properties within given physical communities whereas landmark laws apply only to selected parcels. But, contrary to appellants' suggestions, landmark laws are not like discriminatory, or "reverse spot," zoning: that is, a land-use decision which arbitrarily singles out a particular parcel for different, less favorable treatment than the neighboring ones. In contrast to discriminatory zoning, which is the antithesis of land-use control as part of some comprehensive plan, the New York City law embodies a comprehensive plan to preserve structures of historic or aesthetic interest wherever they might be found in the city, and as noted, over 400 landmarks and 31 historic districts have been designated pursuant to this plan. * * *

In any event, appellants' repeated suggestions that they are solely burdened and unbenefited is factually inaccurate. This contention overlooks the fact that the New York City law applies to vast numbers of structures in the city in addition to the Terminal—all the structures contained in the 31 historic districts and over 400 individual landmarks, many of which are close to the Terminal. Unless we are to reject the judgment of the New York City Council that the preservation of landmarks benefits all New York citizens and all structures, both economically and by improving the quality of life in the city as a whole—which we are unwilling to do—we cannot conclude that the owners of the Terminal have in no sense been benefited by the Landmarks Law. Doubtless appellants believe they are more burdened than benefited by the law, but that must have been true, too, of the property owners in *Miller, Hadacheck, Euclid,* and *Goldblatt.*

Appellants' final broad-based attack would have us treat the law as an instance, like that in *United States v. Causby,* in which government, acting in an enterprise capacity, has appropriated part of their property for some strictly governmental purpose. Apart from the fact that *Causby* was a case of invasion of airspace that destroyed the use of the farm beneath and this New York City law has in nowise impaired the present use of the Terminal, the Landmarks Law neither exploits appellants' parcel for city purposes nor facilitates nor arises from any entrepreneurial operations of the city. The situation is not remotely like that in *Causby* where the airspace above the property was in the flight pattern for military aircraft. The Landmarks Law's effect is simply to prohibit appellants or anyone else from occupying portions of the airspace above the Terminal, while permitting appellants to use the remainder of the parcel in a gainful fashion. This is no more an appropriation of property by government for its own uses than is a zoning law prohibiting, for "aesthetic" reasons, two or more adult theaters within a specified area, or a safety regulation prohibiting excavations below a certain level.

C

Rejection of appellants' broad arguments is not, however, the end of our inquiry, for all we thus far have established is that the New York City law is not rendered invalid by its failure to provide "just compensation" whenever a landmark owner is restricted in the exploitation of property interests, such as air rights, to a greater extent than provided for under applicable zoning laws. We now must consider whether the interference with appellants' property is of such a magnitude that "there must be an exercise of eminent domain and compensation to sustain [it]." That inquiry may be narrowed to the question of the severity of the impact of the law on appellants' parcel, and its resolution in turn requires a careful assessment of the impact of the regulation on the Terminal site.

Unlike the governmental acts in *Goldblatt, Miller, Causby, Griggs,* and *Hadacheck,* the New York City law does not interfere in any way with the present uses of the Terminal. Its designation as a landmark not only permits but contemplates that appellants may continue to use the property precisely as it has been used for the past 65 years: as a railroad terminal containing office space and concessions. So the law does not interfere with what must be regarded as Penn Central's primary expectation concerning the use of the parcel. More importantly, on this record, we must regard the New York City law as permitting Penn Central not only to profit from the Terminal but also to obtain a "reasonable return" on its investment.

Appellants, moreover, exaggerate the effect of the law on their ability to make use of the air rights above the Terminal in two respects. First, it simply cannot be maintained, on this record, that appellants have been prohibited from occupying *any* portion of the airspace above the Terminal. While the Commission's actions in denying applications to construct an office building in excess of 50 stories above the Terminal may indicate that it will refuse to issue a certificate of appropriateness for any comparably sized structure, nothing the Commission has said or done suggests an intention to prohibit *any* construction above the Terminal. The Commission's report emphasized that whether any construction would be allowed depended upon whether the proposed addition "would harmonize in scale, material and character with [the Terminal]." Since appellants have not sought approval for the construction of a smaller structure, we do not know that appellants will be denied any use of any portion of the airspace above the Terminal.

Second, to the extent appellants have been denied the right to build above the Terminal, it is not literally accurate to say that they have been denied *all* use of even those pre-existing air rights. Their ability to use these rights has not been abrogated; they are made transferable to at least eight parcels in the vicinity of the Terminal, one or two of which have been found suitable for the construction of new office buildings. Although appellants and others have argued that New York City's transferable development-rights program is far from ideal, the New York courts here supportably found that, at least in the case of the Terminal, the rights afforded are valuable. While these rights may well not have constituted "just compensation" if a "taking" had occurred, the rights nevertheless undoubtedly mitigate whatever financial burdens the law has imposed on appellants and, for that reason, are to be taken into account in considering the impact of regulation.

On this record, we conclude that the application of New York City's Landmarks Law has not effected a "taking" of appellants' property. The restrictions imposed are substantially related to the promotion of the general welfare and not only permit reasonable beneficial use of the landmark site but also afford appellants opportunities further to enhance not only the Terminal site proper but also other properties.

Affirmed.

MR. JUSTICE REHNQUIST, with whom THE CHIEF JUSTICE and MR. JUSTICE STEVENS join, dissenting [omitted].

NOTES

1. *Penn Central* was the Court's first regulatory takings case arising in a land use context since the 1922 *Pennsylvania Coal v. Mahon* decision. Are the holdings consistent? Looking back to the Brandeis dissent in *Pennsylvania Coal*, do you think it influenced the Court in *Penn Central*? Defining the unit

of property for the purposes of a regulatory takings claim is often outcome determinative. The question may arise in a horizontal, vertical, or temporal context. *See infra* Section B.2. Private Property.

2.   The second *Penn Central* test explores the extent to which the regulation has interfered with "distinct investment-backed expectations." In *Kaiser Aetna v. United States*, 444 U.S. 164, 175 (1979), just a year after *Penn Central*, the Court referred to "reasonable," as opposed to "distinct" investment-backed expectations. While some initially thought the "investment-backed expectations" test would provide "new support for landowner takings claims, * * * , the factor has become, instead, a shield for government." Daniel R. Mandelker, *The Notice Rule in Investment-Backed Expectations* Ch. 2, at 21, in *Taking Sides on Takings Issues: Public and Private Perspectives* (T. Roberts ed.2002).

Assessing "reasonable investment backed expectations" is subjective. One must first ask what investments were made and then ask whether they were reasonable in light of the existing or probable future regulations. Additional questions that might be asked: Did the government make any representations? Did it unfairly lead the property owner to expect to be able to proceed with her intended use? Was reliance reasonable and did the landowner substantially change her position as a result of such reliance? What is the status of other similarly situated property?

Should it matter that the landowner purchased the property knowing that existing wetlands regulation precluded the landowner's expectation to develop the property for a beach club? The Court in *Palazzolo v. Rhode Island*, 533 U.S. 606, 632–33 (2001) held that the "mere fact that title was acquired after the effective date of the state-imposed restriction" does not bar a takings claim under *Penn Central*, but instead is just one of a number of factors to be considered.

While the *Palazzolo* Court protected the landowner from an automatic bar to a taking challenge, the Court rejected the claim that a *Lucas*-type taking had occurred, finding a 93.7% diminution in value was not a categorical taking. The property owner alleged that his property, most of which was wetlands, had a value of $3,150,000 if developed with 74 single-family homes. However, as restricted by the state's wetlands laws, the claimant could only build one home, leaving his parcel with a value of $200,000, or, as he put it, "a few crumbs of value." These "few crumbs," however, were sufficient to render *Lucas* inapplicable, as the Court found that the right "to build a substantial residence on [the whole] parcel does not leave the property 'economically idle.'" 535 U.S. at 631. The Court remanded the case telling the state court to apply the *Penn Central* test.

3.   *Penn Central* says that one factor to consider in a takings claim is the character of the governmental action. It then notes, as an example, that a taking may be more readily found when the government physically invades land than when it regulates land. The *Loretto* case, which followed *Penn Central*, turned this factor into a *"per se"* taking when the character of the

governmental action is a permanent physical occupation of the property at issue.

4. An ordinance can be attacked on its face (asserting that the mere enactment of the ordinance constitutes a taking), or as applied (complaining of the particular impact on property). "The test to be applied in considering [a] facial challenge is fairly straightforward. A statute regulating the uses that can be made of property effects a taking if it 'denies an owner economically viable use of his land * * * .'" *Hodel v. Virginia Surface Mining and Reclamation Ass'n*, 452 U.S. 264, 295–96 (1981). A facial challenge is "an uphill battle." *Keystone Bituminous Coal Ass'n v. DeBenedictis*, 480 U.S. 470, 495 (1987). Does this mean the test is more stringent for facial, compared to as applied, claims? In general, see Richard H. Fallon, Jr., *As-Applied and Facial Challenges and Third-Party Standing*, 113 HARV.L.REV. 1321 (2000).

5. The issues of historic preservation and transferable development rights raised in *Penn Central* are covered in Chapter 2.

A question that has plagued the regulatory takings doctrine from its inception is its relationship to substantive due process. The courts have intermingled and confused the two since *Pennsylvania Coal v. Mahon.* The following case deals with that issue and comprehensively summarizes the Court's jurisprudence for Fifth Amendment takings claims.

LINGLE V. CHEVRON U.S.A. INC.

Supreme Court of the United States, 2005.
544 U.S. 528, 125 S.Ct. 2074, 161 L.Ed.2d 876.

JUSTICE O'CONNOR delivered the opinion of the Court.

On occasion, a would-be doctrinal rule or test finds its way into our case law through simple repetition of a phrase—however fortuitously coined. A quarter century ago, in *Agins v. City of Tiburon*, 447 U.S. 255 (1980), the Court declared that government regulation of private property "effects a taking if [such regulation] does not substantially advance legitimate state interests. . . ." Id., at 260. Through reiteration in a half dozen or so decisions since *Agins*, this language has been ensconced in our Fifth Amendment takings jurisprudence. * * * See *Monterey v. Del Monte Dunes at Monterey, Ltd.*, 526 U.S. 687, 704 (1999) (citing cases).

In the case before us, the lower courts applied *Agins'* "substantially advances" formula to strike down a Hawaii statute that limits the rent that oil companies may charge to dealers who lease service stations owned by the companies. The lower courts held that the rent cap effects an uncompensated taking of private property in violation of the Fifth and Fourteenth Amendments because it does not substantially advance Hawaii's asserted interest in controlling retail gasoline prices. This case requires us to decide whether the "substantially advances" formula announced in *Agins* is an appropriate test for determining whether a regulation effects a Fifth Amendment taking. We conclude that it is not.

[To counteract the effects of market concentration on retail gasoline prices, the Hawaii legislature imposed a cap on the rents that oil companies could charge independent lessee-dealers. Chevron sought to enjoin operation of the act, claiming it effected a facial taking under the 5th Amendment. The district court granted summary judgment to Chevron, holding that the act failed to substantially advance a legitimate state interest because it would not actually reduce lessee-dealers' costs or retail prices. After an appeal and remand, the district court found the expert witness called by Chevron "more persuasive" than the State's expert, and again concluded that oil companies would raise wholesale gasoline prices to offset any rent reduction required by the act, and that the result would be an increase in retail gasoline prices. The 9th Circuit affirmed. *Chevron USA, Inc. v. Bronster*, 363 F.3d 846, 856 (9th Cir.2004). Eds.]

The Takings Clause of the Fifth Amendment, made applicable to the States through the Fourteenth, *see Chicago, B. & Q.R. Co. v. Chicago*, 166 U.S. 226 (1897), provides that private property shall not "be taken for public use, without just compensation." As its text makes plain, the Takings Clause "does not prohibit the taking of private property, but instead places a condition on the exercise of that power." *First English Evangelical Lutheran Church of Glendale v. County of Los Angeles*, 482 U.S. 304, 314 (1987). In other words, it "is designed not to limit the governmental interference with property rights *per se,* but rather to secure *compensation* in the event of otherwise proper interference amounting to a taking." *Id.* (emphasis in original). While scholars have offered various justifications for this regime, we have emphasized its role in "bar[ring] Government from forcing some people alone to bear public burdens which, in all fairness and justice, should be borne by the public as a whole." *Armstrong v. United States*, 364 U.S. 40, 49 (1960); *see also Monongahela Nav. Co. v. United States*, 148 U.S. 312, 325 (1893).

The paradigmatic taking requiring just compensation is a direct government appropriation or physical invasion of private property. *See, e.g., United States v. Pewee Coal Co.*, 341 U.S. 114 (1951) (Government's seizure and operation of a coal mine to prevent a national strike of coal miners effected a taking); *United States v. General Motors Corp.*, 323 U.S. 373 (1945) (Government's occupation of private warehouse effected a taking). Indeed, until the Court's watershed decision in *Pennsylvania Coal Co. v. Mahon*, 260 U.S. 393 (1922), "it was generally thought that the Takings Clause reached *only* a 'direct appropriation' of property, or the functional equivalent of a 'practical ouster of [the owner's] possession.'" *Lucas v. South Carolina Coastal Council*, 505 U.S. 1003, 1014 (1992) (citations omitted and emphasis added; brackets in original); *see also id.* at 1028, n. 15 ("[E]arly constitutional theorists did not believe the Takings Clause embraced regulations of property at all").

Beginning with *Mahon,* however, the Court recognized that government regulation of private property may, in some instances, be so onerous that its effect is tantamount to a direct appropriation or ouster— and that such "regulatory takings" may be compensable under the Fifth Amendment. In Justice Holmes' storied but cryptic formulation, "while property may be regulated to a certain extent, if regulation goes too far it will be recognized as a taking." 260 U.S. at 415. The rub, of course, has been—and remains—how to discern how far is "too far." In answering that question, we must remain cognizant that "government regulation—by definition—involves the adjustment of rights for the public good," *Andrus v. Allard,* 444 U.S. 51, 65 (1979), and that "Government hardly could go on if to some extent values incident to property could not be diminished without paying for every such change in the general law," *Mahon, supra,* at 413. Our precedents stake out two categories of regulatory action that generally will be deemed *per se* takings for Fifth Amendment purposes. First, where government requires an owner to suffer a permanent physical invasion of her property—however minor—it must provide just compensation. *See Loretto v. Teleprompter Manhattan CATV Corp.,* 458 U.S. 419 (1982) (state law requiring landlords to permit cable companies to install cable facilities in apartment buildings effected a taking). A second categorical rule applies to regulations that completely deprive an owner of "*all* economically beneficial us[e]" of her property. *Lucas,* 505 U.S., at 1019 (emphasis in original). We held in *Lucas* that the government must pay just compensation for such "total regulatory takings," except to the extent that "background principles of nuisance and property law" independently restrict the owner's intended use of the property.

Outside these two relatively narrow categories (and the special context of land-use exactions discussed below), regulatory takings challenges are governed by the standards set forth in *Penn Central Transp. Co. v. New York City,* 438 U.S. 104 (1978). The Court in *Penn Central* acknowledged that it had hitherto been "unable to develop any 'set formula' " for evaluating regulatory takings claims, but identified "several factors that have particular significance." Primary among those factors are "[t]he economic impact of the regulation on the claimant and, particularly, the extent to which the regulation has interfered with distinct investment-backed expectations." In addition, the "character of the governmental action"—for instance whether it amounts to a physical invasion or instead merely affects property interests through "some public program adjusting the benefits and burdens of economic life to promote the common good"— may be relevant in discerning whether a taking has occurred. The *Penn Central* factors—though each has given rise to vexing subsidiary questions—have served as the principal guidelines for resolving regulatory takings claims that do not fall within the physical takings or *Lucas* rules. *See, e.g., Palazzolo v. Rhode Island,* 533 U.S. 606, 617–618 (2001); id., at 632–634 (O'CONNOR, J., concurring).

Although our regulatory takings jurisprudence cannot be characterized as unified, these three inquiries (reflected in *Loretto*, *Lucas*, and *Penn Central*) share a common touchstone. Each aims to identify regulatory actions that are functionally equivalent to the classic taking in which government directly appropriates private property or ousts the owner from his domain. Accordingly, each of these tests focuses directly upon the severity of the burden that government imposes upon private property rights. The Court has held that physical takings require compensation because of the unique burden they impose: A permanent physical invasion, however minimal the economic cost it entails, eviscerates the owner's right to exclude others from entering and using her property—perhaps the most fundamental of all property interests. *See Dolan v. City of Tigard*, 512 U.S. 374, 384 (1994); *Nollan v. California Coastal Comm'n*, 483 U.S. 825, 831–832 (1987); *Loretto*, *supra*, at 433; *Kaiser Aetna v. United States*, 444 U.S. 164, 176 (1979). In the *Lucas* context, of course, the complete elimination of a property's value is the determinative factor. *See Lucas*, *supra*, at 1017 (positing that "total deprivation of beneficial use is, from the landowner's point of view, the equivalent of a physical appropriation"). And the *Penn Central* inquiry turns in large part, albeit not exclusively, upon the magnitude of a regulation's economic impact and the degree to which it interferes with legitimate property interests.

In *Agins v. City of Tiburon*, a case involving a facial takings challenge to certain municipal zoning ordinances, the Court declared that "[t]he application of a general zoning law to particular property effects a taking if the ordinance does not substantially advance legitimate state interests, *see Nectow v. Cambridge*, 277 U.S. 183, 188 (1928), or denies an owner economically viable use of his land, *see Penn Central Transp. Co. v. New York City*, 438 U.S. 104, 138, n. 36 (1978)." 447 U.S. at 260. Because this statement is phrased in the disjunctive, *Agins'* "substantially advances" language has been read to announce a stand-alone regulatory takings test that is wholly independent of *Penn Central* or any other test. Indeed, the lower courts in this case struck down Hawaii's rent control statute based solely upon their findings that it does not substantially advance a legitimate state interest. Although a number of our takings precedents have recited the "substantially advances" formula minted in *Agins*, this is our first opportunity to consider its validity as a freestanding takings test. We conclude that this formula prescribes an inquiry in the nature of a due process, not a takings, test, and that it has no proper place in our takings jurisprudence.

There is no question that the "substantially advances" formula was derived from due process, not takings, precedents. In support of this new language, *Agins* cited *Nectow v. Cambridge*, a 1928 case in which the plaintiff claimed that a city zoning ordinance "deprived him of his property without due process of law in contravention of the Fourteenth Amendment,

* * * ." *Agins* then went on to discuss *Village of Euclid v. Ambler Realty Co.*, 272 U.S. 365 (1926), a historic decision holding that a municipal zoning ordinance would survive a substantive due process challenge so long as it was not "clearly arbitrary and unreasonable, having no substantial relation to the public health, safety, morals, or general welfare." Id., at 395, 47 S.Ct. 114 (emphasis added); *see also Nectow, supra*, at 187–188 (quoting the same "substantial relation" language from *Euclid*).

When viewed in historical context, the Court's reliance on *Nectow* and *Euclid* is understandable. *Agins* was the Court's first case involving a challenge to zoning regulations in many decades, so it was natural to turn to these seminal zoning precedents for guidance. * * * Finally, when *Agins* was decided, there had been some history of referring to deprivations of property without due process of law as "takings," *see, e.g., Rowan v. Post Office Dept.*, 397 U.S. 728, 740 (1970), and the Court had yet to clarify whether "regulatory takings" claims were properly cognizable under the Takings Clause or the Due Process Clause, *see Williamson County Regional Planning Comm'n v. Hamilton Bank of Johnson City*, 473 U.S. 172, 197–199 (1985).

* * *

Instead of addressing a challenged regulation's effect on private property, the "substantially advances" inquiry probes the regulation's underlying validity. But such an inquiry is logically prior to and distinct from the question whether a regulation effects a taking, for the Takings Clause presupposes that the government has acted in pursuit of a valid public purpose. The Clause expressly requires compensation where government takes private property "for public use." It does not bar government from interfering with property rights, but rather requires compensation "in the event of *otherwise proper interference* amounting to a taking." *First English Evangelical Lutheran Church*, 482 U.S. at 315 (emphasis added). Conversely, if a government action is found to be impermissible—for instance because it fails to meet the "public use" requirement or is so arbitrary as to violate due process—that is the end of the inquiry. No amount of compensation can authorize such action.

* * *

For the foregoing reasons, we conclude that the "substantially advances" formula announced in *Agins* is not a valid method of identifying regulatory takings for which the Fifth Amendment requires just compensation. Since Chevron argued only a "substantially advances" theory in support of its takings claim, it was not entitled to summary judgment on that claim.

We emphasize that our holding today-that the "substantially advances" formula is not a valid takings test-does not require us to disturb any of our prior holdings. To be sure, we applied a "substantially advances" inquiry in *Agins* itself, (finding that the challenged zoning ordinances "substantially advance[d] legitimate governmental goals"), and arguably also in *Keystone Bituminous Coal Assn. v. DeBenedictis*, 480 U.S. 470, 485–492 (1987) (quoting " 'substantially advance[s]' " language and then finding that the challenged statute was intended to further a substantial public interest). But in no case have we found a compensable taking based on such an inquiry. Indeed, in most of the cases reciting the "substantially advances" formula, the Court has merely assumed its validity when referring to it in dicta. *See Tahoe-Sierra Preservation Council, Inc. v. Tahoe Regional Planning Agency*, 535 U.S. 302, 334 (2002); *Del Monte Dunes*, 526 U.S., at 704; *Lucas*, 505 U.S., at 1016; *Yee v. Escondido*, 503 U.S. 519, 534 (1992); *United States v. Riverside Bayview Homes, Inc.*, 474 U.S. 121, 126 (1985).

It might be argued that this formula played a role in our decisions in *Nollan v. California Coastal Comm'n*, 483 U.S. 825 (1987), and *Dolan v. City of Tigard*, 512 U.S. 374 (1994). But while the Court drew upon the language of *Agins* in these cases, it did not apply the "substantially advances" test that is the subject of today's decision. Both *Nollan* and *Dolan* involved Fifth Amendment takings challenges to adjudicative land-use exactions—specifically, government demands that a landowner dedicate an easement allowing public access to her property as a condition of obtaining a development permit. *See Dolan*, *supra*, (permit to expand a store and parking lot conditioned on the dedication of a portion of the relevant property for a "greenway," including a bike/pedestrian path); *Nollan*, *supra*, (permit to build a larger residence on beachfront property conditioned on dedication of an easement allowing the public to traverse a strip of the property between the owner's seawall and the mean high-tide line).

In each case, the Court began with the premise that, had the government simply appropriated the easement in question, this would have been a *per se* physical taking. The question was whether the government could, without paying the compensation that would otherwise be required upon effecting such a taking, demand the easement as a condition for granting a development permit the government was entitled to deny. The Court in *Nollan* answered in the affirmative, provided that the exaction would substantially advance the same government interest that would furnish a valid ground for denial of the permit. The Court further refined this requirement in *Dolan*, holding that an adjudicative exaction requiring dedication of private property must also be " 'rough[ly] proportiona[l]' . . . both in nature and extent to the impact of the proposed development." 512 U.S., at 391; *see also Del Monte Dunes*, *supra*, at 702 (emphasizing that we have not extended this standard "beyond the special context of [such] exactions").

Although *Nollan* and *Dolan* quoted *Agins'* language, the rule those decisions established is entirely distinct from the "substantially advances" test we address today. Whereas the "substantially advances" inquiry before us now is unconcerned with the degree or type of burden a regulation places upon property, *Nollan* and *Dolan* both involved dedications of property so onerous that, outside the exactions context, they would be deemed *per se* physical takings. In neither case did the Court question whether the exaction would substantially advance some legitimate state interest. Rather, the issue was whether the exactions substantially advanced the same interests that land-use authorities asserted would allow them to deny the permit altogether. As the Court explained in *Dolan*, these cases involve a special application of the "doctrine of 'unconstitutional conditions,'" which provides that "the government may not require a person to give up a constitutional right-here the right to receive just compensation when property is taken for a public use-in exchange for a discretionary benefit conferred by the government where the benefit has little or no relationship to the property." 512 U.S., at 385. That is worlds apart from a rule that says a regulation affecting property constitutes a taking on its face solely because it does not substantially advance a legitimate government interest. In short, *Nollan* and *Dolan* cannot be characterized as applying the "substantially advances" test we address today, and our decision should not be read to disturb these precedents. [Editor's note: we cover *Nollan* and *Dolan* in depth in Chapter 4.H., *infra*.]

* * *

Twenty-five years ago, the Court posited that a regulation of private property "effects a taking if [it] does not substantially advance [a] legitimate state interes[t]." *Agins*, 447 U.S., at 260. The lower courts in this case took that statement to its logical conclusion, and in so doing, revealed its imprecision. Today we correct course. We hold that the "substantially advances" formula is not a valid takings test, and indeed conclude that it has no proper place in our takings jurisprudence. In so doing, we reaffirm that a plaintiff seeking to challenge a government regulation as an uncompensated taking of private property may proceed under one of the other theories discussed above—by alleging a "physical" taking, a Lucas-type "total regulatory taking," a *Penn Central* taking, or a land-use exaction violating the standards set forth in *Nollan* and *Dolan*. Because Chevron argued only a "substantially advances" theory in support of its takings claim, it was not entitled to summary judgment on that claim. Accordingly, we reverse the judgment of the Ninth Circuit and remand the case for further proceedings consistent with this opinion.

It is so ordered.

JUSTICE KENNEDY, concurring.

This separate writing is to note that today's decision does not foreclose the possibility that a regulation might be so arbitrary or irrational as to violate due process. *Eastern Enterprises v. Apfel*, 524 U.S. 498, 539 (1998) (KENNEDY, J., concurring in judgment and dissenting in part). The failure of a regulation to accomplish a stated or obvious objective would be relevant to that inquiry. Chevron voluntarily dismissed its due process claim without prejudice, however, and we have no occasion to consider whether Act 257 of the 1997 Hawaii Session Laws "represents one of the rare instances in which even such a permissive standard has been violated." *Apfel, supra*, at 550. With these observations, I join the opinion of the Court.

NOTES

1.   The prime importance of *Lingle* lies in the doctrinal clarity it brings to the takings issue. While the *Agins* test infrequently affected the result of takings claims, its constant recitation in dicta kept alive the confusion between due process and takings that existed since at least the 1922 *Pennsylvania Coal* decision. *See* Michael B. Kent, Jr., *Construing the Canon: An Exegesis of Regulatory Takings Jurisprudence After* Lingle v. Chevron, 16 N.Y.U.ENVTL.L.J. 63, 107 (2008) ("*Lingle* begins the long overdue process of bringing clarity to the confused realm of regulatory takings.") In addition to the notes that follow, see discussions of *Lingle's* implications in Robert G. Dreher, Lingle's *Legacy: Untangling Substantive Due Process from Takings Doctrine*, 30 HARV.ENVTL.L.REV. 371 (2006); David L. Callies and Christopher T. Goodin, *The Status of* Nollan v. California Coastal Commission *and* Dolan v. City of Tigard *after* Lingle v. Chevron U.S.A., Inc., 40 J.MARSHALL L.REV. 539 (2007), dealing with the continued validity of a state interest investigation in unconstitutional conditions cases.

2.   The *Lingle* Court discusses the types of compensable takings claims. Two are *per se*: (1) a permanent physical occupation under *Loretto*, and (2) a deprivation of all economically beneficial use under *Lucas*. The third type (3) is the *Penn Central* ad hoc claim. Claims (2) and (3) both look to economic impact. Finally, the Court speaks of the "special context of land-use exactions." Is a *Nollan/Dolan* land use exaction claim a separate takings category or part of the first category? If the property owner can make his prima facie case by establishing a permanent physical occupation has occurred, the burden then switches to the state to meet the heightened scrutiny required by the *Nollan/Dolan* nexus test.

3.   Local governments use impact or exaction fees to finance capital improvements and other infrastructure needs. *See, e.g., Home Builders Ass'n of Dayton & Miami Valley v. Beavercreek*, 729 N.E.2d 349 (Ohio 2000), where the court upheld a road fee imposed on residential developers, the money to be used to offset the road costs to the city due to the increase in traffic generated by new residential developments. We cover impact fees in detail in Chapter 4.H.

(d) Judicial Takings

Regulatory takings cases challenge legislative and executive actions. What about judicial action? Can a judicial decision construing state law take property? In *Stop the Beach Renourishment Inc. v. Florida Dept. of Environmental Protection*, 560 U.S. 702 (2010), the United States Supreme Court addressed, but did not decide, the question.

Stop the Beach involved the rights of littoral property owners under Florida law. The state's Beach and Shore Preservation Act provides that the state may restore eroded beaches at public expense. When this is done, the statute provides that the public becomes the owner of the newly-constructed portions of the beach. The statute replaces the ever-changing mean high tide line as the dividing line between private and public beach ownership with a fixed boundary based on the historic mean high tide line. Thus, upland beachfront owners lose the right to have their boundary line touch the water and lose ownership of increases in the beach by the slow build-up of sand, known as accretions.

After an unsuccessful attempt to stop a renourishment project, upland littoral property owners brought suit claiming the loss of these rights constituted a taking. In a lengthy opinion, the Florida Supreme Court slogged through the substantial and complex history of legislative actions and judicial decisions affecting beachfront property rights. In the end, the court ruled that the plaintiffs had no such rights under the common law of the state. 998 So.2d 1102. The plaintiffs asked the Supreme Court to find that the state court ruling effected a judicial taking of their common law rights. Without dissent, the United States Supreme Court found no error in the state court's ruling.

The justices, however, disagreed on what would have happened had they found the state supreme court changed the common law. Writing for a plurality of four, Justice Scalia said:

> The Takings Clause (unlike, for instance, the Ex Post Facto Clauses, *see* Art. I, § 9, cl. 3; § 10, cl. 1) is not addressed to the action of a specific branch or branches. It is concerned simply with the act, and not with the governmental actor ("nor shall private property be taken" (emphasis added)). There is no textual justification for saying that the existence or the scope of a State's power to expropriate private property without just compensation varies according to the branch of government effecting the expropriation. Nor does common sense recommend such a principle. It would be absurd to allow a State to do by judicial decree what the Takings Clause forbids it to do by legislative fiat. 560 U.S. at 713–14.

Concurring, Justice Kennedy wrote:

> The right of the property owner is subject, however, to the rule that the government does have power to take property for a public use, provided that it pays just compensation. This is a vast governmental power * * * In the exercise of their duty to protect the fisc, both the legislative and executive branches monitor, or should monitor, the exercise of this substantial power. Those branches are accountable in their political capacity for the proper discharge of this obligation.
>
> This is just one aspect of the exercise of the power to select what property to condemn and the responsibility to ensure that the taking makes financial sense from the State's point of view. And, as a matter of custom and practice, these are matters for the political branches-the legislature and the executive-not the courts. Courts, unlike the executive or legislature, are not designed to make policy decisions about "the need for, and likely effectiveness of, regulatory actions."
>
> If a judicial decision, as opposed to an act of the executive or the legislature, eliminates an established property right, the judgment could be set aside as a deprivation of property without due process of law. The Due Process Clause, in both its substantive and procedural aspects, is a central limitation upon the exercise of judicial power. And this Court has long recognized that property regulations can be invalidated under the Due Process Clause * * * It is thus natural to read the Due Process Clause as limiting the power of courts to eliminate or change established property rights. 560 U.S. at 734–36.

As to remedy, Justice Kennedy said:

> [I]t is unclear what remedy a reviewing court could enter after finding a judicial taking. It appears under our precedents that a party who suffers a taking is only entitled to damages, not equitable relief: The Court has said that "[e]quitable relief is not available to enjoin an alleged taking of private property for a public use * * * and the Court subsequently held that the Takings Clause requires the availability of a suit for compensation against the States. [Eds. See our discussion of *First English infra* Section B.5. Just Compensation]. It makes perfect sense that the remedy for a Takings Clause violation is only damages, as the Clause "does not proscribe the taking of property; it proscribes taking without just compensation." * * * It is thus questionable whether reviewing courts could invalidate judicial decisions deemed to be judicial takings; they may only be able to order just compensation. 560 U.S. at 740–41.

The plurality responded:

> JUSTICE KENNEDY worries that we may only be able to mandate compensation. That remedy is even rare for a legislative or executive taking, and we see no reason why it would be the exclusive remedy for a judicial taking. If we were to hold that the Florida Supreme Court had effected an uncompensated taking in the present case, we would simply reverse the Florida Supreme Court's judgment that the Beach and Shore Preservation Act can be applied to the property in question. 560 U.S. at 723.

The justices in the plurality, though eager to speak to the question of judicial takings, could not bring themselves to override the Florida court's interpretation of its own law. Presumably the Florida court met the standard set out in *Lucas*, where the Court said that "[t]here is no doubt some leeway in a court's interpretation of what existing state law permits— but not remotely as much, we think, as in a legislative crafting of the reasons for its confiscatory regulation. We stress that an affirmative decree eliminating all economically beneficial uses may be defended only if an objectively reasonable application of relevant precedents would exclude those beneficial uses in the circumstances in which the land is presently found." *See Lucas* n.18.

Beyond the power of the Supreme Court to interpret a state court decision relating to property, note that adoption of a judicial takings doctrine confers significant power on the state courts, which could read state law in such a way as to trigger a compensation award. That would be the remedy, wouldn't it? After all, the Fifth Amendment does not proscribe takings but prescribes compensation.

In one of the quoted passages above, Justice Scalia observed that the compensation remedy "is even rare for a legislative or executive taking." Justice Kennedy, on the other hand, says compensation is the only remedy. The Court in *First English*, see discussion *infra* Section 5.b., said the takings clause was "self-executing." Is awarding compensation in taking cases really rare? *See* John D. Echeverria, *Stop the Beach Renourishment: Why the Judiciary Is Different*, 35 VT.L.REV. 475, 482–83 (2010) ([Justice Scalia's 'even rare'] "statement is self-evidently obscure. If he is saying the Court has only rarely said that compensation is the exclusive remedy for a taking, he is plainly incorrect. If he is saying the courts rarely award compensation in takings cases, that is correct but beside the point, because it merely reflects the high threshold for a successful taking claim and has no bearing on the appropriate remedy if and when a taking actually occurs."). *But see* D. Benjamin Barros, *The Complexities of Judicial Takings*, 45 U.RICH.L.REV. 903, 955 (2011) ("Justice Scalia had the better argument on this issue. A long line of regulatory takings cases have applied or presumed the availability of an invalidation remedy.")

The plurality finds "textual justification" for applying the clause to all branches of government. The plurality says that "where the text [the founders] adopted is clear, what counts is not what they envisioned but what they wrote." 560 U.S. at 722. Should the use of the passive voice in the takings clause necessarily be read to apply to all branches of government? Or should it be read as simply being silent on the matter requiring an examination of original intent? Is Justice Scalia's literal reading justified? Professor Byrne observes that Justice Scalia wrote in *Lucas* that "[p]rior to Justice Holmes' exposition in *Pennsylvania Coal Co. v. Mahon* it was generally thought that the Takings Clause reached only a 'direct appropriation' of property, or the functional equivalent of a practical ouster of [the owner's] possession.' " 505 U.S. at 1014. *See* J. Peter Byrne, *Stop the Stop the Beach Plurality!* 38 ECOLOGY L.Q. 619 (2011). As we saw, *Pennsylvania Coal* held that the word "take" included "to regulate excessively." Also, as we saw in *Hawaii Housing*, the Court reads "public use" to include "public purpose."

There are no successful judicial takings cases in which actual compensation has been awarded. *See Burton v. American Cyanamid Co.*, 775 F.Supp.2d 1093, 1099 (E.D.Wis.2011) ("Defendants cite no authority for the proposition that there can be a judicial taking"); Brace v. United States, 72 Fed.Cl. 337 (2006), *aff'd* 250 F.App'x 359 (Fed.Cir.2007). *See also* Michael C. Blumm & Elizabeth B. Dawson, *The Florida Beach Case and the Road to Judicial Takings*, 35 WM. & MARY ENVTL.L.& POL'Y REV. 713, 770 (2011).

But there is a subsequent cases in which a judicial taking has been accepted as a valid constitutional claim. In *Willits v. Peabody Coal Co., LLC*, 400 S.W.3d 442, 451–52 (Mo.App.2013), the Court held:

> "Judicial takings and due process jurisprudence existed prior to 2010 and *Stop the Beach. See Smith v. United States*, 709 F.3d 1114, 2013 WL 646332, *2–3 (Fed.Cir. Feb.22, 2013) ("it was recognized prior to *Stop the Beach* that judicial action could constitute a taking of property."); *see also* The Debate on Judicial Takings: I Scream, You Scream, We all Scream for Property Rights, 33 No. 7 Zoning and Planning Law Report 1 (July 2010) ("swimming in the depths of [Supreme] Court dicta as far back as the mid-19th century was the notion of a court taking property through its own actions."); *see also* James S. Burling, *Judicial Takings After* Stop the Beach Renourishment v. Florida Department of Environmental Protection, 12 Engage: J. Federalist Soc'y Prac. Groups 41, 42 (2011) ("The idea that a court can be responsible for a taking is not new. It has been around at least since 1897 in Chicago, *Burlington & Quincy Railroad Co. v. Chicago* [, 166 U.S. 226, 17 S.Ct. 581, 41 L.Ed. 979 (1897)] where the Court obliquely referred to a state court being involved in the

taking of private property . . ."); *see e.g.*, *Hughes v. State of Washington*, 389 U.S. 290, 296–97, 298, 88 S.Ct. 438, 19 L.Ed.2d 530 (1967) (J. Stewart concurring) ("the Due Process Clause of the Fourteenth Amendment forbids such confiscation by a State, no less through its court than through its legislature"); *Bonelli Cattle Co. v. Arizona*, 414 U.S. 313, 317, 94 S.Ct. 517, 38 L.Ed.2d 526 (1973) (overruled on other grounds); *Webb's Fabulous Pharmacies, Inc. v. Beckwith*, 449 U.S. 155, 164, 101 S.Ct. 446, 66 L.Ed.2d 358 (1980) (indicating the Takings Clause prohibited a court decision from converting private property into public property without just compensation); *Stevens v. City of Cannon Beach*, 510 U.S. 1207, 114 S.Ct. 1332, 1334, 127 L.Ed.2d 679 (1994) (Scalia, J., dissenting from denial of certiorari) ("No more by judicial decree than by legislative fiat may a State transform private property into public property without compensation."). Therefore, Appellants' constitutional claims (or cause of action) did not emerge or become actionable only after the Supreme Court of the United States issued its *Stop the Beach* decision on June 17, 2010, but, rather, was 'actionable from the filing of their May 28, 2008 petition.

Thus, Appellants could have raised their constitutional claims at the time of filing their *Willits II* petition."

See also, Robinson v. Ariyoshi, 753 F.2d 1468 (9th Cir.1985), another case to hold that a judicial decision that overturned prior case law could be considered a taking. The opinion, however, was vacated and remanded in light of *Williamson County Regional Planning Comm'n v. Hamilton Bank of Johnson City*, 473 U.S. 172 (1985). 887 F.2d 215 (9th Cir.1989). Nonetheless, the case provides a good study of how a judicial takings rule would operate.

Robinson involved the vesting of water rights under Hawaiian law. Landowners challenged a state supreme court decision in federal court. The Ninth Circuit found that in 1931, "[t]he Territorial Court held that Gay and Robinson were the owners of 'normal surplus' water flowing from their Ilis of Koula and Manuahi into the Hanapepe River, and confirmed their right to divert that water for use outside the Hanapepe drainage." 753 F.2d at 1470. All that changed in 1973 when, in *McBryde Sugar Co., Ltd. v. Robinson*, 504 P.2d 1330 (1973), the state supreme court adopted the English common law doctrine of riparian rights, overruling territorial cases to the contrary. The state court also held that there was no such legal category as "normal daily surplus water." 753 F.2d at 1470.

The Ninth Circuit found that the water rights had vested based on several factors: "(1) The water rights which as private property had been bought, sold and leased freely, and which had been the subject of state and local taxation as well as condemnation for ditch rights-of-way; (2) The expenditures by G & R and Olokele of almost one million dollars in building an extensive water transportation system for irrigation of their sugar lands, lands now potentially destined to become pasture; and (3) The interests of McBryde Sugar Company, which stands, if its rights are vested, in the same position as Gay and Robinson. . . . Relying upon the decrees in *Territory I* and *II*, Gay and Robinson proceeded with further development of their plantations. By the time this litigation reached the district court, in *Robinson I*, improvements costing many millions of dollars had been constructed on the affected lands. By any reasonable interpretation of the word 'vested,' Gay and Robinson's rights to the continued use of their water and related engineering works had become vested." *Id.* at 1473–74.

The court noted that "insofar as judicial changes in the law operate prospectively to affect property rights vesting after the law is changed, no specific federal question is presented by the state's choice of implement in changing state law. . . . New law, however, cannot divest rights that were vested before the court announced the new law. . . . In light of the above authorities, the plaintiffs in this case, having acquired through judicial process a de jure vested right to divert water from their lands within the Hanapepe watershed to their own or related lands outside the watershed, cannot now be divested of this right without just compensation." *Id.* at 1474.

As to remedy, the Ninth Circuit said that "[a]s noted, the district court entered a decree granting injunctive relief against named state officials. Because the state officers in these proceedings have taken no steps to interfere with plaintiffs' property, and have denied that they are presently planning to take such steps, the injunction may have been premature. . . . A declaration of the rights of the parties would appear to be sufficient to assure the owners of the rights confirmed in *Territory II*. The state must bring condemnation proceedings before it can interfere with vested water rights and the enjoyment of the improvements made in reliance thereon." *Id.* at 1474–75.

In two subsequent decisions out of Hawaii, *Pele Defense Fund v. Paty*, 837 P.2d 1247 (Haw.1992), *cert. denied*, 507 U.S. 918 (1993), and *PASH v. Hawaii Planning Comm'n*, 903 P.2d 1246 (Haw.1995), *cert. denied*, 517 U.S. 1163 (1996), the Hawaii Supreme Court held that Native Hawaiians may enter any lands in the state, public or private, to engage in largely undefined "customary," cultural, religious and sustenance activities, specifically holding that worshipper of Pele (a Volcano goddess) could enter private land to conduct ceremonies. It makes no difference, said the court, whether such land is developed or undeveloped. The case has been used to rebut charges of trespass and to claim that a local government decision, which permits a series of wooden-platform tents placed on a long hiking "trail" among thousands of acres of private ranch land, should be reviewed to see if the tents interfere with customary native Hawaiian hunting practices. Do the private landowners in these cases have vested right to be free from the exercise of such rights under the reasoning in the *Robinson* decision? If so, what remedies are available to the landowner?

As we have seen above, the idea of judicial takings is not new. See Barton H. Thompson, Jr., *Judicial Takings*, 76 VA.L.REV. 1449 (1990). However, if the concept of judicial takings is eventually adopted, what impact would such a change have on the state action doctrine? See Shelley Ross Saxer, *Judicial State Action:* Shelley v. Kraemer*, State Action, and Judicial Takings,* (Symposium) 21 WIDENER L.J. 847 (2012) (arguing that recognizing a judicial taking would turn a judicial decision that uses common law to resolve private litigation into state action). With four justices expressing support in *Stop the Beach* the commentators have flooded law reviews. In addition to the articles cited above, a few more include: Daniel L. Siegel, *Why We Will Probably Never See a Judicial Takings Doctrine*, 35 VT.L.REV. 459 (2010); Michael C. Blumm & Elizabeth B. Dawson, *The Florida Beach Case and the Road to Judicial Takings*, 35 WM. & MARY ENVTL.L. & POL'Y REV. 713 (2011); Ilya Somin, Stop the Beach Renourishment *and the Problem of Judicial Takings*, 6 DUKE J.CONST.L.& PUB.POL'Y 91 (2011); Robert H. Thomas, Mark M. Murakami, Tred R. Eyerly, *Of Woodchucks and Prune Yards: A View of Judicial Takings from the Trenches*, 35 VT.L.REV. 437 (2010); Julia K. Bramley, *Supreme Foresight: Judicial Takings, Regulatory Takings, and the Public Trust Doctrine*, 38 B.C.ENVTL.AFF.L.REV. 445 (2011).

5.   JUST COMPENSATION

(a) The Compensation Remedy

The Constitution mandates just compensation as the remedy for a taking. Under federal law at least, a remaining issue in eminent domain appears to be compensation. Indeed, questions from some of the Justices during oral argument in *Kelo* appear to indicate that is the "remedy" for overreaching public purpose takings which they would prefer. In light of the difficulties of defining public use in an era of mixed public/private ventures and since private property remains under threat so long as the eminent domain power exists, perhaps we should strengthen the rules of just compensation and thus diminish the number of takings by making it more costly. As it exists now, under federal law and the law of most states, just compensation does not include money for business loss, emotional or subjective losses.

There is some movement towards requiring compensation beyond market value for residential property. *See generally* Katrina M. Wyman, *The Measure of Just Compensation*, 41 U.C.DAVIS L.REV. 239 (2007). See, e.g., the post-*Kelo* amendment to the Michigan Constitution requiring payment of "not less than 125% of fair market value of an individual's principal residence." Mich.Const. art. X, § 2 (amended 2006). See Ind. Code

§ 32–24–4.5–8 (requiring 125% of fair market value for taking of agricultural land and loss of trade or business and 150% for taking of an owner-occupied residence). Such state legislation, if not accomplished by constitutional amendment, can run afoul of the state constitutional public credit clauses, which could prohibit public payments or loaning of credit to private entities on the sale or condemnation of private property above the fair market value of the property. *See The Times of Trenton Pub. Corp. v. Lafayette Yard Community Development Corp.*, 846 A.2d 659, 667 (N.J.App.Div.2004), *aff'd* 874 A.2d 1064 (N.J.2005) ("Under the New Jersey Constitution, Article VIII, Section III, paragraph 3, a governmental entity is prohibited from giving property, lending money, or extending credit to a private entity for private use. This constitutional provision expressed the fundamental principle that public money should be raised and used only for public purposes.") See Murray J. Raff's discussion of such a remedy in Australia in Ch. 1 of Taking Land: Compulsory Purchase and Land Use Regulation in Asian-Pacific Countries (Tsuyoshi Kotaka and David Callies, eds.2002). For more sweeping reform of eminent domain, see the suggestions of James E. Krier and Christopher Serkin, *Public Ruses*, 2004 MICH.ST.L.REV. 859 (2000).

The above discussion assumes that "just compensation" means only money. The Court, however, has not so held. *See* Douglas T. Kendall and James E. Ryan, *"Paying" for the Change: Using Eminent Domain to Secure Exactions and Sidestep* Nollan *and* Dolan, 81 VA.L.REV. 1801 (1995). Could a grant of transferable development rights satisfy the Fifth Amendment? Note the Court's reference to transferable development rights in *Penn Central*. Transferable development rights (known commonly as TDRs) are discussed in the context of *Suitum v. Tahoe Regional Planning Agency*, 520 U.S. 725 (1997), *supra* Chapter 2.

When a regulatory taking is found, how is compensation calculated? The owner's loss, not the taker's gain, is the basic measure of just compensation. *United States v. Miller*, 317 U.S. 369 (1943). Where capable of determination, fair market value is the measure of recovery. *United States ex rel. T.V.A. v. Powelson*, 319 U.S. 266 (1943). Fair market value is what a willing buyer would pay a willing seller. Comparable sales, reproduction or replacement cost, and capitalization of income or rental value are several alternative bases for determining fair market value. Comprehensive examinations of the issue of just compensation appear in 4 Nichols' Law of Eminent Domain (rev. 3d ed.1993). *See* Chapter 6.B.3. *infra*, for a complete analysis of direct condemnation calculation of compensation and damages.

Determining when a taking begins for the purpose of deciding what the compensation period should be is trickier for a regulatory claim than for an inverse condemnation suit based on a physical invasion, such as the flooding of property from construction of a dam downstream. In the latter case, the physical invasion marks the beginning of the taking and the flooding is permanent. In the regulatory setting, there are various possible beginning dates (enactment, application, adjudication of excessiveness). See Gregory M. Stein, *Pinpointing the Beginning and Ending of a Temporary Regulatory Taking*, 70 WASH.L.REV. 953 (1995).

In a facial taking, where it is the "mere enactment" of the law that effects the taking, the answer is easy. But in the as applied context, what if the property owner has no plans to use the land in a manner contrary to the law until three years after it was passed? Was there any harm during that time period? Does the taking not begin until the property owner seeks a permit and is denied? Does a taking not begin until the claim is ripe? See Gregory M. Stein, *Regulatory Takings and Ripeness in the Federal Courts*, 48 VAND.L.REV. 1 (1995); Timothy Sandefur, *The Timing of Facial Challenges*, 43 AKRON L.REV. 51, 77 (2010).

(b) Invalidity or Temporary Taking?

For years debate ensued as to whether the remedy for a *regulatory* taking was just compensation or a declaration of invalidity. *See generally* Robert H. Freilich, *Solving the "Taking" Equation: Making the Whole Equal the Sum of Its Parts*, 15 URB. LAW. 447 (1983); Daniel R. Mandelker, *Land Use Takings: The Compensation Issue*, 8 HASTINGS CONST.L.Q. 491 (1981). The doubt stemmed from the ambiguity of the *Pennsylvania Coal* decision, which, though often viewed as giving birth to the "regulatory taking" doctrine, involved litigation between private parties and did not order compensation. Several courts and many commentators interpreted *Pennsylvania Coal* as a substantive due process decision and dismissed its takings language as "symbolic." *See Williamson County Regional Planning Commission v. Hamilton Bank*, 473 U.S. 172, 197 (1985) (concurring opinion). In *First English Evangelical Lutheran Church v. County of Los Angeles*, 482 U.S. 304 (1987), the Court rejected that view and ended the debate.

First English. Prior to *First English*, several courts had held that "regulatory takings" were not true takings in the sense that a finding that an ordinance had gone "too far" required payment of just compensation. Rather, these courts, including New York, Pennsylvania, and Florida, in addition to California, held that invalidation of an excessive regulation was the proper and constitutionally sufficient remedy. In effect, these courts saw regulatory excesses as Fourteenth Amendment due process matters, not Fifth Amendment takings concerns.

The *First English* Court quickly dispensed with the argument that regulatory takings were not true takings by affirming Justice Holmes famous statement in *Pennsylvania Coal* that " 'if regulation goes too far it will be recognized as a taking.' " 482 U.S. at 316. Without reexamining the substantive arguments about whether these cases ought to be seen as

Fourteenth Amendment due process cases or Fifth Amendment takings cases, the Court simply found the syllogism that a regulatory taking is a taking to be controlling, and like a physical taking, the mandatory and self-executing constitutional remedy is just compensation.

The decision involved an area of Los Angeles County that suffered from extreme flooding in 1978. Rains carried a massive debris flow down Mill Creek. Thirteen people died in the town of Hidden Springs, and Lutherglen, a retreat of the First English Evangelical Lutheran Church that sat in the flood plain of the creek, was destroyed. The county's response to the flood was passage of an interim ordinance, which immediately banned most development activity in a designated interim flood protection area along the creek. This was a temporary measure to preserve the status quo enabling the city to study the problem and determine how best to avoid more deaths and property destruction due to building in the floodplain. After three years of study, the County converted the ordinance into a permanent floodplain restriction.

One month after adoption of the interim ordinance, the church, unable to rebuild in the floodplain, sued the county in inverse condemnation, claiming the ordinance's denial of the right to rebuild entitled it to compensation. The state trial court dismissed the claim on the basis of the rule established by the California Supreme Court that barred the recovery of compensation for a regulation found to be excessive. The issue that went to the U.S. Supreme Court was the propriety of this dismissal. The question was solely the remedial one of whether invalidation was a sufficient and proper remedy for a regulation found to go "too far." The question of whether there had been a taking in fact by either the interim ordinance or the permanent ordinance was not presented.

It had been argued by some, prior to *First English*, that a compensation remedy would have a chilling effect on planners. There was disagreement over whether that would be good or bad. In *San Diego Gas & Electric Co. v. City of San Diego*, 450 U.S. 621 (1981), Justice Brennan, in dissent, answered the question when he penned what has become one of the most well-known lines in takings jurisprudence: "After all, [if] a policeman must know the Constitution, then why not a planner?" 450 U.S. at 661, n.26 Chief Justice Rehnquist, in *First English*, also acknowledged the concern:

> We realize that even our present holding will undoubtedly lessen to some extent the freedom and flexibility of land-use planners and governing bodies of municipal corporations when enacting land-use regulations. But such consequences necessarily flow from any decision upholding a claim of constitutional right; many of the provisions of the Constitution are designed to limit the flexibility and freedom of governmental authorities, and the Just Compensation Clause of the Fifth Amendment is one of them. As

Justice Holmes aptly noted more than 50 years ago, "a strong public desire to improve the public condition is not enough to warrant achieving the desire by a shorter cut than the constitutional way of paying for the change."

482 U.S. at 321–322.

The *First English* Court explained that a governmental entity whose regulation has been found by a court to be excessive, and hence a taking, has a "range of options." 482 U.S. at 321. The government can lift the offending regulation and pay for the period of time the ordinance was in effect (making it a temporary taking) or government can keep the ordinance in effect and pay permanent damages (making it a permanent taking). Whether a taking is temporary or permanent is a decision that rests with the government defendant. Care must be taken in using the "temporary taking" label. The fact that *First English* involved a temporary ordinance led to confusion, as witnessed by the challenge to the temporary ordinance in *Tahoe-Sierra*, discussed below.

Tahoe-Sierra. The decision in *Tahoe-Sierra Preservation Council, Inc. v. Tahoe Regional Planning Agency*, 535 U.S. 302 (2002) was part of a long running dispute between Lake Tahoe area property owners and the Tahoe Regional Planning Agency (TRPA) over the latter's regulatory actions limiting land use to protect the lake. In 1980, TRPA began development of a plan to reverse the deterioration in the quality of the water. In August, 1981, the agency enacted a moratorium effectively freezing new development activity on sensitive parcels while it engaged in the process of creating a permanent plan. The moratorium was to last until a new regional plan was in place. A group of landowners sued TRPA, claiming the 32 month moratoria that lasted from August, 1981 to April, 1984, had, on its face, taken their property.

Examining TRPA's actions in enacting the moratoria and in developing the plan, the federal district court found the intense development activity in the Lake Tahoe area and the ecological sensitivity of the lake made TRPA's planning task complex. The court found that TRPA acted reasonably and did not waste time in enacting a new plan. Nonetheless, the district court interpreted the Supreme Court's 1987 decision in *First English Evangelical Lutheran Church v. County of Los Angeles*, 482 U.S. 304 (1987) and its 1992 *Lucas* decision to find that a moratorium is a categorical taking. The Ninth Circuit Court of Appeals reversed the district court. In a 6–3 decision, the Supreme Court affirmed the Ninth Circuit's determination in favor of TRPA.

While the *First English* mandate that compensation be paid only becomes operative after a court determines that a regulation has effected a taking, language in the opinion to the effect that "temporary takings that deny all use are no different than permanent takings" led to the argument that temporary denials of all use, such as moratoria, were takings. The argument was aided by the happenstance that the regulation challenged in *First English* was also a moratorium. In *Tahoe-Sierra*, the Court rejected this argument.

The Court began with the observation that *First English* was "unambiguously" a remedy case, which expressly disavowed ruling on the merits as to when takings occur. The fact that *First English* involved a moratorium was irrelevant to the holding. To the extent that *First English* spoke to the question of moratoria as takings, it had suggested that the mere denial of all use for a period of time did not, in and of itself, constitute a taking. In addition *First English* had said that property owners must tolerate normal delays in the land use permitting process without compensation.

The *Tahoe-Sierra* Court also rejected the landowners' and district court's reading of *Lucas*. Ignoring the fact that *Lucas* involved a permanent restriction, the Lake Tahoe landowners argued that a moratorium that denies all economically viable use is a *Lucas* taking. The Court concluded that the permanence of the regulation in *Lucas* was critical to the holding. The mere fact that one is delayed for a period of time does not rise to the level of severity required by *Lucas*. Regulations are only to be converted into constructive takings in instances where they are truly excessive, and these instances, *Lucas* and *Tahoe-Sierra* say, will be extremely rare.

Tahoe-Sierra was a facial claim. The burden of the landowners was to show that the mere enactment of this moratorium effected a taking. The inflexibility of the argument, which boiled down to the contention that a moratorium of any length, from 10 minutes to 10 years, was a categorical taking, see transcript oral argument, 2002 WL 43288 at *12, doomed it. The landowners had good reason to bring a facial claim. Prevailing would allow them to avoid the more time consuming process needed to prevail in an as applied claim and they would not have to confront the factual finding that the Agency had acted in good faith and reasonably. But, the claim was too extreme. Its adoption would have led to the wholesale elimination of a valuable land use planning tool despite what might be relatively modest losses by affected landowners. *See infra*, Chapter 7 on the use of moratoria in managing growth. The Court made it clear that a moratorium of unreasonable length could effect a taking. However, the challenge must be an as applied one.

While *Tahoe-Sierra* establishes that a temporary restriction barring all use is not a *per se* taking, in what procedural context might governmental action constitute "a temporary regulatory taking"? First, a permanent restriction may, at the option of the state, become a temporary taking after a judicial finding that the restriction goes "too far." Courts sometimes wrongly speak of such a finding as an invalidation of the law. Properly viewed, the finding converts an exercise of the police power into an exercise of the power of eminent domain. The state then decides whether to keep the law in force, making the taking permanent, or rescind the law, making the taking temporary. In *Lucas*, for example, the state paid Lucas for the lots. But, had the state wanted to, it could have granted a special permit or variance to the landowner allowing him to build and then paid only for the temporary loss of use for the period beginning with the application of the setback to Lucas until the state's lifting of the setback restriction. Second, the regulation, such as a moratorium, may have ended by virtue of its own terms. If there was a taking, it was necessarily temporary. Finally, the government may have subsequently acquired the property in question by purchase or direct condemnation.

(c) Delay as a Temporary Taking?

Assume a city denies a permit. The landowner sues, seeking a determination that the permit denial is based on the city's erroneous view of state law. The court agrees, and orders the city to allow the development. It takes two years for the landowner to secure this judicial victory. Is the two year delay a compensable temporary taking? Citing numerous cases from around the country, the California Supreme Court has held that "a regulatory mistake resulting in delay does *not,* by itself, amount to a taking of property." *Landgate, Inc. v. California Coastal Comm'n*, 953 P.2d 1188, 1195 (Cal. 1998), *cert. denied*, 525 U.S. 876 (1998), where the court found no temporary taking on roughly comparable facts. Citing *Agins,* the court found the delay was part of a reasonable regulatory process designed to advance legitimate government interests. Does *Lingle* affect this holding?

If a city acts in an arbitrary and capricious manner, *Lingle* says it is a due process violation, not a taking. Yet, might the delay suffered under an unconstitutionally applied act be a temporary taking? Following *First English*, the answer is "no," since the trigger for a compensation claim is an "otherwise proper interference" with property rights Unauthorized government action cannot be converted into an exercise of the power of eminent domain since the government could not validly assert eminent domain and would thus not be liable for inverse condemnation. Such an unauthorized delay might result in a damages claim, but would not be entitled to a just compensation remedy. Yet, there is some confusion on the point. See David W. Spohr, *Cleaning Up the Rest of* Agins*: Bringing Coherence to Temporary Takings Jurisprudence and Jettisoning "Extraordinary Delay"*, 41 ENVTL.L.REP. NEWS & ANALYSIS 10435, 10454 (2011); Thomas E. Roberts, *An Analysis of* Tahoe-Sierra *and Its Help and Hindrance in Understanding the Concept of a Temporary Regulatory Taking*, 25 U.HAW.L.REV. 417, 440 (2003).

(d) Measuring Temporary Taking Compensation

In temporary takings cases, various measures have been used to determine just compensation:

(1) Rental return calculates the supposed rent the parties would have negotiated for the period of the take. *See Yuba Natural Resources, Inc. v. United States,* 904 F.2d 1577 (Fed.Cir.1990); *City of Austin v. Teague,* 570 S.W.2d 389 (Tex.1978).

(2) Lost use calculates the amount claimant would have been expected to earn had the money been available for use. *520 East 81st Street Associates v. State,* 780 N.E.2d 518 (N.Y.2002).

(3) Option price equates just compensation to the market value of an option to buy the land during the take. *See Lomarch Corp. v. Mayor of Englewood,* 237 A.2d 881 (N.J.1968).

(4) Before and after valuation compares the value of the property before the taking with the value of the property after the taking and calculates the market rate of return for the time of the taking based on the difference in value. For example, in *Wheeler v. City of Pleasant Grove,* 896 F.2d 1347 (11th Cir.1990), the court's findings were as follows: The property was valued at $2.3 million before the taking. The appellants had a 25% equity interest, thus they were entitled to a return on 25% of the value, or $575,000. After the taking, the property was valued at $200,000 (only the land was left) and 25% of that yielded a $50,000 remaining interest. Thus, they were entitled to the market return on $525,000 (the difference between $575,000 and $50,000). The market rate of return for the fourteen months of the taking was 9.77%, resulting in an award of $59,841.

Lost profits are generally not recoverable. *PDR Development Corp. v. City of Santa Fe,* 900 P.2d 973 (N.M. App. 1995). *See generally* Douglas W. Kmiec, *Regulatory Takings: The Supreme Court Runs Out of Gas in San Diego,* 57 IND.L.J. 45 (1982); Corwin W. Johnson, *Compensation for Invalid Land Use Regulations,* 15 GA.L.REV. 559 (1981), and Cynthia J. Barnes, Comment, *Just Compensation or Just Damages: The Measure of Damages for Temporary Regulatory Takings in* Wheeler v. City of Pleasant Grove, 74 IOWA L.REV. 1243 (1989).

(e) State Statutory Takings

Over the past two decades, many states considered, and a few adopted, legislation commonly labeled "takings legislation." *See generally* Mark W. Cordes, *Leapfrogging the Constitution: The Rise of State Takings Legislation,* 24 ECOLOGY L.Q. 187 (1997). These efforts, often voter-initiated, do not define a constitutional taking, which is a job for the judicial branch, but rather impose procedural steps to be followed in the adoption and application of land use regulations or establish new causes of action for landowners requiring compensation for any reduction in property value or, in some instances, a more modest reduction in property value than required by the courts under the Fifth Amendment. These takings bills generally have been reactions against the takings law developed in the courts, which from the viewpoint of the proponents is perceived as underprotective of the property rights of landowners.

Two distinct types of bills have been considered: takings impact or assessment bills and compensation bills.[3] Compensation bills have been introduced in many states over the past decade, but have passed in only a few. These bills generally require that compensation be paid when property owners suffer any, or a specific percentage of, diminished value as a result of government regulation.

By initiative in 2004, voters in Oregon enacted a statute, known as Measure 37, requiring compensation for the enforcement of a land use regulation that has the effect of causing *any reduction in value.* O.R.S. § 197.352 et seq. Government can opt to waive the law rather than pay. The state supreme court upheld the law, which was challenged on various state and federal grounds, including substantive due process and equal protection. *MacPherson v. Department of Administrative Services*, 130 P.3d 308 (Or.2006). After a few years, the voters in November, 2007, having second thoughts, enacted Measure 49, significantly modifying Measure 37. Measure 49 allows rural landowners to build one to ten houses under various scenarios, but, prohibits larger subdivisions and commercial and industrial development. Section 197.352 (1) now provides that "[i]f a public entity enacts one or more land use regulations that *restrict the residential use of private real property or a farming or forest practice* and that reduce the fair market value of the property, then the owner of the property shall be entitled to just compensation * * * ." (language in italics reflect Measure 49's change).

A review of the short life of Measure 37 concluded that it suffered from two main problems. It was not well thought out and it was poorly drafted. And, the local officials who administered it were often hostile to it and construed it as narrowly as possible. Alex Potapov, *Making Regulatory Takings Reform Work: The Lessons of Oregon's Measure 37*, 39 ENVTL.L.REP.NEWS & ANALYSIS 10516, 10518 (2009) ("This Article is devoted to the question of what went wrong in the administration of Measure 37.") Is a voter initiative the best way to create a new regime for regulating land use? For one answer see Edward J. Sullivan & Jennifer M. Bragar, *The Augean Stables: Measure 49 and the Herculean Task of Correcting an Improvident Initiative Measure in Oregon*, 46 WILLAMETTE L.REV. 577, 620 (2010) ("the substitution of the ham-handed initiative

---

[3]   Impact laws have not had much effect. For a discussion, see Juergensmeyer and Roberts, Land Use Planning and Development Regulation Law § 10.11 (3rd ed.2012).

process in place of a more deliberative legislative process may have advantages on occasion, but often results in multiple unanticipated consequences, such as binary conclusions and lack of discussion or amendment, with attendant costs.")

A resurgence of property-rights advocacy followed the 2005 decision in *Kelo v. City of New London*, 545 U.S. 469 (2005), where, as we saw at the outset of this chapter, the Supreme Court reaffirmed use of deferential judicial review of Fifth Amendment legislative public use determinations. The decision led to "anti-*Kelo*" ballot initiatives in a dozen or so states in the November, 2006 elections, plus a number of changes by state legislatures restricting eminent domain. See discussion *supra* note 2, after *Kelo*. In a few states, regulatory takings measures were piggy-backed onto to these public use issues. They followed generally the 2004 Oregon statute, enhancing compensation requirements. Of these regulatory takings initiatives, the one in Arizona passed and those in Washington, Idaho, and California failed. J. Kusy & A. Stephenson, *Regulatory Takings Initiatives: The Stories Behind the November 2006 Election*, 59 PLANNING & ENVIRONMENTAL LAW 3 (January 2007); and Robert H. Freilich and Seth D. Mennillo, *The* Kelo *Revolution Ends in California*, California Real Estate Journal (2006). *See also* Jeffrey L. Sparks, *Land Use Regulation in Arizona after the Private Property Rights Protection Act*, 51 ARIZ.L.REV. 211 (2009); Hannah Jacobs, Note, *Searching for Balance in the Aftermath of the 2006 Takings Initiatives*, 116 YALE L.J. 1518 (2007) (discussing how states might do more to accommodate community concerns when enacting laws like those of Arizona and Oregon). John D. Echeverria and Thekla Hansen-Young, *The Track Record on Takings Legislation: Lessons from Democracy's Laboratories*, 28 STAN.ENVTL.L.J. 439, 444–45 (2009), examine legislation in Florida, Louisiana, Mississippi, Texas, and Arizona, and conclude that, among other things, such laws "eviscerate regulatory authority," and undermine local government. Is that a surprise? Aren't these the goals of such legislation?

C. DUE PROCESS: SUBSTANTIVE & PROCEDURAL

Many constitutional land use claims are based on the Due Process clause of the Fourteenth Amendment rather than, or in addition to, the Fifth Amendment Takings Clause. While the takings claims discussed in the prior section are Fourteenth Amendment claims in that the Fifth Amendment is being applied to the states through the Fourteenth Amendment by incorporation, *Chicago, B. & Q. R. Co. v. City of Chicago*, 166 U.S. 226 (1897), in this section, we examine due process claims based directly and solely on the Fourteenth Amendment. There are two types of due process claims: *substantive* and *procedural*. The essence of the former is protection against arbitrary state action; the essence of the latter is that a fair process (notice and hearing) accompany deprivations.

While substantive due process is most often expressed as imposing a requirement that a law promote a legitimate public end in a rational manner, the Court has said on occasion, most often a century or more ago, that substantive due process also means that laws ought not be unduly oppressive upon the affected class. *Lawton v. Steele*, 152 U.S. 133, 137 (1894); *Nollan v. California Coastal Commission*, 483 U.S. 825, 845 (1987) (dissenting opinion). In 1922, when the Court in *Pennsylvania Coal* said that otherwise valid regulations that went "too far" could only be sustained as Fifth Amendment takings, it became difficult to separate a takings claim from a substantive due process claim. Query: how do the tests of going "too far" and being "unduly onerous" differ? *Pennsylvania Coal,* in fact, was regarded as a substantive due process case by a few courts, but so long as the remedy for both was a declaration of invalidity, it mattered little how the claim was labeled. That changed when the Court held in the 1987 *First English* decision that the remedy for a regulatory taking was just compensation.

With the mandatory compensation remedy and the higher scrutiny used in some takings claims, there was a need to distinguish between the two claims. Yet, decades of case law, which discussed the two constitutional protections indiscriminately, left attorneys and judges understandably confused. For historical analyses of *Pennsylvania Coal* as a takings or due process case, see Robert Brauneis, *The Foundation of Our "Regulatory Takings" Jurisprudence: The Myth and Meaning of Justice Holmes's Opinion in* Pennsylvania Coal v. Mahon, 106 YALE L.J. 613, 679 (1996), and James W. Ely, Jr., *The Fuller Court and Takings Jurisprudence*, 1996 J.SUP.CT.HIST., vol. II at 120.

Unlike the substantive due process claim that a regulation is unduly oppressive, the arbitrary and capricious substantive due process claim does not assert that a regulation is "unduly oppressive," or goes "too far," but rather contends that the state either has no business regulating the conduct in question or that the state has chosen an irrational or unfair means to regulate. As one court observed, "some things a government cannot do at all, no matter the justification." *Gosnell v. City of Troy*, 59 F.3d 654, 657 (7th Cir.1995).

The arbitrary and capricious claim was addressed in *Lingle*. There, the Court rejected the use of the 1926 *Nectow* due process case as a takings test, but it did not reject the legitimacy of the test for due process claims. Justice O'Connor explained that unlike a takings claim, "if a government action is found to be impermissible-for instance because it fails to meet the 'public use' requirement or is so arbitrary as to violate due process-that is the end of the inquiry. No amount of compensation can authorize such action." Justice Kennedy's concurring opinion makes clear that the arbitrary and capricious claim remains alive.

Still, the arbitrary and capricious claim is often not well received in the courts. Finding themselves inundated with land use claims based on allegedly arbitrary and capricious conduct, courts sometimes belittle what they call "run of the mill, garden variety" zoning disputes. The Seventh Circuit dismissed one such suit declaiming it ought not "displace or postpone consideration of some *worthier object of federal judicial solicitude." Coniston Corp. v. Village of Hoffman Estates*, 844 F.2d 461, 467 (7th Cir.1988). As noted in the next principal case, *Skiles*, only the "most egregious conduct," that which "shocks the conscience," is arbitrary in the constitutional sense. *County of Sacramento v. Lewis*, 523 U.S. 833, 834 (1998).

SKILES V. CITY OF READING

United States Court of Appeals, Third Circuit, 2011.
449 Fed. Appx. 153.

GREENAWAY, JR., CIRCUIT JUDGE:

Brian Skiles ("Skiles") appeals the District Court's January 7, 2011 Order dismissing, with prejudice, his Amended Complaint against the City of Reading (the "City") and certain of its governmental officials (collectively, the "City Defendants"), pursuant to Federal Rule of Civil Procedure 12(b)(6). The Amended Complaint alleged that the City Defendants violated his constitutional rights through the improper enforcement of the City's zoning, housing, and health regulations applicable to his residential and commercial properties. Skiles contends that the District Court applied an improper heightened standard to determine the merits of his substantive due process claim and otherwise failed to consider his well-pled factual allegations. For the reasons that follow, we will affirm the District Court's Order.

Skiles owns multiple residential rental properties throughout the City and one commercial property—the "Scarab" bar and restaurant that is known as "Daddy's Night Club"—located in the City at 724 Franklin Street. Beginning in 2006, Mayor McMahon began implementation of a policy called "Downtown 20/20," designed to "establish a unified vision for improving the quality of life in Greater Reading." The objective of the policy was to reduce the number of rental properties and boarding houses and to revitalize the City's commercial center.

Skiles alleged that the City Defendants sought to destroy the economic viability of his residential and commercial properties through their enforcement of various zoning, residential, and health regulations. Skiles alludes to two instances proving that the policy was inimical to his interest. First, Skiles points to an exchange in May 2008 in which the City Defendants "arbitrarily" changed the zoning approval for one of his residential properties, reducing the number of permissible parking spaces from sixteen to eight. The second instance occurred a month later, when

[margin annotations: "Procedural History", "Background", "Skiles' Argument"]

the City Defendants allegedly misrepresented to two potential buyers of Skiles's residential properties that the properties were zoned for single families when, in fact, they were zoned as multi-family dwellings.

In February 2009, the City Defendants "arbitrarily and unilaterally" sought to redesignate the zoning and housing classifications for several of Skiles's residential properties. Skiles claimed that despite Assistant Solicitor Mayfield's promise in an April 2009 letter to correct the improper redesignations, the requisite corrections were never made. Skiles does not allege, however, that he complied with the prerequisites to the issuance of new permits that Assistant Solicitor Mayfield identified in her letter. Moreover, Skiles acknowledged that he was not the sole target of the City Defendants' efforts to redesignate the zoning and housing classifications for rental properties, as other residential property owners were issued incorrect housing rental permits.

Skiles also alleged that the City Defendants sought to shut down his business, Daddy's Night Club. He maintained that it was widely known that Daddy's Night Club entertained a homosexual clientele. As such, the City Defendants sought to close Daddy's Night Club under the guise of regulatory violations based on the City Defendants' animus towards homosexuals. Since 1982, Skiles has held the title to the property and has operated the business. From 2006–2008, Jose Perez ("Perez"), a business associate of Skiles, was named on the commercial lease for Daddy's Night Club. Both the 2006 and 2007 health permits for the business were held in Perez's name. In March 2007, the zoning permit for Daddy's Night Club was transferred to Perez. Skiles never received an application in 2008 to renew the annual health permit for Daddy's Night Club, as he had in previous years. On May 14, 2008, Skiles attempted to pay for and obtain the health permit at the City's Code Enforcement Office. The office refused to issue the health permit and notified Skiles that Daddy's Night Club would be closed as of that day. Skiles maintained that neither he nor Perez had any prior notice that Daddy's Night Club was subject to closure due to violations of City regulations, though the 2007 health permit for Daddy's Night Club expired on December 31, 2007.

Skiles alleged that the first notice he received came by letter two weeks after the City closed Daddy's Night Club, informing him that the business was closed for failure to obtain a health permit. Skiles also was notified that he had to obtain a valid zoning permit for Daddy's Night Club. In July 2008, Skiles transferred the zoning permit for Daddy's Night Club from Perez back to his name. A month later, Skiles received a detailed letter outlining all of the regulatory violations identified at Daddy's Night Club and an edict that the violations had to be corrected before a health permit could issue. Skiles rectified the health violations and obtained a health permit for Daddy's Night Club, allowing him to reopen the business, in December 2009.

Skiles's federal lawsuit asserted three causes of action: (1) violation of his First Amendment right to freedom of association, pursuant to 42 U.S.C. § 1983; (2) violation of his Fourteenth Amendment due process rights, pursuant to 42 U.S.C. § 1983; and (3) conspiracy to violate his First and Fourteenth Amendment rights, pursuant to 42 U.S.C. §§ 1983 and 1985. The District Court granted the City Defendants' Motion to Dismiss the Amended Complaint, holding that Skiles could not establish a constitutional violation.

* * *

We review a district court's order dismissing a complaint with prejudice for an abuse of discretion. *United States ex rel. Willis v. United Health Grp., Inc.*, 659 F.3d 295, 302 (3d Cir.2011).

To state a Fourteenth Amendment substantive due process claim pursuant to 42 U.S.C. § 1983, a plaintiff must first establish that, as a threshold matter, he has a protected constitutional interest at issue.[5] *See McCurdy v. Dodd*, 352 F.3d 820, 825–26 (3d Cir.2003) (recognizing that § 1983 protects only the deprivation of an individual's constitutional rights). Assuming that this threshold is met, a plaintiff must prove that government employees engaged in conduct that "shocks the conscience." *County of Sacramento v. Lewis*, 523 U.S. 833, 846–47, 118 S.Ct. 1708, 140 L.Ed.2d 1043 (1998); *United Artists Theatre Circuit, Inc. v. Twp. of Warrington*, 316 F.3d 392, 399–400 (3d Cir.2003). This standard reflects the cornerstone of substantive due process that values "protection of the individual against arbitrary action of government." *Lewis*, 523 U.S. at 845, 118 S.Ct. 1708 (quoting *Wolff v. McDonnell*, 418 U.S. 539, 558, 94 S.Ct. 2963, 41 L.Ed.2d 935 (1974)). As a result, this conscience-shocking standard will be satisfied for "only the most egregious official conduct." *Eichenlaub v. Twp. of Indiana*, 385 F.3d 274, 285 (3d Cir.2004) (citations and internal quotation marks omitted).

Governmental conduct that is purposefully injurious is most likely to be indicative of conduct that "shocks the conscience." *Evans v. Sec'y Pa. Dep't of Corrs.*, 645 F.3d 650, 660 (3d Cir.2011); see also *Eichenlaub*, 385 F.3d at 286 (recognizing that allegations of corruption and self-dealing would "shock the conscience"). "The exact degree of wrongfulness necessary to reach the conscience-shocking' level depends upon the circumstances of a particular case." *Miller v. City of Philadelphia*, 174 F.3d 368, 375 (3d Cir.1999). In the zoning and land use context, the "shocks-the-conscience" standard is "designed to avoid converting federal courts into super zoning tribunals." *Eichenlaub*, 385 F.3d at 285.

Skiles argues that the District Court improperly categorized this action as a land-use dispute and then applied a heightened land-use

---

[5] The parties do not dispute that Skiles has a constitutionally protected interest in his residential and commercial land.

version of the conscience-shocking standard. We disagree. The District Court correctly recognized that only governmental conduct that "shocks the conscience" will rise to the level of a substantive due process violation. We have never recognized a heightened standard applicable to those substantive due process claims arising in the land-use context. *See id.* ("The District Court properly held ... that whether a zoning official's actions or inactions violate due process is determined by utilizing a shocks the conscience' test."). Indeed, we have merely recognized that land-use decisions "are matters of local concern, and such disputes should not be transformed into substantive due process claims based only on allegations that government officials acted with improper' motives." *United Artists*, 316 F.3d at 402. That land-use decisions are not matters for federal courts to address, absent conduct that "shocks the conscience," in no way alters, and certainly does not heighten, this substantive due process standard.

But regardless of whether this lawsuit bears the hallmarks of a traditional land-use dispute, taking into account all of Skiles's well-pled allegations, we agree with the District Court that Skiles's substantive due process claim cannot survive a motion to dismiss. Skiles alleged that the City Defendants improperly redesignated the zoning and housing classifications for his residential property. As Skiles acknowledged, the City Defendants corrected certain erroneous designations and, in any event, other residential property owners received similar treatment. These allegations simply do not rise to the level of conduct that "shocks the conscience." Moreover, Mayor McMahon instituted a policy designed to revitalize the City's rental properties—a legitimate governmental interest—that belies Skiles's claim of unfair treatment. *See Nicholas v. Pa. State Univ.*, 227 F.3d 133, 142 (3d Cir.2000).

Skiles's factual assertions are equally insufficient as a matter of law with respect to Daddy's Night Club. Though Skiles claimed that the City Defendants targeted Daddy's Night Club based on personal animus towards its homosexual patrons, Skiles's only evidentiary support for this statement is that City Plumbing Inspector Yourkavitch allegedly referred to Skiles as a "fagot" [sic] during a 2006 inspection of Daddy's Night Club. Even accepting the truth of this factual allegation, it falls woefully short of demonstrating that the City Defendants' treatment of Daddy's Night Club "shocks the conscience." Although the City Defendants closed Daddy's Night Club due to zoning and health code violations, Skiles was able to reopen his business once the violations were rectified. If the City Defendants had been so intent on furthering their discriminatory goal by eradicating Daddy's Night Club, they would not have allowed the business to reopen once the regulatory violations were corrected.

* * *

Because we will affirm the District Court's dismissal of Skiles's substantive due process claim, it follows a fortiori that Skiles cannot succeed on his claim alleging that the City Defendants conspired to violate his civil rights. Accordingly, the District Court also did not err in dismissing the conspiracy count of Skiles's Amended Complaint.

NOTES: SUBSTANTIVE DUE PROCESS

1.   What more would Skiles have needed to show in order to "shock the conscience" of this court? Prevailing on the merits of a substantive due process claim is difficult. The standard of review is the deferential "fairly debatable" test of *Euclid,* and it is not unusual for courts to characterize the standard as one of great deference. "Such claims should * * * be limited to the truly irrational—for example, a zoning board's decision made by flipping a coin * * * ." *Lemke v. Cass County, Neb.*, 846 F.2d 469, 472 (8th Cir.1987).[4] The Supreme Court in *City of Cuyahoga Falls v. Buckeye Community Hope Foundation*, 538 U.S. 188 (2003), rejected the developer's substantive due process claim based on the city's actions in approving a site plan for a low income housing project but refusing to issue a building permit to a developer of low income housing while a citizen referendum was pending. Noting that if the citizen referendum was successful, it would repeal the approval, the Court reasoned that the city's "refusal to issue the permits while the petition was pending in no sense constituted egregious or arbitrary government conduct." 523 U.S. at 198. The case is set out as a principal case in Chapter 2.C.3.

Circuit courts add their own formulas for determining behavior that will violate due process, including "something venal or invidious," "truly irrational," "grave unfairness," and "no conceivable rational relationship." See cases cited in J. Peter Byrne, *Due Process Land Use Claims after* Lingle, 34 ECOLOGY L.Q. 471, 477–478 (2007). Is any one of these better than the others? Or, are they all as subjective as the "shock the conscience" test? What fails to shock one judge's or jury's conscience might shock another's. While judges have thick skins, occasionally their consciences are shocked. *See* Paul D. Wilson & Noah C. Shaw, *The Judge as Cartoon Character Whose Hat Flies into the Air: The "Shocks the Conscience" Standard in Recent Substantive Due Process Land Use Litigation*, 42 URB.LAW. 677 (2010).

2.   The nature of the right affected determines the standard of review. What about a woman's right to an abortion? Assume a municipality allows some medical clinics in an office zone, but excludes clinics that perform abortions. Would that be valid? The court in *Framingham Clinic, Inc. v. Board of Selectmen of Southerborough*, 367 N.E.2d 606 (Mass.1977) invalidated such a zoning law. *West Side Women's Services, Inc. v. City of Cleveland, Ohio*, 573 F.Supp. 504 (N.D.Ohio 1983), exemplifies the lower courts' traditional treatment of zoning regulations that affect the right of a woman to choose to have an abortion. In *West Side*, the district court used a two-step analysis to

---

    4   No doubt the court thought it was being witty, but these things happen. In *Carney v. Warren County Bd. of Com'rs*, 1991 WL 164574, n.1 (Ohio App.1991), the property owner who challenged the denial of his rezoning petition claimed he lost by a coin toss. Apparently that happened, but the courts "review of the record indicates that the coin flip appeared to have been made in jest and was not the reason the board of commissioners rejected the application." For most landowners, however, it is not a laughing matter.

determine that the right was unconstitutionally infringed by the zoning regulation, which prohibited abortion services in the local retail district. The analysis asks whether the ordinance has a "significant impact"—places an undue burden—upon the woman's decision to abort; if it does, the regulatory provision must be narrowly drawn to serve a compelling state interest. *Id.* at 516.

In light of the Supreme Court's decisions regarding a woman's right to choose to abort, however, the standards used to evaluate zoning regulations affecting this right may change. *Planned Parenthood of Southern Pennsylvania v. Casey*, 505 U.S. 833 (1992). In *Casey*, a plurality redefined the right as a "constitutionally protected" liberty and implicitly rejected the established, "fundamental" categorization of that right. *Id.* at 941. Does *Casey* affect zoning? *See Associates in Obstetrics & Gynecology v. Upper Merion Twp.*, 270 F.Supp.2d 633 (E.D.Pa.2003) (abortion clinic operator stated claim that township selectively enforced ordinance out of hostility to abortion in violation of substantive due process rights of operators and patients).

3.   While *Lingle* held substantive due process considerations inappropriate in assessing Fifth Amendment takings claims, the doctrine was not otherwise adversely affected as Justice Kennedy made clear in his concurrence. Yet, *Lingle* seems not to have reinvigorated the doctrine as some had hoped. *See* Nisha Ramachandran, *Realizing Judicial Substantive Due Process in Land Use Claims: The Role of Land Use Statutory Schemes*, 36 ECOLOGY L.Q. 381, 405 (2009) ("Although the Supreme Court's decision in *Lingle* hinted at the potential use of substantive due process in land use, three years after the decision, federal courts have largely maintained their historic resistance in entertaining such claims.")

4.   It is not only difficult for a property owner to prevail on the merits in a substantive due process claim, it is difficult to get to the merits. To do so, one needs a property interest, which the courts make difficult to establish. There is a difference of opinion among the courts as to whether a landowner seeking a building or other permit can rely on her ownership of the land to establish her property right to invoke due process protection, or whether she must establish a property right in the permit she seeks. To do the latter requires an assessment of whether the issuing authority has discretion. If there is any significant discretion, then the applicant is treated as having a mere expectancy (i.e., no property right); if no, or minimal, discretion exists, the applicant has an entitlement (i.e., a property right). Since most land use decisionmaking involves the exercise of discretion, most landowners are deprived of their day in court. *Compare RRI Realty Corp. v. Incorporated Village of Southampton*, 870 F.2d 911 (2d Cir.1989) (requiring landowner to show an entitlement to a permit) *with DeBlasio v. Zoning Bd. of Adj.*, 53 F.3d 592 (3d Cir.1995) abrogated on other grounds, *United Artists Theatre Circuit, Inc. v. Twp. of Warrington*, 316 F.3d 392 (3d Cir.2003). *See also George Washington University v. District of Columbia*, 318 F.3d 203 (D.C.Cir.2003), *cert. denied*, 540 U.S. 824 (2003) (collecting cases). While the entitlement

theory began as an expansion of procedural due process rights, note its effect in the substantive realm.

The Fourth Circuit, in *Gardner v. City of Baltimore*, 969 F.2d 63 (4th Cir.1992), in response to the claim that the denial of subdivision approval was based on the city bowing to politically influential residents, said that "[b]ecause appellants possessed no cognizable property interest, appellees' actions do not constitute a constitutional violation even if their decisions were motivated solely by political considerations. * * * 'The fact that the permit could have been denied on nonarbitrary grounds defeats the federal due process claim.' " *Id.* at 71. Somewhat surprisingly, the Supreme Court has not taken the opportunity to deal with the denigration of land ownership encompassed in the entitlement rule. *See* J. Peter Byrne, *Due Process Land Use Claims after Lingle,* 34 ECOLOGY L.Q. 471, 477 (2007).

5.   The final decision ripeness rule of *Williamson County* is applied by most courts to substantive due process and equal protection claims. *See County Concrete Corp. v. Town of Roxbury*, 442 F.3d 159, 164, 168 (3rd Cir.2006) (to determine whether *as-applied* substantive due process and equal protection challenges are ripe for review, a decision maker must arrive at a definitive position on the issue for the property owner to show an actual, concrete injury; "[t]his rule does not apply, however, to facial attacks on a zoning ordinance, i.e., a claim that the mere enactment of a regulation either constitutes a taking without just compensation, or a substantive violation of due process or equal protection.") There is disagreement as to whether the ripeness rules apply to procedural due process claims. *See Nasierowski Bros. Inv. Co. v. City of Sterling Heights*, 949 F.2d 890 (6th Cir.1991) (no); *Taylor Inv., Ltd. v. Upper Darby TP*, 983 F.2d 1285 (3d Cir.1993) (yes).

6.   What money damages might be awarded for substantive due process violations? In the first place, damages are optional, not mandatory. *See Wheeler v. City of Pleasant Grove*, 833 F.2d 267, 270, n. 3 (11th Cir.1987). In *Herrington v. County of Sonoma*, 834 F.2d 1488 (9th Cir.1987), the court set aside as grossly excessive a jury award of $2.5 million. The Washington Supreme Court takes the position that invalidation is the normal substantive due process remedy, and that there is a higher burden (a showing of irrational or invidious conduct) to receive damages. *See Sintra, Inc. v. City of Seattle*, 829 P.2d 765 (Wash.1992).

NOTES: PROCEDURAL DUE PROCESS

1.   The decisionmaking process in land use cases raises significant concerns with fairness. One problem is the reluctance of some courts to hold that many decisions by city councils are legislative in name but quasi-judicial in fact. If an action is considered legislative, procedural due process requirements do not apply. However, as a general matter, where an action is found adjudicative, the public body must: (1) allow all parties notice and an opportunity to be heard, so that they may adequately present and rebut evidence; (2) act impartially, with a minimum of *ex parte* contact and without substantial pressure from outside interests; (3) keep a record of proceedings;

and (4) make its decisions based upon findings of fact and conclusions of law. These safeguards are not required across the board, and much depends on the kind of decision being made.

2.   Who is entitled to notice, and what kind of notice is sufficient to meet the requirements of procedural due process? The critical question is the character of the action taken. If a rezoning is legislative, due process constraints do not apply. *Bi-Metallic Inv. Co. v. State Bd. of Equalization*, 239 U.S. 441 (1915); *Jacobs, Visconsi & Jacobs, Co. v. City of Lawrence*, 927 F.2d 1111 (10th Cir.1991). If, however, it is quasi-judicial, notice and hearing must be afforded affected persons. See *Nasierowski Bros. Inv. Co. v. City of Sterling Heights*, 949 F.2d 890 (6th Cir.1991) and *Harris v. County of Riverside*, 904 F.2d 497, 501–02 (9th Cir.1990), both finding rezonings quasi-judicial in character and holding that the procedural due process rights of the owners of the land rezoned were violated since they were not given notice. No due process rights attach if the denial of a rezoning request is regarded as legislative. *Petersen v. Riverton City*, 243 P.3d 1261 (Utah 2010).

3.   If a hearing is held, what must it include? In land use proceedings, parties are not entitled to " 'anything like a judicial hearing' with all its adversarial trappings." *Landmark Land Co. of Oklahoma, Inc. v. Buchanan*, 874 F.2d 717, 724 (10th Cir.1989), *overruled on other grounds*; *Federal Lands Legal Consortium ex rel. Robart Estate v. United States*, 195 F.3d 1190 (10th Cir.1999; abrogated by 2016 WL 5720529, see fn. 2). Still, a hearing of some sort is required. For example, unilateral termination of a legal non-conforming use for nonuse violates due process. One city rescinded legal non-conforming use status on property it thought was vacant for six months and only provided after-the-fact notice of its action by posting a sign on the property. The city did allow the property owner to seek a variance to restart the non-conforming use, but that venue did not permit the property owner to contest the city's determination that the property had been vacant. *Mator v. City of Ecorse*, 301 F. App'x 476 (6th Cir.2008).

4.   If an adequate hearing is provided, an incorrect decision is not itself a denial of due process. *Minneapolis Auto Parts Co. v. City of Minneapolis*, 572 F.Supp. 389 (D.Minn.1983), affirmed 739 F.2d 408 (8th Cir.1984). The mere failure to comply with specific state and local notice or hearing requirements does not necessarily constitute a denial of due process as a matter of federal law. *Shanks v. Dressel*, 540 F.3d 1082, 1089 (9th Cir.2008). The U.S. Supreme Court in *Mathews v. Eldridge*, 424 U.S. 319, 335 (1976) applied a balancing test to determine due process requirements based on the circumstances. It identified the following three factors to consider: "First, the private interest that will be affected by the official action; second, the risk of an erroneous deprivation of such interest through the procedures used, and the probable value, if any, of additional or substitute procedural safeguards; and finally, the Government's interest, including the function involved and the fiscal and administrative burdens that the additional or substitute procedural requirement would entail."

5.   With land use matters, the "concept of impartiality is, by necessity and by function, more relaxed and informal." *Hilltop Basic Resources, Inc. v. County of Boone,* 180 S.W.3d 464, 468 (Ky.2005). In *Idaho Historic Pres. Council, Inc. v. City Council of City of Boise*, 8 P.3d 646 (Idaho 2000), the court held that council members are free to take phone calls from concerned citizens prior to a quasi-judicial proceeding so long as the identity of the callers and general description of what each caller said is disclosed. On the other hand, in one case the head of a downtown business association contacted a city council member in an attempt to dissuade her from attempting to change a proposed downtown development plan and suggesting that she try to get four others to vote in the way the downtown association preferred. The court observed that "[s]uch contacts and influence are common and appropriate in the normal legislative functioning of a city council. However, when a council sits in a quasi-judicial capacity, as it must to effect a downzoning, its members must be insulated from such contact." *Albuquerque Commons Partnership v. City Council of City of Albuquerque*, 184 P.3d 411, 422, n.3 (N.M.2008). The failure of a council to act as it should have was expensive. *See Albuquerque Commons Partnership v. City Council of City of Albuquerque*, 248 P.3d 856 (N.Mex.2011) (jury verdict awarding $8.3 million in damages to developer, upheld for violation of due process arising from a quasi-judicial rezoning affecting developer's property).

6.   Everyone is not equal when it comes to determining what due process requires. While parties to a quasi-judicial hearing must be afforded the right to cross examine witnesses and present evidence, non-party participants generally have no such rights. *Carillon Community Residential Association, Inc. v. Seminole County*, 45 So.3d 7 (Fla.App.2010) (adjacent landowner of land rezoned to allow a mixed-use development permitted to participate in the hearing and to pose questions to the board, but not to cross examine witnesses or present evidence).

7.   What due process concerns are raised with respect to permit decisions of zoning enforcement officers or administrators as opposed to boards of adjustment?

> Administrative decisions are routine, nondiscretionary zoning ordinance implementation matters carried out by the staff, including issuance of permits for permitted uses. In general, the zoning administrator is a purely administrative or ministerial agent following the literal provisions of the ordinance. The zoning administrator may well engage in some fact finding, as in making an initial determination as to whether a nonconforming use was in existence at the time a zoning ordinance was adopted. But, in such instances, this involves determining objective facts that do not involve an element of discretion.

County of Lancaster, S.C. v. Mecklenburg County, N.C., 434 S.E.2d 604, 612 (N.C.1993) (citations omitted). In this case, the code authorized the zoning enforcement officer to issue landfill permits as "uses by right subject to special requirements." The court held that the permit issuing decision was an administrative zoning decision rather than quasi-judicial decision since the "special requirements" allowed only objective determinations (e.g., determining yard requirements, screening, hours of operation, access, and notification of adjoining property owners, and reclamation requirements), and did not require an evidentiary hearing.

Typically, when an administrator denies a permit application the decision can be appealed to a board of adjustment where a hearing will be held. At the hearing must the board review the matter de novo or may it defer to findings of the administrator? The West Virginia supreme court found a board is not required to "reconsider each and every aspect of the decisions reached by the zoning administrator and is [not] expressly prohibited from deferring to any determination made by the zoning administrator." *Jefferson Utilities, Inc. v. Jefferson County Bd. of Zoning Appeals*, 624 S.E.2d 873, 874 (W.Va.2005) (exercise of some discretion by a zoning administrator in applying facts to a provision of zoning ordinance is by itself insufficient to invoke due process protections.).

8.   Are federal courts bound by state law characterizations of an action as legislative or quasi-judicial?

9.   Procedural due process claims are subject to the entitlement theory discussed above regarding substantive claims. Further, under *Parratt v. Taylor*, 451 U.S. 527 (1981), there is no federal cause of action for an alleged violation of procedural due process stemming from random, unauthorized actions if there is an adequate remedy provided by the state to protect the victim's rights. *Parratt* was overruled by *Daniels v. Williams*, 474 U.S. 327 (1986), "to the extent that it states that mere lack of due care by a state official may 'deprive' an individual of life, liberty, or property under the Fourteenth Amendment," *Id.* at 330–31. *See* Rosalie Berger Levinson, *Due Challenges to Governmental Actions: The Meaning of* Parratt *and* Hudson, 18 URB.LAW. 189 (1986).

D. EQUAL PROTECTION

Challenges to government treatment of parties seeking development permission can often be framed in equal protection or substantive due process terms. Claims brought pursuant to the Equal Protection clause have a major advantage over substantive due process claims. No property interest need be shown. Nonetheless, equal protection claims that do not involve suspect classes or fundamental rights are subject to the highly deferential rational basis test.[5] Most land use cases fall into this category. Thus, the case that follows came as a bit of a surprise.

---

[5]   *See Village of Belle Terre, infra* Chapter. 5 D.1., for an application of the deferential test. Racial discrimination claims, subject to strict scrutiny, are discussed *infra*, Chapter 5 C.2.

VILLAGE OF WILLOWBROOK V. OLECH

Supreme Court of the United States, 2000.
528 U.S. 562, 120 S.Ct. 1073, 145 L.Ed.2d 1060.

PER CURIAM.

Respondent Grace Olech and her late husband Thaddeus asked petitioner Village of Willowbrook to connect their property to the municipal water supply. The Village at first conditioned the connection on the Olechs granting the Village a 33-foot easement. The Olechs objected, claiming that the Village only required a 15-foot easement from other property owners seeking access to the water supply. After a 3-month delay, the Village relented and agreed to provide water service with only a 15-foot easement.

Olech sued the Village claiming that the Village's demand of an additional 18-foot easement violated the Equal Protection Clause of the Fourteenth Amendment. Olech asserted that the 33-foot easement demand was "irrational and wholly arbitrary"; that the Village's demand was actually motivated by ill will resulting from the Olechs' previous filing of an unrelated, successful lawsuit against the Village; and that the Village acted either with the intent to deprive Olech of her rights or in reckless disregard of her rights.

The District Court dismissed the lawsuit pursuant to Federal Rule of Civil Procedure 12(b)(6) for failure to state a cognizable claim under the Equal Protection Clause. Relying on Circuit precedent, the Court of Appeals for the Seventh Circuit reversed, holding that a plaintiff can allege an equal protection violation by asserting that state action was motivated solely by a " 'spiteful effort to "get" him for reasons wholly unrelated to any legitimate state objective.' " 160 F.3d 386, 387 (C.A.7 1998) (*quoting Esmail v. Macrane*, 53 F.3d 176, 180 (C.A.7 1995)). It determined that Olech's complaint sufficiently alleged such a claim. 160 F.3d at 388. We granted certiorari to determine whether the Equal Protection Clause gives rise to a cause of action on behalf of a "class of one" where the plaintiff did not allege membership in a class or group.

Our cases have recognized successful equal protection claims brought by a "class of one," where the plaintiff alleges that she has been intentionally treated differently from others similarly situated and that there is no rational basis for the difference in treatment. *See Sioux City Bridge Co. v. Dakota County,* 260 U.S. 441 (1923). In so doing, we have explained that " '[t]he purpose of the equal protection clause of the Fourteenth Amendment is to secure every person within the State's jurisdiction against intentional and arbitrary discrimination, whether occasioned by express terms of a statute or by its improper execution through duly constituted agents.' " *Sioux City Bridge Co., supra,* at 445 (*quoting Sunday Lake Iron Co. v. Township of Wakefield*, 247 U.S. 350, 352 (1918)).

That reasoning is applicable to this case. Olech's complaint can fairly be construed as alleging that the Village intentionally demanded a 33-foot easement as a condition of connecting her property to the municipal water supply where the Village required only a 15-foot easement from other similarly situated property owners. The complaint also alleged that the Village's demand was "irrational and wholly arbitrary" and that the Village ultimately connected her property after receiving a clearly adequate 15-foot easement. These allegations, quite apart from the Village's subjective motivation, are sufficient to state a claim for relief under traditional equal protection analysis. We therefore affirm the judgment of the Court of Appeals, but do not reach the alternative theory of "subjective ill will" relied on by that court.

It is so ordered.

JUSTICE BREYER, concurring in the result.

The Solicitor General and the Village of Willowbrook have expressed concern lest we interpret the Equal Protection Clause in this case in a way that would transform many ordinary violations of city or state law into violations of the Constitution. It might be thought that a rule that looks only to an intentional difference in treatment and a lack of a rational basis for that different treatment would work such a transformation. Zoning decisions, for example, will often, perhaps almost always, treat one landowner differently from another, and one might claim that, when a city's zoning authority takes an action that fails to conform to a city zoning regulation, it lacks a "rational basis" for its action (at least if the regulation in question is reasonably clear).

This case, however, does not directly raise the question whether the simple and common instance of a faulty zoning decision would violate the Equal Protection Clause. That is because the Court of Appeals found that in this case respondent had alleged an extra factor as well—a factor that the Court of Appeals called "vindictive action," "illegitimate animus," or "ill will." 160 F.3d 386, 388 (C.A.7 1998). And, in that respect, the court said this case resembled *Esmail v. Macrane*, 53 F.3d 176 (C.A.7 1995), because the Esmail plaintiff had alleged that the municipality's differential treatment "was the result not of prosecutorial discretion honestly (even if ineptly—even if arbitrarily) exercised but of an illegitimate desire to 'get' him." 160 F.3d at 388.

In my view, the presence of that added factor in this case is sufficient to minimize any concern about transforming run-of-the-mill zoning cases into cases of constitutional right. For this reason, along with the others mentioned by the Court, I concur in the result.

NOTES

1.   In this terse per curiam opinion, did the Court rewrite the law of equal protection? Some courts have taken the opinion at face value and assumed that motive is irrelevant, *City Recycling, Inc. v. State*, 778 A.2d 77 (Conn.2001), while others have casually assumed *Olech* presents nothing new in the way of equal protection jurisprudence. *Bryan v. City of Madison, Miss.*, 213 F.3d 267 (5th Cir.2000), *cert. denied* 531 U.S. 1145 (2001). Some courts require illegitimate animus, *Petersen v. Riverton City*, 243 P.3d 1261 (Utah 2010), while others have ducked the question. *Bizzarro v. Miranda*, 394 F.3d 82, 88 (2d Cir.2005). *See* William D. Araiza, *Irrationality and Animus in Class-of-One Equal Protection Cases*, 34 ECOLOGY L.Q. 493 (2007) (courts have split on whether class-of-one claims can be based purely on claims of irrational government action, or whether illegitimate animus is an essential part of the claim). *See also Lindquist v. City of Pasadena*, 656 F.Supp.2d 662, 681 (S.D.Tex.2009) ("most circuits have proceeded cautiously in applying the theory, sensitive to Justice Breyer's warning against turning even quotidian exercises of government discretion into constitutional causes").

Courts can avoid the question by finding that differential treatment did not occur or that the parties were not similarly situated. *Tri County Paving, Inc. v. Ashe County*, 281 F.3d 430 (4th Cir.2002). *See* Paul D. Wilson, *What Hath* Olech *Wrought? The Equal Protection Clause in Recent Land-Use Damages Litigation*, 33 URB.LAW. 729 (2001).

2.   If a landowner can state a class of one equal protection claim simply by alleging differential treatment lacking a rational basis, the Court says her claim falls "under traditional equal protection analysis." Even if the landowner must add an allegation of ill will, does the deferential rational basis test apply? If so, is such a lawsuit a waste of time since it is likely a loser? Perhaps not. Procedurally, such claims may more easily survive a motion to dismiss than has been the case in the past. More significantly, landowners also may survive a summary judgment motion, enabling them to submit their claims to a jury. This occurred in *Cruz v. Town of Cicero*, 275 F.3d 579 (7th Cir.2001). The district court had denied the town's motion for summary judgment despite the fact that the town had conceivable, rational reasons to deny the development permission requested. The town, said the district court, had not offered sufficient proof. The case went to the jury, which awarded the developer $402,000. The Seventh Circuit affirmed the jury verdict on the basis that the jury could have found the town acted for totally illegitimate reasons. *See* Paul D. Wilson, *When Sending Flowers is Not Enough: Developments in Landowner Civil Rights Lawsuits against Municipal Officials*, 34 URB.LAW. 981, 985 (2002).

3.   Claims that fall short of asserting important or fundamental rights or are not brought by members of a suspect or quasi-suspect class fail to obtain strict or intermediate scrutiny. Yet they may receive higher scrutiny than the least protected socio-economic rights. Uses that are unpopular, vulnerable or sensitive (e.g., housing for the mentally retarded) have been subjected to what Justice Kennedy calls "meaningful rational basis review," see his concurring

opinion in *Kelo supra*, or what commentators sometimes call "rationality with a bite." *City of Cleburne v. Cleburne Living Center*, 473 U.S. 432, 440 (1985), is the prime example. *Cleburne* involved a claim by the owner of a group home for the mentally retarded that the city's ordinance illegitimately treated group homes differently from similar uses. The plaintiff sought a declaration by the Court that the mentally retarded were a quasi-suspect class deserving higher scrutiny than rational basis. The Court refused to do this, but nonetheless applying the rational basis test with an atypical searching inquiry into the record, found the ordinance violated equal protection. As Judge Posner has observed, "[t]he majority opinion in *Cleburne* is deficient in candor. * * * We should follow what the Supreme Court does and not just what it says it is doing." *Civil Liberties for Urban Believers v. City of Chicago*, 342 F.3d 752, 768–70 (7th Cir.2003) (Posner, J., dissenting).

4.   Equal protection claims dealing with racial discrimination are dealt with in Chapter 5.

E. THE FIRST AMENDMENT

1. INTRODUCTION

Land use controls frequently implicate First Amendment rights. The three principal activities touched by land use regulations are sexually oriented businesses, billboards and other signs, and religious uses. There is increasingly a fourth claim alleging a violation of the right to petition government when the government retaliates against property owners and developers who seek development permission. Lastly, when codes allow only "single family" use, First and Fourteenth Amendment privacy concerns arise. *See infra* Chapter 5 on regulating nontraditional living arrangements.

When the Supreme Court reentered the land use field in the mid-1970s after a nearly five decade hiatus, see introduction to this chapter, it had no hesitancy sustaining zoning ordinances challenged under the First Amendment. Its initial foray came in *Young v. American Mini Theatres, Inc.*, 427 U.S. 50, 62 (1976), where the Court upheld a Detroit ordinance that regulated location of adult movie theaters. In that case the Court said that "the mere fact that the commercial exploitation of material protected by the First Amendment is subject to zoning * * * is not a sufficient reason for invalidating these ordinances." Rightly or wrongly, that statement led some to think that zoning controls were free from the constraint of the First Amendment. Thus, a state trial court, facing an ordinance that prohibited live entertainment in commercial zones, noted the above statement of *Young* and said that " 'First Amendment guarantees [are] not involved [since the case concerns] solely a zoning ordinance.' " *Schad v. Borough of Mount Ephraim*, 452 U.S. 61, 64 (1981). On appeal, the Supreme Court made it clear that the zoning power "is not infinite and unchallengeable." The standard of review is dictated by the nature of the right affected rather than by the power being exercised, and "when a zoning law infringes upon a protected liberty, it must be narrowly drawn and must further a sufficiently substantial government interest." *Id.* at 68.

2. REGULATING SEXUALLY ORIENTED BUSINESSES

Sexually oriented businesses or "adult entertainment" are extensively regulated. As noted above, in *Young v. American Mini Theatres, Inc.*, the Supreme Court upheld a Detroit ordinance that prohibited adult movie theaters from locating near each other. A plurality of four justices took the position that while non-obscene sexually oriented speech is protected by the First Amendment, it receives less protection than other forms of speech. In a comment that the dissent regarded as "wholly alien" to the First Amendment, the plurality said that:

> few of us would march our sons and daughters off to war to preserve the citizen's right to see "Specified Sexual Activities" exhibited in the theaters of our choice.

427 U.S. at 70. Furthermore, the Detroit ordinance did not seem very burdensome. Despite the limitations, adult theaters enjoyed a "market [that was] essentially unrestrained." 427 U.S. at 62. *City of Renton v. Playtime Theatres, Inc.*, 475 U.S. 41 (1986) decision moved beyond *Young*, determining that the ordinance was a "content-neutral" time-place-manner restriction requiring only that the "ordinance is designed to serve a substantial governmental interest and allows for reasonable alternative avenues of communication." *Id.* at 49. The *Renton* Court found that "the Renton ordinance represents a valid governmental response to the 'admittedly serious problems' created by adult theaters" and thus does not violate the First Amendment. *Id.* at 54–55.

CITY OF LOS ANGELES V. ALAMEDA BOOKS, INC.

Supreme Court of the United States, 2002.
535 U.S. 425, 122 S.Ct. 1728, 152 L.Ed.2d 670.

JUSTICE O'CONNOR announced the judgment of the Court and delivered an opinion, in which THE CHIEF JUSTICE, JUSTICE SCALIA, and JUSTICE THOMAS join.

Los Angeles Municipal Code § 12.70(C) (1983), as amended, prohibits "the establishment or maintenance of more than one adult entertainment business in the same building, structure or portion thereof." Respondents, two adult establishments that each operated an adult bookstore and an adult video arcade in the same building, filed a suit under 42 U.S.C. § 1983, alleging that § 12.70(C) violates the First Amendment and seeking declaratory and injunctive relief. The District Court granted summary judgment to respondents, finding that the city of Los Angeles' prohibition was a content-based regulation of speech that failed strict scrutiny. The

Court of Appeals for the Ninth Circuit affirmed, but on different grounds. It held that, even if § 12.70(C) were a content-neutral regulation, the city failed to demonstrate that the prohibition was designed to serve a substantial government interest. Specifically, the Court of Appeals found that the city failed to present evidence upon which it could reasonably rely to demonstrate a link between multiple-use adult establishments and negative secondary effects. Therefore, the Court of Appeals held the Los Angeles prohibition on such establishments invalid under *Renton v. Playtime Theatres, Inc.*, 475 U.S. 41, 106 S.Ct. 925, 89 L.Ed.2d 29 (1986), and its precedents interpreting that case. 222 F.3d 719, 723–728 (2000). We reverse and remand. The city of Los Angeles may reasonably rely on a study it conducted some years before enacting the present version of § 12.70(C) to demonstrate that its ban on multiple-use adult establishments serves its interest in reducing crime.

I

In 1977, the city of Los Angeles conducted a comprehensive study of adult establishments and concluded that concentrations of adult businesses are associated with higher rates of prostitution, robbery, assaults, and thefts in surrounding communities. Accordingly, the city enacted an ordinance prohibiting the establishment, substantial enlargement, or transfer of ownership of an adult arcade, bookstore, cabaret, motel, theater, or massage parlor or a place for sexual encounters within 1,000 feet of another such enterprise or within 500 feet of any religious institution, school, or public park. See Los Angeles Municipal Code § 12.70(C) (1978).

There is evidence that the intent of the city council when enacting this prohibition was not only to disperse distinct adult establishments housed in separate buildings, but also to disperse distinct adult businesses operated under common ownership and housed in a single structure. Subsequent to enactment, the city realized that this method of calculating distances created a loophole permitting the concentration of multiple adult enterprises in a single structure.

Concerned that allowing an adult-oriented department store to replace a strip of adult establishments could defeat the goal of the original ordinance, the city council amended § 12.70(C) by adding a prohibition on "the establishment or maintenance of more than one adult entertainment business in the same building, structure or portion thereof." Los Angeles Municipal Code § 12.70(C) (1983). The amended ordinance defines an "Adult Entertainment Business" as an adult arcade, bookstore, cabaret, motel, theater, or massage parlor or a place for sexual encounters, and notes that each of these enterprises "shall constitute a separate adult entertainment business even if operated in conjunction with another adult entertainment business at the same establishment." § 12.70(B)(17). The ordinance uses the term "business" to refer to certain types of goods or services sold in adult establishments, rather than the establishment itself. Relevant for purposes of this case are also the ordinance's definitions of adult bookstores and arcades. An "Adult Bookstore" is an operation that "has as a substantial portion of its stock-in-trade and offers for sale" printed matter and videocassettes that emphasize the depiction of specified sexual activities. § 12.70(B)(2)(a). An adult arcade is an operation where, "for any form of consideration," five or fewer patrons together may view films or videocassettes that emphasize the depiction of specified sexual activities. § 12.70(B)(1).

Respondents, Alameda Books, Inc., and Highland Books, Inc., are two adult establishments operating in Los Angeles. Neither is located within 1,000 feet of another adult establishment or 500 feet of any religious institution, public park, or school. Each establishment occupies less than 3,000 square feet. Both respondents rent and sell sexually oriented products, including videocassettes. Additionally, both provide booths where patrons can view videocassettes for a fee. Although respondents are located in different buildings, each operates its retail sales and rental operations in the same commercial space in which its video booths are located. * * * Respondents concede they are openly operating in violation of § 12.70(C) of the city's code, as amended.

After a city building inspector found in 1995 that Alameda Books, Inc., was operating both as an adult bookstore and an adult arcade in violation of the city's adult zoning regulations, respondents joined as plaintiffs and sued under 42 U.S.C. § 1983 for declaratory and injunctive relief to prevent enforcement of the ordinance. At issue in this case is count I of the complaint, which alleges a facial violation of the First Amendment. Both the city and respondents filed cross-motions for summary judgment.

The District Court for the Central District of California initially denied both motions on the First Amendment issues in count I, concluding that there was "a genuine issue of fact whether the operation of a combination video rental and video viewing business leads to the harmful secondary effects associated with a concentration of separate businesses in a single urban area." After respondents filed a motion for reconsideration, however, the District Court found that Los Angeles' prohibition on multiple-use adult establishments was not a content-neutral regulation of speech. It reasoned that neither the city's 1977 study nor a report cited in *Hart Book Stores v. Edmisten*, 612 F.2d 821 (C.A.4 1979) (upholding a North Carolina statute that also banned multiple-use adult establishments), supported a reasonable belief that multiple-use adult establishments produced the secondary effects the city asserted as content-neutral justifications for its prohibition. Therefore, the District Court proceeded to subject the Los Angeles ordinance to strict scrutiny. Because it felt that the city did not offer evidence to demonstrate that its prohibition is necessary to serve a compelling government interest, the District Court granted summary judgment for respondents and issued a permanent injunction enjoining the enforcement of the ordinance against respondents.

The Court of Appeals for the Ninth Circuit affirmed, although on different grounds. The Court of Appeals determined that it did not have to reach the District Court's decision that the Los Angeles ordinance was content based because, even if the ordinance were content neutral, the city failed to present evidence upon which it could reasonably rely to demonstrate that its regulation of multiple-use establishments is "designed to serve" the city's substantial interest in reducing crime. The challenged ordinance was therefore invalid under *Renton*, 475 U.S. 41, 106 S.Ct. 925, 89 L.Ed.2d 29. 222 F.3d, at 723–724. We granted certiorari, 532 U.S. 902, 121 S.Ct. 1223, 149 L.Ed.2d 134 (2001), to clarify the standard for determining whether an ordinance serves a substantial government interest under *Renton, supra.*

II

In *Renton v. Playtime Theatres, Inc., supra,* this Court considered the validity of a municipal ordinance that prohibited any adult movie theater from locating within 1,000 feet of any residential zone, family dwelling, church, park, or school. Our analysis of the ordinance proceeded in three steps. First, we found that the ordinance did not ban adult theaters altogether, but merely required that they be distanced from certain sensitive locations. The ordinance was properly analyzed, therefore, as a time, place, and manner regulation. *Id.*, at 46, 106 S.Ct. 925. We next considered whether the ordinance was content neutral or content based. If the regulation were content based, it would be considered presumptively invalid and subject to strict scrutiny. *Simon & Schuster, Inc. v. Members of N.Y. State Crime Victims Bd.*, 502 U.S. 105, 115, 118, 112 S.Ct. 501, 116 L.Ed.2d 476 (1991); *Arkansas Writers' Project, Inc. v. Ragland*, 481 U.S. 221, 230–231, 107 S.Ct. 1722, 95 L.Ed.2d 209 (1987). We held, however, that the Renton ordinance was aimed not at the content of the films shown at adult theaters, but rather at the secondary effects of such theaters on the surrounding community, namely, at crime rates, property values, and the quality of the city's neighborhoods. Therefore, the ordinance was deemed content neutral. *Renton, supra*, at 47–49, 106 S.Ct. 925. Finally, given this finding, we stated that the ordinance would be upheld so long as the city of Renton showed that its ordinance was designed to serve a substantial government interest and that reasonable alternative avenues of communication remained available. 475 U.S., at 50, 106 S.Ct. 925. We concluded that Renton had met this burden, and we upheld its ordinance. *Id.*, at 51–54, 106 S.Ct. 925.

The Court of Appeals applied the same analysis to evaluate the Los Angeles ordinance challenged in this case. First, the Court of Appeals found that the Los Angeles ordinance was not a complete ban on adult entertainment establishments, but rather a sort of adult zoning regulation, which *Renton* considered a time, place, and manner regulation. 222 F.3d, at 723. The Court of Appeals turned to the second step of the *Renton* analysis, but did not draw any conclusions about whether the Los Angeles ordinance was content based. It explained that, even if the Los Angeles ordinance were content neutral, the city had failed to demonstrate, as required by the third step of the *Renton* analysis, that its prohibition on multiple-use adult establishments was designed to serve its substantial interest in reducing crime. The Court of Appeals noted that the primary evidence relied upon by Los Angeles to demonstrate a link between combination adult businesses and harmful secondary effects was the 1977 study conducted by the city's planning department. The Court of Appeals found, however, that the city could not rely on that study because it did not " 'suppor[t] a reasonable belief that [the] combination [of] businesses . . . produced harmful secondary effects of the type asserted.' " 222 F.3d, at 724. For similar reasons, the Court of Appeals also rejected the city's attempt to rely on a report on health conditions inside adult video arcades described in *Hart Book Stores, supra*, a case that upheld a North Carolina statute similar to the Los Angeles ordinance challenged in this case.

The central component of the 1977 study is a report on city crime patterns provided by the Los Angeles Police Department. That report indicated that, during the period from 1965 to 1975, certain crime rates grew much faster in Hollywood, which had the largest concentration of adult establishments in the city, than in the city of Los Angeles as a whole. For example, robberies increased 3 times faster and prostitution 15 times faster in Hollywood than citywide.

* * *

The Court of Appeals found that the 1977 study did not reasonably support the inference that a concentration of adult operations within a single adult establishment produced greater levels of criminal activity because the study focused on the effect that a concentration of establishments-not a concentration of operations within a single establishment-had on crime rates. The Court of Appeals pointed out that the study treated combination adult bookstore/arcades as single establishments and did not study the effect of any separate-standing adult bookstore or arcade. 222 F.3d, at 724.

The Court of Appeals misunderstood the implications of the 1977 study. While the study reveals that areas with high concentrations of adult establishments are associated with high crime rates, areas with high concentrations of adult establishments are also areas with high concentrations of adult operations, albeit each in separate establishments. It was therefore consistent with the findings of the 1977 study, and thus reasonable, for Los Angeles to suppose that a concentration of adult establishments is correlated with high crime rates because a concentration of operations in one locale draws, for example, a greater concentration of adult consumers to the neighborhood, and a high density of such consumers either attracts or generates criminal activity.

* * *

Respondents' claim assumes that the 1977 study proves that all adult businesses, whether or not they are located near other adult businesses, generate crime. This is a plausible reading of the results from the 1977 study, but respondents do not demonstrate that it is a compelled reading. Nor do they provide evidence that refutes the city's interpretation of the study, under which the city's prohibition should on balance reduce crime. If this Court were nevertheless to accept respondents' speculation, it would effectively require that the city provide evidence that not only supports the claim that its ordinance serves an important government interest, but also does not provide support for any other approach to serve that interest.

In *Renton*, we specifically refused to set such a high bar for municipalities that want to address merely the secondary effects of protected speech. We held that a municipality may rely on any evidence that is "reasonably believed to be relevant" for demonstrating a connection between speech and a substantial, independent government interest. 475 U.S., at 51–52, 106 S.Ct. 925; *see also, e.g., Barnes v. Glen Theatre, Inc.*, 501 U.S. 560, 584, 111 S.Ct. 2456, 115 L.Ed.2d 504 (1991) (SOUTER, J., concurring in judgment) (permitting municipality to use evidence that adult theaters are correlated with harmful secondary effects to support its claim that nude dancing is likely to produce the same effects). This is not to say that a municipality can get away with shoddy data or reasoning. The municipality's evidence must fairly support the municipality's rationale for its ordinance. If plaintiffs fail to cast direct doubt on this rationale, either by demonstrating that the municipality's evidence does not support its rationale or by furnishing evidence that disputes the municipality's factual findings, the municipality meets the standard set forth in *Renton*. If plaintiffs succeed in casting doubt on a municipality's rationale in either manner, the burden shifts back to the municipality to supplement the record with evidence renewing support for a theory that justifies its ordinance. *See, e.g., Erie v. Pap's A.M.*, 529 U.S. 277, 298, 120 S.Ct. 1382, 146 L.Ed.2d 265 (2000) (plurality opinion). This case is at a very early stage in this process. It arrives on a summary judgment motion by respondents defended only by complaints that the 1977 study fails to prove that the city's justification for its ordinance is necessarily correct. Therefore, we conclude that the city, at this stage of the litigation, has complied with the evidentiary requirement in *Renton*.

Our deference to the evidence presented by the city of Los Angeles is the product of a careful balance between competing interests. On the one hand, we have an "obligation to exercise independent judgment when First Amendment rights are implicated." *Turner Broadcasting System, Inc. v. FCC*, 512 U.S. 622, 666, 114 S.Ct. 2445, 129 L.Ed.2d 497 (1994) (plurality opinion); *see also Landmark Communications, Inc. v. Virginia*, 435 U.S. 829, 843–844, 98 S.Ct. 1535, 56 L.Ed.2d 1 (1978). On the other hand, we must acknowledge that the Los Angeles City Council is in a better position than the Judiciary to gather and evaluate data on local problems. *See Turner, supra*, at 665–666, 114 S.Ct. 2445; *Erie, supra*, at 297–298, 120 S.Ct. 1382 (plurality opinion). We are also guided by the fact that *Renton* requires that municipal ordinances receive only intermediate scrutiny if they are content neutral. 475 U.S., at 48–50, 106 S.Ct. 925. There is less reason to be concerned that municipalities will use these ordinances to discriminate against unpopular speech. *See Erie, supra*, at 298–299, 120 S.Ct. 1382.

* * *

Before concluding, it should be noted that respondents argue, as an alternative basis to sustain the Court of Appeals' judgment, that the Los Angeles ordinance is not a typical zoning regulation. Rather, respondents explain, the prohibition on multiuse adult establishments is effectively a ban on adult video arcades because no such business exists independently of an adult bookstore. Respondents request that the Court hold that the Los Angeles ordinance is not a time, place, and manner regulation, and that the Court subject the ordinance to strict scrutiny. This also appears to be the theme of Justice KENNEDY's concurrence. He contends that "[a] city may not assert that it will reduce secondary effects by reducing speech in the same proportion." Post, at 1742 (opinion concurring in judgment). We consider that unobjectionable proposition as simply a reformulation of the requirement that an ordinance warrants intermediate scrutiny only if it is a time, place, and manner regulation and not a ban. The Court of Appeals held, however, that the city's prohibition on the combination of adult bookstores and arcades is not a ban and respondents did not petition for review of that determination.

Accordingly, we reverse the Court of Appeals' judgment granting summary judgment to respondents and remand the case for further proceedings.

It is so ordered.

JUSTICE SOUTER, with whom JUSTICE STEVENS and JUSTICE GINSBURG join, and with whom JUSTICE BREYER joins as to Part II, dissenting.

I

* * *

This ordinance stands or falls on the results of what our cases speak of as intermediate scrutiny, generally contrasted with the demanding standard applied under the First Amendment to a content-based regulation of expression. The variants of middle-tier tests cover a grab bag of restrictive statutes, with a corresponding variety of justifications. While spoken of as content neutral, these regulations are not uniformly distinct from the content-based regulations calling for scrutiny that is strict, and zoning of businesses based on their sales of expressive adult material receives mid-level scrutiny, even though it raises a risk of content-based restriction. It is worth being clear, then, on how close to a content basis adult business zoning can get, and why the application of a middle-tier standard to zoning regulation of adult bookstores calls for particular care.

Because content-based regulation applies to expression by very reason of what is said, it carries a high risk that expressive limits are imposed for the sake of suppressing a message that is disagreeable to listeners or readers, or the government. *See Consolidated Edison Co. of N.Y. v. Public Serv. Comm'n of N.Y.*, 447 U.S. 530, 536, 100 S.Ct. 2326, 65 L.Ed.2d 319 (1980) ("[W]hen regulation is based on the content of speech, governmental action must be scrutinized more carefully to ensure that communication has not been prohibited merely because public officials disapprove the speaker's views" (internal quotation marks omitted)). A restriction based on content survives only on a showing of necessity to serve a legitimate and compelling governmental interest, combined with least restrictive narrow tailoring to serve it*, see United States v. Playboy Entertainment Group, Inc.*, 529 U.S. 803, 813, 120 S.Ct. 1878, 146 L.Ed.2d 865 (2000); since merely protecting listeners from offense at the message is not a legitimate interest of the government, *see Cohen v. California*, 403 U.S. 15, 24–25, 91 S.Ct. 1780, 29 L.Ed.2d 284 (1971), strict scrutiny leaves few survivors.

The comparatively softer intermediate scrutiny is reserved for regulations justified by something other than content of the message, such as a straightforward restriction going only to the time, place, or manner of speech or other expression. It is easy to see why review of such a regulation may be relatively relaxed. No one has to disagree with any message to find something wrong with a loudspeaker at three in the morning, *see Kovacs v. Cooper*, 336 U.S. 77, 69 S.Ct. 448, 93 L.Ed. 513 (1949); the sentiment may not provoke, but being blasted out of a sound sleep does. In such a case, we ask simply whether the regulation is "narrowly tailored to serve a significant governmental interest, and . . . leave[s] open ample alternative channels for communication of the information." *Clark v. Community for Creative Non-Violence*, 468 U.S. 288, 293, 104 S.Ct. 3065, 82 L.Ed.2d 221 (1984). A middle-tier standard is also applied to limits on expression through action that is otherwise subject to regulation for nonexpressive purposes, the best known example being the prohibition on destroying draft cards as an act of protest, *United States v. O'Brien*, 391 U.S. 367, 88 S.Ct. 1673, 20 L.Ed.2d 672 (1968); here a regulation passes muster "if it furthers an important or substantial governmental interest . . . unrelated to the suppression of free expression" by a restriction "no greater than is essential to the furtherance of that interest," *id.*, at 377, 88 S.Ct. 1673. As mentioned already, yet another middle-tier variety is zoning restriction as a means of responding to the "secondary effects" of adult businesses, principally crime and declining property values in the neighborhood. *Renton v. Playtime Theatres, Inc.*, 475 U.S. 41, 49, 106 S.Ct. 925, 89 L.Ed.2d 29 (1986).

Although this type of land-use restriction has even been called a variety of time, place, or manner regulation, *id.*, at 46, 106 S.Ct. 925, equating a secondary-effects zoning regulation with a mere regulation of time, place, or manner jumps over an important difference between them. A restriction on loudspeakers has no obvious relationship to the substance of what is broadcast, while a zoning regulation of businesses in adult expression just as obviously does. And while it may be true that an adult business is burdened only because of its secondary effects, it is clearly burdened only if its expressive products have adult content. Thus, the Court has recognized that this kind of regulation, though called content neutral, occupies a kind of limbo between full-blown, content-based restrictions and regulations that apply without any reference to the substance of what is said. *Id.*, at 47, 106 S.Ct. 925.

It would in fact make sense to give this kind of zoning regulation a First Amendment label of its own, and if we called it content correlated, we would not only describe it for what it is, but keep alert to a risk of content-based regulation that it poses. The risk lies in the fact that when a law applies selectively only to speech of particular content, the more precisely the content is identified, the greater is the opportunity for government censorship. Adult speech refers not merely to sexually explicit content, but to speech reflecting a favorable view of being explicit about sex and a favorable view of the practices it depicts; a restriction on adult content is thus also a restriction turning on a particular viewpoint, of which the government may disapprove.

* * *

II

* * *

And concern with content-based regulation targeting a viewpoint is right to the point here, as witness a fact that involves no guesswork. If we take the city's breakup policy at its face, enforcing it will mean that in every case two establishments will operate instead of the traditional one. Since the city presumably does not wish merely to multiply adult establishments, it makes sense to ask what offsetting gain the city may obtain from its new breakup policy. The answer may lie in the fact that two establishments in place of one will entail two business overheads in place of one: two monthly rents, two electricity bills, two payrolls. Every month business will be more expensive than it used to be, perhaps even twice as much. That sounds like a good strategy for driving out expressive adult businesses. It sounds, in other words, like a policy of content-based regulation.

I respectfully dissent.

NOTES

1.   *Renton* made clear that the regulation of non-obscene, sexually explicit material aimed at secondary effects will not be subjected to strict scrutiny. It reaches that result by its fictional labeling of Renton's ordinance as content neutral. It is a fiction, isn't it? *See generally* Alan C. Weinstein, *The* Renton *Decision: A New Standard for Adult Business Regulation*, 32 WASH.U.J.URB. & CONTEMP.L. 91 (1987); Kimberly K. Smith, Comment, *Zoning Adult Entertainment: A Reassessment of* Renton, 79 CAL.L.REV. 119 (1991); Note, *The Content Distinction in Free Speech Analysis after* Renton, 102 HARV.L.REV. 1904 (1989).

The judicial explanation of the secondary effects doctrine is widely criticized, yet widely applied by the lower courts. Does it apply to other areas of protected speech? If not, what justifies its application only to sexually oriented speech? Professor John Fee, in an informative article, opines that the secondary effects doctrine "is not just coincidentally associated with pornographic speech, but is all about pornographic speech and its predicted effects in society." John Fee, *The Pornographic Secondary Effects Doctrine*, 60 ALA.L.REV. 291, 294 (2009). The Supreme Court, he finds, has not applied the doctrine to other areas of protected speech, but its opinions have the left the matter in an unjustifiably confused state as it "has sometimes entertained secondary effects arguments with respect to non-sexual speech—even political speech—and it has never rejected those arguments on the simple grounds that the doctrine doesn't apply." *Id.* at 304–05. Only rarely has the doctrine been used by lower courts in non-sexual speech cases. *Id.* at 338, n.141.

2.   In one case, a mayor told the press "We're not going to tolerate this kind of filth in this city." In another case, a city attorney sent a memo to his staff asking for an "in depth memo" on the regulation of sexually oriented businesses (SOBs). In a handwritten comment, he added: "Please get together and draft a legal opinion on this-I want to shut these places down! Somehow." *Ambassador Books & Video, Inc. v. City of Little Rock*, 20 F.3d 858 (8th Cir.1994). Does evidence like this present a problem for the city defending a subsequently enacted ordinance? What role, if any, can a purpose related to suppression play?

3.   How good does the secondary impacts study on which the city relies have to be? In *Alameda Books*, the Court upheld an ordinance that banned multiple adult businesses in the same building based on an earlier study that found that concentrations of single use adult businesses in an area (as opposed to within one building) are associated with higher crime rates. Use of the earlier study met with no objection from the Court. The Court said that "a municipality can [not] get away with shoddy data or reasoning."

Should a study showing adverse secondary effects from businesses offering live entertainment support a ban on stores selling adult videos for off-site viewing? *See Encore Videos, Inc. v. City of San Antonio*, 330 F.3d 288 (5th Cir.2003), *cert. denied*, 540 U.S. 982 (2003). Can studies done in urban environments be used in rural environments? *See Abilene Retail #30, Inc. v.*

Board of Commr's, 492 F.3d 1164, 1175 (10th Cir.2007), refusing to allow "prepackaged secondary effects studies from other jurisdictions to regulate any single sexually oriented business, of any type, located in any setting."

A great deal of litigation deals with whether the municipality has satisfactory proof of secondary effects. As these cases and questions suggest, not all sexually oriented uses are equal in terms of the secondary effects they cause. *See* George P. Smith II & Gregory P. Bailey, *Regulating Morality Through the Common Law and Exclusionary Zoning*, 60 CATH.U.L.REV. 403, 444 (2011), observing that "[t]he secondary-effects doctrine places great power, and corresponding responsibility, in the hands of each local community, but it does so at the peril of uniformity," and suggesting that the type and severity of secondary effects that trigger restrictions should be clarified.

4.   *Renton* requires that there be "reasonable alternatives." The City of Renton limited the theaters to 520 acres, and the Court, noting this was "more than five percent" of the city's land area, found this "easily meets this requirement." The test of the reasonableness of the area where the businesses are allowed ignores economic reality. It does not matter that the land is expensive or not on the market. It only must be physically and legally capable of being used for the adult business. *See Tollis, Inc. v. County of San Diego*, 505 F.3d 935 (9th Cir.2007) (holding valid an ordinance requiring relocation to industrial areas).

Would it ever be reasonable to totally exclude adult businesses? What if there are alternatives in neighboring towns? From the city's perspective in zoning land for adult entertainment is it better to err on side of allowing too few sites or too many?

Spacing limitations can pose problems. If an ordinance establishes a minimum buffer protecting sensitive uses from SOBs, what happens if the result is that there are no SOB sites available within the town? Should that be treated as a case of illegitimate total exclusion or should sites outside the town satisfy the Court's requirement? If, in calculating the distance of a proposed SOB from protected sensitive uses, there are sensitive uses outside the city's boundary but within the protected buffer distance, should the SOB be permitted to use the site? See Cal.Govt. Code § 65850.4(a) (city may consider harmful secondary effects on adjacent communities). *See* Chapter 5, *infra*, analyzing cases that hold that a local government's zoning ordinance that totally excludes multi-family housing from the jurisdiction constitutes illegal exclusionary zoning. *In re Appeal of Girsch*, 437 Pa. 237, 263 A.2d 395 (1970). Is the difference that affordable housing promotes a desirable use, while sexually oriented businesses are pernicious?

5.   Can a city that has allowed adult uses to proliferate do much after the fact if it wants to "clean up its image"? Is the use of eminent domain, with its complete deference to the government, a possible tool for closing down adult businesses? *See* Shelley Ross Saxer, *Eminent Domain Actions Targeting First Amendment Land Uses*, 69 MO.L.REV. 653 (2004).

6.   Definitions can be a problem. Assume the ordinance regulates "any business which offers to members of the public entertainment featuring or in any way including specified sexual activities [as further defined]." Would this cover a house in a residential area that hosts an internet web site displaying camera images of nude women where the customers do not come to the house? *Voyeur Dorm, L.C. v. City of Tampa*, 265 F.3d 1232 (11th Cir.2001), *cert. denied*, 534 U.S. 1161 (2002). Could such an operation be excluded from a residential zone not as an adult entertainment facility but simply as a business? *Flava Works, Inc. v. City of Miami*, 609 F.3d 1233 (11th Cir.2010). Or might it qualify as a home occupation?

Overbreadth and vagueness concerns are also present in these cases. *See Entertainment Productions, Inc. v. Shelby County*, 588 F.3d 372 (6th Cir.2009) *cert. denied*, 131 S.Ct. 141 (2010) (definitions of "adult cabaret," "adult-oriented establishment," and "adult entertainment" not unconstitutionally overbroad or impermissibly vague).

7.   Could a municipality use the secondary effects argument to exclude abortion clinics, arguing that the experience of other cities shows that clinics will draw protestors and violence, devaluing nearby properties?

3.   CONTROLS ON THE DISSEMINATION OF INFORMATION

Billboards, portable signs, political posters, and newsracks are ubiquitous as are regulations dealing with them. The billboard in particular triggers strong reactions. To some it is a " 'venerable medium' " of expression, *Metromedia, Inc. v. City of San Diego*, 453 U.S. 490, 501 (1981) (plurality quoting Justice Clark of the California Supreme Court), while to others, it is "distracting and ugly." (Chief Justice Burger, dissenting). *Id.* at 557. For many years, challenges to municipal regulations of billboards and other signs focused on whether they constituted aesthetic controls and, if so, whether such controls were within the police power. Today most state courts recognize aesthetic considerations standing alone as legitimate grounds for police power controls, so there is usually little or no difficulty in establishing a valid state interest in controlling signs and other physical forms of disseminating information. For an elaboration of aesthetics and the police power in the context of sign controls, see Chapter 2.H.

In 1976, the Supreme Court first declared that commercial speech was not "wholly outside" the First Amendment. *Virginia State Board of Pharmacy v. Virginia Citizens Consumer Council*, 425 U.S. 748 (1976). Despite this halfhearted welcome extended to commercial speech, the outdoor advertising industry took to the courts, challenging an ever-intensifying regulatory environment. According to one commentator, the challengers are not faring as well as they should. "Even though the First Amendment extends broad protection for the freedom of speech, when it comes to advertising law, unsympathetic plaintiffs such as pornographers and the Ku Klux Klan enjoy more public support than billboard companies." *Darrel Menthe, Writing on the Wall: The Impending Demise of Modern Sign Regulation Under the First Amendment and State Constitutions,* 18 GEO.MASON U.CIV.RTS.L.J. 1 (2007). After reading the material that follows, consider whether you agree.

In *Metromedia, Inc. v. City of San Diego,* 453 U.S. 490 (1981), the Supreme Court faced a San Diego ordinance that banned all billboards from the city with two categories of exceptions: (1) onsite signs and (2) a mix of various informational signs, such as government signs, for sale signs, time and temperature signs, and historical plaques. A plurality opinion upheld the distinction that favored onsite commercial speech over offsite commercial speech. The Court conceded that the ordinance was underinclusive in that the two types of signs were "equally distracting and unattractive," but noted that it still directly advanced the city's interests by eliminating some signs. Further, it was conceivable that offsite advertising was a "more acute problem," and the city was entitled to favor some types of commercial speech over other types. The relatively low-level protection afforded commercial billboards in *Metromedia* has led most courts to uphold bans similar to San Diego's. *See* Parsons, Comment, *Billboard Regulation after* Metromedia *and* Lucas, 31 HOUS.L.REV. 1555 (1995).

The *Metromedia* plurality, however, objected to the city's preference for one type of commercial speech (onsite signs) over noncommercial speech. Noncommercial speech was to receive greater, not lesser, protection than commercial speech, so that "[i]nsofar as the city tolerate[d] billboards at all, it [could not] choose to limit their content to commercial messages." 453 U.S at 513. There were five opinions in *Metromedia* (one concurrence and three dissents), and according to then Justice Rehnquist, one of the dissenters, "where city planning commissions and zoning boards must regularly confront constitutional claims of this sort, it is a genuine misfortune to have the Court's treatment of the subject be a virtual Tower of Babel, from which no definitive principles can be clearly drawn." *Id.* at 569. One consequence has been a deluge of litigation.

In *City of Cincinnati v. Discovery Network, Inc.,* 507 U.S. 410 (1993), the Court invalidated Cincinnati's ban on commercial newsracks using the intermediate scrutiny test of *Central Hudson Gas & Electric Corp. v. Public Service Comm'n,* 447 U.S. 557 (1980). In 1989, Cincinnati allowed newspapers that contained almost exclusive commercial content to be placed in newsracks on public property. The next year, the city changed its mind, and, concerned for safety and aesthetics, the city began enforcing an "outdated" ordinance against "commercial handbills." Using the intermediate scrutiny test of *Central Hudson,* the Court put the burden on the city to (1) show a reasonable fit between its legitimate safety and aesthetic goals and its means and (2) show that its regulation of speech was no more extensive than necessary. The city failed to carry the burden. Its case was not aided by the fact that the crackdown on commercial newsracks eliminated only 62 of some 2000 newsracks.

Discovery's intermediate scrutiny was limited to ordinances that distinguish between commercial and noncommercial speech. This suggests distinctions between types of commercial speech may not be subjected to higher scrutiny. Thus, bans limited to off-site commercial billboards, such as San Diego's in *Metromedia*, have survived *Discovery's* increased protection of commercial speech. See Juergensmeyer and Roberts, Land Use Planning and Development Regulation Law § 10.16A (3rd ed.2012). In light of Citizen's United v. Federal Election, 558 U.S. 310 (2010) (granting business corporations unlimited rights of political speech under the First Amendment equivalent to the rights of persons), should they? The Court in *Reed v. Town of Gilbert*,135 S.Ct. 2218 (2015) addressed the impact of *Citizen's United* on sign regulation in response to the lower court reasoning that the Town's sign regulation was speaker based and should therefore be treated as content neutral. In reversing the Ninth Circuit's decision, which upheld the Town's sign regulation, the Court noted that content-based laws restricting speech must be subject to strict scrutiny regardless of whether or not they are speaker based. *Id.* at 2230. See below for the principal case.

As to noncommercial speech, the Court in *City of Ladue v. Gilleo*, 512 U.S. 43, 45 (1994) considered a free-speech challenge to an ordinance prohibiting homeowners "from displaying any signs on their property except 'residence identification' signs, 'for sale' signs, and signs warning of safety hazards." However, churches, nonprofit organizations, and commercial establishments were allowed to display some signs that were not permitted for residences. Ms. Gilleo posted an 8.5" by 11" sign in her upstairs window protesting the Persian Gulf War, which sign was explicitly prohibited by the ordinance. The Court subjected the ordinance to a time, place, and manner test, rather than strict scrutiny, by assuming "arguendo, the validity of the City's submission that the various exemptions are free of impermissible content or viewpoint discrimination." *Id.* at 53. Nevertheless, the ordinance was invalidated on the basis that it did not "leave open ample alternative channels of communication" to Ms. Gilleo as "residential signs have long been an important and distinct medium of expression." *Id.* at 54.

Noting the importance of place in free speech challenges, the Court in *City of Ladue* distinguished displaying a sign at your own residence from displaying it someplace else and stated "[p]recisely because of their location, such signs provide information about the identity of the 'speaker.'" *Id.* at 56. Relying on the *City of Ladue* decision, the Ninth Circuit in *Anderson v. City of Hermosa Beach*, 621 F.3d 1051, 1067 (9th Cir. 2010) held that the City's absolute ban on tattoo parlors was not a reasonable time place, or manner restriction because, similar to *City of*

Ladue, it foreclosed an entire medium of expression for "the tattoo itself, the process of tattooing, and the business of tattooing" which were "forms of pure expression fully protected by the First Amendment."

REED V. TOWN OF GILBERT

Supreme Court of the United States, 2015.
135 S.Ct. 2218, 192 L.Ed.2d 236.

JUSTICE THOMAS delivered the opinion of the Court.

The town of Gilbert, Arizona (or Town), has adopted a comprehensive code governing the manner in which people may display outdoor signs. The Sign Code identifies various categories of signs based on the type of information they convey, then subjects each category to different restrictions. One of the categories is "Temporary Directional Signs Relating to a Qualifying Event," loosely defined as signs directing the public to a meeting of a nonprofit group. The Code imposes more stringent restrictions on these signs than it does on signs conveying other messages. We hold that these provisions are content-based regulations of speech that cannot survive strict scrutiny.

* * *

Petitioners Good News Community Church (Church) and its pastor, Clyde Reed, wish to advertise the time and location of their Sunday church services. The Church is a small, cash-strapped entity that owns no building, so it holds its services at elementary schools or other locations in or near the Town. In order to inform the public about its services, which are held in a variety of different locations, the Church began placing 15 to 20 temporary signs around the Town, frequently in the public right-of-way abutting the street. The signs typically displayed the Church's name, along with the time and location of the upcoming service. Church members would post the signs early in the day on Saturday and then remove them around midday on Sunday. The display of these signs requires little money and manpower, and thus has proved to be an economical and effective way for the Church to let the community know where its services are being held each week.

This practice caught the attention of the Town's Sign Code compliance manager, who twice cited the Church for violating the Code. The first citation noted that the Church exceeded the time limits for displaying its temporary directional signs. The second citation referred to the same problem, along with the Church's failure to include the date of the event on the signs. Town officials even confiscated one of the Church's signs, which Reed had to retrieve from the municipal offices.

Reed contacted the Sign Code Compliance Department in an attempt to reach an accommodation. His efforts proved unsuccessful. The Town's

Code compliance manager informed the Church that there would be "no leniency under the Code" and promised to punish any future violations.

Shortly thereafter, petitioners filed a complaint in the United States District Court for the District of Arizona, arguing that the Sign Code abridged their freedom of speech in violation of the First and Fourteenth Amendments. The District Court denied the petitioners' motion for a preliminary injunction. The Court of Appeals for the Ninth Circuit affirmed, holding that the Sign Code's provision regulating temporary directional signs did not regulate speech on the basis of content. It reasoned that, even though an enforcement officer would have to read the sign to determine what provisions of the Sign Code applied to it, the " 'kind of cursory examination' " that would be necessary for an officer to classify it as a temporary directional sign was "not akin to an officer synthesizing the expressive content of the sign." It then remanded for the District Court to determine in the first instance whether the Sign Code's distinctions among temporary directional signs, political signs, and ideological signs nevertheless constituted a content-based regulation of speech.

On remand, the District Court granted summary judgment in favor of the Town. The Court of Appeals again affirmed, holding that the Code's sign categories were content neutral. The court concluded that "the distinctions between Temporary Directional Signs, Ideological Signs, and Political Signs * * * are based on objective factors relevant to Gilbert's creation of the specific exemption from the permit requirement and do not otherwise consider the substance of the sign." * * * As the court explained, "Gilbert did not adopt its regulation of speech because it disagreed with the message conveyed" and its "interests in regulat[ing] temporary signs are unrelated to the content of the sign." Accordingly, the court believed that the Code was "content-neutral as that term [has been] defined by the Supreme Court." In light of that determination, it applied a lower level of scrutiny to the Sign Code and concluded that the law did not violate the First Amendment.

We granted certiorari and now reverse.

The First Amendment, applicable to the States through the Fourteenth Amendment, prohibits the enactment of laws "abridging the freedom of speech." U.S. Const., Amdt. 1. Under that Clause, a government, including a municipal government vested with state authority, "has no power to restrict expression because of its message, its ideas, its subject matter, or its content." *Police Dept. of Chicago v. Mosley*, 408 U.S. 92, 95 (1972). Content-based laws—those that target speech based on its communicative content—are presumptively unconstitutional and may be justified only if the government proves that they are narrowly tailored to serve compelling state interests. *R.A.V. v. St. Paul*, 505 U.S. 377, 395 (1992); *Simon & Schuster, Inc. v. Members of N.Y. State Crime Victims Bd.*, 502 U.S. 105, 115, 118 (1991).

Government regulation of speech is content based if a law applies to particular speech because of the topic discussed or the idea or message expressed. *E.g., Sorrell v. IMS Health, Inc.*, 131 S.Ct. 2653, 2663–2664 (2011); *Carey v. Brown*, 447 U.S. 455, 462 (1980); *Mosley, supra*, at 95. This commonsense meaning of the phrase "content based" requires a court to consider whether a regulation of speech "on its face" draws distinctions based on the message a speaker conveys. *Sorrell, supra*, 131 S.Ct. at 2664. Some facial distinctions based on a message are obvious, defining regulated speech by particular subject matter, and others are more subtle, defining regulated speech by its function or purpose. Both are distinctions drawn based on the message a speaker conveys, and, therefore, are subject to strict scrutiny.

Our precedents have also recognized a separate and additional category of laws that, though facially content neutral, will be considered content-based regulations of speech: laws that cannot be " 'justified without reference to the content of the regulated speech,' " or that were adopted by the government "because of disagreement with the message [the speech] conveys," *Ward v. Rock Against Racism*, 491 U.S. 781, 791 (1989). Those laws, like those that are content based on their face, must also satisfy strict scrutiny.

The Town's Sign Code is content based on its face. It defines "Temporary Directional Signs" on the basis of whether a sign conveys the message of directing the public to church or some other "qualifying event." It defines "Political Signs" on the basis of whether a sign's message is "designed to influence the outcome of an election." And it defines "Ideological Signs" on the basis of whether a sign "communicat[es] a message or ideas" that do not fit within the Code's other categories. It then subjects each of these categories to different restrictions.

The restrictions in the Sign Code that apply to any given sign thus depend entirely on the communicative content of the sign. If a sign informs its reader of the time and place a book club will discuss John Locke's Two Treatises of Government, that sign will be treated differently from a sign expressing the view that one should vote for one of Locke's followers in an upcoming election, and both signs will be treated differently from a sign expressing an ideological view rooted in Locke's theory of government. More to the point, the Church's signs inviting people to attend its worship services are treated differently from signs conveying other types of ideas. On its face, the Sign Code is a content-based regulation of speech. We thus have no need to consider the government's justifications or purposes for enacting the Code to determine whether it is subject to strict scrutiny.

In reaching the contrary conclusion, the Court of Appeals offered several theories to explain why the Town's Sign Code should be deemed content neutral. None is persuasive.

The Court of Appeals first determined that the Sign Code was content neutral because the Town "did not adopt its regulation of speech [based on] disagree[ment] with the message conveyed," and its justifications for regulating temporary directional signs were "unrelated to the content of the sign." * * * But this analysis skips the crucial first step in the content-neutrality analysis: determining whether the law is content neutral on its face. A law that is content based on its face is subject to strict scrutiny regardless of the government's benign motive, content-neutral justification, or lack of "animus toward the ideas contained" in the regulated speech. *Cincinnati v. Discovery Network, Inc.*, 507 U.S. 410, 429 (1993). We have thus made clear that " '[i]llicit legislative intent is not the sine qua non of a violation of the First Amendment,' " and a party opposing the government "need adduce 'no evidence of an improper censorial motive.' " *Simon & Schuster, supra*, at 117. Although "a content-based purpose may be sufficient in certain circumstances to show that a regulation is content based, it is not necessary." *Turner Broadcasting System, Inc. v. FCC*, 512 U.S. 622, 642 (1994). In other words, an innocuous justification cannot transform a facially content-based law into one that is content neutral.

* * *

* * * Because strict scrutiny applies either when a law is content based on its face or when the purpose and justification for the law are content based, a court must evaluate each question before it concludes that the law is content neutral and thus subject to a lower level of scrutiny.

* * *

* * * Accordingly, we have repeatedly "rejected the argument that 'discriminatory . . . treatment is suspect under the First Amendment only when the legislature intends to suppress certain ideas.' " *Discovery Network*, 507 U.S. at 429. We do so again today.

The Court of Appeals next reasoned that the Sign Code was content neutral because it "does not mention any idea or viewpoint, let alone single one out for differential treatment." It reasoned that, for the purpose of the Code provisions, "[i]t makes no difference which candidate is supported, who sponsors the event, or what ideological perspective is asserted." * * *

This analysis conflates two distinct but related limitations that the First Amendment places on government regulation of speech. Government discrimination among viewpoints—or the regulation of speech based on "the specific motivating ideology or the opinion or perspective of the speaker"—is a "more blatant" and "egregious form of content discrimination." *Rosenberger v. Rector and Visitors of Univ. of Va.*, 515 U.S. 819, 829 (1995). But it is well established that "[t]he First Amendment's hostility to content-based regulation extends not only to restrictions on particular viewpoints, but also to prohibition of public discussion of an entire topic." *Consolidated Edison Co. of N.Y. v. Public Serv. Comm'n of N.Y.*, 447 U.S. 530, 537 (1980).

Thus, a speech regulation targeted at specific subject matter is content based even if it does not discriminate among viewpoints within that subject matter. For example, a law banning the use of sound trucks for political speech—and only political speech—would be a content-based regulation, even if it imposed no limits on the political viewpoints that could be expressed. *See Discovery Network, supra,* at 428. The Town's Sign Code likewise singles out specific subject matter for differential treatment, even if it does not target viewpoints within that subject matter. Ideological messages are given more favorable treatment than messages concerning a political candidate, which are themselves given more favorable treatment than messages announcing an assembly of like-minded individuals. That is a paradigmatic example of content-based discrimination.

Finally, the Court of Appeals characterized the Sign Code's distinctions as turning on " 'the content-neutral elements of who is speaking through the sign and whether and when an event is occurring.' " That analysis is mistaken on both factual and legal grounds. To start, the Sign Code's distinctions are not speaker based. The restrictions for political, ideological, and temporary event signs apply equally no matter who sponsors them.

* * *

In any case, the fact that a distinction is speaker based does not, as the Court of Appeals seemed to believe, automatically render the distinction content neutral. Because "[s]peech restrictions based on the identity of the speaker are all too often simply a means to control content," *Citizens United v. Federal Election Comm'n*, 558 U.S. 310, 340 (2010), we have insisted that "laws favoring some speakers over others demand strict scrutiny when the legislature's speaker preference reflects a content preference," *Turner*, 512 U.S. at 658. Thus, a law limiting the content of newspapers, but only newspapers, could not evade strict scrutiny simply because it could be characterized as speaker based. Likewise, a content-based law that restricted the political speech of all corporations would not become content neutral just because it singled out corporations as a class of speakers. *See Citizens United, supra,* at 340–341. Characterizing a distinction as speaker based is only the beginning—not the end—of the inquiry.

* * *

And, just as with speaker-based laws, the fact that a distinction is event based does not render it content neutral. * * * A regulation that targets a sign because it conveys an idea about a specific event is no less content based than a regulation that targets a sign because it conveys some other idea. Here, the Code singles out signs bearing a particular message:

the time and location of a specific event. This type of ordinance may seem like a perfectly rational way to regulate signs, but a clear and firm rule governing content neutrality is an essential means of protecting the freedom of speech, even if laws that might seem "entirely reasonable" will sometimes be "struck down because of their content-based nature." *City of Ladue v. Gilleo*, 512 U.S. 43, 60 (1994) (O'Connor, J., concurring).

Because the Town's Sign Code imposes content-based restrictions on speech, those provisions can stand only if they survive strict scrutiny, " 'which requires the Government to prove that the restriction furthers a compelling interest and is narrowly tailored to achieve that interest,' " *Arizona Free Enterprise Club's Freedom Club PAC v. Bennett*, 131 S.Ct. 2806, 2817 (2011) (quoting *Citizens United*, 558 U.S. at 340). Thus, it is the Town's burden to demonstrate that the Code's differentiation between temporary directional signs and other types of signs, such as political signs and ideological signs, furthers a compelling governmental interest and is narrowly tailored to that end.

The Town cannot do so. It has offered only two governmental interests in support of the distinctions the Sign Code draws: preserving the Town's aesthetic appeal and traffic safety. Assuming for the sake of argument that those are compelling governmental interests, the Code's distinctions fail as hopelessly underinclusive.

Starting with the preservation of aesthetics, temporary directional signs are "no greater an eyesore," *Discovery Network*, 507 U.S. at 425, than ideological or political ones. Yet the Code allows unlimited proliferation of larger ideological signs while strictly limiting the number, size, and duration of smaller directional ones. The Town cannot claim that placing strict limits on temporary directional signs is necessary to beautify the Town while at the same time allowing unlimited numbers of other types of signs that create the same problem.

The Town similarly has not shown that limiting temporary directional signs is necessary to eliminate threats to traffic safety, but that limiting other types of signs is not. The Town has offered no reason to believe that directional signs pose a greater threat to safety than do ideological or political signs. If anything, a sharply worded ideological sign seems more likely to distract a driver than a sign directing the public to a nearby church meeting.

In light of this underinclusiveness, the Town has not met its burden to prove that its Sign Code is narrowly tailored to further a compelling government interest. Because a " 'law cannot be regarded as protecting an interest of the highest order, and thus as justifying a restriction on truthful speech, when it leaves appreciable damage to that supposedly vital interest unprohibited,' " *Republican Party of Minn. v. White*, 536 U.S. 765, 780 (2002), the Sign Code fails strict scrutiny.

Our decision today will not prevent governments from enacting effective sign laws. The Town asserts that an " 'absolutist' " content-neutrality rule would render "virtually all distinctions in sign laws . . . subject to strict scrutiny," but that is not the case. Not "all distinctions" are subject to strict scrutiny, only content-based ones are. Laws that are content neutral are instead subject to lesser scrutiny. *See Clark*, 468 U.S. at 295.

The Town has ample content-neutral options available to resolve problems with safety and aesthetics. For example, its current Code regulates many aspects of signs that have nothing to do with a sign's message: size, building materials, lighting, moving parts, and portability. *See, e.g.*, § 4.402(R). And on public property, the Town may go a long way toward entirely forbidding the posting of signs, so long as it does so in an evenhanded, content-neutral manner. *See Taxpayers for Vincent*, 466 U.S. at 817 (upholding content-neutral ban against posting signs on public property). Indeed, some lower courts have long held that similar content-based sign laws receive strict scrutiny, but there is no evidence that towns in those jurisdictions have suffered catastrophic effects. *See, e.g.*, *Solantic, LLC v. Neptune Beach*, 410 F.3d 1250, 1264–1269 (C.A.11 2005) (sign categories similar to the town of Gilbert's were content based and subject to strict scrutiny); *Matthews v. Needham*, 764 F.2d 58, 59–60 (C.A.1 1985) (law banning political signs but not commercial signs was content based and subject to strict scrutiny).

We acknowledge that a city might reasonably view the general regulation of signs as necessary because signs "take up space and may obstruct views, distract motorists, displace alternative uses for land, and pose other problems that legitimately call for regulation." *City of Ladue*, 512 U.S. at 48. At the same time, the presence of certain signs may be essential, both for vehicles and pedestrians, to guide traffic or to identify hazards and ensure safety. A sign ordinance narrowly tailored to the challenges of protecting the safety of pedestrians, drivers, and passengers—such as warning signs marking hazards on private property, signs directing traffic, or street numbers associated with private houses—well might survive strict scrutiny. The signs at issue in this case, including political and ideological signs and signs for events, are far removed from those purposes. As discussed above, they are facially content based and are neither justified by traditional safety concerns nor narrowly tailored.

* * *

We reverse the judgment of the Court of Appeals and remand the case for proceedings consistent with this opinion.

It is so ordered.

JUSTICE ALITO, with whom JUSTICE KENNEDY and JUSTICE SOTOMAYOR join, concurring.

I join the opinion of the Court but add a few words of further explanation. As the Court holds, what we have termed "content-based" laws must satisfy strict scrutiny. Content-based laws merit this protection because they present, albeit sometimes in a subtler form, the same dangers as laws that regulate speech based on viewpoint. Limiting speech based on its "topic" or "subject" favors those who do not want to disturb the status quo. Such regulations may interfere with democratic self-government and the search for truth. *See Consolidated Edison Co. of N.Y. v. Public Serv. Comm'n of N.Y.*, 447 U.S. 530, 537 (1980).

As the Court shows, the regulations at issue in this case are replete with content-based distinctions, and as a result they must satisfy strict scrutiny. This does not mean, however, that municipalities are powerless to enact and enforce reasonable sign regulations. I will not attempt to provide anything like a comprehensive list, but here are some rules that would not be content based:

Rules regulating the size of signs. These rules may distinguish among signs based on any content-neutral criteria, including any relevant criteria listed below.

Rules regulating the locations in which signs may be placed. These rules may distinguish between free-standing signs and those attached to buildings.

Rules distinguishing between lighted and unlighted signs.

Rules distinguishing between signs with fixed messages and electronic signs with messages that change.

Rules that distinguish between the placement of signs on private and public property.

Rules distinguishing between the placement of signs on commercial and residential property.

Rules distinguishing between on-premises and off-premises signs.

Rules restricting the total number of signs allowed per mile of roadway.

Rules imposing time restrictions on signs advertising a one-time event. Rules of this nature do not discriminate based on topic or subject and are akin to rules restricting the times within which oral speech or music is allowed.

In addition to regulating signs put up by private actors, government entities may also erect their own signs consistent with the principles that allow governmental speech. *See Pleasant Grove City v. Summum*, 555 U.S. 460, 467–469 (2009). They may put up all manner of signs to promote safety, as well as directional signs and signs pointing out historic sites and scenic spots.

Properly understood, today's decision will not prevent cities from regulating signs in a way that fully protects public safety and serves legitimate esthetic objectives.

JUSTICE BREYER, concurring in the judgment. (omitted)

JUSTICE KAGAN, with whom JUSTICE GINSBURG and JUSTICE BREYER join, concurring in the judgment.

Countless cities and towns across America have adopted ordinances regulating the posting of signs, while exempting certain categories of signs based on their subject matter. * * *

Given the Court's analysis, many sign ordinances of that kind are now in jeopardy. * * * Says the majority: When laws "single[ ] out specific subject matter," they are "facially content based"; and when they are facially content based, they are automatically subject to strict scrutiny. And although the majority holds out hope that some sign laws with subject-matter exemptions "might survive" that stringent review, the likelihood is that most will be struck down. After all, it is the "rare case[ ] in which a speech restriction withstands strict scrutiny." *Williams-Yulee v. Florida Bar*, 135 S.Ct. 1656, 1666 (2015). To clear that high bar, the government must show that a content-based distinction "is necessary to serve a compelling state interest and is narrowly drawn to achieve that end." *Arkansas Writers' Project, Inc. v. Ragland*, 481 U.S. 221, 231 (1987). So on the majority's view, courts would have to determine that a town has a compelling interest in informing passersby where George Washington slept. And likewise, courts would have to find that a town has no other way to prevent hidden-driveway mishaps than by specially treating hidden-driveway signs. (Well-placed speed bumps? Lower speed limits? Or how about just a ban on hidden driveways?) The consequence—unless courts water down strict scrutiny to something unrecognizable—is that our communities will find themselves in an unenviable bind: They will have to either repeal the exemptions that allow for helpful signs on streets and sidewalks, or else lift their sign restrictions altogether and resign themselves to the resulting clutter.

* * *

* * * In *City of Ladue v. Gilleo*, 512 U.S. 43 (1994), the Court assumed arguendo that a sign ordinance's exceptions for address signs, safety signs, and for-sale signs in residential areas did not trigger strict scrutiny. *See id.* at 46–47, and n.6 (listing exemptions); *id.* at 53 (noting this assumption). We did not need to, and so did not, decide the level-of-scrutiny question because the law's breadth made it unconstitutional under any standard.

The majority could easily have taken *Ladue*'s tack here. The Town of Gilbert's defense of its sign ordinance—most notably, the law's distinctions between directional signs and others—does not pass strict scrutiny, or intermediate scrutiny, or even the laugh test. The Town, for example, provides no reason at all for prohibiting more than four directional signs on a property while placing no limits on the number of other types of signs. *See* Gilbert, Ariz., Land Development Code, ch. I, §§ 4.402(J), (P)(2) (2014). Similarly, the Town offers no coherent justification for restricting the size of directional signs to 6 square feet while allowing other signs to reach 20 square feet. See §§ 4.402(J), (P)(1). The best the Town could come up with at oral argument was that directional signs "need to be smaller because they need to guide travelers along a route." Why exactly a smaller sign better helps travelers get to where they are going is left a mystery. The absence of any sensible basis for these and other distinctions dooms the Town's ordinance under even the intermediate scrutiny that the Court typically applies to "time, place, or manner" speech regulations. Accordingly, there is no need to decide in this case whether strict scrutiny applies to every sign ordinance in every town across this country containing a subject-matter exemption.

I suspect this Court and others will regret the majority's insistence today on answering that question in the affirmative. As the years go by, courts will discover that thousands of towns have such ordinances, many of them "entirely reasonable." And as the challenges to them mount, courts will have to invalidate one after the other. (This Court may soon find itself a veritable Supreme Board of Sign Review.) And courts will strike down those democratically enacted local laws even though no one—certainly not the majority—has ever explained why the vindication of First Amendment values requires that result. Because I see no reason why such an easy case calls for us to cast a constitutional pall on reasonable regulations quite unlike the law before us, I concur only in the judgment.

NOTES: REGULATION OF COMMERCIAL AND NONCOMMERCIAL SPEECH

1.   After the *Reed* decision, how would you answer these questions about what cities may do with sign regulation? Must cities allow all yard signs? What about commercial yard signs in residential zones? Many cities allow home occupations to post small signs. But, must they allow them?

2.   Almost all cities want to regulate signs, but feel compelled to grant some exceptions and make some distinctions, thus raising the question of whether the city is engaging in invalid content discrimination. Consider some common exemptions: temporary political campaign signs, public and quasi-public institutional advertising, highway directional signs, and religious symbols. Should exceptions for any of these render a statute unconstitutional?

How would a sign regulation, which limited "adult cabarets" within a mile of any state highway to one on-premise sign, which could not exceed 40 sq. ft. in size and could include only the business name, street address, telephone number, and operating hours of the business, fare if challenged?

What about a ban on "immoral signs"? *Union City Board of Zoning Appeals v. Justice Outdoor Displays, Inc.*, 467 S.E.2d 875 (Ga.1996). Is *Renton's* secondary effects rationale available to a city to justify such a ban? *See* John Fee, *The Pornographic Secondary Effects Doctrine*, 60 ALA.L.REV. 291, 294 (2009) (finding that only rarely has the doctrine been used by lower courts in non-sexual speech case).

3.   "*Reed* has left several questions unanswered. As previously noted, treatment of the onsite/offsite and commercial/non-commercial distinctions remains uncertain. *Reed* also failed to provide an answer to how we provide for the public's desire for more signage during election campaigns in a wholly content-neutral manner. We also don't know what, if any, content-based regulations might survive strict scrutiny. In light of these uncertainties, arguably the best course for cities is to err on the side of allowing for less restrictive, rather than more restrictive, sign regulations until the courts provide more guidance on the above questions and others that are certain to be raised." Federal Land Use Law & Litigation § 5:7 (2015 ed.) Brian W. Blaesser & Alan C. Weinstein Chapter 5. Signs, Billboards, and Newsracks. *See also* Brian J. Connolly & Alan C. Weinstein, *Sign Regulation After* Reed: *Suggestions For Coping With Legal Uncertainty*, 47 URB.LAW. 569, 610–11 (2015) (noting that "*Reed*'s outcome increases the level of legal risk associated with many aspects of sign regulation" and recommending that communities "review sign regulations for potential areas of content discrimination and . . . take precautions against potential sign litigation," as well as "consider (or perhaps reconsider) the level of legal risk that the community is willing to tolerate in order to preserve the aesthetic character of the community and to further the safety interests of community members").

4.   Believing "the onsite/offsite distinction will likely be a casualty of the growing pressure in federal jurisprudence to address the differing treatment of 'commercial' and 'non-commercial' speech," one commentator criticizes the distinction between commercial and non-commercial speech.

> [The distinction] was never obvious, and sophisticated advertising techniques can blur the lines even more. To note one example, a billboard operator puts up a sign that reads, "Jesus: The Reason for the Season." While this sign seems indisputably non-commercial, and thus deserving of full First Amendment protection, the sign may actually be part of a commercial advertising program if the color scheme and font indicate a business. The real message is often the subtext that a particular company shares certain values with potential customers. Almost any public-service message can be subtly commercial in this way. Put another way, very few messages that cost several thousand dollars each are actually intended to generate no commercial benefit whatsoever for the speaker.

Darrel Menthe, *Writing on the Wall: The Impending Demise of Modern Sign Regulation Under the First Amendment and State Constitutions*, 18 GEO. MASON U.CIV.RTS.L.J. 1, 6 (2007). The court in *Vono v. Lewis*, 594 F.Supp.2d 189 (D.R.I.2009), reads the writing on the wall, but the overwhelming majority of courts uphold the on-site/off-distinction. Brian W. Blaesser and Alan C. Weinstein, Federal Land Use Law & Litigation § 5:22 (2010). See Steven G. Brody and Bruce E.H. Johnson, *Advertising & Commercial Speech: A First Amendment Guide* § 13:2.1 (Practising Law Institute 2011) for a circuit by circuit listing of decisions.

5.   In addition to First Amendment challenges to billboard bans, Fifth Amendment takings claims are commonly made against sign amortization ordinances. They often fail. *Art Neon Co. v. City and County of Denver*, 488 F.2d 118 (10th Cir.1973) (holding that five years is a reasonable amortization time). When signs are amortized, who loses? The landowner who leases the space for the sign, for one. With respect to the sign company's losses, how is the unit of property defined and what factors go into determining the economic impact? Possible factors include the cost of signs that must be removed, reuse of the signs elsewhere or salvage value, life expectancy of the signs, the lease of land where the signs are placed, and "the percentage of affected signs compared to the remaining signs in the [company's] business unit." *Naegele Outdoor Advertising, Inc. v. City of Durham*, 844 F.2d 172, 178 (4th Cir.1988). Should the court consider the "free ride" that the landowner and advertiser are getting from the state in using the value of adjacency to a public highway, a value that was created with public funds?

6.   The Federal Highway Beautification Act of 1965, 23 U.S.C.A. §§ 131–35 mandated that states either make provision for the control and removal of outdoor advertising signs erected within 660 feet of interstate or primary highway rights-of-way or forfeit federal highway funds. State statutes implementing this congressional policy are in place throughout the country.

The ban does not apply to areas that are zoned for industrial or commercial use or are in "unzoned commercial or industrial areas as may be determined by agreement between the several States and the Secretary." 23 U.S.C.A. § 131(d). *See generally* Roger A. Cunningham, *Billboard Control under the Highway Beautification Act of 1965*, 71 MICH.L.REV. 1296 (1972–73).

Sign control advocates find little in the act to celebrate and regard it as a billboard protection act. As one commentator says, the Act is "at war with itself. Born of a mid-1960s initiative to bring beauty to the nation's roads, the Act today represents a cynical reminder of squandered opportunities because its operation thwarts, rather than promotes, the achievement of its goal." Craig J. Albert, *Your Ad Goes Here: How the Highway Beautification Act of 1965 Thwarts Highway Beautification*, 48 U.KAN.L.REV. 463, 465 (2000). One problem is the exemption of commercial and industrial areas, which invites pressure to rezone bona fide rural areas to industrial or commercial use that will allow billboards. Cities can go too far though in responding to such requests. *See, e.g., L & W Outdoor Advertising Co. v. State*, 539 N.E.2d 497 (Ind.App.1989) (rezoning to commercial to avoid act held to be invalid spot zoning).

COMMENT: RETALIATION, MALLS, AND HOAS

Other situations involving land use regulations that involve the First Amendment:

Government Retaliation: The development process is political. Whether permission is sought from a legislative or administrative body, public hearings are held and public involvement is often great. Behind the scenes maneuvering likewise occurs. The "zoning game" has winners and losers, feathers get ruffled, and, when the government loses, it sometimes retaliates.

Generally, to prevail on a constitutional retaliation claim plaintiff must prove "(1) that she engaged in constitutionally-protected activity; (2) that the government responded with retaliation; and (3) that protected activity caused the retaliation." *Eichenlaub v. Township of Indiana*, 385 F.3d 274, 282 (3rd Cir.2004). Proof of motive is necessary. In *Eichenlaub*, a developer who claimed his protected speech relating to his zoning petition led to the town retaliating against him by removing him from a public meeting and against his family by denying them development permits was found to state a claim. Yet, in another case, a developer alleged that the mayor had retaliated against him because he ran, albeit unsuccessfully, for mayor himself. To prove his allegation, the developer only offered the opinion of a former city official that the mayor influenced and controlled the commission when it denied the developer a permit. This opinion evidence was insufficient to submit the matter to a jury. *Campbell v. Rainbow City*, 434 F.3d 1306 (11th Cir.2006).

Stating a retaliation claim is difficult and many plaintiffs fail at that stage. *Compare, e.g.*, *Baumgardner v. Town of Ruston*, 712 F.Supp.2d 1180 (W.D.Wash.2010) and *Schubert v. City of Rye*, 775 F.Supp.2d 689 (S.D.N.Y. 2011), *with Soundview Associates v. Town of Riverhead*, 725 F.Supp.2d 320, 341 (E.D.N.Y.2010) and *Paeth v. Worth Twp.*, 705 F.Supp.2d 753, 767 (E.D.Mich.2010) (plaintiff alleged that city officials repeatedly denied variance applications and issued a stop work order in retaliation for his criticism of zoning board; the court found the fact that a town clerk issued "a stop work order as a ham-handed method of overriding the adverse judicial decision and punishing the plaintiffs for their successful resort to the courts" sufficient to preclude summary judgment.)

One high profile case involved the federal government. When a proposal was made to convert a motel to a home for recovering substance abusers, neighbors wrote letters to the local government officials and spoke at public meetings. While the neighbors contended that the home as planned lacked adequate staff for proper operation, the proponents accused them of opposing the home because it was to be occupied by disabled persons. The U.S. Department of Housing and Urban Development investigated the neighbors. Claiming their opposition constituted unlawful intimidation under the Fair Housing Act, HUD demanded the neighborhood group's membership list, correspondence, meeting minutes and tapes of meetings and threatened them with fines. While HUD eventually concluded the neighbors had not violated the FHA, the Ninth Circuit found that HUD's activities violated the neighbors'

First Amendment right to petition the government. *White v. Lee*, 227 F.3d 1214 (9th Cir.2000).

Issues of government retaliation may also fall under the Fourteenth Amendment due process or equal protection clauses. In the *Olech* equal protection case, the plaintiff had first prevailed in an unrelated lawsuit against the village. She claimed that when she later sought to connect her property to the public water supply, the excessive easement demanded by the city was in retaliation for her defeating the village in the earlier case. The due process clause may be an option, but less attractive since it requires establishing a property right. In either event, the standard of review under the Fourteenth Amendment is likely to be more deferential than a claim based on the First Amendment.

Shopping Malls: Free speech rights may be implicated where owners of shopping centers wish to exclude petitioners and picketers from their property. While the First Amendment does not protect speech on private property, numerous state courts have held that their state constitutions grant greater protection for freedom of speech, including the right to solicit signatures and picket at private shopping centers. *See Green Party of New Jersey v. Hartz Mountain Industries, Inc.*, 752 A.2d 315 (N.J.2000) (shopping mall's regulations that a political party could not hand out leaflets without providing a $1 million liability insurance policy or signing a hold harmless agreement violated state constitution). Not all courts agree. *State v. Wicklund*, 589 N.W.2d 793 (Minn.1999). If the state law allows only limited and temporary public entry into mall, it does not amount to a Fifth Amendment taking. *PruneYard Shopping Ctr. v. Robins*, 447 U.S. 74 (1980). *See generally* Gregory C. Sisk, *Returning to the* Pruneyard: *The Unconstitutionality of State-Sanctioned Trespass in the Name of Speech*, 32 HARV.J.L. & PUB.POL'Y 389 (2009).

Homeowners' Associations: What about speech limitations imposed by homeowners' associations, such as restrictions on leafleting or the posting of flags? In *Latera v. Isle at Mission Bay Homeowners Ass'n, Inc.*, 655 So.2d 144 (Fla.App.1995), the court found a restrictive covenant of a homeowners' association that banned satellite dishes did not violate the First Amendment because the activity did not qualify as protected speech. Why not simply dismiss the constitutional claim on the basis that state action is lacking? *See Ross v. Hatfield*, 640 F.Supp. 708 (D.Kan.1986). The lack of state action precludes application of the federal due process clause to private covenants. Most state constitutions have similar clauses. One exception is New Jersey, where the free speech guarantee in the state constitution is applied against private parties under a balancing test crafted by the state supreme court. In *Committee for a Better Twin Rivers v. Twin Rivers Homeowners' Ass'n*, 929 A.2d 1060 (N.J.2007), the court held that a homeowners' association did not violate the free speech rights of its members when it banned political signs in yards. The growth and almost unlimited power of homeowners' associations has been heavily criticized. Lisa J. Chadderdon, *No Political Speech Allowed: Common Interest Developments, Homeowners Associations, and Restrictions on*

Free Speech, 21 J.LAND USE & ENVTL.L. 233 (2006); Steven Siegel, *The Public Interest and Private Gated Communities: A Comprehensive Approach to Public Policy That Would Discourage the Establishment of New Gated Communities and Encourage the Removal of Gates from Existing Private Communities*, 55 LOY.L.REV. 805 (2009).

4. RELIGIOUS FREEDOM

The regulation of religious land uses has become increasingly controversial. In zoning's early years, the negative externalities of religious uses were negligible. Buildings devoted to religious use tended to be small, particularly when compared to today's "norms," and congregations served the neighborhoods in which they were located. Some courts viewed religious uses as presumptively or inherently beneficial to residential areas and lessened any burden of proof or shifted the burden on government to justify regulating them. Some still do. *Boyajian v. Gatzunis*, 212 F.3d 1, 7 (1st Cir.2000) (interpreting Massachusetts law); *House of Fire Christian Church v. Zoning Bd. of Adjustment of City of Clifton*, 879 A.2d 1212, 1217 (N.J.App.2005).

Times have changed. Always a religious society, the United States is, increasingly, religiously active and diverse. Activities conducted by many religious organizations are no longer limited to weekends and no longer limited to what many think of as traditional religious services. They may operate day care centers or offer their buildings or grounds as homeless shelters. Multi-complex, multi-use religious organizations with thousands of members and daily activities that range beyond the "traditional" to include restaurants, coffee houses, bookstores, athletic fields, housing for elderly members, and radio and television broadcasting have spread across the country as fast as big box supercenters. They serve regions, not neighborhoods. *See* Sara C. Galvan, Note, *Beyond Worship: The Religious Land Use and Institutionalized Persons Act of 2000 and Religious Institutions' Auxiliary Uses,* 24 YALE L. & POL'Y REV. 207–08 (2006). These so-called "mega-churches" often require substantial acreage and when a new "supersized" project is announced by a religious organization or an existing religious use wants to expand, neighbors invariably will voice concerns. While the objections of neighbors are typically and understandably religious-neutral, relating to the anticipated adverse impact on the community due to the size of buildings and multiplicity of activities that may occur, religious animus is not unknown. Religious orders that are new to a community may be viewed with skepticism. Ignorance or intolerance of those with different religious beliefs and "unusual" practices may well spark a zoning battle.

Economics also plays a role. Cities engaging in urban redevelopment or hoping for urban revitalization may prefer land uses that produce tax revenues and generate economic activity. A storefront, shoestring religious group that leases or buys a decrepit building in the urban center may preclude rehabilitation of the building and the entry of a taxpaying, new chic restaurant. *See* Lucinda Harper, *Storefront Churches: The Neighbors Upscale Stores Don't Love*, WALL ST.J., Mar. 15, 2000, at B1.

Some or all of these factors have led many communities to regulate religious uses more stringently than in the past. This may mean treating religious uses on par with other institutional uses since, as with much land development, they produce problems such as noise, traffic, parking, storm runoff, and erosion. At times, religious organizations may be treated less favorably than other institutional uses. In either event, increasing regulation provokes an increase in First Amendment free exercise challenges, and it has led to congressional intervention into what traditionally has been a matter for local control.

Fearing litigation or believing religious uses should be treated more favorably than other like uses, some communities exempt religious uses from some or most controls. This favoritism may be challenged on establishment clause grounds. The dilemma then for regulators is to deal with the Catch 22: regulating religious uses may lead to free exercise claims but exempting religious uses from regulations others must follow may lead to establishment clause claims.

While it is fundamental that the free exercise clause absolutely protects religious beliefs, government can regulate religious conduct. However, the Court held in *Sherbert v. Verner*, 374 U.S. 398 (1963), that government regulation of conduct that substantially burdens the free exercise of religion cannot be sustained unless it furthers a compelling interest and uses the least restrictive means to advance this interest. In the *Sherbert* era, however, courts consistently found that land use regulations did not substantially burden the free exercise of religion and were thus not subject to the compelling interest test. *See Messiah Baptist Church v. County of Jefferson*, 859 F.2d 820 (10th Cir.1988) (construction of a house of worship on particular tract of land zoned for agricultural use not integrally related to the church's beliefs and church made no showing that alternative sites were unavailable); and *Lakewood, Ohio Congregation of Jehovah's Witnesses, Inc. v. City of Lakewood*, 699 F.2d 303 (6th Cir.1983).

Religious exercise claims in the land use context became even more tenuous in 1990 when the Court held that the strict scrutiny test of *Sherbert* does not apply to claims challenging neutral laws of general applicability. The "right of free exercise does not relieve an individual of the obligation to comply with a 'valid and neutral law of general applicability on the ground that the law proscribes (or prescribes) conduct that his religion prescribes (or proscribes).'" *Id.* at 879.

The Court clarified the reach of *Smith*, where it said that *Smith* did not grant government the power to target religious practices. In *City of Hialeah*, the Court found that a city violated the First Amendment when it applied its zoning, health, and animal cruelty ordinances prohibiting the ritual slaughter of animals to specifically target one church's religious conduct. Applying the compelling interest test, the Court found that the ordinances were not narrowly tailored to achieve the city's interests. Thus, under *City of Hialeah*, an ordinance that is neutral on its face will be subjected to strict scrutiny if shown to have been motivated by religious animus.

In *Rector, Wardens, and Members of Vestry of St. Bartholomew's Church v. City of New York*, 914 F.2d 348 (2d Cir.1990), *cert. denied*, 499 U.S. 905 (1991), the court relied on *Employment Division v. Smith* to deny a free exercise claim by New York City's St. Bartholomew's Church involving the application of New York's historic landmarks law. The church and its adjacent community building were designated historic landmarks in 1967. In 1983, the church wanted to raise revenue for a number of religious purposes and sought permission from the Landmarks Commission to replace its community house with a fifty-nine story office tower. Its request was denied. In the litigation that followed, the court held that the church had to comply with the landmark law, which it found to be a facially neutral regulation of general applicability within the meaning of *Smith*.

Dissatisfied with *Smith*'s perceived narrowing of protection for religious uses, and decisions like *St. Bartholomew's*, Congress enacted the Religious Freedom Restoration Act of 1993 (RFRA), 42 U.S.C. §§ 2000bb et seq., which purported to restore pre-*Smith* First Amendment law. When St. Peter's Catholic Church of Boerne, Texas proposed an addition to its 1923 mission style building, which could not accommodate the growing parish, the city denied its request. The building was a historic landmark, and the proposal would have replaced nearly 80% of it. Such an expansion, the city found, would impermissibly alter the exterior of the structure. The church claimed the denial violated RFRA. The Court, however, held RFRA an unconstitutional exercise of Congress' remedial powers under Section Five of the Fourteenth Amendment. *City of Boerne v. Flores*, 521 U.S. 507 (1997). *See* Alan C. Weinstein, Ch. 4, *Protecting Free Speech and Expression in The First Amendment and Land Use Law* (D. Mandelker and R. Rubin eds.2001).

While almost every member of Congress voted to enact RFRA in 1993, after the *City of Boerne* decision, RFRA could not be imposed to limit state and local laws, but it did continue to apply to federal law. The Religious Land Use and Institutionalized Persons Act (RLUIPA) was enacted in 2000 and "applies the RFRA 'test' to two discrete areas of state law: land use regulation, and the treatment of prisoners and other persons confined in state-operated institutions." Martin S. Lederman, *Reconstructing RFRA: The Contested Legacy of Religious Freedom Restoration*, 125 YALE L.J.FORUM 416, 417 (2016). "More than twenty states have also enacted their own 'mini-RFRAs' that require religious exemptions to state and local laws under certain circumstances—sometimes using language similar or identical to that found in the federal RFRA." *Id.* The coalition of interests in support of state mini-RFRAs has recently fragmented as both non-profit and for-profit corporations have claimed exemption from the so-called "contraception mandate" of the Affordable Care Act. *See, e.g. Burwell v. Hobby Lobby Stores, Inc.,* (holding that closely held for-profit corporations were exempted by RFRA "because the executive agencies had at least one 'less restrictive' way to further the government's compelling interest in ensuring that the companies' female employees (and employee dependents) would have affordable access to effective contraception"). *Id.* at 418. There is also the possibility that federal or state RFRAs will be used to provide religious exemptions from discrimination on the basis of sexual orientation in employment and public accommodations. *Id.* at 419. *See generally* Zachary A. Bray, *RLUIPA and the Limits of Religious Institutionalism,* 2016 UTAH L.REV. 41 (arguing "that the practical application of religious institutionalism to disputes about religious land use will likely make the bad parts of a bad statute even worse, and conclud[ing] with the hope that courts will reject the coming institutional turn in religious land use").

As noted above, Congress enacted the Religious Land Use and Institutionalized Persons Act of 2000 (RLUIPA) in an attempt to overcome the Court's objections to RFRA in *City of Boerne.* 42 U.S.C. §§ 2000cc *et seq. See* Marci A. Hamilton, Federalism and the Public Good: The True Story Behind the Religious Land Use and Institutionalized Persons Act, 78 IND.L.J. 311 (2003). Today, in land use litigation relating to religious activities, religious organizations generally raise the First Amendment free exercise clause, but the claims based on RLUIPA dominate.

WORLD OUTREACH CONFERENCE CENTER V. CITY OF CHICAGO AND TRINITY EVANGELICAL LUTHERAN CHURCH V. CITY OF PEORIA

United States Court of Appeals, Seventh Circuit, 2009.
591 F.3d 531.

POSNER, CIRCUIT JUDGE.

We have consolidated for decision two cases presenting the recurring issue of the rights of religious organizations to avoid having to comply with local land-use regulations. Analysis requires threading our way through a maze of statutory and constitutional provisions and we begin there, which is to say with the Religious Land Use and Institutionalized Persons Act of 2000 (RLUIPA), 42 U.S.C. §§ 2000cc *et seq.,*[2] Illinois's Religious Freedom

---

² [editors' footnote] § 2000cc provides, in relevant part:

(a) Substantial burdens.

(1) General rule. No government shall impose or implement a land use regulation in a manner that imposes a substantial burden on the religious exercise of a person, including a religious

Restoration Act, 775 ILCS 35/1 *et seq.,* and the Constitution's free exercise, establishment, and due process clauses.

The federal Act provides that a government land-use regulation "that imposes a substantial burden on the religious exercise of a . . . religious assembly or institution" is unlawful "unless the government demonstrates that imposition of the burden . . . is in furtherance of a compelling governmental interest; and is the least restrictive means of furthering that compelling governmental interest." 42 U.S.C. § 2000cc(a)(1). The Act also provides that "no government shall impose or implement a land use regulation in a manner that treats a religious assembly or institution on less than equal terms with a nonreligious assembly or institution," or that "discriminates against any assembly or institution on the basis of religion or religious denomination." The Illinois law, is, so far as relates to this case, materially identical to section (a)(1) of the federal law, and so it need not be discussed separately.

The City of Chicago, the defendant in World Outreach's suit, argues that the federal Act exceeds Congress's authority under section 5 of the Fourteenth Amendment. But the Act happens also to be based on Congress's power to regulate commerce. 42 U.S.C. § 2000cc(a)(2)(B); *see Westchester Day School v. Village of Mamaroneck,* 504 F.3d 338, 354 (2d Cir.2007). So the City shifts grounds, and argues that World Outreach's complaint contains "no hint that the application of the zoning ordinance here affected interstate commerce." In fact the complaint alleges that the City prevented World Outreach from renting rooms to refugees from Hurricane Katrina, and if the allegation is correct (the City does not contest

---

assembly or institution, unless the government demonstrates that imposition of the burden on that person, assembly, or institution—

    (A) is in furtherance of a compelling governmental interest; and

    (B) is the least restrictive means of furthering that compelling governmental interest.

  (2) Scope of application. This subsection applies in any case in which . . .

    (C) the substantial burden is imposed in the implementation of a land use regulation or system of land use regulations, under which a government makes, or has in place formal or informal procedures or practices that permit the government to make, individualized assessments of the proposed uses for the property involved.

(b) Discrimination and exclusion.

  (1) Equal terms. No government shall impose or implement a land use regulation in a manner that treats a religious assembly or institution on less than equal terms with a nonreligious assembly or institution.

  (2) Nondiscrimination. No government shall impose or implement a land use regulation that discriminates against any assembly or institution on the basis of religion or religious denomination.

  (3) Exclusions and limits. No government shall impose or implement a land use regulation that—

    (A) totally excludes religious assemblies from a jurisdiction; or

    (B) unreasonably limits religious assemblies, institutions, or structures within a jurisdiction.

it), the City interfered with a "shipment" of persons across states lines, which is a form of interstate commerce.

But we do not mean to concede the City's contention that section 2000cc(a)(1) cannot also be grounded in the authority granted Congress by the enforcement clause. As we explained in *Saints Constantine & Helen Greek Orthodox Church v. City of New Berlin,* 396 F.3d 895, 897 (7th Cir.2005), that section of the Act "codifies *Sherbert v. Verner,*" which *Boerne v. Flores* "reaffirmed . . . insofar as *[Sherbert]* holds that a state that has a system for granting individual exemptions from a general rule must have a compelling reason to deny a religious group an exemption that is sought on the basis of hardship or, in the language of the present Act, of 'a substantial burden on . . . religious exercise.' 521 U.S. at 512–14, 117 S.Ct. 2157. *Sherbert* was an interpretation of the Constitution, and so the creation of a federal judicial remedy for conduct contrary to its doctrine is an uncontroversial use of section 5." (Another constitutional basis of the Religious Land Use and Institutionalized Persons Act is the Constitution's spending clause. The Act creates a remedy for cases in which "the substantial burden is imposed in a program or activity that receives Federal financial assistance, even if the burden results from a rule of general applicability." 42 U.S.C. § 2000cc(a)(2)(A). But it does not appear to be applicable to this case.

If we're right that section 2000cc(a)(1) of RLUIPA codifies *Sherbert v. Verner,* there isn't much point to a plaintiff's adding a claim under 42 U.S.C. § 1983 alleging a *Sherbert*-type violation of the free exercise clause * * * . There are, it is true, other types of violation of the clause. If a state or local government deliberately discriminated against a religious organization (or against religion in general), it would be violating the free exercise clause even if the burden that the discrimination imposed on the plaintiff was not "substantial" within the meaning of RLUIPA. And if it were discriminating in favor of a religious organization or religion in general, it would also be violating the establishment clause. Discrimination by an official body can always be attacked as a violation of the equal protection clause-but that would usually add nothing, when the discrimination was alleged to be based on religion, to a claim under the religion clauses of the First Amendment. But since discrimination against or in favor of a religious organization on religious grounds is expressly prohibited by section 2000cc(b) of RLUIPA, quoted earlier, we cannot see any point in a plaintiff's pitching a religious discrimination claim on *any* provision of the Constitution, rather than just on the statute.

Having cleared some underbrush, we turn to the first of our two cases, the suit by World Outreach. The district court dismissed the suit for failure to state a claim, so we take the facts alleged in the complaint as true for purposes of deciding the appeal.

The World Outreach Conference Center is a Christian sect that operates a community center in a poor area on Chicago's south side called Roseland. World Outreach's mission, according to its home page (www. worldoutreachconferencecenter.org/about.html, visited Oct. 31, 2009), is

> to fulfill the great commission * * * "Go ye into all the world, and preach the gospel to every creature." Our goal will be to prepare the neighborhood and surrounding community for the coming of Jesus Christ and to establish His Kingdom here on earth. . . . Love will be our badge of honor and we will be empowered with the Holy Spirit to live and care for the needy in our community on a personal, one on one basis. We will train, equip and empower the youth in our commuity [sic]. Our goal is to give generous assistance and relief to the needy and suffering in our neighborhood and surrounding community and donate to other organizations that share the same objectives.

The community center consists of a single building, which World Outreach bought from the YMCA in July 2005. The building is not a church as such. The premises mainly contain recreational and living facilities. But there is also space for religious services, and there is no doubt that even the recreational and other nonreligious services provided at the community center are integral to the World Outreach's religious mission, just as the rehabilitation centers operated by the Salvation Army are integral to the Salvation Army's religious mission. Souls aren't saved just in church buildings.

World Outreach wanted to operate the center just the way the YMCA had done for the previous 80 years without any hindrance from the Chicago zoning authorities. In particular, like the YMCA, it wanted to rent the building's 168 apartments as single-room-occupancy units. The YMCA had done that without ever having been told by the City to obtain a Special Use Permit. For the YMCA's use of the building had been what is called a "legal nonconforming use." If a particular land use is begun at a time when the use conformed to the existing zoning regulations, and the zoning regulations are later changed to forbid such use, the user can continue his (no longer) conforming use without a Special Use Permit. See Chicago Zoning Ordinance §§ 17–15–0101, 0103 * * * . The "nonconforming status runs with the land and is not affected by changes of tenancy, ownership, or management." Chicago Zoning Ordinance § 17–15–0106.

The land occupied by the building had been rezoned in 1999 as a Community Shopping District. A community center is a special use in such a district, requiring therefore a Special Use Permit. Chicago Zoning Ordinance § 17–3–0207(I)(1); see also § 17–3–0203. But since the YMCA's center was a legal nonconforming use, the zoning change had no effect on it and should likewise have had no effect on World Outreach when it bought the building.

To provide single-room occupancy, however, World Outreach needed to apply for a single-room-occupancy (SRO) license, for these licenses do not run with the land. Chicago Municipal Code §§ 4–209–010; 4–4–190. It applied in August 2005, the month after its purchase of the building, but was told that it couldn't have the license because it lacked a Special Use Permit to allow it to operate a community center in a Community Shopping District. Yet the City had voluminous files, including files of SRO licenses obtained by the YMCA after the rezoning, which showed that no Special Use Permit was required because the use made of the building, including single-room occupancy, was a legal nonconforming use. But a Chicago alderman named Beale, irate that the building had been sold to World Outreach rather than to a developer who was one of his financial backers, had proposed to the zoning committee of the Chicago City Council that the property on which the building sits be rezoned as a Limited Manufacturing Business Park District. At a hearing before the zoning committee, World Outreach reminded the committee of its legal nonconforming use, but the committee chairman asserted that World Outreach needed to obtain a Special Use Permit if it wanted to continue the YMCA's practice of providing single-room occupancy.

The City Council approved the proposed amendment to the zoning ordinance in October 2005. A community center is not a special use in a limited manufacturing district, which means that no Special Use Permit *could* be granted to permit the World Outreach center to operate. But the operation could still be-and was-a legal nonconforming use, which requires no Special Use Permit. Nevertheless the City in December 2005 filed a suit in state court against World Outreach, in which it claimed that World Outreach had to obtain a Special Use Permit. The suit was frivolous and was voluntarily dismissed by the City, naturally without explanation, in April 2006. But still the City did not issue the SRO license, without indicating that there might be grounds for denying it.

Hurricane Katrina had struck New Orleans in August 2005. The next month the Federal Emergency Management Agency asked World Outreach to house victims of the hurricane in 150 single-room-occupancy units for a year, at a surprisingly high rental of $750 per room per month that would be paid by FEMA. The agreement was conditioned on World Outreach's obtaining an SRO license. The City refused to issue the license even though officials from FEMA, from its Illinois counterpart, and from the Illinois Department of Human Services all urged the City to grant it and no ground for denying it existed.

World Outreach brought the present suit in April 2006, the dismissal of the state court suit having deprived it of that procedural vehicle for challenging the City's insistence on the necessity for a Special Use Permit. In August of the following year, with the suit pending, the City without explanation issued an SRO license to World Outreach even though the organization had not sought or obtained a Special Use Permit.

As a result of the City's actions beginning with the initial denial of the SRO license, World Outreach was impeded in its religious mission of providing living facilities to homeless and other needy people and incurred substantial legal expenses as well. It seeks damages, having abandoned its claim for injunctive relief when the City finally issued the SRO license that world outreach had applied for two years earlier.

The district judge dismissed the complaint on the ground that requiring World Outreach to appeal the denial of a Special Use Permit to the board of zoning appeals did not impose a "substantial burden" on its religious activities. In effect he was ruling that World Outreach had failed to exhaust its administrative remedies. The principle is fine, *Grace Community Church v. Lenox Township,* 544 F.3d 609, 616 (6th Cir.2008), but its application to this case perverse. World Outreach had no legal basis for seeking a Special Use Permit; a community center cannot be a special use in the district in which the center is located, because of its rezoning as a manufacturing district.

It is true that World Outreach was first told that it needed a Special Use Permit three months before the land was rezoned to bar special uses. Had World Outreach obtained the permit before the rezoning, it would have been entitled to continue the permitted use as a lawful nonconforming use. But it was *already* entitled to continue the use of the center for single-room occupancy as a lawful nonconforming use, provided only that it obtained an SRO license, which it had applied for and the City had no grounds for denying. In any event, four months later, by bringing suit against World Outreach, the City chose the forum in which it wanted the organization's rights adjudicated; it can hardly be heard to criticize the organization for accepting that choice. The City then pulled the rug out from under its adversary by voluntarily dismissing its suit, by which time it was too late for World Outreach to seek a Special Use Permit, as the land had been rezoned to preclude a community center from being considered a special use.

World Outreach further alleges that the zoning board of appeals has a fixed policy of not acting on an appeal while an alderman's request for a rezoning is pending. Consistent with this allegation, the chairman of the zoning committee told World Outreach's lawyer at the hearing that World Outreach had two choices: obtain a Special Use Permit or sue the City. World Outreach couldn't obtain a Special Use permit for land that was about to be rezoned to bar special uses, and so it brought this suit. The existence of "aldermanic courtesy" is confirmed in *Biblia Abierta v. Banks,* 129 F.3d 899, 901–02 (7th Cir.1997). One of the aldermen in that case was the chairman of the zoning committee in this one and it was he who told World Outreach to apply for a Special Use Permit.

The picture painted by the complaint is of malicious prosecution of a religious organization by City officials, although the plaintiff doesn't use the term. Malicious prosecution is harassment by frivolous legal claims. * * * That is an exact description of the conduct alleged in the complaint. The burden imposed on a small religious organization catering to the poor was substantial (for burden is relative to the weakness of the burdened), *Saints Constantine & Helen Greek Orthodox Church, Inc. v. City of New Berlin, supra,* 396 F.3d at 899–901; *Westchester Day School v. Village of Mamaroneck, supra,* 504 F.3d at 350–53; Brian W. Blaesser & Alan C. Weinstein, *Federal Land Use Law & Litigation* § 7:18, p. 664 (2009), and there was no possible justification for it. The dismissal of World Outreach's substantial-burden (section 2000cc(a)(1)) claim under the Religious Land Use and Institutionalized Persons Act was therefore error.

World Outreach also makes a claim under section 2000cc(b) of the Act, which forbids discrimination against an organization on religious grounds. The motive that World Outreach alleges for the City's campaign against it was Alderman Beale's desire that the YMCA have sold the property to his supporter; there is no indication that any purchaser, religious or nonreligious, other than the developer would have been treated better than World Outreach was. In other words, there was no discrimination against World Outreach on religious grounds. The City didn't treat the YMCA better than World Outreach on *any* grounds, religious or otherwise; the two organizations were not similarly situated; had the YMCA been in World Outreach's position of buying the center from the previous occupant, it would have been treated just as badly. The discrimination was in favor of a developer on the basis of his financial relationship to a politician. Religion didn't enter the picture.

What is true, however, is that a deliberate, irrational discrimination, even if it is against one person (or other entity) rather than a group, is actionable under the equal protection clause. *Village of Willowbrook v. Olech,* 528 U.S. 562, 564, 120 S.Ct. 1073, 145 L.Ed.2d 1060 (2000) (per curiam). That is one of the claims that World Outreach alleges; the claim is supported by the allegations of the complaint; and so it should not have been dismissed. It has nothing to do with religion, but so what?

The City is correct, however, that the claim of damages for violation of the Chicago Zoning Ordinance is barred by the state's tort immunity act and therefore was properly dismissed. 745 ILCS § 10/2–104; *Village of Bloomingdale v. CDG Enterprises, Inc.,* 196 Ill.2d 484, 256 Ill.Dec. 848, 752 N.E.2d 1090, 1099 (2001). We also do not think that World Outreach had any basis for seeking damages under Illinois Supreme Court Rule 137, which is materially the same as Rule 11 of the federal civil rules, as a sanction for frivolous motions in the state-court case that was dismissed, not in the present case; and Rule 11 does not authorize a judge to impose sanctions in a case in another court unless the case merely originated there and was removed to his court, * * * . World Outreach also seeks sanctions under Rule 11 for the motion to dismiss that the City filed in the present case, but although the motion was weak it was not frivolous or otherwise sanctionable, or so at least the district judge could (and did) conclude without abusing his discretion.

So we move to our second case, which involves a challenge under the Religious Land Use and Institutionalized Persons Act to the application of Peoria's landmark law to the building shown in the photograph at the end of this opinion. The Trinity Evangelical Lutheran Church is located on property at the edge of downtown Peoria. In 1989 it bought an adjacent parcel that contained the building in the photo. Trinity applied to the city in 2000 for a permit to demolish the building. A neighborhood group filed an application to have the building designated a landmark under the City's preservation ordinance. Peoria Municipal Code §§ 16–61, 16–86. The City granted the landmark application. Six years later Trinity again sought the City's permission to demolish the building so that it could build on its site a "Family Life Center." The City refused, and the refusal, Trinity argues, has imposed a substantial burden on its religious activities in violation of section 2000cc(a)(1) because the building is not suitable for the family-life center that Trinity envisages. The district court, disagreeing, granted summary judgment in favor of the City.

Any land-use regulation that a church would like not to have to comply with imposes a "burden" on it, and so the adjective "substantial" must be taken seriously lest RLUIPA be interpreted to grant churches a blanket immunity from land-use regulation. We shall assume that determining whether a burden is substantial (and if so whether it is nevertheless justifiable) is ordinarily an issue of fact (oddly we cannot find a reported opinion that addresses the question) and that substantiality is a relative term-whether a given burden is substantial depends on its magnitude in relation to the needs and resources of the religious organization in question.

The burden imposed on Trinity, a substantial religious organization, by the landmark designation that disables it from demolishing the apartment house is modest. The building has not been rendered uninhabitable by the designation. Trinity can sell it and use the proceeds to finance the construction of its family-life center. It argues that it "lost money renting the building prior to seeking demolition" and that the building is "not economically viable for residential use," but there is no support in the record for these contentions. The prohibition against demolition could harm Trinity only if there were no suitable alternative site for building a family-life center. But there is a 50-foot-by-80-foot empty lot on Trinity's campus. Trinity complains that it would need certain zoning permits to build there which the City might deny it-but the City has committed itself in its brief and at oral argument to granting them. We imagine that the real purpose of this litigation is to extract a commitment from the City to allow Trinity to build the family-life center on the empty lot, and so viewed the suit has succeeded.

The judgment in World Outreach's case is affirmed in part and reversed in part, as explained earlier. The judgment in Trinity Evangelical Lutheran Church is affirmed.

NOTES

1.   The Seventh Circuit heard yet another appeal in the *World Outreach* litigation in 2015 and noted that the "appeal from a district court decision that attempted to resolve a messy and protracted litigation is a sequel to an appeal that we decided five and a half years ago." *World Outreach Conference Center v. City of Chicago*, Nos. 13–3669, 13–3728 (7th Cir.2015). Judge Posner again penned the 2015 decision in response to the district court's finding on remand, which granted summary judgment against all of the World Outreach claims but one. The court affirmed the grant of partial summary judgment in favor of World Outreach, reversed the grant of partial summary judgment to the City, and remanded the case to require a trial. The Seventh Circuit expressed understanding of the district court judge's "desire to end a litigation that will soon have lasted as long as the Trojan War," but also noted that "we do not think that the end is yet in sight."

2.   In the introduction to this section, we pointed out that those claiming land use regulations violated their free exercise rights under *Sherbert v. Verner,* 374 U.S. 398 (1963), did not fare well. Courts consistently found that land use regulations did not substantially burden the free exercise of religion and were thus not subject to the compelling interest test. This remains true. As the Second Circuit said in *Westchester Day School v. Village of Mamaroneck,* 504 F.3d 338, 351 (2d Cir.2007):

> We are, of course, mindful that the Supreme Court's free exercise jurisprudence signals caution in using effect alone to determine substantial burden. * * * This is because an effect focused analysis may run up against the reality that "[t]he freedom asserted by [some may] bring them into collision with [the] rights asserted by" others and that "[i]t is such conflicts which most frequently require intervention of the State to determine where the rights of one end and those of another begin." * * * Accordingly, the Supreme Court has held [in *Employment Division v. Smith*] that generally applicable burdens, neutrally imposed, are not "substantial." This reasoning helps to explain why courts confronting free exercise challenges to zoning restrictions rarely find the substantial burden test satisfied even when the resulting effect is to completely prohibit a religious congregation from building a church on its own land.

504 F.3d at 351 (numerous citations omitted). Today, free exercise claims tend to take a back seat in religious land use cases due to RLUIPA, which is intended to grant greater protection to religious land users. As the court

observed in *World Outreach*, "[i]f we're right that section 2000cc(a)(1) of RLUIPA codifies *Sherbert v. Verner,* there isn't much point to a plaintiff's adding a claim under 42 U.S.C. § 1983 alleging a *Sherbert*-type violation of the free exercise clause."

The legislative history of RLUIPA indicates that the substantial burden test was not to be more broadly interpreted or applied than under *Sherbert*. Yet, the application of *Sherbert* by the Supreme Court has been inconsistent, giving the lower courts little guidance. While establishing a substantial burden remains difficult, considering the prior lack of success under *Sherbert*, under RLUIPA courts have found in favor of religious users more often than one would expect.

3.   In the first federal appellate case interpreting the substantial burden test of RLUIPA, *Civil Liberties for Urban Believers (C.L.U.B.) v. City of Chicago*, 342 F.3d 752 (7th Cir.2003), *cert. denied,* 541 U.S. 1096 (2004), the 7th Circuit adopted a stringent test, holding that the statute required a showing that religious exercise is rendered "effectively impracticable." In *Sts. Constantine and Helen Greek Orthodox Church, Inc. v. City of New Berlin*, 396 F.3d 895 (7th Cir.2005), the court modified *C.L.U.B.'s* strict test, holding that a substantial burden showing can be met where a religious user establishes that it must choose between selling its land and finding another suitable parcel or establishes that it is being subjected to unreasonable delay. Is *World Outreach* an application of this test?

The Eleventh Circuit found the Seventh Circuit's "effectively impracticable" test too onerous. It adopted what it considered to be the majority rule that "a substantial burden is one which actually inhibits religious practice by virtue of a land use decision." *Midrash Sephardi, Inc. v. Town of Surfside*, 366 F.3d 1214, 1227 (11th Cir.2004). While less onerous than the *C.L.U.B.* test, there still must be "significant pressure which directly coerces the religious adherent to conform his or her behavior accordingly." A chilling effect is insufficient. "The governmental conduct being challenged must actually inhibit religious activity in a concrete way." *Id.* In *Midrash*, the court found that a zoning ordinance prohibiting synagogues from locating in a business district, relegating them solely to a two-family residential district, did not constitute a substantial burden. That Orthodox Jews, who do not use automobiles on the Sabbath, would have to walk extra blocks to reach the synagogue was not a substantial burden. *But see DiLaura v. Township of Ann Arbor*, 112 Fed.Appx. 445 (6th Cir.2004) (substantial burden found where, under a bed-and-breakfast permit, a religious retreat would be required to charge visitors and be unable to serve communion wine).

The Ninth Circuit's test holds that for a land use regulation to impose a substantial burden, "it must be 'oppressive' [and] must impose a significantly great restriction or onus upon such exercise." *San Jose Christian College v. City of Morgan Hill*, 360 F.3d 1024, 1034 (9th Cir.2004). *See also Guru Nanak Sikh Society of Yuba City v. County of Sutter*, 456 F.3d 978 (9th Cir.2006) (denial of a conditional use permit was substantial burden where the board had denied the permit despite the applicant's willingness to accept various conditions on use and gave the impression that it would never grant a permit). Other federal and state courts have adopted slightly different tests, but all make the showing of a substantial burden difficult. *See generally* Bram Alden, *Reconsidering RLUIPA: Do Religious Land Use Protections Really Benefit Religious Land Users?*, 57 UCLA L.REV. 1779, 1788–1794 (2010).

4.   Under RLUIPA, the "substantial burden must be imposed in the implementation of a land use regulation or system of land use regulations, under which a government makes, or has in place formal or informal procedures or practices that permit the government to make, individualized assessments of the proposed uses for the property involved." 42 U.S.C.A. § 2000cc (a) (2)(C). This follows from the Court's *Employment Division v. Smith* opinion, where, after holding that "generally applicable burdens, neutrally imposed, are not 'substantial,' " the Court noted that "where the State has in place a system of individual exemptions, it may not refuse to extend that system to cases of 'religious hardship' without compelling reason." 494 U.S. at 884. Thus, as the 9th Circuit says, RLUIPA's substantial burden provision "does not apply directly to land use regulations . . . which typically are written in general and neutral terms. . . . When the Zoning Code is applied to grant or deny a certain use to a particular parcel of land, that application is an 'implementation' under 42 U.S.C. § 2000cc(2)(C)."

Variance and conditional use permit denials constitute the bulk of the substantial burden-individualized assessment cases. *See* Tyson Tamashiro, *RLUIPA and the Individualized Assessment: Special Use Permits and Variances under Strict Congressional Scrutiny*, 31 U.HAW.L.REV. 257 (2008). But are they necessarily individualized assessments? Recall that a variance is a land-based decision that does not properly consider personal hardships. However, looking at the language of the Act, it applies to "individualized assessments of the proposed uses for the property involved." § 2000cc(2)(c). Thus, most courts agree that the variance and special use processes are not neutral laws of general applicability and that RLUIPA applies when the government may take into account the particular details of an applicant's proposed use of land when deciding to permit or deny that use.

Does 42 U.S.C.A. § 2000cc(a)(2)(C) apply to a rezoning or a rezoning denial? In *Greater Bible Way Temple of Jackson v. City of Jackson*, 733 N.W.2d 734 (Mich.2007), a general use rezoning was held not to be an individualized assessment.

5.   A compelling state interest can overcome the finding of a substantial burden. Several courts have found adverse traffic and increased activities were not compelling interests. *Mintz v. Roman Catholic Bishop of Springfield*, 424 F.Supp.2d 309, 323 (D.Mass.2006); *Church of Hills of Twp. of Bedminster v. Township of Bedminster*, 2006 WL 462674 (D.N.J.2006). Whether a compelling interest exists is a case by case matter. *See Westchester Day School v. Village of Mamaroneck*, 504 F.3d 338, 353 (2d Cir.2007) (record did not support claim that traffic concerns amounted to a compelling interest). *But see Peace Lutheran Church & Academy v. Village of Sussex,* 631 N.W.2d 229

(Wis.App.2001) (requiring church to install a sprinkler system advanced a compelling interest in safety).

6. RLUIPA defines religious exercise as "any exercise of religion, whether or not compelled by, or central to, a system of religious belief." 42 U.S.C.A. § 2000cc–5(7)(A). The act also provides that the "use, building, or conversion of real property for the purpose of religious exercise shall be considered to be religious exercise of the person or entity that uses or intends to use the property for that purpose." 42 U.S.C.A. § 2000cc–5(7)(B).

What types of activities are included within that definition? The World Outreach community center was not, according to the court, "a church as such * * * [but] there is no doubt that even the recreational and other nonreligious services provided at the community center are integral to the World Outreach's religious mission." In *Westchester Day School, supra* note 1, the Second Circuit found a private religious school's classroom expansion project was necessary to carry out the school's religious mission where all classrooms were to be used from time to time for religious education and practice. The town's denial of permission to expand imposed a substantial burden. The court went on to say in dicta that not all activities are protected.

> [T]o get immunity from land use regulation, religious schools need to demonstrate more than that the proposed improvement would enhance the overall experience of its students. For example, if a religious school wishes to build a gymnasium to be used exclusively for sporting activities, that kind of expansion would not constitute religious exercise. Or, had the ZBA denied the Westchester Religious Institute's 1986 request for a special permit to construct a headmaster's residence on a portion of the property, such a denial would not have implicated religious exercise. Nor would the school's religious exercise have been burdened by the denial of a permit to build more office space.

504 F.3d at 347–48. *See also Greater Bible Way Temple of Jackson v. City of Jackson*, 733 N.W.2d 734, 746 (Mich.2007) (apartment complex not a "religious exercise" even though the church said it "wishe[d] to further the teachings of Jesus Christ by providing housing and living assistance to the citizens of Jackson.") Though belief in a "higher power" is a central feature of meetings of Alcoholics Anonymous, they have not been protected. *Glenside Center, Inc. v. Abington Twp. Zoning Hearing Bd.*, 973 A.2d 10 (Pa.Cmwlth.2009). *See also St. John's United Church of Christ v. City of Chicago*, 502 F.3d 616, 632 (7th Cir.2007) (finding "nothing inherently religious about a cemetery").

When a religious organization suffers a decrease in membership that threatens its survival, does or should RLUIPA protect non-religious activities necessary to financially support the organization's continued operation? What about holding boxing matches? *See, e.g., Scottish Rite Cathedral Association of Los Angeles v. City of Los Angeles*, 67 Cal.Rptr.3d 207 (Cal.App.2007). Other provisions of the Act may apply.

7. Even if an act does not place a substantial burden on religious exercise, it may run afoul of RLUIPA's "equal terms" section, which provides that "[n]o government shall impose or implement a land use regulation in a manner that treats a religious assembly or institution on less than equal terms with a nonreligious assembly or institution." 42 U.S.C. § 2000cc–(b)(1). The courts have had difficulty in developing a test for an equal terms challenge, as seen in the decisions of the 3rd and 7th Circuits, which vie with the 11th Circuit. *See also Third Church of Christ, Scientist v. City of New York*, 626 F.3d 667 (2d Cir.2010), where a church wanted to host private non-religious catering events to raise money, but was prohibited by the city. The court found the city violated the equal terms provision since it allowed secular institutions to host catered events. *See generally* Patricia E. Salkin, 3 Am. Law of Zoning § 28:7 (5th ed.) (updated May 2011).

The Eleventh Circuit requires a showing that the non-religious use to which the religious use is compared is an assembly as that term is commonly understood by standard dictionary definitions. *Midrash Sephardi, Inc. v. Town of Surfside*, 366 F.3d 1214, 1230 (11th Cir.2004), *cert. denied*, 543 U.S. 1146 (2005). If the religious and non-religious uses are both understood as assemblies then the court applies strict scrutiny to determine whether the uses are treated equally. In *Konikov v. Orange County*, 410 F.3d 1317 (11th Cir.2005), the court held that requiring a group meeting for religious purposes to seek a permit, yet not requiring that of other similar assemblies, such as a Cub Scout group meeting, violated the equal terms provision of RLUIPA.

The Third Circuit holds that "a regulation will violate the Equal Terms provision only if it treats religious assemblies or institutions less well than secular assemblies or institutions that are similarly situated *as to the regulatory purpose*." *Lighthouse Institute for Evangelism, Inc. v. City of Long Branch*, 510 F.3d 253, 266 (3d Cir.2007) (emphasis the court's). The Seventh Circuit follows the Third Circuit, but, finding itself uncomfortable with the subjective nature of the purpose test, changes "as to the regulatory purpose" to "[according] to any accepted zoning criterion." *River of Life Kingdom Ministries v. Village of Hazel Crest,* 611 F.3d 367, 371 (7th Cir.2010). The 3rd and 7th circuit court cases upheld the exclusion of non-commercial uses from areas designated for economic development.

8. While RLUIPA passed Congress unanimously, a number of academic commentators and state and local government organizations have criticized it. *See generally*, Marci A. Hamilton, *Federalism and the Public Good: The True Story Behind the Religious Land Use and Institutionalized Persons Act*, 78 IND.L.J. 311 (2003). Some feared the Act would eviscerate local land use controls. That has not occurred, at least not to any significant extent. In reported cases, religious users lose more often than they win. Still, a number of commentators proclaim that RLUIPA has succeeded in doing what Congress intended it do. *See, e.g.*, Note, *Religious Land Use in the Federal Courts under RLUIPA,* 120 HARV.L.REV. 2178, 2179 (2007), opining that RLUIPA has "succeeded, modestly but clearly, * * * in not only [restoring] the right to religious exemptions from land use laws to its pre-*Smith* status, but also

broadened this right considerably." The Department of Justice, which has intervened in numerous cases on behalf of religious users, reports success as well. *See Report on the Tenth Anniversary of the Religious Land Use and Institutionalized Persons Act* (2010), http://www.justice.gov/opa/pr/2010/September/10–crt–1058.html.

While uncommon, juries have awarded damages. *Reaching Hearts Int'l, Inc. v. Prince George's Cty.*, 584 F.Supp.2d 766 (D.Md.2008), *aff'd* 368 F.App'x 370 (4th Cir.2010) (upholding jury verdict in favor of plaintiff for $3.7 million). Yet, the success of RLUIPA has been questioned. Bram Alden, *Reconsidering RLUIPA: Do Religious Land Use Protections Really Benefit Religious Land Users?*, 57 UCLA L.REV. 1779 (2010). This article contains not only a critical assessment of the claimed success of RLUIPA in the courts but also discusses the practical problems that religious users face in litigating these claims.

9.   Some commentators thought RLUIPA would suffer the same fate as RFRA did in *Boerne* but that has not been the case. The Seventh Circuit in *World Outreach* makes short work of the question of RLUIPA's constitutionality. Also upholding the Act, see *Guru Nanak Sikh Soc. of Yuba City v. County of Sutter*, 456 F.3d 978 (9th Cir.2006); *Midrash Sephardi, Inc. v. Town of Surfside*, 366 F.3d 1214 (11th Cir.2004); *Westchester Day School v. Village of Mamaroneck*, 504 F.3d 338 (2d Cir.2007).

10.   RLUIPA applies to "land use regulations," not, the courts have held, to eminent domain proceedings. *St. John's United Church of Christ v. City of Chicago*, 502 F.3d 616 (7th Cir.2007). Then again, exercises of eminent domain that are a part of a land use plan or zoning matter may be subject to the act. *See Cottonwood Christian Center v. Cypress Redevelopment Agency*, 218 F.Supp.2d 1203 (C.D.Cal.2002), suggesting that "specific eminent domain actions are [covered] where the condemnation proceeding is intertwined with other actions by the city involving zoning regulations." *See also* Shelley Ross Saxer, *Eminent Domain Actions Targeting First Amendment Land Uses*, 69 MO.L.REV. 653 (2004) Are building codes "land use regulations"? *See* Shelley Ross Saxer, *Assessing RLUIPA's Application to Building Codes and Aesthetic Land Use Regulation*, 2 ALB.GOV'T L.REV. 623 (2009).

11.   The First Amendment command is two-edged: neither prohibition nor establishment of religion is allowed. For example, in *Larkin v. Grendel's Den, Inc.*, 459 U.S. 116 (1982), the Court invalidated, on establishment clause grounds, a state statute that conferred upon churches the power to veto applications for liquor licenses within a 500 foot radius. Yet, where favorable zoning treatment has been afforded religious uses, courts have refused to find violations of the establishment clause. *See, e.g., Boyajian v. Gatzunis*, 212 F.3d 1 (1st Cir. 2000), *cert. denied,* 531 U.S. 1070 (2001). See Juergensmeyer and Roberts, Land Use Planning and Development Regulation Law § 10.20 (3rd ed.2012) for other cases. The Supreme Court has held that RLUIPA does not violate the establishment clause in the context of prisoners' religious rights, *Cutter v. Wilkinson*, 544 U.S. 709 (2005), but it has not addressed the land use prong of the statute.

Lower courts have held that RLUIPA does not violate the establishment clause in land use cases. *Westchester Day School v. Village of Mamaroneck*, 504 F.3d 338 (2d Cir.2007); *Vision Church v. Village of Long Grove*, 468 F.3d 975 (7th Cir.2006); and *Midrash Sephardi, Inc. v. Town of Surfside*, 366 F.3d 1214 (11th Cir.2004).

12. Landmark designation of religious structures may raise Fifth Amendment takings issues. How does the takings test work when applied to charitable or religious institutions? *See St. Bartholomew's,* 914 F.2d at 356–57 (concluding that "the Landmarks Law does not effect an unconstitutional taking because the Church can continue its existing charitable and religious activities in its current facilities"). *See* Julia H. Miller, *Regulating Historic Religious Properties Under RLUIPA* (NHTP Preservation Law Reporter Educational Materials, 2007), ALI-ABA, SM056 ALI-ABA 817, presenting a question/answer format on the basic issues.

F. JURISPRUDENTIAL LIMITS AND LAND USE LITIGATION

1. RIPENESS

Courts will not entertain a dispute until it is ripe. The ripeness requirement stems from the justiciability doctrine that courts in our system of jurisprudence are to hear cases only where there is an actual controversy which can be resolved by judicial decree. The facts of a case must be sufficiently defined to assure that the challenger is not presenting a hypothetical or speculative matter to the courts. *B & B Enterprises of Wilson County, LLC v. City of Lebanon,* 318 S.W.3d 839, 848 (Tenn.2010). At its most fundamental, ripeness is a matter of subject matter jurisdiction. *See Iowa Coal Min. Co., Inc. v. Monroe County*, 555 N.W.2d 418, 431 (Iowa 1996). Just as Article III of the federal constitution limits the federal judicial power to actual cases and controversies, most states, by constitution or judicial opinion, similarly limit the judicial power. Yet, courts also employ ripeness in a prudential manner, particularly in regulatory takings cases.

WILLIAMSON COUNTY REGIONAL PLANNING COMMISSION V. HAMILTON BANK OF JOHNSON CITY

Supreme Court of the United States, 1985.
473 U.S. 172, 105 S.Ct. 3108, 87 L.Ed.2d 126.

JUSTICE BLACKMUN delivered the opinion of the Court.

Respondent, the owner of a tract of land it was developing as a residential subdivision, sued petitioners, the Williamson County [Tennessee] Regional Planning Commission and its members and staff, in United States District Court, alleging that petitioners' application of various zoning laws and regulations to respondent's property amounted to a "taking" of that property. At trial, the jury agreed and awarded respondent $350,000 as just compensation for the "taking." Although the jury's verdict was rejected by the District Court, which granted a judgment notwithstanding the verdict to petitioners, the verdict was reinstated on appeal. Petitioners and their *amici* urge this Court to overturn the jury's award on the ground that a temporary regulatory interference with an investor's profit expectation does not constitute a "taking" within the meaning of the Just Compensation Clause of the Fifth Amendment, or, alternatively, on the ground that even if such interference does constitute a taking, the Just Compensation Clause does not require money damages as recompense. Before we reach those contentions, we examine the procedural posture of respondent's claim.

[I—A]

[In 1973, Williamson County adopted a zoning ordinance that allows "cluster" development of residential areas. Thus, housing units can be grouped or "clustered" together, rather than being evenly spaced on uniform lots. The developer received preliminary plat approval in 1973 for a cluster home development from the Planning Commission. The developer then conveyed open space easements to the county and began putting in roads and utility lines. Over the next few years, the commission approved the preliminary plans on several occasions. In 1977, the county changed the density provisions of its zoning ordinance. In 1978, the Commission again approved the plans using the prior ordinance, but in 1979, it reversed itself and advised the developer that the project was subject to the 1977 ordinance. When a revised plat was submitted in 1980, the Commission rejected it. The developer then went to the County Board of Zoning Appeals and sought an interpretation of the applicable law. The Board determined that the 1973 ordinance should apply. Hamilton Bank of Johnson City acquired the property upon foreclosure. In 1981, the bank resubmitted two plats. The Commission, refusing to follow the opinion of the Board of Zoning Appeals, rejected the plans for eight reasons, some based on the new law and some based on the old law. Eds.]

B

Respondent [Hamilton Bank] then filed this suit in the United States District Court for the Middle District of Tennessee, pursuant to 42 U.S.C. § 1983, alleging that the Commission had taken its property without just compensation and asserting that the Commission should be estopped under state law from denying approval of the project. Respondent's expert witnesses testified that the design that would meet each of the Commission's eight objections would allow respondent to build only 67 units, 409 fewer than respondent claims it is entitled to build,[5] and that

---

[5] *Id.*, at 377; Tr. 238–243. Respondent claimed it was entitled to build 476 units: the 736 units allegedly approved in 1973 minus the 212 units already built or given final approval and

the development of only 67 sites would result in a net loss of over $1 million. Petitioners' expert witness, on the other hand, testified that the Commission's eight objections could be overcome by a design that would allow development of approximately 300 units.

After a three-week trial, the jury found that respondent had been denied the "economically viable" use of its property in violation of the Just Compensation Clause, and that the Commission was estopped under state law from requiring respondent to comply with the current zoning ordinance and subdivision regulations rather than those in effect in 1973. The jury awarded damages of $350,000 for the temporary taking of respondent's property. The court entered a permanent injunction requiring the Commission to apply the zoning ordinance and subdivision regulations in effect in 1973 to Temple Hills, and to approve the plat submitted in 1981.

The court then granted judgment notwithstanding the verdict in favor of the Commission on the taking claim, reasoning in part that respondent was unable to derive economic benefit from its property on a temporary basis only, and that such a temporary deprivation, as a matter of law, cannot constitute a taking. In addition, the court modified its permanent injunction to require the Commission merely to apply the zoning ordinance and subdivision regulations in effect in 1973 to the project, rather than requiring approval of the plat, in order to allow the parties to resolve "legitimate technical questions of whether plaintiff meets the requirements of the 1973 regulations," through the applicable state and local appeals procedures.

[III—A]

As the Court has made clear in several recent decisions, a claim that the application of government regulations effects a taking of a property interest is not ripe until the government entity charged with implementing the regulations has reached a final decision regarding the application of the regulations to the property at issue. In *Hodel v. Virginia Surface Mining & Reclamation Assn., Inc.*, 452 U.S. 264 (1981), for example, the Court rejected a claim that the Surface Mining Control and Reclamation Act of 1977, 91 Stat. 447, 30 U.S.C. § 1201 et seq., effected a taking because:

> There is no indication in the record that appellees have availed themselves of the opportunities provided by the Act to obtain administrative relief by requesting either a variance from the approximate—original—contour requirement of § 515(d) or a waiver from the surface mining restrictions in § 522(e). If [the property owners] were to seek administrative relief under these procedures, a mutually acceptable solution might well be reached with regard to individual properties, thereby obviating any need

---

minus 48 units that were no longer available because land had been taken from the subdivision for the parkway.

to address the constitutional questions. The potential for such administrative solutions confirms the conclusion that the taking issue decided by the District Court simply is not ripe for judicial resolution. 452 U.S., at 297 (footnote omitted).

Similarly, in *Agins v. Tiburon, supra*, the Court held that a challenge to the application of a zoning ordinance was not ripe because the property owners had not yet submitted a plan for development of their property. In *Penn Central Transp. Co. v. New York City, supra*, the Court declined to find that the application of New York City's Landmarks Preservation Law to Grand Central Terminal effected a taking because, although the Landmarks Preservation Commission had disapproved a plan for a 50-story office building above the terminal, the property owners had not sought approval for any other plan, and it therefore was not clear whether the Commission would deny approval for all uses that would enable the plaintiffs to derive economic benefit from the property.

Respondent's claim is in a posture similar to the claims the Court held premature in *Hodel*. Respondent has submitted a plan for developing its property, and thus has passed beyond the *Agins* threshold. But, like the *Hodel* plaintiffs, respondent did not then seek variances that would have allowed it to develop the property according to its proposed plat, notwithstanding the Commission's finding that the plat did not comply with the zoning ordinance and subdivision regulations. It appears that variances could have been granted to resolve at least five of the Commission's eight objections to the plat. The Board of Zoning Appeals had the power to grant certain variances from the zoning ordinance, including the ordinance's density requirements and its restriction on placing units on land with slopes having a grade in excess of 25%. The Commission had the power to grant variances from the subdivision regulations, including the cul-de-sac, road grade, and frontage requirements. Indeed, the Temple Hills Committee had recommended that the Commission grant variances from those regulations. Nevertheless, respondent did not seek variances from either the Board or the Commission.

* * *

Indeed, in a letter to the Commission written shortly before its June 18, 1981, meeting to consider the preliminary sketch, respondent took the position that it would not request variances from the Commission until *after* the Commission approved the proposed plat:

[Respondent] stands ready to work with the Planning Commission concerning the necessary variances. Until the initial sketch is renewed, however, and the developer has an opportunity to do detailed engineering work it is impossible to determine the exact nature of any variances that may be needed.

The Commission's regulations clearly indicated that unless a developer applied for a variance in writing and upon notice to other property owners, "any condition shown on the plat which would require a variance will constitute grounds for disapproval of the plat." Thus, in the face of respondent's refusal to follow the procedures for requesting a variance, and its refusal to provide specific information about the variances it would require, respondent hardly can maintain that the Commission's disapproval of the preliminary plat was equivalent to a final decision that no variances would be granted.

As in *Hodel, Agins,* and *Penn Central,* then, respondent has not yet obtained a final decision regarding how it will be allowed to develop its property. Our reluctance to examine taking claims until such a final decision has been made is compelled by the very nature of the inquiry required by the Just Compensation Clause. Although "[t]he question of what constitutes a 'taking' for the purposes of the Fifth Amendment has proved to be a problem of considerable difficulty," *Penn Central Transp. Co. v. New York City*, 438 U.S., at 123, this Court consistently has indicated that among the factors of particular significance in the inquiry are the economic impact of the challenged action and the extent to which it interferes with reasonable investment-backed expectations. * * * Those factors simply cannot be evaluated until the administrative agency has arrived at a final, definitive position regarding how it will apply the regulations at issue to the particular land in question.

* * *

Respondent asserts that it should not be required to seek variances from the regulations because its suit is predicated upon 42 U.S.C. § 1983, and there is no requirement that a plaintiff exhaust administrative remedies before bringing a § 1983 action. *Patsy v. Florida Board of Regents*, 457 U.S. 496 (1982). The question whether administrative remedies must be exhausted is conceptually distinct, however, from the question whether an administrative action must be final before it is judicially reviewable. *See FTC v. Standard Oil Co.*, 449 U.S. 232, 243 (1980); *Bethlehem Steel Corp. v. EPA*, 669 F.2d 903, 908 (C.A.3 1982). *See generally*, C. Wright, A. Miller & E. Cooper, *Federal Practice and Procedure* § 3532.6 (1984). While the policies underlying the two concepts often overlap, the finality requirement is concerned with whether the initial decision-maker has arrived at a definitive position on the issue that inflicts an actual, concrete injury; the exhaustion requirement generally refers to administrative and judicial procedures by which an injured party may seek review of an adverse decision and obtain a remedy if the decision is found to be unlawful or otherwise inappropriate. *Patsy* concerned the latter, not the former.

The difference is best illustrated by comparing the procedure for seeking a variance with the procedures that, under *Patsy,* respondent would not be required to exhaust. While it appears that the State provides procedures by which an aggrieved property owner may seek a declaratory judgment regarding the validity of zoning and planning actions taken by county authorities, see *Fallin v. Knox County Bd. of Comm'rs*, 656 S.W.2d 338 (Tenn.1983); Tenn.Code Ann. §§ 27–8–101, 27–9–101 to 27–9–113, and 29–14–101 to 29–14–113 (1980 and Supp.1984), respondent would not be required to resort to those procedures before bringing its § 1983 action, because those procedures clearly are remedial. Similarly, respondent would not be required to appeal the Commission's rejection of the preliminary plat to the Board of Zoning Appeals, because the Board was empowered, at most, to review that rejection, not to participate in the Commission's decision-making.

Resort to those procedures would result in a judgment whether the Commission's actions violated any of respondent's rights. In contrast, resort to the procedure for obtaining variances would result in a conclusive determination by the Commission whether it would allow respondent to develop the subdivision in the manner respondent proposed. The Commission's refusal to approve the preliminary plat does not determine that issue; it prevents respondent from developing its subdivision without obtaining the necessary variances, but leaves open the possibility that respondent may develop the subdivision according to its plat after obtaining the variances. In short, the Commission's denial of approval does not conclusively determine whether respondent will be denied all reasonable beneficial use of its property, and therefore is not a final, reviewable decision.

B

A second reason the taking claim is not yet ripe is that respondent did not seek compensation through the procedures the State has provided for doing so. The Fifth Amendment does not proscribe the taking of property; it proscribes taking without just compensation. Nor does the Fifth Amendment require that just compensation be paid in advance of, or contemporaneously with, the taking; all that is required is that a " 'reasonable, certain and adequate provision for obtaining compensation' " exist at the time of the taking. If the government has provided an adequate process for obtaining compensation, and if resort to that process "yield[s] just compensation," then the property owner "has no claim against the Government for a taking." Thus, we have held that taking claims against the Federal Government are premature until the property owner has availed itself of the process provided by the Tucker Act, 28 U.S.C. § 1491. Similarly, if a State provides an adequate procedure for seeking just compensation, the property owner cannot claim a violation of the Just Compensation Clause until it has used the procedure and been denied just compensation.

* * *

Under Tennessee law, a property owner may bring an inverse condemnation action to obtain just compensation for an alleged taking of property under certain circumstances. Tenn.Code Ann. § 29–16–123 (1980). The statutory scheme for eminent domain proceedings outlines the procedures by which government entities must exercise the right of eminent domain. The State is prohibited from "enter[ing] upon [condemned] land" until these procedures have been utilized and compensation has been paid the owner, but if a government entity does take possession of the land without following the required procedures,

> the owner of such land may petition for a jury of inquest, in which case the same proceedings may be had, as near as may be, as hereinbefore provided; or he may sue for damages in the ordinary way * * * . § 29–16–123.

The Tennessee state courts have interpreted § 29–16–123 to allow recovery through inverse condemnation where the "taking" is effected by restrictive zoning laws or development regulations. *See Davis v. Metropolitan Gov't of Nashville*, 620 S.W.2d 532, 533–534 (Tenn.App.1981); *Speight v. Lockhart*, 524 S.W.2d 249 (Tenn.App.1975). Respondent has not shown that the inverse condemnation procedure is unavailable or inadequate, and until it has utilized that procedure, its taking claim is premature.

V

In sum, respondent's claim is premature, whether it is analyzed as a deprivation of property without due process under the Fourteenth Amendment, or as a taking under the Just Compensation Clause of the Fifth Amendment. We therefore reverse the judgment of the Court of Appeals and remand the case for further proceedings consistent with this opinion.

It is so ordered.

JUSTICE BRENNAN, with whom JUSTICE MARSHALL joins, concurring. [omitted]

JUSTICE WHITE dissents from the holding that the issues in this case are not ripe for decision at this time.

[JUSTICE STEVENS' concurring opinion is omitted.]

NOTES

1.   The finality requirement is concerned with whether an official, such as a zoning enforcement officer or a board has arrived at a decision that inflicts injury. *Town of Orangetown v. Magee*, 665 N.E.2d 1061, 1067 (N.Y.1996). If the official or board indicates that more information is needed or that modifications in the development plan might suffice for approval, the decision is not final. *Town of Riverhead v. Central Pine Barrens Joint Planning & Policy*

Comm'n, 71 A.D.3d 679, 896 N.Y.S.2d 382 (App.Div.2010) (case unripe where petitioners had failed to provide information requested by commission and had refused to participate in commission's review process).

What more could Hamilton Bank have done to resolve its conflict with the commission? After all that was done, how likely is it that a variance would have been granted? The safe answer from the point of view of the landowner is to apply for a variance if one is available. Likelihood of success is not the test. An expectation that the variance will not be granted due to perceived hostility from city authorities does not excuse one from applying. Still, the rule is not absolute. The Court has said that "useless" and "futile" efforts are not required to make a case ripe. *MacDonald, Sommer & Frates v. Yolo County*, 477 U.S. 340, 353, n.8 (1986). In *Lucas*, the state beachfront management act contained no variance process and the Council stipulated that had Lucas applied for a waiver of the setback, it would not have granted his request. Since it would have been "pointless" to ask, the Court said he did not need to do so.

2. How many times does one have to ask for approval? Recall in *Penn Central* the Court said that denial of proposals for 55 and 53 story towers did not mean that the Commission would not allow anything to be built in the airspace. Does that mean the Railroad should have dropped its request to 40 stories? To 25 stories? In *Palazzolo v. Rhode Island*, 533 U.S. 606 (2001), the landowner twice was denied a permit to fill wetlands. The Court found the state's rejections made it clear that the state would not permit any development activity in its wetlands. Thus, the Court concluded that no further applications were needed. The case was ripe. At a minimum, courts say the decisionmakers ought to have the opportunity to review at least one reasonable or meaningful development proposal, hardly a definitive standard. Note to landowner: get it in writing. *National Advertising Co. v. City of Miami*, 402 F.3d 1329 (11th Cir.2005), *cert. denied*, 546 U.S. 1170 (2006) (oral denial of a permit by an assistant zoning clerk is not a final decision for ripeness purposes).

3. Even if there is no administrative process to follow, there is always the possibility of obtaining a rezoning. Must one seek legislative relief? Generally, no. But, assume the existing zoning classification of a parcel of property was enacted decades ago, and, though reasonable then, changed conditions in the area make the permitted uses highly unattractive at present. Assume also that use variances are not permitted by state law. Should the legislative body get a chance to correct the zoning of the parcel before being dragged into court?

4. The final decision rule of *Williamson County,* a formidable hurdle for litigants, has not been well received by property owners and has been criticized by some commentators. *See* Thomas E. Roberts, *Ripeness and Forum Selection in Fifth Amendment Takings Litigation*, 11 J.LAND USE & ENVTL.L. 37 (1995); Michael M. Berger, *The "Ripeness" Mess in Federal Land Use Cases, or How the Supreme Court Converted Federal Judges into Fruit Peddlers*, Chapter 7, Inst. on Plan., Zoning, and Eminent Domain (1991). *Lucas* and *Palazzolo* show that final decision ripeness can be met. But, if there is uncertainty as to what

is permitted, a claim is apt to be unripe. What message does that send to regulators? Professor Thomas W. Merrill suggests one possible solution to the ripeness mess in his article, *Anticipatory Remedies for Takings*, 128 HARV.L.REV. 1630 (2015). His anticipatory remedies proposal is addressed primarily to regulatory takings claims and encourages courts to principally use the declaratory judgment remedy to "resolve the antecedent question of whether the government action constitutes a taking" while leaving the actual award of just compensation to the appropriate compensatory court. Professor Merrill's article is also a helpful guide to understanding the procedural complexity in takings cases.

5.   The second prong of *Williamson County,* that compensation must be sought in state court to render a federal claim ripe, is even more unpopular in the development community than the final decision prong. The Fifth Amendment does not proscribe the taking of property, only the taking without compensation. But why is the burden on the property owner to bring suit asking for money in order for the cause of action to arise? Why isn't a demand letter to the governmental entity sufficient?

6.   *Williamson County* holds that a property owner is subject to this second prong if the state has an adequate process for obtaining compensation. At the time of the *Williamson County* decision, some states did not provide a compensation remedy. Yet, as we discussed above, two years after *Williamson County* the Court in *First English* interpreted the Fifth Amendment as requiring compensation. From that point on, all states had to provide a compensation remedy. *See Schnuck v. City of Santa Monica*, 935 F.2d 171, 173 (9th Cir.1991). Despite the theoretical availability of a remedy, what if the state courts are hostile to takings claims? Can the property owner then sue in federal court? *Sinaloa Lake Owners Ass'n v. City of Simi Valley*, 882 F.2d 1398, 1403 (9th Cir.1989), *cert. denied*, 494 U.S. 1016 (1990) (rejecting argument that delay and hostility rendered the state process inadequate). What if the state's highest court has recently rejected a takings claim "on all fours" with your claim?

7.   The collective law from *Lingle, First English,* and *Williamson County* is that (1) a challenge to the validity of a law must be brought under the due process clause, (2) a takings claim concedes the validity of a law but claims it goes too far or physically exacts property without justification, (3) the remedy for a Fifth Amendment taking is compensation, and (4) a claimant must seek compensation in state court before filing suit in federal court. How definitive are these?

Are these ripeness requirements jurisdictional or prudential? If jurisdictional, they are non-waivable and can be raised by a party at any time or by the court *sua sponte*. If prudential, they can be waived. The Supreme Court has said on a number of occasions that *Williamson County*'s requirements are prudential. *See, e.g., Lucas* at 1010–13. *See also Guggenheim v. City of Goleta*, 638 F.3d 1111 (9th Cir.2010 en banc), *cert. denied*, 2011 WL 884881 (2011), discussing the issue in depth, and finding sufficient steps taken in state court to waive an additional state court suit. Some aspect of ripeness is clearly jurisdictional (recall the case or controversy requirement of Art. III), yet there is disagreement and confusion in the courts as to when a ripeness issue is jurisdictional and when it is prudential. *See Snaza v. City of Saint Paul*, 548 F.3d 1178 (8th Cir.2008) (Prong 2 is jurisdictional and not waived when city removes case to federal court); *Adam Bros. Farming, Inc. v. County of Santa Barbara*, 604 F.3d 1142 (9th Cir.2010) (waiver of Prong 2 by county in case removed by county due to its failure to raise issue in federal district court).

In cases like *Adam Brothers*, cited above, the plaintiff files for compensation in state court as *Williamson County* requires. The government defendant removes the case to federal court and then moves for dismissal claiming the plaintiff's claim is unripe for not having sued in state court. How can this happen? Is this an abuse of process by the government, or, put another way, an argument you could make in court with a straight face?

8.   Is it misleading to label prong two a matter of "ripeness" since taking the step precludes a subsequent suit in federal court? Rather than ripe, the claim is rotten. After all, every law student learns in the first year civil procedure course that one cannot normally litigate a claim twice. When a property owner seeks compensation from the state court as *Williamson County* demands and the state court finds no taking, or finds a taking but awards compensation in an amount deemed unsatisfactory, standard rules of issue and claim preclusion along with the federal full faith and credit statute bar a subsequent action in federal court. Numerous lower federal courts had so held, and, in 2005, a unanimous Court confirmed this rule *in San Remo Hotel, L.P. v. City and County of San Francisco*, 545 U.S. 323 (2005).

> The continuing vitality of the state compensation requirement is in some doubt. Four justices issued a concurring opinion in *San Remo*, indicating dissatisfaction with it. *Williamson County*'s interpretation of the Fifth Amendment, while defensible, is not unassailable. It is defensible in that while a federal forum is denied, such denial does not violate the constitution. Our dual system presumes state court competency. Furthermore, state courts have greater experience in land use matters than federal courts, and they are interpreting their own law.

> On the other hand, neither the language of the Fifth Amendment nor the rationale of inverse condemnation compels the conclusion that compensation must first be sought from the state by way of litigation. The cause of action could be said to arise when the action complained of is final under prong one of *Williamson County*, or the Court could modify the prong two rule to say that the cause of action arises when the property owner simply demands compensation and the state refuses to pay. Practically it may not matter since those few claimants who manage to get to federal court seem to fare as poorly there as takings claimants do in state court.

Juergensmeyer and Roberts, Land Use Planning and Development Regulation Law, § 10.10 (3rd ed.2012) (footnotes omitted and some citations moved to text).

9.   Courts draw a line between facial and as applied challenges, applying the finality and exhaustion requirements only to the latter. Since a facial claim asserts that the mere existence of a law injures the person, questions of finality and exhaustion are irrelevant. An example is a challenge to a billboard amortization ordinance where the billboard companies suffer an immediate harm upon passage of the ordinance. *See Capital Outdoor Advertising, Inc. v. City of Raleigh*, 446 S.E.2d 289 (N.C.1994). The distinction between facial and as applied claims is often not clear cut, and courts are alert to efforts to characterize as applied challenges as facial in order to avoid finality and exhaustion requirements. *See Hendee v. Putnam Township*, 786 N.W.2d 521, 529 (Mich.2010).

10.   Exhaustion of remedies is required in an as applied case. If an appeal is allowed from an adverse decision of the zoning enforcement officer to the board of adjustment, that path must be pursued. If a further appeal may be taken to the local legislative body, which then sits as a superior administrative body, it too must be followed. In addition, if, as is most often the case, a variance procedure is available, one must be requested. While the exhaustion demanded relates to administrative remedies, in some cases courts have held that a plaintiff must seek legislative relief such as a zoning amendment to establish a ripe claim. A rezoning request may be required when the city has had no opportunity to consider the type of development a landowner wishes to pursue or faces an out-of-date ordinance that ought to be considered for repeal or change. *Hendee v. Putnam Township*, 786 N.W.2d 521 (Mich.2010).

A few cases illustrate application of the ripeness doctrine:

Example 1: In Tartre v. City of Poway, 2010 WL 2477863 (Cal.App.2010), the plaintiffs constructed a fence across a stream without seeking permission from the city. Shortly thereafter, the city notified the Tartres that their land was within a designated flood plain for which a permit was required. Rather than seek a permit, the Tartres disputed the location of the flood plain boundary with the floodplain administrator and, after her adverse decision, appealed to the city council. The council affirmed the administrator's decision, and plaintiffs filed suit contending the city had misapplied its ordinance. The city claimed that the case was unripe due to the plaintiffs' failure to exhaust administrative remedies, namely seeking a permit. The court found the claim ripe. The Tartres had used the procedures to obtain a definitive decision from the city that their land was within the boundary. That was enough. They did not need to seek a permit if their claim that they were exempt from the requirement prevailed. In fact, to have applied for a permit may have resulted in a waiver of their boundary claim.

Example 2: A developer unsuccessfully sought a rezoning of agriculturally zoned land to planned unit development for a 95 unit residential subdivision. The developer sought a variance, which was likewise denied. While administrative proceedings were in progress on the 95 unit development, developer filed a rezoning request to establish a 498 unit manufactured housing community (MHC). Upon being advised by the town that it would not process the MHC rezoning request until it completed its consideration of the 95 unit proposal, the developer withdrew this application. Later, with the proceedings on the initial request completed, the developer brought an action challenging the town's zoning ordinance as unconstitutional on various grounds and in violation of state law prohibiting exclusionary zoning. When the town claimed the case was unripe since the plaintiff had not sought a rezoning to MHC, the developer claimed it would have been futile to do so since the MHC zoning would entail substantially higher density than the PUD. *Hendee v. Putnam Township*, 786 N.W.2d 521 (Mich.2010). The court held the claim unripe based on the failure to seek a rezoning or a use variance for MHC use. The developer could not simply assume the higher density MHC would be rejected due to its higher density.

Example 3: Heavy industrial use of land was found to be incompatible with an adjacent area, which was undergoing revitalization. To protect and expand that revitalization effort, the city downzoned the land zoned heavy industrial to planned unit development zoning. The landowners whose uses became non-conforming sued the city, claiming the rezoning was arbitrary and unreasonable and that the rezoning effected a taking of their property.

The inverse condemnation claim was unripe since the landowners failed to use available administrative remedies to obtain a final decision from the city as to how they could use their land. The ordinance downzoned the land, making the plaintiffs uses non-conforming. While this status generally precludes expansion or change, the city's ordinance gave the zoning administrator authority to allow changes to non-conforming uses if they were compatible with the uses under the new PUD zoning. The code also allowed the landowner an appeal to the board of adjustment if dissatisfied with the administrator's ruling. Separately, the ordinance permitted the board of adjustment to grant variances in cases of hardship. Here, the landowners did not use any of these remedies and their failure to do so meant that the city never had an opportunity to make a final decision on the uses allowed the landowners. *Molo Oil Company v. City of Dubuque*, 692 N.W.2d 686, 691 (Iowa 2005).

11. *A caveat.* It is well established that the exhaustion of administrative remedies is not required in actions based on 42 U.S.C. § 1983. The rule, however, has led many litigants astray in the filing of regulatory takings claims. *See Williamson County, supra,* at 192–93.

2. STANDING

Generally, one who has a legally protected interest and is able to show a substantial or special harm different from that suffered by the public at large is granted standing to challenge a zoning decision. State court standing rules are generally more liberal than those in federal court since the case or controversy requirement imposed on the federal judiciary by Article III of the federal constitution does not apply. *See Suffolk Housing*

Services v. Town of Brookhaven, 397 N.Y.S.2d 302 (Sup.Ct.1977), *aff'd as modified*, 405 N.Y.S.2d 302 (App.Div.1978).

In some states standing requirements vary according to the type of challenge. *Compare Van Renselaar v. City of Springfield*, 787 N.E.2d 1148 (Mass.App.2003) (while standing to challenge administrative decisions requires a showing of a special injury different from the public at large, standing to challenge a legislative zoning decision requires a lesser showing of adverse impact) *with Palmer v. St. Louis County*, 591 S.W.2d 39, 41 (Mo.App.1979) ("Whether dealing with a legislative zoning decision as here, or an administrative one, the test of standing is essentially the same.") and *Massey v. Butts County*, 637 S.E.2d 385, 387–88 (Ga.2006) (using same test for challenges to legislative and administrative acts). Why might use different standards?

Most litigation over standing involves neighbors objecting to grants of variances and special permits by boards of adjustment. Section 7 of the Standard Zoning Enabling Act provides that "[a]ny person * * * aggrieved by any decision of the board of adjustment or any taxpayer" may petition the court. Most states have dropped the phrase "or any taxpayer," or narrowly construed standing for taxpayers. While some states establish specific standing requirements by statute, *see, e.g.*, Vt.Stat.Ann.tit. 24, § 4464 and Ohio Rev. Code Ann. § 713.13, most courts must base their decisions on whether they find the applicant "aggrieved."

KENNER V. ZONING BOARD OF APPEALS OF CHATHAM

Supreme Judicial Court of Massachusetts, 2011.
459 Mass. 115, 944 N.E.2d 163.

SPINA, J.

In June, 2006, the zoning board of appeals of Chatham (board) granted a special permit to Louis and Ellen Hieb (Hiebs) for the demolition, reconstruction, and expansion of their house located at 25 Chatharbor Lane in South Chatham Hieb property). The plaintiffs, Brian and Carol Kenner (Kenners), owners of real property at 18 Chatharbor Lane (Kenner property), challenged the issuance of the permit by filing a complaint in the Land Court against the board and the Hiebs. In their answer, the Hiebs requested that the complaint be dismissed because the Kenners were not "aggrieved" parties within the meaning of G.L. c. 40A, § 17, and, therefore, had no standing to bring their action. After a trial, which included a view of the properties, a judge concluded that the Kenners lacked standing to challenge the issuance of the permit, and, even if they did have standing, they failed to show that the board had acted improperly. Judgment entered for the Hiebs. The Appeals Court reversed in an unpublished memorandum and order issued pursuant to its rule 1:28. See *Kenner v. Zoning Bd. of Appeals of Chatham,* 76 Mass.App.Ct. 1110, 2010 WL 335577 (2010). We granted the joint application for further appellate review filed by the Hiebs and the board. We conclude that the Kenners lacked standing to obtain judicial review of the board's decision and, accordingly, need not reach the merits of this case.

1. *Background.* In considering the Kenners' challenge to the issuance of the special permit, the judge stated that because the Kenners were abutters to the Hieb property, they were presumed to be "aggrieved persons" with standing to seek judicial review of the board's decision. However, the judge continued, once the Hiebs challenged the Kenners' standing, the Kenners were required to present credible evidence to substantiate their particularized claims of harm to their legal rights. This, in the opinion of the judge, the Kenners failed to do. The judge stated that the Kenners' contentions that the increased height of the Hiebs' new house would block light and ocean breezes to the Kenner property and would cause traffic problems in the neighborhood were either generalized concerns, not particular to the Kenners, or were speculative. As to the Kenners' contention that the increased height of the Hiebs' new house would obstruct the Kenners' view of the ocean, the judge agreed that this constituted a claim of individualized harm and stated that § V.B.5 of the Protective By-Law of the Town of Chatham (2007) required the board to consider, when deciding whether to grant a special permit, the impact of a proposed structure on views, vistas, and streetscapes. However, the judge concluded that any impact of the increased height of the Hiebs' new house on the Kenners' view of the ocean was de minimis and, as such, was not sufficient to confer standing on the Kenners. Finally, the judge stated that the Kenners' evidence pertaining to a purported diminution in the value of their property as a consequence of the Hiebs' new house was unsound and speculative, particularly where their alleged loss of view was insignificant.

2. *Standing based on obstruction of ocean view.* The Kenners first contend that the Hiebs' new house, which will be seven feet taller than their existing house, will obstruct the Kenners' view of the ocean. They assert that this negative impact on their property constitutes a particularized harm, separate from the general concerns of the neighborhood as a whole. As such, the Kenners continue, they are "aggrieved persons" and, therefore, have standing to challenge the board's issuance of a special permit to the Hiebs. We disagree.

* * *

"A review of standing based on 'all the evidence' does not require that the factfinder ultimately find a plaintiff's allegations meritorious. To do so would be to deny standing, after the fact, to any unsuccessful plaintiff. Rather, the plaintiff must put forth *credible* evidence to substantiate his allegations" (emphasis added). * * * Standing essentially becomes a question of fact for the judge. "[W]hether a party is 'aggrieved' is a matter of degree . . . and the variety of circumstances which may arise seems to call for the exercise of discretion rather than the imposition of an inflexible rule." The judge's ultimate findings on this issue will not be overturned unless shown to be clearly erroneous.

Here, the Hiebs challenged the standing of the Kenners by offering evidence to rebut the Kenners' presumption of aggrievement based on their claim that the Hiebs' new house would block the Kenners' view of the ocean. There was uncontroverted testimony from Karen Kempton, the Hiebs' architect, that the house was redesigned several times in order to lower the ridge height of the new roof such that it would be only seven feet taller than the structure it replaced. She also provided unrebutted testimony, supported by architectural renderings of the Hiebs' new house that were admitted in evidence, that the ridge height of the new roof would be 34.3 feet above sea level. David Clark, a professional engineer, gave uncontroverted testimony that the site plan for the Kenners' house indicated that the top of its foundation was 32.5 feet above sea level. Moreover, several photographs showing various perspectives on the Hieb and Kenner properties were admitted in evidence. Once the Hiebs offered this evidence to negate the presumption that the Kenners were aggrieved persons with standing to challenge the issuance of the special permit, which the judge concluded the Hiebs had successfully done, the Kenners had the burden of proving, by direct facts and not speculative evidence, that they would suffer a particularized injury as a consequence of the increased height of the Hiebs' house.

A person aggrieved under G.L. c. 40A must assert "a plausible claim of a definite violation of a private right, a private property interest, or a private legal interest." *Harvard Sq. Defense Fund, Inc. v. Planning Bd. of Cambridge,* 27 Mass.App.Ct. 491, 493, 540 N.E.2d 182 (1989). The right or interest asserted by a plaintiff claiming aggrievement must be one that G.L. c. 40A is intended to protect. * * * Generally speaking, concerns about the visual impact of a proposed structure on an abutting property are insufficient to confer standing. *See Martin v. Corporation of the Presiding Bishop of the Church of Jesus Christ of Latter-Day Saints,* 434 Mass. 141, 146, 747 N.E.2d 131 (2001). * * * *See also Sheehan v. Zoning Bd. of Appeals of Plymouth,* 65 Mass.App.Ct. 52, 55, 836 N.E.2d 1103 (2005) (plaintiff's concern about visual impact of condominium development on nearby wooded hill not sufficient to impart standing); * * *

However, where a municipality's zoning bylaw specifically provides that the zoning board of appeals should take into consideration the visual impact of a proposed structure, this "defined protected interest may impart standing to a person whose impaired interest falls within that definition." *Martin, supra* at 146–147, 747 N.E.2d 131 (standing conferred on abutter to challenge issuance of special permit to church for construction of steeple atop temple where Belmont zoning bylaw provided that "[v]iews from public ways and developed properties should be considerately treated in the site arrangement and building design").

* * *

Here, § V.B.5 of the zoning bylaw states that the board, when deciding whether to grant a special permit, shall consider, among other things, the "[i]mpact of scale, siting and mass on neighborhood visual character, including views, vistas and streetscapes." This language does not suggest that the zoning bylaw was designed simply to protect individual homeowners' views of the ocean from their own property. Rather, § V.B.5 addresses the visual impact of a proposed structure, or of changes to an existing structure, on the visual character of the *neighborhood* as a whole. Thus, in order for a plaintiff to establish standing based on the impairment of an interest protected by Chatham's zoning bylaw, the plaintiff would need to show a particularized harm to the plaintiff's own property and a detrimental impact on the neighborhood's visual character. As will be discussed shortly, the Kenners did not put forth credible facts to support their allegation that the increased height of the Hiebs' new house will block their view of the ocean. Moreover, apart from the Kenners' unsubstantiated claims and personal opinions, there was no evidence that the increased height of the Hiebs' new house would have a detrimental impact on the visual character of their neighborhood, the interest that the zoning bylaw is designed to protect.

* * *

Aggrievement requires a showing of more than minimal or slightly appreciable harm. The adverse effect on a plaintiff must be substantial enough to constitute actual aggrievement such that there can be no question that the plaintiff should be afforded the opportunity to seek a remedy. To conclude otherwise would choke the courts with litigation over myriad zoning board decisions where individual plaintiffs have not been, objectively speaking, truly and measurably harmed. Put slightly differently, the analysis is whether the plaintiffs have put forth credible evidence to show that they will be injured or harmed by proposed changes to an abutting property, not whether they simply will be "impacted" by such changes.

* * *

The judge found that the Hiebs' new house would have the same location footprint and setback as the existing structure, and the increase in height of the new house would be only seven feet. The judge stated that the evidence showed that the increased height of the new house would have a de minimis impact on the Kenners' view of the ocean. The judge had the benefit of a view, which put him in a better position than we to evaluate the potential impact of the increased height of the Hiebs' new house on the Kenner property. Based on our review of the record, including the photographs, we cannot conclude that the judge's ultimate finding that the Kenners were not aggrieved persons such that they had standing to challenge the board's issuance of a special permit to the Hiebs was clearly erroneous.

3. *Standing based on diminution in property value.* Related to the Kenners' contention that the increased height of the Hiebs' new house will block their view of the ocean is their claim that an obstructed ocean view diminishes the value of their property. Diminution in the value of real estate is a sufficient basis for standing only where it is "derivative of or related to cognizable interests protected by the applicable zoning scheme." *Standerwick v. Zoning Bd. of Appeals of Andover,* 447 Mass. 20, 31–32, 849 N.E.2d 197 (2006). Zoning legislation "is not designed for the preservation of the economic value of property, except in so far as that end is served by making the community a safe and healthy place in which to live." *Tranfaglia v. Building Comm'r of Winchester,* 306 Mass. 495, 503–504, 28 N.E.2d 537 (1940). * * * Given that, here, the Kenners' view of the ocean is not an interest protected by the town of Chatham's zoning bylaw, and that the judge concluded, in any event, that any impact on their ocean view would be de minimis, the alleged diminution in value of the Kenner property is not a basis for standing.

4. *Standing based on traffic concerns.* The Kenners contend that they have standing to challenge the board's granting of a special permit to the Hiebs based on traffic concerns. More particularly, the Kenners assert that the Hiebs' plan to build a retaining wall along the front of their property will make it impossible for two vehicles to pass each other on Chatharbor Lane such that one will have to back up into the Kenners' driveway or over their property in order to allow the other to pass. Section V.B.8 of the zoning bylaw states that the board, when deciding whether to grant a special permit, shall consider, among other things, the "[i]mpact on traffic flow and safety." As such, the Kenners' traffic concerns are within the scope of the zoning laws. However, the judge found that the Kenners' allegations did not rise above the level of speculation and, therefore, did not constitute a basis for standing.

5. *Conclusion.* The Kenners did not have standing to obtain judicial review of the board's decision to grant the Hiebs a special permit for the demolition, reconstruction, and expansion of their house. As such, the Land Court lacked subject matter jurisdiction over the Kenners' action. The judgment below is vacated, and this case is remanded to the Land Court for entry of a judgment dismissing the Kenners' complaint.

NOTES

1. Should courts be liberal or conservative in deciding standing? Do you agree with the rather heavy burden the court puts on the plaintiffs? After all, standing only allows a person to be heard on the merits. The *Kenner* court demands that "there can be no question that the plaintiff should be afforded the opportunity to seek a remedy. To conclude otherwise would choke the

courts with litigation over myriad zoning board decisions where individual plaintiffs have not been, objectively speaking, truly and measurably harmed." In contrast, Vermont by statute grants automatic standing to persons in the immediate neighborhood. *Appeal of Gadhue*, 149 Vt. 322, 544 A.2d 1151, 1153 (1987) (construing Vt.Stat.Ann.tit. 24, § 4464). In Hawaii, where view, aesthetics, cultural, and recreational interests have been found to confer standing, the guiding principle in assessing the requisite harm is that "standing requirements should not be barriers to justice." *Bremner v. City & County of Honolulu*, 28 P.3d 350, 357 (Haw.App.2001). "Standing should be liberally construed so that land use disputes are settled on their own merits rather than by preclusive, restrictive standing." *Barrett v. Dutchess County Legislature*, 831 N.Y.S.2d 540, 543 (App.Div.2007).

2.   Should the neighbors be content that their interests will be adequately considered since the board must consider the effect the proposed house will have on the neighbors? The problem, as the Illinois Supreme Court notes, is that "a municipality, concerned primarily with the maintaining of the municipality-wide zoning pattern, might inadvertently compromise or neglect the rights of adjoining landowners in such a lawsuit." *Anundson v. City of Chicago*, 256 N.E.2d 1, 3–4 (Ill.1970).

3.   The Kenners' only hope for standing is the town ordinance, which confers upon them an interest that may deserve protection. Had the plaintiffs been forced to rely upon the common law, the court could have dismissed their claim more easily since there is no common law right to a view in Massachusetts and most other states. In *Martin v. Corporation of Presiding Bishop of Church of Jesus Christ of Latter-Day Saints*, 434 Mass. 141, 747 N.E.2d 131, 135 (2001), the plaintiff upset by a proposed 139 foot steeple in view of her home was granted standing because, one, she was within the "scope of the protected interests" created by the ordinance, which directed the board to consider the visual impact of a proposed structure, and two, the size and placement of the steeple would be, according to the trial court, an "enormous structure looming over" her property.

4.   Common experience confirms that those who live closest to a proposed development will be affected the most in terms of zoning's fundamental concerns about noise, traffic, odors, pollution, and, in some states, view and aesthetics. Among possible complainants, those whose property abuts land proposed for development are the most likely to have standing. In some states, standing is automatic; no special injury need be shown. *Appeal of Gadhue*, 544 A.2d 1151 (Vt.1987). Some states, such as Massachusetts, grant a rebuttable presumption that adjacent property owners are aggrieved.

Non-abutting neighbors may also have standing, but the prospect dims as the distance from the land in question increases. *See Downtown Cluster of Congregations v. Dist. of Columbia Bd. of Zoning Adjustment*, 675 A.2d 484 (D.C.1996) (association of churches, three of which were within two blocks of a proposed conversion of a department store to a mixed-use building, granted standing) and *Laughman v. Zoning Hearing Bd. of Newberry Township*, 964

A.2d 19 (Pa.Cmwlth.2009) (owner of property 0.8 miles from a newly created zoning district did not show action would have a detrimental effect on him).

The nature of the proposed use matters more than the distance measurement. While neighbors living 150 feet from a proposed addition to a house lacked standing, *Bagnall v. Town of Beverly Shores*, 726 N.E.2d 782 (Ind.2000), those living 1200 feet to a half mile from proposed CAFO (hog farm) were granted standing. *Sexton v. Jackson County Bd. of Zoning Appeals*, 884 N.E.2d 889 (Ind.App.2008).

5.   In addition to neighbors, other persons and entities that may have standing include local government units and citizen organizations. *See Mississippi Manufactured Housing Ass'n v. Bd. of Aldermen of City of Canton*, 870 So.2d 1189 (Miss.2004) (granting a manufactured home trade association standing and discussing various approaches around the country). Taxpayers and competitors typically do not have standing. In *Regency Outdoor Advertising, Inc. v. City of West Hollywood*, 63 Cal.Rptr.3d 287 (Cal.App.2007), an outdoor advertising corporation lacked standing to demand a California Environmental Quality Act (CEQA) review of a zoning amendment on "tall wall signs." The company was affected as a competitor by the ordinance on buildings, but it had no interest different from the general public with respect to any environmental effects of the ordinance. *See generally* Juergensmeyer and Roberts, § 5.34. Early on courts did not grant standing to extraterritorial litigants, but today they are more receptive to such plaintiffs. In *Wood v. Freeman*, 251 N.Y.S. 2d 996 (Sup.Ct.1964), *aff'd* 24 A.D.2d 704, 262 N.Y.S.2d 431 (App.Div.1965), homeowners whose land abutted a proposed golf course were denied standing since their land was outside the village. Yet, in *Abel v. Planning & Zoning Comm'n of Town of New Canaan*, 998 A.2d 1149 (Conn.2010), New York neighbors, who lived 100 feet from land approved for a subdivision by Connecticut board, had standing to challenge the decision.

For all courts there is a limit to who may challenge zoning decisions. For example, in *Bremner v. City & County of Honolulu*, 28 P.3d 350 (Haw.App.2001), a city planner with extensive involvement in the city's planning and zoning over many years alleged no personal stake in a challenge to void zoning ordinances with which he disagreed, and so he lacked standing.

3. STATUTES OF LIMITATIONS

Statutes of limitations applicable to actions involving land use are often much shorter than those one is accustomed to seeing in other areas. In some states, one statute applies to both administrative and legislative action. In others, there are separate statutes.

The Standard State Zoning Enabling Act, adopted by many states, requires that a challenge to a decision of the board of adjustment be filed within 30 days. SZEA § 7. In some states the period may be as short as ten days. Utah Code Ann. § 10–9a–704. Short statutes of limitations are particularly appropriate for administrative decisions that deal with a multi-stage development process involving the approval of detailed plans.

The economic viability of a project often requires that construction commence as soon as possible after approval is granted, requiring developers to make substantial expenditures. Yet, it is unsafe to proceed until the limitations period has expired, at least where there is an indication that someone may appeal the grant of the permit. The law of vested rights plays a role here. Under the common law, expenditures made with knowledge that suit has been filed are not made in good faith. *Godfrey v. Zoning Board of Adjustment of Union County*, 344 S.E.2d 272 (N.C.1986).

In most states, different statutes of limitation apply to legislative actions but many still use periods of two to three months. Cal. Gov't Code § 65009(c)(1)(B) (90 days); N.C.Gen.Stat. § 1–54.1 (two months). As with administrative decisions, there is concern over the uncertainty that exists with ordinances. The California statute explains that an action "challenging a [legislative] decision of a city, * * * has a chilling effect on the confidence with which property owners and local governments can proceed with projects." Gov't. Code § 65009(c)(1). Thus, as dissatisfaction with the common law vested rights rule led to vested rights statutes and development agreements to provide more certainty, the same is true of statutes of limitations for legislative acts, where the trend has been to shorten them.

Some of the problems that arise in the interpretation of statutes of limitation include determining when a cause of action accrues, whether a discovery rule applies, notice to neighbors and whether a challenge is facial or as applied.

(a) Accrual, the Discovery Rule, and Notice to Neighbors

The statute of limitations to challenge zoning ordinances often accrues upon adoption, and as noted above, the time may be quite short so that the chance of one not knowing of an ordinance's enactment until after the time expires are considerable. This means that despite the fact that the claim may be meritorious, the law will continue in force. The possible consequent injury to the public from enforcement of an assumed invalid law is offset by the certainty achieved. Continued enforcement also may produce harsh results on individuals. For example, in *Thompson v. Town of Warsaw*, 462 S.E.2d 691 (N.C.App.1995), the Thompsons were surprised when their neighbor Wilkins began constructing an industrial garage in their residential zone. Investigating the matter, they discovered that some years earlier, the town's legislative body had enacted an ordinance allowing Wilkins to build a garage. The ordinance was labeled a variance but only the board of adjustment had the power to grant variances. Though state law required public notice of a hearing, none was posted, nor was there notice of the action taken at the hearing. Touting the importance of finality in zoning, the court held that the Thompsons' challenge was time barred, having been brought more than nine months after the ordinance was enacted. That the town enacted the ordinance in violation of state law and its own procedures and that the Thompsons had no way of knowing of the ordinance passed years before construction began did not matter.

Some courts use a discovery rule to avoid such results. In January, 2006, Bret and Tawnya Fox noticed that the three houses being built on a nearby lot appeared to be taller than surrounding homes. Mr. Fox reviewed the plans on file at the city planning office and discovered that the heights allowed in the building permit violated the city code. The Foxes promptly filed an appeal of the planning director's decision to issue the permit with the planning commission. That was too late according to the Planning Commission. The permit had been issued on July 14, 2005, and the time to appeal the decision was 10 days. Notably, the statute did not require notice to neighbors of the issuance of a building permit. The statute also failed to provide when the 10 day period began to run. The court found the suit timely filed, noting that the right to appeal would be meaningless if the time to appeal started to run prior to the time interested persons knew or should have known of their rights. *Fox v. Park City*, 200 P.3d 182 (Utah 2008).

Courts differ over whether the statute of limitations will run against acts that are claimed to be ultra vires. *Schwarz Properties, LLC v. Town of Franklinville*, 693 S.E.2d 271 (N.C.App.2010) (state policy stressing need for finality led a court to apply a two-month statute of limitations to bar a challenge to a zoning ordinance as ultra vires). To similar effect, see *Green v. City of Jacksonville*, 182 S.W.3d 124, 128 (Ark.2004), where a dissenting judge stated:

> I am also deeply concerned that the majority's decision deprives the public of the ability to control unauthorized and even illegal acts of government. I would think that this court would want to protect the ability to bring to light and to correct unauthorized and illegal conduct by government. Under this decision, a city council may now act without authority, beyond authority, or arguably even illegally, and if thirty days pass, the city council is forever protected by Arkansas Inferior Court Rule 9. That is foolish and contrary to law.

In contrast, in *420 Tenants Corp. v. EBM Long Beach, LLC*, 838 N.Y.S.2d 649, 650 (App.Div.2007), the court held that "[w]here a local land use agency acts without jurisdiction in approving or denying a site plan, special permit, or other land use application, a challenge to such an administrative action, as ultra vires, is not subject to the 30-day limitations period * * * ." *See also Glen-Gery Corp. v. Zoning Hearing Bd. of Dover Twp.*, 907 A.2d 1033 (2006) (a claim alleging a procedural defect affecting notice or due process rights in the enactment of an ordinance may be brought notwithstanding 30-day statutory time limit for challenging the ordinance).

(b) Cases Brought Under 42 U.S.C. § 1983

Many land use challenges are brought pursuant to the federal civil rights statute, 42 U.S.C. § 1983. Congress did not create a statute of limitations for such actions. To fill the gap the Supreme Court held that the statute of limitations most appropriate for § 1983 actions is the state limitation period for personal injury actions. *Wilson v. Garcia*, 471 U.S. 261 (1985). State law also generally applies to issues of tolling and extension but, as the Court held in *Wilson*, accrual of the cause of action is a matter of federal law. Most cases hold that the time begins to run when the plaintiff knew or should have known of the injury. *Behavioral Inst. of Indiana, LLC v. Hobart City of Common Council*, 406 F.3d 926 (7th Cir.2005).

Capital Outdoor Advertising. In *Capital Outdoor Advertising, Inc. v. The City of Raleigh*, 337 N.C. 150 (1994), the city enacted a billboard amortization ordinance on October 23, 1983, providing that all billboards above a certain size in specified districts be removed by April 24, 1989. Two years of frequent meetings and hearings, all attended by representatives of several companies engaged in outdoor advertising in the city, preceded the ordinance's adoption. Several companies filed a regulatory takings claim on April 12, 1989, just twelve days short of the removal date.

The federal courts had already considered the same claim against the city brought by another outdoor advertiser. In that case, *National Advertising Co. v. City of Raleigh,* 947 F.2d 1158 (4th Cir.1991), *cert. denied,* 504 U.S. 931 (1992), the sign company filed suit under 42 U.S.C. § 1983, one month after the expiration of the five and one-half year amortization period. The Fourth Circuit upheld the district court's dismissal of the case finding it time barred. Pursuant to *Wilson v. Garcia*, the Fourth Circuit applied the three year period set by N.C.G.S. § 1–52(5)4 relating to personal injury actions.

After reviewing these federal decisions and North Carolina appellate court decisions regarding the statute of limitations to be applied, the *Capital Outdoor Advertising* court held that the plaintiff's challenge to the 1983 zoning law was barred by North Carolina's nine-month statute of limitations for causes of action as to the validity of any zoning ordinance. The court determined that because the cause of action accrued on the date that the zoning law was enacted, 1983, not on the date that the plaintiff sought to enjoin the enforcement, 1989, the action challenging the amortization would be barred under either the three-year or the nine-month statutory time limitation.

NOTES

1.   Assuming the attorneys for the sign companies were retained shortly after the statute was enacted, were they guilty of malpractice or might they knowingly have waited for 5 ½ years to sue?

2.   Does it seem odd that the federal courts and the state courts in North Carolina use different limitations periods in takings claims? Note that this is a difference between the courts as to what federal law is, not a case where state and federal law differ.

Worth mentioning is that we are discussing claims based on federal law brought against state or local laws. A claim brought against the United States in the United States Court of Federal Claims must be filed within six years of its accrual date. However, the statute of limitations may be suspended until the claimant knew or should have known that the claim existed. *Arbelaez v. United States*, 94 Fed.Cl. 753 (2010).

3.   California's statute provides that no action shall be maintained "unless the action or proceeding is commenced and service is made on the legislative body within 90 days after the legislative body's decision: (B) to attack, review, set aside, void, or annul the decision of a legislative body to adopt or amend a zoning ordinance." Cal. Gov't Code § 65009(c)(1)(B). The North Carolina statutes set out in *Capital Outdoor Advertising* similarly provide that the cause of action accrues upon adoption of a statute. It happened that the plaintiffs in *Capital Outdoor Advertising* knew of injury they sustained when the statute was adopted. What happens when the injured party does not know and could not reasonably have discovered the injury within 90 days of the law's adoption?

(c) Facial and as Applied Claims

A law may be challenged on its face or as applied. "When a landowner makes a facial challenge, he or she argues that *any* application of the regulation is unconstitutional; for an as applied challenge, the landowner is attacking only the decision that applied the regulation to his or her property, not the regulation in general." *Eide v. Sarasota County*, 908 F.2d 716, 728, n. 14 (11th Cir.1990).

Two cases we have studied show the distinction between a facial challenge and an as applied challenge. In *Euclid v. Ambler Realty Co.* the property owner contended that the entire zoning ordinance was facially invalid, that its mere enactment had cast a pall over property values in the city, diminishing its property's value as well. The landowner claimed the ordinance was arbitrary in violation of substantive due process. As we have seen, the Court rejected the challenge and found the ordinance valid in its "general scope and dominant features," but warned that a different result might follow when an ordinance came to be applied in a concrete fashion. This occurred two years later. In *Nectow v. City of Cambridge* the property owner, having lost a sale of his land due to the existence of the restrictions placed on it by the zoning ordinance, claimed that the zoning of his parcel failed to advance a legitimate state interest. The Court agreed that in this situation the law was invalidly applied.

The question is whether labeling a claim as facial or as applied matters for the purposes of determining when the claim accrues. The traditional view is that the time to file a facial challenge to an ordinance runs from its adoption and the time to file an as applied challenge runs from the date a permit application is finally denied or an enforcement action is begun. *County of Sonoma v. Superior Court*, 190 Cal.App.4th 1312 (2010); *Templeton v. Town of Boone*, 701 S.E.2d 709 (N.C.App.2010). The effect of this rule may mean that laws become immune from attack merely by the passage of time. Some courts find this unacceptable and have held that if a plaintiff timely files an applied challenge, she may raise a facial claim as well. *Gillmor v. Summit County*, 246 P.3d 102, 111 (2010); *Travis v. County of Santa Cruz*, 94 P.3d 538, 544 (2004). Furthermore, with First Amendment claims, courts often use the continuing injury doctrine in refusing to apply a statute that provides a time limitation running from adoption. *Santa Fe Springs Realty Corp. v. City of Westminster*, 906 F.Supp. 1341, 1364–65 (C.D.Cal.1995) (one year statute used for facial takings claims not applicable to First Amendment facial challenge since the injury is continuing); *3570 E. Foothill Blvd., Inc. v. City of Pasadena*, 912 F.Supp. 1268, 1278 (C.D.Cal.1996). *See generally* Timothy Sandefur, *The Timing of Facial Challenges*, 43 AKRON L.REV. 51 (2010).

Cases challenging the validity of an ordinance should be distinguished from regulatory takings claims, yet courts sometimes write as if these different claims are the same for statute of limitations purposes. Thus a court may proclaim that "[i]f the challenge is to the facial validity of a land-use regulation, the statute of limitations runs from the date the statute becomes effective." *Hensler v. City of Glendale*, 876 P.2d 1043, 1056 (Cal.1994). As the California court later said of its *Hensler* opinion, "[w]hen the court speaks of the time beginning to run on 'facial invalidity,' it must be understood to exclude takings claims since in such a case one concedes the validity and seeks compensation. *Hensler* was a takings claim when the statute will run from the date of injury * * * ." *Travis v. County of Santa Cruz*, 94 P.3d 538, 543–44 (Cal.2004).

A regulatory takings claim accrues on the date of an ordinance's enactment if the ordinance itself severely diminishes the value of property. *Capital Advertising* is an example. *See also Colony Cove Properties, LLC v. City Of Carson*, 640 F.3d 948 (9th Cir.2011) (statute of limitations for facial takings claims runs from the time of adoption since the enactment of the statute is alleged to have reduced the value of the property). In contrast, in an applied regulatory takings claim, the statute of limitations runs from the time the government makes a final decision on the land's use. *Hacienda Valley Mobile Estates v. City of Morgan Hill*, 353 F.3d 651, 657 (9th Cir.2003); *Kottschade v. City of Rochester*, 760 N.W.2d 342 (Minn.App.2009).

4. LAND USE CLAIMS UNDER SECTION 1983 OF THE CIVIL RIGHTS ACT

Section I of the Civil Rights Act of 1871, 42 U.S.C.A. § 1983, is the procedural vehicle for much constitutional land use litigation. Section 1983 provides:

> Every person who, under color of any statute, ordinance, regulation, custom, or usage, of any State or Territory of the District of Columbia, subjects, or causes to be subjected, any citizen of the United States or other person within the jurisdiction thereof to the deprivation of any rights, privileges, or immunities secured by the Constitution and laws, shall be liable to the party injured in an action at law, suit in equity, or other proper proceeding for redress.

The act creates no rights but provides a vehicle which enables one to sue based on federal constitutional or statutory rights that are not self-executing. Wrongs actionable under other federal statutes may not always be actionable under § 1983. In *City of Rancho Palos Verdes v. Abrams*, 544 U.S. 113 (2005), the Court held that a § 1983 action was not available to enforce the rights created by the Telecommunications Act, 47 U.S.C. § 332(c)(7), since it sets out specific remedies. However, the Court's holdings that property rights as well as personal rights were protected by the statute, *Lynch v. Household Finance Corp.*, 405 U.S. 538 (1972), and that municipalities were "persons" covered by the act, *Monell v. Department of Social Services*, 436 U.S. 658 (1978), spurred use of § 1983 by land owners. *See generally* Robert H. Freilich & Richard G. Carlisle, *Section 1983: Sword & Shield* (1983) and Mary Massaron Ross and Edwin Voss, *Sword and Shield Revisited: A Practical Approach to Section 1983* (2nd ed.2006), in particular Ch. 7, The Section 1983 Land Use Case.

The substantive issues in § 1983 land use litigation most often involve allegations that local government has deprived a particular landowner of one or more of the following federal rights: property without just compensation under the Fifth Amendment; denial of procedural or substantive due process or equal protection under the Fourteenth Amendment; and/or freedom of speech or religion under the First Amendment.

While courts sometimes say that there is no direct cause of action under the constitution (except as against federal officials under *Bivens v. Six Unknown Named Agents of the Federal Bureau of Narcotics*, 403 U.S. 388 (1971)), and that § 1983 is the sole remedy for federal constitutional violations by those acting under color of state law, *see, e.g., Murphy v. Zoning Com'n of Town of New Milford*, 223 F.Supp.2d 377 (D.Conn.2002), that is not true of a violation of the Takings Clause is it? After all, as the

Court said in *First English,* the Fifth Amendment's Takings Clause is "self executing."

The Supreme Court has said that "the under-color-of-state-law requirement [of § 1983] does not add anything not already included within the state-action requirement of the Fourteenth Amendment * * * ." *Lugar v. Edmondson Oil Co.,* 457 U.S. 922, 935, n.18 (1982). For all practical purposes, § 1983 land use litigation almost always involves the actions of local governmental entities. Therefore, simply stated, the "state action" or "under color of state law" requirement of the Fourteenth Amendment and § 1983 are usually met, because the actions of a political subdivision of the state constitute state action. Problems, however, can arise in deciding which acts create liability for an individual official or for the government itself (or both). Note that States (in contrast to municipalities and counties) are not "persons" under § 1983. *Will v. Michigan Department of State Police,* 491 U.S. 58 (1989).

The paradigm for governmental liability was created in *Monell v. Department of Social Services,* 436 U.S. 658 (1978). The touchstone of a § 1983 action against a government body is an allegation that "official policy" was responsible for a deprivation of federal rights. In land use cases, the question of the liability of the municipality for decisions by municipal officials in zoning and subdivision related matters may be an issue. A municipality can be liable through the adoption of a zoning ordinance or through the acts of building inspectors, planning officials or the planning commission. *Video Intern. Production, Inc. v. Warner-Amex Cable Communications, Inc.,* 858 F.2d 1075 (5th Cir.1988), *cert. denied,* 491 U.S. 906 (1989).

In *Pembaur v. City of Cincinnati,* 475 U.S. 469 (1986), the Court explained more precisely when an action by a government official on a single occasion may be enough to establish an unconstitutional municipal policy. Although unable to agree on a general standard, the *Pembaur* Court established four principles concerning municipal liability in § 1983 claims:

1)   a municipality is only liable under § 1983 for "acts which the municipality has officially sanctioned or ordered";

2)   only municipal officials who have "final policymaking authority" may subject the municipality to liability;

3)   whether an official has "final policymaking authority is a question of state law"; and,

4)   the challenged action must be in accordance with the policy adopted by the particular official for that official's designated area of the city's business.

Where a mayor vetoed a zoning ordinance in an attempt to bribe a developer, the municipality was not liable. Do you see why? *Manor*

Healthcare Corp. v. Lomelo, 929 F.2d 633 (11th Cir.1991). In *City of St. Louis v. Praprotnik*, 485 U.S. 112 (1988), the Court made it clear that the question of whether a government employee has the authority to establish official policy is a matter of law, and not one for the jury to decide.

The basis for individual liability was established by *Monroe v. Pape*, 365 U.S. 167 (1961) (overruled by *Monroe v. Dept. of Social Services of City of New York*, 436 U.S. 658, 663 (1978) ("insofar as it holds that local governments are wholly immune from suit under § 1983")). The *Monroe* Court found that public officials, sued in their individual capacities, could be liable because "misuse of power, possessed by virtue of state law and made possible only because the wrongdoer is clothed with the authority of state law, is action taken under color of state law." *Monroe*, 365 U.S. at 184 (citing *United States v. Classic*), 313 U.S. 299, 326 (1941) (internal quotation marks omitted).

KAAHUMANU V. COUNTY OF MAUI
United States Court of Appeals, Ninth Circuit, 2003.
315 F.3d 1215.

FISHER, CIRCUIT JUDGE.

This case arises from the Maui County Council's denial of a conditional use permit that would have allowed plaintiffs-appellees ("plaintiffs") to conduct a commercial wedding business on beach-front residential property. Plaintiffs brought suit under 42 U.S.C.A. § 1983 and the Religious Land Use and Institutionalized Persons Act of 2000 (RLUIPA), 42 U.S.C. § 2000cc, against Maui County and members of the Maui County Council in their individual and official capacities after the Council voted not to grant the permit. The defendants-appellants ("defendants") moved to dismiss the claims against the Council members in their individual capacities, arguing that the individual—capacity claims were barred by legislative immunity. The district court denied the motion to dismiss the individual-capacity claims. The defendants now appeal the denial of legislative immunity.

Factual and Procedural Background

Maui may be to weddings in the first decade of this century what Reno was to divorces in the middle decades of the last.[1] As the Maui Visitor's Bureau puts it:

> "Paradise" is a word that takes on special meaning for couples planning to marry or honeymoon in Maui's Magic Isles. What better time for a magical sunset or moonlit walk on a tropical

---

[1]   For evidence of Reno's status as divorce capitol of the United States, *see The Women* (Hunt Stromberg 1939) (Wealthy Mary Haines, played by Norma Shearer, travels to Reno to secure a divorce from her husband after discovering his affair with shop attendant Crystal Allen, played by Joan Crawford.).

beach? What better setting than a tumbling waterfall framed by hillsides carpeted in exotic blooms and gorgeous green rainforest? Candle-lit dinners in a world class restaurant; snorkeling in an underwater garden; hiking the magnificent Haleakala Crater; the list of guaranteed memories goes on and on.

Aloha from Maui Visitors Bureau, *Weddings/Honeymoons, at* http://www. visitmaui.com/index.html (last visited Jan. 6, 2002).

Plaintiff Sandra Barker runs a commercial wedding business, Double S Inc., under the trade name "A Romantic Maui Wedding." Plaintiff Laki Kaahumanu, Pastor of Harvest Chapel Church of God, conducts some of the ceremonies Barker arranges. In 1998, Barker began to arrange wedding ceremonies at her beachfront home. She also provided beach access through her property for wedding ceremonies on the public beach.

On September 3, 1998, Barker applied for a conditional use permit (CUP) so she could continue to use her beachfront property, which is located in a residential district, as a commercial wedding venue.[2] If the proposed use of Barker's property had fallen within one of the "special uses" listed in the Maui County Code (MCC), such as "[c]hurches together with accessory buildings," Barker could have applied to the Maui Planning Commission for a special use permit. MCC §§ 19.08.030, 19.510.070. A special use is one that "meets the intent and purpose of the zoning district but which requires the review and approval of the appropriate planning commission in order to ensure that any adverse impacts on adjacent uses, structures or public services and facilities which may be generated by the use can be, and are, mitigated." *Id.* § 19.04.040. The final authority to grant a special use permit rests with the Planning Commission.

Because Barker's business did not fall within a designated special use, however, she had to apply for a conditional use permit, which can only be granted through the enactment of an ordinance by the Maui County Council. A conditional use permit is intended for uses that are "similar, related or compatible to . . . permitted uses and which ha[ve] some special impact or uniqueness such that [their] effect[s] on the surrounding environment cannot be determined in advance of the use being proposed for a particular location." *Id.* § 19.040.010. The Maui Planning Commission hears and reviews an application for a CUP and makes a recommendation to the Maui County Council. The Council then enacts or declines to enact an ordinance approving the CUP.

On June 17, 1999, after an administrative review of Barker's application, the Maui Planning Commission recommended to the Council that the CUP be approved. On October 20, 2000, a subcommittee of the Council, the Land Use Committee, held a two-hour public meeting at which

---

[2]   Barker's property is located in an A-1 apartment district. Commercial enterprises are neither expressly permitted nor designated as special uses in A-1 apartment districts and are therefore prohibited. Maui County Code (MCC) §§ 19.04.020(B), 19.08.030, 19.12.020.

some members of the public argued against the permit. At the conclusion of the meeting, the Land Use Committee recommended denial of the permit. The Maui County Council voted to reject Barker's application that same day.

On November 24, 2000, Barker and Kaahumanu were cited for "continuing to conduct commercial weddings and other related activities" on the beachfront property and fined $1000.

The plaintiffs filed suit for monetary, declaratory and injunctive relief against the Maui County Council and its members in their individual and official capacities under 42 U.S.C.A. § 1983 for violation of the First, Fifth and Fourteenth Amendments, and under RLUIPA, 42 U.S.C. § 2000cc.

The defendants moved under Rule 12(b)(6) of the Federal Rules of Civil Procedure to dismiss the claims against the Council members in their individual and official capacities. They argued that the individual-capacity claims were barred by legislative immunity and that the official-capacity claims were duplicative of the claims against the County of Maui.

The district court denied the motion to dismiss the individual-capacity claims on the ground of legislative immunity but granted the motion to dismiss the official-capacity claims. The members of the Maui County Council, in their individual capacities, now appeal the district court's denial of legislative immunity.

Discussion

The Supreme Court has long held that state and regional legislators are absolutely immune from liability under § 1983 for their legislative acts. *See Tenney v. Brandhove,* 341 U.S. 367, 376–77 (1951) (state legislators); *Lake Country Estates, Inc. v. Tahoe Reg'l Planning Agency,* 440 U.S. 391, 405 (1979) (regional legislators). They are immune not for the sake of private indulgence, but so they may freely discharge their public duties as legislators. *Tenney,* 341 U.S. at 377. Thus, the immunity attaches only to actions taken "in the sphere of legitimate legislative activity." *Id.* at 376. In *Bogan v. Scott-Harris,* 523 U.S. 44, 49 (1998), the Supreme Court extended this immunity to local legislators, holding them "absolutely immune from suit under § 1983 for their legislative activities."[3]

We have recognized that "not all governmental acts by . . . a local legislature are necessarily legislative in nature." *Cinevision Corp. v. City of Burbank,* 745 F.2d 560, 580 (9th Cir.1984). "Whether an act is legislative turns on the nature of the act, rather than on the motive or intent of the official performing it." *Bogan,* 523 U.S. at 54. The question before us, then, is whether the actions of the Council members, when "stripped of all

---

[3] Because we ultimately conclude that the Council members' action was administrative rather than legislative, and thus not entitled to legislative immunity, we need not reach the question whether legislative immunity extends to suits brought under 42 U.S.C. § 2000cc. The parties did not address this question in their briefs or at oral argument.

considerations of intent and motive," were legislative rather than administrative or executive.

"The Supreme Court 'has generally been quite sparing in its recognition of claims to absolute official immunity.'" *Chateaubriand v. Gaspard,* 97 F.3d 1218, 1220 (9th Cir.1996) (quoting *Forrester v. White,* 484 U.S. 219, 224, 108 S.Ct. 538, 98 L.Ed.2d 555 (1988)). "The burden of proof in establishing absolute immunity is on the individual asserting it." *Trevino v. Gates,* 23 F.3d 1480, 1482 (9th Cir.1994).

We determine whether an action is legislative by considering four factors: (1) "whether the act involves ad hoc decisionmaking, or the formulation of policy"; (2) "whether the act applies to a few individuals, or to the public at large"; (3) "whether the act is formally legislative in character"; and (4) "whether it bears all the hallmarks of traditional legislation." *Bechard v. Rappold,* 287 F.3d 827, 829 (9th Cir.2002) (quoting *San Pedro Hotel,* 159 F.3d at 476, and *Bogan,* 523 U.S. at 55) (internal quotation marks omitted). We consider each factor in turn, but recognize that they are not mutually exclusive.[4]

(1) Ad hoc decision making: The defendants argue that a decision to grant or deny a conditional use permit is an act of public policy rather than an ad hoc decision because it involves the exercise of considerable discretion. They argue that because a CUP authorizes a use that would otherwise be prohibited under the existing comprehensive zoning ordinance, a CUP therefore temporarily modifies and supersedes the policies contained in that ordinance. The plaintiffs respond that such decisions are made on a case-by-case basis, and that as a practical matter, the consequences of each individual permit do not alter the underlying legislative policy.

* * *

We agree with the district court that granting or denying a CUP constitutes ad hoc administration of the existing zoning ordinance rather than the formulation of policy. As the district court observed: "The County of Maui's zoning policy is reflected in the Maui County Code, and as the Code provides a mechanism to 'establish uses not specifically permitted within a given use zone' through obtainment of a CUP, the decision to grant or deny a CUP constitutes administration of the Code." (quoting MCC § 19.40.010). In other words, the Council is carrying out, not changing, the policies embodied in the comprehensive zoning ordinance when it grants or denies a CUP.

---

4   Whether an act is ad hoc can depend on whether it is aimed at a few people or many, and whether an act bears all the hallmarks of traditional legislation can depend on whether it is ad hoc.

* * *

Defendants also argue that the Council's action was not ad hoc by contrasting the procedures for granting conditional and special use permits. The defendants argue that the granting of a special use permit by the Maui Planning Commission is administrative because there has been a prior legislative determination that the special uses listed in the Code meet the intent and purpose of the various zoning districts. They argue that in the case of a conditional use permit, there has been no such prior legislative determination. Instead, they claim, the authority to grant a conditional use permit has been specifically retained by the County's legislative body, the County Council, because the granting of a conditional use permit ultimately involves the reformulation and enactment of zoning policy in derogation of the County's comprehensive zoning ordinance. We cannot accept this professed distinction. The mere fact that the Council has retained the authority to grant conditional use permits does not necessarily imply that granting conditional use permits involves policy-making. The Council's decision to grant or deny a CUP is not a derogation from the comprehensive zoning ordinance; rather, it is an individualized determination that the proposed use is "similar, related or compatible to * * * permitted uses." MCC § 19.40.010. Furthermore, the Code itself seems to distinguish between a conditional use permit and an actual "change of zoning." *Id.* § 19.40.070 (providing that the Maui Planning Commission shall recommend denial of a CUP for "a use which is substantially different from those uses permitted in the use zone," and "may instruct the applicant to seek a *change of zoning* should the facts warrant such an application") (emphasis added).

(2) Whether the act applies to a few individuals or the public at large: When the act in question applies to a few individuals rather than the public at large, legislative immunity is disfavored. * * * We have also recognized, however, that while this factor "may at times be useful, it does not always provide an answer to the question" whether an act is legislative. *Cinevision Corp.,* 745 F.2d at 579 ("Congress, as well as many state and local legislatures, may enact private, or other, bills that affect an individual or a narrowly defined group of individuals. We cannot say that such activities are not legislative.")

A decision to enact or reject an ordinance granting a CUP is made on a case-by-case basis and does not apply to the public at large in Maui County. It is therefore distinguishable from the enactment of a comprehensive zoning ordinance. We do not hold, however, that anything short of a comprehensive zoning ordinance is administrative rather than legislative. The question here is one of degree, and we conclude simply that the very limited impact of the conditional use permit at issue here weighs against absolute immunity. The defendants also argue that the grant of a CUP in this case would have far-reaching prospective implications because the Council would be hard pressed to deny a CUP to the next individual from the same neighborhood who applied for one. Although it may be true that granting one application for a CUP makes it politically difficult for the Council to deny a similar application from someone else, the grant has no legal effect on subsequent Council decisions.

(3) Whether the act is formally legislative in character: The defendants rest their argument for absolute immunity in part on the formally legislative character of their decision. Their "acts of voting . . . were, in form, quintessentially legislative." *Bogan,* 523 U.S. at 55, 118 S.Ct. 966. While this fact weighs in favor of legislative immunity, it does not in itself decide the issue. In *Bogan,* the Supreme Court did not reach the question "whether the formally legislative character of petitioners' actions is alone sufficient to entitle petitioners to legislative immunity, because here the ordinance, in substance, bore all the hallmarks of traditional legislation." *Id.* We, however, reached the question in *Cinevision Corp.* Under *Cinevision,* we must look beyond the formal character of the act to see whether it " 'contain[s] matter which is properly to be regarded as legislative in its character and effect.' " 745 F.2d at 580 (quoting *INS v. Chadha,* 462 U.S. 919, 952, 103 S.Ct. 2764, 77 L.Ed.2d 317 (1983)).

(4) Whether the act bears all the hallmarks of traditional legislation: In *Bogan,* the plaintiff alleged that her discharge, accomplished through an ordinance eliminating the city's health department (of which she was the sole employee), was motivated by racial animus and retaliation for filing a complaint against another employee. *Bogan,* 523 U.S. at 47, 118 S.Ct. 966. The Supreme Court concluded that absolute immunity applied because the ordinance "bore all the hallmarks of traditional legislation." *Id.* at 55. The Court reasoned that the ordinance "reflected a discretionary, policymaking decision implicating the budgetary priorities of the city and the services the city provides to its constituents." *Id.* at 55–56. The Court also found that because the ordinance eliminated a position rather than a particular employee, it "may have prospective implications that reach well beyond the particular occupant of the office." *Id.* at 56. As explained above, the Maui County Council's decision not to grant the CUP was ad hoc rather than one of policy. In denying a single application for a CUP, the Council did not change Maui's comprehensive zoning ordinance or the policies underlying it, nor did it affect the County's budgetary priorities or the services the County provides to residents.

Conclusion

The Maui County Council's decision to deny the CUP was ad hoc, affected only the plaintiffs and did not bear all the hallmarks of traditional legislation. Despite its formally legislative character, the decision was administrative and the individual members of the Maui County Council are therefore not entitled to legislative immunity.[8]

AFFIRMED.

NOTES

1.　Though the defendants lost their bid for absolute immunity, the *Kaahumanu* court notes that the issue of qualified immunity may still shield them from liability. In *Harlow v. Fitzgerald*, 457 U.S. 800 (1982), the Court set out an objective test for qualified immunity: "government officials performing discretionary functions generally are shielded from liability for civil damages insofar as their conduct does not violate clearly established statutory or constitutional rights of which a reasonable person would have known." 457 U.S. at 818. Qualified immunity can be defeated by showing malice, ill will or wanton conduct on the part of the official charged.

2.　Could the defendants in the *Kaahumanu* take advantage of absolute judicial immunity? The court distinguishes between legislative and administrative actions, but suppose the actions of the defendants were considered quasi-judicial? *See Hyatt v. Town of Lake Lure*, 225 F.Supp.2d 647 (W.D.N.C.2002) (town planning board and zoning board members denying landowner appeal from fine imposed by town zoning administrator were acting in quasi-judicial capacity and thus absolutely immune). *See also Jodeco, Inc. v. Hann*, 674 F.Supp. 488 (D.N.J.1987). While courts and commentators often use the terms administrative and quasi-judicial interchangeably, for immunity questions at least, they should be differentiated. But how? Should the administrative label include only executive or ministerial actions?

3.　In contrast to individuals, municipalities can be sued directly under § 1983 for monetary, declaratory, or injunctive relief. *Monell v. Department of Social Services*, 436 U.S. 658 (1978). The state itself, but not municipalities, enjoys Eleventh Amendment immunity, prohibiting federal courts from hearing suits against a state by citizens of another state for retroactive relief. *Lake Country Estates, Inc. v. Tahoe Regional Planning Agency*, 440 U.S. 391, 400–401 (1979).

4.　Section 1983 does not require a plaintiff to exhaust state *judicial* remedies before seeking redress in federal court, as the section provides a remedy supplementary to any state remedies. *Monroe v. Pape*, 365 U.S. 167, 173–74, 183 (1961). Likewise, exhaustion of *administrative* remedies is not a prerequisite to bringing an action under § 1983, since such a requirement would thwart the purpose of the statute. *Patsy v. Board of Regents*, 457 U.S. 496 (1982). The above, however, can be misleading. In effect, a "partial exhaustion" requirement exists for takings claims since the plaintiff must pursue his administrative remedies to the point where an actual taking of a property interest ripens. *See Williamson County Regional Planning Comm'n v. Hamilton Bank*, 473 U.S. 172 (1985). This ripeness rule is also applied by

---

[8]　We have no occasion to address whether the doctrine of qualified immunity applies in this case, nor do we opine on the merits of plaintiffs' claims.

numerous courts to due process claims. Similarly, with respect to allegations of a deprivation of property without procedural due process, availability of post-deprivation remedies may preclude a court from finding a procedural due process violation. *Lujan v. G & G Fire Sprinklers, Inc.*, 532 U.S. 189 (2001).

5.   In actions brought under § 1983, prevailing plaintiffs are entitled to attorney's fees under the Civil Rights Attorney's Fees Awards Act, 42 U.S.C.A. § 1988. For discussions of awards, see *Hensley v. Eckerhart*, 461 U.S. 424 (1983). *See also Farrar v. Hobby*, 506 U.S. 103 (1992) (a prevailing party is only potentially eligible for attorney's fees and the court must consider the extent of the recovery obtained).

6.   Although § 1983 does not require exhaustion of state judicial remedies, a federal court may abstain from exercising jurisdiction if the plaintiff has not sought relief in state court, where state court resolution of a state law matter would avoid decision of a constitutional issue, or if a federal decision would risk interfering with complex state regulatory schemes. Abstention arises frequently in land use cases. *Compare MLC Auto., LLC v. Town of S. Pines*, 532 F.3d 269 (4th Cir.2008) (abstention appropriate) *with Cleveland Housing Renewal Project v. Deutsche Bank Trust Co.*, 621 F.3d 554 (6th Cir.2010) (abstention inappropriate). *See* Brian Blaesser, *Closing the Federal Courthouse Door on Property Owners: The Ripeness and Abstention Doctrines in Section 1983 Land Use Cases*, 2 HOFSTRA PROP.L.J. 73 (1989); Juergensmeyer and Roberts, Land Use Planning and Development Regulation Law § 10.27 (3rd ed.2012).

7.   *Remedies under § 1983:* Choice of remedy is largely a matter of judicial discretion, unless circumscribed by Congress. On its face, § 1983 provides for legal, equitable, or otherwise proper relief. Compensatory damages are available under § 1983. In *Bell v. Hood*, 327 U.S. 678, 684 (1946) the Court held:

> [W]here federally protected rights have been invaded, it has been the rule from the beginning that courts will be alert to adjust their remedies so as to grant necessary relief. And it is also well settled that where legal rights have been invaded, and a federal statute provides for a general right to sue for such invasion, federal courts may use any available remedy to make good the wrong done.

Punitive damages are available against individual defendants on a showing of at least "reckless or callous indifference" toward the federally protected rights of the injured. *Smith v. Wade*, 461 U.S. 30 (1983). They are not available against municipalities. *City of Newport v. Fact Concerts, Inc.*, 453 U.S. 247 (1981).

5. JURISDICTION

Land use litigation typically involves the application and interpretation of state and local regulation because land use law is essentially local in nature. State courts will be more versed in state law and have more experience with land use litigation, while federal courts are resistant to hearing land use cases and have erected procedural barriers such as ripeness and abstention to avoid these cases. ABA-How to Litigate Land Use Cases § 4.H (2000). Therefore, land use litigation is typically handled through the state courts unless it involves takings claims against the federal government, federal constitutional claims under Section 1983, challenges under federal legislation such as RLUIPA or RFRA, discussed above, or diversity of the litigants.

Under the Tucker Act, regulatory takings claims against the federal government for just compensation over $10,000 must be adjudicated by the Court of Federal Claims (CFC), an Article I court. However, claims for injunctive relief or declaratory judgment against the federal government for a regulatory taking, as well as eminent domain actions brought by the federal government, must be adjudicated by an Article III court. *See* Thomas W. Merrill, *Anticipatory Remedies for Takings*, 128 HARV.L.REV. 1630, 1640 (2015). Because a jury trial is not available to litigants seeking just compensation for a takings claim in the Court of Federal Claims, some have argued that the Tucker Act is unconstitutional because it deprives takings litigants of this right. Eric Grant, *A Revolutionary View of the Seventh Amendment and the Just Compensation Clause*, 91 N.W.U.L.REV. 144, 208 (1996) (asserting that "Congress may not strip a property owner of his or her constitutional right to a jury trial by assigning the assessment of just compensation to a non-Article III tribunal that does not employ juries as factfinders").

Abstention: Litigants who file Section 1983 land use actions in both federal and state court may be subject to abstention by the federal court. While federal courts have an obligation to hear such actions, if a stay is placed on the state action or the litigant has made an unreserved submission of all claims to the state court for final resolution, the federal court may abstain or place a stay on its Section 1983 proceedings. *See* Federal Land Use Law & Litigation § 12:11 (2015 ed.). Federal courts have also recognized that abstention may be appropriate when the litigation requires interpreting and applying state and local land use laws. *Burford* abstention is appropriate for federal courts sitting in equity to avoid interfering with complex state regulation that requires the independent exercise of domestic policy by state government. *See Burford v. Sun Wall Co.*, 319 U.S. 315 (1943). *Pullman* abstention encourages federal courts to abstain from hearing cases that require unsettled questions of state law or policy to be resolved before addressing federal constitutional issues. *Railroad Comm'n of Texas v. Pullman Co.*, 312 U.S. 496, 500 (1941). Finally, *Younger* abstention allows a federal court to abstain from hearing a federal claim if there is a state action pending in state court involving the same issues. *Younger v. Harris*, 401 U.S. 37, 40–41 (1971). ABA-How to Litigate Land Use Cases § 4.H (2000).

Res judicata: All claims that arise from the same nucleus of operative facts must be filed in one action. If a land use litigant files federal law claims in federal court, all state law claims that arise from the same facts must also be filed with the federal law claims. Similarly, if state and federal claims are filed in state court, the litigant will be barred from filing claims in federal court after a final decision. ABA-How to Litigate Land Use Cases § 4.H (2000).

Rooker-Feldman *Doctrine:* This doctrine applies to "cases brought by state-court losers complaining of injuries caused by state-court judgments rendered before the district court proceedings commenced and inviting district court review and rejection of those judgments. *Rooker-Feldman* does not otherwise override or supplant preclusion doctrine or augment the circumscribed doctrines that allow federal courts to stay or dismiss proceedings in deference to state-court actions." *Exxon Mobil Corp. v. Saudi Basic Industries Corp.*, 544 U.S. 280, 284 (2005). The *Rooker-Feldman* doctrine causes difficulty when combined with the ripeness rules for takings as a landowner "may not sue for a takings in federal court until he has first sued in state court," and this doctrine would bar a landowner from filing a federal court takings claim if he has already lost in state court. Federal Land Use Law & Litigation § 12:12 (2015 ed.). *See also San Remo Hotel, L.P. v. City and County of San Francisco*, 545 U.S. 323, 351 (2005) (Rehnquist, C.J., concurring in the judgment) (noting that holding "ensures that litigants who go to state court to seek compensation will likely be unable later to assert their federal takings claims in federal court * * * [a]nd, even if preclusion law would not block a litigant's claim, the *Rooker-Feldman* doctrine might, insofar as *Williamson County* can be read to characterize the state courts' denial of compensation as a required element of the Fifth Amendment takings claim").

6. FORMS OF ACTION

The type of government action being challenged—quasi-judicial, executive or administrative, or legislative—dictates the form of action filed. Allowable judicial remedies are highly state-specific. There may be general statutes relating to judicial review, specific zoning enabling act requirements, administrative review acts, and local ordinance provisions that need to be considered. The forms of action most often used in land use disputes include a writ of certiorari to challenge quasi-judicial decisions, a writ of mandamus to challenge executive or administrative decisions, and an action for declaratory judgment to challenges legislative acts.

Certiorari: Certiorari is an extraordinary writ issued typically by an appellate court directing a lower court to deliver the record in the case for review. Since the writ is designed to review decisions of lower judicial bodies, it is appropriately applied to quasi-judicial actions of boards of adjustment. Certiorari is not available to challenge legislation. *Geisler v.*

City Council of City of Cedar Falls, 769 N.W.2d 162 (Iowa 2009). But, as we have seen, nominally legislative bodies may act in a quasi-judicial manner. In that case, a suit in certiorari generally is proper. *Higby v. Bd. of County Com'rs of El Paso County*, 689 P.2d 635 (Colo.App.1984).

Under certiorari as developed at common law, review is based on the record and is discretionary. Today, the writ is issued by right in most states. Most often certiorari review is limited to reviewing whether the board acted within its jurisdiction, committed no errors of law, did not act in an arbitrary manner, and based its decision on substantial evidence of record. Remand is generally the proper remedy allowing local zoning officials the opportunity to correct their error.

Mandamus: A writ of mandamus requires that (1) the petitioner has a clear legal right to the relief sought, (2) the respondent has a ministerial duty to perform the requested act without discretion, and (3) the petitioner has no adequate remedy at law. Parties frequently employ mandamus to seek an order directing the issuance of a building permit or restoration of a revoked permit. For example, after Pigs R Us received a permit to proceed with building swine facility as a permitted use, the town revoked the permit and enacted an interim ordinance making all uses but residential subject to obtaining a special permit. The court held the interim ordinance invalid and said mandamus was appropriate to compel reissuance of the permit. *Pigs R Us, LLC v. Compton Twp.*, 770 N.W.2d 212 (Minn.App.2009).

Variance or special permit decisions are typically discretionary, making mandamus inappropriate for judicial review. However, if the ordinance clearly spells out the standards for a special permit and the applicant definitely meets the standards, a writ of mandamus may be proper. *See, e.g., Smith v. City of Mobile*, 374 So.2d 305 (Ala.1979) (where action of planning commission in disapproving proposed subdivision on grounds that were unrelated to conformance of the proposed subdivision with regulations, mandamus was issued to require approval by city planning commission of proposed subdivision).

As with other actions seeking judicial relief, one must establish that no other adequate remedy exists. In one case, after a property owner obtained a special use permit, he was advised that he must still comply with the city's landscaping requirement. His effort to meet the landscaping requirement was rejected by the zoning enforcement officer. The property owner then sought a writ of mandamus, which the trial court granted, finding the landscaping requirement not applicable. The state supreme court reversed. Since the city code provided that any decision of the zoning enforcement officer could be appealed to the zoning board, the failure to use this plain, adequate, and speedy remedy made the resort to mandamus improper. *Muschiano v. Travers*, 973 A.2d 515 (R.I.2009). *See also DeKalb County v. Cooper Homes*, 657 S.E.2d 206 (Ga.2008).

Where neighbors are unable to get a city to enforce its zoning code, mandamus may be proper. In one Iowa case, for example, mandamus was proper against a city for failing to enforce its zoning code where the code provided that the zoning administrator had a duty to enforce the code. *Paulson v. City of Ventura*, 791 N.W.2d 429 (Iowa App.2010).

Mandamus is usually not available with respect to legislative action or inaction since legislative decisions lie within the discretion of the legislative body. *Mendota Golf, LLP v. City of Mendota Heights*, 708 N.W.2d 162 (Minn.2006). However, if statutorily provided, a party may bring mandamus to require the local legislative body to hold hearings and issue a decision for curative amendments. *Board of Supervisors of East Norriton Township v. Gill Quarries, Inc.*, 53 Pa.Cmwlth. 194, 417 A.2d 277 (1980).

Choosing the wrong action may result in a substantial waste of time and resources but it will not necessarily be fatal. Where a writ of mandamus was sought to have the court declare a legislative zoning action to be unconstitutional, the court said that mandamus was not proper to challenge discretionary decisions. Since the city had not specifically objected to the appropriateness of mandamus, the court decided the case on the merits, choosing not to require the plaintiff to bring a declaratory judgment action. *Mendota Golf, LLP v. City of Mendota Heights*, 708 N.W.2d 162 (Minn.2006).

Declaratory Judgment: A declaratory judgment action, often coupled with a request for injunctive relief, is the typical method of seeking judicial review of legislative actions. There must be an actual controversy to bring an action. Advisory opinions are not rendered in declaratory judgment actions, but a landowner who has been denied a permit or who has been threatened by enforcement of a zoning ordinance is involved in a controversy and can bring a declaratory judgment action. The constitutionality of the ordinance, either on its face or as applied is a proper matter for a declaratory judgment action. *Morgenstern v. Town of Rye*, 794 A.2d 782 (N.H.2002); *Condiotti v. Board of County Com'rs of County of La Plata*, 983 P.2d 184 (Colo.App.1999).

Caution is in order. Since statutes of limitation are so short, a mistake in bringing a plenary proceeding under a general statute of limitations in lieu of a writ can be disastrous. In *Hensler v. City of Glendale*, 876 P.2d 1043 (1994), the court threw out a declaratory judgment action brought under the state's four year general catchall statute of limitations as too late. The appropriate route was to seek a writ of mandamus from the administrative proceeding, which had to be filed within 180 days.

Injunction: The injunction action is also a means of obtaining judicial review of an ordinance, typically in an action for a declaratory judgment. If a person is violating an ordinance or threatening to violate an ordinance, an injunction may be an appropriate mechanism for review. The injunction may also be used where enforcement of the ordinance will result in irreparable damage, such as the threat of being jailed or fined. The injunction can also be used to challenge the constitutionality of the ordinance as applied, or to challenge a development order as being inconsistent with the land use plan. *Baker v. Metropolitan Dade County*, 774 So.2d 14 (Fla.App.2000). Where there is an adequate remedy at law by a certiorari petition to review an administrative decision, an injunction is not proper. *McDonald v. City of Brentwood*, 66 S.W.3d 46, 50 (Mo.App.2001).

Settlement: More land use disputes continue to judgment than might otherwise be the case if there were fewer obstacles to settlement. A major part of the problem is that there are usually three sets of parties involved— the municipality, the developer, and the neighbors. One commentator has suggested that municipal officials should be treated as mediators in disputes between developers and neighbors and that "information and legitimacy concerns would best be addressed by requiring parties who might object to a settlement to intervene in the litigation between developer and municipality rather than retaining the right to challenge any settlement in collateral litigation." Stewart E. Sterk, *Structural Obstacles to Settlement of Land Use Disclosures*, 91 B.U.L.REV. 227, 271– 72 (2011).

CHAPTER 4

SUBDIVISION REGULATION, OFFICIAL MAP, INFRASTRUCTURE FINANCE AND CONSUMER PROTECTION

■ ■ ■

This chapter will discuss the range of planning and implementation techniques used by municipalities to regulate the extension of development into new areas and to provide the necessary facilities or revenues required by new growth generation. It examines the regulatory process of subdivision approval, site planning, the official map, dedication and financing techniques for the provision of off-site capital infrastructure and the protection of the consumer purchasing within the built environment.

A. SUBDIVISION AND SITE PLAN APPROVAL COMPARED

Subdivision is the process that enables a developer to divide land into parcels, tracts or lots for sale after the land has been zoned and all applications for discretionary zoning approvals (conditional or special use permits, exceptions, variances, PUDs, overlay or floating zones) have been secured. Until final subdivision approval and recordation has been completed, land may not be divided and sold, nor may building permits be issued for individual lots.

Site Plan Approval is a similar process that accompanies an application for development approval for plan amendment, rezoning, and other such permits for a parcel that will be developed as an entirety without any subdivision or further division into parcels and lots, such as office buildings, industrial parks, shopping malls, mixed use centers or multi-family buildings or complexes. Whenever this Chapter refers to the standards and processing of subdivisions, the same standards and processing will often be used for site plan approval of a unified parcel, tract or lot. Today, most subdivision and site plan approvals are required to be consistent with the comprehensive plan and with the underlying zoning, unless the underlying zoning itself is inconsistent with the comprehensive plan.

For useful planning, zoning, subdivision, site plan, official map, environmental protection, sustainability, new urbanism, design and improvement standards and other land use definitions, *see* Harvey S. Moskowitz and Carl G. Lindbloom, *The Latest Illustrated Book of*

Development Definitions (Rutgers, Center for Urban Policy Research, 2004); and Michael Davidson and Fay Dolnick, eds., *A Planners Dictionary* (2004).

B. THE HISTORY OF SUBDIVISION REGULATION

A new subdivision of land is not an isolated experience involving only the buyer and seller. The patterns of subdivisions become the pattern of a community, which in turn influence the character of an entire city. If growth is to be orderly and rational, some control over land development, not just the zoning control of use, area dimensions and density, must be appropriately exercised. In the last quarter of the 19th century the American western frontier ended. A new "frontier" of suburbanization and speculative development in southern and western states began.

In 1928 the U.S. Department of Commerce released the Standard City Planning Enabling Act (SPEA) (later extended to counties), and subdivision regulation became a principal tool, alongside of zoning, to fashion development, protect the consumer, preserve the environment, foster sustainability, provide for adequate public facilities and services and control sprawl.

1. THE FIVE PHASES OF SUBDIVISION REGULATION

21ST CENTURY LAND DEVELOPMENT CODE
(American Planning Association, 5–7, 13, 2008)[1].
Robert H. Freilich and S. Mark White.

Prior to 1928, the purpose behind subdivision regulations was to provide a more efficient method for selling land, permitting a seller to record a plat of land by dividing it into blocks and lots, laid out and sequentially lettered and numbered. During this first period of subdivision regulation, plats or maps of a subdivision showed the location of individual lots, public areas and streets and were recorded in the office of the county clerk, or county recorder of deeds. Sales of land and conveyance of easements could then be made by reference to this recorded plat, rather than by more cumbersome metes and bounds description in metes and bounds. The platting of land reduced title and transaction costs and assisted in reducing fraudulent sales of land with conflicting deed descriptions. Uniformity was established in survey methods and boundary and monument descriptions. Real property taxes became easier to assess and collect. The public regulation of land use was rarely contemplated or enacted.

---

[1]   Reprinted with permission from 21st Century Land Development Code, copyright 2008 by the American Planning Association.

A second period of subdivision regulation commenced in 1928 with publication of the SPEA, developed in part as a model act to control problems created by land speculation and premature or inadequate subdivision. The SPEA shifted the concept of subdivision regulation away from a procedure for land recordation to one providing a means to implement the community's master plan.[2] Emphasis was placed on requiring and securing internal improvements for the subdivision prior to recordation. The SPEA included provisions for dealing with the "arrangement of streets in relation to other existing or planned streets and to the master plan, bonding of public facilities, sound engineering standards for design and improvements, adequate and convenient open spaces of traffic, utilities, access of fire fighting apparatus, recreation, light, and air, and avoidance of congestion of population, including minimum width and area of lots." Following state adoption of enabling acts patterned on the SPEA, decisions from state courts across the country readily accepted subdivision regulation as a substantive land use control device, although strictly limited to the terms of the enabling act and the local regulations.

After World War II, the scope of subdivision regulation shifted into a third phase. Communities became aware of the increasing failure of subdivision activity, particularly in the suburbs, to provide adequate on and off-site governmental facilities and services. Concern focused on the demands raised by new subdivision residents for schools, open space, sewer and water systems, parks and recreation facilities and arterial roads. City and county governments added new provisions to their subdivision regulations concerning the mandatory dedication of land for, and construction of, on-site public facilities.

New regulatory devices were added to subdivision regulations creating impact fees, improvement district assessments and utility rates and charges. Where the subdivision did not contain sufficient land to provide and dedicate on-site facilities, "money in lieu of land dedication" provisions were added to state acts and local regulations to permit the off-site development of schools, firehouses, perimeter roads and parks in the vicinity of the subdivision. As long as these powers were expressly granted in the subdivision act, the courts have upheld these provisions. Local governments added provisions in their regulations for "clustering" or "averaging" of density, through conservation subdivision, which required or authorized developers to provide public facilities, dedicate open space and preserve environmentally sensitive lands, while distributing the overall density to the remaining buildable land.

---

[2]   During World War II, almost all states removed the name "master" plan, and replaced it with either "comprehensive" or "general" plan, to avoid any embarrassing similarity to Hitler's "master plan."

These new regulations, however, were inadequate to stem the tide of sprawl that typified suburban America. Major governmental reports in the late 1960s emphasized the need to control urban sprawl as the number one priority in land-use planning. Numerous problems attendant to sprawl were cited: wasteful and inefficient utilization of the land, abandonment of city neighborhoods, downtowns and close-in suburban areas. Deficient facilities and services, increased utility and capital and service costs, rising tax rates, environmental degradation, loss of agricultural land, destruction of rural lifestyle, and racial and socio-economic exclusion were among the most prevalent problems.

In response to an increasing call for control of urban sprawl, a fourth phase of subdivision regulation began to emerge in the 1970s which went far beyond regulating the design and improvement of the subdivision and its immediate perimeter impacts. Communities began to deny subdivision approval where development would cause serious urban sprawl problems, including, conversion of agricultural land, off-site flooding and environmental degradation, and exacerbation of deficient and inadequate off-site public sewer and water, stormwater, arterial roads, parks, schools, fire, police and emergency rescue systems. Ultimately, in the landmark decision of *Golden v. Planning Board of the Town of Ramapo*, 285 N.E.2d 291 (N.Y.1972), appeal dismissed, 409 U.S. 1003 (1972) (discussed in Chapter 7, *infra*), the New York Court of Appeals upheld the constitutionality of growth management regulation to control urban sprawl through timing and sequential controls of residential subdivision activity over the 18 year life of a comprehensive plan and capital improvement program.

This new phase resulted in the development of "concurrency," the linking of zoning, environmental and subdivision regulations through city, county, regional and state "tiered" growth management systems (Tier 1—existing urbanized; Tier IIA—Years 0 to 10 years (Urbanizing and Tier IIB10 to 20 urbanizing; and Tier III—permanent agricultural, environmental and rural) tied to the long term 20 year capital improvements program of the community and the availability adequate public facilities. Statutes authorizing or requiring "concurrency" were adopted in a number of states (Colorado, Florida, Georgia, Hawaii, Maryland, Massachusetts, Nevada, Oregon, New Hampshire and Washington), to assure that development did not impose unreasonable negative impacts on the community's infrastructure. In this fourth period of subdivision regulation, subdivision controls were related to the community and region's external environment through comprehensive planning to organize, pace and phase the development of the community. These efforts came under the rubric of growth management or presently, smart growth.

Finally in the past 20 years, subdivision regulation has evolved into a "sustainability" fifth phase involving incentivizing new building patterns and design consisting of walkable mixed use developments, the "greening" of buildings and sites and the shift to renewable energy use to reduce green house gas emissions and combat global warming."

Sustainable development is an umbrella term that consists of four parts: "smart growth," "new urbanism," "green development" and "renewable energy." Together these umbrella parts are designed with an eye toward: (1) orderly, non-sprawl, walkable mixed use compact, infill, transit corridor, traditional neighborhood or center development; (2) minimizing adverse impacts on the local and global environment by preserving environmentally sensitive, rural and agricultural lands and open space; (3) reducing global warming and green house gas emissions through reduction in vehicle miles travelled and number of daily trips and provision of renewable wind and solar energy systems; and (3) reducing or eliminating long term capital, operational, water and energy costs through establishing "tier systems" tied to federal, state, regional and local transportation and capital facilities financing and planning. *See* Robert H. Freilich, Robert J. Sitkowski and Seth D. Mennillo, *From Sprawl to Sustainability: Smart Growth, New Urbanism, Green Development and Renewable Energy* (American Bar Association, 2010); Joan Fitzgerald, *Emerald Cities: Urban Sustainability and Economic Development* (Oxford University Press, 2010); and Jerry Weitz, *The Next Wave in Growth Management*, 43 URB.LAW. 407 (2011).

2. NEW REFINEMENTS

Smart growth, green and renewable energy development will be fully explored in Chapters 7 & 8 respectively. Other new subdivision refinements are reflected in model planning enabling statutes, state statutory reform and the 21st Century Land Development Code (2008) written by Professor Freilich and Mark White. and being widely promulgated by the American Planning Association. Two other examples are:

(a) In 2002, the American Planning Association published the Growing Smart Legislative Guidebook, which contains model statutes for planning and includes major sections relating to subdivision and site plan approval. The statutes are intended as an update to and rethinking of the Standard City Planning Enabling Act (1928). The model statutes "are intended to provide governors, state legislators, state legislative research bureaus, local elected and appointed officials, planners, citizens, and advocates for statutory change with ideas, principles, methods, procedures, phraseology, and alternative legislative approaches drawn from various states, regions, and local governments across the country." Stuart Meck, ed. *American Planning Association, Growing Smart Legislative Guidebook*, at xli (Jan.2002);

(b) In *New Jersey State League of Municipalities v. Dep't of Cmty. Affairs*, 729 A.2d 21 (N.J.1999), the New Jersey Supreme Court held that new state model subdivision regulations promulgated by the New Jersey Department of Community Affairs (DCA) pursuant to the state Residential Site Improvement Standards Act, were constitutionally valid. The Court concluded that the legislature intended to reduce housing costs by establishing uniform statewide standards for residential site plan and subdivision design and improvements with respect to streets, roads, parking facilities, sidewalks, drainage structures, and utilities. The court held that DCA did not exceed its authority in promulgating these rules.

C. ANTIQUATED SUBDIVISIONS

Standard City Planning Enabling Act (hereinafter, SPEA)

§ 20.   Status of Existing Platting Statutes

From and after the time when a planning commission shall have control over subdivisions as provided in section 13 of this act, the jurisdiction of the planning commission over plats shall be exclusive within the territory under its jurisdiction, and all statutory control over plats or subdivisions of land granted by other statutes shall in so far as in harmony with the provisions of this act be deemed transferred to the planning commission of such municipality, and, in so far as inconsistent with the provisions of this act, are hereby repealed."

GARDNER V. COUNTY OF SONOMA
Supreme Court of California, 2003.
129 Cal.Rptr.2d 869, 62 P.3d 103.

BAXTER, J.

In the matter before us, an owner of property consisting of more than 1,000 acres in the County of Sonoma caused a subdivision map of his land to be recorded in 1865, prior to the earliest origins of California's Subdivision Map Act (hereafter sometimes the Map Act or the Act) (Cal. Gov. Code, § 66410 et seq.). The plaintiffs own 158 acres of that land and seek to establish that their property consists of 12 lawfully subdivided parcels that may be sold, leased, or financed in compliance with the Act. As they see it, the 1865 subdivision map should be given legal recognition under the Act because: (1) the map was recorded and accurately described the property it depicted; and (2) an atlas adopted in 1877 as the "official map" of Sonoma County included the subdivision shown on the 1865 map.

The property in question has remained intact under sequential owners throughout its history.

Our review of the Subdivision Map Act and the relevant case law leads us to conclude that the 1865 recordation of the subdivision map did not establish or create legally cognizable subdivision lots for purposes of the Act, notwithstanding the map's claimed accuracy and its inclusion in the 1877 atlas.

Factual and Procedural Background

In May of 1865, S.H. Greene recorded a map entitled "The Redwood Estate of S.H. Greene" with the Sonoma County Recorder. The map purported to depict a vast subdivision of Greene's property, consisting of nearly 90 rectangular lots in a grid superimposed over more than 1,000 acres of open land. The map divided the lots into four different ranges, with 15 to 28 lots per range. Each lot was labeled with a range number and a lot number, as well as length and width measurements, which appear to be precise to the one-hundredth of an acre.

The Greene map identified two streams flowing through the subdivision, but no other geographic features. It also reflected a county road running along the southeast corner of the grid, but showed no interior roads, easements, access routes, drainage systems, or other subdivision infrastructure.

No applicable subdivision map regulations existed in 1865. Consequently, the Greene map was submitted and accepted for recordation without review or approval by any public entity. The Thompson Atlas of Sonoma County, adopted in 1877 as the "official map" of Sonoma County for township lines and other unspecified county purposes, showed a purported subdivision called "The Redwood Estate of S.H. Greene."

In 1990, approximately 158 acres came into the possession of plaintiffs Jack and Jocelyn Gardner, trustees of the Gardner Family Trust. Plaintiffs' property, located in the south-central area of the so-called Greene subdivision, bears little resemblance to the distinctive rectangular lots depicted on the map Greene recorded in 1865. Although plaintiffs' property includes two of the original rectangular lots in full, its balance consists of only fragments of 10 of the other original lots. The property, which currently is zoned by the County of Sonoma (the County) for "Resource and Rural Development" with a minimum 40-acre [per dwelling unit] density, includes steep slopes and is the subject of a timber harvest plan.

In 1996, plaintiffs applied to the County's permit and resource management department for 12 certificates of compliance with the Subdivision Map Act, pursuant to section 66499.35 of the Government Code, [requesting a development approval] establishing that the County recognize plaintiffs' property as consisting of 12 lawfully created parcels that could be sold, leased, or financed in compliance with the Act. The department denied plaintiffs' application, determining that the Greene map did not create legally cognizable parcels because it was recorded before 1893, the year the Legislature enacted the first subdivision map statute with statewide effect. The planning commission denied plaintiffs' appeal of the department's action, but authorized the department to issue one certificate of compliance recognizing the subject property as a single parcel.

Plaintiffs then appealed the commission's decision to the County Board of Supervisors. The board adopted a resolution upholding the commission's action, finding, as a factual matter, that: (1) plaintiffs' property had been "repeatedly and consistently conveyed as a single unit of land" since 1865 and "generally described in metes and bounds since 1903"; and (2) none of plaintiffs' 12 purported lots had ever been separately conveyed or separately described in a grant deed.

Plaintiffs filed a petition for writ of mandate in superior court to compel the County to issue 12 certificates of compliance for their Greene map lots. The superior court denied the petition. The Court of Appeal affirmed, holding that the legislative intent underlying the Subdivision Map Act precludes legal recognition of subdivision lots shown on antiquated subdivision maps recorded before 1893.

Discussion

The Subdivision Map Act is "the primary regulatory control" governing the subdivision of real property in California. The Act vests the "[r]egulation and control of the design and improvement of subdivisions" in the legislative bodies of local agencies, which must promulgate ordinances on the subject. The Act generally requires all subdividers of property to design their subdivisions in conformity with applicable general and specific plans and to comply with all of the conditions of applicable local ordinances.

As used in the Act, "subdivision" means "the division, by any subdivider, of any unit or units of improved or unimproved land, or any portion thereof, shown on the latest equalized county assessment roll as a unit or as contiguous units, for the purpose of sale, lease or financing, whether immediate or future." Ordinarily, subdivision under the Act may be lawfully accomplished only by obtaining local approval and recordation of a tentative and final map pursuant to section 66426, when five or more parcels are involved, or a parcel map pursuant to section 66428 when four or fewer parcels are involved. A local agency will approve a tentative and final map or a parcel map only after extensive review of the proposed subdivision and consideration of such matters as the property's suitability for development, the adequacy of roads, sewer, drainage, and other services, the preservation of agricultural lands and sensitive natural resources, and dedication issues.

By generally requiring local review and approval of all proposed subdivisions, the Act aims to "control the design of subdivisions for the benefit of adjacent landowners, prospective purchasers and the public in general." More specifically, the Act seeks "to encourage and facilitate orderly community development, coordinate planning with the community pattern established by local authorities, and assure proper improvements are made, so that the area does not become an undue burden on the taxpayer."

Plaintiffs argue, nonetheless, that the Map Act contains two "grandfather" provisions that support legal recognition of the already subdivided nature of their property and compel the issuance of the 12 requested certificates of compliance.

To enforce its important public purposes, the Act generally prohibits the sale, lease, or financing of any parcel of a subdivision until the recordation of an approved map in full compliance with the law. Subdivision (d) of section 66499.30 provides, however, that these prohibitions "do not apply to any parcel or parcels of a subdivision offered for sale or lease, contracted for sale or lease, or sold or leased in compliance with or exempt from any law (including a local ordinance), regulating the design and improvement of subdivisions in effect at the time the subdivision was established."

Before 1893, however, there was no statewide mechanism generally authorizing local agencies to review or approve subdivision maps. In 1865 there was no other subdivision statute, ordinance, or regulation specifically authorizing public agency approval of subdivisions in Sonoma County.

As noted, the first California act providing statewide authorization for the formal recordation of subdivision maps and city and town plats for purposes of lot sales was enacted in 1893, long after the Greene map was recorded in 1865. That early act established standards for mapping by requiring accuracy of maps, identification of public roads and common areas, and specification of each lot's precise length and width. Owners were required to acknowledge subdivision maps and to file them in the county recorder's office prior to sale of the mapped lots.

Although plaintiffs cite a number of judicial decisions for the proposition that subdivision maps recorded before 1893 resulted in the legal creation of parcels under the common law, those decisions merely recognized the principle that subdivision maps could properly supply the legal description of property conveyed by deed.

Consequently, unlike a modern-day final [subdivision] map or parcel map, which upon recordation ordinarily converts what was formerly a single parcel into as many separate lots as appear on the map, the recordation of a subdivision map in Sonoma County in 1865, without something more (such as a conveyance), could not and did not work a legal subdivision of the property shown thereon, and property owners who recorded subdivision maps in Sonoma County in 1865 generally remained free to deed parcels and lots as they desired without regard to the depicted subdivisions.

Section 66451.10(a), commonly known as the "anti-merger provision," prevents local agencies from automatically merging contiguous legal parcels when those parcels come into common ownership: "[T]wo or more contiguous parcels or units of land which have been created under the provisions of this division, or any prior law regulating the division of land, or a local ordinance enacted pursuant thereto, or which were not subject to those provisions at the time of their creation, shall not be deemed merged by virtue of the fact that the contiguous parcels or units are held by the same owner, and no further proceeding under the provisions of this division or a local ordinance enacted pursuant thereto shall be required for the purpose of sale, lease, or financing of the contiguous parcels or units, or any of them."

By its own terms, section 66451.10(a) applies to only those units of land that already were "created" as separate parcels at some point in the past. As we explained nearly a decade ago, the anti-merger protections "sprang from a concern that without them, [the statute] would cause contiguous units of land that had already been qualified as separate parcels under the Act to be automatically merged by virtue of common ownership and thus to require further compliance with the Act before they could be sold separately.

Section 66451.10(a) does not, however, address the creation of parcels in the first instance. Nor does it provide a basis for legal recognition of subdivided lots depicted on antiquated maps. As one court explained, the anti-merger provision has no application if "the lots were not legal subdivisions prior to the Map Act." Because plaintiffs fail to demonstrate through statutory or decisional authority that recordation of the Greene map in 1865 lawfully created the 12 parcels at issue, their reliance on section 66451.10(a) is misplaced.

Not only does the Subdivision Map Act not support plaintiffs' position, but issuing certificates of compliance based on the map Greene filed in 1865 would frustrate the Act's objectives "to encourage and facilitate orderly community development, coordinate planning with the community pattern established by local authorities, and assure proper improvements are made, so that the area does not become an undue burden on the taxpayer."

Because the provisions of the Map Act do not support such a result, and because the Act's objectives and protections would be thwarted if pre-1893 recorded maps such as the Greene map were deemed sufficient by themselves to place parcels into compliance with the Act, we conclude the County properly denied plaintiffs' request for the 12 certificates of compliance.

NOTES

1. *Antiquated Subdivisions.* As illustrated by the *Gardner* case, the term "antiquated subdivision" identifies two distinctly different situations: (1) modern subdivisions whose lot sizes have been made nonconforming by reason of a subsequent change in the zoning laws after the recording of final map approval; and (2) "paper subdivisions," recorded prior to the adoption of modern subdivision regulations. Antiquated subdivisions create many difficult problems for regulating authorities. The problem of premature subdivision is particularly acute in some Sunbelt states and vacation areas, such as Arizona, Colorado, Texas, Florida, New Mexico, and California. *See* Michael M. Schultz & Jeffrey B. Groy, *The Failure of Subdivision Control in the Western United States: A Blueprint for Local Government Action,* 1988 UTAH L.REV. 569; Frank Schnidman & R. Lisle Baker, *Planning for Platted Lands: Land Use Remedies for Lot Sale Subdivisions,* 11 FLA.ST.U.L.REV. 505 (1983). Note that SPEA § 20 above provides that antiquated statutes governing subdivisions prior to the adoption of the SPEA are repealed to the extent they are inconsistent with the SPEA. Does the *Gardner* case carry out this provision?

Resolution of these problems requires some degree of retroactive application of police power controls through subdivision regulation so as to eliminate or change property lines or assemble parcels. Local governments must be careful to act in the best interests of the property owners, or they may be subject to strict nullifying statutory interpretation, *Maselli v. Orange County,* 488 So.2d 904 (Fla.App.1986); may run afoul of due process, *Usery v. Turner Elkhorn Mining Co.,* 428 U.S. 1 (1976); or, the takings clause. (*City of Annapolis v. Waterman,* 745 A.2d 1000 (Md.2000).

2. *Merger Provisions.* Where antiquated lots are too small for use in current day markets, provisions to merge contiguous* substandard lots in common ownership are found in state statutes and local subdivision regulations. *See* Robert H. Freilich and Michael M. Schultz, *Model Subdivision Regulations* (American Planning Association, 1995):

> § 1.5.3: "The *Planning Commission* shall have authority to review * * * the sale * * * of lands:
>
> > (a) where the plat contains contiguous lots in common ownership and one or more of the lots are undeveloped, whether the lots are owned by the original subdivider or an immediate or remote grantee . . . "

Many developers, in the absence of statutory protection, sell off lots through "checker boarding" to prevent merger applying to non-contiguous lots touching only at their points. Would such merger provisions constitute a "taking" of property? See the infamous case of *Fulling v. Palumbo,* 233 N.E.2d 272 (N.Y.1967), where the Court of Appeals (New York's highest court) held that a merger provision applying one acre minimum zoning to two half-acre subdivision lots previously zoned and recorded constituted an "as applied"

---

* Contiguous means touching along a common boundary and not touching at a point. [eds.]

taking to the one unbuilt lot. Do you think the court might have been arbitrarily swayed when the attorney in oral argument on behalf of the owner pointed out that the land was owned by an overly protective father who had purchased the two half acre lots, one in which he built his own house and the second which he reserved for his daughter so that when she married he could closely watch over her? *Fulling* would probably not be decided the same way today under U.S. Supreme Court takings decisions that take into account the entirety of the property and not the individual lot, where the lots are owned by the same owner. *See Tahoe-Sierra Preservation Council v. Tahoe Regional Planning Agency*, 535 U.S. 302 (2002). Most courts have upheld merger provisions as constitutional. *See Natale v. Town of Ridgefield Planning Commission*, 170 F.3d 258 (2d Cir.1999) (merger legislation is not arbitrary or capricious and does not violate substantive due process).

3.   *Anti-Merger Legislation.* Anti-merger provisions such as found in the California Government Code, § 66451.10 (a) are designed to exempt contiguous unbuilt lots in a prior recorded subdivision from new zoning regulations increasing the minimum lot size needed for obtaining building permits to the existing lots. Are such provisions wise? *See, also Morehart v. City of Santa Barbara*, 7 Cal.4th 725, 765, 872 P.2d 143 (1994)(where the Supreme Court of California held that California's anti-merger statute "impliedly preempts zoning ordinances requiring, for issuance of a development permit, the merger of parcels that would not have been eligible subjects of merger . . . ").

4.   *Land Readjustment Techniques.* Techniques for dealing with undersized antiquated subdivision lots vary dramatically. *See* Robert H. Freilich and S. Mark White, *Land Readjustment Techniques, 21st Century Land Development Code* 172 (American Planning Association, 2008):

a.   Offering zoning bonuses for merger of lots, was used in creating the tremendously successful Miami Beach/South Beach Art Deco District. *See* Robert H. Freilich, *Inducing Replatting Through Performance Zoning*, 2 PLATTED LANDS PRESS 5 (Jan.1985). The city used an ascending scale of zoning bonuses for small lot owners to assemble their parcels to usable size for profitable private joint ventures.

b.   Encouraging lot owners to pool lots to create a large usable parcel in which each lot owner will receive an equitable share in the capital investment and profits. *See* Johnson, *Neighborhood Pooling—An Overview*, 3 PLATTED LANDS PRESS 1 (Feb.1986); B. Berns & Y. Chandler, *Neighborhood Buyouts: Balancing Conflicting Interests* (1986).

c.   Authorizing condemnation of antiquated subdivision through redevelopment blight statutes. *See* Mo. Rev. Stat § 353.130 (2003) (permitting private urban redevelopment corporations to exercise governmental condemnation powers); Schultz & Sapp, *Urban Redevelopment and the Elimination of Blight*, 37 J.URB. & CONTEMP.LAW 3 (1990).

d. Permitting landowners within antiquated subdivisions to vacate the plat ("reversions to acreage") against dissenting landowners. *See* Cal. Govt. Code § 66499.12; Ore. Rev. Stat. §§ 92.040, .234; Va. Code Ann. §§ 15.10482(2) & (b); Utah Code Ann. § 57–5–7.1.

e. Creating equity corporations of landowners which develop or sell the unified property remitting proceeds to individual lot owners by percentage of ownership. *See* Northrop, the Farmer's Market District, Urban Land 19 (1984) (discussing commercial redevelopment in Dallas).

For a complete discussion of resubdivision and antiquated subdivisions which predate planning commission review, *see* Michael M. Schultz and Frank Schnidman, *The Potential Application of Land Readjustment in the United States*, 22 URB.LAW. 224–27 (1990); Frank Schnidman, *Resolving Platted Lands Problems: The Florida Experience*, 1 LAND. ASSESSMENT & DEVELOPMENT J. 27, 33–38 (1987).

5. *Plat Vacation.* Most states provide for governmental vacation, altering or amendment of plats only if neither the public nor any lot owner is unilaterally injured by the governmental action. Utah Code Ann. § 57–5–8; Nev. Rev. Stat. §§ 270.160, 270.170; N.M. Stat. Ann. § 47–6–7 (c). Oregon prohibits governmental initiated vacation when one or more lots have been sold. Ore. Rev. Stat. § 92.225 (2) (e). Plat vacation and resubdivision will be approved upon initiation and consent of the property owners, but the property owners may be subject to new design and improvement requirements. *Lampton v. Pinaire*, 610 S.W.2d 915, 921–22 (Ky.App.1980).

D. THE PLANNING CONTEXT FOR SUBDIVISION REGULATION

1. AUTHORITY TO EXERCISE SUBDIVISION CONTROLS

Under the authority of the SPEA, the planning commission regulates subdivision approval. The Act also locates in the planning commission the responsibility for adoption of the comprehensive plan. Every subdivision constitutes an amendment to the comprehensive plan because it lays out new streets and other capital improvements, which are essential functions of the planning process, as follows:

Sec. 12. Subdivision Jurisdiction.

The territorial jurisdiction of any municipal planning commission over the subdivision of land shall include all land located in the municipality and all land lying within 5 miles of the corporate limits of the municipality and not located in any other municipality.

Sec. 13. Scope of Control of Subdivisions.

Whenever a planning commission shall have adopted a [comprehensive] . . . plan of the territory within its subdivision jurisdiction or part thereof . . . then no plat of a subdivision of land within such territory or part shall be filed or recorded until it shall have been approved by such planning commission. . . .

Sec. 14. Subdivision Regulations.

Before exercising the powers referred to in section 13, the planning commission shall adopt regulations governing the subdivision of land within its jurisdiction. Such regulations may provide for the proper arrangement of streets in relation to other existing or planned streets and to the [comprehensive]. . . . plan, for adequate and convenient open spaces for traffic, utilities, access of fire-fighting apparatus, recreation, light and air, and for the avoidance of congestion of population, including minimum width and area of lots.

2. PLANNING CONTEXT

The New Jersey Supreme Court explained the significance of planning to subdivision control 30 years earlier than *Udell v. Haas, supra* Chapter 1. Note the following excerpt from the opinion in *Mansfield & Swett v. Town of West Orange*, 198 A. 225 (N.J.1938), where a developer unsuccessfully challenged the constitutional validity of the state adopted SPEA that empowered the planning board with the authority to create a comprehensive plan and control the subdivision of land:

Planning * * * is as old as government itself; it is of the very essence of civilized society. A comprehensive scheme of physical development is requisite to community efficiency and progress.

* * * Housing, always a problem in congested areas affecting the moral and material life of the people, is necessarily involved in both municipal planning and zoning. And it is essential to adequate planning that there be provision for future community needs reasonably to be anticipated. We are surrounded with the problems of planless growth. The baneful consequences of haphazard development are everywhere apparent. There are evils affecting the health, safety and prosperity of our citizens that are well-nigh insurmountable because of the prohibitive corrective cost. To challenge the power to give proper direction to community growth and development in the particulars mentioned is to deny the vitality of a principle that has brought men together in organized society for their mutual advantage. A sound economy to advance the collective interest in local affairs is the primary aim of municipal government.

198 A. at 229, 232, 233.

NOTE

Local Authority. When a local government regulates subdivision development, it must act strictly pursuant to, and in the manner prescribed by state law. *See Lemm Development Corp. v. Bartlett*, 580 A.2d 1082 (N.H.1990). The traditional rule governing local regulatory authority, known as Dillon's Rule, provides that local governments possess only the powers expressly delegated to them by the state legislature or those powers that are necessarily implied in the express power. *See New Jersey Shore Builders Ass'n v. Twp. of Marlboro*, 591 A.2d 950 (N.J.App.1991) and *Hoepker v. City of Madison Plan Comm'n*, 563 N.W.2d 145 (Wis.1997) (planning commissions are agencies of limited power and must act strictly in accordance with the state subdivision enabling act). *See also Town of Jonesville v. Powell Valley Vill. Ltd. P'ship*, 487 S.E.2d 207 (Va.1997). Once the developer has proven compliance with the design and improvement standards of the subdivision regulations, the Planning Commission has no administrative discretion to deny the plat and is subject to a ministerial writ of mandate. *PTL, LLC v. Chisago County Bd. of Commissioners*, 656 N.W.2d 567 (Minn.App.2003). *See, also Akin v. South Middleton Township Zoning Hearing Bd.*, 120 Pa.Cmwlth. 112, 547 A.2d 883, 884 (1988) (holding that when a subdivision plan complies with all objective provisions of the applicable subdivision ordinance, as well as all other applicable regulations, the plan as filed must be approved as a matter of law); *Montgomery Twp. v. Franchise Realty Interstate Corp.*, 54 Pa.Cmwlth. 535, 422 A.2d 897, 899 (1980) (holding that in order for a condition to properly attach, there must be some requirement of the ordinance that the proposed plan does not meet.

As we saw in Chapter 2, *supra*, this is in contrast to recent judicial acceptance of flexible zoning techniques that confer broader discretion in the utilization of floating zones, planned unit and mixed use developments. Ability to supersede state legislation exists only where the local authority is acting more strictly than the state legislation. For example, in New Hampshire, where a subdivision is defined by local regulation more restrictively than it is by the enabling act, the regulation's narrower definition governs. *Bussiere v. Roberge*, 714 A.2d 894 (N.H.1998) (conversion of an apartment unit into a condominium held not to be a subdivision under limited municipal definition); see also *Sako v. Delsesto*, 688 A.2d 1296 (R.I.1997) (conveyance of a portion of a lot to another lot is not a subdivision under local subdivision regulation). For full development of this thesis, *see* Laurie Reynolds, *Local Subdivision Regulation: Formulaic Constraints in an Age of Discretion*, 24 GA.L.REV. 525 (1990).

This narrow view of local authority has been relaxed somewhat by a number of decisions allowing a broader reading of state enabling acts: *Almquist v. Town of Marshan*, 245 N.W.2d 819 (Minn.1976), a presumption of validity with respect to zoning and planning; *Bounds v. City of Glendale*, 170 Cal.Rptr. 342 (Cal.App.1980); and by the availability of home rule authority. In addition to limitations imposed by state law, a local government's power, however, is also limited by its own ordinances and regulations. *See Akin v. South Middleton Township Zoning Hearing Bd.*, 547 A.2d 883 (Pa.Cmwlth.1988). Local regulations can, however, can further limit the state's minimum requirements. *Burnt Fork Citizens Coalition v. Board of County Commissioners of Ravalli County*, 951 P.2d 1020 (Mont.1997) ("the board may not ignore its own County Regulations and apply just the terms of the [state] Act to review and conditionally approve a proposed subdivision. Rather, we hold that it is bound to follow the County Regulations in effect at the time the proposal is made [especially where the county's eight criteria are *stricter* than the state's five criteria]").

Nevertheless, Planning Commissions have inherent power to deny subdivision approval, or to reconsider prior approvals to prevent fraud and illegal behavior. State statutes are not always necessary to validate provisions which provide for reopening of subdivision/site plan approval, even years later. "An agency, including a planning commission, not otherwise constrained, may reconsider an action previously taken and come to a different conclusion upon a showing that the original action was the product of fraud, surprise, mistake, or inadvertence, or that some new or different factual situation exists that justifies the different conclusion." *See Calvert County Planning Comm'n v. Howlin Realty Mgt., Inc.*, 772 A.2d 1209 (Md.2001).

Powers to fine for subdivision violation and to seek injunctions for violation of the plat or restrictive covenants recorded simultaneously with the plat (known as covenants, conditions and restrictions, "CC&Rs") are regularly included in the enabling statutes. In *Ojavan v. California Coastal Comm'n*, 62 Cal.Rptr.2d 803 (Cal.App.1997), the court upheld a 10 million dollar fine and a cease and desist order where an owner, as a condition of a coastal permit, had recombined an antiquated subdivision of 77 lots to only two lots but a subsequent owner had begun to market 54 of the original 77 lots. The court also upheld an injunction order rescinding sales made in violation of the covenant.

3.   PATTERNS AND USE OF LAND

Subdivision regulations may occasionally control the use of land, which is typically controlled by zoning, and may authorize the division of land into smaller sized lots not permitted as uses by the minimum lot size restrictions in the applicable zoning district, where planned residential development and cluster and conservation subdivision is authorized. Subdivision control of use is often where subdivision regulation is authorized by extraterritoriality statutes that permit city regulation of county unincorporated areas, where no county zoning is in place and the area lies within the city's sphere of influence, established by a regional or state board, or by the subdivision map act. The purpose is to prevent uncontrolled development lacking adequate public facilities in areas that will ultimately be annexed into the city. The following case is illustrative of that practice.

WOOD V. CITY OF MADISON

Supreme Court of Wisconsin, 2003.
260 Wis.2d 71, 659 N.W.2d 31.

We begin with the issue presented by the court of appeals:

> Does Wis. Stat. ch. 236 authorize a municipality to reject a preliminary plat under its extraterritorial jurisdictional authority based on a subdivision ordinance that considers the plat's proposed *use*? (emphasis supplied)

[The landowners in this case sought review of the city's decision to deny the landowners' extraterritorial plat and land division application that included dividing land into lots and rezoning of the land from agricultural to commercial. The landowners argued that the City improperly used its plat approval authority to mandate land use through a subdivision ordinance, which is an area exclusively reserved to zoning (land use and density). Editors' summary.]

Chapter 236 of the Wisconsin Statutes is entitled "Platting Lands and Recording and Vacating Plats." It "regulates intensively the process by which land can be divided into building sites." *See Town of Sun Prairie v. Storms,* 327 N.W.2d 642 (1983). The purpose of the chapter is set out in Wis. Stat. § 236.01:

> The purpose of this chapter is to regulate the subdivision of land to promote public health, safety and general welfare; to further the orderly layout and use of land; to prevent the overcrowding of land; to lessen congestion in the streets and highways; to provide for adequate light and air; to facilitate adequate provision for water, sewerage and other public requirements; to provide for proper ingress and egress; and to promote proper monumenting of land subdivided and conveyancing by accurate legal description. The approvals to be obtained by the subdivider as required in this chapter shall be based on requirements designed to accomplish the aforesaid purposes.

Wisconsin requires that all subdivisions be surveyed and that all plats be approved before they can be recorded. Wis. Stat. § 236.03 (1). Local governments with planning agencies have the power to approve subdivision plats. Plats located within the extraterritorial plat approval jurisdiction of a municipality require approval by the town board, the county planning agency, and the governing body of the municipality or its planning committee or commission. Wis. Stat. §§ 236.10(1) (b)1.3, and 236.10(3).

Approval of any plat is also conditioned on compliance with any subdivision ordinance validly enacted by the appropriate municipality, town, or county. Wis. Stat. § 236.13(1)(b). If multiple governing bodies or agencies with authority to approve or reject a plat have ordinances with conflicting requirements, the plat must comply with the most restrictive requirements. *See* Wis.Stat. § 236.13(4).

In Wis. Stat. § 236.45, the legislature has permitted municipalities, towns, and counties, if they have established planning agencies, to legislate more intensively in the field of subdivision control than provided for the state at large by allowing them to adopt ordinances which are more restrictive than the provisions of ch. 236., Section 236.45(3) which authorizes municipalities to utilize their subdivision ordinances within their extraterritorial plat approval jurisdiction.

Wisconsin Stat. § 236.45(1) explains the legislative intent behind the additional subdivision plat approval authority granted under the section:

> (1) Declaration of legislative intent. *The purpose of this section is to* promote the public health, safety and general welfare of the community and the regulations authorized to be made are designed to . . . *further the orderly layout and use of land;* . . . to prevent the overcrowding of land; to avoid undue concentration of population;. . . . *The regulations provided for by this section shall be made with reasonable consideration, among other things, of the character of the municipality, town or county with a view of* conserving the value of the buildings placed upon land, providing the best possible environment for human habitation, and for *encouraging the most appropriate use of land throughout the municipality, town or county.* Wis. Stat. § 236.45(1) (emphasis added).

The plain language of the declaration of intent in § 236.45(1) leaves no doubt that subdivision regulations and ordinances may consider the use of land. In fact, the statute requires that such ordinances "*shall* be made with reasonable consideration . . . of the character of the municipality, town or county with a view . . . for encouraging the most appropriate use of land throughout the municipality, town or county." Wis. Stat. § 236.45(1) (emphasis added).

Notwithstanding the explicit language in Wis. Stat. § 236.45(1) authorizing the planning agencies of municipalities, towns, and counties to enact subdivision ordinances that consider the "most appropriate use of land," the Woods contend that the use of property may not properly be the subject of subdivision approval authority under chapter 236. They assert that platting authority is inherently different from zoning authority and that only zoning regulations may consider the use of land. In essence, they claim that Wis. Stat. § 62.23 relating to city planning, and in particular subsections (7) and (7a) of the statute, on zoning and extraterritorial zoning, respectively, provide the sole authorization for municipal regulations concerning land use.

The purposes of zoning are listed in § 62.23(7) (c), and apply as well to extraterritorial zoning under Wis. Stat. § 62.23(7a). The listed purposes are remarkably similar to those which underlie subdivision plat approval authority under § 236.45(1). Notably, both zoning and subdivision plat approval authority state that regulation "shall be made with reasonable consideration . . . of the character of the district . . . with a view to . . . encouraging the most appropriate use of land." Wis. Stat. §§ 62.23(7)(c) and 236.45(1).

For these reasons, we conclude, in response to the issue set forth in the certification, that Wis. Stat. ch. 236 does authorize a municipality to reject a preliminary plat under its extraterritorial jurisdictional authority based upon a subdivision ordinance that considers the plat's proposed use.

NOTES

1.   It appears that *Wood* has been superseded by Wis. Stat. § 236.45(3)(b), which provides that "a municipality may not deny approval of a plat or certified survey map . . . on the basis of the proposed use of land within the extraterritorial plat approval jurisdiction of the municipality, unless the denial is based on a plan or regulations, or amendments hereto, adopted by the governing body of the municipality under [Wis. Stat. §] 62.23(7a)(c)[extraterritorial zoning]." *See Lake Delavan Prop. Co., LLC v. City of Delavan*, 353 Wis.2d 173, 844 N.W.2d 632 (2014) (for a Court of Appeals decision noting that *Wood* was called into question under the statute).

2.   The planning commission also has authority to condition subdivision approval on the removal of uses which violate the zoning ordinance. *See In the Matter of Albert Olivieri v. Planning Board of the Town of Greenburgh*, 645 N.Y.S.2d 545 (App.Div.1996).

3.   Subdivision approval can also be denied if the proposed uses for the development are not consistent with the adopted land uses shown on the comprehensive plan, even where the underlying zoning ordinance district classification permits the uses as of right. See the following cases: *S.A.V.E. Centennial Valley Assn. v. Schultz*, 284 N.W.2d 452 (S.D.1979) (approval of a residential subdivision in an agricultural area consistent with the underlying zoning was ruled void, because the planning commission in approving it disregarded the clear intent of the comprehensive plan to preserve the area solely for agricultural use); *Bd. of County Commissioners v. Conder*, 927 P.2d 1339 (Colo.1996) (subdivision can be denied based upon plan inconsistency provided plan is legally adopted by legislative body or compliance with the comprehensive plan is required in the subdivision ordinance).

4.   CLUSTER AND CONSERVATION SUBDIVISION

Planned Residential Development (PRDs), which authorize mixed residential use (*see* Chapter 2, *supra*) are essentially equivalent to a cluster or conservation subdivision in which the minimum lot sizes, authorized by the underlying zoning district, can be reduced in order to preserve sites for public schools, fire, police and emergency response facilities, and significant environmentally sensitive, agricultural, trail, park and open space lands. The number of lots created in the remaining land not preserved usually cannot exceed the number that can be lawfully subdivided without clustering. That is where the combining of PRD and cluster subdivision work well together. Cluster and conservation subdivisions together with their corollary PRD zoning regulations must avoid being indefinite and arbitrary with regard to design and improvement standards and the method and calculation used for the clustering and number of lots. The following case deals with both of these issues.

IN RE PIERCE SUBDIVISION APPLICATION

Supreme Court of Vermont, 2008.
184 Vt. 365, 965 A.2d 468.

BURGESS, J.

Neighbor appeals the Environmental Court's approval of applicant's proposed Planned Residential Development (PRD) adjoining his property in Ferrisburgh, Vermont. Under the Ferrisburgh Zoning Bylaws, a qualified PRD that proposes cluster housing and preservation of open space may be authorized by the Planning Commission by waiver of the standard rules governing single-house lot development. On appeal, neighbor claims that the court erred by concluding that: (1) the proposed subdivision meets the definition of a PRD as specified in the bylaws; (2) the project satisfies the space and density limitations under the bylaws; (3) the bylaws supply adequate standards to guide the court's discretion; and (4) the project complies with the minimum-lot-size requirements of the bylaws. We affirm the project's approval.

Applicant proposed to subdivide a 113-acre [parcel] into a twenty-one lot PRD, with an additional lot reserved for common space. The bylaws define a PRD as "[a]n area of land to be developed as a single entity for a number of dwelling units, the plan for which does not conform to the zoning regulations." Zoning Bylaws for the Town of Ferrisburgh § 2.2. The sizes of the twenty-two lots range from under half an acre to 25.9 acres.

Applicant's 113-acre parcel has varied terrain containing woods, wetlands, Lewis Creek, a stream, and steep slopes. The proposal creates a fifty-foot buffer along Lewis Creek and the stream. Applicant proposes to conserve seventy-six percent of the land in the PRD as open space through perpetual easements once the PRD is approved.

The parcel encompasses three different zoning districts: Rural Residential (RR-2), Rural Agricultural (RA-5), and Conservation (Con-25). Each district has a minimum lot size: RR-2 requires two acres, RA-5 five acres, and Con-25 twenty-five acres. Because zoning regulations for these districts would effectively prevent applicant from clustering houses on the parcel, applicant requested six waivers of the district zoning regulations to reduce the required minimum lot size and acreage per dwelling, along with frontage, width, depth, and setback requirements.

The Planning Commission approved the proposed PRD. Neighbor appealed that decision to the Environmental Court, complaining that the development's compliance with the bylaw definition of PRD could not be determined from applicant's plans; that the Commission improperly included the untraveled portion of the right-of-way as part of the lands subject to subdivision for purposes of calculating allowable density, that the bylaws delegated standardless discretion to the Commission to grant waivers of the district zoning regulations, and that the PRD failed to meet minimum lot size requirements. The Environmental Court rejected neighbor's arguments, affirming the approval of the application. This appeal followed.

I.

Neighbor first contends that the court's conclusion that the project satisfies the definition of a PRD rests upon an erroneous interpretation of Bylaw § 2.2, and, consequently, that the court's decision lacks necessary findings. Section 2.2 defines PRD as an "allowed method of land development" wherein the number of dwelling units "shall not exceed the number which *could be permitted if the land were subdivided into lots in conformance with the zoning regulations.*" Zoning Bylaws § 2.2 (emphasis added). To determine whether the proposed PRD was consistent with this definition, the court used a straightforward mathematical calculation-dividing total acreage of the parcel by minimum lot size as dictated by the three districts involved-to determine how many dwellings "could be permitted" under the bylaws.

Neighbor argues against this determination by simple long division, positing that slope, wetlands and stream characteristics of the parcel "potentially" limit the number of units available to a conforming subdivision, regardless of its aggregate acreage. Neighbor maintains that without a more detailed evaluation of the property vis-à-vis a conforming subdivision plan by which to determine the number of non-PRD units that could actually be built on the parcel, the court's conclusion of compliance with § 2.2 is unsupported by necessary findings. Neighbor characterized the § 2.2 definition as a "hurdle" arising at the outset of a PRD application, overcome only by the applicant engaging in a process before the Planning Commission to achieve approval for an identified number of units in a conventional subdivision plan.

Neighbor's construction of the bylaw is unreasonably burdensome and is not plainly mandated by the language. Since the density inquiry is triggered by an application for a PRD, rather than for a conforming development, the conforming subdivision contemplated by §§ 2.2 and

5.21(C) (2) can be only hypothetical. Nevertheless, neighbor reads both sections to require successive permit applications and proceedings, the first one for an imaginary development and the second one for the real proposal. If such a burden on the landowner was in place, we might question its reasonableness, but its drafters did not write the bylaw to require an applicant to obtain permission to build an unwanted subdivision in order to seek approval for a PRD. As § 2.2 does not plainly intend dual applications, it could, as the Environmental Court reasoned, require only an estimate of allowable density, rather than mandating full scale submission of an unwanted conventional subdivision plan for approval as a precondition to applying for the intended PRD development. That would be if the definition controlled the application at all.

It does not. Neighbor's reliance on § 2.2–a definitional section-to mandate nondiscretionary determination of allowed density is misplaced. While § 2.2 generally describes a PRD as an authorized unconventional development that may not exceed the number of units allowed to a conventional subdivision, the actual determination of allowed units is explicitly vested to the discretion of the Planning Commission under the "General Standards for Review" of PRD proposals, including the condition that before approving a PRD application, the Environmental Court, acting in the Planning Commission's stead, must find that:

> The overall density of the project does not exceed the number of dwelling units which could be permitted, *in the Planning Commission's judgment,* if the land (excluding the area within the boundaries of any proposed road) were subdivided into lots in accordance with the district regulations and other relevant provisions of these bylaws. § 2.2–a.

We disagree with neighbor that the court's summary calculation is insufficient for either the § 2.2 definition or the § 5.21(C) (2) compliance determination. The bylaws require the court to consider the number of units which, in its judgment, could be permitted under the regulations. The court did so and explained its rationale based on the undisputed estimates by applicant's engineer of the acreage in each of the districts involved by the project, as offered to prove that the PRD proposed no more lots than could be achieved by a conventional subdivision conforming to all applicable district regulations. The evidence supported this rationale, and the court's conclusion cannot be overcome by neighbor's speculation that the wetlands, slopes and stream within the parcel could, without more, "potentially" limit the number of units or lots that could have been approved for a conventional subdivision. . . .

III.

We now turn to neighbor's argument that §§ 5.21(C) and 5.21(D) fail to provide sufficient standards to guide the Environmental Court's exercise of discretion when evaluating the PRD. Neighbor contends that the bylaws are so vague that they do not inform applicants, courts or neighbors about what is permitted and what is prohibited. Neighbor further claims that adjoining landowners are denied due process and equal protection when challenging decisions of the Planning Commission because of the absence of standards upon which the court can review decisions.

In the context of land-use regulation, our approach to complaints of standardless and arbitrary discretion focuses on the criteria for due process and equal protection. *See In re Handy,* 764 A.2d 1226, 1235–36 (Vt.2000) ("[T]he power to grant or refuse zoning permits without standards denies applicants equal protection of the laws; and . . . due process of law.")

Zoning ordinances must "provide . . . appropriate conditions and safeguards" to guide the decision maker. While we will invalidate ordinances that "fail [ ] to provide adequate guidance" and therefore lead to "unbridled discrimination," we will uphold standards even if they are general and will look to the entire ordinance, not just the challenged subsection, to determine the standard to be applied. *Id.* at 1236.

Neighbor specifically contends that the bylaw provides no standards for the Planning Commission to approve or deny the six waivers requested by applicant as part of the PRD-approval process. While it is true that § 5.21 provides no concrete standards to consider each individual modification to the zoning regulations, neighbor's argument misunderstands the nature of a PRD. The Legislature authorized PRDs to "encourage flexibility of design and development of land in such a manner as to promote the most appropriate use of land, . . . and to preserve the natural and scenic qualities of the open lands of this state." 24 V.S.A. § 4407(3). In order to achieve these goals, particularly the encouragement of flexible planning, "[t]he modification of zoning regulations by the planning commission . . . may be permitted simultaneously with approval of a subdivision plan." *Id.* Such modifications, or "waivers," are part of the process of approving a PRD-a type of concentrated housing development permitted in exchange for open space which, by its very nature, does not fit the traditional zoning scheme. The consideration of these waivers, therefore, is folded into the Commission's analysis of the PRD itself. The proper inquiry is thus whether the bylaw provides the Commission with sufficient overall standards to grant a PRD permit, and whether the waivers granted comply with these standards.

Subsections (C) and (D) provide standards to guide the Commission's approval of a PRD. Some of the standards in subsection (C) are general:

1. The PRD is consistent with the municipal plan.

. . . .

4. The PRD is an effective and unified treatment of the development possibilities of the site and the development plan makes appropriate provision for preservation of streams, and

stream banks, steep slopes, wet areas and unique natural and manmade features.

5.   The development plan is proposed over a reasonable period of time in order that adequate municipal facilities and services may be provided.

. . . .

8.   Any open space land will be evaluated as to its agricultural, forestry and ecological quality.

By their terms, these tend to be overall objectives and recommendations, rather than specific standards to be measured and met. Other provisions of § 5.21(C) and (D), however, contain more specific standards for the approval of a PRD. Section 5.21(C) requires that:

2.   The overall density of the project does not exceed the number of dwelling units which could be permitted, in the Planning Commission's judgment, if the land were subdivided into lots in accordance with the district regulations and other relevant provisions of these bylaws.

3.   The uses proposed for the project are residential; dwelling units may be of varied types, including one-family, two-family or multifamily construction.

. . . .

7.   Any modification of the zoning regulations approved under this section shall be specifically set forth in terms of standards and criteria for the design, bulk and spacing of buildings and the sizes of lots and open spaces which shall be noted on or appended to the application.

In addition, § 5.21(D) requires that:

1.   District regulations on height and spacing between main buildings shall be met.

2.   To ensure adequate privacy for existing or proposed uses adjacent to the PRD, structures on the perimeter of the PRD shall be set back 50 feet and screening may be required.

3.   Adequate water supply and sewage disposal facilities shall be provided.

4.   Each dwelling unit shall have a minimum two acre lot exclusively associated with it and must comply with the specific standards set forth in Section 4.1 and 4.2 of these bylaws, excluding the lot depth requirement.

5.   The minimum acreage for a PRD shall be 25 acres and a minimum of 60% of the total parcel shall remain undeveloped.

Thus, while some of the bylaws' objectives are general, other provisions impose specific limits to guide and check the Commission's discretion. These requirements provide restrictions on the type of units which may be allowed, the percentage of open space required in a PRD, and the timing and form of applications. As stated in *Handy,* we consider the entire ordinance when evaluating whether it provides sufficient guidance to a decision-making body. By providing both general and specific standards for PRD review, the bylaw strikes an appropriate balance between providing guidance to the Commission and avoiding inflexible requirements which would defeat the creativity and flexibility required to effectuate the goals of the PRD alternative to traditional development. The list of particular requirements set forth in § 5.21(C) and (D) provides sufficient standards for the Commission, and for the court upon review, to evaluate a proposed project's compliance with the bylaws while avoiding, as the Environmental Court put it, the "inflexibility that *Handy* cautioned about."

All six waivers approved as part of the application-lot-size and acreage-per-dwelling minimums, lot frontage, width, and depth requirements, and setback rules-comply with the standards listed in § 5.21(C) and (D). In accordance with § 5.21(C)(7), the waivers were specific, establishing alternative "standards and criteria" for lot sizes, frontage, width, and depth requirements, and setbacks for the units in the PRD. The requested setback waivers did not violate § 5.21(D)(2)'s requirement that structures be set back fifty feet from the perimeter of the PRD. The waivers to minimum-lot-size and acreage-per-dwelling requirements enabled applicant to cluster dwellings in the PRD while also complying with the requirements that "[e]ach dwelling unit [ ] have a minimum two acre lot exclusively associated with it," *id.* § 5.21(D) (4), and that the "overall density of the project [ ] not exceed the number of dwelling units which could be permitted . . . if the land . . . were subdivided . . . in accordance with the district regulations," *id.* § 5.21(C) (2). The lot frontage, width, and depth waivers were similarly in accordance with the standards established by § 5.21(C) and (D). These waivers enabled the flexibility of design needed for the construction of a PRD, yet complied in full with the specific requirements established in § 5.21(C) and (D). As such, we affirm the court's approval of these waivers.

IV.

Neighbor's final argument is that the court erred in concluding that the project complied with § 5.21(D)(4), which requires that: Each dwelling unit shall have a minimum two acre lot exclusively associated with it and must comply with the specific standards set forth in Section 4.1 and 4.2 of these Bylaws, excluding the lot depth requirement. Sections 4.1 and 4.2, respectively, specify dimensional standards in the RR-2 and RA-5 districts for maximum height and lot coverage, together with minimum lot frontage, width, setbacks and lot size. Neighbor is particularly concerned with the subsection's declared minimum lot size and minimum acreage for each dwelling unit of two acres in RR-2, and five acres in RA-5. Many of the unit lots approved by the Commission were significantly smaller than the two and five acres ostensibly required by the bylaws.

The Environmental Court declined to construe the section to require the units themselves to be located on two- and five-acre lots. Instead, the court read the rule to command that there had to be at least the specified number of acres, within the particular district at large, corresponding to each proposed unit in that district. Otherwise, reasoned the court, two- and five-acre building lots would defeat the entire purpose of the PRD, which is to promote cluster housing and open land. Neighbor contends that the court's interpretation was contrary to the plain meaning of the bylaw imposing minimum house-lot areas.

Here, § 5.21(D)(4)'s reference to the district zoning requirements established by §§ 4.1 and 4.2 would appear to require compliance with conventional zoning lot size, but the definition of PRD along with the balance of § 5.21, including the introductory language of subsection (D)(4), indicates the opposite. Section 2.2 defines a PRD as a plan that "does *not* correspond . . . to the zoning regulations established for the district," while § 5.21 establishes standards for evaluating whether the proposed nonconformity is acceptable enough for the Planning Commission to modify the district's zoning rules "*simultaneously* with approval of a site plan." Zoning Bylaws §§ 2.2, 5.21 (emphasis added). The mandate of § 5.21(D) (4), that "[e]ach dwelling unit shall have a minimum two acre lot exclusively associated with it," would be unnecessary if § 4.1 was still to require a minimum unit lot of two acres in RR-2 and similarly irrelevant if companion § 4.2 independently required locating units on five acre lots in RA-5. Reading the bylaws to require units to sit upon two- or five-acre lots would confound the primary objective of the PRD authorization to allow cluster housing and would contradict the bylaws' allowance of clustered units so long as there are at least two acres of land specifically "associated" with each unit in the project as a whole.

Affirmed.

NOTES

1.   Do you agree with the court that only a "hypothetical" subdivision should be used to deter- mine the extent of the open space and environmentally sensitive lands to be preserved, thus automatically and mathematically reducing the size of the lots allowed by the cluster, without any physical site survey and inspection? Wouldn't the planning commission have the authority to require that the on-site open space and environmentally sensitive lands be dedicated to Ferrisburgh, which would reduce the number of lots that could have been built on the remainder of the site, while preserving the 2 and 5 acre minimum lot sizes of the underlying zoning districts? Was the court truly

concerned with protecting the open space and environmentally sensitive lands, or with increasing the number of lots that the developer could build? Perhaps a hidden motive of the court was to deal with the exclusionary aspects of two and five acre minimum lot sizes. We will cover the subject of exclusionary zoning in Chapter 5, *infra.*

2.   Notice that the principal case is up on appeals from Vermont's Environmental Court. Hawai'i recently joined Vermont, becoming only the second state to set up a court devoted exclusively to environmental issues. Do you think that such a specialized court is necessary, desirable, and or /fair? What should be the breadth of such a court's jurisdiction? For a discussion regarding Hawai'i's new environmental court *see* Hon. Michael O. Wilson, *The Hawai'i Environmental Court: A New Judicial Tool to Enforce Hawai'i's Environmental Laws*, HAW.B.J., August 2015, at 4.

3.   In Freilich & White, *21st Century Land Development Code* (American Planning Association, 2008),[3] Chapter 2, Use Patterns, Conservation Subdivisions § 2.2 at 39, the authors set out comprehensive standards for utilizing clustering of development, as follows:

Purpose and findings: The purpose of this section is to provide flexibility in site design in order to allow developers to preserve common open space and natural resources. The specific purposes of this section are to:

- Protect the public health, safety, and general welfare by avoiding surface and groundwater pollution, contaminated run-off, air quality contamination, and urban heat islands that result from the paving and clearing of natural vegetation;

- Protect and preserve natural resources, such as wetlands, streams, lakes, steep slopes, woodlands, and water recharge areas;

- Reduce infrastructure, green house gas emissions and housing costs by reducing the engineering and construction costs produced by conventional subdivision design, which requires more pavement, wetland crossings, grading of trees and natural areas, and maintenance from lawn and landscaping maintenance;

- Protect property values by allowing open space design features that enhance the marketability of the development;

- Provide design flexibility; and

- Promote development on soils that are most suitable for urban densities while preserving soils that are primarily adaptable to other uses, such as woodlands, wildlife habitat, and agriculture.

---

[3]   Reprinted with permission from 21st Century Land Development Code, copyright 2008 by the American Planning Association.

2.2.5   Lot and Block Design

2.2.5.1 *Lot Configurations*

(A) Lots within a conservation subdivision are not subject to the minimum lot size, minimum frontage, or minimum lot width requirements of the zoning district.

(B) In order to provide undivided open space for direct views and access, at least 40 percent of the lots within a conservation subdivision shall abut a conservation area.

(C) Direct pedestrian access to the open space from all lots not adjoining the open space shall be provided through a continuous system of sidewalks and trails. This subsection does not apply to prime farmland, as it is vulnerable to trampling damage and disturbance.

(D) Lots within 100 feet of a primary or secondary conservation area shall front on a conservation access street. Lots shall not front on a collector or higher-order street.

(E) Lots may be arranged in any of the patterns shown in this Chapter.

2.2.6   Transportation

The connectivity ratio for streets does not apply to local streets within a conservation subdivision, except for that portion of the street network that includes the following lot configurations:

(1) Single-family detached and attached homes in traditional neighborhood developments; and

(2) The conservation subdivision shall include a pedestrian circulation system. All sidewalks shall connect to other sidewalks or with trail sidewalks, and trails shall connect to potential areas qualifying as conservation areas on the development parcel, adjoining undeveloped parcels, or with existing parks and open space on adjoining developed parcels.

(3) Streets shall not cross wetlands or existing slopes exceeding 15 percent.

2.2.9   Conservation Areas

2.2.9.1 *Generally*

(A) This section establishes the standards for conservation areas. Conservation areas are the parks, natural features, and passive open space that distinguish this use pattern from other types of development.

(B) Conservation areas shall be designated as permanent open space, not to be further subdivided, and protected through a conservation easement held by the [LOCAL GOVERNMENT] or by a land trust or conservancy.

(C) The conservation easement shall prohibit further development in the conservation areas and may establish other standards safeguarding the site's special resources from negative changes.

2.2.9.2 Set-Aside and Allocation of Conservation Areas

A minimum of 60 percent of the total tract area shall be designated as conservation areas. The following areas shall be designated as conservation areas:

(A) Wetlands;

(B) Woodlands;

(C) Sensitive aquifer recharge features;

(D) All of the floodway and flood fringe within the 100-year floodplain, as shown on the official Federal Emergency Management Agency (FEMA) maps;

(E) All areas within 100 feet of the edge of the 100-year floodplain, as delineated on the FEMA maps, and any Letter of Map Revision;

(F) All areas within 100 feet of the banks of any stream shown as a blue line on the U.S. Geological Survey;

(G) Steep slopes (slopes exceeding 15 percent);

(H) Soils subject to slumping, as indicated on the medium-intensity maps contained in the county soil survey, published by the U.S. Department of Agriculture Natural Resources Conservation Service;

(I) Significant wildlife habitat areas;

(J) Areas with highly permeable (excessively drained) soil;

(K) Prime farmland;

(L) Historic, archaeological, or cultural features listed (or eligible to be listed) on national, state, or local registries or inventories; or

(M) Scenic views into the property from existing public roads."

3. Which standards are more defined and detailed, those of Ferrisburgh or the 21st Century Land Development Code? Can you explain the rationales of the following contradictory cases?

(a) *Void for Vagueness Standards*

(1) "Desirable or advantageous to the community," *Andrews v. Bd. of Supervisors of Loudoun County*, 107 S.E.2d 445 (Va.1959).

(2) "Conservation of natural beauty," *Kosalka v. Town of Georgetown*, 752 A.2d 183 (Me.2000).

(b)   Upheld against Vagueness Challenge to Standards

(1)   "Detrimental to health, safety, morals, comfort and general welfare of the persons residing or working in the neighborhood," *Novi v. City of Pacifica*, 169 Cal.App.3d 678 (Cal.1985).

(2)   "Compatibility assessment," *Hardin County v. Jost*, 897 S.W.2d 592 (Ky.1995).

4.   *Definitions and Exemptions.* In order for a local government's subdivision controls to be activated, a "subdivision" of land must be contemplated by an owner or developer of land. The definition of "subdivision" is, therefore, crucial. Unfortunately, but not surprisingly, there is no simple or single answer to what is an appropriate definition of the subdivision of land. In some states, the legislation provides a specific definition which the local government must incorporate into its subdivision regulations without additions, changes or deletions. *See, e.g., Pennobscot, Inc. v. Board of County Commissioners*, 642 P.2d 915 (Colo.1982) (although the powers conferred on the County were quite broad, the State Land Use Act did not confer the authority to adopt a definition of subdivision which is contrary to the express statutory definition found in the county planning statute). In other states, a local government, granted general power under a state planning enabling act, can adopt under its home rule powers, its own definition of a subdivision. *See Ronning v. Thompson*, 483 N.Y.S.2d 949 (Sup.Ct.1985). The Model Subdivision Regulations recommend a broad definition be adopted by a local government that closes off many loopholes and yet is consistent with most statutes.

> Subdivision: Any land, vacant or improved, which is divided into *two (2)* or more lots, parcels, sites, units, plots, or interests for the purpose of offer, sale, *lease,* or development, either on the installment plan or upon any and all other plans, terms, and conditions, including *resubdivision.* Subdivision includes the division or development of residential and *nonresidential* zoned land, whether by deed, metes and bounds description, *devise, intestacy*, map, plat, or other recorded instrument.

R. Freilich and M. Schultz, *National Model Subdivision Regulations: Planning & Law* 144 (1995) (emphasis added).

This definition *eliminates* most of the following problems which have plagued many communities:

- *Division into lots* does not include division into *parcels* since the former implies "building lots." *See, e.g., Wall v. Ayrshire Corp.*, 352 S.W.2d 496 (Tex.App.1961); *Bloom v. Planning Board of Brookline*, 191 N.E.2d 684 (Mass.1963); *Goldstein v. Planning Board of Lincoln Park*, 144 A.2d 724 (N.J.App.1958).

- *Resubdivision* may be excluded. *See, e.g., Vineyard v. St. Louis County*, 399 S.W.2d 99 (Mo.1966).

- *Number of lots.* In 1991, Utah adopted a version along the lines of the above model approach. Utah Code Ann. § 10–9–103(1)(q).

Still, many statutes and local subdivision regulations define subdivision as being the division of land into *more* than two parcels. *See, e.g.,* Cal. Stat. Ann. § 236.02(12)(a), § 236.45(2)(a) (five or more parcels constitute a subdivision; but a municipality with a planning agency may provide more restrictive provisions); Mass. Gen. Laws Ann. c. 41, § 81(L) (two or more lots but not including a subdivision in which each lot fronts on an existing way). *But see Pasaro Builders, Inc. v. Township of Piscataway,* 446 A.2d 187 (N.J.App.1982) (conveyance of one lot out of more than 20 contiguous lots was not exempt from subdivision approval). Some statutes exempt from municipal review those subdivisions that do not involve the creation of new streets or public improvements. *See, e.g., Dube v. Senter,* 219 A.2d 456 (N.H.1966); *Town of Cherry Hills Village v. Shafroth,* 349 P.2d 368 (Colo.1960).

- *Nonresidential subdivisions* and leases may be partially excluded. Most states, however, provide that commercial, industrial, and other non-residential use subdivisions are handled similarly to residential subdivisions, and subject to the same review system *See Municipality of Anchorage v. Suzuki,* 41 P.3d 147 (Alaska 2002). Regarding commercial development of land, there is clearly a right to require and deny approval of a preliminary plat proposing to subdivide property for commercial use. *See DeKalb County v. Publix Super Markets, Inc.,* 452 S.E.2d 471 (Ga.1994).

- *Utilities.* Some statutes preempt local power to regulate utilities under subdivision regulation.

- *Title* may not be resolved before a Planning Commission but must be resolved in the Courts. *See Borough of Braddock v. Allegheny County Planning Dept.,* 687 A.2d 407 (Pa.Cmwlth.1996) (railroads sought judicial subdivision approval for lands no longer dedicated to railroad purposes). *But see Town of Windham v. Lawrence Savings Bank,* 776 A.2d 730 (N.H.2001) (judicial foreclosure cannot bypass planning commission subdivision approval).

- *Testamentary* (devise) or intestate divisions of property may be excluded. *See In re Estate of Sayewich,* 413 A.2d 581 (N.H.1980) (Testamentary devise of real property into four separate parcels to four children not invalid for failure to receive subdivision approval).

- *Agricultural* land may be excluded. *Metzdorf v. Borough of Rumson,* 170 A.2d 249 (App.Div.1961). *But see HD Dunn & Son LP v. Teton County,* 102 P.3d 1127 (Idaho 2004) (where single-family homes are permitted in the agricultural zone, a 160-acre subdivision obtained by dividing the land twice, first into twenty parcels and second dividing each of the 20 parcels into eight parcels each, does not comply with the *"one-time* only split of one parcel" subdivision exemption made for exclusively for agricultural purposes and was not exempt from subdivision review).

- *Family transfers* of parcels to designated family members may be exempt. New Mexico Stat. Annot. § 47–6–2(J) provides a subdivision exemption for: "(9) the division of land to create a parcel that is sold or donated as a gift to an immediate family member; however, this exception shall be limited to allow the seller or donor to sell or give no more than one parcel per tract of land per immediate family member." To remedy such an irrational evasion of subdivision regulation, especially since the created parcels may then be sold to non-family purchasers, or a family created parcel may be further divided by family transfer, Santa Fe County is considering the following amendment to its Land Development Code:

> Any family transfer, lot or parcel division created through exemption pursuant to NMSA 1978, § 47–6–2(J) shall, prior to receiving ministerial building or grading permit or other discretionary development approval for construction or use, on any tract, parcel or lot of land created by a family transfer, be required to meet all of the non-subdivision and zoning standards of the SLDC through the "site plan" discretionary zoning approval process. No discretionary or ministerial development approval shall be granted for any tract, parcel or lot of land created by an exemption pursuant to NMSA 1978, § 47–6–2(J) until it is demonstrated that such tract, parcel or lot meets all of the requirements of site plan approval pursuant to § 3.22 of the SLDC and additionally meets the requirements of the base zoning district, including but not limited to the zoning uses permitted, minimum lot size, area and yard minimums, and maximum height as set forth in Chapter 9 of the SLDC; the affordable housing requirements set forth in Chapter 11 of the SLDC; the requirements of Chapter 5; and the requirements of Chapter 8, the Official Map (reservation of street, park, trail and public facility right of way), adequate public facilities, impact fees, exactions, dedications, public and private utility fees, charges and rates, and assessments, fees, charges and taxes of assessment and public improvement districts. (Draft, June 6, 2011).

Is this provision compatible with and authorized by the statutory planning and zoning enabling acts? Is the family transfer exemption intended to encompass an end run around zoning as well as subdivision requirements?

To avoid most of these exemption problems, a zoning ordinance provision, similar to Santa Fe's provision above, may require that all land, not subject to subdivision regulation by state law or judicial decision, is required to submit a "site plan" with applications for all discretionary development approvals, or for a building or grading permit, if that is the first development approval following the exempt lot split. Note that a "site plan" would require use, lot size, yards and buffers, environmental, design and improvement, adequate on and off-site public facility provisions and standards, similar to the standards found in local subdivision regulations. How would you improve the Santa Fe provision above, considering the following cases: *Chiplin Enterprises, Inc. v. City of Lebanon*, 411 A.2d 1130 (N.H.1980) (site plan zoning review is authorized by the state zoning enabling act for exempt non-residential projects); and, *Boone v. Board of County Commissioners*, 107 P.3d 1114 (Colo.App.2004) (where parcels of 35 acres or more are exempt from subdivision review, they are nevertheless subject to local zoning regulation).

5. *Major and Minor Subdivision.* Why have states and municipalities allowed these types of exemptions? Presumably, they desire to exempt from regulation the simple lot split where there is no need for public improvements or the division of agricultural or rural land without restriction. Theoretically, the exemption has the salutary purpose of protecting the farmer from onerous bureaucratic regulations and excluding minor divisions of land because of the relatively small impact they are likely to make on patterns of land development. The danger, however, is that they create the potential for legal problems for subsequent purchasers of lots divided without subdivision approval. Some states exempt large parcels from subdivision control even in urban counties. *See, e.g.,* West's Colo.Rev.Stat.Ann. § 30–28–101(10)(a) and (b) (subdivision is defined as "any parcel of land * * * which is to be used for * * * multiple-dwelling units * * * or which is divided into two or more parcels, separate interests, or interests in common * * * " but this definition "shall not apply to any division of land which creates parcels of land each of which comprises *thirty-five or more acres* of land and none of which is intended for use by multiple owners."). This practice negates many of the theories behind the need for subdivision regulation: creation of new streets, shaping the future of municipal utility services, parks, and open spaces, and having a recorded system of plats on file. It cuts up huge valleys of Colorado into 35-acre "ranchettes" disturbing open space, trails, wildlife and flora habitats that could be managed under planned unit development, cluster zoning or minor subdivision approval. *See Bd. of County Commissioners v. O'Dell*, 920 P.2d 48 (Colo.1996) (court upheld commissioners' disapproval of minor subdivision request to divide a 41-acre parcel into two smaller parcels because of concerns about the impact of increased development on wildlife and problems of fire suppression due to lack of water).

An alternative is available which meets the need which subdivision regulation was designed to fulfill but simultaneously lessens the rigors of plat approval for those smaller subdivisions and simple parcel splits. For maximum effectiveness, a "tight" definition of subdivision is preferable; however, a classification of subdivision into major or minor provides for a variation in the review and appeal process that accommodates the differences in detail necessitated by complex versus simple subdivisions. Thus, at the time of sketch plat approval, a subdivision may be classified into a major or minor category as follows:

> *Major subdivision:* All subdivisions not classified as minor subdivisions, including but not limited to subdivisions of four (4) or more lots, or any size subdivision requiring any new street or extension of the local government facilities, or the creation of any public improvements.

> *Minor subdivision:* Any subdivision containing not more than three (3) lots fronting on an existing street, not involving any new street or road, or the extension of municipal facilities, or the creation of any public improvements, and not adversely affecting the remainder of the parcel or adjoining property, and not in conflict with any provision or portion of the Comprehensive Plan, Official Map, Zoning Ordinance or [the subdivision] regulations.

R. Freilich & M. Schultz, *National Model Subdivision Regulations: Planning & Law* 217–18 (1995).

The advantage of being classified as a minor subdivision is that the approval process is abbreviated. Only two steps are required: sketch plat and final approval; but the plat is still reviewed and must be properly recorded. This classification and abbreviated technique has been successfully utilized. *See Graves v. Bloomfield Planning Board*, 235 A.2d 51 (N.J.Super.1967); contra *Kass v. Lewin*, 104 So.2d 572 (Fla.1958) (minor subdivision regulation held unconstitutional as not germane to subdivision control, traffic planning, and as an unreasonable restraint).

The less significant impacts of a minor subdivision should generally minimize the need for extensive review of the proposal, but local governments must take care that developers are not using the process to avoid the more substantial procedures of the major subdivision. For strict control of evasion, see *Orrin Dressler, Inc. v. Burr Ridge*, 527 N.E.2d 1063 (Ill.App.1988); and *Corcoran v. Planning Bd. of Sudbury*, 530 N.E.2d 357 (Mass.App.1988). A related sequence of conveyances and subdivisions constructed so as to use plat exemptions to create an eighteen-parcel plat was held to be an illegal effort to circumvent the purposes of the platting ordinance. *See Gerard v. San Juan County*, 715 P.2d 149 (Wash.App.1986).

6.   *Condominiums and Multi-family Rentals.* The conversion of apartments to condominiums and cooperatives has been especially problematic to municipalities. Does the change of an existing (and approved) multi-family apartment building into a cooperative or condominium require subdivision approval? California's Subdivision Map Act, Cal. Govt. Code § 66424, specifically defines condominium and cooperative projects as subdivisions. California courts have held that a local government may adopt supplementary development and design standards pursuant to the Subdivision Map Act covering condominium conversions which reasonably relate to purposes of the

Act. *Griffin Development Co. v. City of Oxnard*, 703 P.2d 339 (Cal.1985); *Shelter Creek Development Corp. v. City of Oxnard*, 669 P.2d 948 (Cal.1983); *cf. City of West Hollywood v. Beverly Towers, Inc.*, 805 P.2d 329 (Cal.1991) (municipality could not enforce new condominium conversion regulations enacted after real estate developer secured final subdivision map approval and permission from Department of Real Estate to sell individual apartments as condominium units).

Some states have amended the planning enabling act to specifically authorize that condominium projects be treated as a subdivision; Minnesota Uniform Condominium Act Ch. 582; New Hampshire Rev. Stat. Ann. 36.1 VIII; Colorado Rev. Stat. 30–28–101; N.Y. Real Prop. Law § 339f(2). Other states have judicially recognized that condominium development is specifically covered by subdivision approval. *Stillwater Condo. Ass'n v. Town of Salem*, 668 A.2d 38 (N.H.1995); In Alabama the Attorney-General opined that condominiums may be regulated as subdivisions so long as the planning commission also regulates similar physical structures such as multi-family rental units as subdivisions. *See* Op. Att'y-General Solomon, Alabama, October 27, 1997, citing ALA. CODE § 11–52–30 and § 25–8A–106 ("because it involves the division of land into two or more parcels, technically a condominium involves a subdivision of real estate.") The opinion extends the authority to commercial and recreational condominiums. Alabama specifically recognizes subdivision regulation of "sale or building development." Ala. Code § 11–52–1(6).

A few states have adhered to the traditional rule. The Supreme Court of Vermont held that neither a subdivision nor a zoning permit was necessary to convert rental property to condominium ownership. *See In re Lowe*, 666 A.2d 1178 (Vt.1995); *cf. P.O.K. RSA, Inc. v. Vill. of New Paltz*, 555 N.Y.S.2d 476 (App.Div.1990) (finding that law which regulated conversion of property ownership which did not involve alteration in use of property as distinguished from "ownership" was ultra vires and void).

E. SUBDIVISION APPROVAL PROCESS

The procedure for subdivision plat approval is relatively straightforward. The developer meets with the administrative assistants to discuss the proposed development. This mandatory meeting is designed to inform the applicant of current subdivision approval procedures. The administrative assistant indicates the procedures that will be required and directs the developer to contact the other governmental agencies concerned with the development. *See* David Listokin & Carole Walker, *The Subdivision and Site Plan Handbook* 176–77 (Rutgers, 1989). A zoning board of appeals has no power to grant subdivision approval through a variance. *See Eccles v. Zoning Bd. of Appeals of Vill. of Irvington*, 606 N.Y.S.2d 305 (App.Div.1994). The approval of each plat is a prerequisite to the submission of the next one. The three plats, sketch, preliminary, and final, will be looked at individually in this section.

1. SKETCH PLAT

The sketch plat is the first of the three stages of subdivision approval. While the sketch plat is optional under all statutes, if it is required in the local subdivision regulations, the final plat must be consistent with the sketch plat. *See Northfork Citizens for Responsible Dev. v. Bd. of County Commissioners of Park County*, 228 P.3d 838 (Wyo.2010). Once sketch plat review is part of the subdivision approval process, the sketch plat must be based on the design and improvement standards found in the subdivision regulations. *See Croft v. Bd. of Supervisors*, 464 A.2d 625 (Pa.Cmwlth.1983) (holding that where the preliminary plat must conform to sketch plat review, the planning commission must cite with particularity to provisions of the ordinance which the subdivider failed to satisfy).

The sketch plat is used primarily in two scenarios: (1) for complex or controversial subdivisions with many contested issues; or, (2) for minor subdivisions of four lots or fewer, where the statute permits final approval to immediately follow sketch plat approval, skipping the discretionary preliminary or tentative approval stage.

The sketch plat is essentially a rough design map of the proposed subdivision. Included in the plat or accompanying it, is a general layout, without specific metes and bounds, construction specifications and engineering drawings, in order to avoid unnecessary expense of detail before determinations are made as to the overall concept. Proposed reservations of land, street improvements, location of drainage and sewer lines, fire and similar protective matters, availability of existing services, and ownership information of the parcel are furnished and widely distributed to governmental agencies concerned with the plat. This stage allows communication between the planning commission, engineer, developer, and concerned community groups, property owners and governmental bodies which will enable any necessary modifications to occur prior to the developer incurring extensive costs in the preparation of the preliminary or tentative plat. Submission of the sketch plat to regional and state agencies is now often required. *See Eversdyk v. Wyoming City Council*, 421 N.W.2d 574 (Mich.App.1988). The submission of a sketch plat is considered to be "a pre-application procedure" and therefore submission or approval does not create either a vested right to complete the process or to start the running of a "deemed approved" statute. *See Palmer v. City of Ojai*, 178 Cal.App.3d 280 (1986).

2. PRELIMINARY OR TENTATIVE PLAT OR MAP

This is the first formal step of subdivision approval. The preliminary plat shows the detailed plan of the subdivision. The intermediate step of submission of a preliminary plat usually is a local innovation authorized by ordinance but may also be specifically mentioned in state enabling legislation. *See* 4 Anderson, *American Law of Zoning* § 25.13 (4th. ed.2011);

Ill. C.S.A., ch.65, 5/11–12–8; N.J.Stat.Ann. 40:55 D-49. The Standard City Planning Enabling Act § 14, provides: "The regulations or practice of the commission may provide for a tentative approval of the plat previous to such installation, but any such tentative approval shall be revocable and shall not be entered on the plat." Some states like California, as in the *Youngblood* case which follows, designate the preliminary plat as "a tentative map"—but the majority of states use the term "preliminary plat." *See Davidson v. Kitsap County*, 937 P.2d 1309 (Wash.App.1997).

Included in this plat is all the information contained in the sketch plat, but in much greater detail. The plat is reviewed for compliance with all the local requirements and any recommendations derived from the sketch plat. This stage constitutes the major opportunity that regulatory and service agencies have to review the plat for the proposed subdivision. It will also commence the running of deemed approved statutes (see Comment: Deemed Approved Statutes *infra* pg. 550.

Many current statutes require that a public hearing be held with notice to interested parties prior to the approval of a preliminary plat. Furthermore, even in the absence of a statute requiring a public hearing, courts may require one at the preliminary stage. *See Horn v. County of Ventura*, 596 P.2d 1134 (Cal.1979) (approval by a county of a tentative subdivision map is an "adjudicatory function" and thus persons affected by such land use decisions were constitutionally entitled to procedural due process notice and opportunity to be heard before the approval occurs). In addition to gaining approval from the planning commission, a developer may be required to secure approval from other state or local agencies, particularly environmental assessment review. *See Vedanta Soc. of Southern California v. California Quartet Ltd.*, 100 Cal.Rptr.2d 889 (Cal.App.2000). Notice to interested parties may also be required for proceedings held by other agencies which will make recommendations as to plat approval. *See Vitale v. Planning Board of Newburyport*, 409 N.E.2d 237 (Mass.App.1980). The grounds for decision on the preliminary plat is the standard by which the planning authority later acts to grant or deny approval of the final plat. *See Board of Supervisors v. West Chestnut Realty Corp.*, 532 A.2d 942 (Pa.Cmwlth.1987).

As subdivision review is a "quasi-judicial" or "administrative" process, ex parte communications amongst the developer, other interested parties and any member of the planning commission is forbidden. *See Jennings v. Dade County*, 589 So.2d 1337 (Fla.App.1991).

3. FINAL PLAT

After preliminary approval, can the developer be confident that final approval is simply a ministerial act in which it posts its bonds, pays its impact and administrative fees, and prepares its dedications and final map, with full knowledge of certain approval if all conditions imposed at preliminary (or tentative) approval have been met? Suppose that in the interim the zoning ordinance or comprehensive plan applicable to the property has changed? Suppose that additional requirements, fees, or standards for subdivision improvements have been added to the regulations prior to final approval. The following case considers these questions:

YOUNGBLOOD V. BOARD OF SUPERVISORS OF SAN DIEGO COUNTY
Supreme Court of California, 1978.
22 Cal.3d 644, 150 Cal.Rptr. 242, 586 P.2d 556.

TOBRINER, J. These consolidated cases involve the Rancho Del Dios subdivision in West-central San Diego County. On December 10, 1974, the Board of Supervisors of San Diego County approved a tentative [preliminary] subdivision map [plat] providing for one-acre lots, a land use permitted by the then zoning and general plan. On December 31, however, the county amended its general plan to limit density for Rancho Del Dios to one dwelling unit for each two acres; thus when the county approved the final subdivision map on October 25, 1975, the subdivision did not conform to the existing general plan.

Plaintiffs, neighbors of the subdivision, filed two mandamus actions against the board of supervisors; both suits contend that the board acted illegally in approving the tentative and final maps and that it was under a mandatory duty to rezone the subdivision to conform to the new general plan.

While the appeal was pending before this court, the board of supervisors amended the zoning for Rancho Del Dios to conform to the general plan, thus mooting the principal issue of this appeal. The only remaining issue relates to the board's approval of the tentative and final subdivision maps. With respect to those issues, we hold that the board did not act unlawfully in approving the tentative map; once the developer complied with the conditions attached to that approval and submitted a final map corresponding to the tentative map, the board performed a ministerial duty in approving the final map. We therefore affirm the judgment of the superior court.

On June 26, 1974, real party in interest Santa Fe Company filed an application for a tentative subdivision map for Rancho Del Dios. The map divides the 217-acre parcel into 131 lots, many of which would be only 1 acre or slightly larger in size. Because the developer proposed to retain a 40-acre parcel and several smaller parcels in an undeveloped state, the density of the subdivision would approximate .6 dwelling units per acre.

On October 11, 1974, the San Diego County Planning Commission approved the proposed tentative map, expressly finding that it conformed to the existing zoning and general plan. The Planning Commission recommended, however, that a number of conditions be imposed upon approval of a final subdivision map. Although one such condition was that the developer apply for a zoning change from A-4(1) to E-1 (one-acre residential), a zone the commission believed more suitable for a residential subdivision, the Planning Commission refused to require the zoning change as a condition to approval of a final map. On December 10, the board of supervisors approved the tentative map subject to the conditions proposed by the Planning Commission.

* * *

2. *The board of supervisors did not abuse its discretion in approving the tentative subdivision map for Rancho Del Dios.*

Plaintiffs assert that the board abused its discretion when it approved the tentative subdivision map.[1] They first argue that the tentative map was not approved until April 1975, after the enactment of the new San Dieguito Community Plan, and that such approval was ineffective because the tentative map conflicted with the new general plan. The record shows, however, that the board approved the tentative map on December 10, 1974, subject to certain conditions, among which was the condition that Santa Fe Company apply for E-1(B) zoning; on April 24, 1975, the board determined that Santa Fe had fulfilled this condition.

The Subdivision Map Act contemplates that the local agency, when it approves a tentative map, will normally attach conditions to that approval, such as the completion of planned subdivision improvements, and will approve the final map only after certifying that the subdivider has complied with those specified conditions. *This statutory structure* compels the conclusion that the approval of a tentative map subject to conditions is nonetheless an approval for the purpose of determining that map's consistency with the existing general plan. Since the board conditionally approved the tentative subdivision map on December 10, 1974, the features of that map must be measured against the general plan in effect on that date.

* * *

3. *The board of supervisors properly approved the final subdivision map for Rancho Del Dios.*

On October 25, 1975, when the board of supervisors approved the final subdivision map for Rancho Del Dios, the new San Dieguito Community Plan called for two-acre home sites in the area of the subdivision. Plaintiffs contend that the final subdivision map providing for lots of less than two acres conflicted with the general plan then in effect and thus that the

---

[1]   Approval of a tentative subdivision map is a quasi judicial act subject to judicial review for abuse of discretion under Code of Civil Procedure section 1094.5. (*See Woodland Hills Residents Assn., Inc. v. City Council* (1975) 44 Cal.App.3d 825, 838)

board's approval of that map violated Business and Professions Code sections 11526 and 11549.5. The county and the developer in response maintain that under Business and Professions Code sections 11549.6 and 11611 the county *was required* to approve a final map which conformed to a properly approved tentative map if the subdivider had complied with all conditions attached to the approval of the tentative map. We shall explain why we agree with the county's construction of the governing statutes.

* * *

The requirement that subdivision maps conform to a general plan was added by the enactment of Assembly Bill No. 1301 in 1971. When first passed by the Assembly, the bill contained two provisions requiring final maps to conform to a general plan. Section 11526, subdivision (c) stated that "No city or county shall approve a tentative or final subdivision map unless the governing body shall find that the proposed subdivision * * * is consistent with applicable general or specific plans of the city or county." Section 11549.5 then specifically listed all grounds which require the governing body to "deny approval of a final or tentative subdivision map"; the first ground listed, in subdivision (a), is "That the proposed map is not consistent with applicable general and specific plans." Since no statute specified which general plan is "applicable" when the governing body takes up the question of approval of a final map, sections 11526 and 11549.5 could have been construed either to require a final map to conform to the general plan in effect when that map came before the governing body for approval, as plaintiffs contend, or to require it only to conform to the general plan in effect when the tentative map was approved.

* * *

The purpose of section 11549.6, as we perceive it, was to confirm that the date when the tentative map comes before the governing body for approval is the crucial date when that body should decide whether to permit the proposed subdivision. Once the tentative map is approved, the developer often must expend substantial sums to comply with the conditions attached to that approval. These expenditures will result in the construction of improvements consistent with the proposed subdivision, but often inconsistent with alternative uses of the land. Consequently it is only fair to the developer and to the public interest to require the governing body to render its discretionary decision whether and upon what conditions to approve the proposed subdivision when it acts on the tentative map. Approval of the final map thus becomes a ministerial act once the appropriate officials certify that it is in substantial compliance with the previously approved tentative map.

* * *

Plaintiffs do not contend that the final map for Rancho Del Dios does not substantially comply with the tentative map or that Santa Fe Company failed to fulfill the conditions attached to approval of the tentative map. Having held, as we stated earlier, that the board of supervisors properly approved the tentative map, we conclude that the board acted properly in approving the final map.

* * *

NOTES

1. *Final Plat as Non-Discretionary.* The *Youngblood* case establishes the principle that the approval of the preliminary plat for all intents and purposes vests the rights of the developer in whatever is in the preliminary plat against any further subdivision conditions or amendments to the subdivision regulations through to final approval and recordation. See David L. Callies, Daniel J. Curtin, Jr., and Julie A. Tappendorf, *Bargaining for Development*, Ch. V (2003). No new conditions can be added when the plat is submitted for final approval. *See Board of Supervisors v. West Chestnut Realty Corp.*, 532 A.2d 942 (Pa.Cmwlth.1987). Thus preliminary plat is the most important step since it is the only "discretionary" process. *See Commonwealth Properties, Inc. v. Washington County*, 582 P.2d 1384, 1389 (Or.App.1978). While the landowner is protected from future subdivision regulatory change, no vested right to zoning use or density will occur until the issuance of a valid building permit after subdivision recording with substantial construction. *See* Chapter 2, Section G, Vested Rights, *Avco Community Developers, Inc. v. South Coast Regional Commission*, 553 P.2d 546 (Cal.1976).

2. *Changed Conditions.* What happens, however, if a recession causes a developer to reduce the size of the development? Will the developer still be responsible for the conditions agreed to at preliminary and final approval requiring the developer to contribute to the building of off-site road improvements that were sized to the original larger size of the development? In *Toll Brothers v. Board of Chosen Freeholders of Burlington County*, 944 A.2d 1 (N.J.2008), the New Jersey Supreme Court held that the developer would be released from approval conditions if changed conditions necessitated equitable relief:

> At the heart of this case is Toll Brothers' claim that it is entitled to appear before the County Planning Board to request a recalculation of its off-tract improvement obligations due to the substantial downsizing of its original design. We have long recognized that right where "a sufficient change in the application itself or in the conditions surrounding the property" has occurred "to warrant entertainment of the application." *River Vale Planning Bd. v. E & R Office Interiors, Inc.*, 575 A.2d 55 (N.J.App.1990) ("[T]he installation of the improvements contemplated by the Developer's Agreement as a condition of [subdivision] and [site plan approval] was subject to an implied or constructive condition that those improvements were required only if the developer proceeded with the project contemplated by the application and approval." [T]he rule of res

judicata does not bar the making of a new application, or for modification or enlargement of one already granted, or for lifting conditions already imposed in connection with the grant of a [subdivision approval], upon a proper showing of changed circumstances or other good cause warranting a reconsideration by the local authorities.").

3.   *Extensions of Final Plat Submission.* Similar in nature to *Toll Brothers*, *Youngblood* will vest the tentative map to the *benefit of the developer* with regard to a statutory amendment adopted subsequent to tentative map approval. *See California Country Club Homes Association, Inc. v. City of Los Angeles and Twentieth Century Fox Film Corporation*, 18 Cal.App.4th 1425, 1436 (1993), the court upheld the retroactive application of an amendment to the Subdivision Map Act extending the life of a tentative map approval to 13 years before final plat approval is required.

4.   *Effect of Vested Rights Statutes.* The common law rule of late vesting has been changed in a number of states under the recent flurry of property rights legislation to grant vesting upon submission of the first complete discretionary application for development approval.

Some Atlantic Coast states prior to the adoption of these late vesting statutes had already provided that a recorded subdivision is exempt from a subsequent zoning change for a period of two to eight years. N.Y. Gen. City Law § 83–a (3 years); Conn. Gen. Stat. § 8–26a; N.J.S.A. 40:55 D-49 (3 years); Mass. Gen. L. Ch. 40A, § 6 (8 years), enforced in *Heritage Park Development Corp. v. Town of Southbridge*, 674 N.E.2d 233 (Mass.1997).

The State of Washington was one of the first states to enact an early vested rights law requiring that ordinances and regulations in effect at the time of the initial development application govern throughout the review process. *See Association of Rural Residents v. Kitsap County*, 4 P.3d 115 (Wash.2000). Kitsap County argued in this action that a subsequently submitted PUD application should not be part of the previous subdivision application process because it is opening the door to a lengthy negotiated review process. The court disagreed and concluded that when a PUD application is joined with a preliminary plat approval request, the vested right attached to the entire project, including the PUD. However, the court limited the vesting of rights to the uses disclosed in the application, and do not include all conceivable uses allowed by laws in effect at the time of application, citing, *Noble Manor Co. v. Pierce County*, 943 P.2d 1378 (Wash.1997). *See also Pine Forest Owners v. Okanogan County*, 124 Wash.App. 1016 (2004) (holding approval of a PUD application, without an accompanying preliminary plat, insufficient to vest landowner's rights under Washington's vested rights law).

For another example, *see* Tex. Gov't. Code Ann. § 481.143 providing:

The approval, disapproval, or conditional approval of an application for a permit shall be considered by each regulatory agency solely on the basis of any orders, regulations, ordinances, or other duly adopted requirements in effect at the time the original application for the permit is filed. If a series of permits is required for a project, the orders, regulations, ordinances, or other requirements in effect at the time the original application for the first permit in that series is filed shall be the sole basis for consideration of all subsequent permits required for the completion of the project."

In *FM Properties Operating Company v. City of Austin*, 93 F.3d 167 (5th Cir.1996), the plaintiffs, citing the above Texas early vesting statute, brought a federal § 1983 action against the city, contending that because their predecessors in interest had been given preliminary plat approval, the city arbitrarily and capriciously rejected the plaintiff's application for a building permit. The city informed FM Properties that it could not proceed to obtain a building permit until a final subdivision plat had been approved. While the plaintiff prepared for final plat approval, the city's flood ordinance was amended several times, ultimately prohibiting development on the site. The federal 5th Circuit Court of Appeals held that the city's policy of dividing land development activities into two projects, each involving a separate series of permits, did not violate the due process clause and did not vest the project. There was no vested right to have the building permit site plan approved based on the plaintiff's preliminary plat approval under the old ordinance. Similarly, *see Telimar Homes, Inc. v. Miller*, 218 N.Y.S.2d 175 (App.Div.1961), where despite the use of a statutory procedure authorizing the sectionalizing and phasing of subdivision development, the court held that subsequently enacted subdivision regulations increasing the standards for building sidewalks, curbs and other subdivision improvements would apply for the later sections not filed with the county clerk. The court, however, refused to apply new zoning regulations where it was established by conclusive evidence that the drainage and roads were designed for all four sections granting the developer a vested nonconforming use to the whole tract); *see also In re Appeal by Mark-Garner Assoc., Inc.*, 413 A.2d 1142 (Pa.Cmwlth.1980); *Edmonds Shopping Center Associates v. City of Edmonds*, 71 P.3d 233 (Wash.App.2003) (vested rights doctrine does not allow a business to operate exempt from later-enacted police power regulations in furtherance of a legitimate public goal).

5. *Procedural Due Process.* Since subdivision approval is administrative or quasi-judicial, a landowner whose property abuts a parcel seeking subdivision approval has the right to cross-examine witnesses at a public hearing. *People ex rel. Klaeren v. Vill. of Lisle*, 781 N.E.2d 223 (Ill.2002); *see also Weinberg v. Whatcom County*, 241 F.3d 746 (9th Cir.2001). No procedural due process violation was found when a quorum of the Town Council held a site inspection of the applicant's property, where notice of the inspection was posted in the Clerk's office under the Freedom of Information Act, but the Town did not give personal notice to abutting landowners opposing the project. *Grimes v. Conservation Comm'n of Town of Litchfield*, 703 A.2d 101 (Conn.1997). The site inspection was not deemed a "hearing," and the abutting property owner did not have a "cognizable property interest." Even where an unannounced site visit violated the notice requirements of the state's Open Meetings law, the Idaho Supreme Court upheld the visit against a due process

claim because it was not shown to be prejudicial or harmful. *Noble v. Kootenai County*, 231 P.3d 1034 (Idaho 2010).

A procedural due process claim may be improper in other circumstances as well. In *Calvert County Planning Comm'n v. Howlin Realty Mgmt., Inc.*, 772 A.2d 1209 (Md.2001), rescission of a three-year-old plat was deemed "fraud and misrepresentation," not a procedural due process violation, as the planning commission had no rules for reconsideration of subdivision approvals. The failure to have rules violated a statutory mandate, but the statutory violation "did not constitute a lack of due process or preclude the Commission from carrying out its public duties. Due Process is concerned with fundamental fairness in the proceeding, not with whether the agency has failed in some way to comply with a statutory requirement." 772 A.2d at 1221. *But see L.A. Ray Realty v. Town Council of Town of Cumberland*, 698 A.2d 202 (R.I.1997) (official animus and misconduct in denial of developer applications may lead to procedural and substantive due process violations).

6.   *Judicial Review of Final Subdivision Approval: Exhaustion.* Courts will go to great lengths before intervening in a subdivision dispute if a property owner has not exhausted all administrative remedies available. In *Hensler v. City of Glendale*, 876 P.2d 1043 (Cal.1994), the California Supreme Court rejected an inverse condemnation takings claim by a property owner brought 4 years after the City approved the subdivision with a 65% open space dedication requirement. The court reasoned that (1) the property owner was required to raise the constitutional issues at subdivision review before bringing an action for inverse condemnation, and (2) the property owner's action was governed by the California Subdivision Map Act's 90-day limitations period for actions attacking decisions concerning subdivisions. *See also Petrone v. Town of Foster*, 769 A.2d 591 (R.I.2001) (claim by property owners, who subdivided their land without approval from town planning board, that town's refusal to authorize owners to construct buildings on land not approved for subdivision, deprived them of all beneficial use of their land was not ripe, as property owners failed to exhaust their administrative remedies in seeking approval of their proposed use of land).

COMMENT: DEEMED APPROVED STATUTES

Many jurisdictions have statutes requiring the planning commission to make a decision within a specific time frame after the filing of the application for subdivision approval and for other non-legislative development approvals, such as special use permits and site plans. The failure of the planning commission to act within the statutory time frame results in a forfeiture of the right to deny the application, and the plat will be deemed approved. *Bensalem Township v. Blank*, 539 A.2d 948 (Pa.Cmwlth.1988) (final application deemed approved 90 days after the regular meeting of the planning commission); *Paladac Realty Trust v. Rockland Planning Comm'n*, 541 A.2d 919 (Me.1988) (if ordinance does not specify time frame, hearing must be held within a reasonable time). A planning commission can reopen a deemed approval for "good reason" if substantial evidence shows that the planning commission has a statutory basis for denying the subdivision. *See Czyoski v. Planning Board of Truro*, 928 N.E.2d 987 (Mass.App.2010). Similarly, a deemed approval is void if the city can show that the developer is equitably estopped by its own actions in claiming the benefit of the statute. *See Northern States Power v. City of Mendota Heights*, 646 N.W.2d 919, 926 (Minn.App.2002). *See also, Ridge Creek I, Inc. v. City of Shakopee*, No. A09–178, 2010 WL 154632, at *5 (Minn.Ct.App. Jan. 19, 2010). Although an unpublished decision, the court in *Ridge Creek* ultimately found that the property owner was equitably estopped form availing itself to the deemed approved statute, whereas *Northern States Power* did not. The deemed approved status is not gained until the developer submits an application that is complete and contains all of the requirements specified in the preliminary plat regulations. The deemed approved statutes do not apply when the City rejects a developer's plans as being submitted prematurely. *See Miles v. Foley*, 752 A.2d 503 (Conn.2000). The developer brought a mandamus action to compel the city to approve his subdivision plans claiming the rejection as premature was "action" as required by the statute. The developer claimed that the City's failure to take an approved statutory action was the equivalent to no action. The court disagreed and held the City's rejection of the plans as premature constituted an approval, conditional approval, or disapproval as required by the statute.

Since these statutes are for the protection of developers, only developers are entitled to waive the statutory time frame requirements. In *Turnpike Woods, Inc. v. Town of Stony Point*, 514 N.E.2d 380 (N.Y.1987), an action was brought to compel the issuance of a certificate giving final plat approval to a proposed subdivision. The Court of Appeals held that the town's local law which purported to suspend for six months, under an emergency moratorium, its duty to act on an application for a subdivision's final plat approval was ineffective to supersede the state's Town Law which required that the planning board act on applications for final plat approval within a 45 day period, and was therefore invalid.

F. REQUIREMENTS FOR ON-SITE SUBDIVISION IMPROVEMENTS

1. STANDARD PLANNING ENABLING ACT

Standard City Planning Enabling Act (SPEA) § 14. Such regulations may include provisions as to the extent to which streets and other ways shall be graded and improved and to which water and sewer and other utility mains, piping, or other facilities shall be installed as a condition precedent to the approval of the plat. In lieu of the completion of such improvements and utilities prior to the final approval of the plat, the commission may accept a bond with surety to secure to the municipality the actual construction and installation of such improvements or utilities at a time and according to specifications fixed by or in accordance with the regulations of the commission. The municipality is hereby granted the power to enforce such bond by all appropriate legal and equitable remedies.

BROUS V. SMITH

Court of Appeals of New York, 1952.
304 N.Y. 164, 106 N.E.2d 503.

FULD, JUDGE.

Petitioner, a real estate developer and builder, acquired title in 1951 to real estate situated in the Town of Islip, comprising approximately 850 lots as shown upon a map filed in the Suffolk County Clerk's office in the year 1872. Many of the lots abut on existing highways, but many others are located some distance back from those highways, along "paper streets"—streets designated on the map, but not physically in existence. On some of the latter lots, petitioner desired to erect six one-family residences, and he applied to the town's Building and Zoning Inspector, respondent herein, for the requisite building permits. However, respondent refused to grant any permits unless petitioner, pursuant to the provisions of section 280–a of the Town Law, McK. Consol. Laws, c. 62, constructed roads giving access to the proposed structures, or, in the alternative, posted a performance bond to insure the installation of such roads after erection of the buildings. Challenging the validity of section 280–a, petitioner brought this proceeding under article 78 of the Civil Practice Act to compel respondent to issue the permits. From the determination at Special Term, holding the statute constitutional and dismissing the complaint, petitioner appeals directly to this court, Civ. Prac. Act § 588, subd. 4.

"No permit for the erection of any building shall be issued," section 280–a of the Town Law recites, "unless a street or highway giving access to such proposed structure has been duly placed on the official map or plan, or if there be no official map or plan, unless such street or highway is (a) an existing state, county or town highway, or (b) a street shown upon a plat approved by the planning board * * * or (c) [as is the case here] a street on a plat duly filed and recorded in the office of the county clerk or register prior to the appointment of such planning board and the grant to such board of the power to approve plats." Then follows the portion of the statute here under attack. "Before such permit shall be issued," it provides, "such street or highway shall have been suitably improved to the satisfaction of the town board or planning board, if empowered by the town board in accordance with standards and specifications approved by the town board, as adequate in respect to the public health, safety and general welfare for the special circumstances of the particular street or highway." However, the section goes on to specify, "Where the enforcement of the provisions of this section would entail practical difficulty or unnecessary hardship, and where the circumstances of the case do not require the structure to be related to existing or proposed streets or highways," the landowner may appeal to the board of appeals or other board empowered to grant variances or exceptions in zoning regulations. "The board may in passing on such appeal make any reasonable exception and issue the permit subject to conditions that will protect any future street or highway layout." The decision of the board is declared reviewable in the courts by certiorari.

The requirement that a road giving access to the proposed structure be "suitably improved" before a building permit may be issued became a part of the Town Law in 1938, in which year, also, virtually identical provisions were added to the General City Law and the Village Law. Although these three provisions have thus been on the statute books for well over a decade, the present petitioner is the first to complain that any one of them unjustifiably interferes with the proper enjoyment of his property—and this circumstance may itself be of some significance

The challenged regulation is an enactment in that important field of legislation concerned with the problem of community planning and designed to secure the "uniform and harmonious development of the growth" of our villages, towns and cities

* * *

An understanding of the statute under review may be aided, and perspective gained, by a consideration of a related provision enacted at the same time. By that provision, the local planning board is empowered to require, as a condition to the approval of a subdivision plat, "that all streets or other public places shown on such plats shall be suitably graded and paved" and other improvements installed, or alternatively, that a performance bond sufficient to cover the cost of these improvements shall be furnished by the owner. The statute reflects a legislative judgment that the building up of unimproved and undeveloped areas ought to be accompanied by provision for roads and streets and other essential facilities to meet the basic needs of the new residents of the area. "We all know that where subdivision of land is unregulated, lots are sold without paving, water, drainage, or sanitary facilities, and then later the community feels forced to protect the residents and take over the streets and * * * provide for the facilities." Bettman, City and Regional Planning Papers (1946), p. 74. Thus, the regulations benefit both the consumer, who is protected "in purchasing a building site with assurance of its usability for a suitable home," and the community at large, which naturally gains greatly from the use of "sound practices in land use and development." *See* Lautner, *Subdivision Regulations* (1941), p. 238. Similar statutes, enacted in other states * * * have, when questioned in the courts, been upheld as a valid exercise of the police power.

Section 280–a of the Town Law provides for a restriction of the same character. Where adequate roads have not been constructed at the time of subdivision—here, because the plat was filed and recorded long before the development of modern planning legislation—the builder, before he may obtain a building permit, must lay such streets and highways as are necessary to render his dwellings accessible to the outside world. There can be no doubt, in light of the importance of such means of access, that the regulation is reasonable and valid. "In a time of emergency, such as sickness, accident, fire or other catastrophe," the court below pointed out, "a road over which automobiles and fire apparatus can travel safely, must always be available, otherwise great suffering, property damage and even loss of life may result." 109 N.Y.S.2d 289, 290. Nor is it only in time of peril that such roads are essential; in this era of the automobile, modern living as we know it is impossible without improved highways linking people with their jobs, their sources of food and other necessities, their children's schools and their amusements and entertainments. Unimproved or defective roads can cause a complete breakdown of services in a community. The state has a legitimate and real interest in requiring that the means of access to the new construction be properly improved and sufficient for the purpose.

It is petitioner's view, however, that, granting the necessity for such roads, it is a violation of section 7 of article I of the New York State Constitution to compel him or any other landowner to construct them on his land at his expense, without compensation from the town. He points out that, while the statute does not in terms provide that such roads are to become public streets, it is the invariable practice for the owner to dedicate them to the town—among other reasons, because, as public streets, the expenses of maintenance and repair will be shared by other landowners who benefit from them. Of course, no one may question that the town, were it desirous of constructing a road across petitioner's property, would have to condemn the necessary land and compensate petitioner. But the town here has no such desire or design and does not seek to condemn land owned by petitioner. It is petitioner who wishes to construct dwellings on his property, and the town merely conditions its approval of such construction upon his compliance with reasonable conditions designed for the protection both of the ultimate purchasers of the homes and of the public. That the state may empower the town to do this is clear. " * * * the subjection to the police power of all property gives the state the right to forbid the use of property in the way desired save under reasonable conditions, promoting the public welfare. * * * In short, it may regulate any business or the use of any property in the interest of the public health, safety, or welfare, provided this be done reasonably. To that extent the public interest is supreme and the private interest must yield." * * * The courts have accordingly sustained the validity of regulations requiring projected buildings to be set back a certain distance from the street, stipulating that back and side yards of specified area be set aside, and prescribing the minimum area upon which a residence may be built. Not essentially different from these is a regulation requiring the owner to afford access, by suitably improved roads, to the dwellings he proposes to erect.

Situations may, of course, arise where compliance with the requirement would occasion unnecessary hardship. Such may be the case, for example, where the owner of a small plot of land desires merely to construct a dwelling for his own personal use, and the improvement of a road will be an expense far out of proportion to the cost of the building. However, as indicated, section 280–a provides the means for relaxing the requirement. In cases of "practical difficulty" or "unnecessary hardship" and "where the circumstances of the case do not require the structure to be related to existing or proposed streets or highways," the board of appeals is empowered to make a "reasonable exception" in favor of the owner. The validity of the statutory scheme is therefore clear. The order appealed from should be affirmed, with costs.

NOTES

1. *Specification of Standards.* As the foregoing case illustrates, on-site design and public improvement requirements are typically mandated in the subdivision regulations. The regulations must specify these requirements, where possible. Where the standards are required to be supplemented, the planning commission will be responsible for determining the exact requirements usually following the recommendations of a local government engineer. Failure of a developer to provide for continuation of a street to the adjacent property as required in the preliminary plan (as opposed to ending the street in a cul-de-sac) is grounds for denial of a final plat. *See State ex rel. Westside Development Co., Inc. v. Weatherby Lake*, 935 S.W.2d 634 (Mo.App.1996).

2. In *Brous*, the court concluded that the county planning commission could look beyond the internal requirements of the proposed plat itself and consider off-site factors including the safety and general welfare of the entire county. In *Grant's Farm Associates v. Town of Kittery*, 554 A.2d 799 (Me.1989), an enabling act was upheld that authorized the denial of a plat approval if the Planning Board determined that the subdivision would cause off-site traffic congestion or pose a danger to shore land. A county may refuse to vacate a road wholly within a subdivision and deny the subdivision application, if the road is necessary to provide interconnectivity to adjoining land. *See Mattox v. Grimes County Commissioner's Court*, 305 S.W.3d 375 (Tex.App.2010). If an area is unique aesthetically, it is not unreasonable for a city to conclude that it is in the best interests of the general welfare to preserve the beauty and integrity of the land by denying inappropriate subdivision. *See Fleckinger v. Jefferson Parish Council*, 510 So.2d 429 (La.App.1987). In the case of design and aesthetic appearance upgrading off-site roads to the same minimum standard as on-site roads, where the off-site road furnishes access to the subdivision to arterial roads is appropriate. *See Shannondale v. Jefferson County Planning & Zoning Comm'n*, 485 S.E.2d 438 (W.Va.1997).

3. The need for "oversized facilities" to accommodate future growth creates a particular problem. If a subdivision is the first to develop within a planning area, drainage or sewerage basin, it may be required to provide a larger-sized facility or excess capacity to serve the future development in the area. Without providing for equitable distribution of improvement costs, one developer will sustain a "wipeout" while later developers will accrue a

"windfall." Such requirements, where they involve dedication of land or monetary exactions, will be measured by the constitutional test of rough proportionality. *Benchmark Land Company v. City of Battle Ground*, 972 P.2d 944 (Wash.App.1999). *See* Chapter 4.H. *infra*, "Financing of Capital Facilities the Need for Which Is Generated by New Development."

4.   Evidence of the need for such facilities must be contained in the record by the municipality in order to sustain a decision denying development based on inadequate water quality and quantity. *Hurrle v. County of Sherburne*, 594 N.W.2d 246 (Minn.App.1999) (municipality offered no evidence to countermand developer's expert witness testimony and decision to deny plat approval was overturned).

2.   ENSURING COMPLETION

MODEL SUBDIVISION REGULATIONS: PLANNING AND LAW[4]
R. Freilich and M. Schultz, pp. 124–127 (1995).

The planning commission has the authority to require the subdivider to install all of the required public improvements before a subdivision plat is finally approved and recorded. Requiring improvements to be completed before plat approval often causes long delays and expense to a developer who can neither sell lots nor begin the construction of homes until the plat is recorded. Final subdivision plat approval may be granted prior to completion of improvements if the subdivider guarantees to complete the improvements, which takes the form of requiring the subdivider to post a performance bond, a letter of credit or some other type of security for its promise to complete improvements following final plat approval. The performance bond or letter of credit security is limited to only those public improvements or segments of roads, the need for which is generated by the subdivision. *See Homebuilders v. City of LeMoore*, 112 Cal.Rptr.3d 7 (Cal.App.2010).

Acceptable security methods vary by jurisdiction, with the most common requirement being a corporate surety bond "or other adequate security." Where the subdivision is subject to approval by a number of agencies, the developer may be required to post several bonds. Most jurisdictions, however, permit a consolidated bond for all the requirements. The usual term of the bond or security agreement is two years from the date of the final plat approval.

NOTES

1.   *Payment and Performance Bonds.* A municipality might consider requiring both a performance bond and a payment bond. Freilich & Schultz, *Model Subdivision Regulations, Planning and Law*, 2d ed. 1–6 (Am. Planning

---

[4]   Reprinted with permission. Copyright 1995 by the American Planning Association.

Ass'n 1995). The distinction between the two is substantial. The former only ensures that the actual work is completed. There is no assurance that all labor and material costs have been fully paid for the work performed. Under most state statutes, such persons may file a mechanic's or materialman's lien on the improvement, and if the municipality accepts dedication of the improvement, it may find itself liable for payment of the liens in the event of developer insolvency. *Estate of Haselwood v. Bremerton Ice Arena and City of Bremerton*, 210 P.3d 308 (Wash.2009); A municipality may avoid this prior to final plat approval by obtaining and recording an offer of irrevocable dedication with a title search to ensure that there are no prior liens. A provision in the bond which requires dedication of the improvements after construction, free and clear of all liens and encumbrances, makes it a payment as well as performance bond. A performance bond posted by a developer could be used to improve a perimeter road but only as to that part of the road that was directly affected by the proposed residential development. *See Clare v. Town of Hudson*, 999 A.2d 348 (N.H.2010).

2. *Maintenance Bonds.* Still another tool available to ensure even greater fiscal benefit to the local government in addition to performance and payment bonds or security, subdivision approval can be conditioned on the furnishing a maintenance bond (or security), a device used to cover the cost of maintaining improvements until they are accepted by the city or county through dedication. Maintenance bonds have been upheld as an extension of the statutory authority of guaranteeing performance. *See Legion Manor, Inc. v. Township of Wayne*, 231 A.2d 201 (N.J.1967) (approving a maintenance bond equal to ten percent of the performance bond for all defects in material and workmanship occurring within three years after final subdivision approval). *See* Michael M. Schultz and Richard Kelly, *Using, Structuring, and Managing the Standby Letter of Credit to Ensure the Completion of Subdivision Improvements*, 19 URB.LAW. 39 (1987).

G. OFFICIAL MAP

In one of its most far seeing provisions, the SPEA provides for the establishment of a Major Street Plan, separate and apart from the master plan, for the protection of street and public utility rights of way, parks, open spaces, and public buildings and structures. Since the Major Street Plan was a separate document implementing the master plan, the SPEA confers legal status upon the Major Street Plan. It is important to distinguish the "Major Street Plan" from the "Master Plan." To assure that such a distinction is readily apparent, subsequent planning and legal texts have referred to the Major Street Plan as the "Official Map," a term of art that subsequently has been incorporated into state planning statutes. Occasionally, where the municipality's protection is only extended to street and major arterial right of ways, it retains the title of "Major Street Plan" or "Major Thoroughfare Plan." While the SPEA referred to only "municipalities," all subsequent state statutes based on the SPEA include counties as well as cities. We will refer to the term as the "Official Map" in this section. The SPEA sections pertaining to the "Official Map" reads as follows:

Section 21. Reservation of Locations of Mapped Streets for Future Public Acquisition.

> Any planning commission is empowered, after it shall have adopted a major street plan to make or cause to be made, from time to time, surveys for the exact location of the lines of a street or streets and to make a[n] [Official] map of the area or district thus surveyed, showing the land which it recommends be reserved for future acquisition for public streets. The council may approve and adopt or may reject such plat or may modify it with the approval of the planning commission, or, in the event of the planning commission's disapproval, council may, by a favorable vote of not less than two-thirds of its entire membership, modify such map and adopt the modified map. In the resolution of adoption of the map, the council shall fix the period of time for which the street locations shown upon the plat shall be deemed reserved for future taking or acquisition for public use. Such approval and adoption of a map shall not, however, be deemed the opening or establishment of any street, nor the taking of any land for street purposes, nor for public use, nor as a public improvement, but solely as a reservation of the street locations shown thereon, for the period specified in the council

The American Planning Association, in its Growing Smart Legislative Guidebook, at 7–246, 8–65 (Jan.2002) describes the functions of the Official Map as being far broader than the preservation of major street right-of-ways. Sixty years ago, two important legal commentators, who were responsible for the resurgence of the Official Map in Wisconsin, described its functions in a famous article as follows:

> "In essence the official map is a simple device. It is one way, but not the only way, to fix building lines. The official map may plat future as well as existing streets. Where future streets are mapped, subdividers must conform to the mapped street lay-out, unless they can prevail upon the proper officials to amend the map. Public sewer and water will be installed only in the bed of the mapped streets. Even more important, a landowner who builds in the bed of the mapped street may be refused compensation for his building when the street is ultimately opened and the mapped land taken.

> The official map of future streets has obvious advantages in terms of the public coffers. It assures that land needed for future streets will be available at bare land prices. Mapping of future streets also gives direction and pattern to future growth of the

community, though some feel that the map casts the mold too inflexibly, especially if minor as well as major streets are mapped.

Where existing streets have been officially mapped, the map will often set widening lines (set-backs) warning that new structures must be located in conformance with their lines, and these also have obvious advantages in cutting costs of street widening.

Joseph C. Kucirek and J.H. Beuscher, *Wisconsin's Official Map Law*, 1957 W.L.REV. 176, 177.

As cities and counties began to implement Official Maps, they widened the scope of the Official Map from a street plan to include mapping of parks, trails, habitat corridors, environmentally sensitive lands, open spaces and public buildings. New methods of implementing official maps to avoid classification as regulatory takings have been very successful. Consider the flexibility of the following Florida Supreme Court decision in refusing to find that such official maps were facial takings.

PALM BEACH COUNTY V. WRIGHT
Supreme Court of Florida, 1994.
641 So.2d 50.

GRIMES, CHIEF JUSTICE.

We review *Palm Beach County v. Wright*, 612 So.2d 709 (Fla.4th DCA 1993), in which the court certified the following as a question of great public importance:

> Is a county thoroughfare map designating corridors for future roadways, and which forbids land use activity that would impede future construction of a roadway, adopted incident to a comprehensive county land use plan enacted under the local government comprehensive planning and land development regulation act, facially unconstitutional under *Joint Ventures, Inc. v. Department of Transportation*, 563 So.2d 622 (Fla.1990)?

The thoroughfare map referred to in the certified question is a portion of the traffic circulation element of the Palm Beach County Comprehensive Plan as adopted in Ordinance 89–17. The map defines certain transportation corridors along specified roadways throughout Palm Beach County as well as certain other locations designated for future roadway construction. The traffic circulation element of the Comprehensive Plan provides that the "County shall provide for protection and acquisition of existing and future right-of-way consistent with the adopted Thoroughfare Right-of-Way Protection Map." The traffic circulation element continues by providing that the "Map is designed to protect identified transportation corridors from encroachment by other land use activities." The map applies to all land development activities within unincorporated Palm Beach County. The land development activities are defined as including but not limited to residential, commercial, institutional, or industrial purposes. All development is required to be consistent with and provide for the transportation right-of-way shown on the thoroughfare map. The land use element of the Comprehensive Plan provides that no land use activity may be permitted within any roadway designated on the thoroughfare map that would impede future construction of the roadway. The land use element further provides that all development approvals and actions by the county must be consistent with the provisions contained in the Comprehensive Plan.

The roadway corridors are located on the thoroughfare map in varying widths from 80 to 240 feet. The thoroughfare map contains a 220-foot right-of-way corridor which includes Southern Boulevard, an existing roadway in Palm Beach County. Respondents own property on the north side of Southern Boulevard. Therefore, a portion of their property lies within the corridor of the thoroughfare map.

The respondents filed suit attacking the constitutionality of the thoroughfare map. The trial court entered summary judgment against the county finding that the map as implemented by the land use element and traffic circulation element of the Comprehensive Plan was facially unconstitutional. The court determined that the map was in violation of the Fifth Amendment of the United States Constitution and article X, section 6 of the Florida Constitution. The court reasoned that the map was not a valid police regulation furthering the county's planning function for future growth and that it did not substantially advance a legitimate state interest. The court also held that the adoption of the map constituted a temporary taking of the respondents' property within the right-of-way corridor and ordered a jury trial to determine compensation for the taking. In a split decision, the district court of appeal affirmed the judgment. The appellate court reasoned that the thoroughfare map was functionally indistinguishable from the reservation map this Court declared invalid in *Joint Ventures, Inc. v. Department of Transportation*, 563 So.2d 622 (Fla.1990). The court also agreed that a taking had occurred.

Subsequent to the decision of the district court of appeal, this Court issued its opinion in *Tampa-Hillsborough County Expressway Authority v. A.G.W.S. Corp.*, 640 So.2d 54 (Fla.1994), which has a substantial bearing on this case. In A.G.W.S., we held that landowners with property inside the boundaries of maps of reservation invalidated by Joint Ventures, Inc., are not legally entitled to receive per se declarations of taking. We explained that subsections 337.241(2) and (3), Florida Statutes (1987), which authorized the filing of the maps of reservation, were held invalid because they did not meet the requirements of due process, not because the filing of such a map always resulted in a taking. Whether the filing of a map of reservation resulted in a taking of particular property would depend upon whether its effect was to deny the owner of substantially all of the economically beneficial or productive use of the land.

If the filing of a map of reservation under subsections 337.241(2) and (3) did not constitute a per se taking, it is clear that the adoption of the Palm Beach County thoroughfare map which designates corridors for future roadways would not constitute a per se taking. Therefore, at least one portion of the final judgment will have to be reversed. There remains, however, the question of whether the thoroughfare map is unconstitutional. On this point, the parties differ with respect to the applicability of Joint Ventures, Inc.

The respondents assert that the practical effect of the thoroughfare map is the same as that of the maps of reservation held invalid in Joint Ventures in that the thoroughfare map does not permit land use or activity within the designated corridors which would impede future roadway construction. However, the county argues that section 337.241, which prohibited construction within the limits of [state] recorded maps of reservation, was enacted for the sole purpose of reducing the future acquisition costs of roads. By contrast, the county's thoroughfare map is an unrecorded long-range planning tool tied to a comprehensive plan that outlines general roadway corridors and does not on its face delineate the exact routes of future roadways.

The county contends that the plan provides sufficient flexibility so that it cannot be determined whether a taking has occurred within the roadway corridors until the property owner submits a development approval application. When this occurs, the county asserts that it will be in the position to work with the property owner to (1) assure the best routes through the land that maximize the development potential; (2) offer development opportunities for clustering densities at key nodes and parcels off the corridors; (3) grant alternative and more valuable uses; (4) avoid loss of value that results in taking by using development rights transfer and credit for impact fees; and, if necessary, (5) alter or change the road pattern.

The county points out that the effect of designating road corridors is to increase most property values. Often, the increase in value of abutting property will more than offset any loss occasioned by the owner's inability to use land within the corridor. Therefore, the county argues that a determination of whether a taking has occurred within the corridor can only be made when a county has acted upon an application for development approval.

Palm Beach County's comprehensive plan was adopted pursuant to the requirements of the Local Government Comprehensive Planning and Land Development Regulation Act. Section 163.3177(6)(b), Florida Statutes (1991), requires the comprehensive plan to contain "[a] traffic circulation element consisting of the types, locations, and extent of existing and proposed major thoroughfares and transportation routes." Palm Beach County was further required to place measures in the comprehensive plan to protect existing and future rights-of-way from building encroachments and to preserve and acquire existing and future rights-of-way. One of the purposes of the thoroughfare map is to place property owners on notice as to the necessity and location of future roads. According to the comprehensive plan, this "allows land developers adequate time to plan their developments with proper road interfacing requirements."

There are many public benefits to be achieved through comprehensive planning of future road development. Since the infrastructure of many of America's cities demands extensive redevelopment along sewer and transportation networks, the opportunity arises for a comprehensive integration of land use and transportation planning. Where mass and rapid transit is envisioned, the area from one-quarter to one-half of a mile in radius from stops should be planned for redevelopment. These areas should be developed at densities sufficient to sustain the planned transportation facility. Additionally, commercial and industrial siting should follow this pattern so that sites may be concentrated along transportation corridors and thus facilitate access to employment and decreased energy consumption and automobile usage. The resulting pattern of community development would allow transit and other aspects of the infrastructure to take advantage of economies of scale. *See* James A. Kushner, *Urban Transportation Planning*, 4 URBAN LAW & POL'Y 161, 173 (1981). Thus, there can be no question that the planning for future growth must include designation of the areas where roads are likely to be widened and future roads are to be built.

We are persuaded that the Palm Beach County thoroughfare map as implemented by the comprehensive plan is not facially invalid. At least with respect to existing streets, the roadway corridors are analogous to set-back requirements. Many years ago this Court held that a city may establish building set-back lines through the exercise of police power and without compensation to the property owners. Furthermore, the owners most likely to benefit from planned road construction are those whose properties are adjacent to transportation corridors. Under the concurrency requirements of section 163.3177(10)(h), Florida Statutes (1991), development will be curtailed unless roads are available to accommodate the impact of such development. Therefore, projects closest to new roads are likely to benefit the most from construction of the roads even if a portion of the owner's property must be reserved for road construction.

The thoroughfare map differs in several ways from the maps of reservation invalidated by Joint Ventures. The thoroughfare map only limits development to the extent necessary to ensure compatibility with future land use. The thoroughfare map is not recorded as were maps of reservation and may be amended twice a year. The road locations within the transportation corridors shown on the thoroughfare map have not been finally determined. Unlike the Department of Transportation which recorded the maps of reservation, Palm Beach County is a permitting authority which has the flexibility to ameliorate some of the hardships of a person owning land within the corridor. Section 337.241 precluded the issuance of all development permits for land within the recorded map. Moreover, the only purpose of that statute was to freeze property so as to depress land values in anticipation of eminent domain proceedings. While the Palm Beach County thoroughfare map can have the effect of adversely affecting land values of some property, it also serves as an invaluable tool for planning purposes. Thus, we hold that the adoption of the thoroughfare map is the proper subject of the county's police power which substantially advances a legitimate state interest. In fact, the county's ability to plan for future growth would be seriously impeded without the thoroughfare map.

At the same time, we recognize that as applied to certain property, the thoroughfare map may result in a taking. In rejecting a facial challenge to certain restrictive mining regulations in favor of "an applied" determination, the United States Supreme Court aptly noted:

> "[T]his Court has generally 'been unable to develop any "set formula" for determining when "justice and fairness" require that economic injuries caused by public action be compensated by the government, rather than remain disproportionately concentrated on a few persons.' Rather, it has examined the 'taking' question by engaging in essentially ad hoc, factual inquiries that have identified several factors—such as the economic impact of the regulation, its interference with reasonable investment backed expectations, and the character of the government action—that have particular significance."

Hodel v. Virginia Surface Mining & Reclamation Ass'n, 452 U.S. 264, 295 (1981) (quoting *Kaiser Aetna v. United States*, 444 U.S. 164, 175 (1979).

Therefore, we are convinced that the taking issue may only be determined upon an individualized basis because the various property owners' interests will be different and will be affected by the thoroughfare map in a differing manner. As noted by the Court in *Penn Central Transportation Co. v. City of New York*, 438 U.S. 104, 130 (1978), " '[t]aking' jurisprudence does not divide a single parcel into discrete segments and attempt to determine whether rights in a particular segment have been entirely abrogated." *See Department of Transp. v. Weisenfeld*, 617 So.2d 1071 (Fla.5th DCA 1993) (In deciding whether a governmental regulation deprives an owner of substantially all economically beneficial use of land, the owner's affected property interest must be viewed as a whole.), approved, 640 So.2d 73 (Fla.1994). Normally, we would expect the issue to be precipitated by a property owner's application for a development permit. By virtue of the county's response, the owner will then know what can be done with the property. In any event, an aggrieved owner may always bring an inverse condemnation proceeding which if successful will result in a payment for the taking as well as the recovery of attorney's fees.

We answer the certified question in the negative and quash the decision below.

It is so ordered.

NOTES: OFFICIAL MAPS AND THE TAKINGS ISSUE

1. As demonstrated by the *Wright* case, Florida has had a great deal of official map litigation in recent years. In *Joint Ventures, Inc.*, discussed within *Wright*, the Florida Department of Transportation recorded a reservation map of specific right-of-way in the public land records of a county pursuant to a statute that granted such authority. Under that statute, once the map was recorded, construction for improvements could not occur and development permits could not be issued for a period of five years within the transportation corridor shown on the map. The Florida Supreme Court found the statute that authorized the use of a reservation map to be facially unconstitutional. The court likened the use of the state's recorded official map to the illegal freezing of property values in an attempt to depress land values in anticipation of eminent domain proceedings. The court explained that the government may act as a neutral arbiter through the use of its police powers by adopting such measures as zoning ordinances and building codes, "[b]ut where the purpose of the governmental action is the prevention of the development of land that would increase the cost of a planned future acquisition of such land by government * * * it can no longer pretend to be acting as a neutral arbiter." 563 So.2d 622 at 626.

2. Contrary to Florida, the Illinois Supreme Court in *Davis v. Brown*, 851 N.E.2d 1198 (Ill.2006) held that a statute allowing the state to reserve indefinitely rights of way for future additions to the state highway system, with owners of land in reserved rights of way required to give the state notice of their intent to develop, with the state required to condemn the land within 165 days, did not constitute a facial regulatory taking.

3. In *Ward v. Bennett*, 625 N.Y.S.2d 609 (App.Div.1995) the court held that the city's refusal of a building permit in the bed of a 50-year-old mapped street constituted a regulatory taking of the property, since the General City Law allowed the City of New York a period of 10 years to either condemn the property or allow a building to be erected. The court did opine that a temporary restriction on the land without compensation for the purpose of conducting studies toward a comprehensive regulatory scheme would be constitutional, citing *Matter of Rubin v. McAlevey*, 288 N.Y.S.2d 519 (App.Div.1968). Interim development controls are discussed in Chapter 7.

4. If compliance with the official map regulations will not leave the landowner reasonable, economically beneficial use, then either the government must condemn and pay compensation or issue a variance, use of clustering or

transfer of development rights. To what extent will such regulations be held to leave the landowner with a reasonable use?

5.   In *Kottschade v. City of Rochester*, 537 N.W.2d 301 (Minn.App.1995), a property owner refused to convey his land for street right-of-way as a condition of development approval for a Target store, restaurants and a shopping center. These widened street right-of-ways were designated on the official map. The landowner brought suit, and the Minnesota Court of Appeals held that there was no constitutional deprivation where the need for the widened right-of-way dedication was generated by the proposed development. This concept is fully discussed in Section F, *infra*.

6.   When might a set-back provision amount to a taking?

7.   While the law is well settled that a reasonable official map regulation will be upheld under the police power and the government will not be required to pay compensation until it condemns, what about a reservation that requires a landowner to hold any portion of his land that is shown on the official map until the municipality decides whether to acquire it by purchase or condemnation? May a government reserve an area for a park, street improvements or school site without paying compensation to the landowner? For how long a period of time can a government take in making its decision to condemn? Should there be a difference in the treatment of official map regulations and recorded maps of reservation? What remedies does the landowner have? In *Urbanizadora Versalles, Inc. v. Rivera Rios*, 701 F.2d 993 (1st Cir.1983), the court held that 14 years was an unreasonable reservation period. Can a clear line be drawn as to when the court will declare a reservation period a taking? Referring to a five year period which was found to be unconstitutionally unreasonable by the federal Court of Claims in *Benenson v. United States*, 548 F.2d 939, 947 (Ct.Cl.1977), the court in *Urbanizadora* said: "We need not decide * * * whether we would find so short a period to be unconstitutional." 701 F.2d at 997. In *Miller v. City of Beaver Falls*, 82 A.2d 34 (Pa.1951), the court held that a state statute and city ordinance enacted under it which gave the city three years to decide whether to condemn property for a park was an unconstitutional taking without compensation.

8.   In *Lomarch Corp. v. Mayor and Common Council of City of Englewood*, 237 A.2d 881 (N.J.1968), the New Jersey Supreme Court had an opportunity to rule on a one year reservation ordinance. The plaintiff owner of 16 acres of land applied for subdivision approval. While his application was pending, the council, pursuant to state statute, placed the land on the city official map and designated it as land reserved for use as a park. The statute allowed the city one year after final plat approval to decide whether it would condemn the land. The plaintiff filed suit challenging the constitutionality of the state statute. The court upheld the statute by reading into it intent to compensate the landowner during the interim period. The court concluded plaintiff was entitled to compensation which should equal the value of an "option" to purchase the land for the year, including taxes accruing during the "option" period. *But see Lord Calvert Theatre v. Mayor and City Council of Baltimore*, 119 A.2d 415 (Md.1956) (holding a twenty-five-year reservation to

widen a street not a taking, absent facts showing bad faith or de facto control of the site even after twenty-five years). Why should park reservations be subject to stricter review than street reservations?

After the *Lomarch* decision, the New Jersey statute was amended to include a compensation requirement for actual loss during reservation periods. *See* N.J.Stat.Ann. § 40:55D–44. Subsequent to adoption of the statute, an appellate court held that a 120 day120-day reservation would not constitute a temporary taking which would entitle a landowner to compensation. *See Kingston East Realty Co. v. State Commissioner of Transportation*, 336 A.2d 40 (N.J.App.1975).

9.   Suppose that the street widening, proposed street or reserved park, open space, trail, or school site is shown solely on the comprehensive plan and not on an official map. Whether such designation will be legally binding on the landowner and/or municipality will depend on whether the state makes the plan a legally binding instrument. In *Platt v. City of New York*, 93 N.Y.S.2d 738 (App.Div.1949), Ms. Platt brought an action against the City of New York to recover damages for allegedly causing her property to become unsalable. The property was shown on the City's Master Plan as lying within the boundaries of a proposed parkway. It was alleged that the city had instructed the Building Department not to issue any building permits within the street boundaries and made public statements to the effect that such permits would not be issued. In dismissing the complaint, the court noted that since the lots were not shown on an adopted separate Official Map and no actual permit had been refused, there was no authority to maintain the action.

10.   Where a statute provides that an "official map shall be deemed conclusive with respect to the location * * * of streets," N.J.Stat.Ann. § 40:55 D-32, is a planning board bound to follow the map in ruling on subdivision applications? In *Nigro v. Planning Bd.*, 584 A.2d 1350, 1358 (N.J.1991), the court held that:

> An official map deserves substantial but not absolute deference in planning board decision-making regarding subdivision approvals. Although a clear conflict with a street proposed on a municipality's official map may provide a basis for a planning board to reject a subdivision application, the official map should not be seen as immutable.

Does that make any sense if the very purpose of the Official Map is to legally protect the right-of-way?

11.   *Access to, and Repair of, Streets and Roads Shown on the Official Map.* It is important to distinguish between the denial of inverse condemnation relief to owners when government acts to prevent development on the bed of a proposed right-of-way shown on an adopted Official Map, and the failure of the government to maintain the street in good repair or to provide access to the street when there is no other reasonable access. In *Jordan v. St. Johns County*, 63 So.3d 835 (Fla.App.2011), the Court held that:

There is a right to be compensated through inverse condemnation when governmental action causes a substantial loss of access to one's property from an existing street shown on the Official Map. Even though there is no physical appropriation of the property itself. It is not necessary that there be a complete loss of access to the property. However, the fact that a portion or even all of one's access to an abutting road is destroyed does not constitute a taking unless, when considered in light of the remaining access to the property, it can be said that the property owner's right of access was substantially diminished. The loss of the most convenient access is not compensable where other suitable access continues to exist. *Palm Beach County v. Tessler,* 538 So.2d 846, 849 (Fla.1989)".

Similarly, the court held that once a county accepts a road into its street system, it has a duty to maintain the street in reasonably good repair no matter what the cost or difficulty. We will consider the impairment of the fiscal wellbeing of counties that unthinkingly accept the road infrastructure of ever increasing sprawl development in Chapter 7, *infra.*

H. FINANCING OF CAPITAL FACILITIES THE NEED FOR WHICH IS GENERATED BY NEW DEVELOPMENT

1. INTRODUCTION: INFRASTRUCTURE DEFICIENCIES

Consider the customary process of development. Development *A,* the first built in a new city, constructs a thousand homes and pays for 100% of the cost of building off-site roads, parks, schools and other public infrastructure facilities, since the cost, $24,000 per development unit, will be 100% borne by Developer A, either as a regulatory exaction directly laid on Developer A, or paid for through the city's general property tax, since the city and the developer are one and the same. Now when Developer *B* comes along and builds a second thousand homes and asserts that the off-site public improvements, the need for which has been generated by Development B, are "community facilities" and must be paid for by the city's general property tax, rather than exacted directly on Developer *B,* the occupants of *A's* houses will have to pay for 50% of the cost of the facilities. Now imagine that Developer *C* arrives and builds a third thousand homes. The same scenario arises with the same result: *A* and *B* pay for two-thirds of C's off-site facilities, resulting in an exportation of city general revenue to the new growth area and the concomitant lack of city revenue for maintenance and improvement of the facilities built by A and B's developments. Two results obtain: (1) since city general revenue is being used to subsidize B and C's developments, there is little likelihood that those facilities will ever be built to full capacity and massive deficiencies will begin to build up in the city; and (2) the city's revenue payments to new growth areas incentivizes, subsidizes and stimulates wasteful urban sprawl and penalizes the city's built up existing neighborhoods, leading to urban blight.

We will cover the sprawl issues in Chapter 7 and the blight issues in Chapter 6. This section of Chapter 4 will deal with the methods (dedication of land, money in lieu of land, impact fees, affordable housing linkage fees and capital improvement programming) needed to properly exact either land or money from new development to cover the costs of off-site capital facilities, the need for which has been generated by the new development. As we have seen earlier in Chapter 4, the on-site capital costs will be borne by the development through the subdivision process.

Homes	A	B	C
1000	$24,000		
2000	$12,000	$12,000	
3000	$8,000	$8,000	$8,000

Recent studies of our country's crumbling infrastructure testify to the urgent need for our nation to expend large sums to repair and upgrade capital facilities within our existing communities, and to prevent sprawl development from creating further massive deficiencies in capital infrastructure, where adequate off-site capital facilities or services, the need for which is generated by new development, will not be built or provided to appropriate levels of service defined in the comprehensive plan or long term capital improvements program.

The continuing exportation of capital to new development, shown in the diagram above, promotes deterioration of closer-in neighborhoods and subsidizes the process of urban sprawl. In light of the massive economic and fiscal crises facing our states and cities from the recessions of 2001 to 2004 and 2008 to the present, coupled with major tax reductions passed over the past decade, it is critical to charge new development and new residents for the full cost of providing those facilities. Will these charges raise housing costs beyond the reach of low and moderate-income households, a subject we will discuss in Chapter 5? The answer appears to be "no". *See* Arthur C. Nelson, Liza K. Bowles, Julian C. Juergensmeyer, and James C. Nicholas, *A Guide to Impact Fees and Housing Affordability* 99 (2008) (citing to extensive studies in Florida from 1993 to 2003); Franklin James, *Evaluation of Local Impact Fees as a Source of Infrastructure Finance*, 11 MUN.FIN.J. 407 (1990).

In 1984, the National Infrastructure Advisory Committee of the Joint Economic Committee of the United States Congress published its report entitled Hard Choices, Summary Report of the National Infrastructure Study prepared for the Joint Economic Committee of the United States Congress, 98th Cong., 2d Sess. (1984). The report inventoried our nation's infrastructure needs and predicted that the shortfall between the total national needs and available revenue through the year 2000 would be over $400 billion. The report severely underestimated the problem. By 2003, the American Society of Civil Engineers reported that the infrastructure deficiencies had grown to $1.6 trillion dollars just for the next five years. Local water and sewer systems alone will need an extra $535 billion dollars over the next twenty years simply to keep waterways from becoming more polluted. The federal government spent $3.7 billion in taxpayer money to rebuild Iraq's water and sewer systems compared to just $1.8 billion for EPA's sewer and water grants for the entire nation in fiscal year 2004, dropping from $2.2 billion in fiscal year 2003.

These reports, however, have received limited exposure, and their central thesis—that the federal government has become a less significant partner in rebuilding and expanding the nation's infrastructure—has been largely ignored. This is in part due to a new focus on bringing down the national deficit and severely downsizing federal government employment and programs. For an excellent analysis of the deteriorating infrastructure, *see* Felix G. Rohatyn and Everett Ehrlich, *A New Bank to Save Our Infrastructure* (New York Review of Books, November 11, 2010).

This severe problem has forced local governments to examine and experiment with alternate ways to fund its infrastructural needs. One of the primary mechanisms local governments have used to assist in the funding and provision of public facilities generated by new development has been the development exaction which may consist of a number of different implementing financing techniques: (1) dedication of land; (2) money-in lieu of land dedication; impact fees; mitigation fees; excise taxes; increasing use of public improvement district assessment, bonding and taxation; and public utility rate structures.

The National Council on Public Works Improvement, in its final report (Feb.1988), suggested that the basic strategy for funding public works should include *increased reliance on beneficiaries financing public works at all levels of government and encouragement of developer financing of new infrastructure investments.* The development exaction, as a means of financing necessary public facilities and infrastructure in an era of reduced availability of traditional sources of revenue for such activities, is clearly an important regulatory tool for counties and local governments and should be integrated into each government's comprehensive plan financing element and capital improvements program (CIP) methodology for funding the construction of public facilities, the demand for which is generated by growth, as well as for maintaining and repairing its existing infrastructure. *Id.* at 3.

2. EXACTIONS: REASONABLY RELATED, UNIQUELY ATTRIBUTABLE, RATIONAL NEXUS AND ROUGH PROPORTIONALITY: THE STATE CONSTITUTIONAL QUADRUPLETS

(a) Authority

Exactions may falter because express statutory authority is lacking. *See New Jersey Builders Ass'n v. Bernards Twp.*, 528 A.2d 555 (N.J.1987) (holding a requirement that new development pay pro rata share of town's $20 million road improvement plan exceeded authority granted by the state's enabling act). Still, many courts have implied the authority to impose exactions for public utilities, both from the need to protect citizens from the hazards the public facilities are designed to mitigate, and from specific authority to provide directly for such facilities, often as part of a municipal plan function. *See* Frona Powell, *Challenging Authority for Municipal Subdivision Exactions: The Ultra Vires Attack*, 39 DEPAUL L.REV. 635 (1990). In *Call v. City of West Jordan*, 606 P.2d 217 (Utah 1979), the court upheld an ordinance requiring subdividers to dedicate 7% of the land or the equivalent value in cash to be used for flood control and/or park and recreation facilities as within the implied authority of the city:

> It is not questioned that cities have no inherent sovereign power, but only those granted by the legislature. But it must be realized that it is impractical for statutes to spell out to the last detail all of the things city governments must do to perform the functions imposed upon them by law. This Court has in numerous cases recognized this and has held that cities have those powers which are expressly granted and also those necessarily implied to carry out such responsibilities. * * * The Municipal Planning Enabling Act empowers a city to have a planning commission which may "adopt and certify to the legislative body, a master plan for the physical development of the municipality." Section 10–9–22 states that the planning commission "shall have such powers as may be necessary to enable it to perform its functions and promote municipal planning." * * * In modern times of ever-increasing population and congestion, real estate developers buy land at high prices. From the combined pressures of competition and desire for gain, they often squeeze every lot they can into some labyrinthian plan, with only the barest minimum for tortious and circuitous streets, without any arterial ways through such subdivisions, and with little or no provision for parks, recreation areas, or even for reasonable "elbow room." The need for some general planning and control is apparent, and makes manifest the wisdom underlying the delegation of powers to the cities, as is done in the statutes above referred to.

Id. at 218–19.

(b) Nexus

NOLLAN V. CALIFORNIA COASTAL COMMISSION
Supreme Court of the United States, 1987.
483 U.S. 825, 107 S.Ct. 3141, 97 L.Ed.2d 677.

JUSTICE SCALIA delivered the opinion of the Court

James and Marilyn Nollan appeal from a decision of the California Court of Appeal ruling that the California Coastal Commission could condition its grant of permission to rebuild their house on their transfer to the public of an easement across their beachfront property. The California court rejected their claim that imposition of that condition violates the Takings Clause of the Fifth Amendment, as incorporated against the States by the Fourteenth Amendment. We noted probable jurisdiction.

The Nollans own a beachfront lot in Ventura County, California. A quarter-mile north of their property is Faria County Park, an oceanside public park with a public beach and recreation area. Another public beach area, known locally as "the Cove," lies 1,800 feet south of their lot. A concrete seawall approximately eight feet high separates the beach portion of the Nollans' property from the rest of the lot. The historic mean high tide line determines the lot's oceanside boundary.

The Nollans originally leased their property with an option to buy. The building on the lot was a small bungalow, totaling 504 square feet, which for a time they rented to summer vacationers. After years of rental use, however, the building had fallen into disrepair, and could no longer be rented out.

The Nollans' option to purchase was conditioned on their promise to demolish the bungalow and replace it. In order to do so, under Cal. Pub. Res. Code Ann. §§ 30106, 30212, and 30600 (West 1986), they were required to obtain a coastal development permit from the California Coastal Commission. On February 25, 1982, they submitted a permit application to the Commission in which they proposed to demolish the existing structure and replace it with a three-bedroom house in keeping with the rest of the neighborhood.

The Nollans were informed that their application had been placed on the administrative calendar, and that the Commission staff had recommended that the permit be granted subject to the condition that they allow the public an easement to pass across a portion of their property bounded by the mean high tide line on one side, and their seawall on the other side. This would make it easier for the public to get to Faria County Park and the Cove. The Nollans protested imposition of the condition, but the Commission overruled their objections and granted the permit subject to their recordation of a deed restriction granting the easement.

On June 3, 1982, the Nollans filed a petition for writ of administrative mandamus asking the Ventura County Superior Court to invalidate the access condition. They argued that the condition could not be imposed absent evidence that their proposed development would have a direct adverse impact on public access to the beach. The court agreed, and remanded the case to the Commission for a full evidentiary hearing on that issue.

On remand, the Commission held a public hearing, after which it made further factual findings and reaffirmed its imposition of the condition. It found that the new house would increase blockage of the view of the ocean, thus contributing to the development of "a 'wall' of residential structures" that would prevent the public "psychologically .psychologically . . . from realizing a stretch of coastline exists nearby that they have every right to visit." The new house would also increase private use of the shorefront. These effects of construction of the house, along with other area development, would cumulatively "burden the public's ability to traverse to and along the shorefront." Therefore the Commission could properly require the Nollans to offset that burden by providing additional lateral access to the public beaches in the form of an easement across their property. The Commission also noted that it had similarly conditioned 43 out of 60 coastal development permits along the same tract of land, and that of the 17 not so conditioned, 14 had been approved when the Commission did not have administrative regulations in place allowing imposition of the condition, and the remaining 3 had not involved shorefront property.

The Nollans filed a supplemental petition for a writ of administrative mandamus with the Superior Court, in which they argued that imposition of the access condition violated the Takings Clause of the Fifth Amendment, as incorporated against the States by the Fourteenth Amendment. The Superior Court ruled in their favor on statutory grounds, finding, in part to avoid "issues of constitutionality," that the California Coastal Act of 1976, Cal. Pub. Res. Code Ann. § 30000 *et seq.* (West 1986), authorized the Commission to impose public access conditions on coastal development permits for the replacement of an existing single-family home with a new one only where the proposed development would have an adverse impact on public access to the sea. In the court's view, the administrative record did not provide an adequate factual basis for concluding that replacement of the bungalow with the house would create a direct or cumulative burden on public access to the sea. Accordingly, the Superior Court granted the writ of mandamus and directed that the permit condition be struck.

The Commission appealed to the California Court of Appeal. While that appeal was pending, the Nollans satisfied the condition on their option to purchase by tearing down the bungalow and building the new house, and bought the property. They did not notify the Commission that they were taking that action.

The Court of Appeal reversed the Superior Court. It disagreed with the Superior Court's interpretation of the Coastal Act, finding that it required that a coastal permit for the construction of a new house whose floor area, height or bulk was more than 10% larger than that of the house it was replacing be conditioned on a grant of access. It also ruled that the requirement did not violate the Constitution under the reasoning of an earlier case of the Court of Appeal, *Grupe v. California Coastal Comm'n,* 166 Cal.App.3d 148, 212 Cal.Rptr. 578 (1985). In that case, the court had found that so long as a project contributed to the need for public access, even if the project standing alone had not created the need for access, and even if there was only an indirect relationship between the access exacted and the need to which the project contributed, imposition of an access condition on a development permit was sufficiently related to burdens created by the project to be constitutional. The Court of Appeal ruled that the record established that that was the situation with respect to the Nollans' house. It ruled that the Nollans' taking claim also failed because, although the condition diminished the value of the Nollans' lot, it did not deprive them of all reasonable use of their property. Since, in the Court of Appeal's view, there was no statutory or constitutional obstacle to imposition of the access condition, the Superior Court erred in granting the writ of mandamus. The Nollans appealed to this Court, raising only the constitutional question.

II

Had California simply required the Nollans to make an easement across their beachfront available to the public on a permanent basis in order to increase public access to the beach, rather than conditioning their permit to rebuild their house on their agreeing to do so, we have no doubt there would have been a taking. To say that the appropriation of a public easement across a landowner's premises does not constitute the taking of a property interest but rather (as Justice Brennan contends) "a mere restriction on its use," is to use words in a manner that deprives them of all their ordinary meaning. Indeed, one of the principal uses of the eminent domain power is to assure that the government be able to require conveyance of just such interests, so long as it pays for them. * * * Perhaps because the point is so obvious, we have never been confronted with a controversy that required us to rule upon it, but our cases' analysis of the effect of other governmental action leads to the same conclusion. We have repeatedly held that, as to property reserved by its owner for private use, "the right to exclude [others is] 'one of the most essential sticks in the bundle of rights that are commonly characterized as property.'" *Loretto v. Teleprompter Manhattan CATV Corp.*, 458 U.S. 419, 433 (1982), quoting *Kaiser Aetna v. United States*, 444 U.S. 164, 176 (1979). In *Loretto* we observed that where governmental action results in "[a] permanent physical occupation" of the property, by the government itself or by others, "our cases uniformly have found a taking to the extent of the occupation, without regard to whether the action achieves an important public benefit or has only minimal economic impact on the owner." We think a "permanent physical occupation" has occurred, for purposes of that rule, where individuals are given a permanent and continuous right to pass to and fro, so that the real property may continuously be traversed, even though no particular individual is permitted to station himself permanently upon the premises.

Justice Brennan argues that while this might ordinarily be the case, the California Constitution's prohibition on any individual's "exclu[ding] the right of way to [any navigable] water whenever it is required for any public purpose," Art. X, § 4, produces a different result here. There are a number of difficulties with that argument. Most obviously, the right of way sought here is not naturally described as one to navigable water (from the street to the sea) but *along* it; it is at least highly questionable whether the text of the California Constitution has any prima facie application to the situation before us. Even if it does, however, several California cases suggest that Justice Brennan's interpretation of the effect of the clause is erroneous, and that to obtain easements of access across private property the State must proceed through its eminent domain power. * * *)[2]

Given, then, that requiring uncompensated conveyance of the easement outright would violate the Fourteenth Amendment, the question becomes whether requiring it to be conveyed as a condition for issuing a land-use permit alters the outcome. We have long recognized that land-use regulation does not effect a taking if it "substantially advance[s] legitimate state interests" and does not "den[y] an owner economically viable use of

---

[2] Justice Brennan also suggests that the Commission's public announcement of its intention to condition the rebuilding of houses on the transfer of easements of access caused the Nollans to have "no reasonable claim to any expectation of being able to exclude members of the public" from walking across their beach. He cites our opinion in *Ruckelshaus v. Monsanto Co.*, 467 U.S. 986 (1984), as support for the peculiar proposition that a unilateral claim of entitlement by the government can alter property rights. In *Monsanto*, however, we found merely that the Takings Clause was not violated by giving effect to the Government's announcement that application for "*the right to [the] valuable Government benefit*," (emphasis added), of obtaining registration of an insecticide would confer upon the Government a license to use and disclose the trade secrets contained in the application. But the right to build on one's own property—even though its exercise can be subjected to legitimate permitting requirements—cannot remotely be described as a "governmental benefit." And thus the announcement that the application for (or granting of) the permit will entail the yielding of a property interest cannot be regarded as establishing the voluntary "exchange," that we found to have occurred in Monsanto. Nor are the Nollans' rights altered because they acquired the land well after the Commission had begun to implement its policy. So long as the Commission could not have deprived the prior owners of the easement without compensating them, the prior owners must be understood to have transferred their full property rights in conveying the lot.

his land," *Agins v. Tiburon*, 447 U.S. 255, 260 (1980). *See also Penn Central Transportation Co. v. New York City,* 438 U.S. 104 (1978) ("[A] use restriction may constitute a 'taking' if not reasonably necessary to the effectuation of a substantial government purpose"). Our cases have not elaborated on the standards for determining what constitutes a "legitimate state interest" or what type of connection between the regulation and the state interest satisfies the requirement that the former "substantially advance" the latter.[3] They have made clear, however, that a broad range of governmental purposes and regulations satisfies these requirements. *See Agins v. Tiburon, supra,* 447 U.S., at 260–262 (scenic zoning); *Penn Central Transportation Co. v. New York City, supra* (landmark preservation); *Euclid v. Ambler Realty Co.,* 272 U.S. 365 (1926) (residential zoning); Laitos & Westfall, *Government Interference with Private Interests in Public Resources,* 11 HARV.ENVTL.L.REV. 1, 66 (1987). The Commission argues that among these permissible purposes are protecting the public's ability to see the beach, assisting the public in overcoming the "psychological barrier" to using the beach created by a developed shorefront, and preventing congestion on the public beaches. We assume, without deciding, that this is so—in which case the Commission unquestionably would be able to deny the Nollans their permit outright if their new house (alone, or by reason of the cumulative impact produced in conjunction with other construction)[4] would substantially impede these purposes, unless the denial would interfere so drastically with the Nollans' use of their property as to constitute a taking.

The Commission argues that a permit condition that serves the same legitimate police-power purpose as a refusal to issue the permit should not

---

[3]   Contrary to Justice Brennan's claim, our opinions do not establish that these standards are the same as those applied to due process or equal protection claims. To the contrary, our verbal formulations in the takings field have generally been quite different. We have required that the regulation "substantially advance" the "legitimate state interest" sought to be achieved, *Agins v. Tiburon,* 447 U.S. 255, 260 (1980), not that "the State '*could rationally have decided*' that the measure adopted might achieve the State's objective." Justice BRENNAN relies principally on an equal protection case, *Minnesota v. Clover Leaf Creamery Co., supra,* and two substantive due process cases, *Williamson v. Lee Optical of Oklahoma, Inc.,* 348 U.S. 483, 487–488 (1955), and *Day-Brite Lighting, Inc. v. Missouri,* 342 U.S. 421 (1952), in support of the standards he would adopt. But there is no reason to believe (and the language of our cases gives some reason to disbelieve) that so long as the regulation of property is at issue the standards for takings challenges, due process challenges, and equal protection challenges are identical; any more than there is any reason to believe that so long as the regulation of speech is at issue the standards for due process challenges, equal protection challenges, and First Amendment challenges are identical. *Goldblatt v. Hempstead,* 369 U.S. 590 (1962), does appear to assume that the inquiries are the same, but that assumption is inconsistent with the formulations of our later cases.

[4]   If the Nollans were being singled out to bear the burden of California's attempt to remedy these problems, although they had not contributed to it more than other coastal landowners, the State's action, even if otherwise valid, might violate either the incorporated Takings Clause or the Equal Protection Clause. One of the principal purposes of the Takings Clause is "to bar Government from forcing some people alone to bear public burdens which, in all fairness and justice, should be borne by the public as a whole." *Armstrong v. United States,* 364 U.S. 40, 49 (1960); *see also San Diego Gas & Electric Co. v. San Diego,* 450 U.S. 621, 656 (1981) (BRENNAN, J., dissenting); *Penn Central Transportation Co. v. New York City,* 438 U.S. 104 (1978). But that is not the basis of the Nollans' challenge here.

be found to be a taking if the refusal to issue the permit would not constitute a taking. We agree. Thus, if the Commission attached to the permit some condition that would have protected the public's ability to see the beach notwithstanding construction of the new house—for example, a height limitation, a width restriction, or a ban on fences—so long as the Commission could have exercised its police power (as we have assumed it could) to forbid construction of the house altogether, imposition of the condition would also be constitutional. Moreover (and here we come closer to the facts of the present case), the condition would be constitutional even if it consisted of the requirement that the Nollans provide a viewing spot on their property for passersby with whose sighting of the ocean their new house would interfere. Although such a requirement, constituting a permanent grant of continuous access to the property, would have to be considered a taking if it were not attached to a development permit, the Commission's assumed power to forbid construction of the house in order to protect the public's view of the beach must surely include the power to condition construction upon some concession by the owner, even a concession of property rights, that serves the same end. If a prohibition designed to accomplish that purpose would be a legitimate exercise of the police power rather than a taking, it would be strange to conclude that providing the owner an alternative to that prohibition which accomplishes the same purpose is not.

The evident constitutional propriety disappears, however, if the condition substituted for the prohibition utterly fails to further the end advanced as the justification for the prohibition. When that essential nexus is eliminated, the situation becomes the same as if California law forbade shouting fire in a crowded theater, but granted dispensations to those willing to contribute $100 to the state treasury. While a ban on shouting fire can be a core exercise of the State's police power to protect the public safety, and can thus meet even our stringent standards for regulation of speech, adding the unrelated condition alters the purpose to one which, while it may be legitimate, is inadequate to sustain the ban. Therefore, even though, in a sense, requiring a $100 tax contribution in order to shout fire is a lesser restriction on speech than an outright ban, it would not pass constitutional muster. Similarly, here, the lack of nexus between the condition and the original purpose of the building restriction converts that purpose to something other than what it was. The purpose then becomes, quite simply, the obtaining of an easement to serve some valid governmental purpose, but without payment of compensation. Whatever may be the outer limits of "legitimate state interests" in the takings and land-use context, this is not one of them. In short, unless the permit condition serves the same governmental purpose as the development ban, the building restriction is not a valid regulation of land use but "an out-

and-out plan of extortion." *J.E.D. Associates, Inc. v. Atkinson*, 121 N.H. 581, 584, 432 A.2d 12, 14–15 (1981). * * *[5]

III

The Commission claims that it concedes as much, and that we may sustain the condition at issue here by finding that it is reasonably related to the public need or burden that the Nollans' new house creates or to which it contributes. We can accept, for purposes of discussion, the Commission's proposed test as to how close a "fit" between the condition and the burden is required, because we find that this case does not meet even the most untailored standards. The Commission's principal contention to the contrary essentially turns on a play on the word "access." The Nollans' new house, the Commission found, will interfere with "visual access" to the beach. That in turn (along with other shorefront development) will interfere with the desire of people who drive past the Nollans' house to use the beach, thus creating a "psychological barrier" to "access." The Nollans' new house will also, by a process not altogether clear from the Commission's opinion but presumably potent enough to more than offset the effects of the psychological barrier, increase the use of the public beaches, thus creating the need for more "access." These burdens on "access" would be alleviated by a requirement that the Nollans provide "lateral access" to the beach.

Rewriting the argument to eliminate the play on words makes clear that there is nothing to it. It is quite impossible to understand how a requirement that people already on the public beaches be able to walk across the Nollans' property reduces any obstacles to viewing the beach created by the new house. It is also impossible to understand how it lowers any "psychological barrier" to using the public beaches, or how it helps to remedy any additional congestion on them caused by construction of the Nollans' new house. We therefore find that the Commission's imposition of the permit condition cannot be treated as an exercise of its land-use power for any of these purposes.[6] Our conclusion on this point is consistent with

---

[5]   One would expect that a regime in which this kind of leveraging of the police power is allowed would produce stringent land-use regulation which the State then waives to accomplish other purposes, leading to lesser realization of the land-use goals purportedly sought to be served than would result from more lenient (but non-tradable) development restrictions. Thus, the importance of the purpose underlying the prohibition not only does not *justify* the imposition of unrelated conditions for eliminating the prohibition, but positively militates against the practice.

[6]   As Justice Brennan notes, the Commission also argued that the construction of the new house would " 'increase private use immediately adjacent to public tidelands,' " which in turn might result in more disputes between the Nollans and the public as to the location of the boundary. That risk of boundary disputes, however, is inherent in the right to exclude others from one's property, and the construction here can no more justify mandatory dedication of a sort of "buffer zone" in order to avoid boundary disputes than can the construction of an addition to a single-family house near a public street. Moreover, a buffer zone has a boundary as well, and unless that zone is a "no-man's land" that is off limits for both neighbors (which is of course not the case here) its creation achieves nothing except to shift the location of the boundary dispute further on to the private owner's land. It is true that in the distinctive situation of the Nollans' property the seawall could be established as a clear demarcation of the public easement. But since not all of the lands to which this land-use condition applies have such a convenient reference point,

the approach taken by every other court that has considered the question, with the exception of the California state courts.

Justice Brennan argues that imposition of the access requirement is not irrational. In his version of the Commission's argument, the reason for the requirement is that in its absence, a person looking toward the beach from the road will see a street of residential structures including the Nollans' new home and conclude that there is no public beach nearby. If, however, that person sees people passing and repassing along the dry sand behind the Nollans' home, he will realize that there is a public beach somewhere in the vicinity. The Commission's action, however, was based on the opposite factual finding that the wall of houses completely blocked the view of the beach and that a person looking from the road would not be able to see it at all.

Even if the Commission had made the finding that Justice Brennan proposes, however, it is not certain that it would suffice. We do not share Justice Brennan's confidence that the Commission "should have little difficulty in the future in utilizing its expertise to demonstrate a specific connection between provisions for access and burdens on access," that will avoid the effect of today's decision. We view the Fifth Amendment's Property Clause to be more than a pleading requirement, and compliance with it to be more than an exercise in cleverness and imagination. As indicated earlier, our cases describe the condition for abridgement of property rights through the police power as a "*substantial* advanc[ing]" of a legitimate state interest. We are inclined to be particularly careful about the adjective where the actual conveyance of property is made a condition to the lifting of a land-use restriction, since in that context there is heightened risk that the purpose is avoidance of the compensation requirement, rather than the stated police-power objective.

We are left, then, with the Commission's justification for the access requirement unrelated to land-use regulation: "Finally, the Commission notes that there are several existing provisions of pass and repass lateral access benefits already given by past Faria Beach Tract applicants as a result of prior coastal permit decisions. The access required as a condition of this permit is part of a comprehensive program to provide continuous public access along Faria Beach as the lots undergo development or redevelopment." That is simply an expression of the Commission's belief that the public interest will be served by a continuous strip of publicly accessible beach along the coast. The Commission may well be right that it is a good idea, but that does not establish that the Nollans (and other coastal residents) alone can be compelled to contribute to its realization. Rather, California is free to advance its "comprehensive program," if it wishes, by using its power of eminent domain for this "public purpose," see

---

the avoidance of boundary disputes is, even more obviously than the others, a made-up purpose of the regulation.

U.S. Const., Amdt. 5; but if it wants an easement across the Nollans' property, it must pay for it.

Reversed.

JUSTICE BRENNAN, with whom JUSTICE MARSHALL joins, dissenting. [omitted]

NOTES: NOLLAN AND PLANNING

1.   The Court's "essential nexus" requirement establishes "a remoteness test where a court inquires into whether there exists a reasonable causal connection between the prevention of the perceived adverse impacts of the development project and the health, safety and general welfare condition the government has imposed on the permit." Robert H. Freilich and Terry Morgan, *Municipal Strategies for Imposing Valid Development Exactions: Responding to* Nollan, 10 ZONING AND PLANNING L.REP., No.11 at 170 (Dec.1987). How this decision radically affected the law is suggested in Vicki Been, *"Exit" As a Constraint on Land Use Exactions: Rethinking the Unconstitutional Conditions Doctrine*, 91 COLUM.L.REV. 473 (1991).

2.   The *Nollan* opinion does not address a second constitutional issue as to when an exaction will be regarded as excessive. For example, had the remoteness test been met in *Nollan*, there still would have been a question as to whether the required dedication was disproportionate to the needs generated by the development. See also footnote 4 of the Court's opinion. The Court returned to the proportionality requirement in the following case.

(c) Proportionality

DOLAN v. CITY OF TIGARD
Supreme Court of the United States, 1994.
512 U.S. 374, 114 S.Ct. 2309, 129 L.Ed.2d 304.

CHIEF JUSTICE REHNQUIST delivered the opinion of the Court.

The State of Oregon enacted a comprehensive land use management program in 1973. The program required all Oregon cities and counties to adopt new comprehensive land use plans that were consistent with the statewide planning goals. The plans are implemented by land use regulations which are part of an integrated hierarchy of legally binding goals, plans, and regulations. Pursuant to the State's requirements, the city of Tigard, a community of some 30,000 residents on the southwest edge of Portland, developed a comprehensive plan and codified it in its Community Development Code (CDC). The CDC requires property owners in the area zoned Central Business District to comply with a 15% open space and landscaping requirement, which limits total site coverage, including all structures and paved parking, to 85% of the parcel. After the completion of a transportation study that identified congestion in the Central Business District as a particular problem, the city adopted a plan for a pedestrian/bicycle pathway intended to encourage alternatives to automobile transportation for short trips. The CDC requires that new development facilitate this plan by dedicating land for pedestrian pathways where provided for in the pedestrian/bicycle pathway plan.

The city also adopted a Master Drainage Plan (Drainage Plan). The Drainage Plan noted that flooding occurred in several areas along Fanno Creek, including areas near petitioner's property. The Drainage Plan also established that the increase in impervious surfaces associated with continued urbanization would exacerbate these flooding problems. To combat these risks, the Drainage Plan suggested a series of improvements to the Fanno Creek Basin, including channel excavation in the area next to petitioner's property. Other recommendations included ensuring that the floodplain remains free of structures and that it be preserved as greenways to minimize flood damage to structures. The Drainage Plan concluded that the cost of these improvements should be shared based on both direct and indirect benefits, with property owners along the waterways paying more due to the direct benefit that they would receive. The CDC and the Tigard Park Plan carry out these recommendations.

Petitioner Florence Dolan owns a plumbing and electric supply store located on Main Street in the Central Business District of the city. The store covers approximately 9,700 square feet on the eastern side of a 1.67 acre parcel, which includes a gravel parking lot. Fanno Creek flows through the southwestern corner of the lot and along its western boundary. The year round flow of the creek renders the area within the creek's 100 year floodplain virtually unusable for commercial development. The city's comprehensive plan includes the Fanno Creek floodplain as part of the city's greenway system.

Petitioner applied to the city for a permit to redevelop the site. Her proposed plans called for nearly doubling the size of the store to 17,600 square feet, and paving a 39 space parking lot. The existing store, located on the opposite side of the parcel, would be razed in sections as construction progressed on the new building. In the second phase of the project, petitioner proposed to build an additional structure on the northeast side of the site for complementary businesses, and to provide more parking. The proposed expansion and intensified use are consistent with the city's zoning scheme in the Central Business District.

The City Planning Commission granted petitioner's permit application subject to conditions imposed by the city's CDC. The Commission required that petitioner dedicate the portion of her property lying within the 100 year floodplain for improvement of a storm drainage system along Fanno Creek and that she dedicate an additional 15 foot strip of land adjacent to the floodplain as a pedestrian/bicycle pathway. The dedication required by that condition encompasses approximately 7,000 square feet, or roughly 10% of the property. In accordance with city practice, petitioner could rely on the dedicated property to meet the 15% open space and landscaping requirement mandated by the city's zoning scheme. The city would bear the cost of maintaining a landscaped buffer between the dedicated area and the new store.

II

The Takings Clause of the Fifth Amendment of the United States Constitution, made applicable to the States through the Fourteenth Amendment, provides: "[N]or shall private property be taken for public use, without just compensation." One of the principal purposes of the Takings Clause is "to bar Government from forcing some people alone to bear public burdens which, in all fairness and justice, should be borne by the public as a whole." *Armstrong v. United States*. Without question, had the city simply required petitioner to dedicate a strip of land along Fanno Creek for public use, rather than conditioning the grant of her permit to redevelop her property on such a dedication, a taking would have occurred. Such public access would deprive petitioner of the right to exclude others, "one of the most essential sticks in the bundle of rights that are commonly characterized as property." *Kaiser Aetna v. United States*.

On the other side of the ledger, the authority of state and local governments to engage in land use planning has been sustained against constitutional challenge as long ago as our decision in *Euclid v. Ambler Realty Co.* "Government hardly could go on if to some extent values incident to property could not be diminished without paying for every such change in the general law." *Pennsylvania Coal Co. v. Mahon*. A land use regulation does not effect a taking if it "substantially advance[s] legitimate state interests" and does not "den[y] an owner economically viable use of his land." *Agins v. Tiburon*.

The sort of land use regulations discussed in the cases just cited, however, differ in two relevant particulars from the present case. First, they involved essentially legislative determinations classifying entire areas of the city, whereas here the city made an adjudicative decision to condition petitioner's application for a building permit on an individual parcel. Second, the conditions imposed were not simply a limitation on the use petitioner might make of her own parcel, but a requirement that she deed portions of the property to the city. In *Nollan, supra*, we held that governmental authority to exact such a condition was circumscribed by the Fifth and Fourteenth Amendments. Under the well settled doctrine of "unconstitutional conditions," the government may not require a person to give up a constitutional right—here the right to receive just compensation when property is taken for a public use—in exchange for a discretionary benefit conferred by the government where the property sought has little or no relationship to the benefit.

Petitioner contends that the city has forced her to choose between the building permit and her right under the Fifth Amendment to just compensation for the public easements. Petitioner does not quarrel with the city's authority to exact some forms of dedication as a condition for the grant of a building permit, but challenges the showing made by the city to justify these exactions. She argues that the city has identified "no special benefits" conferred on her, and has not identified any "special quantifiable burdens" created by her new store that would justify the particular dedications required from her which are not required from the public at large.

III

In evaluating petitioner's claim, we must first determine whether the "essential nexus" exists between the "legitimate state interest" and the permit condition exacted by the city. If we find that a nexus exists, we must then decide the required degree of connection between the exactions and the projected impact of the proposed development. We were not required to reach this question in *Nollan*, because we concluded that the connection did not meet even the loosest standard. Here, however, we must decide this question.

A

[The Court summarizes *Nollan* and its holding.]

No such gimmicks are associated with the permit conditions imposed by the city in this case. Undoubtedly, the prevention of flooding along Fanno Creek and the reduction of traffic congestion in the Central Business District qualify as the type of legitimate public purposes we have upheld. It seems equally obvious that a nexus exists between preventing flooding along Fanno Creek and limiting development within the creek's 100 year floodplain. Petitioner proposes to double the size of her retail store and to pave her now gravel parking lot, thereby expanding the impervious surface on the property and increasing the amount of stormwater run off into Fanno Creek.

The same may be said for the city's attempt to reduce traffic congestion by providing for alternative means of transportation. In theory, a pedestrian/bicycle pathway provides a useful alternative means of transportation for workers and shoppers: "Pedestrians and bicyclists occupying dedicated spaces for walking and/or bicycling ... remove potential vehicles from streets, resulting in an overall improvement in total transportation system flow." A. Nelson, *Public Provision of Pedestrian and Bicycle Access Ways: Public Policy Rationale and the Nature of Private Benefits 11,* Center for Planning Development, Georgia Institute of Technology, Working Paper Series (Jan. 1994).

B

The second part of our analysis requires us to determine whether the degree of the exactions demanded by the city's permit conditions bear the required relationship to the projected impact of petitioner's proposed development. Here the Oregon Supreme Court deferred to what it termed the "city's unchallenged factual findings" supporting the dedication conditions and found them to be reasonably related to the impact of the expansion of petitioner's business.

The city required that petitioner dedicate "to the city as Greenway all portions of the site that fall within the existing 100 year floodplain [of Fanno Creek] . . . and all property 15 feet above [the floodplain] boundary." In addition, the city demanded that the retail store be designed so as not to intrude into the greenway area. The city relies on the Commission's rather tentative findings that increased stormwater flow from petitioner's property "can only add to the public need to manage the [floodplain] for drainage purposes" to support its conclusion that the "requirement of dedication of the floodplain area on the site is related to the applicant's plan to intensify development on the site."

The question for us is whether these findings are constitutionally sufficient to justify the conditions imposed by the city on petitioner's building permit. Since state courts have been dealing with this question a good deal longer than we have, we turn to representative decisions made by them.

In some States, very generalized statements as to the necessary connection between the required dedication and the proposed development seem to suffice. We think this standard is too lax to adequately protect petitioner's right to just compensation if her property is taken for a public purpose.

Other state courts require a very exacting correspondence, described as the "specifi[c] and uniquely attributable" test. Under this standard, if the local government cannot demonstrate that its exaction is directly proportional to the specifically created need, the exaction becomes "a veiled exercise of the power of eminent domain and a confiscation of private property behind the defense of police regulations." We do not think the Federal Constitution requires such exacting scrutiny, given the nature of the interests involved.

A number of state courts have taken an intermediate position, requiring the municipality to show a "reasonable relationship" between the required dedication and the impact of the proposed development. Typical is the Supreme Court of Nebraska's opinion in *Simpson v. North Platte*, where that court stated:

> The distinction, therefore, which must be made between an appropriate exercise of the police power and an improper exercise of eminent domain is whether the requirement has some reasonable relationship or nexus to the use to which the property is being made or is merely being used as an excuse for taking

property simply because at that particular moment the landowner is asking the city for some license or permit.

Thus, the court held that a city may not require a property owner to dedicate private property for some future public use as a condition of obtaining a building permit when such future use is not "occasioned by the construction sought to be permitted."

We think the "reasonable relationship" test adopted by a majority of the state courts is closer to the federal constitutional norm than either of those previously discussed. But we do not adopt it as such, partly because the term "reasonable relationship" seems confusingly similar to the term "rational basis" which describes the minimal level of scrutiny under the Equal Protection Clause of the Fourteenth Amendment. We think a term such as "rough proportionality" best encapsulates what we hold to be the requirement of the Fifth Amendment. No precise mathematical calculation is required, but the city must make some sort of individualized determination that the required dedication is related both in nature and extent to the impact of the proposed development.[8]

Justice Stevens' dissent relies upon a law review article for the proposition that the city's conditional demands for part of petitioner's property are "a species of business regulation that heretofore warranted a strong presumption of constitutional validity." But simply denominating a governmental measure as a "business regulation" does not immunize it from constitutional challenge on the grounds that it violates a provision of the Bill of Rights. In *Marshall v. Barlow's, Inc.*, we held that a statute authorizing a warrantless search of business premises in order to detect OSHA violations violated the Fourth Amendment. And in *Central Hudson Gas & Electric Corp. v. Public Service Comm'n of N.Y.*, we held that an order of the New York Public Service Commission, designed to cut down the use of electricity because of a fuel shortage, violated the First Amendment insofar as it prohibited advertising by a utility company to promote the use of electricity. We see no reason why the Takings Clause of the Fifth Amendment, as much a part of the Bill of Rights as the First Amendment or Fourth Amendment, should be relegated to the status of a poor relation in these comparable circumstances. We turn now to analysis of whether the findings relied upon by the city here, first with respect to the floodplain easement, and second with respect to the pedestrian/bicycle path, satisfied these requirements.

It is axiomatic that increasing the amount of impervious surface will increase the quantity and rate of storm water flow from petitioner's

---

[8] Justice Stevens' dissent takes us to task for placing the burden on the city to justify the required dedication. He is correct in arguing that in evaluating most generally applicable zoning regulations, the burden properly rests on the party challenging the regulation to prove that it constitutes an arbitrary regulation of property rights. Here, by contrast, the city made an adjudicative decision to condition petitioner's application for a building permit on an individual parcel. In this situation, the burden properly rests on the city.

property. Therefore, keeping the floodplain open and free from development would likely confine the pressures on Fanno Creek created by petitioner's development. In fact, because petitioner's property lies within the Central Business District, the Community Development Code already required that petitioner leave 15% of it as open space and the undeveloped floodplain would have nearly satisfied that requirement. But the city demanded more—it not only wanted petitioner not to build in the floodplain, but it also wanted petitioner's property along Fanno Creek for its greenway system. The city has never said why a public greenway, as opposed to a private one, was required in the interest of flood control.

The difference to petitioner, of course, is the loss of her ability to exclude others. As we have noted, this right to exclude others is "one of the most essential sticks in the bundle of rights that are commonly characterized as property." *Kaiser Aetna*. It is difficult to see why recreational visitors trampling along petitioner's floodplain easement are sufficiently related to the city's legitimate interest in reducing flooding problems along Fanno Creek, and the city has not attempted to make any individualized determination to support this part of its request.

The city contends that recreational easement along the greenway is only ancillary to the city's chief purpose in controlling flood hazards. It further asserts that unlike the residential property at issue in Nollan, petitioner's property is commercial in character and therefore, her right to exclude others is compromised. " 'The Constitution extends special safeguards to the privacy of the home[.]' " The city maintains that "[t]here is nothing to suggest that preventing [petitioner] from prohibiting [the easements] will unreasonably impair the value of [her] property as a [retail store]."

Admittedly, petitioner wants to build a bigger store to attract members of the public to her property. She also wants, however, to be able to control the time and manner in which they enter. The recreational easement on the greenway is different in character from the exercise of state protected rights of free expression and petition that we permitted in *PruneYard*. In *PruneYard*, we held that a major private shopping center that attracted more than 25,000 daily patrons had to provide access to persons exercising their state constitutional rights to distribute pamphlets and ask passersby to sign their petitions. We based our decision, in part, on the fact that the shopping center "may restrict expressive activity by adopting time, place, and manner regulations that will minimize any interference with its commercial functions." By contrast, the city wants to impose a permanent recreational easement upon petitioner's property that borders Fanno Creek. Petitioner would lose all rights to regulate the time in which the public entered onto the greenway, regardless of any interference it might pose with her retail store. Her right to exclude would not be regulated, it would be eviscerated.

If petitioner's proposed development had somehow encroached on existing greenway space in the city, it would have been reasonable to require petitioner to provide some alternative greenway space for the public either on her property or elsewhere. But that is not the case here. We conclude that the findings upon which the city relies do not show the required reasonable relationship between the floodplain easement and the petitioner's proposed new building.

With respect to the pedestrian/bicycle pathway, we have no doubt that the city was correct in finding that the larger retail sales facility proposed by petitioner will increase traffic on the streets of the Central Business District. The city estimates that the proposed development would generate roughly 435 additional trips per day. Dedications for streets, sidewalks, and other public ways are generally reasonable exactions to avoid excessive congestion from a proposed property use. But on the record before us, the city has not met its burden of demonstrating that the additional number of vehicle and bicycle trips generated by the petitioner's development reasonably relate to the city's requirement for a dedication of the pedestrian/bicycle pathway easement. The city simply found that the creation of the pathway "could offset some of the traffic demand . . . and lessen the increase in traffic congestion."

No precise mathematical calculation is required, but the city must make some effort to quantify its findings in support of the dedication for the pedestrian/bicycle pathway beyond the conclusory statement that it could offset some of the traffic demand generated.

IV

Cities have long engaged in the commendable task of land use planning, made necessary by increasing urbanization particularly in metropolitan areas such as Portland. The city's goals of reducing flooding hazards and traffic congestion, and providing for public greenways, are laudable, but there are outer limits to how this may be done. "A strong public desire to improve the public condition [will not] warrant achieving the desire by a shorter cut than the constitutional way of paying for the change." *Pennsylvania Coal.*

The judgment of the Supreme Court of Oregon is reversed, and the case is remanded for further proceedings consistent with this opinion.

[The dissenting opinion of JUSTICE STEVENS, in which JUSTICES BLACKMUN and GINSBURG joined, and the dissenting opinion of JUSTICE SOUTER are omitted.]

NOTES: NOLLAN/DOLAN

1.   Note that the Supreme Court used substantive due process theory in *Nollan* (citing *Euclid* and *Nectow*'s use of the substantive due process irrational nexus or arbitrary and capricious behavior to weigh the validity of

zoning). *Nollan* determined that the ad hoc administrative bargaining by the Coastal Commission, lacking a valid nexus to the purpose of the regulatory approval process, invalidated the mandatory dedication condition requiring a beachfront easement. *Nollan,* however, utilized a substantive due process test based on *Agins v. City of Tiburon,* 447 U.S. 255 (1980), where the Court had said, in dicta, that the failure to substantially advance a legitimate state interest constitutes a taking. In 2005, the Supreme Court overturned the *Agins* decision on the basis that the failure to advance a substantial state interest did not properly constitute a regulatory taking test and belonged only in a substantive due process case. See *Lingle v. Chevron U.S.A., Inc.,* 544 U.S. 528 (2005), discussed in Chapter 3. The *Lingle* Court referred to *Nollan* and *Dolan* "as special applications of the doctrine of 'unconstitutional conditions' " and noted that both cases arose in the context of ad hoc administrative bargaining. Did the Court mean to exclude legislative conditions from *Nollan/Dolan* scrutiny? If so, why? For differing opinions, *see* James S. Burling & Graham Owen, *The Implications of* Lingle *on Inclusionary Zoning and Other Legislative and Monetary Exactions,* 28 STAN.ENVTL.L.J. 397 (2009) and Daniel L. Siegel, *Exactions after* Lingle*: How Basing* Nollan *and* Dolan *on the Unconstitutional Conditions Doctrine Limits Their Scope,* 28 STAN.ENVTL.L.J. 577 (2009). While most courts do limit *Nollan/Dolan* to administratively imposed conditions, some do not. For a listing of cases, *see* Juergensmeyer and Roberts, *Land Use Planning and Development Regulation Law* § 10.5 (2012).

So long as an action promotes a legitimate public purpose within the meaning of *Kelo,* does a property owner have any recourse under the takings clause other than to seek compensation? Can a court enjoin what a landowner contends is an unconstitutional condition imposed as the price for the government granting a permit? See the discussion *supra,* In *Alto Eldorado Partnership LLC v. County of Santa Fe,* 634 F.3d 1170 (10th Cir.2011), *cert. denied* 132 S.Ct. 246 (2011), the court dealt with an ordinance that required developers of residential subdivisions to develop and sell a certain percentage of the homes as affordable housing. The developers brought a facial takings claim in federal court seeking injunctive relief. The court held the claim unripe on the basis of *Willamson County,* see discussion *supra* Ch. 3, since the developers had not sought compensation in state court. Addressing the developers claim the court stated:

> The developers argue that *Nollan* and *Dolan* limit the power of the state to interfere with property rights, regardless of compensation, by requiring permitting exactions to "substantially advance" the same interest that would allow denial of the permit. According to the developers, *Nollan* and *Dolan* thus authorize facial challenges seeking to invalidate [or enjoin] an alleged taking when the taking arises in the context of a permitting requirement, akin to the now-defunct "substantially advances" theory previously available to challenge any regulatory taking.
>
> The developers misunderstand *Nollan* and *Dolan.* The premise of the challenge in both cases was that the takings were uncompensated.

There was no contention the state could not properly exercise its right to appropriate the land use rights at issue in *Nollan* and *Dolan* if such takings were compensated; rather, the question presented was whether the state could permissibly achieve the same result without compensation by exacting the land use rights in exchange for granting a permit it was otherwise entitled to deny.

Arguing that *Nollan* and *Dolan* provide a cause of action to facially invalidate land-use exactions, rather than to invalidate those exactions only where compensation is denied, the developers cite the Supreme Court's reliance on the unconstitutional conditions doctrine. As the Court stated in *Dolan,* however, under this doctrine, "the government may not require a person to give up a constitutional right—*here the right to receive just compensation* when property is taken for a public use" to receive an unrelated discretionary benefit. 512 U.S. at 385 (emphasis the court's). That is, the right a property owner cannot be forced to give up is the right to compensation; had the state justly compensated the plaintiffs in *Nollan* and *Dolan,* no Takings Clause violations could have been alleged even under the unconstitutional conditions doctrine.

In essence, the developers attempt to turn *Nollan* and *Dolan* into loopholes in the *Lingle* rule that challenges to regulation as not substantially advancing a legitimate governmental interest are not appropriate under the Takings Clause. *Nollan* and *Dolan* do not authorize challenges to permitting decisions as alleged unconstitutional takings without first seeking compensation if the state has provided the means to seek compensation.

Finally, neither *Nollan* nor *Dolan* presented a facial challenge to a regulation and the ripeness concerns at issue here were not present in those cases. * * * In both cases, the way in which the regulation would affect a particular piece of land was finally decided by the administrative body implementing the regulation, and the challenge was an as-applied challenge to the way the regulation interfered with the property.

634 F.3d at 1178–79.

With respect to the court's conclusion that *Nollan/Dolan* scrutiny is applicable to only conditions imposed in an adjudicative context, some courts, as we note above, disagree. Consider Justice Thomas' view:

It is hardly surprising that some courts have applied [*Dolan*]'s rough proportionality test even when considering a legislative enactment. It is not clear why the existence of a taking should turn on the type of governmental entity responsible for the taking. A city council can take property just as well as a planning commission can. Moreover, the general applicability of the ordinance should not be relevant in a takings analysis. If Atlanta had seized several hundred homes in order to build a freeway, there would be no doubt that Atlanta had taken property. The distinction between sweeping legislative takings and particularized administrative takings appears to be a distinction without a constitutional difference.

Parking Ass'n of Georgia, Inc. v. City of Atlanta, 450 S.E.2d 200 (Ga.1994), *cert. denied*, 515 U.S. 1116, 1118 (1995) (Thomas, J., joined by O'Connor, J., dissenting from denial of certiorari). Which view do you think is correct?

2.   Under state constitutional law there are three tests for the proportionality of conditioning development approval with regulatory exactions (dedication of land, money in lieu of land and impact fees) prior to and subsequent to *Dolan*.

Specifically and uniquely attributable test. A few state courts follow the specifically and uniquely attributable test, rejected by the Supreme Court in *Dolan*. An Illinois case illustrates this test. Under a formula that called for the dedication of at least one acre for each 60 residential sites, a developer was required to dedicate 6.7 acres of land to be used as an elementary school site. Upon challenge, the Supreme Court of Illinois in *Pioneer Trust and Savings Bank v. Village of Mount Prospect*, 176 N.E.2d 799 (Ill.1961), said:

> If * * * the burden cast upon the subdivider is specifically and uniquely attributable to his activity, then the requirement is permissible; if not, it is forbidden and amounts to a confiscation of private property in contravention of the constitutional prohibitions rather than reasonable regulation under the police power. * * * There can be no controversy about the obvious fact that the orderly development of a municipality must necessarily include a consideration of the present and future need for school and public recreational facilities. * * * The question is not one of the desirability of education or recreation, * * * [but, rather,] who shall pay for such improvements. Is it reasonable that a subdivider should be required under the guise of a police power regulation to dedicate a portion of his property to public use; or does this amount to a veiled exercise of the power of eminent domain and a confiscation of private property behind the defense of police regulations?

> That the addition by this subdivision of some 250 residential units to the municipality would of course aggravate the existing need for additional school and recreational facilities is admitted * * * However, this record does not establish that the need for recreational and educational facilities in the event that said subdivision plat is permitted to be filed, is one that is specifically and uniquely attributable to the addition of the subdivision and which should be cast upon the subdivider as his sole financial burden. The agreed statement of facts shows that the present school facilities of Mount Prospect are near capacity. This is the result of the total development of the community. If this whole community had not developed to such an extent or if the existing school facilities were greater, the purported need supposedly would not be present. Therefore, on the

record in this case the school problem which allegedly exists here is one which the subdivider should not be obliged to pay the total cost of remedying, and to so construe the statute would amount to an exercise of the power of eminent domain without compensation. 176 N.E.2d at 802.

Did the court in the *Pioneer Trust* case fail to grasp the difference between requiring the developer to pay for existing deficiencies that the new development did not create the need for and the needs the developer did create? This distinction is fundamental to the constitutional validity of all exactions.

3. *Calculating Dedication or the Money in Lieu of Dedication Exaction.* Two principal formulas have been used by communities to determine the amount of land that is required to be dedicated, or the amount of money that may be paid in lieu of dedication by the developer:

(a) *Dedication of Land.* The most common approach is to require a fixed percentage of the total amount of land in the subdivision—varying from 3 per cent to 15 per cent or more. The fixed percentage approach has several disadvantages. It imposes the same burden on all development, irrespective of density or whether the subdivision contains multi-family or single-family units. It is obvious that a high-density development requires a greater percentage of land to be devoted to open space. A variable formula is based on the amount of needed open space per inhabitant—not per acre. Without a variable formula, it is questionable whether the land to be dedicated in any way relates to the needs generated by the subdivision for open space, park, and school sites. In *Frank Ansuini, Inc. v. City of Cranston*, 264 A.2d 910 (R.I.1970), the court upheld the constitutionality of dedication provisions but ruled that a seven per cent fixed percentage requirement, regardless of density, was fatally arbitrary. *See also* Robert L. Dolbeare, *Mandatory Dedication of Public Sites as a Condition in the Subdivision Process in Virginia*, 9 U.RICH.L.REV. 435, 459 (1975). Dolbeare notes that fixed percentage dedications penalize subdivisions with large lots. He suggests a sliding scale based on density which would recognize "that it is the people living in the subdivision that create the needs." *Id.* at 459.

(b) *Money in Lieu.* The money in lieu of land approach is valuable when the subdivision is small and there is insufficient land to dedicate for parks or recreational facilities, where the land or topography is not well suited for park or recreational purposes, or where the comprehensive plan indicates a needed park or recreation site on land situated outside the boundaries of the subdivision. If the alternative of money in lieu of land is not provided for, small parcels of land or fractional portions of land unfit for suitable municipal purposes have to be dedicated. If, on the other hand, these small subdivisions are exempt from dedication requirements, incentives exist for large developers to evade subdivision requirements through utilization of checkerboarding into small subdivisions. This results in a fragmentation of the development process with a serious reduction in the efficiency with which municipal services can be provided.

The "money in lieu of land" technique has met mixed reactions from the judiciary. Many jurisdictions have approved the approach: *Weingarten v. Town of Lewisboro*, 542 N.Y.S.2d 1012 (Sup.Ct.1989), *aff'd* 559 N.Y.S.2d 807 (1990) (court upholds a $5000 per lot fee for park use); *City of College Station v. Turtle Rock Corp.*, 680 S.W.2d 802 (Tex.1984) (an ordinance requiring park land dedication or money in lieu thereof as a condition of subdivision plat approval was not unconstitutionally arbitrary or unreasonable on its face). A few jurisdictions have found fault with the "money in lieu" approach: *Enchanting Homes, Inc. v. Rapanos*, 143 N.W.2d 618 (Mich.App.1966) (no statutory authority to require money in lieu of land); *City of Montgomery v. Crossroads Land Co.*, 355 So.2d 363 (Ala.1978) (without specific legislative authorization, city had no power to require money in lieu of land for public parks; state enabling statute for "open spaces" insufficient).

4. *Double Taxation.* Money in lieu of land requirements have been challenged as imposing a special burden on the future residents of the subdivision, in essence imposing a double tax. Developers assert that the new residents must not only pay for the initial cost of the park but will also be required to assume property taxes which will be used for its maintenance. Consider the court's response in *Associated Home Builders of Greater East Bay v. City of Walnut Creek*, 484 P.2d 606 (Cal.1971):

> double taxation occurs only when "two taxes of the same character are imposed on the same property, for the same purpose, by the same taxing authority within the same jurisdiction, during the same taxing period." * * * Obviously the dedication or fee required of the subdivider and the property taxes paid by the later residents of the subdivision do not meet this definition. *Id.* at 613.

5. *Impact Fees and Assessments.* The latest step in the continuum of land use financing techniques is the impact fee. Functionally, it is similar to dedication of land and the fee in lieu of land in that both are imposed to pay for capital improvements. Some courts use the terms interchangeably.

Money in lieu of dedication payments are currently being assimilated into the impact fee concept. Both are fees used to fund schools, parks and other facilities located outside the subdivision. Because in lieu fees may only be imposed as an alternative to actual dedication, however, they must meet the same legal tests as the dedication requirements. Impact fees have characteristics which distinguish them from both special assessments and subdivision exactions and allow them to be a more flexible device to shift the costs of new development to the development itself.

KOONTZ V. ST. JOHNS RIVER MGMT. DIST.
Supreme Court of the United States, 2013.
133 S.Ct. 2586, 186 L.Ed.2d 697.

JUSTICE ALITO delivered the opinion of the Court.

Our decisions in *Nollan v. California Coastal Comm'n.*, 483 U.S. 825 (1987), and *Dolan v. City of Tigard*, 512 U.S. 374 (1994), provide important protection against the misuse of the power of land-use regulation. In those cases, we held that a unit of government may not condition the approval of a land-use permit of the owner's relinquishment of a portion of his property unless there is a "nexus" and "rough proportionality" between the government's demand and the effects of the proposed land use. In this case, the St. Johns Water Management District (District) believes that it circumvented *Nollan* and *Dolan* because of the way in which it structured its handling of a permit application submitted by Coy Koontz, Sr., whose estate is represented in this Court by Coy Koontz, Jr.[1] The District did not approve his application on the condition that he surrender an interest in his land. Instead, the District, after suggesting that he could obtain approval by signing over such an interest, denied his application because he refused to yield. The Florida Supreme Court blessed this maneuver and thus effectively interred those important decisions. Because we conclude that *Nollan* and *Dolan* cannot be evaded in this way, the Florida Supreme Court's decision must be reversed.

In 1972, petitioner purchased an undeveloped 14.9-acre tract of land on the south side of Florida State Road 50, a divided four-lane highway east of Orlando. The property is located less than 1,000 feet from that road's intersection with Florida State Road 408, a tolled expressway that is one of Orlando's major thoroughfares.

A drainage ditch runs along the property's western edge, and high-voltage power lines bisect it into northern and southern sections. The combined effect of the ditch, a 100-foot wide area kept clear for the power lines, the highways, and other construction on nearby parcels is to isolate the northern section of petitioner's property from any other undeveloped land. Although largely classified as wetlands by the State, the northern section drains well; the most significant standing water forms in ruts in an unpaved road used to access the power lines. The natural topography of the property's southern section is somewhat more diverse, with a small creek, forested uplands, and wetlands that sometimes have water as much as a foot deep. A wildlife survey found evidence of animals that often frequent developed areas: raccoons, rabbits, several species of bird, and a turtle. The record also indicates that the land may be a suitable habitat for opossums.

The same year that petitioner purchased his property, Florida enacted the Water Resources Act, which divided the Sate into five water

---

[1]   For case of reference, this opinion refers to both men as "petitioner."

management districts and authorized each district to regulate "construction that connects to, draws water from, drains water into, or is placed in or across the waters in the state." 1972 Fla. Laws cit. 72–299, pt. IV. § 1(5), pp. 1115, 1116 (codified as amended at Fla. Stat. § 373, 403(5)(2010)). Under the Act, a landowner wishing to undertake such construction must obtain from the relevant district a Management and Storage of Surface Water (MSSW) permit, which may impose "such reasonable conditions" on the permit as are "necessary to assure" that construction will "not be harmful to the water resources of the district." 1972 Fla. Laws, § 4(1), at 1118 (codified as amended to Fla. Stat. § 373.413(1)).

In 1984, in an attempt to protect the State's rapidly diminishing wetlands, the Florida Legislature passed the Warren S. Henderson Wetlands Protection Act, which made it illegal for anyone to "dredge or fill in, on, or over surface waters" without a Wetlands Resources Management (WRM) permit. 1984 Fla. Laws ch. 84–79, pt. VII, § 403.905(1), pp. 204– 205. Under the Henderson Act, permit applicants are required to provide "reasonable assurance" that proposed construction on wetlands is "not contrary to the public interest," as defined by an enumerated list of criteria. *See* Fla. Stat. § 373.414(1). Consistent with the Henderson Act, the St. Johns River Water Management District, the district with jurisdiction over petitioner's, requires that permit applicants wishing to build on wetlands offset the resulting environmental damage by creating, enhancing, or preserving wetlands elsewhere.

Petitioner decided to develop the 3.7-acre northern section of his property, and in 1994 he applied to the District for MSSW and WRM permits. Under his proposal, petitioner would have raised the elevation of the northernmost section of his land to make it suitable for a building, graded the land from the southern edge of the building site down to the elevation of the high-voltage electrical lines, and installed a dry-bed pond for retaining and gradually releasing stormwater runoff from the building and its parking lot. To mitigate the environmental effects of his proposal, petitioner offered to foreclose any possible future development of the approximately 11-acre southern section of his land by deeding to the District a conservation easement on that portion of his property.

The District considered the 11-acre conservation easement to be inadequate, and it informed petitioner that it would approve construction only if he agreed to one of two concessions. First, the District proposed that petitioner reduce the size of his development to 1 acre and deed to the District a conservation easement on the remaining 13.9 acres. To reduce the development area, the District suggested that petitioner could eliminate the dry-bed pond from his proposal and instead install a more costly subsurface stormwater management system beneath the building site. The District also suggested that petitioner install retaining walls rather than gradually sloping the land from the building site down to the elevation of the rest of his property to the south.

In the alternative, the District told petitioner that he could proceed with the development as proposed, building on 3.7 acres and deeding a conservation easement to the government on the remainder of the property, if he also agreed to hire contractors to make improvements to District-owned land several miles away. Specifically, petitioner could pay to replace culverts on one parcel or fill in ditches on another. Either of those projects would have enhanced approximately 50 acres of District-owned wetlands. When the District asks permit applicants to fund offset mitigation work, its policy is never to require any particular offset project, and it did not do so here. Instead, the District said that it "would also favorably consider" alternatives to its suggested offsite mitigation projects if petitioner proposed something "equivalent." App. 75.

Believing the District's demands for mitigation to be excessive in light of the environmental effects that his building proposal would have caused, petitioner filed suit in state court. Among other claims, he argued that he was entitled to relief under Fla. Stat. § 373.617(2), which allows owners to recover "monetary damages" if a state agency's action is "an unreasonable exercise of the state's police power constituting a taking without just compensation."

We have said in a variety of contexts that "the government may not deny a benefit to a person because he exercised a constitutional right" *Regan v. Taxation With Representation of Wash.*, 461 U.S. 540, 545 (1983). *See also, e.g. Rumsfeld v. Forum for Academic and Institutional Rights, Inc.*, 547 U.S. 47, 59–60 (2006); *Rutan v. Republican Party of Ill.*, 497 U.S. 62, 78 (1990). In *Perry v. Sindermann*, 408 U.S. 593 (1972), for example, we held that a public college would violate a professor's freedom of speech if it declined to renew his contract because he was an outspoken critic of the college's administration. And in *Memorial Hospital v. Maricopa County*, 415 U.S. 250 (1974), we concluded that a county impermissibly burdened the right to travel by extending healthcare benefits only to those indigent sick who had been residents of the county for at least one year. Those cases reflect an overarching principle, known as the unconstitutional conditions doctrine, which vindicates the Constitution's enumerated rights by preventing the government from coercing people into giving them up.

Nollan and *Dolan* "involve a special application" of this doctrine that protects the Fifth Amendment right to just compensation for property the government takes when owners apply for land-use permits. *Lingle v. Chevron U.S.A., Inc.*, 544 U.S. 528, 547 (2005); *Dolan*, 512 U.S. at 385 (invoking "the well-settled doctrine of "unconstitutional conditions""). Our decisions in those cases reflect two realities of the permitting process. The first is that land-use permit applicants are especially vulnerable to the type of coercion that the unconstitutional conditions doctrine prohibits because the government often has broad discretion to deny a permit that is worth far more than property it would like to take. By conditioning a building permit on the owner's deeding over a public right-of-way, for example, the government can pressure an owner into voluntarily giving up property for which the Fifth Amendment would otherwise require just compensation. *See* id., at 384; *Nollan*, 483 U.S. So long as the building permit is more valuable than any just compensation the owner could hope to receive for the right-of-way, the owner is likely to accede to the government's demand, no matter how unreasonable. Extortionate demands of this sort frustrate the Fifth Amendment right to just compensation, and the unconstitutional conditions doctrine prohibits them.

A second reality of the permitting process is that many proposed land uses threaten to impose costs on the public that dedications of property can offset. Where a building proposal would substantially increase traffic congestion, for example, officials might condition permit approval on the owner's agreement to deed over the land needed to widen a public road. Respondent argues that a similar rational justifies the exaction at issue here: petitioner's proposed construction project, it submits, would destroy wetlands on his property, and in order to compensate for this loss, respondent demands that he enhance wetlands elsewhere. Insisting that landowners internalize the negative externalities of their conduct is a hallmark of responsible land-use policy, and we have long sustained such regulations against constitutional attack. *See Village of Euclid v. Ambler Realty Co.*, 272 U.S. 365 (1926).

Nollan and *Dolan* accommodate both realities by allowing the government to condition approval of a permit on the dedication of property to the public so long as there is a "nexus" and "rough proportionality" between the property that the government demands and the social costs of the applicant's proposal. *Dolan, supra*, at 391; *Nollan*, 483 U.S., at 837. Our precedents thus enable permitting authorities to insist that applicants bear the full cost of their proposals while still forbidding the government from engaging in "out-and-out . . . extortion" that would thwart the Fifth Amendment right to just compensation. *Ibid.* (internal quotation marks omitted). Under *Nollan* and *Dolan* the government may choose whether and how a permit applicant is required to mitigate the impacts of a proposed development, but it may not leverage its legitimate interest in mitigation to pursue governmental ends that lack an essential nexus and rough proportionality to those impacts.

The principles that undergird our decisions in *Nollan* and *Dolan* do not change depending on whether the government *approves* a permit on the condition that the applicant turn over property or *denies* a permit because the applicant refuses to do so. We have often concluded that denials of governmental benefits were impermissible under the unconstitutional conditions doctrine. *See, e.g., Perry*, 408 U.S., at 597 (explaining that the government *may not deny* a benefit to a person on a basis that infringes his constitutionally protected interests" (emphasis added); *Memorial Hospital*, 415 U.S. 250 (finding unconstitutional condition where government denied healthcare benefits). In so holding, we have recognized that regardless of whether the government ultimately succeeds in pressuring someone into forfeiting a constitutional right, the unconstitutional conditions doctrine forbids burdening the Constitution's enumerated rights by coercively withholding benefits from those who exercise them.

A contrary rule would be especially untenable in this case because it would enable the government to evade the limitations of *Nollan* and *Dolan* simply by phrasing its demands for property as conditions precedent to permit approval. Under the Florida Supreme Court's approach, a government order stating that a permit is "approved of" if the owner turns over property would be subject to *Nollan* and *Dolan*, but an identical order that uses the words "denied until" would not. Our unconstitutional conditions cases have long refused to attach significance to the distinction between conditions precedent and conditions subsequent. *See Frost & Frost Trucking Co. v. Railroad Comm'n of Cal.*, 271 U.S. 583, 592–593 (1926) (invalidating "regulation that required the petitioner to give up a constitutional right "as a condition precedent to the enjoyment of a privilege""); *Southern Pacific Co. v. Denton*, 146 U.S. 202, 207 (1892) (invalidating statute "requiring the corporation, as a condition precedent to obtaining a permit to do business within the State, to surrender a right and privilege secured to it by the Constitution."). *See also Flower Mound*, 135 S.W.3d, at 639 ("The government cannot sidestep constitutional protections merely by rephrasing its decision from only 'if' to 'not unless' "). To do so here would effectively render *Nollan* and *Dolan* a dead letter.

The Florida Supreme Court puzzled over how the government's demand for property can violate the Takings Clause even though "no property of any kind was ever taken." 77 So.3d, at 1225 (quoting 5 So.3d, at 20 (Griffin, J., dissenting)); see also 77 So.3d, at 1229–1230, but the unconstitutional conditions doctrine provides a ready answer. Extortionate demands for property in the land-use permitting context run afoul of the Takings Clause not because they take property but because they impermissibly burden the right not to have property taken without just compensation. As in other unconstitutional conditions cases in which someone refuses to cede a constitutional right in the face of coercive pressure, the impermissible denial of a governmental benefit is a constitutionally cognizable injury.

Nor does it make a difference, as respondent suggests, that the government might have been able to deny petitioner's application outright without giving him the option of securing a permit by agreeing to spend money to improve public lands. *See Penn Central Trans. Co. v. New York*

City, 438 U.S. 104 (1978). Virtually all of our unconstitutional conditions cases involve a gratuitous governmental benefit of some kind. *See, e.g. Regan,* 461 U.S. 540 (tax benefits); *Memorial Hospital,* 415 U.S. 250 (healthcare); *Perry,* 408 U.S. 593 (employment); *United States v. Butler,* 297 U.S. 1, 71 (1936) (crop-payments); *Frost, supra* (business license). Yet we have repeatedly rejected the argument that if the government need not confer a benefit at all, it can withhold the benefit because someone refuses to give in to unconstitutional rights. E.g., *United States v. American Library Assn., Inc.,* 539 U.S. 194, 210 (2003) ("[T]he government may not deny a benefit to a person on a basis that infringes his constitutionally protected . . . freedom of speech *even if he has no entitlement to that benefit.*" (emphasis added and internal quotation marks omitted)); *Wieman v. Updegraff,* 344 U.S. 183, 191 (1952) (explaining in unconstitutional conditions case that to focus on "the facile generalization that there is no constitutionally protected right to public employment is to obscure the issue"). Even if respondent would have been entirely within its rights in denying the permit for some other reason, that greater authority does not imply a lesser power to condition permit approval on petitioner's forfeiture of his constitutional rights. *See Nollan,* 483 U.S. at 836–837 (explaining that "[t]he evident constitutional propriety" of prohibiting a land use "disappears . . . if the condition substituted for the prohibition utterly fails to further the end advanced as the justification for the prohibition").

That is not to say, however, that there is *no* relevant difference between a consummated taking and the denial of a permit based on an unconstitutionally extortionate demand. Where the permit is denied and the condition is never imposed, nothing has been taken. While the unconstitutional conditions doctrine recognizes that this *burdens* a constitutional right, the Fifth Amendment mandates a particular remedy—just compensation—only for takings. In cases where there is an excessive demand but no taking, whether money damages are available is not a question of federal constitutional law but of the cause of action— whether state or federal—on which the landowner relies. Because petitioner brought his claim pursuant to a state law cause of action, the Court has no occasion to discuss what remedies might be available for a *Nollan/Dolan* unconstitutional conditions violation either here or in other cases.

We turn to the Florida Supreme Court's alternative holding that petitioner's claim fails because respondent asked him to spend money rather than give up an easement on his land. A predicate for any unconstitutional conditions claim is that the government could not have constitutionally ordered the person asserting the claim to do what it attempted to pressure that person into doing. *See Rumsfeld,* 547 U.S., at 59–60). For that reason, we began our analysis in both *Nollan* and *Dolan* by observing that if the government had directly seized the easements it sought to obtain through the permitting process, it would have committed a *per se* taking. *See Dolan*, 512 U.S., at 384; *Nollan*, 483 U.S. at 831. The Florida Supreme Court held that petitioner's claim fails at this first step because the subject of the exaction at issue here was money rather than a more tangible interest in real property. 77 So. 3d at 1230. Respondent and the dissent take the same position, citing the concurring and dissenting opinions in *Eastern Enterprises v. Apfel*, 524 U.S. 498 (1998), for the preposition that an obligation to spend money can never provide the basis for a takings claim. *See post*, at 5–8 (opinion of KAGAN, J.)

We note as an initial matter that if we accepted this argument it would be very easy for land-use permitting officials to evade the limitation of *Nollan* and *Dolan*. Because the government need only provide a permit applicant with one alternative that satisfies the nexus and rough proportionality standards, a permitting authority wishing to exact an easement could simply give the owner a choice of either surrendering an easement or making a payment equal to the easement's value. Such so-called "in lieu of fees" are utterly commonplace. Rosenberg, *The Changing Culture of American Land Use Regulation: Paying for Growth with Impact Fees*, 59 S.M.U.L.REV. 177, 202–203 (2006), and they are functionally equivalent to other types of land use exactions. For that reason and those that follow, we reject respondent's argument and hold that so-called "monetary exactions" must satisfy the nexus and rough proportionality requirements of *Nollan* and *Dolan*.

Respondent and the dissent argue that if monetary exactions are made subject to scrutiny under *Nollan* and *Dolan*, then there will be no principled way of distinguishing impermissible land-use exactions from property taxes. See *post*, at 9–10. We think they exaggerate both the extent to which that problem is unique to the land-use permitting context and the practical difficulty of distinguishing between the power to tax and the power to take by eminent domain.

It is beyond dispute that "[t]axes and user fees . . . are not takings." *Brown, supra*, at 243, n. 2 (SCALIA, J., dissenting). We said much in *County of Mobile v. Kimball*, 102 U.S. 691, 703 (1881), and our cases have been clear on that point ever since. *United States v. Sperry Corp.*, 493 U.S. 52, 62, n. 9 (1989); *see A. Magnano Co. v. Hamilton*, 292 U.S. 40, 44 (1934); *Dane v. Jackson*, 256 U.S. 589, 599 (1921); *Henderson Bridge Co. v. Henderson City*, 173 U.S. 592, 614–615 (1899). This case therefore does not affect the ability of governments to impose property taxes, user fees, and similar laws and regulations that may impose financial burdens on property owners.

At the same time, we have repeatedly found takings where the government, by confiscating financial obligations, achieved a result that could have been obtained by imposing a tax. Most recently, in *Brown, supra* at 232, we were unanimous in concluding that a State Supreme Court's seizure of the interest on client funds held in escrow was a taking despite the unquestionable constitutional propriety of a tax that would have raised exactly the same revenue. Our holding in *Brown* followed from *Phillips v. Washington Legal Foundation*, 524 U.S. 156 (1998), and *Webb's Fabulous Pharmacies, Inc. v. Beckwith*, 449 U.S. 115 (1980), two earlier cases in which we treated confiscations of money as takings despite their functional similarity to a tax. Perhaps most closely analogous to the present case, we have repeatedly held that the government takes property when it seizes liens, and in so ruling we have never considered whether the government could have achieved an economically equivalent result through taxation. *Armstrong*, 364 U.S. 40; *Louisville Joint Stock Land Bank*, 295 U.S. 555.

Two facts emerge from those cases. The first is that the need to distinguish taxes from takings is not a creature of our holding today that monetary exactions are subject to scrutiny under *Nollan* and *Dolan*. Rather, the problem is inherent in this Court's long-settled view that property the government could constitutionally demand through its taxing power can also be taken by eminent domain.

Second, our cases show that teasing out the different between taxes and takings is more difficult in theory than in practice. *Brown* is illustrative. Similar to respondent in this case, the respondents in *Brown* argued that extending the protection of the Takings Clause to a bank account would open a Pandora's Box of constitutional challenges to taxes. Brief for Respondents Washington Legal Foundation, *et al.* and Brief for Respondent Justices of the Washington Supreme Court, 22, in *Brown v. Legal Foundation of Wash.*, O.T. 2002, *No. 01–1325*. But also likely respondent here, the *Brown* respondents never claimed that they were exercising their power to levy taxes when they took the petitioners' property. Any such argument would have been implausible under state law; in Washington, taxes are levied by the legislature, not the courts. *See* 538 U.S., at 242, n. 2 (SCALIA, J., dissenting).

The same dynamic is at work in this case because Florida law greatly circumscribes respondent's power to tax. *See* Fla. Stat. Ann. § 373.503 (authorizing respondent to impose *ad valorem* tax on properties within its jurisdiction); § 373.109 (authorizing respondent to charge permit application fees but providing that such fees "shall not exceed the cost . . . for processing, monitoring, and inspecting for compliance with the permit.") If respondent had argued that its demand for money was a tax, it would have effectively conceded that its denial of petitioner's permit was improper under Florida law. Far from making that concession, respondent has maintained throughout this litigation that it considered petitioner's money to be a substitute for his deeding to the public a conservation easement on a larger parcel of undeveloped land.[3]

---

[3]   Citing cases in which state courts have treated similar governmental demands for money differently, the dissent predicts that courts will "struggle to draw a coherent boundary" between taxes and excessive demands for money that violate *Nollan* and *Dolan*. *Post*, at 9–10. But the cases

This case does not require us to say more. We need not decide at precisely what point a land-use permitting charge denominated by the government as a "tax" becomes "so arbitrary . . . that it was not the exertion of taxation but a confiscation of property." *Brushaber v. Union Pacific* "the power of taxation should not be confused with the power of eminent domain," *Houck v. Little River Drainage Dist.*, 239 U.S. 254, 264 (1915), we have had little trouble distinguishing between the two.

Finally, we disagree with the dissent's forecast that our decision will work a revolution in land use law by depriving local governments of the ability to charge reasonable permitting fees. *Post*, at 8. Numerous courts—including courts in many of our Nation's most populous States—have confronted constitutional challenges to monetary exactions over the last two decades and applied the standard from *Nollan* and *Dolan* or something like it. *See, e.g., Northern Ill. Home Builders Assn v. County of DuPage*, 165 Ill.2d 25, 31–32, 649 N.E. 2d 384, 388–389 (1995); *Home Builders Assn v. Beavercreek*, 89 Ohio St.3d 121, 128, 729 N.E.2d 349, 356 (2000); *Flower Mound*, 135 S.W.3d at 640–641. Yet the "significant practical harm" the dissent predicts has not come to pass. *Post*, at 8. That is hardly surprising, for the dissent is correct that state law normally provides an independent check on excessive land use permitting fees. *Post*, at 11.

The dissent criticizes the notion that the Federal Constitution places any meaningful limits on "whether one town is overcharging for sewage, or another is setting the price to sell liquor too high." *Post*, at 9. But only two pages later, it identifies three constraints on land use permitting fees that it says the Federal Constitution imposes and suggests that the additional protection of *Nollan* and *Dolan* are not needed. *Post*, at 11. In any event, the dissent's argument that land use permit applicants need no further protection when the government demands money is really an argument for overruling *Nollan* and *Dolan*. After all, the Due Process Clause protected the Nollans from an unfair allocation of public burdens, and they too could have argued that the government's demand for property amounted to a taking under the *Penn Central* framework. See *Nollan*, 483 U.S., at 838. We have repeatedly rejected the dissent's contention that other constitutional doctrines leave no room for the nexus and rough proportionality requirements of *Nollan* and *Dolan*. Mindful of the special vulnerability of land use permit applicants to extortionate demands for money, we do so again today.

We hold that the government's demand for property from a land-use permit applicant must satisfy the requirements of *Nollan* and *Dolan* even when the government denies the permit and even when its demand is for money. The Court expresses no view on the merits of petitioner's claim that

---

the dissent cites illustrates how the frequent need to decide whether a particular parcel demand for money qualifies as a tax under state law, and the resulting state statutes and judicial precedents on point, greatly reduce the practical difficulty of resolving the same issue in federal constitutional cases like this one.

respondent's actions here fail to comply with the principles set forth in this opinion and those two cases. The Florida Supreme Court's judgement is reversed, and this case is remanded for further proceedings not inconsistent with this opinion.

It is so ordered.

NOTES AND QUESTIONS

1.   At a minimum, *Nollan* and *Dolan* established a form of heightened scrutiny for regulations that constituted physical exactions. Thus, a traditional right of way dedication of a strip of land bordering a highway as a condition for a permit was invalidated in *Unlimited v. Kitsap County*, 750 P.2d 651 (Wash.App.1988), where the court found a causal connection lacking. For other examples of courts trying to come to grips with the requirements of *Nollan* and *Dolan*, *see Sintra, Inc., v. City of Seattle*, 829 P.2d 765, 773 n. 7 (Wash.1992) (demolition fee for low income housing not subject to Nollan nexus because exaction was not physical); *Christopher Lake Dev. Co. v. St. Louis County*, 35 F.3d 1269 (8th Cir.1994) (state mandated design specifications for disposal of storm water could be a taking of developer's property); *Walz v. Town of Smithtown*, 46 F.3d 162 (2d Cir.1995) (plaintiff entitled to damages when town refused to issue an evacuation permit to which the plaintiff was entitled); *Burton v. Clark County*, 958 P.2d 343 (Wash.App.1998) (county's decision to condition approval of plat plan on developer's willingness to construct a road for public use through his property constituted a taking of his property).

2.   *Non-Physical Exactions.* Following *Koontz*, the heightened scrutiny requirement applies as well to non-physical exactions, like fees in lieu of land or impact fees where property owners or developers are required to make additional payments as a prerequisite to development.

3.   *Heightened Scrutiny and the Legislative v. Administrative Distinction.* What about "legislative" acts as opposed to administrative acts of agencies as in *Koontz, Nollan* and *Dolan*? While some courts agree with Justice Thomas that "a city can take property just as well as a planning commission," *Parking Assoc. v. City of Atlanta*, 515 U.S. 1116, 1117 (1995) (dissenting to denial of certiorari), many restrict application of intermediate scrutiny of the type applied in *Nollan* and *Dolan* to administrative decisions only. *See, e.g., Homebuilders Association of Metropolitan Portland v. Tualatin Hills Park and Recreation District*, 62 P.3d 404 (Or.App.2003) (heightened scrutiny not applicable to legislative exaction). *See also,* Shelley Ross Saxer, *When Local Government Misbehaves,* 2016 UTAH L.REV. 105 (advocating for Nollan and Dolan to be applied to administrative decisions only). Some courts, however, have imposed *Nollan/Dolan* scrutiny on legislative decision. For a listing of such cases, *see* Juergensmeyer and Roberts, *Land Use Planning and Development Regulation Law* § 10.5 (2012) and David L. Callies, *Through A Glass Clearly: Predicting the Future in Land Use Takings Cases*, 54 WASHBURN L.REV. 43 (2012), at 48–49.

4. *Exactions and Rezoning.* Exactions involving land dedication or facility construction as a condition of plan approval or rezoning are treated as immediately suspect both because they involve appropriation of property and because rezoning and plan approval do not generate a need for public facilities. When such exactions are imposed simply to conform to a community's general regulations, rather than to respond to specific project impacts on public facilities, they may fail to meet the Dolan proportionality test. *But see* the California Supreme Court's decision in *California Building Industry Association v. City of San Jose,* 351 P.3d 974.

These types of exactions (which might seek to improve arterial streets or major park systems, for example) are hard to allocate to individual developments that yield incremental impacts because reasonably priced measurements of impacts are needed. In these cases, municipalities may use impact fees, which distribute costs for such improvements over many developments. Dedications can still be used as credits toward fee payments.

Furthermore, may states require land dedication or cash payments to mitigate adverse environmental impacts of development projects such as the one at issue in *Nollan* and *Dolan.* Under *Nollan's* standards, these exactions logically come under greater scrutiny, although no doubt exists that their purposes are valid police-power objectives. The problem with imposing exactions for such purposes lies in the difficulty of quantifying adverse development impacts. Nevertheless, to satisfy the *Nollan* remoteness test, government agencies must document the relationship between development and the need for mitigating conditions, and incorporate the documentation into standards that govern the conditioning of development permits. *See Takings: Land Development Conditions and Regulatory Takings After* Nollan *and* Lucas 20–26 (Callies Ed.1996).

5. *Collection of Fees.* Impact fees are usually collected at the latest stage of the development approval process when building permits or certificates of occupancy are issued, rather than at the subdivision approval stage, which results in several advantages, for both municipalities and developers. The fees become available at the same time the need for new services is generated and new capital funding is required. If funds were collected at subdivision approval, the developer would have to borrow the funds. If payable on issuance of the certificate of occupancy, the cost can be passed directly to the consumer. Moreover payment at certificate of occupancy prevents developers from avoiding the fees for projects which have received building permits but have not completed construction. *See* Arthur C. Nelson, Liza K. Bowles, Julian C. Juergensmeyer and James C. Nicholas, *A Guide to Impact Fees and Housing Affordability, Collection of Fees* 42–43 (2008). Since the fees, as opposed to the exactions, are collected nearer to the time that units are actually sold, developers need not finance and carry the fees over a long period of time. *See* James C. Nicholas, *Impact Exactions: Economic Theory, Practice, and Incidence,* 50 LAW & CONTEMP.PROB. 85 (1987). *See City of Key West v. R.L.J.S. Corp.,* 537 So.2d 641(Fla.App.1989) (impact fees may be collected at the certificate of occupancy stage).

6.   *Site Plan Approval*. Impact fees result in other advantages for developing cities. Impact fees can be applied through site plan approval to apartments, condominiums, industrial and commercial development which generate the need for capital facilities but often avoid payment of exactions and impact fees because of the inapplicability of subdivision regulation to single tracts of land that are not being subdivided.

7.   *Vested Rights*. A developer is not immune from having new impact fees imposed even after he acquires a building permit. In *City of Key West v. R.L.J.S. Corp.*, 537 So.2d 641 (Fla.App.1989), the city issued building permits for 76 condominium units, then declined to issue permits for 92 new units because the developers had failed to pay impact fees for sewers, solid waste, and traffic that were imposed on the developer after the first 76 certificates of occupancy were granted.

The developers, claiming the city's actions were unconstitutional, relied on *Contractors and Builders Association v. City of Dunedin*, 329 So.2d 314 (Fla.1976), which held that "an opportunity to pass on such fees to the ultimate user who causes the impact on the community is necessary for the law to meet constitutional muster." *Key West*, 537 So.2d at 644. However, the court declined to follow the developers' interpretation of *Dunedin* that the ability of the developer to pass on the fee to the new occupants is a constitutional requirement. The court characterized *Dunedin's* use of the word "user" to mean anyone who derives a benefit from a service, including a developer who seeks to sell condominium units. *Dunedin* was interpreted by the court to draw a distinction only between all the taxpayers of a municipality and a specific group of taxpayers in an impacted area, and not between a developer and the purchasers of the developer's units.

The developers also argued that the doctrine of vested rights prevented the city from imposing the impact fees after the first set of certificates was granted. The court explained that

> [T]he doctrine of vested rights limits local governments in the exercise of their zoning powers when a property owner relying in good faith upon some act or omission of the government has substantially changed position or incurred such excessive obligations and expenses that it would be highly inequitable and unjust to destroy the rights that the owner has acquired. 537 So.2d at 644.

The court declined to use this doctrine to invalidate the impact fees, stating "we do not believe that a requisite to the validity of an impact fee is that the possibility that it will be imposed at some future time be made an express condition of a building permit." *Id*. at 646. The court justified this reasoning by drawing a distinction between 1) a situation where a city imposes one requirement and then in the course of construction imposes a different requirement, and 2) a city issues a building permit and then later, under its taxing authority, increases taxes upon the property being built on, or imposes fees for municipal services which will be required when the construction is complete.

In *Russ Bldg. Partnership v. City and County of San Francisco*, 750 P.2d 324 (Cal.1988), the court held that San Francisco's Transit Impact Development Fee (TIDF) ordinance may be applied retroactively to projects which, at the time of the enactment, were in the course of construction pursuant to building permits conditioned on the developers' participation "in a downtown assessment district, or similar fair and appropriate mechanism, to provide funds for maintaining and augmenting transportation service. . . ." The court concluded that the condition in the building permit encompassed the subsequently adopted TIDF, and therefore held that the TIDF may be imposed on the projects without impairing the developers' vested rights.

For another instance in which a vesting argument lost, *see Arenstam v. Planning Bd.*, 560 N.E.2d 142 (Mass.App.1990) (developer tardiness in resubmission of preliminary plan voided vested rights argument). Regardless of who is determined to be the "ultimate user" for purposes of imposing an impact fee, the ultimate users are not the only beneficiaries of the fee. As one commentator has stated, "[i]mpact fees have normative merit as sources of local government revenue, because they allocate the costs of new infrastructure to the beneficiaries of the infrastructure: landowners, developers, and consumers of the new development." Franklin James, *Evaluation of Local Impact Fees as a Source of Infrastructure Finance*, 11 MUN.FIN.J. 407, 413 (1990).

8. *Authority to Impose Impact Fees.*

(a) *Implied Authority.* The authority to impose impact fees may be express or, in some states, implied. *See City of Mesa v. Home Builders Ass'n*, 523 P.2d 57 (Ariz.1974) (Mesa's charter implies home rule power to enact residential development tax) and *Home Builders Association v. Provo City*, 503 P.2d 451 (Utah 1972) (sewer connection charge statute). Even without a specific grant of authority, municipalities have been allowed to charge impact fees as a valid exercise of their home rule police power. *See, e.g., Coulter v. City of Rawlins*, 662 P.2d 888 (Wyo.1983) (power to impose impact fees for sewer connections was fairly and necessarily implied from powers expressly granted to the City to carry out its duty to regulate, maintain, construct and operate a sewer system) and *Hollywood, Inc. v. Broward County*, 431 So.2d 606 (Fla.App.1983) (impact fee as a condition of plat approval, to be used in expanding county level park system to accommodate new residents was a reasonable regulation under the police power). Without enabling legislation, impact fees have also been adopted pursuant to home rule powers or standard planning, zoning, and subdivision legislation. Terry Morgan, *State Impact Fee Legislation: Guidelines for Analysis*, (pts. 1 & 2), Land Use L. & Zoning Dig. (Mar. 1990 at 3, Apr.1990 at 3).

(b) *Express Authority.* The use of impact fees is expanding throughout the country, and the adoption of state impact fee enabling legislation has grown in response, as Martin L. Leitner and Susan P. Schoettle explain in their article, *A Survey of State Impact Fee Enabling Legislation*, 25 URB.LAW. 491, 492–495 (1993):

Since 1986, seventeen (17) states have adopted express impact fee enabling legislation. In some states, the state legislation places limits on the independent home rule authority of local governments, while other legislation provides a limited grant of authority to impose impact fees. Once initiated, proposed legislation has typically generated vigorous debate as the local government representatives and the development industry representatives each strive to achieve their objectives: the former seeking the greatest flexibility and the latter seeking the greatest restrictions on the use and application of impact fees.

Since 1983, a substantial body of case law on impact fees has developed, which provides significant guidance for two major issues: (1) does the local government have authority to enact the impact fee, and (2) does the impact fee comply with state and federal constitutional limitations. The adoption of state impact fee enabling legislation has obviated challenges to local impact fee ordinances based on the issue of authority, and have established a framework for ensuring compliance with constitutional standards. Three state court tests of the constitutionality of impact fees have emerged from the case law: (1) the specifically and uniquely attributable test, which requires that the burden placed on a developer must be directly and uniquely attributable to that development; (2) the rational nexus test which requires that there must be proportionality between the amount of the fee and the type and amount of facilities demand generated by the development and that there must be a reasonable connection between the use of the fees and the benefits accruing to new development; and (3) the reasonable relationship test which requires that there be a reasonable connection between the burden placed on the developer and the needs generated by that development.

Regardless of which of the three tests a court may deem to be applicable, the reasonableness of an impact fee is generally analyzed by reference to the following six factors: (1) spatial (the distance between the development paying the impact fee and the facilities constructed with the impact fees paid, (2) temporal (the length of time elapsing between collection of the impact fee and construction of the facilities), (3) amount (the amount of the impact fee in relation to the actual costs of the facilities), (4) need (the relationship between the burden created by the development and the increased facility needs), (5) benefit (the ability of the facilities constructed to satisfy the facility needs resulting from the development, and (6) earmarking (an assurance that the impact fees collected from the development are restricted solely for the provision of capital facilities of the type for which the fees were collected and for facilities serving the new development).

See also Terry Morgan, *Recent Developments in the Law of Impact Fees With Special Attention to Legislation*, 1990 INSTITUTE ON PLANNING, ZONING, AND EMINENT DOMAIN, 4.1 (1990); Brian Blaesser and Christine Kentoff, *Impact Fees: The "Second Generation,"* 38 WASH.U.J.URB. & CONTEMP.LAW 55 (1990); *Home Builders of Central Arizona v. City of Apache Junction*, 11 P.3d 1032 (Ariz.App.2000) (school fees were not authorized by statute).

(c) *Strict Construction.* Not all courts are willing to liberally construe impact fee authority. *New Jersey Builders Ass'n v. Bernards Township*, 528 A.2d 555 (N.J.1987), exemplifies the important role the specific language of the enabling statute plays in a judicial determination of the validity of impact fees. A provision in Bernards Township's ordinance required new developers to pay their pro rata share of the township's entire transportation network improvement program without carefully examining which roads within the Township were generated by their development. N.J.S.A. 40:55D–42 permits municipalities to require developers to pay their "reasonable and necessary" share of off-site improvements. Placing emphasis on the use of the word "necessary" the court held that the ordinance violated the limited grant of authority that permitted municipalities to require developers to pay their share of reasonable and necessary off-site improvements.

(d) *Standards.* The standard by which courts judge the validity of impact fees is often not clearly articulated. An important question is whether the fee accurately reflects the new development's proportionate share of the cost of the new facility. *Cameron & Cameron v. Planning Bd.*, 593 A.2d 1250 (N.J.App.1991) (under New Jersey statute, landowners are required to pay for on-site improvements and only a proportionate share of the off-site improvements). Many courts simply judge impact fees by the same standard applied to subdivision exactions. Recent decisions have judged impact fees by a "reasonableness" test, as illustrated by the following:

> to comply with the standard of reasonableness, a municipal fee * * * must not require newly developed properties to bear more than their equitable share of the capital costs in relation to benefits conferred. * * *

> [A] municipality should determine the relative burdens previously borne and yet to be borne by those properties in comparison with other properties in the municipality as a whole; the fee in question should not exceed the amount sufficient to equalize the relative burden of newly developed and other properties.

Banberry Development Corp. v. South Jordan City, 631 P.2d 899, 903 (Utah 1981).

The Utah Supreme Court in *Banberry* enunciated a series of factors to be used in determining whether the fee meets the test of reasonableness:

> (1) the cost of existing capital facilities; (2) the manner of financing existing capital facilities (such as user charges, special assessments, bonded indebtedness, general taxes, or federal grants); (3) the relative extent to which the newly developed properties and the other

properties in the municipality have already contributed to the cost of existing capital facilities (by such means as user charges, special assessments, or payments from the proceeds of general taxes); (4) the relative extent to which the newly developed properties and the other properties in the municipality will contribute to the cost of existing capital facilities in the future; (5) the extent to which the newly developed properties are entitled to a credit because the municipality is requiring their developers or owners (by contractual arrangement or otherwise) to provide common facilities (inside or outside the proposed development) that have been provided by the municipality and financed through general taxation or other means (apart from user charges) in other parts of the municipality; (6) extraordinary costs, if any, in servicing the newly developed properties; and (7) the time-price differential inherent in fair comparisons of amounts paid at different times.

Id. at 904 (Citations omitted). The court also emphasized the need for "flexibility" to deal realistically with impact fees since they are "not susceptible [to] * * * exact measurement." *Id.* at 904. As long as an authority's methodology is not wholly arbitrary and is reasonably related to objectives of enabling legislation, fees are acceptable without mathematical precision. *Warrenville Plaza, Inc. v. Warren Twp. Sewerage Auth.*, 553 A.2d 874 (N.J.App.1989).

9.   *Taxation v. Police Power.* While there is no requirement of mathematical precision, if the fees are substantially in excess of the proportionate cost of new facilities, the fee may be characterized as a revenue measure and held invalid as a tax lacking statutory authorization. Taxes are distinguished from impact fees by the objectives for which they are imposed. If the imposition is primarily for the purpose of raising general revenue it is a tax, but if the purpose is regulating development activity under the police power it is a regulatory fee. *S & P Enters., Inc. v. City of Memphis*, 672 S.W.2d 213 (Tenn.App.1983). This distinction is widely accepted and would seem self-evident despite language to the contrary, in the *Koontz* dissent.

In *Homebuilders Association of Mississippi v. City of Ocean Springs*, 932 So.2d 44 (Miss.2006), the Court held that the state does not have a specific constitutional provision or statute regarding implementation of development impact fees, nor can authority be found in the common law. Nor did the municipal planning statutes, which granted city authority to adopt and carry out a comprehensive plan for the purposes of bringing about coordinated physical development, grant city authority to adopt impact fees or other revenue raising mechanisms to implement city's comprehensive plan, despite case law authority that cities have implied authority to implement the comprehensive plan. *But see, Almquist v. Town of Marshan*, 245 N.W.2d 819 (Minn.1976) holding that local governments can adopt emergency interim development moratoria, based on the authority of the SPEA in order to implement the comprehensive plan. The *Homebuilders* court further held that the city could not use its home rule police power to adopt impact fees since such fees are taxes used to raise general public improvements, unless they cover only the administrative expenses of reviewing the development approval.

Most courts refuse to strike impact fees as invalid taxes. The following comprehensive explanation, upholding the impact fee as a police power measure and not a tax, comes from the decision of the Supreme Court of Colorado in *Bloom v. City of Fort Collins*, 784 P.2d 304, 307–08 (Colo.1989):

> There are several measures for generating revenue available to a municipality for the purpose of deriving funds to carry out the city's public functions. The more common types, and the ones against which the transportation utility fee in this case must be measured, are an ad valorem tax, an excise tax, a special assessment, and a special fee.
>
> An ad valorem tax is a tax upon various classes of real and personal property located within the territorial limits of the taxing authority. * * * Traditionally, the ad valorem property tax has been one of the mainstays of municipal revenue-raising. The Colorado Constitution expressly grants home rule municipalities "all powers necessary, requisite or proper for the government and administration of its local and municipal matters," including the power to legislate upon "[t]he assessment of property in such city or town for municipal taxation and the levy and collection of taxes thereon for municipal purposes." Colo. Const. art. XX, § 6(g). Article X, section 3 of the Colorado Constitution requires any direct tax upon real or personal property to be "uniform," which means that the tax must be imposed uniformly or in like manner upon both real and personal property of the same class, according to assessed evaluation of the property. [Most states have similar uniformity requirements: Editors.] * * * In contrast to a direct tax on property, an excise tax is not based on the assessed value of the property subject to the tax but, instead, is imposed on a particular act, event, or occurrence. The object of an excise tax, like that of an ad valorem property tax, is to provide revenue for the general expenses of government, but, unlike the ad valorem property tax, the payment of the excise tax is made a condition precedent to the act, event, or occurrence on which the tax is based. * * *
>
> To be distinguished from both a property tax and an excise tax is a special assessment. The essential characteristic of a special assessment is that it must confer some special benefit to the property assessed. *See* Oswald Reynolds, Jr., *Local Government Law* § 99 (1982). A special assessment is "based on the premise that the property assessed is enhanced in value at least to the amount of the levy." The burden of the assessment falls on the property owners because "the benefits they receive from the particular improvements are different from the benefits they enjoy in common with other property owners." A special assessment for a local improvement, therefore, must specifically benefit or enhance the value of the premises assessed "in an amount at least equal to the burden imposed." The funds generated by a special assessment cannot be

diverted to other purposes, since the imposition of the assessment "upon a particular class of taxpayers can be justified only to the extent that such taxes are equivalent to special benefits conferred upon those taxpayers."

Unlike a tax, a special fee is not designed to raise revenues to defray the general expenses of government, but rather is a charge imposed upon persons or property for the purpose of defraying the cost of a particular governmental service. The amount of a special fee must be reasonably related to the overall cost of the service. Mathematical exactitude, however, is not required, and the particular mode adopted by a city in assessing the fee is generally a matter of legislative discretion. An ordinance creating a special service fee, therefore, generally will be upheld as long as the ordinance is reasonably designed to defray the cost of the particular service rendered by the municipality.

10. *Preemption*. Impact fees, even though authorized by home rule power, may nevertheless be overridden by state occupation of the field. *See Albany Area Builders Ass'n v. Town of Guilderland*, 546 N.E.2d 920 (N.Y.1989), where the court found that a transportation impact fee was preempted by the state transportation finance act.

11. *Methodology*. Several courts have comprehensively addressed the methodology required to meet nexus and proportionality requirements, utilizing either the rational relationship test or the reasonable relationship test.

(a) *Rational Relationship. See F & W Associates v. County of Somerset*, 648 A.2d 482 (N.J.App.1994), holding that traffic impact fees assessed against a developer met the rational nexus test:

> The developer's pro-rata share must be "necessitated or required by the construction or improvements within such subdivision . . . [citation omitted]. The statute is a codification which focused on the "rational nexus" between the needs created by, and the benefits conferred upon, the subdivision and the cost of the off-tract improvements. 648 A.2d at 486–87.

Noting that the ordinance assessing the impact fees was adopted "only after a comprehensive study of such factors as existing road facilities, current zoning, projected population growth, and existing commercial uses in the area," the court dismissed the notion that

> A causal nexus between the necessity for off-tract improvements and the development must be measured with precision. * * * What must be demonstrated is a "rational" nexus, not mathematical certainty. For example, the assessment should not be invalidated simply because there may be residual benefit conferred to the general public in its use of the off-tract road improvement. An assessment is subject to challenge only if the developer is required to pay a "disproportionate share of the cost of the improvements that also benefit other persons." *Id.* at 487.

The court set out in detail what the acceptable comprehensive study contained:

> The study devised a volume-capacity ratio, measuring the demand volume and Mountain Boulevard's capacity. Based on projected full development of potential residential, retail and office use, the study adopted vehicle "trip generation" methodology and from this model, predicted incremental traffic impact resulting from future development of the land. The study estimated how much extra traffic would be generated by each development in the target area (Mountain Boulevard and surrounding roadways). The estimates were grounded on industrial standards, observations and empirical data obtained from traffic counts. The study then suggested what roadway improvements would be needed to accommodate the increased demands, and estimated the cost of those improvements. Id.

Noting that the township ordinance adopted the results of this "exacting study," the court observed that the ordinance authorized traffic-impact fees according to the formula for calculating each developer's share of the cost of the needed off-tract improvements. Not only does the ordinance provide for adjustment of the developer's pro rata share if conditions change, but it also exempts a developer from the fee altogether if the developer's off-tract impact is negligible, or if the developer does not benefit from the highway improvement.

(b) *Reasonable Relationship*. Where the local government has performed the requisite studies to establish a level of service and then determined the need generated by the development, the impact fees may be upheld on a reasonable relationship basis. *See Homebuilders Association of Tulare/Kings Counties v. City of Lemoore, California*, 112 Cal.Rptr.3d 7 (Cal.App.2010), the Court of Appeals analyzed an entire range of impact fees and found that they satisfied the substantial judicial deference test of reasonable relationship between the development generation of the need for additional community facilities. The fees generated $3.2 million dollars of a needed $5.0 million dollars of capital facilities due to population growth

12. *Computation of Need Generated by the Development*. Impact fees may be computed in one of two ways: (1) a fixed fee based on a unit of development. *See City of Mesa, supra* (residential development tax of $150 charged for each new dwelling unit, mobile home or trailer space); (2) a variable formula calculated on a standard relative to the need for facilities generated by the development within the impact fee area. Professors Nicholas Nelson and Juergensmeyer have has written extensively about the issue. *See* James C. Nicholas, Arthur Nelson and Julian C. Juergensmeyer, *A Practitioner's Guide to Development Impact Fees* (1991); James C. Nicholas and Dan Davidson, *Impact Fees in Hawaii: Implementing the State Law* (1992). A sample formula of a road impact fee is as follows:

Attributable New Travel in Vehicular Miles per Day =

[(Trip Rate X Trip Length)/2] X New Trips

New Lane Miles =

Attributable Travel/Capacity per Lane – Mile in Vehicles per Day

Construction Cost =

New Lane – Miles X Construction Cost per Lane – Mile

Right-of-Way Cost =

New Lane – Miles of Roads X Right-of-Way Cost per Lane – Mile

Total Cost = Construction Cost + Right-of-Way Cost

Credits =

[(Attributable Travel X Days per Year)/Miles per Gallon] X

Capital Portion of Motor Fuels Tax[ ] X Present Value Factor

Present Value Factor =

Sum from 1 to 25 of $(1/(1.06n)$, Where n is the Year from 1 to 25

Net Cost = Total Cost – Credits

Impact Fee = New Cost – Discount

Martin County, Florida, Road Impact Fee from James Nicholas, Arthur Nelson and Julian Juergensmeyer, *A Practitioner's Guide to Development Impact Fees* at 127–28.

Most fees are of the fixed variety and take the form of a per unit charge, often based on the number of bedrooms, rather than a percentage of acreage or assessed valuation. The formula approach has the advantage of being able to more accurately reflect the proportionate costs of public facilities attributable to specific types of new development. Regardless of which method is used, the fee must relate to the cost of the additional facilities necessitated by the new development to withstand attack. To fashion a valid development fee, *Bixel Associates v. City of Los Angeles*, 265 Cal.Rptr. 347 (Cal.App.1989) demonstrates the dual nexus that a city must calculate when drafting a development fee ordinance: (1) the need generated by the development; and (2) that the facilities built will benefit back the development. The City of Los Angeles was faced with a constitutional challenge of its fire hydrant fee ordinance as imposed on a new development. Proposition 13 of the California Constitution prohibits any "special taxes" unless approved by a two-thirds public vote, but "development fees" may be imposed without such a vote.

The court found that the fee was invalid as a "development fee" first because the amount charged did not bear a reasonable relationship to the need generated by the development, and the method of calculating the fee was a percentage based on the new development's relationship to the entire amount spent by the city on fire hydrants and water main improvements. The correct calculation should have computed the costs that would be incurred to the city as a result of the new development, and allocate those costs to the new development.

Similarly, the court in *Building Industry Ass'n of Central California v. City of Patterson*, 171 Cal.App.4th 886 (2009), the court held that the City's increased in-lieu affordable housing development fee of $20,946 per market rate unit violated a subdivision development agreement stating that developer agreed to be bound by the revised fee schedule if it was "reasonably justified." Since the amount of the increased fee was not based on the need generated by the subdivision, but rather, the per-unit fee was reached by dividing the cost of bridging the city's "affordability gap" for the cost of the total number of affordable units needed citywide, and the cost of new market rate units the city did not demonstrate any connection between the city's total need for affordable housing and the need for affordable housing associated with new market rate development.

13. *Deficiencies*. Exactions normally are confined to charges related to facilities, the need for which is generated by new growth, and may not be used for existing infrastructure deficiencies, *Marblehead v. City of San Clemente*, 277 Cal.Rptr. 550 (Cal.App.1991), or regional needs, *Anema v. Transit Construction Auth.*, 788 P.2d 1261 (Colo.1990). Nevertheless, in *Building Industry Ass'n v. City of Oxnard*, 267 Cal.Rptr. 769 (Cal.App.1990), the court upheld the city's use of the existing deficient standards as the basis for determining the level of service and requisite facilities for impact fees for the new growth related facilities for the future. Deficiencies must be financed by the general fund property or sales tax or through special assessment, although the latter will not be politically popular. Does this not suggest that the proper use of impact fee financing is to avoid the creation of new deficiencies by utilizing the new level of service established in its comprehensive plan that the City wishes to attain?

14. *Operation and Maintenance*. Operation and maintenance costs after facilities have been built pose major difficulties. Since these are not capital costs, neither impact fees nor special assessments can be used. Is there a way that "utilities" can be created for traditional municipal functions such as road and drainage? *Bloom v. City of Fort Collins*, 784 P.2d 304 (Colo.1989) involved a "transportation utility" fee imposed on owners or occupants of property to be used to maintain roadways. The court upheld the fee as a "special fee" reasonably related to expenses incurred by city maintaining streets. See the *Bloom* quote, *supra*, regarding special fees versus other types of revenue raising measures.

15. *Assessments v. Impact Fees*. Constitutional restrictions requiring supra-majority general election votes, such as California's Proposition 13, have led to the development of techniques such as the facilities benefit assessment used by San Diego and upheld in *J.W. Jones Cos. v. City of San Diego*, 203 Cal.Rptr. 580 (Cal.App.1984). San Diego imposed a special assessment, styled a facilities benefit assessment (FBA), on undeveloped land to pay for future public facilities based on projected need. The ordinance required owners of parcels of land falling within the benefit area of the planned public facilities to

pay the assessment based proportionately on the benefit each would receive. Projected need was determined by using the maximum number of identical housing units that a developer could build on a given parcel of land based on current zoning regulations. The Court of Appeals rejected a developer's challenge that the ordinance was a tax falling under Proposition 13 requiring voter approval. *Jones* is noteworthy in that it upheld a single assessment for multiple integral area-wide public improvements. It also upheld the FBAs against a challenge to the Special assessments as being subject to Proposition 13. *See also Knox v. City of Orland*, 841 P.2d 144 (Cal.1992).

16. *Equal Protection.* Is there an equal protection issue if the facilities are used by both new and old residents with only the former contributing to the financing? Most courts uphold impact fees if the charges against new developments are limited to the proportion of costs for facilities necessitated by such development. *See Home Builders & Contractors Ass'n v. Bd. of County Comm'rs*, 446 So.2d 140 (Fla.App.1983) (charges against new development are reasonable because the new development creates the necessity for new road construction). Stated another way, the facilities would not have been required but for the new development and the older residents are only incidentally using the facilities. *See also J.W. Jones Cos. v. City of San Diego*, 203 Cal.Rptr. 580 (Cal.App.1984) (holding that the fact that the new facilities financed by the FBAs incidentally benefitted existing development did not constitute an equal protection violation).

Although impact fees are often challenged on the grounds that they result in double charging, courts usually avoid the issue since the charges are normally less than the proportionate system cost. *See City of Mesa v. Home Builders Ass'n*, 523 P.2d 57, 60 (Ariz.1974), where the court, in conclusory fashion, simply stated that the charge did not "result in double taxation of new residents * * * even assuming that the $150.00 tax is passed on to the purchaser, the new resident, and that he has to pay an ad valorem tax levied against the property in the same taxable year."

17. *Linkage Fees and Affordable Housing.* Impact fees do increase the cost of housing, but scholars debate whether that cost is borne by the developer, *see* Franklin James, *Evaluation of Local Impact Fees as a Source of Infrastructure Finance*, 11 MUN.FIN.J. 407 (1990), or increases the value of the housing more than the cost of the fees due to availability of the facilities and services by reason of the impact fees. *See* Arthur C. Nelson, Liza K. Bowles, Julian C. Juergensmeyer, and James C. Nicholas, *A Guide to Impact Fees and Housing Affordability* 99 (2008) (citing to extensive studies in Florida from 1993 to 2003). In the rare cases that an impact fee itself may raise the cost of housing from within affordability to above affordability, the impact fee legislation may exempt the lower cost housing. *See* S. Mark White, *Development Fees and Exemptions for Affordable Housing: Tailoring Regulations to Achieve Multiple Public Objectives*, 6 J.LAND USE & ENVTL.LAW 25 (1990). Impact fees can also be used in an inclusionary manner. *See* Ch. 5.B.2.

Linkage fees charge nonresidential developers an affordable housing fee to provide for the percentage of new employees who will require low or moderate income housing. In *Commercial Builders v. City of Sacramento*, 941 F.2d 872 (9th Cir.1991), *cert. denied*, 504 U.S. 931 (1992), the court upheld a city ordinance which conditioned nonresidential building permits upon the payment of a fee for housing to offset expenses associated with the influx of low-income workers for the new project. The developers argued that the ordinance was a taking because it placed the burden of paying for the housing upon the new development without a sufficient showing that nonresidential development contributed to the need for new low-income housing in proportion to that burden. The court found no taking, however, as the fee was enacted only after a study revealed that the need for low-income housing would rise as a direct result of demand from workers on the new development. "The burden assessed against the developers thus bears a rational relationship to a public cost closely associated with such development." *Id.* at 874. The court seemingly broadened its holding beyond the imposition of a fee for low-income housing when it stated that "[a] purely financial exaction, then, will not constitute a taking if it is made for the purpose of paying a social cost that is reasonably related to the activity against which the fee is assessed." *Id.* at 876.

However, *see Building Industry Ass'n of Central California v. City of Patterson*, 90 Cal.Rptr.3d 63 (Cal.App.2009), in which the court found no reasonable connection between a substantial affordable housing in-lieu fee and a market-rate single family development: "the fee calculations . . . do not support a finding that the fees to be borne by Developer's project bore any reasonable relationship to any deleterious impact associated with the project." *Id.* at 74. The California Supreme Court sided with the *Napa* and not the *Patterson* decision in *California Building Industry Ass'n v. City of San Jose*, 351 P.3d 974 (2015), *cert. denied*, 136 S.Ct. 928 (2016), which upheld a city inclusionary zoning ordinance requiring that 15 percent of the dwelling units in a new development be set aside for affordable or workforce housing. See discussion in Chapter 5, pg. 642 regarding Inclusionary Zoning. Alternatively, the landowner could construct affordable housing units off-site equal to 20 percent of the total projected market-rate units, or pay an in-lieu fee. While the decision only applies to California, the case has been widely reported in national media. Moreover, it holds lessons for planner nationwide.

First, a bit of background. The ordinance requires landowner-provided affordable housing units as a condition on the development of land. It is therefore at first glance a land development condition (also called an exaction, impact fee, etc.), subject to nexus and proportionality requirements set out in three U.S. Supreme Court decisions. First, in *Nollan v. California Coastal Commission*, the Court held that a government imposing land development conditions must demonstrate a close connection, or nexus to the needs or problems that the development causes. Second, in *Dolan v. City of Tigard*, the Court further required that a government demonstrate that such conditions bear a rough proportionality to such demonstrated needs or problems.

Third, in *Koontz v. St. Johns River Water Management District*, the Court in 2013 held that both the *Nollan* and *Dolan* nexus and proportionality requirements apply to monetary exactions like mitigation fees, in-lieu fees, and impact fees, as well as government-required dedication of land or interests in land (like easements). Thus, for example, government could constitutionally require a landowner to provide a public school site or in-lieu fee as a condition for approval of a large residential development, or a fee representing a development's fair share of the cost of such a school site on a small residential development. However, it could not require either a site of a fee from a commercial center development for lack of a nexus: commercial developments do not drive a need for schools, but residential developments do.

Applying these cases and the standards they represented to the San Jose ordinance would seem to be clear: requiring a percentage of workforce housing as a condition for approving a land development would be constitutional if—but only if—San Jose could demonstrate that a development caused a need for affordable housing. Thus, for example, a hotel development would likely be subject to such a requirement since it would presumably generate low-paying jobs and, consequently, a need to house those workers.

Indeed, the 9th Circuit Court of Appeals—with jurisdiction over California, by the way—so held, applying a version of the federal nexus and proportionality standards in *Commercial Builders of N. Cal v. City of Sacramento*, 941 F.2d 872 (1991). There, the court upheld a workforce housing mandatory set-aside after the city undertook a detailed study of the workforce housing needs a hotel complex would generate.

The California Supreme Court ignored all of the above, specifically holding that nexus and proportionality do not apply to mandatory affordable housing requirements. Instead, the court agreed with the lower court of appeals that since California's planning statutes require each local government to formulate a comprehensive plan and to include an affordable housing element, the San Jose ordinance was no different from any zoning ordinance regulation like use, yard, and set-back regulations. Moreover, the court further held that the mandatory housing requirement was no more than the equivalent of a rent-controlled ordinance most of which have been approved where litigated, especially in California.

The court's demonstrated ignorance of basic zoning law—indeed local land-use controls generally—is breathtaking. Zoning ordinances are regulatory: They prevent certain uses or limits the size of permitted structures through bulk requirements such as height, set-back, and yard maximums and minimums. By contrast, the mandatory workforce housing requirement in San Jose requires a landowner to affirmatively provide a public need or benefit—affordable housing—just as other land development conditions require water and sewer systems, road, schools, parks, and other public facilities, provided the development drives a need for them. There is no such need for affordable housing driven by or caused by a residential development for market-rate housing.

Planners outside California should be wary of adopting the rationale of the California Supreme Court for requiring mandatory affordable housing as a land development condition. First, the statutory planning scheme in California is different from that in most states. The *San Jose* decision is anchored on the plan consistency requirements and housing element in California. Second, developers in California are entitled by statute to density bonuses that commence at four percent affordable housing set-asides and escalate substantially as the percentage increases.

Finally, the principle federal case on set-asides involving Sacramento lays out clearly government's responsibility for such workforce housing requirements:

- Undertake a detailed study of the precise need for workforce housing on a project-by-project basis.

- Calculate the precise fee or set-aside each project requires.

- Cut that fee in half before applying it to a given project.

- Provide meaningful density bonuses, expedited permitting and grants.

For commentary critical of housing set-asides, see David L. Callies, *Mandatory Set-Asides as Land Development Conditions*, 42/43 URB.LAW. 307 (2010), and James D. O'Donnell, *Affordable Housing Ordinances: Exactions or Use Restrictions in the Post-Koontz Era?*, 48 THE URBAN LAWYER 899 (2016).

VOLUSIA COUNTY V. ABERDEEN AT ORMOND BEACH, L.P.

Supreme Court of Florida, 2000.
760 So.2d 126.

QUINCE, J.

Aberdeen at Ormond Beach, L.P., owns Aberdeen at Ormond Beach Manufactured Housing Community (Aberdeen), a mobile home park in Ormond Beach that provides housing for persons at least 55 years of age or older. Aberdeen brought suit against Volusia County and the Volusia County School Board (Volusia County) to challenge the constitutionality of public school impact fees assessed on new homes constructed at Aberdeen.

As a mobile home park, Aberdeen is regulated by Chapter 723, Florida Statutes. Its minimum age requirements comply with the "housing for older persons" exemption of the Federal Fair Housing Act. See 42 U.S.C. § 3607 (1994 & Supp. I 1996). Aberdeen's Supplemental Declaration of Covenants, Conditions and Restrictions (Supplemental Declaration) contains the following provisions: exceptions to the minimum age requirement are permitted under limited circumstances; persons under eighteen are prohibited from permanently residing in any dwelling unit; the developer reserves the absolute right to modify or revoke all other covenants; and restrictions are binding upon owners for thirty years from the date of recordation.

Effective October 1, 1992, Volusia County enacted Ordinance No. 92–9, imposing countywide public school impact fees on new dwelling units constructed in Volusia County. The ordinance's definition of "dwelling unit" ("living quarters for one family only") included single and multi-family housing, but excluded nursing homes, adult congregate living facilities and group homes. See, Volusia County, Fla., Ordinance 92–9, art. 1, § 4, (July 2, 1992). In addition, the ordinance furthered the County's policy of ensuring "that new development should bear a proportionate share of the cost of facility expansion necessitated by such new development." *Id.* art. 1, § 2(l).

The impact fee represents the cost per dwelling unit of providing new facilities. Ordinance 97–7 lowered the impact fee and permitted adjustments "to reflect any inflation or deflation in school construction costs." *Id.* § VII, (enacting code § 70–175(d)). In calculating the fee, the County utilized the student generation rate, which is the average number of public school students per dwelling unit. Pursuant to the Volusia County impact fee ordinances, Aberdeen has paid $86,984.07 under protest for 84 homes as of July 31, 1998.

Aberdeen filed suit against Volusia County, claiming, inter alia, that public school impact fees were unconstitutional as applied to Aberdeen because of the deed restrictions prohibiting minors from living on the property. In response, the County argued that exempting Aberdeen would convert the impact fee into a "user fee," thereby violating the state constitutional guarantee of a free public school system. Although both parties filed motions for summary judgment, the trial court denied Volusia County's motion and granted Aberdeen's motion.

Volusia County further contends that *Florida Home Builders Ass'n Inc. v. County of Volusia*, No 93–10992–CIDL, Div. 02 (Fla. 7th Cir. Nov. 21, 1996) and *St. Johns County v. Northeast Florida Builders Ass'n, Inc.*, 583 So.2d 635 (Fla.1991) control the outcome of this dispute. In Florida Home Builders, the plaintiffs challenged the number of tax credits used in calculating the impact fee. In settling the dispute, Volusia County agreed to utilize a more liberal standard to determine the permissible credits for other funding. Volusia County argues that it should not have to relitigate the calculation of the fee with every homeowner. Specifically, the County contends that Aberdeen's claims are barred because both Florida Home Builders and the instant case involve challenges to the methodology used in determining the feepayer's proportionate share of the impact fee. This purported similarity, however, oversimplifies Aberdeen's claims. While the plaintiffs in Florida Home Builders disputed the calculation used to determine the amount of the fee, Aberdeen argues that it is exempt from the fee. In short, Florida Home Builders involved a challenge to the methodology; the instant case involves a challenge to the fee's constitutionality as applied to Aberdeen.

Therefore, Florida Home Builders is not controlling precedent. Similarly, St. Johns County does not preclude review of Aberdeen's claims. In St. Johns County, the plaintiffs attacked the impact fee ordinance as unconstitutional on its face. *See St. Johns County*, 583 So.2d at 637. The ordinance allocated the cost of new schools to each new unit of residential development. In addition, the ordinance permitted households to adjust the fee in individual cases. The Court rejected the argument that dwelling units without children did not have an impact on the school system, noting that occupants would change and children would "come and go." *Id.* at 638. The Court likewise rejected the argument that the "benefits" prong of the dual rational nexus test requires that "every new unit of development benefit from the impact fee in the sense that there must be a child residing in that unit who will attend public school." *Id.* at 639. However, the Court ultimately found that the ordinance was defective because fee funds could be spent within municipalities whose residents were not subject to the fee. The St. Johns County plaintiffs also attacked the ordinance on the ground that it violated the state constitutional guarantee of a uniform system of free public schools. The Court opined that the adjustment provision for individual households would turn into a user fee paid primarily by families with children in school. Thus, the Court invalidated the alternative provision, but noted that exemptions for adult housing where land use restrictions prohibited minors from residing were permissible.

Volusia County contends that St. Johns County and the instant case involve the same issues of law. It notes that the plaintiffs in St. Johns County contested the constitutionality of the fee because a portion of the county was excluded, while Aberdeen similarly contests the constitutionality of the fee because it is included. Although the plaintiffs seek opposite results, argues Volusia County, the issues of law remain the same. This argument, however, overlooks the unique issue that Aberdeen's claims raise. The Court in St. Johns County approved the methodology used in the impact fee ordinance. Additionally, the Court articulated the constitutional prohibition against assessing fees based on whether children actually lived in the dwelling unit. Aberdeen, however, is neither attacking the fundamental validity of the ordinance nor arguing that fees should be assessed solely based on use. Instead, Aberdeen challenges the imposition of school impact fees on a development that is closed to children. Thus, Aberdeen's "as applied" challenge raises the question of whether St. Johns County's rationale is applicable to its deed-restricted adult community. Although the Court's dicta addressed this scenario, the Court's holding simply did not reach this issue. Therefore, St. Johns County does not bar Aberdeen's claims.

In an effort to thwart the foregoing analysis, Volusia County contends that Aberdeen has disguised its challenge to the methodology as an "as applied" claim. In effect, Volusia County argues that the application cannot be challenged without contesting the methodology. To bolster its argument,

Volusia County discusses in depth cases where the "as applied" challenge was successful because the underlying methodology was defective. *See Contractors & Builders Ass'n v. City of Dunedin*, 329 So.2d 314 (Fla.1976); *Westwood Lake, Inc. v. Dade County*, 264 So.2d 7 (Fla.1972); *Florida Keys Aqueduct Auth. v. Pier House Joint Venture*, 601 So.2d 1270 (Fla. 3d DCA 1992); *City of Tarpon Springs v. Tarpon Springs Arcade Ltd.*, 585 So.2d 324 (Fla. 2d DCA 1991). This aspect of the cited cases, however, is irrelevant. It is well settled that an ordinance that is constitutional on its face may be unconstitutional as applied to a particular party. *See City of Miami v. Stegemann*, 158 So.2d 583 (Fla. 3d DCA 1963). That the underlying methodology may be invalidated in other cases does not transform the nature of Aberdeen's claims. As previously mentioned, Aberdeen is not challenging the fundamental validity of the ordinance; it challenges the assessment of the fee only as it is applied to Aberdeen. Therefore, we hold that stare decisis does not preclude review of Aberdeen's claims.

The parties dispute the proper application of the dual rational nexus test. In St. Johns County, the Court expressly adopted the dual rational nexus test for determining the constitutionality of impact fees: the local government must demonstrate reasonable connections between (1) "the need for additional capital facilities and the growth in population generated by the subdivision" and (2) "the expenditures of the funds collected and the benefits accruing to the subdivision." *St. Johns County*, 583 So.2d at 637 (quoting *Hollywood, Inc. v. Broward County*, 431 So.2d 606, 611–12 (Fla. 4th DCA 1983)). Volusia County argues that the test requires needs and benefits to be assessed based on countywide growth, and that the specific-need/special-benefit analysis is limited to the water and sewer line context. This argument, however, is without merit.

The language of the test itself belies the assertion that a countywide standard should be employed. The first prong of the test explicitly requires a nexus between the County's need and the "growth in population generated by the subdivision." 583 So.2d at 637. Similarly, the test's second prong ensures that "benefits accru[e] to the subdivision." *Id.* Thus, the explicit references to subdivisions indicate that the standard is not tailored to countywide growth, but to growth of a particular subdivision.

Furthermore, this Court in St. Johns County adopted the dual rational nexus test exactly as it was enunciated in *Hollywood, Inc. v. Broward County*, 431 So.2d 606 (Fla. 4th DCA 1983), which applied the test to parks. The test ensures that the Broward County requirements—the fee must "offset needs sufficiently attributable to the subdivision" and the fee revenue must be "sufficiently earmarked for the substantial benefit of the subdivision residents"—are satisfied. *Id.* at 611. Moreover, this Court in St. Johns County reaffirmed the Dunedin requirement that the fees must "be spent to benefit those who have paid the fees." *St. Johns County*, 583

So.2d at 639. Thus, the Court's use of the dual rational nexus test has not been limited to the water and sewer line context.

Additionally, in *Collier County v. State*, 733 So.2d 1012 (Fla.1999), we reaffirmed the specific-need/special-benefit standard. Construing St. Johns County, we said, "[T]he fee in St. Johns County was invalid because it did not provide a unique benefit to those paying the fee." *Id.* at 1019. We further explained that the fee at issue in Collier County was an invalid tax because "the services to be funded by the fee are the same general police-power services provided to all County residents." *Id.* Thus, we expressly repudiated a countywide standard for determining the constitutionality of impact fees.

This nexus is significant because of the distinction between taxes and fees. As this Court noted in Collier County, "[T]here is no requirement that taxes provide any specific benefit to the property; instead, they may be levied throughout the particular taxing unit for the general benefit of residents and property." *Collier County*, 733 So.2d at 1016 (quoting *City of Boca Raton v. State*, 595 So.2d 25, 29 (Fla.1992)). Fees, by contrast, must confer a special benefit on fee payers "in a manner not shared by those not paying the fee." *Id.* at 1019. We likewise noted in *State v. City of Port Orange*, 650 So.2d 1, 3 (Fla.1994), that "the power of a municipality to tax should not be broadened by semantics which would be the effect of labeling what the City is here collecting a fee rather than a tax." Thus, a liberal reading of the dual rational nexus test would obliterate the distinction between an unconstitutional tax and a valid fee.

The issue, however, is not whether Aberdeen influences the student generation rate or the amount of the impact fee, but whether Aberdeen increases the need for new schools. Indeed, Ordinance 97–7 defines "land development activity" as "any change in land use or any construction or installation of a dwelling unit, or any change in the use of any structure that will result in additional students in the public schools of the District." In addition, the test itself clearly frames the issue: whether there is a "need for additional capital facilities." *St. Johns County*, 583 So.2d at 637. Moreover, the student generation rate has remained unchanged since the impact fee was initially assessed in 1992. The ordinance provides that it will be adjusted only to "reflect any inflation or deflation in school construction costs." It does not contemplate adjustments based on variations in countywide demographics. As Aberdeen correctly points out, even if adjustments to the student generation rate were correlative to developmental growth, it would not change the fact that Aberdeen does not generate any students. That all residential units were included in the initial student generation rate is insufficient to establish a substantial nexus between Aberdeen's growth and the need for new schools. Thus, Aberdeen's purported effect on the student generation rate does not satisfy the dual rational nexus test.

Volusia County is unable to satisfy the "benefits" prong of the dual rational nexus test. Because no children can live at Aberdeen, impact fees collected at Aberdeen will not be spent for Aberdeen's benefit, but for the benefit of children living in other developments. Volusia County contends that Aberdeen benefits from the construction of new schools because they also serve as emergency shelters and sites for adult education classes. However, the connection between the expenditure of impact fee funds for the construction of new schools and the tangential benefit of having places of refuge in natural disasters is too attenuated to demonstrate a substantial nexus. Put another way, the schools are built primarily for the educational benefit of school-age children and, to the extent that Aberdeen derives any incidental benefit from their construction, it is insufficient to satisfy the dual rational nexus test.

In sum, Aberdeen neither contributes to the need for additional schools nor benefits from their construction. Accordingly, the imposition of impact fees as applied to Aberdeen does not satisfy the dual rational nexus test.

For the foregoing reasons, we hold that Volusia County's public school impact fees are unconstitutional as applied to Aberdeen. Accordingly, we affirm the trial court's decision.

NOTE

See *Home Builders Association of Dayton and the Miami Valley v. City of Beavercreek*, 729 N.E.2d 349 (Ohio 2000), upholding the application of the dual nexus test as gleaned from *Nollan and Dolan* as applied by the Florida Court in *Volusia*. The court held that a reviewing court must determine: "(1) whether there is a reasonable connection between the need for additional capital facilities and the growth in population generated by the subdivision; and (2) if a reasonable connection exists, whether there is a reasonable connection between the expenditure of funds collected through the imposition of an impact fee and the benefits accruing to the subdivision." *Id.* at 354.

I. CONSUMER REMEDIES: INTERSTATE LAND SALES AND BLUE SKIES CONSUMER PROTECTION

The case of *Rodriguez v. Banco Central Corp.*, 990 F.2d 7 (1st Cir.1993), presents the dilemma that purchasers of lots in subdivisions sometimes face. Plaintiffs, looking for retirement home sites, purchased lots based on promotional materials and oral representations that plaintiffs say promised them a development with all the perquisites: schools, churches, stores, recreational facilities, and so forth. The icing on the cake was the land's proximity to Disney World. It turned out that the lots plaintiffs bought were undevelopable swamp land. What can they do?

In order to protect the consumer from land sales frauds, various statutory measures have been enacted. The most widely utilized federal initiative in the consumer protection field relating to real estate subdivision is the Interstate Land Sales Full Disclosure Act. States also regulate such sales to some degree through their Blue Sky Laws.

1. FEDERAL INTERSTATE LAND SALES FULL DISCLOSURE ACT

STEVE AN V. LEVIEV FULTON CLUB, LLC

United States District Court, S.D. New York, 2010.
2010 WL 3291402.
Cited By Griffith v. Steiner Williamsburg, 760 F.Supp.2d 345 (S.D.N.Y.2010).

GEORGE B. DANIELS, DISTRICT JUDGE.

Steve An, (Plaintiff) brings this action against Defendant Leviev Fulton Club, LLC ("LFC") to rescind his condominium purchase agreement. Plaintiff moves for summary judgment contending that he has a right to rescission and the return of his deposit due to Defendant's failure to comply with the registration and disclosure requirements of the Interstate Land Sales Full Disclosure Act ("ILSFDA"), 15 U.S.C. § 1701 *et seq.* Defendant moves for summary judgment contending that the purchase agreement required construction of the unit to be completed within two years of signing, qualifying the condominium for the Improved Lot Exemption of the ILSFDA, 15 U.S.C. § 1702(a) (2). Defendant's motion for summary judgment is denied. Plaintiff's motion for summary judgment is granted.

The ILSFDA was "designed to prevent false and deceptive practices in the interstate sale of unimproved tracts of land by requiring developers to disclose information needed by potential purchasers." *See Flint Ridge Dev. Co. v. Scenic Rivers Ass'n of Okla.*, 426 U.S. 776, 778 (1976): "Congress, in passing the statute, desired to protect purchasers from unscrupulous sales of undeveloped home sites, frequently involving out-of-state sales of subdivided land purportedly suitable for development but actually under water or useful only for grazing". *See Beauford v. Helmsley*, 740 F.Supp. 201, 209 (S.D.N.Y.1990). Although concerned principally with the sale of raw land, Congress made the statute applicable to all lots. *See Winter v. Hollingsworth Properties*, 777 F.2d 1444, 1447 (11th Cir.1985) (noting that "[Congress] struck a balance by making the statute applicable to all lots and providing an exemption, not for all improved land, but for improved land on which a residential, commercial, condominium, or industrial building exists or where the contract of sale obligates the seller to erect such a structure within two years."). As such, condominium sales are within the scope of the statute and the protections of the ILSFDA are to be construed broadly, while the exemptions are to be construed narrowly. The Improved Lot Exemption, at issue here, provides that:

> Unless the method of disposition is adopted for the purpose of evasion of this title [15 U.S.C. §§ 1701 et seq.], the provisions of this title shall not apply to . . . the sale or lease of any improved land on which there is a residential, commercial, condominium, or industrial building, or the sale or lease of land under a contract obligating the seller or lessor to erect such a building thereon within a period of two years.

In the absence of certain exemptions, like the Improved Lot Exemption, the ILSFDA requires developers to file a statement of record with the Department of Housing and Urban Development ("HUD"), and to provide purchasers or lessees with a printed property report before the signing of any contract. Any contract or agreement for the sale of a lot that does not meet these requirements, and is not exempt under 15 U.S.C. § 1702, may be revoked within two years of signing at the option of the purchaser or lessee. See 15 U.S.C. § 1703(c) (d). A purchaser or lessee has a right of rescission and is entitled to the return of his or her deposit. In addition, "the court may order damages, specific performance, or such other relief as the court deems fair, just, and equitable." See 15 U.S.C. § 1709.

Here, Defendant is the sponsor of the LFC condominium development located at 111Fulton Street, New York, New York. The condominium development consists of one hundred sixty three residential units which were open for sale to the general public after June 1, 2007. On August 24, 2007, Plaintiff entered into a contract to purchase Unit 312 for $820,000.00 and paid a deposit of $82,000.00.

In order for the Defendant to be exempt under the Improved Lot Exemption, the contract must obligate the Defendant to erect the condominium units within two years of the purchaser's signing of the contract. *Long v. Merrifield Town Ctr. L.P.*, 611 F.3d 240 (4th Cir.2010) (holding "that to qualify for the Improved Lot Exemption under § 1702(a)(2) . . . the sales contract must obligate the seller to build and deliver the required structure within two years of the date that the purchaser signs the contract and incurs obligations"). Therefore, Defendant's contract with Plaintiff must obligate the Defendant to construct Unit 312 by August 24, 2009.

Each purchase agreement incorporated the Offering Plan, which details in part the "Procedure to Purchase" and the "Rights and Obligations of Sponsor" (LFC). The Rights and Obligations of Sponsor section provides in relevant part that:

> Under the present construction schedule, it is anticipated that a first temporary certificate of occupancy could be issued on or about April 1, 2008 and the Building will be substantially completed on

or about April 1, 2008, subject to Unavoidable Delays. Neither Sponsor nor its principals, managers, members, agents, designees, employees or affiliates, however, make any warranty or representation as to the date of substantial completion or the issuance of the first temporary certificate of occupancy.

The Procedure to Purchase section of the Offering Plan further provides that:

It is anticipated that the First Closing will occur by [April 1, 2008]. In the event the project commencement date of Condominium operation is twelve (12) months or later than the anticipated date of the First Closing, Sponsor will offer all Purchasers the right to rescind their Purchase Agreements and have their Down Payments refunded to them. In the event that the project commencement date of Condominium operation is six (6) months later than the anticipated date of the First Closing, the Plan will be amended to include a revised budget disclosing the then current budget projections.

Defendant failed to file or provide the required disclosure requirements pursuant to the ILSFDA before the signing of the purchase agreement by Plaintiff. However, Defendant subsequently scheduled a closing with Plaintiff individually via certified mail and first class mail. Plaintiff did not attend his closing. Thereafter, Plaintiff sent written notification from his attorneys indicating his intent to rescind his purchase agreement due to Defendant's failure to comply with reporting and disclosure requirements of the ILSFDA. Defendant responded to this notification by sending written notice informing Plaintiff that if he did not close by a certain date, Defendant could cancel the purchase agreement at its option and retain all the down payments as liquidated damages. Plaintiff again failed to close by the second closing date indicated by this notification. In response, Defendant refused to return Plaintiff's deposit despite demands to do so.

Plaintiff filed a complaint in this Court seeking rescission of his purchase agreement and the return of his deposit. Defendant initially presented counterclaims against Plaintiff arguing that sections of the Offering Plan (the Procedure to Purchase and the Rights and Obligations of Sponsor sections) obligated Defendant to build the condominiums within two years. Defendant has since conceded that the "Rights and Obligations of Sponsor" section of the Offering Plan (where one would expect such an obligation to be) does not unambiguously obligate Defendant to build the unit within two years. However, Defendant still argues that the Procedure to Purchase section of the Offering Plan obligates the Defendant to build the unit within two years of signing. Defendant solely relies on the sentence which reads:

[i]n the event the project commencement date of the Condominium operation is twelve (12) months or later than the anticipated date of the First Closing, Sponsor will offer all Purchasers the right to rescind their Purchase Agreements and have their Down Payments refunded to them.

Defendant contends that the Procedure to Purchase section required the Defendant to "build all units and to substantially complete the Condominium on or about April 1, 2008." Defendant further argues that in the event that this first April 1, deadline was not met, the Defendant had up to an additional year (by April 1, 2009) to complete construction of the Condominium, otherwise all purchasers had the "additional" right to rescind their respective agreements, "at their own election." Defendant contends that the Procedure to Purchase section contains an "unambiguous" obligation on the Defendant to complete construction of the unit by April 1, 2009.

Defendant further contends that because the contract language does not waive any of the purchasers' rights or limit their rights solely to specific performance, Defendant qualifies for the Improved Lot Exemption. Indeed, Defendant argues that the unambiguous obligation to build by April 1, 2009 does not waive any of the purchasers' rights, nor does the liquidated damages provision bar the purchasers' remedy of specific performance. Additionally, Defendant argues, in the alternative that should this Court find "that the subject agreement is ambiguous, in that it does not provide for a time for performance for the obligation to build, then under the contract interpretation laws of New York, a reasonable time for performance [is] to be imputed into the agreement. Defendant also notes that in fact all the condominium units were ultimately completed within the two year requirements of the ILSFDA.

Plaintiff counter-argues that whether construction was ultimately completed within two years is irrelevant in determining whether Defendant is entitled to the Improved Lot Exemption. Plaintiff contends that in order for Defendant to be entitled to the exemption, this Court must determine that the purchase agreement "unconditionally obligates" Defendant to complete the condominium unit within two years. If such an obligation does exist, Defendant is entitled to the Improved Lot Exemption, and is exempt from all the requirements of the ILSFDA. At issue here is whether the terms of the Procedure to Purchase section, incorporated into Plaintiff's Purchase Agreement, imposed such an unconditional obligation on Defendant to complete construction of the units within two years.

Defendant must show that the plain meaning of the alleged "unambiguous" obligation created by the Procedure to Purchase section automatically triggers the rights and remedies afforded purchasers under the ILSFDA. It must create both a legal duty to meet the deadline where the Plaintiff has the right to require the Defendant to timely perform. It must also offer all remedies the ILSFDA provides for failure to meet that deadline. The language of the "Rights and Obligation of Sponsor" and the "Procedure to Purchase" sections both say that completion is only "anticipated." No language in the Procedure to Purchase section creates an unconditional obligation or legal duty to build the units by April 1, 2009. The First Closing date is "anticipated" to occur by April 1, 2008, and "in the event that the project commencement date of the Condominium operation is twelve months or later than the anticipated date of the First Closing, Sponsor will offer all purchasers the right to rescind their purchase agreements and have their down payments refunded to them." An offered remedy for nonperformance does not equate to a legally enforceable duty to timely perform. No contract language legally obligates the Defendant to construct the units by April 1, 2009. While the Procedure to Purchase section offers a remedy for purchasers if Defendant decides not to meet that deadline, this section provides no legal compulsion upon the Defendant to construct the units within two years of purchase. As the HUD guidelines appropriately indicate, "the contract must not allow nonperformance by the seller at the seller's discretion." The contract provides no legal right for Plaintiff to force Defendant to build within two years. Plaintiff cannot legally compel such a timely result. As such, the Procedure to Purchase section does not provide an unconditional legal obligation for the Defendant to construct the units within two years of signing, so as to qualify for the ILSFDA exemption.

Defendant's motion for summary judgment is denied. Plaintiff's motion for summary judgment is granted.

NOTE

In *An v. Leviev Fulton Club, LLC,* No. 09 CV 1937 GBD, 2010 WL 3291402 (S.D.N.Y. Aug. 10, 2010), the Court focused on the interpretation of the Interstate Land Sales Full Disclosure Act ("ILSFDA"), particularly with respect to the disclosure requirements for condominium sales.

The ILSFDA was amended in 2013 to clarify how the Act applies to condominiums. The amendment became effective on September 26, 2014, lessening the disclosure requirements for condominium sales given the inherent different between condominium sales and the sale of lots of land contemplated when the ILSFDA was enacted. Congress amended the ILSFDA in 2014 to specifically exempt condominiums from the registration and disclosure requirements under the ILSFDA. *Beaver v. Tarsadia Hotels,* 29 F.Supp.3d 1332–4 (S.D.Cal.2014), leave to appeal granted (Jan. 14, 2015), followed.

BEAVER V. TARSADIA HOTELS

United States District Court, S.D. California, 2014.
29 F.Supp.3d 1323.

GONZALO P. CURIEL, DISTRICT JUDGE.

On September 26, 2014, a bill that amended the Interstate Land Sales Disclosure Act ("ILSA") to exclude condominiums from the registration and disclosure requirements was enacted. As a result, the liability of Tarsadia Defendants depends on whether the amendment applies to the pending case.

The bill is entitled, "To amend the Interstate Land Sales Full Disclosure Act to clarify how the Act applies to condominiums." (*Id.*). If the recent amendment applies to the instant case, it would affect the Court's recent decision granting Plaintiff's motion for summary judgement on the UCL cause of action for violations of the registration and disclosure requirements. Plaintiffs support the position that the presumption against retroactivity applies in this case while Tarsadia Defendants assert that the amendment is a clarification of prior law which should be applied retrospectively to this case. Accordingly, the Court must determine whether the amendment should be applied retroactively to the instant case.

A careful look at the recent amendment reveals that it added condominiums as an exemption under the registration and disclosure requirements under the ILSA. In essence, the amendment changes the liability provisions of the ILSA where condominiums that were previously not exempted are now exempt from the registration and disclosure requirements. *See* 15 U.S.C. § 1702(b). The amendment increased the number of exemptions for purposes of the registration and disclosure requirements to include all condominiums. The parties do not provide any analysis as to how the added exemption to exclude condominiums from the registration and disclosure requirements under the ILSA clarifies the prior law. It is clear that the prior statute did not exclude condominiums from the registration and disclosure requirement. Moreover, there is no split in authority on whether the disclosure and registration requirements of the preamendment ILSA applied to condominiums. The Court concludes that there is no ambiguity in the prior law as to whether an exemption existed for condominiums that were exempt only for the registration and disclosure requirements. Accordingly, this factor weights in favor of the amendment being a substantive change in law.

Legislative History

Plaintiffs assert that the legislative history reveals no "clear" and "unambiguous directive" as to retroactively required by *Landgraf*. Tarsadia Defendants maintain that the legislative history reinforces the clarifying purpose of the amendment.

Based on the Court's review, the legislative history is limited to the introductory remarks from a sponsor, Carolyn Maloney and three statements prior to a vote in the House of Representatives. No statements were made by the Senators. It does not appear that there are many committee reports, conference reports, or floor debates.

Carolyn Maloney, one of the sponsors of the bill, made introductory remarks on the measure on June 28, 2013. Congressional Record E1004–1005 (June 28, 2013). In those remarks, she stated that ILSA was intended to protect out-of-state buyers who were sold land that was not what was advertised and provides a right of action to rescind the contract but courts have ruled over the years that ILSA applies to condominiums which required developers to file redundant paperwork that was unnecessary and not relevant. *Id.* at 1004. She noted that the law needed a "technical fix" to distinguish condominium sales from other types of land sales. *Id.* at 1005. The Court notes that there are no statements as to "clarification" in these introductory remarks.

On September 25, 2013, the House moved to suspend the rules and pass the bill. H.R. 2600. The House proceeded with comments by the sponsors on September 25, 2014 prior to voting. Representative Patrick T. McHenry, from North Carolina stated,

> I want to begin by commending my colleague Congresswoman Carolyn Maloney of New York for introducing NO. 2600 in an effort to clarify the intent and purpose of the Interstate Land Sales Full Disclosure Act, or ILSA.

> ILSA was signed into law almost a half century ago to regulate fastbuck operators who were bilking investors, especially the elderly, through blatantly fraudulent sales of raw land often located in swamps and deserts.

> It was land sales, not condo units, which were the intended target of the ILSA disclosures, which is quite evident in the fact that the required disclosures relate to land issues, such as access to roads and water supply, and make no sense in the context of more urban vertical developments. Nevertheless, in the 1980's, the Federal courts started to apply WSA to vertical condominiums based on HUD's broad interpretation and Congress' failure to expressly exempt condominiums.

> The fact is that purchasers of vertical condominiums units do not need the additional disclosures of that act. To the extent that any of the act's disclosures relate to condo developments, they are generally duplicative of more extensive information already contained in State-mandated disclosures to purchasers.

> The private use of ILSA was practically nonexistent for 40 years, until 2008, when the real estate market crashed and purchasers'

lawyers starting looking for ways to escape re-crash contracts. As the recession continued, plaintiffs' lawyers began seeking out purchaser clients to file lawsuits under that act, demanding the full rescission of contracts with such Web sites as "No-Condo.com."

Courts generally acknowledge that ILSA has become "an increasingly popular means of channeling buyer's remorse"; but while courts have expressed sympathy for the developers' position, many courts have felt compelled to apply the language of the statute literally, allowing buyers to escape valid contracts.

Therefore I stand in strong support of H.R. 2600, which puts an end to the exploitation of ILSA and allows residential condominium sales to make a return to the marketplace. I want to urge my colleagues to support this bill. . . .

Representative Carolyn B. Maloney stated,

The Interstate Land Sales Full Disclosure Act, known as ILSA was enacted in 1969 to protect consumers from being cheated in land deals. It was originally intended to protect out-of-State buyers who were sold land that was not what it was advertised to be and to provide a right of action to rescind the contract and walk away from the deal. However, due to *ambiguities* in the original law, courts have ruled over the years that ILSA applies to condominiums and that developers are required to file redundant paperwork and make disclosures that are completely nonsensical when applied to condo units.

This has led to absurd results. For example, ILSA requires condo developers to file a report that discloses, among other things, information about the condo unit's topography, how much of the condo is covered by water, whether there is any soil erosion, and whether the condominium has any oil and gas rights.

I, for one, don't know of any high-rise condo units that are covered by water. Requiring condo developers to file these types of nonsensical disclosures provides no consumer protection whatsoever and simply generates unnecessary paperwork.

Unfortunately, during the economic down turn in 2008, some buyers used the recording requirements of ILSA to rescind otherwise valid contracts for economic reasons, an unintended consequence of the act and its intent. The law now needs a technical fix to distinguish condominium sales from other types of land sales and to recognize the unique conditions under which these units are sold in today's market. . . .

Representative Jerrold Nadler stated,

Mr. Speaker, I rise in support of H.R. 2600, a commonsense *clarification* to the Interstate Land Sales Full Disclosure Act, ILSA, to preserve consumer protections while keeping our economic recovery on track.

More than 40 years ago, Congress passed ILSA to prevent real estate developers from bilking unsuspecting buyers out of their life savings by selling them parcels of land in the middle of a swamp or of a desert.

ILSA requires sellers to disclose critical information about the land being sold, including automobile access to the property, the availability of water on a lot, and access for emergency personnel. These disclosure requirements are clearly necessary and appropriate for individuals who are buying land sight unseen.

They do not make sense, however, when you try to apply them to purchases of condominiums in urban high-rise developments. Clearly, a condo in downtown Manhattan or in downtown Dallas will have access to water and emergency services, and purchasers do not need to know about the risk of soil erosion or about the presence of mobile homes within their units on the 15th floor.

Although common sense would dictate otherwise, courts have interpreted the vague statutory and regulatory language of ILSA to apply to condo purchases. While that interpretation has been disputed and discussed over the years, ILSA was rarely an issue in private condo sales until the economy collapsed in 2008; and as mentioned by Mrs. Maloney, in facing tough financial times and underwater mortgages, many condo and co-op buyers began to use a developer's failure to comply with ILSA to void otherwise valid contracts for condo purchases and receive full refunds of their pre-cash down payments. These suits slowed the housing recovery and left many large developments in New York, Florida, and in other States unfurnished or unoccupied.

We can all agree that ILSA provides vital consumer protections for land purchasers, but the law should not be used to void valid contracts because of buyer's remorse.

The bill before us today provides a simple *clarification* to explicitly exempt condominium sales from the law's disclosure requirements. To ensure that ILSA continues to provide the highest level of consumer protection, condominium developers will still be required to comply with the law's antifraud provisions. Developers will also be required to continue complying with all State and local disclosure requirements for condominiums. . . .

Congressional Record H5821–5823 (Sept. 25, 2013) (emphasis added). On September 18, 2014, the Senate passed the bill unanimously. Congressional Record 5862 (Sept. 18, 2013).

Based on the above, the Court concludes that the 2014 amendment to the ILSA does not apply to the instant case. The hearing set for October 31, 2014 shall be *vacated*. The Court, *sua sponte*, certifies this Order and the Court's Orders filed on October 16, 2013 and July 2, 2014 for interlocutory appeal. In line with the Court's *sua sponte* certification order, the Court also GRANTS in part Tarsadia Defendants' motion for certificate of appealability on these same issues (Dkt. No. 158.)

IT IS SO ORDERED.

NOTES

1.   In *Stein v. Paradigm Mirasol, LLC*, 586 F.3d 849 (11th Cir.2009) the Court of Appeals noted the reason why so many purchasers were recently using the ILSFDA to walk away from condominium purchases:

> In a market-based economy the price of housing, like other goods, is subject to swings. There was a sharp upward swing in housing prices between late 2000 and the end of 2005, and the resulting bubble was bigger in Florida than it was in most other states. Home prices there rose eighty-two percent in absolute terms during that short period, outstripping the national increase by thirty-one percent. *See* Gabriel Montes Rojas et al., *The Florida Housing Boom,* 3 FLA.FOCUS 1, 2 (2007). All bubbles eventually burst, as this one did. The bigger the bubble, the bigger the pop. The bigger the pop, the bigger the losses. And the bigger the losses, the more likely litigation will ensue. Hence this ILSFDA case.

2.   There are two separate commonly used exemptions from the ILSFDA which concern the number of lots in the subdivision or condominium. In *Griffith v. Steiner Williamsburg, LLC,* 760 F.Supp.2d 345, 358, 359 (S.D.N.Y.2010), the court examined the exemptions for subdivisions or condominiums of fewer than 25 or 100 lots, explaining the statute as follows:

> There are two types of ILSA exemptions: (1) full exemptions, listed in 15 U.S.C. § 1702(a), which relieve a developer, of fewer than 25 lots, from all of ILSFDA's provisions; and (2) partial exemptions, listed in 15 U.S.C. § 1702(b) (1), which relieve a developer of fewer than 100 lots of ILSFDA's registration and disclosure requirements, but not its anti-fraud provisions.

> [Steiner's condominium subdivision consisted of 135 units]. Steiner argues that because it did not sell ninety-nine units before obtaining a temporary certificate of occupancy for all the units, and because all the unsold units now qualify for the improved lot exemption, the 100 lot exemption applies. In determining whether the 100 lot exemption applies here, this Court will consider how many non-exempt lots the

developer publicly was offering to sell at the time plaintiffs entered into their Purchase Agreements. *See, e.g., Long v. Merrifield Town Ctr. Ltd. P'ship*, 611 F.3d at 240, 248 (Where purchase agreements did not satisfy the two year exemption, "the 100 Lot Exemption also could not have applied to the plaintiffs' contracts because there were more than 100 non-exempt units."); *First Global Corp. v. Mansiana Ocean Residences, LLC*, 2010 WL 2163756 at 4 ("For purposes of the 100-lot exemption, the relevant number is the number of units communicated by the developer to the buyer and the purchasing public" and the developer was not entitled to the 100 lot exemption because "at the time that [the purchaser] contracted to purchase its unit, the only information communicated to [the purchaser], and to the public at-large, was that the [condominium] would consist of 135 units.")

3.   The Interstate Land Sales Full Disclosure Act, 15 U.S.C. § 1701 et seq., requires that a subdivider, using the mails or instrumentalities of interstate commerce, file a Property Report with the Secretary of Housing and Urban Development when she offers to sell, sells or leases fifty or more unimproved lots. The inherent weakness of the act is that it is merely a disclosure statute and does not regulate the quality of an offering. As seen above, the act's impact is great if the developer fails to file and deliver to the purchaser the Property Report. The act's impact is minimal where a developer, once having disclosed all material facts concerning an offering in the Property Report, proceeds to sell a lot in the Okefenokee Swamp or the Mojave Desert and not be responsible for the lack of improvements or facilities accompanying the lot.

The Act provides registration and disclosure requirements only for subdivisions that fall under the Act. In addition to self-executing statutory exemptions explored in the *Steve An* case, the Secretary of HUD has discretionary power to grant additional exemptions under 15 U.S.C. § 1702(c).

The provisions of the Act apply to "any developer or agent." *See* 15 U.S.C. § 1703(a). Lenders who only finance the purchases of subdivision lots are not covered by the statute. *See Adema v. Great Northern Development Co.*, 374 F.Supp. 318 (N.D.Ga.1973).

The information that is required to be disclosed to prospective purchasers is for their benefit; therefore, any omission or untrue statements about material facts will trigger liability. Would failure to disclose to subdivision lot purchasers the possibility of loss on their investment constitute a material omission? *See Hester v. Hidden Valley Lakes, Inc.*, 495 F.Supp. 48 (N.D.Miss.1980). Is reliance by the purchaser necessary? *See Bryan v. Amrep Corp.*, 429 F.Supp. 313 (S.D.N.Y.1977).

Once a subdivision falls under the Act, any lease or contract for sale must contain a provision informing the lessee or buyer of their right to revoke the contract within seven days of signing. States have a right to extend this period of time. *See* 15 U.S.C. § 1703(b).

The Interstate Land Sales Full Disclosure Act was patterned after the Federal Securities Act of 1933. *See* 15 U.S.C. §§ 77a et seq. Under the Securities Act, full disclosure of all material facts relating to a public offering of securities must be made to all prospective purchasers. Since the Act is designed to protect purchasers of securities, its application to subdivision purchasers is limited to land sales classified as either an "investment contract" or some form of third-party profit-making device.

2. STATE PROTECTION: BLUE SKY LAWS

Kansas enacted the first state "blue sky" law in 1911. It required companies selling securities in Kansas to register with the bank commissioner and disclose information about their operations. Stockbrokers were required to be registered. Louis Loss & Edward M. Cowett, *Blue Sky Law* 4 (1958). By the time Congress passed the Federal Securities Act of 1933, every state except Nevada had enacted a "blue sky law" to regulate the sale of securities. Although how the state statutes came to be known as "blue sky" laws is uncertain, certain accounts contend that the name arose from the type of problems addressed by the statutes: either "speculative schemes which have no more basis than so many feet of blue sky," 69A Am.Jur.2d Sec. Reg. Stat. § 1 (1993), or "fast talking eastern industrialists selling everything under the blue sky." 1 Thomas Lee Hazen, *Treatise on the Law of Securities Regulation* § 8.1, at 490–492 (3d ed.1995); *See In re WorldCom*, 293 Bank Rptr. 308, n.25 (S.D.N.Y.2003). While these state laws purport to protect investors from fraud, they were adopted in part from pressure by banks, farmers, and small businessmen to limit competition for capital by restricting securities sales. Richard W. Painter, *Responding to a False Alarm: Federal Preemption of State Securities Fraud Causes of Action*, 84 CORN.L.REV. 1, 22 (1998); see Jonathan R. Macey & Geoffrey P. Miller, *Origin of the Blue Sky Laws*, 70 TEX.L.REV. 347, 364–70 (1991). In *Florida Realty, Inc. v. Kirkpatrick*, 509 S.W.2d 114 (Mo.1974), the court upheld a statute that categorized the sale of out-of-state subdivision lots using a deferred payment method as securities within the meaning of Missouri's Blue Sky Law. Restricting the law to the sale of land outside the state of Missouri was reasonable in that "a Missouri resident might reasonably be expected to have the ability * * * to personally view land lying within the state of his residence * * * whereas it might be difficult or impossible for the prospective purchaser to travel long distances for these purposes." *Id.* at 118. Similarly, out of state purchases are deemed "securities" under California law. *See Diamond Multimedia Systems, Inc. v. Superior Court*, 968 P.2d 539 (Cal.1999).

Every effort should be made to protect the ordinary purchaser from a potential land swindle. While Missouri and several other states may bring sales of foreign real estate within the ambit of securities regulation, such minimal protection is not enough. If a developer dealt strictly in cash sales which are not securities, there would be little if any protection. If the state in which the land is located has minimal subdivision or other type of regulation to ensure that the land is properly developed and adequate public facilities provided, then mere disclosure under a securities law is of little help to the purchaser who will later find no roads, sewers or water utilities. Some of the better state regulations will provide, in addition to classifying foreign real estate as a security, that there be on-site inspection by the appropriate commission, or even more, that performance bonds be put up to ensure that the necessary amenities are provided. *See, e.g.,* West's Ann.Cal.Bus. & Prof.Code §§ 11000 et seq.

A state Blue Sky law regulates the sale of securities in order to protect the public from deceptive or fraudulent practices. The states have generally construed certain real estate transactions to be a security, when, as in the federal law, there exists an overall scheme or plan where money is invested with the expectation that the investor will receive a return on his investment from the effort provided by a third party or promoter. In interpreting whether a transaction is a security, the courts look through form to substance and consider the facts and circumstances surrounding the transaction to ascertain the true intent of the parties. Blue Sky laws usually fall within one of four classifications. (1) Certain acts are directed at securities fraud. A violation arises if a registered security is found to perpetrate a fraud. No licensing or "qualifying" by meeting minimum standards provisions exist under this type of Blue Sky law. *See* Ariz.Rev.Stat. §§ 44–1801 to 44–2037; Minn.Stat.Ann. §§ 83.01 et seq.; Neb.Rev.Stat. §§ 81–1101 et seq.; *see also* Loss and Cowett, *Blue Sky Law* 19 (1958). (2) Other statutes are concerned with the licensing of dealers and do not provide specific requirements for the security. *See* Colo.Rev.Stat. 11–51–101 et seq. (3) Certain laws set up minimum requirements for the security involved. *See* 32 Me.Rev.Stat.Ann. §§ 751–891; and Tenn.Code Ann. §§ 48–2–101 et seq. (4) Finally, certain statutes combine the requirements of (2) and (3).

Many real estate transactions are not covered under state Blue Sky laws either because the transaction does not fit within the securities definition or because the type of transaction is not covered by the particular classification of law. Once a real estate transaction meets the requirements of the state's definition of a security, it constitutes an effective source of protection as criminal, and multiple civil sanctions may be imposed (attorneys' fees, damages, interest, etc.).

The states have also entered the field of consumer protection involving the disclosure of credit terms. The most notable example of state action is the Uniform Consumer Credit Code (UCCC) covering real estate transactions involving the extension of credit. A credit sale of any interest in land occurs when credit is extended by someone regularly engaged in the business and the buyer is an individual other than a corporation, partnership, or trust. The borrower must be purchasing primarily for personal, family, household, or agricultural purposes. Should the creditor violate the disclosure requirements of the UCCC, he is liable to the buyer for twice the amount of the credit service or loan finance charge plus reasonable attorney's fees. The liability cannot be less than $100 or more than $1000. *See* UCCC § 5–203(1)(a). The UCCC also offers a right of rescission in the credit sale of an interest in land.

The common law will also provide protection in both contract and tort to house purchasers and homeowner associations against defaulting developers. *See Chesus v. Watts*, 967 S.W.2d 97 (Mo.App.1998) (sustaining lot purchaser recovery in contract and fraud for failure to carry out development plans, including road and drainage; and granting standing to home owners association on promissory estoppel binding developer to promises that induce purchase relating to transfer of common areas in good repair).

CHAPTER 5

ZONING AND HOUSING

▪ ▪ ▪

A. EXCLUSIONARY ZONING

1. THE STATE OF HOUSING

James Truslow Adams, who coined the "American Dream" phrase in his 1931 book, *The Epic of America,* wrote of the "dream of a land in which life should be better and richer and fuller for everyone * * * It is not a dream of motor cars and high wages merely, but a dream of social order in which each man and each woman shall be able to attain to the fullest stature of which they are innately capable, and be recognized by others for what they are, regardless of the fortuitous circumstances of birth or position."

Owning a home is a major component of the dream. It has been a dream of not only a place to live but of a long-term investment that will grow in value. For many, it has been a "dream come true." In 1920, 46% of homes in the country were owner-occupied. The Great Depression was a setback, and by 1940 the rate had dropped to 44%. However, after World War II, housing boomed. Massive construction answered the pent-up demand for housing. By 1950 home ownership rates had increased to 62%. By 2000, two-thirds of American households were owner-occupied. http://www.census.gov/housing/census/data/HousingBriefs/c2kbr01-13.pdf

The price of housing increased as well. In the last years of the twentieth century, many people, overly eager to become homeowners and aided and abetted by lax lending practices, bought houses they could not afford. Then, in the first few years of this century, the housing market turned frantic. For some, buying a house became more of a short-term investment than a place to live. Houses were bought to flip. Some markets saw annual price increases of 20%. Based on the conviction that houses always increased in value, caution went out the window. As we know, that which seemed too good to be true wasn't. The housing bubble burst in 2007. Prices declined and record numbers of home mortgages were foreclosed. By 2016, the housing market had reportedly recovered, with a median home price in the U.S. reported as $231,000 as compared to the previous record high of $228,000 in July 2005. However, this increase in median home price only exacerbates the problem of affordability when wages have remained relatively stagnant over this same time period. http://money.cnn.com/ 2016/07/28/real_estate/record-home-prices-2016/.

Zoning, which began in earnest only a few years before Adams wrote of the American Dream, has played a significant role in the housing available to Americans. For those who study housing markets, there is disagreement as to whether the effect of land regulation has been positive or negative. The answer to that question is complicated because the housing market is regional, not national. Conditions can vary greatly by region. Dense urban areas differ from rural and suburban areas. Overarching influences of the general economy make it difficult to pin point with certainty the degree to which any individual factor has affected housing prices.

The balance of this chapter examines land use regulation of housing. First, we will examine exclusionary zoning practices, then inclusionary zoning and finally, zoning's role in defining the American household.

2.   EXCLUSIONARY ZONING AND THE STATES

"Zoning thy name is exclusion." *

The use of land use controls to promote racial and economic discrimination has been noted from their beginning. The federal district judge who first considered the ordinance of the Village of Euclid found it invalid because it classified "the population and segregate[d] them according to their income or situation in life." *Ambler Realty Co. v. Village of Euclid*, 297 Fed. 307, 316 (D.C.Ohio 1924). The police power, the court held, could not be used to that end. The Supreme Court reversed with the none too flattering observation that apartments were parasites and could be kept away from "private" homes.

Exclusionary practices are well-documented and much criticized. *See, e.g.*, Charles Haar, *Suburbs Under Siege: Race, Space, and Audacious Judges* (1995); David Kirp, John P. Dwyer, and Larry A. Rosenthal, *Our Town: Race, Housing, and the Soul of Suburbia* (1996); Sarah Schindler, *Architectural Exclusion: Discrimination and Segregation Through Physical Design of the Built Environment*, 124 YALE L.J. 1934 (2015); Jerry Frug, *The Geography of Community*, 48 STAN.L.REV. 1047 (1996); Richard Thompson Ford, *The Boundaries of Race: Political Geography in Legal Analysis*, 107 HARV.L.REV. 1841 (1994).

This section deals with the principal techniques of exclusionary zoning. It also examines the *de minimis* role that the United States Supreme Court plays in the area, and closes with an examination of the Federal Fair Housing Act (FHA).

---

*   Donald Hagman, *Taking Care of One's Own Through Inclusionary Zoning: Bootstrapping Low- and Moderate-Income Housing by Local Government*, 5 URB.L. & POL'Y 169 (1982).

Local governments are most imaginative in regulating land use in facially innocuous ways that have the effect of excluding, and have all too often been intended to exclude, racial, religious and economic minorities. *See* Richard F. Babcock and David L. Callies, *Virtues in Conflict: Environment and Housing, in Modernizing Land Policy* (Clawson ed.1973). Among the more common techniques: minimum lot area requirements, minimum floor area requirements, limitations on multifamily dwellings and manufactured housing, minimum yard, setback and other extraordinary bulk requirements, and growth caps. Initially, courts found such techniques a sound method to preserve a community's character. Commencing in the 1960s, however, a few state high courts, most notably Pennsylvania and New Jersey, began to invalidate them as exclusionary.

Minimum Lot Size: Generally, the larger the lot, the more expensive the home. Courts have sustained large minimum lot size regulations of one to three acres in suburban areas. (Note: an acre has 43,560 sq. ft.; a football field excluding the end zones has 48,000 sq. ft.). However, in the 1960s, the tide turned as courts began to question whether deferential review was proper in exclusionary zoning cases. *See National Land & Inv. Co. v. Kohn*, 215 A.2d 597 (Pa.1965) (holding unconstitutional a four- acre minimum lot size, observing that the town, in the path of development from Philadelphia and the King of Prussia-Valley Forge area, could not use the zoning power to advance private goals contrary to the public interest). *See also* Gavin L. Phillips, *Validity of Zoning Laws Setting Minimum Lot Size Requirements*, 1 A.L.R.5th 622 (1992, updated to 2016).

Large minimum lot sizes in agricultural and other preservation areas are treated more favorably. Courts have upheld minimum lot sizes of 50 to 80 acres for agricultural preservation. *See Codorus Township v. Rodgers*, 492 A.2d 73 (Pa.Cmwlth.1985) (50 acres); *County of Ada v. Henry*, 668 P.2d 994 (Idaho 1983) (80 acres); *Ketchel v. Bainbridge Twp.*, 52 Ohio St.3d 239, 557 N.E.2d 779 (1990) (upholding three acre minimum lot size where challengers could not disprove town's claim that more dense development would strain the town's water supply); *but see Hopewell Township Bd. of Supervisors v. Golla*, 452 A.2d 1337 (Pa.1982) (ordinance allowing only five houses on 140 acre farm invalid). Perhaps the record belongs to Carbon County, Wyoming, with a minimum lot size of *one square mile*. How big is that? 640 acres. Central Park in New York City is only a bit larger. Mead Gruver, *Home on the Range: Square-Mile Minimum for Lots Enacted*, Caspar Star Tribune, April 7, 2003.

Even where a court customarily defers to legislative zoning ordinances, a town must offer a plausible rationale. In *C & M Developers, Inc. v. Bedminster Twp. Zoning Hearing Bd.*, 573 Pa. 2, 820 A.2d 143, 151, 159 (2002), the court held a one-acre minimum lot size purportedly to preserve agricultural lands unreasonable when the only reason proffered was the town's "belief that one acre was a 'good number' which would forestall the development of large houses on small lots."

Multi-Family Housing: How much land is typically zoned for high density housing? Generally none or very little, and then perhaps only by special permit or variance. In some cases, multi-family housing is only allowed where it can serve to buffer single-family houses from commercial or industrial uses. *See Village of Arlington Heights v. Metropolitan Housing Development Corp.*, 429 U.S. 252 (1977).

Manufactured Homes: They are likely not allowed at all or, if allowed, are relegated to "planned manufactured home communities" or "mobile home parks." What are the objections to manufactured or mobile homes? Safety? Aesthetics? Or, are the objections to the occupants? As one court stated, "[t]railer folk for the most part are nomads at heart." *Streyle v. Board of Property Assessment*, 98 A.2d 410, 412 (Pa.Super.1953). The perception that the occupants of such housing are undesirable and transient neighbors persists despite evidence to the contrary. For example, in Malibu, California, some mobile homes in Paradise Cove sell for several million dollars. http://www.today.com/home/malibu-mobile-home-lists-3-75-million-1D79930658.

Off-site built, or manufactured, houses, on average cost half that of site-built houses. Though not cheap, such housing represents, in relative terms, affordable housing without need of governmental subsidy. Increasingly, courts and legislatures around the country have enacted limitations on the ability of municipalities to exclude off-site built homes.

Fiscal Motivations: In addition to elitist motivations (such zoning is sometimes labeled "snob zoning"), exclusionary practices also have fiscal motivations. Growth cuts two ways: it brings in new revenues but it increases municipal costs. A major factor is the number of bedrooms. More bedrooms mean more children, and hence, more schools. *See* George Sternlieb, *Housing Development and Municipal Costs*, (Center for Urban Policy Research, Rutgers University, 1973).

House Size: Average house size increased over the past half-century. Estimates of the average house size in 1970 range from 1300 to 1500 square feet. In 2006, estimated average house size ranged from 2100 to 2300 square feet and increased to 2600 square feet in 2014. money.cnn.com/2014/06/04/real_estate/american-home-size/. Ironically, the growth in house size coincided with a reduction in household size from 3.1 persons in 1970 to 2.6 in 2015.

As large as a 2600 square foot house is, it is modest alongside many houses built over the past fifteen to twenty years in the higher price segment of the market. These homes go by such names as "monster homes," "trophy homes," and "starter castles." However, "McMansions" has come to be the most popular label. The labels are not complimentary. Though

McMansions lack a precise definition or minimum size, they commonly are built on relatively small lots and boast a footprint of 5000 square feet or more. Such development may reduce the supply of affordable housing. *See Bjorklund v. Zoning Bd. of Appeals of Norwell*, 878 N.E.2d 915, 919 (Mass.2008), where an owner sought to replace a 675 square foot house with a 3600 square foot house, the court opined that:

> many municipalities do not welcome the building of structures that represent the popular trend of 'mansionization.' This is especially so when the structures involve reconstruction on nonconforming lots. The expansion of smaller houses into significantly larger ones decreases the availability of would-be 'starter' homes in a community, perhaps excluding families of low to moderate income from neighborhoods. Municipalities may permissibly exercise their police power to attempt to limit these potential adverse effects. Doing so is consistent with the Legislature's concern for the critical need for affordable housing
> * * *

Larger houses may not only be unattractive, they may come with other issues. Some McMansions are used as boardinghouses for unrelated persons, some of whom are college students and "others [who] appear to be immigrants." Ovetta Wiggins, *"McMansions Turn 'McApartments,' Stirring Ire,"* Washington Post, B02, Sept. 4, 2007. For trends and issues, see Nancy Kubasek, *MegaMansions: A New Source of Conflict Between Environmentalists and Developers*, 35 REAL ESTATE L.J. 173 (2006).

One solution is to impose *maximum* house size restrictions. Reported cases are few, but courts that have addressed these matters have sustained such controls. *See Board of County Commissioners of Teton County v. Crow*, 65 P.3d 720 (Wyo.2003) (8000 square foot limit upheld) and *Rumson Estates, Inc. v. Mayor & Council of Borough of Fair Haven*, 828 A.2d 317 (N.J.2003) (2200 square feet). A proposed 29-bedroom, 40-bathroom, 55,000 square foot home with a 75 car garage and a 10,000 square foot playhouse on a 63 acre tract prompted the adoption of an ordinance limiting houses to 20,000 square feet. Alas, the court found the owner had a vested right to complete his "house." *In the Matter of Association of Friends of Sagaponack v. Zoning Bd. of Appeals of the Town of Southampton*, 731 N.Y.S.2d 851 (App.Div.2001). The City of Los Angeles has attempted for years to stop mansionization, but "[e]xisting rules to curb mansionization have 'a lot of loopholes and shortcomings' " according to advocates of the restrictions. http://www.latimes.com/local/lanow/la-me-ln-mansionization-law-201607 14-snap-story.html. *See generally* Elizabeth A. Garvin and Glen S. LeRoy, *Design Guidelines: The Law of Aesthetic Controls*, 55 LAND USE LAW & ZONING DIG. 3 (Apr. 2003). Beyond aesthetics, maximum house size ordinances may also be adopted to preserve lower cost housing.

The trend in increasing house size has reversed itself. Beginning in 2008, buyers began demanding smaller houses. The economy and the real estate crash are the major causes of the reversal. Larger houses generally cost more and many who could afford such homes can no longer do so. In addition to harsh economic realities, many people want smaller homes. Lifestyles have changed. Studies show that younger homebuyers want to live in an urban setting. They want to walk to work and to shop. The National Association of HomeBuilders (NAHB) reports that walkability, as well as energy efficiency and sustainability are important factors for Millennials entering the housing market. http//www.nahb.org *NIMBYism*: Increasing housing supply requires cities to upzone for higher density. Yet today, one can expect neighbors to object to any such suggestion. These neighbors are well described by several pejorative acronyms. First, there is the well-known NIMBY (Not in My Back Yard) syndrome, followed by the increasingly popular CAVE people (Citizens against Virtually Everything) and the BANANA bloc ("Build Absolutely Nothing Anywhere Near Anything") syndrome. If communities remain underzoned, where do those in need of lower cost housing go? Not to the suburbs, unless the state court or state legislature has intervened to curb exclusionary practices. Increasingly, however, such curbs have been put in place.

B. INCLUSIONARY ZONING

1. FAIR SHARE OBLIGATIONS

In *Euclid,* the Supreme Court said that there might be "cases where the general public interest would so far outweigh the interest of the municipality that the municipality would not be allowed to stand in the way." 272 U.S. at 390. Lurking behind this warning is the concept that a municipality exercises the state's police power, not its own, and that the regional effects of local zoning are relevant to zoning validity. Some state courts use this principle to impose fair share obligations on cities.

In the same year that the Pennsylvania and New York courts adopted a fair share requirement, the New Jersey Supreme Court handed down the most famous exclusionary-inclusionary zoning case*, Southern Burlington County NAACP v. Township of Mt. Laurel*, 336 A.2d 713 (N.J.1975) (now known as *Mt. Laurel I*). The case involved a developing community in New Jersey near Philadelphia and Camden. The residential zoning essentially was for large lot, low density housing. No land was zoned for multi-family housing or for mobile homes. Viewing the right to housing as fundamental, the New Jersey Supreme Court found the ordinance violated the state constitution's substantive due process and equal protection guarantees. The court ordered the township to affirmatively plan and provide reasonable opportunities for a variety of housing. That was 1975. What happened? Read on.

SOUTHERN BURLINGTON COUNTY N.A.A.C.P. V. TOWNSHIP OF MT. LAUREL

Supreme Court of New Jersey, 1983.
92 N.J. 158, 456 A.2d 390.

WILENTZ, C.J.

This is the return, eight years later, of Southern Burlington County N.A.A.C.P. v. Township of Mount Laurel, 67 N.J. 151, 336 A.2d 713 (1975) (*Mount Laurel I*). We set forth in that case, for the first time, the doctrine requiring that municipalities' land use regulations provide a realistic opportunity for low and moderate income housing. The doctrine has become famous. The *Mount Laurel* case itself threatens to become infamous. After all this time, ten years after the trial court's initial order invalidating its zoning ordinance, Mount Laurel remains afflicted with a blatantly exclusionary ordinance. Papered over with studies, rationalized by hired experts, the ordinance at its core is true to nothing but Mount Laurel's determination to exclude the poor. Mount Laurel is not alone; we believe that there is widespread non-compliance with the constitutional mandate of our original opinion in this case.

To the best of our ability, we shall not allow it to continue. This Court is more firmly committed to the original *Mount Laurel* doctrine than ever, and we are determined, within appropriate judicial bounds, to make it work. The obligation is to provide a realistic opportunity for housing, not litigation. We have learned from experience, however, that unless a strong judicial hand is used, *Mount Laurel* will not result in housing, but in paper, process, witnesses, trials and appeals. We intend by this decision to strengthen it, clarify it, and make it easier for public officials, including judges, to apply it.

* * *

In *Mount Laurel I,* this Court held that a zoning ordinance that contravened the general welfare was unconstitutional. We pointed out that a developing municipality violated that constitutional mandate by excluding housing for lower income people; that it would satisfy that constitutional obligation by affirmatively affording a realistic opportunity for the construction of its fair share of the present and prospective regional need for low and moderate income housing. This is the core of the *Mount Laurel* doctrine. * * *

The constitutional basis for the *Mount Laurel* doctrine remains the same. The constitutional power to zone, delegated to the municipalities subject to legislation, is but one portion of the police power and, as such, must be exercised for the general welfare. When the exercise of that power by a municipality affects something as fundamental as housing, the general welfare includes more than the welfare of that municipality and its citizens: it also includes the general welfare—in this case the housing needs—of those residing outside of the municipality but within the region that contributes to the housing demand within the municipality. Municipal land use regulations that conflict with the general welfare thus defined abuse the police power and are unconstitutional. In particular, those regulations that do not provide the requisite opportunity for a fair share of the region's need for low and moderate income housing conflict with the general welfare and violate the state constitutional requirements of substantive due process and equal protection.

* * *

The clarity of the constitutional obligation is seen most simply by imagining what this state could be like were this claim never to be recognized and enforced: poor people forever zoned out of substantial areas of the state, not because housing could not be built for them but because they are not wanted; poor people forced to live in urban slums forever not because suburbia, developing rural areas, fully developed residential sections, seashore resorts, and other attractive locations could not accommodate them, but simply because they are not wanted. It is a vision not only at variance with the requirement that the zoning power be used for the general welfare but with all concepts of fundamental fairness and decency that underpin many constitutional obligations.

Subject to the clear obligation to preserve open space and prime agricultural land, a builder in New Jersey who finds it economically feasible to provide decent housing for lower income groups will no longer find it governmentally impossible. Builders may not be able to build just where they want—our parks, farms, and conservation areas are not a land bank for housing speculators. But if sound planning of an area allows the rich and middle class to live there, it must also realistically and practically allow the poor. And if the area will accommodate factories, it must also find space for workers. The specific location of such housing will of course continue to depend on sound municipal land use planning. * * *

No one has challenged the *Mount Laurel* doctrine on these appeals. Nevertheless, a brief reminder of the judicial role in this sensitive area is appropriate, since powerful reasons suggest, and we agree, that the matter is better left to the Legislature. We act first and foremost because the Constitution of our State requires protection of the interests involved and because the Legislature has not protected them. We recognize the social and economic controversy (and its political consequences) that has resulted in relatively little legislative action in this field. We understand the enormous difficulty of achieving a political consensus that might lead to significant legislation enforcing the constitutional mandate better than we can, legislation that might completely remove this Court from those controversies. But enforcement of constitutional rights cannot await a supporting political consensus. So while we have always preferred legislative to judicial action in this field, we shall continue—until the Legislature acts—to do our best to uphold the constitutional obligation that underlies the *Mount Laurel* doctrine. That is our duty. We may not build houses, but we do enforce the Constitution.

* * *

Our rulings today have several purposes. First, we intend to encourage voluntary compliance with the constitutional obligation by defining it more clearly. We believe that the use of the State Development Guide Plan and the confinement of all *Mount Laurel* litigation to a small group of judges, selected by the Chief Justice with the approval of the Court, will tend to serve that purpose. Second, we hope to simplify litigation in this area. While we are not overly optimistic, we think that the remedial use of the SDGP may achieve that purpose, given the significance accorded it in this opinion. Third, the decisions are intended to increase substantially the effectiveness of the judicial remedy. In most cases, upon determination that the municipality has not fulfilled its constitutional obligation, the trial court will retain jurisdiction, order an immediate revision of the ordinance (including, if necessary, supervision of the revision through a court appointed master), and require the use of effective affirmative planning and zoning devices. The long delays of interminable appellate review will be discouraged, if not completely ended, and the opportunity for low and moderate income housing found in the new ordinance will be as realistic as judicial remedies can make it. We hope to achieve all of these purposes while preserving the fundamental legitimate control of municipalities over their own zoning and, indeed, their destiny.

The following is a summary of the more significant rulings of these cases:

(1) *Every* municipality's land use regulations should provide a realistic opportunity for decent housing for at least some part of its resident poor who now occupy dilapidated housing. The zoning power is no more abused by keeping out the region's poor than by forcing out the resident poor. In other words, each municipality must provide a realistic opportunity for decent housing for its indigenous poor except where they represent a disproportionately large segment of the population as compared with the rest of the region. This is the case in many of our urban areas.

(2) The existence of a municipal obligation to provide a realistic opportunity for a fair share of the region's present and prospective low and moderate income housing need will no longer be determined by whether or not a municipality is "developing." The obligation extends, instead, to every municipality, any portion of which is designated by the State, through the SDGP as a "growth area." This obligation, imposed as a remedial measure, does not extend to those areas where the SDGP discourages growth—

namely, open spaces, rural areas, prime farmland, conservation areas, limited growth areas, parts of the Pinelands and certain Coastal Zone areas.

* * *

Moreover, the fact that a municipality is fully developed does not eliminate this obligation although, obviously, it may affect the extent of the obligation and the timing of its satisfaction. The remedial obligation of municipalities that consist of both "growth areas" and other areas may be reduced, based on many factors, as compared to a municipality completely within a "growth area."

There shall be a heavy burden on any party seeking to vary the foregoing remedial consequences of the SDGP designations.

(3) *Mount Laurel* litigation will ordinarily include proof of the municipality's fair share of low and moderate income housing in terms of the number of units needed immediately, as well as the number needed for a reasonable period of time in the future. "Numberless" resolution of the issue based upon a conclusion that the ordinance provides a realistic opportunity for *some* low and moderate income housing will be insufficient. Plaintiffs, however, will still be able to prove a *prima facie* case, without proving the precise fair share of the municipality, by proving that the zoning ordinance is substantially affected by restrictive devices, that proof creating a presumption that the ordinance is invalid.

The municipal obligation to provide a realistic opportunity for low and moderate income housing is not satisfied by a good faith attempt. The housing opportunity provided must, in fact, be the substantial equivalent of the fair share.

(4) Any future *Mount Laurel* litigation shall be assigned only to those judges selected by the Chief Justice with the approval of the Supreme Court. * * *

(5) The municipal obligation to provide a realistic opportunity for the construction of its fair share of low and moderate income housing may require more than the elimination of unnecessary cost-producing requirements and restrictions. Affirmative governmental devices should be used to make that opportunity realistic, including lower-income density bonuses and mandatory set-asides. Furthermore the municipality should cooperate with the developer's attempts to obtain federal subsidies. * * * Mobile homes may not be prohibited, unless there is solid proof that sound planning in a particular municipality requires such prohibition.

(6) The lower income regional housing need is comprised of both low and moderate income housing. A municipality's fair share should include both in such proportion as reflects consideration of all relevant factors,

including the proportion of low and moderate income housing that make up the regional need.

(7) Providing a realistic opportunity for the construction of least-cost housing will satisfy a municipality's *Mount Laurel* obligation if, and only if, it cannot otherwise be satisfied. In other words, it is only after *all* alternatives have been explored, *all* affirmative devices considered, including, where appropriate, a reasonable period of time to determine whether low and moderate income housing is produced, only when everything has been considered and tried in order to produce a realistic opportunity for low and moderate income housing that least-cost housing will provide an adequate substitute. Least-cost housing means what it says, namely, housing that can be produced at the lowest possible price consistent with minimal standards of health and safety.

(8) Builder's remedies will be afforded to plaintiffs in *Mount Laurel* litigation where appropriate, on a case-by-case basis. Where the plaintiff has acted in good faith, attempted to obtain relief without litigation, and thereafter vindicates the constitutional obligation in *Mount Laurel*-type litigation, ordinarily a builder's remedy will be granted, provided that the proposed project includes an appropriate portion of low and moderate income housing, and provided further that it is located and designed in accordance with sound zoning and planning concepts, including its environmental impact.

(9) The judiciary should manage *Mount Laurel* litigation to dispose of a case in all of its aspects with one trial and one appeal, unless substantial considerations indicate some other course.

* * *

(10) The *Mount Laurel* obligation to meet the prospective lower income housing need of the region is, by definition, one that is met year after year in the future, throughout the years of the particular projection used in calculating prospective need. In this sense the affirmative obligation to provide a realistic opportunity to construct a fair share of lower income housing is met by a "phase-in" over those years; it need not be provided immediately. * * *

We reassure all concerned that *Mount Laurel* is not designed to sweep away all land use restrictions or leave our open spaces and natural resources prey to speculators. Municipalities consisting largely of conservation, agricultural, or environmentally sensitive areas will not be required to grow because of *Mount Laurel*. No forests or small towns need be paved over and covered with high-rise apartments as a result of today's decision.

As for those municipalities that may have to make adjustments in their lifestyles to provide for their fair share of low and moderate income housing, they should remember that they are not being required to provide more than their *fair* share. No one community need be concerned that it will be radically transformed by a deluge of low and moderate income developments. Nor should any community conclude that its residents will move to other suburbs as a result of this decision, for those "other suburbs" may very well be required to do their part to provide the same housing. Finally, once a community has satisfied its fair share obligation, the *Mount Laurel* doctrine will not restrict other measures, including large-lot and open area zoning, that would maintain its beauty and communal character.

Many of these points will be discussed later in this opinion. We mention them now only to reassure all concerned that any changes brought about by this opinion need not be drastic or destructive. Our scenic and rural areas will remain essentially scenic and rural, and our suburban communities will retain their basic suburban character. But there will be *some* change, as there must be if the constitutional rights of our lower income citizens are ever to be protected. That change will be much less painful for us than the status quo has been for them.

* * *

D. Meeting the Mount Laurel Obligation

1. *Removing Excessive Restrictions and Exactions*

In order to meet their *Mount Laurel* obligations, municipalities, at the very least, must remove all municipally created barriers to the construction of their fair share of lower income housing. Thus, to the extent necessary to meet their prospective fair share and provide for their indigenous poor (and, in some cases, a portion of the region's poor), municipalities must remove zoning and subdivision restrictions and exactions that are not necessary to protect health and safety.

* * *

Once a municipality has revised its land use regulations and taken other steps affirmatively to provide a realistic opportunity for the construction of its fair share of lower income housing, the *Mount Laurel* doctrine requires it to do no more. For instance, a municipality having thus complied, the fact that its land use regulations contain restrictive provisions incompatible with lower income housing, such as bedroom restrictions, large lot zoning, prohibition against mobile homes, and the like, does not render those provisions invalid under *Mount Laurel*. Obviously, if they are otherwise invalid—for instance if they bear no reasonable relationship to any legitimate governmental goal—they may be declared void on those other grounds. But they are not void because of *Mount Laurel* under those circumstances. *Mount Laurel* is not an indiscriminate broom designed to sweep away all distinctions in the use of land. Municipalities may continue to reserve areas for upper income housing, may continue to require certain community amenities in certain areas, may continue to zone with some regard to their fiscal obligations: they may do all of this, provided that they have otherwise complied with their *Mount Laurel* obligations.

2. Using Affirmative Measures

Despite the emphasis in *Mount Laurel I* on the *affirmative* nature of the fair share obligation, the obligation has been sometimes construed (after *Madison*) as requiring in effect no more than a theoretical, rather than realistic, opportunity. As noted later, the alleged realistic opportunity for lower income housing in *Mount Laurel II* is provided through three zones owned entirely by three individuals. There is absolutely no assurance that there is anything realistic in this "opportunity": the individuals may, for many different reasons, simply not desire to build lower income housing. They may not want to build any housing at all, they may want to use the land for industry, for business, or just leave it vacant. * * * "Affirmative," in the *Mount Laurel* rule, suggests that the *municipality* is going to do something, and "realistic opportunity" suggests that what it is going to do will make it *realistically* possible for lower income housing to be built. Satisfaction of the *Mount Laurel* doctrine cannot depend on the inclination of developers to help the poor. It has to depend on affirmative inducements to make the opportunity real.

* * *

Therefore, unless removal of restrictive barriers will, without more, afford a realistic opportunity for the construction of the municipality's fair share of the region's lower income housing need, affirmative measures will be required.

There are two basic types of affirmative measures that a municipality can use to make the opportunity for lower income housing realistic: (1) encouraging or requiring the use of available state or federal housing subsidies, and (2) providing incentives for or requiring private developers to set aside a portion of their developments for lower income housing. Which, if either, of these devices will be necessary in any particular municipality to assure compliance with the constitutional mandate will be initially up to the municipality itself. Where necessary, the trial court overseeing compliance may require their use. We note again that least-cost housing will not ordinarily satisfy a municipality's fair share obligation to provide low and moderate income housing unless and until it has attempted the inclusionary devices outlined below or otherwise has proven the futility of the attempt.

A. Subsidies

Because the kinds of lower income housing subsidies available are subject to change—and have in fact changed often—it is more important to establish the municipality's general *Mount Laurel* obligation concerning subsidies than its required role as to any particular existing subsidy. The importance of defining that obligation may depend at any particular time on the then extent and impact of available subsidies; if anything, the quantity of housing subsidies varies even more than the kind. * * * They are, nevertheless, apparently a permanent part of the housing scene; the long-term importance of defining the municipality's *Mount Laurel* obligation in relation to such subsidies is that the construction of lower income housing is practically impossible without some kind of governmental subsidy.

* * *

The implication of the observation that lower income housing cannot be built without subsidies is that if the *Mount Laurel* principle requires municipalities to provide a realistic opportunity for such housing through their land use regulations but leaves them free to prevent subsidies through non-action, that obligation is a charade. *Mount Laurel* was never intended to produce the perfect model of a just zoning ordinance; it was intended to provide a realistic opportunity for the construction of lower income housing.

* * *

In evaluating the obligation that the municipality might be required to undertake to make a federal or state subsidy available to a lower income housing developer, the fact that some financial detriment may be incurred is not dispositive. Satisfaction of the *Mount Laurel* obligation imposes many financial obligations on municipalities, some of which are potentially substantial. By contrast, a tax abatement for a low or moderate income housing project will have only a minimal effect on the public fisc. Thus viewed, the asserted fiscal reasons justifying the failure to provide a tax abatement may be nothing more than a red herring. * * * The trial court in a *Mount Laurel* case, therefore, shall have the power to require a municipality to cooperate in good faith with a developer's attempt to obtain a subsidy and to require that a tax abatement be granted for that purpose pursuant to applicable New Jersey statutes where that abatement does not conflict with other municipal interests of greater importance.

B.   Inclusionary Zoning Devices

There are several inclusionary zoning techniques that municipalities must use if they cannot otherwise assure the construction of their fair share of lower income housing. Although we will discuss some of them here, we in no way intend our list to be exhaustive; municipalities and trial courts are encouraged to create other devices and methods for meeting fair share obligations.

* * *

(I) Incentive Zoning

Incentive zoning is usually accomplished either through a sliding scale density bonus that increases the permitted density as the amount of lower income housing provided is increased, or through a set bonus for participation in a lower income housing program.

Incentive zoning leaves a developer free to build only upper income housing if it so chooses. Fox and Davis, in their survey of municipalities using inclusionary devices, found that while developers sometimes profited through density bonuses, they were usually reluctant to cooperate with incentive zoning programs; and that therefore those municipalities that relied exclusively on such programs were not very successful in actually providing lower income housing.

Sole reliance on "incentive" techniques (or, indeed, reliance exclusively on any one affirmative device) may prove in a particular case to be insufficient to achieve compliance with the constitutional mandate.

(II) Mandatory Set-Asides

A more effective inclusionary device that municipalities must use if they cannot otherwise meet their fair share obligations is the mandatory set-aside.[30] According to the Department of Community Affairs, as of 1976 there were six municipalities in New Jersey with mandatory set-aside programs, which varied from a requirement that 5 percent of developments in a certain zone be composed of low and moderate income units (Cherry Hill, Camden County) to a requirement that between 15 and 25 percent of all PUDs be reserved for low and moderate income housing (East Windsor, Mercer County). Apparently, judging from the Handbook itself and from responses to our inquiries at oral argument, lower income housing is in fact being built pursuant to these mandatory requirements.

The use of mandatory set-asides is not without its problems: dealing with the scarcity of federal subsidies, maintaining the rent or sales price of lower income units at lower income levels over time, and assuring developers an adequate return on their investments. Fox and Davis found

---

[30] Mandatory set-asides do not give rise to the legal issues treated in *Property Owners Ass'n of N. Bergen v. Twp. of N. Bergen*, 74 N.J. 327, 378 A.2d 25 (1977). We held in that case that rent control ordinances that exempted units occupied by senior citizens from future rent increases were confiscatory as to the landlord, unfair as to the tenants, and unconstitutional on both grounds. No one suggests here that units created by mandatory set-asides be exempt thereafter from rent increases under a rent control ordinance. Such increases, one aspect of an inflationary economy, generally parallel increases in the median income of lower income families. They would not ordinarily result in rentals beyond the lower income range. As for confiscation, the builder who undertakes a project that includes a mandatory set-aside voluntarily assumes the financial burden, if there is any, of that condition. There may very well be no "subsidy" in the sense of either the landlord or other tenants bearing some burden for the benefit of the lower income units: those units may be priced low not because someone else is subsidizing the price, but because of realistic considerations of cost, amenities, and therefore underlying values.

that the scarcity of federal subsidies has greatly undermined the effectiveness of mandatory set-asides where they are triggered only when a developer is able to obtain such subsidies. Where practical, a municipality should use mandatory set-asides even where subsidies are not available.

* * *

Mandatory set-asides can be rendered ineffective if a developer builds all its conventional units first and then reneges on the obligation to build the lower income units. To avoid this problem, municipalities and courts should require that a developer phase-in the lower income units as the development progresses. That is, if a developer is required to set aside 20 percent of a development for lower income units, 20 percent of *each* stage of the development should be lower income, to the extent this is practical.

In addition to the mechanisms we have just described, municipalities and trial courts must consider such other affirmative devices as zoning substantial areas for mobile homes and for other types of low cost housing and establishing maximum square footage zones, i.e., zones where developers cannot build units with *more* than a certain footage or build anything other than lower income housing or housing that includes a specified portion of lower income housing. In some cases, a realistic opportunity to provide the municipality's fair share may require over-zoning, i.e., zoning to allow for *more* than the fair share if it is likely, as it usually is, that not all of the property made available for lower income housing will actually result in such housing.

Although several of the defendants concede that simply removing restrictions and exactions is unlikely to result in the construction of lower income housing, they maintain that requiring the municipality to use affirmative measures is beyond the scope of the courts' authority. We disagree. * * *

* * *

The specific contentions are that inclusionary measures amount to a taking without just compensation and an impermissible socio-economic use of the zoning power, one not substantially related to the use of land. Reliance is placed to some extent on *Board of Supervisors v. DeGroff Enterprises, Inc.,* that effect. We disagree with that decision. We now resolve the matter that we left open in *Madison.* We hold that where the *Mount Laurel* obligation cannot be satisfied by removal of restrictive barriers, inclusionary devices such as density bonuses and mandatory set-asides keyed to the construction of lower income housing, are constitutional and within the zoning power of a municipality.

* * *

The contention that generally these devices are beyond the municipal power because they are "socio-economic" is particularly inappropriate. The very basis for the constitutional obligation underlying *Mount Laurel* is a belief, fundamental, that excluding a class of citizens from housing on an economic basis (one that substantially corresponds to a socio-economic basis) distinctly disserves the general welfare. That premise is essential to the conclusion that such zoning ordinances are an abuse of the zoning power and are therefore unconstitutional.

It is nonsense to single out inclusionary zoning (providing a realistic opportunity for the construction of lower income housing) and label it "socio-economic" if that is meant to imply that other aspects of zoning are not. Detached single family residential zones, high-rise multi-family zones of any kind, factory zones, "clean" research and development zones, recreational, open space, conservation, and agricultural zones, regional shopping mall zones, indeed practically any significant kind of zoning now used, has a substantial socio-economic impact and, in some cases, a socio-economic motivation. It would be ironic if inclusionary zoning to encourage the construction of lower income housing were ruled beyond the power of a municipality because it is "socio-economic" when its need has arisen from the socio-economic zoning of the past that excluded it.

Looked at somewhat differently, having concluded that the constitutional obligation can sometimes be satisfied only through the use of these inclusionary devices, it would take a clear contrary constitutional provision to lead us to conclude that that which is necessary to achieve the constitutional mandate is prohibited by the same Constitution. In other words, we would find it difficult to conclude that our Constitution both requires and prohibits these measures.

We find the distinction between the exercise of the zoning power that is "directly tied to the physical use of the property," and its exercise tied to the income level of those who use the property artificial in connection with the *Mount Laurel* obligation, although it obviously troubled us in *Madison*.[34] The prohibition of this kind of affirmative device seems unfair when we have for so long allowed large lot single family residence districts, a form of zoning keyed, in effect, to income levels. The constitutional obligation itself is not to build three bedroom units, or single family residences on very small lots, or high-rise multi-family apartments, but

---

[34] In any event the relationship of lower income units to "the physical use of the land" (i.e., their mandatory inclusion as part of a multi-family project) appears as substantial as the relationship of units for the elderly to a mobile home district. *See Weymouth*, 80 N.J. 6, 364 A.2d 1016 (1976). The inclusion of some lower income units in a multi-family housing project that may also house families with other income levels may be socially beneficial and an economic prerequisite to the creation of lower income units.

This problem does not arise when a municipality wants to create upper income housing since the physical requirements of the zoning district ("directly tied to the land") combined with housing market forces are sufficient. The *explicit* requirement of lower income units in a zoning provision may be necessary if the municipality's social goals are to prevail over neutral market forces. Zoning does not require that land be used for maximum profitability, and on occasion the goals of zoning may require something less.

rather to provide through the zoning ordinance a realistic opportunity to construct *lower income housing.* * * *

3.   Zoning for Mobile Homes

As the cost of ordinary housing skyrockets for purchasers and renters, mobile homes become increasingly important as a source of low cost housing. The evidence clearly supports a finding that mobile homes are significantly less expensive than site-built housing. * * * We agree fully with the finding of Judge Wood in *Mount Laurel II* that mobile homes are "economically available for persons of low and moderate income." Therefore, subject to the qualifications noted hereafter, we rule that municipalities that cannot otherwise meet their fair share obligations must provide zoning for low-cost mobile homes as an affirmative device in their zoning ordinances.

* * *

Lest we be misunderstood, we do *not* hold that every municipality must allow the use of mobile homes as an affirmative device to meet its *Mount Laurel* obligation, or that any ordinance that totally excludes mobile homes is *per se* invalid. Insofar as the *Mount Laurel* doctrine is concerned, whether mobile homes must be permitted as an affirmative device will depend upon the overall effectiveness of the municipality's attempts to comply: if compliance can be just as effectively assured without allowing mobile homes, *Mount Laurel* does not command them; if not, then assuming a suitable site is available, they must be allowed.

Insofar as the arbitrariness of a total exclusion is concerned, such conclusion will depend upon the facts and circumstances of each case, regardless of the *Mount Laurel* doctrine. While the question is not directly before us, there may be municipalities whose development is such that the otherwise inoffensive appearance of a mobile home park may be quite offensive. There may be municipalities whose only vacant land has been legitimately set aside for commercial, industrial or residential uses other than mobile homes, where such planning is quite legitimate. But just as *Vickers* is hereby overruled to the extent that it held that *any* developing municipality may totally exclude mobile homes, we hold that such attempt at a total exclusion will have to be justified by the same doctrines that would justify a total exclusion of apartment houses, townhouses, or even single family residences. We recognize the propriety of aesthetic considerations in zoning, but the "subjective sensibilities" of present residents are not a sufficient basis for the exclusion.

4.   Providing "Least Cost" Housing

There may be municipalities where special conditions such as extremely high land costs make it impossible for the fair share obligation to be met even after all excessive restrictions and exactions, i.e., those not essential for safety and health, have been removed and all affirmative measures have been attempted. In such cases, *and only in such cases,* the *Mount Laurel* obligation can be met by supplementing whatever lower income housing can be built with enough "least cost" housing to satisfy the fair share. * * * Least cost housing means the least expensive housing that builders can provide after removal by a municipality of *all* excessive restrictions and exactions and after thorough use by a municipality of all affirmative devices that might lower costs. Presumably, such housing, though unaffordable by those in the lower income brackets, will be inexpensive enough to provide shelter for families who could not afford housing in the conventional suburban housing market. At the very minimum, provision of least cost housing will make certain that municipalities in "growth" areas of this state do not "grow" only for the well-to-do.

The form that "least cost" housing will take can vary with the particular characteristics of individual municipalities. Municipalities that must resort to "least cost" housing to meet their *Mount Laurel* obligations should, if appropriate, zone significant areas for housing that most closely approaches lower income housing, e.g., mobile homes. Furthermore, "overzoning" for such housing will greatly increase the likelihood that some of these units, even if not "lower income," will be affordable by those close to the top of the moderate income bracket.

It is important for us to emphasize here that unless it meets the stringent "least cost" requirements set out above, middle income housing will not satisfy the *Mount Laurel* obligation. This is so despite claims by some defendant-municipalities that the provision of such middle income housing will allow less expensive housing to "filter down" to lower income families. The problem with this theory is that the housing that has been built and is now being built in suburbs such as Mount Laurel is rapidly *appreciating* in value so that none of *it* will "filter down" to poor people. Instead, if the only housing constructed in municipalities like Mount Laurel continues to be middle and upper income, the only "filter down" effect that will occur will be that housing on the fringes of our inner cities will "filter down" to the poor as more of the middle class leave for suburbs, thereby exacerbating the economic segregation of our cities and suburbs. * * * Only if municipalities like Mount Laurel begin now to build lower income or least cost housing will some part of *their* housing stock ever "filter down" to New Jersey's poorer families.

NOTES: INCLUSIONARY ZONING AND FAIR SHARE

1. The portion of the *Mt. Laurel II* opinion printed here is significantly edited. The entire opinion runs to some 120 pages of text in the Atlantic Reporter, making it most likely the longest zoning opinion ever written.

2. The reaction to *Mt. Laurel II* was vociferous. The governor labeled it communistic, and a mayor threatened to go to jail rather than comply. John M. Payne, *Rethinking Fair Share: The Judicial Enforcement of Affordable Housing Policies*, 16 REAL EST.L.J. 20, 22 (1987). Why? "Where *Mount Laurel I* could be ignored because it was ineffective, *Mount Laurel II* worked and it stirred up a firestorm." *Id*.

After the uproar died down, the New Jersey legislature in 1985 accepted the court's invitation and enacted the Fair Housing Act (not to be confused with the federal act of the same name) to deal with the *Mt. Laurel* issue. N.J. Stat. Ann. §§ 52.27D–301 to 52.27D–329. The act created a state agency to define housing regions and needs, and, upon request, to decide whether a municipality's plan met the fair share requirement. The act expressly approves of, and directs municipalities to consider, mandatory set-asides. N.J. Rev. Stat. Ann. § 52.27D–311(a)(1). One unusual aspect of the act is the authority given to municipalities to transfer up to 50% of their fair share obligation to other municipalities within their region pursuant to contract. *See* Rachel Fox, *The Selling Out of Mount Laurel: Regional Contribution Agreements in New Jersey's Fair Housing Act*, 16 FORDAM URB.L.J. 535, 572 (1988) concluding that the act creates units of housing but that it "abandons [*Mount Laurel's*] goals of economic and racial deconcentration."

In April, 1997, moving "with all deliberate speed," twenty-six years after the complaint was filed the Mt. Laurel Planning Board approved a development of a rental complex of 140 townhouses for low-and moderate-income persons. A unanimous and favorable planning board vote followed immediately on the heels of the angry objections of some 200 of the neighbors-to-be. Actual construction of the project depended on the non-profit developer securing limited federal tax credits. Ronald Smothers, *Affluent Suburb Approves Building of Homes for Poor*, New York Times, April 12, 1997, at 6. Financing was obtained, and by the fall of 1998, construction was under way.

3. Pennsylvania's approach differs from New Jersey's. Pennsylvania's enabling act states that zoning authorities are to provide for

> "housing of various dwelling types encompassing all basic forms of housing, including single-family and two-family dwellings, and a reasonable range of multifamily dwellings in various arrangements, mobile homes and mobile home parks [and is] to accommodate reasonable overall community growth, including population and employment growth."

Pa.Stat. 53 P.S. § 10604(4) and (5). The courts, however, view this as requiring only that municipalities zone for all uses, not for all income classes. Affordable multi-family housing for those with low to moderate incomes is not required. *See Heritage Bldg. Group, Inc. v. Plumstead Twp. Bd. of Sup'rs*, 833 A.2d 1205 (Pa.Cmwlth.2003).

Courts in other states have also embraced the view that a zoning ordinance should reflect a balanced consideration of regional housing needs.

See Associated Home Builders v. City of Livermore, 135 Cal.Rptr. 41, 557 P.2d 473 (1976); *S.A.V.E. v. City of Bothell*, 576 P.2d 401 (Wash.1978); and *Britton v. Town of Chester*, 595 A.2d 492 (N.H.1991).

4. Legislatures, too, have imposed fair share requirements. Since 1969, Massachusetts has had state legislation, referred to as the anti-snob zoning act, which can override local exclusionary zoning. In 2004, Massachusetts adopted a voluntary program, which rewards municipalities that create affordable housing districts by giving them money. Cities may get up to $600,000 for creating an affordable housing district, and $3,000 for each building permit issued. *See John Boothroyd v. Zoning Board of Appeals of Amherst*, 868 N.E.2d 83 (Mass.2007) (town that meets 10% affordable housing requirement may continue to issue fast track permits to affordable housing developers).

California imposes a fair share requirement by statute. West's Ann. Cal. Govt. Code § 65584(a). Communities are obligated, as part of the housing element of their general plan, to identify the housing needs of all persons, designate land where affordable housing can be built, and assist developers in building such housing. *See generally* Cecily T. Talbert, *California's Response to the Affordable Housing Crisis*, SN005 ALI-ABA 1491 (ALI-ABA Aug. 2007).

Legislation in Florida, Connecticut, and Rhode Island also requires that the housing elements of municipal plans address regional housing needs. *See* Juergensmeyer and Roberts, *Land Use Planning and Development Regulation Law* § 6.6 (3rd ed. 2012).

5. Private parties may be able to do what government will not, or cannot, do. Some new communities literally build walls to insulate themselves from the masses. Existing communities within urban areas may also wall themselves in, blocking off previously public streets. Those who are wealthy enough to afford homes in such communities may be seeking security from the threat of crime, but these mini-fiefdoms, known as gated communities, raise concerns of social disintegration that threaten to balkanize urban areas. That concern, plus the fact that such communities create traffic burdens by adding cars to the roads but not aiding traffic flow, has led to bans on gated communities. *See* Joel Burgess, Asheville *[North Carolina] Bans Gated-Communities*, Citizen-Times, June 13, 2007. While many of the excluded criticize, and perhaps resent, such communities, others defend them, contending that people are attracted to gated communities because of distrust and dissatisfaction with local government, and not base motives.

Covenants imposed on the residents of restricted communities, in terms of land use and privacy, and on outsiders, in terms of access for free speech purposes, generally are not restricted by the constitution since state action is lacking. For example, if the communities provide their own security forces, the Fourth Amendment would not apply to protect against unreasonable searches or seizures committed by those forces, would it? *See* John B. Owens, *Westec Story: Gated Communities and the Fourth Amendment*, 34 AM.CRIM.L.REV. 1127 (1997). *See generally* David J. Kennedy, Note, *Residential Associations as*

State Actors: Regulating the Impact of Gated Communities on Nonmembers, 105 YALE L.J. 761 (1995); David L. Callies, Paula A. Franzese, and Heidi Kai Guth, Ramapo *Looking Forward: Gated Communities, Covenants, and Concerns*, 35 URB.LAW. 177 (2003).

2.   INCLUSIONARY SET-ASIDES

The problem of providing adequate shelter for low- and moderate-income families has bedeviled urban planners, lawyers and governmental officials for some time. *See* Herbert M. Franklin, David Faulk, and Arthur J. Levin, *In-Zoning: A Guide for Policy-Makers on Inclusionary Land Use Programs* (1974). The relative lack of success of more traditional programs such as subsidized housing has led to the use of inclusionary zoning and other techniques. Essentially, inclusionary housing techniques are directed at encouraging or, in some instances, forcing the private sector to provide housing that is "affordable" to the lower-income segments of the resident or resident-to-be population as part of the land development process. The principal techniques are to provide density, area, or other land development bonuses for the construction of such affordable housing (whether on or offsite) or the payment of money in lieu thereof, or to simply require a developer to set aside a certain percentage of units as a cost of development on much the same basis as local governments exact park site, school site and infrastructure improvements as conditions for subdivision approval. Such positive housing construction requirements are generally called "mandatory set-asides."

Inclusionary housing ordinances present two legal issues, statutory authority and constitutionality:

1.   Does state enabling legislation (or, in the case of a home-rule unit of local government, a charter) provide an adequate basis for using mandatory set-asides of affordable housing or impact fees to pay for such housing?

2.   Does such an ordinance go beyond the limits of the police power, and amount to a taking of property without compensation? How might the presence or absence of density bonuses affect this issue?

More specifically, are the needs that these techniques address attributable to the development upon which they are being levied? If not, does that render the requirement unconstitutional? A developer of a commercial project, like a resort hotel or a shopping center, generates a spectrum of housing needs that includes low-and moderate-income families (store clerks, maintenance personnel, hotel service employees, and so forth). Is that a sufficient reason to impose a burden on the developer to pay, or at least help pay, for the needed housing? What of the residential developer? How does such a development affect the need for housing in the community in a fashion that justifies having the developer provide less profitable units of affordable housing? Will this cost, if not absorbed by bonuses, be passed on in terms of increased "market" housing prices, or be passed back to the landowner in terms of lower land prices?

In New Jersey, communities are obligated pursuant to the state constitution and state statutory law to consider using mandatory set-asides. Some communities in other states have voluntarily decided to use mandatory set-asides. What happens then?

CALIFORNIA BUILDING INDUSTRY ASSOCIATION V. CITY OF SAN JOSE

Supreme Court of California, 2015.
61 Cal.4th 435, 189 Cal.Rptr.3d 475, cert. denied, 136 S.Ct. 928 (2016).

CANTIL-SAKAUYE, C.J.

Health and Safety Code section 50003, subdivision (a), currently provides: "The Legislature finds and declares that * * * there exists within the urban and rural areas of the state a serious shortage of decent, safe, and sanitary housing which persons and families of low or moderate income * * * can afford. This situation creates an absolute present and future shortage of supply in relation to demand * * * and also creates inflation in the cost of housing, by reason of its scarcity, which tends to decrease the relative affordability of the state's housing supply for all its residents."

This statutory language was first enacted by the Legislature *over 35 years ago,* in the late 1970s. (Stats.1975, 1st Ex.Sess., ch. 1, § 7, pp. 3859–3861, adding Health & Saf.Code, former § 41003; Stats.1979, ch. 97, § 2, p. 225, amending Health & Saf.Code, § 50003.) It will come as no surprise to anyone familiar with California's current housing market that the significant problems arising from a scarcity of affordable housing have not been solved over the past three decades. Rather, these problems have become more severe and have reached what might be described as epic proportions in many of the state's localities. All parties in this proceeding agree that the lack of affordable housing is a very significant problem in this state.

As one means of addressing the lack of a sufficient number of housing units that are affordable to low and moderate income households, more than 170 California municipalities have adopted what are commonly referred to as "inclusionary zoning" or "inclusionary housing" programs. (Non-Profit Housing Association of Northern California, Affordable by Choice: Trends in California Inclusionary Housing Programs (2007) p. 3 (hereafter NPH Affordable by Choice).) As a 2013 publication of the United States Department of Housing and Urban Development (HUD) explains, inclusionary zoning or housing programs "require or encourage developers to set aside a certain percentage of housing units in new or rehabilitated projects for low- and moderate-income residents. This integration of affordable units into market-rate projects creates opportunities for households with diverse socioeconomic backgrounds to live in the same developments and have access to [the] same types of community services and amenities * * * " (U.S. Dept. of Housing and Urban Development, *Inclusionary Zoning and Mixed-Income Communities* (Spring 2013) Evidence Matters, p. 1, fn. omitted (hereafter *2013 HUD Inclusionary Zoning*).

In 2010, after considerable study and outreach to all segments of the community, the City of San Jose (hereafter sometimes referred to as the city or San Jose) enacted an inclusionary housing ordinance that, among other features, requires all new residential development projects of 20 or more units to sell at least 15 percent of the for-sale units at a price that is affordable to low or moderate income households. (The ordinance is described in greater detail in pt. II., *post.*)

Very shortly after the ordinance was enacted and before it took effect, plaintiff California Building Industry Association (CBIA) filed this lawsuit in superior court, maintaining that the ordinance was invalid on its face on the ground that the city, in enacting the ordinance, failed to provide a sufficient evidentiary basis "to demonstrate a reasonable relationship between any adverse public impacts or needs for additional subsidized housing units in the City ostensibly caused by or reasonably attributed to the development of new residential developments of 20 units or more and the new affordable housing exactions and conditions imposed on residential development by the Ordinance."

* * *

The complaint maintained that under the "controlling state and federal constitutional standards governing such exactions and conditions of development approval, and the requirements applicable to such housing exactions as set forth in *San Remo Hotel v. City And County Of San Francisco* (2002) 27 Cal.4th 643, 117 Cal.Rptr.2d 269, 41 P.3d 87, and *Building Industry Assn. of Central California v. City of Patterson* (2009) 171 Cal.App.4th 886, 90 Cal.Rptr.3d 63" the conditions imposed by the city's inclusionary housing ordinance would be valid only if the city produced evidence demonstrating that the requirements were reasonably related to the adverse impact on the city's affordable housing problem *that was caused by or attributable to the proposed new developments that are subject to the ordinance's requirements,* and that the materials relied on by the city in enacting the ordinance did not demonstrate such a relationship. Although the complaint did not explicitly spell out the specific nature of its constitutional claim, CBIA has subsequently clarified that its challenge rests on "the unconstitutional conditions doctrine, as applied to development exactions" under the takings clauses (or, as they are sometimes denominated, the just compensation clauses) of the United

States and California Constitutions. CBIA's challenge is based on the premise that the conditions imposed by the San Jose ordinance constitute "exactions" for purposes of that doctrine. The superior court agreed with CBIA's contention and issued a judgment enjoining the city from enforcing the challenged ordinance.

The Court of Appeal reversed the superior court judgment, concluding that the superior court had erred (1) in finding that the San Jose ordinance requires a developer to dedicate property to the public within the meaning of the takings clause, and (2) in interpreting the controlling constitutional principles and the decision in *San Remo Hotel v. City and County Of San Francisco, supra*, 27 Cal.4th 643, 117 Cal.Rptr.2d 269, 41 P.3d 87 (*San Remo Hotel*), as limiting the conditions that may be imposed by such an ordinance to only those conditions that are reasonably related to the adverse impact the development projects that are subject to the ordinance themselves impose on the city's affordable housing problem. Distinguishing the prior appellate court decision in *Building Industry Assn. of Central California v. City of Patterson, supra*, 171 Cal.App.4th 886, 90 Cal.Rptr.3d 63 (*City of Patterson*), the Court of Appeal held that the appropriate legal standard by which the validity of the ordinance is to be judged is the ordinary standard that past California decisions have uniformly applied in evaluating claims that an ordinance regulating the use of land exceeds a municipality's police power authority, namely, whether the ordinance bears a real and substantial relationship to a legitimate public interest. The Court of Appeal concluded that the matter should be remanded to the trial court for application of this traditional standard.

CBIA sought review of the Court of Appeal decision in this court, maintaining that the appellate court's decision conflicts with the prior Court of Appeal decision in *City of Patterson, supra*, 171 Cal.App.4th 886, 90 Cal.Rptr.3d 63, and that *City of Patterson* was correctly decided and should control here. We granted review to determine the soundness of the Court of Appeal's ruling in this case.

For the reasons discussed below, we conclude that the Court of Appeal decision in the present case should be upheld. As explained hereafter, contrary to CBIA's contention, the conditions that the San Jose ordinance imposes upon future developments do not impose "exactions" upon the developers' property so as to bring into play the unconstitutional conditions doctrine under the takings clause of the federal or state Constitution. Furthermore, unlike the condition that was at issue in *San Remo Hotel, supra*, 27 Cal.4th 643, 117 Cal.Rptr.2d 269, 41 P.3d 87, and to which the passage in that opinion upon which CBIA relies was addressed—namely, an in lieu monetary fee that is imposed to mitigate a particular adverse effect of the development proposal under consideration—the conditions imposed by the San Jose ordinance at issue here do not require a developer to pay a monetary fee but rather place a limit on the way a developer may use its property. In addition, the conditions are intended not only to mitigate the effect that the covered development projects will have on the city's affordable housing problem but also to serve the distinct, but nonetheless constitutionally legitimate, purposes of (1) *increasing the number of affordable housing units in the city* in recognition of the insufficient number of existing affordable housing units in relation to the city's current and future needs, and (2) assuring that new affordable housing units that are constructed *are distributed throughout the city as part of mixed-income developments* in order to obtain the benefits that flow from economically diverse communities and avoid the problems that have historically been associated with isolated low income housing. Properly understood, the passage in *San Remo Hotel* upon which CBIA relies does not apply to the conditions imposed by San Jose's inclusionary housing ordinance.

Accordingly, we conclude that the judgment of the Court of Appeal in this case should be affirmed.

I.   Statutory background

We begin with a brief summary of the California statutes that form the background to the San Jose ordinance challenged in this case.

Nearly 50 years ago, the California Legislature enacted a broad measure requiring all counties and cities in California to "adopt a comprehensive, long-term general plan for the physical development of the county or city." (Gov.Code, § 65300 et seq., enacted by Stats.1965, ch. 1880, § 5, pp. 4334, 4336, operative Jan. 1, 1967.) Each municipality's general plan is to contain a variety of mandatory and optional elements, including a mandatory housing element consisting of standards and plans for housing sites in the municipality that "shall endeavor to make adequate provision for the housing needs of all economic segments of the community." (Gov.Code, former § 65302, subd. (c), as amended by Stats.1967, ch. 1658, § 1, p. 4033; see now Gov.Code, § 65580.)

* * *

Although to date the California Legislature has not adopted a statewide statute that requires every municipality to adopt a mandatory inclusionary housing ordinance if needed to meet the municipality's obligations under the Housing Element Law, in recent decades more than 170 California cities and counties have adopted such inclusionary housing ordinances in an effort to meet such obligations. * * * The provisions and legislative history of the affordable housing statutes make it clear that the California Legislature is unquestionably aware of these numerous local mandatory inclusionary housing ordinances and that the existing state legislation is neither inconsistent with nor intended to preempt these local measures.

II. Background and description of challenged San Jose inclusionary housing ordinance

It is within the context of the foregoing statutory framework that San Jose began considering the need and desirability of adopting an inclusionary housing ordinance. As noted, the statewide Housing Element Law places responsibility upon a city to use its powers to facilitate the development of housing that makes adequate provision for all economic segments of the community, in particular extremely low, very low, lower and moderate income households, including the city's allocation of the regional housing need as determined by the applicable regional council of governments. (Gov.Code, §§ 65580, subd. (d), 65583, 65584.)

* * *

Prior to the adoption of the challenged citywide ordinance in 2010, San Jose's experience with a mandatory inclusionary housing policy was limited to residential development projects that were undertaken within the redevelopment areas of the city. (At that time, redevelopment areas comprised almost 20 percent of the city's territory and included one-third of the city's population.) As noted, redevelopment areas were one of the two types of locations within which the Legislature had directed that any new residential development must include some affordable housing units. Under the applicable statute, at least 15 percent of all new or substantially rehabilitated dwelling units in a redevelopment project undertaken by a public or private entity other than the redevelopment agency were required to be made available at an affordable housing cost and to be occupied by persons and families of low or moderate income. (Health & Saf.Code, § 33413, subd. (b)(2)(A)(i)).

* * *

III. Lower court proceedings

On March 24, 2010, just two months after the ordinance was enacted, CBIA filed the underlying lawsuit in this proceeding in superior court, seeking invalidation of the ordinance. The complaint alleged that the ordinance was invalid on its face because at no time prior to the adoption of the ordinance had the city provided substantial evidence "to demonstrate a reasonable relationship between any adverse public impacts or needs for additional subsidized housing units in the City ostensibly caused by or reasonably attributed to the development of new residential developments of 20 units or more and the new affordable housing exactions and conditions imposed on residential development by the Ordinance." The complaint maintained that the city's actions in enacting the ordinance were "unlawful, unconstitutional, and in violation of controlling state and federal constitutional standards governing such exactions and conditions of development approval, and the requirements applicable to such housing exactions as set forth in *San Remo Hotel L.P. v. City & County of San*

Francisco (2002) 27 Cal.4th 643 [117 Cal.Rptr.2d 269, 41 P.3d 87], and *Building Industry Association of Central California v. City of Patterson* (5th Dist.2009) 171 Cal.App.4th 886 [90 Cal.Rptr.3d 63]." The complaint sought a judicial declaration that the ordinance is invalid, and injunctive relief prohibiting the city from enforcing the ordinance.

* * *

After extensive briefing, the superior court agreed with CBIA's legal contentions, concluding that the ordinance was constitutionally invalid and enjoining its enforcement. In its order, the court rejected the city's position that the inclusionary ordinance did not require a developer to dedicate or convey property, and struck down the ordinance. * * *

The Court of Appeal reversed the superior court judgment. Initially, the appellate court rejected CBIA's contention that the ordinance requires a developer seeking a permit to " 'dedicate or convey property (new homes) for public purposes,' or alternatively, pay a fee in lieu of 'such compelled transfers of property,' " concluding that the ordinance "does not prescribe a dedication." The appellate court then went on to agree with the city and interveners that the ordinance's inclusionary housing requirements must properly be evaluated under the standard ordinarily applicable to general, legislatively imposed land use regulations, namely whether the ordinance's requirements bear a real and substantial relation to the public welfare. The Court of Appeal determined that the matter should be remanded to the trial court to permit that court to review CBIA's challenge under the proper legal standard.

* * *

After the Court of Appeal decision, CBIA sought review in this court, maintaining that the appellate opinion in this case directly conflicted with the Court of Appeal decision in *City of Patterson, supra,* 171 Cal.App.4th 886, 90 Cal.Rptr.3d 63, and that *City of Patterson* was correctly decided. We granted review to determine the soundness of the appellate court's ruling in this case.

In analyzing this question, we first consider an initial point that divided the lower court decisions in this case—whether the conditions imposed by the San Jose ordinance constitute "exactions" for purposes of the federal and state takings clauses and thus trigger the applicability of the unconstitutional conditions doctrine. (*See* pt. IV., *post.*) Thereafter, we consider whether the passage in this court's decision in *San Remo Hotel,* upon which CBIA relies, applies to the conditions imposed by the challenged inclusionary housing ordinance. (*See* pt. V., *post.*)

IV. Does the San Jose inclusionary housing ordinance, in requiring new residential developments to sell some of the proposed new units at an affordable housing price, impose an

"exaction" on developers' property under the takings clauses of the federal and California Constitutions, so as to bring into play the unconstitutional conditions doctrine?

We begin with the well-established principle that under the California Constitution a municipality has broad authority, under its general police power, to regulate the development and use of real property within its jurisdiction to promote the public welfare. (Cal. Const., art. XI, § 7; *Big Creek Lumber Co. v. County of Santa Cruz* (2006) 38 Cal.4th 1139, 1151–1152, 45 Cal.Rptr.3d 21, 136 P.3d 821.) * * *

We review challenges to the exercise of such power deferentially. "In deciding whether a challenged [land use] ordinance reasonably relates to the public welfare, the courts recognize that such ordinances are presumed to be constitutional, and come before the court with every intendment in their favor." (*City of Livermore, supra,* 18 Cal.3d at pp. 604–605, 135 Cal.Rptr. 41, 557 P.2d 473.) Accordingly, a party challenging the facial validity of a legislative land use measure ordinarily bears the burden of demonstrating that the measure lacks a reasonable relationship to the public welfare. (*See, e.g., Goldblatt v. Hempstead* (1962) 369 U.S. 590, 596, 82 S.Ct. 987, 8 L.Ed.2d 130; *Building Industry Assn. of Central California v. County of Stanislaus* (2010) 190 Cal.App.4th 582, 591, 118 Cal.Rptr.3d 467.) Nonetheless, as this court explained in *City of Livermore, supra,* 18 Cal.3d at p. 609, 135 Cal.Rptr. 41, 557 P.2d 473, although land use regulations are generally entitled to deference, "judicial deference is not judicial abdication. The ordinance must have a *real and substantial* relation to the public welfare. There must be a reasonable basis in fact, not in fancy, to support the legislative determination. Although in many cases it will be 'fairly debatable' that the ordinance reasonably relates to the regional welfare, it cannot be assumed that a land use ordinance can *never* be invalidated as an enactment in excess of the police power." (*See also McKay Jewelers v. Bowron* (1942) 19 Cal.2d 595, 600–601, 122 P.2d 543; *Skalko v. City of Sunnyvale* (1939) 14 Cal.2d 213, 215–216, 93 P.2d 93.)

In the present case, however, CBIA contends that this traditional standard of judicial review is not applicable and that the conditions that the ordinance imposes upon a proposed new development are valid only if those conditions bear a reasonable relationship to the amount of the city's need for affordable housing that is attributable to the proposed development itself, rather than that the ordinance's conditions bear a reasonable relationship to the public welfare of the city and region as a whole. It also contends that the city, rather than the party challenging the ordinance, bears the burden of proof regarding the validity of the ordinance.

As already noted, although the precise nature and source of CBIA's constitutional claim was somewhat opaque in earlier stages of this litigation, in its briefing in this court CBIA has clarified that its facial constitutional challenge rests upon the takings clauses of the United States and California Constitutions (U.S. Const., 5th and 14th Amends.; Cal. Const., art. I, § 19), and, more specifically, on the claim "that the Ordinance violates the unconstitutional conditions doctrine, as applied to development exactions." As we shall explain, however, there can be no valid unconstitutional-conditions takings claim without a government exaction of property, and the ordinance in the present case does not effect an exaction. Rather, the ordinance is an example of a municipality's permissible regulation of the use of land under its broad police power.

* * *

Rather than being an exaction, the ordinance falls within what we have already described as municipalities' general broad discretion to regulate the use of real property to serve the legitimate interests of the general public and the community at large. * * * Similarly, if a municipality determines that a particular neighborhood or the community in general is in special need of a specific type of residential development or business establishment—such as a multiunit residential project or a retail shopping center—it may adopt land use regulations to serve such a need. (*See, e.g., Ensign Bickford Realty Corp. v. City Council* (1977) 68 Cal.App.3d 467, 477–478, 137 Cal.Rptr. 304.)

* * *

As a general matter, so long as a land use regulation does not constitute a physical taking or deprive a property owner of all viable economic use of the property, such a restriction does not violate the takings clause insofar as it governs a property owner's future use of his or her property, except in the unusual circumstance in which the use restriction is properly found to go "too far" and to constitute a "regulatory taking" under the ad hoc, multifactored test discussed by the United States Supreme Court in *Penn Central Transp. Co. v. New York City* (1978) 438 U.S. 104, 98 S.Ct. 2646, 57 L.Ed.2d 631 (*Penn Central*). (*See Lingle, supra,* 544 U.S. at pp. 538–539, 125 S.Ct. 2074.) Where a restriction on the use of property would not constitute a taking of property without just compensation if imposed outside of the permit process, a permit condition imposing such a use restriction does not require a permit applicant to give up the constitutional right to just compensation in order to obtain the permit and thus does not constitute "an exaction" so as to bring into play the unconstitutional conditions doctrine. (*See, e.g., Powell v. County of Humboldt* (2014) 222 Cal.App.4th 1424, 1435–1441, 166 Cal.Rptr.3d 747.)

* * *

There are a variety of conditions or restrictions that a municipality could impose on new residential development in an effort to increase the community's stock of affordable housing and promote economically diverse residential developments. For example, a municipality might attempt to achieve these objectives by requiring all new residential developments to include a specified percentage of studio, one-bedroom, or small-square-footage units, on the theory that smaller units are more likely to be affordable to low or moderate income households than larger units. Although such use restrictions might well reduce the value of undeveloped property or lessen the profits a developer could obtain in the absence of such requirements, CBIA cites no authority, and we are aware of none, suggesting that such use restrictions would constitute a taking of property outside the permit process or that a permit condition that imposes such use restrictions on a proposed development would constitute an exaction under the takings clause that would be subject to the *Nollan/Dolan* test.

* * *

As we have explained, an ordinance that places nonconfiscatory price controls on the sale of residential units and does not amount to a regulatory taking would not constitute a taking of property without just compensation even if the price controls were applied to a property owner who had not sought a land use permit. Accordingly, the inclusionary housing ordinance's imposition of such price controls as a condition of a development permit does not constitute the imposition of an exaction for purposes of the unconstitutional conditions doctrine under the takings clause.

* * *

In sum, for all of the foregoing reasons, the basic requirement imposed by the challenged ordinance—conditioning the grant of a development permit for new developments of more than 20 units upon a developer's agreement to offer for sale at an affordable housing price at least 15 percent of the on-site for-sale units—does not constitute an exaction for purposes of the takings clause so as to bring into play the unconstitutional conditions doctrine under the *Nollan, Dolan*, and *Koontz* decisions.

* * *

V. Does the passage in San Remo Hotel, supra, 27 Cal.4th 643, 671, relied on by CBIA, apply to the affordable housing condition imposed by San Jose's inclusionary housing ordinance?

CBIA also rests its facial challenge to the validity of the San Jose ordinance upon a passage in this court's decision in *San Remo Hotel, supra,* 27 Cal.4th at page 671, 117 Cal.Rptr.2d 269, 41 P.3d 87. CBIA characterizes this portion of the *San Remo Hotel* decision as resting upon an application of the unconstitutional conditions doctrine, but we have demonstrated that doctrine is not applicable here because the ordinance does not effect an exaction. We note, however, that the passage in question in *San Remo Hotel* did not itself refer to that doctrine and the Court of

Appeal decision in *City of Patterson, supra,* 171 Cal.App.4th 886, 90 Cal.Rptr.3d 63, upon which CBIA also relies, did not analyze the passage in *San Remo Hotel* as an aspect of the unconstitutional conditions doctrine. Accordingly, notwithstanding our rejection of CBIA's unconstitutional conditions claim, we shall consider whether the passage in *San Remo Hotel* upon which CBIA relies should properly be interpreted as applicable to the challenged inclusionary housing ordinance.

* * *

Unlike the decision in *San Remo Hotel,* in which we addressed a development fee that was intended solely to mitigate the adverse effect of the proposed conversion of long-term rental units to tourist units, in this court's earlier decision in *Ehrlich, supra,* 12 Cal.4th 854, 50 Cal.Rptr.2d 242, 911 P.2d 429, we had occasion to consider, among other issues, the validity of a land use permit condition or requirement that was intended, like the affordable housing condition at issue here, to serve a constitutionally permissible public purpose other than mitigating the impact of the proposed development project. For this reason, the *Ehrlich* decision provides useful guidance in ascertaining the standard under which the validity of the San Jose inclusionary housing ordinance is properly evaluated.

In *Ehrlich, supra,* 12 Cal.4th 854, 50 Cal.Rptr.2d 242, 911 P.2d 429, the developer challenged the validity of two different types of development conditions that the defendant city had imposed as a condition of the plaintiff's proposed development: (1) a recreational-facility replacement fee and (2) a public art requirement. The court in *Ehrlich* first held that the ad hoc recreational-facility replacement fee that had been imposed in that case should properly be evaluated under the *Nollan/Dolan* standard (*Ehrlich, supra,* at pp. 874–881, 50 Cal.Rptr.2d 242, 911 P.2d 429 (plur. opn. of Arabian, J.); *id.* at pp. 899–901, 50 Cal.Rptr.2d 242, 911 P.2d 429 (conc. opn. of Mosk, J.)), and, as such, the amount of the fee was required to be roughly proportional to the adverse public impact attributable to the loss of property reserved for private recreational use that would result from the developer's proposed project. (Id. at pp. 882–885, 50 Cal.Rptr.2d 242, 911 P.2d 429 (plur. opn. of Arabian, J.); *id.* at pp. 901–902, 50 Cal.Rptr.2d 242, 911 P.2d 429 (conc. opn. of Mosk, J.).) Applying the *Nollan/Dolan* standard, the court in *Ehrlich* concluded that the record was insufficient to support the amount of the recreational-facility replacement fee that had been imposed in that case. (Id. at pp. 884–885, 50 Cal.Rptr.2d 242, 911 P.2d 429 (plur. opn. of Arabian, J.); *id.* at pp. 901–902, 50 Cal.Rptr.2d 242, 911 P.2d 429 (conc. opn. of Mosk, J.).)

By contrast, with respect to the public art condition—which required the developer either (1) to pay into the city art fund a fee equal to 1 percent of the total building valuation, or (2) to contribute an approved work of public art of an equivalent value that could be placed on site or donated to the city for placement elsewhere—the court in *Ehrlich* did not evaluate the validity of the condition by asking whether or not the amount of the required fee or value of the work of art was reasonably related to the adverse impact that the proposed development would have on the existing state of public art in the city. Instead, in *Ehrlich* this court upheld the validity of the public art requirement (including the related in lieu public art fee) upon finding that the requirement (and related in lieu fee) was reasonably related to the constitutionally legitimate public purpose of increasing the amount of publicly accessible works of art for the benefit of the community and the public as a whole.

* * *

In sum, we conclude that the requirements of the inclusionary housing ordinance at issue here do not conflict with the passage in *San Remo Hotel* upon which CBIA relies. Accordingly, there is no merit to CBIA's contention that, under *San Remo Hotel,* the ordinance is invalid on its face because the city failed to show that the ordinance's inclusionary housing requirements are reasonably related to the impact on affordable housing attributable to such developments.

* * *

Although the affordable-housing in lieu fee at issue in *City of Patterson*, *supra*, 171 Cal.App.4th 886, 90 Cal.Rptr.3d 63, and the long-term rental replacement fee at issue in *San Remo Hotel*, *supra*, 27 Cal.4th 643, 117 Cal.Rptr.2d 269, 41 P.3d 87, shared the characteristics noted by the Court of Appeal in *City of Patterson* (both were formulaic, legislatively mandated fees), the court in *City of Patterson* overlooked a critical difference between the two. Unlike the long-term rental replacement in lieu fee in *San Remo Hotel,* the affordable-housing in lieu fee in *City of Patterson* was not imposed for the purpose of mitigating an adverse effect that was caused by the developer but was imposed to further the very different public purpose of increasing the stock of affordable housing in the city to meet the need for affordable housing as determined by the relevant county council of governments. (171 Cal.App.4th at p. 892, 90 Cal.Rptr.3d 63.)

* * *

For the reasons discussed above, we disapprove the decision in *Building Industry Assn. of Central California v. City of Patterson, supra*, 171 Cal.App.4th 886, 90 Cal.Rptr.3d 63, to the extent it indicates that the conditions imposed by an inclusionary zoning ordinance are valid only if they are reasonably related to the need for affordable housing attributable to the projects to which the ordinance applies. At the same time, because the question is not before us, we express no opinion regarding the validity of the amount of the particular in lieu fee at issue in *City of Patterson* or of the methodology utilized in arriving at that fee. (See *id.* at pp. 891–893, 90 Cal.Rptr.3d 63.)

VI. Is this court's recent decision in Sterling Park, supra, 57 Cal.4th 1193, inconsistent with the conclusions reached above?

Finally, CBIA asserts that this court's recent decision in *Sterling Park*, *supra*, 57 Cal.4th 1193, 163 Cal.Rptr.3d 2, 310 P.3d 925, supports its contention that the test set forth in *San Remo Hotel, supra*, 27 Cal.4th 643, 117 Cal.Rptr.2d 269, 41 P.3d 87, applies to the affordable housing requirement of the San Jose inclusionary housing ordinance at issue here. As we explain, the legal issue that was presented and decided in *Sterling Park* bears no relationship to the issue presented here, and we conclude the *Sterling Park* decision does not support CBIA's position in this case.

In *Sterling Park, supra*, 57 Cal.4th 1193, 163 Cal.Rptr.3d 2, 310 P.3d 925, the issue before this court was which of two statutes of limitation applied to the lawsuit at issue in that case. * * *

* * *

In *Sterling Park* we concluded that the statute of limitations provisions of Government Code section 66020 (part of the Mitigation Fee Act) should properly be interpreted to apply to the affordable housing requirements imposed by the Palo Alto inclusionary housing ordinance. * * *

* * *

In the course of the *Sterling Park* opinion, we rejected the city's contention that the requirements of its inclusionary housing ordinance should not be considered "exactions" as that term is used in Government Code section 66020. * * *

* * * But whether or not the affordable housing requirements of the San Jose ordinance should be considered "exactions" as that term is used in Government Code section 66020, and thus are subject to the procedural protest and statute of limitations provisions of that statute—an issue we need not and do not decide—it is clear that our decision in *Sterling Park* did not address or intend to express any view whatsoever with regard to the legal test that applies in evaluating the substantive validity of the affordable housing requirements imposed by an inclusionary housing ordinance. The opinion in *Sterling Park* focused exclusively on the procedural issue presented in that case and made no mention of the passage in *San Remo Hotel, supra*, 27 Cal.4th 643, 117 Cal.Rptr.2d 269, 41 P.3d 87, or any other substantive legal test. Nothing in *Sterling Park* supports CBIA's claim that the challenged San Jose ordinance is subject to a judicial standard of review different from that traditionally applied to other legislatively mandated land use development requirements.

VII. Conclusion

As noted at the outset of this opinion, for many decades California statutes and judicial decisions have recognized the critical need for more affordable housing in this state. Over the years, a variety of means have been advanced and undertaken to address this challenging need. We emphasize that the legal question before our court in this case is not the wisdom or efficacy of the particular tool or method that the City of San Jose has adopted, but simply whether, as the Court of Appeal held, the San Jose ordinance is subject to the ordinary standard of judicial review to which legislative land use regulations have traditionally been subjected.

For the reasons discussed above, the judgment of the Court of Appeal is affirmed.

NOTES: SET-ASIDES, LINKAGE AND RELOCATION FEES

1. The San Jose decision was denied cert. by the U.S.S.C., 136 S.Ct. 928 (2016) with Justice Thomas explaining that while the "case implicates an important and unsettled issue under the Takings Clause," it "does not present an opportunity to resolve the conflict." The conflict he refers to is that "lower courts have divided over whether the *Nollan / Dolan* test applies in cases where the alleged taking arises from a legislatively imposed condition rather than an administrative one." Following the *San Jose* decision, the appellate court in *616 Croft Ave, LLC v. City of West Hollywood*, No. B266660 (Cal.App. Sep. 23, 2016) held that a legislatively-imposed requirement for low-income housing was not an exaction because "as in *San Jose*, the purpose of the in-lieu housing fee here is not to defray the cost of increased demand on public services resulting from Croft's specific development project, but rather to combat the overall lack of affordable housing." What about the exaction tests discussed *supra* in Chapter 4 regarding subdivision exactions and impact fees? *See* David L. Callies, *Mandatory Set-Asides as Land Development Conditions*, 42/43 URB.LAW. 307 (2010). *See also* Shelley Ross Saxer, *When Local Government Misbehaves*, 2016 UTAH L.REV. 105 (arguing that the *Nollan / Dolan* test should not apply to legislatively imposed conditions).

2. Inclusionary set-asides are most heavily used in New Jersey and California. A 2006 survey found 121 inclusionary ordinances in California. Cecily T. Talbert, Nadia L. Costa and Alison L. Krumbein, *Recent Developments in Inclusionary Zoning*, 38 URB.LAW. 701, 703 (2006). Montgomery County, Maryland has used inclusionary zoning since 1973. Set-asides are used, albeit less extensively, in Colorado, Florida, Maryland, Massachusetts, New Mexico, South Carolina, Texas, and Virginia. *Id. See also* Barbara Ehrlich Kautz, *In Defense of Inclusionary Zoning: Successfully Creating Affordable Housing*, 36 U.S.F.L.REV. 971 (2002).

Whether these programs are worth the legal/constitutional risks as set out in the following notes is increasingly questionable given the relative paucity of affordable/workforce housing actually yielded. Not only does that yield depend upon a robust housing construction market, but studies indicate that even so, the yield is comparatively small. *See* Douglas Porter, *Inclusionary Zoning for Affordable Housing* (2004).

3.   States pursue a variety of programs to encourage affordable housing. For analysis of the efforts in California, Connecticut, Massachusetts, Illinois and New Jersey, *see* Julie A. Tappendorf, *State Laws, Policies, and Programs for Affordable Housing*, ALI-ABA 1481 (ALI-ABA Aug. 2007). *See also* Brian Stromberg & Lisa Sturtevant, *What Makes Inclusionary Zoning Happen?* National Housing Conference (NHC) (May 2016) (describing local inclusionary programs and noting that in 2014 the NHC with the help of others assembled a database of local inclusionary housing programs in the U.S.). California has encouraged density bonuses since 1979. Cal.Gov.Code § 65915. Under the statute, if a developer agrees to construct a certain percentage of affordable housing units, a city must grant a density bonus. Over the years, the state has made bonuses more attractive to developers. Under a 2005 amendment to the statute, developers can obtain density bonuses up to 35%, based on the percentage of affordable units they offer to build. *See also* Inclusionary Housing in California: 30 Years of Experience, California Coalition for Rural Housing and Non-Profit Housing Association of Northern California (2004). In 2007, California amended the housing element of its planning laws to address the housing needs of the homeless, including requiring cities to identify zones where emergency shelters are a permitted use without a conditional use permit. *See* Cal.Govt.Code §§ 65582, 65583, and 65589.5.

4.   Can new high cost housing be shown to exacerbate the affordable housing supply so that it is fair to make the developer build, or pay, for some? Some say there is only so much land and that the construction of high cost housing means there is less land now available for affordable housing. Others say new high cost housing actually increases the supply of affordable housing by the trickle down process. For contrasting views on the economic efficiency of inclusionary zoning, *see* Robert C. Ellickson, *The Irony of "Inclusionary" Zoning*, 54 S.CAL.L.REV. 1167 (1981), and Andrew G. Dietderich, *An Egalitarian's Market: The Economics of Inclusionary Zoning Reclaimed*, 24 FORDHAM URB.L.J. 23 (1996). *See also*, Murtaza Baxamusa, *The Real Reasons Affordable Housing Isn't Being Built in California*, National Housing Institute: The Shelterforce blog (July 17, 2016); Claude Gruen, *Getting Inclusionary Zoning Right,* LandWrites pg. 78 (July/August 2016). http: //www.ggassoc.com/publications/LandWritesJuly-Aug2016.pdf.

5.   Fees on non-residential builders to pay for affordable housing, frequently called *linkage fees*, are increasingly common. It is easier to show a nexus between commercial development and the problem of affordable housing than it is for high cost residential housing. For an article supporting the imposition of inclusionary fees on commercial development, see Jane E. Schukoske, *Housing Linkage: Regulating Development Impact on Housing Costs*, 76 IOWA L.REV. 1011 (1991). For arguments against such commercial fees, see Theodore C. Taub, *Exactions, Linkages, and Regulatory Takings: The Developer's Perspective*, 20 URB.LAW. 515 (1988).

Cities are increasingly turning their attention to so-called "workforce housing" to hold onto key municipal workers, particularly police and firefighters and in some instances, public school teachers, all of whom, along with many other municipal employees, are often priced out of housing in the city where they work. *See* Tim Iglesias, *Our Pluralist Housing Ethics and the Struggle for Affordability*, 42 WAKE FOREST L.REV. 511, 581 (2007). In 2016, the Palo Alto city council voted to study a housing proposal to subsidize housing for families making from $150,000 to $250,000 in the Silicon Valley to help out teachers, firefighters, and other government employees. http:// sanfrancisco.cbslocal.com/2016/03/22/250k-per-year-salary-could-qualify-for-subsidized-housing-under-new-palo-alto-plan/.

A linkage fee may be treated as a revenue measure, rather than a regulatory one. If so, it must meet state law regarding the levying of taxes. *See Sintra, Inc. v. City of Seattle*, 829 P.2d 765 (Wash.1992). Specific enabling legislation for linkage fees may be required. *See* William W. Merrill and Robert K. Lincoln, *Linkage Fees and Fair Share Regulations: Law and Method*, 25 URB.LAW. 223 (1993).

6.   Who should be given the opportunity to buy or rent inclusionary units? Should a town take care of its own first and grant a preference to those who live or work in the town? *See* Donald Hagman, *Taking Care of One's Own Through Inclusionary Zoning: Bootstrapping Low-and Moderate-Income Housing by Local Government*, 5 URB.LAW & POL'Y 169 (1982). Is this a ploy to prevent those from the urban centers from moving into the community? If current low and moderate income residents are white, and the urban applicants black, might a preference for local residents or workers be viewed as an illegitimate racial exclusion? *See In re Petition for Substantive Certification*, 622 A.2d 1257 (N.J.1993), where the New Jersey Supreme Court held that preferences for residents violated the *Mt. Laurel* obligation.

7.   *Housing Trust Funds.* Some cities impose relocation fees on developers who plan to demolish or convert low cost housing, usually single-room occupancy units, or to close mobile home parks. The money is then earmarked for the construction of affordable housing. Many states fund their housing trust funds in whole or in part by dedicating the revenue gained from real estate transfer taxes or recording fees to them. *See* Cecily T. Talbert, Nadia L. Costa and Alison L. Krumbein, *Recent Developments in Inclusionary Zoning*, 38 URB.LAW. 701, 706 (2006), listing sixteen state statutes.

C. FEDERAL EXCLUSIONARY ZONING ISSUES: CONSTITUTIONAL ASPECTS AND LEGISLATIVE INTERVENTION

The federal government has played both a proactive and reactive role in exclusionary housing practices. It has done its share to promote segregated living patterns in several ways. The combination of the interstate highway system, the income tax deduction, and guarantees on mortgage loans contributes to urban sprawl by making it easier for the wealthier to leave the urban center. Also, in the 1930s, when the federal government began loan guarantees to save the housing industry, it required that racially restrictive covenants be put in deeds, and "discouraged the movement of 'inharmonious racial or nationality groups' into all-white communities." Robert F. Drinan, S.J., *Untying the White Noose*, 94 YALE L.J. 435, 437 (1993). *See also* James A. Kushner, *Apartheid in America: An Historical and Legal Analysis of Contemporary Racial Residential Segregation in the United States*, 22 HOW.L.J. 547 (1979).

The Supreme Court has also reviewed racially and economically based exclusionary practices of state and local governments. The Court initially addressed racially exclusionary zoning in 1917 in *Buchanan v. Warley*, 245 U.S. 60 (1917), where it invalidated on due process grounds an ordinance that set aside areas of town on a racial basis. *See* James W. Ely, Jr., *Reflections on Buchanan v. Warley, Property Rights, and Race*, 51 VAND.L.REV. 953 (1998). In 1926, however, in *Euclid* the Court endorsed the use of zoning for economic segregation, but it also said that there may be "cases where the general public interest would so far outweigh the interest of the municipality that the municipality would not be allowed to stand in the way." 272 U.S. at 390.

1.   THE EQUAL PROTECTION CLAUSE

VILLAGE OF ARLINGTON HEIGHTS V. METROPOLITAN HOUSING DEVELOPMENT CORPORATION

Supreme Court of the United States, 1977.
429 U.S. 252, 97 S.Ct. 555, 50 L.Ed.2d 450.

MR. JUSTICE POWELL delivered the opinion of the Court.

* * *

Arlington Heights is a suburb of Chicago, located about 26 miles northwest of the downtown Loop area. Most of the land in Arlington Heights is zoned for detached single-family homes, and this is in fact the prevailing land use. The Village experienced substantial growth during the 1960's, but, like other communities in northwest Cook County, its population of racial minority groups remained quite low. According to the 1970 census, only 27 of the Village's 64,000 residents were black.

The Clerics of St. Viator, a religious order (Order), own an 80-acre parcel just east of the center of Arlington Heights. Part of the site is occupied by the Viatorian high school, and part by the Order's three-story novitiate building, which houses dormitories and a Montessori school. Much of the site, however, remains vacant. Since 1959, when the Village first adopted a zoning ordinance, all the land surrounding the Viatorian property has been zoned R-3, a single-family specification with relatively small minimum lot-size requirements. On three sides of the Viatorian land there are single-family homes just across a street; to the east the Viatorian property directly adjoins the backyards of other single-family homes.

The Order decided in 1970 to devote some of its land to low-and moderate-income housing. Investigation revealed that the most expeditious way to build such housing was to work through a nonprofit developer experienced in the use of federal housing subsidies under § 236 of the National Housing Act, 48 Stat. 1246, as added and amended, 12 U.S.C. § 1715z–1.

MHDC is such a developer. It was organized in 1968 by several prominent Chicago citizens for the purpose of building low-and moderate-income housing throughout the Chicago area. In 1970 MHDC was in the process of building one § 236 development near Arlington Heights and already had provided some federally assisted housing on a smaller scale in other parts of the Chicago area.

After some negotiation, MHDC and the Order entered into a 99-year lease and an accompanying agreement of sale covering a 15-acre site in the southeast corner of the Viatorian property. MHDC became the lessee immediately, but the sale agreement was contingent upon MHDC's securing zoning clearances from the Village and § 236 housing assistance from the Federal Government. If MHDC proved unsuccessful in securing either, both the lease and the contract of sale would lapse. The agreement established a bargain purchase price of $300,000, low enough to comply with federal limitations governing land-acquisition costs for § 236 housing.

MHDC engaged an architect and proceeded with the project, to be known as Lincoln Green. The plans called for 20 two-story buildings with a total of 190 units, each unit having its own private entrance from outside. One hundred of the units would have a single bedroom, thought likely to attract elderly citizens. The remainder would have two, three, or four bedrooms. A large portion of the site would remain open, with shrubs and trees to screen the homes abutting the property to the east.

* * *

During the spring of 1971, the Plan Commission considered the proposal at a series of three public meetings, which drew large crowds. Although many of those attending were quite vocal and demonstrative in opposition to Lincoln Green, a number of individuals and representatives of community groups spoke in support of rezoning. Some of the comments, both from opponents and supporters, addressed what was referred to as the "social issue"—the desirability or undesirability of introducing at this location in Arlington Heights low-and moderate-income housing, housing that would probably be racially integrated.

Many of the opponents, however, focused on the zoning aspects of the petition, stressing two arguments. First, the area always had been zoned single-family, and the neighboring citizens had built or purchased there in reliance on that classification. Rezoning threatened to cause a measurable drop in property value for neighboring sites. Second, the Village's apartment policy, adopted by the Village Board in 1962 and amended in 1970, called for R-5 zoning primarily to serve as a buffer between single-family development and land uses thought incompatible, such as commercial or manufacturing districts. Lincoln Green did not meet this requirement, as it adjoined no commercial or manufacturing district.

At the close of the third meeting, the Plan Commission adopted a motion to recommend to the Village's Board of Trustees that it deny the request. * * * The Village Board met on September 28, 1971, to consider MHDC's request and the recommendation of the Plan Commission. After a public hearing, the Board denied the rezoning by a 6–1 vote.

The following June MHDC and three Negro individuals filed this lawsuit against the Village, seeking declaratory and injunctive relief. A second nonprofit corporation and an individual of Mexican-American descent intervened as plaintiffs. The trial resulted in a judgment for petitioners. Assuming that MHDC had standing to bring the suit, the District Court held that the petitioners were not motivated by racial discrimination or intent to discriminate against low-income groups when they denied rezoning, but rather by a desire "to protect property values and the integrity of the Village's zoning plan." 373 F.Supp. at 211. The District Court concluded also that the denial would not have a racially discriminatory effect.

A divided Court of Appeals reversed.

* * *

[T]he Court of Appeals ruled that the denial of the Lincoln Green proposal had racially discriminatory effects and could be tolerated only if it served compelling interests. Neither the buffer policy nor the desire to protect property values met this exacting standard. The court therefore concluded that the denial violated the Equal Protection Clause of the Fourteenth Amendment. * * *

II

[Editors' note: The Court then considered, and rejected, petitioners challenge to respondents' standing. Under Warth v. Seldin, 422 U.S. 490 (1975), discussed in note 4 following this opinion, the Court enacted stringent standing rules in exclusionary zoning cases. The Court found, however, that MHDC met the *Warth* standards since the "challenged action of the petitioners stands as an absolute barrier to constructing the housing MHDC had contracted to place on the Viatorian site. If MHDC secures the injunctive relief it seeks, that barrier will be removed. * * * When a project is as detailed and specific as Lincoln Green, a court is not required to engage in undue speculation as a predicate for finding that the plaintiff has the requisite personal stake in the controversy."]

Clearly MHDC has met the constitutional requirements, and it therefore has standing to assert its own rights. Foremost among them is MHDC's right to be free of arbitrary or irrational zoning actions. *See Euclid v. Ambler Realty Co.*, 272 U.S. 365 (1926); *Nectow v. City of Cambridge*, 277 U.S. 183 (1928); *Village of Belle Terre v. Boraas*, 416 U.S. 1 (1974). But the heart of this litigation has never been the claim that the Village's decision fails the generous *Euclid* test, recently reaffirmed in *Belle Terre*. Instead it has been the claim that the Village's refusal to rezone discriminates against racial minorities in violation of the Fourteenth Amendment. As a corporation, MHDC has no racial identity and cannot be the direct target of the petitioners' alleged discrimination. In the ordinary case, a party is denied standing to assert the rights of third persons. But we need not decide whether the circumstances of this case would justify departure from that prudential limitation and permit MHDC to assert the constitutional rights of its prospective minority tenants. For we have at least one individual plaintiff who has demonstrated standing to assert these rights as his own.

Respondent Ransom, a Negro, works at the Honeywell factory in Arlington Heights and lives approximately 20 miles away in Evanston in a 5-room house with his mother and his son. The complaint alleged that he seeks and would qualify for the housing MHDC wants to build in Arlington Heights. Ransom testified at trial that if Lincoln Green were built he would probably move there, since it is closer to his job.

The injury Ransom asserts is that his quest for housing nearer his employment has been thwarted by official action that is racially discriminatory. If a court grants the relief he seeks, there is at least a "substantial probability," that the Lincoln Green project will materialize, affording Ransom the housing opportunity he desires in Arlington Heights. His is not a generalized grievance. Instead, as we suggested in *Warth*, it focuses on a particular project and is not dependent on speculation about the possible actions of third parties not before the court. Unlike the individual plaintiffs in *Warth*, Ransom has adequately averred an "actionable causal relationship" between Arlington Heights' zoning practices and his asserted injury. We therefore proceed to the merits.

III

Our decision last Term in *Washington v. Davis*, 426 U.S. 229 (1976), made it clear that official action will not be held unconstitutional solely because it results in a racially disproportionate impact. "Disproportionate impact is not irrelevant, but it is not the sole touchstone of an invidious racial discrimination." Proof of racially discriminatory intent or purpose is required to show a violation of the Equal Protection Clause. Although some contrary indications may be drawn from some of our cases, the holding in *Davis* reaffirmed a principle well established in a variety of contexts. (Citations omitted).

* * *

Determining whether invidious discriminatory purpose was a motivating factor demands a sensitive inquiry into such circumstantial and direct evidence of intent as may be available. The impact of the official action—whether it "bears more heavily on one race than another," *Washington v. Davis, supra*, 426 U.S., at 242—may provide an important starting point. Sometimes a clear pattern, unexplainable on grounds other than race, emerges from the effect of the state action even when the governing legislation appears neutral on its face. The evidentiary inquiry is then relatively easy. But such cases are rare. Absent a pattern as stark as that in *Gomillion* or *Yick Wo,* impact alone is not determinative, and the Court must look to other evidence.

The historical background of the decision is one evidentiary source, particularly if it reveals a series of official actions taken for invidious purposes. The specific sequence of events leading up the challenged decision also may shed some light on the decisionmaker's purposes. *Reitman v. Mulkey*, 387 U.S. 369, 373–376 (1967). For example, if the property involved here always had been zoned R-5 but suddenly was changed to R-3 when the town learned of MHDC's plans to erect integrated housing, we would have a far different case. Departures from the normal procedural sequence also might afford evidence that improper purposes are playing a role. Substantive departures too may be relevant, particularly if the factors usually considered important by the decisionmaker strongly favor a decision contrary to the one reached.

The legislative or administrative history may be highly relevant, especially where there are contemporary statements by members of the decisionmaking body, minutes of its meetings, or reports. In some extraordinary instances the members might be called to the stand at trial to testify concerning the purpose of the official action, although even then such testimony frequently will be barred by privilege. *See Tenney v. Brandhove*, 341 U.S. 367 (1951); *United States v. Nixon*, 418 U.S. 683, 705 (1974).

The foregoing summary identifies, without purporting to be exhaustive, subjects of proper inquiry in determining whether racially discriminatory intent existed. * * *

* * *

We also have reviewed the evidence. The impact of the Village's decision does arguably bear more heavily on racial minorities. * * * But there is little about the sequence of events leading up to the decision that would spark suspicion. * * * The rezoning request progressed according to the usual procedures. The Plan Commission even scheduled two additional hearings, at least in part to accommodate MHDC and permit it to supplement its presentation with answers to questions generated at the first hearing.

The statements by the Plan Commission and Village Board members, as reflected in the official minutes, focused almost exclusively on the zoning aspects of the MHDC petition, and the zoning factors on which they relied are not novel criteria in the Village's rezoning decisions. There is no reason to doubt that there has been reliance by some neighboring property owners on the maintenance of single-family zoning in the vicinity. The Village originally adopted its buffer policy long before MHDC entered the picture and has applied the policy too consistently for us to infer discriminatory purpose from its application in this case. Finally, MHDC called one member of the Village Board to the stand at trial. Nothing in her testimony supports an inference of invidious purpose.

In sum, the evidence does not warrant overturning the concurrent findings of both courts below. Respondents simply failed to carry their burden of proving that discriminatory purpose was a motivating factor in the Village's decision.[21] This conclusion ends the constitutional inquiry. The Court of Appeals' further finding that the Village's decision carried a discriminatory "ultimate effect" is without independent constitutional significance.

V

Respondents' complaint also alleged that the refusal to rezone violated the Fair Housing Act of 1968, 42 U.S.C. § 3601 et seq. They continue to urge here that a zoning decision made by a public body may, and that petitioners' action did, violate § 3604 or § 3617. The Court of Appeals, however, proceeding in a somewhat unorthodox fashion, did not decide the statutory question. We remand the case for further consideration of respondents' statutory claims.

Reversed and remanded.

---

[21] Proof that the decision by the Village was motivated in part by a racially discriminatory purpose would not necessarily have required invalidation of the challenged decision. Such proof would, however, have shifted to the Village the burden of establishing that the same decision would have resulted even had the impermissible purpose not been considered. If this were established, the complaining party in a case of this kind no longer fairly could attribute the injury complained of to improper consideration of a discriminatory purpose. In such circumstances, there would be no justification for judicial interference with the challenged decision. But in this case respondents failed to make the required threshold showing. *See Mt. Healthy City School Dist. Bd. of Education v. Doyle*, 429 U.S. 274.

NOTES

1.   Upon remand, the Seventh Circuit determined that the Village of Arlington Heights had violated the Fair Housing Act. In 1980, a consent decree approved by the district court was affirmed by the Seventh Circuit. *Metropolitan Housing Dev. Corp. v. Village of Arlington Heights*, 616 F.2d 1006 (7th Cir.1980). The Village and the plaintiffs agreed upon an alternate site of twenty-six acres of vacant land which the Village annexed and rezoned in an unincorporated area of Cook County. In 1983, a 190-unit Section 8 housing development was dedicated.

2.   Poverty is not a suspect classification, *San Antonio Indep. School Dist. v. Rodriguez*, 411 U.S. 1 (1973), and housing is not a fundamental right, *Lindsey v. Normet*, 405 U.S. 56 (1972), therefore *Arlington Heights'* implicit endorsement of economic exclusionary zoning is not surprising. Regarding *Arlington Heights*, see David L. Callies and Clifford L. Weaver, *The Arlington Heights Case: The Exclusion of Exclusionary Zoning Challenges*, 2 REAL ESTATE ISSUES 37 (1978) and Daniel R. Mandelker, *Racial Discrimination and Exclusionary Zoning: A Perspective on Arlington Heights*, 55 TEX.L.REV. 1217 (1977).

3.   Is it right to put the burden on the challenger to show racial motivation? Doesn't reality suggest that a showing of impact should be sufficient to switch the burden? Consider Professor Perry's comment:

> In such a case, who ought to get the benefit of the doubt—the challenging or the defending party? Principally, because racism is still a pervasive feature of American life, infecting more official decisionmaking than we like to admit, the doubt should be resolved in the challenging party's favor; the presumption should be that the decision *is* race-dependent.

See Michael J. Perry, *Modern Equal Protection: A Conceptualization and Appraisal*, 79 COLUM.L.REV. 1023, 1039 (1979). Is Perry's 1979 comment accurate today? What happens if racial motivation is shown? See footnote 21 in the Court's opinion.

4.   Restrictive standing rules limit the ability of federal courts to hear exclusionary zoning cases. In *Warth v. Seldin*, 422 U.S. 490 (1975), several groups charged the town of Penfield, a suburb of Rochester, New York, with practicing exclusionary zoning. The Court denied standing to four categories of plaintiffs: low income non-residents unable to find housing in the community; taxpayers in the central city bearing a disproportionate share of low income costs; suburban residents denied benefits of living in an integrated community; and associations representing contractors unable to construct low-income housing in the suburbs. As Justice Brennan commented in dissent, the *Warth* decision "tosses out of court almost every conceivable kind of plaintiff * * * ." *Id.* at 520. With respect to the non-residents who found no affordable housing in the area, the Court noted that there was inadequate proof that the injury they suffered would be remedied by the Court intervening. Elimination

of exclusionary zoning practices would not necessarily lead to the construction of affordable housing. *Arlington Heights* was rare in that standing was found since there was a low-income minority person who was a potential resident of a specific housing project which had been denied approval. (Most of the standing discussion is omitted from the *Arlington Heights* opinion in the text).

A plaintiff may be able to take advantage of broader state court standing rules since state courts are not obligated to follow *Warth*. In *Stocks v. City of Irvine*, 170 Cal.Rptr. 724 (Cal.App.1981), the state court granted standing to non-resident low-income persons to challenge the City of Irvine's land use ordinance and regulations. Plaintiffs alleged that the city injured them by preventing them from obtaining affordable housing in the city and the entire region. The court held that the federal standing requirements enunciated in *Warth* were not applicable in California state courts.

COMMENT: CONSENT DECREES AND LAND USE

The resolution of complex legal issues after filing a complaint based on a judicially approved settlement in the form of a consent decree is relatively common. Such a decree has the advantage of judicial enforceability often lacking in other forms of dispute resolution. This enforceability, together with the consent of the parties, makes the consent decree a form of contract with the extra oomph of a judicial decree, taking it several steps beyond mere settlement of litigation.

The nature of the consent decree is critical to an analysis of its use in settling complex environmental and land use law disputes. Is it a contract or is it a judgment? According to some authorities, it is merely a private contract between the litigating parties. Others view it as a judgment of the court. According to one commentator, the "dominant modern view is that a consent decree is a hybrid, with elements of both contract and judgment," Which would require a court to decide whether a particular problem implicates the contract or the judgment aspects of the decree. Larry Kramer, *Consent Decrees and the Rights of Third Parties*, 87 MICH.L.REV. 321, 324 (1988). A settlement by consent decree has several advantages. First, if either party breaches the agreement, the other party can enforce it by means of contempt sanctions without having to file an independent lawsuit. No waiting and no expense of a separate suit is required. Second, the court will likely take an active role in seeing that the settlement is carried out. This is particularly true in complicated settlements that are to be worked out over a period of years, such as the settlement of environmental litigation involving the implementation of pollution controls either by rule or by construction of facilities. Third, the consent decree may be more easily modified during the course of settlement activity than a simple contract. Fourth, the consent decree, as a judgment of a court, is res judicata, binding the parties so they may not file a fresh lawsuit. Finally, from the perspective of the court rather than the litigants, the consent decree has the obvious advantage of calendar-clearing; it facilitates the settlement of complex litigation without lengthy trials even though court supervision of its terms may be necessary. In short, the consent decree is cheaper and more expeditious for the parties, and it ends complex litigation for the court.

Used increasingly in the settlement of complex environmental and land use disputes, the consent decree nevertheless raises several troublesome issues. *First*, to what extent can the consent decree authorize local government action that is contrary to normal legal procedures? Does it make a difference if the court issuing the consent decree is a federal or state court? Does the subject matter of the litigation make a difference? Does it make a difference if the abbreviated or eliminated legal process is enshrined in state statute or local ordinance, regulation, or rule? *Second*, what is the effect of a consent decree on the due process rights of non-parties, such as neighbors or intervenors? Can a consent decree involving only the local government and the property owner eliminate a public hearing that would normally be required for a zoning change or a particular project approval?

The potential conflict between federal, state, and local laws is illustrated by *League of Residential Neighborhood Advocates v. City of Los Angeles*, 498 F.3d 1052 (9th Cir.2007), where a synagogue sued, complaining that the city's permit denial violated the Religious Land Use and Institutionalized Persons Act (RLUIPA). RLUIPA is covered *supra* in Ch. 3.E.4. The district court approved a settlement entered into by the city and the synagogue, without public notice or hearing, which allowed the synagogue to be built. In approving the agreement, the district court authorized the city to disregard its zoning regulations based on finding "a *potential* violation of federal law." "This was incorrect," said the Court of Appeals. "Before approving any settlement agreement that authorizes a state or municipal entity to disregard its own statutes in the name of federal law, a district court must find that there has been or will be an *actual* violation of that federal law." *Id.* at 1057. "Even if such a finding is made, a district court would then have to consider the appropriateness of the agreed-to remedy under federal law." *Id.* at 1057, n.3.

The federal courts appear to be most likely to accept those aspects of the consent decree that direct action outside of, if not in contravention of, state and local processes for dealing with the use of land. This is particularly true in the fields of housing discrimination and environmental law, but the interest of the federal courts in settling any complex litigation appears also to be a compelling reason. In state courts, the situation is by no means so clear. Many state courts still refuse to permit the use of the consent decree to circumscribe state and local land use or environmental procedures. However, it is possible to explain away the difference solely on the basis of separation of powers. State courts are coequal with the state legislature, which, either directly or through local governments, sets out certain provisions that the court is loath to tamper with through the consent decree.

The matter of procedural due process rights of third parties is murkier still, with both federal and state courts in disagreement over whether such rights can be cut off. Clearly the courts should and do require some measure of due process. But to the extent the affected parties are permitted to intervene in court proceedings in a meaningful fashion prior to the consent decree, then whether or not it is to their liking, courts appear to be willing to cut off intervenors' rights to collaterally attack the consent judgment that results, particularly given the courts' predilection for ending complex and expensive litigation.

The use of the consent decree to settle complex litigation thus presents a problem and opportunity: the avoidance of complex and lengthy land use and environmental impact approvals. There is theoretically little to prevent the local government and landowner from agreeing to settle litigation by means of a consent decree granting approval of development without all the procedures and permits required by state or local law, including lengthy hearing requirements, so long as due process rights of third parties are honored to some extent in the judicial process. On the other hand, it behooves the courts to take special care that they do not become an unwilling substitute for local land use and environmental permit agencies simply for the sake of convenience and expediency. *See* David L. Callies, *The Use of Consent Decrees in Settling Land Use and Environmental Disputes*, 21 STETSON L.REV. 871 (1992). Since settlements between the government and the landowner/developer omit the neighbors who may object to the agreement, the neighbors' only option is to sue to void the agreement. Would it not be better to require them to intervene? *See* Stewart E. Sterk, *Structural Obstacles to Settlement of Land Use Disputes*, 91 B.U.L.REV. 227 (2011).

2. THE FEDERAL FAIR HOUSING ACT AND RACIAL DISCRIMINATION

DEPARTMENT OF HOUSING AND COMMUNITY AFFAIRS V. THE INCLUSIVE COMMUNITIES PROJECT, INC.

Supreme Court of the United States, 2015.
135 S.Ct. 2507, 192 L.Ed.2d 514.

JUSTICE KENNEDY delivered the opinion of the Court.

The underlying dispute in this case concerns where housing for low-income persons should be constructed in Dallas, Texas—that is, whether the housing should be built in the inner city or in the suburbs. This dispute comes to the Court on a disparate impact theory of liability. In contrast to a disparate-treatment case, where a "plaintiff must establish that the defendant had a discriminatory intent or motive," a plaintiff bringing a disparate impact claim challenges practices that have a "disproportionately adverse effect on minorities" and are otherwise unjustified by a legitimate rationale. *Ricci v. DeStefano*, 557 U.S. 557, 577 (2009). The question presented for the Court's determination is whether disparate impact claims are cognizable under the Fair Housing Act (or FHA), 82 Stat. 81, as amended, 42 U.S.C. § 3601 *et seq.*

I

Before turning to the question presented, it is necessary to discuss a different federal statute that gives rise to this dispute. The Federal Government provides low-income housing tax credits that are distributed to developers through designated state agencies. 26 U.S.C. § 42. Congress has directed States to develop plans identifying selection criteria for distributing the credits.

* * *

In the State of Texas these federal credits are distributed by the Texas Department of Housing and Community Affairs (Department). Under Texas law, a developer's application for the tax credits is scored under a point system that gives priority to statutory criteria, such as the financial feasibility of the development project and the income level of tenants. The Texas Attorney General has interpreted state law to permit the consideration of additional criteria, such as whether the housing units will be built in a neighborhood with good schools. Those criteria cannot be awarded more points than statutorily mandated criteria.

The Inclusive Communities Project, Inc. (ICP) is a Texas-based nonprofit corporation that assists low-income families in obtaining affordable housing. In 2008, the ICP brought this suit against the Department and its officers in the United States District Court for the Northern District of Texas. As relevant here, it brought a disparate impact claim under §§ 804(a) and 805(a) of the FHA. The ICP alleged the Department has caused continued segregated housing patterns by its disproportionate allocation of the tax credits, granting too many credits for housing in predominantly black inner-city areas and too few in predominantly white suburban neighborhoods. The ICP contended that the Department must modify its selection criteria in order to encourage the construction of low-income housing in suburban communities.

The District Court concluded that the ICP had established a prima facie case of disparate impact. It relied on two pieces of statistical evidence. First, it found "from 1999–2008, [the Department] approved tax credits for 49.7% of proposed non-elderly units in 0% to 9.9% Caucasian areas, but only approved 37.4% of proposed non-elderly units in 90% to 100% Caucasian areas." 749 F.Supp.2d 486, 499 (N.D. Tex. 2010). Second, it found "92.29% of [low-income housing tax credit] units in the city of Dallas were located in census tracts with less than 50% Caucasian residents." *Id.*

The District Court then placed the burden on the Department to rebut the ICP's prima facie showing of disparate impact. 860 F.Supp.2d 312, 322–323 (2012). After assuming the Department's proffered interests were legitimate, the District Court held that a defendant—here the Department—must prove "that there are no other less discriminatory alternatives to advancing their proffered interests." Because, in its view, the Department "failed to meet [its] burden of proving that there are no less discriminatory alternatives," the District Court ruled for the ICP.

* * *

While the Department's appeal was pending, the Secretary of Housing and Urban Development (HUD) issued a regulation interpreting the FHA to encompass disparate-impact liability. *See* Implementation of the Fair Housing Act's Discriminatory Effects Standard, 78 Fed. Reg. 11460 (2013). The regulation also established a burden-shifting framework for adjudicating disparate impact claims. Under the regulation, a plaintiff first must make a prima facie showing of disparate impact. That is, the plaintiff "has the burden of proving that a challenged practice caused or predictably will cause a discriminatory effect." If a statistical discrepancy is caused by factors other than the defendant's policy, a plaintiff cannot establish a prima facie case, and there is no liability. After a plaintiff does establish a prima facie showing of disparate impact, the burden shifts to the defendant to "prov[e] that the challenged practice is necessary to achieve one or more substantial, legitimate, nondiscriminatory interests." HUD has clarified that this step of the analysis "is analogous to the Title VII requirement that an employer's interest in an employment practice with a disparate impact be job related." 78 Fed. Reg. 11470. Once a defendant has satisfied its burden at step two, a plaintiff may "prevail upon proving that the substantial, legitimate, nondiscriminatory interests supporting the challenged practice could be served by another practice that has a less discriminatory effect."

The Court of Appeals for the Fifth Circuit held, consistent with its precedent, that disparate impact claims are cognizable under the FHA. 747 F.3d 275, 280 (2014). On the merits, however, the Court of Appeals reversed and remanded. Relying on HUD's regulation, the Court of Appeals held that it was improper for the District Court to have placed the burden on the Department to prove there were no less discriminatory alternatives for allocating low-income housing tax credits. In a concurring opinion, Judge Jones stated that on remand the District Court should reexamine whether the ICP had made out a prima facie case of disparate impact. She suggested the District Court incorrectly relied on bare statistical evidence without engaging in any analysis about causation. She further observed that, if the federal law providing for the distribution of low-income housing tax credits ties the Department's hands to such an extent that it lacks a meaningful choice, then there is no disparate impact liability.

The Department filed a petition for a writ of certiorari on the question whether disparate impact claims are cognizable under the FHA. The question was one of first impression, and certiorari followed. It is now appropriate to provide a brief history of the FHA's enactment and its later amendment.

De jure residential segregation by race was declared unconstitutional almost a century ago, *Buchanan v. Warley*, 245 U.S. 60 (1917), but its vestiges remain today, intertwined with the country's economic and social life. Some segregated housing patterns can be traced to conditions that arose in the mid-20th century. Rapid urbanization, concomitant with the rise of suburban developments accessible by car, led many white families to leave the inner cities. This often left minority families concentrated in the center of the Nation's cities. During this time, various practices were followed, sometimes with governmental support, to encourage and maintain the separation of the races: racially restrictive covenants prevented the conveyance of property to minorities, *see Shelley v. Kraemer*, 334 U.S. 1 (1948); steering by real-estate agents led potential buyers to consider homes in racially homogenous areas; and discriminatory lending practices, often referred to as redlining, precluded minority families from purchasing homes in affluent areas. *See, e.g.*, M. Klarman, *Unfinished Business: Racial Equality in American History* 140–141 (2007); Brief for Housing Scholars as Amici Curiae 22–23. By the 1960's, these policies, practices, and prejudices had created many predominantly black inner cities surrounded by mostly white suburbs. *See* K. Clark, *Dark Ghetto: Dilemmas of Social Power* 11, 21–26 (1965).

The mid-1960's was a period of considerable social unrest; and, in response, President Lyndon Johnson established the National Advisory Commission on Civil Disorders, commonly known as the Kerner Commission. After extensive fact-finding, the Commission identified residential segregation and unequal housing and economic conditions in the inner cities as significant, underlying causes of the social unrest. *See* Report of the National Advisory Commission on Civil Disorders 91 (1968) (Kerner Commission Report). * * * The Commission concluded that "[o]ur Nation is moving toward two societies, one black, one white—separate and unequal." *Id.* at 1. To reverse "[t]his deepening racial division," it recommended enactment of "a comprehensive and enforceable open-occupancy law making it an offense to discriminate in the sale or rental of any housing . . . on the basis of race, creed, color, or national origin." *Id.* at 263.

In April 1968, Dr. Martin Luther King, Jr., was assassinated in Memphis, Tennessee, and the Nation faced a new urgency to resolve the social unrest in the inner cities. Congress responded by adopting the Kerner Commission's recommendation and passing the Fair Housing Act. The statute addressed the denial of housing opportunities on the basis of "race, color, religion, or national origin." Then, in 1988, Congress amended the FHA. Among other provisions, it created certain exemptions from liability and added "familial status" as a protected characteristic. *See* Fair Housing Amendments Act of 1988, 102 Stat. 1619.

II

The issue here is whether, under a proper interpretation of the FHA, housing decisions with a disparate impact are prohibited. Before turning to the FHA, however, it is necessary to consider two other antidiscrimination statutes that preceded it.

The first relevant statute is § 703(a) of Title VII of the Civil Rights Act of 1964, 78 Stat. 255. The Court addressed the concept of disparate impact under this statute in *Griggs v. Duke Power Co.*, 401 U.S. 424 (1971). There, the employer had a policy requiring its manual laborers to possess a high school diploma and to obtain satisfactory scores on two intelligence tests. The Court of Appeals held the employer had not adopted these job requirements for a racially discriminatory purpose, and the plaintiffs did not challenge that holding in this Court. Instead, the plaintiffs argued § 703(a)(2) covers the discriminatory effect of a practice as well as the motivation behind the practice.

* * *

* * * the Court held § 703(a)(2) of Title VII must be interpreted to allow disparate impact claims. *Id.* at 429–430.

* * *

The second relevant statute that bears on the proper interpretation of the FHA is the Age Discrimination in Employment Act of 1967 (ADEA), 81 Stat. 602 et seq., as amended. * * *

The Court first addressed whether this provision allows disparate impact claims in *Smith v. City of Jackson*, 544 U.S. 228 (2005). There, a group of older employees challenged their employer's decision to give proportionately greater raises to employees with less than five years of experience.

* * * As the plurality observed, the text of these provisions "focuses on the effects of the action on the employee rather than the motivation for the action of the employer" and therefore compels recognition of disparate impact liability. *Id.* at 236. * * *

* * *

Together, *Griggs* holds and the plurality in *Smith* instructs that antidiscrimination laws must be construed to encompass disparate impact claims when their text refers to the consequences of actions and not just to the mindset of actors, and where that interpretation is consistent with statutory purpose. These cases also teach that disparate impact liability must be limited so employers and other regulated entities are able to make the practical business choices and profit-related decisions that sustain a vibrant and dynamic free-enterprise system. And before rejecting a business justification—or, in the case of a governmental entity, an analogous public interest—a court must determine that a plaintiff has shown that there is "an available alternative . . . practice that has less disparate impact and serves the [entity's] legitimate needs." Ricci, *supra*, at 578. The cases interpreting Title VII and the ADEA provide essential background and instruction in the case now before the Court.

* * *

Recognition of disparate impact claims is consistent with the FHA's central purpose. The FHA, like Title VII and the ADEA, was enacted to eradicate discriminatory practices within a sector of our Nation's economy. See 42 U.S.C. § 3601 ("It is the policy of the United States to provide, within constitutional limitations, for fair housing throughout the United States"); H.R. Rep., at 15 (explaining the FHA "provides a clear national policy against discrimination in housing").

These unlawful practices include zoning laws and other housing restrictions that function unfairly to exclude minorities from certain neighborhoods without any sufficient justification. Suits targeting such practices reside at the heartland of disparate impact liability. The availability of disparate impact liability, furthermore, has allowed private developers to vindicate the FHA's objectives and to protect their property rights by stopping municipalities from enforcing arbitrary and, in practice, discriminatory ordinances barring the construction of certain types of housing units. Recognition of disparate impact liability under the FHA also plays a role in uncovering discriminatory intent: It permits plaintiffs to counteract unconscious prejudices and disguised animus that escape easy classification as disparate treatment. In this way disparate impact liability may prevent segregated housing patterns that might otherwise result from covert and illicit stereotyping.

* * *

Unlike the heartland of disparate impact suits targeting artificial barriers to housing, the underlying dispute in this case involves a novel theory of liability. This case, on remand, may be seen simply as an attempt to second-guess which of two reasonable approaches a housing authority should follow in the sound exercise of its discretion in allocating tax credits for low-income housing.

An important and appropriate means of ensuring that disparate impact liability is properly limited is to give housing authorities and private developers leeway to state and explain the valid interest served by their policies. This step of the analysis is analogous to the business necessity standard under Title VII and provides a defense against disparate-impact liability. *See* 78 Fed.Reg. 11470 (explaining that HUD did not use the phrase "business necessity" because that "phrase may not be easily understood to cover the full scope of practices covered by the Fair

Housing Act, which applies to individuals, businesses, nonprofit organizations, and public entities").

* * *

It would be paradoxical to construe the FHA to impose onerous costs on actors who encourage revitalizing dilapidated housing in our Nation's cities merely because some other priority might seem preferable. Entrepreneurs must be given latitude to consider market factors. Zoning officials, moreover, must often make decisions based on a mix of factors, both objective (such as cost and traffic patterns) and, at least to some extent, subjective (such as preserving historic architecture). These factors contribute to a community's quality of life and are legitimate concerns for housing authorities. The FHA does not decree a particular vision of urban development; and it does not put housing authorities and private developers in a double bind of liability, subject to suit whether they choose to rejuvenate a city core or to promote new low-income housing in suburban communities. As HUD itself recognized in its recent rulemaking, disparate impact liability "does not mandate that affordable housing be located in neighborhoods with any particular characteristic." 78 Fed.Reg. 11476.

In a similar vein, a disparate-impact claim that relies on a statistical disparity must fail if the plaintiff cannot point to a defendant's policy or policies causing that disparity. A robust causality requirement ensures that "[r]acial imbalance . . . does not, without more, establish a prima facie case of disparate impact" and thus protects defendants from being held liable for racial disparities they did not create. *Wards Cove Packing Co. v. Atonio*, 490 U.S. 642, 653 (1989), superseded by statute on other grounds, 42 U.S.C. § 2000e–2(k). Without adequate safeguards at the prima facie stage, disparate impact liability might cause race to be used and considered in a pervasive way and "would almost inexorably lead" governmental or private entities to use "numerical quotas," and serious constitutional questions then could arise. 490 U.S. at 653.

* * *

Courts must therefore examine with care whether a plaintiff has made out a prima facie case of disparate impact and prompt resolution of these cases is important. A plaintiff who fails to allege facts at the pleading stage or produce statistical evidence demonstrating a causal connection cannot make out a prima facie case of disparate impact. For instance, a plaintiff challenging the decision of a private developer to construct a new building in one location rather than another will not easily be able to show this is a policy causing a disparate impact because such a one-time decision may not be a policy at all. It may also be difficult to establish causation because of the multiple factors that go into investment decisions about where to construct or renovate housing units. And as Judge Jones observed below, if the ICP cannot show a causal connection between the Department's policy and a disparate impact—for instance, because federal law substantially limits the Department's discretion—that should result in dismissal of this case.

* * *

The limitations on disparate impact liability discussed here are also necessary to protect potential defendants against abusive disparate impact claims. If the specter of disparate impact litigation causes private developers to no longer construct or renovate housing units for low-income individuals, then the FHA would have undermined its own purpose as well as the free-market system. And as to governmental entities, they must not be prevented from achieving legitimate objectives, such as ensuring compliance with health and safety codes.

* * *

Were standards for proceeding with disparate impact suits not to incorporate at least the safeguards discussed here, then disparate impact liability might displace valid governmental and private priorities, rather than solely "remov[ing] . . . artificial, arbitrary, and unnecessary barriers." *Griggs*, 401 U.S. at 431. And that, in turn, would set our Nation back in its quest to reduce the salience of race in our social and economic system.

It must be noted further that, even when courts do find liability under a disparate impact theory, their remedial orders must be consistent with the Constitution. Remedial orders in disparate impact cases should concentrate on the elimination of the offending practice that "arbitrar[ily] . . . operate[s] invidiously to discriminate on the basis of rac[e]." *Id*. If additional measures are adopted, courts should strive to design them to eliminate racial disparities through race-neutral means. *See Richmond v. J.A. Croson Co.*, 488 U.S. 469, 510 (1989) (plurality opinion) ("[T]he city has at its disposal a whole array of race-neutral devices to increase the accessibility of city contracting opportunities to small entrepreneurs of all races"). Remedial orders that impose racial targets or quotas might raise more difficult constitutional questions.

While the automatic or pervasive injection of race into public and private transactions covered by the FHA has special dangers, it is also true that race may be considered in certain circumstances and in a proper fashion. *Cf. Parents Involved in Community Schools v. Seattle School Dist. No. 1*, 551 U.S. 701, 789 (2007) (KENNEDY, J., concurring in part and concurring in judgment) ("School boards may pursue the goal of bringing together students of diverse backgrounds and races through other means, including strategic site selection of new schools; [and] drawing attendance zones with general recognition of the demographics of neighborhoods"). Just as this Court has not "question[ed] an employer's affirmative efforts to ensure that all groups have a fair opportunity to apply for promotions and to participate in the [promotion] process," *Ricci*, 557 U.S. at 585, it likewise does not impugn housing authorities' race-neutral efforts to encourage revitalization of communities that have long suffered the harsh consequences of segregated housing patterns. When setting their larger goals, local housing authorities may choose to foster diversity and combat racial isolation with race-neutral tools, and mere awareness of race in attempting to solve the problems facing inner cities does not doom that endeavor at the outset.

* * *

III

In light of the longstanding judicial interpretation of the FHA to encompass disparate impact claims and congressional reaffirmation of that result, residents and policymakers have come to rely on the availability of disparate impact claims. Indeed, many of our Nation's largest cities— entities that are potential defendants in disparate-impact suits—have submitted an amicus brief in this case supporting disparate-impact liability under the FHA. The existence of disparate-impact liability in the substantial majority of the Courts of Appeals for the last several decades "has not given rise to . . . dire consequences." *Hosanna-Tabor Evangelical Lutheran Church and School v. EEOC*, 132 S.Ct. 694, 710 (2012).

Much progress remains to be made in our Nation's continuing struggle against racial isolation. In striving to achieve our "historic commitment to creating an integrated society," *Parents Involved, supra*, at 797 (KENNEDY, J., concurring in part and concurring in judgment), we must remain wary of policies that reduce homeowners to nothing more than their race. But since the passage of the Fair Housing Act in 1968 and against the backdrop of disparate-impact liability in nearly every jurisdiction, many cities have become more diverse. The FHA must play an important part in avoiding the Kerner Commission's grim prophecy that "[o]ur Nation is moving toward two societies, one black, one white—separate and unequal." Kerner Commission Report 1. The Court acknowledges the Fair Housing Act's continuing role in moving the Nation toward a more integrated society.

The judgment of the Court of Appeals for the Fifth Circuit is affirmed, and the case is remanded for further proceedings consistent with this opinion.

It is so ordered.

* * *

JUSTICE ALITO, with whom THE CHIEF JUSTICE, JUSTICE SCALIA, and JUSTICE THOMAS join, dissenting (omitted).

NOTES

1.   The Fair Housing Act makes it unlawful to make housing unavailable *"because of* race, color, religion, sex, familial status, or national origin [or handicap]." (emphasis added) 42 U.S.C. § 3604. This has now been interpreted by the Supreme Court to allow liability for both intentional acts and acts that have a discriminatory impact. Making a case under the FHA based on intent is difficult but by no means impossible. In rebuilding the Louisiana coast after Hurricane Katrina, several parishes excluded or imposed moratoria on multi-family and rental housing with racially discriminatory intent to exclude African Americans. *See Greater New Orleans Fair Housing Action Center. v. St. Bernard Parish*, 641 F.Supp.2d 563 (E.D.La.2009) (moratoria violated the FHA). *See also* Stacy E. Seicshnaydre, *How Government Housing Perpetuates Racial Segregation: Lessons from Post-Katrina New Orleans*, 60 CATH.U.L.REV. 661 (2011).

2.   Once a plaintiff establishes a *prima facie* case under a disparate impact theory, the burden shifts to the defendant to prove that its actions furthered a legitimate, bona fide governmental interest and that no alternative would serve that interest with less discriminatory effect. This three-step process requires: 1) plaintiff to show that the government policy or practice has a disparate impact on a protected class under the FHA; 2) defendant to rebut a charge of discrimination by showing that the challenged practice or policy is not for discriminatory purposes, but is instead benign and neutral to achieve a public goal; and 3) plaintiff may show that there are other, less burdensome means to achieve the benign and neutral goals of the government. In the *Inclusive Communities* decision, Justice Kennedy primarily focused on the first step and pointed out that governmental liability could not be based solely on showing statistical disparity. Instead, the Court applied a "robust causality requirement" demanding that the plaintiff identify the government policy causing the disparity and that the plaintiff distinguish between "artificial, arbitrary and unnecessary barriers" and "displacement of valid governmental policies."

3.   Lower courts may construe *Inclusive Communities* as requiring an elevated burden for plaintiffs, particularly at the *prima facie* stage. On remand of this case to the district court, the court noted that it had not previously "give[n] the prima facie requirement the same emphasis the Supreme Court had given it." *Inclusive Communities Project, Inc. (ICP) v. Texas Dep't of Hous. & Cmty. Affairs (TDHCA)*, 2015 WL 5916220, at *3 (N.D.Tex. Oct. 8, 2015). The court concluded that, based upon the Supreme Court's decision, TDHCA should be allowed to challenge the ICP's *prima facie* showing even though TDHCA had not contested the *prima facie* case. *See* David L. Callies and Derek Simon, *Fair Housing, Discrimination and Inclusionary Zoning in the United States* 3J INT'L COMPAR. L. ____ (2017) and Brian J. Connolly, *Promise Unfulfilled? Zoning, Disparate Impact, and Affirmatively Furthering Fair Housing*, 48 THE URBAN LAWYER 785 (2016). *See also, Azam v. City of Columbia Heights*, 2016 WL 424966, at *1, 10–11 (D.Minn. Feb. 3, 2016) (holding that plaintiff failed to establish a *prima facie* case of disparate impact under the

"robust causality requirement"); *City of Los Angeles v. Wells Fargo & Co.*, 2015 WL 4398858, at *1, 7–8 (D.C.Cal. July 17, 2015) (defendant entitled to summary judgment because city failed to present sufficient "statistical disparity evidence" and failed to identify a policy causing the disparate impact); *Ellis v. City of Minneapolis*, 2015 WL 5009341, at *1, 8–12 (D.Minn. Aug. 24, 2015) (citing Justice Kennedy's "cautionary standards" and concluding plaintiffs failed to plead a *prima facie* case of disparate impact and failed to plead facts showing a causal link between the challenged policies and the disparity). *But see Rhode Island Comm'n for Human Rights v. Graul*, 2015 WL 4868904, at *1, 8–13 (D.R.I. Aug. 13, 2015) (granting plaintiff's motion for summary judgment as to liability and concluding, without citing ICP's burden-shifting standard, plaintiff satisfied three-step analysis).

4.   Standing under the federal Fair Housing Act has been interpreted to extend to the fullest limits of Article III, which requires injury in fact and the likelihood that court action can redress the injury. In *Huntington Branch, N.A.A.C.P. v. Town of Huntington*, 689 F.2d 391 (2d Cir.1982), *cert. denied,* 460 U.S. 1069 (1983), the court held plaintiffs had standing to bring an action, even though no federal housing monies under Section 8 were currently available to finance the proposed project; the possibility of monies being available at a later date could not be excluded.

5.   As noted in the statutory language quoted in Note 1, the Fair Housing Act is also available to challenge zoning decisions on other grounds such as familial status or disability. See discussion in Section D of this Chapter.

COMMENT: ENVIRONMENTAL JUSTICE

The environmental justice movement charges that locally unwanted land uses (LULUs), primarily waste facilities, are disproportionately sited in communities of color. A major aim of the movement is to rectify the siting process to equitably distribute LULUs among the broader population. *See generally* Juergensmeyer and Roberts, *Land Use Planning and Development Regulation Law* § 6.9 (3rd ed.2012).

The movement had its beginnings in 1979 when Dr. Robert Bullard published a report on disproportionate siting of solid waste facilities in Houston. Then, in 1982, Reverend Ben Chavis helped publicize the siting of a toxic waste landfill in rural Warren County, North Carolina, a predominantly black area. The movement gained national prominence in 1987, with the release of a report by the Commission for Racial Justice of the United Church of Christ. The commission reported that while socio-economic status played a role in the siting of LULUS, race was the most significant factor. *See generally* Robert D. Bullard and Jim Motavalli, *Some People Don't Have "The Complexion for Protection,"* Network, Inc., vol. 9, no. 4, Jul/Aug 1998, 1998 WL 16883680.

Studies produce conflicting conclusions as to whether low-income minority neighborhoods are disproportionately burdened by LULUs, and, if so, whether it is the siting process that causes this result. The United Church of Christ's

1987 report, updated in 1994, concludes that such evidence exists. Others disagree. Professor Vicki Been, who has studied and written on the matter extensively, observes that market forces, rather than the siting process, may be responsible for the problem. *See* Vicki Been, *Locally Undesirable Land Uses in Minority Neighborhoods: Disproportionate Siting or Market Dynamics?*, 103 YALE L.J. 1383 (1994); Vicki Been and Francis Gupta, *Coming to the Nuisance or Going to the Barrios?, A Longitudinal Analysis of Environmental Justice Claims*, 24 ECOLOGY L.Q. 1 (1997); Vicki Been, *Analyzing Evidence of Environmental Justice*, 11 J.LAND USE & ENVTL.L. 1 (1995).

Legal remedies to resist, or seek damages from, the siting of LULUs in communities of color have been difficult to come by. Equal protection is not likely to work. Poverty-based claims are not likely to succeed since poverty is not a suspect class. If racial discrimination is the basis for the suit, discriminatory intent must be shown, and that is difficult to do, as *Arlington Heights* demonstrates.

Efforts to use various federal civil rights statutes have not fared well. Initially, Title VI of the Civil Rights Act of 1964, 42 U.S.C.A. § 2000d, which prohibits racial discrimination in programs that receive federal assistance, showed promise of success. In one case, a court ordered that a city provide minorities with services equal to those provided whites pursuant to Title VI. *Johnson v. City of Arcadia*, 450 F.Supp. 1363 (M.D.Fla.1978). Then in *Alexander v. Sandoval*, 532 U.S. 275 (2001), the Court held that there is no private right of action under Title VI. Following that decision, the Third Circuit held that § 1983 could not be used to enforce a regulation purporting to create a disparate impact cause of action. *South Camden Citizens in Action v. New Jersey Depart. of Environmental Protection*, 274 F.3d 771 (3d Cir.2001), *cert. denied*, 536 U.S. 939 (2002). *See generally* Tara Ulezalka, *Race and Waste: The Quest for Environmental Justice*, TEMP.J.SCI.TECH. & ENVTL.L. 51 (2007) (assessing federal, state, and common law remedies); Melissa A. Hoffer, *Closing the Door on Private Enforcement of Title VI and EPA's Discriminatory Effects Regulations: Strategies for Environmental Justice Stakeholders after Sandoval and Gonzaga,* 38 NEW ENG.L.REV. 971 (2004).

The lack of reported successful cases may not, however, tell the whole story. Publicity about the issue has led to an increased level of consciousness in regulators, industry, and residents about the potential adverse health effects of living near waste facilities and the unfairness of subjecting communities of color to a disproportionate burden. This has caused a tightening of the site selection and permitting processes as demonstrated by the fact that permitting authorities have turned away several proposed sitings around the country after local residents complained. *See supra, Bullard and Motavalli.* Furthermore, President Clinton issued an executive order requiring federal agencies to identify and address disproportionately high adverse health effects from LULUs in communities of color. Exec. Order No. 12,898, 59 Fed.Reg. 7,629 (1994). The order does not create a private right of action, but studies done are subject to judicial review. *Saint Paul Branch of N.A.A.C.P. v. United States D.O.T.*, 764 F.Supp.2d 1092 (D.Minn.2011) (Final

Environmental Impact Statement (FEIS) for a light rail transit construction project adequately addressed mitigation of the displacement of businesses and residents caused by gentrification). According to one court, "[t]he opportunity for meaningful public involvement is the most important consideration in an environmental justice review." *Hinds County v. Mississippi Comm'n on Envtl. Quality*, 61 So.3d 877, 886 (Miss.2011). *See also* Rachael E. Salcido, *Reviving the Environmental Justice Agenda*, 91 CHI.-KENT REV. 115 (2016) (discussing the limits and tensions between environmental laws protecting the quality of the environment and environmental justice concerns about the distributional harms to minority and low-income communities).

Putting aside legal constraints, what about ethics? Consider:

> Whether anticoncentration or siting laws, permitting rules, public notice-and-comment requirements, administrative staffing policies, mapping, or enforcement strategies are utilized to curb the impacts of environmental justice issues, it is imperative that regulatory agencies be prepared to address the ethical issues noted above in order to develop successful environmental justice law and policy.

Julia C. Rinne & Carol E. Dinkins, *Environmental Justice: Merging Environmental Law and Ethics*, NAT.RESOURCES & ENV'T, Winter 2011, at 7.

Consider the effects of using eminent domain to condemn property of the poor. Recall in *Kelo v. City of New London*, *supra* Ch. 3, the Court held that a city could take property of middle class homeowners for the public purpose of economic development. In dissent, Justice Thomas said:

> The consequences of today's decision are not difficult to predict, and promise to be harmful. So-called "urban renewal" programs provide some compensation for the properties they take, but no compensation is possible for the subjective value of these lands to the individuals displaced and the indignity inflicted by uprooting them from their homes. Allowing the government to take property solely for public purposes is bad enough, but extending the concept of public purpose to encompass any economically beneficial goal guarantees that these losses will fall disproportionately on poor communities. Those communities are not only systematically less likely to put their lands to the highest and best social use, but are also the least politically powerful. If ever there were justification for intrusive judicial review of constitutional provisions that protect "discrete and insular minorities," *United States v. Carolene Products Co.,* 304 U.S. 144, 152, n.4 (1938), surely that principle would apply with great force to the powerless groups and individuals the Public Use Clause protects. The deferential standard this Court has adopted for the Public Use Clause is therefore deeply perverse. It encourages "those citizens with disproportionate influence and power in the political process, including large corporations and development firms" to victimize the weak.

125 S.Ct. at 2686–87. Do you agree? Professor Byrne's take on the matter differs. *See* J. Peter Byrne, *Condemnation of Low Income Residential Communities Under the Takings Clause*, 23 UCLA J.ENVTL.L. & POL'Y 131 (2005). *See also* Catherine E. Beideman, Note, *Eminent Domain and Environmental Justice: A New Standard of Review in Discrimination Cases*, 34 B.C.ENVTL.AFF.L.REV. 273 (2007).

State reforms that have followed *Kelo* have not benefited poor, predominantly minority, communities because the reforms, by and large, continue to allow condemnation of blighted areas. *See* David A. Dana, *The Law and Expressive Meaning of Condemning the Poor After* Kelo, 101 NW.U.L.REV. 365 (2007) and Audrey G. McFarlane, *The New Inner City: Class Transformation, Concentrated Affluence and the Obligations of the Police Power*, 8 U.PA.J.CONST.L. 1, 38–50 (2006).

D. REGULATING NONTRADITIONAL LIVING ARRANGEMENTS

From its inception, zoning has been obsessed with protecting the single family home from higher density or more intensive land use. Recall the *Euclid* Court's likening of apartments to parasites in areas set aside for "detached private house purposes," and the California Supreme Court's endorsement of zoning to "promote and perpetuate the American home" in the *Miller* case. *See* note 9 *supra* following *Euclid*, pg. 82. Zoning has also been concerned with not only how the land was used but also who used it. From its inception, zoning reflected a view, consistent with the times but now dated, of what constituted a family who could occupy those single family homes: mother, father, and their biological or adopted children.

Various non-traditional living arrangements have made their way into the traditional single family neighborhood. These include groups of college students renting houses to escape college dorm life, people banding together for religious reasons, people opening their homes to accept foster children, and private or governmental social agencies establishing homes for persons requiring assistance in independent living: the disabled, battered spouses, recovering substance abusers, and halfway houses for those on the path to release from prison.

Neighbors have mightily resisted the introduction of these living arrangements in traditional neighborhoods. To fight the entry of non-traditional housing arrangements neighbors rely on existing zoning laws, their ability to bring political pressure on local officials to create, if need be, new exclusionary zoning rules, the common law of nuisance, and private covenants.

In turn, proponents of non-traditional housing sometimes find they are able to trump local law with state and federal constitutional protections or state and federal fair housing acts. As the following cases indicate, they have had mixed success.

1. CONSTITUTIONAL CONSIDERATIONS

VILLAGE OF BELLE TERRE V. BORAAS

Supreme Court of the United States, 1974.
416 U.S. 1, 94 S.Ct. 1536, 39 L.Ed.2d 797.

MR. JUSTICE DOUGLAS delivered the opinion of the Court.

Belle Terre is a village on Long Island's north shore of about 220 homes inhabited by 700 people. Its total area is less than one square mile. It has restricted land use to one-family dwellings excluding lodging houses, boarding houses, fraternity houses, or multiple-dwelling houses. The word 'family' as used in the ordinance means, "(o)ne or more persons related by blood, adoption, or marriage, living and cooking together as a single housekeeping unit, exclusive of household servants. A number of persons but not exceeding two (2) living and cooking together as a single housekeeping unit though not related by blood, adoption, or marriage shall be deemed to constitute a family."

Appellees, the Dickmans, are owners of a house in the village and leased it in December 1971 for a term of 18 months to Michael Truman. Later Bruce Boraas became a colessee. Then Anne Parish moved into the house along with three others. These six are students at nearby State University at Stony Brook and none is related to the other by blood, adoption, or marriage. When the village served the Dickmans with an 'Order to Remedy Violations' of the ordinance,[1] the owners plus three tenants thereupon brought this action under 42 U.S.C. § 1983 for an injunction and a judgment declaring the ordinance unconstitutional. The District Court held the ordinance constitutional, and the Court of Appeals reversed.

* * *

The present ordinance is challenged on several grounds: that it interferes with a person's right to travel; that it interferes with the right to migrate to and settle within a State; that it bars people who are uncongenial to the present residents; that it expresses the social preferences of the residents for groups that will be congenial to them; that social homogeneity is not a legitimate interest of government; that the restriction of those whom the neighbors do not like trenches on the newcomers' rights of privacy; that it is of no rightful concern to villagers whether the residents are married or unmarried; that the ordinance is

---

[1] * * * During the litigation the lease expired and it was extended. Anne Parish moved out. Thereafter the other five students left and the owners now hold the home out for sale or rent, including to student groups.

antithetical to the Nation's experience, ideology, and self-perception as an open, egalitarian, and integrated society.[4]

We find none of these reasons in the record before us. It is not aimed at transients. *Cf. Shapiro v. Thompson*, 394 U.S. 618. It involves no procedural disparity inflicted on some but not on others such as was presented by *Griffin v. Illinois*, 351 U.S. 12. It involves no "fundamental" right guaranteed by the Constitution, such as voting, *Harper v. Virginia State Board*, 383 U.S. 663; the right of association, *NAACP v. Alabama ex rel. Patterson*, 357 U.S. 449; the right of access to the courts, *NAACP v. Button*, 371 U.S. 415; or any rights of privacy, *cf. Griswold v. Connecticut*, 381 U.S. 479; *Eisenstadt v. Baird*, 405 U.S. 438, 453–454. We deal with economic and social legislation where legislatures have historically drawn lines which we respect against the charge of violation of the Equal Protection Clause if the law be "reasonable, not arbitrary" (*quoting F.S. Royster Guano Co. v. Virginia*, 253 U.S. 412, 415) and bears "a rational relationship to a (permissible) state objective." *Reed v. Reed*, 404 U.S. 71, 76.

It is said, however, that if two unmarried people can constitute a "family," there is no reason why three or four may not. But every line drawn by a legislature leaves some out that might well have been included. That exercise of discretion, however, is a legislative, not a judicial, function.

It is said that the Belle Terre ordinance reeks with an animosity to unmarried couples who live together. There is no evidence to support it; and the provision of the ordinance bringing within the definition of a 'family' two unmarried people belies the charge.

The ordinance places no ban on other forms of association, for a "family" may, so far as the ordinance is concerned, entertain whomever it likes.

The regimes of boarding houses, fraternity houses, and the like present urban problems. More people occupy a given space; more cars rather continuously pass by; more cars are parked; noise travels with crowds.

A quiet place where yards are wide, people few, and motor vehicles restricted are legitimate guidelines in a land-use project addressed to family needs. This goal is a permissible one within *Berman v. Parker*, *supra*. The police power is not confined to elimination of filth, stench, and unhealthy places. It is ample to lay out zones where family values, youth values, and the blessings of quiet seclusion and clean air make the area a sanctuary for people.

---

[4]   Many references in the development of this thesis are made to F. Turner, *The Frontier in American History* (1920), with emphasis on his theory that "democracy (is) born of free land." *Id.*, at 32.

The suggestion that the case may be moot need not detain us. A zoning ordinance usually has an impact on the value of the property which it regulates. But in spite of the fact that the precise impact of the ordinance sustained in *Euclid* on a given piece of property was not known, 272 U.S., at 397, the Court, considering the matter a controversy in the realm of city planning, sustained the ordinance. Here we are a step closer to the impact of the ordinance on the value of the lessor's property. He has not only lost six tenants and acquired only two in their place; it is obvious that the scale of rental values rides on what we decide today. * * *

Reversed.

MR. JUSTICE BRENNAN, dissenting. [omitted].

MR. JUSTICE MARSHALL, dissenting.

* * * [I]t is appropriate that we afford zoning authorities considerable latitude in choosing the means by which to implement such purposes. But deference does not mean abdication. This Court has an obligation to ensure that zoning ordinances, even when adopted in furtherance of such legitimate aims, do not infringe upon fundamental constitutional rights.

* * *

My disagreement with the Court today is based upon my view that the ordinance in this case unnecessarily burdens appellees' First Amendment freedom of association and their constitutionally guaranteed right to privacy. Our decisions establish that the First and Fourteenth Amendments protect the freedom to choose one's associates. *NAACP v. Button*, 371 U.S. 415, 430 (1963). * * * The selection of one's living companions involves similar choices as to the emotional, social, or economic benefits to be derived from alternative living arrangements.

The freedom of association is often inextricably entwined with the constitutionally guaranteed right of privacy. The right to "establish a home" is an essential part of the liberty guaranteed by the Fourteenth Amendment. *Meyer v. Nebraska*, 262 U.S. 390, 399 (1923); *Griswold v. Connecticut*, 381 U.S. 479, 495 (1965) (GOLDBERG, J., concurring). And the Constitution secures to an individual a freedom "to satisfy his intellectual and emotional needs in the privacy of his own home." *Stanley v. Georgia*, 394 U.S. 557, 565 (1969). * * *

* * * Belle Terre imposes upon those who deviate from the community norm in their choice of living companions significantly greater restrictions than are applied to residential groups who are related by blood or marriage, and compose the established order within the community. The village has, in effect, acted to fence out those individuals whose choice of lifestyle differs from that of its current residents.

* * *

NOTES

1.   If the group in *Belle Terre* had been six nuns, would the Court have reached the same conclusion? A man and woman with four foster children? Two women each with two children living together for economic reasons? What if the *Belle Terre* ordinance had "reek[ed] with an animosity to unmarried couples?" *See City of Ladue v. Horn*, 720 S.W.2d 745 (Mo.App.1986) (zoning ordinance, with purpose of promoting marriage and the integrity of family values, could constitutionally exclude unmarried man and woman).

2.   The City of East Cleveland, Ohio, adopted an ordinance that allowed only single families. The ordinance defined family to include the head of household and spouse but it allowed them to have their unmarried children living with them only if there were no grandchildren. An exception provided that the head of the household and spouse could have one dependent child and the dependent children of that child live with them. Mrs. Moore lived with her son Dale, and Dale's son, Dale, Jr. A second grandson, John, came to live with Moore following his mother's death. At that point, the city notified Moore that she housed an illegal occupant (because John had a different parent than Dale, Jr.). When Moore failed to evict the child, criminal charges were filed against her. She was convicted, fined $25, and sentenced to five days in jail. Under *Belle Terre*, Moore's conviction would likely have been upheld. However, in a 5–4 decision, the Court found *Belle Terre* inapplicable and reversed the conviction. *Moore v. City of East Cleveland*, 431 U.S. 494 (1977). For the majority, Justice Powell reasoned:

> The city argues that our decision in *Village of Belle Terre v. Boraas*, 416 U.S. 1 (1974), requires us to sustain the ordinance attacked here. * * * But one overriding factor sets this case apart from *Belle Terre*. The ordinance there affected only unrelated individuals. It expressly allowed all who were related by "blood, adoption, or marriage" to live together, and in sustaining the ordinance we were careful to note that it promoted "family needs" and "family values." East Cleveland, in contrast, has chosen to regulate the occupancy of its housing by slicing deeply into the family itself. This is no mere incidental result of the ordinance. On its face it selects certain categories of relatives who may live together and declares that others may not. In particular, it makes a crime of a grandmother's choice to live with her grandson in circumstances like those presented here.
>
> When a city undertakes such intrusive regulation of the family, neither *Belle Terre* nor *Euclid* governs; the usual judicial deference to the legislature is inappropriate. "This Court has long recognized that freedom of personal choice in matters of marriage and family life is one of the liberties protected by the Due Process Clause of the Fourteenth Amendment." *Cleveland Board of Education v. LaFleur*, 414 U.S. 632, 639–640 (1974). * * * But when the government intrudes on choices concerning family living arrangements, this Court must examine carefully the importance of the governmental

interests advanced and the extent to which they are served by the challenged regulation. *See Poe v. Ullman, supra*, 367 U.S., at 554 (Harlan, J., dissenting).

431 U.S. at 499.

3.   To give its permanent residents some peace and quiet, Ames, Iowa, home to Iowa State University, defined a "family" as any number of related persons or no more than three unrelated persons. The court rejected equal protection claims under the state and federal constitutions. With regard to *Belle Terre*, the plaintiffs argued that "the Supreme Court will likely overturn *Belle Terre* if given the opportunity to do so." The court declined to "be so presumptuous to predict how the Supreme Court would rule if presented with this case." *Ames Rental Property Ass'n v. City of Ames*, 736 N.W.2d 255, 258 (Iowa 2007), *cert. denied*, 552 U.S. 1099, 128 S.Ct. 908, 169 L.Ed.2d 729 (2008). Have you seen any indications in the cases studied to lead you to think the Supreme Court would overrule *Belle Terre*? Have notions of "family" changed since 1974 such that the Court should reexamine its opinion?

The Iowa court found the notion of requiring cities to allow an "Animal House hubbub" in single-family zones unreasonable. Discussing the ordinance's underinclusiveness, the court said "sure, the ordinance would allow the Beverly Hillbillies to live in a single-family zone while prohibiting four judges from doing so. However, neither hypothetical is typical of reality." *Id.* at 260–261, 262.

Several state courts interpret their constitutions to invalidate ordinances like Belle Terre's. Generally, they rely on substantive due process or privacy to find a right of persons to choose their living companions without regard to blood, marriage, or adoption. *See City of Santa Barbara v. Adamson*, 164 Cal.Rptr. 539, 610 P.2d 436 (1980); *New Jersey v. Baker*, 405 A.2d 368 (N.J.1979); *Charter Township of Delta v. Dinolfo*, 351 N.W.2d 831 (Mich.1984). *But see Dvorak v. City of Bloomington*, 796 N.E.2d 236 (Ind.2003) (ordinance prohibiting occupancy by more than three unrelated adults did not violate state privileges and immunities clause); *State v. Champoux*, 555 N.W.2d 69 (Neb.App.1996) *aff'd*, 566 N.W.2d 763 (Neb.1997).

4.   Widespread flooding following Hurricane Katrina in 2005 created a severe housing shortage in St. Bernard Parish, Louisiana. In 2006, the council responded to the shortage by enacting an ordinance prohibiting "persons from renting, leasing, loaning, or otherwise allowing occupancy or use of any single-family residence other than by family members related by blood, without first obtaining a Permissive Use Permit." Do you see how the ordinance would solve the problems created by the storm?

A fair housing organization promptly sued in federal district court to enjoin enforcement of this "blood relative" law. The court invalidated the law, and enjoined the parish from re-enacting it. The parish did enact the same ordinance, deleting the blood relative exception and limiting the prohibition to rental without a permit. The council then notified the plaintiffs, who had purchased at least 50 houses for rental purposes before enactment of the rental prohibition, that they were in violation of the law. The plaintiffs challenged the ordinance on several constitutional grounds. What arguments might they have made?

5.   In *City of Cleburne v. Cleburne Living Center*, 473 U.S. 432 (1985), the Texas city's zoning ordinance required a special use permit for a group home for mentally disabled. The Court reviewed the Fifth Circuit's decision that mental retardation is a "quasi-suspect" classification and that the ordinance violated Equal Protection. The Court instead applied a lesser standard of scrutiny—the rational basis test—but nevertheless concluded that the ordinance violated Equal Protection as applied in this case. The Court concluded that "requiring the permit in this case appears to us to rest on an irrational prejudice against the mentally retarded." *Id.* at 450. Justice Marshall concurred in the judgment in part and dissented in part, noting that "[t]he Court holds the ordinance invalid on rational-basis grounds and disclaims that anything special, in the form of heightened scrutiny, is taking place. Yet Cleburne's ordinance surely would be valid under the traditional rational-basis test applicable to economic and commercial regulation."

Would the *Belle Terre* ordinance have failed if the Court had employed the kind of rational basis scrutiny it used in *Cleburne*? Should *Cleburne*-type scrutiny be used in such cases?

6.   When does *Cleburne* rational basis apply and when does *Belle Terre* rational basis apply? In *Jacobs, Visconsi & Jacobs, Co. v. City of Lawrence*, 927 F.2d 1111 (10th Cir.1991), the court refused to apply *Cleburne*-type scrutiny in favor of a shopping center developer. The court said *Cleburne's* "exacting rational basis" scrutiny focused on "politically unpopular groups" and shopping center developers did not qualify. 927 F.2d at 1119, n.6. Regulation of a residential substance abuse center was protected by *Cleburne* scrutiny, *see Open Homes Fellowship, Inc. v. Orange County*, 325 F.Supp.2d 1349 (M.D.Fla.2004), but a shelter for battered women was not. *Doe v. City of Butler*, 892 F.2d 315 (3d Cir.1989).

7.   After *Cleburne*, could a village like Belle Terre, consistent with the equal protection clause, exclude a home for the mentally retarded? If the answer is yes, the village still must contend with the federal Fair Housing Amendments Act of 1988, as the following case demonstrates.

2.   DISCRIMINATION AGAINST THE DISABLED UNDER THE FEDERAL FAIR HOUSING ACT

In 1988 Congress amended the Fair Housing Act to ban discrimination against persons who are "handicapped." 42 U.S.C.A. § 3602(h).[1] An explosion of litigation, most of it dealing with the handicap provision,

---

[1]   The amendments also prohibit discrimination on the basis of "familial status," i.e., discrimination against parents or other custodial persons domiciled with children under the age of 18. 42 U.S.C. § 3602(k). See also discussion of such a claim, supra *Cuyahoga Falls v. Buckeye*.

followed. Under the act "[h]andicap" means, with respect to a person—(1) a physical or mental impairment which substantially limits one or more of such person's major life activities, (2) a record of having such an impairment, or (3) being regarded as having such an impairment, but such term does not include current, illegal use of or addiction to a controlled substance (as defined in section 802 of Title 21). 42 U.S.C.A. § 3602 (h). The Act uses the term "handicapped," but the regulations use the term "disabled," reflecting currently accepted terminology to avoid stereotypes and patronizing attitudes that accompany the word "handicapped." 28 C.F.R., § 36.104, Pt. 36, App. B.

CITY OF EDMONDS v. OXFORD HOUSE, INC.
Supreme Court of the United States, 1995.
514 U.S. 725, 115 S.Ct. 1776, 131 L.Ed.2d 801.

JUSTICE GINSBURG delivered the opinion of the Court.

The Fair Housing Act (FHA or Act) prohibits discrimination in housing against, *inter alios*, persons with handicaps.[1] Section 3607(b)(1) of the Act entirely exempts from the FHA's compass "any reasonable local, State, or Federal restrictions regarding the maximum number of occupants permitted to occupy a dwelling." 42 U.S.C. § 3607(b)(1). This case presents the question whether a provision in petitioner City of Edmonds' zoning code qualifies for § 3607(b)(1)'s complete exemption from FHA scrutiny. The provision, governing areas zoned for single-family dwelling units, defines "family" as "persons [without regard to number] related by genetics, adoption, or marriage, or a group of five or fewer [unrelated] persons." Edmonds Community Development Code (ECDC) § 21.30.010 (1991).

The defining provision at issue describes who may compose a family unit; it does not prescribe "*the* maximum number of occupants" a dwelling unit may house. We hold that § 3607(b)(1) does not exempt prescriptions of the family-defining kind, *i.e.*, provisions designed to foster the family character of a neighborhood. Instead, § 3607(b)(1)'s absolute exemption removes from the FHA's scope only total occupancy limits, *i.e.*, numerical ceilings that serve to prevent overcrowding in living quarters.

In the summer of 1990, respondent Oxford House opened a group home in the City of Edmonds, Washington for 10 to 12 adults recovering from alcoholism and drug addiction. The group home, called Oxford House-Edmonds, is located in a neighborhood zoned for single-family residences. Upon learning that Oxford House had leased and was operating a home in

---

[1] The FHA, as originally enacted in 1968, prohibited discrimination based on race, color, religion, or national origin. *See* 82 Stat. 83. Proscription of discrimination based on sex was added in 1974. See Housing and Community Development Act of 1974, § 808(b), 88 Stat. 729. In 1988, Congress extended coverage to persons with handicaps and also prohibited "familial status" discrimination, i.e., discrimination against parents or other custodial persons domiciled with children under the age of 18. 42 U.S.C. § 3602(k).

Edmonds, the City issued criminal citations to the owner and a resident of the house. The citations charged violation of the zoning code rule that defines who may live in single-family dwelling units. The occupants of such units must compose a "family," and family, under the City's defining rule, "means an individual or two or more persons related by genetics, adoption, or marriage, or a group of five or fewer persons who are not related by genetics, adoption, or marriage." Edmonds Community Development Code (ECDC) § 21.30.010. Oxford House-Edmonds houses more than five unrelated persons, and therefore does not conform to the code.

Oxford House asserted reliance on the Fair Housing Act, 42 U.S.C. § 3601 et seq., which declares it unlawful "[t]o discriminate in the sale or rental, or to otherwise make unavailable or deny, a dwelling to any buyer or renter because of a handicap of . . . that buyer or a renter." § 3604(f)(1)(A). The parties have stipulated, for purposes of this litigation, that the residents of Oxford House-Edmonds "are recovering alcoholics and drug addicts and are handicapped persons within the meaning" of the Act.

Discrimination covered by the FHA includes "a refusal to make reasonable accommodations in rules, policies, practices, or services, when such accommodations may be necessary to afford [handicapped] person[s] equal opportunity to use and enjoy a dwelling." § 3604(f)(3)(B). Oxford House asked Edmonds to make a "reasonable accommodation" by allowing it to remain in the single-family dwelling it had leased. Group homes for recovering substance abusers, Oxford urged, need 8 to 12 residents to be financially and therapeutically viable. Edmonds declined to permit Oxford House to stay in a single-family residential zone, but passed an ordinance listing group homes as permitted uses in multifamily and general commercial zones.

* * *

The sole question before the Court is whether Edmonds' family composition rule qualifies as a "restrictio[n] regarding the maximum number of occupants permitted to occupy a dwelling" within the meaning of the FHA's absolute exemption. 42 U.S.C. § 3607(b)(1).[4] In answering this question, we are mindful of the Act's stated policy "to provide, within constitutional limitations, for fair housing throughout the United States." § 3601. We also note precedent recognizing the FHA's "broad and inclusive" compass, and therefore according a "generous construction" to the Act's complaint-filing provision. Accordingly, we regard this case as an instance in which an exception to "a general statement of policy" is sensibly read "narrowly in order to preserve the primary operation of the [policy]."

---

[4]   Like the District Court and the Ninth Circuit, we do not decide whether Edmonds' zoning code provision defining "family," as the City would apply it against Oxford House, violates the FHA's prohibitions against discrimination set out in 42 U.S.C. §§ 3604(f)(1)(A) and (f)(3)(B).

Congress enacted § 3607(b)(1) against the backdrop of an evident distinction between municipal land use restrictions and maximum occupancy restrictions.

* * *

Land use restrictions aim to prevent problems caused by the "pig in the parlor instead of the barnyard." *Village of Euclid v. Ambler Realty Co.* In particular, reserving land for single-family residences preserves the character of neighborhoods, securing "zones where family values, youth values, and the blessings of quiet seclusion and clean air make the area a sanctuary for people." *Village of Belle Terre v. Boraas; see also Moore v. City of East Cleveland*, 431 U.S. 494, 521 (1977) (Burger, C.J., dissenting) (purpose of East Cleveland's single-family zoning ordinance "is the traditional one of preserving certain areas as family residential communities"). To limit land use to single-family residences, a municipality must define the term "family"; thus family composition rules are an essential component of single-family residential use restrictions.

Maximum occupancy restrictions, in contradistinction, cap the number of occupants per dwelling, typically in relation to available floor space or the number and type of rooms. * * * These restrictions ordinarily apply uniformly to all residents of all dwelling units. Their purpose is to protect health and safety by preventing dwelling overcrowding. *See, e.g.,* BOCA Code §§ PM–101.3, PM–405.3, PM–405.5 and commentary; *Abbott, Housing Policy, Housing Codes and Tenant Remedies*, 56 B.U.L.REV. 1, 41–45 (1976).

We recognized this distinction between maximum occupancy restrictions and land use restrictions in *Moore v. City of East Cleveland*. In *Moore*, the Court held unconstitutional the constricted definition of "family" contained in East Cleveland's housing ordinance. East Cleveland's ordinance "select[ed] certain categories of relatives who may live together and declare[d] that others may not"; in particular, East Cleveland's definition of "family" made "a crime of a grandmother's choice to live with her grandson." In response to East Cleveland's argument that its aim was to prevent overcrowded dwellings, streets, and schools, we observed that the municipality's restrictive definition of family served the asserted, and undeniably legitimate, goals "marginally, at best." Another East Cleveland ordinance, we noted, "specifically addressed * * * the problem of overcrowding"; that ordinance tied "the maximum permissible occupancy of a dwelling to the habitable floor area." * * *

Section 3607(b)(1)'s language—"restrictions regarding the maximum number of occupants permitted to occupy a dwelling"—surely encompasses maximum occupancy restrictions.[8] But the formulation does not fit family

---

[8]   The plain import of the statutory language is reinforced by the House Committee Report, which observes: "A number of jurisdictions limit the number of occupants per unit based on a

composition rules typically tied to land use restrictions. In sum, rules that cap the total number of occupants in order to prevent overcrowding of a dwelling "plainly and unmistakably," fall within § 3607(b)(1)'s absolute exemption from the FHA's governance; rules designed to preserve the family character of a neighborhood, fastening on the composition of households rather than on the total number of occupants living quarters can contain, do not.

* * *

Edmonds nevertheless argues that its family composition rule, ECDC § 21.30.010, falls within § 3607(b)(1), the FHA exemption for maximum occupancy restrictions, because the rule caps at five the number of unrelated persons allowed to occupy a single-family dwelling. But Edmonds' family composition rule surely does not answer the question: "What is the maximum number of occupants permitted to occupy a house?" So long as they are related "by genetics, adoption, or marriage," any number of people can live in a house. Ten siblings, their parents and grandparents, for example, could dwell in a house in Edmonds' single-family residential zone without offending Edmonds' family composition rule.

Family living, not living space per occupant, is what ECDC § 21.30.010 describes. Defining family primarily by biological and legal relationships, the provision also accommodates another group association: five or fewer unrelated people are allowed to live together as though they were family. This accommodation is the peg on which Edmonds rests its plea for § 3607(b)(1) exemption. Had the City defined a family solely by biological and legal links, § 3607(b)(1) would not have been the ground on which Edmonds staked its case. It is curious reasoning indeed that converts a family values preserver into a maximum occupancy restriction once a town adds to a related persons prescription "and also two unrelated persons."[11]

* * *

The parties have presented, and we have decided, only a threshold question: Edmonds' zoning code provision describing who may compose a "family" is not a maximum occupancy restriction exempt from the FHA under § 3607(b)(1). It remains for the lower courts to decide whether Edmonds' actions against Oxford House violate the FHA's prohibitions

---

minimum number of square feet in the unit or the sleeping areas of the unit. Reasonable limitations by governments would be allowed to continue, as long as they were applied to all occupants, and did not operate to discriminate on the basis of race, color, religion, sex, national origin, handicap or familial status." H.R.Rep. No. 100–711, p. 31 (1988).

[11] This curious reasoning drives the dissent. If Edmonds allowed only related persons (whatever their number) to dwell in a house in a single-family zone, then the dissent, it appears, would agree that the § 3607(b)(1) exemption is unavailable. But so long as the City introduces a specific number—any number (two will do)—the City can insulate its single-family zone entirely from FHA coverage. The exception-takes-the-rule reading the dissent advances is hardly the "generous construction" warranted for antidiscrimination prescriptions.

against discrimination set out in §§ 3604(f)(1)(A) and (f)(3)(B). For the reasons stated, the judgment of the United States Court of Appeals for the Ninth Circuit is *affirmed.*

JUSTICE THOMAS, with whom JUSTICE SCALIA and JUSTICE KENNEDY join, dissenting (omitted).

NOTES

1.   For a critique of how the 1988 Amendments "dramatically expanded the influence of federal law on local land use regulatory power," see Peter W. Salsich, Jr., *Federal Influence on Local Land Use Regulations: The Fair Housing Act Amendments*, 9 J. AFFORDABLE HOUSING & COMMUN.DEV.L. 228) (2000). Reported case law overturning municipal exclusion of the disabled is extensive. *See, e.g., First Step, Inc. v. City of New London*, 247 F.Supp.2d 135 (D.Conn.2003) (city's reasons pretextual).

2.   While the *Edmonds* Court eschews a narrow construction of the statutory exemption, its holding is narrow. In its closing paragraph, the majority notes that it still must be decided whether the town has discriminated against protected persons. Precisely what question must be answered?

3.   Discrimination covered by the FHA includes "a refusal to make reasonable accommodations in rules, policies, practices, or services, when such accommodations may be necessary to afford [handicapped] person[s] equal opportunity to use and enjoy a dwelling." 42 U.S.C.§ 3604(3)(B). What is a "reasonable accommodation"? Can group homes of unrelated, disabled persons be excluded from zones where persons who are related and who reside as single families are permitted? Is it enough of an accommodation to allow group homes somewhere in town? *See Tsombanidis v. West Haven Fire Dept.*, 352 F.3d 565 (2d Cir.2003) (Superseded by regulation; *see Mhany Management, Inc. v. County of Nassau*, 819 F.3d 581, 619 (2d Cir.2016, notes new HUD regulations)(where ordinance prohibited more than three unrelated persons to live together, city should have accommodated housing for seven men in recovery from alcohol and drug addiction under the FHAA and ADA).

4.   Can group homes be subjected to a special permit process under the Act? Under the Constitution? *See Cleburne. See generally* Robert L. Schonfeld, *"Reasonable Accommodation" Under the Federal Fair Housing Amendments Act*, 25 FORDHAM URB.L.J. 413–41 (1998); Louise C. Malkin, Comment, *Troubles at the Doorstep: The Fair Housing Act of 1988 and Group Homes for Recovering Substance Abusers*, 144 U.PA.L.REV. 759 (1995). A city need only accommodate therapeutic needs, not economic needs. See *Sanghvi v. City of Claremont*, 328 F.3d 532 (9th Cir.2003), where, the city refused to extend sewer service to an Alzheimer's care facility in an unincorporated area. This was held to be reasonable in part because the owners refused to be annexed (a city condition for sewer service) because they wished to avoid complying with city codes.

5.   What if such homes are allowed but are subject to a requirement that they cannot be placed within a quarter of a mile of similar facilities? *Compare*

Larkin v. Michigan Dept. of Social Services, 89 F.3d 285 (6th Cir.1996) (violative of Act) *with Familystyle of St. Paul, Inc. v. City of St. Paul*, 923 F.2d 91 (8th Cir.1991) (not violative of Act).

6.   In *Edmonds*, Oxford House opened its doors without seeking a variance from the code. Why do you suppose it did that? Was it ignorant of the law or was this an act of civil disobedience? If a provider like Oxford House decides to seek approval before opening where the ordinance, like that of *Edmonds*, on its face precludes the use it intends to pursue, what avenue of relief should it seek?

7.   As the large number of reported cases and the many stories in the local section of almost any newspaper attest, the 1988 amendment adding protection of the handicapped to the FHA exposed a raw nerve in the traditional American neighborhood. Does the FHA threaten the traditional single family neighborhood? If it does, is that a good or bad thing? *See* Brian E. Davis, *The State Giveth and the Court Taketh Away: Preserving the Municipality's Ability to Zone for Group Homes*, 59 U.PITT.L.REV. 193 (1997). One community went so far as to attempt to condemn land for a park to prevent a facility for disabled persons from locating there. *See Borough of Essex Fells v. Kessler Institute for Rehabilitation, Inc.*, 673 A.2d 856 (N.J.Super.1995) (holding that this effort was an unlawful use of the eminent domain power.

8.   Should federal law protect group homes for mentally disabled children while leaving group homes for orphans unprotected? *See* Michael J. Davis and Karen L. Gaus, *Protecting Group Homes for the Non-Handicapped: Zoning in the Post-*Edmonds *Era*, 46 U.KAN.L.REV. 777 (1998).

9.   In addition to the FHA, the Americans with Disabilities Act can be used to challenge municipal zoning actions, and its availability is vital in non-housing cases, where the FHA is inapplicable. The ADA provides that no person with a qualifying disability shall, "by reason of such disability, * * * be denied the benefits of the services, programs, or activities of a public entity, or be subjected to discrimination by such entity." 42 U.S.C.A. 12132. *See Bay Area Addiction Research and Treatment, Inc. v. City of Antioch*, 179 F.3d 725 (9th Cir.1999) and *Innovative Health Sys., Inc. v. City of White Plains*, 117 F.3d 37 (2d Cir.1997), *overruled on other grounds*; *Zervos v. Verizon New York, Inc.*, 252 F.3d 163, 171 n.7 (2d Cir.2001) (court preliminarily enjoined city from enforcing its zoning against an outpatient drug and alcohol rehabilitation treatment center that sought to locate in a business district).

As with the FHA, government must make reasonable modifications in policies when necessary to avoid discrimination on the basis of disability, unless it can demonstrate that to do so would fundamentally alter the nature of its activity. The legal analysis is essentially the same under the FHA and the ADA. *See, e.g., McGary v. City of Portland*, 386 F.3d 1259 (9th Cir.2004) (claim stated under the FHA and the ADA where the city was alleged to have failed to reasonably accommodate disability by denying plaintiff additional time to clean his yard in order to comply with city's nuisance abatement ordinance). *See also Forest City Daly Housing, Inc. v. Town of N. Hempstead,*

175 F.3d 144 (2d Cir.1999) (city need not permit construction of an assisted living facility on land zoned for commercial use where the evidence showed that a special use permit would not be granted to any residence of similar size whether intended for persons without disabilities or not). A "but for" causation standard is used to show the requested accommodation is necessary, meaning that without the accommodation, the plaintiff will be denied an equal opportunity to obtain the housing of her choice. *Wisconsin Community Services, Inc. v. City of Milwaukee*, 465 F.3d 737, 749 (7th Cir.2006).

Some builders and architects, particularly new urbanist practitioners, find the ADA unduly impinges on their creativity. New urbanism is discussed *infra* Ch. 2.J. The "visitability" issue, as it is known, pits these builders and architects against accessibility advocates. How much accessibility is acceptable, and at what cost? The greater the degree of visitability, the easier life is for disabled persons, particularly wheelchair users and the more difficult it is for urban building design. For a comprehensive examination of planning for accessibility, see Robin Paul Malloy, *Land Use Law and Disability: Planning and Zoning for Accessible Communities*, Cambridge University Press, 2015.

10. In the absence of zoning obstructions to group housing, can neighbors achieve similar results by entering into private covenants? The FHA applies to both state and private conduct. *See* Juergensmeyer and Roberts, *Land Use Planning and Development Regulation Law* § 15.11 (3rd ed.2012).

11. The 1988 amendments to the FHA also ban discrimination based on "familial status," which "means one or more individuals (who have not attained the age of 18 years) being domiciled with (1) a parent or another person having legal custody of such individual or individuals; or (2) the designee of such parent or other person having such custody, with the written permission of such parent or other person." 42 U.S.C.A. § 3602(k). Thus, the provision is directed towards discrimination against children, and does not apply to groups of unrelated persons seeking to avoid a *Belle Terre* type ordinance. Bona fide housing projects for the elderly are exempt from the ban on discrimination against families.

CHAPTER 6

REVITALIZING THE URBAN CORE

■ ■ ■

A. INTRODUCTION

Urban core revitalization, whether it consists of slum clearance, redevelopment, rehabilitation, historic preservation, housing code enforcement, new urbanist traditional neighborhood, transit oriented development, mixed use centers, gentrification or infill, requires a basic understanding of many complex tools and techniques involving both the public and private sectors. In earlier chapters we explored land use regulation over the use and form of land. The revitalization of downtown areas and existing built-up neighborhoods of cities and first ring suburbs, requires the use of an entirely different approach to development—the carrot as well as the stick. Government cannot by regulation alone compel private development to locate in areas where market economics are contra-indicated, or where land cannot be purchased because of fragmented or unwilling ownership.

The primary technique, and the one with which we begin this chapter, involves condemnation of land and interests in property to enable the assembly of parcels. As we saw with "antiquated subdivisions" in Chapter 4, assemblage and merger of parcels are critical to stimulate development activity. Other techniques, including tax increment financing and tax abatement, will be examined to determine the level of subsidy required to overcome lower cost suburban land. Federal and state grants, loans and subsidies, although of lesser magnitude in recent years, can assist in leveraging private capital. Incentives and bonuses to increase the density or FAR of development can be leveraged in exchange for amenity packages of development with open spaces or plazas, transit stations, architectural features or contributions for the building of affordable housing and cultural facilities.

The public and private sectors can be linked together in public-private partnerships in which each side brings important assets into the union. The government can authorize zoning, speed development approval, assemble parcels, prepare environmental impact reports and provide tax relief and bonuses. The private sector can furnish benefits available through hedge fund investment pools, investment tax credits, depreciation, historic preservation tax credits and construction, marketing and financing. The world of urban redevelopment and revitalization has come

711

a long way from the early days of urban renewal and slum clearance that followed World War II.

B. REDEVELOPMENT THROUGH EMINENT DOMAIN (PUBLIC PURPOSE)

One of the basic techniques of achieving urban revitalization may require that the government exercise the power of eminent domain, or direct condemnation, if landowners hold out for exorbitant prices for the land, or if fragmented ownership prevents the sale of the property. The leading case upholding the use of eminent domain to condemn blighted urban property for development is *Berman v. Parker*, 348 U.S. 26 (1954). Berman involved the District of Columbia's Redevelopment Act, which directed the National Capital Planning Commission to acquire blighted property in the District for urban renewal purposes. After setting aside land for streets, utilities, schools, and recreational facilities, the Planning Commission was authorized to lease or sell the balance of the land acquired by condemnation to private parties, who agree to develop the property in accord with the commission's plan. Under Title I (Urban Renewal) of the National Housing Act, 42 U.S.C. § 1441 (1949), the federal government paid 2/3 of the write down loss occasioned by acquiring and re-selling or leasing the property to a private developer at below market value.

Unfortunately, the times were not ripe for renewed development in central city core neighborhoods due to white flight to the suburbs incentivized by the following countervailing federal policies: (1) the FHA subsidization of suburban single family mortgages; (2) federal tax deductions of mortgage interest and property taxes for single family homes but not for rental apartments; and (3) interstate highway construction destroying and dividing inner city neighborhoods while building suburban ring roads attracting commercial, office and industrial uses to the intersections of north-south and east-west interstates with interstate perimeter ring roads. For a brilliant analysis of the catastrophe of the Federal Urban Renewal Program, see Martin Anderson, *The Federal Bulldozer: A Critical Analysis of Urban Renewal*, 1949 to 1962 (1965).

KELO V. CITY OF NEW LONDON
Supreme Court of the United States, 2005.
545 U.S. 469, 125 S.Ct. 2655, 162 L.Ed.2d 439.

JUSTICE STEVENS delivered the opinion of the Court.

In 2000, the city of New London approved a development plan that, in the words of the Supreme Court of Connecticut, was "projected to create in excess of 1,000 jobs, to increase tax and other revenues, and to revitalize an economically distressed city, including its downtown and waterfront areas." 268 Conn. 1, 5, 843 A.2d 500, 507 (2004). In assembling the land needed for this project, the city's development agent has purchased property from willing sellers and proposes to use the power of eminent domain to acquire the remainder of the property from unwilling owners in exchange for just compensation. The question presented is whether the city's proposed disposition of this property qualifies as a "public use" within the meaning of the Takings Clause of the Fifth Amendment to the Constitution.

I

The city of New London (hereinafter City) sits at the junction of the Thames River and the Long Island Sound in southeastern Connecticut. Decades of economic decline led a state agency in 1990 to designate the City a "distressed municipality." In 1996, the Federal Government closed the Naval Undersea Warfare Center, which had been located in the Fort Trumbull area of the City and had employed over 1,500 people. In 1998, the City's unemployment rate was nearly double that of the State, and its population of just under 24,000 residents was at its lowest since 1920.

These conditions prompted state and local officials to target New London, and particularly its Fort Trumbull area, for economic revitalization. To this end, respondent New London Development Corporation (NLDC), a private nonprofit entity established some years earlier to assist the City in planning economic development, was reactivated. In January 1998, the State authorized a $5.35 million bond issue to support the NLDC's planning activities and a $10 million bond issue toward the creation of a Fort Trumbull State Park. In February, the pharmaceutical company Pfizer Inc. announced that it would build a $300 million research facility on a site immediately adjacent to Fort Trumbull; local planners hoped that Pfizer would draw new business to the area, thereby serving as a catalyst to the area's rejuvenation. After receiving initial approval from the city council, the NLDC continued its planning activities and held a series of neighborhood meetings to educate the public about the process. In May, the city council authorized the NLDC to formally submit its plans to the relevant state agencies for review. Upon obtaining state-level approval, the NLDC finalized an integrated development plan focused on 90 acres of the Fort Trumbull area.

* * *

The NLDC intended the development plan to capitalize on the arrival of the Pfizer facility and the new commerce it was expected to attract. In addition to creating jobs, generating tax revenue, and helping to "build momentum for the revitalization of downtown New London," the plan was also designed to make the City more attractive and to create leisure and recreational opportunities on the waterfront and in the park.

The city council approved the plan in January 2000, and designated the NLDC as its development agent in charge of implementation. The city council also authorized the NLDC to purchase property or to acquire property by exercising eminent domain in the City's name. The NLDC successfully negotiated the purchase of most of the real estate in the 90-acre area, but its negotiations with petitioners failed. As a consequence, in November 2000, the NLDC initiated the condemnation proceedings that gave rise to this case.

II

Petitioner Susette Kelo has lived in the Fort Trumbull area since 1997. She has made extensive improvements to her house, which she prizes for its water view. Petitioner Wilhelmina Dery was born in her Fort Trumbull house in 1918 and has lived there her entire life. Her husband Charles (also a petitioner) has lived in the house since they married some 60 years ago. In all, the nine petitioners own 15 properties in Fort Trumbull—4 in parcel 3 of the development plan and 11 in parcel 4A. Ten of the parcels are occupied by the owner or a family member; the other five are held as investment properties. There is no allegation that any of these properties is blighted or otherwise in poor condition; rather, they were condemned only because they happen to be located in the development area.

In December 2000, petitioners brought this action in the New London Superior Court. They claimed, among other things, that the taking of their properties would violate the "public use" restriction in the Fifth Amendment. After a 7-day bench trial, the Superior Court granted a permanent restraining order prohibiting the taking of the properties located in parcel 4A (park or marina support). It, however, denied petitioners relief as to the properties located in parcel 3 (office space).

After the Superior Court ruled, both sides took appeals to the Supreme Court of Connecticut. That court held, over a dissent, that all of the City's proposed takings were valid. It began by upholding the lower court's determination that the takings were authorized by chapter 132, the State's municipal development statute. See Conn.Gen.Stat. § 8–186 et seq. (2005). That statute expresses a legislative determination that the taking of land, even developed land, as part of an economic development project is a "public use" and in the "public interest." Next, relying on cases such as Hawaii Housing Authority v. Midkiff, 467 U.S. 229 (1984), and Berman v. Parker, 348 U.S. 26 (1954), the court held that such economic development qualified as a valid public use under both the Federal and State Constitutions.

* * *

The three dissenting justices would have imposed a "heightened" standard of judicial review for takings justified by economic development. Although they agreed that the plan was intended to serve a valid public use, they would have found all the takings unconstitutional because the

City had failed to adduce "clear and convincing evidence" that the economic benefits of the plan would in fact come to pass.

We granted certiorari to determine whether a city's decision to take property for the purpose of economic development satisfies the "public use" requirement of the Fifth Amendment.

III

Two polar propositions are perfectly clear. On the one hand, it has long been accepted that the sovereign may not take the property of *A* for the sole purpose of transferring it to another private party *B*, even though *A* is paid just compensation. On the other hand, it is equally clear that a State may transfer property from one private party to another if future "use by the public" is the purpose of the taking; the condemnation of land for a railroad with common-carrier duties is a familiar example. Neither of these propositions, however, determines the disposition of this case.

As for the first proposition, the City would no doubt be forbidden from taking petitioners' land for the purpose of conferring a private benefit on a particular private party. *See Midkiff,* 467 U.S., at 245 ("A purely private taking could not withstand the scrutiny of the public use requirement; it would serve no legitimate purpose of government and would thus be void"); Nor would the City be allowed to take property under the mere pretext of a public purpose, when its actual purpose was to bestow a private benefit. The takings before us, however, would be executed pursuant to a "carefully considered" development plan. The trial judge and all the members of the Supreme Court of Connecticut agreed that there was no evidence of an illegitimate purpose in this case. Therefore, as was true of the statute challenged in *Midkiff,* 467 U.S., at 245, the City's development plan was not adopted "to benefit a particular class of identifiable individuals."

On the other hand, this is not a case in which the City is planning to open the condemned land—at least not in its entirety—to use by the general public. Nor will the private lessees of the land in any sense be required to operate like common carriers, making their services available to all comers. But although such a projected use would be sufficient to satisfy the public use requirement, this "Court long ago rejected any literal requirement that condemned property be put into use for the general public." *Midkiff* at 244. Indeed, while many state courts in the mid-19th century endorsed "use by the public" as the proper definition of public use, that narrow view steadily eroded over time. * * *

The disposition of this case therefore turns on the question whether the City's development plan serves a "public purpose." Without exception, our cases have defined that concept broadly, reflecting our longstanding policy of deference to legislative judgments in this field.

In *Berman v. Parker,* 348 U.S. 26 (1954), this Court upheld a redevelopment plan targeting a blighted area of Washington, D. C., in which most of the housing for the area's 5,000 inhabitants was beyond repair. Under the plan, the area would be condemned and part of it utilized for the construction of streets, schools, and other public facilities. The remainder of the land would be leased or sold to private parties for the purpose of redevelopment, including the construction of low-cost housing.

The owner of a department store located in the area challenged the condemnation, pointing out that his store was not itself blighted and arguing that the creation of a "better balanced, more attractive community" was not a valid public use. Writing for a unanimous Court, Justice Douglas refused to evaluate this claim in isolation, deferring instead to the legislative and agency judgment that the area "must be planned as a whole" for the plan to be successful. The Court explained that "community redevelopment programs need not, by force of the Constitution, be on a piecemeal basis—lot by lot, building by building." The public use underlying the taking was unequivocally affirmed:

> "We do not sit to determine whether a particular housing project is or is not desirable. The concept of the public welfare is broad and inclusive. . . . The values it represents are spiritual as well as physical, aesthetic as well as monetary. It is within the power of the legislature to determine that the community should be beautiful as well as healthy, spacious as well as clean, well-balanced as well as carefully patrolled. In the present case, the Congress and its authorized agencies have made determinations that take into account a wide variety of values. It is not for us to reappraise them. If those who govern the District of Columbia decide that the Nation's Capital should be beautiful as well as sanitary, there is nothing in the Fifth Amendment that stands in the way." *Id.,* at 33, 75 S.Ct. 98.

In *Hawaii Housing Authority v. Midkiff,* 467 U.S. 229 (1984), the Court considered a Hawaii statute whereby fee title was taken from lessors and transferred to lessees (for just compensation) in order to reduce the concentration of land ownership. We unanimously upheld the statute and rejected the Ninth Circuit's view that it was "a naked attempt on the part of the state of Hawaii to take the property of A and transfer it to B solely for B's private use and benefit." Reaffirming *Berman's* deferential approach to legislative judgments in this field, we concluded that the State's purpose of eliminating the "social and economic evils of a land oligopoly" qualified as a valid public use. 467 U.S., at 241–242. Our opinion also rejected the contention that the mere fact that the State immediately transferred the properties to private individuals upon condemnation somehow diminished the public character of the taking. "[I]t is only the taking's purpose, and not its mechanics," we explained, that matters in determining public use.

* * *

IV

Those who govern the City were not confronted with the need to remove blight in the Fort Trumbull area, but their determination that the area was sufficiently distressed to justify a program of economic rejuvenation is entitled to our deference. The City has carefully formulated an economic development plan that it believes will provide appreciable benefits to the community, including—but by no means limited to—new jobs and increased tax revenue. As with other exercises in urban planning and development, the City is endeavoring to coordinate a variety of commercial, residential, and recreational uses of land, with the hope that they will form a whole greater than the sum of its parts. To effectuate this plan, the City has invoked a state statute that specifically authorizes the use of eminent domain to promote economic development. Given the comprehensive character of the plan, the thorough deliberation that preceded its adoption, and the limited scope of our review, it is appropriate for us, as it was in *Berman,* to resolve the challenges of the individual owners, not on a piecemeal basis, but rather in light of the entire plan. Because that plan unquestionably serves a public purpose, the takings challenged here satisfy the public use requirement of the Fifth Amendment.

To avoid this result, petitioners urge us to adopt a new bright-line rule that economic development does not qualify as a public use. Putting aside the unpersuasive suggestion that the City's plan will provide only purely economic benefits, neither precedent nor logic supports petitioners' proposal. Promoting economic development is a traditional and long accepted function of government. There is, moreover, no principled way of distinguishing economic development from the other public purposes that we have recognized. In our cases upholding takings that facilitated agriculture and mining, for example, we emphasized the importance of those industries to the welfare of the States in question, *see, e.g., Strickley,* 200 U.S. 527; in *Berman,* we endorsed the purpose of transforming a blighted area into a "well-balanced" community through redevelopment, 348 U.S., at 33;[13] in *Midkiff,* we upheld the interest in breaking up a land oligopoly that "created artificial deterrents to the normal functioning of the State's residential land market," and in *Ruckelshaus v. Monsanto*, 467 U.S 986 (1984), we accepted Congress' purpose of eliminating a "significant

---

[13] It is a misreading of Berman to suggest that the only public use upheld in that case was the initial removal of blight. The public use described in Berman extended beyond that to encompass the purpose of developing that area to create conditions that would prevent a reversion to blight in the future. *See* 348 U.S., at 34–35 ("It was not enough, [the experts] believed, to remove existing buildings that were insanitary or unsightly. It was important to redesign the whole area so as to eliminate the conditions that cause slums. . . . The entire area needed redesigning so that a balanced, integrated plan could be developed for the region, including not only new homes, but also schools, churches, parks, streets, and shopping centers. In this way it was hoped that the cycle of decay of the area could be controlled and the birth of future slums prevented"). Had the public use in Berman been defined more narrowly, it would have been difficult to justify the taking of the plaintiff's nonblighted department store.

barrier to entry in the pesticide market." It would be incongruous to hold that the City's interest in the economic benefits to be derived from the development of the Fort Trumbull area has less of a public character than any of those other interests. Clearly, there is no basis for exempting economic development from our traditionally broad understanding of public purpose.

Petitioners contend that using eminent domain for economic development impermissibly blurs the boundary between public and private takings. Again, our cases foreclose this objection. Quite simply, the government's pursuit of a public purpose will often benefit individual private parties. For example, in *Midkiff,* the forced transfer of property conferred a direct and significant benefit on those lessees who were previously unable to purchase their homes. * * * The owner of the department store in *Berman* objected to "taking from one businessman for the benefit of another businessman," referring to the fact that under the redevelopment plan land would be leased or sold to private developers for redevelopment.[15] Our rejection of that contention has particular relevance to the instant case: "The public end may be as well or better served through an agency of private enterprise than through a department of government—or so the Congress might conclude. We cannot say that public ownership is the sole method of promoting the public purposes of community redevelopment projects." *Id.,* at 34.[16]

It is further argued that without a bright-line rule nothing would stop a city from transferring citizen *A*'s property to citizen *B* for the sole reason that citizen *B* will put the property to a more productive use and thus pay more taxes. Such a one-to-one transfer of property, executed outside the confines of an integrated development plan, is not presented in this case. While such an unusual exercise of government power would certainly raise a suspicion that a private purpose was afoot,[17] the hypothetical cases

---

[15]   Notably, as in the instant case, the private developers in Berman were required by contract to use the property to carry out the redevelopment plan.

[16]   Nor do our cases support Justice O'CONNOR's novel theory that the government may only take property and transfer it to private parties when the initial taking eliminates some "harmful property use." (dissenting opinion). There was nothing "harmful" about the nonblighted department store at issue in *Berman,* 348 U.S. 26; see also n. 13, *supra*; nothing "harmful" about the lands at issue in the mining and agriculture cases, *see, e.g., Strickley,* 200 U.S. 527; see also nn. 9, 11, *supra;* and certainly nothing "harmful" about the trade secrets owned by the pesticide manufacturers in *Monsanto,* 467 U.S. 986. In each case, the public purpose we upheld depended on a private party's future use of the concededly nonharmful property that was taken. By focusing on a property's future use, as opposed to its past use, our cases are faithful to the text of the Takings Clause. See U.S. Const., Amdt. 5. ("[N]or shall private property be taken for public use, without just compensation"). Justice O'CONNOR's intimation that a "public purpose" may not be achieved by the action of private parties confuses the purpose of a taking with its mechanics, a mistake we warned of in *Midkiff,* 467 U.S., at 244. *See also Berman,* 348 U.S., at 33–34 ("The public end may be as well or better served through an agency of private enterprise than through a department of government").

[17]   Courts have viewed such aberrations with a skeptical eye. *See, e.g., 99 Cents Only Stores v. Lancaster Redevelopment Agency,* 237 F.Supp.2d 1123 (C.D.Cal.2001); cf. *Cincinnati v. Vester,* 281 U.S. 439, 448 (1930) (taking invalid under state eminent domain statute for lack of a reasoned

posited by petitioners can be confronted if and when they arise. They do not warrant the crafting of an artificial restriction on the concept of public use.

Alternatively, petitioners maintain that for takings of this kind we should require a "reasonable certainty" that the expected public benefits will actually accrue. Such a rule, however, would represent an even greater departure from our precedent. * * * A constitutional rule that required postponement of the judicial approval of every condemnation until the likelihood of success of the plan had been assured would unquestionably impose a significant impediment to the successful consummation of many such plans.

Just as we decline to second-guess the City's considered judgments about the efficacy of its development plan, we also decline to second-guess the City's determinations as to what lands it needs to acquire in order to effectuate the project. "It is not for the courts to oversee the choice of the boundary line nor to sit in review on the size of a particular project area. Once the question of the public purpose has been decided, the amount and character of land to be taken for the project and the need for a particular tract to complete the integrated plan rests in the discretion of the legislative branch." *Berman,* 348 U.S., at 35–36.

In affirming the City's authority to take petitioners' properties, we do not minimize the hardship that condemnations may entail, notwithstanding the payment of just compensation. We emphasize that nothing in our opinion precludes any State from placing further restrictions on its exercise of the takings power. Indeed, many States already impose "public use" requirements that are stricter than the federal baseline. Some of these requirements have been established as a matter of state constitutional law, while others are expressed in state eminent domain statutes that carefully limit the grounds upon which takings may be exercised. As the submissions of the parties and their *amici* make clear, the necessity and wisdom of using eminent domain to promote economic development are certainly matters of legitimate public debate. This Court's authority, however, extends only to determining whether the City's proposed condemnations are for a "public use" within the meaning of the Fifth Amendment to the Federal Constitution. Because over a century of our case law interpreting that provision dictates an affirmative answer to that question, we may not grant petitioners the relief that they seek.

The judgment of the Supreme Court of Connecticut is affirmed.

JUSTICE KENNEDY, concurring.

I join the opinion for the Court and add these further observations.

---

explanation). These types of takings may also implicate other constitutional guarantees. *See Village of Willowbrook v. Olech,* 528 U.S. 562 (2000) (per curiam).

* * * The determination that a rational-basis standard of review is appropriate does not, however, alter the fact that transfers intended to confer benefits on particular, favored private entities, and with only incidental or pretextual public benefits, are forbidden by the Public Use Clause.

A court applying rational-basis review under the Public Use Clause should strike down a taking that, by a clear showing, is intended to favor a particular private party, with only incidental or pretextual public benefits, just as a court applying rational-basis review under the Equal Protection Clause must strike down a government classification that is clearly intended to injure a particular class of private parties, with only incidental or pretextual public justifications. *See Cleburne v. Cleburne Living Center, Inc.,* 473 U.S. 432, 446–447, 450 (1985).

* * *

For the foregoing reasons, I join in the Court's opinion.

NOTE

A furious public reaction arose in the states immediately following *Kelo*, leading to major state legislation, constitutional amendments and judicial decisions challenging the use of eminent domain for urban redevelopment where the public purpose was primarily to advance economic development but only "pretextually" to eliminate community blight. For the most part, as the following case reveals, these state actions do no preclude the use of condemnation for redevelopment so long as statutory blight exists, following Berman v. Parker, regardless of whether there will be collateral advancement of economic development or economic benefit to the purchaser of the condemned property.

1. FINDING OF BLIGHT IS ESSENTIAL TO EXERCISE EMINENT DOMAIN AUTHORITY FOR REDEVELOPMENT PURPOSES

KAUR V. NEW YORK STATE URBAN DEVELOPMENT CORPORATION

Court of Appeals of New York, 2010.
15 N.Y.3d 235, 907 N.Y.S.2d 122, 933 N.E.2d 721.

CIPARICK, J.

In this appeal, we are called upon to determine whether respondent's exercise of its power of eminent domain to acquire petitioner's property for the development of a new Columbia University campus was support by a sufficient public use, benefit or purpose (*see* N.Y. Const., art. I, § 7[a]; Eminent Domain Procedural Law ("EDPL") 207[C][4]). We answer this question in the affirmative and conclude, pursuant to our recent holding in

Matter of Goldstein v. New York State Urban Dev. Corp., 921 N.E.2d 164 (2009), (See initial discussion of Goldstein in Chapter 4, *supra*) that the Empire State Development Corporation's ESDC finding of blight and determination that the condemnation of petitioners' property qualified as a "land use improvement project" were rationally based and entitled to deference. Significantly, the Columbia Plan [also] recognized that neighboring institutions such as Columbia's Morningside Heights campus, the main campus of City College, and the Columbia Presbyterian Medical Center can be key catalysts in the economic development of West Harlem. These institutions will provide the day-to-day presence that will enliven the area as a regional attraction and act as partners in job creation.

In 2003, ESDC hired Urbitran Associates (Urbitran), an engineering, architecture and planning firm, to conduct a separate study, examining the neighborhood conditions of West Harlem. Urbitran documented and photographed the area of the Project site as well as the surrounding area and focused its analysis on four major criteria: (1) signs of deterioration, (2) substandard or unsanitary conditions, (3) adequacy of infrastructure and (4) indications of the impairment of sound growth in the surrounding community. The study, issued by ESDC in August 2004, determined that the conditions in the study area merited a designation of blight. Specifically, the study revealed that several of the buildings throughout West Harlem were dilapidated. Urbitran also concluded that numerous buildings evidenced poor exterior conditions and structural degradation. According to this study, two of the blocks with the highest number of deficient buildings and lots are within the Project site.

Meanwhile, as Urbitran performed its neighborhood conditions study of West Harlem, Columbia began to purchase property located within the Project site. In September 2006, notwithstanding the results of the Urbitran study, ESDC retained AKRF to perform a neighborhood conditions report of the Project site on its behalf. AKRF photographed and conducted detailed inspections of each of the individual lots in the Project site. It documented structural conditions, vacancy rates, site utilization, property ownership, and crime data. For each building on the Project site, it also documented the physical and structural conditions, health and safety concerns, building code violations, underutilization, and environmental hazards. AKRF said it selected these factors "because they are generally accepted indicators of disinvestment in a neighborhood. The widespread presence of one or more of these factors can also demonstrate the need for revitalization and redevelopment of an area." Based on these factors, on November 1, 2007, AKRF issued its Manhattanville Neighborhood Conditions Study. This study concluded that the Project site was "substantially unsafe, unsanitary, substandard, and deteriorated" or, in short, blighted. Nonetheless, on February 20, 2009, petitioners challenged ESDC's findings and determination in the Appellate Division. A plurality of that court concluded that "ESDC's determination that the project has a public use, benefit or purpose is wholly unsupported by record and precedent" (72 A.D.3d 1, 9, 2009]). Respondent appealed as of right, pursuant to CPLR 5601(a) and (b), and we now reverse.

With the "blight studies" of both AKRF and Urbitran in hand and with the knowledge that the City Council had approved the Project site for rezoning, on July 17, 2008, ESDC adopted a General Project Plan (GPP) that would enable Columbia to move forward with its plan to build an urban campus in West Harlem. Petitioners submitted two legal memoranda and thousands of pages of materials in opposition to the Project during the comment period of the public environmental impact assessment of the GPP. ESDC, in turn, prepared a comprehensive 75-page document entitled "Response to Comments," which thoroughly addressed the concerns raised by petitioners and others. Taking into consideration the questions raised by the petitioners during the hearing and their substantial written submissions that followed, ESDC adopted a modified GPP and authorized the issuance of its findings and determination.

In eliminating the blighted conditions plaguing the area of the Project site, ESDC noted that the Project would create 14,000 jobs during the construction of the new campus as well as 6,000 permanent jobs following the Project's completion. ESDC found that The Project would generate substantial revenue, estimating that "tax revenue derived from construction expenditures and total personal income during this period" at $122 million for the State and $87 million for New York City. Moreover, ESDC indicated that another purpose of the Project was the creation of much needed public space. Specifically, it found that the Project site would create "approximately 94,000 square feet of accessible open space and maintained as such in perpetuity that will be punctuated by trees, open vistas, paths, landscaping and street furniture and an additional well-lit 28,000 square feet of space of widened sidewalks that will invite east-west pedestrian traffic." In addition to the open space created, ESDC highlighted that the Project made provision for infrastructure improvements—most notably to the 125th Street subway station—as well as substantial financial commitment by Columbia to the maintenance of West Harlem Piers Park. ESDC further acknowledged that Columbia would open its facilities—including its libraries and computer centers—to students attending a new public school that Columbia is supplying the land to rent-free for 49 years. Columbia would also open its new swimming facilities to the public.

Petitioners' main argument on this appeal is that the Project approved by ESDC is unconstitutional because the condemnation is not for the purpose of putting properties to "public use" within the meaning of article I, § 7(a) of the N.Y. Constitution, which provides that "[p]rivate property shall not be taken for public use without just compensation." First, petitioners vociferously contend that ESDC's blight findings were made in bad faith and the Project only serves the private interests of Columbia. ESDC counters that the duly approved Project qualifies as a "land use improvement project" within the meaning of the UDC Act and that the Appellate Division plurality erred as a matter of law when it conducted a de novo review of the administrative record and concluded that the Project site was not blighted. We agree with ESDC.

"[I]t is indisputable that the removal of urban blight is a proper, and, indeed constitutionally sanctioned, predicate for the exercise of the power of eminent domain. It has been deemed a 'public use' within the meaning of the State Constitution's Takings Clause at least since *Matter of New York City Housing Authority v. Muller*, 270 N.Y. 333 (1936) and is expressly recognized by the Constitution as a ground for condemnation" (*Matter of Goldstein*, 921 N.E.2d 164 (N.Y.2009).

In Matter of Goldstein, we reaffirmed the long-standing doctrine that the role of the Judiciary is limited in reviewing findings of blight in eminent domain proceedings. Because the determinations of blight and public purpose are the province of the Legislature, and are entitled to deference by the Judiciary, we stated that:

> * * * It is only where there is *no room for reasonable difference of opinion* as to whether an area is blighted, that judges may substitute their views as to the adequacy with which the public purpose of blight removal has been made out for that of the legislatively designated agencies" *Id.* (emphasis added).

Thus, a court may only substitute its own judgment for that of the legislative body authorizing the project when such judgment is irrational or baseless (*see* Matter of Goldstein, 921 N.E.2d 164).

Applying this standard of review, as we must, we now look to the relevant statute.

The UDC Act provides that, in the case of land use improvement projects, ESDC must find:

> (1) That the area in which the project is to be located is a substandard or insanitary area, or is in danger of becoming a substandard or insanitary area and tends to impair or arrest the sound growth and development of the municipality;
>
> (2) That the project consists of a plan or undertaking for the clearance, re-planning, reconstruction and rehabilitation of such area and for recreational and other facilities incidental or appurtenant thereto;
>
> (3) That the plan or undertaking affords maximum opportunity for participation by private enterprise, consistent with the sound needs of the municipality as a whole" (§ 6260[c] [UDC Act § 10(c)]).

The term "substandard or insanitary area" is defined as "a slum, blighted, deteriorated or deteriorating area, or an area which has a blighting influence on the surrounding area" (§ 6253[12] [UDC Act § 3(12)]). Here, the two reports prepared by ESDC consultants-consisting of a voluminous compilation of documents and photographs of property conditions-arrive at the conclusion that the area of the Project site is blighted. Just as in Matter of Goldstein, "all that is at issue is a reasonable difference of opinion as to whether the area in question is in fact substandard and insanitary," which is "not a sufficient predicate to supplant [ESDC's] determination" (921 N.E.2d 164).

Thus, given our precedent, the de novo review of the record undertaken by the plurality of the Appellate Division was improper. On the "record upon which the ESDC determination was based and by which we are bound," it cannot be said that ESDC's finding of blight was irrational or baseless. Indeed, ESDC considered a wide range of factors including the physical, economic, engineering and environmental conditions at the Project site. Its decision was not based on any one of these factors, but on the Project site conditions as a whole. Accordingly, since there is record support—"extensively documented photographically and otherwise on a lot-by-lot basis" (245 N.E.2d 804)—for ESDC's determination that the Project site was blighted, the Appellate Division plurality erred when it substituted its view for that of the legislatively designated agency.

In the context of eminent domain cases, we have held that, to guard against discriminatory application of the law, it is not necessary that "the degree of deterioration or precise percentage of obsolescence or mathematical measurement of other factors be arrived at with precision" (*Yonkers Community Dev. Agency*, 37 N.Y.2d at 484, 373 N.Y.S.2d 112, 335 N.E.2d 327).

Indeed, in Yonkers Community Dev. Agency, we recognized that "[m]any factors and interrelationships of factors may be significant" for a blight finding and "may include such diverse matters as irregularity of the plots, inadequacy of the streets, diversity of land ownership making assemblage of property difficult, incompatibility of the existing mixture of residential and industrial property, overcrowding, the incidence of crime, lack of sanitation, the drain an area makes on municipal services, fire hazards, traffic congestion, and pollution" (id. at 483).

Not only this Court, but the Supreme Court has consistently held that blight is an elastic concept that does not call for an inflexible, one-size-fits-all definition, *See Berman v. Parker*, 348 U.S. 26, 33–34 [1954]). Rather, blight or "substandard or insanitary areas," as we held in Matter of Goldstein and Yonkers Community Dev. Agency, must be viewed on a case-by-case basis. Accordingly, because the UDC Act provides adequate meaning to the term "substandard or insanitary area," we reject petitioners' argument that the statute is unconstitutionally vague on its face.

In determining that Columbia created the blighted conditions in West Harlem, the plurality of the Appellate Division disregarded the Urbitran blight study commenced in 2003. That study, was based on a survey of the Project site and surrounding neighborhood at a time when Columbia was only beginning to purchase property in the area. Indeed, the Urbitran study unequivocally concluded that there was "ample evidence of deterioration of the building stock in the study area" and that "[s]substandard and unsanitary conditions were detected in the study area." Moreover, Earth Tech found that, since 1961, the neighborhood has suffered from a long-standing lack of investment interest. Thus, since there is record support that the Project site was blighted before Columbia began to acquire property in the area, the issue is beyond our further review.

Accordingly, the order of the Appellate Division should be reversed, with costs.

NOTES

1.   The post-Kelo actions of state legislatures and courts limiting public purpose was due to the rising use of condemnation to facilitate large scale economic development projects in outlying suburbs, originated by banks and entrepreneurs, in which the elimination of blight appeared to be only a secondary or pre-textual purpose for the primary purpose of economic development and profit. Indeed, that was the decision of the Appellate Division plurality that was overruled by the Court of Appeals in Kaur. After this post-Kelo hubbub, the smoke has cleared and some state courts, as in Kaur, have returned to the principle that proper elimination of blight does serve as a primary purpose, overriding any incidental, secondary purpose of economic development. The Kaur court seems to have achieved a rational balancing of elimination of blight and economic benefits achieved by such elimination.

2.   In an effort to establish a reasonable balance between protecting private property rights and rehabilitating urban slums, state courts and legislatures have paid significant attention to the meaning of "blight" and "economic development" as restraints on governmental power. In *City of Stockton v. Marina Towers LLC*, 171 Cal.App.4th 93, 105 (2009), the Court of Appeals held that "the essential prerequisite for identifying a project area is that there be blight within the area. The blight conditions must predominate in such a way as to impact proper utilization of the area, causing a physical and economic burden on the community." Other decisions, such as the one in *State ex. rel. Jackson v. Dolan*, 398 S.W.3d 472 (Mo.2013), reflect the legislature's interest in curbing eminent domain abuse in those instances where it is used for "solely economic development purposes." The Missouri statute under scrutiny in Jackson had defined economic development as "use of a specific piece of property or properties which would provide an increase in the tax base, tax revenues, employment and general economic health."

3.   The post-Kelo Ohio Supreme Court decision in *City of Norwood v. Horney*, 853 N.E.2d 1115 (Ohio 2006), while overturning the condemnation action by the City, did so only because the City had found "deteriorating conditions" and not "blight." In such a case the court said, the economic development purpose became primary and could not sustain on its own the public purpose of the condemnation. The court stated:

> "Although we have permitted economic concerns to be considered in addition to other factors, such as slum clearance, when determining whether the public-use requirement is sufficient, we have never found economic benefits alone to be a sufficient public use for a valid taking. We decline to do so now.

> Rather, we find that the analysis by the Supreme Court of Michigan in *Hathcock*, 684 N.W.2d 765 (Mich.2004), and those presented by the dissenting judges of the Supreme Court of Connecticut and the dissenting justices of the United States Supreme Court in Kelo are better models for interpreting Section 19, Article I of Ohio's Constitution. In Hathcock, the court overruled its prior holding in *Poletown Neighborhood Council v. Detroit*, 304 N.W.2d 455, a case that the court characterized as a "radical and unabashed departure" from eminent-domain jurisprudence. Poletown had found that a generalized economic benefit constituted a valid public purpose for exercising eminent domain. In overturning Poletown, the court in Hathcock correctly observed:

>> "Every business, every productive unit in society, * * * contribute[s] in some way to the commonwealth. To justify the exercise of eminent domain solely on the basis of the fact that the use of that property by a private entity seeking its own profit might contribute to the economy's health is to render impotent our constitutional limitations on the government's power of eminent domain. Poletown's 'economic benefit' rationale would validate practically any exercise of the power of eminent domain on behalf of a private entity. After all, if one's ownership of private property is forever subject to the government's determination that another private party would put one's land to better use, then the ownership of real property is perpetually threatened by the expansion plans of any large discount retailer, 'mega- store,' or the like. Indeed, it is for precisely this reason that this Court has approved the transfer of condemned property to private entities only when certain other conditions [blight] * * * are present." 853 N.E.2d at 1141.

Is there any real difference between Kaur and City of Norwood? *See* Hudson Hayes Luce, *The Meaning of Blight: A Survey of Statutory and Case Law*, 35 REAL PROP.PROB. & TR.J. 389, 401 (2000) (noting that only a small minority of state eminent-domain statutes permit the consideration of lack of viable economic use in determining whether property is blighted). What appears to be significantly different in result, is *City of Las Vegas Downtown*

Redevelopment Agency v. Pappas, 76 P.3d 1 (Nev.2003) (economic development is a sufficient public purpose to support a finding of blight).

4. *Bailey v. Myers*, 76 P.3d 898 (Ariz.Ct.App.2003), is an important pre-Kelo case raising a number of inquiries that might be used to determine whether condemnation for redevelopment has a valid public purpose. Reversing an order of possession, the Court of Appeals held that the state constitution prohibits using eminent domain to take property of one owner and transfer it to another owner, unless public benefits substantially predominate over private gain. The court relied upon the following factors, in addition to finding blight, in determining whether a public use has been established in a redevelopment project:

a. Will title be held by a public entity?

b. Will property be used for private profit, non-profit, or public purposes?

c. Will the end use of the property provide needed public services?

d. What are the anticipated public uses or benefits?

e. What control will the condemning authority retain over property use?

f. What is the ratio of public to private funds to be expended?

g. Is there true slum or blight to be removed?

h. Who stands to gain most—private parties or the public?

i. Are private developers the driving force behind the project?

In other states where condemnation has been used to unilaterally transfer property between private landowners, courts have expressly prohibited private benefits from being conferred on private parties. *See Reading Area Water Auth. v. Schuylkill River Greenway Ass'n*, 100 A.3d 572 (Pa.2014) where the state Supreme Court adhered to the principle that eminent domain may not be used to confer a private benefit on a particular private party, even if there is an incidental benefit to the public, utilizing the state's post-Kelo legislation, the Property Right's Protection Act and not the constitutional public use limitation. Contrast Reading with *City of Chicago v. Eychaner*, 26 N.E.3d 501 (Ill.App.Ct.2015) where the court upheld the Redevelopment taking of private land in order to sell it to a private chocolate factory for one dollar, because the City had created a Planned Manufacturing District with tax increment financing power, and there was some blight in the area but not on the chocolate factory land. For criticism of the Eychaner decision, *see* Robert H. Thomas, *Recent Developments in Eminent Domain*, 47 URB.LAW. 501, 504–507 (2015).

5. In an unusual opinion, in which the appellate court virtually ignored the legislature's findings and analyzed what is required to demonstrate blight findings themselves, the California Court of Appeals rejected a redevelopment project. *See County of Los Angeles v. City of Glendora Redevelopment Project*, 185 Cal.App.4th 817 (2010), holding that the attempt to add a new fifth area

to four previous blighted areas within a redevelopment project area required that a new legislative finding of blight had to be prepared

6.   The findings of "blight" and "substandardness" often required in redevelopment statutes as a precondition for condemnation can be attacked on a number of other grounds. In *Aposporos v. Urban Redevelopment Comm'n*, 790 A.2d 1167 (Conn.2002), the court addressed common abuses in the redevelopment process. The city wanted to condemn land on the basis of a 1963 redevelopment plan. In 1997 the city entered into a "Land Disposition Agreement" with a redeveloper and the owners sued to enjoin the taking. The trial court denied the injunction but the Connecticut Supreme Court of Errors reversed. The court found that the attempted taking was illegal because the city made no renewed finding of blight and the old 1963 finding was stale and did not relate to the development area as defined in 1988. The court held that while the city need not re-determine blight at each stage of its plans, it may not rely on a prior finding of blight, particularly where the property was not targeted for acquisition when the blight finding was made. *See* Robert M. Fogelson, *Downtown: Its Rise and Fall*, 1880 (2001), particularly Chapter 7 at pp. 317–380, entitled "Inventing Blight: Downtown and the Origins of Urban Redevelopment."

7.   States vary on whether or not blight elimination should constitute a valid public purpose for a taking, but can one local subdivision have authority to exercise eminent domain for redevelopment while another locality in the same state is denied that power? Depending on state constitutions and enabling statutes, the answer may be yes, depending on whether the local government is a home rule city or a general law city. Missouri's constitution, for example, requires that the power to eliminate blight through redevelopment be delegated either by statute or by constitutional home rule. *See City of North Kansas City v. K.C. Beaton Holding Co.*, 417 S.W.3d 825 (Mo.Ct.App.2014) (holding that the City did not have the power to use redevelopment to remove blight because the Missouri Legislature never expressly delegated the power to non-home rule cities).

8.   Is a subsequent change in the public purpose through amendment of the Redevelopment Plan void? *See Powerhouse Arts District Neighborhood Ass'n v. City Council of City of Jersey City*, 994 A.2d 1054 (N.J.Super.App.Div.2010) (City's adoption of amendment to redevelopment plan that was inconsistent with initial plan because the area was no longer blighted, did not have to show continuing blight, and had adequate support in the record created before the planning board and the city council demonstrating the greater likelihood of success of new types of uses, and therefore was not arbitrary or capricious; city appropriately explained its reasons for adopting the amendment, and the adoption was not the product of favoritism, as asserted by objectors.) What differentiates this case from the Glendora case?

9.   Besides compensation what are the rights of the owners of land being taken for private redevelopment? The California Code provides:

> "Every redevelopment plan shall provide for participation in the redevelopment of property in the project area by the owners of all or part of such property if the owners agree to participate in the redevelopment in conformity with the redevelopment plan adopted by the legislative body for the area."

Cal. Health & Safety Code § 33339. *See Huntington Park Redevelopment Agency v. Duncan*, 190 Cal.Rptr. 744 (Cal.App.1983), *cert. denied*, 464 U.S. 895 (1983) (a redevelopment agency may take the property of a landowner, notwithstanding the owner's right to participate in the project, if the land-owner refuses to conform to the plan). If the redevelopment agency selects a redeveloper by entering into a disposition agreement to develop the entire site, which fails to give the existing property owner an opportunity to develop its own project, consistent with the plan, the taking will be set aside. *See Cottonwood Christian Center v. City of Cypress*, 218 F.Supp.2d 1203 (C.D.Cal.2002) (setting aside the condemnation of land for a Costco project when the church had its own major proposal for the site, citing *Sweetwater Valley Civic Ass'n v. City of National City*, 555 P.2d 1099 (Cal.1976), where the court stated, "One man's land cannot be seized by the government and sold to another man in order that the purchaser may build upon it a better house or a house which better meets the government's idea of what is appropriate or better designed. [The powers of redevelopment and eminent domain] can never be used just because the public agency considers that it can make better use or planning than its present use or plan." *See also* (*Friends of Mammoth v. Town of Mammoth Lakes Redevelopment Agency*, 98 Cal.Rptr.2d 334 (Cal.App.2000); *Pequounock Yacht Club v. City of Bridgeport*, 790 A.2d 1178 (Conn.2002) denying the right to take where the city arbitrarily failed to integrate the current use of the property (a private yacht club with 196 boat slips, a gas dock, a boat storage area, and parking) into the redevelopment project.—NOTE: Superseded by statute).

10. Following the bursting of the housing bubble in mid-2007, underwater mortgages became commonplace, setting off a wave of foreclosures that negatively impacted property and contributed to systemic blight. City governments whose communities were hit hard by the crisis began searching for ways to provide immediate relief to homeowners. One popular rescue strategy involved applying the power of direct condemnation to intangible property. The City of Richmond, California, was the first municipality in the country to devise a plan to acquire underwater mortgages at fair market value and help borrowers refinance into more affordable loans. Aside from providing just compensation, the city claimed that the public purpose of the program is to prevent the blight that typically follows once a large supply of vacant properties has flooded the market. The mortgage and investment industries argued against the measure stating that the plan would undermine the durability of contracts and would discourage banks from lending in these towns in the future, potentially inflicting more serious damage to the housing market in the long-run. .The FHFA also issued warnings that it may initiate legal action against any local governments that approve such plans. For more on the

California city's plan to bail out homeowners, *see* Shaila Dewan, *Eminent Domain: A Long-Shot Against Blight*, N.Y. Times, Jan. 11, 2014.

11. Pursuant to Section 220 of the National Housing Act (12 U.S.C. § 1715k) and FHA Regulations at 24 CFR part 200, subpart A, and part 220, FHA mortgage insurance is issued to finance mortgages for housing in urban renewal areas, areas in which concentrated revitalization activities have been undertaken by local government, or to alter, repair, or improve housing in those areas. FHA insures mortgages on new or rehabilitated homes or multifamily structures located in designated urban renewal areas and areas with concentrated programs of code enforcement and neighborhood development. Insured mortgages may be used to finance construction or rehabilitation of detached, semidetached, row, walk-up, or elevator-type rental housing or to finance the purchase of properties that have been rehabilitated by a local public agency. Properties must be located in an urban renewal area, an urban development project, code enforcement program area, urban area receiving rehabilitation assistance as a result of natural disaster, or area where concentrated housing, physical development, or public service activities are being carried out in a coordinated manner. For substantial rehabilitation projects, the maximum mortgage amount is 90 percent of the estimated cost of repair and rehabilitation and the estimated value of the property before the repair and rehabilitation project. The maximum mortgage term is 40 years, or not in excess of three-fourths of the remaining economic life of the project, whichever is less.

2. PUBLIC NECESSITY

Generally, an exercise of the power of eminent domain must not only be for a public use; it also must be reasonably necessary for that use. *See Proffitt v. Louisville and Jefferson County Metropolitan Sewer District*, 850 S.W.2d 852 (Ky.1993). A resolution of necessity by the condemnor is frequently required by statute. *See e.g.* Cal.Civ.Proc. Code § 1245.220. When such a resolution of necessity is adopted by the governing body, the general view is that necessity is not judicially reviewable in the absence of fraud, bad faith, or abuse of discretion. *See Anderson v. Teco Pipeline Co.*, 985 S.W.2d 559, 565 (Tex.App.1998); Nichols, The Law of Eminent Domain, § 4.11 (2016). If the condemnor has failed to evaluate the environmental consequences of the proposed taking, would that be an abuse of discretion? *See Florida Power and Light Co. v. Berman*, 429 So.2d 79 (Fla.Dist.Ct.App.1983). In a number of states, a landlocked private owner may bring a direct condemnation proceeding against a neighboring private landowner in order to obtain a right-of-way of necessity to a public road, so long as that authorization is contained in the state constitution.

In fulfilling the necessity requirement there must be a finding of a reasonable commitment in time and funds to complete the proposed project. Where property to be condemned was to be used for parking facilities, the court held that the condemnor city must not only show that the extent of parking is needed for the public, but also the probability that the structures, which the parking is designed to serve, will be constructed within a reasonable period of time. The city was unable to meet this burden in *City of Helena v. Dewolf*, 508 P.2d 122 (Mont.1973). In California, a condemnor may exercise the power of eminent domain to acquire property to be used in the future for a particular public use, but the statute requires a reasonable probability that the date of use will occur within seven years from the date the eminent domain complaint is filed, or within such longer period as is judicially held to be reasonable.

If the land sought to be condemned is already being used for a public purpose, courts employ a higher level of scrutiny in considering the issue of necessity. The courts consider: (1) whether the public use has been abandoned; (2) whether the taking is being initiated by a higher sovereign authority; (3) if the taking is authorized by express legislative authority; (4) whether the new use is consistent with the prior use or whether the land being taken is essential to the current public use; and (5) balancing in favor of the greater public use. *See* Nichols, *The Law of Eminent Domain*, §§ 2.2–2.2[9] [2016].

In the event that the state condemns land for a specific project which is never built, there is a potential remedy for suing the government for extrinsic fraud. There are four cases in California all of which, however, failed to succeed. Examples of failed or unbuilt projects abound. *See Arechiga v. Housing Auth.*, 159 Cal.App. 2d 657 (1958) on remand, 183 Cal.App.2d 835, 838–839 (1960) (land taken for public housing that was never built was turned over to Brooklyn Dodgers to induce them to move to Los Angeles); *Capron v. State*, 247 Cal.App.2d 212 (1966) (land taken for state mental hospital that was never built); *Lavine v. Jessup*, 161 Cal.App.2d 59 (1958) (land taken for domestic relations courthouse that was never built); *County of Los Angeles v. Anthony*, 224 Cal.App.2d 103 (1964) (land taken for county motion picture museum that was never built); *Beistline v. San Diego*, 256 F.2d 421 (9th Cir.1958) (land taken for redevelopment not used for the project but resold to private party). Note that the courts denied relief in all of these cases.

Yet all of these cases state that the landowner would be successful if extrinsic fraud resulted from the condemnation. *Lopez v. Lopez*, 408 P.2d 744 (Cal.1965), *see, United States v. Throckmorton*, 98 U.S. 61 (1878), in which the U.S. Supreme Court defined extrinsic fraud as the circumstances in which 'the unsuccessful party has been prevented from exhibiting fully his case, by fraud or deception practiced on him by his opponent, * * * these, and similar cases which show that there has never been a real contest in the trial or hearing of the case, are reason for which a new suit may be sustained to set aside and annul the former judgment or decree, and open the case for a new and fair hearing.' This rule is restated in the Restatement of Judgments, section 121:

" 'Subject to general equitable considerations, equitable relief from a valid judgment will be granted to a party to the action injured thereby if the judgment was based upon a fraudulent claim or defense which he did not contest because he was: (a) fraudulently misled by the other party to the action to believe that he had no claim or defense; or (b) prevented by duress from contesting it.' "

What would constitute bad faith or an abuse of discretion? In *City of Stockton v. Marina Towers*, 171 Cal.App.4th 93, 105 (2009), the court held that providing a vague description of a project in the resolution of necessity constituted a gross abuse of discretion. Evidence that an agency irrevocably committed itself to the taking of private property without considering less harmful alternatives may also provide grounds for overturning a resolution of necessity. *See Council of San Benito County Governments v. Hollister Inn, Inc.*, 209 Cal.App.4th 473, 485 (2012). Congress has provided statutory restrictions which require findings of necessity in certain federal funding programs. Section 4(f) of the Department of Transportation Act, 49 U.S.C.A. § 3303(c) (1982), prohibits the Secretary of Transportation from using federal funds to finance construction of highways through public parks "if a feasible and prudent" alternate route exists. *See Citizens to Preserve Overton Park, Inc. v. Volpe*, 401 U.S. 402 (1971).

3. VALUATION—STANDARDS OF JUST COMPENSATION

(a) Fair Market Value

Normally, just compensation means paying the fair market value of the property. *See United States v. 50 Acres of Land*, 469 U.S. 24 (1984). This requires determining what a willing buyer would pay a willing seller. Fair market value is measured by three alternative formulae: (1) sale of comparable lands, (2) replacement cost minus depreciation or (3) the income from the property, usually measured by rents. The sale of comparable lands is the preferred method of valuation. Replacement cost is primarily used for unique non-residential buildings that have no income and no comparable sales data. Uses which fit into this category are hospitals, schools, churches and other non-profit uses. The income method is used for rental properties (multi-family or commercial and industrial facilities). Absent a statutory remedy, as in (d) 2 below, compensatory damages may not be claimed for the taking, only the loss of the fair market value of the land taken. *See* 4 Nichols, Law of Eminent Domain §§ 12.2, 12.311(3), and 12.312.

(b) Business Loss

Nothing in the United States Constitution requires compensation for the loss of business profit or goodwill due to a diminution of profits caused by a governmental taking. *See Kimball Laundry Co. v. United States*, 338 U.S. 1 (1949). Compensation for goodwill is not constitutionally required, and historically it was not an element of damages under California's eminent domain law. *See City of San Diego v. Sobke*, 65 Cal.App.4th 379, 387 (1998). In 1975, however, the California Legislature enacted a comprehensive revision of eminent domain law in response to a widespread criticism of the injustice wrought by the Legislature's historic refusal to compensate condemnees whose ongoing businesses were diminished in value by a forced relocation. The purpose of the statute was unquestionably to provide monetary compensation for the kind of losses which typically occur when an ongoing small business is forced to move and give up the benefits of its former location. *See Redevelopment Agency of City of San Diego v. Attisha*, 128 Cal.App.4th 357 (2005). Similarly, despite the general eminent domain rule that business damages are intangible, consequential injuries, which the government is not constitutionally required to compensate, Florida has elected to provide such compensation through statute since 1933, Fla.Stats.Ann. § 73.071(3)(b). *See System Components Corp. v. Florida Department of Transportation*, 14 So.3d 967 (Fla.2009).

An exception to the common law rule, applicable to express lease- hold agreements, provides that in the absence of a specific statute, a leasehold agreement can provide for the payment for the loss of goodwill and business profits. *See City of Roeland Park v. Jasan Trust*, 132 P.3d 943, 946–47 (Kan.2006): "BCB cites cases dating back to 1914 for the proposition that only the value of the unexpired lease, and not the profits of the business or the inconvenience of moving the business, are compensable in a condemnation case. Instead of controverting BCB's recitation of Kansas common law regarding the general rule, Payless observes: 'Ordinarily, the court turns to the lease for guidance on allocating the award.'" It notes that Kansas courts have long held that a lease provision governing the rights of the parties is controlling.

(c) Severance Damages

Severance damages are available for the untaken remainder of the land when a partial taking has occurred. There are three required elements to allow a property owner to recover severance damages; (1) unity of title, (2) contiguity, and (3) unity of use. *Commonwealth Transp. Commissioner of Virginia v. Glass*, 613 S.E.2d 411 (Va.2005). The condemnee must show that the condemned property and the remaining property are necessary and mutually dependent elements of one enterprise, *Winooski Hydroelectric Co. v. Five Acres of Land in East Montpelier and Berlin, Vt.*, 769 F.2d 79 (2d Cir.1985), and that the land remaining has been diminished in value as a result of the taking. *See City of San Diego v. Rancho Penasquitos*, 105 Cal.App.4th 1013 (2003). Once severance damages have been proved, the burden shifts to the condemnor to prove the existence and quantum of any special benefit received by the property which may be available as an offset against the severance damages. *Louisiana Dept. of Highways v. Modica*, 514 So.2d 22 (La.Ct.App.1987), writ denied, 515 So.2d 449 (La.1987). A simple example of how severance damages works comes from the following Kansas Supreme Court case. In *Riddle v. State Highway Commission*, 339 P.2d 301 (Kan.1959), the commission condemned 4.32 acres at the back of a tract to locate a new highway. As a result, the tract's motel was facing away from the new highway and had no direct access to it. The value of the 4.32 acres was $4,000; the value of the entire tract of 6.82 acres was $45,820. After the taking, the remaining 2.5 acres (upon which the motel was located) was worth $17,500. The Supreme Court affirmed a judgment of $23,887 in severance damages. *See Eminent Domain: A Handbook of Condemnation Law*, Chapters 2–4 (Scheiderich, Fraser, and Callies, eds. 2011) for a discussion of damages and valuation.

(d) Relocation Benefits

1.   Federal Legislation. Congress has addressed this problem in passing the Uniform Relocation Assistance and Real Property Acquisition Policies Act of 1970 (URA) (42 U.S.C.A. §§ 4601 to 4655). The House reported:

The need for such legislation arises from the increasing impact of Federal and federally assisted programs. * * * In a less complex time, Federal and federally assisted public works projects seldom involved major displacements of people. There was relatively little taking of residential or commercial property for farm-to-market routes or for reservoirs or public buildings. * * * However, with the growth and development of an economy which is increasingly urban and metropolitan, the demand for public facilities and services has increasingly centered on such urban areas, and the acquisition of land for such projects has become the most difficult facet of many undertakings by public agencies.

H.R.Rep. No. 1656, 91st Cong., 2d Sess. 3, reprinted in 1970 U.S. Code Congressional. & Administrative News 5850.

2.   There are basically two requirements under the URA. They are: (a) being a displaced person as defined under 42 U.S.C.A. § 4601; and (b) that displacement occur as a result of "acquisition" or the "written order of the acquiring agency to vacate." *See* 42 U.S.C.A. § 4601(6) (b) (federal involvement).

Generally, "displaced person" means a human person rather than a corporate person. 42 U.S.C.A. § 4601(6) purports to define "displaced person," but the focus of the definition is on what is meant by "displaced," rather than what is meant by "person." The Supreme Court considered the definition of "person" in *Norfolk Redevelopment & Housing Auth. v. Chesapeake & Potomac Tel. Co.*, 464 U.S. 30 (1983). The Court held that a telephone company, forced to relocate some of its transmission facilities because of a street realignment, is not a "displaced person" within the meaning of the Uniform Relocation Act of 1970 and is thus not entitled to relocation benefits. The Court held that the "displaced persons" protected in the Relocation Act are: "residential and business tenants and owners, living and working in buildings that would be bulldozed by federal and federally-funded programs." *See* 464 U.S. at 41.

3.   The URA does not cover persons displaced by programs operated by private persons receiving Federal funds. *See Moorer v. HUD*, 561 F.2d 175 (8th Cir.1977). In *Parlane Sportswear Co. v. Weinberger*, 513 F.2d 835 (1st Cir.1975), *cert. denied*, 423 U.S. 925 (1975), the plaintiff, a manufacturer of women's sportswear, leased a building which was purchased by Tufts University. A few years later, Tufts obtained a grant from the National Institute of Health, then a subsidiary of the Department of Health, Education and Welfare. Using this money, Tufts set up a program in the space which Parlane had been occupying. Parlane sought relocation assistance under the URA and, when rejected, brought the action. The court held that: (a) the statute was intended for displacement caused by public work or improvement programs; and (b) although URA was intended to include displacement caused by Federal financial assistance, such was only intended to cover dislocation caused directly by such assistance to state agencies. In this case the displacement was caused by a Federal subsidy to a private source and the dislocation which occurred was not covered by the URA. 513 F.2d at 837.

4.   Benefits provided include moving and related expenses. Homeowners may obtain replacement housing payments for comparable replacement dwellings up to $22,500. 42 U.S.C.A. § 4623. *See generally*, 6A Powell on Real Property ¶ 876.6.

5.   State Relocation Act Benefits May Exceed Federal Benefits. In *Beaty v. Imperial Irrigation District*, 186 Cal.App.3d 897, 911–12 (1987), the Court held: "Before adoption of the State Relocation Act in 1971, California provided for relocation assistance to displaced persons only in a limited number of circumstances. Such assistance was then available if a person was displaced by a redevelopment agency taking land for a redevelopment project (Health & Saf. Code, § 33415). In responding to the Federal Act, the California Legislature chose to extend relocation benefits beyond those required by Congress. In framing the definition of "displaced person," the California Legislature rejected the narrow definition used in the Federal Act. The Federal Act limits the definition of a displaced person to

> "any person who moves from real property as a result of an acquisition of such real property, or as the result of the written order of the acquiring agency to vacate for a program or project undertaken by a Federal agency, or with Federal financial assistance" 42 U.S.C., § 4601, subd. (6).

By limiting relocation assistance under the Federal Act to persons forced to move by a federal "program or project," it is clear Congress contemplated limiting benefits to those persons displaced by government initiated action, i.e., eminent domain or negotiated purchase."

Significantly, the California Legislature, having the Federal Act before it, did not adopt Congress' language of "a program or project undertaken" by the government, but instead broadly defined a "displaced person" as "any person who moves from real property as a result of the acquisition of such real property by a public entity for public use." (Gov't Code § 7260, subd. (c)). This language is broad enough to include certain inverse condemnees within its scope. The Legislature's concern about inverse condemnees when it was adopting the relocation assistance provisions, is also reflected in section 7267.6. Section 7267.6 provides:

> "If any interest in real property is to be acquired by exercise of the power of eminent domain, the public entity shall institute formal condemnation proceedings. No public entity shall intentionally make it necessary for an owner to institute legal proceedings to prove the fact of the taking of his real property."

Compare the following. In a 2003 amendment to the Minnesota Urban Redevelopment Act, (MURA), the Minnesota legislature adopted the federal URA's definition of displaced person. *See* Minn.Stat. § 117.50, subd. 3 (Supp.2003) (displaced person' means any person who, notwithstanding the lack of federal financial participation, meets the definition of a displaced person under 42 USCA §§ 4601 to 4655, and regulations adopted under those sections). This legislative amendment superseded and limited the holding of *Application for Relocation Benefits of James Bros. Furniture, Inc.*, 642 N.W.2d 91, 96–7 (Minn.App.2002), which rejected an interpretation of MURA that would mirror the federal act and specifically concluded that the MURA definition of "displaced person" was broader than its federal counterpart. Under the rationale of James Bros., a person is displaced under the MURA if the person moves from real property as a result of an acquisition by an acquiring authority. The acquisition may be by negotiation or by eminent domain, Minn.Stat. § 117.50, subd. 4, and need not have been be causally connected to a state-funded project or program, James Bros., 642 N.W.2d at 99. For a comparative law view, see T. Kotaka and David Callies, *Moving Experiences: How the U.S and Japan Handle Mass Relocations*, Plan. Mag., Nov. 2006, at 42–44.

6.   The URA also requires Federal agencies and other public entities using federal funding to condemn private land to abide by policies that "assure consistent treatment of owners" and "promote public confidence in Federal land acquisition policies." 42 U.S.C. § 4651. Does the Act, however, provide a private right of action to enforce those policies? In *Clear Sky Car Wash LLC v. City of Chesapeake, Va.*, 743 F.3d 438 (4th Cir.2014), the Court of Appeals found it did not. The owner of a carwash whose land was

being condemned by the Virginia Department of Transportation (VDOT) asserted that the agency's "quick take" action violated § 4651 and its fair treatment principles. The Fourth Circuit clarified that the URA did not confer enforcement rights on landowners. Instead, Congress intended § 4651 to function more as a directive to guide federal agencies in overseeing the land acquisition process. Although the URA is supposed to help people relocate, it provides no right for the intended beneficiaries to enforce it themselves.

4. CONDEMNATION BLIGHT

"Condemnation blight" is integrally related to the late twentieth century and early 21st Century trend towards major development projects—airports, toll roads, freeways, arenas, convention centers, industrial parks, downtown redevelopment, waterfront parks and recreation, transit lines and public-private transit oriented development, university research centers, hospital office complexes and many others. The long delay in the planning, announcement, public acceptance, adoption, and implementation of these complex projects through condemnation of the affected lands, often causes damage to properties that are scheduled to be condemned in the future, but for which no formal eminent domain proceeding has been commenced.

When urban renewal (or other major project) plans are announced, "condemnation blight" may occur if the value of property, stated to be targeted for condemnation in the redevelopment plan or announcement of the project, falls prior to the time the redevelopment agency formally begins condemnation of the site. Areas targeted for redevelopment are frequently older areas with intense rental use of both housing and businesses. When a redevelopment project is announced and the notice specifically identifies the property to be taken, tenants of the targeted property may move out, creating losses in rental income and increases in crime and dilapidation. The time between the announcement of the project and the actual condemnation of the targeted land may also leave the targeted landowner with a substantial interim loss (both in rental income and in the decrease in value of the property between the project announcement and actual condemnation) and calling into question whether that loss should be considered in assessing the value of the property at the time of condemnation. Condemnation blight therefore applies to the availability of increased pre-condemnation damages when the redevelopment agency subsequently commences eminent domain proceedings against the targeted property.

Normally the valuation of the condemned property is fixed at the time of commencement of the eminent domain proceeding, the deposit of money after the suit is commenced or at the time the jury trial commences, and is known as the de jure take. Where there is condemnation blight, the courts have adopted a variety of means to establish a different date for valuation of the property than the de jure date. Some courts choose to value the property at the time of the de jure take, but compute compensation as if the property had not been subjected to the debilitating effect of condemnation blight. Most courts have been willing to measure compensation at a date prior to the de jure taking. Another approach is to fix the date of the taking at the time in which the acts of the condemning authority can be said to have deprived the owner of the beneficial use and enjoyment of the property. Other courts have declared that the date of the taking is the first time the owner could have justifiably relied upon the actions of the condemnor as leading to the loss of her property. *See* Robert H. Freilich, *Condemnation Blight: Analysis and Solutions, Chapter 5 in Current Condemnation Law: Takings, Compensation and Benefits*, Ackerman and Dynkowski, eds. 83, 91 (American Bar Association, Section of Real Property, Probate and Trust Law, 2006).

Condemnation blight is not applicable to "generalized blight," consisting of the preparation of plans or drawings for a public works improvement, as well as the adoption of measures by a public entity possessing the power of condemnation in preparation for public improvements, without the specific targeting of a tract of land. *See Border Business Park v. City of San Diego*, 142 Cal.App.4th 1538 (2006). For instance, the proposed construction of a highway, contemplated expansion of an airport, or enactment of a transportation corridor map as a portion of the traffic circulation element of a comprehensive plan, are all examples of pre-improvement planning. Mere planning by a government body in anticipation of taking land for public use and preliminary steps to accomplish this, without filing of condemnation proceedings, a physical taking or actual invasion, or specific targeting of land for condemnation, is considered "generalized blight" and is not actionable by the landowner as in contravention of the U.S. or state Constitution. *See City of Los Angeles v. Superior Court*, 194 Cal.App.4th 210 (2011).

Condemnation blight must be distinguished from "inverse condemnation" which was studied in Chapter 3. Where a property is designated for formal condemnation pursuant to a planned, prospective, public improvement, adverse interim consequences caused to the property by the prospect of condemnation will not constitute an inverse condemnation unless those interim consequences are such that the owner is deprived of the use and enjoyment of the property, or is subjected to the loss of the property before formal condemnation can provide compensation. If there has been such an interim deprivation of use, or exposure to loss, then the principle of de facto taking becomes applicable to accelerate the time when the governmental authority must make compensation and the affected landowner may bring an inverse condemnation action without awaiting the commencement of a formal condemnation action by the authority. *See McElwee v. Southeastern Transportation Authority*, 948 A.2d 762 (Pa.2008).

5. EXCESS CONDEMNATION

DEPARTMENT OF TRANSPORTATION V. FORTUNE FEDERAL SAVINGS AND LOAN ASSOCIATION

Supreme Court of Florida, 1988.
532 So.2d 1267.

KOGAN, JUSTICE.

We have for review the Second District Court of Appeal opinion in *Department of Transportation v. Fortune Federal Savings and Loan Ass'n*, 507 So.2d 1172 (Fla.2d DCA 1987), in which section 337.27(3), Florida Statute (1985) was held invalid. The district court certified the following question to this Court as one of great public importance:

> Whether section 337.27(3), Florida Statutes (1985), which limits acquisition costs in eminent domain cases by allowing the state to condemn more property than is necessary to implement a valid public purpose, contravenes the Florida Constitution?

Id. at 1178. Because we see the central issue before this Court differently than did the district court, we deem it necessary to restate the certified question as follows:

> Whether the public purpose of limiting acquisition costs under section 337.27(3), Florida Statutes (1985), which allows the state to condemn more property than is presently needed where it would cost more to condemn only part of the property, contravenes the Florida Constitution?

As restated, we answer the certified question in the negative and quash the opinion of the district court.

These proceedings began when the Florida Department of Transportation (DOT) filed a petition to acquire a parcel of land through the state's power of eminent domain. The parcel, owned by Fortune Federal Savings and Loan Association (Fortune), was needed for a road widening project planned by DOT. A bank branch owned by Fortune sits on the parcel, and it is undisputed that a taking of the whole or part of the parcel will destroy the banking business. DOT admittedly only needs a portion of the parcel to complete its project.

At the hearing conducted pursuant to DOT's eminent domain petition, testimony indicated that if only a portion of the property were taken, Fortune would be entitled to $2,000,000 in business damages under section 73.071(3)(b), Florida Statutes (1985). DOT attempted to invoke section 337.27(3) which allows the state agency to take an entire parcel of land when it would cost the state less money than if only part of the tract were taken. Fortune contested the taking of the unneeded tract, arguing that to do so would violate the state constitutional prohibition against taking private property except for a public purpose and with full compensation Art. X, § 6, Fla. Const. If DOT were only permitted to condemn the needed portion of the property, Fortune would be entitled to $2,225,000. That number represents the value of the condemned land ($225,000) plus business damages ($2,000,000). If DOT is permitted to take the entire tract, including the unneeded portion, Fortune would be entitled only to $480,000, representing the value of the entire, undivided tract of land. The trial court granted only the petition for the taking of that portion of the tract needed by DOT to complete its project. It did not reach the constitutional issues raised by Fortune.

On appeal the Second District Court of Appeal held section 337.27(3) unconstitutional as allowing a taking without a valid public purpose. The court ruled that saving the state money, in itself, was not a valid public purpose under the state constitutional guidelines. The court reasoned that allowing the state agency to take more property than necessary to complete its project in order to avoid the payment of business damages would deprive the owner of his private property without full compensation and without a valid public purpose.

Before analyzing the constitutional issues presented, we will examine the statutory provisions involved to discern precisely what is required or allowed by the legislation. Section 73.071(3)(b), Florida Statutes (1985), part of the chapter entitled "Eminent Domain," states:

> Where less than the entire property is sought to be appropriated, any business damages to the remainder caused by the taking, including, when the action is by the Department of Transportation TTT for the condemnation of a right-of-way, and the effect of the taking of the property involved may damage or destroy an established business of more than 5 years' standing, owned by the party whose lands are being so taken, located upon adjoining lands owned or held by such party, the probable damages to such business which the denial of the use of the property so taken may reasonably cause; any person claiming the right to recover such special damages shall set forth in his written defenses the nature and extent of such damages.

This provision entitles Fortune to recover $2,000,000 in damages if DOT is permitted to take only part of the property. If DOT takes the entire parcel, Fortune is not entitled to business damages under the statute.

The statute under scrutiny here, section 337.27(3), Florida Statutes (1985), permits the state agency to condemn more property than is necessary when the state agency saves money by doing so. The statute, enacted in 1984, states:

In the acquisition of lands and property, the department [of
transportation] may acquire an entire lot, block, or tract of land
if, by doing so, the acquisition costs to the department will be
equal to or less than the cost of acquiring a portion of the property.
This subsection shall be construed as a specific recognition by the
Legislature that this means of limiting the rising costs to the state
of property acquisition is a public purpose and that, without this
limitation, the viability of many public projects will be threatened.

§ 337.27(3), Fla.Stat. (1985). The second sentence of the provision
states the legislature's determination that limiting the rising cost of
property acquisition is a public purpose. The pivotal issue before this Court
is whether that public purpose is valid.

While it is true, as DOT argues, that the legislative statement of public
purpose deserves some degree of deference, *State v. Housing Finance
Authority of Polk County*, 376 So.2d 1158 (Fla.1979), the ultimate question
of the validity of that public purpose is a judicial question to be decided by
a court of competent jurisdiction. *See Canal Authority v. Miller*, 243 So.2d
131 (Fla.1970); *Wilton v. St. Johns County*, 123 So. 527 (Fla.1929).
Nonetheless, the role of the judiciary in determining whether the power of
eminent domain is exercised in furtherance of a public purpose is narrow.
See Berman v. Parker, 348 U.S. 26 (1954). With this limited standard of
review in mind, we must examine the statute, as well as the enunciated
public purpose, to determine whether each fulfills the requirements of the
Florida Constitution.

In order to invalidate a statute that has a stated public purpose, the
party challenging that statute must show that the stated purpose is
arbitrary and capricious. The determination by the legislature of a public
purpose, "while not conclusive, is presumed valid and should be upheld
unless it is arbitrary or unfounded—unless it is so clearly erroneous as to
be beyond the power of the legislature." *See State v. Miami Beach
Redevelopment Agency*, 392 So.2d 875, 886 (Fla.1980). Thus, the
legislature's statement that section 337.27(3) reflects the public purpose of
limiting property acquisition costs must be upheld unless that purpose is
beyond the power of the legislature and is clearly erroneous.

In attempting to show that section 337.27(3) has no valid public
purpose, Fortune argues that it is improper to require one private business
to finance a public project, and thus reducing property acquisition costs at
the expense of one business is beyond the power of the legislature. We
cannot agree. It should be recognized that the full compensation demanded
by our state constitution requires only that the condemning authority
compensate the property owner for the full market value of the property
taken. It is only by the will of the legislature that business damages may
be awarded in certain situations which are properly limited by the
legislature. In other words, the legislature has created a right to business

damages, so it may also limit that right. There is no constitution- al right to business damages. As the district court noted, business damages are a matter of legislative grace. The legislature may award them in one statute and take them away in another. Fortune has no vested right to those damages. Therefore, it can hardly be said that the forfeiting of business damages requires Fortune to shoulder the burden of financing a public project.

Accordingly, the only remaining question is whether reducing the cost of property acquisition is a valid public purpose in the context of eminent domain when the entire parcel in question is not needed for a present public project. To resolve this question, it is important to distinguish between "public use" and "public purpose."

The term "public purpose" does not mean simply that the land is used for a specific public function, i.e. a road or other right of way. Rather, the concept of public purpose must be read more broadly to include projects which benefit the state in a tangible, foreseeable way. We believe that the purpose of cutting acquisition costs to expand the financial base for further public projects constitutes a valid public purpose under this definition. We find no reasonable justification for limiting, as Fortune argues we should, the definition of public purpose to that of public use. On the contrary, we believe that our decision is supported by the legislature's recognition of the need to reduce the costs of financing the vast growth this state will endure over the next several years. *Baycol, Inc. v. Downtown Development Authority*, 315 So.2d 451 (Fla.1975). This decision does present us with one standard which we must employ: "Eminent Domain cannot be employed to take private property for a predominantly private use" 315 So.2d at 455 (emphasis in original). Thus, if the condemning authority uses the property for an essentially nonpublic use, the condemnation is invalid. In this case, there is no evidence that DOT intends to subject the property to a private use. Indeed, the evidence suggests that DOT has no present plans for the land not used in the highway widening project. In any event, Fortune has certainly not shown that the property will be privately used.

Accordingly, because Fortune has not sustained its burden of demonstrating that the public purpose stated by the legislature is clearly erroneous or arbitrary and unfounded, we uphold the constitutionality of section 337.27(3), Florida Statutes (1985).

It is so ordered.

Notes: Remnant, Recoupment and Protective Theories

There are three justifications for excess condemnation: remnant, recoupment and protective bases. *See* David L. Callies, *A Hypothetical Case: Value Capture/Joint Development Techniques*, 16 Urb.L.Ann. 155 (1979). In addition, the Kelo revolution has added the constitutional test of public use to the exercise of excess condemnation. *See, Utah Department of Transportation*

(UDOT) v. Carlson, 332 P.3d 900, 901 (Utah 2014). The transportation authority condemned 15 acres of private land, even though it only planned to utilize 1.2 acres for the project, apparently to avoid litigation over potential severance damages. UDOT, however, never expressly articulated its plans or purposes for the excess property. The case was remanded to the trial court to decide if UDOT's condemnation of excess property satisfies the public use element in an eminent domain action. While the lower court was given the discretion to allow the parties to further develop the factual record, the Utah Supreme Court observed that Kelo never effectively resolved the public use question, leaving it unclear as to whether excess takings are constitutional. The three justifications for the use of excess condemnation are as follows:

1. Remnants. The remnant theory applies when a portion of private land is taken for a public improvement, leaving a remainder of such a size and shape as to be virtually worthless. *See Piedmont Triad Regional Water Authority v. Sumner Hills Incorporated*, 543 S.E.2d 844, 846 (N.C.2001) ("The question raised by the instant appeal is whether the Water Authority may condemn the entire tract of property, including the 97 unneeded acres, under North Carolina law. Section 40A–7(a) of our General Statutes provides:

(a) When the proposed project requires condemnation of only a portion of a parcel of land leaving a remainder of such shape, size or condition that it is of little value, a condemnor may acquire the entire parcel by purchase or condemnation. If the remainder is to be condemned the petition filed under the provisions of G.S. 40A–20 or the complaint filed under the provisions of G.S. 40A–41 shall include:

(1) A determination by the condemnor that a partial taking of the land would substantially destroy the economic value or utility of the remainder; or (2) A determination by the condemnor that an economy in the expenditure of public funds will be promoted by taking the entire parcel; or (3) A determination by the condemnor that the interest of the public will be best served by acquiring the entire parcel. N.C.Gen.Stat. § 40A–7(a) (1999) (emphasis added).")

Remnants are allowed by statute to be taken even when the condemnation of an entire parcel is only slightly more expensive than the condemnation of the needed land. *See State by State Highway Commissioner v. Buck*, 226 A.2d 840 (N.J.App.1967). *See People ex rel. Department of Public Works v. Superior Court*, 436 P.2d 342 (Cal.1968), the court held that even a "remnant" as large as 54 acres could be condemned:

Although a parcel of 54 landlocked acres is not a physical remnant, it is a financial remnant: its value as a landlocked parcel is such that severance damages might equal its value. Remnant takings have long been considered proper. *Id.* at 346.

2. Recoupment is a means of financing public improvements by condemning more land than is needed, and then selling the surplus to private individuals at a price enhanced by the improvement. In *Cincinnati v. Vester*, 281 U.S. 439 (1930), the City of Cincinnati sought to acquire excess land by

condemnation with the design of reselling it at a profit to private individuals as a method of financing a costly road widening project. The United States Supreme Court held such a taking to be violative of constitutional rights absent a state legislative declaration authorizing such public use. The Fortune Federal case demonstrates the use of financial recoupment where there is such a statutory directive. The escalating costs of land assembly for public "mega" projects, together with increased awareness of the impacts of such undertakings on surrounding land uses, have led to efforts to integrate the financial, social and land use planning required to bring these projects into being. Particular concern focuses around freeway interchanges and mass transit stations. Recapture of the value "created" in an area by the vast expenditure of public funds can achieve a number of objectives:

    (a)   lessen the financial burden on public agencies;

    (b)   increase the community benefits resulting from the project;

    (c)   provide for special social needs of those in the project area for housing and access.

What happens if the condemning authority refuses to condemn the entire parcel? Severance damages will be available but the court will limit the damages to the parcel by excluding any added value that the project brings. Is it fair to limit the landowner's damages to pre-condemnation value, while allowing the condemnor to acquire excess land and then sell it for the value added by the project? Protective Theory permits the condemnor to take the needed parcel plus excess land to protect the public improvement. The authority for protective excess condemnation, as well as recoupment, must be based upon a statutory authorization. *See* N.J.Stat.Ann. § 27:7–22.6; West's Rev. Code Ann. § 47.12.250; R.I. Const. Amend. 17, § 1. The protective theory has been used to condemn excess land around dams and reservoirs to enhance the safety and beauty of the area. *See Department of Public Works v. Lagiss*, 223 Cal.App.2d 23 (1963); *Culley v. Pearl River Industrial Commission*, 108 So.2d 390, 400 (Miss.1959) ("the one-quarter mile perimeter is necessary for the public use in the protection and development of the reservoir").

    3.   Under the protective theory excess land adjacent to the public improvement but unnecessary to its construction is taken to prevent undesirable development or activity in the project's vicinity. Protective excess condemnation permits a condemnor to control the use of tangential property, either by holding it or conveying it subject to appropriate restrictions. By controlling the use of adjacent land, a condemnor is able to preserve or enhance the appearance, value or utility of a project, as well as ensure the achievement of project objectives. The preservation and protection of public improvements have long been held to be public uses; thus, the constitutionality of excess condemnation under the protective theory is well settled. The major concern of the courts in permitting this type of excess condemnation is whether the excess condemnation is reasonably related to the achievement of the purposes of the original condemnation.

Application of the protective theory most often occurs in cases involving highway projects, urban redevelopment, or dam and reservoir construction. Property adjacent to the public improvement is taken to protect the public from safety hazards or health hazards or to preserve the scenic beauty of the area surrounding the improvement. The factors of safety and aesthetics have also been considered justifications for the taking of excess land to protect or preserve various other types of public improvements. *See* Robert H. Freilich and Stephen P. Chinn, *Transportation Corridors: Shaping and Financing Urbanization*, 55 UMKC L.REV. 153, 203–04 (1987).

C. TAX TECHNIQUES OF REDEVELOPMENT

In the early days of urban redevelopment, known as "Urban Renewal," the redevelopment agency was able to acquire property through eminent domain and then resell the property to a private developer at a substantial write-down, the sale price being only 1/4 of the acquisition price. The federal government, through Title I of the National Housing Act of 1949, would reimburse the agency for 3/4 of the write-down loss plus all expenses of preparing and implementing the redevelopment plan, together with all consultant costs. The local government's 1/3 share of the write-down was not paid in cash but was calculated by valuing the sewer, water and road improvements that the government brought to the site. The scale of this enormous federal subsidy to local government and private redevelopers resulted in wholesale abuse of the power of eminent domain and a swath of destruction swept across the urban landscape. *See* Martin Anderson, *The Federal Bulldozer: A Critical Analysis of Urban Renewal*, 1949 to 1962 (1965). For a valuable description of the 1949 National Housing Act programs, *see* Peter Salsich, Jr., *A Decent Home for Every American, Can the 1949 Goal be Met*, 71 N.C.L.REV. 1619 (1993).

By 1974, over 400 federal grant programs, including urban renewal, housing code enforcement, demolition and community planning grants were eliminated and a new consolidated "Community Block Grant Program" was substituted at a loss of over 3/4 of the former grant revenue to local government. The subsidy to the private redeveloper disappeared and new subsidies had to be found or the urban renewal program would become moribund. The substitute was no surprise. Local governments, buttressed by state enabling acts, allowed the private developer, who now had to pay closer to 100% of the acquisition price, the ability to capture the increased property taxes flowing from the new development and use it to offset parking, utilities and construction costs. As the programs became more sophisticated the anticipated tax increment realized from the project became bondable and the developer never had to advance any equity capital on the project. The programs involved either total tax abatement or tax increment financing, commonly known as "TIF." *See* George Lefcoe, *Redevelopment Takings After* Kelo: *What's Blight Got to Do With It?*, 17

S.CAL.REV. OF LAW & SOCIAL JUSTICE 803 (2008) [Reprinted in 2009 Zoning and Planning Law Handbook (Thomson Reuters-West Publishing)].

1. TAX ABATEMENT

Tax abatement and tax increment financing are both rooted in the concept of teaming government powers with private enterprise to do that which neither could do alone—hence, the oft used phrase "public-private" partnership. The private side does not possess the government powers necessary to undertake large-scale projects requiring eminent domain, provision of public utilities and financing through taxation, special district assessments and tax exempt bonding. The government, on the other hand, does not generally act in a proprietary capacity designed to efficiently execute a large-scale urban development. Together, however, such projects are made possible. *See* Robert H Freilich & Brenda J. Nichols, *Public-Private Partnerships in Joint Development: The Legal and Financial Anatomy of Large-Scale Urban Development Projects*, 7 MUN.FINANCE J. 5 (1986).

While tax abatement and tax increment financing may be used by private enterprise, one should not assume that all projects which make use of these tools are money-making ventures. Often, the entities are nonprofit corporations established solely to improve the area.

Both mechanisms generally operate on the premise that offering certain incentives will prompt private parties to develop deteriorating or blighted areas, and/or generate economic productivity in areas which are underproductive or idle. Since investment in such areas is risky, the incentives are often quite valuable. Monetary incentives, discussed below, usually weigh most heavily. Lower on the scale, but perhaps generating as much debate, is the use of eminent domain in redevelopment projects. Often this power is delegated to private entities, but more frequently the power is actually exercised by or in conjunction with the local government. In any event, quick land assembly is needed in order to execute a redevelopment project successfully, so acquisition of lands by eminent domain remains a key corollary element of tax abatement and tax increment financing projects. *See* Elizabeth A. Taylor, *The Dudley Street Neighborhood Initiative and the Power of Eminent Domain*, 36 B.C.L.REV. 1061 (1996); Kenneth A. Porro and Sheri K. Siegelbaum, *Redevelopment through Condemnation: The Key to Municipal Revitalization*, 168 N.J.LAW. 29 (April 1995).

Tax-abated redevelopment provides an incentive for private enterprise to develop within a deteriorating area by freezing the assessed value of the project area at its pre-development assessment, thus permitting the developer to pay only those taxes at the frozen assessed valuation even while property values substantially increase. The abatement of the tax exists only for a set statutory period, subsequent to which the owners pay tax on the full assessed value.

Under the New York scheme, qualifying property owners pay a 'mini tax' which is calculated not on the assessed value of the new improvement but by applying the current tax rate to the assessed value of the property in the year before construction began. *See D.S. Alamo Associates v. Commissioner of Finance of the City of New York*, 520 N.E.2d 542 (N.Y.1988) where the Court of Appeals held that: (1) entitlement to exemption did not depend on the nature of the building's ownership; (2) entitlement of commercial uses to the benefit of the exemption was not limited to the extent that such uses were "incidental" to residential use; and (3) an entire 32-story mixed-use condominium building, which included commercial space comprising less than 12% of the building's aggregate floor area, was eligible for the full range of statutory tax benefits. Missouri's tax abatement is accomplished with a constitutional provision and a statutory procedure delegating condemnation and redevelopment powers to private redevelopment corporations. *See* Vernon's Ann.Mo.Stat. Ch. 353. Article 10, Section 7 of the Missouri Constitution, entitled, "Relief from Taxation—Forest Lands—Obsolete, Decadent, or Blighted Areas—Limitations—Exception," providing:

For the purpose of encouraging the reconstruction, redevelopment, and rehabilitation of obsolete, decadent, or blighted areas, the general assembly by general law may provide for such partial relief from taxation of the lands devoted to any such purpose, and of the improvements thereon, by such method or methods, for such period or periods of time, not exceeding twenty-five years in any instance, and upon such terms, conditions, and restrictions as it may prescribe. *See* Robert L. Zoeckler, *The Tax Abatement Program for Historic Properties in Georgia*, 28 GA.ST.BAR J. 129 (1992); and Susan Mead, *"Incentives for Downtown Revitalization," Southwest Legal Foundation Institute for Planning, Zoning, & Eminent Domain* (Matthew Bender 2000). Tax abatement (because the tax is not paid on the differential between the frozen and fair market values) usually requires a state constitutional amendment to avoid the problem of uniformity of taxation requirements. *See Annbar Associates v. West Side Redevelopment Corp.*, 397 S.W.2d 635 (Mo.1965).

2. TAX INCREMENT FINANCING

Tax increment financing (TIF) statutes authorize the governing body of a municipality to adopt a redevelopment plan providing for the redevelopment of a designated area. The municipality is authorized to issue bonds or other obligations which are secured by a pledge of payments in lieu of taxes (PILOTs), attributable to the increase in assessed valuation of taxable real property within the designated area resulting from redevelopment improvements.

The theory of TIF is that by encouraging redevelopment projects, the value of real property in a redevelopment area will increase. When a TIF plan is adopted, the assessed value of real property in the redevelopment area is frozen for tax purposes at the current base level prior to construction of improvements. The owner of the property continues to pay taxes at this base level. As the property is improved, the assessed value of real property in the redevelopment area increases above the base level. By applying the tax rate of all taxing districts having taxing power over the base level, a "tax increment" is produced. The tax increments are paid by the property owner in the same manner as regular property taxes. The payments, however, are not transferred to the general fund, but are transferred by the collecting agency to the treasurer of the municipality and deposited in a special allocation trust fund. The fund is then used to pay directly for redevelopment or to retire bonds or other obligations issued to pay project costs at the outset. *See generally Tax Increment Financing* (David L. Callies and W. Andrew Gowder, Jr., eds. 2012); Robert H. Freilich & Brenda A. Nichols, *Public Private Partner-ships in Joint Development: The Legal and Financial Anatomy of Largescale Urban Development Projects*, 7 MUN.FIN.J. 5 (1986). With tax increment financing, the developer receives the subsidy at the beginning of the project rather than over the life of the project as with tax abatement. Tax increment financing has become the technique of choice over tax abatement because the full tax is paid although diverted to the redevelopment area through a trust fund. TIFs based on property taxes have now been extended to capture of sales and gross receipts taxes and are known as "Super TIFs."

Many tax increment finance statutes require a showing of "blight" in the area as the triggering device for redevelopment. A conservative definition of blight is "a portion of a city which the legislative authority of the city determines by reason of age, obsolescence, or physical deterioration, has become economic and social liabilities and that such conditions are conducive to ill health, transmission of disease, crime, or the inability to pay reasonable taxes." *See* Mo.Rev.Stat. § 353.020(2). The Washington statute emphasizes substandard housing conditions as a trigger for blight including substantial physical dilapidation, deterioration, age or obsolescence of buildings, insanitary and unsafe conditions, inadequate ventilation, danger to person and property, and detriment to public health, safety, morals and welfare. *See* West's Rev. Code Wash.Ann. 35.81.010. The California Health and Safety Code lists the following factors to be considered when determining blight: defective design and character of physical construction; faulty interior arrangement and exterior spacing; high density of population and overcrowding; inadequate provision of ventilation, light, sanitation, open spaces and recreational facilities; age, obsolescence, mixed character, and shifting use. *See In re Bunker Hill Urban Renewal Project 1B*, 389 P.2d 538 (Cal.1964); *see also State v. Miami*

Beach Redevelopment Agency, 392 So.2d 875 (Fla.1980), which illustrates the use of tax increment finance bonds in severely blighted area.

(a) The "But For" Requirement

In a minority of states, at the time public officials designate a project area for tax increment financing, local governments are obliged by statute to make a special finding that without government assistance, private developers would not have undertaken the project on their own. A second type of "but for" test calls for local officials to determine that the proposed project could not reasonably be expected to proceed with the same public benefits, on the same timetable, at the designated location, and still be financially feasible for the developer without the public contribution. Unfortunately, the blight and "but for" tests are for the most part totally evaded by the developers, the governments and the courts. The following case is illustrative.

BOARD OF EDUCATION, PLEASANTDALE SCHOOL DISTRICT NO. 107 V. VILLAGE OF BURR RIDGE

Court of Appeals of Illinois, 2003.
341 Ill.App.3d 1004, 793 N.E.2d 856.

The Subject Property (Property) consists of approximately 85 acres of vacant land located immediately south of Interstate 55 and east of the County Line Road interchange, which divides Cook and DuPage Counties. The Village of Burr Ridge lies in both counties, but the Property lies solely in Cook County. There is no dispute that establishing the Property as a TIF district would enable the Village to more rapidly develop the Property by allowing the Village to provide various financial incentives to selected developers to offset the higher Cook County commercial real estate taxes.

Prior to the present litigation, the Village had been advised that the Property did not qualify as a TIF district. Steven Stricker, the Village administrator, sent a memo dated December 8, 1995, to the Village president and board, stating that he had spoken with Phil McKenna from the consulting firm of Kane, McKenna & Associates in order to "once again discuss the possibility of implementing a T.I.F. District in the Burr Ridge Corporate Park." In the memo, Stricker informed the Village that, "after reviewing the statutes we have determined once and for all that the Village of Burr Ridge would not be eligible to implement a T.I.F. District on the Corporate Park property."

[Despite that Report] the economic development committee recommended that the Village consider creating a TIF district for the Subject Property in order to create parity between Cook and DuPage Counties real estate taxes. The committee generated a chart illustrating the inequities of the tax structure between commercial property in Cook County and DuPage County, showing that businesses locating in Cook

County pay almost double in taxes what they would pay in DuPage County. On April 13, 1998, the Village accepted Barton's request and awarded Camiros, Ltd., a contract to prepare a TIF eligibility study and a redevelopment plan and project for the Property.

The Camiros eligibility study was undertaken in April and May 1998, and completed in July 1998. The Camiros study found that pursuant to the TIF Act, growth and development of the Property had been impeded by four blighting factors: diversity of ownership, flooding, obsolete platting, and tax delinquencies.

The Village also claimed that the Property should be deemed blighted on the ground that immediately prior to becoming vacant it qualified as a blighted improved area under the statute. Thus, under the factual circumstances in this case, the Property would be eligible for TIF financing if at least two or more of the blight factors were established or the Property qualified as a blighted improved area before becoming vacant.

The Village next contends that the trial court erred in granting the School District's motion for summary judgment where the conflicting expert opinion testimony created issues of fact regarding whether the four statutory blighting factors were established. In addition, the Village maintains that there is a genuine issue of fact regarding whether the Property qualified as a blighted area before it became vacant. Again, we must reject the Village's contentions.

In the instant case, the facts did not support the Village expert's opinion testimony that four statutory blight conditions existed on the Property. In support of these assertions, the Village presented the Camiros eligibility study and the expert testimony of urban planner John Brancaglione. To counter the Village's assertions, the School District presented the expert testimony of urban planner Theodore R. Johnson, who in turn relied on the guidelines promulgated by the Illinois Department of Revenue as set forth in the 1988 TIF compliance manual (TIF Guide).

Under the TIF Act, obsolete platting is one of the relevant factors in determining whether vacant land is blighted within the meaning of the Act. 65 ILCS 5/11–74.4–3(a) (1) (West 1994). The TIF guide defines obsolete platting of vacant land as follows:

> "Obsolete platting of vacant land would include parcels of limited or narrow size and configuration or parcels of irregular size or shape that would be difficult to develop on planned basis and in a manner compatible with contemporary standards and requirements."

The Subject Property consists of seven vacant parcels ranging in size from approximately 3 acres to 31 acres. At his deposition, the Village's expert, Brancaglione, testified that the Subject Property satisfied the obsolete platting criteria for blighted property because two of the seven parcels were too large. Brancaglione conceded that these large parcels could be readily subdivided, but opined that this was not a reasonable solution because it would be inconvenient and expensive to accomplish.

In an affidavit dated January 1, 2000, the School District's expert, Theodore R. Johnson, averred that the Subject Property was not affected by obsolete platting. He stated that the two parcels at issue were not of limited or narrow size and were accessible from Frontage Road. He further stated that the fact that these parcels had not been subdivided into smaller parcels did not represent an impediment to development. The facts in this case do not show that obsolete platting interfered with the development of the Property. No evidence was presented that the shape or size of the parcels at issue ever interfered with the economic development of the Subject Property.

In the present case, evidence indicates that portions of the proposed TIF district are located in a flood plain. However, the only report of flooding regarding the Subject Property came from a 1933 report by the Department of Corrections which indicated that some flooding occurred on the property in the 1930s, more than 50 years before the Burr Ridge Corporate Park was developed.

The evidence shows that the Subject Property was developed as part of the Burr Ridge Corporate Park in the early 1980s by EMRO, a unit of the Marathon Oil Company. The EMRO development included, among other things, sewers and infrastructure improvements relating to drainage and flood detention. The Subject Property contains a storm water management easement around the retention areas that was designed to account for the 100-year flood plain.

In concluding that there was sufficient evidence of flooding to support a finding of blight with respect to the Property, the Village relied on Brancaglione's opinion that if any portion of the Subject Property appeared on a FEMA (Federal Emergency Management Agency) or FIRM (Flood Insurance Rate Map) flood plain map, the flooding criterion of the TIF Act was satisfied. The evidence, however, reveals that the flood plain maps Brancaglione relied on in forming his opinion had not been updated to reflect drainage improvements on the Subject Property.

In addition, the TIF guide does not provide that the inclusion of property on a flood map is per se evidence of flooding. Rather, the TIF guide provides that evidence of flooding may be derived from secondary source information that satisfactorily documents the condition of flooding. Here, the flood plain maps did not document any conditions of flooding on the Subject Property and the maps did not include several drainage improvements on the Subject Property. The TIF guide refers to conditions of flooding and not the mere possibility of future flooding.

Under the TIF Act, tax and special delinquencies on a parcel of vacant land is one of the relevant factors in determining whether the parcel of land is blighted within the meaning of the Act. In regard to tax and special delinquencies, the TIF guide provides that "[e]vidence of nonpayment of real estate property taxes and/or special assessments for an unreasonable period of time must be shown to document the presence of this factor. This could also include evidence of forfeiture."

No evidence was presented that the previous tax delinquencies impaired the development of the Subject Property. Rather, the evidence shows that no tax delinquencies existed on the Subject Property at the time the Village enacted the TIF ordinances.

The trial court also found that development of the Subject Property would occur without the aid of TIF designation. The TIF Act requires a showing that the Subject Property "would not reasonably be anticipated to be developed without the adoption of the redevelopment plan." This is the "but-for" test.

The Village contends that the trial court's but-for finding was in error because the court failed to consider that the development of property within the proposed TIF district has been stagnated while properties outside the TIF area have continued to develop. The Village is incorrect. An examination of the trial court's order granting the School District's motion for summary judgment shows that the court was aware that economic development in the proposed TIF district had been stagnated. The trial court, however, determined that this stagnation was not attributable to any alleged blighting factors on the Property but, rather, was due to the tax disparities between Cook and DuPage Counties. The trial court also noted that, in spite of the large tax impediment, a 30-screen movie complex and a residential townhome development had been proposed for the Subject Property but was denied by the Village planning commission after a large number of residents actively campaigned against the two projects.

The record shows that the absence of TIF financing did not discourage other developers from being interested in the Property. For example, a company called Care Matrix was willing to proceed with a development on 19 acres of the Subject Property without TIF financing. Moreover, the course of development in the area immediately surrounding the Property supports the trial court's finding that the lack of development on the Property is due to the tax disparities between Cook and DuPage Counties rather than any statutory blighting factors. The record shows that during the early to mid-1990s, three banks, two office buildings and a restaurant were developed in the immediate area of the Property. The record also shows that Barton proceeded with his project before the Village actually adopted the ordinances establishing the TIF district.

Given the evidence showing that developers were interested in the Subject Property without TIF financing and the evidence that growth and development were occurring in the immediate area of the Property, there is no basis in the record to overturn the trial court's finding that the Village failed to meet the "but-for" test articulated in the TIF Act. *See Castel Properties v. City of Marion*, 631 N.E.2d 459 (Ill.App.1994) (affirming the trial court's finding that the city therein failed to meet the but-for test, highlighting the extensive evidence of growth and redevelopment occurring in the area and noting that a project was being developed without the TIF issue having been determined).

Accordingly, for the reasons set forth above, the judgments of the circuit court of Cook County are affirmed.

NOTES

1.   In another "but for" case the Illinois Court of Appeals found that a large agricultural tract was not blighted. *See Henry County Board v. Village of Orion*, 663 N.E.2d 1076 (Ill.App.1996). Does it surprise you that suburban cities and rural villages will try to claim that they are "blighted" in order to capture tax revenue from the county, school districts and adjacent small towns?

2.   Tax increment financing legislation has been enacted in 49 states and the District of Columbia. *See* Council of Dev. Fin. Agencies, 2008 Tax Increment Financing State-By-State Report (2008). Nevertheless, TIF is a process that has, in the large, not favored the urban redevelopment of blighted land and has, under loose city findings of "near blight," been rarely challenged in the courts, which has permitted its predominant use to be suburban shopping centers, large scale entertainment, office blocks and big box retail entities to thrive upon hapless owners of land. *See* Robert Denlow, *Tax Increment Finance from the Property Owner's View*, ABA Section of State and Local Government Newsletter, October 1999. In the St. Louis, Missouri metropolitan area, for example, there are approximately fifty (50) TIF projects. Only a few are in the City of St. Louis, an older city with substantial decay. The rest are in St. Louis County, an affluent area surrounding the City. Most of the TIF projects involve strip shopping centers or some form of commercial development). For a report on TIF in the St. Louis region, See East-West Gateway Council of Governments, An Assessment of the Effectiveness and Fiscal Impacts of the Use of Development Incentives in the St. Louis Region, Interim Report IV (Jan. 2009). Denlow also points out that State enabling legislation does not mandate that projects in seriously blighted areas must be designed to improve the wellbeing of its dislocated small business owners or poorly housed residents. Displaced property owners have rights to compensation and in a few states displaced residents to relocation payments as well, but often they are denied compensation for the loss of business profit and goodwill. They have no constitutional or statutory right to prevent the redevelopment of the project area for the benefit of others.

3. TIF offers distinct advantages over the financing of capital improvements to attract new private development through: (a) tax abatements, (b) general obligation bonds and (c) special district assessment.

(a) Tax abatements. Local governments can grant tax abatements to induce firms to build new taxable facilities. Tax abatements are not contingent on the tax base increasing. However, since the taxes do not accrue and are uncertain until they have been collected, local governments cannot issue bonds at the commencement to finance the project. Revenue bonds can be issued using TIF financing since the extent of the funds placed in a TIF trust fund are known immediately.

(b) General obligation bonds. TIF financing is easier to arrange than general obligation financing, the way that most local governments finance capital improvements, because in most states it escapes constitutional debt limits and majority or supermajority voter approval.

(c) Special district assessment. A special assessment is more akin to a user fee than a tax because it is based on the benefit conferred upon the taxpayer. The special assessment will be levied in addition to the regular ad valorem tax. Affected property owners have to approve the formation of a special assessment district which, during a period of discontent with government and tax revenue, has little chance of success.

(b) Uses and Abuses of TIF

The following article comprehensively assesses the current status of TIF, both as an excellent tool for creating new urbanism spaces and traditional neighborhood and downtown development and as a continued sad exponent of local government fiscal cannibalism in metropolitan settings.

(1) Excerpts from George Lefcoe, *Competing for the Next Hundred Million Americans: The Uses and Abuses of Tax Increment Financing*, 43 URBAN LAWYER 424 (2011).

The Use of TIF to Support Walkable Urbanism

A number of communities across the country, including Virginia Beach, Virginia and Lakewood, Colorado, have used tax increment financing to successfully achieve mixed use walkable downtowns and neighborhoods. See Dep't of Finance, City of Virginia Beach, Report on the Tax Increment Financing districts and special service districts in the City of Virginia Beach 11 (2009), finding assessed property values in the city center climbed steadily from $150,000,000 in 1998 to over $800,000,000 in 2009. Besides producing over $5,000,000 a year in property taxes, the project area also generates $5,700,000 in other business taxes (hotel, meal and admission taxes, business property and license fees, and sales taxes).

Outer Suburbs Use TIF to Lure Employers from Center Cities and First Ring Suburbs

While a number of cities are using TIF in its traditional manner to redevelop city neighborhoods and downtowns, most cities use TIF money to outbid each other for jobs. Minnesota is a perfect example. TIF is the most commonly used economic development tool in Minnesota. Because TIF is available to all the cities and counties within the state, they compete against each other for jobs. Two researchers decided to take advantage of excellent available data in Minnesota to see whether TIF- subsidized employment helped where it was most needed, within easy reach of minority, low income, and transit dependent big city populations. The study faulted Minnesota's program for enabling prosperous outer suburbs sometimes to lure employers from the poverty-burdened cities of Minneapolis and St. Paul and their inner suburbs.

State Law Reforms Inadequate to Curb TIF Use for Retailing

State legislators have done little to curb inter-municipal competition for retail activity for reasons outlined later in the text. A handful of states have enacted limitations on TIF funding of retail development. The most aggressive can be found in Utah and Minnesota. Utah bars the collection or expenditure of TIF for retail development in an economic development area if development of retail is the project area's 'primary objective.' Utah Code Ann. § 17C–1–407(1)(a) (West 2010) ("If the development of retail sales of goods is the primary objective of an urban renewal project area, tax increment from the urban renewal project area may not be paid to or used by an agency unless a finding of blight is made under Chapter 2, Part 3, Blight Determination in Urban Renewal Project Areas." It only allows TIF to be used for retail development in a blighted urban renewal area. In Minnesota, economic development districts generally cannot be used for retail, office, or similar commercial developments.

Other Taxing Entities Are Affected

Only the state can confer upon a city the right to utilize property tax increments that otherwise belong to counties, schools, and special districts. The basis for legislative concern is clear. Other taxing entities need to make up the revenue by service cutbacks, or increased fees and taxes, to the extent states allow development agencies to tap into their revenue streams. *See Meaney v. Sacramento Housing & Redevelopment Agency*, 13 Cal.App.4th 566 (1993) (Where four school districts and the Superintendent of Schools in the Sacramento area sued the Sacramento Housing & Redevelopment Agency, the city of Sacramento, and its council alleging improper diversion of tax revenue to build a courthouse that would have otherwise gone to the schools.). Counties may have to cut back on health clinics, drug treatment centers, sheriff patrol officers, jail beds, and library services. Schools are particularly burdened by TIF and tax abatements to business firms. These firms often bring new families to the area without contributing to the property taxes that schools need "to increase school capacity to serve the new enrollment." In California, Governor Brown has called for the elimination of TIF programs and has called for the return of $1.6 billion dollars stashed in redevelopment agency TIF trust funds.

A handful of states allow schools, counties and other taxing entities the choice of opting in or out of sharing their tax increments for any particular redevelopment or economic development plan. Ga. Code Ann. 36–44–8 (1) (2010) (consent needed from independent taxing entities); Ohio Rev. Code Ann. § 5709.40(D)(1) (2010) (need school board approval if TIF district is to last for more than 10 years); 53 Pa.Cons.Stat. § 6930.5(a)(7) (2010) (each entity can opt out of the plan); and Texas Tax Code Ann. § 311.013(f) (2010) (each taxing unit can opt out).

Taxing entities with the option of withholding their revenues from TIF projects frequently negotiate the terms of their participation through agreements with sponsoring city jurisdictions. Deal points usually include the duration of participation, the percentage of increment to be withheld and other contributions to school district needs. Council of Development Finance Agencies, Advanced Tax Increment Finance Guide 18 (2009).

Failure of Statutory "But For" Tests

(a) As in the Burr Ridge case, in Illinois and twenty-one states and the District of Columbia, local governments must make a finding that redevelopment would not reasonably be expected to occur solely through private investment within the reasonably foreseeable future, or that no significant private development would have been likely to be built at the target site 'but for' the public role. Enforcement, though, is scant, left entirely to the discretion of the same local officials responsible for initiating the TIF effort, with no one specifically empowered to stop them from proceeding on the basis of cursory, poorly supported 'but for' findings.

(b) The Individual Project 'but for' Test: Once a jurisdiction selects a private redeveloper, and negotiates a deal, a second type of 'but for' test calls for local officials to determine that the proposed project could not reasonably be expected to proceed with the same public benefits, on the same timetable, at the designated location, and still be financially feasible for the developer without the public contribution. In Minneapolis, for instance, TIF applicants are expected to provide the basic financial data from which city officials can assess how much public support, if any, their projects require to be viable.

Public agencies and developers negotiate, often for months, over the appropriate rate of return the project should yield the developer. They pour over the developer's estimates of project expenses and costs, consider the cost implications of different site plans and architectural treatments, and study the rates of return developers are earning on comparable projects. A thorough analysis takes into account the track record, solvency and capacity of the developer, the timing of the agency's and developer's respective contributions, and unusual or extraordinary costs that made the project financially unfeasible in the marketplace, and public infrastructure to remedy existing deficiencies or provide adequate capacity to support the proposed project.

Though the industry lacks policies, procedures, and guidelines, one of the industry's leading trade associations, the Council of Development Finance Agencies (CDFA), strongly recommends project specific 'but for' studies as a best practice. (1) This is an opportunity for local governments to articulate precisely why TIF is needed, to identify the aspects of the project that justify public assistance; (2) to make the most efficient use of public funds, not to squander public funds by over compensating developers; and (3) to justify public subsidies for private development.

Skeptics may challenge the utility of these types of inquiries, likely to be expensive and inconclusive because opinions will vary on whether an area is likely to be redeveloped without public assistance, and how large a rate of return the developer of any proposed subsidized project should receive. If forced to make these determinations against their will, public officials can be expected to select consultants likely to give them the results they are looking for.

Judicial Review of 'But For' Determinations

Some courts, unlike the principal Illinois case we reviewed, display little interest in the local public agency's 'but for' analysis. *See Great Rivers Habitat Alliance v. City of St. Peters*, 246 S.W.3d 556, 562–63 (Mo.App.2008) (applying the 'fairly debatable' standard of review to a local government's finding that but for the city's intervention, private development is not reasonably anticipated to occur in the designated redevelopment site without the adoption of TIF). As Professor Briffault rightly observes, "state courts generally treat 'but for' determinations as legislative matters deserving great judicial deference without much evidence being required."

For another comprehensive analysis of "TIF," *see* Richard Briffault, *The Most Popular Tool: Tax Increment Financing and the Political Economy of Local Government*, 77 U.CHI.L.REV. 65, 80 (2010).

The Demise of Tax Increment Financing and Redevelopment Agencies in California

Examples of the diversion of tax funds from county and school district revenue, crippling state functions and local government police, fire and educational services have led a number of states to consider the dissolution of Community Redevelopment Agencies ending the diversion of tax revenue from the State through TIF incentives. California dissolved all of its redevelopment agencies in 2011 as elucidated in the following case:

CITY OF CERRITOS V. STATE OF CALIFORNIA

Court of Appeals of California, 2015.
239 Cal.App.4th 1020, 191 Cal.Rptr.3d 611.

Briefly summarized, since the 1940's, the Community Redevelopment Law allowed sponsoring cities and counties to establish redevelopment agencies to address urban blight. (See Legis. Analyst's Off., Governor's Redevelopment Proposal (Jan. 18, 2011) p. 1; see also the Community Redevelopment Law, Health & Saf. Code, § 33000 et seq.]. A redevelopment agency was a separate legal entity from the city or county that established it. (*County of Solano v. Vallejo Redevelopment Agency* (1999) 75 Cal.App.4th 1262, 1267 ["A redevelopment agency is a public body, corporate and politic, which may sue, be sued, and make contracts," and is a separate legal entity from its sponsoring agency].)

Redevelopment agencies generally could not levy taxes, and, instead, relied primarily on tax increment financing as a funding source as authorized by Article XVI, section 16 of the California Constitution and Health and Safety Code section 33670. Under that funding mechanism, redevelopment agencies received the growth in property taxes from a designated redevelopment plan area, known as the property tax increment, while the other public entities entitled to receive property tax revenue in the redevelopment area were only allocated a portion based on the assessed value of the property prior to the effective date of the redevelopment plan (known as the frozen base). (Cal.Const., art. XVI, § 16, subds. (a), (b); § 33670.)

By 2011, California's redevelopment agencies were receiving approximately 12 percent of statewide property tax revenues. (See Legis. Analyst's Off., Governor's Redevelopment Proposal (Jan. 18, 2011) p. 1.) It was further estimated that redevelopment agencies would divert approximately $5 billion of property tax revenue annually that would otherwise fund school districts, cities, counties, and special districts. Under negotiated agreements and state statute, redevelopment agencies "passed through" about $1.1 billion to local agencies; a portion of this amount was passed to schools. The state General Fund, however, had to backfill the remaining property tax revenues diverted from K-14 schools, at a cost of over $2 billion annually.

Faced with a budget gap of more than $25 billion, on January 20, 2011 Governor Brown proposed eliminating redevelopment agencies entirely. Governor's Budget Summary—2011–2012 (Jan. 10, 2011) p. 171 ["The Budget prohibits existing [redevelopment] agencies from creating new contracts or obligations effective upon enactment of urgency legislation. By July 1, existing agencies would be disestablished and successor local agencies would be required to use the property tax that RDAs would otherwise have received to retire RDA debts and contractual obligations in accordance with existing payment schedules"].)

It was projected that dissolving redevelopment agencies would produce approximately $1.7 billion in revenue to offset State general fund costs for the 2011–2012 fiscal year.

Responding to the declared fiscal emergency, the Legislature passed Assembly Bill 1X 26 and Assembly Bill 1X 27 during the special legislative session. Among other things, Assembly Bill 1X 26 barred redevelopment agencies from incurring new or expanding existing monetary or legal obligations. (*See* Health & Saf. Code, Part 1.8 (§§ 34161 to 34169.5) [the freeze component restricting redevelopment agency powers].) It also provided for their windup and dissolution. (*See* Health & Saf. Code, Part 1.85 (§§ 34170 to 34191) [the dissolution component dissolving redevelopment agencies and transferring control of their assets to successor agencies].) We address relevant portions of Assembly Bill 1X 26 in more detail below.

Assembly Bill 1X 27 offered an exemption from dissolution for sponsoring agencies that agreed to make specified payments to both the applicable county educational revenue augmentation funds (ERAF's) and a new county special district augmentation fund on behalf of their redevelopment agencies. (*See* Health & Saf. Code, Part 1.9 (§§ 34192 to 34196).) If the payments were timely made, the sponsoring agency's redevelopment agency would be permitted to continue operating under the Community Redevelopment Law. (§ 34193, subd. (a)). Failure to make timely payments resulted in a redevelopment agency's dissolution. (§ 34195.)

The California Redevelopment Association, the League of California Cities and other affected parties challenged the constitutionality of Assembly Bill 1X 26 and Assembly Bill 1X 27. (California Redevelopment Association v. Matosantos, (Matosantos I), 267 P.3d 580, 53 Cal.4th 231, 241–242 (2011). The Supreme Court upheld Assembly Bill 1X 26 as a valid exercise of the Legislature's power but struck down Assembly Bill 1X 27 as unconstitutional. California Redevelopment Association v. Matosantos I, ibid.) Regarding Assembly Bill 1X 26, the Supreme Court specifically found it did not violate either Article XVI, section 16, or Proposition 22, which added Article XIII, section 25.5, subdivision (a)(7) to the California Constitution.

Shortly after the Supreme Court decided Matosantos I, plaintiffs filed a motion for preliminary injunction to stay the enforcement of Assembly Bill 1X 26 in the present proceedings. Plaintiffs argued Assembly Bill 1X 26 was unconstitutional under Article XIII, Section 25.5(a)(3)—Pro Rata Share of Ad Valorem Property Taxes.

Plaintiffs' primary contention on appeal is that Assembly Bill 1X 26 violates Proposition 1A, which the electorate approved at the general election in November 2004. (Stats. 2004, Ch. 133.) Proposition 1A added Article XIII, section 25.5(a)(3) to the state Constitution. (*California*

Redevelopment Association v. Matosantos, (Matosantos II, 212 Cal. App. 4th 1457, 1467 (2013).) That section generally "prohibits the Legislature from raiding local property tax allocations to help balance the budget." (Ibid.) It provides in relevant part: "(a) On or after November 3, 2004, the Legislature shall not enact a statute . . . changing for any fiscal year the pro rata shares in which ad valorem property tax revenues are allocated among local agencies in a county other than pursuant to a bill passed in each house of the Legislature by rollcall vote entered in the journal, two-thirds of the membership concurring." (Cal.Const., art. XIII, § 25.5, subd. (a)(3).) Its protections, however, do not apply to redevelopment agencies. (*Matosantos I, supra*, 53 Cal.4th at 249; Cal.Const., art. XIII, § 25.5, subd. (b)(2); Rev. & Tax. Code, § 95, subds. (a) [omitting redevelopment agencies from the definition of local agency] & subd. (m) [excluding from the definition of "special district" "any agency that is not authorized by statute to levy a property tax rate"].)

Despite this, plaintiffs claim Assembly Bill 1X 26, which governs the dissolution and wind down of redevelopment agencies, allocates ad valorem property taxes to local agencies on a non-pro rata basis without having been passed by a two-thirds supermajority as Article XIII, section 25.5(a)(3) requires. * * *

To determine whether Assembly Bill 1X 26 violates Proposition 1A, plaintiffs contend we must resolve a single legal question: does redevelopment agency tax increment survive the dissolution of redevelopment agencies?

According to plaintiffs, if tax increment survives redevelopment agency dissolution, then Assembly Bill 1X 26 violates Article XVI, section 16, which authorizes tax increment financing for redevelopment plans, and Article XIII, section 25.5, subdivision (a)(7), which limits what the Legislature may do with an operating redevelopment agency's tax increment. (*Matosantos I, supra*, 53 Cal.4th at pp. 246, 249, 263.) If redevelopment agency tax increment no longer exists after dissolution, which plaintiffs argue is apparent from several provisions in Assembly Bill 1X 26, then, the argument goes, the law purportedly violates Proposition 1A because all taxes redevelopment agencies would have received are now ad valorem property taxes that must be allocated to local agencies on a pro rata basis.

Plaintiffs, however, ask and answer the wrong question. Even if redevelopment agency tax increment no longer exists after redevelopment agency dissolution, the proper inquiry, we believe, is whether Assembly Bill 1X 26 changed the pro rata shares of any taxing entities that receive ad valorem property taxes within the meaning of Proposition 1A. Because we find that Assembly Bill 1X 26 did not affect any such change, we conclude the Legislature's statutory scheme to dissolve and wind down redevelopment agencies does not violate Proposition 1A * * *

When read in context, Assembly Bill 1X 26 simply dissolved redevelopment agencies, provided for their wind up, and disbursed any remaining funds to local agencies in accordance with their AB 8 allocations. As a result of Assembly Bill 1X 26, local agencies receive more revenue than they otherwise would have been entitled to had redevelopment agencies not been dissolved. (Cal.Const., art. XVI, § 16, subd. (b).) Their pro rata shares of property taxes were not changed under the statutory scheme, and, therefore, Assembly Bill 1X 26 does not violate Proposition 1A * * *

The trial court's order denying the motion for a preliminary injunction is affirmed. The case is remanded for further proceedings consistent with the foregoing opinion.

NOTES

1. *Post-Redevelopment Litigation.* As of January 2016, more than 180 redevelopment lawsuits have been filed in the aftermath of Matosantos and the "wind-down laws". Some arose from disputes with the Department of Finance over specific expenses made by redevelopment agencies before dissolution, while others like Cerritos have broader implications and risk billions for the state. While AB–1x–26 may have delivered the death-blow to the RDAs, one particular piece of legislation has been decried by some as a political act of tomb robbing. Signed into law on June 27, 2012, AB 1484 was enacted to accelerate and ensure an orderly wind-up process of the RDAs. See Josh Stephens, Redevelopment Cleanup Bill Sparks Relief, Outrage Among Cities, http://www.cp-dr.com/node/3237 (2012). The legislation offers several benefits to successor agencies that have returned any money owed to state or local entities and have received a Finding of Completion. The state promises to honor pre-existing loan agreements signed before June 1, 2011, allow proceeds from bonds issued before 2011 to be used for their original purposes, and permit the retention of any real property assets that serve a public purpose, including redevelopment. Despite this show of good will towards local governments, AB 1484 nonetheless imposes hefty sanctions on successor agencies that fail to relinquish any share of the 2011 property tax distribution that pertains to local taxing entities.

2. *Site Specific Tax Revenue.* After the redevelopment agencies were dissolved and California became one of only two states in the country without property tax increment financing, site specific tax revenue (SSTR) became a popular tool for funding new development in their cities. It is similar to a Super-TIF (adding sales tax and property) with the exception that it does not subsidize redevelopment with property tax increments. Local government agencies and developers will typically enter into a subvention agreement, which allows SSTR to be used to bridge the feasibility gap in construction costs to build the project. In Los Angeles, the local policy is that only up to 50% of net new revenue generated by a project may be used to assist a project through subvention. The city defines "net new revenue" as the sales tax money the city would not receive unless the project was built. Is this restriction an effort to

comply with the "but for" test? Sale tax rebates and SSTR, like TIF, are also subject to abuse. A recent bidding war between two cities to lure Amazon to build a shipping center in their town is emblematic of this problem. See Marc Lifsher, Amazon Poised to Get a Cut of California Sales Taxes, L.A. Times, May 9, 2012. Cities have also traditionally provided large subsidies to automobile dealerships because they generate hefty sales-tax revenue. What often results is a race to the bottom with the private enterprise coming out on top. In October of 2013, Governor Brown signed AB 562 (now Gov. Code § 53083) to curb this type of abuse. It imposes transparency requirements on economic development subsidies of $100,000 or more and prohibits financial assistance of any type to a vehicle dealer or big box retailer that is relocating from one jurisdiction of a local agency to another when the relocation is within the same market area.

3.   Efforts to restore the RDAs in some form have succeeded in California. Cal.Gov't Code, 62000 (2015) authorizes local governments to create Community Revitalization and Investment Authorities to use property tax increment revenue to improve infrastructure, assist businesses, and support affordable housing in disadvantaged communities. This act is modelled after the Florida Tax Increment Funded Deficiency Area and Transportation Development Authority Act, F.S.A. § 163.3182 (2015) allows Counties or Municipalities to establish Transportation Deficiency Areas (TDAs) discussed *supra*.

D. TRANSIT ORIENTED DEVELOPMENT

1. TOD INFRASTRUCTURE FINANCE NEEDS

In Chapter 2 we explored the first two facets of New Urbanism (traditional neighborhood development and form bases codes). With the growth of rail transit, many central core cities have introduced a third facet, "transit oriented development" consisting of high density mixed use transit villages comprising a 1/4-mile radius around transit stations.

As New Urbanism evolved, a form of New Urbanist development emerged known as Transit-Oriented Development (TOD). TODs place greater emphasis on the integration of land development around public transit stations and provide opportunities for denser mixed use development. The cost-benefit analysis of TODs essential for attracting investment necessitates the use of many infrastructure tools as the following article reveals:

> Metropolitan areas form economic regions that benefit from passenger rail systems. Communities have learned that the benefits of public transport can be enhanced when station-area planning makes it easier for people to walk or bike as well as take transit or drive, provides affordable housing options, and offers businesses greater access to potential employees and customers from across the region. This type of planning, known as transit-

oriented development (TOD), brings together housing, transportation, and jobs.

But while transit and TOD can offer a community a host of advantages, the infrastructure is costly. A street network is required to get people to their local destinations. This street network must also have infrastructure and facilities to support drivers, transit users, bikes, and pedestrians. Sidewalks and on street parking will be needed, and commuters, residents, and commercial users often need parking garages. Energy, water, and stormwater must be addressed and managed. Regardless of who delivers the infrastructure, it must be funded, and a municipal commitment might be needed to instill market confidence.

Rail projects and TOD are long-term economic commitments. Whether a particular market is expanding or contracting, passenger rail and TOD can catalyze economic prosperity. A municipality does not want to pass up long-term transportation investments for lack of funding or financing. In many cases, places with or considering passenger rail already have professional staff with experience in sophisticated financial transactions for various types of infrastructure and transportation finance. Yet funding might already be allocated to other projects, or existing sources of funding such as revenue, formula funds, or grants might no longer be available at past levels. This raises the troubling issue of how to balance investments for long-term growth and development when the ability to fund these projects is limited.

This report provides information about funding mechanisms and strategies that communities can use to provide innovative financing options for TOD. It explains dozens of tools that provide traditional financing as well as new tools. The tools are broadly categorized under:

- Direct fees, including user and utility fees and congestion pricing.

- Debt tools, including private debt, bond financing, and federal and state infrastructure debt mechanisms.

- Credit assistance, including federal and state credit assistance tools and the Transportation Infrastructure Finance and Innovation Act (TIFIA).

- Equity, including public-private partnerships and infrastructure investment funds.

- Value capture, including developer fees and exactions, special districts, tax increment financing, and joint development.

- Grants and other philanthropic sources, including federal transportation and community and economic development grants and foundation grants and investments.

- Emerging tools, including structured funds, land banks, redfields to greenfields, and a national infrastructure bank.

Report on Infrastructure Financing Options for TOD (National League of Cities Sustainable Cities Institute, 2013)

2. PUBLIC-PRIVATE PARTNERSHIPS AND TOD

In the United States, non-profit and governmental entities have begun to shed their passive roles as providers of public services or regulators of private land, and now often share in the profits generated by private development on land the public sector has made available. If a project is managed carefully, the public entity need not pay unrelated business income tax and can control the entire transaction through a long term lease arrangement, in which public benefits can accrue or profit shared on the basis of gross revenue. The land also returns to the municipality after the developer has reaped the tax benefits of depreciation write-offs and tax credits. As we saw at the beginning of the Chapter, traditionally, the public sector's involvement with development was limited to the urban renewal process. The city's role was to eliminate blight and deterioration in central cities and to utilize grant and incentive funds to stimulate the process of distributing la newer approach expands the public sector role to include risk sharing; participation in loan commitments and mortgages on the site; sharing operating as well as capital costs; participation in sale/leaseback arrangements; assisting the private sector by reducing administrative red tape and regulation problems; encouraging cooperation among the state, regional authorities, counties and special districts; creating special redevelopment authorities; and directly participating in development ownership activities in the planning, design, financing and ultimate marketing of redevelopment, transit-oriented and large scale mixed use projects.

The private sector, through impact fees and exactions, or tax increment financing can directly fund the financing, design, construction, ownership and operation of the public facilities which serve the site such as roads, schools, fire, police, sewer, water and drainage. See discussion of financing capital infrastructure in Chapter 4, *supra. See also* Freilich & Nichols, *Public-Private Partnerships in Joint Development: The Legal and Financial Anatomy of Large-Scale Urban Development Projects*, 7 MUN.FINANCE J. 5 (1986).

Prior to carrying out joint development, a public agency must assess a number of factors which will determine the level of public involvement and stimulation which will be required. These include: (1) the amenities desired and the extent to which these amenities will generate a return on investment; (2) the degree of risk associated with the development; (3) the availability of private sources of capital; (4) the extent to which infrastructure will be required to support and mitigate the project; and (5) the extent of long-term maintenance requirements.

The greater the cost and the more the risk to a private developer, the greater the return and the longer the public sector contribution will be required to lure developers into the marketplace. However, the government entity contributing significant land or capital to a risky venture can, through the structure of the transaction, ensure that it will realize upside potential on its investment. * * * Michael S. Bernick and Amy E. Freilich, *Transit Villages and Transit-Based Development: The Rules Are Becoming More Flexible—How Government Can Work with the Private Sector to Make It Happen*, 30 URB.L. 1, 14 (1998).

The role of the private sector has expanded to include developer participation in the planning, design, financing and ultimate marketing of redevelopment, transit-oriented and large scale mixed use projects. The private sector, through impact fees and exactions, or tax increment financing can directly fund the financing, design, construction, ownership and operation of the public facilities which serve the site such as roads, schools, fire, police, sewer, water and drainage. See discussion of financing capital infrastructure in Chapter 4, *supra. See also* Freilich & Nichols, *Public-Private Partnerships in Joint Development: The Legal and Financial Anatomy of Large-Scale Urban Development Projects*, 7 MUN.FINANCE J. 5 (1986).

Prior to carrying out joint development, a public agency must assess a number of factors which will determine the level of public involvement and stimulation which will be required. These include: (1) the amenities desired and the extent to which these amenities will generate a return on investment; (2) the degree of risk associated with the development; (3) the availability of private sources of capital; (4) the extent to which infrastructure will be required to support and mitigate the project; (5) the extent of long-term maintenance requirements; and (6) the constitutionality of the public grants, loans and incentives.

The greater the cost and the more the risk to a private developer, the greater the return and the longer the public sector contribution will be required to lure developers into the marketplace. However, the government entity contributing significant land or capital to a risky venture can, through the structure of the transaction, ensure that it will realize upside potential on its investment. * * *

Is the public/private combination a sound one? Is there a fundamental conflict between the government's role as entrepreneur and its role as regulator? For insightful analyses *see* Richard Babcock, *The City as Entrepreneur: Fiscal Wisdom or Folly*, 29 SANTA CLARA L.REV. 931 (1989); and Judith W. Wegner, *Utopian Visions: Cooperation without Conflicts in Public/Private Ventures*, 31 SANTA CLARA L.REV. 931 (1989).

Legislation to implement the urban infrastructure needs of TODs has been adopted in Florida: F.S.A. 287.05712 (2015). Public-private Partnerships:

For a detailed description of the vast scope of the Florida legislation, *see* Chasity H. O'Steen & John R. Jenkins, *We Built It, and They Came! Now What? Public-Private Partnerships in the Replacement Era*, 41 STETSON L.REV. 249, 268–71 (2012).

3. TOD URBAN PLANNING LEGISLATION

Local governments must utilize and implement strategic planning to successfully achieve TOD projects.

This requires the following steps:

- Adopt a comprehensive plan that establishes a broad, long-term vision for a TOD area yet is flexible enough to respond to a changing market cycle, funding opportunities, and other conditions;

- Constant monitoring and proactive coordination allows local governments to take advantage of new opportunities as they emerge;

- Think strategically about prioritizing public investments and public funds. Starting with small steps and moving forward incrementally helps to build market confidence and attract other sources of capital;

- Look for multiple funding sources;

- Look for a broad funding base, both to generate the most funding possible and to create a more stable revenue stream, which could allow the project to get a lower interest rate;

- Look for synergies among infrastructure projects. By grouping projects together, communities might be able to create efficiencies; and,

- Look for public-private partnerships to fill the gaps left by traditional funding sources.

See, Cal.Gov't Code § 65460 et seq., The Transit Village Development Planning Act of 1994, which authorizes local governments to enact plans for TODs on land within a quarter mile of the parcel on which rail transit stations lie, with a mix of housing types and uses and designed so that residents, workers, shoppers and others find it convenient and attractive to patronize transit,

Utilizing the new Act, Los Angeles enabled remarkable investment in rail transit. Over just a few years, the various divisions of the Los Angeles County Metropolitan Transportation Authority (MTA) opened and expanded numerous routes throughout the system. Policymakers recognized in the mid-nineties that they could leverage these transit expansions to address some of the crises threatening the City of Los Angeles by coordinating land development with transit build-out. By integrating the principles of New Urbanism into its long-term strategy for land use and development, the city aspired to maximize the benefits of new development and curtail the harms of the existing urban form.

The General Plan Framework encourages the retention of the City's stable residential neighborhoods while channeling growth into higher-intensity commercial and mixed-use targeted growth areas around stations. Thus, the Framework calls for any growth that occurs to take the form of Transit-Oriented Development. The primary focal point of development is proposed for areas in proximity to transportation corridors and transit stations. The highest development intensities are targeted generally within one-quarter mile of the transit stations, accommodating a considerable mix of uses, both residential and commercial, that serve both transit users and local residents, providing population support and enhanced activity near the stations, in accordance with the Land Use/Transportation Policy. In coordination with MTA, Community Plans are being revised as additional rail transit routes are funded.

Today, Los Angeles is undergoing a second renaissance of transit investment. Various rail, bus and subway upgrades and extensions are creating new opportunities for TOD throughout the city. Transit expansion is likely to accelerate due to the Metro's recent support for the "30/10 Initiative." In November 2008, L.A. County's commuters approved Measure R, which increased their sales tax by a half-cent on the dollar over the next 30 years to generate roughly $35 billion for electric rail systems. Former Mayor Antonio Villaraigosa then began the 30/10 Initiative to "use long-term revenue from the Measure R sales tax as collateral for long-term bonds and a federal loan which will allow Metro to build 12 key mass transit projects in 10 years, rather than 30." See LACMTA, Metro's 30/10 Initiative, 2010. In October 2010, the U.S. Dept. of Transportation awarded Los Angeles with a $546 million loan, bringing Angelenos closer to a twenty-first century transportation system. Los Angeles Metro authorities also received in fiscal year 2014 a $1.25 billion grant and a $856 million loan from the federal TIFIA program to further accelerate the county's transit growth, affording new opportunities to reshape its urban form, so long as the city is prepared and committed to doing so.

In the fall of 2016 a second Measure M was approved adding an additional half-cent sales tax and extending the existing Measure R half-cent increase passed by voters in 2008. The Los Angeles Metropolitan Transportation Authority estimates the tax increase will generate $120 billion over 40 years, funding massive rail expansions, highway improvements, biking and walking infrastructure and local street repairs. See, Meghan McCarty and Aaron Mendelson, LA says "Yes" to Tax Increase for Transportation, KPCC News (November 9, 2016).

Transit Oriented Development PowerPoint by Stefanos Polyzoides, Moule & Polyzoides, Pasadena California (2016). Reprinted with permission. *See also*, Brian Ohm and Robert Sitkowski, *The Influence of New Urbanism on Local Ordinances: The Twilight of Zoning?*, 35 URB.LAW. 738, 784 (2003).

4.   CONSTITUTIONAL ISSUES

TURKEN V. GORDON, MAYOR OF THE CITY OF PHOENIX

Supreme Court of Arizona, En Banc, 2010.
223 Ariz. 342, 224 P.3d 158.

HURWITZ, VICE CHIEF JUSTICE.

Does an agreement by the City of Phoenix to pay a developer as much as $97.4 million for the use of garage parking spaces violate the Gift Clause, Ariz.Const. art. 9, § 7?

City North is the proposed commercial core of Desert Ridge, a Phoenix master-planned community. City North is projected to contain office space, luxury hotels, residences, several parking garages, and more than one million square feet of high-end retail space. City North's developer, NPP City North L.L.C. ("NPP"), approached the City of Phoenix, claiming it could not complete the project as planned without financial assistance. The City became concerned that absent such aid, the development might not contain the full proposed retail component and potential sales tax revenues would be lost, perhaps to neighboring Scottsdale.

In response to NPP's request, the City Council adopted Ordinance No. S–33743, authorizing the City to enter into a "Parking Space Development and Use Agreement" (the "Parking Agreement") with NPP. The Ordinance contained findings, as required by A.R.S. § 9–500.11(D) (2008), that tax revenue generated by the City North project would exceed the amount to be paid to NPP under the Agreement and that without a tax incentive, the project would not locate in the City in the same time, place, or manner. The Ordinance provided, as required by § 9–500.11(H), that the City not enter into the Parking Agreement until these findings were independently verified.

After a consultant verified the findings, the City and NPP executed the Parking Agreement. The Agreement required NPP to set aside, for 45 years, 2,980 parking garage spaces for the non-exclusive use of the general public and 200 spaces for the exclusive use of drivers participating in commuting, Meyer Turken and several other Phoenix taxpayers and business owners (collectively, "Turken") sued the City to enjoin payments to NPP under the Parking Agreement. Turken alleged that the Agreement violated the Gift Clause, which provides:

> Neither the state, nor any county, city, town, municipality, or other subdivision of the state shall ever give or loan its credit in the aid of, or make any donation or grant, by subsidy or otherwise, to any individual, association, or corporation, or become a subscriber to, or a shareholder in, any company or corporation, or become a joint owner with any person, company, or corporation.

Ariz.Const. art. 9, § 7. Turken also alleged that the Parking Agreement violated the Equal Privileges and Immunities Clause, Ariz.Const. art. 2, § 13; and the Special Laws Clause, Ariz.Const. art. 4, pt. 2, § 19.

The superior court granted summary judgment to the defendants. In rejecting Turken's Gift Clause arguments, the court relied upon the two-pronged test set forth in *Wistuber v. Paradise Valley School District*, 687 P.2d 354, 357 (Ariz. En Banc, 1984). Wistuber provides that a governmental expenditure does not violate the Gift Clause if (1) it has a public purpose, and (2) in return for its expenditure the consideration received by the City, compared to the expenditure, is "not so inequitable and unreasonable that it amounts to an abuse of discretion, thus providing a subsidy to the private entity."

The Court of Appeals reversed and its opinion below concluded that, [based on two previous] Court of Appeals decisions, "Wistuber did not adopt [a] definitive two-prong test." "[W]e conclude that the Supreme Court itself did not adopt that test."). In focusing on whether a public expenditure "unduly promotes private interests," the opinion below effectively adopted Justice Cameron's dissent in Wistuber which proposed a "primary/incidental benefit" Gift Clause test, forbidding transactions in which the private entity is the primary beneficiary. The Court of Appeals held that the Parking Agreement was invalid because it will directly promote City North's private purposes, with only indirect benefits to the City.

The City and NPP petitioned for review. We granted review because interpretation of the Gift Clause is an issue of statewide importance.

In Wistuber, this Court rejected the approach [of a "primary/incidental benefit"] in favor of a simpler question: Does the expenditure, even if for a public purpose, amount to a subsidy because "[t]he public benefit to be obtained from the private entity as consideration far exceeded by the consideration being paid by the public"? 687 P.2d at 357. Kromko took a similar approach, analyzing the adequacy of consideration issue only after finding the requisite public purpose. 718 P.2d at 480–81. We adhere to that straightforward approach today. When a public entity purchases something from a private entity, the most objective and reliable way to determine whether the private party has received a forbidden subsidy is to compare the public expenditure to what the government receives under the contract. When government payment is grossly disproportionate to what is received in return, the payment violates the Gift Clause. We therefore analyze whether the Parking Agreement violates the Gift Clause under the two-pronged Wistuber test. When public funds are used to purchase something from a private entity, finding a public purpose only begins the constitutional inquiry. Wistuber also requires us to examine the "consideration" received from the private entity. The Gift Clause is violated when that consideration, compared to the expenditure, is "so inequitable and unreasonable that it amounts to an abuse of discretion, thus providing a subsidy to the private entity." *Wistuber*, 687 P.2d at 357.

Under contract law, courts do not ordinarily examine the proportionality of consideration between parties contracting at arm's length, leaving such issues to the marketplace. In contrast, our Gift Clause jurisprudence quite appropriately focuses on adequacy of consideration because paying far too much for something effectively creates a subsidy from the public to the seller. The potential for a subsidy is heightened when, as occurred here, a public entity enters into the contract without the benefit of competitive proposals.

In finding that the Parking Agreement satisfied the Wistuber test, the superior court viewed the relevant consideration as not only the value of the parking places obtained by the City, but also indirect benefits, such as projected sales tax revenue. The court erred in that analysis. Although anticipated indirect benefits may well be relevant in evaluating whether spending serves a public purpose, when not bargained for as part of the contracting party's promised performance, such benefits are not consideration under contract law or the Wistuber test. In evaluating a contract like the Parking Agreement, analysis of adequacy of consideration for Gift Clause purposes focuses instead on the objective fair market value of what the private party has promised to provide in return for the public entity's payment.

A hypothetical illustrates the point. Assume that a municipality must repair a sewer line. If the line is not repaired, disease will likely break out and spread quickly, causing deaths and significant public health care expenditures. Several competent contractors are willing to do the repair for $5,000. Under the City's reasoning, the municipality could pay a contractor $5 million without violating the Gift Clause because the indirect benefits from the repair-saved lives and avoided health care costs- exceed the $5 million payment. We disagree that this should be the result. The Gift Clause prohibits subsidies to private entities, and paying far more than the fair market value for the repair plainly would be a subsidy to the contractor. Similarly, if the City's payments to NPP under the Parking Agreement are grossly disproportionate to the objective value of what NPP has promised to provide in return, the consideration prong of the Wistuber test has not been satisfied.

We therefore turn to the consideration provided for in the Parking Agreement. The Agreement is clear—the City has agreed to pay up to $97.4 million for the non-exclusive use of some 2,980 parking garage spaces and the exclusive use of 200 park-and-ride spaces. NPP made no other promises. To be sure, the City's obligation to make payments under the Agreement does not commence until NPP has developed a specified amount of retail space. However, the Agreement makes plain that NPP has no contractual obligation to build the retail component, characterizing retail construction as "a condition precedent of the City's obligation to pay the Use Payment and not a covenant of the Developer." As the City notes, the payments for the parking spaces under the Agreement are based on the taxes generated at the development. But the Agreement does not obligate NPP to produce a penny of tax revenue for the City. Rather, the duty of City North and its tenants to pay taxes arises from law applicable to all, not out of contract. In short, the only consideration flowing to the City from NPP under the Parking Agreement is the right to use the parking spaces. Under Wistuber, the relevant inquiry is whether the amount the City has agreed to pay for use of those spaces is grossly disproportionate to what it will receive.

The Parking Agreement obligates the City to pay up to $97.4 million for the parking spaces. The City argues that its payments cannot be a gift or subsidy under the Gift Clause, because they will be offset by tax revenues from the City North project. But this argument misses the point. Once collected, these tax revenues are public funds. Whether the subsequent expenditure of those funds is consistent with the Gift Clause depends on what the City receives in return under the Parking Agreement.

Thus, the remaining question is whether the $97.4 million that the City has promised to pay far exceeds the value of the parking places promised in return. Turken has conceded that $97.4 million might well be a fair payment for exclusive use of 3,180 spaces over the next 45 years. The Parking Agreement, however, gives the City exclusive use of only 200 spaces. Nothing in the Agreement prevents City North customers from filling up the other 2,980 spaces when other members of the public might most want to use them.

We find it difficult to believe that the 3,180 parking places have a value anywhere near the payment potentially required under the Agreement. The Agreement therefore quite likely violates the Gift Clause. However, because the superior court viewed projected sales tax revenue and other indirect benefits as consideration for Wistuber purposes, it never separately addressed the value of the parking places. We are not finders of fact, and our intuitions as to proportionality, however strong, cannot substitute for specific findings of fact.

Thus, under normal circumstances, we would be constrained to remand to the superior court. However, due to the confusion created in a number of prior Court of Appeal decisions by the statement in Kromko that "perpetuation of the critical educational relationship between the hospital and the University of Arizona College of Medicine" can be counted as consideration. 718 P.2d at 481. Read out of context, this language could suggest that indirect public benefits are consideration. In Kromko, however, the perpetuation of the educational relationship was directly contracted for in exchange for the conveyance of the hospital to the nonprofit corporation, *id.* at 320, 718 P.2d at 479, and thus plainly qualified as traditional consideration.

In short, although neither Wistuber nor Kromko held that indirect benefits enjoyed by a public agency as a result of buying something from a private entity constitute consideration, we understand how that notion might have been mistakenly inferred from language in our opinions. We therefore believe it appropriate to limit today's clarification of the consideration test to transactions occurring after the date of this opinion.

For the reasons above, we vacate the opinion of the court of appeals. Because we apply our clarification of the Wistuber consideration test prospectively, we affirm the superior court's dismissal of Turken's Gift Clause claim. The Court of Appeals did not reach Turken's other constitutional arguments, and we therefore remand to the court of appeals to consider those issues in the first instance.

COMMENT: FAST-TRACKING TRANSIT-ORIENTED DEVELOPMENT THROUGH ENVIRONMENTAL REVIEW

Within the last decade, California has made remarkable progress in adjusting its environmental, transportation and land-use policies to address the issue of global climate change. Key among these is the state's express prioritization of infill development in its plan to meet the AB 32 mandate of reducing greenhouse gas emissions and improving environmental quality. Challenging this effort, however, are slow-growth supporters and private-sector competitors who increasingly rely on CEQA litigation to put a stop to new development. As three former California governors pointed out, these types of frivolous "lawsuits are frequently filed . . . for reasons having nothing to do with environmental protection."

To help offset these procedural challenges, California enacted several bills equipped with their own set of incentives to lure development back to the urban core and away from low-density suburbs and undeveloped open space. The common denominator among these "carrots" is the promise of fewer burdens under CEQA for infill developers. This can occur in the form of a complete exemption from the Act, permission to forego analysis of certain impacts or alternatives in an EIR, reduction of circulation and review periods, requiring fewer documents for a CEQA filing, or tiering under plan-level EIRs.

SB 375—Transit Priority Projects

Also known as the Sustainable Communities and Climate Protection Act of 2008, SB 375 gave developers three new streamlining tools for infill projects: the "Residential or Mixed-Use Residential Project," "Transit-Priority Project," and "Sustainable Communities Project." The Transit-Priority Project (TTP) is particularly geared towards building compact TOD projects at key transit points identified in a regional transportation plan. To qualify for the TTP label, a project must be consistent with the general use designation, density, building intensity, and the applicable policies specified for the project area in a Sustainable Communities Strategy (SCS) or Alternative Planning Strategy (APS) document. At least fifty percent of the project's total building square footage must be set aside for residential use, with a floor area ratio of no less than 0.75 (if the project has less than seventy-five percent residential use) and a minimum net density of at least twenty dwelling units per acre. In addition to these requirements, the project must be within one-half mile of a major transit stop or high-quality transit corridor.

TPPs offer three streamlining perks. First, a CEQA document need not reference any growth-inducing impacts nor discuss specific or cumulative impacts from car and light truck traffic induced by the project. An EIR is also not required to include a "reduced residential density alternative" to offset any car or light-duty truck trip impacts. These growth-inducing impact exemptions are a great relief for infill developers because "virtually any proposed development in most California cities can add to local traffic congestion and air pollution, and for this reason, can be rejected under CEQA." Secondly, so long as the project complies with all feasible mitigation measures, performance standards and other criteria set forth in a plan-level EIR, it is eligible for review under a Sustainable Communities Environmental Assessment (SCEA). The SCEA is the functional equivalent of a negative declaration or mitigated negative declaration. The initial study does not have to identify any of the significant or potentially significant impacts listed in Cal.Pub.Res. Code § 21159.28. Perhaps the most helpful part of the SCEA process is that it raises the burden of proof for opponents challenging a lead agency's project approval from the fair argument to the substantial evidence standard. Lastly, if the project poses potential impacts not addressed in a plan-level EIR and not exempted from a SCEA, the TPP can prepare a limited EIR analyzing only project-specific impacts without having to include any off-site alternatives in the study. The lead agency's decision to approve a limited EIR is presumably given the same deferential treatment as regular EIRs, in which case the court will find no abuse of discretion unless 1) the agency did not proceed in a manner required by or 2) the agency decision is not supported by substantial evidence.

Critics of the TPP tool are most concerned with the difficulty of demonstrating consistency between the project and plan-level documents, particularly with a SCS or APS package since many were still being prepared under the SB 375 mandate. Fortunately, most Metropolitan Planning Organizations have already adopted a CARB-certified SCS. The real challenge for TPPs is more likely to be the potential inconsistencies between the regional plan and local ordinances since SCS implementation has only begun to take effect. Furthermore, the traffic impact analysis process for the TPP does not absolve it of locally-imposed traffic mitigation measures. Given some of the uncertainties that still loom over the new SB 375 framework, developers may decide the risks outweigh the potential rewards.

SB 743—Urban Infill Exemption

In 2013, SB 743 was enacted to help implement SB 375 and provide additional incentives for fast-tracking urban infill development and TODs in particular. One of those streamlining tools is the urban infill exemption. It provides broader specific plan tiering for residential, employment center or mixed-use projects located in a transit priority area, which includes locations within one-half mile of a major transit stop, existing or planned. A "major transit stop" is further defined as "a site containing an existing rail station, a ferry terminal served by either a bus or rail transit service, or the intersection of two or more major bus routes with a frequency of service interval of fifteen minutes or less during the morning and afternoon peak commute periods." Projects applying for this infill exemption must be consistent with a specific plan for which a certified EIR has been prepared and, like the TPP, must also be consistent with the general use designation, density, building intensity and applicable policies specified for the project area in a SCS or APS. The type of CEQA streamlining Cal.Pub.Res. Code § 21155.4 offers is generally similar to the plan-level tiering provided under the SCEA and limited EIR mechanisms for TPPs, with the exception that it can be applied to a broader range of uses.

Unlike the TPP provisions, however, § 21155.4 does not elaborate on the standard of review to be used by the courts. Dublin Citizens v. City of Dublin (Cap. App. 2013) ultimately resolved this issue. The case involved the residential infill exemption permitted in Cal. Govt. Code § 65457. Developer AvalonBay sought approval to build a 7.2-acre parcel within the larger Dublin Transit Village Center. The City of Dublin issued a finding of consistency with the Eastern Dublin Specific Plan and then approved the project pursuant to § 65457, which exempts residential development from environmental review if it is consistent with a specific plan and its certified EIR. Project opponents appealed the decision through writ of mandamus, challenging the public agency's authority to grant the exemption. The court ruled in favor of the city, holding that statutory exemptions like § 65457 are subject to the substantial evidence test and that the agency did not abuse its discretion. Furthermore, an exemption determination itself qualifies as environmental review for purposes of program EIR tiering. This extra coating of discretion adds tremendous bite to the residential infill exemption, but its impact will resonate the most under § 21155.4 since the urban infill exemption applies to a wider array of product types. Deemphasizing the residential component should also gratify sustainable living advocates who would argue that incentivizing the potential oversupply of housing in an urban neighborhood is inapposite to SB 375's policy of promoting compact, urban development that minimizes the need to commute for work, shopping and other commercial essentials.

See, George Deukmejian, Pete Wilson, and Gray Davis, *Keeping California Green with CEQA Reforms*, U-T San Diego, July 12, 2012. http://www.utsandiego.com/news/2012/jul/12/keep-california-green-and-golden-with-ceqa-reforms/ (last visited Apr. 3, 2015).

SB 743—Reforming Traffic Impact Analysis

The other streamlining tool SB 743 provides for transit-oriented development relates to traffic impact analysis. These provisions are codified in Cal.Pub.Res. Code § 21099. First, if any residential, mixed-use residential or employment center project is located within a transit priority area, aesthetic and parking impacts will not be treated as significant for purposes of environmental review. This is a positive change in CEQA regulation because parking and aesthetic impacts tend to grow in significance as traffic congestion intensifies from the production of new development. Developers are then required to invest in costly mitigation measures while project opponents have another avenue for initiating a CEQA lawsuit. The result was a direct clash with SB 375's method of using transit-oriented development to address the more serious problem of reducing greenhouse gas emissions at the regional level.

PRC § 21099 also set into motion what has become one of the more controversial topics in CEQA reform today. It compels the Office of Planning and Research (OPR) to devise a new method of analyzing transportation impacts and recommend criteria for determining significance levels and modeling the impacts. What the legislature is ultimately after is shifting the focus of transportation impact analysis from levels of service (LOS) to other considerations such as "the amount and distance of automobile travel associated with the project." Automobile delay no longer constitutes a significant impact under the new provision, although local agencies must still analyze transportation impacts related to air quality, noise, safety or other indirect effects. Given the high costs associated with addressing automobile delays through expensive LOS studies and mitigation measures like roadway improvements, removing this segment should indirectly promote higher-density projects in urban infill areas and reduce regional travel. Also, by not forcing developers to create additional roadway capacity to minimize automobile delays, commuters are discouraged from driving to these destinations because of traffic congestion, and thereby contribute to the cause of reducing regional greenhouse gas emissions. *See* Mitchell M. Tsai, *Concerns*

About a CEQA Reform that Favors Multimodal Transportation, Los Angeles Law., p. 36 (Jan. 2015):

> "The change is positive. LOS analyzes auto congestion, not the environmental impacts of motor vehicle travel, including air pollution and greenhouse gas emissions. The LOS standard discourages urban infill and multimodal transportation network, requires costly roadway expansion to maintain existing LOS levels and impedes projects that lower roadway capacity, including bike lanes and public transit."

The text to the newly proposed CEQA Guideline § 15064.3 indicates that OPR currently plans to replace LOS analysis with vehicle miles traveled (VMT) as the new standard of transportation impact analysis for all land use projects. The guideline further adds that projects located in transit priority areas are generally to be treated as having a less than significant transportation impact, whereas projects that are not otherwise exempted and result in a VMT greater than the regional average for the land use type "may indicate a significant impact." All other projects resulting in net decreases in VMT when measured to existing conditions as well as those proposed in land use plans that are consistent with a SCS or APS are deemed to have a less than significant impact on traffic. Critics of the metric show greatest concern with the fact that there is no widely accepted standard for estimating VMT. With about twenty different models in use for calculating VMT, OPR is allowing local agencies to select their methodology of choice. The proposed guideline also permits local agencies to adopt their own thresholds of significance. With no consistent thresholds or widely accepted VMT methodology in place, project opponents have several more bullets in their chamber for trying to delay or kill a project.

OPR's list of recommended VMT mitigation measures also increases the risk of litigation unless more reliable methods of quantifying their impacts become available. Mitigations such as "improving the jobs/housing fit of a community," "incorporating affordable housing into the project," or "increasing access to common goods and services" are improvements known to reduce automobile travel when studied at an aggregate level, but it would be an incredible feat of modern-day traffic engineering to be able to precisely predict the impact that one of these project-level mitigation measures would have on the regional system. There is also no telling how difficult it can be for developers to properly monitor mitigations that escape quantification. One critic believes the proposed guidelines can potentially lead to situations where property owners are required to track tenant VMT and secure bonding to ensure compliance. Furthermore, developers may still have to pay for LOS studies since it remains the go-to-method for evaluating other impacts related to traffic congestion, such air quality, noise and safety, and it is still required outside the CEQA context under congestion management plans and impact fees analysis. If one metric cannot be had without the other, the new VMT reform might well be more of a penalty than a reward.

The proposed guideline is currently scheduled to start applying to projects within transit priority areas as soon as the Natural Resources Air Agency adopts them, while all other projects must comply with the new rules beginning January 1, 2016. Assuming the guideline is not substantially revised in 2015, developers of non-exempted projects will continue to underwrite the cost and time of using LOS, a "traffic analysis [that] consumes more time and attention than anything else in a CEQA analysis."

Despite the legislature's recent attempts to level the environmental review landscape for urban infill and transit-oriented development, there may remain considerable uncertainty and dissatisfaction with the results. Do the streamlining incentives resolve the procedural miasma, litigation risks and costs incurred from CEQA compliance, when the legislation provides local opponents with new tools to defeat projects or extract concessions unrelated to their environmental impacts? Would you advise your clients to shelve the streamlining tools and prepare full-blown EIRs to avoid a lawsuit arising? The level of uncertainty and litigation risk could be high enough to justify paying a premium for an EIR that may cost anywhere from several hundred thousand dollars to five million or more for larger projects. Nevertheless, innovative development attorneys, should find that most agency determinations involving one of these incentives will be given significant judicial deference under the substantial evidence standard. So long as the potential reductions in project costs and delays outweigh the effort of preparing an administrative record that passes the substantial evidence test, the incentives provide better options than the standard EIR framework and should promote the kind of development that is good for the environmental and economic sustainability of the state.

E. BUSINESS IMPROVEMENT DISTRICTS

The Business Improvement District (BID) is rapidly succeeding in rejuvenating commercial areas of the urban core. BIDs are essentially creatures of local government, where large urban cities, pursuant to state enabling acts, authorize the creation of smaller internal special improvement districts which provide additional services to commercial, mixed use, entertainment and offices over and above the services provided by the city. Nationwide, there are over 1500 business improvement districts designed with similar goals in mind—in essence providing higher levels of service to the businesses located within them. The services are funded with assessments on local businesses within the district, which are collected in the same manner as property taxes. BIDs have been extremely successful in many of America's major cities, Baltimore, Cleveland, Denver, Los Angeles, New York, Philadelphia, San Francisco, Washington, D.C. among many others. *See* Robert H. Nelson, Kyle R. McKenzie and Eileen Norcross, *Lessons from Business Improvement Districts: Building on Past Successes*, Mercatus Policy Series Primer No. 5, June 2008 at 2–3.

A Business Improvement District is a formal organization made up of commercial property owners who are dedicated to promoting business development and improving an area's quality of life. BIDs deliver supplemental services such as sanitation and maintenance, public safety and visitor services, marketing and promotional programs, capital improvements, and beautification for the area. *See* Carole Jean Becker, *Self-Determination, Accountability Mechanisms, and Quasi-Governmental Status of Business Improvement Districts in the United States*, 33 PUBLIC PERFORMANCE AND MANAGEMENT REV. 413 (Mar. 2010). BIDs are not private entities but a distinct hybrid of public and private elements, which while theoretically subject to municipal control, provide a public-private mechanism for providing the public services and investment that financially strapped cities need if they are to survive. *See* Richard Briffault, *A Government for Our Time? Business Improvement Districts and Urban Governance*, 99 COLUM.L.REV. 365 (1999). Nevertheless, there are a number of major concerns that have never been satisfactorily resolved when turning over public power to private parties.

The first concerns whether the special assessments are fairly distributed over the district. To rectify this situation, the City of Long Beach, California, calculates the assessment by dividing the district into five zones that are based on differing benefit levels of improvements and supplemental services rendered to the zone, with each owner paying the value assigned to the zone multiplied by the frontage and square foot area of the property. Note in that case, the assessment is not based on the assessed value of the property, so higher valued properties pay proportionally less than their poorer cousins.

The second raises the issue as to whether a BID represents the undemocratic privatization of government. Lessee businesses and offices, which pay the assessment through their rents, non-business property owners and residential tenants question whether it is proper for a private organization, whose board consists exclusively of business owners, to act in a public governmental capacity, benefitting business ownership over tenants and non-business owners and residents, with few checks and balances from a city government that is grateful for the removal of the service burden and delighted with the additional revenues generated. A BID's unelected board is handed significant authority, power that was traditionally in the hands of a democratically elected municipal government.

Do the special assessments constitute unauthorized taxes under state law? See *Zimmerman v. City of Memphis*, 67 S.W.3d 798 (Tenn.2001) (holding that the city levy on property owners in the city's central business district was a special assessment, rather than a tax, where the city council annually determined the costs and expenses to be paid from the levy; the city council reviewed and approved apportionments; the assessment was necessary to improve the safety and welfare of the city; and, the money from the assessment was used solely to benefit properties in the business district and was not paid into general public treasury or used for general public expenses.) Should *Dolan* rough proportionality be applicable?

Supposing they are special assessments and the Board is elected only by owners of property in the BID, do they violate the equal protection clause if they do not provide for non-ownership tenant voting rights? The following case explores that issue:

KESSLER V. GRAND CENT. DIST. MANAGEMENT ASS'N, INC.

United States Court of Appeals, Second Circuit, 1998.
158 F.3d 92.

A.   Establishment and Functions of BIDs

The Grand Central BID was established in 1988, and its territory was extended in June 1995, pursuant to the procedures set forth in the Act and the corresponding City ordinances. As extended, the Grand Central BID encompasses 337 properties on sections of 75 blocks in midtown Manhattan, including the Grand Central Terminal railroad station. There are 242 owners of property within the GCBID. These property owners (Class "A") are the only persons who vote for the Board and on approval of any special assessments. Non-owners and tenants (Class "B") do not have any voting rights. That property includes approximately 71 million square feet of commercial space, constituting approximately 19% of the total commercial space in Manhattan. The office space in the GCBID "exceeds the entire space inventory of the Central Business District in such cities as Houston, San Francisco, Dallas, Denver, and Boston." (District Plan, as Amended, for the Grand Central BID dated June 30, 1994 ("District Plan"), § II.B.). The GCBID also contains approximately 897,000 square feet of residential space, occupied by approximately 930 residents.

The District Plan authorizes the construction of capital improvements (the "Improvements") and the provision of additional services (the "Services") in the GCBID. The Improvements include the renovation of sidewalks and crosswalks; the planting of trees; the installation of new lighting, street signs, bus shelters, news kiosks, and trash receptacles; contributions to the renovation of Grand Central Terminal; and the services include security guards and sanitation workers.

B.   "One Person, One Vote"

In the landmark case of *Reynolds v. Sims*, 377 U.S. 533 (1964), the Supreme Court announced that "as a basic constitutional standard, the Equal Protection Clause requires" that the seats in a state legislature "be apportioned on a population basis." *Id.* at 568. This principle, generally referred to as the principle of "one person, one vote," *Gray v. Sanders,* 372 U.S. 368 (1963), is based on the propositions that "people govern themselves through their elected representatives and that 'each and every citizen has an inalienable right to full and effective participation in the political processes.' (1989) (quoting *Reynolds*, 377 U.S. at 565). The Court in *Reynolds* concluded that population-based apportionment was necessary in state legislative elections to ensure that each voter had an equal vote, and hence an "equally effective voice." 377 U.S. at 565, 84 S.Ct. 1362. Thus, in such cases, "[p]opulation is, of necessity, the starting point for consideration and the controlling criterion for judgment." *Id.* at 567.

This principle applies as well to elections for units of local government. *See, e.g., Board of Estimate,* 489 U.S. at 692–93, 1433; *Hadley v. Junior College District,* 397 U.S. 50, 54, 90 S.Ct. 791, 25 L.Ed.2d 45 (1970); *Avery v. Midland County,* 390 U.S. 474, 480–81.

C. Special Purpose Districts Having Disproportionate Effects

Nonetheless, "nothing in the Constitution . . . prevent[s] experimentation." *Hadley,* 397 U.S. at 59 (internal quotation marks omitted); see *Avery,* 390 U.S. at 485, 488 (Constitution is not a "roadblock [ ] in the path of innovation, experiment, and development among units of local government").

Viable local governments may need many innovations, numerous combinations of old and new devices, great flexibility in municipal arrangements to meet changing urban conditions. *Sailors v. Board of Education,* 387 U.S. 105, 110–11.

The Equal Protection Clause simply establishes a "ground rule" for such innovation and experimentation: that citizens may not be denied equal voting power in elections for "units with general governmental powers over an entire geographic area." *Avery,* 390 U.S. at 485–86. Thus, in *Avery,* the first Supreme Court case to apply the one-person-one-vote rule to a local government having such general power, the Court held open the possibility that the rule might not apply to a special-purpose unit of government assigned the performance of functions affecting definable groups of constituents more than other constituents. *Id.* at 483–84, 88 S.Ct. 1114; see also *Hadley* ("there might be some case in which a State elects certain functionaries whose duties are so far removed from normal governmental activities and so disproportionately affect different groups that a popular election in compliance with Reynolds [v. Sims] might not be required").

In *Salyer Land Co. v. Tulare Lake Basin Water Storage District,* 410 U.S. 719 (1973), the Court was presented with this question and upheld recognition of an exception to the one-person-one-vote rule with respect to a special-purpose district that assessed and benefited some constituents more than others. *See also Associated Enterprises, Inc. v. Toltec Watershed Improvement District,* 410 U.S. 743 (1973) (per curiam) (same). At issue in Salyer was an entity created under California law to manage the storage of water. The affected property consisted of 193,000 acres of sparsely populated farmland, and the district's primary goal was to ensure that all property owners would have the water needed to make productive use of that farmland. The district was authorized principally to plan projects and, upon approval by the district landowners and the state, to execute projects "for the acquisition, appropriation, diversion, storage, conservation, and distribution of water." *Id.* at 723, (internal quotation marks omitted). The costs of district projects were assessed against land in the district "in accordance with the benefits accruing to each [separately owned] tract." *Id.* at 724, 93 S.Ct. 1224. In addition, the district could "fix tolls and charges for the use of water and collect them from all persons receiving the benefit of the water or other services in proportion to the services rendered." *Id.* The district was managed by a board of directors chosen in weighted voting in an election open only to district landowners. *See id.* at 725.

Nonlandowning residents of the district at issue in Salyer contended that the Equal Protection Clause entitled them to a vote in board elections, arguing that they "ha[d] as much interest in the operations of [the] district as landowners." *Id.* at 726. The Supreme Court disagreed, holding that elections for the district board were not subject to the one-person-one-vote requirement "by reason of [the district's] special limited purpose and of the disproportionate effect of its activities on landowners as a group." *Id.* at 728. Though the water storage district possessed "some typical governmental powers," the Court concluded that the district had "relatively limited authority." *Id.* Its primary purpose, indeed the reason for its existence, is to provide for the acquisition, storage, and distribution of water for farming. . . . It provides no other general public services such as schools, housing, transportation, utilities, roads, or anything else of the type ordinarily financed by a municipal body. . . . There are no towns, shops, hospitals or other facilities designed to improve the quality of life within the district boundaries, and it does not have a fire department, police, buses, or trains.

With respect to the disproportionate effect of district activities on landowners, the Court noted that all costs and charges were assessed "in proportion to the benefits received" by the land, that delinquency in payment would result in a lien on the land, and that "the operations of the district[ ] primarily affect the land." *Id.* at 729.

The Salyer Court thus held the district exempt from the one-person-one-vote requirement. Accordingly, it reviewed the voting restrictions to determine only whether they were "wholly irrelevant to achievement of the regulation's objectives." *Id.* at 730 (internal quotation marks omitted). Under this deferential standard, the Court held that the Constitution did not require that district elections be open to nonlandowners. *See id.* at 729–30 ("it is quite understandable that the statutory framework for election of directors of the [district] focuses on the land benefited, rather than on people as such").

Four years later, the Court summarized the exception it had created in Salyer, stating that "the electorate of a special-purpose unit of government . . . may be apportioned to give greater influence to the constituent groups found to be most affected by the governmental unit's functions." *Town of Lockport v. Citizens for Community Action at the Local Level, Inc.*, 430 U.S. 259, 266 (1977); and in *Ball v. James*, 451 U.S. 355, 101 S.Ct. 1811, 68 L.Ed.2d 150 (1981), the Court was again presented with a governmental unit to which it found the exception applicable. The unit whose voting scheme was challenged was again a water storage district, but one whose functions were "more diverse and affect[ed] far more people" than the district in Salyer, for it included "almost half the population of the State [of Arizona], including large parts of Phoenix and other cities." *Ball*, 451 U.S. at 365, 101 S.Ct. 1811. The district was a "nominal public entit[y]," *id.* at 368, 101 S.Ct. 1811, so designated in order to permit it to raise money inexpensively through the issuance of public bonds; it also "exercised its statutory power to generate and sell electric power," *id.* at 365, 101 S.Ct. 1811. The Court nonetheless concluded that the district was "essentially [a] business enterprise[ ]," *id.* at 368, 101 S.Ct. 1811, that had the special limited purpose of "stor[ing], conserv[ing], and deliver[ing] water," *id.* at 369, 101 S.Ct. 1811, and was not a general governmental body in light of the limited scope of its purpose and powers: . . . .

[T]he District simply does not exercise the sort of governmental powers that invoke the strict demands of Reynolds [v. Sims]. The District cannot impose ad valorem property taxes or sales taxes. It cannot enact any laws governing the conduct of citizens, nor does it administer such normal functions of government as the maintenance of streets, the operation of schools, or sanitation, health, or welfare services. *Ball*, 451 U.S. at 366, 101 S.Ct. 1811.

For the foregoing reasons, we conclude that the Grand Central BID is a district that exists for a special limited purpose, that GCDMA's activities have a disproportionate effect on property owners, and that GCDMA has no primary responsibilities or general powers typical of a governmental entity. Accordingly, we conclude that the GCBID falls within the exception to the one-person-one-vote requirement. Since the Act's guarantee of majority Board representation to property owners has a reasonable relationship to the purpose of the BID, we conclude that the weighted voting system for electing GCDMA's Board does not violate the Equal Protection Clause.

NOTES

1.   Do you agree with the majority in Kessler which held that the largest BID in the United States, in the largest city in the nation, containing the largest transportation terminal in the world, fits the description of the type of rural district that the Salyer court had in mind?

2.   *The Homeless and BIDs.* The New York City 2009 Business Improvement Districts Fiscal Year Annual Report, contained the following:

Established by district property owners in 1988, the Grand Central Partnership (GCP) was primarily a response to the physical and economic deterioration of an area recognized as one of the city's largest homeless encampments. To address the homeless condition, the GCP commenced a 'clean and safe' program aimed at moving the homeless off the streets and into shelters.

To achieve this goal, formerly homeless men were hired to persuade the homeless to take advantage of a GCP social service program held at a local church, which included shelter, meals, and job placement services. The GCP estimates that 150 homeless individuals were placed in full-time jobs. They also claim a 50% reduction in crime.

The GCP clean and safe program came under scrutiny in 1995 when a small scandal erupted over allegations that 'goon squads' were using force to remove homeless individuals that would not willingly leave. Whether or not violent tactics were used, the GCP was exposed for exercising poor judgment in the use of untrained formerly homeless men as social service workers. Further scandals emerged over the $1.15 hourly rate paid to social service workers, which was justified as having been established as an outreach program.

The Department of Housing and Urban Development (HUD) and the City's Department of Homeless Services both conducted investigations into these allegations. Ultimately, HUD rescinded its $547,000 grant, and Chase Manhattan Bank cancelled its $450,000 contract with the GCP. Soon afterwards the city comptroller issued a critical audit of the Grand Central BID and in the summer of 1998, citing 'persistent noncompliance with municipal directives' the city of New York declined to renew the Grand Central District Management Agency's (GCDMA) contract to manage the BID.

The finance committee's own review found that two independent incidents (1990, 1992) had been reported in which Grand Central Partnership Social Services Corporation (GCSSC) workers were alleged to have used excessive force in removing homeless individuals. Both cases resulted in $5 million lawsuits against the GCSSC and in neither case were the allegations formally detailed, documented or reported to the board of directors. Furthermore, the GCSSC was unable to prevent further incidents/ allegations because the documentation process was inadequate to provide a reasonable level of accountability for staff members. The failure to implement an adequate complaint resolution process limits understanding of how many complaints have been made against the BID or the nature of those complaints.

This information was available to the trial court in Kessler. Does this not discredit the district court and the court of appeals findings that the City government had sufficient supervisory powers over the BID? Does an issue concerning the treatment of the homeless provide a sufficient rationale for the proposition that the BID board should have been elected by the citizens of the district?

3.   *Management Problems.* While the BIDs have obviously played an important role in the maintenance and upkeep of business districts, they have also been criticized. *See* Berman and Vallone, *Cities within Cities: Business Improvement Districts and the Emergence of the Micropolis*, the Council of the City of New York Staff Report to the Finance Committee, November 8, 1995. In this report, results showed that a number of businesses located within BIDs were under informed on important issues, including where their money was going, who was running the BIDs, whether they had any say in the BID's activities and who the officers were, how they were being assessed, what the BID's district manager was paid or who that person even was. It further showed a complete lack of internal procedures for performance review and administrative functions, such as contracting procedures. Perhaps the most serious finding, was the lack of control over issuance of bonds to service debt undertaken by the BIDs. This, the investigation showed, may result in a perpetual life for the BIDs, leaving the businesses locked into debt with little or no knowledge of the services that were undertaken.

Such difficulties led the New York City Council to rethink the regulations governing BIDs. Among some of the proposed regulations would be tighter controls on the issuance of bonds, better reporting procedures and tighter administrative procedures, for example allowing individuals to be president of only one BID, rather than several, as has occurred recently. *See Further Restraint is Sought for Business Improvement Districts: City Council Report to be Released Today*, The New York Times, Wednesday, November 12, 1997. For a comprehensive discussion of BIDs, *see* Mark S. Davies, *Business Improvement Districts*, 52 WASH.U.J.URB. & CONTEMP.L. 187 (1997); *see also* N.Y. Times, April 3, 1998, at A22. As a result of a major overhaul of the city's procedures in holding BIDs accountable, in 2009, New York City was home to the nation's largest and most comprehensive network of Business Improvement Districts in the country. The City's 64 BIDs annually invest close to $100 million worth of programs and services in neighborhoods across the five boroughs. Since 1999, the NYC Department of Small Business Services is responsible for managing the City's relationship with each BID and works to ensure BIDs carry out services efficiently by liaising with City agencies, promoting best practices and aggregating information about the programs, services and goals of each BID.

F. BROWNFIELDS

A brownfield is an abandoned urban industrial site with existing environmental problems. The federal Government Affairs Office estimates that 450,000 brownfields exist as of 2010.

The Brownfield movement focuses on cleaning up these urban environmental sites and at the same time fights against urban blight by making already existing urban sites more attractive to developers. The movement creates a larger tax base for cities, more jobs, a more stable community and a reason for companies not to relocate in outlying areas and contribute to suburban sprawl. In the past, when industrial and manufacturing plants became outdated with the advent of new technologies, they were abandoned to rust. In 1976, federal environmental laws made current and even future owners of these properties responsible for cleaning up any pollution detected. These laws have deterred developers from buying these properties for fear of costs of the cleanup, which are high and difficult to measure. *See* Stephanie B. Goldberg, *Let's Make a Deal: Cooperation, Not Litigation*, ABA JOURNAL (March 1997).

Federal and state governments have decided to take a practical approach to cleaning up brownfields. Since the 2002 Brownfields Revitalization Act, the EPA has stepped in to lower standards for brownfields to decrease the costs surrounding clean up. The standard has gone from ridding the site of all contamination to doing what is necessary to make the property compatible with its intended use and to protect the public health.

There are many different schemes for promoting the cleanup of brownfields; some are solely private ventures, others are public-private partnerships, but most contain government tax incentive packages at state, local and federal levels. *See* Andrea Wortzel, *Greening the Inner Cities: Can Federal Tax Incentives Solve the Brownfields Problem?*, 29 URB.LAW. 309 (1997).

On January 11, 2002, President Bush signed the Small Business Liability Relief and Brownfields Revitalization Act (Pub. L. No. 107–118, 115 stat. 2356, "the Brownfields Law"). The Brownfields Law amended the Comprehensive Environmental Response, Compensation, and Liability Act (CERCLA or Superfund) by providing funds to assess and clean up brownfields in urban areas; clarified CERCLA liability protections; and provided funds to enhance state and tribal response programs. Other related laws and regulations have been amended to incentivize brownfields cleanup and reuse through the following financial incentives and regulatory requirements such as the:

Small Business Liability Relief and Brownfields Revitalization Act: Provides relief for small businesses from liability under the

Comprehension Environmental Response, Compensation, and Liability Act of 1980;

Related Law: Amends CERCLA, Resource Conservation and Recovery Act (RCRA), Community Reinvestment Act (CRA), Superfund Amendments and Reauthorization Act (SARA) to ease the way for brown- fields redevelopment;

Brownfields Tax Incentive: Contiguous property owners ("CPOs"), bona fide prospective purchasers ("BFPPs"), or innocent landowners ("ILOs") qualify for the liability limitations provided in the Brown- fields Law. The Taxpayer Relief Act provides for tax credits to spur the cleanup and redevelopment of brownfields in distressed urban and rural areas.

In redeveloping sites under the 2002 law, it is critical that BFPPs not do anything to disturb or further release contaminants. In *United States v. Honeywell Int'l, Inc.*, 542 F.Supp.2d 1188, 1200 (E.D.Cal.2008), the District Court for the Eastern District of California denied a party the innocent landowner defense because the party's affirmative steps in grading and excavating the property, and extending water and sewer lines through the site, agitated the soil, causing new releases of hazardous substances and caused the release of further contaminants.

Contiguous property owners and easement owners running rail- roads or utilities through the site are not subject to CERCLA operator liability for cleanup of hazardous waste on easement property, where they had no control over the polluter's internal decisions regarding waste disposal and storage, had no hands-on involvement contributing to release, and never assumed control of disposal or storage of waste. Comprehensive Environmental Response, Compensation, and Liability Act of 1980, § 107(a), 42 U.S.C.A. § 9607(a). *Grand Trunk Western Railway Co. v. Acme Belt Recoating, Inc.*, 859 F.Supp. 1125 (W.D.Mich.1994).

Obtaining financing from banks to develop these sites, even after the cleanup process, was difficult for investors and developers. In the past, courts found lenders liable for environmental costs if they have significantly participated in the company's management. *See United States v. Fleet Factors Corp.*, 901 F.2d 1550 (11th Cir.1990). Congress responded by enacting the Lender Liability Act of 1996, which limits the scope of lender liability for environmental cleanups to make financing more readily available. *See* 42 U.S.C.A. § 9601(20).

HUD Programs

HUD's 2015 Brownfields Economic Development Initiative (BEDI) is a competitive grant program designed to assist cities with the redevelopment of brownfield abandoned and underused industrial and commercial facilities, where expansion and redevelopment is burdened by real or potential environmental contamination. BEDI provides competitive economic development grants to Community Development Block Grant (CDBG) recipients, in connection with notes or other obligations guaranteed under Section 108 of the Housing and Community Development Act of 1974, for the purposes of enhancing either the security of the guaranteed loans or the viability of the projects financed with these Section 108 loans. BEDI grants and Section 108 loan funds must be used in conjunction with the same economic development project. Section 108(q) of the Housing and Community Development Act of 1974 (42 U.S.C. 5308(q)), 24 CFR part 570, Subpart M.

G.   DEMOLITION, LAND BANKING AND REHABILITATION IN ABANDONED AREAS OF INDUSTRIAL CITIES

1.   ABANDONMENT

MOORE V. CITY OF DETROIT
Court of Appeals of Michigan, 1987.
159 Mich.App. 199, 406 N.W.2d 488.

KELLY, JUDGE.

This case is before us on remand from the Supreme Court for a decision on whether Detroit City Ordinance No. 556–H "unconstitutionally deprives property owners of their property interests without due process of law or just compensation." We hold that Ord. 556–H does not deprive property owners of a property interest within the prohibitions of the state or federal due process clauses.

Moore argues that Ord. 556–H authorizes the city to confiscate privately owned property for a public purpose, and thus involves the exercise of the city's power of eminent domain rather than its police powers. Moore then concludes that the omission of a provision in the ordinance requiring just compensation renders the ordinance violative of the property owners' due process rights. We earlier held that Ord. 556–H was enacted under the police powers granted to Detroit as a home rule city. We again conclude that Ord. 556–H represents an exercise of the city's police powers and we reject Moore's reliance on the law of eminent domain.

Section 12–11–46.1 of Ord. 556–H sets forth the legislative findings on which the Detroit city council relied in enacting the nuisance abatement ordinance:

> (a) Scattered throughout the city are a large number of unoccupied dwellings which are constantly broken into, vandalized, used for unsanitary or immoral purposes and are potential fire hazards.

(b) There are many unoccupied dwellings in the city which, because of their vacant status, constitute hazards to the health, safety, and welfare of the public.

(c) Certain vacant dwellings have reached a state of disrepair and deterioration which create a public nuisance or exert a downgrading or blighting influence on the surrounding neighborhood, resulting in discouraging neighbors from making improvements to properties and thus adversely affecting the tax revenue of the city.

(d) Throughout the city, the number of vacant and deteriorated dwellings constituting public nuisances has become so high that traditional means of abating such nuisances have been ineffectual, and blight and deterioration of emergency proportions have resulted.

(e) Currently, tax delinquent abandoned dwellings revert to the state and are then deeded to the city through the state tax reversion process. However, this process takes several years, during which time many dwellings are lost through vandalism and deterioration.

(f) Permitting families to repair and move into abandoned homes within the city will preserve the residential housing stock of the city, increase neighborhood stability and provide needed homes for Detroit families.

These stated purposes fall within the city's powers to "provide for the public peace and health of its citizenry and promote the safety of persons and properties within its boundaries." *Butcher v. Detroit*, 347 N.W.2d 702 (Mich.App.1984). Although these goals, if achieved, will no doubt benefit the public, we are not persuaded that the taking authorized under Ord. 556–H is for a "public purpose" as that term has evolved under the law of eminent domain. Most significantly, Ord. 556–H does not impose upon the property owner a burden which should be borne by the public. In a disordered society, vacant houses develop into public nuisances, as that term is defined in Ord. 556–H, partly because of the action or inaction of their owners. It is neither unfair nor unjust for the city to impose the burden of abating these nuisances upon the individual owners rather than upon the public as a whole. Neighborhoods don't blight overnight.

Although we reject Moore's reliance on the law of eminent domain, our conclusion that Ord. 556–H represents an exercise of the city's police powers does not entirely resolve the issue of whether the ordinance unconstitutionally deprives property owners of their property interests without adequate compensation. *See Loretto v. Teleprompter Manhattan CATV Corp.*, 458 U.S. 419 (1982). A statute or ordinance authorizing physical occupancy of property without compensation to the property owner must be reasonable under the surrounding circumstances. Before considering the reasonableness of the occupancy authorized under Ord. 556–H, we find it helpful to visit a few of its procedural provisions.

Ord. 556–H does not by itself transfer title of property to the city or to the nuisance abatement contractor. Transfer of title must be achieved by the city through an action to quiet title, or through delinquent tax proceedings. Ord. 556–H simply creates a temporary right in third parties to enter, occupy and repair a vacant home which has been declared by lawful authority to be an unlawful nuisance. At the end of the abatement period, the city will have obtained title to the property through prescribed judicial proceedings so that the property may then be sold by the city to the nuisance abatement contractor. We note that the property owner is notified of the activity on his or her property at all stages of the abatement process and is provided numerous opportunities to assert ownership of the property, thereby terminating the nuisance abatement contract. It is significant that defendants in this case do not assert any due process challenge to the notice and hearing provisions of Ord. 556–H.

Since Ord. 556–H does not authorize permanent occupancy of private property by third persons, Moore's reliance on *Loretto, supra* is not dispositive. The Supreme Court in Loretto repeatedly emphasized that its decision is based upon the "permanency" of the government-authorized occupancy challenged therein. Defendants' reliance on Loretto stems from an erroneous interpretation of Ord. 556–H as authorizing the city to take title to real property.

Correctly interpreted, Ord. 556–H simply amends the city's original building code and creates an alternative to demolition or costly repairs by government or third persons who do not gain rights to occupy the property. Plaintiff agrees that the city may authorize a third party to enter private property in order to demolish a building identified as a public nuisance and that the property owner has no right to just compensation for this taking. Moore further admits that just compensation is not required where the city contracts with a third party to repair a building identified as a public nuisance. It is the nuisance abatement contractor's occupancy of the property while making repairs which defendants now challenge as unconstitutional.

Defendants, however, fail to adequately distinguish between a taking authorized under the original building code and the taking authorized under Ord. 556–H. Under both the original building code and Ord. 556–H, third parties are authorized by the city to enter onto private property for the purpose of abating a public nuisance. Although the entry and physical possession authorized under Ord. 556–H extends the duration of the physical occupancy and allows the third party to make general use of the property while abating the nuisance, obviously such possession is not more intrusive than demolition.

In any event, the dispositive inquiry is whether this extended physical possession is reasonable under the circumstances. We believe that it is. As noted by Justice Stevens in *Young v. American Mini Theatres, Inc.*, 427 U.S. 50, 71 (1976), cities "must be allowed a reasonable opportunity to experiment with solutions to admittedly serious problems." After having determined that existing mechanisms were ineffective in attacking the perils of abandoned homes scarring its neighborhoods, the city's legislative body enacted Ord. 556–H as an alternative method of abating these public nuisances. Defendants have failed to carry their burden of proving that this alternative is unreasonable and, therefore, unconstitutional. Ord. 556–H authorizes only a temporary physical possession of property for the purpose of abating a public nuisance and relies upon other, well established judicial processes in providing for the transfer of title to property. Built into the ordinance are ample notice and opportunity provisions which protect the right of the property owner to terminate the nuisance abatement contract at any point. Given the nature of the intrusion, the purpose sought to be accomplished and the ease with which a property owner may terminate a nuisance abatement contract, we cannot say that Ord. 556–H constitutes an unreasonable exercise of the city's police powers.

Moore briefly argues that Ord. 556–H is arbitrary and discriminatory because property owners will be treated differently based on the whims of nuisance abatement contractors regarding which houses will be occupied. While it is true that some houses capable of rehabilitation will be the subject of nuisance abatement contracts while others will be demolished or repaired by non-occupant third parties, this difference in treatment is neither arbitrary nor unfair. We hold that it is a reasonable effort to solve a difficult problem. It may not work but it should be tried.

Defendants raise several other issues on appeal which we decline to address because the Supreme Court remanded this case to us for the sole purpose of considering defendants' due process challenge.

Affirmed.

NOTE

The Court's next to concluding paragraph presciently states "It may not work but it should be tried." The following article indicates that the temporary occupation of abandoned residences policies in Detroit as shown in the above case was unable to stem the tide.

Detroit Free Press editorial, March 23, 2011:

> Stop arguing about what happened and start focusing on what to do now. If there is a single, unifying message to be found in Detroit's population count from the 2010 census, this is it:

> The city lost more than 200,000 residents over the past decade. Among U.S. cities, only flood-ravaged New Orleans hemorrhaged a

larger percentage of its population. They had a hurricane. We had a near-biblical exodus of people who were home dwellers, school attendees and taxpayers. At 713,000 residents, the city has about 5,000 residents for each one of its 139 square miles. That's just a little denser than Manhattan— the eighth-largest city in Kansas.

Why so many people left Detroit doesn't matter anymore. Neither does who's at fault. The important thing now is for everyone to accept that this is a fundamentally changed city, a hollowed-out version of the Detroit that boasted 1.8 million people in the mid-1950s.

New Orleans is not distracted by squabbling over how to rebuild that city to accommodate all the people who have left. Detroiters and their leaders must similarly focus on making their city work for the folks who are still here. Density is a big part of that. If there was any question about the city's ability to maintain its sprawling infrastructure in the face of a continuing population slide, the sharp decline in the 2010 census numbers put it to rest.

The census numbers prove that the city's nearly depopulated acreage is growing, not shrinking. [Mayor] Bing and the City Council must focus on creating critical mass in the areas that still have solid population bases, and come up with a credible plan to abandon the infrastructure in other areas, or find suitable, low-impact uses for them. The census numbers mean large-scale farming is no longer some pipe dream, but an imperative part of the discussion about land use. Homesteading, which could also facilitate the low-cost repurposing of the city's 80,000 abandoned homes and businesses, also deserves serious consideration.

At the same time, city leadership must continue to build on the things that are going right. While people were leaving at a rate of one every 20 minutes, the decade from 2001–10 was also one that saw the city re- establish itself as the cultural and economic hub of the region. Three casinos and two stadiums opened downtown; the city hosted a baseball All-Star game and a football Super Bowl, and attracted thousands of suburbanites and expatriates to celebrate its 300th anniversary. Two major employers moved into the city, and General Motors decided to stay.

Downtown and Midtown, which are attracting new workers and residents have to be girded with services that will continue to attract and retain people. And services won't get better until they're not spread over such a large, depopulated area.

2. LAND BANKING

Cleveland, Baltimore, Philadelphia and New York State Cities outside of New York City and other large eastern cities are experiencing to a lesser extent the same problems as Detroit.

(a) Cleveland Land Banking and Neighborhood Revitalization

One of the most serious of central city problems is the widespread tax delinquency and abandonment of inner-city land. Nearly every city, particularly older industrial cities in the Northeast and Midwest, has neighborhoods blighted by large tracts of abandoned land. Urban planners in these cities have the responsibility to measure the extent of the problem, manage the situation through improved legal and administrative procedures, and plan for the recycling of abandoned parcels to productive reuse. This case study details the roles played by many different Cleveland planners in establishing a land bank to revitalize neighborhoods. It suggests strategies other planners might adopt when faced with similar problems.

Planners in the city of Cleveland began outlining the extent of this problem in the early 1970s while tracking population decline, housing abandonment, and tax delinquency. They found that the city had more than 11,000 delinquent parcels and that existing state laws and local procedures for handling tax delinquent properties were slow, expensive, and not effective. Existing foreclosure procedures were actually counterproductive, as sales prices at auctions rarely covered back taxes, liens, and administrative costs.

By 1978, Cleveland's planners had completed a detailed research project resulting in a book, Olson and Lachmann, Tax Delinquency in the Inner City (1978), which developed a strategy for dealing with extensive tax delinquency, and succeeded in changing Ohio's laws regarding tax delinquent property. It also had established the state's first land bank, which is still in operation today. Thousands of abandoned parcels flowed into the land bank to be administered by the city's Community Development Department. In the last two decades, cheap properties with cleared, marketable titles available through the land bank have been responsible for much of the new development and revitalization taking place in many Cleveland neighborhoods.

(b) Baltimore

Thousands of vacant buildings in Baltimore will be demolished over the next four years, officials said Tuesday. The demolitions will start in the neighborhood where Freddie Gray was fatally injured in police custody, prompting civil unrest that highlighted the urban decay. The plan includes $75 million in state funding to demolish blocks of abandoned buildings to create space for affordable housing, businesses and parks, Gov. Larry Hogan of Maryland and Mayor Stephanie Rawlings-Blake said. The city will provide nearly $19 million worth of administrative services, and the state will offer more than $600 million in financing opportunities for private-sector development. *Baltimore Plans Extensive Demolitions*, The N.Y. Times, Jan. 6, 2016 at A-16.

(c) Philadelphia

Abandoned properties, numbering an estimated 32,000 owned by both private and public sectors citywide, may be tempting targets for developers during a current real estate boom in some areas of Philadelphia. But potential buyers have often been deterred by delinquent taxes or by having to locate absent owners or determine that the owners are deceased.

Developers and city officials hope that the Philadelphia Land Bank, a recently created city program, will help sift through the labyrinth of records on vacant and abandoned lots like the Eubanks property and make them available for sale and redevelopment.

But some neighborhood residents and activists worry that developers' efforts will lead to higher taxes and gentrification, forcing out longtime homeowners.

On Dec. 9, Philadelphia's mayor, Michael A. Nutter, announced the transfer of deeds for 150 properties owned by the Philadelphia Housing Development Corporation, a city agency, to the Land Bank. The transfer represented the first set of buildings or lots to be taken over by the new entity.

A further 1,135 city-owned properties have been transferred to the Land Bank by the end of 2015, beginning a process that could shift about 8,500 publicly owned vacant properties from a number of city agencies to a single entity that would become a "one-stop shop" for developers.

While other United States cities have operated land banks for years, Philadelphia, with a population of about 1.5 million, is the largest to do so. Its program, created by a City Council resolution in December 2013, is expected to contain more properties than the others when it is fully operational.

If a private property becomes tax-delinquent, the Land Bank will get a right of first refusal to acquire it without a cash payment before it goes to a sheriff's sale. Any acquisition by the Land Bank will be subject to negotiation with other city agencies, especially the Department of Revenue, which may wish to prevent the property from entering the Land Bank in an effort to obtain unpaid taxes.

The Land Bank's first acquisitions from the public sector include 18 properties in the 1400 block of North Marston Street in the Brewerytown section of Philadelphia. The street once contained 59 of the city's characteristic rowhouses but now has only 12 structures, six of which are occupied. The other six are boarded up and derelict. A total of 26 properties on the street are tax-delinquent.

The street's privately owned properties include No. 1432, now a vacant lot, which was last sold for $3,750 in 1961, is now valued at $3,400, and owes city property taxes of $8,281, according to city records.

The blighted landscape, only two miles from the gleaming skyscrapers of downtown Philadelphia, became an increasingly familiar sight as the decline of manufacturing drove out many residents starting in the 1960s, and it has become a longstanding challenge for city officials seeking to return large areas of the city to productive use.

By consolidating vacant property, the Land Bank aims to free up adjoining lots that can be put together to create market-rate or low-income housing, commercial developments or green space.

The Land Bank will determine whether developers' plans are appropriate to local needs such as more affordable units in neighborhoods dominated by market-rate housing, or more market-rate development in a neighborhood that already has a good stock of subsidized properties, said Beth McConnell, policy director for the Philadelphia Association of Community Development Corporations, which advocates for the Land Bank.

Ms. McConnell said the Land Bank had the potential to clear urban blight and return land to productive use in a way that conforms with neighborhood and citywide plans.

"It's different than the alternative of just making everything available at the market rate, and whoever the highest bidder is gets it," she said.

The Land Bank will not stop developers from acquiring private property, but it could make it easier for them to do so, Ms. McConnell said. "Market-rate developers can continue to do what they do now," she said. If the developers can find the owners, they can buy the properties "if the Land Bank doesn't get access to them first," she added.

City officials hope that the new availability of property on streets like North Marston will spread development from adjoining neighborhoods that are already seeing new construction, and higher prices, as a real estate boom in central Philadelphia ripples outward.

But on Etting Street, whose houses back onto North Marston, Lee Chamblis, a resident, fears that the arrival of developers will eventually drive out longtime residents.

"Improvement is a good thing but I really don't believe they are going to leave it as a community like it is," said Mr. Chamblis, 48, who inherited the house he has lived in all his life. he blighted landscape, only two miles from the gleaming skyscrapers of downtown Philadelphia, became an increasingly familiar sight as the decline of manufacturing drove out many residents starting in the 1960s, and it has become a longstanding challenge for city officials seeking to return large areas of the city to productive use. Jon Hurdle, *A Plan to Untangle Philadelphia's Daunting Decay*, The New York Times, Dec. 29, 2015 at A-1.

(d) New York State Cities

New York State is a late entry in approving local government land banks for vacant and abandoned properties. The Land Bank Act, Not-for-Profit Corp. Law, Ch. 35, §§ 1600 et seq., became effective July 29, 2011:

§ 1601 Legislative Intent.

The legislature finds and declares that New York's communities are important to the social and economic vitality of the state. Urban, suburban, or rural communities are struggling to cope with vacant, abandoned, and tax-delinquent properties. There exists a crisis in many cities and their metro areas caused by disinvestment in real property and resulting in a significant amount of vacant and abandoned property. For example, Cornell Cooperative Extension Association of Erie County estimates that the City of Buffalo [whose population has dropped from 580,000 to 250,000] has thirteen thousand vacant parcels, four thousand vacant structures and an estimated twenty-two thousand two hundred ninety vacant residential units. This condition of vacant and abandoned property represents lost revenue to local governments and large costs ranging from the costs of removing safety hazards and the spreading deterioration of neighborhoods including resulting mortgage foreclosures.

The Land Bank Act [S663A–2011, Pub. Auth. Law §§ 1600 et seq.] will give localities across New York State new tools for redeveloping vacant and abandoned properties. The "land banks" [which will be non-profit 501C3 corporations will be created and run by local authorities [with foreclosing of tax lien powers] pursuant to an intergovernmental agreement with [the county, cities and school districts or any one of them] with the purpose of reducing the high number of vacant properties in many upstate towns and cities and returning those abandoned parcels to a more productive use. As the Governor noted in his urban agenda, blighted properties bring despair to communities and land banks are an innovative way to restore struggling neighborhoods. Albany, Binghamton, Buffalo, Rochester, Schenectady, Syracuse, Troy and Utica all face vacancy rates over ten percent, according to recent census data. Vacant properties pose a serious threat to New York communities by lowering surrounding property values, attracting crime, cutting into local tax revenues and perpetuating cycles of disinvestment.

Establish a hierarchical ranking of Priorities for the Use of Real Property Conveyed by a Land Bank including but not limited to:

The Land Bank will receive funds from the federal, state and local governments; will have the ability to acquire properties (except by eminent domain); issue revenue bonds, will be subject to the supervision of the New York State Urban Development Corporation; and will be required to prepare redevelopment plans and strategies for new growth for the following priorities to be established by the creating local governments:

(1)   Use for Purely Public Spaces and Places;

(2)   Use for Retail, Commercial and Industrial Activities;

(3)   Use as Wildlife Conservation Areas; and

(4)   Such other Uses and in such Hierarchical Order as Determined by the Foreclosing County, City or School District Governmental Units.

McKinney's Consol. Laws of NY, Not-for-Profit Corp. Ch. 35, Art. 16 § 1609 (2015). Abigail Gardner, Smart Growth America Applauds Governor Cuomo for Signing Land Bank Act into Law, Effective July 29, 2011, Posted on August 1, 2011.

(e) Other States

Georgia, Michigan, Ohio and Pennsylvania have passed similar legislation. For several interesting critiques of the Land Bank approach, see Darren M. Belajac, Comment, *The Pennsylvania Legislature Takes A Significant, Though Insufficient, Step Toward Addressing Blight And Tax Delinquency: House Bill 712, The Land Bank Act*, 49 DUQUESNE. L.REV. 79 (2011); and Nigel Griswold and Patricia E. Norris, *Economic Impacts of Residential Property Abandonment and the Genesee County Land Bank in Flint, Michigan: An Urban Revitalization Report*, The Michigan St. U. Land Pol'y Inst., East Lansing, Michigan (2007).

3. DEMOLITION AND REHABILITATION

(a) *Demolition.* Should a violation of housing or building codes require demolition? The question has been answered in the negative in *Horton v. Gulledge*, 177 S.E.2d 885 (N.C.1970), overruled on other grounds in *State v. Jones*, 290 S.E.2d 675 (N.C.1982). The North Carolina Supreme Court held that an ordinance which prescribed mandatory demolition of substandard or code violating buildings without the alternative of repairs was not within the police power of the City of Greensboro to enact. The court suggested that the city-ordered demolition might be proper if the owner was given the opportunity but failed to make repairs.

Demolition has been particularly important for abandoned and vacated buildings which cast a blighting influence on the neighborhood. Community Development Block Grant and Section 108 Loan Funds can be used for demolition programs as the successor of HUD's categorical grant demolition program. *See* Section 116(b) of the Housing and Urban Development Act of 1965, P.L. 89–117. Could an ordinance be drafted to treat abandoned buildings as an implied dedication to the city so they may immediately be turned over for rehabilitation and occupancy?

(b) *Rehabilitation. See City and County of San Francisco v. Municipal Court*, 213 Cal.Rptr. 477 (Cal.App.1985) stating:

> The Marks-Foran Residential Rehabilitation Act of 1973 (Health & Saf. Code, Section 37910 et seq.) authorizes cities, counties, and their redevelopment agencies and housing authorities to make long-term, low-interest loans to finance residential rehabilitation in depressed residential areas in order to encourage the upgrading of property in such areas (Health & Safety Code section 37911) and to issue bonds for the purpose of financing such residential rehabilitation (Health & Safety Code, section 37916). Before issuing bonds, the local agency is required to adopt a comprehensive residential rehabilitation financing program. *Id.* at 478.

> Under this program the city conducts a feasibility study to determine which neighborhoods need improved housing conditions. The program requires an inspection of a designated area to determine whether the properties are in compliance with the San Francisco Housing code section 301A. This section requires the Bureau of Building Inspection to inspect every building and structure in an area designated for area-wide concentrated code enforcement. The Court of Appeal held that there were reasonable legislative or administrative standards for conducting an inspection pursuant to rehabilitation assistance programs and affidavits in support of inspection warrants provided for probable cause for warrants to be issued.

H. HOUSING CODES

A housing code is an application of state police power implemented by a local ordinance setting minimum housing standards. The requirements of the Housing Act of 1954, 42 U.S.C.A. §§ 1450–60, required communities seeking urban renewal funds to adopt a "workable program for community improvement," which was interpreted to include the adoption of local housing codes and formulation of a plan of code enforcement. *See* Wexler, *Housing and Local Government* (1975). Both the Housing and Community Development Act of 1974, 42 U.S.C.A. § 1451(c), and the Housing and Urban Development Act of 1965, 12 U.S.C. § 1701, provided further incentives for housing code enactment and enforcement. In 1956, only about fifty-six communities had housing codes. By 1969, the National Commission on Urban Problems counted 4,904 communities with housing codes, not including statewide codes. *See National Commission on Urban Problems, Building the American City*, H.R.Doc. No. 91–34, 91st Congress, 1st Sess. The Workable Program requirement was repealed in 1974 with the passage of the Housing and Community Development Act of 1974, 42 U.S.C.A. 5301–5308. *See* Jane McGrew and John Bates, *Code Enforcement: The Federal Role*, 14 URBAN LAWYER 1 (1982).

The traditional purpose of housing codes is to prevent the deterioration of neighborhoods by establishing standards for a healthful and safe housing environment.

Housing codes generally cover three main areas:

1.   The supplied facilities in the structure.

2.   The level of maintenance, which includes both structural and sanitary maintenance.

3.   Occupancy, which concerns the size of dwelling units and of rooms of different types, the number of people who can occupy them, and other issues concerned on the whole with the usability and amenity of interior space.

When inspections reveal code violations, the owner must repair the structure (utilizing the city's latest building) or face the prospect of the city: (1) appointing a receiver for the property to collect rents and make the repairs; (2) having the City make the repairs and foreclose a lien on the property for the cost of the repairs; or, (3) for the city to enforce an order to demolish the property.

1.   MANDATORY INSPECTION REQUIREMENTS

Today almost every city in America has a housing code ordinance. The problem with housing code enforcement is that without the authority to enter buildings, the city is forced to rely on tenant complaints in order to inspect the interior of buildings. To prevent pervasive decline in rental buildings, cities have adopted multifamily and condominium rental licensing ordinances, as companion ordinances to the housing code, which require inspections whenever an apartment or the building itself is sold or rented. At the time of licensing, owners are required to post a bond ensuring that required repairs will be funded. Limiting inspections to the time of sale or lease of the building or unit has the added advantage of inspection occurring at a time when funds are available for the necessary repairs. *See McSwain v. Commonwealth*, 520 A.2d 527 (Pa.Cmwlth.1987) (court upheld as constitutional under due process and equal protection, a city ordinance requiring a housing code inspection and certification prior to each rental of a unit). Licensing procedures can include code inspection as a necessary adjunct to issuance of certificates of occupancy, particularly for multiple family units. *See generally* Otto Hetzel, *The Search for Effective and Cost-Efficient Housing Strategies: Enforcing Housing Condition Standards through Code Inspections at Time of Sale or Transfer*, 36 J.URB. & CONTEMP.L. 25 (1989). These mandatory inspection requirements run into problems with the Fourth Amendment search and seizure protections. The following case is illustrative.

MANN V. CALUMET CITY
United States Court of Appeals, Seventh Circuit, 2009.
588 F.3d 949.

POSNER, CIRCUIT JUDGE.

These consolidated appeals bring before us a challenge to the constitutionality of an ordinance of Calumet City, Illinois, that forbids the sale of a house without an inspection to determine whether it is in compliance with the City's building code. Calumet City Code § 14–1. The suit challenges the constitutionality of the ordinance "on its face," a phrase of uncertain meaning, as we pointed out in *A Woman's Choice—East Side Women's Clinic v. Newman*, 305 F.3d 684, 687 (7th Cir.2002). What the plaintiffs seem to mean by it is that "no set of circumstances exists under which the [ordinance] would be valid," which is the definition in *United States v. Salerno*, 481 U.S. 739, 745 (1987); *see also United States v. Nagel*, 559 F.3d 756, 764–65 (7th Cir.2009); and *Rancho Viejo, LLC v. Norton*, 323 F.3d 1062, 1077–78 (D.C.Cir.2003). One way to think of condemning a statute "on its face" is as an exception to the principle that a statute should if possible be interpreted in such a way as to avoid its being held unconstitutional. *See e.g., Rancho Viejo, LLC v. Norton, supra*, 323 F.3d at 1077–78.

It is always an option for a plaintiff to challenge a statute without dwelling on particulars of his case that might invalidate the application of the statute to him. That is the course that the plaintiffs in these cases have chosen. They don't argue that the City unreasonably delayed the sale of their property or unreasonably prevented the sale; they argue that even punctilious compliance with the procedural safeguards created by the ordinance cannot protect their constitutional rights. They are challenging the ordinance as written.

They have an uphill fight. "Point of sale" ordinances such as this one are common and have withstood constitutional attack in all cases that we know of in which the ordinance avoided invalidation under the Fourth Amendment by requiring that the city's inspectors obtain a warrant to inspect a house over the owner's objection. *Joy Management Co. v. City of Detroit*, 455 N.W.2d 55, 57–58 (1990); *Butcher v. City of Detroit*, 347 N.W.2d 702, 707–08 (Mich.App.1984); *Currier v. City of Pasadena*, 48 Cal.App.3d 810 (1975); *Greater New Haven Property Owners Ass'n v. City of New Haven*, 951 A.2d 551, 562–66 (Conn.2008); *Dome Realty, Inc. v. City of Paterson*, 416 A.2d 334, 349–50 (N.J.1980). That means all cases other than *Wilson v. City of Cincinnati*, 46 Ohio St.2d 138, 346 N.E.2d 666, 671 (1976), and *Hometown Co-operative Apartments v. City of Hometown*, 495 F.Supp.

55, 60 (N.D.Ill.1980). Calumet City's ordinance contains such a requirement.

The plaintiffs appeal mainly to the due process clause of the Fourteenth Amendment, which, so far as bears on their case, forbids a state or local government to deprive a person of property without due process of law. No court thinks, however, that this means the state can't regulate property-can't for example enact building codes and zoning regulations even though such measures limit the property owner's right to do what he wants with his property. *Village of Euclid v. Ambler Realty Co.*, 272 U.S. 365, 394–95 (1926), so held and has been followed in innumerable cases. *See e.g., Town of Rhine v. Bizzell*, 751 N.W.2d 780, 793–96 (Wis.2008); *Napleton v. Village of Hinsdale*, 891 N.E.2d 839, 853 (Ill.2008); *General Auto Service Station v. City of Chicago*, 526 F.3d 991, 1000–01 (7th Cir.2008); *Davet v. City of Cleveland*, 456 F.3d 549, 552–53 (6th Cir.2006). The principle is illustrated by a notable recent decision upholding the validity of an ordinance that prohibited keeping more than three dogs on property in a residential district. *Luper v. City of Wasilla*, 215 P.3d 342, 348–49 (Alaska 2009); *see also Greater Chicago Combine & Center, Inc. v. Chicago*, 431 F.3d 1065, 1072 (7th Cir.2005) (keeping pigeons in residential areas); *Hull v. Scruggs*, 2 So.2d 543 (Miss.1941) (property owner can kill a trespassing dog that has an irresistible urge to suck eggs).

What is true is that a regulation may so constrict the rights of a property owner as to be deemed a "regulatory taking," entitling the owner to compensation under the takings clause of the Fifth Amendment for the diminution of the market value of his property. But our plaintiffs aren't proceeding under the takings clause. Their argument is that the restrictions that the ordinance places on their property rights are irrational and therefore deprive them of property without due process of law, entitling them to enjoin the ordinance rather than just insist on compensation. *See Lingle v. Chevron U.S.A. Inc.*, 544 U.S. 528, 536–37, 540–43 (2005); *Cavel International, Inc. v. Madigan*, 500 F.3d 551, 556 (7th Cir.2007); and, *Guggenheim v. City of Goleta*, 582 F.3d 996, 1030–31 (9th Cir.2009).

But building [and housing] codes, to which the challenged ordinance is ancillary, cannot be thought irrational. They do increase the cost of property (as do other conventional regulations of property), but if reasonably well designed they also increase its value. Without them more buildings would catch fire, collapse, become unsightly, attract squatters, or cause environmental damage and by doing any of these things reduce the value of other buildings in the neighborhood. Assuring full compliance with building codes is difficult after a building is built, because most violations are committed inside the building and thus out of sight until a violation results in damage visible from the outside. Hence the ordinance, another objective of which is to prevent the surreptitious conversion of single-family into multi-family residences (for example by the owner's constructing a second kitchen or additional bathrooms), in violation of zoning codes the constitutionality of which is not questioned.

All this seems eminently reasonable (as reasonable as conditioning the transfer of title to real estate on payment of any real estate taxes due on the property-another common restriction on the sale of property), and indeed the plaintiffs do not, except in passing, challenge the principle of point of sale ordinances. Their focus is on the procedural adequacy of the method by which Calumet City's ordinance is enforced. They say it fails to protect a homeowner from unreasonable limitations on his property rights; one of those rights is the right to sell the property. But they fail to indicate concretely what the ordinance would have to provide in order to pass a workable test of reasonableness. It provides the conventional procedural safeguards and if these are inadequate we don't know what adequacy requires. The ordinance requires a property owner to notify the City government of a proposed sale of his property. The City has 28 days after receiving the notice to conduct a compliance inspection. During that period, it must notify the owner of its intention to conduct the inspection. If he responds that he won't consent to an inspection, the City has 10 days within which to get a warrant from a judge, limited to authorizing an inspection for compliance with the building code. The City's building code is a standard such code (not an invention of Calumet City) called the "2006 International Property Maintenance Code."

Within three business days after conducting the inspection (whether or not pursuant to a warrant) the City must notify the owner whether the house is in compliance with the building code and, if not, what repairs are required to bring it into compliance. (If the inspection discloses an unlawful conversion of the house to a multifamily dwelling, the order, instead of being a repair order, will order deconversion.) After the City is notified that the repairs have been made or deconversion effected, it has three business days within which to reinspect. An owner who is in a hurry to sell the house can do so before completing the ordered repairs or deconversion if his buyer posts a bond equal to the expected cost of bringing the house into compliance. The buyer then has 180 days to complete the repairs or deconversion; if he fails to do so, the City can ask a court to order him to.

The owner can appeal a repair or deconversion order to the City's Zoning Board of Appeals, where he is entitled to a full hearing. The appeal stays the City's order. An owner who loses in the board of appeals is entitled to judicial review in the Illinois state court system in the usual manner.

We cannot think of what more could reasonably be required to protect the homeowner's rights, including his Fourth Amendment rights, which the ordinance's warrant provisions fully protect. *Currier v. City of Pasadena, supra,* 121 Cal.Rptr. at 917–18; *Hometown Co-operative*

Apartments v. City of Hometown, supra, 515 F.Supp. at 504; cf. *Tobin v. City of Peoria, supra,* 939 F.Supp. at 631–33; *see generally Camara v. Municipal Court of City and County of San Francisco,* 387 U.S. 523, 538–40 (1967). The plaintiffs' arguments are either frivolous or pertinent only to a challenge to how the ordinance is applied in particular cases by the City or its board of zoning appeals or the state courts, and that as we know is not the nature of their challenge.

The plaintiffs' challenges to how the ordinance might be applied include claims that the City may order purely cosmetic changes to the property and that the board of zoning appeals might not allow cross-examination. Such challenges are premature until and unless a homeowner challenges the ordinance on the ground that it has been applied to him in a way, not foreordained by the text of the ordinance, that deprives him of property. Unwilling to complain about the specifics of the application of the order to their planned sales, the plaintiffs insist that the ordinance be so detailed as to anticipate and provide for every possible abuse or irregularity in enforcement. To satisfy them the ordinance would have to be a thousand pages long. The Constitution does not require such detail.

There are some other issues, but no need to discuss them. The judgments are affirmed.

NOTES

1. *Rental License Ordinances.* In *People v. LaRoche,* 902 N.Y.S.2d 878 (N.Y.App.2010), the court found that a rental license ordinance which made it unlawful to erect, alter or maintain any rental building or structure until the license was obtained was not unconstitutionally vague. The court also upheld the constitutionality of the ordinance under the Fourth Amendment because there was a provision requiring consent or obtaining a judicial search warrant. The search warrant may be issued by a municipal or administrative judge. *See Frech v. City of Columbia,* 693 S.W.2d 813 (Mo. En banc, 1985).

2. *Flexible Housing Codes.* A fundamental problem exists with the enforcement of a single standard housing code in all areas of the city regardless of the condition of the housing or neighborhood. Buildings with violations of the housing code are required to reconstruct in accordance with the latest building code criteria, causing extreme hardship to older existing structures lacking major modern technology. Consideration should be given to revising the housing code in order to make it more flexible and to establish differential standards to limit repairs to economically affordable limits in the gray areas of the city. *See* Adopt "Rehab Codes" to Facilitate Rehabilitation of Older Homes, Housing Policy.org (July 5, 2011):

> In communities that use conventional building codes, the level of building upgrades required in a rehabilitation project is typically based on the estimated cost of the project, rather than the type or

scope of work proposed. The more expensive the project, the greater the degree to which the building must comply with current standards. Use of this system can trigger requirements for extensive renovation in rehabilitation projects that make only minimal structural changes—a scenario that increases costs and may discourage the redevelopment of affordable homes.

In contrast, rehabilitation codes match the level of required compliance to the type of work proposed. This shift can lead to substantial savings in time and money and may be the key to making a particular rehab project feasible.

Indeed, there is a worldwide movement to encourage "flexible housing construction" for new buildings to assure that these buildings have the structural capacity to adapt to new technological changes in energy conservation, rainwater capture, plumbing, electrical, solar and wind systems and green development design.

3.   The origins of "flexible housing codes" stem from a number of innovative articles: (a) Peter W. Salsich, Jr., *Housing and the States*, 2 URB.LAW. 40 (1970); (b) Eugenia Landman, *The Flexible Housing Code—The Mystique of the Single Standard: A Critical Analysis and Comparison of Model and Selected Housing Codes Leading to the Development of a Proposed Model Flexible Housing Code*, 18 HOWARD L.J. 251, 255 (1974); and (c) Note, *Municipal Housing Codes*, 69 HARV.L.REV. 1115 (1956) (using a flexible housing code, the local governing body designates areas for "protection," "rehabilitation," and "demolition," corresponding to what is frequently termed the "good," "gray" and "worst" areas of the community).

4.   *Equal Protection*. A housing code which creates differing requirements for disparate areas runs some risk of violating the equal protection clause. The classification of a city into housing code zones may be upheld as reasonably related to the ultimate legislative purposes of health, safety, and slum prevention. Equal protection is not denied when different methods are employed to obtain validly differentiated objectives. *See Anderson v. Provo City Corp.*, 108 P.3d 701 (Utah 2005) (zoning amendment for university district that restricted leasing of "accessory" apartments by owners who occupied the residence did not violate uniform operation of law provision of state Constitution, even though amendment created two classes of occupying and non-occupying homeowners; the disparity in treatment was reasonably justified by the city's stated objective of balancing city's competing interests in accommodating student housing needs. West's U.C.A. Const. Art. 1, § 24); *but see Brennan v. Milwaukee*, 60 N.W.2d 704 (Wis.1953) (action by apartment owners to enjoin city and city's commissioner of health from enforcing city ordinance requiring installation of bathtub or shower in apartments containing more than three rooms. The Supreme Court held that the ordinance was not based upon a substantial distinction which make one class really different from another or which bore reasonably upon object to be sought, and, therefore, was violative of the equal protection clause of the Federal Constitution).

2. REMEDIES FOR HOUSING CODE VIOLATIONS

ELSMERE PARK CLUB, L.P. v. TOWN OF ELSMERE

United States Court of Appeals, Third Circuit, 2008.
542 F.3d 412.

AMBRO, CIRCUIT JUDGE.

We decide whether the Town of Elsmere, Delaware, violated Elsmere Park Club's procedural due process rights under the Fourteenth Amendment to our Constitution when the Town condemned the Club's apartment complex without offering a pre-deprivation hearing. We hold that the Town did not run afoul of the Constitution because post-deprivation process was all that was required given the circumstances of this case. Because the Town provided adequate post-deprivation process by way of an administrative appeal, and the Club failed to avail itself of that process, we affirm the District Court's grant of summary judgment against the Club.

The Club is the former owner of the Elsmere Park Apartments ("Apartments"). The Apartments are a complex of thirty-nine buildings, arranged in nine separate groups. They contain a total of 156 garden-style apartments, including one basement unit in each of the thirty-nine buildings. After severe flooding from Hurricane Hugo in 1989, the Town prohibited the Club from renting out its basement apartments, but allowed continued use of the above-ground units. The Club then boarded up the basement apartments with plywood. In 1996, after increasing incidents of vandalism, the Town instructed the Club to brick over the basement windows and seal the basement apartments.

All was relatively quiet between the Town and the Club between 1996 and 2002. Then, on Tuesday, October 1, 2002, while conducting a routine pre-rental inspection of the Apartments, the Town's Code Inspector, Ellis Blomquist, detected a strong smell of mold. Blomquist returned to the Apartments on Friday, October 4, with Kenneth Belmont, a representative from the State of Delaware Department of Public Health. They inspected two of the sealed basement units and found mold, water leaks, and raw sewage, amounting to various violations of the Elsmere Town Building Code. After observing the mold, Blomquist and Belmont sought the advice of Gerald Llewellyn, Chief Toxicologist for the State of Delaware. Llewellyn concluded that the conditions in the basements posed a serious health threat to the buildings' residents due to what he saw as the likelihood that mold spores were migrating up to the occupied units through openings such as pipe chases and ventilation ducts. Together, Llewellyn and Belmont recommended that the two buildings be condemned and vacated immediately. Blomquist agreed, and, after informing the Apartment's on-site manager of his decision, proceeded to condemn the buildings and vacate the residents.

On Monday, October 7, the inspections of the basements resumed. Blomquist, Belmont, Llewellyn and George Yocher, an environmental epidemiologist for the State of Delaware, proceeded to go through the remaining basements, along with several stairways and some unoccupied apartments, condemning each building they inspected. By Thursday, October 10, 2002, every building except the one housing the complex's rental management office had been condemned. It appears that no time in the Town's inspection did it examine any occupied apartments, and the record does not note what category of mold was present in the basements. As the condemnations were occurring, the Club filed a motion for a temporary restraining order in the Delaware Court of Chancery, asserting, inter alia, that the Town had effected an unconstitutional taking by condemning the thirty-eight buildings without compensating the Club. After a hearing, the Chancery Court denied relief. In so holding, the Court found that the Town had been justified in invoking its emergency powers to condemn the property.

At the end of October 2002, the Club notified the Town that it intended to appeal the condemnation of the Apartments. It sent a letter to the Town asking for a hearing before the "Board of Building Appeals," which was listed in the Elsmere Town Code as the appropriate body for hearing such appeals. In correspondence with the Town Solicitor, the Club was told that the Town actually referred to its appellate body as the Board of Adjustment. The Town Solicitor explained that the "Board of Building Appeals" reference came from a code section that had been borrowed from the National Building Code and incorporated into the Town's Code without being adjusted to reflect the Town's particular usage. In January 2003, the Club and the Town Solicitor executed an agreement to stay the Club's administrative appeal, and the Club, by its own admission, "abandoned its administrative appeal." In April 2003, the Club sold the Apartments at a fire-sale price.

A year and a half later, the Club brought an action under 42 U.S.C. § 1983 in the United States District Court for the District of Delaware against the Town and several of its agents. In its complaint, the Club alleged that the Town deprived it of due process when the Town condemned and evacuated the Apartments without first affording the Club the opportunity for a hearing or the chance to cure the alleged code violations. The District Court concluded that the Town "failed to present sufficient evidence of exigent circumstances to justify the absence of any pre-deprivation due process [rights]." *See Elsmere Park Club, L.P. v. Town of Elsmere*, 474 F.Supp.2d 638, 647 (D.Del.2007). The Court found it significant that Blomquist and other Town representatives made the decision to condemn the apartments without first inspecting any of the occupied units or taking air samples. Moreover, it noted that the record contains no evidence that any residents actually complained of, or suffered from, mold-related ailments or conditions in their units. As such, the Court concluded that Town had violated the Club's due process rights in not offering a pre-deprivation opportunity to oppose the condemnation. Despite having found a procedural due process violation, the Court went on to conclude that the Club was ineligible for relief because it had failed to avail itself of the Town's post-deprivation hearing procedure (citing *Alvin v. Suzuki*, 227 F.3d 107, 116 (3d Cir.2000), for the proposition that a plaintiff alleging a procedural due process violation must have taken advantage of all available local process in order to claim a constitutional injury). It therefore entered summary judgment in favor of the Town. We affirm.

The Club contends that the Town violated its rights to procedural due process in two ways: first, in failing to provide a hearing before condemning the Apartments, and, second, in offering what the Club argues were inadequate means for challenging the condemnations after they occurred. The Fourteenth Amendment prohibits a state from "depriving any person of life, liberty, or property, without due process of law". "A fundamental requirement of due process is the opportunity to be heard." *Armstrong v. Manzo*, 380 U.S. 545, 552 (1965). That opportunity "must be granted at a meaningful time and in a meaningful manner." In the typical situation, the hearing should come before the Government deprives a person of his property. This makes practical sense, "[f]or when a person has an opportunity to speak up in his own defense, and when the State must listen to what he has to say, substantively unfair and simply mistaken deprivations of property interests can be prevented." *Fuentes v. Shevin*, 407 U.S. 67, 81 (1972). Nonetheless, the Supreme Court has held that, in special circumstances, a state may satisfy the requirements of procedural due process merely by making available "some meaningful means by which to assess the propriety of the State's action at some time after the initial taking." *See Parratt v. Taylor*, 451 U.S. 527, 539 (1981). Where there is "the necessity of quick action by the State," or where "providing any meaningful pre-deprivation process" would be impractical, the Government is relieved of the usual obligation to provide a pre-deprivation hearing. Our first task, then, is to determine whether the Town was faced with circumstances in which it was required to provide a pre-deprivation hearing. If so, then no amount of post-deprivation process could cure the Town's initial failure to provide a hearing.

It is beyond question "that summary administrative action may be justified in emergency situations." *Hodel v. Va. Surface Mining & Reclamation Ass'n*, 452 U.S. 264, 300 (1981); *see also Herwins v. City of Revere*, 163 F.3d 15, 18 (1st Cir.1998) ("No one can seriously doubt that emergency conditions may exist (e.g., a severe fire hazard) that would warrant a peremptory shutdown of a residential building."). The Club, however, is not disputing that, where there is a threat to public health or safety requiring prompt action, the Government may act quickly to eliminate that threat. Rather, the Club argues that the mold situation did not amount to an emergency, and that, regardless, the Town did not conduct a thorough enough investigation at the time to justify its belief that emergency action was warranted.

To assess this argument, we ask what sort of scrutiny we should apply to an official decision that emergency action is required. Other courts of appeals have held that such decisions must be analyzed very deferentially. *See Catanzaro v. Weiden*, 188 F.3d 56, 62–63 (2d Cir.1999); *Herwins*, 163 F.3d at 19; *Harris v. City of Akron*, 20 F.3d 1396, 1404 (6th Cir.1994). This makes basic sense. As the Court of Appeals for the Second Circuit has explained:

> "The law should not discourage officials from taking prompt action to insure the public safety. By subjecting a decision to invoke an emergency procedure to an exacting hindsight analysis, where every mistake, even if made in good faith, becomes a constitutional violation, we encourage delay and thereby potentially increase the public's exposure to dangerous conditions. This quandary is exactly what these emergency procedures are designed to prevent, and is the primary reason they are constitutionally acceptable". Yet, it is important to avoid the opposite trap. That is, we cannot apply so much deference as to allow "the government [to] avoid affording due process to citizens by arbitrarily invoking emergency procedures." Accordingly, we adopt the test laid out by our colleagues in the Second Circuit: "where there is competent evidence allowing the official to reasonably believe that an emergency does in fact exist. The discretionary invocation of an emergency procedure results in a constitutional violation only where such invocation is arbitrary or amounts to an abuse of discretion. *See Armendariz v. Penman*, 31 F.3d 860, 866 (9th Cir.1994) ("[T]he rationale for permitting government officials to act summarily in emergency situations does not apply where the officials know no emergency exists, or where they act with reckless disregard of the actual circumstances."), vacated in part on other grounds, 75 F.3d 1311 (9th Cir.1996) (en banc).

Thus, in analyzing the Town's decision to condemn summarily the apartments, we look to whether there was "competent evidence" supporting the reasonable belief that the mold situation presented an "emergency," and to whether the Town's actions were otherwise "arbitrary" or an "abuse of discretion." We conclude that, under that standard, the Town's failure to provide a pre-deprivation hearing did not amount to a constitutional violation.

It is undisputed that the sealed-off basement apartments were overrun with mold. It is also undisputed that Blomquist consulted several state experts who told him that the mold potentially posed a substantial and immediate threat to the health and welfare of the Apartments' residents.

Given that, we cannot say that the Town acted unreasonably in summarily condemning the Apartments. It is true that the investigation of the mold situation was far from perfect. We are particularly troubled, as was the District Court, by the failure to inspect any of the occupied units to determine whether toxic mold was in fact spreading up from the basements. Nonetheless, we are reluctant to second guess the decision to act on an urgent basis. Where government officials are faced with a situation in which a failure to act quickly could have serious health consequences, perfection or near perfection is not the standard. Given the mold problem in the sealed basement apartments, and the Town's reliance on the advice of experts, the Town's actions cannot be characterized as arbitrary or an abuse of its discretion. We therefore hold that due process did not require a pre-deprivation hearing before the Town condemned the Apartments.

Having concluded that a pre-deprivation hearing was not required, we must nevertheless determine whether the post-deprivation remedy the Town offered was adequate. Even where exigent circumstances exist, it is still necessary to make available "some meaningful means by which to assess the propriety of the State's action at some time after the initial taking" in order to "satisfy the requirements of procedural due process." *Parratt*, 451 U.S. at 539. If an adequate post-deprivation remedy existed, and the Club failed to avail itself of it, then we must affirm the District Court's grant of summary judgment. *Cf. Alvin*, 227 F.3d at 116 ("In order to state a claim for failure to provide due process, a plaintiff must have taken advantage of the processes that are available to him or her, unless those processes are unavailable or patently inadequate.").

There was an adequate post-deprivation remedy in this case—that of administrative appeal—and the Club concedes that it failed to take such an appeal. We have held that "[i]n order to state a claim for failure to provide due process, a plaintiff must have taken advantage of the processes that are available to him or her, unless those processes are unavailable or patently inadequate." *Alvin*, 227 F.3d at 116. Thus, the Club's failure to take advantage of that process means that it cannot claim a constitutional injury.

This requirement that a plaintiff avail itself of the processes available differs from the administrative exhaustion requirements that appear in other civil rights contexts. Administrative exhaustion is not generally required in § 1983 suits. *See McGreevy v. Stroup*, 413 F.3d 359, 369 (3d Cir.2005). However, as we explained in Alvin, "exhaustion is analytically distinct from the requirement that the harm alleged has occurred. [A] procedural due process violation cannot have occurred when the governmental actor provides apparently adequate procedural remedies and the plaintiff has not availed himself of those remedies." *See Alvin*, 227 F.3d at 116. Thus, it is not that the Club lost its claim because it failed to litigate it fully through local procedures before seeking federal relief. Rather, because the constitutional injury alleged is the Town's failure to provide adequate procedures to the Club, no such injury could have occurred where the Club has failed to take advantage of the procedures actually offered, at least not absent a showing that the process offered was "patently inadequate."

Having failed to take advantage of the available process, the Club has not demonstrated a violation of the Due Process Clause of the Fourteenth Amendment and thus cannot maintain a successful § 1983 action in federal court.

For these reasons, we affirm the District Court's grant of summary judgment.

NOTES

1.   As shown in the principal case, buildings that are public nuisances in fact may be abated or condemned by cities, irrespective of the fact that they were constructed prior to the enactment of the law under which public authorities are proceeding. A building must be a nuisance in fact before it can be abated or condemned as such without municipal liability for destruction or damages. *See Mohilef v. Janovici*, 51 Cal.App.4th 267 (1996); and *City of Kansas City v. New York-Kansas Bldg. Associates, L.P.*, 96 S.W.3d 846 (Mo.App.2002). Demolition has been particularly important for abandoned and vacated buildings which cast a blighting influence on the neighborhood. Community Development Block Grant funds can be used for demolition programs as the successor of HUD's categorical grant demolition program. See Section 116(b) of the Housing and Urban Development Act. Could an ordinance be drafted to treat abandoned buildings as an implied dedication to the city so they may immediately be turned over for rehabilitation and occupancy? *See Horton v. Gulledge*, 177 S.E.2d 885 (N.C.1970), overruled on other grounds in *State v. Jones*, 290 S.E.2d 675 (N.C.1982). The North Carolina Supreme Court held that an ordinance which prescribed mandatory demolition of substandard or code violating buildings without the alternative of repairs was not within the police power of the City of Greensboro to enact. The court suggested that the city-ordered demolition might be proper if the owner was given the opportunity but failed to make repairs.

2.   The action of a local legislative body in condemning a structure has been deemed to be quasi-judicial in nature. While the abatement may be administrative without judicial process in some instances and while it may require destruction or removal of a building, depending on applicable law and circumstances, summary or administrative abatement risks municipal liability where the building is not a nuisance in fact. An ordinance authorizing a suit to abate the nuisance seems to be more appropriate and reasonable process. Except where a threat to public health or safety exists, a municipal ordinance which required a building owner to demolish an unsafe structure if the costs of repair would exceed 100% of the property's appraised value was

unconstitutional because there was no rational reason for the city not to allow the building owner to abate a nuisance on his or her property. *See Herrit v. Code Management Appeal Bd. of City of Butler*, 704 A.2d 186 (Pa.Cmwlth.1997). However, a statute providing that repairs shall be presumed unreasonable if their cost exceeded 50% of stated formula value, merely created a rebuttable presumption, and did not foreclose the possibility, under severe health and safety circumstances, warranting repair of a building at a cost in excess of 50% of the formula value. *See Posnanski v. City of West Allis*, 213 N.W.2d 51 (Wis.1973). In *Knapp v. Newport Beach*, 9 Cal.Rptr. 90 (Cal.App.1960) the owner was ordered to virtually reconstruct the building at a cost equal to twice its present value. Nevertheless, even after earthquake damage, the court in *Rose v. City of Coalinga*, 190 Cal.App.3d 1627 (1987) held that "when private property is wrongfully damaged or destroyed in the course of governmental action and the government has not first undertaken procedures to guarantee due process to the owner, such as an action in eminent domain or proceedings to declare a condition a nuisance, then, absent an emergency giving rise to the proper exercise of the police power, an action in inverse condemnation by the owner against the governmental agency will lie to establish the damages suffered by the owner."

3. The best approach is to treat the code violations as a continuing public nuisance and seek civil injunctive relief, which can tailor the remedy to the specific circumstances and be enforced by civil contempt. *See City of Kansas City v. Mary Don Co.*, 606 S.W.2d 411 (Mo.App.1980). Generally, this process runs into the legal principle that a court of equity will not permit itself to be used as a medium for the enforcement of the criminal laws or quasi-criminal ordinances. This principle is not applicable if the action involves enjoining the maintenance of a public nuisance. *See City of Independence v. DeWitt*, 550 S.W.2d 840 (Mo.App.1977).

4. Use of a specialized "housing" court which enables chronic violators to be identified has been in use in major cities for over 30 years. Code enforcement cases have traditionally been heard by courts of limited jurisdiction, which handle traffic violations, landlord-tenant disputes and a mass of minor violations of municipal ordinances. Consequently, the importance placed on, and the prosecution of, housing code violations is minimized. Establishment of specialized housing courts is an alternative in which particularized treatment can be given to the numerous problems which arise. A specialized housing court in Pittsburgh has been especially successful through the use of fines, supervised probation and close cooperation with the code agencies themselves. Other types of housing courts, established in Chicago and Boston, have broader subject matter jurisdiction and availability of civil and equitable powers. Existing court rules and procedures can also be reformed to meet the specialized needs of housing law. For example, special dockets and judges can be formed for code cases and greater communication can be established with prosecuting attorneys and code agencies. *See* Miller and Brannigan, *Code Enforcement: Courts, Prosecutors, and Code Agencies, A Report of the Special Committee on Housing and Urban Development Law of the American Bar Association* (1982) and Sarah H. Ramsey and Frederick

Zolna, *A Piece in the Puzzle of Providing Adequate Housing: Court Effectiveness in Code Enforcement*, 18 FORD.URB.L.J. 605 (1991).

5.   Receivership. Several states have enacted statutes which provide for the appointment of a receiver to collect the rents and make the necessary repairs. *See* 65 Ill. Consolidated Statutes, § 11–31–2:

> If the appropriate official of any municipality determines, upon due investigation, that any building or structure therein fails to conform to the minimum standards of health and safety as set forth in the applicable ordinances of such municipality * * * the municipality may make application to the circuit court for an injunction requiring compliance * * * or for such other order as the court may deem necessary or appropriate to secure such compliance.

In Missouri, the court may "appoint the code enforcement agency * * * licensed attorney or real estate broker * * * as a receiver * * * ." Vernon's Ann.Mo.Stat. § 441.590(1), (2).

In *Central Savings Bank v. New York*, 18 N.E.2d 151 (N.Y.1938) the Court of Appeals held the first New York receivership statute to be unconstitutional due to the procedural due process defect of lack of notice and hearing to mortgagees whose liens were subordinated to the lien of the receiver. *In re Department of Bldgs.*, 200 N.E.2d 432 (N.Y.1964), upheld a revised statute which established the priority of the lien of the receiver on the building but not on the rents. Note that Illinois gives priority to the receiver's lien for both the rents and the structure.

In New York and Missouri, appointment of a receiver is based on a finding of nuisance. In *City of St. Louis v. Golden Gate Corporation*, 421 S.W.2d 4 (Mo.1967), the court refused to grant injunctive relief and the appointment of a receiver where an ordinance and not a state statute was utilized.

I.   PUBLIC HOUSING: FROM DESPAIR TO HOPE

1.   HISTORY

In 1937 the United States Housing Act was enacted to provide decent and safe rental housing for eligible low-income families, the elderly, and persons with disabilities. The program was very simple. Public Housing Authorities PHAs, sold general obligation bonds to buy land and build low income housing projects. Public housing comes in all sizes and types, from scattered single family houses to high rise apartments for elderly families. There are approximately 1.2 million households living in public housing units, managed by some 3,300 PHAs. Between 1937 and 1970, the major achievement of the federal government under the act, in concert with local PHAs, was to build segregated dense high rise public housing projects in urban cores cleared by the urban renewal bulldozer. Never popular with political conservatives and a disillusionment to liberals, public housing starts began to decline in the late 1960s. Perhaps the most notorious of all public housing projects was the Pruitt-Igoe Project in St. Louis, Missouri. Ten thousand people lived in what one writer called a "federally built and supported slum." *See* Lee Rainwater, *Behind Ghetto Walls* (1970). The Project contained 33 eleven-story buildings near downtown St. Louis. Though the Project was touted as a national showpiece of what public housing could do, it was a failure almost from its dedication. Elevators stopped only at the fourth, seventh, and tenth floors; children were impossible to supervise outdoors; crime and vandalism were as high as anywhere in the country, and one in four units remained vacant. Finally, the Project was demolished. In some ways, the Pruitt-Igoe experience is symbolic of American public housing.

The decline of federally built public housing projects also coincided with the enforcement of the federal Fair Housing Act through preventing site location discrimination.

In *Shannon v. United States Dept. of Housing & Urban Dev.*, 436 F.2d 809 (3d Cir.1970), HUD chose to locate another public housing-interest subsidized project in a predominantly black area. Both white and black residents brought an action against HUD. The court noted that some "institutionalized methods" were necessary for use by HUD in making decisions regarding the location of subsidized housing. The Shannon court set out the rules and factors that HUD must consider in selecting a site for a public housing project:

1.   What procedures were used by the LPA (local public authority) in considering the effects on racial concentration when it made a choice of site or of type of housing?

2.   What tenant selection methods will be employed with respect to the proposed project?

3.   How has the LPA or the local governing body historically reacted to proposals for low income housing outside areas of racial concentration?

4.   Where is low income housing, both public and publicly assisted, now located in the geographic area of the LPA?

5.   Where is middle income and luxury housing, in particular middle income and luxury housing with federal mortgage insurance guarantees, located in the geographic area of the LPA?

6.   Are some low income housing projects in the geographic area of the LPA occupied primarily by tenants of one race, and if so, where are they located?

7.   What is the projected racial composition of tenants of the proposed project?

8.   Will the project house school age children and if so what schools will they attend and what is the racial balance in those schools?

9.   Have the zoning and other land use regulations of the local governing body in the geographic area of the LPA had the effect of confining low income housing to certain areas, and if so how has this effected racial concentration?

10.   Are there alternative available sites?

11.   At the site selected by the LPA how severe is the need for restoration, and are other alternative means of restoration available which would have preferable effects on racial concentration in that area?

Id. at 821–22. These site selection criteria were codified in 1971 in 24 C.F.R. § 200.700 and are still used today. Under what circumstances will HUD itself be liable for site selection violations? HUD has an affirmative obligation under the Fair Housing Act to end discrimination in public housing, *see Garrett v. City of Hamtramck*, 503 F.2d 1236 (6th Cir.1974) (HUD will be liable where it has disbursed federal funds to local housing authorities that will "establish and add to segregation in housing patterns.")

The net result of Shannon and Garrett was to proscribe high rise public housing projects in urban core neighborhoods with concentrated minority populations. In one last ditch effort, the Dallas Housing Authority persisted in building public housing projects in segregated African-American minority areas. In a series of cases, the Dallas Housing Authority (DHA) and HUD were found to be responsible for racial segregation in low-income public housing by selecting sites for low-income housing projects in minority areas despite alternative locations. In *Walker v. HUD*, 734 F.Supp. 1231, 1244 (N.D.Tex.1989) (Walker I) the court ordered the use of sites only in non-segregated areas. In *Walker v. United States Dept. of Housing and Urban Dev.*, 734 F.Supp. 1289 (N.D.Tex.1989), the court issued an order requiring DHA to disperse housing units to other parts of the city and suburbs by entering into consent agreements with the suburban cities. The city of Dallas was required to contact annually surrounding suburban cities and request them to enter into cooperation agreements with the Dallas Housing Authority to develop a reasonable number of low income family housing units in such cities in order to further desegregation efforts. Finally, in 1997 HUD selected a site that was located in the non-minority areas of far North Dallas. The homeowners in the area filed suit protesting the housing project. The court rejected the homeowners' attempts to enjoin the construction and approved two small public housing apartment buildings. *Walker v. Department of HUD*, 169 F.3d 973 (5th Cir. 1999), *cert. denied*, 528 U.S. 1131 (2000). The District

Court implemented the Court of Appeals order in 326 F.Supp.2d 780 (N.D.Tex.2004), *aff'd* 402 F.3d 532 (5th Cir.2005).

In its latest housing discrimination decision, recognizing disparate impact claims, in lieu of intentional discrimination, the U.S. Supreme Court set aside a state low income housing tax credit program on the basis that the state provided the tax credits on a discriminatory basis by limiting black and Latino inhabited projects receiving the tax credits to minority concentrated areas. *Texas Department of Housing and Community Affairs v. Inclusive Communities Project, Inc.*, 135 S.Ct. 2507, 2521–22 (2015):

"These unlawful practices include zoning laws and other housing restrictions that function unfairly to exclude minorities from certain neighborhoods without any sufficient justification. Suits targeting such practices reside at the heartland of disparate-impact liability. *See, e.g. Greater New Orleans Fair Housing Action Center v. St. Bernard Parish*, 641 F.Supp.2d 563, 569, 577–578 (E.D.La.2009) (invalidating post-Hurricane Katrina ordinance restricting the rental of housing units to only " 'blood relative[s]' " in an area of the city that was 88.3% white and 7.6% black).

The availability of disparate-impact liability, furthermore, has allowed private developers to vindicate the FHA's objectives and to protect their property rights by stopping municipalities from enforcing arbitrary and, in practice, discriminatory ordinances barring the construction of certain types of housing units. . . . Recognition of disparate-impact liability under the FHA also plays a role in uncovering discriminatory intent: It permits plaintiffs to counteract unconscious prejudices and disguised animus that escape easy classification as disparate treatment. In this way disparate-impact liability may prevent segregated housing patterns that might otherwise result from covert and illicit stereotyping."

2.   FEDERAL HOUSING PROGRAMS

Today PHAs build very little new housing due to Congress's failure to provide funding for direct housing construction. Nevertheless, there are a number of programs that provide rental, tax credit, grant and loan assistance in lieu of direct construction. In all forms of public housing assistance, applicants must have very low-, low- or moderate incomes. Very low-income is defined as below 50 percent of the area median income (AMI). Other programs are available to low-income families, between 50 and 80 percent of AMI; or moderate income families below 115 percent of AMI. These income limitations are universally used by state and local for their own affordable housing programs. In lieu of public construction, in 1993 the Congress enacted the HOPE VI program in which all existing housing projects were to be demolished and replaced with smaller workable housing units. In addition, the Section 8 program provides for rental assistance for public housing eligible families in privately owned apartment facilities and federal low income tax credits are made available for buildings constructed or converted to low income housing.

(a) HOPE VI

The Robert Taylor Homes housing project located in Chicago was also considered one of the worst slum areas in the United States. It is one of several of the nation's worst public housing projects that are being razed under the Federal program HOPE VI. Section 24 of the U.S. Housing Act, Urban Revitalization Demonstration Program. Pub.L.No. 102–389, 106 Stat. 1579 (1993). The HOPE VI, initiated in 1992, replaces obsolete high-rise public housing project buildings with smaller traditional neighborhood developments that are safer and have mixed-income residents. HUD estimates that as of 2000, it approved approximately 100,000 units of substandard public housing for demolition. The demolition of Robert Taylor Homes razed 28 high-rises with 4,321 apartments displacing 11,000 people. A difficult task is relocating and educating the residents of these high-rises. In Robert Taylor, 96% of the adult residents were unemployed and some of the families face problems with drug abuse or gang affiliation. Atlanta, which pioneered the Hope VI program, is considering the demolition of its last three public housing projects. *See* Jenny Jarvie, *Atlanta Rethinks Housing Changes*, Los Angeles Times, January 31, 2008, A-10. The HOPE VI Program was developed as a result of recommendations by National Commission on Severely Distressed Public Housing, which was charged with proposing a National Action Plan to eradicate severely distressed public housing. Since the inception of the HOPE VI program, there have been a total of 262 revitalization grants awarded between FYs 1993–2010, totaling approximately $6.3 billion. The HOPE VI program serves a vital role in the Department of Housing and Urban Development's efforts to transform Public Housing. In October of 2000, HOPE VI was honored with national recognition as a recipient of an Innovation in American Government Award. HOPE VI was recognized for its Mixed-Finance Public Housing Program, "an innovative approach that is transforming some of the nation's most severely distressed public housing from sources of urban blight to engines of neighborhood renewal." HOPE VI is a major HUD plan meant to revitalize the worst public housing projects into mixed-income developments whose philosophy is largely based on new urbanism and the concept of defensible space. It is now used as a tremendous funding source, together with the Low Income Housing Tax Credit, for the revitalization of today's inner core cities with traditional neighborhood development.

The program began in 1992, with formal recognition in law in 1998. As of 2005, the program had distributed $5.8 billion through 446 federal block grants to cities for the developments, with the highest individual grant being $67.7 million, awarded to Arvene/Edgemere Houses in New York City. HOPE VI has included a variety of grant programs including:

Revitalization, Demolition, Main Street, and Planning grant programs. As of June 1, 2010 there have been 254 HOPE VI Revitalization grants awarded to 132 housing authorities since 1993—totaling more than $6.1 billion.

The specific elements of public housing transformation that have proven key to HOPE VI include:

- Changing the physical shape of public housing.

- Establishing positive incentives for resident self-sufficiency and comprehensive services that empower residents.

- Lessening concentrations of poverty by placing public housing in non-poverty neighborhoods and promoting mixed-income and mixed use communities.

- Forging partnerships with other agencies, local governments, nonprofit organizations, and private businesses to leverage support and resources.

- Demolishing severely distressed public housing projects.

(b) Section 8 Housing Assistance

Section 8 of the United States Housing Act of 1937 (often simply known as Section 8), as repeatedly amended, authorizes the payment of rental housing assistance to private landlords on behalf of approximately 3.1 million low-income households. It operates through several programs, the largest of which, the Housing Choice Voucher program, pays a large portion of the rents and utilities of about 2.1 million households. The US Department of Housing and Urban Development manages the Section 8 programs.

The Housing Choice Voucher Program provides "tenant-based" rental assistance, so an assisted low income tenant can move with assistance from one unit of minimum housing quality to another. It is the key for tenants leaving HOPE VI demolished public housing projects for the private housing market. It grants a priority for those low-income families moving to mixed income and use traditional neighborhood development replacement on HOPE VI sites. Section 8 also authorizes a variety of "project-based" rental assistance programs, under which the owner reserves some or all of the units in a building for low-income tenants, in return for a Federal government guarantee to make up the difference between the tenant's contribution and the rent specified in the owner's contract with the government. *See* Shaun Donovan, *Secretary of HUD, Housing Choice Vouchers Fact Sheet*, U.S. Dep't of HUD, July 5, 2011.

The housing must also comply with the PHA health and safety codes. The income levels are limited to very low income families with income below 50% of median income for the metropolitan area.

(c) Low-Income Housing Tax Credits

The federal low-income housing tax credit program has been successful since 1987 A tax credit property is an apartment complex owned or constructed by a landlord who participates in the federal low-income housing tax credit program. These landlords get to claim 25% income tax credits for eligible buildings in return for renting some or all of the apartments to low-income tenants at a restricted rent. The Low-Income Housing Tax Credit (LIHTC) is the most important resource for creating affordable housing to implement the HOPE VI program (and other state inclusionary housing programs) in the United States today. The LIHTC program, created by HUD and available to the public since Hope VI was initiated in 1997, has completed 31,251 projects and placed over 1,843,000 housing units in service between 1987 and 2007. Created by the Tax Reform Act of 1986, the LIHTC program gives State and local LIHTC allocating agencies the equivalent of nearly $8 billion in annual budget authority to issue tax credits for the acquisition, rehabilitation, or new construction of rental housing targeted to lower-income households. The HUD database includes project address, number of units and low-income units, number of bedrooms, year the credit was allocated, year the project was placed in service, whether the project was new construction or rehab, type of credit provided, and other sources of project financing. The database helps to show how incentives to locate projects in low-income areas and other underserved markets are working.

An average of almost 1,450 projects and 108,000 units were placed in service in each year of the 1995 to 2007 period. See HUD's National Low Income Housing Tax Credit (LIHTC) Database, Projects Placed in Service through 2007 (February 16, 2010).

(d) Rural Very Low-Income Housing Repair

This program provides loans and grants to very low-income homeowners in rural areas to repair, improve, or modernize their dwellings or to remove health and safety hazards. Grant funds are only available to homeowners aged 62 or older. This includes repairs or replacement of heating, plumbing or electrical services, roof or basic structure as well as water and waste disposal systems, and weatherization. Loans bear an interest rate of one percent and are repaid over a period up to 20 years.

In addition to the above purpose, loan funds may be used to modernize the dwelling. Maximum loan amount cannot exceed a cumulative total of $20,000 to any eligible person and a maximum lifetime grant assistance is $7,500 to any eligible person. The house must be located in an eligible rural area which does not exceed 10,000 population. Some places with population between 10,000 and 25,000 may be eligible if not within a Metropolitan Statistical Area (MSA).

Direct and guaranteed loans may also be used to buy, build, or improve the applicant's permanent residence. New manufactured homes may be financed when they are on a permanent site, purchased from an approved dealer or contractor, and meet certain other requirements. Under very limited circumstances, homes may be re-financed with direct loans. Dwellings financed must be modest, decent, safe, and sanitary. The value of a home financed with a direct loan may not exceed the area limit. The property must be located in an eligible rural area.

(e) Community Block Grants

Most other federal categorical housing grant programs, have been merged into a single Community Development Block Grant which can be used for subsidizing interest rates, and providing grants to local governments for housing code enforcement, demolition, planning, urban renewal and rehabilitation. The local communities have discretion as to the use of these monies within the parameters of the fair housing laws and use for community development.

3.   HOMELESS HOUSING

(a) Federal Programs

HUD serves over 1 million people through emergency, transitional and permanent housing programs each year. The total number of people who experience homelessness could be twice as high. There are five federally defined categories under which individuals and families might qualify as homeless:

- Literally homeless;
- Imminent risk of homelessness;
- Homeless under other Federal statutes; and
- Fleeing/attempting to flee domestic violence.

HUD's Office of Special Needs Assistance Programs (SNAPS) supports the nationwide commitment to ending homelessness by providing funding opportunities to nonprofit organizations and State and local governments to quickly rehouse homeless individuals and families. Through these opportunities, SNAPS advocates self-sufficiency and promotes the effective utilization of mainstream resources available to individuals and families experiencing homelessness. HUD also maintains a Continuum of Care Homeless Assistance Program that links housing to other social and medical assistance. Nevertheless, as the following case demonstrates, there is no procedural mechanism to provide standing for a homeless veteran or person to gain access to these programs:

ELIAS MORALES V. RELATED MANAGEMENT COMPANY, LP D/B/A/ ARMORY PLAZA SENIOR HOUSING

U.S. District Court, Southern District of New York, December 2, 2015.
2015 WL 7779297.

Pro se Plaintiff Elias Morales ("Plaintiff") filed the instant Amended Complaint against Related Management Company, LP, d/b/a/ Armory Plaza Senior Housing, Armory Manager, as individual and other members of Related Management Company LP, and Armory Plaza Senior Housing (collectively, the "Armory Defendants"); Denise Velez ("Velez"); and the Department of Housing and Urban Development ("HUD") and Robin Bell ("Bell") (collectively, the "Federal Defendants"), alleging various constitutional and statutory violations arising from the rejection of Plaintiff's application for an apartment at Armory Plaza, an affordable housing complex in White Plains, New York.1 Liberally construed, the Amended Complaint alleges violations of Plaintiff's due process rights, violations of the Fair Housing Act of 1968, as amended by the Fair Housing Amendments Act of 1988, 42 U.S.C. § 3601, et seq. (the "FHA"), and a claim for relief pursuant to the Administrative Procedure Act, 5 U.S.C. §§ 551 et seq., 701 et seq. (the "APA"). (See Pl.'s Am. Compl. ("Am. Compl.") (Dkt. No. 6).) Before the Court is the Federal Defendants' Motion To Dismiss the Amended Complaint pursuant to Federal Rules of Civil Procedure 12(b)(1) and 12(b)(6). (See Mot. To Dismiss ("Mot.") (Dkt. No. 41).)

Plaintiff's claim is based on Armory Plaza's rejection of his application for an apartment. In other words, Plaintiff asserts a property interest in a specific apartment. To determine whether a plaintiff has a property interest, "a court must focus on the applicable statute, contract, or regulation that purports to establish the benefit." *Martz v. Village of Valley Stream*, 22 F.3d 26, 30 (2d Cir.1994)). Plaintiff's claim concerns his Section 8 assistance in connection with the HUD-VASH program. Accordingly, the Court looks to the applicable statute and regulations governing this assistance. The United States Housing Act, 42 U.S.C. § 1437, et seq. ("The Housing Act"), was enacted to provide housing assistance for low-income families. "The HUD-VASH program combines HUD rental assistance for homeless veterans with case management and clinical services provided by the VA at its medical centers" and is "generally administered pursuant to the HUD Housing Choice Voucher Program (HCV)." *Smart v. U.S. Dep't of Veteran Affairs*, 759 F.Supp.2d 867, 872 (W.D.Tex.2010). The HCV, which is "generally administered by State or local governmental entities called public housing agencies (PHAs)," in turn, provides rental subsidies to tenants who choose to rent housing units in the private market. 24 C.F.R. § 982.1(a)(1).

[The court granted the Motion to dismiss because the court found that Plaintiff has no property interest in specific property in federal housing projects, but only a right to apply for assistance, that may not be granted for years because of long waiting lists and awarding of the application is at the absolute discretion of the housing agency.]

(b) Legal Status of Homeless Persons Under State and Local Law

In a fascinating article, Professor Mark L. Roark takes up the legal status of homeless persons with regard to the community's allocation, or lack thereof, of public space. Because of the lack of "property identity", (as in the case above), the homeless are deprived of access to public space. *See, Homelessness in the Cathedral*, 80 MO.L.REV. 53 (2015). The dominant forces in the community aggregate public space for parks, sidewalks and recreational areas for owners and tenants, excluding participation by the homeless. Roark catalogs and explains different categories of public space conflicts or concerns related to homelessness:

- Regulating activities of public space for purposes of sleeping, storing property and living.

- Criminalizing trespass by virtue of state laws and local ordinances relating to public nuisances and granting injunctive relief to adjoining private property.

- Determining how the local government mistreats non-profit organizations which service the needs of the homeless.

- Requiring environmental assessment and justice for development project impacts upon the homeless.

The article calls for granting legal status to the homeless with respect to protecting their personal property right to a fair access to public space. *See*, 30 Probate and Property 22 (ABA Section of Real Property, Trust and Estate law, January-February 2016).

(c) Local Programs

Since federal programs are meeting only a small portion of the need to house the homeless and is falling further and further behind the rapidly growing homeless population nationwide, the burden has shifted to local cities and counties, which despite herculean efforts, are unable to meet current and future needs. Note the following article West Bausmith, *How Should L.A. Spend its $100-million Homelessness Emergency Fund?* Los Angeles Times, Op-Ed, October 29, 2015:

> "Last month, Mayor Eric Garcetti and seven City Council members in Los Angeles said they would devote up to $100 million to eradicate homeless in Los Angeles. What they didn't say was how, exactly, they would spend the money. We are not going to build our way out of homelessness in Los Angeles, even with the $100 million that Mayor Eric Garcetti and the City Council have allocated to deal with a declared "state of emergency." We have

asked seven different homeless advocates to offer the city's elected officials some free advice.. The views of these advocates are summarized as follows:

In 2015, we do not have a homeless crisis. We have a housing crisis. Los Angeles County needs 527,722 additional affordable rental units to meet the housing needs of the 44,359 homeless people and the 26% of residents who live in poverty—and who are falling into homelessness at the rate of 13,000 a month.

One in every 267 Angelenos is living on our sidewalks, under freeways, along street medians, in hospital emergency rooms. Many of them have survived out there for years, and their encampments do provide some security and privacy. But as these individuals age and weaken from stress, exposure and lack of available behavioral health treatment, we have been busy counting, surveying, categorizing and criminalizing them rather than solving the crisis.

What will a $100-million investment accomplish? A brief flurry of attention; planning summits; a renewed effort to coordinate outreach, services and data. This has merit, but it's how we have responded to the homeless crisis for 40 years. For decades we have approached housing by building low-income projects. The average cost of housing one person in a 300-square-foot studio apartment in Los Angeles is $468,000. That means we would need nearly $25 billion to provide homes to all the homeless here—53,000 people by one estimate.

It's time to stop relying on emergency response efforts. The poor and homeless residents have a right to decent, affordable housing. We have the resources to invest in real, long-term, life-sustaining solutions. But do we have the political and moral will?"

The "housing first" model, which aims to move individuals experiencing homelessness into private apartments, has been touted by President Obama, HUD, L.A. County and city, the L.A. Homeless Services Authority, United Way, the Chamber of Commerce and many other local organizations. It has been pushed so strongly that a vast majority of resources have shifted to permanent housing and away from shelters. There's a major drawback to this approach: It's extremely expensive on a per-unit basis, meaning "housing first" helps the few while leaving the many out on the streets. For instance, it took nearly $40 million and seven years to build a homeless complex on skid row with 102 units.

That $40 million could have been used to establish two Union Rescue Missions and provide a roof, shelter, safety, security, a sober environment and 24/7 comprehensive services to 1,600 people experiencing homelessness. If non-profit agencies had $100 million, plus empty county/city facilities for a lease of $1 a year, this is what they could do with it: provide shelter and services to 3,900 people daily for one year, assist 2,000 into permanent housing and graduate an estimated 650 from a one-year recovery program.

We need to focus on housing people rather than building units. Not all homeless people are without income. About 40% have mental and physical disabilities, which means they either collect Social Security disability or are eligible for it. And the Los Angeles County Department of Public Social Services provides housing subsidies to eligible people during the wait time to receive Social Security. Everyone with Social Security or equivalent income could be placed immediately into shared housing, using a portion of that income".

(d) Property Tax Exemption

ASSOCIATION FOR NEIGHBORHOOD REHABILITATION V. BOARD OF ASSESSORS OF THE CITY OF OGDENSBURG

Appellate Division of New York, 2011.
81 App.Div.3d 1214, 917 N.Y.S. 2d 734.

Appeals from those parts of an order and judgment of the Supreme Court (trial court) (Demarest, J.), entered August 25, 2009 in St. Lawrence County, which granted seven of petitioner's applications, in 10 proceedings pursuant to RPTL article 7, to declare certain real property tax exempt.

Petitioner is a not-for-profit corporation that has as one of its primary missions to provide housing to people who are at high risk of becoming homeless, including, among others, the mentally infirm or disabled, people who are drug or alcohol dependent, domestic violence victims and low-income individuals. As part of this mission, petitioner renovates properties, some of which it then rents to individuals in accordance with criteria established by various governmental entities. Funding for the properties and the programs does not come uniformly from one governmental aid program and, thus, the properties are subject to varying requirements. Most units where a tenant is unable to pay the full rent are subsidized, resulting in petitioner often receiving amounts at or near market rent for the region.

Next, we consider the property referred to as Gaslight Village, where homeless families (rather than homeless individuals) were housed by petitioner. The record did not establish as high a level of poverty at Gaslight Village as at the SRO properties and, while programs to address the tenants' problems that contributed to their homelessness were made available, the programs were not mandatory as in *Matter of Adult Home at Erie Sta., Inc. v. Assessor & Bd. of Assessment Review of City of Middletown*, 10 N.Y.3d at 215–216, 856 N.Y.S.2d 515, 886 N.E.2d 137. These facts alone are not necessarily dispositive since all germane circumstances must be considered in light of the stated charitable goal. For example, since homelessness results from a confluence of factors, the fact that sometimes an at-risk person can afford housing may not, by itself, adequately address the person's problem. Moreover, while mandatory participation in programs designed to address the underlying causes of homelessness is certainly an easier case for an exemption, a property is not necessarily ineligible for an exemption where it clearly serves a narrowly tailored at-risk population by successfully integrating a host of optional programs.

Gaslight Village was funded by the New York State Homeless Housing and Assistance Corporation, a public benefit corporation that administers the Homeless Housing Assistance Program and works in conjunction with the State Office of Temporary Disability Assistance. Referrals of tenants typically come from the state Department of Social Services (DSS) or similar agencies and only families who meet the requirement of being homeless or at risk of homelessness are accepted. No one is turned away for inability to pay. There are no other similar housing projects in St. Lawrence County for homeless families. Like SRO housing, rent is set by DSS allowances, with a maximum of 30% of income. The length of stays at Gaslight Village is longer than the SRO program, with average periods of three to four years. There was testimony that many of the families at Gaslight Village often come from "intergenerational poverty" with "multiple barriers to their self-sufficiency" and, significantly, that simply supplying them with a rent subsidy for living at another location would not adequately address their underlying problems; however, those problems can be addressed at Gaslight Village through the various programs made readily available to tenants by petitioner in conjunction with other agencies. While the issue is closer for the property used to assist families as opposed to individuals, we are unpersuaded that Supreme Court erred in its determination.

CHAPTER 7

FROM SPRAWL TO SUSTAINABILITY: GROWTH MANAGEMENT AND SMART GROWTH[1]

■ ■ ■

A. INTRODUCTION

1. THE NATIONALIZATION OF SPRAWL

FROM SPRAWL TO SUSTAINABILITY: GROWTH MANAGEMENT, SMART GROWTH, NEW URBANISM, GREEN DEVELOPMENT AND RENEWABLE ENERGY

Robert H. Freilich, Robert J. Sitkowski and Seth D. Mennillo.
Section of State and Local Government, American Bar Association, 2010.
Chapter 2, page 23.

Sprawl, as ingrained in our national myth as baseball and apple pie once were, has become an institutionalized facet of American life. Sprawl is accelerated by the predominant American desire for an imagined rural lifestyle coupled with an urban income, while ignoring the catastrophic economic, environmental, traffic and fiscal impacts that such living patterns create. See Eugenie Birch, From Town to Metropolis, in Local Planning Contemporary Principles and Practices 20 (Gary Hack, Eugenie Birch and Paul Sedway, eds., International City Managers Association, 2009). A major influence has been the political power of special interests, which have obtained federal and state legislative mandates in two significant areas: (1) by creating income tax deductions for single-family mortgage interest payments and property taxes; and (2) by having existing urban areas subsidize new growth, because of inadequate developer

---

[1] "Growth management" which originated in 1972 with the New York Court of Appeals decision in *Golden v. Planning Board of the Town of Ramapo,* 285 N.E.2d 291 (1972), appeal dismissed, 409 U.S. 1003, upheld the constitutionality of timing and sequencing of growth in the suburbs over an 18 year period tied to the availability of adequate public facilities scheduled in 18 year capital improvement plan. "Smart Growth", a moniker for growth management at the state level, began in Maryland in 1997 as an effort to use state funds as incentives to direct growth. The general goals of Maryland's 1997 Smart Growth initiative were to enhance the state's existing communities and other locally-designated growth areas; identify and protect the state's most valuable farmland and other natural resources; and save taxpayers from the cost of building new infrastructure to support poorly planned development. The initiative was centered on two primary efforts, the Smart Growth Areas Act and the Rural Legacy Program. Through these measures, the State finances infrastructure development in designated Priority Areas.

funding of infrastructure, the need for which is generated by new development. These governmental fiscal and legislative policies contribute to sprawl by perpetuating a reduction of resources in urban areas; and creating huge deficiencies in public facilities and services in the suburbs, which have led to mounting city, county and state deficits that have become cancers that attacking metropolitan regions from the inside out and outside in.

Every twenty years we seek to revolt from this pattern. In the 1950s we talked about "The City of Man."(Christopher Tunnard, The City of Man 362–85, (1953). In the 1960s and 1970s we played with building mixed use "new towns" in the suburbs. *See* Kenneth L. Kraemer, *Developing Governmental Institutions in New Communities*, 1 URBAN LAWYER 268 (1969). In the 1980s and 1990s we began envisioning new urbanism walkable "neo-traditional neighborhoods", and transit oriented development in both the suburbs and cities. S. Mark White and Dawn Jourdan, *Neo-traditional Development: A Legal Analysis*, 49 LAND USE L. & ZONING DIGEST 3 (1997). In the early years of this century, we are seeing a surge towards LEED (Leadership in Energy and Environmental Design) green development projects and neighborhood sustainable infill development. Nevertheless, because these efforts have so far been limited in scope and geography, there has been an increasing awareness that the federal government, states, regional planning organizations and local governments have not dealt effectively with the problems of sprawl that are national in scope. Time will tell whether new legislation to secure renewable energy, multi-transit alternatives, land use coordination and environmental sustainability will bear fruit.

"For heaven's sake — the father of suburban sprawl!"

———

Controlling sprawl through growth management benefits central city dwellers through rehabilitation and revitalization of the central city, is environmentally beneficial by reducing greenhouse gas emissions, preserving agricultural land and open space, and aiding in reducing energy consumption. By limiting the area over which services must be extended, it reduces the cost of services to suburbanites and aids in the fiscal solvency of local governments. Because so many various interest groups can be benefited by effective growth management, it should now be possible to form coalitions to combat this hydra-headed problem.

The first major national effort to control sprawl was the report of The National Commission on Urban Problems (Douglas Commission), which recognized the limitations of traditional zoning techniques in 1968:

At the metropolitan scale, the present techniques of development guidance have not effectively controlled the timing and location of development. Under traditional zoning, jurisdictions are theoretically called upon to determine in advance the sites needed for various types of development. * * * In doing so, however, they have continued to rely on techniques which were never designed as timing devices and which do not function well in controlling timing. The attempt to use large-lot zoning, for example, to control timing has all too often resulted in scattered development on large lots, prematurely establishing the character of much later development—the very effect sought to be avoided. New types of controls are needed if the basic metropolitan scale problems are to be solved.

The prevention of urban sprawl should therefore qualify as a valid public purpose justifying the use of valid zoning and timing regulations * * *. The Commission recommends that * * * local governments establish holding zones in order to postpone urban development in areas that are inappropriate for development * * *.

The Report of the National Commission on Urban Problems, Building the American City 245 (1968). *See also* Robert H. Freilich, *Development Timing, Moratoria and Controlled Growth*, 1974 INSTITUTE OF PLANNING, ZONING AND EMINENT DOMAIN 147, 148–49 n. 3 (citing *National Commission on Urban Problems, Alternatives to Urban Sprawl* 45 (Res. Report No. 15, 1968)).

Urban sprawl has had a particularly devastating effect upon rural and agricultural America. Robert H. Freilich Linda K. Davis, *Saving the Land: The Utilization of Modern Techniques of Growth Management to Preserve Rural and Agricultural America*, 13 URBAN LAWYER 27, 29 (1981). *See also* Robert H. Freilich and Bruce Peshoff, *The Social Costs of Sprawl*, 29 URBAN LAWYER 183 (1997); Eric D. Kelly, *Managing Community Growth: Policies, Techniques, and Impacts* (1993). One study on urban sprawl commissioned by the New Jersey legislature concluded that sprawl development between 1993 and 2010, would consume 292,000 acres of prime agricultural land, whereas only 165,000 acres would be used under compact development controls. *See* Amer. Planning Ass'n Planning Advisory Service Memo, Feb. 1993.

The cost of sprawl has been detailed by a glittering array of the nation's leading fiscal land economists: Robert Burchell, William Dolphin, Arthur Nelson, Reid Ewing, James C. Nicholas, Lazar Spasovic and Bransilav Dimitnjevic, in *Calculating Development Impacts: The Transportation Costs of New Development* (Island Press, 2011). The costs and benefits that stem from controlling sprawl can best be understood by referring to the chart below:

Relative Cost of Planned Development v. Sprawl

Facility Sprawl		Planned Development			
		A	B	C	Synthesis
Roads	100%	40%	76%	73%	75%
Schools	100%	93%	97%	99%	95%
Utilities	100%	60%	92%	66%	85%
Other	100%	102%	N/A	100%	N/A

For a decidedly different view on sprawl, *see* Robert Bruegmann, *Sprawl: A Compact History* (2005).

2. GROWTH MANAGEMENT AND SMART GROWTH

In the past few years, widespread frustration with sprawling development patterns has led to the "growth management" and "smart growth" movements, which contend that the shape and quality of metropolitan growth in America is no longer desirable—or sustainable. It asserts that current growth patterns are fiscally wasteful, competitively unwise, environmentally damaging, and racially and socially divisive. It argues that these growth patterns are not inevitable but rather the result, in part, of major government policies that distort the market and facilitate the excessive decentralization of people and jobs.

Across the country, a growing chorus of constituencies—corporations, local elected officials, environmentalists, ordinary citizens—are demanding that the market and the government change the way they do business and take actions to curb sprawl, promote urban reinvestment, and build communities of quality and distinction. Governors and state legislatures are responding to these demands by proposing and enacting significant reforms in governance, land use, and infrastructure policies. Voters at the ballot box regularly are approving measures to address the consequences of sprawling development patterns.

Major forces—the changing demographics of the country, the restructuring of the market economy, the rise of congestion, the backlash to excessive suburbanization—fuel a desire for a different pattern of growth from the one that has dominated the American landscape since the end of World War II. However, the potential to reshape metropolitan America will be achieved only if a series of political, policy, and social challenges are addressed head-on. Bruce Katz, *the Permanent Campaign, Urban Land*, May 2003. *See also* Arthur C. Nelson and Robert E. Lang, *Megapolitan America: A New Vision for Understanding America's Metropolitan Geography* (APA Press, 2011).

Growth management and smart growth reduce the consumption of land for roads, houses and commercial buildings by channeling development to areas with existing infrastructure. It centers growth around urban and older suburban areas and preserves green space, wetlands, and farm land. The goal is to reap the benefits of growth and development, such as jobs, tax revenues, and other amenities, while limiting the disasters of growth, such as degradation of the environment, escalation of local taxes and worsening traffic congestion. "While there is no special formula for growth management and smart growth, there are common features in each of the communities that have adopted them. Wherever it occurs, growth management and smart growth: (1) enhances a sense of community; (2) protects investment in existing neighborhoods; (3) provides a greater certainty in the development process; (4) protects environmental quality; (5) rewards developers with profitable products, financing and flexibility; (6) decreases congestion by providing alternative modes of transportation; and (7) makes efficient use of public money." Maryann Froelich, *Smart Growth: Why Local Governments Are Taking a New Approach to Managing Growth in Their Communities*, Public Mgmt. 5 (May 1998), 1998 WL 10328353.

Smart Growth efforts have taken place on national, state, regional and local levels. In 1997, the Smart Growth Network was created by the U.S. Environmental Protection Agency to allow local government officials across the nation to share growth strategies and exchange information on the latest and best trends in sustainable development. The American Planning Association produced in 2002 the Growing Smart Legislative Guidebook which offers models for comprehensive planning and neighborhood planning. For more information about the network *see* http:// www.smartgrowth.org and for more information about the guidebook see www.planning.org/plnginfo/growsmar/gsindex.html#7. Voters generally respond positively to smart growth programs. In recent years, voters have approved plans to preserve historical sites, parks, farmland and open space and approved an estimated $7 billion for conservation, urban revitalization and smart-growth initiatives. *See* Daniel Curtin, *Battling Sprawl in Northern California: Initiatives, Referenda, Interim Development Ordinances, Adequate Public Facilities and Population Controls*, Inst. on Planning, Zoning, and Eminent Domain (Matthew Bender 2000). Alabama, Arizona, California, Colorado, Florida, Georgia, Maryland, Michigan, Minnesota, New Jersey, Oregon, Rhode Island and Washington are some of the states which have passed smart growth plans. *See* Patricia E. Salkin, *Squaring The Circles on Sprawl: What More Can We Do? Progress Towards Sustainable Land Use in the States*, 16 WIDENER L.J. 787 (2007).

Some growth management and smart growth regulations have been criticized as "dumb" where government simply places arbitrary caps on the number of building permits. *See* Dwight Merriam and Gurdon H. Buck, *Smart Growth, Dumb Takings*, 29 ELR 10746 (1999); and Timothy J. Dowling, *Reflections on Urban Sprawl, Smart Growth, and the Fifth Amendment*, 148 U.Pa.L.Rev. 873 (2000).

3. STATE SMART GROWTH SOLUTIONS TO CONTROL URBAN SPRAWL

In many instances local plans and regulations are inadequate to control sprawl in metropolitan regions. Over the past forty years, since *Ramapo*, states have attempted to assume jurisdiction to develop smart growth solutions over the entire state (Florida, Hawaii, Maryland, New Jersey and Oregon) or in major environmental areas (Colorado and Vermont) or metropolitan regions (California, Minnesota, Nevada Washington, and Wisconsin).

Edward J. Sullivan and Jessica Yeh, *Smart Growth: State Strategies in Managing Sprawl*, 45 URBAN LAWYER 349 (2013):

> "In order for smart growth programs to succeed, proactive state involvement in land use planning is needed. Smart growth policies and enforcement mechanisms can have measureable effects on sustainable growth management. State oversight and enforcement in certain aspects of land use are critical to the success of any smart growth program. Factors such as strong implementation methods, public participation, and coordinated legislation can contribute to the success of smart growth programs".

4. PLANS AND TECHNIQUES TO MANAGE GROWTH

A key underpinning to an effective and legally defensible growth management or smart growth system, whether statewide, regional or local, is proper planning supported by detailed studies. Note the statement in Fred Bosselman, David L. Callies & John Banta, *The Taking Issue* 290 (1973):

> The importance of a sound factual presentation is apparent in the urban context as well. The town of Ramapo, on the outskirts of the New York Metropolitan area, successfully defended a growth control ordinance before New York's highest court with success due in no small part to a thorough presentation of their case. * * *

> The town was able to present a vast array of planning data in their defense. In its statement of the facts in Golden v. Planning Board of the Town of Ramapo, * * * the Court of Appeals pointed to the Town Master Plan, whose "preparation included a four volume study of the existing land uses, public facilities, transportation, industry and commerce, housing needs, and projected population trends. * * * Additional sewage district and drainage studies were undertaken which culminated in the adoption of a Capital Budget. * * * " Thus, not only could the town rely upon a large number of formal municipal actions, adoption of a Master Plan, a Capital Budget, zoning and subdivision ordinances and the like, but they

could also document each with thorough and detailed planning studies.

In *Stoney-Brook Development Corp. v. Town of Fremont*, 474 A.2d 561 (N.H.1984), the New Hampshire Supreme Court ruled a growth control ordinance invalid because it failed to follow the requirement that assessments of community development needs must be carefully studied. *See also* Julian Juergensmeyer and Thomas E. Roberts, *Land Use Planning and Development Regulation Law* §§ 9.5–9.9 (2016); John DeGrove, *Balanced Growth: A Planning Guide for Local Government* (1991); Eric D. Kelly, *Managing Community Growth: Policies, Techniques, and Impacts* (1993).

B. INTERIM DEVELOPMENT CONTROLS AND MORATORIA

An interim development control ordinance temporarily restricts the rezoning of land, approval of new subdivisions, issuance of conditional, special use and building permits for a reasonable period of time in certain areas of a city or county which will be affected by a pending plan or zoning amendment. A practical function of interim controls is providing a framework or structure for the planning process. Interim controls represent timetables and operate as an organizing system for an extremely complex process. A second function is the protection of the planning or plan amendment process, ensuring that planning itself takes place. Third, and a corollary to the function of protecting the planning process, is the prevention of new non-conforming uses during the process. Thus, interim controls ensure that the effectiveness of the planning is not destroyed before it has a chance to be implemented by preventing the vesting of developers' rights.

Generally, when the nature of plan revisions or proposed zoning changes become apparent, landowners and developers begin seeking building permits based on existing zoning, hoping to obtain approval before the changes are enacted. The municipality in response is pressed into making a hasty determination to adopt a permanent zoning ordinance. These competing behaviors have been termed "a race of diligence." Interim controls eliminate this "race." A fourth major function is the promotion of public debate on the issues, goals and policies of the plan and development techniques proposed to implement the plan. Essential public involvement will often prevent the kind of planless implementation too often found in communities when action is precipitated without the public's and landowner's participation. *See* Robert H. Freilich, *Interim Development Controls: Essential Tools for Implementing Flexible Planning and Zoning*, 49 J.URBAN LAWYER 65 (1971). Elizabeth A. Garvin and Martin L. Leitner, *Drafting Interim Development Ordinances: Creating Time to Plan, Land Use Law and Zoning Digest* (June 1996) (both articles were cited by the

U.S. Supreme Court in *Tahoe Sierra* as a strong basis for supporting the constitutionality of interim development controls).

BRADFORDVILLE PHIPPS LIMITED PARTNERSHIP v. LEON COUNTY

District Court of Appeal of Florida, 2001.
804 So.2d 464.

Appellant Bradfordville Phipps Limited Partnership (Partnership), challenges an order rendered by the Second Judicial Circuit Court denying its motion for summary judgment in favor of Appellee, Leon County (County). The Partnership, which owns property in a part of Leon County known as the Bradfordville Study Area (BSA), had filed an inverse condemnation action against the County following the imposition of a temporary injunction that prohibited the County from issuing certain permits for development in the BSA. We affirm.

I.

The record reveals that effective December 3, 1998, the circuit court imposed an injunction in another proceeding, prohibiting the County "from issuing any future building permits or other development permits authorizing construction within the Bradfordville Study Area until such time as the County comes into compliance with 8.1, 8.3, 8.3.1, and 8.5.2 of the Land Use Element of the Tallahassee/Leon County Comprehensive Plan." Land Use Goal 8 concerned the development and implementation of a comprehensive stormwater plan for the BSA. On January 12, 1999, the plaintiffs in the other proceeding and the County entered an interim settlement agreement, pursuant to which the County agreed not to appeal the injunction order. The next day, the court entered another order, amending the injunction order to exclude from its scope certain property and projects.

On April 5, 1999, the Partnership brought this action against the County. In the complaint, the Partnership alleged, among other things, that the County's actions "resulted in the [Partnership's] inability to move forward with the development and use of its property and has deprived the [Partnership] of all reasonable economic use of its property." The Partnership alleged that it "has expended substantial efforts and substantial sums of money and has incurred great expense in pursuing its plan of development' of the property. The Partnership further alleged that, in December 1998, it had submitted "a completed Environmental Permit application relating to the development of its project," but this application was rejected by the County due to the injunction. The Partnership alleged that this permit application was a prerequisite to the issuance of any building permit and "[t]he denial of the application for such permit prohibits [the Partnership] from proceeding with the development of its property." The complaint summarized the Partnership's basis for a claim of inverse condemnation:

The acts and omissions of the County as alleged herein, including: (a) agreeing to the entry of an Order enjoining the County from issuing any further permits for development; and (b) agreeing not to appeal any order which may be entered enjoining issuance of permits for the development of the subject property, constitute a substantial deprivation of the beneficial use of the Plaintiff's property rights and constitutes a taking of Plaintiff's property for a public purpose without payment or compensation.

On December 14, 1999, as part of its effort to comply with the injunction and the Comprehensive Plan, the County adopted Ordnance No. 99–31, an Interim Development Ordinance (IDO). Pursuant to the IDO, the County restricted the issuance of development permits for land in the BSA:

1. Development Permits. Notwithstanding any provision of the Land Development Regulations to the contrary, no development permit shall be issued and no Application for Land Use Approval shall be approved in the Bradfordville Study Area during the term of this Ordinance, except as provided in paragraph 4, below.

* * *

4. Types of Uses and Development Permits Affected. This Ordinance shall apply, as and to the extent set forth herein, to all applications for land use approval submitted after the Effective Date of this Ordinance not otherwise excepted by the Court Orders being the Injunction Order dated December 15, 1998, the Interim Settlement Agreement of January 12, 1999, and the modified Injunction Order dated January 13, 1999.

The IDO also listed several "Types of Uses and Development Permits Not Affected." The term of the IDO was limited to seven months, unless extended by a majority voted of the Board of County Commissioners.

On July 11, 2000, the County adopted Ordinance No. 00–31. This ordinance implemented the provisions of Land Use Goal 8 of the Comprehensive Plan and evidently constituted the requisite action to comply with the court-ordered injunction. By order dated October 23, 2000, the circuit court dissolved the injunction.

On October 5, 2000, the Partnership and the County each filed motions for summary judgment. By an order rendered December 4, 2000, the circuit court granted the County's motion and denied the Partnership's motion, and entered final summary judgment in favor of the County.

III.

We find that the trial court properly concluded the Partnership had not shown it was deprived of all or substantially all economically beneficial use of its property such that a temporary regulatory taking had occurred under the test set forth in *Lucas v. South Carolina Coastal Council*, 505

U.S. 1003, 112 S.Ct. 2886, 120 L.Ed.2d 798 (1992). In Lucas, the United States Supreme Court explained that "when the owner of real property has been called upon to sacrifice all economically beneficial uses in the name of the common good, that is, to leave his property economically idle, he has suffered a taking." 505 U.S. at 1019, 112 S.Ct. 2886. The Court indicated, however, that the situations are "relatively rare" where the government deprives a landowner of "all economically beneficial uses." *Id.* at 1018, 112 S.Ct. 2886. We note that the Partnership has proceeded in its temporary regulatory taking claim only on the theory that a temporary taking occurred under the Lucas test, arguing that the injunction effectively deprived it of all economically beneficial use of its property.

* * *

The First English discussion of temporary takings referred to "retrospectively temporary takings," that is, "the Court used the term 'temporary taking' to refer to the period before a regulatory taking is invalidated . . ." Keshbro, 801 So.2d at 873. Indeed, as explained above, "First English really involved a question of remedies . . ." *Id.*

In Keshbro, however, the Florida Supreme Court had before it the threshold issue of whether a compensable talking could occur under Lucas when nuisance abatement boards ordered, prospectively, temporary takings" for purposes of applying the Lucas analysis to nuisance cases. Nevertheless, the court noted that, in cases involving land use and planning concerns, courts have refused to extend First English beyond a situation involving retrospectively temporary takings:

> [T]he courts refusing to extend First English beyond its remedial genesis to prospectively temporary regulations have done so in the land use and planning arena, where an entirely different set of considerations are implicated from those in the context of nuisance abatement where a landowner is being deprived of a property's dedicated use. The concerns specific to the regulation of land use and planning were noted by the Ninth Circuit in declining to apply Lucas's categorical takings analysis to the temporary takings claims of landowners in the Lake Tahoe region with regard to a temporary moratorium on development instituted in an effort to stem the environmental degradation of Lake Tahoe.

> [T]he widespread invalidation of temporary planning moratoria would deprive state and local governments of an important land-use planning tool with a well-established tradition. Land-use planning is necessarily a complex, time-consuming undertaking for a community, especially in a situation as unique as this. In several ways, temporary development moratoria promote effective planning. First, by preserving the status quo during the planning process, temporary moratoria ensure that a community's

problems are not exacerbated during the time it takes to formulate a regulatory scheme. Relatedly, temporary development moratoria prevent developers and landowners from racing to carry out development that is destructive of the community's interests before a new plan goes into effect. Such a race-to-development would permit property owners to evade the land-use plan and undermine its goals. Finally, the breathing room provided by temporary moratoria helps ensure that the planning process is responsive to the property owners and citizens who will be affected by the resulting land-use regulations.

Id. (quoting *Tahoe-Sierra Pres. Council v. Tahoe Reg'l Planning Agency*, 216 F.3d 764, 777 (9th Cir.2000) (citations and footnote omitted), *cert. granted in part*, 533 U.S. 948, 121 S.Ct. 2589, 150 L.Ed.2d 749 (2001) (granting certiorari petition on the following question: "Whether the Court of Appeals properly determined that a temporary moratorium on land development does not constitute a taking of property requiring compensation under the taking of property requiring compensation under the Takings Clause of the United States Constitution?"). The reference to land planning moratoria is more helpful in the present case than is Keshbro. We acknowledge the Keshbro rule allowing a prospective taking, but note that the factual impetuses for that case-nuisance abatement boards' actions in temporarily closing motels and apartments where criminal activity had occurred-are far removed from those now before us.

In Tahoe-Sierra, the Ninth Circuit held that a temporary moratorium on development did not amount to a categorical taking under Lucas because it did not result in the deprivation of all of the value or use of the property. Under the Tahoe-Sierra analysis, no temporary taking is wrought by virtue of a development moratorium where the future use of property has a substantial present value. In that case, the moratorium lasted thirty-two months. Here, the injunction lasted twenty-two months. In light of Lucas, we agree with the reasoning of the Ninth Circuit that a temporary land use regulation could rarely, if ever, completely deprive the owner of all economically beneficial use:

> Of course, were a temporary moratorium designed to be in force so long as to eliminate all present value of a property's future use, we might be compelled to conclude that a categorical taking had occurred. We doubt, however, that a true temporary moratorium would ever be designed to last for so long a period.

Like the situation in Tahoe-Sierra, the injunction here was designed to suspend certain development only until the County completed the stormwater study required by the Comprehensive Plan. *See id.* Even though a moratorium may restrict or delay temporarily the use of property for development purposes, it can hardly be said that a moratorium that was temporary from the outset destroys the economic value of the property.

Indeed, nothing in the present record suggests that the property owned by the Partnership completely, or even substantially, lost its present value by virtue of the temporary injunction. Thus, our conclusion, similar to the result in Tahoe-Sierra, does not conflict with Lucas.

IV.

A truly temporary land use injunction or moratorium looks more like a permitting delay than a compensable regulatory taking. Many communities have, through state and local elected officials, expressed a preference for strict land use control. In such locales, a developer may labor months or years to obtain all necessary approval for a substantial development. This is essentially what the circuit judge observed in his order when he noted "the general restrictive environment for commercial development in Leon County." In such an environment, the timetable established by a commercial developer must anticipate delays, whether occasioned by holdups in the permitting process, litigation by neighboring land owners, or a temporary development injunction or moratorium.

Our decision here, as well as that of the trial court, reflects the role of courts versus the role of local bodies in these types of disputes. Courts do not generally interfere with local regulatory bodies in matters, including land use regulation, simply because legislation or regulation may be unwise or economically unsound. Courts constrain such bodies only where regulations are illegal or unconstitutional. As the Court indicated in Lucas, the situations are "relatively rare" where the government deprives a landowner of "all economically beneficial uses." 505 U.S. at 1018, 112 S.Ct. 2886. Close regulation by local government that is merely expensive or time consuming for developers does not arise to a taking. Such regulation presumably expresses the will of local citizens who have elected governing boards such as county and city commissions. Thus, the question of regulation in situations such as the one now before us, presents a political rather than a justiciable issue. The regulatory taking analysis of Lucas is consistent with this view.

AFFIRMED.

NOTES

1. The United States Supreme Court affirmed the Ninth Circuit opinion in *Tahoe-Sierra* one year after the decision in *Bradfordville. See Tahoe-Sierra Preservation Council, Inc. v. Tahoe Regional Planning Agency*, 535 U.S. 302 (2002), *supra* in Chapter 3.

2. Justice Stevens, in his dissent in the 1987 *First English* case, *supra* Chapter 3, attached significance to the duration of the restriction as a critical factor in determining whether a taking has occurred and he categorized regulations as:

three dimensional; they have depth, width, and length. As for depth, regulations define the extent to which the owner may not use the property in question. With respect to width, regulations define the amount of property encompassed by the restriction. Finally, and for purposes of this case, essentially, regulations set forth the duration of the restrictions. It is obvious that no one of these elements can be analyzed alone to evaluate the impact of a regulation, and hence to determine whether a taking has occurred.

482 U.S. 304, 330 (1987). His dissent ultimately became the majority position in *Tahoe-Sierra*.

As the Supreme Court held in *Tahoe-Sierra*, if the regulation is not permanent, time is a factor to be used in determining whether a taking has occurred. Only if there is a taking will compensation be payable for the period of the restriction. The reasonable use of land left by a temporary regulation depends on whether the regulation left a reasonable use over a reasonable period of time. *See Golden v. Planning Bd. of Town of Ramapo*, 285 N.E.2d 291 (1972), *appeal dismissed*, 409 U.S. 1003, 93 S.Ct. 436, 34 L.Ed.2d 294 (1972). For a complete review of state cases with respect to determinations of the reasonableness of the time duration of interim development controls, *see* Robert H. Freilich, *Time, Space, and Value in Inverse Condemnation: A Unified Theory for Partial Takings Analysis*, 24 U.HAW.L.REV. 589 (2002). On remand, the California Court of Appeals upheld the Los Angeles moratorium in *First English* (discussed *supra* Ch. 3.C.2(c)):

> The interim ordinance is further justified as a reasonable temporary limitation on construction to maintain the status quo while the county determined what, if any, structures were compatible with public safety. (all caps in original).

> As an independent and sufficient ground for our decision, we further hold the interim ordinance did not constitute a "temporary unconstitutional taking" even were we to assume its restrictions were too broad if permanently imposed on First English. This interim ordinance was by design a temporary measure—in effect a total moratorium on any construction on First English's property—while the County conducted a study to determine what uses and what structure, if any, could be permitted on this property consistent with considerations of safety. We do not read the U.S. Supreme Court's decision in First English as converting moratoriums and other interim land use restrictions into unconstitutional "temporary takings" requiring compensation unless, perhaps, if these interim measures are unreasonable in purpose, duration or scope. On its face, Ordinance 11,855 is reasonable in all these dimensions.

> The ordinance had the legitimate avowed purpose of preserving the status quo while the County studied the problem and devised a permanent ordinance which would allow only safe uses and the construction of safe structures in and near the river bed. The

restrictions in Ordinance 11,855 were reasonably related to the achievement of this objective. Given the seriousness of the safety concerns raised by the presence of any structures on this property, we find it was entirely reasonable to ban the construction or reconstruction of any structures for the period necessary to conduct an extensive study and fully develop persuasive evidence about what, if any, structures and uses would be compatible with the preservation of life and health of future occupants of this property and other properties in this geographic area.

We do not find the ordinance remained in effect for an unreasonable period of time beyond that which would be justified to conduct the necessary studies of this situation and devise a suitable permanent ordinance. The study was completed and a report containing recommended restrictions submitted in less than two years. County decision-makers took another six months to hold hearings, ponder and pass the somewhat less restrictive permanent ordinance. These periods are reasonable especially given the complexity of the issues to be studied and resolved. Nor were the restrictions imposed by the interim ordinance unreasonable in scope given the seriousness of the danger posed by the construction of new structures in Lutherglen and nearby properties. We cannot say that without a thorough-going study it would have been reasonably feasible to identify any structure which could be safely permitted on these properties. Thus we find the time taken by this study and the time this interim ordinance remained in effect to be well within the bounds of reason. The County owed this landowner no special duty to give priority to the study of Lutherglen over the study of other properties which might pose a danger to safety. Nor did it owe any of these landowners a duty to cut any corners in the study or take any risks that anything might be overlooked which could produce a permanent ordinance less restrictive than public safety concerns demanded.

258 Cal.Rptr. 893, 906 (1989).

3. *Valley View Indus. Park v. City of Redmond*, 733 P.2d 182 (Wash.1987), considered time as a factor in determining that a delay which occurred in processing a building permit application did not justify damages for an interim taking, where the delay did not extend beyond a reasonable period for issuance of a permit. *See also Gisler v. Deschutes County*, 945 P.2d 1051 (Or.App.1997) and *Guinnane v. City & County of San Francisco*, 197 Cal.App.3d 862 (1987), *cert. denied*, 488 U.S. 823 (1988), which held that delaying action on a building permit application in excess of one year was not so "excessive" as to constitute a compensable temporary taking. Compare *Lakeview Apartments v. Town of Stanford*, 108 A.D.2d 914 (N.Y.1985), which invalidated a seven-year moratorium on multifamily, commercial, and industrial development which was reviewed annually.

4.   Although most cases have addressed the validity of interim development controls in the context of a city or county developing a comprehensive, specific, area, or redevelopment plan, interim controls serve the same function when the local government is amending and updating its zoning regulations, undertaking an historic preservation project, constructing new capital projects, or evaluating the necessity of restricting development on a flood plain area, *See Woodbury Place Partners v. City of Woodbury*, 492 N.W.2d 258 (Minn.App.1992) (a 2 year interim development ordinance adopted in order to determine the appropriate location of a freeway interchange).

5.   Where does a municipality, county, or regional entity find the authority to enact interim development ordinances? Several sources have been identified and used by the courts to uphold interim controls. A number of states have enacted specific enabling legislation which permits a municipality to enact interim zoning ordinances with constraints as to time and requiring diligent action by the municipality to enact new or revised regulations. Minnesota law provides:

> If a county is conducting, or in good faith intends to conduct studies within a reasonable time, or has held or is holding a hearing for the purpose of considering a comprehensive plan or official controls or an amendment, extension, or addition to either, or in the event new territory for which no zoning may have been adopted, may be annexed to a municipality, the board in order to protect the public health, safety, and general welfare may adopt as an emergency measure a temporary interim zoning map or temporary interim zoning ordinance, the purpose of which shall be to classify and regulate uses and related matters as constitutes the emergency. Such interim resolution shall be limited to one year from the date it becomes effective and to one year to renewal thereafter.

Minn.Stat.Ann. § 394.34.

New Jersey confers very limited authority as it only allows a moratorium "where the municipality demonstrates on the basis of a written opinion by a qualified health professional that a clear imminent danger to the health of the inhabitants of the municipality exists * * * ." N.J.Stat.Ann. 40:55D–90. In *New Jersey Shore Builders Association v. Mayor and Township of Middletown*, 561 A.2d 319 (N.J.Super.1989), the court invalidated a six month moratorium on major site plans and subdivision applications because it was not convinced by the expert's testimony that water shortage problems constituted a clear and imminent danger. *See also, Toll Brothers, Inc. v. West Windsor TP*, 712 A.2d 266 (N.J.App.1998) (holding that a timing and sequencing ordinance also conflicted with the same statute).

Holding that a timing and sequencing growth management provision violated the state's statute on moratorium duration.

6.   Where specific statutory authority does not exist, the courts have relied on implied authority to exercise the police power to protect statutory planning processes or looked to the general language in the state's zoning

enabling act. *See Collura v. Town of Arlington*, 329 N.E.2d 733 (Mass.1975) (court found authority to adopt interim zoning provisions implied from the general language of the zoning enabling act which represented a broad delegation of police power to cities and towns and the court found a second source of local zoning authority in a home rule amendment to the state constitution) and *Almquist v. Town of Marshan*, 245 N.W.2d 819 (Minn.1976) (broad reading of Standard Planning Enabling Act negates requirement for a more specific statutory authorization). *See also Bittinger v. Corporation of Bolivar*, 395 S.E.2d 554 (W.Va.1990); *Rubin v. McAlevey*, 282 N.Y.S.2d 564 (Sup.Ct.1967), *affirmed*, 288 N.Y.S.2d 519 (App.Div.1968) (interim ordinances enacted by the Town of Ramapo while developing its landmark timing and sequencing plan were upheld under enabling act). In other eastern states, interim controls have been struck down for reasons of insufficient statutory authority. *See Naylor v. Township of Hellam*, 773 A.2d 770 (Pa.2001); *Schrader v. Guilford Planning and Zoning Comm'n*, 418 A.2d 93 (Conn.App.1980); and *Matthews v. Board of Zoning Appeals of Greene County*, 237 S.E.2d 128 (Va.1977).

7.   Interim controls can also be achieved through informal techniques of administrative processing. Under the "administrative control theory" or pending ordinance rule a municipality can deny administratively the issuance of a building permit where the proposed use would conflict with a pending change in the zoning ordinance. A principle of administrative law prohibits an administrative officer from granting a permit in violation of a proposed law. Even though the Pennsylvania court found insufficient statutory authority for interim control ordinances in *Kline v. City of Harrisburg*, 68 A.2d 182, 190 (Pa.1949), the court upheld a municipality's administrative procedures accomplishing the same objective in *A.J. Aberman, Inc. v. City of New Kensington*, 105 A.2d 586 (Pa.1954) (a municipality may properly refuse a building permit for a land use repugnant to a pending and later enacted zoning ordinance even though applied for when the intended use conforms to existing regulations). *Foothills of Fernley, LLC v. City of Fernley*, 355 Fed.Appx. 109 (9th Cir.2009) and *Russian Hill Improvement Association v. Board of Permit Appeals*, 423 P.2d 824 (Cal.App.1967).

8.   Assuming legislative authorization, the validity of any given control depends on the reasonableness of the approach. The duration of the ordinance is of critical importance. Most statutes allow freezes for a period of six months to one year with extensions. Without statutory limits, the courts have determined the reasonableness of the time period on a case-by-case basis. A primary determinant appears to be the complexity and scope of the plan being prepared. Compare *Conway v. Town of Stratham*, 414 A.2d 539 (N.H.1980) (upholding interim controls on condition that the town implement master plan within one year) with *Campana v. Clark*, 197 A.2d 711 (N.J.Law.Div.1964) (sustaining an interim control ordinance for 31 months) and *Peacock v. County of Sacramento*, 77 Cal.Rptr. 391 (Cal.App.1969) (finding that an interim ordinance which prevented development for three years gave the county reasonable time to complete its study, but was a taking without compensation when it extended beyond that time). Longer periods of growth management

controls including 18 and 20 year delays have been upheld. *See Golden v. Town of Ramapo*, 285 N.E.2d 291 (N.Y.1972) and *Long Beach Equities v. County of Ventura*, 282 Cal.Rptr. 877 (Cal.App.1991).

Tahoe-Sierra held that the 32 month interim development control did not constitute a per se taking.

9.   Many states require that the same procedures be followed when enacting an interim control as when enacting permanent zoning; that is, notice to the public and a hearing must take place before the legislative body can enact a valid ordinance. *See Collura v. Town of Arlington, supra*, note 7; and *Lancaster Development, Ltd. v. Village of River Forest*, 228 N.E.2d 526 (Ill.App.1967). However, other states have upheld interim ordinances without requiring compliance with procedural aspects of permanent zoning. *See Metro Realty v. County of El Dorado*, 35 Cal.Rptr. 480 (Cal.App.1963) (no notice required before adopting ordinance because it was an emergency measure necessary to preserve the status quo while county was formulating a water development and conservation plan) and *Jablinske v. Snohomish County*, 626 P.2d 543 (Wash.App.1981) (notice and hearing requirements not applicable to emergency zoning measures designed to preserve status quo pending adoption of comprehensive zoning plan). Note that the Minnesota statute cited in note 5 above grants counties the authority to enact the control as "an emergency measure." Other statutes do the same. *See* West's Colo.Rev.Stat.Ann. § 30–28–121. The problem of enactment without hearing is greater in states where the authority must be implied. *See* Roberts, 3 *Zoning and Land Use Controls* § 22.02[3][ii] (Rohan ed.2016). In the light of "the race of diligence," and the disadvantages of requiring notice and hearing before enacting interim development ordinances, might a City Council in advance incorporate a permanent chapter in its zoning ordinance which allows the designation of interim development areas by resolution?

10.   Courts require municipalities to act in good faith and are more likely to strike down interim development controls that are unfairly directed at specific proposals. In *Charles v. Diamond*, 392 N.Y.S.2d 594, 360 N.E.2d 1295 (N.Y.1977) (remanding case to the trial court for determination of whether a ten-year delay by the city in making remedial sewer improvements was unreasonable, dilatory and in bad faith, where during the delay, all development was barred by an interim development ordinance). In *Medical Services, Inc. v. City of Savage*, 487 N.W.2d 263 (Minn.App.1992), a landowner submitted a building permit application for a proposed infectious waste facility in its industrial district. Questions existed as to whether it was a permitted use, yet it was not until 1991 that, in closed session and after the applicant had filed an action against the city, the council imposed a moratorium on permits. The court found the moratorium on the issuance of a building permit for the applicant to be arbitrary, capricious and in bad faith. In most jurisdictions, however, the mere fact that a specific proposed use stimulates the enactment of a freeze is not enough to invalidate it. *See Almquist v. Town of Marshan*, 245 N.W.2d 819 (Minn.1976) (an interim development ordinance was upheld, where its purpose was to restrict residential subdivisions in prime

agricultural areas pending amendments of the Town's comprehensive plan and zoning ordinance in conformance to the Regional Development Framework of the Metropolitan Council of the Minneapolis-St. Paul seven county region, even though the IDO was precipitated by a specific proposal).

The "pending ordinance" rule discussed *supra* in note 7 is another example of good faith approval of municipal action, if the proposed zoning ordinance amendment was pending prior to the time the permit was sought. David Heeter has pointed out potential abuses of interim development controls. He notes: "It is far more difficult to rationalize interim zoning restrictions and moratoriums that are adopted in response to specific development proposals. In far too many instances, the alleged need for such controls arises from the community's failure to adequately plan for its future—not from the proposed development." David Heeter, *Interim Zoning Controls: Some Thoughts on Their Uses and Abuses, in Management & Control of Growth* 409, 411 (Scott ed. 1975).

COMMENT: ENVIRONMENTAL AND PUBLIC SERVICES MORATORIA TO CORRECT CAPITAL DEFICIENCIES

(a) Inadequate sewer and water treatment facilities, which pose threats to the environment, often lead municipalities to enact moratoria on new development pending corrective action. These environmental or public service moratoria differ from the interim development ordinance imposed for planning purposes in that they are based on the general police power, as distinguished from zoning enabling authority. The purpose of such moratoria is not to prevent the vesting of rights (since they prevent further development even when the owner's rights are vested), but to protect the environment and the public health and safety. *See Belle Harbor Realty Corp. v. Kerr*, 323 N.E.2d 697 (N.Y.1974).

(b) The court in *Westwood Forest Estates, Inc. v. Village of South Nyack*, 244 N.E.2d 700 (N.Y.1969) identified three criteria by which to evaluate the reasonableness of a short term environmental moratorium: (1) it must be temporary, (2) it must be within limits of necessity, and (3) it must be directed at community needs rather than individual property owners. In *Westwood Forest*, the ordinance was found invalid because the village had adequate capacity in its sewer system but had failed over a period of several years to provide adequate treatment of sewage effluent; the impact of the village's failure was unfairly placed on one individual by refusing to allow him any reasonable use of his land. *Belle Harbor Realty*, *supra*, upheld revocation of a permit for construction of a nursing home upon evidence that sewers were grossly inadequate for current use and revocation was necessary to prevent a condition dangerous to the public health and welfare. The court pointed out that the municipality's action must be reasonably calculated to prevent a crisis condition and, further, that it must be taking steps to alleviate the problem. *See also Swanson v. Marin Municipal Water District*, 128 Cal.Rptr. 485 (Cal.App.1976) (a moratorium on new water service was reasonable in light of threatened water shortage but recognizing a continuing obligation on the part of the district to "exert every reasonable effort to augment its available water supply in order to meet increasing demands").

(c)   As with interim development ordinances, enacted moratoria must be rational and in good faith. In *Wincamp Partnership v. Anne Arundel County*, 458 F.Supp. 1009 (D.Md.1978), both the state statute and the local ordinance prohibited issuance of building permits in the absence of adequate sewer capacity. For a comprehensive discussion *see* Julie Biggs, *No Drip, No Flush, No Growth: How Cities Can Control Growth Beyond Their Boundaries by Refusing to Extend Utility Services*, 22 URBAN LAWYER 285 (1990).

COMMENT: UTILITY EXTENSIONS

The primary duty of a public utility is to serve on reasonable terms all those who desire the service that it renders. *See United Fuel Gas Co. v. Railroad Commission of Kentucky*, 278 U.S. 300 (1929); *City of Winter Park v. Southern States Utilities, Inc.*, 540 So.2d 178 (Fla.App.1989); *Planning Bd. of Braintree v. Department of Public Utilities*, 647 N.E.2d 1186 (Mass.1995). It may not choose to serve only the portion of the territory covered by its franchise that is presently profitable for it to serve. *See People of State of New York ex rel. New York & Queens Gas Co. v. McCall*, 245 U.S. 345 (1917); *State ex rel. Toledo Edison Co. v. Clyde*, 668 N.E.2d 498 (Ohio 1996).

A public service commission can require a utility to provide unprofitable services to some customers as long as the utility is allowed a reasonable opportunity to earn its authorized rate of return on its overall investment. *United States West Communications, Inc. v. Public Service Com'n of Utah*, 882 P.2d 141 (Utah 1994). The right to provide utility services to the public carries with it a concomitant duty to promptly and efficiently provide those same services. *See City of Mount Dora v. JJ's Mobile Homes, Inc.*, 579 So.2d 219 (Fla.App.1991).

Where the public utility is controlled by a city or county, and not a private utility, the ability of a city to control growth by the denial of utility extension depends in large part on whether public utility law and the police power are viewed as the source of the city's authority. The provision of capital facilities is a critical aspect of growth control. As the problem and notes above on public services moratoria indicate, utility extension denial is one way for a municipality to control urban sprawl on an interim basis. It can also be used as a long term control. The city's comprehensive plan can include processes and rules governing utility extension. If the comprehensive plan does control the location and timing of utilities, a municipality can avoid extension where to do so would be inconsistent with the plan. In *Dateline Builders, Inc. v. City of Santa Rosa*, 194 Cal.Rptr. 258 (Cal.App.1983), the court upheld a city's decision refusing to extend sewerage connections to a development beyond a city's corporate boundaries, but within its utility boundaries. The proposed development was in an agricultural area and was inconsistent with the city and county regional general plan.

Public Utility Law: If a city's provision of water or sewer is authorized solely under public utility law, the city may deny service for a utility-related reason, but little discretion is afforded to the utility to decide when and whether to extend service. *See Reid Development Corp. v. Parsippany-Troy Hills TP*, 89 A.2d 667 (N.J.1952) (township is unable to condition service extension on developer's willingness to increase minimum lot size). While a city cannot be required to extend utility services outside its border, if it does so and secures a monopoly in, or "stakes out," a service area, courts may require that it impartially serve all those reasonably within reach of its supply system. One way a municipality may avoid the harshness of this rule is to extend services only under contract. *See City of Milwaukee v. Public Service Commission*, 66 N.W.2d 716 (Wis.1954).

Municipal service refusal to new users must be based on a utility-related reason. The court in *Mayor & City Council of Cumberland v. Powles*, 258 A.2d 410 (Md.1969), noted that a water shortage or financial crisis would justify refusal. *See also Reid Development Corp. v. Parsippany-Troy Hills TP*, 107 A.2d 20 (N.J.App.Div.1954) (utility extension as growth control allowed so long as reasonable utility related reasons alleged). Such reasons include: limited financial resources, *Rose v. Plymouth Town*, 173 P.2d 285 (Utah 1946); insufficient facilities or shortage of capacity, *Swanson v. Marin Municipal Water District*, 128 Cal.Rptr. 485 (Cal.App.1976); and environmental concerns, *Capture Realty Corp. v. Board of Adjustment*, 336 A.2d 30 (N.J.App.1975). *But see Robinson v. City of Boulder*, 547 P.2d 228 (Colo.1976) (city providing extraterritorial utility service cannot deny service based on its land use growth policies)(NOTE: Englewood test used in Robinson overturned in 718 P.2d 235, 243). Similarly, a water district or other public utility will not be able to exert total control over local land use policy. Some people may be able to develop their own private water supplies, despite the difficulty and expense. A public water district clearly could not adopt a blanket restriction on private water supplies while simultaneously refusing to look for new public sources of water. *Cf. Charles v. Diamond*, 360 N.E.2d 1295, 1303 (1977) (stating that once a landowner has established that an ordinance requiring hookup to public sewers has caused an unreasonable delay in development, the landowner may construct a private sewer system).

Police Power: In contrast, if a city's provision of utility service viewed as an exercise of the police power, it will have greater discretion and more likely will be able to use growth related reasons to deny service extension. *See Dateline, supra. See* Stuart Deutsch, *Capital Improvement Controls as Land Use Devices*, 9 ENVTL.LAW 61 (1978); and Julie Biggs, *No Drip, No Flush, No Growth: How Cities Can Control Growth Beyond Their Boundaries By Refusing to Extend Utility Services*, 22 URBAN LAWYER 285 (1990) (county or city water or sewer districts can also be formed for the purpose of controlling growth). *See Wilson v. Hidden Valley Municipal Water District*, 63 Cal.Rptr. 889 (Cal.App.1967); and Herman, Note, *Sometimes There's Nothing Left to Give: The Justification for Denying Water Service to New Consumers to Control Growth*, 44 STAN.L.REV. 429 (1992). *But see Swanson v. Marin Municipal Water District*, 128 Cal.Rptr. 485 (Cal.App.1976) (recognizing a continuing obligation on the part of the district to "exert every reasonable effort to augment its available water supply in order to meet increasing demands").

Adequate Water Availability: Utilities may also be regulated by state agencies. In *Gilbert v. State of California Department of Health*, 266 Cal.Rptr. 891 (Cal.App.1990), the court held that the State Department of Health had authority to condition issuance of a water permit to a public water district on condition that the district continue its 20 year moratorium on new or additional service connections, due to drought conditions, until it developed an adequate water supply, and the Department of Health had discretion to order the water district to take measures to comply with water standards, including measures designed to take into account availability of sufficient water to meet maximum demand for current users. Cal. Health & Safety Code §§ 4011, 4013, and 4014. California now requires that a "water assessment" be performed by subdivisions of over 500 homes and large commercial and industrial projects to assure availability of a secure 50 year water supply. S.B. 610, Cal. Gov't Code 66473. Infill projects are exempt. *Id.* at 66473.7. The water assessment is enforced through the CEQA environmental review process. *See California Water Impact Network v. Newhall County Water District*, 75 Cal.Rptr.3d 393 (Cal.App.2008).

What if local government provides unequal distribution of utility services and capital facilities to black and white neighborhoods within its borders? *See Hawkins v. Town of Shaw*, 437 F.2d 1286 (5th Cir.1971) and *Ammons v. Dade City*, 783 F.2d 982 (11th Cir.1986).

C. TIMING AND SEQUENCING CONTROLS

GOLDEN V. PLANNING BOARD OF TOWN OF RAMAPO

Court of Appeals of New York, 1972.
30 N.Y.2d 359, 285 N.E.2d 291, appeal dismissed, 409 U.S. 1003.

SCILEPPI, JUDGE.

Both cases arise out of the 1969 amendments to the Town of Ramapo's Zoning Ordinance. In Golden, petitioners, the owner of record and contract vendee, by way of a proceeding pursuant to CPLR article 78 [writ of certiorari] sought an order reviewing and annulling a decision and determination of the Planning Board of the Town of Ramapo which denied their application for preliminary approval of a residential subdivision plat because of an admitted failure to secure a special permit as required by section 46–13.1 of the Town zoning ordinance prohibiting subdivision approval except where the residential developer has secured, prior to the application for plat approval, a special permit or a variance pursuant to section F of the ordinance. Special Term sustained the amendments and granted summary judgment. On appeal, the Appellate Division elected, since all necessary parties were before the court, to treat the proceeding as an action for declaratory judgment and reversed, 37 A.D.2d 236, 324 N.Y.S.2d 178.

The plaintiffs in Rockland County Builders Association, on the other hand, sought, in an action for declaratory judgment, to set aside the ordinance as unconstitutional and commenced the present action after the Planning Board had denied plaintiff Mildred Rhodes preliminary plat approval for her parcel of property because of a conceded failure on her part to obtain a special permit as required under the challenged ordinance.

Experiencing the pressures of an increase in population and the ancillary problem of providing municipal facilities and services,[1] the Town of Ramapo, as early as 1964, made application for grant under section 801 of the Housing Act of 1964 (78 U.S. Stat. 769) to develop a master plan. The plan's preparation included a four-volume study of the existing land uses, public facilities, transportation, industry and commerce, housing needs and projected population trends. The proposals appearing in the studies were subsequently adopted pursuant to section 272–a of the Town Law, Consol. Laws, c. 62, in July, 1966 and implemented by way of a master plan. The master plan was followed by the adoption of a comprehensive zoning ordinance. Additional sewage district and drainage studies were undertaken which culminated in the adoption of a capital budget, providing for the development of the improvements specified in the master plan within the next six years. Pursuant to section 271 of the Town Law, authorizing comprehensive planning, and as a supplement to the capital budget, the Town Board adopted a capital program which provides for the location and sequence of additional capital improvements for the 12 years following the life of the capital budget. The two plans, covering a period of 18 years, detail the capital improvements projected for maximum development and conform to the specifications set forth in the master plan, the official map and drainage plan.

Based upon these criteria, the Town subsequently adopted the subject amendments for the alleged purpose of eliminating premature subdivision and urban sprawl. Residential development is to proceed according to the provision of adequate municipal facilities and services, with the assurance that any concomitant restraint upon property use is to be of a "temporary"

---

[1] The Town's allegations that present facilities are inadequate to service increasing demands goes uncontested. We must assume, therefore, that the proposed improvements, both as to their nature and extent, reflect legitimate community needs and are not veiled efforts at exclusion (see National Land & Inv. Co. v. Easttown Twp. Bd. of Adj., 215 A.2d 597). In the period 1940–1968 population in the unincorporated areas of the Town increased 285.9%. Between the years of 1950–1960 the increase again in unincorporated areas, was 130.8%; from 1960–1966 some 78.5%; and from the years 1966–1969 20.4%. In terms of real numbers, population figures compare at 58,626 as of 1966 with the largest increment of growth since the decennial census occurring in the undeveloped areas. Projected figures, assuming current land use and zoning trends, approximate a total Town population of 120,000 by 1985. Growth is expected to be heaviest in the currently undeveloped western and northern tiers of the Town, predominantly in the form of subdivision development with some apartment construction. A growth rate of some 1,000 residential units per annum has been experienced in the unincorporated areas of the Town.

nature and that other private uses, including the construction of individual housing, are authorized.

The amendments did not rezone or reclassify any land into different residential or use districts,[2] but, for the purposes of implementing the proposals appearing in the comprehensive plan, consist, in the main, of additions to the definitional sections of the ordinance, section 46–3, and the adoption of a new class of "Special Permit Uses", designated "Residential Development Use." "Residential Development Use" is defined as "The erection or construction of dwellings or any vacant plots, lots or parcels of land" (§ 46–3); and, any person who acts so as to come within that definition, "shall be deemed to be engaged in residential development which shall be a separate use classification under this ordinance and subject to the requirement of obtaining a special permit from the Town Board" (§ 46–3).

The standards for the issuance of special permits are framed in terms of the availability to the proposed subdivision plat of five essential facilities or services: specifically (1) public sanitary sewers or approved substitutes; (2) drainage facilities; (3) improved public parks or recreation facilities, including public schools; (4) State, county or town roads—major, secondary or collector; and, (5) firehouses. No special permit shall issue unless the proposed residential development has accumulated 15 development points, to be computed on a sliding scale of values assigned to the specified improvements under the statute. Subdivision is thus a function of immediate availability to the proposed plat of certain municipal improvements; the avowed purpose of the amendments being to phase residential development to the Town's ability to provide the above facilities or services.

[Author's note: The fifteen development points were computed on the following scale of values:]

---

[2]   As of July, 1966, the only available figures, six residential zoning districts with varying lot size and density requirements accounted for in excess of nine tenths of the Town's unincorporated land area. Of these the RR classification (80,000 square feet minimum lot area) plus R-35 zone (35,000 square feet minimum lot area) comprise over one half of all zoned areas. The subject sites are presently zoned RR-50 (50,000 square feet minimum lot area). The reasonableness of these minimum lot requirements are not presently controverted, though we are referred to no compelling need in their behalf. Under present zoning regulations, the population of the unincorporated areas could be increased by about 14,600 families (3.5 people) when all suitable vacant land is occupied. Housing values as of 1960 in the unincorporated areas range from a modest $15,000 (approx. 30%) to higher than $25,000 (25%), with the undeveloped western tier of Town showing the highest percentage of values in excess of $25,000 (41%). Significantly, for the same year only about one half of one percent of all housing units were occupied by nonwhite families. Efforts at adjusting this disparity are reflected in the creation of a public housing authority and the authority's proposal to construct biracial low-income family housing.

"(1) Sewers
 (a) Public sewers available in RR-
       50, R-40, R-35, R-25, R-15 and
       R-15S districts . . . .   5 points
 (b) Package Sewer Plants . . . .   3 points
 (c) County approved septic system
       in an RR-80 district . . . .   3 points
 (d) All others . . . .   0 points
"(2) Drainage
       Percentage of Required
       Drainage Capacity Available
 (a) 100% or more . . . .   5 points
 (b) 90% to 99.9% . . . .   4 points
 (c) 80% to 89.9% . . . .   3 points
 (d) 65% to 79.9% . . . .   2 points
 (e) 50% to 64.9% . . . .   1 point
 (f) Less than 50% . . . .   0 points
"(3) Improved Public Park or
       Recreation Facility Including
       Public School Site
 (a) Within ¼ mile . . . .   5 points
 (b) Within ½ mile . . . .   3 points
 (c) Within 1 mile . . . .   1 point
 (d) Further than 1 mile . . . .   0 points
"(4) State, County or Town Major,
       Secondary or Collector Road(s)
       Improved with Curbs and
       Sidewalks
 (a) Direct Access . . . .   5 points
 (b) Within ½ mile . . . .   3 points
 (c) Within 1 mile . . . .   1 point
 (d) Further than 1 mile . . . .   0 points
"(5) Fire House
 (a) Within 1 mile . . . .   3 points
 (b) Within 2 miles . . . .   1 point
 (c) Further than 2 miles . . . .   0 points

The undisputed effect of these integrated efforts in land use planning and development is to provide an over-all program of orderly growth and adequate facilities through a sequential development policy commensurate with progressing availability and capacity of public facilities. While its goals are clear and its purposes indisputably laudatory, serious questions are raised as to the manner in which these ends are to be effected, not the least of which relates to their legal viability under present zoning enabling legislation, particularly sections 261 and 263 of the Town Law. The owners of the subject premises argue, and the Appellate Division has sustained the proposition, that the primary purpose of the amending ordinance is to control or regulate population growth within the Town and as such is not within the authorized objectives of the zoning enabling legislation. We disagree.

In enacting the challenged amendments, the Town Board has sought to control subdivision in all residential districts, pending the provision (public or private) at some future date of various services and facilities. A reading of the relevant statutory provisions reveals that there is no specific authorization for the "sequential" and "timing" controls adopted here. That, of course, cannot be said to end the matter, for the additional inquiry remains as to whether the challenged amendments find their basis within the perimeters of the devices authorized and purposes sanctioned under current enabling legislation. Our concern is, as it should be, with the effects of the statutory scheme taken as a whole and its role in the propagation of a viable policy of land use and planning.

Considering the activities enumerated by section 261 of the Town Law, and relating those powers to the authorized purposes detailed in section 263, the challenged amendments are proper zoning techniques, exercised for legitimate zoning purposes. The power to restrict and regulate conferred under section 261 includes within its grant, by way of necessary implication, the authority to direct the growth of population for the purposes indicated, within the confines of the township. It is the matrix of land use restrictions, common to each of the enumerated powers and sanctioned goals, a necessary concomitant to the municipalities' recognized authority to determine the lines along which local development shall proceed, though it may divert it from its natural course.

Of course, zoning historically has assumed the development of individual plats and has proven characteristically ineffective in treating with the problems attending subdivision and development of larger parcels, involving as it invariably does, the provision of adequate public services and facilities. To this end, subdivision control (Town Law, §§ 276, 277) purports to guide community development in the directions outlined here, while at the same time encouraging the provision of adequate facilities for the housing, distribution, comfort and convenience of local residents. It reflects in essence, a legislative judgment that the development of unimproved areas be accompanied by provision of essential facilities. And though it may not, in a definitional or conceptual sense be identified with the power to zone, it is designed to complement other land use restrictions, which, taken together, seek to implement a broader, comprehensive plan for community development.

It is argued, nevertheless, that the timing controls currently in issue are not legislatively authorized since their effect is to prohibit subdivision absent precedent or concurrent action of the Town, and hence constitutes an unauthorized blanket interdiction against subdivision.

It is, indeed, true that the Planning Board is not in an absolute sense statutorily authorized to deny the right to subdivide. That is not, however, what is sought to be accomplished here. The Planning Board has the right to refuse approval of subdivision plats in the absence of those improvements specified in section 277, and the fact that it is the Town and not the subdividing owner or land developer who is required to make those improvements before the plat will be approved cannot be said to transform the scheme into an absolute prohibition any more than it would be so where it was the developer who refused to provide the facilities required for plat approval.[7] Denial of subdivision plat approval, invariably amounts to a prohibition against subdivision, albeit a conditional one and to say that the Planning Board lacks the authority to deny subdivision rights is to mistake the nature of our inquiry which is essentially whether development may be conditioned pending the provision by the municipality of specified services and facilities. Whether it is the municipality or the developer who is to provide the improvements, the objective is the same—to provide adequate facilities, off-site and on-site; and in either case subdivision rights are conditioned, not denied.

Experience, over the last quarter century, however, with greater technological integration and drastic shifts in population distribution has pointed up serious defects and community autonomy in land use controls has come under increasing attack by legal commentators, and students of urban problems alike, because of its pronounced insularism and its correlative role in producing distortions in metropolitan growth patterns, and perhaps more importantly, in crippling efforts toward regional and

---

[7]   The difference between the ordinary situation and the situation said to subsist here resides in the fact that where plat approval is denied for want of various improvements, the developer is free to provide those improvements at his own expense. In the ordinary case where the proposed improvements will not be completed before the plat is filed the developer's obligation is secured by a performance bond (Town Law, § 277). On the other hand, in the present case, plat approval is conditioned upon the Town's obligation to undertake improvements in roads, sewers and recreational facilities. As the Town may not be held to its program, practices do vary from year to year "and fiscal needs cannot be frozen beyond review and recall" (concurring opn. Hopkins, J., 37 A.D.2d 244, 324 N.Y.S.2d 178), the "patient owner" who relied on the capital program for qualification then is said to face the prospect that the improvements will be delayed and the impediments established by the ordinance further extended by the Town's failure to adhere to its own schedule.

The reasoning, as far as it goes, cannot be challenged. Yet, in passing on the validity of the ordinance on its face, we must assume not only the Town's good faith, but its assiduous adherence to the program's scheduled implementation. We cannot, it is true, adjudicate in a vacuum and we would be remiss not to consider the substantial risk that the Town may eventually default in its obligations. Yet, those are future events, the staple of a clairvoyant, not of a court in its deliberations. The threat of default is not so imminent or likely that it would warrant our prognosticating and striking down these amendments as invalid on their face. When and if the danger should materialize, the aggrieved landowner can seek relief by way of an article 78 proceeding, declaring the ordinance unconstitutional as applied to his property. Alternatively, should it arise at some future point in time that the Town must fail in its enterprise, an action for a declaratory judgment will indeed prove the most effective vehicle for relieving property owners of what would constitute absolute prohibitions.

State-wide problem solving, be it pollution, decent housing, or public transportation.

Recognition of communal and regional interdependence, in turn, has resulted in proposals for schemes of regional and State-wide planning, in the hope that decisions would then correspond roughly to their level of impact. Yet, as salutary as such proposals may be, the power to zone under current law is vested in local municipalities, and we are constrained to resolve the issues accordingly. What does become more apparent in treating with the problem, however, is that though the issues are framed in terms of the developer's due process rights, those rights cannot, realistically speaking, be viewed separately and apart from the rights of others " 'in search of a [more] comfortable place to live.' "

There is, then, something inherently suspect in a scheme which, apart from its professed purposes, effects a restriction upon the free mobility of a people until sometime in the future when projected facilities are available to meet increased demands. Although zoning must include schemes designed to allow municipalities to more effectively contend with the increased demands of evolving and growing communities, under its guise, townships have been wont to try their hand at an array of exclusionary devices in the hope of avoiding the very burden which growth must inevitably bring.

* * *

Though the conflict engendered by such tactics is certainly real, and its implications vast, accumulated evidence, scientific and social, points circumspectly at the hazards of undirected growth and the naive, somewhat nostalgic imperative that egalitarianism is a function of growth.

Hence, unless we are to ignore the plain meaning of the statutory delegation, this much is clear: phased growth is well within the ambit of existing enabling legislation. And, of course, it is no answer to point to emergent problems to buttress the conclusion that such innovative schemes are beyond the perimeters of statutory authorization. These considerations, admittedly real, to the extent which they are relevant, bear solely upon the continued viability of "localism" in land use regulation; obviously, they can neither add nor detract from the initial grant of authority, obsolescent though it may be. The answer which Ramapo has posed can by no means be termed definitive; it is, however, a first practical step toward controlled growth achieved without forsaking broader social purposes.

The subject ordinance is said to advance legitimate zoning purposes as it assures that each new home built in the township will have at least a minimum of public services in the categories regulated by the ordinance. The Town argues that various public facilities are presently being constructed but that for want of time and money it has been unable to provide such services and facilities at a pace commensurate with increased public need. It is urged that although the zoning power includes reasonable restrictions upon the private use of property, exacted in the hope of development according to well-laid plans, calculated to advance the public welfare of the community in the future, the subject regulations go further and seek to avoid the increased responsibilities and economic burdens which time and growth must ultimately bring.

It is the nature of all land use and development regulations to circumscribe the course of growth within a particular town or district and to that extent such restrictions invariably impede the forces of natural growth.

What we will not countenance, then, under any guise, is community efforts at immunization or exclusion. But, far from being exclusionary, the present amendments merely seek, by the implementation of sequential development and timed growth, to provide a balanced cohesive community dedicated to the efficient utilization of land. The restrictions conform to the community's considered land use policies as expressed in its comprehensive plan and represent a bona fide effort to maximize population density consistent with orderly growth. True other alternatives, such as requiring off-site improvements as a prerequisite to subdivision, may be available, but the choice as how best to proceed, in view of the difficulties attending such exactions cannot be faulted.

We only require that communities confront the challenge of population growth with open doors. Where in grappling with that problem, the community undertakes, by imposing temporary restrictions upon development, to provide required municipal services in a rational manner, courts are rightfully reluctant to strike down such schemes. The timing controls challenged here parallel recent proposals put forth by various study groups and have their genesis in certain of the pronouncements of this and the courts of sister States * * * . [T]he preeminent protection against their abuse resides in the mandatory on-going planning and development requirement, present here, which attends their implementation and use.

We may assume, therefore, that the present amendments are the product of foresighted planning calculated to promote the welfare of the township. The Town has imposed temporary restrictions upon land use in residential areas while committing itself to a program of development. It has utilized its comprehensive plan to implement its timing controls and has coupled with these restrictions provisions for low and moderate income housing on a large scale. Considered as a whole, it represents both in its inception and implementation a reasonable attempt to provide for the sequential, orderly development of land in conjunction with the needs of the community, as well as individual parcels of land, while simultaneously obviating the blighted aftermath which the initial failure to provide needed facilities so often brings.

The proposed amendments have the effect of restricting development for onwards to 18 years in certain areas. Whether the subject parcels will be so restricted for the full term is not clear, for it is equally probable that the proposed facilities will be brought into these areas well before that time. Assuming, however, that the restrictions will remain outstanding for the life of the program, they still fall short of a confiscation within the meaning of the Constitution.

An ordinance which seeks to permanently restrict the use of property so that it may not be used for any reasonable purpose must be recognized as a taking: The only difference between the restriction and an outright taking in such a case "is that the restriction leaves the owner subject to the burden of payment of taxation, while outright confiscation would relieve him of that burden". An appreciably different situation obtains where the restriction constitutes a temporary restriction, promising that the property may be put to a profitable use within a reasonable time. The hardship of holding unproductive property for some time might be compensated for by the ultimate benefit inuring to the individual owner in the form of a substantial increase in valuation; or, for that matter, the landowner, might be compelled to chafe under the temporary restriction, without the benefit of such compensation, when that burden serves to promote the public good.

Every restriction on the use of property entails hardships for some individual owners. Those difficulties are invariably the product of police regulation and the pecuniary profits of the individual must in the long run be subordinated to the needs of the community. The fact that the ordinance limits the use of, and may depreciate the value of the property will not render it unconstitutional, however, unless it can be shown that the measure is either unreasonable in terms of necessity or the diminution in value is such as to be tantamount to a confiscation. Diminution, in turn, is a relative factor and though its magnitude is an indicia of a taking, it does not of itself establish a confiscation.

In sum, where it is clear that the existing physical and financial resources of the community are inadequate to furnish the essential services and facilities which a substantial increase in population requires, there is a rational basis for "phased growth" and hence, the challenged ordinance is not violative of the Federal and State Constitutions. Accordingly, the order appealed from should be reversed and the actions remitted to Special Term for entry of a judgment declaring section 46–13.1 of the Town Ordinance constitutional.

FULD, C.J., and BURKE, BERGAN and GIBSON, JJ., concur with SCILEPPI, J.

BREITEL, J., dissents and votes to affirm in a separate opinion in which JASEN, J., concurs [omitted.]

In each case: Order reversed, with costs, and the case remitted to Special Term for further proceedings in accordance with the opinion herein.

NOTES: TIMING AND SEQUENCING OF DEVELOPMENT TO COINCIDE WITH PROVISION OF CAPITAL IMPROVEMENTS

1.   The critical constitutional principle of the case was to enlarge the concept of "reasonable use" enunciated by *Euclid* and *Nectow* to "reasonable use over a reasonable period of time as measured by a comprehensive plan." Professor Freilich, who was the author of the Ramapo plan, drafted the ordinance and argued the case through the courts, has elaborated on the development of the case and its constitutional significance in Robert H. Freilich and David Greis, *Timing and Sequencing Development: Controlling Growth, in Future Land Use, Energy, Environment and Legal Constraints* 59–106 (Burchell and Listokin ed., 1975).

Will the developments in takings law evinced in the *Tahoe-Sierra* case have an effect on the validity of growth controls? *See* Robert H. Freilich and Elizabeth A. Garvin, *Takings After* Lucas: *Growth Management, Planning, and Regulatory Implementation Will Work Better Than Before*, Chapter 3, in After Lucas: Land Use Regulation and the Taking of Property Without Compensation (Callies ed., 1993); Robert H. Freilich, *Time, Space, and Value in Inverse Condemnation: A Unified Theory for Partial Takings Analysis*, 24 HAW.L.REV. 589 (2002).

2.   A noted treatise on zoning and land use controls made the following observation regarding the significance of *Ramapo*:

> The *Ramapo* decision shifted the balance of power from the developer to public land use agencies. The developer no longer has an absolute right to proceed with development, irrespective of whether public facilities can reasonably accommodate the development. Instead, the developer can be made to wait a reasonable period to allow public facilities to catch up or be forced to expend funds to ripen the land for development. At the same time, the *Ramapo* case has expanded the judicial view of just what incidental public costs affiliated with development may be shifted to the developer * * * . The *Ramapo* decision and rationale also permanently altered the courts' perception of the land use regulatory process, and paved the way for subsequent decisions that have favored public regulation over the developer or landowner's immediate right to develop property (irrespective of the harm such development might inflict upon the public good.) * * *

Rohan, 1 *Zoning and Land Use Controls* § 4.05 (1984). Copyright © 1984 by Matthew Bender & Co., Inc., reprinted with permission from Zoning & Land Use Controls.

3.   After fourteen years elapsed of the eighteen year Ramapo plan, a newly elected Town Board decided in March of 1983 to eliminate the point system due to a combination of factors: (1) the unincorporated town had since been carved into thirteen villages (nine additional villages together with the original four), which made implementation of the plan totally impracticable. The town had adopted a Village Incorporation Law to prevent multiple incorporations unless they were "in the overall interest of the town as a whole." The New York Court of Appeals held that the local law was preempted by the state's village incorporation law. *Marcus v. Baron*, 442 N.E.2d 437 (N.Y.1982), (overturning a lengthy analysis in the Appellate Division, 445 N.Y.S.2d 587 (1981), which had held that Ramapo's law was a proper exercise of home rule authority and regional planning statutes).

See John R. Nolon, *Golden and Its Emanations: The Surprising Origins of Smart Growth*, 35 URBAN LAWYER 15 (2003), and Robert H. Freilich, Robert J. Sitkowski and Seth D. Mennillo, *From Sprawl to Sustainability: Smart Growth, New Urbanism, Green Development and Renewable Energy* (ABA 2010); Geneslaw & Raymond, *Planning* (June 1983) at 8. For historical discussions and comments on the plan and its techniques, *see* Elliot and Marcus, *From Euclid to Ramapo: New Directions in Land Development Controls*, 1 HOFSTRA L.REV. 56 (1973); Herbert Franklin, *Controlling Growth: But for Whom? The Social Implications of Development Timing* (1973) reprinted in 2 Management and Control of Growth 78 (Scott ed., 1975); Fred Bosselman, *Can the Town of Ramapo Pass a Law to Bind the Rights of the Whole World?*, 1 FLA.ST.U.L.REV. 234 (1973); Note, *Phased Zoning: Regulation of the Tempo and Sequence of Land Development*, 26 STAN.L.REV. 585 (1974); Manual Emanuel, *Ramapo's Managed Growth Program: After Five Years Experience*, 4 Planning Notebook, No. 5 (1974), reprinted in 3 Management and Control of Growth 302 (Scott ed., 1975).

4.   Ramapo's requirement that links development approval with the availability of public facilities went statewide in Florida. In 1985, Florida became the first state to impose so-called "concurrency" requirements as part of its mandatory planning law, West's Fla.Stat.Ann. § 163.3177 (10)(h). *See* Thomas Pelham, *From the Ramapo Plan to Florida's Statewide Concurrency System: Ramapo's Influence on Infrastructure Planning*, 35 URBAN LAWYER 113 (2003) ("[P]ublic facilities and services needed to support development shall be concurrent with the impacts of such development." In 1990, Washington became the second state to require local governments to link development approval and provision of adequate public facilities. West's RCWA § 36.70A. *See* Larry Smith, *Planning for Growth, Washington Style, in State and Regional Comprehensive Planning: Implementing New Methods for Growth Management* (Peter Buchsbaum and Smith eds.1993). *See also* John DeGrove, *The New Frontier for Land Policy: Planning and Growth Management in the States* (with Mines, 1992); and Boggs and Apgar, *Concurrency and Growth Management: A Lawyer's Primer*, 7 J.LAND USE & ENVTL.L. 1 (1991).

5. Later systems have built on the Ramapo model by tying development approvals to level of service (LOS) standards. LOS standards measure the ratio of public facility capacity to the need for the facility. This deceptively simple concept incorporates several features missing from the point system. First, the LOS measure takes into account all demand for the facilities, including existing demand as well as the additional population added by new development proposals. By contrast, the point system only accounts for those facilities available to the project under review. Second, an adopted LOS standard reflects a policy decision concerning the appropriate equilibrium between population and public facilities that would achieve a standardized review process for new development and a regulated capital budgeting process. *See* S. Mark White, *Adequate Public Facilities Ordinances and Transportation Management* (APA, 1996).

6. The most controversial issues raised by the Court of Appeals in the *Ramapo* case were the alleged exclusionary effects and whether timing and sequencing met regional general welfare. The court in *Ramapo* found that the plan was not exclusionary:

> What we will not countenance, then, under any guise, is community efforts at immunization or exclusion. But, far from being exclusionary, the present amendments merely seek, by the implementation of sequential development and timed growth, to provide a balanced cohesive community dedicated to the efficient utilization of land. The restrictions conform to the community's considered land use policies as expressed in its comprehensive plan and represent a bona fide effort to maximize population density consistent with orderly growth. True other alternatives * * * may be available, but the choice as how best to proceed, in view of the difficulties attending such exactions * * * cannot be faulted.

334 N.Y.S.2d at 152.

The court noted that Ramapo "utilized its comprehensive plan to implement its timing controls and has coupled with these restrictions provisions for low and moderate income housing on a large scale." *Id.* at 153. Ramapo was the first suburban town in New York State to voluntarily develop, as part of its planning, integrated public housing for low income families, over the objection of thousands of its citizens. In order for Ramapo to develop two public housing areas with hundreds of low income units, the town had to fight several lawsuits. *See Greenwald v. Town of Ramapo*, 317 N.Y.S.2d 839 (App.Div.1970); *Farrelly v. Town of Ramapo*, 317 N.Y.S.2d 837 (App.Div.1970); and *Fletcher v. Romney, Secretary of HUD*, 323 F.Supp. 189 (S.D.N.Y.1971). In addition, the Villages of Spring Valley and Suffern, located within the town, had provided for thousands of multi-family apartment units.

GOLDEN AND ITS EMANATIONS: THE SURPRISING
ORIGINS OF SMART GROWTH

John R. Nolon.
35 Urban Lawyer 15 (2003).**

I.   Introduction

How effectively can local governments prevent the effects of sprawl?
Are they empowered to adopt smart growth strategies? Can they, acting
alone, create balanced and orderly land use patterns? Does danger lurk in
empowering local governments to act aggressively regarding such matters,
in the absence of statewide or regional planning? These questions, despite
their contemporary relevance, are not new. Thirty years ago, land use
practitioners and scholars hotly debated growth management, regionalism,
and the preemption of local land use authority. A 1972 case decided by New
York's highest court catalyzed this national debate. A hesitant court of
appeals ceded Ramapo, a single town in the path of metropolitan area
development, authority to control growth. In doing so, it set in motion three
decades of experimentation and creativity responsible for a plethora of
techniques now available to fight sprawl: the toolbox practitioners use to
achieve smart growth at the local level. The court's ambivalence was
palpable: New York's zoning regime, it said, "is burdened by the largely
antiquated notion which deigns that the regulation of land use and
development is uniquely a function of local government. . . ."

At precisely the same time, a revolution to wrest land use control from
local governments was begun. It was one fueled by the understanding that
local control of land use creates serious inefficiencies and inequities. A
report entitled "The Quiet Revolution," prepared for the Council of
Environmental Quality in 1971, contained a powerful statement of the
problems caused by the delegation of land use control to towns, villages,
boroughs, cities, and townships: "This country is in the midst of a
revolution in the way we regulate the use of our land. . . . The ancient
regime being overthrown is the feudal system under which the entire
pattern of land development has been controlled by thousands of individual
local governments, each seeking to maximize its tax base and minimize its
social problems, and caring less what happens to all the others."[2] The
revolution has not succeeded, despite all the attention given to the efforts
of states to create statewide, counter-regimes under the rubrics of growth
management, sustainable development, and, recently, smart growth. After
analyzing recent state planning and smart growth legislation, a
preeminent practitioner and scholar concludes that one of the major

---

** Reprinted with permission from the author and the American Bar Association, copyright
2003.

   2 Fred Bosselman and David Callies, *The Quiet Revolution* (Council on Envtl. Quality 1971).

problems in fighting sprawl today is "the states' failure to reclaim some of their authority delegated early on to localities in the land use field. . . ."[3]

In November, 2002, the Land Use Law Center of Pace University Law School, the Government Law Center of Albany Law School, The Urban Lawyer, the National Law Journal, and the American Bar Association Section of Local and State Government Law hosted a national conference on the Ramapo case and its extraordinary contemporary relevance. The event was a reunion for the architects of the Ramapo Plan, including the town's chief elected official, professional planner, zoning enforcement officer, and its special counsel, Professor Robert H. Freilich, whose extraordinary career and legacy as the founder and, for over thirty years, the editor of The Urban Lawyer was enthusiastically celebrated as part of the event. The conference was a retrospective for practitioners who reflected on the debt owed the Ramapo case for jump-starting local smart growth strategies, and for scholars who wondered at the wisdom of the continued devolution of land use authority to local governments.

This article provides the background for the adoption of the Ramapo ordinance, explains its precocious inventions in some detail, and describes other dramatic local inventions emanating from the Ramapo approach to smart growth.

II.   Background and Summary of Ramapo's Current Relevance

Professor Robert H. Freilich was Ramapo's legal advisor during the 1960s when it was experiencing the type of rapid growth that causes so much concern today. Like many suburban communities, Ramapo was zoned predominantly for residential development, mostly single-family homes. Low-density suburban zoning of this type causes sprawl to the great consternation of local residents. Throughout the land, local officials struggle to change zoning ordinances and master plans to absorb growth in a more creative and responsible manner. A look at how the town of Ramapo and the judiciary responded to growth pressures thirty years ago is instructive. The 1972 opinion of the New York Court of Appeals was nothing short of prescient. It has been sustained by thirty years of extensive land use and regulatory takings litigation, including several recent decisions of the U.S. Supreme Court. The Ramapo decision has been examined and discussed in over 100 major decisions by subsequent courts in dozens of states and evaluated in over 150 law review and journal articles. In New York, the cases that relay on *Golden v. Ramapo* are among the most influential land use cases decided by its appellate courts.

The planning literature of the time was full of excitement about growth management, but there was little evidence, on the ground, of its legal adoption. Ramapo's law preceded by several years the passage of the

---

[3]   Robert H. Freilich, *From Sprawl to Smart Growth: Successful Legal, Planning and Environmental Systems* (ABA 1999).

much-heralded urban growth boundaries legislation in Oregon, the creation of the Adirondack Park Agency in New York, and Florida's infrastructure concurrency law.

As a more basic matter, Ramapo's investment in comprehensive planning put it solidly on the "pro-adoption" side of a debate emerging in the 1960s about the wisdom of adopting comprehensive plans in the majority of states where local governments have the option of doing so. Some advocates, even today, think local comprehensive plans unduly constrain local governments and are ineffective documents, not worth the high cost of preparation. Others believe that land use laws that conform to objectives contained in adopted comprehensive plans are highly successful in overcoming legal challenges. They strongly urge communities to adopt, and regularly update, truly comprehensive plans, backed up by detailed studies.

To implement its master plan, Ramapo adopted several amendments to its zoning ordinance. It also adopted a six-year capital budget and a capital plan for the following twelve years that committed the town to providing supportive infrastructure to all parts of the community over an eighteen-year period. No changes were made in the town's zoning districts or in the land uses allowed in each district. Instead, residential subdivision was designated a new class of land use, called "Residential Development Use," and prospective subdividers were required to obtain a special permit. The permit could not be issued unless a critical mass of infrastructure was in place to serve the subdivision, including roads, sewers, drainage, parks, and firehouses. This provision created a temporary suspension of the right to develop, similar to the effect of a development moratorium, which has become a popular technique in many states.

Several provisions of the Ramapo amendments softened the effect of the temporary restraint on development: Development of unsubdivided land was not prohibited, leaving all property owners some current land use. Variances could be provided to landowners who could show that their plans were consistent with the town's strategy. A special permit could be obtained vesting a landowner's right to develop the parcel in the future when infrastructure is in place. Developers were permitted to advance infrastructure to qualify for a special permit. A development easement acquisition commission was established to provide property tax relief to landowners not able to develop their parcels for several years.

Judge Scileppi, writing for the majority of the New York Court of Appeals, upheld Ramapo's land use amendments as being within the delegated authority of local governments, decided that the eighteen-year suspension of the right to develop did not constitute a regulatory taking, dismissed the town's argument that some of the landowners' claims were not ripe, established the concept that local zoning may not be exclusionary, carefully defined the role of the courts in land use matters versus that of the state legislature, and deferred to fact-based determinations of local lawmakers. In all these respects, the decision clearly forecast the ensuing thirty years of land use policy and litigation. The threads used by the Town of Ramapo and the Ramapo court to weave the fabric of our modern land use law are as follows:

Regulatory Takings: In upholding Ramapo's temporary restrictions on the right to develop, the New York Court of Appeals anticipated the U.S. Supreme Court's most recent regulatory takings decision: Tahoe-Sierra Preservation Council, Inc. v. Tahoe Regional Planning Agency. In Tahoe, the Court held that a moratorium on all development lasting thirty-two months was not, in itself, a taking. The landowners argued for a categorical rule that would classify a development moratorium as a taking without considering the moratorium's length, the severity of the problems addressed, or the good faith of the agency involved. The Ramapo court's rationale parallels that used in the Tahoe opinion in rejecting these arguments. Both indicate that property may not be segmented in time or estate for takings purposes, that benefits accrue to burdened property owners during moratoria, and that temporary suspensions of the right to develop can be in the public interest.

Total Takings: The measures adopted by the Town of Ramapo to mitigate the regulation's effect on property owners (variances, vested right permits, limited as-of-right development, self-help options, and tax relief), anticipated the U.S. Supreme Court's view in another seminal regulatory takings case: Lucas v. South Carolina Coastal Council. The absence of a hardship variance provision in the South Carolina beachfront management act led the Lucas Court to characterize a 1,000 foot setback provision, prohibiting all development on the plaintiff's parcels, as a total taking requiring compensation to the landowner. The Ramapo softening provisions prevented the ordinance from effecting a "total taking," established by Lucas as a per se violation of the Fifth Amendment's Taking Clause.

Affordable Housing and the Exclusion of Growth: The Ramapo decision established the fundamental proposition that the rights of citizens in search of a place to live are bound in the [regional general welfare state constitutional] due process rights of developers who bring actions challenging the exclusionary effect of local zoning. This notion underlies the court's subsequent decision in Berenson v. New Castle, holding that local zoning must accommodate present and future housing needs of the community and region. In the Ramapo court's words, "What we will not countenance, then, under any guise, is community efforts at immunization or exclusion." It was important to the court that the Ramapo Plan did not attempt "to freeze population at present levels but to maximize growth by the efficient use of the land, and in so doing testify to this community's continuing role in population assimilation." This is cautionary advice to communities that attempt to use their delegated land use power to resist, rather than to accommodate, growth.

Empowering Local Land Use Inventions—the Birth of Smart Growth: Perhaps Ramapo's greatest relevance lies in its reliance on local governments to achieve smart growth and the degree to which it endorsed the local power of invention. Doctrinally, the New York Court of Appeals held that the state legislature had delegated vast implied powers to municipalities to time growth, to achieve the most appropriate use of the land, and to invent the mechanisms for doing so. Pragmatically, the court left balls in two courts: local officials were told to pick up theirs and invent land use controls in their self-interest, while the state legislature was admonished to create regional and statewide solutions to hedge against the risks of parochialism run amok.

D. CITY-COUNTY-REGIONAL TIER SYSTEMS

The following sections demonstrate how quickly Ramapo evolved into city, county, regional and state growth management systems.

The principles and techniques upheld in Ramapo linking timing and sequencing of development to availability of off-site capital improvements and public services, while integrating the comprehensive plan, the capital improvement budget, affordable housing, subdivision regulations and the zoning ordinance, stimulated an expanded view of the planning, management and channeling of growth not only in small suburban towns on the developing fringe but as a major basis for structuring entire metropolitan regions.

1. PATTERNS OF TIERED GROWTH

Future urban growth can take a variety of forms related to the existence of transportation networks, water availability, topography, and historic development of the region. As growth management emerged in the mid to late 70s from the Ramapo Plan, a three tier pattern emerged: (1) Tier I, existing built up areas; (2) Tier II (urbanizing tier) covering development over the next 20 years, based on the Ramapo the timed and sequenced three CIP areas (1–6; 7 to 12; and 13 to 18; and (3) a rural and agricultural, non-development tier). The three tier concept, derived from the Ramapo Plan, has now become the key organizing principle used by regions, states, and the federal transportation act in enacting growth management and sustainability legislation. The urbanizing tier (Tier II) concept can be accomplished through either of three alternative patterns of growth:

    (a) Concentric growth through use of compact and limited urban service areas adjacent to Tier I infill areas (as in Ramapo). See Minneapolis-St. Paul; and Portland, Oregon;

(b) Linear transportation corridors (Puget Sound, Washington [Seattle-Tacoma]; Montgomery County, Maryland [Washington, D.C.] (extending from tier I through tiers II and III); and

(c) Freestanding "new towns" and "major mixed use centers" (Baltimore County, Maryland; and San Diego, California)

(a) Pattern I: Concentric Growth and Urban Service Area Boundaries

A. Minnesota Metropolitan Council. This pattern was evident in the Minneapolis/St. Paul Metropolitan Plan with the downtown areas (Tier I) and the established neighborhoods (Tier II), surrounded by a concentric timed and sequenced urbanizing fringe and with outside free standing cities having their own growth areas (Tier III). Rural and agricultural areas (Tier IV) were outside of the concentric growth rings.

Linking specific growth management techniques to regional geographical and functional areas with common problems and goals was incorporated in the Metropolitan Development Framework of Minneapolis-St. Paul; two years after the Ramapo decisions came down. The regional comprehensive plan divided the region into four "tiers": Tier I was the central city and downtown business area; Tier II included existing urban and suburban developed areas; Tier III included both the area of active urbanization (similar to the area where Ramapo's timing and sequencing controls were applied) and free standing small cities outside the tier boundary; and Tier IV consisted of rural and agricultural areas. Densities in Tier IV were as low as one unit per forty acres in order to prevent conversion to housing within viable agricultural lands. *See* Chapter 9, *infra.* The Ramapo timing and sequencing controls played a significant role in Tier III. The development of this area of active urbanization was regulated by a 20-year capital improvement program separating the existing urban tiers (I and II) from the rural, agricultural and open space Tier IV. Landowners in Tier IV could not suffer a *Penn Central* taking because agricultural and rural housing uses were reasonable since development in Tier III was timed and sequenced over the 20-year life of the plan and Tier IV had no projected urban capital facilities during the 20 year plan period. For a detailed analysis of the Metropolitan Plan, *see* Robert H. Freilich and John Ragsdale, *Timing and Sequential Controls, the Essential Basis for Effective Regional Planning: An Analysis of the New Directions for Land Use Control in the Minneapolis-St. Paul Metropolitan Region,* 58 MINN.L.REV. 1009 (1974).

B. Alameda County, California . . . California has judicially approved urban growth boundaries for many years. Alameda County adopted an urban growth boundary in May of 1994 covering some 418 square miles as part of the county's general plan. In November of 2000 the electorate approved an initiative ordinance that revised the general plan by shifting the urban growth boundary to lessen the amount of developable land, and shifted the removed lands to agricultural use. In *Shea Homes Ltd. Partnership v. County of Alameda*, 2 Cal.Rptr.3d 739 (Cal.App.2003), the court upheld the initiative as a valid measure to preserve agricultural and open space lands. The court rejected an exclusionary zoning challenge finding that state law provisions relating to housing requirements were fully met by the land remaining within the urban growth boundary including the channeling of development into already populated infill areas that have additional capacity to receive housing.

C.   In *Long Beach Equities, Inc. v. County of Ventura*, 282 Cal.Rptr. 877 (Cal.App.1991), Long Beach Equities (LBE) sought to build 249 single-family residences on a 250 acre parcel land it owned adjacent to the City of Simi Valley (City). LBE contended that the land use regulations of Ventura County (County) and the City, on their face and as applied, so greatly delayed its development plans as to render them economically infeasible. The County general plan guidelines established an Urban Growth Boundary, with urban development permitted inside of cities, while rural-agricultural uses with very low densities were located outside of the Urban Growth Boundary for all of the unincorporated area of the county. The general plan guidelines also incorporated adequate public facility requirements. In order to develop at non-rural higher urban densities, unincorporated land owners were required to petition for annexation within a city. Long Beach Equities applied for annexation to the City of Simi Valley and was turned down. They then applied to the County for a change of zone to allow high density uses. The rezoning was turned down. Long Beach Equities then sued the County for a taking of all or substantially all of its beneficial use and value. The California Court of Appeal held in favor of the County, finding validity in the urban/rural growth boundary distinction created by the City and County:

> "Both the County's Guidelines and the City's Growth Management Ordinance satisfy all taking tests. The County enacted the Guidelines to promote efficient and effective delivery of community services and to conserve the resources of County by encouraging urban development to occur within cities and growth outside of cities to remain rural in character with low density uses. The County's Guidelines emphasize annexation to the City as a means for developers to accomplish these purposes. The City enacted its ordinance "to protect the unique, hill-surrounded environment; enhance the quality of life; promote public health, safety or welfare and the general well-being of the community. . . ." By limiting the rate, distribution, quality and type of urban residential development on an annual basis, to the availability of adequate public services and facilities, with periodic reviews of the ongoing situation, the City seeks "to improve local air quality, reduce traffic demands . . . and ensure

that future demands for such essential services as water, sewers and the like are met. . . ." *Id.* at 885.

Fig. 7.1.

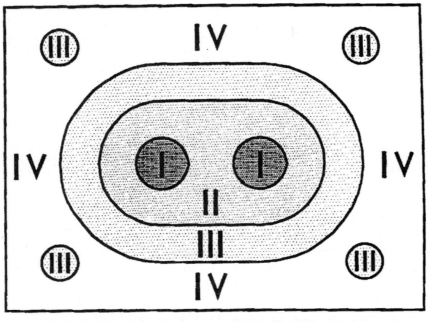

SOURCE: Peggy A Reichert, Growth Management in the Twin Cities Metropolitan Area: The Development Framework Planning Process (1976).

(b) Pattern II: Transportation Corridors

The transportation corridor is a geographic and functional area which becomes Tier II. Transportation corridors are the rapidly urbanizing areas in most communities. They provide an excellent framework for the application of established precepts of growth management and the sound integration of multi-disciplinary and intergovernmental planning. Transportation facilities are the most effective and significant growth and land use determinant. If creatively harnessed, such facilities can serve as the centerpiece for a well-conceived regional growth management system. They provide a perspective which is broader than the one from which the problem of explosive population growth is traditionally viewed—the local government. Major transportation corridors are, by nature, regional. The focus is the development of a comprehensive plan, which allows for the coordination of local, regional and state planning objectives to assure the rational and orderly development of a regional corridor, the backbone of which is a specified transportation road or transit facility.

* * * The encouragement of high density development within the corridor is a key element of the overall transportation corridor concept. By promoting high density development adjacent to transportation facilities within the corridor, the use of mass transportation and multimodal transportation facilities is encouraged and a sufficient client base is established to help make the massive expenditures required to construct high speed or rapid transit more feasible. High speed and mass transit reduce the dependency of the automobile as a source of travel, effectively reducing energy needs and despoliation of the environment.

As the situs of high density development, the corridor becomes the focus for the state's developmental activity where major commercial, office, industrial and high density residential development occurs, assuring that employment and a proper mix of housing is available within the state. By encouraging high density residential development of property immediately adjacent to transportation facilities, the unique transportation needs of the elderly and the handicapped are more easily met. By the promotion of high density development within the corridor through joint development and other governmental techniques such as transfer of development rights and bonus and incentive zoning, the public sector is more easily able to protect non-corridor environmentally sensitive land, agricultural lands and provide for open space to break urban sprawl and maintain an urban-rural balance within the state.

Robert H. Freilich and Stephen P. Chinn, *Transportation Corridors: Shaping and Financing Urbanization Through Integration of Eminent Domain, Zoning and Growth Management Techniques*, 55 UMKC L.REV. 153 (1987); Robert H. Freilich and S. Mark White, *Transportation Congestion and Growth Management: Comprehensive Approaches to Resolving America's Major Quality of Life Crisis*, 24 LOY.L.A.L.REV. 915 (1991), and Robert H. Freilich and S. Mark White, *The Interaction of Land Use Planning and Transportation Management: Lessons from the American Experience*, Transport Policy 101–115 (1994).

A.   The Washington, D.C., Regional Radial Transportation Corridors Plan

Subsequent to World War II, as with many regions, the Washington, D.C., area experienced a surge of outward suburban growth. In 1969 the Metro Washington Council of Governments adopted "The Radial Corridor Year 2000 Plan" to channel growth. In lieu of a compact urban growth boundary, the Urbanizing Tier II would become transportation corridors.

Fig. 7.2.

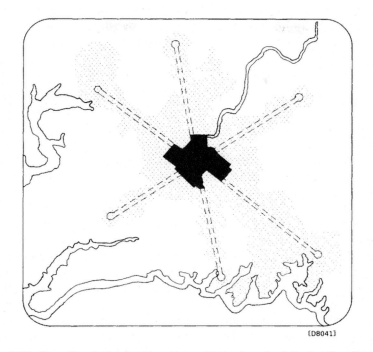

[D8041]

Year 2000 Plan—The Radial Corridor, Metro. Wash. Council of Gov'ts, The Changing Regions: A Comparison of Plans and Policies With Development Trends (1969).

B.   Montgomery County, Maryland

Lying directly north of the District of Columbia, Montgomery County utilized the I-270 transportation corridor as the base for its growth management system and tied the system to Ramapo's adequate public facility timed and phased growth program (see fig. 7.1). Similar to the system used in Ramapo, Montgomery County's adequate public facilities ordinance (APFO) requirements are enforced through the subdivision process; but, unlike Ramapo, it was based on level of service (LOS) standards rather than a point system. Montgomery County utilized adequate public facilities not only to regulate the timing of development in the Urbanizing Transportation Corridor Tier but also to achieve a balance between jobs and housing and to preserve its agricultural lands through transfers of development rights to high density projects within the corridor.

The Montgomery County ordinance, (Montgomery County, Maryland, Code ch. 50, § 50–35(k)) divides the county into policy areas in which growth ceilings are established for jobs and housing. Flexible growth ceilings and LOS standards are established for areas served by public transit and for affordable housing. Similar to Ramapo's adequate public facilities requirement, Montgomery County enforces its APFO through the subdivision process, imposing adequate public facilities requirements at the preliminary plat stage. The APFO allows a lower roadway LOS where public transit is available. This technique maintains the integrity of the APFO system while encouraging development to occur in the Urbanizing Tier where alternative transportation capacity is available.

Specifically, the LOS standards are assigned within "policy areas," which are aggregations of traffic zones. A "staging ceiling" is established for the policy area. The staging ceiling is the maximum amount of residential and employment growth that may occur within the policy area without exceeding the adopted LOS. LOS standards apply to the entire policy area and are used to calculate the maximum level of congestion and development that can occur without exceeding the assigned LOS. Separate staging ceilings are calculated for residential and employment-generating growth to effectuate an appropriate jobs-housing balance. Where ceiling limits are exceeded by approved, and/or approved-but-unbuilt ("pipeline") traffic, a moratorium is declared for subdivision applications for that type of use. LOS standards are assigned to reflect the availability of public transportation. Local area review is applied where (1) the project is above a certain threshold size and (2) the project is near a congested intersection (level of service D), or if the policy area is within 5 percent of the staging ceiling. The APFO is monitored annually through the adoption of an "annual growth policy" in which various political subdivisions of the county interested in its enforcement review the staging ceiling and administrative reform.

An important feature is the use of joint public-private development along its three major I-270 interstate corridor interchanges. The transportation corridor includes both vehicular transportation (I-270) and the major rail line coming out of Washington, D.C. The county has been able to assemble land around the interchanges; install sewer, water, and other essential public facilities; and lease the land out to private development, retaining a percentage of revenue earned. All corridor improvements are financed by an excise tax on the square footage of new buildings and structures, which was upheld in *Eastern Diversified Properties v. Montgomery County*, 570 A.2d 850 (Md.1990). Excise taxes are far superior to impact fees since neither *Nollan* nexus, nor and *Dolan* rough proportionality is required. *Bloom v. City of Fort Collins*, 784 P.2d 304 (Colo.1989) (identifies five methods of raising funds for infrastructure finance: utility fees, charges and rates; excise tax; special assessment; impact fees, and ad valorem property taxation). *See* Eric J. Strauss and Martin L. Leitner, *Financing Public Facilities with Development Excise Taxes: An Alternative to Exaction and Impact Fees*, 11 ZONING & PLAN.L.REP. 1, 17–22 (Mar. 1988).

Fig. 7.3

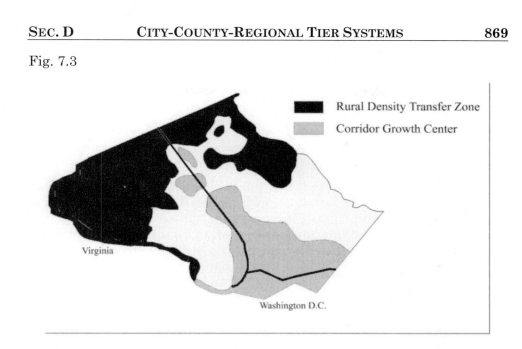

C.   Central Puget Sound, Washington, Transportation Corridor Regional Rail System: Seattle to Tacoma

Rapid growth in the Central Puget Sound Metropolitan Area threatened to destroy the area's quality of life and, with it, the jobs and industrial base needed to sustain future growth. *See* Metropolitan Washington Council of Governments, Task Force on Growth and Transportation: A Legacy of Excellence for the Washington Region, Task Force Report on Growth and Transportation (June 1991). In response to these issues, the Washington state legislature adopted a planning framework for harnessing this growth and simultaneously encouraging the potential for economic development. Statewide growth management and planning legislation was passed to incorporate the *Ramapo* techniques of timing and phasing of development in accordance with adequate public facilities by establishing the following three goals:

1.   Reduce urban sprawl by encouraging growth to occur where "adequate public facilities and services can be provided in an efficient manner."

2.   Provide "efficient multimodal transportation systems."

3.   "Ensure that those public facilities and services necessary to support development shall be adequate to serve the development at the time the development is available for occupancy and use without decreasing current service levels below locally established minimum standards."

See Richard L. Settle & Charles G. Gavigan, *The Growth Management Revolution in Washington: Past, Present, and Future*, 16 U.PUGET SOUND

L.REV. 867, 869 (1993); and Robert H. Freilich, Elizabeth A. Garvin & S. Mark White, *Economic Development and Public Transit: Making the Most of the Washington Growth Management Act*, 16 U.PUGET SOUND L.REV. 949, 954 (1993).

The 1990 Growth Management Act (GMA), Wash.Rev.Code § 36.70A.040, requires all levels of government to adopt comprehensive growth management plans and implementing regulations.

Counties required to plan (the 4 Puget Sound Counties) are required to delineate twenty-year urban growth areas (UGAs). The legislation requires transportation concurrency, a policy that requires the cities or counties to identify funding for transportation facilities, transportation facility deficits, and the future needs on a ten-year time frame. Thus, the Washington legislation recognized the Ramapo adequate public facilities (also referred to as "concurrency") concept and its implementation at the local level of government.

Using a set of targeted incentives designed to encourage development around transit station stops, Professor Freilich recommended that the region utilize a transportation corridor center approach running down the spine of I-5, which would ultimately grow into a full-fledged transit corridor system (see fig. 7–3). These incentives would target development in two key geographic locations: transit corridor centers and infill development areas, in order to control sprawl beyond the urbanizing tier.

Fig. 7.4.

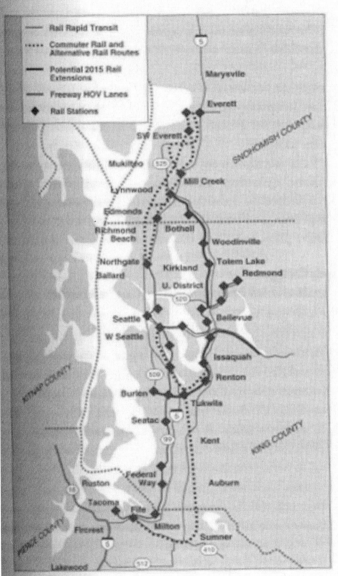

2. FREESTANDING URBAN CENTERS AND NEW TOWNS

(a) Baltimore County, Maryland

Maryland's population has increased by twenty-two percent over the last twenty years. The population is expected to increase by 1 million by the year 2020. Much of Maryland's population lies within heavily traveled transportation corridors, near major passenger and freight railroads and interstate highways which cover its length on the east coast. *See* David L. Winstead, Secretary of Transportation-Maryland, *Smart Growth, Smart Transportation: A New Program to Manage Growth in Maryland*, 30 URBAN LAWYER 537 (1998). While the older central cities and urban areas have declined in population, much farm land and forest has been devoured by suburban sprawl development. Abandoned urban areas and loss of open space created great concern for Maryland. In 1997, the legislature reacted, adopting a "Smart Growth" initiative. *See* Chapter 759, Md.Code Ann. (1997). Maryland actually coined the term "Smart Growth" in its innovative 1997 legislation. Because transportation is a prevalent factor in controlling growth in Maryland, the new program emphasizes system maintenance to achieve greater mobility from highway and other modal systems. The legislation also has a provision to encourage redevelopment of contaminated sites and tax incentives to create a better mix of housing and jobs. *See* Maryann Froehlich, *Smart Growth: Why Local Governments Are Taking a New Approach to Managing Growth in Their Communities*, Public Mgmt. 5 (May 1998), 1998 WL 10328353. Nevertheless, the Maryland counties have weakened the backbone of the Smart Growth program by failing to enforce transportation concurrency, *see* J. Celeste Sakowicz, *Urban Sprawl: Florida's and Maryland's Approaches*, 19 J.LAND USE & ENVTL.L. 377, 405 (2004) (stating that "The effect of softening the rigidity of transportation concurrency is to sacrifice traffic congestion for policies preferred by the current local government.").

While Maryland is a home-rule state, where local governments have much control over land-use decisions, the State has given itself a new role in controlling urban sprawl. Maryland's Smart Growth initiative is designed to encourage compact development and direct capital facilities financing to "priority funding areas." *See* Md.Code Ann. State Fin. & Proc. §§ 5–7B–10. Under the Smart Growth initiative, localities have the power to designate these funding areas within state mandated restrictions that generally require the areas be capable of supporting growth (be industrial in nature or already served by sewer systems). Similar to the Ramapo system, discussed *supra*, the Smart Growth initiative allows Maryland the opportunity to influence, if not control, local land decisions by only funding projects in priority and smart locations—those in urbanized areas where adequate public facilities are prevalent or can be easily provided. For a discussion of Maryland's growth initiative, *see* Frece and Leahy-Fucheck,

Smart Growth and Neighborhood Conservation, 13 NAT.RES. & ENV'T 319 (1998). Much of the direction for the "Smart Growth" state initiative came from Baltimore County's innovative growth management program.

Baltimore County, Maryland in undertaking its growth management program stressed four major New Town Urban Centers as its Tier II urbanizing areas for accelerated growth. These centers included existing or designated commercial and town centers and their surrounding residential areas. The county was divided into the following tiers: (1) Tier I—Existing Communities (all areas of the county that are already built-up or urbanized); (2) Tier II—Urbanizing Growth areas (areas presently sewered or planned to be sewered within 10 years); and (3) Tier III—Rural and Agricultural Areas (areas not planned for sewer extensions or with soils with high agricultural productivity). New Development Areas within Tier II recommended for staged accelerated growth included three major urban "new towns" which were particularly suited as mixed use active development centers, Owings Mills, Reisterstown, and White Marsh. See Baltimore County Growth Management Program, 1979–2009, Baltimore County, Maryland.

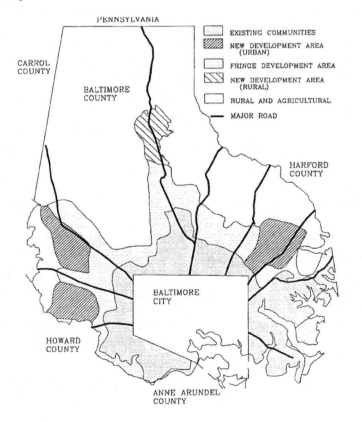

(b) City of San Diego, California (Transportation Corridors and Freestanding "New Towns")

Techniques selected to manage growth on the urbanizing fringe will often stimulate growth in the central city and vacant areas in the urban service area. A prime example of this phenomenon is found in the San Diego experience. In its Progress Guide and General Plan, the City of San Diego (520 square miles), in 1979 adopted a transportation corridor-major activity "new town" mixed use centers tier approach, coupled tied to 30-year growth management program. The general plan established three major tiers: Tier I, the Urbanized Area (UA), 167 square miles of downtown and existing built up adjacent neighborhoods; Tier II, the Planned Urbanizing Area (PUA); and Tier III (FUA), the permanent open space and urban reserve areas. Tier II followed of the San Diego-Tijuana light rail trolley and the I-5, I-8 and I-15 transportation corridors, emphasizing large mixed use "new town" communities at the major intersections of the corridors. The growth management system was designed to redistribute growth with a specific objective to transfer a greater proportion of new growth to the Tier! Urbanized Area, reversing the prior 30 year sprawl pattern of growth. Objectives for the UA included strengthening the viability of the central areas through renewal, redevelopment, and new construction; attracting more intensive and varied land uses including office, administrative, residential and entertainment; and conserving the socio-economic character of older neighborhoods.

Prior to 1979, the estimated distribution of growth was 90% in the PUA and 10% in the UA and FUA. A goal was established to change the percentages to 50% in the PUA and 50% in the UA in order to more efficiently utilize existing public facilities and services. These goals were met in only 4 years, according to a June 24, 1983 Planning Department Information Report (No. 83–289):

1979–1983 Population Growth				1979–1983 Housing Units Added		
	46,233	UA	(60%)		15,921	UA	(62%)
	28,216	PUA	(36%)		9,958	PUA	(38%)
	2,951	FUA	(4%)				
Total	77,400			Total	25,879	

The major factor contributing to the dramatic reversal in the location of growth was the fiscal incentive favoring the Urbanized Area, Tier I. Building in older areas where public services were available, reduced housing costs in comparison to new growth areas where development was required to finance needed capital infrastructure.

The FUA was zoned rural and agricultural and consisted of primarily vacant land which was part of the open space and urban reserve for the 30-year life of the Plan. Subsequent general plan amendments and city-wide initiatives have changed the FUA to permanent open space and rural. Tax relief is provided to landowners in the FUA by preferential tax assessment under the state's Williamson Act. *See* Chapter 9D3, *infra*.

The PUA and the UA together provide sufficient land for development of the city according to the 30 year projected population growth. In the PUA, additional public investment is necessary to complete development and to allow growth of communities to be served by capital facilities over the life of the plan. Land is to be opened for urbanization in a timed, phased and contiguous manner through orderly extension of adequate public facilities. Developers are required to bear the prime responsibility for financing the infrastructure through facilities benefit assessments as was discussed in Chapter 4, *supra*.

Growth along the I-5 Corridor in the Planned Urbanizing Area was to be concentrated in two major freestanding mixed use communities (North City West and University City) whose new town planning had already begun prior to the 1979 plan adoption, and was adopted into the General Plan Growth Management Progress Guide. The following case illustrates the dramatic change from low density suburban to high density "new town" mixed use activity center. The outrage of the wealthy low density suburban city of Del Mar to the north culminated in one of the nation's great regional general welfare cases following *Mount Laurel* and *Livermore* which we analyzed in Chapter 5. The litigation hastened the judicial recognition of growth management, new urbanism, high density sustainability, by extending the doctrine of regional general welfare outside of the exclusionary zoning arena.

CITY OF DEL MAR v. CITY OF SAN DIEGO
Court of Appeal, Fourth District, California, 1982.
133 Cal.App.3d 401, 183 Cal.Rptr. 898.

WIENER, ASSOCIATE JUSTICE.

This appeal by the City of Del Mar (Del Mar) describes the negative, almost frightening, physical, social and financial costs imposed upon society by the further urbanization of the City of San Diego (San Diego) in its creation of the new community called North City West. Del Mar's emotionally compelling narrative challenges San Diego's willingness to extend its megalopolis northward changing the sparse development of approximately 4,286 acres of agricultural land located 20 miles from downtown San Diego to a bustling urban enclave consisting at completion of about 40,000 people from the upper and middle classes living in expensive homes. The record reveals the dynamic political process extending for more than a decade which has culminated in this litigation. Public hearings relating to the policy of growth management of San Diego, including the meaning, significance and implementation of maintaining what is blithely described as the "quality of life," has consumed innumerable hours involving various interested segments of society over the last several years. The voluminous and complex reports from the various consultants and planning departments on diverse subjects all related to urban planning have been reviewed, re-examined, argued and voted upon. Now, as was probably inevitable from the start, the almost irresolvable question of whether San Diego acted correctly in giving its threshold approval for the first phase of implementation of North City West rests with the courts. Understandably, the judicial function differs considerably from that of other branches of government. The trial court approved San Diego's actions. Our analysis, provided the trial court applied the correct legal standards, is necessarily limited to whether substantial evidence supports that judgment. As we shall explain, although it is undisputed the project will have numerous adverse environmental impacts on the region, we nevertheless conclude that San Diego did not abuse its discretion in approving the steps at issue here as a rational accommodation of the social, economic and environmental interests with which the city must concern itself. We will, therefore, affirm the trial court's decision denying a writ of mandate and declaratory relief.

Planning for North City West began over 12 years ago. On June 8, 1971, a "Statement of Planning Principles" governing the North City planning program was adopted by the San Diego City Council. In August of 1972, a study by the planning department of the City of San Diego entitled "New Communities, Background Study Considerations for New Communities" was presented to the city council. Nine development phases are planned, with completion of the entire project estimated near the year 2000. Although primarily residential, North City West, located near the northern boundary of the City of San Diego, is designed to incorporate many self-contained community concepts; one of the nine development phases is scheduled to be an employment center and commercial service centers will be located at various points in the project. Plans call for developers and landowners to finance the capital costs associated with providing needed governmental services for the community. Carmel Valley is the first of the nine phases scheduled for development. Situated on 358 acres, it will contain 2,065 units of various types including single family, duplex, cluster and garden apartments. Population for the phase is projected at approximately 5,000 persons.

In 1979, the San Diego City Council approved the North City West Planned District Ordinance, the Carmel Valley Precise Plan, and the Carmel Valley Precise Plan Design Element which provide the necessary zoning, regulations and procedures for the submission of subdivision maps and development plans of the Carmel Valley phase [which were incorporated into the City's new General Plan Progress Guide and Growth Management Element.

Within weeks of San Diego's action, Del Mar sought a writ of mandate and declaratory relief challenging San Diego's approval of the North City

West Planned District Ordinance, the Carmel Valley Precise Plan, and the Carmel Valley Precise Plan Design Element on three grounds. It claimed (1) San Diego failed to comply with the mandates of the California Environmental Quality Act (CEQA); (2) San Diego's approval of the project failed to adequately consider the welfare of the entire San Diego region as required by *Associated Home Builders etc., Inc. v. City of Livermore*, 557 P.2d 473 (1976); and (3) the approvals were inconsistent with the San Diego General Plan objective to provide adequate housing opportunities for persons of low and moderate incomes.

Earlier we touched upon the enormity of the problem in resolving the relevant considerations of urban planning to the satisfaction of all concerned. What is so easily stated as a goal is in reality a difficult and trying process of accommodating environmental interests and housing needs in an ever-burgeoning population. Here, several critical issues and considerations cut across the specific legal causes of action brought by Del Mar. Legal challenges to such an approval, regardless of the label, generally take issue with the nature of the balance struck between those interests. The discussion which follows will first analyze Del Mar's Livermore challenge.

The Livermore Challenge:

North City West and the Regional Welfare

Del Mar challenges the North City West approvals as an improper exercise of San Diego's police power. Recognizing that any zoning decision involves a cost-benefit accommodation of competing interests, Del Mar's attack is two-pronged. On the cost side, Del Mar points to the substantial adverse environmental impacts on the San Diego region which will result from the North City West development. Del Mar argues that San Diego improperly ignored numerous opportunities to mitigate the effect of the development on air pollution levels, water supplies, sewage treatment capabilities and energy consumption. On the benefits side, Del Mar contends that North City West is an ineffective contribution to solution of the regional housing need because attempts to provide low and moderate income housing opportunities within the development are inadequate. Thus, by focusing upon the regional cost and questioning the regional benefit, Del Mar argues that the North City West approvals are unreasonable.

* * * Land use regulation was and is an attempt to mitigate these "spillover" effects for the overall benefit of the community. Just as persons have congregated in increasing numbers within municipalities, so too have municipalities become clustered within expansive urban regions. San Diego County, for instance, encompasses 16 municipalities. And in some parts of the state, these regions cut across the boundaries of several counties. But just as land use decisions by individual property owners often have effects on their neighbors, so too do the effects of land use decisions by individual municipalities "spill over" into the entire urban region. In *Associated Home Builders, etc., Inc. v. City of Livermore*, 557 P.2d 473 (1976), the California Supreme Court reviewed the validity of a municipal land use ordinance which had significant spillover effects on the entire San Francisco Bay region. Pursuant to an initiative, the citizens of Livermore enacted an ordinance which imposed a moratorium on the issuance of residential building permits until local educational, sewage treatment and water supply facilities met specified standards. Since the initiative precluded new residential construction within the city, it had the effect of shifting the burden of providing new housing to other communities in the San Francisco Bay area—a substantial spillover. In determining whether the initiative was a legitimate exercise of Livermore's police power, the court noted, "[M]unicipalities are not isolated islands remote from the needs and problems of the area in which they are located; thus an ordinance, superficially reasonable from the limited viewpoint of the municipality, may be disclosed as unreasonable when viewed from a larger perspective." Although rejecting an argument that spillover ordinances should be subject to strict scrutiny—invalid unless necessary to achieve a compelling state interest—the court nonetheless required municipalities to evaluate more than their local self-interest in enacting such land use regulations.

* * *

Although Livermore and the instant case are similar in that both involve significant regional spillovers, it is also important to recognize some relevant distinctions. The Livermore ordinance was exclusionary in character. In Justice Mosk's words, Livermore sought to "build a Chinese Wall to insulate itself from growth problems. . . .". By refusing to permit new housing construction, Livermore was able to shift the entire burden of the regional need for new housing to other localities in the region. By contrast, the North City West approvals are inclusionary in nature. San Diego has attempted to provide for its share of regional new housing need. Although Del Mar argues that substantial adverse environmental impacts will beset the region as a result of the construction of North City West, San Diego is in no way shielded from these impacts. There are clearly regional spillovers which San Diego must take into account, but unlike Livermore, San Diego is not able to shift the entire burden of its zoning decision to other municipalities in the region. In that sense, the San Diego action is considerably less suspect.

* * *

The approvals by the City of San Diego of the Carmel Valley Precise Plan, the Carmel Valley Design Element and the Planned District Ordinance whether viewed alone, or in conjunction with City of San Diego [growth management] land-use policies, promote the general welfare of the region significantly affected thereby in that:

"a. They provide needed housing in the region and in the north San Diego area and serve to satisfy housing demand in those areas;

"b. They aid in the reasonable distribution of new development along major transportation corridors and from a geographical standpoint within San Diego and the region;

"c. They provide for residences near employment centers;

"d. They will provide employment opportunities in the region and generally benefit the economy of the region;

"e. The north city and north county areas will probably experience substantial population growth without the approvals and may undergo incremental growth of negative patterns without an overall plan."

Del Mar proceeds on the premise that North City West will cause all the various regional impacts which it documents, or that in other words, but for North City West, the articulated impacts would not occur. San Diego, on the other hand, views itself as merely planning for the inevitable population growth of the north city region. Under San Diego's approach, North City West will cause few if any of the impacts cited by Del Mar. In fact, the planned foundation of the North City West community will in many cases mitigate the adverse impacts which would otherwise be caused by unplanned piecemeal development.

* * *

Within our purview, the evidence includes the County of San Diego's estimate that north county population in the year 2000 will be 26,000 persons less if North City West is built. This constitutes more than substantial evidence to support the trial court's finding that "[i]f the North City West community planning area were not built as planned, residents would still come to live in the areas of the north county and north City. . . ." Moreover, the addition of 26,000 additional persons to north county would create many if not most of the same adverse regional impacts which North City West's 40,000 residents will. By accepting growth within the city rather than shifting it to smaller municipalities and the unincorporated areas of the county, San Diego can hardly be accused of pursuing its own self-interest at the expense of the regional welfare. Moreover, the self-contained community concepts utilized in the North City West design tend to mitigate the adverse air quality effects by reducing the need for automobiles and lessening trip distances.

* * *

In conclusion, applying the standard enunciated in *Associated Home Builders etc., Inc. v. City of Livermore, supra,* we conclude that San Diego's approval of the North City West Planned District Ordinance and the

Carmel Valley Precise Plan and Design Element bears a real and substantial relationship to the general welfare of the entire San Diego region. We will not presume that San Diego will act unreasonably in the future, and we therefore affirm the judgment of the trial court. * * *

COMMENT: NEW TOWNS

New Towns have long been part of sound urban planning, in effect, the early embodiment of what is today called "smart growth." In the early twentieth century, the British "Garden City" movement, which was the genesis of modern-day new towns, was started by Sir Ebenezer Howard, ("Garden Cities of Tomorrow", 1898). This movement was a reaction against the dirty, crowded cities associated with the industrial revolution. Howard's three pre-World War I English garden cities, Welwyn Garden City, Letchworth and Stevenage, were located well away from urban centers, and emphasized open space buffers around the community to maintain individuality, while separating commercial and industrial activities.

In the American adaptation, neighborhoods were typically based on quarter sections (160 acres) with major streets bounding neighborhoods one-half mile apart with no through traffic. Americans adapting his garden city concept did not consider his vision to be one of "sprawl and scatter." A key element of Howard's vision involved the "planned dispersal" of employment and population to these self-contained new towns that provide a mix of industry, services and residential dwelling types.

1.   New Towns in America (1925–1929)

Clarence Stein and Henry Wright imported Howard's "garden city" concept to the United States. Beginning in 1923 Stein and Wright collaborated on the plan for Sunnyside Gardens, a neighborhood of the New York City borough of Queens. The 77-acre low-rise pedestrian-oriented development was constructed between 1924 and 1929. It took the garden city ideas of Sir Ebenezer Howard as a model. This neighborhood has retained its special character and has been listed on the National Register of Historical Places.

In Radburn (Fair Lawn, New Jersey), the designers incorporated a series of individual subdivisions known as superblocks in order to address America's "automobile-based suburban market." The superblock involved long cul-de-sacs to the front of homes, with sidewalks connecting the homes at the rear. The sidewalks framed an internalized open space system and the entire community was separated by a greenbelt from adjacent development. Unfortunately, Radburn was never completely finished because of the depression and after World War II melded into the surrounding suburban sprawl. Radburn is listed on the National Register of Historical Places. For a complete analysis of the 1920s new towns, see Clarence Stein, *Towards New Towns in America* (1951).

2.   New Deal New Towns (1934–1941)

Stein's ideals were incorporated into three New Towns built during the Depression, with depressing bureaucratic names: Greenbelt, Maryland; Greenhills, Ohio; and Greendale, Wisconsin. These towns were built simultaneously by the New Deal's Resettlement Administration, but were never fully implemented and were eventually sold to private entities. *See* Frederick J. Osborne, *Greenbelt Cities* 29 (2d ed.1971). Unfortunately, much of Greenhills, Ohio is being torn down despite its classification on the National Register of Historic Places. *See* Tracie Rozhon, *New Deal Architecture Faces Bulldozer*, N.Y. Times, February 9, 2009 at A-1.

3.   World War II New Towns (1941–1945)

New Towns during the World War II era were prompted by the federal government's wartime initiatives for creation of the Atomic bomb. These include the small towns of the Tennessee Valley Authority ("TVA") and the "atomic cities" of Los Alamos, Richland, Oak Ridge, and Hanford. These communities were established by the Atomic Energy Commission to provide employee housing. The hydroelectric plants and atomic energy facilities of these towns provided a local economic base. These were essentially government "company towns," but were eventually sold to the private sector as the result of the complexities of government ownership.

4.   Private New Towns (1960–1968)

Private new towns emerged during 1960–1968 with the development of Reston, Virginia; Columbia, Maryland; and Irvine, California. These are large-scale, mixed use communities with neighborhoods organized around villages and town centers. These developments emerged as a response to market demands and developers' visions, and are continuing their buildout today. These communities have achieved many of their objectives. For example, Reston has excellent jobs-housing balance with 40,000 jobs and 63,000 residents, while the "new town-in town" at the Stapleton Airport area in Denver on 4,000 acres will have 35,000 jobs with 30,000 residents, an even more impressive ratio. *See* Ann Forsyth, *Planning Lessons from Three New Towns of the 1960s and 1970s*, 68 J.AM.PLAN.ASS'N 387 (2002).

5.   Public-Private Towns (1967–1972)

Public-private New Towns from 1967–1972 were developed under the New Communities Act of 1968 (formerly 42 U.S.C. §§ 3901–14). The concepts of the New Communities Act were carried forward by the Urban Growth and New Community Development Act of 1970 (formerly 42 U.S.C. § 4511), which increased federal incentives for new town development. Communities developed under the federal new town legislation included Jonathan, Minnesota; The Woodlands; Texas; St. Charles Communities, Maryland; and Park Forest South, Illinois. *See* Ann Forsyth, *Planning Lessons from Three New Towns of the 1960s and 1970s*, 68 J.AM.PLAN.ASS'N 387 (2002).

6.   Modern Day "New Towns" and "New-Towns-In-Town"

Patterns of growth have been dramatically changed in the past three decades by a consortium of ideas on developing more compact, walkable, mixed land use, energy/environmentally sustainable communities designed to combat urban sprawl and promote revitalization of cities and older suburbs. Building upon the history and ideas of the New Town movement as well as modern day realities of the need to accommodate growth near existing communities of varying sizes, a modern day New-Town has the following characteristics:

- new urban activity centers and communities designated on the future land use map and located within an existing city or geographically separated from existing urban areas and other New Towns.

- sufficient size, population and use composition to support a variety of economic and social activities consistent with an urban area designation.

- incorporates basic economic activities; all major land use categories, with the possible exception of agriculture and heavy industry; and a centrally provided full range of public facilities and services.

- designation on a future land use map as a new urban activity center and master planned community located within or adjacent to an existing city or urban area.

- memorialized by a specific development plan that sets forth compatible land uses and design guidelines and balances the distribution of land uses to provide for jobs-housing balance, preservation of environmentally sensitive lands and open spaces.

- located along a transportation corridor.

- encourages residents and workers to walk, ride bicycles, or use public transit to addition to automobiles as a means of transportation.

- concentrate development around transportation nodes within developed areas, thus preserving rural, open space, agricultural, and environmental lands.

See H. Pike Oliver and D. Scott Middleton, *Developing Successful New Communities* (1991).

New-Towns-In-Town differ slightly from New Towns in that they are not located in isolation, but are within or adjacent to an existing community. Their design and development is necessarily within the context of the existing city and considers the social and economic circumstances of not only the new residents of the development but also those of the existing city. However, the New Town concepts of creating community with a balance of land uses and building forms, from apartments to town houses, local commercial and public facilities, remains the same in the New-Town-In-Town. Indeed, the New-Town-In-Town is a confluence of the concepts of smart growth and new urbanism with New Town principles when located adjacent to existing communities. For a comprehensive treatment of new towns, *see* Robert H. Freilich, Robert J. Sitkowski and Seth D. Mennillo, *From Sprawl to Sustainability: Smart Growth, New Urbanism, Green Development and Renewable Energy* 157–168 (ABA, Section of State and Local Government 2010).

7.   Stapleton Airport—Denver, Colorado, New-Town-In-Town

The community of Stapleton in Denver, Colorado, is now recognized as a regional and national model for sustainable growth in the twenty-first century. Stapleton is a master-planned new-town-in-town on the 4,700-acre former Stapleton International Airport in Denver. Redevelopment of the site began in 2001, and Stapleton is already home to more than 6,000 residents and 13,000 jobs. Build-out of the community is expected in 2020 and will include

- 30,000 residents,
- 12,000 homes and apartments,
- 13 million square feet of commercial uses,
- 35,000 jobs, and
- 1,100 acres of new parks and open space.

Plans to build Stapleton began in the early 1990s. The Stapleton Development Foundation, a nonprofit group financed by private philanthropy, was created in 1990 as a civic vehicle to develop a public/private partnership that would maximize public benefits of redevelopment. The Foundation worked with the City in defining a long-term management structure for the Stapleton program.

In 1995, after two years of extensive community outreach, the Foundation produced the Stapleton Development Plan, which was adopted a short while later by the Denver City Council. In November of that same year, the nonprofit Stapleton Development Corporation (SDC) was formed as a vehicle to lease and sell Stapleton Property. Forest City Enterprises, Inc., a national real estate company with a commitment to mixed use urban infill projects, was selected to be SDC's development partner.

Since then, Forest City has purchased portions of Stapleton and has worked with the City of Denver, citizens' groups, and scores of design, financial, and legal experts to make the Stapleton Development Plan become a reality. As planned, Stapleton echoes the design elements found in Denver's older neighborhoods and the principles promoted by the Congress of New Urbanism. Stapleton homes feature front porches and smaller lots with public open space as gathering places. Sidewalks and greenbelts now encourage pedestrian activity, as village shops and restaurants are within walking distance of most residences. Less than half complete, Stapleton has already become an economic boon for the area, generating $5.7 billion for the Metro Denver region. At build-out Stapleton is expected to generate upwards of $36.3 billion. The community has also received international acclaim as one of the most desirable and successful new urban communities in the nation. For a complete description of Denver-Stapleton Airport, *see* Francesca Ortiz, *Smart Growth and Innovative Design: An Analysis of the New Community*, 34 ENVT'L L.RPTR. 10003 (2004).

E. STATES WITH BINDING SMART GROWTH PLANNING

1. INTRODUCTION

Since the promulgation of the Standard City Zoning Enabling Act in 1926, the use of planning and land use regulatory power, which constitutionally resides in the states, was historically transferred to cities and counties. *See* Clifford L. Weaver and Richard F. Babcock, *City Zoning: The Once and Future Frontier* (1980); Stuart Meck, ed. *Growing Smart Legislative Guidebook: Model Statutes for Planning and the Management of Change* (American Planning Assoc. 2002). Undoubtedly it is better to have some growth management of development located here and there, rather than none, but a cohesive and strategic plan of land use goals, policies and regulations borne out of state-required or incentivized inter-governmental cooperation would likely produce a sum greater than its parts. Governments cooperating in this manner could identify and assess the relative priorities of local, regional and statewide concerns, needs and desires regarding, among other things, public utilities, capital facilities, roads, and preservation of agricultural and environmentally sensitive lands. A noted legal scholar, James A. Kushner, has stated that states are in a powerful position to advance sustainable planning and development:

> Smart Growth policies would include mandating a statewide plan for open space, forestation, food supply, and most importantly transportation by public transit and rail development. Planning laws can mandate local and regional governments [to undertake] sustainable master plans that call for dense, mixed use neighborhoods around transit stops—sitting of retail, industry and office centers would be limited to transit serve land.

James A Kushner, *Global Climate Change and the Road to Extinction: The Legal and Planning Response*, Carolina Academic Press (2009).

Currently, a threefold approach is utilized by states consisting of growth management, environmental sustainability and new urbanism legislation for controlling sprawl and unplanned sprawl development, which has come to be known under the umbrella of sustainability. *See* Patricia E. Salkin, *Squaring The Circles on Sprawl: Sustainable Land Use In The States*, 16 WIDENER L.J. 787 (2007); Steven G. Davidson, *Regulation of Emission of Greenhouse Gases and Hazardous Air Pollutants From Motor Vehicles*, 1 PITT.J.ENVT'L PUB.HEALTH 1 (2006); J.R. DeShazo and Jody Freeman, *Timing and Form of Federal Regulation: The Case of*

Climate Change, 155 U.PA.L.REV. 1499 (2007) (supporting state regulation to speed up federal climate control regulation). *See also* Conn.Gen.Stat. Ann. § 16(a)–27 (2005), requiring every local government to include a planning element in its comprehensive plan providing for integrating transportation and land use to create high density housing and mixed use development around transit stops.

This Section explores the variety of state planning and sustainability legislation, much of it focusing on the use of regional "tiered" growth strategies stemming from the *Ramapo* case. *See* Thomas G. Pelham, *From the Ramapo Plan to Florida's Statewide Concurrency System: Ramapo's Influence on Infrastructure Planning*, 35 URBAN LAWYER 113 (2003). State legislation in green development and sustainability will be considered in Chapter 8, *infra*. Such legislation coordinates local planning with state goals, and often involves joint city-county and regional transportation-land use-greenhouse gas emission planning. The Urbanizing Tier becomes the most critical area of importance for controlling sprawl, largely because utilizing the Ramapo system of timing and sequencing of adequate public facilities and services ultimately controls the pace and location of development in metropolitan areas. A common foundation shared by each state's legislation, and ultimately its sustainability strategy, is the utilization of creative and flexible programs developed by regional and metropolitan planning agencies embedded in land use, air quality, environmental and transportation plans. New state legislation conjoins smart growth, renewable energy, global warming, sustainability, and new urbanism strategies with regional land use, transportation, air quality, affordable housing, and infrastructure provision. *See* Robert H. Freilich and Neil M. Popowitz, *The Umbrella of Sustainability: Smart Growth, New Urbanism, Renewable Energy and Green Development in the 21st Century*, 42 URBAN LAWYER 1 (2010).

2. CALIFORNIA'S 2008 SUSTAINABLE GROWTH MANAGEMENT LEGISLATION COMBINING LAND USE, TRANSPORTATION, ENVIRONMENTAL QUALITY AND GLOBAL WARMING (SB 375)

(a) Early State Policy and Legislative Initiatives

California started early with innovative legislation relating to coastal zone management, Cal. Coastal Zone Management Act, Public Resources Code §§ 30600 et seq., and mandatory environmental review. California Environmental Quality Act, Public. Resources Code §§ 15125 et seq. (CEQA). CEQA has become the main source of state judicial review of city and county plans, regulation and development approvals. The definition of environmental impact requiring review was so broadly interpreted by the courts that the state foolishly thought it unnecessary to adopt substantive state or regional planning. Indeed, the failure to confront sprawl led to a condemnatory report by the Southern California Studies Center and Brookings Institution Center on Urban and Metropolitan Policy: Sprawl Hits the Wall: Confronting The Realities of Metropolitan Los Angeles, 10 (2001).

The first emerging sign of state involvement was the development of the State's Strategic Growth Plan commissioned by Governor Wilson in 1991 pursuant to Executive Order W–2–91. The resultant 1993 Strategic Growth Plan in part prepared in part by Professor Freilich for the State Office of Planning and Research, established a number of planning policies to address California's rapid growth demands:

> Plan strategies shall include establishing efficient growth patterns that link job growth and housing within regions or sub regions. This includes voluntary statewide growth guidelines that encourage more sensible land-use patterns including orderly growth, provision of housing, protecting the environment and natural resources, cost effective provision and use of necessary infrastructure, and closely integrating transportation, housing, air quality, and energy. The growth guidelines suggest resource identification and conservation, removing barriers to housing, local permit streamlining, consultation with neighbors, infill/densification, efficient infrastructure (funding and capacity), jobs/housing balance, and transit/housing integration. This expressly encourages sustainable development contiguous to existing urban areas by fully utilizing available and existing infrastructure. The plan acknowledges the importance of establishing higher densities with compact development, as well as a balance between jobs and housing. Governor's Office of Planning and Research, Strategic Growth: Taking Charge of the Future, Report of the Growth Management Council to Governor Wilson (January 1993).

- Preventing urban development patterns that unnecessarily compromise the agricultural industry by keeping development contiguous to existing urban area, while building new areas of development that promote the efficient delivery of public services.

- Requiring state infrastructure investments to support cost efficient growth and development patterns that direct and encourage growth in areas where it is environmentally and economically desirable. The plan suggests that priority growth areas should be designated to control the location of new state funded infrastructure.

(b) The State Planning Act (AB 857)

AB 857 (State Planning Act, Cal. Gov't Code § 65041.1.) adopted on September 28, 2002, formally established state planning policy priorities for growth and development. These policies are used to select infrastructure and to guide state expenditures as set forth in the comprehensive State Environmental Goals and Policy Report. AB 857 establishes statewide policies for sound infrastructure planning (priorities and funding), promoting development with existing infrastructure, encouraging development within existing built up areas with services that minimizes costs to taxpayers, and protect agricultural land. *See also* Robert H. Freilich, *Sprawl or Smart Growth Analysis of the Proposed High Speed Rail Alignments prepared for the California High Speed Rail Authority* (July 26, 2004) (saving over one million acres of prime farmland in the Central Valley).

(c) Global Warming Solutions Act (AB 32)

California's Global Warming Solutions Act of 2006, AB 32, Cal. Health & Safety Code § 38500 et seq.; sets high enforceable limits on greenhouse gas emissions from stationary sources. *See* Lora Lucero, *The Lawyers Confront Hot Air, Zoning and Planning Law Report* (American Planning Assoc. July/August 2007).

(d) Transportation Planning, Environmental Quality, Traffic Demand Modeling and Sustainable Communities Strategy Act of 2008 (SB 375)

SB 375, amending transportation planning (Cal. Gov't Code §§ 65080 et seq.) and environmental quality (Cal. Pub. Res. Code § 21159.28), is a landmark piece of anti-sprawl legislation that promises to achieve the type of sustainable smart growth land use planning and development at the state, regional and local level that will be widely emulated in other states. The bill is succinctly described as "providing [vehicle] emissions-reduction goals around which regions can plan—integrating disjointed planning activities and providing incentives for local governments and developers to follow new conscientiously-planned growth patterns."

SB 375 will be implemented through the state's 17 metropolitan planning organizations ("MPOs"), which are federally mandated transportation policy-making organizations composed of representatives from local government entities, state agencies and transportation authorities. MPOs are currently charged with, among other things, developing regional transportation plans which guide federal and state transportation funding decisions. The bill will require each MPO to incorporate into this plan a sustainable community strategy ("SCS"), designed to achieve AB 32 vehicle emissions-reduction goals—which were assigned by the California State Air Resources Board to the MPOs in

2010—by tying plans for existing and future transportation infrastructure to anticipated rates and patterns of regional development updated every four years until 2050. Each SCS must devise strategies for promoting transit-oriented development and jobs-housing within its region that will mitigate sprawl by reducing the length and number of vehicle trips and emissions.

SB 375 stopped short of requiring cities and counties to bring their general plans and zoning into conformity with the SCS. Although most of the provisions are currently voluntary, these planning strategies will require local governments to incorporate the SCS strategies in land use planning and development plans, regulations and decisions through a combination of mandates and incentives. First, existing state housing law requires each regional council of governments to allocate to its constituent cities and counties their "fair share" of existing and projected regional housing need for all income groups. Cities and counties must then incorporate policies and measures into their general plans to satisfy those housing needs. SB 375 will require this regional allocation to be consistent with the development pattern set forth in the region's SCS. Second, the bill provides incentives to real estate developers whose so-called transit oriented projects—fundamentally dense, transit-oriented and residential or mixed-use projects—comply with an SCS. Such projects will be either exempt from environmental review under the California Environmental Quality Act or will qualify for limited review. This incentive alone could prove to be a significant driver of sustainable development, given the staggering amounts of time and money that are often devoted to CEQA compliance. Third, federal and state transportation funds will be routed to priority growth areas shown in the SCS plans. Everything still depends on the political willingness of the MPOs to come up with meaningful sustainable smart growth strategies. The first indications are that control of the MPOs by local cities and counties will produce bland results; *see* Ethan Elkind, *So Much for California's Anti Sprawl Law*, Legal Planet (July 5, 2011) (http://legalplanet.wordpress.com/2001/07/05/so-much-for-califonias-anti-sprawl-law/).

CLEVELAND NATIONAL FOREST FOUNDATION V. SAN DIEGO ASSOCIATION OF GOVERNMENTS
Court of Appeal of California, 2014.
231 Cal.App.4th 1056, 180 Cal.Rptr.3d 548.

After the San Diego Association of Governments (SANDAG) certified an environmental impact report (EIR) for its 2050 Regional Transportation Plan/Sustainable Communities Strategy (transportation plan), CREED-21 and Affordable Housing Coalition of San Diego filed a petition for writ of mandate challenging the EIR's adequacy under the California Environmental Quality Act (CEQA) (Pub. Resources Code, § 21000 et seq.). Cleveland National Forest Foundation and the Center for Biological

Diversity filed a similar petition, in which Sierra Club and the People later joined.

The superior court granted the petitions in part, finding the EIR failed to carry out its role as an informational document because it did not analyze the inconsistency between the state's policy goals reflected in Executive Order S–3–05 (Executive Order) and the transportation plan's greenhouse gas emissions impacts after 2020. The court also found the EIR failed to adequately address mitigation measures for the transportation plan's greenhouse gas emissions impacts. Given these findings, the court declined to decide any of the other challenges raised in the petitions.

SANDAG appeals, contending the EIR complied with CEQA in both respects. Cleveland National Forest Foundation and Sierra Club (collectively, Cleveland) cross-appeal, contending the EIR further violated CEQA by failing to analyze a reasonable range of project alternatives, failing to adequately analyze and mitigate the transportation plan's air quality impacts, and understating the transportation plan's impacts on agricultural lands. We conclude the EIR failed to comply with CEQA in all identified respects. We, therefore, modify the judgment to incorporate our decision on the cross-appeals and affirm. In doing so, we are upholding the right of the public and our public officials to be well informed about the potential environmental consequences of their planning decisions, which CEQA requires and the public deserves, before approving long-term plans that may have irreversible environmental impacts.

In 2005 then Governor Arnold Schwarzenegger issued the Executive Order establishing greenhouse gas emissions reduction targets for California. Specifically, the Executive Order required reduction of greenhouse gas emissions to 2000 levels by 2010, to 1990 levels by 2020, and to 80 percent below 1990 levels by 2050.

The Legislature subsequently enacted the California Global Warming Solutions Act of 2006 (Health & Saf.Code, § 38500 et seq.), referred to by the parties as Assembly Bill No. 32 (AB 32). Among its provisions, AB 32 tasked the California Air Resources Board (CARB) with determining the state's 1990 greenhouse gas emissions level and approving an equivalent emissions level to be achieved by 2020. (Health & Saf.Code, § 38550.)

Bolstering this conclusion, the Legislature also enacted the Sustainable Communities and Climate Protection Act of 2008 (Stats. 2008, ch. 728; Stats. 2009, ch. 354, § 5), referred to by the parties as Senate Bill No. 375 (SB 375). In enacting SB 375, the Legislature found automobiles and light trucks are responsible for 30 percent of the state's greenhouse gas emissions. (Stats. 2008, ch. 728, § 1, subd. (a).) Accordingly, SB 375 directed CARB to develop regional greenhouse gas emission reduction targets for automobiles and light trucks for 2020 and 2035. (Gov.Code, § 65080, subd. (b)(2)(A).) The targets established by CARB for the San Diego region require a 7 percent per capita reduction in carbon dioxide emissions by 2020 and a 13 percent per capita reduction by 2035 (compared to a 2005 baseline). CARB must update these targets every eight years until 2050, and may update the targets every four years based on changing factors. (Gov.Code, § 65080, subd. (b)(2)(A)(iv).)

The transportation plan, which SANDAG must prepare every four years (23 U.S.C. § 134, subd. (c); Gov.Code, § 65080, subds. (a) & (d)), "serves as the long-range plan designed to coordinate and manage future regional transportation improvements, services, and programs among the various agencies operating within the San Diego region." In enacting SB 375, the Legislature found the state's emissions reductions goals cannot be met without improved land use and transportation policy. Consequently, SB 375 (Gov.Code, § 65080, subd. (b)(2)(B)) mandates the transportation plan include a sustainable communities strategy to, as the EIR states, "guide the San Diego region toward a more sustainable future by integrating land use, housing, and transportation planning to create more sustainable, walkable, transit-oriented, compact development patterns and communities that meet [CARB's greenhouse gas] emissions targets for passenger cars and light-duty trucks." Once the sustainable communities strategy is approved, some transit priority projects consistent with the strategy are exempt from CEQA requirements. Other transit priority projects, residential projects, and mixed-use projects consistent with the strategy are subject to streamlined CEQA requirements.

In this case, SANDAG's decision to omit an analysis of the transportation plan's consistency with the Executive Order did not reflect a reasonable, good faith effort at full disclosure and is not supported by substantial evidence because SANDAG's decision ignored the Executive Order's role in shaping state climate policy. The Executive Order underpins all of the state's current efforts to reduce greenhouse gas emissions. As SANDAG itself noted in its Climate Action Strategy, the Executive emissions reduction goal "is based on the scientifically-supported level of emissions reduction needed to avoid significant disruption of the climate and is used as the long-term driver for state climate change policy development." (Italics added.)

Indeed, the Executive Order led directly to the enactment of AB 32, which validated and ratified the Executive Order's overarching goal of ongoing emissions reductions, recognized the Governor's Climate Action Team as the coordinator of the state's overall climate policy, and tasked CARB with establishing overall emissions reduction targets for 2020 and beyond. The Executive Order also led directly to the enactment of SB 375, which tasked CARB with establishing regional automobile and light truck emissions reduction targets for 2020 and 2035. CARB is required to revisit these targets every eight years through 2050, or sooner if warranted by changing circumstances. (Gov. Code, § 65080, subd. (b)(2)(A)(iv).) Thus, the Executive Order, with the Legislature's unqualified endorsement, will continue to underpin the state's efforts to reduce greenhouse gas emissions throughout the life of the transportation plan. The EIR's failure to analyze the transportation plan's consistency with the Executive Order, or more particularly with the Executive Order's overarching goal of ongoing greenhouse gas emissions reductions, was therefore a failure to analyze the transportation plan's consistency with state climate policy. As evidence in the record indicates the transportation plan would actually be inconsistent with state climate policy over the long term, the omission deprived the public and decision makers of relevant information about the transportation plan's environmental consequences. The omission was prejudicial because it precluded informed decisionmaking and public participation. (*Smart Rail, supra*, 57 Cal.4th at p. 463, 160 Cal.Rptr.3d 1, 304 P.3d 499; *City of Long Beach, supra*, 176 Cal.App.4th at p. 898, 98 Cal.Rptr.3d 137.)

By disregarding the Executive Order's overarching goal of ongoing emissions reductions, the EIR's analysis of the transportation plan's greenhouse gas emissions makes it falsely appear as if the transportation plan is furthering state climate policy when, in fact, the trajectory of the transportation plan's post-2020 emissions directly contravenes it. "[O]mitting material necessary to informed decisionmaking and informed public participation" subverts the purposes of CEQA and "precludes both identification of potential environmental consequences arising from the project and also thoughtful analysis of the sufficiency of measures to mitigate those consequences." (*Lotus v. Department of Transportation* (2014) 223 Cal.App.4th 645, 658, 167 Cal.Rptr.3d 382.) Such an omission is particularly troubling where, as here, the project under review involves long-term, planned expenditures of billions of taxpayer dollars. No one can reasonably suggest it would be prudent to go forward with planned expenditures of this magnitude before the public and decision makers have been provided with all reasonably available information bearing on the project's impacts to the health, safety, and welfare of the region's inhabitants. We, therefore, conclude SANDAG prejudicially abused its discretion by omitting from the EIR an analysis of the transportation plan's consistency with the state climate policy, reflected in the Executive Order, of continual greenhouse gas emissions reductions.9

The EIR analyzed seven project alternatives. They were:

1.   A no project alternative, which assumed the transportation plan would not be adopted and only transportation improvements under construction or development would be built (Alternative 1);

2.   A modified funding strategy alternative, which deleted some highway improvements, delayed other highway improvements, added some transit projects, advanced other transit projects, and increased some transit service frequencies (Alternative 2a);

3. The same modified funding strategy alternative coupled with a modified "smart growth" land use pattern, which assumed added infill and redevelopment to increase residential development density in urban and town center areas and increased employment within job centers (Alternative 2b);

4. A transit emphasis alternative, which advanced the development of some transit projects, but did not add any new transit projects (Alternative 3a);

5. The same transit emphasis alternative, but assuming the modified smart growth land use pattern (Alternative 3b);

6. An alternative implementing the transportation plan's transportation network, but assuming the modified smart growth land use pattern (Alternative 4); and

7. A slow growth alternative, which assumed the application of regulations and/or economic disincentives to slow population and employment and delayed the complete implementation of the transportation plan by five years (Alternative 5).

Cleveland contends the EIR fails to comply with CEQA because the EIR did not analyze a reasonable range of project alternatives. As the focus of this contention is whether the analysis was reasonable and not whether it occurred, the contention presents a predominately factual question and our review is for substantial evidence. (*Vineyard, supra*, 40 Cal.4th at p. 435, 53 Cal.Rptr.3d 821, 150 P.3d 709.)

"CEQA requires that an EIR, in addition to analyzing the environmental effects of a proposed project, also consider and analyze project alternatives that would reduce adverse environmental impacts. The [Guidelines] state that an EIR must 'describe a range of reasonable alternatives to the project . . . which would feasibly attain most of the basic objectives of the project but would avoid or substantially lessen any of the significant effects of the project. . . .' An EIR need not consider every conceivable alternative to a project or alternatives that are infeasible.

In this case, the EIR's discussion of project alternatives is deficient because it does not discuss an alternative which could significantly reduce total vehicle miles traveled. Although Alternatives 3a and 3b are labeled "transit emphasis" alternatives, the labeling is a misnomer. These alternatives mainly advance certain rapid bus projects, but leave the planned rail and trolley projects largely unchanged. In addition, these alternatives do not provide any new transit projects or significant service increases. In fact, the "transit emphasis" alternatives include fewer transit projects than some of the other non-"transit-emphasis" alternatives.

The omission of an alternative which could significantly reduce total vehicle miles traveled is inexplicable given SANDAG's acknowledgment in its Climate Action Strategy that the state's efforts to reduce greenhouse gas emissions from on-road transportation will not succeed if the amount of driving, or vehicle miles traveled, is not significantly reduced. The Climate Action Strategy explained, "Lowering vehicle miles traveled means providing high-quality opportunities to make trips by alternative means to driving alone such as walking, bicycling, ridesharing, and public transit, and by shortening vehicle trips that are made. This can be accomplished through improved land use and transportation planning and related measures, policies and investments that increase the options people have when they travel." Accordingly, the Climate Action Strategy recommended policy measures to increase and prioritize funding and system investments for public transit and transit operations, increase the level of service on existing routes and provide new public transit service through expanded investments, and improve the performance of public transit with infrastructure upgrades. Given these recommendations, their purpose, and their source, it is reasonable to expect at least one project alternative to have been focused primarily on significantly reducing vehicle trips.

The matter is remanded to the superior court with directions to modify the judgment and writ of mandate to incorporate our decision on the cross-appeals. The judgment is affirmed as so modified."

NOTES

1.   The court in the Cleveland case also remanded the issue that the EIR failed to properly evaluate the impacts of the Plan upon preservation of agriculture. Cleveland had set forth the agricultural issue in the trial court as follows: "It is not clear how the [EIR] could use current planning assumptions for growth and determine that there will be only 10,500 acres of agricultural land impacted, when the current plans on which it bases its assumptions assume there will be more than five times as many acres impacted. SANDAG must explain if there is a basis for this discrepancy. Without any such explanation, the [EIR] appears to severely underestimate the amount of agricultural land that will be impacted, in contravention of CEQA. [¶] In sum, the [EIR's] failure to accurately account for impacts to agricultural land renders it inadequate as a matter of law."

2.   The California Supreme Court has taken review of the case, 343 P.3d 903 (March15, 2015).

3.   HUD provides funds for regional planning in its Sustainable Communities Regional Planning Grants Support to metropolitan and multijurisdictional planning efforts to consider challenges of economics, energy use, public health, and the environment. The grants program is closely coordinated with the U.S. Department of Transportation (DOT) and the U.S. Environmental Protection Agency (EPA), supports metropolitan and multijurisdictional planning efforts that integrate housing, land use, economic and workforce development, transportation, and infrastructure investments in

a manner that empowers jurisdictions to consider the interdependent challenges of: (1) economic competitiveness and revitalization; (2) social equity, inclusion, and access to opportunity; (3) energy use and climate change; and (4) public health and environmental impact. Sustainable Communities and Regional Planning Grants place a priority on investing in partnerships, including nontraditional partnerships (e.g., arts and culture, recreation, public health, food systems, regional planning agencies and public education entities) that generate strategies that direct long-term development and reinvestment, demonstrate a commitment to addressing issues of regional significance, use data to set and monitor progress toward performance goals, and engage stakeholders and residents in meaningful decision-making roles. Consolidated Appropriations Act, Division A, Title II; FY 2011 Department of Defense and Full-Year Continuing Appropriations Act (Public Law 112–10).

3. OTHER STATE GROWTH MANAGEMENT LAWS INCORPORATING CONCURRENCY REQUIREMENTS AND URBAN GROWTH BOUNDARIES

(a) Hawaii

Hawaii in 1961 became the first state to institute statewide land use control. *See* Haw.Rev.Stat. § 205–12–18. The state legislature created the State Land Use Commission (Goodin, *The Honolulu Development Plans: An Analysis of Land Use for Oahu*, 6 U.HAW.L.REV. 33 (1984)), which determines what lands will be developed classifying "urban," "agricultural," "conservation," or "rural" lands. Considered one of the most sophisticated land use management systems in the country, Hawaii's plan consists of detailed development plans with common provision text, land use maps, and public facilities maps covering every inch of the Island of Oahu County charters forbid even the "initiation" of a subdivision or zoning change unless it conforms to the development plan with adequate public facilities. The issues that spurred the government in Hawaii to adopt a state plan in 1961 included a desire to preserve rural, natural resource, and agricultural lands from rapid urban encroachment and to promote economic development. By 1975, the system had been in place for fifteen years, but urban encroachment was continuing to occur as well as depletion agricultural and natural resource lands depletion. David L. Callies, Regulating *Paradise: Land Use Controls in Hawaii*, Introduction and Chapter One (2nd ed.2011).

The Hawaii State Growth Management System authorizes an appointed State Land Use Commission to establish the boundaries of four land use districts and hear and decide most petitions for "boundary assessments" (reclassification to another district). An Office of State Planning theoretically conducts a review of district boundaries every five years. There are four districts: an urban, a rural, an agricultural, and a conservation district. The state controls the conservation district, the local governments control the urban district, and the state and local governments split the control of land use in the remaining rural and agricultural districts. The districts may be viewed as a combination of urban growth boundaries and tiered development. Each urban district also is surrounded by-an urban growth boundary, the intervening land being usually classified in the agricultural district. Reclassification to urban from agriculture within the urban growth boundary to accommodate urban needs for housing and commercial development is commonplace and has been sustained by Hawai'i's high court. *See Sierra Club v. The Land Use Commission of the State of Hawai'i*, ___ P.3d ___ (Hawai'i 2015). The permitted uses in the rural district are generally low-density residential uses (that is, minimum lot size of one dwelling unit per half acre), agricultural uses, and public facilities. Boundary amendments to the urban, rural, or agricultural districts may be approved by the county if the amendment involves fewer than fifteen acres. All boundary amendments in the conservation district and amendments involving greater than fifteen acres in the other districts require approval by the State Land Use Commission. Because the state defines the permitted uses and retains control of special uses for proposals over fifteen acres in three of the districts, the state assumes the majority of control of the land in Hawaii. *See* David L. Callies, *It All Began in* Hawai'i, 45 JOHN MARSHALL L.REV. 317 (2012).

(b) Oregon

Oregon's Urban Growth Boundary (UGB) program is the first statewide legislative requirement that local governments designate enforceable UGBs. Local governments are required to design, phase and locate transportation facilities, (including air, marine, rail, mass transit, highways, bicycle and pedestrian facilities) in such a manner as to encourage growth in urbanized areas while discouraging growth in rural areas. As a general rule, a local government is not permitted to establish an urban growth boundary containing more land than the locality "needs" for future growth. *See Milne v. City of* Canby, 96 P.3d 1267 (Or.Ct.App.2004).

With its longstanding urban growth boundary (UGB) and well-developed transit system, Portland, Oregon is one of the most frequently cited and best examples of smart growth, which has developed under Oregon's system of statewide land use management goals and is truly one of the pioneers of state-directed regional growth management planning. Thirty years ago in 1979, the Oregon legislature enacted a comprehensive growth management system using urban growth boundaries to protect environmentally sensitive areas, including agricultural, forest and coastlands, to conserve natural resources to provide public facilities and services, and to prevent urban sprawl. *See* Or.Rev.Stat. § 197.005. Oregon's urban growth boundary system established in Goal 14 was the first statewide requirement mandating local governments to designate enforceable UGBs. The Oregon system is based on nineteen state goals or policies that serve as legislative standards that state agencies, local governments, and regional authorities must comply with in their planning efforts. *See 1000 Friends of Oregon v. LCDC of Lane County*, 752 P.2d 271 (Or.1988).

The Oregon legislation established the State Land Conservation and Development Commission (LCDC), which adopts the state goals, reviews the local, regional, and state agency plans for consistency with state goals and for compliance with other planning and regulatory requirements, and enforces the state planning requirements. Another state agency the Land Use Board of Appeals (LUBA) was established and granted exclusive jurisdiction over land use decisions made by state agencies, special districts, local governments, and regional entities. *See* Edward J. Sullivan, *Reviewing the Reviewer: The Impact of the Land Use Board of Appeals on the Oregon Land Use Program*, 36 WILLAMETTE L.REV. 441, 447 (2000).

In 1978, voters in Multnomah, Washington and Clackamas counties created an elected regional government called the "metropolitan service district" to oversee issues that confronted the traditional city and county boundaries. It became popularly known as Metro. See the Regional Framework Plan—Portland, Oregon (Dec. 11, 1997). Metro's partners in the region are 25 cities, three counties and more than 130 special service districts, the State of Oregon, Tri-Met, the Port of Portland and the Portland Area Boundary Commission. Metro was established in an effort to eliminate duplication of services and overlapping jurisdictions by consolidating the regional governments into an elected governing body to allow accountability and responsiveness to the citizenry. *See* Or.Rev.Stat. § 268.015 (NOTE: Repealed by Laws 1997 (833, § 27). Metro's responsibilities include amending the regional Urban Growth Boundary (UGB) and adopting planning goals and objectives for the region.

The primary growth management techniques used in Oregon's growth management system are urban growth boundaries and intergovernmental coordination. The urban growth boundaries separate urban lands from agricultural, forest or other nonurban uses. In connection with amending the urban growth boundary, several factors must be considered including the need for housing, employment opportunities, and orderly, timed and sequenced provisions for public facilities and services. These Ramapo principles have contributed to Oregon's success in growth control. Oregon has strictly defined and limited amendments to the UGB to those that demonstrate that additional land us proven to be "needed" to meet actual future growth. *See*, Edward J. Sullivan, *Urbanization in Oregon: Goal 14 and the Urban Growth Boundary*, 47 URB.LAW. 165 (2015). A recent case decided by the Oregon Court of Appeals reveals that strictness:

1000 FRIENDS OF OREGON V. LAND CONSERVATION AND DEVELOPMENT COMMISSION

Court of Appeals of Oregon, 2015.
260 Or.App. 444, 317 P.3d 927.

Under Oregon's land use laws, local governments may (and, in some cases, must) engage in periodic review of their comprehensive land use plans. *See* ORS 197.628 to 197.636. As a result of a periodic-review process, the City of Woodburn amended its urban growth boundary (UGB) to include additional land—409 gross acres or about 362 net buildable acres—for industrial use. The city submitted that amendment to the state Land Conservation and Development Commission (LCDC) for review. ORS 197.626(1)(b). LCDC approved the city's amendment of its UGB. Petitioners sought judicial review of LCDC's order of approval. We concluded that LCDC's order was inadequate for judicial review and, accordingly, reversed the order and remanded the case to LCDC for reconsideration. *1000 Friends of Oregon v. LCDC,* 237 Or.App. 213, 239 P.3d 272 (2010) (*Woodburn I*). LCDC has now completed that reconsideration and issued a new order approving the city's UGB expansion.

Petitioners again seek judicial review. Petitioners challenge two aspects of LCDC's order: its approval of the amount of industrial land in the UGB amendment and its approval of the inclusion of particular high-value farmland within the UGB as industrial land. Petitioners contend that the city included more industrial land within its UGB than will be developed within the 20-year planning period and that LCDC did not adequately explain why that inclusion is consistent with Statewide Land Use Planning Goals 9 and 14 and other rules.

In the target-industries approach developed here, the city aimed to promote economic growth by pursuing development that would create higher-paying jobs to attract new residents who would both live and work in Woodburn. To facilitate that goal, the city identified high-wage target industries that it believed might locate in Woodburn because of its location on I-5 between Portland and Salem. The city then identified the site and building requirements and preferences of the targeted industries. The city also adopted an employment-growth forecast. In light of academic and federal population estimates and forecasts, the city predicted a 20-year employment-growth rate of 3 percent, leading to a projected increase of 8,374 jobs. Ultimately, the city determined that, to further its economic-development strategy and accommodate the volume of job growth that it projected, it needed 42 total industrial sites, 23 of which were available on land within the existing UGB and 19 of which it decided to provide by expanding its UGB into its Southwest Industrial Reserve (SWIR).

Petitioners objected to the UGB amendment, and LCDC considered those objections. Petitioners contended, among other things, that the city had included more industrial land within its amended boundary than was needed to accommodate projected industrial job growth or the needs of its target industries and, accordingly, more industrial land than the city expected to develop over the 20-year planning period, in violation of Goal 9, the land use planning goal that addresses economic development. *Woodburn I,* 237 Or.App. at 222, 239 P.3d 272. Petitioners further argued that the city's target-industries approach "inflate[d]" the number of acres that needed to be included within the UGB to accommodate industrial job growth and did not address the demonstrated need for any additional industrial land to be included in the proposed UGB expansion as required by Goal 14, the land use planning goal that addresses urbanization.

LCDC approved the city's expansion of its UGB. LCDC reasoned as follows in rejecting petitioners' objections:

"[The city's UGB Justification Report] identified the total number of sites required for all the site size needs, and found 42 total sites needed for all targeted industries. According to 1000 Friends, this is an oversupply of sites that leads to more land than is justified. *However, the city has designated these sites* to provide for the required short-term supply as well as *to provide market choice among sites. The Commission finds that this is a key component of a successful industrial development strategy, and is required by OAR 660–009–0025.* In addition, the objection states that the city acknowledges that 'not all of the industrial land proposed for inclusion is expected to develop by 2020.' This is due to the fact that industrial users often choose to purchase a site larger than their immediate need in order to ensure that they have adequate land for future expansion, and the statement referred to by the objector is recognition of that fact. Additionally, OAR 660–009–[0] 025(2) specifies that plans must designate serviceable land suitable to meet the site needs identified in Section (1) of this rule. Except as provided for in Section (5) of this rule, the total acreage of land designated must at least equal the total projected land needs for each industrial or other employment use category identified in the plan during the 20-year planning period.

"In conclusion, the Commission finds that Woodburn's plans for economic development comply with the Goal 9 and Goal 14 rules. The city's employment projection and land needs assessment are reasonable, for the reasons explained in these findings and more particularly described in the Woodburn UGB Justification Report."

In *Woodburn I,* 237 Or. App. at 222–23, 239 P.3d 272, Petitioners sought judicial review of LCDC's approval of the city's UGB amendments. As we characterized petitioners' arguments in our original opinion, they contended that the city had included more land in the UGB than it would need during the 20-year planning period in violation of Goals 9 and 14, and that LCDC's justification for affirming that inclusion—*i.e.,* that the inclusion is required by OAR 660–009–0025 to provide market choice among sites—is not allowed under Goals 9 or 14. *Id.* at 223–24, 239 P.3d 272.

We concluded that LCDC's order did not provide an adequate basis for us to review petitioners' contentions. We noted that, "although LCDC discussed Goal 9 and its implementing rules and concluded that the UGB amendment complies with both Goals 9 and 14, LCDC provided essentially no reasoning as to that conclusion with respect to Goal 14. In particular, LCDC offered no explanation concerning the reasons that the need factors of Goal 14 are satisfied under the circumstances of this case." *Id.* at 223, 239 P.3d 272.

In conclusion, we stated:

"[B]ecause LCDC did not adequately explain the reasons that the UGB amendment—which included more industrial land than will be developed during the planning period so that the city could provide for market choice among sites—was consistent with Goals 9 and 14, its order failed to respond to petitioners' objections and [was] inadequate for judicial review * * * concerning the propriety of the UGB amendment."

Id. at 226–27, 239 P.3d 272.

On remand, LCDC circulated a draft revised order to the parties and considered written and oral arguments. On March 16, 2011, LCDC issued a revised order again approving the city's amendment of its UGB. LCDC's analysis rests on two foundations: first, what it characterized as a "close correlation" between the need for industrial land calculated using the employees-per-acre approach and the need for industrial land determined using the target-industries approach, and second, the city's analysis of population, employment, target industries, and site requirements, which LCDC concluded provided a factual and analytical base to establish that the city's decision was consistent with Goal 14, Goal 9, and ORS 197.712 (setting out comprehensive plan requirements). For the reasons explained below, we again conclude that LCDC's analysis is not supported by substantial reason.[3]

LCDC began its analysis by comparing the projected land need (in buildable acres) based on employment projections and an employee-per-acre calculation—*viz.,* 311 acres—with the projected land need based on the target-industries approach used by the city—*viz.,* 362 acres. LCDC stated that "the relatively close correlation" between those two numbers "provide[d] important corroboration for the city's ultimate decision concerning the amount of land needed for industrial and office uses."

In its order on remand, LCDC concluded that the city's analysis of population, employment, target industries, and site requirements provided a factual and analytical base to establish that the city's decision was consistent with Goal 14, Goal 9, and ORS 197.712. LCDC thoroughly reiterated the steps undertaken by the city and its consultant in order to arrive at the conclusion that, under a target-industries analysis and to support the economic opportunities that the city wished to offer, the city needed to add 409 gross acres of land for industrial use. The city indeed engaged in a lengthy process, resulting in a voluminous record, in this periodic-review process. Similarly, LCDC, in its order on remand, recounted in detail the steps that the city took in engaging in and documenting its process. LCDC also walked through applicable goals and other legal provisions, and concluded that the city's expansion of its UGB was consistent with each. What is lacking, however, is a meaningful explanation of *why* the steps taken by the city satisfy those legal standards. Instead, LCDC recounted all the steps that the city took and then concluded—without analysis—that those steps are factually and analytically supported, and are consistent with the law.

That discussion, while lengthy, does not include reasoning. It includes findings of fact (including facts about what the city or its consultant did during the periodic-review process) and statements of law or policy. It also includes conclusions that the facts in this case satisfy the law. It does not include the reasoning that led LCDC from the facts to its conclusion

To the extent that LCDC intended to base its conclusion that the city's actions complied with Goal 14, factor 2, on the proposition that the city had engaged in a particular process that is insufficient. If it were sufficient, local governments could establish compliance with Goal 14, factor 2, simply by verifying that they had engaged in the correct process, regardless of their conclusions. Substantial reason requires, at the least, an explanation of why the process in which a local government engaged *and* the results that it reached are consistent with the law.

We have carefully reviewed LCDC's entire order on remand, and we conclude that LCDC did not adequately explain the reasons that led it to conclude the city's UGB amendment complied with applicable law. As noted, in light of that disposition, we do not address petitioners' arguments regarding the inclusion of certain high-value farmland within the UGB as industrial land.

Reversed and remanded for reconsideration.

NOTE

Oregon's system has been somewhat jeopardized by statewide ballot Measure 37 adopted in 2004. Measure 37 requires government to compensate landowners for any reduction in land value due to land use regulations or to modify, remove or not apply such regulations. *See MacPherson v. Department of Administrative Services*, 130 P.3d 308 (Or.2006) (approving the constitutionality of Measure 37 against a broad range of attacks.) The effect of Measure 37 was to bring the state's growth management system to a virtual halt. *See* Edward J. Sullivan, *Year Zero: The Aftermath of Measure* 37, 38 URBAN LAWYER 237 (2006).

(c) Washington

The Washington Growth Management Act (GMA), Wash.Rev. Code Ann. § 36.70A.020, delineates several goals and issues including urban sprawl, transportation needs, and concurrency of public facilities and services. Involving all levels of government, it mandates planning by some cities and counties and by certain multicounty areas. Wash.Rev. Code Ann. § 36.70A.210(7) (multicounty regions that must develop planning policies; currently applies to the central Puget Sound Region, which encompasses King, Kitsap, Pierce, and Snohomish counties). The multicounty area and counties required to plan must adopt countywide planning policies that serve as the framework for the county and city comprehensive plans. The state mandates specific elements in the comprehensive plans of cities and counties. All counties are required to adopt development regulations that protect critical areas. The GMA outlines consistency requirements for planning, including:

1. city and county plans must be consistent with state goals;

2. city and county plans must be internally consistent; and

3. city and county plans must be consistent with neighboring city and county plans.

The two growth management techniques that are predominant in the Washington system are urban growth boundaries and concurrency management of transportation facilities. Counties that are required to plan must also delineate twenty-year urban growth areas (UGAs). The cities propose the boundary of their UGA, the county consults with cities, and finally the county designates the boundary of the UGA. Urban growth is encouraged within the UGA, and growth outside the boundary is allowed only if it is considered "not urban in nature." The UGA is determined through population projections and is to provide adequate land to accommodate growth at urban densities for a twenty-year period as well as to provide a greenbelt and open space.

Mandatory concurrency and timing for infrastructure is required. The Washington Growth Management Act has explicit provisions for adequate public facility compliance:

1. Urban growth. Encourage development in urban areas where adequate public facilities and services exist or can be provided in an efficient manner. (§ 36.70A.020 (1)); and

2. Public facilities and services. Ensure that those public facilities and services necessary to support development shall be adequate to serve the development at the time the development is available for occupancy and use without decreasing current service levels below locally established minimum standards. (§ 36.70A.020 (12)).

This policy requires the cities or counties to identify funding for transportation facilities, transportation facility deficits, a capital improvement program, and other future needs on a ten-year frame. Larry G. Smith, *Planning for Growth, Washington Style, in State and Regional Comprehensive Planning: Implementing New Methods for Growth Management* 145 (Buchsbaum & Smith eds., ABA 1993).

Metropolitan Planning Organizations (MPOs) are then charged with the coordination of city and county transportation plans within a region. The MPO certifies the transportation portion of local comprehensive plans, develops and adopts a regional transportation plan, and identifies and plans for transportation improvements for corridors of regional significance. *See* Robert H. Freilich, Elizabeth A. Garvin and S. Mark White, *Economic Development and Public Transit: Making the Most of the Washington Growth Management Act* (with Elizabeth A. Garvin and S. Mark White), 16 U.PUGET SOUND L.REV. 949 (1993).

Other regional entities are involved, including three regional planning boards that hear appeals concerning consistency or UGAs, and are authorized to reject a plan and require the submission of a new plan. The State Department of Community Development reviews plans and development regulations for consistency and for required elements. The growth management system requires local governments to adopt and enface ordinances that allow development only if the affected transportation or other public facility will not decline below the predetermined level of services, unless those improvements or strategies for providing the facilities are made concurrent with the development. The legislature defines concurrency as improvements or strategies that are in place at the time of development or that a financial commitment is in place to complete the improvements or strategies within six years.

Unlike its neighbor Oregon, Washington voters rejected in 2006 an initiative proposing enactments of a Private Property Rights Protection Act which would have required compensation if the state's growth management system's regulations created any loss in the value of regulated land.

(d) Florida

Commencing with the Environmental Land and Water Management Act in 1972, Fla.Stat.Ann. § 380.012–10, Florida began its foray into statewide land-use controls by protecting areas of critical state concern through state designation; and regulation of developments of regional impact through oversight by the state Department of Community Affairs. In 1985 Florida enacted the State and Local Government Comprehensive Growth Management Act, Fla.Stat.Ann. § 163.3167, which requires the formulation of city and county programs for providing infrastructure (need and location of public facilities, as well as their projected costs) and forbids the granting of any land development permits unless public facilities will be concurrently available to meet the needs generated by that development. *Id.* at § 163.3202(2)(g). *See* Thomas G. Pelham, *The Florida Experience: Creating a State, Regional and Local Comprehensive Planning Process, in State and Regional Comprehensive Planning: Implementing New Methods For Growth Management*, 102, 107, 109, 110 (Buchsbaum & Smith eds., 1993). If a proposed development cannot meet a level of service standard established by the local government across the full range of public facilities delineated in the comprehensive plan, then the proposed development must be rejected unless the local government itself is willing and able to maintain that service level. *See* Robert M. Rhodes, *Florida Growth Management: Past, Present and Future*, 9 FLA.COASTAL L.REV. 107 (2007).

The State Act mandates local comprehensive planning, local plan consistency with regional and state plans, and oversight by the state Department of Community Affairs to assure the integration of local capital improvements program with the local land development regulatory process on a statewide, regional, and local basis similar to the Ramapo program. James C. Nicholas, *The Ups and Downs of Growth Management in Florida*, 12 U.FLA.L.J. & PUB.POL'Y 213 (2001).

In 2011 a newly elected property rights legislature saw the removed critical elements of the growth management policy. *See* Valerie J. Hubbard, *Florida's New Community Planning Act, Legal Update EXTRA, International Council of Shopping Centers*, August, 2011:[4]

> On June 2, a landmark change to Florida's growth management laws became effective. The "Community Planning Act" (2011–139, Laws of Florida) returns more control of growth management decisions to local governments, focuses the state's review of local comprehensive plans and amendments on "important state facilities and resources," streamlines comprehensive plan review processes and contains other measures to reduce the regulatory burden and provide relief to Florida's ailing development industry.
>
> The legislation addresses many factors that have created difficulties for development projects, including:

---

[4] Valerie J. Hubbard, FAICP, LEED AP, Director of Planning Services, Akerman Senterfitt, Tallahassee, FL. Reprinted with permission of the author and the ICSC.

Removal of the requirement to establish that there is a "need" for additional land to accommodate growth before approving land use amendments. The "need" criteria now focuses instead on providing sufficient land for development.

Repeal of state-mandated "concurrency" for transportation, public school facilities and parks and recreation. Concurrency is a type of adequate public facilities requirement. This change allows local governments to choose whether to retain these concurrency requirements.

Revised requirements for calculating and applying transportation proportionate share mitigation, to ensure that development is not required to pay for existing deficiencies or more than its fair share of needed improvements.

Repeal of the requirement that local plans be "financially feasible." Many plan amendments have been challenged for not demonstrating the financial feasibility of funding infrastructure needed to support proposed growth.

https://www.icsc.org/pub/legal_update_extra/0811_legalUpdateExtra.pdf

The concurrency provisions—what's now left of these as noted above—are the "teeth" of the growth management system, requiring that every comprehensive plan include the availability of adequate public facilities when a development order is issued and that the requirement be enforced at the development order stage.

The predominant growth management techniques used through the Florida State Plan include Ramapo's concurrency management for adequate public facilities provision, impact analysis for development with regional impact, and projects proposed in critical concern areas. The Florida legislature has since decided the concurrency requirement is deemed satisfied "[i]f the public facilities and services for a development are phased, or the development is phased, so that the public facilities and those related services which are deemed necessary by the local government to operate the facilities necessitated by that development are available concurrent with the impacts of the development." While Florida's growth management efforts further the utilization of concurrency, they have failed to revitalize the older urban central cities. Florida's growth management techniques need to be timed and sequenced within the Urbanized Tier and with the appropriate planning basis. *See* Thomas G. Pelham, *From the Ramapo Plan to Florida's Statewide Concurrency System: Ramapo's Influence on Infrastructure Planning*, 35 URBAN LAWYER 113–114 (2003).

Finally, the 2013 Legislative Session in Florida passed some interesting changes to the existing growth management legislation. HB 319 encourages local governments that repeal transportation concurrency as a result of the CPA to adopt a mobility fee system that will reduce vehicle miles traveled, encourage urban and mixed use development, incorporate strategies that encourage multimodal and pedestrian development and other mobility techniques. HB 319 also provides that local governments that maintain transportation concurrency requirements allow an applicant to satisfy transportation concurrency with a proportionate share contribution. Fla.Stat. § 163.3180(5)(h) (2013). HB 537 was passed to clarify confusion surrounding the ban on development referenda contained in the CPA and the subsequent local interpretations of the 2011 legislation. HB 537 clarifies that initiative and referendum processes for development orders, comprehensive plan amendments or map amendments are prohibited. Fla.Stat. § 163.3167(8) (2013).

While land use regulation is generally local, Florida's legislature has found that certain types of activities affect the state as a whole. There are several regions in Florida that have developed effective programs based on mandatory conformance with the statewide comprehensive legislation. Growth management has been necessary, especially to southern Florida. The current plan addresses critical problems such as the restoration of the Everglades, Florida's future water supply, the loss of agricultural lands, and the need to preserve and restore Florida's environmental systems. Florida's southeast coast is now implementing growth management techniques designed to provide a meaningful channel for growth in southeast Florida to lands other than those adjacent to the Everglades, thereby protecting the environment, encouraging more compact energy-efficient development patterns, and redirecting growth to the older coastal cities requiring revitalization and infill. § 163.3202(2)(g). *See* Thomas G. Pelham, *The Florida Experience: Creating a State, Regional and Local Comprehensive Planning Process, in State & Regional Comprehensive Planning: Implementing New Methods For Growth Management*, 102, 107, 109, 110 (Buchsbaum & Smith eds.1993).

4. STATES WITH NON-BINDING SMART GROWTH PLANNING

(a) Colorado

See, Edward J. Sullivan and Jessica Yeh, *Smart Growth: State Strategies in Managing Sprawl*, 45 URBAN LAWYER 349, 535 (2013): "Colorado and Virginia are examples of states where as a result of inconsistent requirements for a state comprehensive plan and a lack of enforceable "sticks" or enticing "carrots", smart growth policies are ineffective. Colorado has no statewide growth management system. Its land use system is characterized by delegation to local governments, which engage in planning with minimal standards. The few obligations the state imposes reflect federal requirements, and are entrusted to local governments to meet."

See also, Gregory K. Ingram et al., *Lincoln Inst. of Land Policy, Smart Growth Policies: An Evaluation of Programs and Outcomes, Executive Summary*, 205 (2009), available at http://www.lincolninst.edu/pubs/smart-growth-policies-executivesummary.pdf (evaluating the success of smart growth factors for states with mandatory smart growth programs and those without such programs). There is virtually no state enforcement, and the state relies on voluntary regional collaboration to manage growth. While there are regulations in place relating to environmental conservation programs, these have largely been the result of local initiative, not state legislation. Further, long-range transportation planning is carried out at the regional level with little state review. The state requires regional planning only in areas of "critical state interest" and cross-regional planning is voluntary. Counties with a certain population level or growth rate must prepare and adopt a master (comprehensive) plan, which is reviewed and commented on by a state agency". Colo.Rev.Stat. § 24–65.1–101 (2012)."

(b) New Jersey

The State Plan, adopted in 1992, is the result of a cross-acceptance process that included thousands of New Jersey citizens in hundreds of public forums, discussing all of the major aspects of the plan—its goals, strategies, policies and application. The legislated purpose of the State Plan (State Planning Act) is to:

- Identify areas for growth, limited growth, agricultural and open space preservation;

- Encourage development and economic growth in locations that are well situated with respect to present or anticipated public service facilities; and

- Discourage development where it may impair or destroy natural resources or environmental qualities. State Planning Act, N.J.Stat.Ann. § 52:18A–196.

Another section of the Act provides that:

> "The State Plan shall coordinate planning activities and establish Statewide planning objectives in the following areas: land use, housing, economic development, transportation, natural resource conservation, agriculture and farmland retention, recreation, urban and suburban redevelopment, historic preservation, public facilities and services, and intergovernmental coordination." (N.J.S.A. 52:18A–200(f))."

After considering four alternative systems for managing growth, the State Planning Commission concluded that the Ramapo tier system would most effectively provide the growth management mandates of the State

Planning Act. The primary objectives of the State Plan were to reduce sprawl, protect natural resources, stimulate development in urban infill and contiguous growth and to channel growth into nodes within designated transportation corridors. The state was divided into five tiers, tiers one through three were designated as growth areas, while tiers four and five were designated as limited growth areas. *See,* the report of the Plan's principal consultants, Robert H. Freilich and Martin L. Leitner, *New Jersey Development Standards for Limited Growth Areas* (January 27, 1988).

On June 29, 2011, Governor Chris Christie issued a Reorganization Plan, No. 002–2011 (the "Plan") reiterated the role of the State Planning Commission as "coordinating long-term and short-term planning for growth, economic development, urban renewal, agriculture, natural resource preservation, open space conservation, and other appropriate land uses throughout the State. The State Planning Commission's responsibilities include working closely with stakeholders at the State and local levels and coordinating with principal departments of State government to target and coordinate the State's resources and funding in ways that enhance the quality of life for residents of New Jersey." [New Jersey Register at 43 N.J.R. 16220 (a) 002–2011].

The 1992 State Plan was working well until two court decisions emasculated the binding mandate of the State Plan. In the most recent decision, *Griepenburg v. Township of Ocean,* 2013 WL 4554621 (N.J.App.2013)(NOTE: Judgment overturned by 105 A.3d 1082 (2015)), the court overturned a rural township zoning of property as a limited growth area and an environmentally sensitive area, following the State Planning Commission's designations.

Beginning in 2004, Ocean became interested in concentrating development in a town center and slowing development outside the center. The Planning Board recommended rezoning Ocean's industrial zoning districts located west of the Garden State Parkway, as well as some properties located east of the Garden State Parkway, to an environmentally sensitive land use designation. This area included the subject property owned by the Griepenburgs and consisting of 26 acres of wooded land.

Ocean requested from the State Planning Commission, changes to the planning area boundaries in the State Development & Redevelopment Plan (State Plan). The State Plan is the product of the State Planning Act, *N.J.S.A.* 52:18A–196 to –207. The Act charges the State Planning Commission with the task of adopting and revising a State Plan providing for a "coordinated, integrated and comprehensive plan for the growth, development, renewal and conservation of the State and its regions and which shall identify areas for growth, agriculture, open space conservation and other appropriate designations." *N.J.S.A.* 52:18A–199(a). The Plan generally divides the State into five planning areas: PA-1 (metropolitan or urban); PA-2 (developed suburban); PA-3 (fringe suburban); PA-4 (rural); and PA-5 (environmentally sensitive). The subject property had been within PA-2 but following Ocean's request the PA-5 designation area was expanded in the Township to encompass the subject property. The State Plan does not provide for a minimum acreage requirement for parcels within PA-5.

On September 21, 2006, Ocean adopted Ordinance 2006–34 (ordinance) which established the boundaries, design regulations, and standards for a new EC Zone. The ordinance stated: "It is the intent of this area to act as the low density environs of the center. Given the environmentally sensitive characteristics for the area, only very low intensity uses are allowed. Protection of the area is the principle objective of the EC district." Additionally, Ocean's expert professional planner Stan Slachetka testified that aside from protecting the environmentally sensitive nature of the land, Ordinance 2006–34's purpose was "to create a very, very distinct and clear boundary between" the town center and lands. . . .

Ocean maintains that since the ordinance is consistent with PA-5 under the State Plan, that its designation of the subject property as EC Zone was not arbitrary and capricious. However, in *Mount Olive Complex v. Township of Mount Olive,* 340 N.J.Super. 511, 541 (App.Div.2001) (citing *N.J.A.C.* 17:32–6.1(b)) *remanded on other grounds,* 174 N.J. 359 (2002), **we noted that the State "[P]lan is not intended to validate or invalidate any municipal code or zoning ordinance."** Thus Ocean cannot rely on the designation of the subject property as PA-5 under the State Plan to validate its downzoning of the property.

In light of existing development in the areas surrounding the subject property, we conclude that Ocean has not shown that the limitation of development to one unit per twenty acres is required to serve the stated purposes of the zoning ordinances. In view of the nearby residential development and the absence of any significant environmental constraints upon development, the limitation of potential future residential development of the subject property to one unit per twenty acres is arbitrary and unreasonable.

While the rezoning of the subject property for lower density development will result in preservation of a greater amount of open space, Ocean may not compel private property to be devoted to preservation for open space by restrictive zoning that is not justified by environmental constraints or other legitimate reasons. *See Pheasant Bridge, supra,* 169 N.J. at 294–95. Instead, Ocean must acquire any properties that it deems necessary for open space preservation by payment of fair market value to the owners. *See Mount Laurel Twp. v. Mipro Homes, L.L.C.,* 379 N.J.Super. 358, 371–74 (App.Div.2005), *aff'd,* 188 N.J. 531 (2006), *cert. denied,* 552 U.S. 940, 128 S.Ct. 46, 169 L.Ed.2d 242 (2007).

NOTES

1.   The court in Griepenburg found that the designation of the land as environmental conservation failed to meet the criteria for wetlands preservation and completely brushed aside the limited growth designation of the State Plan. Indeed, it never discussed the importance of growth management as set forth in the State Plan, the State Planning Act and the Governor's 2011 Executive Order. The court found that zoning to implement the state plan objective to preserve open space was tantamount to a taking.

2.   As attorney for the Township would you have placed the property in an environmental protection zone or into a Limited Growth Zone of one unit per twenty acres. Would this have required the court to focus on the growth management aspects of the case? Whether or not the court would have found that the State Plan was not binding, would its actions have made the rezoning reasonable and not arbitrary?

F. OTHER TECHNIQUES TO LIMIT OR STOP GROWTH: QUOTAS AND POPULATION CAPS

CONSTRUCTION INDUSTRY ASSOCIATION OF SONOMA COUNTY V. CITY OF PETALUMA

United States Court of Appeals, Ninth Circuit, 1975.
522 F.2d 897.

CHOY, CIRCUIT JUDGE:

The City of Petaluma (the City) appeals from a district court decision voiding as unconstitutional certain aspects of its five-year housing and zoning plan. We reverse.

The City is located in southern Sonoma County, about 40 miles north of San Francisco. In the 1950's and 1960's, Petaluma was a relatively self-sufficient town. It experienced a steady population growth from 10,315 in 1950 to 24,870 in 1970. Eventually, the City was drawn into the Bay Area metropolitan housing market as people working in San Francisco and San Rafael became willing to commute longer distances to secure relatively inexpensive housing available there. By November 1972, according to unofficial figures, Petaluma's population was at 30,500, a dramatic increase of almost 25 per cent in little over two years.

The increase in the City's population, not surprisingly, is reflected in the increase in the number of its housing units. From 1964 to 1971, the following number of residential housing units were completed:

Year	Units	Year	Units
1964	270	1968	379
1965	440	1969	358
1966	321	1970	591
1967	234	1971	891

In 1970 and 1971, the years of the most rapid growth, demand for housing in the City was even greater than above indicated. Taking 1970 and 1971 together, builders won approval of a total of 2000 permits although only 1482 were actually completed by the end of 1971.

Alarmed by the accelerated rate of growth in 1970 and 1971, the demand for even more housing, and the sprawl of the City eastward, the City adopted a temporary freeze on development in early 1971. The construction and zoning change moratorium was intended to give the City Council and the City planners an opportunity to study the housing and zoning situation and to develop short and long range plans. The Council made specific findings with respect to housing patterns and availability in Petaluma, including the following: That from 1960–1970 housing had been in almost unvarying 6000 square-foot lots laid out in regular grid patterns; that there was a density of approximately 4.5 housing units per acre in the single-family home areas; that during 1960–1970, 88 percent of housing permits issued were for single-family detached homes; that in 1970, 83 percent of Petaluma's housing was single-family dwellings; that the bulk of recent development (largely single-family homes) occurred in the eastern portion of the City, causing a large deficiency in moderately priced multi-family and apartment units on the east side.

To correct the imbalance between single-family and multi-family dwellings, curb the sprawl of the City on the east, and retard the accelerating growth of the City, the Council in 1972 adopted several resolutions, which collectively are called the "Petaluma Plan" (the Plan).

The Plan, on its face limited to a five-year period (1972–1977), fixes a housing development growth rate not to exceed 500 dwelling units per year.[2] Each dwelling unit represents approximately three people. The 500-unit figure is somewhat misleading, however, because it applies only to housing units (hereinafter referred to as "development-units") that are part of projects involving five units or more. Thus, the 500-unit figure does not reflect any housing and population growth due to construction of single-family homes or even four-unit apartment buildings not part of any larger project.

The Plan also positions a 200-foot wide "greenbelt" around the City,[3] to serve as a boundary for urban expansion for at least five years, and with respect to the east and north sides of the City, for perhaps ten to fifteen years. One of the most innovative features of the Plan is the Residential Development Control System which provides procedures and criteria for the award of the annual 500 development-unit permits. At the heart of the

---

[2]   The allotment for each year is not an inflexible limitation. The Plan does provide for a 10 percent variance (50 units) below or above the 500 unit annual figure, but the expectation of the Council is that not more than 2500 units will be constructed during the five-year period.

[3]   At some points this urban extension line is about one-quarter of a mile beyond the present City limits.

allocation procedure is an intricate point system, whereby a builder accumulates points for conformity by his projects with the City's general plan and environmental design plans, for good architectural design, and for providing low and moderate income dwelling units and various recreational facilities. The Plan further directs that allocations of building permits are to be divided as evenly as feasible between the west and east sections of the City and between single-family dwellings and multiple residential units (including rental units),[4] that the sections of the City closest to the center are to be developed first in order to cause "infilling" of vacant area, and that 8 to 12 percent of the housing units approved be for low and moderate income persons.

In a provision of the Plan, intended to maintain the close-in rural space outside and surrounding Petaluma, the City solicited Sonoma County to establish stringent subdivision and appropriate acreage parcel controls for the areas outside the urban extension line of the City and to limit severely further residential infilling.

Purpose of the Plan

The purpose of the Plan is much disputed in this case. According to general statements in the Plan itself, the Plan was devised to ensure that "development in the next five years, will take place in a reasonable, orderly, attractive manner, rather than in a completely haphazard and unattractive manner." The controversial 500-unit limitation on residential development-units was adopted by the City "(i)n order to protect its small town character and surrounding open space."[5] The other features of the Plan were designed to encourage an east-west balance in development, to provide for variety in densities and building types and wide ranges in prices and rents, to ensure infilling of close-in vacant areas, and to prevent the sprawl of the City to the east and north. The Construction Industry Association of Sonoma County (the Association) argues and the district court found, however, that the Plan was primarily enacted "to limit Petaluma's demographic and market growth rate in housing and in the immigration of new residents."

Market Demand and Effect of the Plan

In 1970 and 1971, housing permits were allotted at the rate of 1000 annually, and there was no indication that without some governmental

---

[4] By providing for the increase of multi-family dwellings (including townhouses as well as rental apartments), the Plan allows increased density. Whereas, during the years just preceding the Plan, housing density was about 4.5 units per acre, under the Plan single-family housing will consist of not only low (4.5 units per acre) but also medium density (4.5 to 10 units per acre). And multi-family housing, to comprise about half of the housing under the Plan, will be built at a density of 10 or more units per acre.

[5] After the appellees initiated this suit, the City attempted to show that the Plan was implemented to prevent the over-taxing of available water and sewage facilities. We find it unnecessary, however, to consider the claim that sewage and water problems justified implementation of the Plan.

control on growth consumer demand would subside or even remain at the 1000-unit per year level. Thus, if Petaluma had imposed a flat 500-unit limitation on all residential housing, the effect of the Plan would clearly be to retard to a substantial degree the natural growth rate of the City. Petaluma, however, did not apply the 500-unit limitation across the board, but instead exempted all projects of four units or less. Because Appellees failed to introduce any evidence whatsoever as to the number of exempt units expected to be built during the five-year period, the effect of the 500 development-unit limitation on the natural growth in housing is uncertain. For purposes of this decision, however, we will assume that the 500 development-unit growth rate is in fact below the reasonably anticipated market demand for such units and that absent the Petaluma Plan, the City would grow at a faster rate.

According to undisputed expert testimony at trial, if the Plan (limiting housing starts to approximately 6 percent of existing housing stock each year) were to be adopted by municipalities throughout the region, the impact on the housing market would be substantial. For the decade 1970 to 1980, the shortfall in needed housing in the region would be about 105,000 units (or 25 per cent of the units needed). Further, the aggregate effect of a proliferation of the Plan throughout the San Francisco region would be a decline in regional housing stock quality, a loss of the mobility of current and prospective residents and a deterioration in the quality and choice of housing available to income earners with real incomes of $14,000 per year or less. If, however, the Plan were considered by itself and with respect to Petaluma only, there is no evidence to suggest that there would be a deterioration in the quality and choice of housing available there to persons in the lower and middle income brackets. Actually, the Plan increases the availability of multi-family units (owner-occupied and rental units) and low-income units which were rarely constructed in the pre-Plan days.

Court Proceedings

Two landowners (the Landowners) and the Association instituted this suit under 28 U.S.C. §§ 1331, 1343 and 42 U.S.C. § 1983 against the City and its officers and council members, claiming that the Petaluma Plan was unconstitutional. The district court ruled that certain aspects of the Plan unconstitutionally denied the right to travel insofar as they tended "to limit the natural population growth of the area." The court enjoined the City and its agents from implementing the unconstitutional elements of the Plan, but the order was stayed by Justice Douglas pending this appeal.

[Editor's note: The Ninth Circuit held that while the builders' association and individual landowners suffered injuries in fact from the plan, they could not raise the right to travel argument for unknown third parties who might be excluded from Petaluma by the plan.]

Although we conclude that Appellees lack standing to assert the rights of third parties, they nonetheless having standing to maintain claims based on violations of rights personal to them. Accordingly, Appellees have standing to challenge the Petaluma Plan on the grounds asserted in their complaint that the Plan is arbitrary and thus violative of their due process rights guaranteed by the Fourteenth Amendment and that the Plan poses an unreasonable burden on interstate commerce. The fact that one of the Landowner's property lies wholly outside the present City boundaries and that the other's property lies mostly outside the boundaries is no bar to their challenging the City's Plan which has a direct, intended and immediate effect on the property.

Other Challenges to the Plan

Although the district court rested its decision solely on the right to travel claim, all the facts and legal conclusions necessary to resolve Appellees' other claims are part of the record. Thus, in order to promote judicial economy, we now dispose of the other challenges to the Plan.

Substantive Due Process

Appellees claim that the Plan is arbitrary and unreasonable and, thus, violative of the due process clause of the Fourteenth Amendment. According to Appellees, the Plan is nothing more than an exclusionary zoning device, designed solely to insulate Petaluma from the urban complex in which it finds itself. The Association and the Landowners reject, as falling outside the scope of any legitimate governmental interest, the City's avowed purposes in implementing the Plan the preservation of Petaluma's small town character and the avoidance of the social and environmental problems caused by an uncontrolled growth rate.

In attacking the validity of the Plan, Appellees rely heavily on the district court's finding that the express purpose and the actual effect of the Plan is to exclude substantial numbers of people who would otherwise elect to move to the City. The existence of an exclusionary purpose and effect reflects, however, only one side of the zoning regulation. Practically all zoning restrictions have as a purpose and effect the exclusion of some activity or type of structure or a certain density of inhabitants. And in reviewing the reasonableness of a zoning ordinance, our inquiry does not terminate with a finding that it is for an exclusionary purpose. We must determine further whether the exclusion bears any rational relationship to a legitimate state interest. If it does not, then the zoning regulation is invalid. If, on the other hand, a legitimate state interest is furthered by the zoning regulation, we must defer to the legislative act. Being neither a super legislature nor a zoning board of appeal, a federal court is without authority to weigh and reappraise the factors considered or ignored by the legislative body in passing the challenged zoning regulation. The reasonableness, not the wisdom, of the Petaluma Plan is at issue in this suit.

It is well settled that zoning regulations "must find their justification in some aspect of the police power, asserted for the public welfare." See *Village of Euclid v. Ambler Realty Co.*, 272 U.S. 365, 387 (1926). The concept of the public welfare, however, is not limited to the regulation of noxious activities or dangerous structures. * * *

In determining whether the City's interest in preserving its small town character and in avoiding uncontrolled and rapid growth falls within the broad concept of "public welfare," we are considerably assisted by two recent cases. *See Belle Terre, supra*, and *Ybarra v. City of Town of Los Altos Hills*, 503 F.2d 250 (9th Cir.1974), each of which upheld as not unreasonable a zoning regulation much more restrictive than the Petaluma Plan, are dispositive of the due process issue in this case.

In Belle Terre the Supreme Court rejected numerous challenges to a village's restricting land use to one-family dwellings excluding lodging houses, boarding houses, fraternity houses or multiple-dwelling houses. By absolutely prohibiting the construction of or conversion of a building to other than single-family dwelling, the village ensured that it would never grow, if at all, much larger than its population of 700 living in 220 residences. Nonetheless, the Court found that the prohibition of boarding houses and other multi-family dwellings was reasonable and within the public welfare because such dwellings present urban problems, such as the occupation of a given space by more people, the increase in traffic and parked cars and the noise that comes with increased crowds. According to the Court,

> A quiet place where yards are wide, people few, and motor vehicles restricted are legitimate guidelines in a land-use project addressed to family needs. This goal is a permissible one within *Berman v. Parker, supra*. The police power is not confined to elimination of filth, stench, and unhealthy places. It is ample to lay out zones where family values, youth values, and the blessings of quiet seclusion, and clean air make the area a sanctuary for people.

416 U.S. at 9. While dissenting from the majority opinion in Belle Terre on the ground that the regulation unreasonably burdened the exercise of First Amendment associational rights, Mr. Justice Marshall concurred in the Court's express holding that a local entity's zoning power is extremely broad:

> [L]ocal zoning authorities may properly act in furtherance of the objectives asserted to be served by the ordinance at issue here: restricting uncontrolled growth, solving traffic problems, keeping rental costs at a reasonable level, and making the community attractive to families. The police power which provides the justification for zoning is not narrowly confined. And, it is appropriate that we afford zoning authorities considerable

latitude in choosing the means by which to implement such purposes.

416 U.S. at 13–14, 94 S.Ct. at 1543 (Marshall, J., dissenting) (emphasis added) (citations omitted).

Following the Belle Terre decision, this court in Los Altos Hills had an opportunity to review a zoning ordinance providing that a housing lot shall contain not less than one acre and that no lot shall be occupied by more than one primary dwelling unit. The ordinance as a practical matter prevented poor people from living in Los Altos Hills and restricted the density, and thus the population, of the town. This court, nonetheless, found that the ordinance was rationally related to a legitimate governmental interest—the preservation of the town's rural environment—and, thus, did not violate the equal protection clause of the Fourteenth Amendment.

Both the Belle Terre ordinance and the Los Altos Hills regulation had the purpose and effect of permanently restricting growth; nonetheless, the court in each case upheld the particular law before it on the ground that the regulation served a legitimate governmental interest falling within the concept of the public welfare: the preservation of quiet family neighborhoods (Belle Terre) and the preservation of a rural environment (Los Altos Hills). Even less restrictive or exclusionary than the above zoning ordinances is the Petaluma Plan which, unlike those ordinances, does not freeze the population at present or near-present levels. Further, unlike the Los Altos Hills ordinance and the various zoning regulations struck down by state courts in recent years, the Petaluma Plan does not have the undesirable effect of walling out any particular income class nor any racial minority group.

Although we assume that some persons desirous of living in Petaluma will be excluded under the housing permit limitation and that, thus, the Plan may frustrate some legitimate regional housing needs, the Plan is not arbitrary or unreasonable. We agree with Appellees that unlike the situation in the past most municipalities today are neither isolated nor wholly independent from neighboring municipalities and that, consequently, unilateral land use decisions by one local entity affect the needs and resources of an entire region. *See e.g., Golden v. Planning Board of Town of Ramapo*, 30 N.Y.2d 359, 334 N.Y.S.2d 138, 285 N.E.2d 291, appeal dismissed, 409 U.S. 1003, 93 S.Ct. 436, 34 L.Ed.2d 294 (1972); *National Land & Investment Co. v. Kohn*, 419 Pa. 504, 215 A.2d 597 (1965); Note, *Phased Zoning: Regulation of the Tempo and Sequence of Land Development*, 26 STAN.L.REV. 585, 605 (1974). It does not necessarily follow, however, that the due process rights of builders and landowners are violated merely because a local entity exercises in its own self-interest the police power lawfully delegated to it by the state. *See Belle Terre, supra; Los Altos Hills, supra.* If the present system of delegated zoning power does not effectively serve the state interest in furthering the general welfare of the region or entire state, it is the state legislature's and not the federal courts' role to intervene and adjust the system. As stated supra, the federal court is not a super zoning board and should not be called on to mark the point at which legitimate local interests in promoting the welfare of the community are outweighed by legitimate regional interests.

We conclude therefore that under Belle Terre and Los Altos Hills the concept of the public welfare is sufficiently broad to uphold Petaluma's desire to preserve its small town character, its open spaces and low density of population, and to grow at an orderly and deliberate pace.

Reversed.

NOTES: POPULATION QUOTAS

1.   A unique aspect of Petaluma's plan was its annual design competition by which the 500 building permits were issued. Although design criteria might be subject to abuse because of the subjectivity of some of the standards, they do have the advantages of encouraging better planning in the layout and character of residential development and providing the community with the opportunity to examine all proposed developments at one time, providing a broader perspective for evaluating their impact. *See* Gray, *The City of Petaluma: Residential Development Control*, in 2 MANAGEMENT & CONTROL OF GROWTH 149, 154 (Scott ed.1975). In addition to these environmental and physical considerations, Petaluma developed social and fiscal goals. *See* Hart, *The Petaluma Case, Cry California*, Spring 1974, reprinted in 2 MANAGEMENT & CONTROL OF GROWTH 127 (Scott ed.1975).

2.   Pitkin County (Aspen), Colorado has implemented a Growth Management Quota System by regulation, under its Land Use Act that provides for the regulation of population density, phased development of services and facilities and land use regulations based upon the impact on the community or surrounding areas. It establishes an annual quota system for new building permits based on a formula against which each development application was tested and scored. The applications are granted on the basis of their score, the high score is granted a permit first, and then the rest are granted in descending order until the annual growth management quota is filled. This elaborate system for phasing development was upheld in *Wilkinson v. Pitkin County*, 872 P.2d 1269 (Colo.App.1993).

3.   In addition to limiting the issuance of building permits to 500 dwelling units per year for a 5 year period, the Petaluma Plan also established, and the court upheld, an urban extension or "greenbelt" line around the city as a boundary for urban expansion for a stated number of years. A similar plan was upheld in *Norbeck Village Joint Venture v. Montgomery County Council*, 254 A.2d 700 (Md.1969), which established a greenbelt of open spaces and parks to shield the area from the "ever-lengthening and overcrowding suburban sprawl" coming from Washington, D.C., and rezoned appellants' lands from 1/2 acre lots to 2 acre lots. The court upheld the plan, noting that it

was in conformity with the regional General Plan and was a "carefully thought out, carefully implemented policy" to preserve a suitable area as a self-identifiable community. 254 A.2d at 705.

4.   In *Pardee Construction Company v. Camarillo*, 208 Cal.Rptr. 228, 690 P.2d 701 (1984), the Supreme Court of California, in a strongly worded opinion, upheld a growth control ordinance with an annual quota of building permits despite the fact that the City and developer had entered into a consent judgment vesting the developer's zoning under the general plan. The Supreme Court found that neither the judgment nor the general plan referred to any time schedule or rate of development. The judgment reserved to the City the police power to adopt any ordinances not inconsistent with the judgment. The court held that the growth control ordinance, adopted by an initiative measure after entry of the judgment, regulated the rate of development but did not change the underlying zoning or alter the general plan. Thus it did not infringe on the company's rights under the judgment.

5.   The validity of quotas often depends on the quality of the planning effort used to justify a need to limit development and the rationality of distinctions drawn by the controls. See for example, *Rancourt v. Town of Barnstead*, 523 A.2d 55 (N.H.1986), where a denial of a subdivision application based on a three percent growth rate contained in a master plan was overturned. The town had not enacted a capital improvements program and the court was not convinced that the town's decision was based on solid scientific, statistical data. *Sturges v. Town of Chilmark*, 402 N.E.2d 1346, 1354 n. 16 (Mass.1980), upheld a rate of development by-law "in the absence of a contrary showing, that a period of ten years is reasonably necessary to complete all necessary studies and implement recommendations and that the town will proceed with its studies in good faith." *Begin v. Inhabitants of Sabattus*, 409 A.2d 1269 (Me.1979), recognized the validity of restrictions limiting the number of construction permits in the light of availability of municipal service. The court, however, struck down the ordinance because it applied only to mobile homes with no rational basis for such distinction. In *Giuliano v. Town of Edgartown*, 531 F.Supp. 1076 (D.Mass.1982), an ordinance limiting to ten the number of lots in a subdivision which could be conveyed or built upon without a special permit in any one year was upheld. The planning board balanced the benefits of subdivision versus burdens on schools, public facilities, traffic and pedestrian travel, availability of public water and sewer, recreational facilities, open spaces, agricultural resources, preservation of unique natural features, the planned rate of development, and housing for senior citizens and people of moderate income.

Twenty years after Petaluma the federal courts continue to uphold population quota systems.

SCHENCK V. CITY OF HUDSON

United States Court of Appeals, Sixth Circuit, 1997.
114 F.3d 590.

OPINION

RUSSELL, DISTRICT JUDGE.

This case involves a slow-growth zoning ordinance enacted by the Defendant City of Hudson. The Plaintiffs, primarily developers who already own land in Hudson, brought this action seeking a permanent injunction against the enforcement of the ordinance. After a two-day hearing, the district court granted a preliminary injunction and this appeal ensued. Upon review, we find that the plaintiffs have failed to show a likelihood of success on the merits and, therefore, dissolve the preliminary injunction and remand this case for further proceedings.

The City of Hudson, located in northern Ohio, is the result of a 1994 merger between the City of Hudson Village and Hudson Township. The City covers 25 square miles and has an estimated population of 21,000. Over the last thirty years the City and the Township have grown very rapidly, increasing by more than 50 percent in the 1970s and more than 35 percent in the 1980s. In a part of the state where the population has generally been declining, the area that is now the City of Hudson has had a rate of growth of 3.5 percent each year for the past 15 years.

In accordance with its conditions of merger, the City established a Comprehensive Plan (the "Plan"). The Plan, developed in conjunction with community input, public meetings, and the commission of studies on the City's infrastructure, concerns land use, recreation, community facilities, transportation, historic preservation, and growth management. Among the goals set forth in the Plan are the following: to manage the City's growth rate so that it does not exceed the capabilities of its infrastructure; to avoid the need for new infrastructure so that the City can meet current needs; and to protect the City's "unique" character. In addition, the Plan suggested that the City encourage nonresidential development to decrease the disparity between residential and nonresidential growth.

The City passed several zoning ordinances to implement the Plan's proposals, including Chapter 1207, the provision at issue in this case. In enacting these ordinances, the City relied upon studies that indicated the following: The City's sewer facilities were operating beyond capacity; the City's water treatment and distribution systems are inadequate; the City's roads are insufficient for existing traffic needs; emergency services are unable to meet the City's current needs, both in personnel and equipment; and The property taxes collected from new home construction are less than the costs to the City generated by the home's construction.

Under Chapter 1207, an applicant for a zoning certificate to construct a "residential dwelling unit" must receive a residential development allotment first. Each year the City Council determines how many residential allotments will be issued in that year, based upon the level of residential development for the previous year and the ability of the City's infrastructure to cope with new development. In July 1996, the first allotment after the ordinance's enactment, the number of allotments to be awarded for the year was set at 100 with 30 more allotments to be granted by the City Council for special projects, such as housing with 25% of the units reserved for the elderly and disabled and those with mixed commercial and residential uses that are located in the downtown area. Under the ordinance's provisions, the City can award thirty additional allotments for applicants who are denied allotments in the lottery. An unsuccessful applicant can apply for one of these allotments by showing hardship. An applicant denied allotments in the lottery can also appeal to the City Council. The allotments are distributed twice a year by a lottery system. Eighty percent of each distribution is reserved for the "priority development pool," which includes the following:

(1) Affordable housing;

(2) Housing reserved for the disabled and those over the age of sixty-two;

(3) Lots that were created and received preliminary or final plat approval before the ordinance's effective date; and

(4) Lots of five acres or more with access to a public street, public water, and sewer systems.

§ 1207.03(c)(2).

All of the plaintiffs in this action qualified for the priority development pool. However, the City of Hudson has 350–375 lots that have already received preliminary or final plat approval and are, therefore, qualified for the priority pool. As a result, all 84 applicants in the July 1996 distribution were priority applicants, and the distribution was determined by a lottery, in which no applicant received more than one allotment. After the July 1996 distribution the plaintiffs filed this action.

We review the district court's grant of a preliminary injunction for abuse of discretion. The reviewing court should consider four factors when determining whether the district court's grant of a preliminary injunction was an abuse of discretion: (1) the likelihood of success on the merits of the action; (2) the irreparable harm which could result without the relief requested; (3) the impact on the public interest; and (4) the possibility of substantial harm to others. *See L.P. Acquisition Co. v. Tyson*, 772 F.2d 201, 205 (6th Cir.1985).

The power of local governments to zone and control land use is undoubtedly broad and its proper exercise is an essential aspect of achieving a satisfactory quality of life. . . ." *Schad v. Borough of Mount*

Ephraim, 452 U.S. 61, 68 (1981). A legislative body need not even select the best or the least restrictive method of attaining its goals so long as the means selected are rationally related to those goals. *See National Paint & Coatings Ass'n v. City of Chicago*, 45 F.3d 1124, 1129 (7th Cir.1995) ("If there are alternative ways of solving a problem, [the federal courts] do not sit to determine which of them is best suited to achieve a valid state objective."), *cert. denied*, 515 U.S. 1143 (1995). Likewise, despite the temptation it is not the province of a federal court to act as a super-zoning board. *Exxon Corp. v. Governor of Maryland*, 437 U.S. 117, 124 (1978) ("[T]he Due Process Clause does not empower the judiciary 'to sit as a super legislature to weigh the wisdom of legislation.'" (quoting *Ferguson v. Skrupa*, 372 U.S. 726, 731 (1963)).

It is clear that the City of Hudson had a proper purpose, land use. As noted above, Chapter 1207 of the City's zoning code has several stated land use goals, which are based on enumerated findings of fact. The Supreme Court has specifically recognized similar goals as legitimate state interests. *See, e.g., Village of Belle Terre v. Boraas*, 416 U.S. 1 (1974) (holding goals of reducing traffic, noise and parking problems legitimate state interests);*Village of Euclid v. Ambler Realty Co.*, 272 U.S. 365, 393–94 (1926) (holding desire to decrease traffic congestion, increase safety and security, and economic administration legitimate purposes); *Construction Indus. Ass'n v. City of Petaluma*, 522 F.2d 897, 909 (9th Cir.1975) (holding desire to preserve small town character, open spaces, and low density and to grow at "an orderly and deliberate pace" legitimate governmental interests), *cert. denied*, 424 U.S. 934 (1976). Therefore, to survive a substantive due process challenge, Chapter 1207 must merely be rationally related to its purpose.

We conclude that it is. "Federal court review of a zoning ordinance may only determine whether it is clearly arbitrary and unreasonable, in the very restricted sense that it 'has no substantial relation to the public health, safety, morals or general welfare.'" *Pearson*, 961 F.2d at 1223 (quoting *Village of Belle Terre v. Boraas*, 416 U.S. 1, 7–8 (1974)). The City of Hudson wishes to control growth of residential areas until such time as its infrastructure is able to meet current and future needs. A cap on the number of homes built in the City unquestionably bears a rational relationship to this concern.

Even though the City of Hudson will have to remedy existing infrastructure problems regardless of whether another house is built, Chapter 1207 is rationally related to the City's legitimate concerns. Slowing the rate of growth will allow the City to improve its infrastructure to meet existing and future needs without straining resources. At the same time the City's system is designed to accommodate its changing needs. For example, the number of allotments available is reviewed annually by the City Council to ensure that growth occurs in tandem with infrastructure improvements. In addition, landowners who had obtained preliminary or final platting approval when the ordinance was enacted are granted "priority" status when allotments are assigned. In the event that there are more applicants than allotments in a given year, the lottery system is certainly a rational means of distribution because it avoids beauty contests between property owners and is more efficient for the City to administer. A system which weighs the merits of each development in determining the distribution of allotments would be more cumbersome and could exclude developments for subjective reasons. The City's lottery system promotes efficiency and allows every applicant an equal chance at obtaining one of the allotments. Finally, the ordinance contains a provision for landowners who have not received an allotment after one year to petition the City Council for compensation due to hardship.

Chapter 1207 clearly has a substantial relationship to the City's welfare because it will slow the City's growth until such time as the City believes it is equipped to sustain a more rapid growth rate. It is not our place to judge the wisdom of such a provision because "[t]he Constitution presumes that, absent some reason to infer antipathy, even improvident decisions will eventually be rectified by the democratic process and that judicial intervention is generally unwarranted no matter how unwisely we may think a political branch has acted." *See Vance v. Bradley*, 440 U.S. 93, 97 (1979). As such, the district court abused its discretion by granting plaintiffs' request for a preliminary injunction.

The preliminary injunction is DISSOLVED and this case is REMANDED for proceedings on the merits.

ALAN E. NORRIS, CIRCUIT JUDGE, dissenting.

Although one might posit a slow-growth ordinance which is sufficiently narrow and prospective to meet the test of rationality, we are not favored with such an ordinance in this appeal.

Plaintiffs are not individuals who contemplate purchasing lots in Hudson with full knowledge of the restrictions imposed by the slow-growth ordinance at issue in this case. Rather, they are, for the most part, individuals and business entities which have already invested substantial time and money in improving lots for development. Furthermore, they made these investments in good faith reliance upon platting approval received from the appropriate governmental bodies.

The majority's analysis fails to distinguish between the legitimate expectations of these property owners, and those of future developers of lots located in Hudson. The district court recognized that the two groups are not similarly situated, declining to enjoin the prospective application of Chapter 1207. Instead, it limited the scope of the injunction to those lots which had obtained preliminary or final plat approval, and which enjoyed access to existing infrastructure. In my view, the distinction drawn by the district court is proper: forcing the owners of the lots covered by the injunction to comply with the scheme set forth by Chapter 1207 is not rationally related to the stated purpose of the slow-growth ordinance.

First, the primary rationale advanced by the City in defense of this ordinance concerns the rate at which new building threatens to outpace existing infrastructure. Given this concern, one would expect that exceptions to the allotment scheme would be made approved lots with existing water, sewer, and road access. This is not the case. Although such lots are accorded "priority" status, that designation is effectively meaningless because every allotment granted during the period under review went to a "priority" applicant. Second, limiting owners of multiple improved lots to the same, single allotment as owners of one lot strikes me as irrational on its face, particularly where, as here, owners of multiple lots have invested significant sums in infrastructure, the very problem Chapter 1207 purports to address.

In short, although deferential, our review of zoning ordinances such as that enacted by Hudson does not end once the city articulates a legitimate land use concern. Rather, we must make sure that the ordinance is rationally related to the alleviation of that concern. When its practical effect is to impose harm on a class of property owners which is clearly arbitrary and unreasonable, the ordinance runs afoul of substantive due process. *Pearson v. City of Grand Blanc*, 961 F.2d 1211, 1223 (6th Cir.1992). Because that is the case here, I believe the district court properly granted injunctive relief to those individuals who own lots that have received either preliminary or final plat approval.

Accordingly, I respectfully dissent.

NOTES

1. Would you have drafted a lottery as the ultimate method for distribution of building permits? Is a lottery the same as "flipping a coin"?

2. *See also Boulder Builders Group v. City of Boulder*, 759 P.2d 752 (Colo.App.1988), described in Pollock, *Controlling Sprawl in Boulder: Benefits and Pitfalls*, 10 LAND LINES (Jan.1998), (Lincoln Inst. of Land Policy) ("This approach owed much to the phased growth control ordinance pioneered in 1969 by the Town of Ramapo, New York").

3. Several articles have discussed the Petaluma Plan and its place in growth management systems. *See* Larry Smith, *Does Petaluma Lie at the End of the Road From Ramapo?*, 19 VILL.L.REV. 739 (1974); Dawson, *Management of Residential Growth*, in 1981 Zoning and Planning Law Handbook 145 (Strom ed.) and Malcolm Misuraca, Petaluma vs. the T.J. Hooper: *Must the Suburbs be Seaworthy?*, 2 MANAGEMENT & CONTROL OF GROWTH 187 (Scott ed., 1975) (the author was the attorney for the Construction Industry Association in the Petaluma case).

4.   What about the right to travel argument that was not addressed in Petaluma due to lack of standing? *See Associated Home Builders of the Greater Eastbay, Inc. v. Livermore*, 557 P.2d 473 (Cal.1976) (holding the indirect effect of growth controls on the right to travel does not call for strict scrutiny and finding no constitutional violation). *See* Note, *That Old Due Process Magic: Growth Control and the Federal Constitution*, 88 MICH.L.REV. 1245 (1990) (arguing that the right to travel, the privileges and immunities clause and the commerce clause, not due process, are the appropriate constitutional measures to test growth controls).

5.   Boca Raton, Florida attempted to control its growth by placing an absolute limit on its population. In lieu of a limit on the number of permits it would issue annually over a limited number of years, Boca Raton used a population cap limiting the number of building permits it would ever issue. The numerical cap in Boca Raton was arrived at "backwards." Citizens who were concerned about the rapid growth of the city, used initiative and referendum provisions to submit to the voters a charter amendment question limiting the total number of units to 40,000. Once the voters then passed the charter amendment, the city was faced with implementing the "cap." Almost 17 months later, the city council enacted new zoning ordinances. Although the city used the services of two consultants to aid in developing techniques to implement the cap, the final result was a simple across-the-board 50 percent downzoning density reduction. Furthermore, most of the studies cited to support the cap were undertaken after the cap was established; there was no convincing evidence of utility shortages. The court invalidated the cap. *See City of Boca Raton v. Boca Villas Corporation*, 371 So.2d 154 (Fla.App.1979).

6.   Compare a cap instituted on the number of permits allowed over a ten-year span, which was instituted by Monroe County, Florida. Monroe County is situated at the southern tip of the Florida Peninsula in the Gulf of Mexico and includes the low-lying chain of small islands known as the Florida Keys. Numerous problems have evolved from the unchecked overwhelming explosion of population growth and development in Monroe County and the Florida Keys. One major problem has been damage to the unique tropical environment. The islands host over seventy-five plant and animal species listed as endangered, threatened, or under some other form of protected status. Another problem from the population growth was the hurricane evacuation time, which was one of the longest in the country. In a place where hurricane threats are very real, the consequences of a long evacuation time are exacerbated by the elongated configuration of the Keys and the fact that the 12 mile evacuation route is a low-lying highway prone to flooding before the hurricane even arrives. To resolve these problems Monroe County had to reduce its growth rate and better plan for future growth, which it attempted to do by following the Ramapo recipe of consistency, concurrency and compactness. The County adopted a Permit Allocation System in 1992, which limited the number of dwelling units allowed from 1992 to 2002 to 2,552, approximately 255 units per year. At the time of adoption there were approximately 14,500 existing platted lots, each with an allocated development

right for one dwelling unit. In a short per curiam opinion, the Court of Appeals upheld the constitutionality of the ROGO (rate of growth system).

BURNHAM V. MONROE COUNTY

District Court of Appeal of Florida, 1999.
738 So.2d 471.

Opinion: PER CURIAM.

Property owners in Monroe County appeal from a final judgment declaring that Monroe County had not taken their property in an inverse condemnation proceeding, and that Monroe County's "Rate of Growth Ordinance" is constitutional. We affirm.

The Burnhams have owned their property in Monroe since 1967; they submitted their application for a building permit in July, 1992, after Monroe County's "Rate of Growth Ordinance", commonly referred to as "ROGO" became effective. See Monroe County, Fla., Ordinance 16-1992 (June 23, 1992). Under ROGO, Monroe County awards points for certain [sustainable] design features included in building plans. Building permits are allocated to applicants who have accumulated the most points. Building features for which points are awarded include, but [are not limited to] [location adjacent to U.S. Highway 1 to reduce transportation congestion], solar hot water heaters; high-efficiency air conditioning systems; hurricane-strength structural wind loads; and low-flow plumbing fixtures.

The owners' construction plans did not include enough of the features that ROGO sought to encourage to entitle them to a building permit. The County repeatedly informed them that they could obtain a ROGO allocation, and the ensuing building permit, at any time simply by incorporating a few basic additions to their plans. At no time did the owners make those changes; they instead chose to challenge the ordinance and sued the County for inverse condemnation. The trial court ruled that no taking had occurred because the County had not deprived the owners of all beneficial use of their property. The trial court further found that the ordinance was constitutional. We agree.

It is clear from the record that no taking occurred; all that the owners had to do in order to obtain the necessary points for their building permit was make a few minor changes to their plans. To establish a taking by inverse condemnation, a plaintiff must show that the challenged regulation denies all [or substantially all] economically beneficial or productive use of land. See *Lucas v. South Carolina Coastal Council*, 505 U.S. 1003 (1992); *Jacobi v. City of Miami Beach*, 678 So.2d 1365 (Fla.1996). The owners made no such showing in this case.

Moreover, the trial court correctly determined that the ROGO ordinance was constitutional, as it substantially advances the legitimate state interests of promoting water conservation, windstorm protection, energy efficiency, growth control, and habitat protection. (emphasis supplied) *See Nollan v. California Coastal Comm'n*, 483 U.S. 825 (1987).

AFFIRMED.

NOTES

1.   The Rate of Growth (ROGO) Permit Allocation System has been successful at cutting the historical growth rate for Monroe County by more than half since its enactment in 1992. *See* Lorenzo Aghemo, *Adequate Public Facilities and Concurrency in Florida: The Case of the Florida Keys, Annual Institute of Planning, Zoning and Eminent Domain*, Matthew Bender, Ch. 9 (1996).

2.   In later decision, the Florida District Court of Appeals endorsed the County's 1992 ROGO system with the following language: "The first land development regulations were adopted in 1986 pursuant to Sections 380.05(6) and (8), Florida Statutes (1985). In 1992, the Rate of Growth Ordinance ("ROGO") was adopted as part of a state emergency rule. Finally, in January of 1996, Monroe County adopted its 2010 comprehensive plan measures to add environmental and infrastructure standards on residential growth in a sensitive island chain." *See Monroe County v. Ambrose*, 866 So.2d 707 (Fla.App.2003).

3.   For additional reading regarding population curbs and caps and their relationship to constitutional issues *see* John Nolon, *Comprehensive Land Use Planning: Learning How and Where to Grow*, 13 PACE L.REV. 351 (1993); Johnstone, *Government Control of Urban Land Use: A Comparative Major Program Analysis*, 39 N.Y.L.SCH.L.REV. 373 (1994); Rachel Alterman, *Land Use Law in the Face of a Rapid-Growth Crisis: The Case of Mass-Immigration to Israel in the 1990s*, 3 WASH.U.J.L. & POL'Y 773 (2000).

CHAPTER 8

GLOBAL WARMING, CLIMATE CHANGE AND LAND USE

■ ■ ■

A. INTRODUCTION

We earlier learned from Chapter 7, that land use law is actively involved in combating global warming and climate change by: utilizing growth management tiered systems with transportation corridors, mixed use higher density transit oriented and traditional neighborhood development and priority urban growth areas that reduce greenhouse gas emissions, by shortening trip lengths, reducing the number of trips taken per day, and by shifting patterns of growth to walkable developments within free standing centers.

The focus of this Chapter is to analyze and implement land use regulation of global warming and climate change through: (a) state environmental assessment acts; (b) reducing stationary and mobile sources of greenhouse gas emissions, through cap and trade market options; (c) using rainwater capture and groundwater management to overcome drought and flooding; (d) adopting "green development" codes and standards; (e) utilizing nuclear, solar and wind renewable energy systems; and (f) interim natural gas fracking to replace dirtier coal and oil for electrical utilities and home heating and air-conditioning, until renewable sources of energy are universal.

B. GLOBAL WARMING AND CLIMATE CHANGE

"Global Warming" refers only to the Earth's rising surface temperature, while "Climate Change" includes warming and the "side effects" of warming—melting glaciers, rising seas, heavier rainstorms, drought and flooding, destruction of agricultural land and human-caused climate change.

Your results are back. It's climate change. Just how
many greenhouse gases have you been consuming?

https://www.climate.gov/sites/default/files/Q&A_GWvsCC_comic_lrg.png

When scientists or public leaders talk about global warming they mean human caused warming—warming due to the rapid increase in carbon dioxide, methane and other greenhouse gases from the burning of coal, oil, gasoline and natural gas.

Climate change, on the other hand, means both human-caused changes or natural ones. Besides burning fossil fuels, humans cause climate changes by emitting aerosol pollution—the tiny particles that reflect sunlight and cool the climate—into the atmosphere, or by transforming the Earth's landscape, for instance, from carbon-storing forests to farmland. The planet has experienced climate change before: the Earth's average temperature has fluctuated throughout the planet's 4.54 billion-year history. The planet has experienced long cold periods ("ice ages") and warm periods ("inter-glacials") on 100,000-year cycles for at least the last million years.

Previous warming episodes were triggered by small increases in sunlight that reached Earth's surface and then amplified by large releases of carbon dioxide from the oceans as they warmed. Today's global warming is overwhelmingly due to the increase in heat-trapping gases that humans are adding to the atmosphere by burning fossil fuels. In fact, over the last five decades, natural factors (solar forcing and volcanoes) would actually have led to a slight cooling of Earth's surface temperature.

Global warming is also different from past warming in its rate. The current increase in global average temperature over the past 160 years appears to be occurring much faster than at any point since modern civilization and agriculture developed 11,000 years or so—and probably faster than any interglacial warm periods over the last million years. Today's global warming is an unprecedented type of climate change, and it is driving a cascade of side effects in our climate system. It's these side effects, such as rising changes in sea level along heavily populated coastlines and the worldwide retreat of mountain glaciers that millions of people depend on for clean air, drinking water, and agriculture. *See*, Jerry M. Melillo, Terese Richmond, and Gary W. Yohe, eds., *2014 Climate Change Impacts in the United States: The Third National Climate Assessment*, U.S Global Change Research Program; online at nca2014. globalchange.gov.

Recent evidence only confirms the trend:

Justin Gillis, 2015 Was Hottest Year in Historical Record, Scientists Say, New York Times, January 20, 2016 at A 1.

"Scientists reported Wednesday that 2015 was the hottest year in the historical record by far, breaking a mark set only the year before—a burst of heat that has continued into the new year and is roiling weather patterns all over the world.

In the contiguous United States, the year was the second warmest on record, punctuated by a December that was both the hottest and the wettest since record keeping began. One result has been a wave of unusual winter floods coursing down the Mississippi River watershed.

Scientists started predicting a global temperature record a month ago, in part because an El Niño weather pattern, one of the largest in a century, is releasing an immense amount of heat from the Pacific Ocean into the atmosphere. But the bulk of the record-setting heat, they say, is a consequence of the long-term planetary warming caused by human emissions of greenhouse gases.

"The whole system is warming up, relentlessly," said Gerald A. Meehl, a scientist at the National Center for Atmospheric Research in Boulder, Colo. It will take, he said, a few more years to know for certain, but the back-to-back records of 2014 and 2015 may have put the world back onto a trajectory of rapid global warming, after a period of relatively slow warming dating to the last powerful El Niño, in 1998.

Politicians attempting to claim that greenhouse gases are not a problem seized on that slow period to argue that "global warming stopped in 1998," with these claims and similar statements reappearing recently on the Republican 2016 presidential campaign trail. Statistical analysis suggested all along that those claims were false, and that the slowdown was, at most, a minor blip in an inexorable trend, perhaps caused by a temporary increase in the absorption of heat by the Pacific Ocean.

"Is there any evidence for a pause in the long-term global warming rate?" said Gavin A. Schmidt, head of NASA's climate science unit, the Goddard Institute for Space Studies, in Manhattan. "The answer is no. That was true before last year, but it's much more obvious now."

Two American government agencies—NASA, the National Aeronautics and Space Administration, and NOAA, the National Oceanic and Atmospheric Administration released figures on Wednesday showing that 2015 was the warmest year in a global record that began, in their data, in 1880. British scientists released figures showing 2015 as the warmest in a record dating to 1850. The Japan Meteorological Agency had already released preliminary results showing 2015 as the warmest year in a record beginning in 1891.

When temperatures are averaged at a global scale, the differences between years are usually measured in fractions of a degree. In the NOAA data set, 2015 was 0.29 degrees Fahrenheit warmer than 2014, the largest jump ever over a previous record. NASA calculated a slightly smaller figure, but still described it as an unusual one year increase. The intense warmth of 2015 contributed to a heat wave in India last spring that turns out to have been the second worst in that country's history, killing an estimated 2,500 people. The long term global warming trend has exacted a severe toll from extreme heat, with eight of the world's 10 deadliest heat waves occurring since 1997.

C. INTERNATIONAL EFFORTS TO CONTROL GLOBAL WARMING

The United States praised a landmark climate change agreement approved Saturday in Paris, saying it could be "a turning point for the world."

Though the plan was hailed as a milestone in the battle to keep Earth hospitable to human life, critics say it is short on specifics, such as how the plan will be enforced or how improvements will be measured.

The accord achieved one major goal. It limits average global warming to 2 degrees Celsius (3.6 degrees Fahrenheit) above pre-industrial temperatures and strives for a limit of 1.5 degrees Celsius (2.7 degrees Fahrenheit) if possible.

The agreement, put together at the 21st Conference of Parties, or COP21, doesn't mandate exactly how much each country must reduce its greenhouse gas emissions. Rather, it sets up a bottom-up system in which each country sets its own goal—which the agreement calls a "nationally determined contribution"—and then must explain how it plans to reach that objective. Those pledges must be increased over time, and starting in 2018 each country will have to submit new plans every five years.

Many countries actually submitted their new plans before climate change conference, known as COP21, started last month—but those pledges aren't enough to keep warming below the 2-degree target. But the participants' hope is that over time, countries will aim for more ambitious goals and ratchet up their commitments, [in that regard] the agreement calls for the creation of a committee of experts to "facilitate implementation" and "promote compliance" with the agreement, but it won't have the power to punish violators.

The U.S. Climate Action Plan, presented to COP21, calls for leadership abroad. To support this objective, the 2016 Budget provides $1.29 billion, a significant increase above the 2015 enacted level, to advance the goals of the Global Climate Change Initiative (GCCI) by supporting important multilateral and bilateral engagement with major and emerging economies. This funding includes $500 million for U.S. contributions to the new international Green Climate Fund (GCF), established at COP21, which will help developing countries leverage public and private finance and invest in reducing carbon pollution and strengthening resilience to climate change. By reducing the most catastrophic risks of climate change, the GCF will help promote smart, sustainable long-term economic growth and preserve stability and security in fragile regions of strategic importance to the United States. These investments will build on the best practices and lessons learned from previous Climate Investment Funds (CIFs). More GCCI funding enables the U.S. to provide international leadership through the Department of State (State), the U.S. Agency for International Development (USAID), and the Department of the Treasury.

Nevertheless, the fall in the price of oil and natural gas will test the will of nations to maintain the transition to solar and wind clean energy. *See,* Clifford Krauss and Diane Cardwell, *Climate Deal's First Big Hurdle: The Draw of Cheap Oils,* New York Times, January 26, 2016, at A1:

> Steady improvements in the fuel economy of new vehicles have stalled recently as consumers, buoyed by low gas prices, snap up lower-mileage trucks and sport utility vehicles. Barely a month after world leaders signed a sweeping agreement to reduce carbon emissions, renewable energy sources face their first big test as the price of oil collapses.

> Americans are largely eschewing electric cars in favor of lower-mileage trucks and sport utility vehicles. Yet the Obama administration has shown no signs of backing off its requirement that automakers nearly double the fuel economy of their vehicles by 2025.

> In China, government officials are also taking steps to ensure that the recent plunge in oil prices to under $30 a barrel does not undermine its programs to improve energy efficiency. Earlier this month, the country's top economic planning agency introduced a

new regulation, effective immediately, aimed at deterring oil consumption.

For the climate accord to work, governments must resist the lure of cheap fossil fuels in favor of policies that encourage and, in many cases, require the use of zero-carbon energy sources. But those policies can be expensive and politically unpopular, especially as traditional fuels become ever more affordable."

D. FEDERAL ACTION AND GLOBAL WARMING

PEOPLE OF THE STATE OF CALIFORNIA V. GENERAL MOTORS

U.S. District Court, Northern District of California, 2007.
2007 WL 2726871.

The court summarized the history of Congressional and Presidential action with respect to Global Warming:

"A chronology of the relevant environmental policy on global warming is helpful in setting the stage for the issues now before the Court. Congress and the Executive Branch have taken several actions to understand and address the complex issue of global warming. *See Connecticut v. American Elec. Power Co.*, 406 F.Supp.2d 265, 269 (S.D.N.Y.2005) ("AEP").

In 1978, Congress established a "national climate program" to improve understanding of global climate change through research, data collection, assessments, information dissemination, and international cooperation. See National Climate Program Act of 1978, 15 U.S.C. §§ 2901, et seq. Two years later, Congress directed the Office of Science and Technology Policy to engage the National Academy of Sciences in a study of the "projected impact, on the level of carbon dioxide in the atmosphere, of fossil fuel combustion, coal-conversion and related synthetic fuels activities" authorized by the Energy Security Act. See Energy Security Act (1980).

Congress next addressed the issue in 1987, when it enacted the Global Climate Protection Act, 15 U.S.C. § 2901. Finding that "manmade pollution—the release of carbon dioxide, chlorofluorocarbons, methane, and other trace gases into the atmosphere—may be producing a long-term and substantial increase in the average temperature on Earth," Congress directed EPA to propose to Congress a "coordinated national policy on global climate change," and ordered the Secretary of State to work "through the channels of multilateral diplomacy" and coordinate diplomatic efforts to combat global warming. Congress emphasized that "ongoing pollution and deforestation may be contributing now to an irreversible process" and that "necessary actions must be identified and implemented in time to protect the climate."

In 1990, Congress enacted the Global Change Research Act. 15 U.S.C. §§ 2931–2938. This Act established a ten-year research program for global climate issues. § 2932. One of the Act's provisions directed the President to establish a research program to "improve understanding of global change," § 2933, and provided for scientific assessments every four years that "analyze current trends in global change," § 2936(3)."

Turning to the current legislative landscape, Congress established a comprehensive state and federal scheme to control air pollution in the United States in the Clean Air Act, 42 U.S.C. § 7401 et seq. ("CAA"). *See National Audubon Society v. Dept. of Water*, 869 F.2d 1196, 1201 (9th Cir.1988). The central elements of this comprehensive scheme are the Act's provisions for uniform national standards of performance for new stationary sources of air pollution. *See* 42 U.S.C. § 7411. The Act's provisions provide for uniform national emission standards for hazardous air pollutants likely to cause an increase in mortality or serious illness, § 7412, for promulgation of primary and secondary national ambient air quality standards (NAAQS), §§ 7408–09, and for the development of national ambient air quality standards for motor vehicle emissions. § 7521; National Audubon Society, 869 F.2d at 1202."

Continuing on with current federal developments, in 2015 in response to *Massachusetts v. E.P.A.*, 549 U.S. 497 (2007), the U.S. Environmental Protection Agency (EPA) released a permanent rule to limit greenhouse gas emissions from new power plants on August 3, 2015 (Technical Support Document (TSD) the Final Carbon Pollution Emission Guidelines for Existing Stationary Sources: Electric Utility Generating Units. CO_2 Emission Performance Rate and Goal Computation). The final "Carbon Pollution Standard for New Power Plants" replaces earlier proposals from September 2013 and March 2012. It establishes New Source Performance Standards (NSPS) under the Clean Air Act, Section 111(b) to limit emissions of carbon dioxide (CO_2) from coal and natural gas-fired power plants and officially recognizes global warming.

In an act of bi-partisanship, Congress passed the 2016 Omnibus Budget Bill which officially recognized global warming and reauthorized investment tax credits for renewable solar and wind energy. The 2016 federal budget invests heavily in the world Green Climate Fund to lead efforts to cut carbon pollution and enhance climate change resilience.

However, on March 27, 2017, President Trump ordered the federal government to retreat from the battle against climate change launched by President Obama, issuing a directive aimed at dismantling the core policies that have made the U.S. a global leader in curbing emissions.

The plan unveiled by President Trump reflects an about-face for the U.S. on energy, and it puts into jeopardy the nation's ability to meet the obligations it agreed to under the global warming pact signed in Paris with 194 other nations. It would shelve the landmark Clean Power Plan that mandates electricity companies reduce their emissions. It seeks to dislodge consideration of climate throughout the federal government, where it has been a factor in every relevant decision in recent years.

"My administration is putting an end to the war on coal," Trump said. "I am taking historic steps to lift the restrictions on American energy to reverse government intrusions and to cancel job killing regulations."

Under the order, the government will abandon the "social cost of carbon" that regulators had painstakingly calculated and begun factoring into their decision on permit applications and rulemaking. Restrictions on methane releases at oil and gas drilling facilities would be eased.

Agencies will also stop contemplating climate impacts as they launch into new projects, and restrictions on coal leasing and fracking on federal lands will be lifted. Evan Halper, *Trump Orders Government to Dismantle Obama's Climate Change Policies*, Los Angeles Times, March 28, 2017.

E. STATE ENVIRONMENTAL QUALITY ACTS AND GLOBAL WARMING

1. CALIFORNIA ENVIRONMENTAL QUALITY ACT (CEQA)

On November 29, 2010, the California Building Industry Association (CBIA) filed suit challenging the Bay Area Quality Management Air District's (BAAQMD's) environmental review guidelines for greenhouse gases (GHGs) and toxic air contaminants related to urban development projects and conflicts between CEQA, SB 375, New Urbanism and Affordable Housing. *California Building Industry v. Bay Area Air Quality Mgmt.*, 2012 WL 9172278 (Cal.Super). The CBIA asserted that recently established guidelines, which focus on projects planned near major freeways, conflict with the state's overarching climate change goals, such as those found in the 2008 law SB 375, of reducing sprawl and encouraging infill and transit-oriented development. The guidelines set lower thresholds of significance for pollutants such as ozone, nitrogen oxide and particulate matter that must be evaluated under the California Environmental Quality Act (CEQA).

The lawsuit specifically alleged that the BAAQMD failed to analyze the potential environmental impacts of adjacent district toxic air contaminant "thresholds of significance" under CEQA. According to the BAAQMD, the guidelines provide tools for local agencies to use in making smart development decisions that protect residents from harmful air emissions and greenhouse gases. However, one consequence of the protections found in the guidelines is that stricter emission standards for certain pollutants makes it difficult to approve infill residential development adjacent to freeways and major roadways, where diesel soot and other pollutants from adjacent properties and areas are typically quite high.

In addition to the building industry, these implications have caused concern among some advocates for affordable housing, such as the San Francisco Housing Action Coalition and new urbanists, because of fears that prime urban locations for affordable housing and traditional neighborhood development will be unable to meet the requirements of the new guidelines. While the new regulations will not bar development in the more polluted areas, they would require builders to spend time and money studying and addressing the pollution. District officials have stated that they plan to closely monitor proposals for infill development projects to ensure they are not negatively impacted by the guidelines, and that it does not become more difficult for infill projects to advance.

Do these guideline thresholds contribute to greater greenhouse gas emissions by replacing housing in inner cities with large scale urban sprawl to outlying areas with resulting increased trip distances and numbers of trips? The conflict between protecting the health and safety of residents of homes built close to freeway corridors and the health and safety of the residents of the world, nation, city and neighborhood as a result of rapidly advancing global warming is just one of the problems of dealing with global warming.

Does the decision in *California Building Industry Association v. Bay Area Air Quality Management District*, 362 P.3d 792 (Cal.2015) below help solve these infill concerns?

CALIFORNIA BUILDING INDUSTRY ASSOCIATION V. BAY AREA AIR QUALITY MANAGEMENT DISTRICT
Supreme Court of California, 2015.
62 Cal.4th 369, 196 Cal.Rptr.3d 94, 362 P.3d 792.

We granted review to address the following question: Under what circumstances, if any, does the California Environmental Quality Act (CEQA) (Pub. Resources Code, 1 § 21000 et seq.) require an analysis of how existing off-site environmental conditions will impact future residents or users of a proposed residential project?

In light of CEQA's text, statutory structure, and purpose, we conclude that agencies subject to CEQA generally are not required to analyze the impact of existing off-site environmental conditions on a project's future users or residents. But when a proposed project risks exacerbating those environmental hazards or conditions that already exist, an agency must analyze the potential impact of such hazards on future residents or users. In those specific instances, it is the project's impact on the environment—and not the off-site environment's impact on the project—that compels an evaluation of how future residents or users could be affected by exacerbated conditions. Our reading is consistent with certain portions of administrative guidelines issued by the California Natural Resources Agency (Resources Agency), to whom we owe a measure of deference in a case such as this one.

Moreover, special CEQA requirements apply to certain airport, school, and housing construction projects. In such situations, CEQA requires agencies to evaluate a project site's environmental conditions regardless of whether the project risks exacerbating existing conditions. The environmental review must take into account—and a negative declaration or exemption cannot issue without considering—how existing environmental risks such as noise, hazardous waste, or wildland fire hazard will impact future residents or users of a project. That these exceptions exist, however, does not alter our conclusion that ordinary CEQA analysis is concerned with a project's impact on the environment, rather than with the environment's impact of existing off-site environmental conditions on a project and its users or residents.

We reverse the Court of Appeal's judgment and remand for proceedings consistent with our decision.

The Bay Area Air Quality Management District (District) is a regional agency authorized to adopt and enforce regulations governing air pollutants from stationary sources such as factories, refineries, power plants, and gas stations in the San Francisco Bay Area. The District's purpose is to achieve and maintain compliance, in its regional jurisdiction, with state and federal ambient air quality standards. (Health & Saf. Code, §§ 39002, 40000, 40001, subd. (a), 40200.) To fulfill this purpose, the District monitors air quality, issues permits to certain emitters of air pollution, and promulgates rules to control emissions. (Id., §§ 40001, 42300, 42301.5, 42315.)

The Resources Agency, meanwhile, is the agency with primary responsibility for statewide implementation of CEQA. It carries out this task in part by adopting administrative guidelines (Cal. Code Regs., tit. 14, § 15000 et seq.) that call for other agencies subject to CEQA, such as the District, to develop "thresholds of significance" for determining "the significance of environmental effects." (Guidelines, § 15064.7, subd. (a)). In 1999, the District published thresholds of significance for certain air pollutants, along with its own regional guidelines concerning the use of the thresholds and CEQA air quality issues in general, in order to guide those preparing or evaluating air quality impact analyses for projects in the San Francisco Bay Area. The thresholds set levels at which toxic air contaminants (TACs) and certain types of particulate matter would be deemed environmentally significant requiring full environmental assessment and review.

A decade later, in 2009, the District drafted new proposed thresholds of significance partly in response to the Legislature's adoption of laws addressing greenhouse gases (GHGs). The District cited three factors to justify the new thresholds: (1) the existence of more stringent state and federal air quality standards that took effect after the District adopted its earlier thresholds, (2) the discovery that greenhouse gas emissions (GHGs) present a greater health risk than previously thought, and (3) growing concerns over global climate change.

During the public hearing process, the California Building Industry Association (CBIA) expressed concern that the District's proposed thresholds and guidelines were too stringent and would make it difficult to complete urban infill projects located near existing sources of air pollution. CBIA claimed the proposed thresholds would require environmental impact reports (EIRs) for many more projects than before, and would result in non-approval of other projects. If these infill projects were not feasible, CBIA argued, development would occur in more suburban areas and result in even more GHG pollution from automobile commuter traffic.

The District was not persuaded. In June 2010, the District's board of directors passed resolution No. 2010–06, adopting new thresholds of significance for air pollutants, including "receptor thresholds" and thresholds for GHGs and PM2.5 (particulate matter with a diameter of 2.5 microns or less). The District also published new CEQA air quality guidelines, which include the new thresholds and suggest methods of assessing and mitigating impacts found to be significant. (District, Cal Environmental Quality Act: Air Quality Guidelines (June 2010).)

CBIA filed a petition for writ of mandate challenging these thresholds. (Code Civ. Proc. § 1085.) After rejecting CBIA's contentions that state law preempts the thresholds, the superior court conducted a hearing on the merits of the following claims: (1) the District should have conducted a CEQA review of the thresholds before their promulgation because they constitute a "project" within the meaning of CEQA; (2) the risk and hazard thresholds are arbitrary and capricious to the extent they unlawfully require an evaluation of the impacts the environment would have on a given project; (3) aspects of the thresholds are not based on substantial evidence; and (4) the thresholds fail the "rational basis" test because sufficient evidence does not exist for their approval.

The superior court determined that the District's promulgation of the 2010 thresholds was indeed a "project" under CEQA, and that the District was therefore bound to evaluate the thresholds' potential impact on the environment. Because the District issued the thresholds without the required CEQA review, the court entered judgment in favor of CBIA without addressing CBIA's other arguments. The court then issued a writ of mandate directing the District to set aside its approval of the thresholds, without addressing CBIA's claim that the District's thresholds were arbitrary and capricious because they required an analysis of how a project would impact future residents or users.

The Court of Appeal reversed. In ordering the superior court to vacate its writ of mandate, the Court of Appeal concluded, among other things, that the District's promulgation of the 2010 thresholds was not a project subject to CEQA review. It also rejected CBIA's various challenges to the substance of the thresholds. The Court of Appeal more narrowly determined that the thresholds have valid applications irrespective of whether CEQA requires an analysis of how existing environmental conditions impact a project's future residents or users, and therefore are "not invalid on their face."

We then granted CBIA's petition for review, but limited the scope of our review to the following question: Under what circumstances, if any, does CEQA require an analysis of how existing off-site environmental conditions will impact future residents or users (receptors) of a proposed project?

CEQA was enacted to advance four related purposes: to (1) inform the government and public about a proposed activity's potential environmental impacts; (2) identify ways to reduce, or avoid, environmental damage; (3) prevent environmental damage by requiring project changes via alternatives or mitigation measures when feasible; and (4) disclose to the public the rationale for governmental approval of a project that may significantly impact the environment. (*Tomlinson v. County of Alameda*, 278 P.3d 803 (Cal.2012) (Tomlinson).

To further these goals, CEQA requires that agencies follow a three-step process when planning an activity that could fall within its scope. First, the public agency must determine whether a proposed activity is a "project," i.e., an activity that is undertaken, supported, or approved by a public agency and that "may cause either a direct physical change in the environment, or a reasonably foreseeable indirect physical change in the environment." (§ 21065.)

Second, if the agency determines the project is not exempt, it must then decide whether the project may have a significant environmental effect. And where the project will not have such an effect, the agency "must 'adopt a negative declaration to that effect.

Third, if the agency finds the project "may have a significant effect on the environment," it must prepare an EIR before approving the project. It is quite clear that an EIR is required even if the project's ultimate effect on the environment is far from certain. (*Communities for a Better Environment v. California Resources Agency*, 103 Cal.App.4th 98, 110 (2002) [EIR is required " ' "whenever it can be fairly argued on the basis of substantial evidence that the project may have significant environmental impact," ' regardless of whether other substantial evidence supports the opposite conclusion"], disapproved on another ground in *Berkeley Hillside Preservation v. City of Berkeley*, 343 P.3d 834 (Cal.2015). Determining environmental significance "calls for careful judgment on the part of the public agency involved, based to the extent possible on scientific and factual data." The Guidelines encourage public agencies to develop and publish "thresholds of significance" which generally promote predictability and efficiency when the agencies determine whether to prepare an EIR.

When an agency prepares an EIR, it provides public officials and the general public with details about a proposed project's consequences. The EIR also lists the ways to potentially minimize any significant environmental effects, and presents alternatives to the project. (§ 21061; see § 21002.1, subd. (a).) By making this information available to decision makers and the public at a crucial moment when the merits of a project and its alternatives are under discussion, an EIR advances not only the goal of environmental protection but of informed self-government. (*In re Bay-Delta*, 184 P.3d 709 (Cal.2008), [an EIR "give[s] the public and government agencies the information needed to make informed decisions, thus protecting ' "not only the environment but also informed self-government" ' "].

In light of CEQA's text and structure, we conclude that CEQA generally does not require an analysis of how existing off-site environmental conditions will impact a project's future users or residents. The District emphasizes, correctly, that CEQA addresses human health and safety. Section 21083(b)(3)'s express language, for example, requires a finding of a " 'significant effect on the environment' " (§ 21083(b)) whenever the "environmental effects of a project will cause substantial adverse effects on human beings, either directly or indirectly." (§ 21083(b)(3), and the Legislature has made clear—in declarations accompanying CEQA's enactment—that public health and safety are of great importance in the statutory scheme. (E.g., §§ 21000, subds. (b), (c), (d), (g), 21001, subds. (b), (d) [emphasizing the need to provide for the public's welfare, health, safety, enjoyment, and living environment].) Still, the District reads too much into the phrase "environmental effects of a project."

The District's reading of that phrase goes too far despite all the reasons for us to give the Resources Agency's interpretation special weight. The phrase in question is best interpreted as limited to those impacts on a project's users or residents that arise from the project's effects on the environment. CEQA does not contain language directing agencies to analyze the off-site environment's effects on a project. Requiring such an evaluation in all circumstances would impermissibly expand the scope of CEQA.

With this holding in mind, we must distinguish between requirements that consider the environment's effects on a project and those that contemplate the project's impacts on the existing environment. The former, in light of our analysis of section 21083 and other relevant language in CEQA, are invalid. . . . Similarly, the EIR should evaluate any potentially significant impacts of locating development in other areas susceptible to hazardous conditions (e.g., floodplains, coastlines, wildfire risk areas) as identified in authoritative hazard maps, risk assessments or in land use plans addressing such hazards areas."

For the foregoing reasons, we hold that CEQA does not generally require an agency to consider the effects of existing environmental conditions on a proposed project's future users or residents. What CEQA does mandate, consistent with a key element of the Resources Agency's interpretation, is an analysis of how a project might exacerbate existing environmental hazards. CEQA also requires such an analysis where the project in question falls into certain specific statutory categories governing school, airport, and certain housing projects under sections 21151.8, 21096, 21159.21, 21159.22, 21159.23, 21159.24, and 21155.1. Accordingly, we find Guidelines section 15126.2(a) valid only in part.

We reverse the Court of Appeal's judgment and remand so that it may have an opportunity to address these issues to the extent necessary in light of today's holding.

NOTES

1.   In reading California EIR cases, seven fundamental principles guide the environmental assessment process: (a) analysis of the project, i.e., whether environmental review is statutorily required or the project is exempt; (b) the extent of review, i.e. whether a full environmental report (EIR) is required, or, a negative declaration is sufficient; (c) analysis of all feasible project alternatives; (d) the baseline determination of the existing environmental condition before review, in order to determine mitigation required above the baseline; (e) considerations of cumulative impacts; (f) program or tiered environmental review, the capacity to incorporate prior regional, county or city environmental reviews on plans and policies into EIRs or negative declarations for narrower projects emanating from the plan or policy; and (g) the ability of the lead agency preparing the EIR to override required mitigation for the project if it adopts a finding of overriding social and economic circumstances. For more detailed discussions of the above, *see* Longtin's *California Land Use*, Chapter 4, California Environmental Quality Act (2015); and Curtin's *Land*

Use and Planning Law, Chapter 6, California Environmental Quality Act, Chapter 6 (2015).

(a) *Analysis of the Project.* The first step in CEQA analysis is whether the activity in question amounts to a "project." (*Muzzy Ranch Co. v. Solano County Airport Land Use Commission*, 160 P.3d 116, 125 (Cal.2007) (a CEQA project falls into one of three categories of activity which may cause either a direct physical change in the environment, or a reasonably foreseeable indirect physical change in the environment). They are: (a) a private development project requiring discretionary development approval; (b) adoption of a governmental plan, ordinance or administrative regulation; or (c) a public facility or project built by a governmental authority).

(b) *Negative Declaration.* A public agency pursuing or approving a project need not prepare an EIR unless the project may result in a significant effect on the environment. Cal. Pub. Res. Code (CEQA) § 21100(a) defines significant effect as a substantial, or potentially substantial, adverse change in the environment. If the agency's initial study of a project produces substantial evidence supporting "a fair argument" that the project may have significant adverse effects, the agency must prepare an EIR. Where there is no "fair argument" supported by substantial evidence, in light of the whole record, that the project may have a significant effect on the environment, the agency may adopt a negative declaration. This is sometimes also known as the "common sense" exemption, which applies where it can be seen with certainty that there is no possibility that there will be a significant effect on the environment. *See No Oil, Inc. v. City of Los Angeles*, 529 P.2d 66 (Cal.1974).

(c) *Project Alternatives.* Subject to a "rule of reason," the EIR must contain a meaningful discussion of all project alternatives that (a) offer environmental advantages over the project, including not building the project; and (b) accomplish most of the basic objectives of the project, although alternatives that are costlier must be included. *Planning and Conservation League v. Department of Water Resources*, 83 Cal.App.4th 892, 100 Cal.Rptr.2d 173 (2000).

(d) *Baseline Determinations.* The EIR measures only the significant effects that the project will create over the existing environmental effects, prior to the project being built. This helps the applicant by eliminating prior environmental deficiencies from any mitigation requirements, similar to the rule for impact fees that we studied in Chapter 4, i.e., that impact fees cannot be exacted for existing deficiencies. The baseline rule is well summed up in *Communities for a Better Environment v. South Coast Air Quality Management Dist.*, 226 P.3d 985, 989, 990 (Cal.2010):

> "The California Environmental Quality Act requires a public agency to prepare an environmental impact report (EIR) only on projects that may have significant environmental effects. To decide whether a given project's environmental effects are likely to be significant, the agency must use some measure of the environment's state absent the project, a measure sometimes referred to as the "baseline" for

environmental analysis. According to an administrative guideline for CEQA's application, the baseline "normally" consists of "the physical environmental conditions in the vicinity of the project, as they exist at the time environmental analysis is commenced."

(e) *Cumulative Impacts.* An EIR must discuss significant cumulative individual impacts from other existing, pending or proposed projects that when considered together with the pending project, compound or increase environmental effects or impacts. *See Friends of the Eel River v. Sonoma County Water Agency*, 108 Cal.App.4th 859, 134 Cal.Rptr.2d 322 (2003). The purpose of this requirement is to avoid piecemeal approval of projects without considering the total environmental effects that all of the projects would have when taken together. *San Joaquin Raptor/Wildlife Center v. County of Stanislaus*, 27 Cal.App.4th 713, 740, 32 Cal.Rptr.2d 704 (1994).

(f) *Programmatic or Tiered Environmental Review.* In *Cleveland National Forest Foundation v. San Diego Association of Governments*, 180 Cal.Rptr.3d 548, 557 (Cal.App.2014), the Court of Appeals defined the benefit of using a "programmatic" or "tiered" EIR:

> "The EIR at issue in this case is a program EIR. A "program EIR" is "an EIR which may be prepared on a series of actions that can be characterized as one large project" and are related in specified ways. (Guidelines, § 15168, subd. (a); *Town of Atherton v. California High-Speed Rail Authority*, 175 Cal.Rptr.3d 145 (Cal.App.2014). The use of a program EIR can: "(1) Provide an occasion for a more exhaustive consideration of effects and alternatives than would be practical in an EIR on an individual action; (2) Ensure consideration of cumulative impacts that might be slighted in a case-by-case analysis; (3) Avoid duplicative reconsideration of basic policy considerations; (4) Allow the lead agency to consider broad policy alternatives and program wide mitigation measures at an early time when the agency has greater flexibility to deal with basic problems or cumulative impacts, [and] (5) Allow reduction in paperwork."

> "[W]here an agency prepares a 'program EIR' for a broad policy document . . . , Guidelines section 15168, subdivision (c)(2) allows agencies to limit future environmental review for later activities that are found to be 'within the scope' of the program EIR." (*Latinos Unidos de Napa v. City of Napa*, 164 Cal.Rptr.3d 274 (Cal.App.2013); *Citizens Against Airport Pollution v. City of San Jose* (2014) 227 Cal.App.4th 788, 801–802 (2014). Further environmental review for such activities is required only where: "(a) substantial changes are proposed in the project which will require major revisions of the EIR. (b) substantial changes occur with respect to the circumstances under which the project is being undertaken which will require major revisions in the EIR; and (c) new information, which was not known or could not have been known at the time the EIR was certified as complete, becomes available."

Because of these important simplifications of the process, once an EIR is finally approved, a court generally cannot compel an agency to perform further environmental review for any known or knowable information about the project's impacts omitted from the EIR, *Citizens for–Responsible Equitable Environmental Development v. City of San Diego*, 196 Cal.App.4th 515, 129 Cal.Rptr.3d 512, 524–525 (2011); it also generally cannot compel an agency to perform further environmental review if new regulations or guidelines for evaluating the project's impacts are adopted in the future.

Thus a project specific EIR was not required for a proposed hotel in a redevelopment area that had previously been the subject of a "program" EIR for the entire redevelopment specific plan. A secondary study concluded that all of the potential significant impacts that would be caused by the hotel project had been sufficiently analyzed in the prior programmatic EIR. *See Citizens for Responsible Equitable Environmental Development v. City of San Diego Redevelopment Agency*, 134 Cal.App.4th 598, 36 Cal.Rptr.3d 249 (2005).

Similar to a program EIR is a "tiered" EIR. Tiering refers to the process of preparing a broad EIR for a general plan or policy, with later EIRs or negative declarations reserved for narrower specific projects arising under the policy or plan. Mitigation measures in an EIR prepared for a proposed retail super-store, adequately addressed air quality concerns, where the EIR was "tiered" from an earlier EIR that addressed the air quality concerns of large scale retail uses in the shopping center as a whole. *See Natural Resources Defense Council, Inc. v. City of Los Angeles*, 103 Cal.App.4th 268 (2002). An earlier tiered EIR must address the water supply availability for all future phases of the project, but does not need to require absolute assurance, in order for an EIR for a later specific project to borrow from the earlier tiered EIR. *See Vineyard Area Citizens for Responsible Growth, Inc. v. City of Rancho Cordova*, 150 P.3d 709, 721 (Cal.2007): CEQA should not be understood to require assurances of certainty regarding long-term future water supplies at an early phase of planning for large land development projects, within a tiered EIR, but simply consideration of all available water sources, in order for a later EIR for a specific detailed project to borrow from the tiered EIR).

Note that the use of program and tiered EIRs can be instrumental in reducing the cost of EIRs for higher density new urbanist mixed use walkable TND or TOD projects, because the most expensive cost studies involve off-site air quality and transportation impacts. Lead agencies can use program and tiered EIRs prepared for the regional sustainable community strategies under California's SB 375 legislation that we studied in Chapter 7, State Solutions.

(g) *Overriding Considerations.* CEQA is not a substantive but a procedural statute. It is designed to assure that an EIR evaluates all feasible project alternatives so that the lead agency can make an informed decision on project approval with appropriate mitigating conditions. The lead agency may still approve the project, however, despite the fact that the environmental impacts of the project may not be fully mitigated, where the lead agency determines in written findings, based on substantial evidence in the record, that there are overriding social, economic or other considerations that dictate that the project be approved. *See No Oil, Inc. v. City of Los Angeles*, 529 P.2d 66 (Cal.1974); and such overriding considerations can even justify approval of the project even where it is inconsistent with the general plan, *Gray v. County of Madera*, 167 Cal.App.4th 1099, 85 Cal.Rptr.3d 50 (2008). The decision to override full mitigation of the project is not appropriate, however where the override is based on an erroneous legal assumption.

In *City of San Diego v. Board of Trustees of California State University*, 352 P.3d 883 (Cal.2005) the Supreme Court held:

> "As noted, our decision in *Marina v. Board of Trustees of California State University*, 138 P.3d 692 (Cal.2006), addressed a challenge to California State University (CSU) Board's EIR for an earlier campus expansion project. In that EIR, the Board had found that to expand would significantly affect drainage, water supply, traffic, wastewater management and fire protection throughout Fort Ord, the former military base on which the campus was located, as well as vehicular traffic in the neighboring municipalities of Seaside and the City of Marina. (*Id.* at pp. 349–350, 46 Cal.Rptr.3d 355, 349–350, 138 P.3d 692.) Nevertheless, the Board refused to share the cost of mitigating these impacts with the public entities responsible for undertaking the necessary infrastructure improvements. Any payment for that purpose, the Board asserted in its EIR, would amount to an unlawful assessment of CSU or a gift of public funds. (*Id.* at pp. 352–353, 46 Cal.Rptr.3d 355, 138 P.3d 692.) Based on these legal assumptions, the Board found that mitigation was infeasible and that overriding considerations justified certifying the EIR and approving the Master Plan despite the unmitigated effects. (*Id.* at pp. 351–354, 46 Cal.Rptr.3d 355, 138 P.3d 692.)

> We concluded the Board had abused its discretion in certifying the EIR because the finding of infeasibility and statement of overriding considerations depended on erroneous legal assumptions. Prominent among those assumptions was that the campus's geographical boundaries defined the extent of the Board's duty to mitigate. To the contrary, as we explained, "CEQA requires a public agency to mitigate or avoid its projects' significant effects not just on the agency's own property but 'on the environment' (Pub. Resources Code, § 21002.1, subd. (b)), with 'environment' defined for these purposes as 'the physical conditions which exist within the area which will be affected by a proposed project' (id., § 21060.5, italics added)." (*Marina*, at p. 360, 46 Cal.Rptr.3d 355, 138 P.3d 692.) The same erroneous assumption had also led the Board to find that off-site mitigation was the responsibility of other agencies. (*Marina*, 39 Cal.4th at p. 366, 46 Cal.Rptr.3d 355, 138 P.3d 692).

(h) *Critiques of Strict Environmental Assessment.* CEQA with its extraordinarily complicated environmental assessment process has always drawn critical analyses from the business community.

The following L.A. Times Op-Ed, written by Bill Allen, CEO of the Los Angeles Economic Development Corporation (LAEDC), and former San Diego Mayor, Maureen O'Connor, chairwoman of the LAEDC, makes the case for CEQA reform as a potential economic driver. According to the LAEDC, too many good projects are delayed by frivolous exploitation of CEQA's good intentions and reforming the law would be a critical driver for the revitalization of the state's economy.

"So why then do some of our elected officials still act as though we don't have a serious jobs crisis? Why are they refusing to examine certain politically untouchable, "third rail" laws, even though the original intent of some of these laws has been twisted and abused? One of the worst examples of this "don't dare broach the subject" form of policymaking is the misuse of the California Environmental Quality Act, or CEQA.

Enacted in the 1970s, the goal of CEQA was—and continues to be—a noble one: to make sure that the public is provided with a good-faith assessment of the reasonably foreseeable environmental impact of a proposed project. This information would be considered by the permitting agency before it approved or disapproved the project. However, CEQA has expanded from a thoughtful review for environmental purposes to an unruly set of laws and regulations that add complexity, cost, delay and, most problematic, unpredictability, and too frequently have been exploited for non-environmental purposes. All of this hinders job creation and tax revenue generation.

It is not uncommon for businesses, such as retailers, to organize and fund groups to oppose developments by their competitors under the guise of CEQA. It's also become fairly common for groups with union ties to oppose projects on CEQA grounds in order to extract labor-friendly promises.

Finally, a cottage industry of CEQA lawyers and groups has emerged that oppose far too many developments, threatening or bringing litigation in hopes of simply exacting a financial settlement or "go away" money from the developer of a given project. This is using CEQA to manipulate the law for purposes that have absolutely nothing to do with protecting the environment. The purpose of CEQA was never to help businesses block competitors; help unions squeeze businesses for concessions; or help CEQA lawyers enrich themselves. * * *

The "CEQA gone wild" state of affairs in California has deterred businesses from developing or expanding in the state. Just as important, non-environmental CEQA challenges significantly slow previously approved public infrastructure projects. All of this costs Californians jobs.

Just like treating cancer, our most adept lawmakers should perform careful surgery on the law to remove the malignant parts of CEQA that enable the worst abuses of this important and well-intentioned statute. A careful, reasonable approach should make two changes.

The first would be to improve transparency. Every person or group supporting or opposing a proposed project should have to disclose to the permitting agency its identity and that of its members, as well as who is paying its costs to support or oppose the project. This would allow the agency to evaluate whether opposition to a project actually helps protect the environment or attempts to use CEQA for non-environmental purposes.

Second, the state attorney general, as the "people's attorney," should be responsible for CEQA challenges, with the exclusive right to file suit once a project has been certified by its lead agency. This would eliminate the uncontrolled prerogative of any person or group to litigate a permitting agency's decision to approve a project. This would cull those parties who are intent on exacting nuisance settlements from developers, while still protecting a project opponent's right to comment during the very lengthy public review process and to petition the attorney general to file a suit once a project has been approved.

With these changes, the fundamental purpose of the law—to ensure the informed consideration of the environmental impacts of any project by the permitting agency—would remain strong. But the abuses of CEQA—its use for non-environmental purposes—would be greatly reduced".

The Los Angeles County Economic Development Corporation (LAEDC) Requests Changes to CEQA, The California Planning & Development Report, April 2011, quoting from http://articles.latimes.com/2011/mar/30/opinion/la-oe-allen-ceqa–20110330.

Note particularly the bitter animosity towards the clique of lawyers that specialize in bringing and defending CEQA lawsuits. Should CEQA be resolved before a state or regional administrative agency with environmental expertise, without recourse to non-expert courts? Is legal analysis overwhelming the resolution of environmental impacts? Aside from the alleged amelioration of the jobs crisis, do you agree with the suggested reforms above? What additional reforms would you suggest for CEQA?

2. OTHER STATE ENVIRONMENTAL ASSESSMENT ACTS AND GLOBAL WARMING

Three states, Massachusetts, New York and Washington, also incorporate consideration of greenhouse gas emissions and global warming into their environmental review statutes, often referred to as "Little NEPAs," out of 15 states that have environmental policy acts modeled to varying degrees after the National Environmental Policy Act (NEPA). The Massachusetts Environmental Policy Act, Mass.Ann. Laws, §§ 61 to 62 (MEPA) requires state agencies or state applicants to prepare an EIR for actions or development projects that are likely to create environmental impact. The Act applies to any project (a) where the state is the proponent, (b) provides financial assistance, or, (c) a private project requires state air quality or vehicular access permits. In 2007, Massachusetts issued a MEPA Greenhouse Gas Emissions Policy and Protocol (see Stephanie Ebbert, Massachusetts Steps Up Climate Rules for Developers, Boston Globe, April 22, 2007 at A1) that determined that "damage to the environment as used in MEPA includes the emission of greenhouse gases caused by projects subject to MEPA review."

Similarly, under Washington's State Environmental Policy Act, Wash.Rev. Code Ann. § 43.21C.010 (2), the environment is specifically defined to include "climate." *See* Wash.Admin. Code § 197–11–444(1) (b) (iii) (2007). *See,* Judi Brawer and Matthew Vespa, *Thinking Globally, Acting Locally: The Role of Local Government in Minimizing Greenhouse Gas Emissions from New Development,* 44 IDAHO L.REV. 589 (2008), reprinted in Zoning and Planning Law Handbook, Chap. 12 at 671, 709– 712 (Patricia E. Salkin, ed. West 2009).

3. THE NATIONAL ENVIRONMENTAL POLICY ACT

The National Environmental Policy Act, 42 U.S.C. § 4321 et seq. (1972) (NEPA) established the broad national framework for protecting the environment. NEPA's basic policy is to assure that all branches of the federal government give proper consideration to the environment prior to undertaking any major federal action that significantly affects the environment.

NEPA does not require a substantive result, but only requires that mitigation be discussed in sufficient detail. *Desert Protective Council v. U.S. Dep't of the Interior*, 927 F.Supp.2d 949, 971 (S.D.Cal.2013) *aff'd,* 2015 WL 7292969 (9th Cir. Nov. 19, 2015); *Pac. Coast Fed. of Fishermen's Association v. Blank*, 693 F.3d 1084, 1103 (9th Cir.2012) ("There is a fundamental distinction, however, between a requirement that mitigation be discussed in sufficient detail to ensure that environmental consequences have been fairly evaluated, on the one hand, and a substantive requirement that a complete mitigation plan be actually formulated and adopted, on the other.").

NEPA requirements are invoked when airports, buildings, military complexes, highways, parkland purchases, and other federal activities are proposed, or a private project intersects with federal agency overview, under the Endangered Species Act, (administered by the U.S. Fish and Wildlife Service) or, the Clean Water Act wetlands assessment (administered by the U.S. Corps of Engineers). Environmental Assessments (EAs) and Environmental Impact Statements (EISs), which are assessments of the likelihood of impacts from alternative courses of action, are required from all federal agencies and are the most visible NEPA requirements. These federal Acts are considered in Chapter 9.

Whenever a project requires both an EIR under CEQA and an EIS under NEPA, the lead agency shall use the federal EIS as the environmental report. Where the best available science points to environmental impacts to an endangered species as a result of climate change, those impacts must be evaluated in the federal EIS as part of the "consultation" process between local, state and federal agencies pursuant to Section 7 of the Endangered Species Act, 16 U.S.C. § 1536 (the implementation section afforded to listed species). *See Natural Resources Defense Council v. Kempthorne*, 506 F.Supp.2d 322, 367–370 (E.D.Cal.2007).

F. CAP AND TRADE SYSTEMS

OUR CHILDREN'S EARTH FOUNDATION V. CALIFORNIA AIR RESOURCES BOARD
Court of Appeals of California, 2015.
234 Cal.App.4th 870, 184 Cal.Rptr.3d 365.

The California Air Resources Board ("CARB") is charged with implementing the California Global Warming Solutions Act of 2006. (Health & Safety Code, §§ 38500 et seq.) "AB 32".

In this case, appellant challenges CARB's regulations implementing a market-based compliance mechanism for achieving reductions in GHG emissions, which is referred to by the parties as the "Cap-and-Trade" program. Pursuant to a petition for writ of mandate, appellant alleged that one component of this program which affords offset credits for voluntary reductions in GHG emissions violates the 2006 Act by failing to ensure that these credited reductions are "in addition to" any GHG emission reduction that is otherwise required by law or that would otherwise occur. (§ 38562, subd. (d) (§ 38562(d)).) The trial court rejected this claim and denied the petition. Appellant contends on appeal, as it did in the trial court, that CARB exceeded its power under the 2006 Act by implementing regulations that violate this "additionality" requirement. We affirm.

The AB 32 is supported by legislative findings that global warming poses a "serious threat" to the "economic well-being, public health, natural resources, and the environment of California," and that global warming will have "detrimental effects on some of California's largest industries." (§ 38501, subds. (a), (b).) The Legislature also found that California has long been a leader with respect to energy conservation and environmental protection, and that programs established under the AB 32 would "continue this tradition of environmental leadership by placing California at the forefront of national and international efforts to reduce emissions of greenhouse gases." (§ 38501, subd. (c).)

The present case pertains to the legislative directive that CARB adopt rules and regulations to "achieve the maximum technologically feasible and cost-effective reductions in greenhouse gas emissions. . . ." (§ 38560.) To comply with that directive, CARB was required to "adopt greenhouse gas emission limits and emission reductions measures by regulation . . . in furtherance of achieving the statewide greenhouse gas emissions limit, to become operative beginning on January 1, 2012." (§ 38562, subd. (a).)

The Legislature expressly authorized CARB to adopt regulations which establish market-based compliance mechanisms "in furtherance of achieving the statewide [GHG] emissions limit. AB 32 requires that every CARB regulation adopting GHG emission limits and emission measures "shall ensure" that the GHG "emission reductions achieved are real, permanent, quantifiable, verifiable, and enforceable by the state board." (§ 38562, subd. (d)(1).) Regulations adopting market-based compliance mechanisms are subject to a further requirement that the "reduction is in addition to any greenhouse gas emission reduction otherwise required by law or regulation, and any other greenhouse gas emission reduction that otherwise would occur." This section 38562(d)(2) "additionality" requirement is the subject of this appeal.

In January 2012, CARB implemented the "California Cap on Greenhouse Gas Emissions and Market-Based Compliance Mechanisms" pursuant to its authority under the 2006 Act. (Cal. Code Regs., tit. 17 [17 CCR] §§ 95801–96022.) The purpose of this "Cap-and-Trade" program regulation is "to reduce emissions of greenhouse gases" from sources covered by the program "by applying an aggregate greenhouse gas allowance budget on covered entities and providing a trading mechanism for compliance instruments." (17 CCR § 95801.) Entities covered by the program are from a broad spectrum of industries, including electricity, natural gas and fuel suppliers, each of whom has previously reported GHG emissions that exceed a threshold established by the Board for that industry. (*Id.* at §§ 95811–95812.)

The program imposes a "cap" on the aggregate GHG emissions these covered entities may emit during the annual compliance period. (17 CCR §§ 95801, 95802, subd. (a)(53).) CARB enforces the cap, which is lowered over time, by issuing a limited number of compliance instruments referred to as "allowances," the total value of which is equal to the amount of the cap. (*Id.* at § 95820.) Each allowance represents a limited authorization to emit up to one metric ton of carbon dioxide equivalent of greenhouse gases (CO2e), subject to stated restrictions. (Ibid.) Covered entities demonstrate compliance with the program by the timely surrender of allowances which correspond to that entity's compliance obligation during the relevant compliance period which is calculated pursuant to a formula set forth in the program regulation. (*Id.* at §§ 95854–95856.) Subject to restrictions and limitations, allowances are tradable, which means that individual participants can buy, bank or sell allowances which are used by the covered entities to satisfy their compliance obligations.

A covered entity can also use offsets to meet a percentage of its compliance obligation under the program. An offset is a voluntary GHG emissions reduction from a source that is not directly covered by the Cap-and-Trade program which is used by a covered entity to comply with the program's GHG emissions cap.

As noted above, the Cap-and-Trade program regulation requires that an offset credit result from the use of a "Compliance Offset Protocol" that has been approved by CARB. One of the qualification requirements addressed by the Board protocols is that the GHG emissions reduction has to be "additional."

Petitioners alleged that the Compliance Offset Protocols incorporate a flawed approach for evaluating additionality which fails to satisfy the integrity standards imposed by the 2006 Act. According to the petition, each protocol is based on a "Performance Standard" which purports to ensure additionality but inherently fails to do so for at least two reasons. First, the standard attempts to exclude activities that otherwise would occur by setting a threshold for GHG emission reductions for a specified activity at a level that is only "significantly better than average," and/or "beyond 'common practice' " for that specified activity. According to petitioners, this approach is inherently defective because it necessarily includes activities which otherwise would occur.

There is no dispute in this case that the Cap-and-Trade program requires that GHG emission reductions that generate offset credits are in addition to GHG emission reductions otherwise required by law or regulation. Rather, appellant's claim is that CARB exceeded its authority under the 2006 Act by adopting a market-based compliance mechanism which fails to ensure that offset credits are in addition to "any" GHG emission reductions that "otherwise would occur." (§ 38562(d)(2).)

The real dispute in this case pertains to a different phrase in section 38562(d)(2) which requires that reductions generated by a market-based compliance mechanism must be in addition to reductions "that otherwise would occur."

Within this authority, CARB established rules and protocols which give sufficient meaning to the concept of additionality so that the statutory requirement is capable of enforcement. By developing these rules and protocols CARB did not exceed its power, but rather exercised the legislative authority delegated to it by the Legislature.

Although we find no case law that interprets section 38562(d), our conclusion is consistent with authority construing other provisions of the 2006 Act. In *Irritated Residents, supra*, 206 Cal.App.4th 1487, 143 Cal.Rptr.3d 65, the petitioner alleged that the Board's "Climate Change Scoping Plan" (which authorized the development of the Cap-and-Trade program) failed to comply with the requirements of the 2006 Act. (*Id.* at p. 1489, 143 Cal.Rptr.3d 65.) The trial court rejected that contention and Division Three of this court affirmed the judgment, holding that CARB did not disregard statutory requirements or act arbitrarily or capriciously. The Irritated Residents court found, among other things, that the directives imposed on CARB by the 2006 Act are all "exceptionally broad and open-ended," leaving "virtually all decisions to the discretion of the Board. . . ." (*Id.* at p. 1495, 143 Cal.Rptr.3d 65.) We agree with that conclusion.

These provisions of the 2006 Act reflect that the Legislature contemplated that there could be incentives for voluntary early reductions even before the Act was passed, and that it authorized CARB to credit those early actions. Implicitly acknowledging this fact in its reply brief, appellant contends that the Board exceeded its authority under these statutory provisions by implementing an early action offset program that incorporates the Reserve protocols because they suffer from the same alleged defects as CARB's other protocols. According to appellant, "both sets of protocols fail to weed out activity that 'otherwise would occur,' relying instead on predetermined findings that the type of activity is beyond 'common practice.' " (Fn. omitted.) In other words, appellant challenges the early action offset program on the same ground that it challenges the other offset provisions of the Cap-and-Trade program— because it does not mandate proof of an unknown. We have already explained why that challenge fails.

Here, the administrative record demonstrates that CARB engaged in an extensive regulatory process in order to establish a working definition of additionality that (1) furthers the purposes of the 2006 Act and (2) can be implemented through the use of offset protocols incorporated into the Cap-and-Trade program. That process included soliciting input from the public, pertinent industries, and relevant experts.

The judgment is affirmed.

NOTES

1.   The "Cap-and-Trade" program was one of 73 measures identified in a "Scoping Plan" CARB prepared and approved in December 2008 pursuant to another legislative directive in the 2006 Act. (§ 38561.) "The process for developing and approving the scoping plan in compliance with the statutory mandate was extensive and rigorous." (*Association of Irritated Residents v. State Air Resources Bd.*, 206 Cal.App.4th 1487, 143 Cal.Rptr.3d 65 (2012).

2.   For an excellent analysis of California's Cap and Trade and offset forest protection protocol programs, *see,* Ellis Raskin, *Urban Forests as Weapons against Climate Change: Lessons from California's Global Warming Solutions Act*, 47 URBAN LAWYER 387 (Summer 2015).

G. GREEN DEVELOPMENT

Promoting Green Buildings: Green buildings are high performance buildings that (1) use energy, water, and materials more efficiently and (2) use measures related to siting, design, construction, operation, maintenance, and removal to reduce the building's impacts on human health and the environment. The large use of energy, water and other resources by buildings demonstrates the compelling need to use green building practices to foster sustainability and reduce global warming impacts.

Currently, traditional buildings:

(1) use about 40% of all the energy consumed and 72% of all the electricity used in the country;

(2) are responsible for about 40% of the country's carbon dioxide emissions;

(3) account for 52% of sulfur dioxide emissions, 19% of nitrous oxide emissions, and 12% of particulate emissions, all of which degrade air quality;

(4) produce 136 million tons of construction and demolition waste annually; and

(5) represent 40% of the raw materials consumed in the United States.

Green building can greatly contribute to easy and cost-effective climate change mitigation. There are more than 82 million residential buildings and about 75 billion square feet of commercial floor space in buildings in the United States. Cost-effective energy efficiency retrofits to this existing building stock can result in major energy savings. For an excellent summary of Green Development Codes in the U.S., see the following excerpt from Edna Sussman, *Reshaping Municipal and County Laws to Foster Green Building, Energy Efficiency, and Renewable Energy*, 16 N.Y.U.ENVT'L L.J. 1, 8, 10–13 (2008):

1. GREEN DEVELOPMENT CODES AND STANDARDS

There are many avenues that can be pursued to promote green building. The following sections will describe the Leadership in Energy and Environmental Design (LEED) rating system, mandatory use of green building standards, revised energy and building codes, requiring specific design elements, and non-monetary incentives.

The United States Green Building Council and LEED:[1] The United States Green Building Council (USGBC) has emerged as the leader and has been central to the progress of the green building movement in the United States. Using a membership consensus process, the USGBC developed a green rating system for new commercial construction and

---

[1] LEED, or Leadership in Energy and Environmental Design, is a private green building certification system. Developed by the U.S. Green Building Council (USGBC), LEED provides building owners with a framework to implement practical and measurable green building design and construction. LEED certification is very costly but a development that has silver, gold or platinum certification is worth many times more than the certificate cost.

major renovations that is increasingly utilized as the national standard for green buildings.

The LEED Green Building Rating System ranks buildings as Certified, Silver, Gold, or Platinum depending on the level of sustainability achieved by construction and renovation projects. This system serves the critical purposes of promoting sustainable design features and creating a standard that can be applied universally and credibly. The system has gained wide acceptance.

It is considerably easier for a community to adopt an established green building rating system than to develop its own and to provide its own mechanisms and staff to certify compliance. Thus LEED is a remarkably useful tool to assure that the building is truly sustainable and not just the product of a "green washed" sales exercise. At the same time, LEED obviates the need for additional staff for review. However, concerns have been expressed by some that the LEED certification drives up the price of construction and several communities have opted to develop their own system of green building credits or to simply require that the buildings be LEED certifiable without actually requiring LEED certification.

Mandating Green Building: Recognizing the many benefits of green building, communities all over the country have focused on how they can capitalize on this opportunity. Numerous communities have now bound themselves to building new construction and major renovations to LEED standards. Many have also included in this requirement construction that obtains public funding. The individual mandates vary as to the minimum size of the building as to which a commitment is made and what level of LEED must be achieved. Typically, a minimum of 5,000 square feet is specified and LEED Silver is the certification level to be achieved. Since LEED is a framework for all aspects of sustainability and its credits are not restricted to energy concerns, to assure that adequate energy improvements are included, some communities have specified that a certain number of LEED credits be earned from the energy credit category.

In a growing trend, communities have begun to mandate green building for larger projects in the private sector as well. The City of Boston, Massachusetts enacted regulations requiring buildings of over 50,000 square feet to be LEED certifiable. The City of Washington, D.C., enacted a Green Building Act that requires a non-residential privately owned project of over 50,000 square feet to be verified as having fulfilled LEED standard certification requirements starting in 2012. Some communities are beginning to require LEED or LEED equivalency even for smaller scale projects. The Town of Babylon, New York requires all new construction of commercial, office, industrial or multi-family residences of over 4,000 square feet to complete a LEED checklist or comparable mechanism acceptable to the building inspector and no building permit is issued unless the proposed building will be able to attain LEED certified status. A certificate of occupancy is not issued unless proof is produced that the standard has been met.

To move towards more energy efficient home construction several communities turned to the Energy Star Homes program, EPA's national program offering assessment tools and certifiers. To earn the Energy Star label, a home must meet guidelines for energy efficiency set by EPA. These homes are at least 15% more energy efficient than homes built to the 2014 International Residential Code, and include additional energy-saving features that typically make them 20–30% more efficient than standard homes. The Green Building program in Frisco, Texas prescribes the EPA's "Energy Star" program requirements as the minimum building standard for new homes. Brookhaven, New York, requires that any new single or multi-family residence of four or fewer units and of not more than three stories be built to comply with the New York Energy Star labeled home program, and that a home energy rating be submitted.

2.   ENERGY AND BUILDING CODES

The most direct and comprehensive way to achieve greener building is through changing energy and building codes. These codes can serve to promote or impede green building development. The development and enforcement of energy codes is a shared responsibility of state and local government. Prior to 1992, states enacted energy codes on a voluntary basis but the U.S. Department of Energy (DOE) required all states to adopt commercial energy codes at least as stringent as a specified ASHRAE/IES standard by 2004, and most states have complied. The actual standards adopted vary from state to state. Since new technologies are always emerging, frequent code upgrades are necessary and the DOE continues to work on developing more stringent model codes.

3.   FEDERAL PREEMPTION OF GREEN BUILDING AND ENERGY CODES

BUILDING INDUSTRY ASSOCIATION OF WASHINGTON V. WASHINGTON STATE BUILDING CODE COUNCIL

United States Court of Appeals, Ninth Circuit, 2012.
683 F.3d 1144.

The Energy Policy and Conservation Act of 1975 ("EPCA"), 42 U.S.C. § 6295 et seq., as amended, establishes nationwide energy efficiency standards for certain residential home appliances, and expressly preempts state standards requiring greater efficiency than the federal standards. It nonetheless exempts from preemption state building codes promoting energy efficiency, so long as those codes meet certain statutory conditions. § 6297(f)(3). As initially enacted in 1975, EPCA provided that federal energy efficiency standards be established for covered products, and it preempted all state "efficiency standard[s] or similar requirement[s]" for covered products. Energy Policy and Conservation Act of 1975, Pub. L. No. 94–163, sec. 327, 89 Stat. 871, 926–27. Congress modified the blanket preemption in 1987, when it amended EPCA to carve out an explicit exemption from preemption for certain efficiency standards in state and local building codes. See National Appliance Energy Conservation Act of 1987, Pub. L. No. 100–12, sec. 7, 101 Stat. 103, 117–22 (codified as amended at 42 U.S.C. § 6297). EPCA thus now expressly exempts from preemption any regulation or other requirement contained in a state or local building code for new construction concerning the energy efficiency or energy use of covered products, but only if the provisions of the code satisfy seven statutory conditions. 42 U.S.C. § 6297(f)(3).

This case is a challenge to the State of Washington's Building Code, see Wash. Admin. Code § 51–11–0100 et seq., brought by the Building Industry Association of Washington ("BIAW"), along with individual builders and contractors. The impetus for this challenge is the State's 2009 requirement that new building construction meet heightened energy conservation goals. This is the first case at the appellate level to consider EPCA's preemption-exemption provision. Plaintiffs-Appellants ("Plaintiffs") argue that the Building Code does not satisfy EPCA's conditions for exemption. The district court, however, held that Washington had satisfied EPCA's conditions, and therefore was not preempted. We affirm.

To escape preemption, a state's building code must satisfy the seven conditions codified in 42 U.S.C. § 6297(f)(3). The two at issue here are § 6297(f)(3)(B) and (C). Under subsection (B), a state's building code cannot require a covered product—energy consuming fixtures such as water heaters and refrigerators—to be more efficient than the standards established by the United States Department of Energy ("DOE"). The State of Washington's Building Code requires builders to reduce a building's energy use by a certain amount, and provides a number of options from which a builder may choose how to meet that requirement. Some of the options involve the installation of products that have an efficiency that exceeds the federal standards. These options, according to the builders, also happen to be cheaper than the other options. The builders contend that they are therefore being "required" to use products that exceed the federal standards, in violation of subsection (B). We hold that a builder is not "required" to select an option, within the meaning of subsection (B), simply because there is an economic incentive to do so. Section 6297(f)(3)(B) is violated when the code requires a builder, as a matter of law, to select a particular product or option. The Supreme Court has recognized this to be what a requirement entails. *See Bates v. Dow Agrosciences LLC*, 544 U.S. 431, 445 (2005) (rejecting a preemption challenge, and holding that the term "requirement" in a different statute means "a rule of law that must be obeyed"). Plaintiffs in this case are thus not "required" to choose the less expensive, more efficient option.

The evidence that is in the record supports the district court's conclusion that the state-assigned credit values satisfy the "one-for-one equivalent energy use" requirement of subsection (C). The district court admitted the State's expert testimony and documentation because the court found the State's computer models for assigning credit values used sound data and methodology, and that they were reliably applied. *See Daubert v. Merrell Dow Pharmaceuticals*, 509 U.S. 579, 113 S.Ct. 2786, 125 L.Ed.2d 469 (1993). The district court properly held that Plaintiffs could not show that the Building Code violated subsection (C).

We therefore hold that the Washington Building Code satisfies the conditions Congress established for enforcement of state and local building codes consistent with federal energy law and we affirm the judgment of the district court in favor of the State.

The state would effectively require higher efficiency products, in violation of subsection (B), if the code itself imposed a penalty for not using higher efficiency products. This is what a building code ordinance for the city of Albuquerque, New Mexico did. The federal district court for the District of New Mexico therefore granted a preliminary injunction against enforcing that ordinance. *See Air Conditioning, Heating, and Refrigeration Institute v. City of Albuquerque*, 2008 WL 5586316 (D.N.M.2008). That court held, in relevant part, that the ordinance did not satisfy EPCA's subsection (B), because the ordinance itself had created a situation in which the builder had no choice. Albuquerque's ordinance imposed costs, as a matter of law, on builders who installed certain covered products meeting federal standards, by requiring the builder to install additional products that would compensate for not using a higher efficiency product. *Id.* at *2. As the court explained, "if products at the federal efficiency standard are used, a building owner must make other modifications to the home to increase its energy efficiency." *Id.* at *9. The Albuquerque ordinance thus effectively required use of higher efficiency products by imposing a penalty through the code itself.

Here, by contrast, the Washington Building Code itself imposes no additional costs on builders. The district court noted that there are "substantial differences" between the Washington Building Code and Albuquerque's ordinance. It correctly rejected the Plaintiffs' argument concerning subsection (B), explaining that the Washington Building Code created no penalties, and did not require higher efficiency products as the "only way to comply with the code." We hold the Washington Building Code complies with subsection (B) because it does not create any penalty or legal compulsion to use higher efficiency products.

NOTE

In *Air Conditioning, Heating and Refrigeration Institute v. City of Albuquerque (AHRI)*, 2008 WL 5586316 (D.N.Mex.2008), the district court ruled in favor of a motion for summary judgment filed by the plaintiffs who represented HVAC manufacturers, distributors, and installers. The judge agreed with the HVAC industry's claim that since the federal government requires all air conditioners manufactured in the U.S. to be at a minimum of 13 SEER, a city or state cannot mandate a more stringent requirement. The LEED for Homes program requires a 14.5 SEER and will continue to require that all homes also be certified to ENERGY STAR. Beginning in 2011, however, the EPA requires that homes certified to its ENERGY STAR program must have at least 14.5 SEER air conditioners.

14.5 SEER is greater than the federal minimum requirement of 13 SEER that the court in AHRI said cities could not exceed by mandate. Therefore, it could be illegal for a city to mandate ENERGY STAR and/or LEED for Homes. A mandate of either of these programs in 2011 or beyond would present a similar fact pattern as in AHRI. Note that EPCA governs only state and local government regulations, statutes and ordinances. LEED as a private organization can require any standard for its certifications. It is only where local governments incorporate LEED standards into their codes that conflict with EPCA appears. See http://www.energystar.gov/.

4. LEED FOR NEIGHBORHOOD DEVELOPMENT

One of the great deficiencies of the initial LEED certification program was the focus on individual development sites that failed to take into account the reduction in greenhouse gas emissions from building within Smart Growth priority growth areas, infill sites or within new urban traditional neighborhood or transit oriented developments, in order to achieve regional benefits from reduced vehicle miles travelled and trips generated. The following is an account of LEED-ND from Robert H. Freilich, Robert J Sitkowski and Seth D. Mennillo, *From Sprawl to Sustainability: Smart Growth, New Urbanism, Green Development and Renewable Energy*, Chapter 6, 186–189 (American Bar Association, Section of State and Local Government Law, 2010):[2]

The Latest Leadership in Energy and Environmental Design Program: LEED for Neighborhood Developments (LEED-ND)

In February 2006, a partnership between three organizations—the U.S. Green Building Council ("USGBC"), the Congress for the New Urbanism ("CNU") and the Natural Resources Defense Council ("NRDC")—announced that it would be seeking up to 120 projects volunteering to be rated in the test phase of a new Leadership in Energy

---

[2] © 2010 American Bar Association. Reprinted with permission. All rights reserved. This information or any or portion thereof may not be copied or disseminated in any form or by any means or stored in an electronic database or retrieval system without the express written consent of the American Bar Association.

and Environmental Design ("LEED") program: the LEED for Neighborhood Developments ("LEED-ND") Rating System. The LEED-ND pilot program, which actually tested nearly 240 projects, led to its adoption as an official LEED system in 2009.

LEED-ND is the latest expansion of the now-familiar LEED system developed by the USGBC, which has become the national benchmark for high-performance green buildings. The LEED-ND is a rating system that combines the elements of smart growth, new urbanism, and green building. In contrast with other LEED certification systems governing building construction and green building practices, LEED-ND will certify neighborhood design and construction techniques that create what is best described as "Sustainable Urbanism." (See Douglas Farr, Sustainable Urbanism: Urban Design with Nature (Wiley, 2008)). The USGBC explains that the primary benefits of developing a LEED-ND community are to: reduce urban sprawl; encourage healthy living; protect threatened species; increase transportation choice; and decrease automobile dependence.

How Does LEED-ND Work?

The LEED-ND, as presented in the 94-page 1st Public Comment Draft: LEED for Neighborhood Developments Rating System, is broken into three major categories in which it is possible to achieve 100 total points (before bonuses) toward LEED certification. These are:

- Smart Location & Linkage;

- Neighborhood Pattern & Design; and

- Green Infrastructure & Buildings.

As with other LEED programs, projects can achieve various certification levels: Certified (40–49 points); Silver (50–59 points); Gold (60–79 points); and Platinum (80–106 points). With certification comes three tiers of fees tied to the size of the project.

In order for a project to achieve certification, it must meet each prerequisite and accumulate various point totals largely based on the amount of credits achieved. The first two major categories address neighborhood location and design, which together account for close to 70% of the total possible points, as well as all but one of the prerequisites. This is predictable given the USGBC's explanation under the heading of "Reduce Urban Sprawl" in the list of benefits of the LEED-ND system:

In order to reduce the impacts of urban sprawl, or unplanned, uncontrolled spreading of urban development into areas outside of the metropolitan region, and create more livable communities, LEED for Neighborhood Development communities are:

- locations that are closer to existing town and city centers

- areas with good transit access

- infill sites

- previously developed sites

- sites adjacent to existing development

Each of the prerequisite and credit types are comprehensively described in the text of the LEED for Neighborhood Developments Rating System, and the component parts of each prerequisite and credit type are presented under the headings of Intent, Requirements, and Submittals. A review of the mechanics of the rating system shows that the primary target for LEED-ND is developers who would propose specific projects. However, local governments are likely a secondary audience. Various panelists in the full-day session on LEED-ND at the June 2007 Congress for the New Urbanism in Philadelphia (primarily members of the Core Committee) mentioned that local governments might use these standards, not by adopting them wholesale as regulatory tools, but rather by showing a preference in permitting processes or timing for LEED-ND-certified projects.

5. LOCAL GOVERNMENT GREEN BUILDING AND ENERGY CODES: MAINTAINING EFFICIENCY

REFINING GREEN BUILDING REGULATIONS AND FUNDING GREEN BUILDINGS IN ORDER TO ACHIEVE GREENHOUSE GAS REDUCTIONS

Erin Elizabeth Burg Hupp.
42 Urban Lawyer 639, 640, 644 (2010).[3]

Recent Changes in City and State mandates for Green Building Certification are being enacted. Cities are refining green building regulations to account for latent deficiencies and ambiguities in existing codes. Issues with commissioning, audits, and performance bonds have been principal concerns in these code refinements.

Many of the long-term benefits of green building retrofits are contingent upon the ability of green buildings to maintain their energy efficiency once built, certified, and operating. Greening existing buildings may save anywhere from 4–20% over a 20-year building lifespan, but may cost anywhere from 1–2% of the building's up-front costs. It is important for green building regulations to include commissioning requirements in order to ensure full capture of a green building's cost savings over the long-term. Commissioning has been described as a systematic, forensic approach to quality assurance. Existing buildings that are retrofitted to increase energy efficiency may be later commissioned in order to determine

---

whether they continue to perform at the efficiency level at which they were designed, since inevitably a building "drifts" away from its intended efficiency level. There have been growing concerns with green building performance and whether the high initial costs of green building are truly recovered as projections indicate.

New York City recently dealt with these national concerns that green building does not provide long-term energy savings by enacting an impressive code that requires commissioning. For example, New York City's Code (New York City Municipal Code § 28–308 (2010)), requires that all buildings greater than 50,000 square feet (a significant number of buildings in the city) monitor energy and water usage and undergo energy audits and retro-commissioning every ten years. The New York City Code also closes a loophole in the city's previous code that allowed renovations comprising less than fifty percent of the building area to remain non-compliant. Now all renovations must comply with the International Energy Conservation Code (IECC).

Performance bonds are another mechanism by which cities are ensuring that a green building will live up to long-term expectations for energy and water savings. In December, 2009, Washington D.C. updated its green building ordinance (Washington D.C. Code § 6–1451.05 (2009) to clarify performance bond requirements. Until recently, no bond, security, or insurance instruments existed to guarantee LEED® or other green building certification. In this case, if a city requires LEED certification and the building fails to achieve such requirements, additional money would be needed for final greening of the building. Washington D.C.'s code previously had no guarantee that a building would achieve LEED certification because it required a performance bond and there is no bond or security instrument on the market that could be substituted for the city's "performance bond" requirement. See Chris Cheatham, White Paper: Revisions to Performance Bond Requirement of the D.C. Green Building Act, available at: http://www.greenbuildinglawupdate.com/uploads/file/DC%20White%20Paper%20FINAL%20PDF.pdf.

Thus, if a building did not follow green building requirements, a surety or building owner must complete the project, and cover any related costs to complete. Washington D.C.'s recent amendments may hold promise as an example for other cities to use when requiring bond instruments that guarantee green building certification, plans and specifications.

Other cities are still focusing on implementing existing green building requirements. San Francisco's 2008 regulations, (San Francisco, Cal., Building Code § 1302C (2008), include the strictest requirements for green retrofits in the nation. San Francisco's green building requirements apply only to commercial buildings with areas of over 5,000 gross square feet and residential structures. In order to complete major alterations (in excess of 25,000 gross square feet)—specifically the existing structural, mechanical, electrical, or plumbing components of the buildings—developers must submit documentation of a LEED Silver rating by 2009 and a LEED Gold rating by 2012. Los Angeles is the largest city to have implemented a green building retrofit program, which it enacted in 2009 (Los Angeles, Cal., MUNICIPAL Code § 16.10B). Los Angeles' regulations apply to green building retrofits of at least 50 dwelling units in an existing mixed-use or residential building, if those alterations comprise at least 50,000 gross square feet of floor area and for which construction value is fifty percent or more of the replacement cost of the building. Boston has not amended its 2007 green building law, which requires that all rehabilitations over 50,000 square feet achieve LEED certification.

Until recently, cities have been leading the green building trend by requiring third-party green building verification; however, states are also now entering the green building regulation arena. For example, as of January 2010, Hawaii's 2008 legislation requiring solar hot water heaters in all new homes went into effect. In the last year, Massachusetts updated its green building code, while California drafted and enacted a mandatory green building code that includes the strictest state-level requirements. In February of 2010, the California Building Standards Commission unanimously approved the new state building code (the "2010 CalGreen") that has taken effect on January 2011. Pursuant to 2010 CalGreen, some previously voluntary regulations will become mandatory. A tier system, similar to LEED, divides requirements into Tier 1 and Tier 2, which require certain buildings to exceed current California Energy Commission requirements by 15% and 30%, respectively. Some commentators have claimed the 2010 CalGreen to be the most stringent and environmentally friendly state building code yet. A coalition of environmental and green building certification groups, however, have criticized the 2010 CalGreen as a step backward, because its requirements are less strict than both LEED standards and existing California city building code standards, including those of Los Angeles and San Francisco. All commentators seem to agree, however, that the mandatory basic requirements of the 2010 CalGreen are at least a step toward a greener California. The 2010 CalGreen requires that new construction will reduce water consumption by 20%, divert 50% of construction waste from landfills, and install low pollutant-emitting materials such as paints and carpets. The California Air Resources Board estimates that the Code's mandatory provisions will reduce greenhouse gas emissions by three million metric tons equivalent by 2020.

Several international and national green building models have also been recently published. Instead of requiring LEED certification, cities may choose to use these model codes as a basis for local green building requirements. For example, the International Green Construction Code (IGCC), released in March 2010, will be published in final form in 2012. The IGCC focuses on reducing the carbon footprints for commercial buildings. The 2008 National Green Building Standard, as approved by the National Association of Homebuilders (NAHB), defines green building for newly constructed single and multi-family homes and residential remodeling projects.

Cities also have the option of adopting a broader standard recently announced and adopted by the American Society of Heating, Refrigerating, and Air-Conditioning Engineers (ASHRAE), Standard 189.1. Standard 189.1, the first comprehensive code for green building standards in the United States, will cover standard green building issues such as siting, design, construction, and planning for operation of high performance, green buildings. Although comprehensive, ASHRAE's Standard 189.1 will not apply to single-family houses, multi-family structures of three stories or fewer above grade, manufactured houses (mobile homes), and manufactured houses (modular). The standard includes requirements for site sustainability, water use efficiency, energy efficiency, indoor environmental quality, and the building's impact on the atmosphere, materials, and resources. ASHRAE's Standard 189.1 will achieve a 25% energy savings and a broader scope over in the 2007 ASHRAE Standard 90.1. ASHRAE's intent is for cities to adopt Standard 189.1 into their local codes.

6. OTHER THIRD-PARTY RATING SYSTEMS FOR GREEN BUILDING REGULATIONS

REFINING GREEN BUILDING REGULATIONS AND FUNDING GREEN BUILDINGS IN ORDER TO ACHIEVE GREENHOUSE GAS REDUCTIONS

Erin Elizabeth Burg Hupp.
42 Urban Lawyer 639, 640, 644 (2010).[4]

Which System to Choose:

The question that many cities now face is which code or standard to adopt: a third-party rating system or a set of local green building standards. Many cities have chosen to implement point systems put forward by third-party rating entities. The benefits of such third-party rating systems include independent verification of green building measures, committee experts devoted to providing quality green building requirements, and some of the strictest regulations in the country. Currently, LEED is the most popular third-party rating system. LEED has put forward a set of very stringent standards at the Gold and Platinum rating level. As discussed above, cities such as San Francisco and Los

---

Angeles have chosen LEED due to its popularity and because of its reputation for quality requirements. Despite its solid reputation, LEED is attempting to address recent concerns about its rating process. For example, LEED is beginning to institute commissioning and paper auditing requirements. Until recertification standards are developed, uncertainty involved in LEED could result in an increase of construction litigation over building performance. LEED certification requirements and points are not very clear. To make matters worse, as of the summer of 2009, USGBC halted publication of LEED Credit Interpretation Requests (CIR), which interpret and explain LEED requirements to those entities implementing LEED. This increased ambiguity as to what measures will satisfy LEED requirements will likely result in confusion and increased litigation over LEED accreditation.

Other government entities have opted to create their own green building regulations or adopt national or international standards instead of third-party rating systems. As an example, California created the CalGreen three-tier system, as discussed above. California claims that its standards surpass a third-party rating system for several reasons, including: its standards are less costly, since LEED accreditation can range from $30,000 to $50,000, and California's standards are not based on private membership like LEED but instead include an open public process. The state emphasizes that CalGreen includes in-person auditing rather than LEED paper audits, and contains uniformity throughout since there is one set of standards for all localities and for all types of buildings (whereas LEED has several point-based systems for each type of building). Whichever type of green building standard a locality chooses, there are now several examples of well-developed codes to choose from.

7. GREEN BUILDING OPPORTUNITIES AND LIMITATIONS

FROM SPRAWL TO SUSTAINABILITY

Robert H. Freilich, Robert J. Sitkowski and Seth D. Mennillo.
Chapter 7, pp. 208–210 (ABA, 2010).[5]

Despite its meteoric rise over the last decade, green building activity still represents a small but growing segment of new commercial construction—from 2 percent each year at the beginning of the decade to 10–12 percent at the end. Two roadblocks preventing even greater acceptance are the perceived or actual upfront cost premium over traditional building design and construction and the disconnect between those who pay these costs and those who benefit. Many decision makers in the real estate world still believe that green projects will cost substantially more than code-based projects. In the survey discussed above, more than half of the real estate executives polled attributed 5 percent or greater premiums to green buildings, and 22 percent attributed 10 percent or greater premiums. Only 9 percent of the respondents believed that costs would be the same or less for green buildings.

Numerous case studies have questioned the existence or magnitude of such cost premiums. A 2003 California study that looked at thirty-three LEED-registered projects with available cost data estimated this "green premium" to be about 2 percent, on average, ranging from less than 1 percent for projects certified at the basic LEED level to more than 6 percent for LEED Platinum-rated projects." However, with so little green building data available at the time, the report acknowledged that its conclusions were somewhat speculative. The report also noted a lack of data comparing what individual traditional projects would have cost compared to green projects, and vice versa. A similar cost increase has been shown in other recent studies.

The rapid pace of sustainable development over the last few years has produced a much larger set of available green project data from which to draw more accurate cost comparisons. One recent study compared 221 projects—83 at various LEED rating levels and 138 traditional projects—varying in locality, size, and use (schools, hospitals, etc.). *See* Davis Langdon, *Cost of Green Revisited: Reexamining the Feasibility and Cost Impact of Sustainable Design in the Light of Increased Market Adoption* (July 2007), available at http://www.davislangdon.com/USA/Research. For each use, the study analyzed the cost per square foot of construction for the green projects versus the traditional projects, while endeavoring to maximize relevancy by normalizing costs for time and location and adjusting project checklists to LEED for New Construction version 2.2. The comparisons still revealed a "very large variation in costs of buildings," and thus failed to "provide any meaningful data for any individual project to assess what-if any-cost impact there might be for incorporating LEED and sustainable design." However, the report noted that a majority of the projects analyzed were able to achieve LEED certification without any additional funding, and found that for each cost, construction costs for the green buildings fell into the existing cost range for traditional projects.

If the studies were to reflect LEED-ND as well as LEED for New Construction, the results would come out sharply in favor of sustainable projects. A recent study conducted for the EPA revealed cost comparisons of various development scenarios for a South Carolina site. The research indicated that a rectilinear grid favored by LEED-ND would lower per unit infrastructure costs by 35 to 40 percent compared to conventional suburban development. *See* Robert Steuteville, *The Case for the Simple Grid*, NEW URB. NEWS, Mar. 2009, at 1. The costs of infrastructure are similarly reduced for smart growth development patterns over sprawl growth, leaving local governments with available funds to provide incentives for sustainable LEED-ND development.

H. RENEWABLE ENERGY

1. SOLAR ENERGY

(a) Assuring Access

Many states have enacted solar easement statutes, which define solar easements and provide a voluntary contractual structure for their creation and protection but preempt the use of private nuisance litigation to protect solar energy systems. Usually, the statute itself does not create private rights. Rather, it provides a framework for future implementation, either by private bargaining for conveyances or by state or local legislation. One example is the Illinois Comprehensive Solar Energy Act of 1977, Ill Compiled Stat Ch. 30, §§ 725/1 to 725/8.2. *See O'Neill v. Brown*, 609 N.E.2d 835 (Ill.App.1993) (Solar Energy Act, which defines "solar sky-space easement," does not create such easement to protect solar access to greenhouse from neighbor's addition of second story to house). *See* James C. Smith & Jacqueline P. Hand, *Common Law Property Rights*, § 5:5 Rights to Prevent Development of Adjacent Airspace (West 2010):

> A number of states have passed statutes that facilitate the development of solar energy systems by limiting the ability of local governments to use their zoning powers to exclude them. *E.g.,* Cal. Gov. Code § 65850.5(c) ("A city or county may not deny an application for a use permit to install a solar energy system unless it makes written findings based upon substantial evidence in the record that the proposed installation would have a specific, adverse impact upon the public health or safety, and there is no feasible method to satisfactorily mitigate or avoid the specific, adverse impact"); Fla.Stat. § 163.04(2) ("A deed restriction, covenant, declaration, or similar binding agreement may not prohibit or have the effect of prohibiting solar collectors, clotheslines, or other energy devices based on renewable resources from being installed on buildings erected on the lots or parcels covered by the deed restriction, covenant, declaration, or binding agreement"); Wis.Stat. § 66.0401(1) ("No county, city, town, or village may place any restriction, either directly or in effect, on the installation or use of a solar energy system ... or a wind energy system ... unless the restriction satisfies one of the following conditions:
>
> (a)   Serves to preserve or protect the public health or safety,

(b) Does not significantly increase the cost of the system or significantly decrease its efficiency [or]

(c) Allows for an alternative system of comparable cost and efficiency").

See State ex rel. Numrich v. City of Mequon Bd. of Zoning Appeals, 626 N.W.2d 366 (Wis.App.2001) (applicant for conditional use permit from local government does not have to satisfy criteria for issuance of permit under § 66.0403 that restricts neighbors from interfering with operation of system). Similarly, some states have statutes that override covenants and other private restrictions. *E.g.*, Ariz.Rev.Stat. § 33–439(A); Col.Rev.Stat. § 38–30–168(1)(a); Fla.Stat. § 163.04(2) ("A deed restriction, covenant, declaration, or similar binding agreement may not prohibit or have the effect of prohibiting solar collectors, clotheslines, or other energy devices based on renewable resources from being installed on buildings erected on the lots or parcels covered by the deed restriction, covenant, declaration, or binding agreement"); Nev.Rev.Stat. § 111.239 ("Any covenant, restriction or condition contained in a deed, contract or other legal instrument which affects the transfer or sale of, or any other interest in, real property and which prohibits or unreasonably restricts or has the effect of prohibiting or unreasonably restricting the owner of the property from using a system for obtaining solar energy on his property is void and unenforceable").

(b) Solar Rights Acts

California has gone further and adopted a Solar Rights Act that prevents adjoining property owners from erecting structures or growing trees that block adjoining solar systems. *See* Cal. Civil Code § 801.5. Solar easement and solar energy system defined; minimum description in instrument

(a) The right of receiving sunlight as specified in subdivision 18 of Section 801 shall be referred to as a solar easement. "Solar easement" means the right of receiving sunlight across real property of another for any solar energy system.

As used in this section, "solar energy system" means either of the following:

(1) Any solar collector or other solar energy device whose primary purpose is to provide for the collection, storage, and distribution of solar energy for space heating, space cooling, electric generation, or water heating.

(2) Any structural design feature of a building, whose primary purpose is to provide for the collection, storage, and distribution of solar

energy for electricity generation, space heating or cooling, or for water heating.

(b) Any instrument creating a solar easement shall include, at a minimum, all of the following:

(1) A description of the dimensions of the easement expressed in measurable terms, such as vertical or horizontal angles measured in degrees, or the hours of the day on specified dates during which direct sunlight to a specified surface of a solar collector, device, or structural design feature may not be obstructed, or a combination of these descriptions.

(2) The restrictions placed upon vegetation, structures, and other objects that would impair or obstruct the passage of sunlight through the easement.

(3) The terms or conditions, if any, under which the easement may be revised or terminated. Cal. Civ. Code § 801.5 (West)

C. For an interesting article suggesting that economic efficiency and cost-benefit analysis resulting from solar power should be a factor in the balancing of interests, *see* Richard O. Zerbe, Jr., *Justice and the Evolution of the Common Law, X Sunlight and the Law of Nuisance,* 3 J.L.ECON. & POL'Y 81, 115–116 (2007).

(c) Financing Green Development, Solar and Wind Renewable Energy: Property Assessed Clean Energy (PACE) Bonds

Since green building improvements and installation of solar rooftop systems are on the rise and produce energy cost savings, private and public landowners are able to finance the high initial cost of energy retrofits. A study performed by the California Sustainable Building Task Force found that only 2% of a building's market value up-front costs for renewable energy yield 20% savings over a twenty-year building life. In response to front-loaded costs for solar energy, states, cities, and counties are able to offer Property Assessed Clean Energy (PACE) Bonds. PACE bond proceeds are lent to private commercial and residential property owners for the financing of solar renewable energy retrofits and repaid through a tax or assessment lien over five, ten, or twenty years. Although the PACE bond financing mechanisms are by no means a one-stop solution to the costs of green retrofits, they are an example of one type of creative financing for green retrofits. Importantly, PACE bonds also include front-end funding for the installation of energy-saving devices, provide municipal flexibility in implementing such funding, and allow owners to contract directly with contractors. PACE bonds, therefore, a judicial validated avenue for local governments in the financial battle against the high up-front cost of certain green building retrofits so long as they forego judicial foreclosure and rely on tax foreclosures.

THOMAS V. CLEAN ENERGY COASTAL CORRIDOR

Supreme Court of Florida, 2015.
176 So.3d 249.

This case is before the Court on appeal from a circuit court judgment validating a proposed bond issue by Clean Energy Coastal Corridor (Clean Energy). We affirm the circuit court's decision to validate the bonds, but remand for the circuit court to require Clean Energy to amend the financing agreement as described herein.

Clean Energy was created pursuant to section 163.01(7), Florida Statutes, by interlocal agreement between three municipalities located in Miami-Dade County, Florida. Clean Energy is a separate legal entity from the municipalities that created it, and its purpose is to finance through the issuance of bonds certain qualifying improvements to real property authorized by section 163.08, Florida Statutes, commonly referred to as the Property Assessed Clean Energy (PACE) Act.

Participation in Clean Energy's PACE Program by property owners within the area covered by the interlocal agreement is voluntary, and in exchange for receiving financing for qualifying improvements, including those related to renewable energy, energy efficiency and conservation, and wind resistance, property owners agree to the imposition of non-ad valorem assessments on the benefitted property. The PACE Act requires these non-ad valorem assessments to be collected on the tax bill pursuant to the uniform method of collection authorized by section 197.3632, Florida Statutes.

After Clean Energy's creation, its governing board adopted a bond resolution authorizing the issuance of revenue bonds in an amount not to exceed $500,000,000 for the purpose of financing qualifying improvements. Clean Energy then filed a complaint to validate those bonds and the non-ad valorem assessments securing them in the Circuit Court for Leon County, Florida, as specified in section 163.01(7)(d), Florida Statutes.

The only argument regarding Clean Energy's authority to issue the bonds raised below that is repeated in this appeal is that the bonds cannot be validated because the financing agreement to be signed by Clean Energy and property owners participating in the PACE Program purports to authorize a remedy for the collection of unpaid assessments that is not authorized by Florida law, namely judicial foreclosure.

This Court has explained the standard of review for bond validation cases where the bond issuance is funded by special assessments:

> This Court performs expedited review in bond validation cases to "facilitate an adjudication as to the validity of bonds so as to provide assurance of the marketability of the bonds." *City of Oldsmar v. State*, 790 So.2d 1042, 1050 (Fla.2001). Our review authority in these cases is "circumscribed in scope and purpose,"

id. at 1049, and is generally limited to three issues: (1) whether the public body has the authority to issue bonds; (2) whether the purpose of the obligation is legal; and (3) whether the bond issuance complies with the requirements of law. *See Keys Citizens for Responsible Gov't, Inc. v. Fla. Keys Aqueduct Auth.*, 795 So.2d 940, 944 (Fla.2001); *State v. Osceola County*, 752 So.2d 530, 533 (Fla.1999). However, where, as here, a bond issuance is funded by special assessments, we will apply an additional two-pronged test to evaluate whether those special assessments meet the requirements of the law. The Court in *City of Winter Springs v. State*, 776 So.2d 255[, 257] (Fla.2001), explained:

> To comply with the requirements of the law, a special assessment funding a bond issuance must satisfy the following two-prong test: (1) the property burdened by the assessment must derive a special benefit from the service provided by the assessment; and (2) the assessment for the services must be properly apportioned among the properties receiving the benefit. *See Lake County v. Water Oak Management Corp.*, 695 So.2d 667, 668 (Fla.1997) (citing *City of Boca Raton v. State*, 595 So.2d 25, 30 (Fla.1992)) and, *Citizens Advocating Responsible Envtl. Solutions, Inc. v. City of Marco Island*, 959 So.2d 203, 206 (Fla.2007).

We have further explained that "subsumed within the inquiry as to whether the public body has the authority to issue the subject bond is the legality of the financing agreement upon which the bond is secured." *State v. City of Port Orange*, 650 So.2d 1, 3 (Fla.1994).

In this case, the financing agreement's references to judicial foreclosure are inconsistent with its requirement—and Florida law—that collection of non-ad valorem assessments must be accomplished pursuant to chapter 197's uniform method. *See generally* § 197.3632, Fla.Stat. (providing for the collection of assessments on the same bill as property taxes and for the issuance and sale of tax certificates and, ultimately, tax deeds if assessments are not paid); *see also* § 163.08(4), Fla.Stat. (providing that financing costs for qualifying PACE program improvements "may be collected as a non-ad valorem assessment [which] shall be collected pursuant to s. 197.3632"). However, as the circuit court noted, the financing agreement limits Clean Energy to "appropriate legal remedies" for collecting unpaid assessments, and as Clean Energy concedes, judicial foreclosure is not an appropriate legal remedy.

Because judicial foreclosure is not an appropriate legal remedy for collecting the non-ad valorem assessments, we find no error in the circuit court's decision to read the financing agreement in a manner that effectively severs this inappropriate remedy and limits Clean Energy to the appropriate legal remedy—also provided by the financing agreement—of collecting assessments pursuant to the uniform method. *See Fonte v. AT &*

T Wireless Servs., Inc., 903 So.2d 1019, 1024 (Fla. 4th DCA 2005) ("As a general rule, contractual provisions are severable, where the illegal portion of the contract does not go to its essence, and, with the illegal portion eliminated, there remain valid legal obligations.").

While we agree with the circuit court that judicial foreclosure is not an appropriate remedy, we conclude that additional steps are required to implement the circuit court's ruling since the financing agreement will serve as the form for all financing agreements between Clean Energy and the property owners who participate in its PACE Program. Specifically, we remand with instructions for the circuit court to require Clean Energy to amend the financing agreement to remove all references to judicial foreclosure and to file the amended agreement in the circuit court following its approval by Clean Energy's governing board. *Cf. State v. City of Venice*, 147 Fla. 70, 2 So.2d 365, 367–68 (1941) (remanding to circuit court "with directions to require the amendment of the resolution and the bonds" to correct language regarding the pledged funds that was "too broad to be sustained" and stating that "when the same are so amended the decree of validation . . . will stand affirmed").

For the foregoing reasons, we affirm the circuit court's final judgment validating Clean Energy's bonds, but remand with instructions for the circuit court to require Clean Energy to amend the financing agreement as described herein.

It is so ordered.

(d) Resolving FHA Problems with PACE Financing

Because PACE involves local government assessments or taxes, these municipal obligations have lien priority over other creditors in the event of foreclosure, thus allowing for lower borrowing costs due to the higher certainty of repayment. It was this lien priority feature that prompted the Federal Housing Finance Administration (FHFA) to halt federal guarantees of loans on residential properties with PACE assessments (commercial properties were unaffected). This action effectively killed PACE across the country from 2009 to 2015. The problem has been solved by a recent agreement between FHA, banks and municipalities. *See*, Kate Berry, *Banks Win FHA Support in Lien Fight with Pace Lenders*, National News, August 25, 2015:

> "The Federal Housing Administration has resolved a long-standing conflict with municipalities and private companies that back "green energy" loans and also will allow higher loan amounts for energy improvements.

Property Assessed Clean Energy loans help borrowers finance environmentally-friendly home improvement projects such as solar panels. A major sticking point has been that FHA mortgage lenders and PACE lenders have both staked first priority claims to the same collateral—the borrower's homes—if their loans go bad. The policy question has been which side should get repaid first in the event of default.

The PACE loans, made by municipalities, are repaid by the homeowner as a line item on their property tax bills. Mortgage lenders have raised concerns that since PACE loans are essentially tax assessments they have a "super lien" status that take precedence over the first-lien mortgage, creating an impediment to the sale and refinancing of properties.

The FHA has developed lender guidance that says PACE loans are subordinate to a first lien mortgage. In exchange FHA will allow borrowers with FHA loans to refinance or sell their properties instead of having to pay off the PACE loan as a condition of getting a new mortgage. In addition, the FHA has launched an initiative with the Department of Energy that allows borrowers to obtain larger loans, of roughly 2% more than the loan amount, to finance energy improvements.

California has taken the lead in the proliferation of municipally financed green retrofits through PACE bonds with the implementation of California's Assembly Bill 811 (AB 811) (Cal. Streets & Highway Code § 5898.12(a)–(d) (2008). AB 811 enables all California cities and counties to create assessment districts, which may encompass a portion or all of a city. Within that assessment district, the city or county is authorized by AB 811 to provide low-cost financial assistance to property owners in the form of contractual assessments for the installation or purchase of renewable energy sources that are permanently affixed to residential, commercial, and industrial property (such as solar panels). AB 811 requires that the property be already developed in order to ensure that the funds are used for the retrofitting of existing buildings rather than the construction of new buildings. These assessments are then recorded on the property's tax roll as liens on the property and paid by the property owner as a contractual assessment. The liens run with the property and are carried over to subsequent property owners. In order to provide these loans, AB 811 requires that the city: (i) designate the boundary of the area where these loans are available; (ii) draft a specific contract specifying the terms and conditions of the loan; (iii) create a method for prioritizing property owners' requests; and (iv) create a plan for raising capital through bond funds.

Similarly, Berkeley, California enacted a PACE-type program called Berkeley Financing Initiative for Renewable and Solar Technology (FIRST), through California Mello-Roos Act, a slightly different channel than the AB 811-authorized assessment districts. Through FIRST, a property-owner agrees to annex into a special city tax district, and then the city provides up-front costs for residential and commercial property owners to install electric and thermal solar systems. These costs are repaid to the city over twenty years through a special tax on the property.

Following California's lead, Colorado has also passed a PACE bond law that allows cities to grant property liens for energy efficient fixtures, such as solar panels, on both commercial and residential property. Boulder County's ClimateSmart Loan Program implements efficient energy fixture funding city-wide through loans financed by publicly offered bonds.

(e) Monetary Incentives for Green Building

(1) General

Jason R. Busch, Rosemary A. Collins and Janet F. Jacobs, *Tax and Financial Incentives for Green Building*, 15 LOS ANGELES LAWYER 15 (2008)

Twenty years ago, when green building was first conceived, this innovative construction concept received little public notice. Today, however, developers acknowledge that green building offers an opportunity to reduce adverse effects on the environment while improving the bottom line. By integrating siting, design, construction, operation, maintenance, and waste management practices, developers can realize long-term positive returns from improved efficiencies. Developers are also taking advantage of short-term financial incentives provided by federal tax law and state and local governments to promote green buildings.

The concept of green building has expanded beyond design and materials to include integrated systems and life cycle analyses, site selection and use of passive elements, energy efficiency and renewable energy production, water conservation, waste reduction, indoor environment improvement, and smart growth and sustainable development.

While green building may have once been more expensive than traditional building techniques, this is no longer necessarily true. On the contrary, "[t]he financial payoff from green building will be multifaceted, comprising direct savings from reduced energy use, higher value in the real estate market (including resale value), increased employee retention and productivity, and potential carbon credits from reduced CO2 emissions." To realize these benefits, however, owners and developers must retain professionals who understand the many evolving options available for green building projects and can apply the appropriate choices to the project at hand.

(2) Federal Tax Incentives

Internal Revenue Code Section 179D allows a commercial building owner to deduct all or a portion of the cost of certain "energy efficient commercial building property" placed in service.

In order for the building to qualify for the credit, it must be designed according to a plan that achieves a reduction of 50 percent or more in total annual energy costs, attained solely from interior lighting and heating, cooling, ventilation, and hot water systems, as compared to a reference building meeting the minimum requirements of Standard 90.1–2001.

The amount of the tax deduction varies depending on the energy reductions that are achieved. If the building meets or exceeds the 50 percent threshold, the deduction equates to the cost of the energy efficient commercial building property placed in service during the taxable year subject to a limit of $1.80 per square foot. For buildings that achieve a documented savings of 16 percent but less than 50 percent, the deduction is set at $.60 per square foot.

Residential property builders may take a one-time tax credit of up to $2,000 under IRC Section 45L for "qualified new energy efficient homes," including manufactured homes meeting the Federal Manufactured Home Construction and Safety Standards.

A home qualifies for the entire credit if 1) the building is certified as reducing energy consumption by 50 percent compared to a home constructed in accordance with certain national and international standards, and 2) building envelope improvements (e.g., thermal resistance of the outer structural materials, window placement and coatings or glazing, and roof strategies such as reductions to the heat island effect through the use of light or reflective materials) account for at least one-fifth of the 50 percent reduction. A manufactured home may qualify for a $1,000 credit if it is certified as reducing energy consumption by at least 30 percent and building envelope improvements account for at least one-third of the 30 percent reduction or if the home complies with requirements under the Energy Star Labeled Homes program.

For any commercial or residential building that incorporates solar energy equipment, the property may also qualify for enhanced tax benefits that help offset the overall cost of the equipment. IRC Section 48 provides a nonrefundable income tax credit equal to 30 percent of the tax basis of any energy property, including certain solar energy equipment.

Solar energy property may also qualify for greatly accelerated depreciation deductions. A deduction may be taken over five years using the double declining balance method for solar energy property qualifying for the tax credit, which can also create significant tax savings.

(3) California Tax Incentives

California currently offers two incentives in the Revenue and Taxation Code to encourage green building. The first permits the entire cash value of a solar energy system to be excluded for purposes of calculating property taxes. While the addition of a solar energy system increases the appraised value of the property on which it is installed, state law provides that no corresponding increase will be recognized in the property's assessed value for tax purposes over the system's operational life. A qualifying system or "active solar energy system" is one that uses solar devices that are "thermally isolated from living space or any other area where the energy is used, to provide for the collection, storage, or distribution of solar energy." Energy systems used to support the production of electricity, heat, mechanical energy, air conditioning, and domestic, recreational, therapeutic, or service water heating are each acceptable. Storage devices, power conditioning, and transfer equipment are also eligible for the exemption.

The second incentive entitles residential property owners to deduct interest paid on loans taken out with investor-owned utilities to purchase energy-efficient systems or products. This includes energy-efficient heating systems, ventilation, air conditioning, lighting, solar systems, advanced metering of energy usage, windows, insulation, zone heating products, and weatherization systems. Consumers whose utilities do not offer such financing may be able to deduct the interest on home equity or improvement loans used to make similar purchases. To claim the deduction, the utility must issue an IRS Form 1098 or similar document notifying customers of their eligibility for this deduction. Further, the credit may not be taken if another tax credit is taken for purchasing the same equipment.

(f) Solar Power Rebates (Renewable Energy Credits)

In January 2006, the CPUC adopted a state rebate program called the California Solar Initiative (CSI). With a program budget of $3.3 billion for 10 years for solar projects, the CSI's objective is to provide 3,000 MW of solar capacity by 2017. CSI will first fund solar photovoltaics and then other solar technologies. The initiative is divided into two separate programs. The CPUC manages the program for nonresidential and existing residential customers, while the California Energy Commission oversees the New Solar Homes Partnership targeting the residential new construction market. CSI has already been expanded and now requires that municipal utilities offer incentives beginning this year (nearly $800 million). The CPUC authorized the use of tradable renewable energy credits on March 11, 2010, http://docs.cpuc.ca.gov/PUBLISHED/ AGENDA_DECISION/114750.htm.

Renewable Energy Credits (RECs) represent the environmental benefits of solar rooftop power and can be sold separately from the cost of electricity saved. RECs can be sold at substantial values only by the owners of the solar facilities. Industrial companies that are required to mitigate their greenhouse gas emissions can purchase RECs to reduce the extent of their mitigation. Unbridled REC sales grew to 36 million MWH in 2014, increasing 15% from 2013. U.S. Department of Energy, Energy Efficiency and Renewable Energy, The Green Power Network, (2015). Most solar rooftop installations are constructed by private solar companies that lease the solar facility to the building owner. Thus it is the lessor company that gets to sell the RECs and not the building owner. This demonstrates the advantage of a city or county using a PACE program to finance the installation so that the owner can directly sell the REC for additional saving.

(g) Alternatives to Property Tax Incentives: Monetization of Renewable Energy & Rainwater Capture Through Public Improvement District and Public Utility Special Assessments

FROM SPRAWL TO SUSTAINABILITY: SMART GROWTH, NEW URBANISM, GREEN DEVELOPMENT AND RENEWABLE ENERGY

Robert H. Freilich, Robert J. Sitkowski & Seth D. Mennillo.
Chapter 7, pp. 210–211 (ABA, 2010).

"The initial costs of a number of green building features can be overcome by use of simple financing techniques. An exhaustive study conducted by California's Sustainable Building Task Force established that incorporating green features into a building's design would generate a tenfold return on investment over the life of the building. The findings were substantial; even without solar energy, green buildings consume 30 percent less energy. Green buildings with solar energy consumed 80 percent less energy and 30–50 percent less water and produced 50–75 percent less construction waste." The key is to monetize the initial cost over the lifetime of the building. This can readily be done for the solar energy and rainwater-capture-system components of green development by amortizing the savings resulting from reductions in electricity, natural gas, and water utility rates and charges.

Solar power has extraordinary potential; in the United States alone, the unused capacity of solar energy amounts to 10,000 times as much electric power as is currently consumed in the country. Solar domestic hot water collectors are affordable and efficient, can be paid off in ten years, and replace the second most expensive element of home utilities after heating and air conditioning.

The cost of a single-family 10K solar facility, capable of providing all of the electrical energy required by a home, is currently about $35,000, with monthly utility rates of electricity averaging $400 in many states. An 80 percent savings of $320 per month from solar energy would take only ten years to recoup the solar investment. The savings over the life of a thirty-year mortgage loan would amount to $90,240.

One of the major problems with building green or renewable solar facilities is the requirement that a housing developer must pay the upfront $35,000 per dwelling unit cost, while state and federal subsidies are paid directly to the homeowner. Rainwater capture systems represent extraordinary potential. The cost of water is rising rapidly, especially in the drought-ridden Southeast and Southwest. By installing cisterns, pervious driveways, and swales in place of culverts, rainwater retention, treatment, and reuse results in huge savings in the amount of water purchased from water utilities. Costs can be lowered by 50–80 percent even under semi-arid rainfall conditions of eleven to thirteen inches a year. Basic water and electricity conservation methods coupled with public information on average use of water and electricity will further save money. But as with solar energy installation, developers must pay the initial cost of rainwater capture systems and are fearful that they will not be able to recoup their investment from the sale of the unit.

A simple solution is to monetize the cost of solar and rainwater systems through grants or loans to the developer by the electric or water utility, a public improvement district, or the homeowner's association, which will be amortized by the savings from the lowered utility rate charges, special district assessments, or homeowner's association dues. If water rates are $400 per month, the savings of $200 to $320 per month in water rates will easily amortize the rainwater system with large amounts left over for the homeowner. Special assessments and utility rates are normally used for public capital facilities, but the courts and state legislatures are opening the door for public and/or special district assessments for solar energy and rainwater capture. A New Mexico court recently ruled that a municipality or utility had the authority to impose rate surcharges on a property owner's use of water to pay for the cost of purchasing available water in addition to providing hard physical treatment plants and distribution lines. *See Stennis v. City of Santa Fe*, 143 P.3d 756 (N.M.App.2006). In *Board of Trustees of Washington County Water Conservancy Dist. v. Keystone Conversions*, 103 P.3d 686 (Utah 2004), the court held that a fee levied for developing secondary water sources did not violate the Impact Fees Act, Utah Code Ann. §§ 11–36–101 to 11–36–501).

The same result has been achieved to pay for the costs of conservation to meet the stringent stormwater discharge regulations issued by the EPA under the 1987 Water Quality Act. *See* David Bergman, *A Utility Approach to Storm Water Management, Pas Memo/Public Investment* (American Planning Ass'n, June 1991). Communities have created "storm water utilities" and "transportation utilities" that pass the cost of construction, operation, maintenance, and repair directly to the property owners served by the system through monthly assessments, using a concept of equivalent dwelling units (EDUs) and trip generation. *See Bloom v. City of Fort Collins*, 784 P.2d 304 (Colo.1989) (upholding creation of a transportation utility for repair and maintenance of arterial and collector roads utilizing rates imposed on existing development). Direct assessments can be levied against the homeowners by the homeowner's association. These assessments are used to amortize the utility or special district's grant or loan to the developer.

2. WIND ENERGY

DESERT PROTECTIVE COUNCIL V. U.S. DEPARTMENT OF THE INTERIOR

United States District Court, S.D. California, 2013.
927 F.Supp.2d 949.

Plaintiffs appeal the district court's judgment denying Plaintiffs' motion for summary judgment and granting Defendants' motion for summary judgment. We have jurisdiction pursuant to 28 U.S.C. § 1291, and we affirm.

NEPA requires federal agencies to follow certain procedures and take a "hard look" at environmental consequences. *Idaho Conservation League v. Mumma*, 956 F.2d 1508, 1519 (9th Cir.1992). NEPA regulations require agencies to make "environmental information . . . available to public officials and citizens before decisions are made," 40 C.F.R. § 1500.1(b), and "insure the . . . scientific integrity[ ] of the discussions and analyses in environmental impact statements [("EIS")]," § 1502.24. NEPA also requires agencies to discuss appropriate mitigation measures in an EIS "in sufficient detail to ensure that environmental consequences have been fairly evaluated." *Robertson v. Methow Valley Citizens Council*, 490 U.S. 332, 352 (1989).

The district court did not err in determining that the BLM complied with NEPA, because the BLM sufficiently evaluated and disclosed the environmental impacts of the Ocotillo wind energy facility project (the "Project"). Plaintiffs contend that they were not provided with an opportunity for public comment on 34 raptor studies that were cited in the final Avian and Bat Protection Plan ("ABPP"), but not in the draft ABPP. A mitigation plan, such as the ABPP, does not need to be in final form to comply with NEPA's procedural requirements. *See Nat'l Parks & Conservation Ass'n v. U.S. Dep't of Transp.*, 222 F.3d 677, 681 n. 4 (9th Cir.2000). The draft EIS concluded that raptor use of the Project site was low and provided supporting evidence. Plaintiffs commented on the draft EIS and did not take issue with this conclusion.

Similarly, Plaintiffs have not shown that the methodologies used by the BLM in conducting migration surveys were arbitrary or capricious. While Plaintiffs question the BLM's methodologies as they relate to the timing of raptor migration surveys, the final EIS contains a reasoned analysis of the migration and presence of Swainson's hawks and other raptors at the Project site. We are "most deferential when reviewing scientific judgments and technical analyses within the agency's expertise under NEPA" and will not "impose [ourselves] as a panel of scientists." *See*

Native Ecosystems Council v. Weldon, 697 F.3d 1043, 1051 (9th Cir.2012) (internal citations and quotation marks omitted). Further, the BLM included a reasonably complete discussion of mitigation measures in the final EIS. It was not arbitrary and capricious for the final EIS to require turbine curtailment for golden eagles and not other raptors, because the special legal status of golden eagles justified different mitigation measures.

FLPMA authorizes the Department of Interior to grant rights-of-way across public lands for various purposes, including for "systems for generation, transmission, and distribution of electric energy." 43 U.S.C. § 1761(a)(4). These grants must "require compliance with State standards for . . . environmental protection . . . if those standards are more stringent than applicable Federal standards." § 1765(a)(iv). The grants must also include terms and conditions that "minimize damage to . . . fish and wildlife habitat and otherwise protect the environment." § 1765(a)(ii).

The BLM did not act arbitrarily and capriciously in granting a right-of-way for the Project. The right-of-way explicitly requires compliance with state law. Contrary to Plaintiffs' argument, the California Department of Fish and Wildlife has not interpreted the California Fish and Game Code as requiring wind energy facilities to prevent all bird and bat fatalities. The right-of-way also includes terms and conditions minimizing damage to wildlife habitat and protecting the environment. The right-of-way was not required to include turbine curtailment for all raptor species as a mitigation measure. The Project adopted sufficient mitigation measures designed to minimize damage to wildlife habitat.

Affirmed.

NOTES

1.   In an important decision, *Piedmont Environmental Council v. Federal Energy Regulatory Commission*, 558 F.3d 304 (4th Cir.2009), the federal Court of Appeals held that the Federal Energy Regulatory Commission (FERC) does not have statutory authority under the Federal Power Act to override state administrative licensing of wind farms and electrical transmission lines, as long as the state final decision is made within one year of the filing of the licensing application.

2.   Major problems arise for wind power because the prime location in the west for wind farms lies in the deserts of Arizona, New Mexico and California. These wind farms, together with solar facilities, require new electrical transmission lines to cross the Rocky and Sierra mountains to reach the Pacific coastal urban areas. However, unlike the interstate highway system, the federal government has had little to do with the interstate electric transmission grid. Common law property rules and multiple, overlapping local and state authorities hinder the formation of these developable renewable wind parcels. Professor Wiseman argues that creation of regional agencies capable of facilitating such formation is necessary if we are to achieve

meaningful renewable energy production. *See* Hannah Wiseman, *Expanding Regional Renewable Governance*, 35 HARV.ENVTL.L.REV. 477 (2011).

3. The major threats to the growth of remote wind farms and the concomitant transmission lines needed to convey the power are the environmental impacts to wildlife and plant habitats in wilderness preserves and national forests. A recent proposal by the City of Los Angeles to secure 40 percent of its electricity from renewable energy, particularly wind and solar power from the remote Salton Sea and Imperial County, was withdrawn to study six other alternative routes that would avoid the natural flora and fauna wildlife habits in the Big Morongo Wildlife Preserve, Pioneertown in Yucca Valley, Pipes Canyon Wilderness Reserve, and a corner of the San Bernardino National Forest. Where some see unwelcome invasion of the wilderness, others see green energy that will save the entire world's environment from destruction by global warming. Is there a direct conflict between the priorities of two segments of the environmental movement, i.e. those that seek to solve global warming as a first priority on one hand and those who desire to preserve pristine areas as the first priority?

4. With regard to continued assertions by renewable energy producers that local opposition constitutes a new variation of NIMBYism, *see* Jeffrey Swofford & Michael Slattery, *Public Attitudes of Wind Energy in Texas: Local Communities in Close Proximity to Wind Farms and Their Effect on Decision-Making*, 38 ENERGY POL'Y 2508 (2010). Wind farms have also been challenged under public trust doctrine theories. The environmental nonprofit CBD sued the operators of the controversial Altamont Pass Wind Farm in the Bay Area for violation of the public trust doctrine because the turbines killed off bats and birds. *See Center for Biological Diversity v. FPL Group, Inc.*, 83 Cal.Rptr.3d 588 (2008). Because the state (or relevant agency actor) has the affirmative duty to consider the public trust in managing resources and sovereign supervision over commonly held resources, the court found that the state was the appropriate party to be challenged. However, the court found that judicial abstention was appropriate in the case, because CBD's appropriate avenue for challenging the permits had long passed. The court also opined on the agency's careful consideration and awareness of the wind turbine's impact on wildlife and the balancing of interests in developing wind power in the region as "complex and value laden and outside proper judicial intervention." FPL Group, at 1371. While the public trust doctrine clearly creates opportunity for public involvement in state resource allocation decisions, this area of law may have limited application for environmental challenges to wind projects. *See* Alexa Burt Engelman, *Against the Wind: Conflict Over Wind Energy Siting*, 41 ENVTL.L.REP.NEWS & ANALYSIS 10549 (2011).

5. Since the 1990s, wind power has grown rapidly in the United States. In Texas, for example, almost 10 percent of electricity supplied to the main electrical grid was generated by wind energy in 2013. Other states similarly aspire to move their energy production to wind power and other renewable energy sources in the near future. Governments, from the federal level to the local, have enacted policies to address constituent concerns about the potential

negative environmental consequences of burning fossil fuels. The perceived environmental benefits of wind power include increased sustainability, reduced carbon emissions, and reduced potential for catastrophic human-caused climate change. In 2012 wind energy represented 43 percent of all new electricity-generating capacity, more than any other type of energy.

6.   As much new generating power came from wind as from natural gas. Jad Mouawad, *Wind Power Grows 39% for the Year*, N.Y. TIMES, January 26, 2010. Wind power has increased 700 percent since 2002 and now represents more than 4 percent of the nation's total electrical output. It is expected to grow to 6 percent by 2020, and will probably reach 25 percent by 2020 to 2025. The cost of wind, wave and hydroelectric power is less than seven cents per kilowatt hour (kwh) and by 2020 will drop to four cents per kwh Most of this growth surge comes from the federal Production tax credit and the Energy Investment Tax Credit. Randy T. Simmons, Ryan M. Yonk and Megan E. Hansen *The True Cost of Energy: Wind Power, Institute of Political Economy* (2015). The 2016 Federal Budget reinvigorated these tax credits but phases them out by 2020. Will the rise of wind power continue its rapid growth after these tax credits are eliminated?

3   CLEAN COAL

(a) The Problem

According to United Nations Intergovernmental Panel on Climate Change, the burning of coal, a fossil fuel, is a major contributor to global warming. (See the UN IPCC Fourth Assessment Report, 2014) producing 25.5% of the world's electrical generation in 2004. Coal is the second largest domestic contributor to carbon dioxide emissions in the USA. *See*, Sean O'Hara, *The Importance of the United States Staying the Course While Implementing Environmental Policy in Accordance with the American Recovery and Reinvestment Act of 2009*, 17 U.BALT.J.ENVTL.L. 85, 88 (2009).

Emissions from coal generators are hazardous to the health of the entire ecosystem. These emissions contain toxic sulfur oxides, nitrogen oxides, carbon oxides, and particulate matter, all regulated criteria pollutants under the Clean Air Act. These poisons damage crops, vegetation, human health and the atmosphere. Acid rain only widens this devastation as the sulfites and nitrates react with the rain and spread the environmental impact of coal plants longer distances. Further, coal generators are one of the most significant sources of GHG emissions. Human production of GHGs is believed to cause or accelerate global warming, and an associated rise in ocean temperatures and levels threatens to create 56 million environmental refugees by century's end. Bradford C. Mank, *Standing and Global Warming: Is Injury to All Injury to None?*, 35 ENVTL.L. 1, 3 (2005).

(b) Obama Administration Regulations

On October 23, 2015 the EPA enacted a final rule, effective December 22, 2015, implementing the President's Climate Action Plan, 40 CFR Part 60, Carbon Pollution Emission Guidelines for Existing Stationary Source Electric Utility Generating Plants:

"This final rule is a significant step forward in implementing the President's Climate Action Plan. To address the far-reaching harmful consequences and real economic costs of climate change, the President's Climate Action Plan details a broad array of actions to reduce GHG emissions that contribute to climate change and its harmful impacts on public health and the environment. Climate change is already occurring in this country, affecting the health, economic well-being and quality of life of Americans across the country, and especially those in the most vulnerable communities. This Clean Air Act (CAA) section 111(d) rulemaking to reduce GHG emissions from existing [coal] power plants, and the concurrent CAA section 111(b) rulemaking to reduce GHG emissions from new, modified, and reconstructed power plants, implement one of the strategies of the Climate Action Plan. Nationwide, by 2030, this final CAA section 111(d) existing source rule will achieve CO2 emission reductions from the utility power sector of approximately 32 percent from CO2 emission levels in 2005."

The Rule also requires every state to achieve that drastic reduction in their regional air pollution plans.

This Rule and the President's Climate Action Plan was immediately challenged in the federal courts as beyond the EPA's rule-making authority. In a severe blow to the 27 states that originated the case, the D.C. Circuit Court of Appeals, on January 21, 2016 denied a stay of the rule until the case reaches trial and final appeal, so that the rule is in immediate effect. See, West Virginia et al. v. Environmental Protection Agency (D.C.Cir. January 21, 2016). *See*, Brent Kendall and Amy Harder, *Appeals Court declines to Block EPA Carbon Rule During Litigation*, Wall Street Journal, January 21, 2016 ("States, utilities, coal producers and business groups say they face immediate burdens from compliance").

(c) Trump Executive Order

On March 28, 2017, President Trump signed the "Promoting Energy Independence and Economic Growth" Executive Order attempting to roll back the Obama initiatives on the Climate Action Plan, 40 CFR Part 60, Carbon Pollution Emission Guidelines for Existing Stationary Source Electric Utility Generating Plants. The President's Executive Order initiated a repeal of the EPA's Clean Power Plan, while also ending the Interior Department's moratorium on new coal mining on federal land. Among other things, the executive order also instructs federal agencies to abandon their policy of factoring the impacts on climate change into government decisions. And it orders the EPA and the Department of the Interior to dismantle Obama administration rules that reduce methane emissions from the coal, oil and gas sector and regulate fracking on public land. He told friendly crowds in coal-producing states that lifting carbon restrictions would not only keep energy costs affordable but also help revitalize the coal industry and the communities economically ravaged by environmental regulations.

(d) How Effective Will the New Executive Order Be?

Two before and after comments assess the effectiveness of the Trump Executive Order:

(1)   Devashree Saha and Sifan Liu, The Avenue, December 19, 2006:

"The appointment of Scott Pruitt to head the Environmental Protection Agency (EPA) reveals that President-elect Trump is dead serious about his campaign promises to rein in environmental regulations and revive the coal industry. Pruitt is a vocal critic of the EPA's Clean Power Plan (CPP), which seeks to cut carbon dioxide emissions from power plants, and he has threatened to dismantle CPP to end the "war on coal".

The war on coal is a false narrative that oversimplifies what is happening in the energy economy. In blaming environmental regulations under the Obama administration as the sole reason for the recent turmoil in the coal industry, Trump and Pruitt are ignoring fundamental market realities that are buffeting the industry.

A December 2016 Brookings paper shows how the ongoing large-scale switch in the power sector from coal to cheaper and abundant natural gas—a trend driven more by investors and market forces than by environmental regulations—is playing a huge role in states' increased ability to "decouple" their economic growth from growth in carbon emissions. The natural gas glut has reshaped how we get electricity across the board, with natural gas-fired generation expected to surpass coal generation in the United States for the first time in 2016.

At the same time, renewable energy is continuing to increase its market share aided by declining costs, increasing efficiency, and economies of scale. Renewables, including hydro, wind, solar, biomass, and geothermal, provided 16.9 percent of electricity generated in the first half of 2016. That compares with 13.7 percent in all of 2015.

The wave of coal plant retirements in recent years, therefore, is not surprising as utilities continue to move away from coal to burn cheaper natural gas and increase their renewable capacity. The latest data from Energy Information Administration's (EIA) September Monthly Electric Generator Inventory shows that in 2015 alone, utilities retired power plants generating 22.2 gigawatts of electricity. Coal-fired plants accounted for 67 percent (14.8 gigawatts) of the retirements. The loss in coal energy represents 5 percent of the nation's total coal-fired electrical generation capacity, a significant number in a single year. The industry retired another 6.5 gigawatts of coal-fired generation in the first half of 2016."

(2) *See also* Aaron Bernstein, *Why Donald Trump Can't Save the Coal Industry*, Newsweek, March 30, 2017:

Everybody needs to calm down. Trump's executive order reversing the Obama administration's Clean Power Plan designed to cut carbon pollution from power plants is meaningless. Washington has far less ability to change the direction of economic forces than politicians and the public seem to believe. Laws could be passed providing new federal support for the buggy whip industry, but that business is not coming back. The same goes for coal; the world has simply changed too much. Coal, by any reasonable measure, is on life support and won't be recovering no matter what Trump and Congress do. A revitalization of the industry—which would push up the pollution generated by this dirty fuel—is not going to happen.

Coal plants have been closing year after year. In 2005, there were 619 coal-fired power plants in the United States; that number dropped to 427 by 2015—long before the Obama administration announced the Clean Power Plan. In fact, since Trump won the presidency, six more coal-fired power plants have closed or announced they will. Over the same time, the number of natural gas plants climbed from 1,664 to 1,779. (And don't forget the many non-hydroelectric plants running on renewable energy like solar. Those climbed from 781 to 3,043. Such renewables, which generated next to nothing in 1990, now account for almost 10 percent of total power generated in the U.S.)

(e) Clean Coal

The coal industry's only hope of continuance is to develop "clean coal" technologies. The coal industry has spent more than $50 billion towards the development and deployment of "traditional" clean coal technologies over the past 30 years; and promises $500 million towards carbon capture and storage research and development. Clean Coal Technology, http://en.wikipedia.org/wiki/Clean_coal_technology.

The U.S. Department of Energy refer to carbon capture and sequestration (CCS) as the latest in "clean coal" technologies. CCS is a means to capture carbon dioxide from any source, compress it to a dense liquid-like state, and inject and permanently store it underground. Currently, there are more than 80 carbon capture and sequestration projects underway in the United States. All components of CCS technology have been used for decades in conjunction with enhanced oil recovery and other applications; commercial-scale CCS is currently being tested in the U.S. and other countries. Proposed CCS sites are subjected to extensive investigation and monitoring to avoid potential hazards, which could include leakage of sequestered CO2 to the atmosphere, induced geological instability, or contamination of aquifers used for drinking water supplies. Gregory B. Foote, *Considering Alternatives: The Case for Limiting CO2 Emissions from New Power Plants through New Source Review*, 34 ENVTL.L.REP. 10642, 10659–60 (2004).

Theoretically, it is possible to use CCS to remove pollutants from emissions and store them underground in geologic formations. The American Recovery and Reinvestment Act of 2009 ("ARRA") provides $1.5 billion for geologic sequestration projects. Sean O'Hara, *The Importance of the United States Staying the Course While Implementing Environmental Policy in Accordance with the American Recovery and Reinvestment Act of 2009*, 17 U.BALT.J.ENVTL.L. 85, 88 (2009).

Yet, while CCS may be feasible, broader circumstantial considerations render resort to this technology infeasible. *See, In Clean Coal We Trust, or Do We*, Paris Tech Review (October 15, 2014).

CCS technology, while achievable, is not an economically efficient redress to the harms of coal. Uncertainties regarding storage capacity and prohibitive costs are overly burdensome at present. The National Academy of Sciences, while conceding CCS is possible, cautions that the US will require five to twenty times more underground reservoir volume than currently anticipated. Christine Ehlig-Economides & Michael J. Economides, *Sequestering Carbon Dioxide in a Closed Underground Volume, Journal of Petroleum Sci. & Engineering* 70, 130 (2010).

Sequestered carbon may be geologically stored in as much as one percent of available pore space within a rock formation. Therefore, adequate storage requires a volume of rock larger than the volume of liquefied carbons by a magnitude of one hundred to one. Considering, the daily generation of carbon monoxide, when compressed, amounts to 28 million barrels, storage will require an immense amount of suitable rock.

Practically speaking, a 500 MW, medium-sized, coal generator requires a geologic reservoir the "size of a small US state."

Carbon capture and sequestration is also presently uncompetitive. CCS technology can easily double the construction price of a modern IGCC generation facility. Widespread introduction of this technology will potentially increase the end retail price of electricity up to 50%. Howard Herzog & Koen Smekens, *Cost and Economic Potential, Carbon Dioxide Capture and Storage* 339, 341 (2005), http://www.ipcc.ch/pdf/special-reports/srccs/srccs_chapter8.pdf.

Clean coal technology is making great strides, but is presently too costly and uncertain to fully address the extent of the harm at issue. Investment into research and design of cutting edge clean coal technologies should undoubtedly continue, but the technology is not yet evolved, or certain enough, to become economically viable. Therefore, clean coal technologies should not be regarded as a present solution to the ills of coal. Clean coal just doesn't cut it.

I. WATER SUPPLIES

1. THE DROUGHT PROBLEM

(a) Eduardo Porter, In California and The South-West, Water Has Limits, N.Y. Times, April 7, 2015

Most scientists agree there is little evidence to conclusively tie the recent instances of extreme weather to human-driven climate change. But there is little question that climate change will have a big impact on the weather and the availability of water, in the not-so-distant future.

A new study by three researchers from Stanford University concluded that human emissions of carbon dioxide had increased the odds that California will suffer repeated combinations of warm temperature and low precipitation, "the co-occurring warm-dry conditions that have created the acute human and ecosystem impacts associated with the 'exceptional' 2012—2014 drought in California."

And if such emissions continue growing throughout the century, researchers from the NASA Goddard Institute for Space Studies, the Lamont-Doherty Earth Observatory at Columbia University and Cornell University estimated that the entire American Southwest would face at least an 80 percent chance of suffering a multi-decade "mega-drought" from 2050 through 2099.

In a nutshell, climate change is expected to increase rain or snowfall in areas that are already relatively wet and reduce it in areas that are already relatively dry, like the Southwest, Mexico and Australia. Dry areas, moreover, will be warmer, increasing loss of water through evaporation and transpiration.

"Climate change will steadily and fundamentally lower the baseline for water availability in the West," said Benjamin Cook, a co-author of the study affiliated with the Goddard Institute and Columbia's observatory.

The state relies on a water cycle that has remained roughly stable for decades: Heavy snow falling in the Sierra in the winter accumulates as snowpack, holding water until it is needed in the dry summer. The state built a sophisticated conveyance and storage infrastructure based on these patterns.

They are unlikely to hold in the future. Snowpack in the Sierra is at only 5 percent of its historical average. Less precipitation is falling as snow, and snow is melting five to 30 days earlier than in the last half-century. The risk is that water will fill reservoirs too soon, perhaps overflowing or evaporating early, leaving too little water available for the most critical months.

Even if carbon emissions were to peak before midcentury, calculations by Mr. Cook and his colleagues suggest that the South-west will still face an exceptionally high risk of suffering a mega-drought. "Our results point to a remarkably drier future that falls far outside the contemporary experience of natural and human systems in Western North America," wrote the researchers.

(b) Extent of Drought on Agriculture

Though originally considered to be the worst drought in the history of recorded rainfall (approximately 163 years), recent analysis of tree-ring cores throughout the state has concluded that that it is, in fact, California's worst in 1,200 years. While the low precipitation levels alone are not entirely unprecedented, when combined with water use, the situation has turned dire.

Though the root cause is up for debate, as well as speculation of its connection to human-induced climate change, the consequences are remarkably certain, including increased wild fires, landslides, floods, and poor water quality. Most immediately apparent, however, are diminished water supplies and shortages throughout the state, as heavily relied upon water sources, such as the Colorado River, are dwindling at an alarming rate. With over 9 million acres of prime, irrigated farmland throughout the state, the industry requires 34 million acre-feet of water per year, or roughly 80% of the state's human water supply. In non-drought years, up to two thirds of this water is supplied by surface water coming from rivers and lakes, and governed by state riparian water laws. However, this source is drastically short in supply, as 2014 agricultural surface water was reduced by 6.6 million acre-feet, or roughly 20% of agriculture's overall water needs. After enduring years of abnormally dry conditions, California is in the midst of an ongoing, four-year drought. Currently, 67% of the state is in "extreme" or "exceptional" drought, while the rest of the state is in "severe" drought. Laura Poppick, *California Droughts Could have Dangerous Ripple Effects*, LIVESCIENCE (Dec. 30, 2014) http://www. livescience.com/49287-california-droughts-ripple-effects.html.

2. SOLUTIONS

(a) Conservation

Matt Stevens, *California Water Use Declines 13.5%, State Board Reports*, Los Angeles Times, June 2, 2015

Californians used 13.5% less water in April compared to the same month in 2013 in response to Gov. Jerry Brown's historic executive order (Cal. Exec. Order No. B–29–15 (Apr. 1, 2015), http://gov.ca.gov/docs/4.1.15 _Executive_Order.pdf) requiring increased conservation in the fourth year of drought, the State Water Resources Board reported Tuesday.

The decline in water use comes as local water officials statewide have scrambled to implement new watering restrictions aimed at achieving the 25% urban water-use reduction.

In the three previous months, the data released Tuesday also showed that the state has a long way to go before it meets Brown's target. Cumulative water savings since summer totaled only 9% compared with the same 11-month period in 2013, the board said.

The new conservation figures come as California water agencies try to figure out how to slash water consumption even further during the hot, dry summer months ahead. Water board officials have stressed the need to reduce outdoor water usage.

The water board spent much of April developing a push to implement Brown's water-saving plan and increase conservation. The plan, as approved last month, as-signs conservation targets to each of the state's water suppliers and requires cuts in consumption ranging from 8% to 36% compared with 2013 levels.

The level of water savings each district must attain is based on residential per capita use in July, August and September of 2014. Cities and water districts with the lowest consumption during that period have to cut the least. Heavy users have to cut the most.

Many water suppliers have been relying on education and outreach to help eliminate water waste. But in some cases, regulators have hired more water "cops," installed smart meters and taken other action to enforce water rules.

(b) Desalination

Amanda Little, Can Desalination Counter the Drought? The New Yorker, July 22, 2015

The waves of the Pacific seem to taunt the thirsty landscape of California. The state has eight hundred and forty miles of coastline adjoining the world's largest ocean—an oversupply of brine at a time when drought has left fallow more than half a million acres of farmland, claimed some twenty thousand jobs, and cost the economy billions of dollars. To Mark Lambert, though, the state's water-rich coast is the overwhelming answer to its problems.

"Thirty-five thousand gallons a minute!" Lambert shouted recently, over the sound of water gushing from a fat pipe into a lagoon at the edge of the Pacific. He was showing me the discharge site of a billion-dollar desalination plant now under construction in Carlsbad, California. "Desal," as it's known in industry vernacular, converts ocean water into pure, delicious tap water. The fat pipe, also known as the brine pit, is where the salt that's been removed from the drinking water is returned to the ocean.

Lambert heads up the North American division of IDE Technologies, an Israeli company that designs and operates mega-scale desalination plants worldwide. IDE's Carlsbad facility will be the largest desalination plant in the Western Hemi-sphere. Built in collaboration with the San Diego County Water Authority and Poseidon, a private developer of water infrastructure, the plant will come online in early fall, and is currently in the early stages of startup. Nearly a tenth of the San Diego County's total water supply—enough for about four hundred thousand county residents—will come from this facility. A hundred million gallons of ocean water will be pumped through the plant per day; half will become drinking water, the other half will flow back into the ocean carrying the removed salt.

Twelve years in the making, the project is now uncannily well timed. "This is as good an entry into the U.S. market as we could have hoped for," Avshalom Felber, the C.E.O. of IDE, told me.

But desalinization has a troubled history in the United States. Engineering problems at a Tampa Bay, Florida, plant reduced the facility's operating capacity by eighty per cent for years, costing the city millions more than it had budgeted. A plant in Santa Barbara, California, has been mothballed for more than two decades, after a devastating drought in the nine-teen-nineties. It just became too expensive to operate after rainfall returned and filled local reservoirs. Today, the total volume of desal production from seawater in the U.S. doesn't amount to much—less than the Carlsbad plant will yield on its own.

Still, the technology has gained traction in other parts of the world. Roughly fourteen billion gallons of desalinated drinking water are produced each day, by thousands of plants scattered along the coastlines of

China, India, Australia, Spain, and other countries with scarce freshwater supplies. According to the International Desalination Association, Ras Al-Khair, in Saudi Arabia, is the largest desal plant in the world, producing two hundred and seventy-three million gallons of drinking water per day, more than five times the capacity of Carlsbad. In Israel, the technology produces about a quarter of the nation's water supply.

Part of the problem in the United States has been that we just haven't needed it. The land where Israel is situated has been dealing with chronic water scarcity since the Iron Age, but the U.S. is filled with rivers and lakes—and some regions of the country still get plenty of rain. Average water prices in United States cities are notably (and, many argue, ludicrously) low: on average, about ten dollars per thousand gallons, less than half of the prices in Australia and European nations. Another part of the problem is that, in the U.S., environmental groups generally don't like desalination, citing concerns about utilities and customers not conserving if they perceive there being an endless supply of clean water from the ocean. Furthermore, according to Sara Aminzadeh, the executive director of the California Coastkeeper Alliance, "It's just not a good option from a cost and energy standpoint." She went on, "Desalination may seem like a panacea, but it's the worst deal out there."

Environmental groups in California have filed fourteen legal challenges against the Carlsbad plant; all have been denied, but many Californians still wonder about the impact of the technology on both marine life and the atmosphere. The environmentalists assert that it would be counterproductive, after all, to try to solve problems created by drought with a technology that would contribute to climate change—and, arguably, drive more drought.

In *Capistrano Taxpayers Association v. City of San Juan Capistrano*, 235 Cal.App.4th 1493, 186 Cal.Rptr.3d 362 (2015) the court held:

> "Under the statute providing that an agency providing water service may adopt a schedule of fees or charges authorizing automatic adjustments that pass through increases in wholesale charges for water for a period not to exceed five years, within a five-year period a water agency might develop a capital-intensive means of production of what is effectively new water, such as recycling or desalinization, and pass on the costs of developing that new water to those customers whose marginal or incremental extra usage requires such new water to be produced. Cal. Water Code § 31020; Cal. Gov't Code § 53755".

(c) Rainwater Capture

The cost of water is rising rapidly especially in the drought ridden southwest. By installing rooftop drains connecting to underground cisterns, using pervious driveways and swales in place of culverts, major rainwater capture and retention, treatment and reuse results in huge savings of cost and supply. Cities currently lay that extra cost on the developer but reward the purchaser with the federal and state tax credits and incentives. A simple solution is to monetize the cost of rainwater capture and reuse systems through grants or loans to the developer by the electric or water utility, a special district or the homeowner's association which will be amortized by utility rate surcharges, special district assessments, or homeowner association dues on the homeowner that are paid from the savings on water utility rates and charges. Normally special assessments and utility rates are used for public capital facilities but the courts and state legislatures are opening the door for public and/ or special district assessments for rainwater capture. *See, Stennis v. City of Santa Fe*, 143 P.3d 756 (N.M.Ct.App.2006); *Board of Trustees of Washington County Water Conservancy District v. Keystone Conversions*, 103 P.3d 686 (Utah 2004) (fee levied for developing secondary water sources did not violate Impact Fees Act, Utah Code Ann. § 11–36–101–501 (2003)); Dennis J. Herman, Note, *Sometimes There's Nothing Left to Give: The Justification for Denying Water Service to New Consumers to Control Growth*, 44 Stan.L.Rev. 429 (1992).

State court decisions have held that a city, county or public utility has the authority to impose rate surcharges on a property owner's use of water to pay for the cost of purchasing or conserving available water in addition to providing hard physical treatment plants and distribution lines. *Bloom v. City of Fort Collins*, 784 P.2d 304 (Colo.1989) (upholding creation of transportation utility for repair and maintenance of arterial and collector roads through utility rates imposed on existing development); Public Investment, A Utility Approach to Stormwater Management, PAS Memo, American Planning Association, (June 1991); Parking Benefit Districts Make Headway in Texas and the West, New Urban News at 9, March 2006.

The same result has been achieved to pay for the costs of conservation to recapture storm water discharge. Communities have created "storm water utilities" which pass the cost of construction directly to the property owners served by the system through monthly assessments, using a concept of equivalent residential uses (ERUs). *See* Steven Siegel, *The Public Role In Establishing Private Residential Communities Towards a New Formulation of Local Government Land Use Policies that Eliminates the Legal Requirements to Privatize New Communities in the United States*, 38 URBAN LAWYER 859, 861 (2006) (public service homeowner exactions).

(d) Recycling of Water Supply

CAPISTRANO TAXPAYERS ASSOCIATION V. CITY OF SAN JUAN CAPISTRANO

Court of Appeals of California, 2014.
235 Cal.App.4th 1493, 186 Cal.Rptr.3d 362.

A.   Capital Costs and Proposition 218

[2] We first review the constitutional text. Article XIII D, section 6, subdivision (b)(4) provides: "No fee or charge may be imposed for a service unless that service is actually used by, or immediately available to, the owner of the property in question. Fees or charges based on potential or future use of a service are not permitted. Standby charges, whether characterized as charges or assessments, shall be classified as assessments and shall not be imposed without compliance with Section 4."

The trial court ruled City Water had violated this provision by "charging certain ratepayers for recycled water that they do not actually use and that is not immediately available to them." The trial judge specifically found, in his statement of decision, that "City [Water] imposed a fee on all ratepayers for recycled water services and delivery of recycled water services, despite the fact that not all ratepayers used recycled water or have it immediately available to them or would ever be able to use it."

But the trial court assumed that providing recycled water is a fundamentally different kind of service from providing traditional potable water. We think not. When each kind of water is provided by a single local agency that provides water to different kinds of users, some of whom can make use of recycled water (for example, cities irrigating park land) while others, such as private residences, can only make use of traditional potable water, providing each kind of water is providing the same service. Both are getting water that meets their needs. Non-potable water for some customers frees up potable water for others. And since water service is already immediately available to all customers of City Water, there is no contravention of subdivision (b)(4) in including charges to construct and provide recycled water to some customers."

(e) Pipeline from Seattle? Cloud Seeding? Any Other Ideas?

3. REGULATION OF SURFACE WATERS AFFECTING TRADITIONAL WATER RIGHTS

LIGHT V. STATE WATER RESOURCES CONTROL BOARD
Court of Appeals of California, 2014.
226 Cal.App.4th 1463, 173 Cal.Rptr.3d 200.

Following a series of hearings and the preparation of an environmental impact report, the State Water Resources Control Board (Board) adopted a regulation that is likely to require a reduction in diversion of water from the stream system for frost protection, at least under certain circumstances. The regulation itself contains no substantive regulation of water use, instead delegating the task of formulating regulatory programs to local governing bodies composed of the diverting growers themselves. The regulation declares that any water use inconsistent with the programs, once they have been formulated and approved by the Board, is unreasonable and therefore prohibited. The trial court granted a writ of mandate invalidating the regulation on several grounds. We reverse.

Ownership of California's water is vested generally in the state's residents, but individuals and entities can acquire "water rights," the right to divert water from its natural course for public or private use. (Water.Code, 6 § 102; *see generally United States v. State Water Resources Control Bd.* (1986) 182 Cal.App.3d 82 (1986). California maintains a "dual system" of water rights, which distinguishes between the rights of "riparian" users, those who possess water rights by virtue of owning the land by or through which flowing water passes, and "appropriators," those who hold the right to divert such water for use on noncontiguous lands. (*See El Dorado Irrigation Dist. v. State Water Resources Control Bd.,* 142 Cal.App.4th 937, 961 (2006).

For historical reasons, California further subdivides appropriators into those whose water rights were established before and after 1914. Post-1914 appropriators may possess water rights only through a permit or license issued by the Board, and their rights are circumscribed by the terms of the permit or license. Riparian users and pre-1914 appropriators need neither a permit nor other govern-mental authorization to exercise their water rights. (*California Farm Bureau Federation v. State Water Resources Control Bd.* (2011), 247 P.3d 112 (Cal. 2011). Inevitably, given the nature of the resource, "water rights are limited and uncertain. The available supply of water is largely determined by natural forces." *See* Gray, *The Uncertain Future of Water Rights in California: Reflections on the Governor's Commission Report,* 36 McGEORGE L.REV. 43, 49–51 (2005).

The differences between and among riparian users and appropriators become most pronounced when the available supply of water is inadequate to satisfy the needs of all those holding water rights. Under the "rule of priority," which governs diversion in such circumstances, the rights of riparian users are para-mount. Although riparian users must curtail their use proportionately among themselves in times of short-age, they are entitled to satisfy their reasonable needs first, before appropriators can even begin to divert water. (*United States, supra*, 182 Cal.App.3d at p. 104, 227 Cal.Rptr. 161.) As a result, appropriators may be deprived of all use of water when the supply is short. In turn, senior appropriators—those who acquired their rights first in time—are entitled to satisfy their reasonable needs, up to their full appropriation, before more junior appropriators become entitled to any water. (*Id.* at pp. 104–105, 227 Cal.Rptr. 161; *North Kern Water Storage Dist. v. Kern Delta Water Dist.* (2007) 147 Cal.App.4th 555, 561 [54 Cal.Rptr.3d 578])

Water use by both riparian users and appropriators is constrained by the rule of reasonableness, which has been preserved in the state Constitution since 1928. (Cal.Const., art. X, § 2; hereafter Article X, Section 2.) Article X, Section 2 was a direct response to a 1926 judicial decision, *Herminghaus v. South. California Edison Co.* (1926) 200 Cal. 81 [252 P. 607], in which the Supreme Court affirmed an injunction that pre-vented the diversion of San Joaquin River water to Southern California. The court reasoned there was no water to spare because riparian users of the river were entitled to receive its "usual and ordinary flow," which the court found to include even its floodwaters, of which the users made little use. (The Constitution was amended two years later effectively to overrule Herminghaus by adding what is now codified as Article X, Section 2. (*Joslin v. Marin Mun. Water District*, 429 P.2d 889 (1967). Article X, Section 2 states, in relevant part: "The right to water or to the use or flow of water in or from any natural stream or water course in this State is and shall be limited to such water as shall be reasonably required for the beneficial use to be served, and such right does not and shall not extend to the waste or unreasonable use or unreasonable method of use or unreasonable method of diversion of water. Riparian rights in a stream or water course at-tach to, but to no more than so much of the flow thereof as may be required or used consistently with this section, for the purposes for which such lands are, or may be made adaptable, in view of such reasonable and beneficial uses. . . ." (Cal.Const., art. X, § 2.) As the Supreme Court recognized soon after Article X, Section 2 was added, the rule limiting water use to that reasonably necessary "applies to the use of all water, under whatever right the use may be enjoyed." (*Peabody v. City of Vallejo* (1935) 2 Cal.2d 351, 367–368, 40 P.2d 486 (1935). The rule of reasonableness is now "the overriding principle governing the use of water in California." (*People ex rel. State Water Resources Control Bd. v. Forni* (1976) 54 Cal.App.3d 743, 750 (1976).

California courts have never defined, nor as far as we have been able to determine, even attempted to define what constitutes an unreasonable use of water, perhaps because the reasonableness of any particular use depends largely on the circumstances. (*Peabody, supra*, 2 Cal.2d at p. 368, 40 P.2d 486.) "What may be a reasonable beneficial use, where water is present in excess of all needs, would not be a reasonable beneficial use in an area of great scarcity and great need. What is a beneficial use at one time may, because of changed conditions, become a waste of water at a later time." (*Tulare Dist. v. Lindsay-Strathmore Dist.* (1935) 3 Cal.2d 489, 567 [45 P.2d 972].) In this regard, the Joslin court commented, "Although, as we have said, what is a reasonable use of water depends on the circumstances of each case, such an inquiry cannot be resolved in vacuo isolated from statewide considerations of transcendent importance. Paramount among these we see the ever increasing need for the conservation of water in this state, an inescapable reality of life quite apart from its express recognition in [Article X, Section 2]." (*Joslin, supra*, 67 Cal.2d at p. 140, 60 Cal.Rptr. 377, 429 P.2d 889, fn. omitted; *see similarly In re Waters of Long Valley Creek Stream System* (1979) 25 Cal.3d 339, 354, 158 Cal.Rptr. 350, 599 P.2d 656 ["it appears self-evident that the reasonableness of a riparian use cannot be determined without considering the effect of such use on all the needs of those in the stream system [citation], nor can it be made 'in vacuo isolated from statewide considerations of transcendent importance' "].) Few decisions have ruled on the reasonableness of a specific use of water, but in separate cases the Supreme Court has concluded, essentially as self-evident, that the use of water for the sole purpose of flooding the land to kill gophers and squirrels is unreasonable (*Tulare Dist.*, at p. 568, 45 P.2d 972), as is the use of floodwaters solely to deposit sand and gravel on flooded land (*Joslin*, at p. 141, 60 Cal.Rptr. 377, 429 P.2d 889).

Existing alongside the rule of reasonableness is a second doctrine imposing at least a potential limit on private uses of water. As the Supreme Court has explained that doctrine, the state holds the navigable waterways in "public trust" for the benefit of state residents. (*National Audubon Society v. Superior Court* (1983) 33 Cal.3d 419, 434, 437 [189 Cal.Rptr. 346, 658 P.2d 709] (Audubon Society).) In Audubon Society, the plaintiffs challenged long-standing water use permits issued by the Board that, by allowing the diversion of water from streams feeding Lake Mono, had resulted in an environmentally destructive decrease in the lake's level. In declining to reconsider the permits, the Board concluded it was required to allocate all available water for beneficial use by appropriators, notwithstanding the potential environmental harm such diversions would cause. (*Id.* at p. 427, 189 Cal.Rptr. 346, 658 P.2d 709.) The Audubon Society court required the Board to re-consider the permits, taking into account the public trust doctrine. (*Id.* at pp. 446–447, 189 Cal.Rptr. 346, 658 P.2d 709.)

In contending the Board exceeded its authority, plaintiffs cite the time-honored exemption of riparian users and pre-1914 appropriators from the permitting authority of the Board. (*E.g., Farm Bureau, supra*, 51 Cal.4th at p. 429, 121 Cal.Rptr.3d 37, 247 P.3d 112.) While such users cannot be required to obtain permits as a condition of exercising their right to divert, that does not mean their use of California's waters is free from Board regulation. "[N]o water rights are inviolable; all water rights are subject to governmental regulation." (*United States, supra*, 182 Cal.App.3d 82, 106, 227 Cal.Rptr. 161.) The Supreme Court recognized as much in Farm Bureau; immediately after noting the Board "has no permitting or licensing authority over riparian . . . rights, or over appropriative rights acquired before 1914," the court observed the Board "does have authority to prevent illegal diversions and to prevent waste or unreasonable use of water, regardless of the basis under which the right is held." (*Farm Bureau*, at p. 429, 121 Cal.Rptr.3d 37, 247 P.3d 112, fn. omitted.)

The order granting a preliminary injunction and the judgment granting a writ of mandate are reversed, and the preliminary injunction is dissolved.

NOTES

1.   Bettina Boxall, *California Moves to Restrict Water Pumping by pre-1914 Rights Holders*, L.A. Times June 12, 2015:

"For the first time in nearly 40 years, state regulators are telling more than 100 growers and irrigation districts with some of the oldest water rights in California that they have to stop drawing supplies from drought starved rivers and streams in the Central Valley. The curtailment order, issued Friday by the State Water Resources Control Board, has been expected for weeks. Earlier this spring, the board halted diversions under some 8,700 junior rights. With snowmelt reduced to a trickle this year, there simply isn't enough water flowing in rivers to meet the demand of all those with even older rights predating 1914. And as flows continue to decline this summer, board officials said, they expect to issue more curtailments, stopping river pumping by more senior diverters".

2.   With over 9 million acres of prime, irrigated farmland throughout the state, the industry requires 34 million acre-feet of water per year, or roughly 80% of the state's human water supply. In non-drought years, up to two thirds of this water is supplied by surface water coming from rivers and lakes, and governed by state riparian water laws. However, this source is drastically short in sup-ply, as 2014 agricultural surface water was reduced by 6.6 million acre-feet, or roughly 20% of agriculture's overall water needs. Agricultural Water Use, Department of Water Resources, http://www.water.ca.gov/wateruse efficiency/agricultural/ (last visited Apr. 30, 2015).

3.   Most farmers, however, are making up the shortfall by turning to groundwater pumping. This source of water is derived from underground porous earth, or aquifers, which can absorb and store water from rainfall and snowmelt, and are then tapped by wells with electronic pumps. Ordinarily such

water sources account for 30–40% of agricultural needs, however, in 2014 an additional 5 million acre-feet were pumped, bringing the overall reliance closer to 60%. Janny Choy & Geoff McGhee, *Understanding California's Groundwater, Water in the West* (Jul. 31, 2014).

4.   GROUNDWATER MANAGEMENT

(a) The Problem

Most farmers are making up the shortfall in surface water by turning to groundwater pumping. This source of water is derived from underground porous earth, or aquifers, which can absorb and store water from rainfall and snowmelt, and are then tapped by wells with electronic pumps. Ordinarily such water sources account for 30–40% of agricultural needs, however, in 2014 an additional 5 million acre-feet were pumped, bringing the overall reliance closer to 60%. Janny Choy & Geoff McGhee, Understanding California's Groundwater, Water in the West (Jul. 31, 2014).

Though aquifers are replenished through natural processes, the current overreliance is worrisome as groundwater sources are being depleted at twice the rate that they can be replenished. For example, well drillers in the Central Valley often must bore holes 1,000 or even 2,000 feet deep in order to reach water, whereas 500 feet used to be more than sufficient. Moreover, such rapid groundwater depletion can lead to "land subsidence," or a compaction of subterranean aquifers that reduces the pore volume. This subsidence is troubling as it can lead to sudden and catastrophic sink-holes, increased risk of flooding, and, most detrimental, a permanent reduction of the aquifers total water storage capacity, depleting future groundwater supplies. Brian Clark Howard, *California Drought Spurs Groundwater Drilling Boom in Central Valley*, National Geographic (Aug. 16, 2014), http://news.nationalgeographic.com/news/ 2014/08/140815-central-valley-california-drilling-boom-groundwater-drought-wells. (such wells can cost upwards of $350,000). In total, an additional $454 million was spent in groundwater pumping in 2014. *Howitt, supra* note 28, at ii.

Additionally, heavy depletion often means one must extract water from deeper sections of an aquifer, which is often heavily saturated with various minerals, and can be unsafe to drink. Overall, aquifers in the Central Valley have lost an estimated 60 million acre-feet since the 1960's, and, in many regions, the water table has fallen by 60 feet in the past year alone. Brian Clark Howard, *California Drought Spurs Groundwater Drilling Boom in Central Valley*, National Geographic (Aug. 16, 2014), http://news.nationalgeographic.com/news/2014/08/140815-central-valley-california-drilling-boom-groundwater-drought-wells. (such wells can cost upwards of $350,000). In total, an additional $454 million was spent in groundwater pumping in 2014. *Howitt, supra* note 28, at ii.

(b) Groundwater Management Legislation

As of 2014 California was the only state in the U.S. with no legal infrastructure in place to regulate groundwater use, and as no groundwater meters were required, it was unclear how much individual farmers were pumping. However, in late 2014, California legislature passed historic and much-needed ground-water legislation, the Sustainable Groundwater Management Act (SGMA) (Cal. Water Code section 10720 et seq.). Under the SGMA, local water agencies will have the authority to monitor and restrict groundwater pumping, shut down wells, and impose fines. The Act specifically authorizes local agencies, which can be cities, counties or regional conglomerations of cities and counties, after adopting a groundwater sustainability plan for a groundwater basin, pursuant to approval by the state Department of Water Resources to:

- Require registration of wells within its management area;

- Require every well in the management area be measured by a water measuring device, at the expense of the well owner;

- Require a well owner or operator to file an annual statement setting forth the total extraction of groundwater from that well for the previous year;

- Acquire, hold, use, enjoy, sell, let and dispose of real and personal property including lands and water rights and construct, maintain, alter and operate any works or improvements within or outside the GSA as necessary and proper to carry out the Act;

- Appropriate, acquire, import, conserve and store surface water and groundwater and surface and groundwater rights as necessary and proper to carry out the Act;

- Establish a program for voluntary fallowing of agricultural lands;

- Perform acts necessary to enable the GSA to purchase, transfer, deliver or exchange water or water rights; and

- Transport, reclaim, purify, desalinate, treat or otherwise manage and control polluted water and wastewater.

The Act has been criticized for not giving the state a more affirmative role, since it is unclear whether the state Department of Water Resources (DWR) can reject plans after evaluating them. The DWR has the authority to designate a basin as a probationary basin if it finds that after June 30, 2017, none of the following has occurred (Water Code § 10735.2(a)):

- A local agency has decided to become a GSA that intends to develop a GSP for the entire basin.

- A collection of local agencies has formed a GSA or prepared agreements to develop one or more GSPs that will collectively serve as a GSP for the entire basin.

- A local agency has submitted an alternative that has been approved or is pending approval pursuant to Section 10733.6.

- If unmanaged areas of a basin exist on July 1, 2017, those areas shall be subject to groundwater ex-traction reporting to the DWR in accordance with Part 5.2 (commencing with § 5200) of Division 2 of the Water Code and could be subject to fees listed in § 1529.5.

5. TIERED WATER RATES

Unfortunately, in a pair of appellate cases the courts have restricted local agencies from using a major implementation tool, that of tiered water rates, to discourage excessive water use that was recommended by Governor Brown in his historic order to cut water use by 25% statewide. The Order directed water agencies to use pricing structures that encourage conservation by charging higher rates to people who use the most water. About two-thirds of California Water Agencies use some type of tiered structure.

CAPISTRANO TAXPAYERS ASSOCIATION V. CITY OF SAN JUAN CAPISTRANO

Court of Appeals of California, 2015.
235 Cal.App.4th 1493, 186 Cal.Rptr.3d 362.

We conclude the trial court erred in holding that Proposition 218 does not allow public water agencies to pass on to their customers the capital costs of improvements to provide additional increments of water—such as building a recycling plant. Its findings were that future water provided by the improvement is not immediately available to customers. (*See* Cal.Const., art. XIII D, § 6, subd. (b)(4)) [no fees "may be imposed for a service unless that service is actually used by, or immediately available to, the owner of the property in question"].) But, as applied to water delivery, the phrase "a service" cannot be read to differentiate between recycled water and traditional, potable water. Water service is already "immediately available" to all customers, and continued water service is assured by such capital improvements as water recycling plants. That satisfies the constitutional and statutory requirements.

However, the trial court did not err in ruling that Proposition 218 requires public water agencies to calculate the actual costs of providing water at various tiered levels of usage. Article XIII D, section 6, subdivision (b)(3) of the California Constitution, as interpreted by our Supreme Court in *Bighorn-Desert View Water Agency v. Verjil* (2006) 39 Cal.4th 205, 226,

46 Cal.Rptr.3d 73, 138 P.3d 220 (Bighorn) provides that water rates must reflect the "cost of service attributable" to a given parcel. While tiered, or inclined rates that go up progressively in relation to usage are perfectly consonant with article XIII D, section 6, subdivision (b)(3) and Bighorn, the tiers must still correspond to the actual cost of providing service at a given level of usage. The water agency here did not try to calculate the cost of actually providing water at its various tier levels. It merely allocated all its costs among the price tier levels, based not on costs, but on pre-determined usage budgets. Accordingly, the trial court correctly determined the agency had failed to carry the burden imposed on it by another part of Proposition 218 (art. XIII D, § 6, subd. (b)(5)) of showing it had complied with the requirement water fees not exceed the cost of service attributable to a parcel—at least without a vote of the electorate. That part of the judgment must be affirmed.

NOTES

1. Since the court ruled in favor of the residents, water agencies could still justify using tiered rates by tying them to a specific water source, such as the Colorado River or a local aquifer. Then, agencies could charge customers based on the varying costs of getting water from those sources. The key would be ensuring the rates are not what the Court called "arbitrary," Water lawyers have also suggested that agencies that receive water from wholesalers, such as the Metropolitan Water District of Southern California, could tie increased costs to sur-charges imposed during rationing. The MWD has on a plan to cut its water allocations by 15%. Water districts that use more than they are allocated would be hit with expensive surcharges, costs they are likely to pass on to customers who use large amounts of water. *See*, Matt Stevens, *Court Case Could be Blow for California Drought Fight*, Los Angeles Times, April, 14, 2015.

2. *Newhall County Water District v. Castaic Lake Water Agency*, 197 Cal.Rptr.3d 429

"In 2001, the Legislature required the Agency to begin preparation of a groundwater management plan, and provided for the formation of an advisory council consisting of representatives from the retail water purveyors and other major extractors. (Water Code Appendix., § 103–15.1, subd. (e)(1) & (2)(A).) The Legislature required the Agency to "regularly consult with the council regarding all aspects of the proposed groundwater management plan." (Id., subd. (e)(2)(A).)

Under this legislative authority, the Agency spearheaded preparation of the 2003 Groundwater Management Plan for the Basin, and more recently the 2010 Santa Clarita Valley Urban Water Management Plan. These plans were approved by the retailers, including Newhall.

The 2003 Groundwater Management Plan states the overall management objectives for the Basin as: (1) development of an integrated surface water, groundwater, and recycled water supply to meet existing and projected demands for municipal, agricultural and other water uses; (2) assessment of groundwater basin conditions "to determine a range of operational yield values that will make use of local groundwater conjunctively with [State Water Project] and recycled water to avoid groundwater overdraft"; (3) preservation of groundwater quality; and (4) preservation of interrelated surface water resources. The 2010 Santa Clarita Valley Urban Water Management Plan, as the trial court described it, is "an area-wide management planning tool that promotes active management of urban water demands and efficient water usage by looking to long-range planning to ensure adequate water supplies to serve existing customers and future demands. . . ."

The Agency's primary source of imported water is the State Water Project. The Agency purchases that water under a contract with the Department of Water Resources. The Agency also acquires water under an acquisition agreement with the Buena Vista Water Storage District and the Rosedale-Rio Bravo Water Storage District, and other water sources include recycled water and water stored through groundwater banking agreements. Among the Agency's powers are the power to "[s]tore and recover water from groundwater basins" (Water. Code Appendix, § 103–15.2, subd. (b)), and "[t]o restrict the use of agency water during any emergency caused by drought, or other threatened or existing water shortage, and to prohibit the wastage of agency water" (§ 103–15, subd. (k)). Nevertheless, the Agency charged Newhall rates for groundwater that Newhall drilled wells for and which did not come from the Agency. The Agency had no authority to impose rates based on the use of groundwater that the Agency does not provide, and that conversely, Newhall's use of its groundwater rights does not burden the Agency's system for delivery of imported water. Thus the rates bore no reasonable relationship to Newhall's burden on, or benefit received from, the Agency's service. The rates also violated Government Code section 54999.7 (providing that a fee for public utility service "shall not exceed the reasonable cost of providing the public utility service" (Gov.Code, § 54999.7, subd. (a)), and violated common law requiring utility charges to be fair, reasonable and proportionate to benefits received by ratepayers. We order the Agency to revert to the rates previously in effect until the adoption of new lawful rates, and order it to refund to Newhall the difference between the monies paid under the challenged rates and the monies that would have been paid under the previous rates.

We affirm.

6. SEA LEVEL RISE

Sea level rise is one of the more widely acknowledged results of climate change. Indeed, as part of the Intergovernmental Panel on Climate Change's ("IPCC") 2014 Fifth Assessment Report, the Working Group on the physical science basis of climate change reported in 2013 "high confidence" that the rates of sea level rise in-creased in the late 19th and early 20th centuries compared to the prior two millennia.83 Moreover, the Working Group concluded that it was "very likely" that mean rates of global average sea level rise had increased from a rate of 1.7 millimeters (mm) per year between 1901 and 2010 to a rate of 2.0 mm per year between 1971 and 2010 to a mean rate of 3.2 mm per year between 1993 and 2010.84 In total, sea level has risen about 0.19 meters since 1901,85 and the Working Group projects that: Global mean sea level will continue to rise during the 21st century. Under all RCP scenarios, the rate of sea level rise will very likely exceed that observed during 1971 to 2010 due to increased ocean warming and increased loss of mass from glaciers and ice sheets. Robin Kundis Craig, of Sea Level Rise and Superstorms: The Public Health Police Power as a Means of Defending against "Takings" Challenges to Coastal Regulation, 22 N.Y.U. Environmental Law Journal 84 (2014).

(a) Elizabeth Kolbert, The Siege of Miami: As Temperatures Climb, So, Too, Will Sea Levels, The New Yorker, December 21 & 28, 2015

The City of Miami Beach floods on such a predictable basis that if, out of curiosity or sheer perversity, a person wants to she can plan a visit to coincide with an inundation. Knowing the tides would be high around the time of the "super blood moon," in late September, I arranged to meet up with Hal Wanless, the chairman of the University of Miami's geological-sciences department. Wanless, who is seventy-three, has spent nearly half a century studying how South Florida came into being. From this, he's concluded that much of the region may have less than half a century more to go. According to the Intergovernmental Panel on Climate Change, sea levels could rise by more than three feet by the end of this century. The United States Army Corps of Engineers pro-jects that they could rise by as much as five feet; the National Oceanic and Atmospheric Administration predicts up to six and a half feet.

We'd come to a neighborhood of multimillion dollar homes where the water was creeping under the security gates and up the driveways. Porsches and Mercedes's sat flooded up to their chassis." To cope with its recur-rent flooding, Miami Beach has already spent something like a hundred million dollars. It is planning on spending several hundred million more. Such efforts are, in Wanless's view, so much money down the drain. Sooner or later—and probably sooner—the city will have too much water to deal with. Even before that happens, Wanless believes, insurers will stop selling policies on the luxury condos that line Biscayne Bay. Banks will stop writing mortgages.

The latest data from the Arctic, gathered by a pair of exquisitely sensitive satellites, show that in the past decade Greenland has been losing more ice each year. In August, NASA announced that, to supplement the satellites, it was launching a new monitoring program called—provocatively—Oceans Melting Greenland, or O.M.G. In November, researchers reported that, owing to the loss of an ice shelf off northeastern Greenland, a new "floodgate" on the ice sheet had opened. All told, Greenland's ice holds enough water to raise global sea levels by twenty feet.

Many of the world's largest cities sit along a coast, and all of them are, to one degree or another, threatened by rising seas. Entire countries are endangered—the Maldives, for instance, and the Marshall Islands. Globally, it's estimated that a hundred million people live within three feet of mean high tide and another hundred million or so live within six feet of it. Hundreds of millions more live in areas likely to be affected by increasingly destructive storm surges.

Against this backdrop, South Florida still stands out. The region has been called "ground zero when it comes to sea-level rise." It has also been described as "the poster child for the impacts of climate change," the "epicenter for studying the effects of sea-level rise," a "disaster scenario," and "the New Atlantis." Of all the world's cities, Miami ranks second in terms of assets vulnerable to rising seas—No. 1 is Guangzhou—and in terms of population it ranks fourth, after Guangzhou, Mumbai, and Shanghai. A recent report on storm surges in the Unit-ed States listed four Florida cities among the eight most at risk. (On that list, Tampa came in at No. 1.) For the past several years, the daily high-water mark in the Miami area has been racing up at the rate of almost an inch a year, nearly ten times the rate of average global sea-level rise. It's unclear exactly why this is happening, but it's been speculated that it has to do with changes in ocean currents which are causing water to pile up along the coast. Talking about climate change in the Everglades this past Earth Day, President Obama said, "Nowhere is it going to have a bigger impact than here in South Florida."

The region's troubles start with its topography. In Miami-Dade County, the average elevation is just six feet above sea level. But South Florida's problems also run deeper. The whole region—indeed, most of the state—consists of limestone that was laid down over the millions of years Florida sat at the bottom of a shallow sea. The limestone is filled with holes, and the holes are, for the most part, filled with water. (Near the surface, this is generally freshwater, which has a lower density than saltwater.) The South Florida Water Management District, a state agency, claims that it operates the "world's largest water control system," which includes twenty-three hundred miles of canals, sixty-one pump stations, and more than two thousand "water control structures." Floridians south of Orlando depend on this system to prevent their lawns from drowning and their front steps from becoming docks. When the system was designed—redesigned, really—in the nineteen-fifties, the water level in the canals could be maintained at least a foot and a half higher than the level of high tide. Thanks to this difference in elevation, water flowed off the land toward the sea. At the same time, there was enough freshwater pushing out to prevent saltwater from pressing in. Owing in part to sea-level rise, the gap has since been cut by about eight inches, and the region faces the discomfiting prospect that, during storms, it will be inundated not just along the coasts but also inland, by rainwater that has nowhere to go. Researchers at

Florida Atlantic University have found that with just six more inches of sea-level rise the district will lose almost half its flood-control capacity. Mean-while, what's known as the saltwater front is advancing. One city—Hallandale Beach, just north of Miami—has already had to close most of its drinking wells, because the water is too salty. Many other cities are worried that they will have to do the same.

(b) Strategies for Adaptation Are Doomed and Retreat Measures Must Be Taken

As NOAA's Management Retreat report below points out, flooding during high tides is now common in many places on the East and Gulf coasts of the U.S., and is projected to worsen as sea level rises. In addition, rising seas are also contributing to worsening flood risks and damage from storm surge, and increasing coastal erosion. Simultaneously, growing development in the floodplain is increasing exposure to flood damages. Hurricane Sandy showed how devastating storm surge in a densely developed area can be. It is estimated that the storm caused $165 billion in damages and 159 deaths, damaged 650,000 homes and left 8.5 million customers without power.

Municipalities, with state and federal help, should prioritize and incentivize flood-proofing of homes, neighborhoods, and key infrastructure; curtail development in areas subject to tidal flooding; consider the risks and benefits of adaptation measures such as sea walls and natural buffers; establish height standards of at least 3 feet above 20 year projected mean high tide lines and develop long-term plans based on the best available science. Sales of coastal property should include a disclosure requirement that informs prospective purchasers.

There is a hard truth about adaptation, however. It has fundamental limits—whether physical, economic, or social—and it can only fend off the impacts of sea level rise to a point. Better yet communities must resort to legally sound retreat strategies. The NOAA website explains the concept of managed retreat as an adaptation strategy to address issues caused by sea-level rise and increased storm surge and erosion. It describes two case studies of managed retreat projects in Pacifica and Ventura California. According to NOAA: "a managed retreat approach typically involves establishing thresholds to trigger demolition or relocation of structures threatened by erosion. Therefore, this approach is frequently coupled with several other planning and regulatory techniques including: shoreline planning, to identify high-risk areas where this type of policy would be the only cost-effective, long-term solution; regulating the type of structure allowed near the shore to ensure that buildings are small enough and constructed in a way to facilitate relocation when needed; and instituting relocation assistance and/or buy-back programs to help with relocation costs or compensate property owners when their property be-comes unusable." Georgetown Climate Center Report on Managed Retreat

Strategies, NOAA Office of Coastal Resource Management (2015) http://coastalmanagement.noaa.gov/initiatives/shoreline_ppr_retreat.html

As Debbie M. Cjizewer and A. Dan Tarlock astutely analyze:

> "The real problem facing government today is the legacy of past local, state and federal flood control strategies. The country's investment in levees, dams and floodways have prevented damage, but they also have had a perverse effect: structural flood plain protection encourages more settlement, which in turn increases the number of people and property impacted when a flood occurs. The result is a classic moral hazard problem. A moral hazard is a socially undesirable, often inefficient, behavior encouraged by the expectation that it will not be punished and often will be rewarded.

> The moral hazard problem is especially acute in flood prone areas where the existence of levees often leads to an illusionary sense of safety for flood plain residents. The illusion is a dangerous one, because our infrastructure is old and increasingly unsafe. Congress acknowledged this problem when, in 2007, it ordered the United States Army Corps of Engineers (the Corps) to undertake an assessment of levees over which it has oversight, including levees initially constructed by the Corps and subsequently turned over to the states. A 2013 follow-up Associated Press article, based on Freedom of Information Act requests, found that "inspectors taking the first-ever inventory of flood control systems overseen by the federal government have found hundreds of structures at risk of failing and endangering people and property in 35 states." Many dams are al-so unsafe. Post-flood compensation available through flood insurance and ad hoc disaster payments from the federal government feed the illusion and subsidize the cost of moral hazard behavior. The rub is that "since lump-sum government-relief payments usually do not relate to risk, no incentives are provided to potential victims to take effective preventative measures." New Challenges for Urban Areas Facing Flood Risks, 40 Fordham Urban L. J. 1739 (2013)

7. SEA RISE LITIGATION

GOVE v. ZONING BOARD OF APPEALS OF CHATHAM

Supreme Judicial Court of Massachusetts, 2005.
444 Mass. 754, 831 N.E.2d 865.

Roberta Gove owns "lot 93," an undeveloped parcel of land within a "coastal conservancy district" (conservancy district) in Chatham. In 1998, Ann and Donald J. Grenier agreed to buy lot 93 from Gove, contingent on regulatory approval for the construction of a single-family house on the property. Because Chatham prohibits construction of new residences in the conservancy district, the zoning board of appeals of Chatham (board) denied the Greniers a building permit. Gove and the Greniers sought relief in the Superior Court on statutory and constitutional grounds, contending that the prohibition against residential construction on lot 93 had effected a taking of lot 93, without compensation, in violation of the Fifth and Fourteenth Amendments to the United States Constitution and art. 10 of the Massachusetts Declaration of Rights. After a two-day bench trial, a judge in the Superior Court ruled in favor of the defendants on all counts. The Appeals Court affirmed. 814 N.E.2d 1154 (2004). We granted Gove's application for further appellate review, and now affirm the judgment of the Superior Court.

Lot 93 is located in the Little Beach section of Chatham. Little Beach is part of a narrow, low-lying peninsula, bounded by Chatham Harbor and Stage Harbor, at the extreme southeastern corner of Cape Cod. In recent years, a "breach" has formed in the barrier island that long separated Chatham Harbor from the open ocean. The breach, which is widening, lies directly across the harbor from Little Beach, and a land surveyor familiar with the area testified that Little Beach is now "wide open to the Atlantic Ocean" and prone to northeasterly storm tides. Chatham is known for its vulnerability to storms, and, according to an expert retained by Gove and the Greniers, in recent years Chatham has "as a direct result of the breach" experienced a "significant erosion problem," including "[h]ouses falling into the sea." The same expert testified that, since the appearance of the breach, "there had been a significant rise in the mean high water [near lot 93] along Chatham Harbor."

The bylaw governing the conservancy district bars without exception the construction of new residential dwellings. The bylaw does allow specified nonresidential uses, either as of right or by special permit. The zoning officer testified that the nonresidential uses are less likely to create a danger in the event of a flood than are residential structures, in part because structures "ancillary" to homes "tend to break off" in storms and "do a lot of collateral damage to other structures and property," whereas such damage is less likely when nonresidential structures, normally more firmly anchored to the ground, are built. A zoning officer denied the Greniers a permit to build a house on the property. The board upheld the decision of the zoning officer. Gove and the Greniers then filed one suit against the selectmen and board and another against the conservation commission of Chat-ham.

Here, the facts are no more indicative of a total taking than those considered by the Supreme Court in Palazzolo. Even if we limit our analysis to lot 93, Gove has failed to prove that the challenged regulation left her property "economically idle." Her own expert testified that the property was worth $23,000, a value that itself suggests more than a "token interest" in the property. In *Palazzolo v. Rhode Island*, 533 U.S. 606, 630–631, 121 S.Ct. 2448, 150 L.Ed.2d 592 (2001) the Supreme Court further explained that, to prove a total regulatory taking, a plaintiff must demonstrate that the challenged regulation leaves "the property 'economically idle'" and that she retains no more than "a token interest." *Id.* at 631, 121 S.Ct. 2448, quoting *Lucas, supra* at 1019. The plaintiff in Palazzolo was unable to prove a total taking by showing that an eighteen-acre property appraised for $3,150,000 had been limited, by regulation, to use as a single residence with "$200,000 in development value." *Id.* at 616, 631. *See, Rith Energy, Inc. v. United States*, 270 F.3d 1347, 1349 (Fed.Cir.2001), *cert. denied*, 536 U.S. 958 (2002) (discussing "token interest"). Moreover, the expert's $23,000 valuation did not take into account uses allowed in the conservancy district, either as of right or by special permit, which she admitted could make the property "an income producing proposition.". The judge's finding that lot 93 retained significant value despite the challenged regulation invalidates Gove's theory: she cannot prove a total taking by proving only that one potential use of her property—i.e., as the site of a house—is prohibited. *Lucas, supra* at 1019, requires that the challenged regulation "denies all economically beneficial use" of land. *See, Lingle, supra* at 2082 (in Lucas context "the complete elimination of a property's value is the determinative factor").

We now turn to the Penn Central inquiry. Considering all of the evidence at trial, we agree with the judge that Gove failed to show that the conservancy district regulations had a substantial "economic impact" on her or deprived her of "distinct investment-backed expectations" in lot 93. *Lingle v. Chevron U.S.A. Inc.*, 544 U.S. 528; 125 S.Ct. 2074, 2082 (2005), quoting *Penn Central* at 98 S.Ct. 2646.

We add that "the character of the governmental action" here, *Lingle, supra* at 2082, quoting *Penn Central, supra* at 124, 98 S.Ct. 2646, is the type of limited protection against harmful private land use that routinely has withstood allegations of regulatory takings. It is not at all clear that Gove has "legitimate property interests" in building a house on lot 93. *Lingle, supra*. The judge found that "it is undisputed that [lot 93] lies in the flood plain and that its potential flooding would adversely affect the surrounding areas" if the property were developed with a house.18 Reasonable government action mitigating such harm, at the very least when it does not involve a "total" regulatory taking or a physical invasion, typically does not require compensation. *See Agins v. Tiburon*, 447 U.S. 255, 261 (1980) (regulation reducing "ill effects of urbanization"); *Penn Central, supra* at 98 S.Ct. 2646 (regulation restricting alteration of historic landmarks); *Goldblatt v. Hempstead, supra* (regulation restricting extent of excavation below ground water level); *Miller v. Schoene*, 276 U.S. 272, 48 S.Ct. 246, 72 L.Ed. 568 (1928) (statute requiring landowner to destroy disease-harboring trees).

NOTES

1.   As Robin Kundis points out in her excellent article, this erudite case demonstrates that there is a "recent growing recognition among the courts in coastal states that coastal properties are inherently vulnerable and that this vulnerability has bearing both on the regulatory takings analysis and the compensation owed for any kind of governmental taking of coastal properties". Robin Kundis, *Of Sea Level Rise and Superstorms: The Public Health Police Power as a Means of Defending against "Takings" Challenges to Coastal Regulation*, 22 N.Y.U.ENVIRONMENTAL L.J. 84 (2014).

2.   Active efforts by state and local governments to protect threatened properties, rather than retreat, will often require condemnation of a partial site in order to provide dune or seawall protection. Yet the courts are beginning to formulate judicial concepts that recognize that the compensation due should reflect a credit for the benefit that the property owner realizes from the enhanced value of the property resulting from the public project. *Borough of Harvey Cedars v. Karan*, 70 A.3d 524 (N.J.2013).

3.   Indeed, courts have only held regulations invalid in a few of the more than 125 appellate state and federal cases addressing floodplain regulations including many challenges to regulations as a taking of private property. For cases upholding regulations, *see*, for example *Beverly Bank v. Illinois Department of Transportation*, 579 N.E.2d 815 (Ill.1991) (Court held that Illinois legislature had the authority to prohibit the construction of new residences in the 100-year floodway and that a taking claim was premature.). *State of Wisconsin v. Outagamie County Board of Adjustment*, 532 N.W.2d 147 (Wis.App.1995) (Court held that variance for a replacement of fishing cottage in the floodway of the Wolf River was barred by county shore-land zoning ordinance.). *Bonnie Briar Syndicate, Inc. v. Town of Mamaroneck, et al.*, 94 N.Y.2d 96 (N.Y.1999) (Court rejected claim that the rezoning of 150-acre golf course property important for flood storage from residential to solely recreational use was a taking of private property.). *Wyer v. Board of Environmental Protection*, 747 A.2d 192 (Me.2000) (Court held that denial of a variance under sand dune laws not a taking because property could be used for parking, picnics, barbecues, and other recreational uses). John A. Kusler, *Ass'n of State Floodplain Managers, Common Legal Questions about Floodplain Regulations in the Courts* 2 (2003), cited in Debbie Chizewer and A. Dan Tarlock, *New Challenges for Urban Areas Facing Flood Risks*, 40 FORDHAM URBAN L.J. 1739 (2013).

4.   Nevertheless, a few courts continue to assess takings liability where states and local governments take either a proactive stance to affirmatively improve the coastal property, or by failing to act to protect property, using the principles laid down in *Lucas v. South Carolina Coastal Council*, 505 U.S. 1003 (1992), which we studied in Chapter 3. *See*, Christopher Serkin, *Passive Takings: The State's Affirmative Duty to Protect Property*, 113 MICH.L.REV. 345 (2014).

5.   Finally, for those skeptics who see Climate Change as only interesting to environmentalists and engineers, think again. *See*, Marc L. Miller and Jonathan Overpeck, *Climate Change and the Practice of Law*, 47 ARIZONA ATTORNEY 30 (2010):

> "On some reflection, there seem to be more areas of practice where climate change might generate independent claims or issues, or otherwise affect the advice given to clients. Some of the most immediate areas of practice are those representing regulated clients such as power, water and transportation companies and utilities, where the state and federal governments are increasingly incorporating (or proposing to incorporate) climate change in regulatory policy. Energy clients are balancing "old" and "new" energy and the development of new transmission and storage capacities. Emerging carbon trading regimes and clean businesses will generate significant new and ongoing work for lawyers. Environmental practitioners doing work on public lands and natural resources, including topics such as forest plans and endangered species, al-ready wrestle with climate change. In this article we explore the relevance of climate change to many areas of practice, including general business, real estate, insurance, land use, public utilities, state and local law, transportation, as well as power and water. Our hypothesis is that through change in the "facts on the ground", current and emerging impacts, and through active discussions of legal and regulatory reforms, climate change is fast becoming an issue of significant importance to legal practice."

J. OIL AND GAS FRACKING

1. GENERAL BACKGROUND

OIL AND GAS FRACKING: STATE AND FEDERAL REGULATION DOES NOT PREEMPT NEEDED LOCAL GOVERNMENT REGULATION

Robert H. Freilich & Neil M. Popowitz.
44 Urban Lawyer 533 (2012).

Increasing onshore oil and gas activity, resulting from the new technology of hydraulic fracturing, commonly known as "fracking," ranging from the Wattenberg Field in Colorado, the Bakken Field in North Dakota and Montana, the Marcellus Field underlying portions of Maryland, New York, Ohio, Pennsylvania, and West Virginia, to the Barnett and Eagle Ford Fields of Texas, has stirred the imagination of the American people, allowing them to believe in the possibility of achieving energy self-sufficiency. Despite environmental risks, a gas boom brings important environmental benefits because burning natural gas emits half as much carbon dioxide as coal. The United States' emissions reportedly have accordingly dropped by 450 million tons in the past five years.

On the other hand, the recent boom in oil and natural gas drilling resulting from the technological advance of fracking has overwhelmed many small communities. Workers seeking employment in the oil and gas fields of North Dakota, together with their families, have created a population explosion in a part of the country best known for open plains and rural solitude. Between April 2010 and June 2011, the Williston, North Dakota area population grew 8.8%, while Dickinson and Minot, North Dakota count among the top eight fastest-growing micropolitan regions in the United States. The existing roads, schools, police, fire, and emergency rescue services are simply inadequate for the number of people flocking to these communities, leading to greatly increased traffic and crime. Inadequate housing has left people sleeping in cars and trucks, or living in "man camps."

In Texas, where oil and gas output is expanding exponentially, the construction of every new well requires the transportation of as much as 1,000 truckloads of materiel and equipment, each weighing up to 80,000 pounds. In LaSalle County, TX, the cost of improving the county's 230 miles of rural roads to withstand the inflow of drilling related traffic exceeds $100 million while the entire budget of the county is about $6 million. The State of Texas benefits from the surge in drilling because its energy production taxes have amounted to $3.1 billion, while county government property tax revenues can only rise 8% per year. Other states, such as Louisiana, North Dakota, and Pennsylvania, have been similarly struggling with the wear and tear on rural roads from the national drilling boom.

The need for local zoning to address impact fees and adequate public facilities dedications is critical to maintaining health, welfare, and the quality of life in states where oil and gas resources can be reached by fracking. Proper usage of adequate public facilities ordinances can deny development approval of permits for oil and gas drilling, unless the developers agree to enter into development agreements providing adequate capacity of roads leading to and from the sites. Such development agreements are not subject to the Nollan/Dolan heightened scrutiny standard.

Local governments, in cooperation with the state government, must manage the influx of people and the attendant impacts resulting from booming oil and gas growth due to fracking. A proper role for state government is the regulation of the on-site drilling, chemicals used in the fracking and production process. It is the role of local government, on the other hand, to guarantee that adequate off-site infrastructure, services, affordable housing, and environmental protection are provided to assure the health and safety of the community through the use of comprehensive planning and zoning tailored to the unique needs of each community. As oil and gas money fills state coffers, however, many state legislatures are considering the adoption of statutes that purport to preempt local government regulation of expanded oil and gas operations, masking, in part, the true purpose of avoidance of critical off-site consequences and needed mitigation. While failing to require state resolution of these comprehensive off-site issues, these state legislatures are unreasonably preempting local communities from dealing with those very same issues, resulting in the barring of supplemental regulation of oil and gas operations by cities and counties. Appropriate public policy should provide that states not preempt or occupy the field to the exclusion of local government supplemental oversight.

Traditional Oil and Gas Regulation at the State Level.

Absent federal statutes comprehensively governing fracking, the question of whether to regulate fracking is left wholly to state and local governments.[6] In Texas, for example, "neither the Legislature nor the [Railroad] Commission has ever seen fit to regulate [hydro-fracturing]." Although states like New York had relatively comprehensive regulations that cover fracking, it has not seen fit to totally preempt local government land use regulation in the field. Traditionally, state regulation has been achieved through favored industry oil and gas commissions. Regulations were generally limited to the "rule of capture" and those pertaining to the drill site itself. The rule of capture "gives a mineral rights owner title to the oil and gas produced from a lawful well bottomed on the property, even if the oil and gas flows to the well from beneath another owner's tract." Functioning as a rule similar to the principle of adverse possession, it encourages economic development over property rights. To combat the rule of capture, other states have statutes offering owners the correlative right to pool their oil and gas holdings with those of neighboring owners actually drilling oil and gas wells that draw down on the adjacent owners' oil and gas reserves. *Hegarty v. Bd. of Oil, Gas & Mining*, 57 P.3d 1042, 1048 (Utah 2002). These concerns have resulted in rules that:

> wells shall be drilled, cased, operated, and plugged in such manner, through well permitting and financial security so as to prevent: escape of oil, gas, or water out of the reservoir in which they are found into another formation; detrimental intrusion of

---

[6]   The bi-partisan 2016 federal Budget supports implementation of the Bureau of Land Management's (BLM) forthcoming regulations on hydraulic fracturing on public lands. The Budget also invests in research to ensure safe and responsible natural gas production. Specifically, it includes $47 million to support an interagency Research and Development (R&D) initiative aimed at understanding and minimizing potential environmental, health, and safety impacts of unconventional gas resource development and production through hydraulic fracturing. This research is being coordinated between the Department of Energy (DOE), Department of the Interior's (DOI) U.S. Geological Survey, and the Environmental Protection Agency (EPA) and will focus on timely, policy-relevant science to ensure prudent development while protecting human health and the environment. Additionally, in FY 2016, the Budget supports new R&D at DOE focused on mitigating and more accurately quantifying fugitive methane emissions from natural gas infrastructure.

water into an oil or gas reservoir; pollution of fresh water supplies by oil, gas, or salt water; blowouts; cavings; seepages; fires; unreasonable loss of a surface land owner's crops on surface land; [unreasonable] loss of value of existing improvements owned by a surface landowner on surface land; and [unreasonable] permanent damage to surface land. UTAH CODE ANN. § 40–6–5 (2011), amended by Surface Owner Protection Act, 2012 Utah Laws ch. 342 § 40–6–5.

Thus, the traditional state concerns have primarily focused on three issues: prevention of waste, protection of correlative rights, and the conservation of oil and gas natural resources. N.M. Oil and Gas Act, N.M. STAT.ANN. §§ 70–2–1 to –38 (2015). To the extent that local government regulation focuses on matters relating to land use, financing of critical off-site infrastructure and services, environmental impact on adjacent lands, noise, traffic congestion, and conformity with the comprehensive plan, these areas are matters of local concern and not occupied within the exclusive "field" of state regulation.

Nevertheless, numerous court decisions have dealt with the issue of state preemption and occupation of the field, prohibiting any local government regulation. Particularly the issue of whether a local government may use its zoning or home rule powers to ban oil and gas fracking within the jurisdiction despite ever increasing and pervasive state law regulation of oil and gas sites and production.

2.   STATE PREEMPTION

MATTER OF WALLACH V. TOWN OF DRYDEN
Court of Appeals of New York, 2014.
23 N.Y.3d 728, 992 N.Y.S.2d 710, 16 N.E.3d 1188.

We are asked in these two appeals whether towns may ban oil and gas production activities, including hydrofracking, within municipal boundaries through the adoption of local zoning laws. We conclude that they may because the supersession clause in the statewide Oil, Gas and Solution Mining Law (OGSML) does not preempt the home rule authority vested in municipalities to regulate land use. The orders of the Appellate Division should therefore be affirmed.

Respondent Town of Dryden is a rural community located in Tompkins County, New York. Land use in Dryden is governed by a comprehensive plan and zoning ordinance. The underlying goal of the comprehensive plan is to "[p]reserve the rural and small town character of the Town of Dryden, and the quality of life its residents enjoy, as the town continues to grow in the coming decades." Despite the fact that oil and gas drilling has not historically been associated with Dryden, its location within the Marcellus Shale region has piqued the interest of the natural gas industry.

The Marcellus Shale formation covers a vast area across sections of a number of states, including New York, Pennsylvania, Ohio and West Virginia. Natural gas—primarily methane—is found in shale deposits buried thousands of feet below the surface and can be extracted through the combined use of horizontal drilling and hydrofracking. To access the natural gas, a well is drilled vertically to a location just above the target depth, at which point the well becomes a horizontal tunnel in order to maximize the number of pathways through which the gas may be removed. The process of hydraulic fracturing—commonly referred to as hydrofracking—can then commence. Hydrofracking involves the injection of large amounts of pressurized fluids (water and chemicals) to stimulate or fracture the shale formations, causing the release of the natural gas (see generally U.S. Dept. of Energy, Natural Gas from Shale: Questions and Answers [Apr. 2013], available at http://www.energy.gov/sites/prod/files/2013/04/f0/complete_brochure.pdf [accessed June 18, 2014]).

In 2006, petitioner Norse Energy Corp. USA (Norse), through its predecessors, began acquiring oil and gas leases from landowners in Dryden for the purpose of exploring and developing natural gas resources. The Town Board took the position that gas extraction activities were prohibited in Dryden because such operations fell within the catch-all provision of its zoning ordinance that precluded any uses not specifically allowed. Nevertheless, the Town Board decided to engage in a "clarification" of the issue. After holding a public hearing and reviewing a number of relevant scientific studies, the Town Board unanimously voted to amend the zoning ordinance in August 2011 to specify that all oil and gas exploration, extraction and storage activities were not permitted in Dryden. The amendment also purported to invalidate any oil and gas permit issued by a state or federal agency. In adopting the amendment, the Town Board declared that the industrial use of land in the "rural environment of Dryden" for natural gas purposes "would endanger the health, safety and general welfare of the community through the deposit of toxins into the air, soil, water, environment, and in the bodies of residents."

A month later, Norse commenced this hybrid CPLR article 78 proceeding and declaratory judgment action to challenge the validity of the zoning amendment. Norse asserted that Dryden lacked the authority to prohibit natural gas exploration and extraction activities because section 23–0303(2) of the Environmental Conservation Law (ECL)—the supersession clause in the Oil, Gas and Solution Mining Law—demonstrated that the state legislature intended to preempt local zoning laws that curtailed energy production. In response, Dryden moved for summary judgment, seeking a declaration that the zoning amendment was a valid exercise of its home rule powers.

The trial court granted Dryden's motion and declared the amendment valid with one exception—it struck down the provision invalidating state and federal permits). The Appellate Division affirmed, rejecting Norse's claim that the OGSML preempted Dryden's zoning amendment (108 A.D.3d 25, 964 N.Y.S.2d 714 [3d Dept.2013]). We granted Norse leave to appeal (21 N.Y.3d 863, 2013 WL 4562930 [2013]).

On appeal, Norse and CHC, supported by several amici curiae, press their contention that Dryden lacked the authority to proscribe hydrofracking and associated natural gas activities within their town boundaries. They assert that the energy policy of New York, as exemplified by the statewide OGSML, requires a uniform approach and cannot be subject to regulation by a mélange of the state's 932 towns. They maintain that the OGSML contains a supersession clause that expressly preempts all local zoning laws, like those enacted by the Town, which restrict or forbid oil and gas operations on real property within a municipality. The Town, joined by other amici curiae, respond that the courts below correctly concluded that they acted within their home rule authority in adopting the challenged local laws. They urge that the ability of localities to restrict the industrial use of land with the aims of preserving the characteristics of their communities and protecting the health, safety and general welfare of their citizens implicates the very essence of municipal governance. They further contend that, when analyzed under the principles set forth in our precedent, the OGSML and its supersession clause do not extinguish their zoning powers. Unlike our dissenting colleagues, we believe that the Towns have the better argument.

Our analysis begins with a review of the source of municipal authority to regulate land use and the limits the State may impose on this power. Article IX, the "home rule" provision of the New York Constitution, states that "every local government shall have power to adopt and amend local laws not inconsistent with the provisions of this constitution or any general law . . . except to the extent that the legislature shall restrict the adoption of such a local law" (N.Y.Const., art. IX, § 2[c][ii]). To implement this constitutional mandate, the state legislature enacted the Municipal Home Rule Law, which empowers local governments to pass laws both for the "protection and enhancement of [their] physical and visual environment" (Municipal Home Rule Law § 10[1][ii][a][11]) and for the "government, protection, order, conduct, safety, health and well-being of persons or property therein" (Municipal Home Rule Law § 10[1][ii][a][12]). The legislature likewise authorized towns to enact zoning laws for the purpose of fostering "the health, safety, morals, or the general welfare of the community" (Town Law § 261; *see also* Statute of Local Governments § 10[6] [granting towns "the power to adopt, amend and repeal zoning regulations"]). As a fundamental precept, the legislature has recognized that the local regulation of land use is "among the most important powers and duties granted . . . to a town government" (Town Law § 272–a [1][b]).

We, too, have designated the regulation of land use through the adoption of zoning ordinances as one of the core powers of local governance (see *DJL Rest. Corp. v. City of New York*, 749 N.E.2d 186 [2001]). Without question, municipalities may "enact land-use restrictions or controls to enhance the quality of life by preserving the character and desirable aesthetic features of [the community]" (*Trustees of Union Coll. in Town of Schenectady in State of N.Y. v. Members of Schenectady City Council*, 690 N.E.2d 862 [1997] And we have repeatedly highlighted the breadth of a municipality's zoning powers to "provide for the development of a balanced, cohesive community" in consideration of "regional needs and requirements" (*Matter of Gernatt Asphalt Prods. v. Town of Sardinia*, 664 N.E.2d 1226 [1996]; *see also Udell v. Haas*, 235 N.E.2d 897 [1968] ["Underlying the entire concept of zoning is the assumption that zoning can be a vital tool for maintaining a civilized form of existence"]).

That being said, as a political subdivision of the State, a town may not enact ordinances that conflict with the State Constitution or any general law (*see* Municipal Home Rule Law § 10 [1][i], [ii]). Under the preemption doctrine, a local law promulgated under a municipality's home rule authority must yield to an inconsistent state law as a consequence of "the untrammeled primacy of the Legislature to act with respect to matters of State concern" (*Albany Area Bldrs. Assn. v. Town of Guilderland*, 538 N.E.2d 356 [1989] But we do not lightly presume preemption where the preeminent power of a locality to regulate land use is at stake. Rather, we will invalidate a zoning law only where there is a "clear expression of legislative intent to preempt local control over land use" (*Gernatt*, 664 N.E.2d 1226).

We do not examine the preemptive sweep of this supersession clause on a blank slate. This question may be answered by considering three factors: (1) the plain language of the supersession clause; (2) the statutory scheme as a whole; and (3) the relevant legislative history. The goal of this three-part inquiry, as with any statutory interpretation analysis, is to discern the legislature's intent.

Guided by these principles, we now apply Frew Run's three-part inquiry to the OGSML's supersession clause.

The operative text of the OGSML's supersession clause is quite close to the provision we analyzed in Frew Run, preempting local laws "relating to the regulation of the oil, gas and solution mining industries" (ECL 23–0303[2]; compare ECL 23–2703 [former (2)] [preempting local laws "relating to the extractive mining industry"]). Based on the similarities between the two state statutes, we decline the invitation of Norse and CHC to ascribe a broader meaning to the language used in the OGSML. To the contrary, the distinction we drew in Frew Run applies with equal force here, such that ECL 23–0303(2) is most naturally read as preempting only local laws that purport to regulate the actual operations of oil and gas activities, not zoning ordinances that restrict or prohibit certain land uses within town boundaries. Plainly, the zoning laws in these cases are directed at regulating land use generally and do not attempt to govern the details, procedures or operations of the oil and gas industries. Although the zoning laws will undeniably have an impact on oil and gas enterprises, as in Frew Run, " this incidental control resulting from the municipality's exercise of its right to regulate land use through zoning is not the type of regulatory enactment relating to the [oil, gas and solution mining industries] which the Legislature could have envisioned as being within the prohibition of the statute" (*Frew Run*, 71 N.Y.2d at 131, 524 N.Y.S.2d 25, 518 N.E.2d 920).

Nevertheless, Norse and CHC, relying on the secondary clause in the OGSML's supersession provision—preserving "local government jurisdiction over local roads or the rights of local governments under the real property tax law" (ECL 23–0303[2])—contend that the operative text cannot be limited to local laws that purport to regulate the actual operations of oil and gas companies. They submit that the secondary clause's exemption of local jurisdiction over roads and taxes makes sense only if the preemptive span of the operative text is broader than we have allowed because roads and taxes are not associated with "operations." Consequently, they argue that there would have been no need for the legislature to exclude them from the operative language if supersession was limited to local laws aimed at oil and gas operations.

We find this textual argument misplaced because local regulation of roads and taxes can fairly be characterized as touching on the operations of the oil and gas industries and would have been preempted absent the secondary savings clause. The state legislature's decision to preserve "local government jurisdiction over local roads" was appropriate given the heavy truck and equipment traffic typically associated with oil and gas production, including water and wastewater hauling. Local laws dictating the number of daily truck trips or the weight and length of vehicles bear directly on industry operations and would otherwise be preempted absent the secondary clause. Similarly, the preservation of "the rights of local governments under the real property tax law" must be read in conjunction with section 594 of the Real Property Tax Law, which allows municipalities to impose taxes on oil and gas businesses. Because these special taxes are based on the level of production, they can be viewed as affecting the operations of the oil and gas industry, such that it was reasonable for the legislature to carve out an exception from the preemptive scope of the operative text. We are therefore unpersuaded by the claim of Norse and CHC that the plain language of ECL 23–0303(2) as a whole supports preemption of the Towns' zoning laws.

In sum, the plain language of ECL 23–0303(2) does not support preemption with respect to the Towns' zoning laws.

The second factor relevant to discerning whether a supersession clause preempts local zoning powers involves an assessment of the clause's role in the statutory framework as a whole. We therefore turn to the OGSML—article 23 of the Environmental Conservation Law.

And contrary to the position advanced by Norse and CHC, we see no inconsistency between the preservation of local zoning authority and the OGSML's policies of preventing "waste" and promoting a "greater ultimate recovery of oil and gas" (ECL 23–0301), or the statute's spacing provisions for wells (*see* ECL 23–0501, 23–0503). Waste is used as a term of art in the OGSML meaning, among other things, the "inefficient, excessive or improper use of, or the unnecessary dissipation of reservoir energy" and the "locating, spacing, drilling, equipping, operating, or producing of any oil or gas well or wells in a manner which causes or tends to cause reduction in the quantity of oil or gas ultimately recoverable" (ECL 23–0101[20][b], [c]). The OGSML's overriding concern with preventing waste is limited to inefficient or improper drilling activities that result in the unnecessary waste of natural resources. Nothing in the statute points to the conclusion that a municipality's decision not to permit drilling equates to waste. The OGSML's related goal of ensuring a "greater ultimate recovery" and its well-spacing provisions—designed to limit the number of wells that may be drilled into an underground pool of oil or gas—are likewise directly related to the concept of waste prevention and do not compel a different result. As the Appellate Division below aptly observed in the Dryden case:

> "the well-spacing provisions of the OGSML concern technical, operational aspects of drilling and are separate and distinct from a municipality's zoning authority, such that the two do not conflict, but rather, may harmoniously coexist; the zoning law will dictate in which, if any, districts drilling may occur, while the OGSML instructs operators as to the proper spacing of the units within those districts in order to prevent waste" (108 A.D.3d at 37, 964 N.Y.S.2d 714).

The third and final factor for review in deciding whether the supersession clause preempts local zoning powers requires that we examine the OGSML's legislative history.

Nothing in the legislative history undermines our view that the supersession clause does not interfere with local zoning laws regulating the permissible and prohibited uses of municipal land. Indeed, the pertinent passages make no mention of zoning at all, much less evince an intent to take away local land use powers. Rather, the history of the OGSML and its predecessor makes clear that the state legislature's primary concern was with preventing wasteful oil and gas practices and ensuring that the Department had the means to regulate the technical operations of the industry.

In sum, application of the three Frew Run factors—the plain language, statutory scheme and legislative history—to these appeals leads us to conclude that the Towns appropriately acted within their home rule authority in adopting the challenged zoning laws. We can find no legislative intent, much less a requisite "clear expression," requiring the preemption of local land use regulations.

At the heart of these cases lies the relationship between the State and its local government subdivisions, and their respective exercise of legislative power. These appeals are not about whether hydrofracking is beneficial or detrimental to the economy, environment or energy needs of New York, and we pass no judgment on its merits. These are major policy questions for the coordinate branches of government to resolve. The discrete issue before us, and the only one we resolve today, is whether the state legislature eliminated the home rule capacity of municipalities to pass zoning laws that exclude oil, gas and hydrofracking activities in order to preserve the existing character of their communities. There is no dispute that the state legislature has this right if it chooses to exercise it. But in light of ECL 23–0303(2)'s plain language, its place within the OGSML's framework and the legislative background, we cannot say that the supersession clause—added long before the current debate over high-volume hydrofracking and horizontal drilling ignited—evinces a clear expression of preemptive intent. The zoning laws of Dryden and Middlefield are therefore valid.

Accordingly, in each case, the order of the Appellate Division should be affirmed, with costs.

NOTES

1.   Governor Andrew Cuomo banned hydraulic fracturing in December 2014, a few months after New York's high court held that state regulation of the oil and gas industry did not preempt local governments' attempts to prohibit activities inconsistent with municipal land use laws, including oil and gas development. Cuomo cited a New York Department of Health report that found a high level of uncertainty about the safety of hydraulic fracturing and the potential for significant negative health impacts. Pro-gas development groups protested the loss of revenue and jobs while environmentalists lauded the ban as a key victory for human and environmental health. *See,* Beth Kinne, *Community Impacts Beyond Fracking: Midstream Challenges of Natural Gas Development,* 39 STATE & LOCAL LAW NEWS 9 (Fall, 2015).

2.   The Pennsylvania Supreme Court, in *Robinson Township, Washington County v. Commonwealth of Pennsylvania,* 83 A.3d 901 (Pa.2013), found that Pennsylvania's state constitutional Environmental Rights Amendment, Const. Art. 1, § 27, overrode the state legislature's preemptive statute: "According to the plain language of Section 27, the provision establishes two separate rights in the people of the Commonwealth. The first— in the initial, prohibitory clause of Section 27—is the declared "right" of

citizens to clean air and pure water, and to the preservation of natural, scenic, historic and esthetic values of the environment. This clause affirms a limitation on the state's power to act contrary to this right. While the subject of the right certainly may be regulated by the Commonwealth, any regulation is "subordinate to the enjoyment of the right . . . [and] must be regulation purely, not destruction"; laws of the Commonwealth that unreasonably impair the right are unconstitutional. *See Hartford Accident & Indemnity Co. v. Insurance Commissioner*, 482 A.2d 542, 548–49 (Pa.1984).

3.   In Colorado, *Town of Milliken v. Kerr-McGee Oil & Gas Onshore LP*, 2013 WL 1908965 (Colo.App.2013) *review denied* 2014 WL 1465027 (Colo.Sup.Ct.2014), the court found that:

> "we note that this case does not concern the Town's authority to conduct safety and security inspections of oil and gas well sites within its boundaries. Indeed, section 34–60–106(15)'s last sentence "supports the conclusion that the General Assembly did not intend to preempt all local regulation of oil and gas operations." *Town of Frederick v. North American Resources Co.*, 60 P.3d 758, 763 (Colo.App.2002); *see* § 31–15–401, C.R.S.2012 (outlining municipalities' general police powers); *cf. City of Golden v. Ford*, 348 P.2d 951, 954 (Colo.1960) ("Nor do we imply any limitation upon the traditional but statutory rights of municipalities to prevent disturbances of the peace and to maintain law and order by appropriate police action. It is only when the city's acts or regulations attempt to interfere with or cover, as here, a field preempted by the state or which is of state-wide concern that they must fail.")."

In Colorado, local governments can supplement state regulation of mineral processing by regulating the location of the use and its offsite impacts. Colo.Rev.Stat. §§ 34–32–109(6), 34–32–115(4)(c)(I) (2011). However, a locality will overstep its land use authority when it specifically regulates the on-site use of chemicals involved in the extraction process which is also regulated by the state or creates an outright ban on oil and gas drilling, fracking, or production within the boundaries of the local government. *Colo. Mining Ass'n v. Bd. of County Commissioners*, 199 P.3d 718 (Colo.2009). The Colorado Supreme Court specifically held that the Summit County ordinance before it granted the county broad powers which were improper, but it acknowledged that valid regulation of mine siting and impacts consistent with the Mined Land Reclamation Act could be enacted.

The 2009 Colorado Mining Association decision was followed by significant local government activity to address the effects of oil and gas fracking on local communities. Pursuant to Executive Order B 2012–002, the Governor established a Task Force to develop cooperative state and local government strategies regarding the regulation of oil and gas development in Colorado. The Task Force discussed jurisdictional issues regarding substantive regulations but determined that drawing bright lines between state and local jurisdictional authority was neither realistic nor productive. Despite the Task Force recommendations, in July 2012, the Colorado Oil and Gas Conservation

Commission filed suit against the City of Longmont seeking a declaratory order invalidating portions of a recent City of Longmont ordinance the Commission believes to be preempted by the Colorado Oil and Gas Commission Act. The Colorado Oil and Gas Association, a private industry group, moved to intervene on the side of the Commission. See Colo. Oil and Gas Comm'n v. City of Longmont, Boulder, in which the Colorado Supreme Court held:

> "Applying well-established preemption principles, this court concludes that the City of Longmont's ban on fracking and the storage and disposal of fracking wastes within its city limits operationally conflicts with applicable state law. Accordingly, the court holds that Longmont's fracking ban is preempted by state law and, therefore, is invalid and unenforceable. The court further holds that the inalienable rights provision of the Colorado Constitution does not save the fracking ban from preemption by state law. The court thus affirms the district court's order enjoining Longmont from enforcing the fracking ban and remands this case for further proceedings consistent with this opinion."

3. MODEL LOCAL GOVERNMENT FRACKING ORDINANCE

Santa Fe County, New Mexico, adopted an Oil and Gas Element of its General Plan and an Oil and Gas Ordinance incorporating the following goals, policies, and recommendations as necessary to address the challenges facing Santa Fe County because of potential oil and gas drilling through the process of hydrological fracturing:

- Planning and regulation. Oil and gas development in the Galisteo Basin has created a desire to protect against "negative impacts to the environment, cultural and archeological sites . . . and to preserve the public health, safety and welfare of the communities." This has created a need for planning and regulation to protect the "surface property owners, existing land uses and environmental and cultural features, while fairly treating oil and gas mineral estates owners and lessees . . . ."

- Cumulative impacts of oil and gas development. The approach to planning and development regulation must be comprehensive, avoiding the treatment of each individual oil and gas project as an individual entity because it is the cumulative effect of the development that impacts the character of the county.

- Control of sprawl. Because oil and gas development on the edges of the county would create a physical and social barrier to preservation and enhancement of the areas and would require costly extension of capital facilities, infrastructure, and services, the County should ensure that oil and gas development does not hinder smart growth.

- Natural and cultural resources. Because the Galisteo Basin contains an "abundance of prime ranching, agricultural, natural resource and environmentally sensitive lands, together with important historical, archeological and cultural sites" the county must identify the most effective regulatory and mitigation techniques to reduce negative impacts of oil and gas development.

- Traffic congestion. Due to the number and extent of increasing trips, trip loads, and vehicle miles travelled by heavy trucks, tankers, and drilling equipment, "roadways must be improved and maintained to standards that allow oil and gas, residential, agriculture and ranching users to interact safely and for adequate police, fire and emergency response."

- Water quantity and quality. The county needs to maintain and protect currently available water, as well as "the aquifer recharge areas and the ability of the natural water system to maintain its function and refresh its supply."

- Adequate police, fire, and emergency response. To maintain the existing levels of service for emergency response services, oil and gas developers should pay for facility and service improvements and for the enhancement necessary to adequately respond to oil and gas emergencies resulting from drilling and production.

- Fiscal balance and responsibility. The county must balance environmental protection concerns with county costs. Consequently, it should employ "development agreements, mitigation and impact fees, improvement district assessments, rates and charges" to reduce negative fiscal effects and improve the long term fiscal health of the county and its residents.

- Consistency with federal and state legislation. To avoid state or federal preemption or statutory conflict, the ordinance must be supplementary, to enhance and not replace laws, and be consistent with federal and state statutes, executive orders, and regulations.

- Nuisance protection. With owners of mineral estates and oil and gas leases having rights and privileges to use pieces of the surface estate reasonably required to extract and develop the subsurface mineral or oil and gas resources and with surface estate owners having protection under the common law (nuisance) and statute, both deserve protection.

The plan implementation program included within the Oil and Gas Plan Element identifies a number of tools available to the county to be employed to bring the goals, policies, and strategies of the plan to fruition. The following implementation tools are interrelated and work together providing continuity and breadth to the implementation program:

(1) Adoption of an Oil and Natural Gas Ordinance, implementing the Oil and Gas Plan Element.

(2) Requirements that all future oil and gas legislative and quasi-judicial discretionary development approvals be consistent with the goals, objectives, policies, and strategies of the Oil and Gas Element to the General Plan.

(3) Creating a three-step process for approval of oil and gas project applications including: obtaining a legislative overlay zoning district classification; a quasi-judicial special use and development permit; and ministerial grading and building permits and a certificate of completion.

(4) Developer preparation of the following reports, studies, and assessments to be utilized in determining approval of the legislative overlay zoning district classification (plan consistency report); environmental impact report; fiscal impact assessment; adequate public facilities and services assessment; water availability assessment; police, fire, and emergency service preparedness studies; traffic impact assessment; and a geo-hydrological report.

(5) Provision of standards governing the issuance of the quasi-judicial special permit and ministerial permits and the certificate of completion, supplementary to and consistent with applicable state permit standards and conditions, for equipment, operations, emergency service and response plans, site remediation, grading and soil disturbance, spills and leaks, lighting, buffers, landscaping and screening, closed loop systems, operating hours, and temporary and permanent abandonment.

(6) Establishment of a Land Environmental Suitability Analysis and Maps that will control the number and spacing of drilling wells per thousand acres based on environmental capacity.

(7) Preparing a prioritized 20-Year Capital Improvements and Services Plan to address the needs generated by oil and gas drilling, production and transportation, to be financed by adequate public facility and service ordinance provisions; development agreements; environmental mitigation and facility impact fees; and special improvement district creation financed by rates, fees, charges, taxes, and bonds.

(8)   Provisions for eliminating takings litigation through use of a beneficial use and value determination process, transfers of development rights, clustering, co-generation at well sites, and variances.

See Santa Fe County, N.M., Ordinance 2008–19.

Each of these processes utilizes the zoning, environmental analysis, impact fees and assessments, and capital improvement programming that we have studied throughout this casebook and constitutes an excellent review of all of that material.

Note that the Santa Fe County ordinance does not regulate the off-site storage of excess methane gas. The Federal Energy and Resource Commission (FERC) has preempted the regulation of gas storage as part of gas pipeline transportation. Any storage facility that connects to an interstate pipeline grants FERC exclusive jurisdiction, under sections 7(c) and (e) of the Natural Gas Act. The City of Arlington N.Y.'s storage project will connect via Arlington's 20-mile Seneca Lake pipeline to the interstate Dominion and Millennium pipelines.

Before granting a certificate of public convenience and necessity allowing a project to proceed, FERC must determine that the benefits of the project outweigh the negative impacts. In this case, the benefits of the project include increased storage located between the Marcellus Shale region is producing large quantities of gas, and the northeast United States, which has a large demand. FERC accepted Arlington's evidence of interest from prospective buyers for more than 11 times the gas this project will store as compelling evidence of need.

FERC rejected Arlington's initial NEPA environmental impact assessment and required additional information concerning, cumulative environmental impacts related to current and proposed projects within a five-mile radius of the site. FERC's final order found that specific noise concerns and impacts on landowners from construction and operations of the facility would be temporary or non-problematic, and that Arlington's engineers had adequately and comprehensively addressed concerns over faults in or near the salt caverns. FERC, Order Issuing Certificate and Confirming Market-based Rates, Arlington Gas Storage, LLC, No. CP13–83–000 (May 15, 2014), https://www.ferc.gov/whats-new/comm-meet/2014/051514/C-1.pdf.

CHAPTER 9

CONTROLLING THE USE OF ECOLOGICALLY SENSITIVE LANDS

■ ■ ■

It is often impossible to use private land without complying with a plethora of environmental laws. This Chapter first addresses the most common federal statutory requirements affecting land use: the Endangered Species Act, the Clean Water Act and the Coastal Zone Management Act. Next, the chapter deals with the regulation of development in floodplains and on steep hillsides. Finally, we cover the preservation of agricultural land and the use of public lands.

A. WILDLIFE HABITAT AND THE ENDANGERED SPECIES ACT

Many state and federal laws exist to preserve land or protect particular species of wildlife, flora and fauna. Several federal statutes are species-related, like the Bald Eagle Protection Act, 16 U.S.C.A. § 668, the Wild-Free Roaming Horses and Burros Act, 16 U.S.C.A. § 1331, and the Migratory Bird Treaty Act, 16 U.S.C.A. § 703. The Marine Mammal Protection Act, 16 U.S.C.A. § 1361, and the Fisheries Conservation Act, 16 U.S.C.A. § 1801, protect fish habitat. The federal Wilderness Act of 1964 16 U.S.C.A. § 1131, is an early example of land preservation, but it is limited to federal public lands.

The Endangered Species act (ESA), 16 U.S.C.A. §§ 1531–1543, controls land use activities on federal, state, and private land by prohibiting activities that may affect endangered or threatened species. The United States Supreme Court has described the Act as "the most comprehensive legislation for the preservation of Endangered Species ever enacted by any Nation." *Tennessee Valley Authority v. Hill*, 437 U.S. 153, 180 (1978). *TVA v. Hill* was an early test of the ESA. To the surprise of many, the Court applied the act literally and enjoined the operation of a virtually completed federal dam on the Tellico River in Tennessee when it was determined that closing the dam would eradicate the snail darter, an endangered species.

Congress enacted the ESA to:

Provide a means whereby the ecosystems upon which endangered species and the threatened species depend may be conserved, to provide a program for the conservation of such endangered species and threatened species, and to take such steps as may be appropriate to achieve the purposes of the treaties and conventions set forth [in the act]. 16 USC § 1531(b).

The act directs the Secretary of the Interior to list species of plants, fish, and wildlife as threatened or endangered. An endangered species is one "in danger of extinction throughout all or a significant portion of its range." A threatened species is one that "is likely to become an endangered species within the foreseeable future throughout all or a significant portion of its range." 16 U.S.C.A. § 1532(6) and (20). Whether a particular species falls within one of these categories is determined on "the basis of the best scientific and commercial data available." The Act does not protect species that present an overwhelming risk to humans. Some 1300 species are listed as either threatened or endangered. For listed plants and animals, see http://www.fws.gov/endangered/. The Fish and Wildlife Service (FWS) of the Department of the Interior and the National Marine Fisheries Service (NMFS) of the Department of Commerce administer the ESA.

NATIONAL ASSOCIATION OF HOME BUILDERS V. BABBITT

United States Court of Appeals, District of Columbia Circuit, 1997.
130 F.3d 1041, cert. denied, 524 U.S. 937, 118 S.Ct. 2340, 141 L.Ed.2d 712 (1998).

WALD, CIRCUIT JUDGE:

The National Association of Home Builders of the United States, the Building Industry Legal Defense Fund, the County of San Bernardino, and the City of Colton, California brought this action in the United States District Court for the District of Columbia to challenge an application of section 9(a)(1) of the Endangered Species Act ("ESA"), 16 U.S.C. § 1538(a)(1), which makes it unlawful for any person to "take"—*i.e.,* "to harass, harm, pursue, hunt, shoot, wound, kill, trap, capture, or collect, or attempt to engage in any such conduct," 16 U.S.C. § 1532(19)-any endangered species. The plaintiffs sought a declaration that the application of section 9 of the ESA to the Delhi Sands Flower-Loving Fly ("the Fly"), which is located only in California, exceeds Congress' Commerce Clause power and an injunction against application of the section to the plaintiff's construction activities in areas containing Fly habitat.

This dispute arose when the Fish and Wildlife Service ("FWS") placed the Fly, an insect that is native to the San Bernardino area of California, on the endangered species list. The listing of the Fly, the habitat of which is located entirely within an eight mile radius in southwestern San Bernardino County and northwestern Riverside County, California, forced San Bernardino County to alter plans to construct a new hospital on a recently purchased site that the FWS had determined contained Fly habitat. The FWS and San Bernardino County agreed on a plan that would allow the County to build the hospital and a power plant in the area designated as Fly habitat in return for modification of the construction plans and purchase and set aside of nearby land as Fly habitat. In November 1995, FWS issued a permit to allow construction of the power plant. During the same month, however, the County notified the FWS that it planned to redesign a nearby intersection to improve emergency vehicle access to the hospital. The FWS informed the County that expansion of the intersection as planned would likely lead to a "taking" of the Fly in violation of ESA section 9(a). After brief unsuccessful negotiations between the County and FWS, the County filed suit in district court challenging the application of section 9(a)(1) to the Fly.

The district court held that application of section 9(a)(1) of the Endangered Species Act to the Fly is a valid exercise of Congress' power pursuant to the Commerce Clause. Accordingly, the court entered summary judgment on behalf of the government. Because we also find that the application of section 9(a)(1) of the Endangered Species Act to the Fly does not exceed Congress' Commerce Clause power, we affirm the district court's decision to grant the government's motion for summary judgment.

I. FACTUAL AND PROCEDURAL BACKGROUND

The Delhi Sands Flower-Loving Fly, which lives only in the "Delhi series" soils found in southwestern San Bernardino County and northwestern Riverside County, California, is the only remaining subspecies of its species. The other subspecies, the El Segundo Flower-Loving Fly, is believed to be extinct due to destruction of its habitat through urban development. The Fly is also one of only a few North American species in the "mydas flies" family and one of only a few species in that family that visit flowers in search of nectar, thereby pollinating native plant species.

Over 97 percent of the historic habitat of the Fly has been eliminated, and, prior to its listing as endangered, its remaining habitat was threatened by urban development, unauthorized trash dumping, and off-road vehicle use. There are currently 11 known populations of the Fly, all of which occur within an eight mile radius of one another. The size of the entire population of Flies was recently estimated in the low hundreds.

In 1990, after receiving two petitions asking that the Fly be placed on the endangered species list, the FWS began an investigation into whether listing of the Fly as endangered was warranted. Soon thereafter, the FWS found that substantial information had been presented to indicate that the Fly was an endangered species. Two years later, the FWS published its final determination that the Fly is "in imminent danger of extinction due to extensive habitat loss and degradation that has reduced its range by 97 percent." 58 Fed.Reg. at 49,881. The listing of the Fly as endangered triggered the automatic statutory prohibitions of section 9(a)(1) of the ESA, 16 U.S.C. § 1538(a)(1). As a result, commercial trade in the species could no longer occur lawfully and no person could "take" individuals of the species without a permit or an exemption.

For several years prior to the listing of the Fly as endangered, the County of San Bernardino had been planning to build a $470 million earthquake-proof "state of the art" hospital to serve as the central emergency medical center for the San Bernardino County area in the event of an earthquake and to serve as a primary burn care center and teaching facility. In July 1992, two years after the FWS had published its notice that sufficient information had been presented to justify listing the Fly as endangered but before the Fly was actually so listed, the Board of the new San Bernardino County hospital acquired the final site parcels for the hospital. The 76-acre site that the board acquired contained habitat of the Fly.

In November 1992, the FWS notified the County that the Fly was likely to be listed as endangered, and in May 1993—after the Fly was listed—the FWS advised the County that the hospital site was occupied by the Fly and that construction of the facility as then proposed would likely "take" members of the species in violation of the ESA. The County decided to modify the layout and design of the hospital to eliminate direct and indirect impacts to the Fly and to eliminate the need for a section 10 "incidental take permit."[1] One of the modifications to the original design for the hospital included in the plan was to move the hospital 250 feet north to "avoid[ ] direct impact to the entire area identified as occupied or suitable Delhi Fly habitat." Habitat Preservation, Habitat Enchangement [sic] and Impact Avoidance Plan for the Delhi Sands Flower-Loving Fly at the San Bernardino County Hospital Replacement Site 8 (Dec. 1, 1993). This resulted in an 8.35 acre Delhi Fly habitat preserve. *Id.* The plan also created a 100-foot wide corridor to link two Fly habitat areas and permit interbreeding between Fly colonies.

In October 1994, the County approached FWS with a proposal to construct a substation to power the hospital on "the best remaining habitat" for the Fly. The County submitted an application for incidental "take" of the Fly, which would permit it to build on about 4 acres of Fly habitat. To offset this reduction in Fly habitat, the County proposed to acquire and manage a nearby 7.5 acre site as Fly habitat. In November 1995, the FWS issued the section 10 permit for the substation and construction began shortly thereafter.

In November 1995, the County informed FWS of its plans to redesign an intersection near the hospital that the County argues is critical to emergency vehicle access to the new hospital. The FWS determined that

---

[1] [fn 2] Under section 10 of the ESA, the Secretary of the FWS may permit a taking of an endangered species otherwise prohibited by section 9(a)(1) if the taking is incidental to carrying out an otherwise lawful activity. No permit may be issued until after the applicant submits a conservation plan, the Secretary offers opportunity for public comment on the plan, and the Secretary finds, among other things, that the taking will be incidental, the impacts of the taking will be minimized to the extent practicable, adequate funding for the plan is available, and the taking will not appreciably reduce the likelihood of the survival and recovery of the species. *See* 16 U.S.C. § 1539(a).

the plan, which called for a reduction of the 100 foot wide corridor to an 18 foot wide corridor, a reduction of 70 to 80 percent, would "greatly reduce, if not effectively eliminate, the entire corridor area set aside as a critical part of the County's efforts to avoid a take" of the Fly. The FWS advised the County that the redesign of the intersection would probably cause a "take" of the Fly in violation of section 9 of the ESA.

On October 20, 1995, the National Association of Home Builders of the United States, the Building Industry Legal Defense Fund, the County of San Bernardino, and the City of Colton, California filed a complaint seeking a declaration that the taking prohibition of section 9 of the ESA was unconstitutional as applied to "takes" of the Fly and asking for an injunction barring application of the provision. An amended complaint later added the California Building Industry Association and the City of Fontana as plaintiffs. On December 6, 1996, the district court granted the government's motion for summary judgment. This appeal ensued.

Appellants challenge the application of section 9(a)(1) of the ESA, which makes it unlawful for any person to "take any [endangered or threatened] species within the United States or the territorial sea of the United States," 16 U.S.C. § 1538(a)(1), to the Delhi Sands Flower-Loving Fly. *See also Babbitt v. Sweet Home Chapter of Communities for a Great Oregon,* 515 U.S. 687 (1995) (upholding agency's interpretation of the term "take" to include significant habitat degradation). Appellants argue that the federal government does not have the authority to regulate the use of non-federal lands in order to protect the Fly, which is found only within a single state. Indeed, they claim that "the Constitution of the United States does not grant the federal government the authority to regulate wildlife, nor does it authorize federal regulation of nonfederal lands."

The district court held that the application of section 9(a)(1) of the ESA to the Fly is constitutional. It concluded that the federal government's "limited and enumerated" powers include the power to regulate wildlife and non-federal lands that serve as the habitat for endangered species. The court also concluded that the ESA provides for a regulatory scheme that is within the bounds of Congress' power under the Commerce Clause. The district court thus granted the government's motion for summary judgment. We affirm the district court's decision.

The ESA's prohibition on takings of endangered species can be justified as a necessary aid to the prohibitions in the ESA on transporting and selling endangered species in interstate commerce. In this sense, the prohibition against takings of endangered species is analogous to the prohibition against transfer and possession of machine guns (including purely intrastate possession) of 18 U.S.C. § 922(*o*), which has been upheld by the Fifth, Sixth, Ninth, and Eleventh Circuits as a regulation of the channels of interstate commerce. In *United States v. Rambo,* 74 F.3d 948, 951 (9th Cir.), *cert. denied,* 519 U.S. 819 (1996), for instance, the Ninth

Circuit upheld section 922(*o*) against a *Lopez*-inspired Commerce Clause challenge. Similarly, the prohibition on "taking" endangered species is properly classified as a first category regulation because one of the most effective ways to prevent traffic in endangered species is to secure the habitat of the species from predatory invasion and destruction. Therefore, like section 922(*o*), section 9(a)(1) of the ESA can be properly upheld as a regulation of the use of the channels of interstate commerce.

The prohibition on takings of endangered animals also falls under Congress' authority to prevent the channels of interstate commerce from being used for immoral or injurious purposes. This authority was perhaps best described by the Supreme Court in *Heart of Atlanta,* 379 U.S. 241, which the *Lopez* Court cited and quoted in its reference to Congress' power to regulate the use of the "channels of interstate commerce." In *Heart of Atlanta,* the Supreme Court upheld a prohibition on racial discrimination in places of public accommodation serving interstate travelers against a Commerce Clause challenge. * * *

This same reasoning that the Supreme Court applied in *Heart of Atlanta* is applicable to the case at hand. In those cases as well as here, Congress used its authority to rid the channels of interstate commerce of injurious uses to regulate the conditions under which goods are produced for interstate commerce. In *Heart of Atlanta,* Congress used this authority to prevent racial discrimination by a hotel serving an interstate clientele. Similarly, in this case, Congress used this authority to prevent the eradication of an endangered species by a hospital that is presumably being constructed using materials and people from outside the state and which will attract employees, patients, and students from both inside and outside the state. Thus, like regulations preventing racial discrimination or labor exploitation, regulations preventing the taking of endangered species prohibit interstate actors from using the channels of interstate commerce to "promot[e] or spread[ ] evil, whether of a physical, moral or economic nature."

B.   *Substantially Affects Interstate Commerce*

The takings clause in the ESA can also be viewed as a regulation of the third category of activity that Congress may regulate under its commerce power. According to *Lopez,* the test of whether section 9(a)(1) of the ESA is within this category of activity "requires an analysis of whether the regulated activity 'substantially affects' interstate commerce." 514 U.S. at 559. A class of activities can substantially affect interstate commerce regardless of whether the activity at issue-in this case the taking of endangered species-is commercial or noncommercial. * * *

The Committee Reports on the ESA reveal that one of the primary reasons that Congress sought to protect endangered species from "takings" was the importance of the continuing availability of a wide variety of species to interstate commerce. As the House Report explained:

. . . As we homogenize the habitats in which these plants and animals evolved, and as we increase the pressure for products that they are in a position to supply (usually unwillingly) we threaten their-and our own-genetic heritage.

The value of this genetic heritage is, quite literally, incalculable. . . .

* * *

From the most narrow possible point of view, it is in the best interests of mankind to minimize the losses of genetic variations. The reason is simple: they are potential resources. They are keys to puzzles which we cannot solve, and may provide answers to questions which we have not yet learned to ask.

* * *

Who knows, or can say, what potential cures for cancer or other scourges, present or future, may lie locked up in the structures of plants which may yet be undiscovered, much less analyzed? More to the point, who is prepared to risk being [sic] those potential cures by eliminating those plants for all time? Sheer self interest impels us to be cautious.

H.R.REP. NO. 93–412, at 4–5 (1973).

This legislative history distinguishes the ESA from the statute at issue in *Lopez*. In *Lopez,* the Court noted that "as part of our independent evaluation of constitutionality under the Commerce Clause we of course consider legislative findings, and indeed even congressional committee findings regarding effect on interstate commerce." 514 U.S. at 562 (citations omitted). The *Lopez* Court found, however, that there were no "congressional findings [that] would enable [it] to evaluate the legislative judgment that the activity in question substantially affected interstate commerce." In this case, in contrast, the committee reports on the ESA discuss the value of preserving genetic diversity and the potential for future commerce related to that diversity. * * *

1. *Biodiversity*

Approximately 521 of the 1082 species in the United States currently designated as threatened or endangered are found in only one state. The elimination of all or even some of these endangered species would have a staggering effect on biodiversity—defined as the presence of a large number of species of animals and plants—in the United States and, thereby, on the current and future interstate commerce that relies on the availability of a diverse array of species.

The variety of plants and animals in this country are, in a sense, a natural resource that commercial actors can use to produce marketable products. In the most narrow view of economic value, endangered plants and animals are valuable as sources of medicine and genes. Fifty percent of the most frequently prescribed medicines are derived from wild plant and animal species. Such medicines were estimated in 1983 to be worth over $15 billion a year. In addition, the genetic material of wild species of plants and animals is inbred into domestic crops and animals to improve their commercial value and productivity. As *Amici Curiae* explained: "Fortifying the genetic diversity of U.S. crops played a large part in the explosive growth in farm production since the 1930s, accounting for at least one-half of the doubling in yields of rice, soybeans, wheat, and sugarcane, and a three-fold increase in corn and potatoes. Genetic diversity provided by wild plants also protects domestic crops from disease and pest damage." Similar genetic engineering can be used with animals. For instance, it is not beyond the realm of possibility that the genes of a wild pollinator species like the Fly might be inbred with the honeybee, which currently pollinates most major U.S. crops, to produce a pollinator that is more disease resistant.

Each time a species becomes extinct, the pool of wild species diminishes. This, in turn, has a substantial effect on interstate commerce by diminishing a natural resource that could otherwise be used for present and future commercial purposes. Unlike most other natural resources, however, the full value of the variety of plant and animal life that currently exists is uncertain. Plants and animals that are lost through extinction undoubtedly have economic uses that are, in some cases, as yet unknown but which could prove vitally important in the future. A species whose worth is still unmeasured has what economists call an "option value"-the value of the possibility that a future discovery will make useful a species that is currently thought of as useless. *See* Bryan Nolan, *Commodity, Amenity, and Morality: The Limits of Quantification in Valuing Biodiversity, in* BIODIVERSITY 200, 202 (Edward O. Wilson ed., 1988). To allow even a single species whose value is not currently apparent to become extinct therefore deprives the economy of the option value of that species. Because our current knowledge of each species and its possible uses is limited, it is impossible to calculate the exact impact that the loss of the option value of a single species might have on interstate commerce. *See* Alan Randall, *What Mainstream Economists Have to Say about the Value of Biodiversity, in* BIODIVERSITY, *supra,* at 217. In the aggregate, however, we can be certain that the extinction of species and the attendant decline in biodiversity will have a real and predictable effect on interstate commerce.

We hold that the section 9(a)(1) of the Endangered Species Act is within Congress' Commerce Clause power and that the Fish and Wildlife Service's application of the provision to the Delhi Sands Flower-Loving Fly was therefore constitutional. The district court's decision granting the Government's motion for summary judgment is therefore *Affirmed.*

KAREN LECRAFT HENDERSON, CIRCUIT JUDGE, concurring: [omitted]

SENTELLE, CIRCUIT JUDGE, dissenting: [omitted]

NOTES

1. In addition to NAHB, a handful of cases in other circuits have dealt with and upheld the constitutionality of the take prohibition of the ESA on grounds ranging from the Commerce Clause to the Necessary and Proper Clause. These include: *San Luis & Delta-Mendota Water Auth. v. Salazar*, 638 F.3d 1163 (9th Cir.2011); *Ala. Tombigbee Rivers Coal. v. Kempthorne*, 477 F.3d 1250 (11th Cir.2007); *GDF Realty Inv. v. Norton*, 326 F.3d 622 (5th Cir.2003); *Rancho Viejo, LLC v. Norton*, 323 F.3d 1062 (D.C.Cir.2003); *Gibbs v. Babbitt*, 214 F.3d 483 (4th Cir.2000); *Nat'l Ass'n of Home Builders v. Babbitt*, 130 F.3d 1041 (D.C.Cir.1997). In 2014, however, a Federal District Court ruled that prairie dog takes in Utah had only intrastate impacts, and therefore could not be regulated under the Commerce Clause. *People for the Ethical Treatment of Property Owner v. U.S. Fish and Wildlife Service*, 57 F.Supp.3d 1337 (D.Utah 2014). For the argument by the attorney who represented People for the Ethical Treatment of Property Owners that the scope of the ESA is limited under the Necessary and Proper Clause to protecting only species that have a tie to interstate commerce, *see* Jonathan Wood, *A Federal Crime Against Nature? The Federal Government Cannot Prohibit Harm to All Endangered Species Under the Necessary and Proper Clause*, 29 TUL.ENVTL.L.J. 65.

For a further review of the constitutionality of the ESA, *see generally* Michael C. Blumm and George Kimbrell, *Flies, Spiders, Toads, Wolves and the Constitutionality of the Endangered Species Act's Take Provision*, 34 ENVTL. L. 309 (2004); Bradford C. Mank, *After Gonzales v. Raich: Is the Endangered Species Act Constitutional Under the Commerce Clause?*, 788 U. COL.L.REV. 375 (2007).

2. Habitat protection is essential if the purpose of the ESA is to be achieved. There is no use protecting a plant or wildlife species if that species has no place to live, yet for years the Fish and Wildlife Service lagged in designating critical habitat. It was forced to accelerate the pace of designation in a series of lawsuits. See, e.g., *Natural Resources Defense Council v. United States Dept. of the Interior*, 113 F.3d 1121 (9th Cir.1997), finding that a state natural communities conservation program was no substitute for the Service's statutory duty to designate critical habitat for the California gnatcatcher. Critical habitat designation affects primarily federal activities on public land. Of what concern to owners is such designation on private land? In both Hawaii and California where the Service initially proposed designating hundreds of thousands of acres of private land in several counties to protect a tree frog (California) and two subterranean cave-dwelling insects (Hawaii), landowners mounted major efforts to substantially reduce the designated areas. One clue is language in Hawaii's state land use law which provides that "Conservation districts shall include areas necessary for * * * conserving indigenous or endemic plants, fish, and wildlife, including those which are threatened or endangered." HRS 205–2(a) and other statutory language which requires the

state Department of Land and Natural Resources to "initiate amendments to the conservation district boundaries in order to include . . . the habitat of rare native species of flora and fauna within the conservation district." HRS 195D–5.1. Once so included, all local land use controls are preempted and virtually no economically beneficial use of any kind is permitted. Is this constitutional under *Lucas*?

The Tenth Circuit has held that the FWS must use a "co-extensive" approach, which "would take into account all of the economic impact of the [critical habitat designation], regardless of whether those impacts are caused co-extensively by any other agency action (such as listing) and even if those impacts would remain in the absence of the [designation]." *New Mexico Cattle Growers Ass'n v. United States Fish & Wildlife Serv.*, 248 F.3d 1277 (10th Cir.2001). The ESA requires the consideration of economic impact before the designation of critical habitat, ESA § 4(b)(2), 16 U.S.C. § 1533(b)(2). In 2014, the Departments of Interior and Commerce issued a final rule to resolve a longstanding circuit split over the methodology used to carry out this mandate in favor of a "baseline" or "incremental" approach. This approach compares the state of affairs at the time of a species' listing to how things would look after designation of critical habitat, and is more favored by conservationists. 50 C.F.R. § 424.19. The competing co-extensive approach "take[s] into account all of the economic impact of the [critical habitat designation], regardless of whether those impacts are caused co-extensively by any other agency action (such as listing) and even if those impacts would remain in the absence of the [designation]." *New Mexico Cattle Growers Ass'n v. United States Fish & Wildlife Serv.*, 248 F.3d 1277 (10th Cir.2001). For review in favor of adoption of the baseline approach and the legal challenges it still may face, *see generally* Sheila Baynes, *Cost Considerations and the Endangered Species Act*, 90 N.Y.U.L.REV. 961 (2015).

3.   In addition to Section 4 critical habitat designations, Sections 7 and 9 also affect land use.

(a)   Section 7 directs federal agencies to consider the impact proposed actions may have on protected species. Working with the FWS, agencies must conduct biological assessments if the FWS determines that protected or proposed species are present. 16 U.S.C.A § 1536.

(b)   Section 9 affects private development by its prohibition against the "taking" of protected species. 16 U.S.C.A. § 1538(a)(1). "Take" means to "harass, harm, pursue, hunt, shoot, wound, kill, trap, capture, or collect, or attempt to engage in any such conduct." 16 U.S.C.A. § 1532(19). Within those proscribed actions, the most significant is "harm," defined not only as an act that actually kills or injures a species, but also any habitat modification or degradation which actually kills or injures wildlife by significantly impairing essential behavioral patterns, including breeding, feeding, or sheltering. 50 C.F.R. § 17.3. Thus, for example, the grazing of wild sheep introduced on public land for the benefit of sport hunters constitutes a threat to a six-inch-long, finchbill endangered bird because the grazing sheep destroy the bird's habitat. *Palila v. Hawaii Department of Land & Natural Resources*, 852 F.2d 1106 (9th

Cir.1988). The United States Supreme Court upheld this definition of "harm," but limited its application to circumstances where there is substantial evidence linking the habitat modification and the actual death or injury to the protected species. *See Babbitt v. Sweet Home Chapter of Communities for a Great Oregon*, 515 U.S. 687 (1995).

The "take" provision of the act does not always prevent all activity. *See Defenders of Wildlife v. Bernal*, 204 F.3d 920 (9th Cir.2000), where the court held the pigmy owl could tolerate a high degree of human presence, and therefore construction of a school complex in an area where the owl had been spotted would not illegally "take" the owl by affecting its habitat. Other landowners have been successful in fighting "incidental take" statements under the ESA in the course of development where the FWS could not show sufficient damage to the habitat of a listed species. *See, e.g., Arizona Cattle Growers' Association v. United States Fish and Wildlife*, 273 F.3d 1229 (9th Cir.2001).

4.   The ESA provides some flexibility to its otherwise apparent ban on actions that affect protected species through its allowance, of so-called "Section 10 incidental takings." An incidental taking is "a taking that is otherwise prohibited, if such taking is incidental to, and not the purpose of, carrying out of an otherwise lawful activity." 16 U.S.C.A. § 1539. *See also Friends of Endangered Species, Inc. v. Jantzen*, 760 F.2d 976 (9th Cir.1985). The process of attaining an incidental taking permit differs slightly between a taking involving a federal action and involving a private action.

Section 10 of the Act applies to private activity, and requires the private landowner to submit a habitat conservation plan (HCP) to the FWS seeking an incidental taking permit. 16 U.S.C.A. § 1539(a)(2)(A). The conservation plan must show the expected effects of the proposed act, the steps that will be taken to minimize and mitigate any takings that will or might occur, show that the taking will not appreciably reduce the likelihood of the survival of the species, and what alternative actions were considered and why they were not used. The Service must also be assured that there will be adequate funding for the conservation plan, and it may issue the permit subject to conditions.

5.   The Fifth Amendment takings implications of the ESA are an often discussed, but little litigated, topic. With Section 9's prohibition against taking an endangered species three types of cases may arise: (1) the loss of livestock or damage to real property by protected species, (2) a physical invasion by the government and (3) the inability to engage in economically viable uses of land due to the presence of a protected species.[2]

In the first type of case, the physical invasion by the protected animal (e.g., a grizzly bear killing cattle), courts have held that where protected species injures private property, no taking occurs since the state does not own or control the wild animals. *See Christy v. Hodel*, 857 F.2d 1324 (9th Cir.1988),

---

[2]   A fourth type of claim is that the ESA's prohibition against sale of endangered species is a taking. These claims have failed. *United States v. Hill*, 896 F.Supp. 1057 (D.Colo.1995) (ESA) and *Andrus v. Allard*, 444 U.S. 51 (1979) (Migratory Bird Treaty Act).

cert. denied 490 U.S. 1114 (1989). The argument has its weaknesses. See Justice White's dissent in *Christy*, 490 U.S. at 1115. In actions involving other federal and state laws protective of animals, damage to land has also been held not to be a taking. *See Mountain States Legal Foundation v. Hodel*, 799 F.2d 1423 (10th Cir.1986), *cert. denied* 480 U.S. 951 (1987) (damage to private lands caused by wild horses and burros protected by federal law did not constitute a taking; animals' grazing did not deprive owners of all economically viable use of the lands); *Moerman v. California*, 21 Cal.Rptr.2d 329 (Cal.App.1993), *cert. denied* 511 U.S. 1031 (1994). *See also Southview Associates, Ltd. v. Bongartz*, 980 F.2d 84 (2d Cir.1992), *cert. denied* 507 U.S. 987 (1993).

Regulations affecting water use raise the second category. In order to maintain stream flow for protected fish species, the government at times diverts water that farmers and ranchers rely upon or order them to curtail their water use. When the water rights rise to the level of property rights, there is the question of whether a taking has occurred. In 1956, the government granted the Casitas Municipal Water District the perpetual right to divert water from the Ventura River. In 1997, after the NFMS listed the steelhead trout as endangered, the Bureau of Reclamation ordered the Water District to construct a fish ladder necessary for the survival of the steelhead trout and to decrease its diversion of water from the river for the operation of the ladder. The water district complained that the loss of water was a physical taking. The Federal Circuit agreed, holding *Loretto* controlled. The government had "commandeer[ed] the water for a public use-preservation of an endangered species. [In so doing,] Casitas' right to use that water is forever gone." *Casitas Municipal Water District v. United States*, 543 F.3d 1276, 1294 (Fed.Cir.2008). *But see CRV Enterprises, Inc. v. United States*, 626 F.3d 1241 (Fed.Cir.2010) *cert. denied*, 131 S.Ct. 2459 (U.S. 2011) (government installation of a log boom that restricted property owners' use of slough was not a physical taking) and *Allegretti & Co. v. County of Imperial*, 42 Cal.Rptr.3d 122 (Ct.App.2006). For an unfavorable view of *Casitas, see* Raymond Dake, *Trout of Bounds: The Effects of the Federal Circuit Court of Appeals' Misguided Fifth Amendment Takings Analysis in* Casitas Municipal Water District v. United States, 36 Colum.J.Envtl.L. 59 (2011).

The third category requires application of the *Lucas* and *Penn Central* tests. In *Casitas*, for example, the dissent argued the BORs action was a mere regulation of water use and subject to the *Penn Central* test. When the issue is treated as a regulatory taking, different results ensue. In light of the "horror stories" of landowners being compelled to leave their land unused due to the presence of protected species, reported takings claims have been few compared to other claims regarding ecologically sensitive lands such as wetlands and forests. The whole parcel analysis has defeated some claims. *See Seiber v. State ex rel. Bd. of Forestry*, 149 P.3d 1243 (Or.App.2006), *cert. denied*, 552 U.S. 1061, 128 S.Ct. 706 (2007) (state wildlife regulation, temporarily preventing landowners from harvesting timber from 40 acres of a 200-acre parcel that were identified as nesting site for spotted owls, did not effect a taking under the "whole parcel" rule); *Coast Range Conifers LLC v. State Board of Forestry*,

117 P.3d 990 (Or.2005) (40 acre tract used as denominator rather than the 9 acres which could not be logged to protect bald eagle habitat).

6. Critics of the Endangered Species Act point to the perverse incentive the Act provides for property owners to "shoot, shovel, and shut up." Jonathan Wood, *A Federal Crime Against Nature? The Federal Government Cannot Prohibit Harm to All Endangered Species Under the Necessary and Proper Clause*, 29 TUL.ENVTL.L.J. 65, 74 (2015). For a comparative review of how both the Endangered Species Act and the Historical Preservation Act may encourage destruction of "the very resources that these laws seek to protect," *see generally* J. Peter Byrne, *Precipice Regulations and Perverse Incentives: Comparing Historic Preservation Designation and Endangered Species Listing*, 27 GEO.INT'L.ENT'L L.REV. 343 (2015).

7. Can the ESA be used to curb anthropogenic nitrogen emissions? Some scholars believe so. *See generally* Zravka Tzankova, *et. al., Can the ESA Address the Threats of Atmospheric Nitrogen Deposition? Insights from the Case of the Bay Checkerspot Butterfly*, 35 HARV.ENVTL.L.REV. 443 (2011). Tzankova explores how the ESA may be used to curb nitrogen emissions and nitrogen deposition that are the most significant threat to the checker spot butterfly's serpentine grassland habitat. Specifically, nitrogen deposits encourage and facilitate growth of non-native grass species displacing the grasses that the butterfly needs to survive. Could nitrogen-emitting activities, such as the operation of power plants, engagement in agricultural activities and use of motor vehicles constitute a 'take' under Section 9 of the ESA? What would the impact of expanding the scope of the ESA to include nitrogen emissions be on property owners? Could it be extended to cover all greenhouse gas emissions?

B. CLEAN WATER AND LAND USE

It is difficult to make effective use of land without discharging something into a waterway. Therefore, the repeated attempts by Congress to see that the United States—and in particular its states and local governments—does what is possible to clean up the nation's waterways has had significant land use consequences. The Federal Water Pollution Control Act, as amended by the Clean Water Act of 1977 (the "Clean Water Act"), is the complex legislation that was passed to implement the Congressional intent.

The Clean Water Act contains several parts that have a particularly strong bearing on the use of land: Section 208 wastewater planning, pollution discharge (point and nonpoint source), U.S. Army Corps of Engineers' dredge and fill permit programs applicable to wetlands, and wastewater treatment plant construction. Drinking water preservation is the subject of separate legislation, closely related to the Clean Water Act. With clean air, coastal zone, flood hazard, and other programs, the federal government drastically affects land use control, long considered to be the domain of state and local government.

The Clean Water Act has as its principal purpose the cleaning and maintenance of the nation's waters. It attacks the problem broadly by means of so-called "structural" and "nonstructural" techniques. The structural techniques pertain to the financing and construction of wastewater treatment plants and ancillary facilities. Nonstructural techniques pertain primarily to regulatory mechanisms, such as planning and land use controls. *See, e.g.,* William L. Andreen, *No Virtue Like Necessity: Dealing with Nonpoint Source Pollution and Environmental Flows in the Face of Climate Change,* 34 VIRG.ENT'L L.J. 255 (2016). The purpose of both is to eliminate the discharge of pollutants into the nation's waterways. Initially, most federal money went into the former category, even though there was little, if any, early planning or consideration of the growth-generating potential of large municipal wastewater treatment plants. It became increasingly apparent that all the hardware the federal government could afford for the treatment of pollutants discharged into individual waterway segments was not going to significantly improve the nation's waterways without plans required by other sections of the Clean Water Act. The shift in emphasis, together with the increased role of the Corps of Engineers in granting or not granting permits to dredge and fill navigable waterways, appears to represent current EPA policy.

Inherent in the federal programs, both structural and nonstructural, is the emphasis on their implementation by state and local governments. While it is the federal government that provides most of the money for municipal wastewater treatment facilities, it is the local government unit—city, county, village, special district—that constructs, operates, and maintains the facility and attempts to implement the various rules and regulations concerning connections, pretreatment of effluent, and the like, which come with the money. It is also a regional unit of state or local government that is to do the planning—especially the wastewater management planning upon which much regulatory implementation depends. To state and local governments also falls the job of monitoring, regulating, and enforcing compliance.

1. THE ROLE OF NPDES PERMITTING IN REGULATING THE USE OF LAND

The National Pollution Discharge Elimination System (NPDES) permit requirements under the Clean Water Act affect virtually every conceivable use of land except where exempted by Congress. The following case considers whether or not feathers and debris dispersed by a ventilation fan from a Confined Animal Feeding Operation and swept off the land due to rainfall into a waterway fits into an agricultural storm water runoff exemption. The effect on the use of land is obvious.

ALT V. UNITED STATES ENVIRONMENTAL PROTECTION AGENCY

United States District Court, N.D. West Virginia, 2013.
979 F.Supp.2d 701.

JOHN PRESTON BAILEY, CHIEF JUDGE.

This civil action was filed by the plaintiff, Lois Alt, on June 14, 2012, seeking declaratory and other relief due to the issuance by the United States Environmental Protection Agency ("EPA"), of a November 14, 2011, "Findings of Violation and Order for Compliance" under the Clean Water Act ("CWA"), 33 U.S.C. § 1251 *et seq.* [Doc. 1]. By Order entered October 9, 2012, this Court permitted the American Farm Bureau and West Virginia Farm Bureau (collectively "Farm Bureaus" or "Plaintiff Intervenors") to intervene in the action [Doc. 27].

Lois Alt operates a concentrated animal feeding operation ("CAFO") at Old Fields, Hardy County, West Virginia, for raising poultry [AR1; AR2 at 3]. The facility consists of eight poultry confinement houses equipped with ventilation fans, a little storage shed, a compost shed and feed storage bins [AR2 at 4]. All poultry growing operations, manure and little storage, and raw material storage at Lois Alt's CAFO are under roof [AR2 at 4–5].

Some particles of manure and litter from Ms. Alt's confinement houses have been tracked or spilled in Ms. Alt's farmyard [AR1 at 4; AR2 at 4–5]. Some dust composed of manure, litter and dander, and some feathers, have been blown by the ventilation fans from the confinement houses into Ms. Alt's farmyard where they have settled on the ground [AR1 at 3; AR2 at 4].

Precipitation has fallen on Ms. Alt's farmyard, where it contacted the particles, dust and feathers from the confinement houses, creating runoff that carried such particles, dust and feathers across a neighboring grassy pasture and into Mudlick Run, a water of the United States [AR1 at 3–4; AR2 at 4–5; AR3].

Ms. Alt does not have a permit pursuant to the CWA or corresponding law of the State of West Virginia authorizing discharges into Mudlick Run [AR1 at 4; AR2 at 3].

EPA asserted its regulatory authority over stormwater runoff from Lois Alt's farmyard by issuing its November 14, 2011, Findings of Violation and Order for Region 3 (hereinafter, the "Order) [AR1]. In its Order, EPA found that Ms. Alt's poultry production facility is a "concentrated animal feeding operation" (CAFO) that "has discharged pollutants from man-made ditches via sheet flow to Mudlick Run during rain events generating runoff without having obtained an NPDES." [AR1, ¶¶ 30, 32]. On that basis, EPA concluded as a matter of law that Ms. Alt is in violation of the CWA and EPA's implementing regulations [AR1 ¶ 33]. EPA said that it could bring a civil action against Ms. Alt for this violation, in which case Ms. Alt "will be subject to civil penalties of up to $37,500 per day of violation . . . "[AR1

¶ 38]. EPA added that a criminal action could be initiated, and that if Ms. Alt were to be convicted she "may be subject to a monetary fine and/or imprisonment . . . " [AR1 ¶¶ 38, 39]. EPA also ordered Ms. Alt to apply for a permit [AR1 ¶ 34].

Plaintiff and Plaintiff-Intervenors move for summary judgment that EPA lacks the authority to issue its Order finding that Ms. Alt violated the CWA when precipitation on her farmyard picked up dust and poultry manure emitted from her poultry house ventilation fans and/or particles of poultry little tracked or spilled from her poultry houses and caused a discharge to Mudlick Run.

The central issue presented by the case is whether the litter found on Ms. Alt's farmyard that could be picked up by rainwater, washed two hundred yards across a grassy cow pasture, and discharged into a creek named Mudlick Run is exempted from liability under the agricultural stormwater exception to the definition of a point source. This issue necessitates a review of the statutory and regulatory history of the Clean Water Act.

"In 1948, Congress enacted the Federal Water Pollution Control Act (FWPCA). FWPCA encouraged states to enact uniform laws to combat water pollution, recognizing 'that water pollution control was primarily the responsibility of state and local governments.' The state-run regulation of discharges 'involved a complex process in which the government was required to trace in-stream pollution back to specific discharges, and, given the difficulty of this task, enforcement was largely nonexistent.' The federal government's power to curtail water pollution was also limited under FWPCA. Thus, federal action against a discharger could only proceed 'with the approval of state officials in the state where the discharge originated and after a complicated series of notices, warnings, hearings, and conference recommendations.'" *National Pork Producers Council v. USEPA*, 635 F.3d 738, 742 (5th Cir.2011)(internal footnotes omitted).

"In 1972, FWPCA was amended to replace the state-run regulation of discharges with an obligation to obtain and comply with a federally-mandated National Pollutant Discharge Elimination System (NPDES) permit program. These amendments also transformed FWPCA into what is known today as the CWA." *Id.* at 742–43. The Clean Water Act "was a dramatic response to accelerating environmental degradation of rivers, lakes and streams in this country. The Act's stated goal is to eliminate the discharge of pollutants into the Nation's waters by 1985. This goal [was] to be achieved through the enforcement of the strict timetables and technology-based effluent limitations established by the Act." *Natural Resources Def. Council v. Costle*, 568 F.2d 1369, 1371 (D.C.Cir.1977).

"The NPDES permit program, which is primarily articulated in 33 U.S.C. § 1342, allows the EPA to 'issue a permit for the discharge of any pollutant, or combination of pollutants. . .' 33 U.S.C. § 1342(a)(1). To be clear, the CWA prohibits the discharge of pollutants into navigable waters. 33 U.S.C. § 1311. However, if a facility requests a permit, it can discharge within certain parameters called effluent limitations and will be deemed a point source. 33 U.S.C. §§ 1342, 1362 (14). Accordingly, the point source will be regulated pursuant to the NPDES permit issued by the EPA or one of 46 States authorized to issue permits." *Pork Producers, supra* at 73.

The term "point source" was originally defined in § 1362(14) as "any discernible, confined and discrete conveyance, including but not limited to any pipe, ditch, channel, tunnel, conduit, well, discrete fissure, container, rolling stock, concentrated animal feeding operation, or vessel or other floating craft, from which pollutants are or may be discharged." *Costle*, at 1373.

In 1987, Congress amended § 1362 (14) to add an exemption to the statutory definition of a point source. As amended, § 1362(14) defined "point source" as "any discernible, confined and discrete conveyance, including but not limited to any pipe, ditch, channel, tunnel, conduit, well, discrete fissure, container, rolling stock, concentrated animal feeding operation, or vessel or other floating craft, from which pollutants are or may be discharged. **This term does not include agricultural stormwater discharges** and return flows from irrigated agriculture." (emphasis added). Nowhere did Congress define the term "agricultural stormwater" nor did the EPA promulgate any regulations defining the term.

For a number of years, this section was interpreted in accordance with its plain meaning. For example, in *Concerned Area Residents for the Environment v. Southview Farm*, 34 F.3d 114 (2nd Cir.1994), the Second Circuit found that liquid manure spreading operations of a large dairy farm were a point source discharge. The Court stated that the real issue was whether the discharges were the result of precipitation.

Similarly, in *Fishermen Against the Destruction of the Environment v. Closer Farms, Inc.*, 300 F.3d 1294 (11th Cir.2002), the Eleventh Circuit found that waters pumped into Lake Okeechobee by Closer Farms was agricultural stormwater.

It appears to be a central assumption of the EPA's position that the agricultural stormwater discharge exemption had no meaning whatsoever from the time the exemption was added to the statute in 1987 until the EPA promulgated its new regulations in 2003. This is an assumption that this Court simply cannot accept.

The term "agricultural stormwater discharge" was not and has not been defined in the statute. The fact that Congress found it unnecessary to define the term indicates that the term should be given its ordinary meaning.

The Act defines "discharge of a pollutant" to mean "any addition of any pollutant to navigable waters from any point source." § 1362(12). Thus, the basic prohibition in section 1311(a) and the requirement to obtain an NPDES permit pursuant to section 1342 apply only to discharges from a *point source.*

The Act defines "point source" as follows:

The term "point source" means any discernible, confined and discrete conveyance, including but not limited to any pipe, ditch, channel, tunnel, conduit, well, discrete fissure, container, rolling stock, *concentrated animal feeding operation,* or vessel or other floating craft, from which pollutants are or may be discharged. The term *does not include agricultural stormwater* discharges and return flows from irrigated agriculture.

§ 1362(14) (emphasis added).

The term generally includes a CAFO, but specifically excludes "agricultural stormwater discharges," even if they are associated with a CAFO or any other type of point source. Therefore, the discharge of pollutants from a CAFO requires an NPDES permit *unless* that discharge is an "agricultural stormwater discharge." Because neither the Act nor EPA's implementing regulations has defined "agricultural stormwater discharges" within the context of CAFO farmyard runoff, it falls to this Court to interpret this statutory term.

This Court must decide the issued based upon the statutory text. The terms "agricultural" and "stormwater" should be given their ordinary meaning in accordance with common usage. *BP v. Burton,* 549 U.S. 84, 91, 127 S.Ct. 638, 166 L.Ed.2d 494 (2006); *Perrin v. United States,* 444 U.S. 37, 42, 100 S.Ct. 311, 62 L.Ed.2d 199 (1979).

Common sense and plain English lead to the inescapable conclusion that Ms. Alt's poultry operation is "agricultural" in nature and that the precipitation-caused runoff from her farmyard is "stormwater."

In 2005 the Second Circuit took the same approach when it reviewed EPA's interpretation of the agricultural stormwater exemption in the context of CAFO land application areas. Examining the term "agricultural," that court said:

Dictionaries from the period in which the agricultural stormwater exemption was adopted define "agriculture" or "agricultural" in a way that can permissibly be construed to encompass CAFOs. For example, Webster's New World Dictionary defined the term "agriculture" to include, *inter alia,* "work of cultivating the soil, producing crops, *and raising livestock.*" WEBSTER'S NEW WORLD DICTIONARY OF AMERICAN ENGLISH 26 (3rd College Ed. 1988). The Oxford English Dictionary similarly defined agriculture to include, *inter alia*, "cultivating the soil, "including the allied pursuits of gathering in the crops and *rearing livestock.*" I The Oxford English Dictionary 267 (2d ed. 1989). Here, there is no question that CAFOs "rais[e]" or "rear" livestock. . . .

Waterkeeper Alliance, Inc. v. EPA, 399 F.3d 486, 509 (2d Cir.2005) (emphases added).

With respect to the term "stormwater," the court agreed with EPA that this should mean "precipitation-related discharge[s]." *Id.* at 508.

Contrary to EPA's present position, it is clear that the agricultural stormwater discharge exemption existed prior to the promulgation of the 2003 regulations.

It is clear, then, that the agricultural stormwater exemption existed prior to the 2003 regulations. Congress, however, has not seen fit to define the term. The EPA, however, has not promulgated any regulations defining the term other than the land application regulations, which was and is an expansion of the preexisting exemption. In fact, in the preamble to the 2003 Rule, the EPA stated that *"EPA does not intend its discussion* of how the scope of point source discharges from a CAFO is limited by the agricultural storm water exemption to apply *to discharges that do not occur as a result of land application* of manure, litter, or process wastewater by a CAFO to land areas under its control . . . " 68 Fed.Reg. at 7,198.

This Court declares that the litter and manure which is washed from the Alt farmyard to navigable waters by a precipitation event is an agricultural stormwater discharge and therefore not a point source discharge, thereby rendering it exempt from the NPDES permit requirement of the Clean Water Act.

NOTES

1.   Federal Clean Water Act regulation does not stop with controls at the (point) source. Other detailed regulations control the amount of pollutants in a defined portion or "segment" of a stream or river in terms of "total maximum daily loads" (TMDLs) of named pollutants, whether from point or non-point sources of pollution. *See Pronsolino v. Nastri*, 291 F.3d 1123 (9th Cir.2002). For the relationship between NPDES permitting and TMDLs, *see Friends of Pinto Creek v. United States EPA*, 504 F.3d 1007 (9th Cir.2007). There, a citizen group sued the EPA for issuing a NPDES permit for a copper mine. The mine adjoined a river that was already contaminated with copper from historical mining activities, and was on Arizona's list of impaired waterways. Although the EPA set TMDLs in the process of granting the permits, there was no compliance schedule for the waterway in place. Hence, the EPA was essentially allowing additional copper to be discharged into an impaired waterway with no plan to bring the waterway into compliance. The court vacated the permit on the basis that "no permit may be issued to a new discharger if the discharge will contribute to the violation of water quality standards." This is not a ban

on discharge of pollution into impaired waters; it is a requirement for a schedule "designed to bring the segment into compliance" before the permit issues.

2.   For the effect of TMDLs on agriculture and subdivision development, *see Hawes v. Oregon*, 125 P.3d 778 (Or.Ct.App.2005), and *Croton Watershed Clean Water Coal. Inc. v. Planning Bd. of Town of Southeast*, 798 N.Y.S.2d 708 (Sup.Ct.2004). In the former, Oregon farmers and ranchers sued the Oregon Department of Environmental Quality, alleging TMDLs imposed by the agency would limit agricultural activities on their waterway-adjacent property. They challenged the agency's authority to impose limits on nonpoint sources. The court dismissed on jurisdictional grounds, holding that the agreement between the DEQ and EPA was only a blueprint for how the state would adopt load limits, not the final agency action implementing that policy. Because the Oregon circuit courts only have jurisdiction to review final agency orders, the court declined to reach the merits of the claim. In the latter, a planning board in upstate New York gave preliminary resubdivision approval for a development located in the watershed for New York City drinking water. Where the board made a finding that post-development pollutant loadings would be reduced to below pre-construction level, the court found that the board adequately considered the development's impact on water quality, and complied with the state-imposed requirements. Hence, the board's decision allowing resubdivision approval was upheld.

2.   WETLANDS AND 404 PERMITS

To many people the idea of "wetlands" conjures up images of dismal, dank, mosquito-ridden, snake-infested, miasmic swamps to either be avoided or paved over. Indeed, this notion has been so prevalent in our nation's collective subconscious that we have destroyed over fifty percent of our wetland resources. They were lost beneath the crunching blow of drag lines and dredges making way for subdivisions, trailer parks, agribusiness and dumps. For those with the above delusion this turn of events may seem just fine; the best swamp is a drained swamp. Yet as a nation, we are just now beginning to realize that wetlands may be the most important (economically, as well as ecologically) of all environmentally sensitive lands.

Juergensmeyer and Roberts, *Land Use Planning and Development Regulation Law* § 11.2 (3rd ed.2012).

The federal agencies charged with enforcing federal wetlands law, the Environmental Protection Agency and the Army Corps of Engineers, define wetlands as "those areas that are inundated or saturated by surface or ground water at a frequency and duration sufficient to support, and that under normal circumstances do support, a prevalence of vegetation typically adapted for life in saturated soil conditions." 33 CFR § 328.3(b)(c)(4). As this definition suggests, wetlands include areas well beyond swamps like the Okefenokee. There are, in fact, many different types of wetlands. Some stay wet year round, some only for a matter of weeks each year, and yet others, affected by tide, are both wet and dry twice a day. Each wetland, regardless of type, provides important services to the surrounding ecosystem, mainly flood control, pollution control, and wildlife habitat. Wetlands often constitute a buffer zone between open bodies of water and uplands. They soak up rainwater like a sponge and limit downstream flooding. Erosion caused by waves also can be slowed by wetlands. Wetlands purify water by providing a bed where pollutants can settle. They are an important wildlife habitat as they provide spawning grounds for fish and shellfish and are home to reptiles and mammals that depend on them for food and shelter. Wetlands are also prime attraction spots for recreation. *See* David A. Salvesen, *Wetlands: Mitigating and Regulating Development Impacts* (1990); William J. Mitsch & James G. Gosselink, *Wetlands* 173 (1986).

Over the past several decades efforts to limit wetland loss have gradually increased. Preservation efforts involve purchase and regulation. Purchasing wetlands typically is the technique employed by private groups, like The Nature Conservancy. In contrast, the federal and state governments, though they possess the power to condemn, generally preserve wetlands by regulation. Professor Malone notes that 21 coastal states regulate tidal wetlands, and 17 states regulate freshwater wetlands. These regulations fall under various statutory rubrics, such as shoreline protection acts, stream encroachment rules, or the regulation of developments of regional impact. See Linda Malone, *Environmental Regulation of Land Use* § 4.29[1] (2002). Since wetlands regulations often severely limit use, takings challenges are common. Such claims are not unique and our coverage of regulatory takings in Chapter 3 covers this issue. The two recurring questions that arise in many wetlands takings cases are (1) defining the unit of property against which to measure the economic loss, i.e., whether to use the "whole parcel" approach, and (2) if a showing of a total loss is made, whether the landowner's proposed alteration of the wetlands violates a background principle of property or nuisance law. *See Palazzolo v. Rhode Island*, 533 U.S. 606 (2001).

SOLID WASTE AGENCY OF NORTHERN COOK COUNTY V. UNITED STATES ARMY CORPS OF ENGINEERS

Supreme Court of the United States, 2001.
531 U.S. 159, 121 S.Ct. 675, 148 L.Ed.2d 576.

CHIEF JUSTICE REHNQUIST delivered the opinion of the Court.

Section 404(a) of the Clean Water Act (CWA or Act), 86 Stat. 884, as amended, 33 U.S.C. § 1344(a), regulates the discharge of dredged or fill material into "navigable waters." The United States Army Corps of Engineers (Corps) has interpreted § 404(a) to confer federal authority over an abandoned sand and gravel pit in northern Illinois which provides habitat for migratory birds. We are asked to decide whether the provisions of § 404(a) may be fairly extended to these waters, and, if so, whether Congress could exercise such authority consistent with the Commerce Clause, U.S. Const., Art. I, § 8, cl.3. We answer the first question in the negative and therefore do not reach the second.

Petitioner, the Solid Waste Agency of Northern Cook County (SWANCC), is a consortium of 23 suburban Chicago cities and villages that united in an effort to locate and develop a disposal site for baled nonhazardous solid waste. The Chicago Gravel Company informed the municipalities of the availability of a 533-acre parcel, bestriding the Illinois counties Cook and Kane, which had been the site of a sand and gravel pit mining operation for three decades up until about 1960. Long since abandoned, the old mining site eventually gave way to a successional stage forest, with its remnant excavation trenches evolving into a scattering of permanent and seasonal ponds of varying size (from under one-tenth of an acre to several acres) and depth (from several inches to several feet).

The municipalities decided to purchase the site for disposal of their baled nonhazardous solid waste. By law, SWANCC was required to file for various permits from Cook County and the State of Illinois before it could begin operation of its balefill project. In addition, because the operation called for the filling of some of the permanent and seasonal ponds, SWANCC contacted federal respondents (hereinafter respondents), including the Corps, to determine if a federal landfill permit was required under § 404(a) of the CWA, 33 U.S.C. § 1344(a).

Section 404(a) grants the Corps authority to issue permits "for the discharge of dredged or fill material into the navigable waters at specified disposal sites." The term "navigable waters" is defined under the Act as "the waters of the United States, including the territorial seas." § 1362(7). The Corps has issued regulations defining the term "waters of the United States" to include

> "waters such as intrastate lakes, rivers, streams (including intermittent streams), mudflats, sandflats, wetlands, sloughs, prairie potholes, wet meadows, playa lakes, or natural ponds, the use, degradation or destruction of which could affect interstate or foreign commerce. . . ." 33 CFR § 328.3(a)(3) (1999).

In 1986, in an attempt to "clarify" the reach of its jurisdiction, the Corps stated that § 404(a) extends to intrastate waters:

> "a. Which are or would be used as habitat by birds protected by Migratory Bird Treaties; or
>
> "b. Which are or would be used as habitat by other migratory birds which cross state lines; or

"c. Which are or would be used as habitat for endangered species; or

"d. Used to irrigate crops sold in interstate commerce." 51 Fed.Reg. 41217.

This last promulgation has been dubbed the "Migratory Bird Rule."[3]

The Corps initially concluded that it had no jurisdiction over the site because it contained no "wetlands," or areas which support "vegetation typically adapted for life in saturated soil conditions," 33 CFR § 328.3(b) (1999). However, after the Illinois Nature Preserves Commission informed the Corps that a number of migratory bird species had been observed at the site, the Corps reconsidered and ultimately asserted jurisdiction over the balefill site pursuant to subpart (b) of the "Migratory Bird Rule." The Corps found that approximately 121 bird species had been observed at the site, including several known to depend upon aquatic environments for a significant portion of their life requirements. Thus, on November 16, 1987, the Corps formally "determined that the seasonally ponded, abandoned gravel mining depressions located on the project site, while not wetlands, did qualify as 'waters of the United States' . . . based upon the following criteria: (1) the proposed site had been abandoned as a gravel mining operation; (2) the water areas and spoil piles had developed a natural character; and (3) the water areas are used as habitat by migratory bird [sic] which cross state lines."

During the application process, SWANCC made several proposals to mitigate the likely displacement of the migratory birds and to preserve a great blue heron rookery located on the site. Its balefill project ultimately received the necessary local and state approval. By 1993, SWANCC had received a special use planned development permit from the Cook County Board of Appeals, a landfill development permit from the Illinois Environmental Protection Agency, and approval from the Illinois Department of Conservation.

Despite SWANCC's securing the required water quality certification from the Illinois Environmental Protection Agency, the Corps refused to issue a § 404(a) permit. The Corps found that SWANCC had not established that its proposal was the "least environmentally damaging, most practicable alternative" for disposal of nonhazardous solid waste; that SWANCC's failure to set aside sufficient funds to remediate leaks posed an "unacceptable risk to the public's drinking water supply"; and that the impact of the project upon area-sensitive species was "unmitigatable since a landfill surface cannot be redeveloped into a forested habitat."

Petitioner filed suit under the Administrative Procedure Act, 5 U.S.C. § 701 et seq., in the Northern District of Illinois challenging both the Corps'

---

3   [Ct's fn 1] The Corps issued the "Migratory Bird Rule" without following the notice and comment procedures outlined in the Administrative Procedure Act, 5 U.S.C. § 553.

jurisdiction over the site and the merits of its denial of the § 404(a) permit. The District Court granted summary judgment to respondents on the jurisdictional issue, and petitioner abandoned its challenge to the Corps' permit decision. On appeal to the Court of Appeals for the Seventh Circuit, petitioner renewed its attack on respondents' use of the "Migratory Bird Rule" to assert jurisdiction over the site. Petitioner argued that respondents had exceeded their statutory authority in interpreting the CWA to cover nonnavigable, isolated, intrastate waters based upon the presence of migratory birds and, in the alternative, that Congress lacked the power under the Commerce Clause to grant such regulatory jurisdiction.

The Court of Appeals began its analysis with the constitutional question, holding that Congress has the authority to regulate such waters based upon "the cumulative impact doctrine, under which a single activity that itself has no discernible effect on interstate commerce may still be regulated if the aggregate effect of that class of activity has a substantial impact on interstate commerce." 191 F.3d 845, 850 (C.A.7 1999). The aggregate effect of the "destruction of the natural habitat of migratory birds" on interstate commerce, the court held, was substantial because each year millions of Americans cross state lines and spend over a billion dollars to hunt and observe migratory birds.[4] The Court of Appeals then turned to the regulatory question. The court held that the CWA reaches as many waters as the Commerce Clause allows and, given its earlier Commerce Clause ruling, it therefore followed that respondents' "Migratory Bird Rule" was a reasonable interpretation of the Act.

Congress passed the CWA for the stated purpose of "restor[ing] and maintain[ing] the chemical, physical, and biological integrity of the Nation's waters." 33 U.S.C. § 1251(a). In so doing, Congress chose to "recognize, preserve, and protect the primary responsibilities and rights of States to prevent, reduce, and eliminate pollution, to plan the development and use (including restoration, preservation, and enhancement) of land and water resources, and to consult with the Administrator in the exercise of his authority under this chapter." § 1251(b). Relevant here, § 404(a) authorizes respondents to regulate the discharge of fill material into "navigable waters," 33 U.S.C. § 1344(a), which the statute defines as "the waters of the United States, including the territorial seas," § 1362(7). Respondents have interpreted these words to cover the abandoned gravel pit at issue here because it is used as habitat for migratory birds. We conclude that the "Migratory Bird Rule" is not fairly supported by the CWA.

---

⁴ [Ct's fn 2] Relying upon its earlier decision in *Hoffman Homes, Inc. v. EPA,* 999 F.2d 256 (C.A.7 1993), and a report from the United States Census Bureau, the Court of Appeals found that in 1996 approximately 3.1 million Americans spent $1.3 billion to hunt migratory birds (with 11 percent crossing state lines to do so) as another 17.7 million Americans observed migratory birds (with 9.5 million traveling for the purpose of observing shorebirds). See 191 F.3d, at 850.

This is not the first time we have been called upon to evaluate the meaning of § 404(a). In *United States v. Riverside Bayview Homes, Inc.*, 474 U.S. 121 (1985), we held that the Corps had § 404(a) jurisdiction over wetlands that actually abutted on a navigable waterway. In so doing, we noted that the term "navigable" is of "limited import" and that Congress evidenced its intent to "regulate at least some waters that would not be deemed 'navigable' under the classical understanding of that term." But our holding was based in large measure upon Congress' unequivocal acquiescence to, and approval of, the Corps' regulations interpreting the CWA to cover wetlands adjacent to navigable waters. We found that Congress' concern for the protection of water quality and aquatic ecosystems indicated its intent to regulate wetlands "inseparably bound up with the 'waters' of the United States."

It was the significant nexus between the wetlands and "navigable waters" that informed our reading of the CWA in Riverside Bayview Homes. Indeed, we did not "express any opinion" on the "question of the authority of the Corps to regulate discharges of fill material into wetlands that are not adjacent to bodies of open water. . . ." In order to rule for respondents here, we would have to hold that the jurisdiction of the Corps extends to ponds that are not adjacent to open water. But we conclude that the text of the statute will not allow this.

Indeed, the Corps' original interpretation of the CWA, promulgated two years after its enactment, is inconsistent with that which it espouses here. Its 1974 regulations defined § 404(a)'s "navigable waters" to mean "those waters of the United States which are subject to the ebb and flow of the tide, and/or are presently, or have been in the past, or may be in the future susceptible for use for purposes of interstate or foreign commerce." 33 CFR § 209.120(d)(1). The Corps emphasized that "[i]t is the water body's capability of use by the public for purposes of transportation or commerce which is the determinative factor." § 209.260(e)(1). Respondents put forward no persuasive evidence that the Corps mistook Congress' intent in 1974.[5]

Respondents next contend that whatever its original aim in 1972, Congress charted a new course five years later when it approved the more expansive definition of "navigable waters" found in the Corps' 1977 regulations. In July 1977, the Corps formally adopted 33 CFR § 323.2(a)(5) (1978), which defined "waters of the United States" to include "isolated wetlands and lakes, intermittent streams, prairie potholes, and other

---

[5]   [Ct's fn 3] Respondents refer us to portions of the legislative history that they believe indicate Congress' intent to expand the definition of "navigable waters." Although the Conference Report includes the statement that the conferees "intend that the term 'navigable waters' be given the broadest possible constitutional interpretation," S.Conf.Rep. No. 92 (1236, p. 144 (1972), U.S.Code Cong. & Admin.News 1972 pp. 3668, 3822, neither this, nor anything else in the legislative history to which respondents point, signifies that Congress intended to exert anything more than its commerce power over navigation. Indeed, respondents admit that the legislative history is somewhat ambiguous.

waters that are not part of a tributary system to interstate waters or to navigable waters of the United States, the degradation or destruction of which could affect interstate commerce." Respondents argue that Congress was aware of this more expansive interpretation during its 1977 amendments to the CWA. Specifically, respondents point to a failed House bill, H.R. 3199, that would have defined "navigable waters" as "all waters which are presently used, or are susceptible to use in their natural condition or by reasonable improvement as a means to transport interstate or foreign commerce." 123 Cong. Rec. 10420, 10434 (1977). They also point to the passage in § 404(g)(1) that authorizes a State to apply to the Environmental Protection Agency for permission "to administer its own individual and general permit program for the discharge of dredged or fill material into the navigable waters (other than those waters which are presently used, or are susceptible to use in their natural condition or by reasonable improvement as a means to transport interstate or foreign commerce . . . , including wetlands adjacent thereto) within its jurisdiction. . . ." 33 U.S.C. § 1344(g)(1). The failure to pass legislation that would have overturned the Corps' 1977 regulations and the extension of jurisdiction in § 404(g) to waters "other than" traditional "navigable waters," respondents submit, indicate that Congress recognized and accepted a broad definition of "navigable waters" that includes nonnavigable, isolated, intrastate waters.

Although we have recognized congressional acquiescence to administrative interpretations of a statute in some situations, we have done so with extreme care. "[F]ailed legislative proposals are 'a particularly dangerous ground on which to rest an interpretation of a prior statute.'" *Central Bank of Denver, N.A. v. First Interstate Bank of Denver, N.A.*, 511 U.S. 164, 187 (1994) (quoting *Pension Benefit Guaranty Corporation v. LTV Corp.*, 496 U.S. 633, 650 (1990)). A bill can be proposed for any number of reasons, and it can be rejected for just as many others. The relationship between the actions and inactions of the 95th Congress and the intent of the 92d Congress in passing § 404(a) is also considerably attenuated. Because "subsequent history is less illuminating than the contemporaneous evidence," *Hagen v. Utah*, 510 U.S. 399, 420 (1994), respondents face a difficult task in overcoming the plain text and import of § 404(a).

We conclude that respondents have failed to make the necessary showing that the failure of the 1977 House bill demonstrates Congress' acquiescence to the Corps' regulations or the "Migratory Bird Rule," which, of course, did not first appear until 1986. Although respondents cite some legislative history showing Congress' recognition of the Corps' assertion of jurisdiction over "isolated waters,"[6] as we explained in Riverside Bayview

---

6   [Ct's fn 4] Respondents cite, for example, the Senate Report on S.1952, which referred to the Corps' "isolated waters" regulation. See S.Rep. No. 95–370, p. 75 (1977), U.S.Code Cong. &

Homes, "[i]n both Chambers, debate on the proposals to narrow the definition of navigable waters centered largely on the issue of wetlands preservation." Beyond Congress' desire to regulate wetlands adjacent to "navigable waters," respondents point us to no persuasive evidence that the House bill was proposed in response to the Corps' claim of jurisdiction over nonnavigable, isolated, intrastate waters or that its failure indicated congressional acquiescence to such jurisdiction.

Section 404(g) is equally unenlightening. In Riverside Bayview Homes we recognized that Congress intended the phrase "navigable waters" to include "at least some waters that would not be deemed 'navigable' under the classical understanding of that term." But § 404(g) gives no intimation of what those waters might be; it simply refers to them as "other . . . waters." Respondents conjecture that "other . . . waters" must incorporate the Corps' 1977 regulations, but it is also plausible, as petitioner contends, that Congress simply wanted to include all waters adjacent to "navigable waters," such as nonnavigable tributaries and streams. The exact meaning of § 404(g) is not before us and we express no opinion on it, but for present purposes it is sufficient to say, as we did in Riverside Bayview Homes, that "§ 404(g)(1) does not conclusively determine the construction to be placed on the use of the term 'waters' elsewhere in the Act (particularly in § 502(7), which contains the relevant definition of 'navigable waters'). . . ."

We thus decline respondents' invitation to take what they see as the next ineluctable step after Riverside Bayview Homes: holding that isolated ponds, some only seasonal, wholly located within two Illinois counties, fall under § 404(a)'s definition of "navigable waters" because they serve as habitat for migratory birds. As counsel for respondents conceded at oral argument, such a ruling would assume that "the use of the word navigable in the statute . . . does not have any independent significance." We cannot agree that Congress' separate definitional use of the phrase "waters of the United States" constitutes a basis for reading the term "navigable waters" out of the statute. We said in Riverside Bayview Homes that the word "navigable" in the statute was of "limited import" 474 U.S., at 133, and went on to hold that § 404(a) extended to nonnavigable wetlands adjacent to open waters. But it is one thing to give a word limited effect and quite another to give it no effect whatever. The term "navigable" has at least the import of showing us what Congress had in mind as its authority for enacting the CWA: its traditional jurisdiction over waters that were or had been navigable in fact or which could reasonably be so made.

Respondents—relying upon all of the arguments addressed above—contend that, at the very least, it must be said that Congress did not address the precise question of § 404(a)'s scope with regard to nonnavigable, isolated, intrastate waters, and that, therefore, we should

---

Admin.News 1977 pp. 4326, 4400. However, the same report reiterated that "[t]he committee amendment does not redefine navigable waters."

give deference to the "Migratory Bird Rule." See, e.g., *Chevron U.S.A., Inc. v. Natural Resources Defense Council, Inc.*, 467 U.S. 837 (1984). We find § 404(a) to be clear, but even were we to agree with respondents, we would not extend Chevron deference here.

Where an administrative interpretation of a statute invokes the outer limits of Congress' power, we expect a clear indication that Congress intended that result. *See Edward J. DeBartolo Corp. v. Florida Gulf Coast Building & Constr. Trades Council*, 485 U.S. 568, 575 (1988). This requirement stems from our prudential desire not to needlessly reach constitutional issues and our assumption that Congress does not casually authorize administrative agencies to interpret a statute to push the limit of congressional authority. This concern is heightened where the administrative interpretation alters the federal-state framework by permitting federal encroachment upon a traditional state power. * * *

Twice in the past six years we have reaffirmed the proposition that the grant of authority to Congress under the Commerce Clause, though broad, is not unlimited. *See United States v. Morrison*, 529 U.S. 598 (2000); *United States v. Lopez*, 514 U.S. 549 (1995). Respondents argue that the "Migratory Bird Rule" falls within Congress' power to regulate intrastate activities that "substantially affect" inter-state commerce. They note that the protection of migratory birds is a "national interest of very nearly the first magnitude," *Missouri v. Holland*, 252 U.S. 416, 435 (1920), and that, as the Court of Appeals found, millions of people spend over a billion dollars annually on recreational pursuits relating to migratory birds. These arguments raise significant constitutional questions. For example, we would have to evaluate the precise object or activity that, in the aggregate, substantially affects interstate commerce. This is not clear, for although the Corps has claimed jurisdiction over petitioner's land because it contains water areas used as habitat by migratory birds, respondents now, post litem motam, focus upon the fact that the regulated activity is petitioner's municipal landfill, which is "plainly of a commercial nature." But this is a far cry, indeed, from the "navigable waters" and "waters of the United States" to which the statute by its terms extends.

These are significant constitutional questions raised by respondents' application of their regulations, and yet we find nothing approaching a clear statement from Congress that it intended § 404(a) to reach an abandoned sand and gravel pit such as we have here. Permitting respondents to claim federal jurisdiction over ponds and mudflats falling within the "Migratory Bird Rule" would result in a significant impingement of the States' traditional and primary power over land and water use. *See, e.g., Hess v. Port Authority Trans-Hudson Corporation*, 513 U.S. 30, 44 (1994) ("[R]egulation of land use [is] a function traditionally performed by local governments"). Rather than expressing a desire to readjust the federal-state balance in this manner, Congress chose to "recognize, preserve, and protect the primary responsibilities and rights of States . . . to plan the development and use . . . of land and water resources. . . ." 33 U.S.C. § 1251(b). We thus read the statute as written to avoid the significant constitutional and federalism questions raised by respondents' interpretation, and therefore reject the request for administrative deference.

We hold that 33 CFR § 328.3(a)(3) (1999), as clarified and applied to petitioner's balefill site pursuant to the "Migratory Bird Rule," 51 Fed.Reg. 41217 (1986), exceeds the authority granted to respondents under § 404(a) of the CWA. The judgment of the Court of Appeals for the Seventh Circuit is therefore REVERSED.

JUSTICE STEVENS, with whom JUSTICE SOUTER, JUSTICE GINSBURG, and JUSTICE BREYER join, dissenting.

In 1969, the Cuyahoga River in Cleveland, Ohio, coated with a slick of industrial waste, caught fire. Congress responded to that dramatic event, and to others like it, by enacting the Federal Water Pollution Control Act (FWPCA) Amendments of 1972, commonly known as the Clean Water Act (Clean Water Act, CWA, or Act). The Act proclaimed the ambitious goal of ending water pollution by 1985. § 1251(a). The Court's past interpretations of the CWA have been fully consistent with that goal. Although Congress' vision of zero pollution remains unfulfilled, its pursuit has unquestionably retarded the destruction of the aquatic environment. Our Nation's waters no longer burn. Today, however, the Court takes an unfortunate step that needlessly weakens our principal safeguard against toxic water.

It is fair to characterize the Clean Water Act as "watershed" legislation. The statute endorsed fundamental changes in both the purpose and the scope of federal regulation of the Nation's waters. In § 13 of the Rivers and Harbors Appropriation Act of 1899 (RHA), 30 Stat. 1152, as amended, 33 U.S.C. § 407, Congress had assigned to the Army Corps of Engineers (Corps) the mission of regulating discharges into certain waters in order to protect their use as highways for the transportation of interstate and foreign commerce; the scope of the Corps' jurisdiction under the RHA accordingly extended only to waters that were "navigable." In the CWA, however, Congress broadened the Corps' mission to include the purpose of protecting the quality of our Nation's waters for esthetic, health, recreational, and environmental uses. The scope of its jurisdiction was therefore redefined to encompass all of "the waters of the United States, including the territorial seas." § 1362(7). That definition requires neither actual nor potential navigability.

The Court has previously held that the Corps' broadened jurisdiction under the CWA properly included an 80-acre parcel of low-lying marshy land that was not itself navigable, directly adjacent to navigable water, or even hydrologically connected to navigable water, but which was part of a larger area, characterized by poor drainage, that ultimately abutted a navigable creek. *United States v. Riverside Bayview Homes, Inc.*, 474 U.S. 121 (1985). Our broad finding in Riverside Bayview that the 1977 Congress had acquiesced in the Corps' understanding of its jurisdiction applies equally to the 410-acre parcel at issue here. Moreover, once Congress crossed the legal watershed that separates navigable streams of commerce from marshes and inland lakes, there is no principled reason for limiting the statute's protection to those waters or wetlands that happen to lie near a navigable stream.

In its decision today, the Court draws a new jurisdictional line, one that invalidates the 1986 migratory bird regulation as well as the Corps' assertion of jurisdiction over all waters except for actually navigable waters, their tributaries, and wetlands adjacent to each. Its holding rests on two equally untenable premises: (1) that when Congress passed the 1972 CWA, it did not intend "to exert anything more than its commerce power over navigation," and (2) that in 1972 Congress drew the boundary defining the Corps' jurisdiction at the odd line on which the Court today settles.

As I explain, the text of the 1972 amendments affords no support for the Court's holding, and amendments Congress adopted in 1977 do support the Corps' present interpretation of its mission as extending to so-called "isolated" waters. Indeed, simple common sense cuts against the particular definition of the Corps' jurisdiction favored by the majority.

Because I would affirm the judgment of the Court of Appeals, I respectfully dissent.

NOTES

1. The majority's charge that there "are significant constitutional questions raised by" the Corps' application of its regulation to isolated waters is particularly ominous after the groundbreaking Commerce Clause cases of *Lopez* and *Morrison* described by the dissent. Is the regulation of wetlands a local land use issue or a national environmental issue? Does it make sense to distinguish between regulations by using the labels "land use" and "environmental"? See the controversial attempt by the U.S. Supreme Court to so distinguish in *California Coastal Comm'n v. Granite Rock Co.*, 480 U.S. 572 (1987). For recent decisions testing the validity of the Endangered Species Act under the Commerce Clause, see note 1 following National Association of Home Builders v. Babbitt in Section A. Are the Commerce Clause connections of endangered plants and wildlife similar to wetlands?

2. Does *SWANCC* limit the Corps' jurisdiction under the CWA to navigable waters and waters adjacent to them? Certainly, a non-navigable tributary of a navigable stream is covered. But what about a man-made ditch? Is that a tributary?

Lower courts have differed on the impact of *SWANCC*. In addition to the Fourth Circuit in Deaton, at least three other circuits have given *SWANCC* a narrow reading, allowing the Corps to exercise jurisdiction where there is an indirect hydrologic connection: the Sixth, *United States v. Rapanos*, 339 F.3d 447 (6th Cir.2003), Seventh, *United States v. Krilich*, 303 F.3d 784 (7th Cir.2002), and Ninth, *Headwaters, Inc. v. Talent Irrigation Dist.*, 243 F.3d 526 (9th Cir.2001). The Fifth Circuit has disagreed, finding *SWANCC* requires a navigable waterway or adjacency to navigable waterway. *Rice v. Harken Exploration Co.*, 250 F.3d 264 (5th Cir.2001). See Lawrence Liebesman, *Judicial, Administrative, and Congressional Responses to SWANCC*, 33 ENVTL.L.REP. 10899 (2003). In the face of continued Corps intransigence over the limits of its jurisdiction as suggested in *SWANCC*, the U.S. Supreme Court attempted to tighten the definition of wetlands subject to Corps regulation in *Rapanos v. United States*, 547 U.S. 715 (2006). However, the Court was unable to concur on much beyond the need for a "nexus" between a wetland and a waterway, leaving the entire field so fact-specific that anything beyond *SWANCC's* holding remains speculative.

3.   Regulating wetlands based on the discharge language of § 404 results in less than comprehensive protection. The language does not cover the draining of a wetland, a major loophole. *See Save Our Community v. United States Envtl. Protection Agency*, 971 F.2d 1155, 1158, n. 5 (5th Cir.1992). The Corps of Engineers adopted a rule in 1993 that partially closed this loophole by defining a discharge as "any addition of dredged material * * * including any redeposit of dredged material" into a wetland. C.F.R. § 323.2(d)(1). The rule covered so-called incidental "fallback," the inevitable redeposit of some material that occurs with any dredging. This so-call Tulloch rule (named after a settlement in *North Carolina Wildlife Federation v. Tulloch*, Civ. No. C90–713–CIV–5–BO (E.D.N.C.1992)) was held invalid in *National Mining Association v. United States Army Corps of Engineers*, 145 F.3d 1399 (D.C.Cir.1998). *See* Joseph J. Kalo, *"Now Open for Development?": The Present State of Regulation of Activities in North Carolina Wetlands*, 79 N.C.L.REV. 1667 (2001). After the National Mining decision, the Corps issued a new rule that gave the decision a narrow reading. The new regulations replaced "any redeposit of dredged material" with "redeposit of dredged material other than incidental fallback." Then, in a footnote, the Corps stated that "incidental fallback results in the return of dredged material to virtually the spot from which it came." 33 C.F.R. § 323.2(d)(2). *See Greenfield Mills, Inc. v. O'Bannon*, 189 F.Supp.2d 893 (N.D.Ind.2002), applying the new regulation. *See also* J. Juergensmeyer & T. Roberts, *Land Use Planning and Development Regulation Law* § 11.11 (2003).

4.   As the previous cases discussed, however, the consequences of discharging pollutants into the "waters of the United States" without a permit are high and can include both civil and criminal penalties. As a safeguard, landowners may request a jurisdictional determination ("JD") from the Army Corps of Engineers before engaging in activity on the land. The agency may issue either a "preliminary" or "approved" JD. Preliminary JD's conclude only that waters may be present, and binds the landowner and both the Army Corps of Engineers and the Environmental Protection Agency to that determination

for five years. *United States Army Corps of Engineers v. Hawkes Co., Inc., et. al.*, 136 S.Ct. 1807, 578 U.S. ____ (2016).

Until *United States Army Corps of Engineers v. Hawkes Co., Inc., et. al.*, property owners could not seek judicial review of an approved JD and were forced to either proceed with the activity on their land and risk an enforcement action, or complete the full permitting process and then appeal the agency's decision. 578 U.S. ____ (2016). In *Hawkes*, the Army Corps of Engineers issued three peat-mining companies an approved JD for a 530-acre tract they owned that contained wetlands. The Corps determined that the wetlands "had a significant nexus" to a river located 120 miles away. In order to obtain judicial review of the decision, the companies would be required to complete the full NPDES permitting process at a cost estimated over $100,000. Upon Writ of Certiorari, the Supreme Court held that the issuance of an approved JD is a final agency action subject to administrative review under the Administrative Procedure Act, enabling land owners to resolve JD issues without expending significant sums to complete the permitting process or risking civil and criminal penalties for non-compliance. *United States Army Corps of Engineers v. Hawks Co., Inc., et. al.*, 136 S.Ct. 1807, 578 U.S. ____ (2016).

5.   In 2015, the United States Army Corps of Engineers and the Environmental Protection Agency published a new definitional rule purporting "through increased use of bright-lined boundaries" to make "the process of identifying waters protected under the Clean Water Act easier to understand, more predictable and consistent with the law and peer reviewed science, while protecting the streams and wetlands that form the foundation of our nation's water resources." 80 Fed.Reg. 37,054 (June 29, 2015).

Eighteen states challenged the validity of the rule on the basis that the definitional changes "effect an expansion of respondent agencies' regulatory jurisdiction and dramatically alter the existing balance of federal-state collaboration in restoring and maintaining the integrity of the nation's waters." The petitioners further argued that the new "bright-line tests" for establishing a nexus to waters of the United States is not in line with prior Supreme Court holdings and that the agency did not follow the proper rulemaking procedure. While the Sixth Circuit only reached jurisdictional issues, it noted that the "practical effect" of the new rule will be "to *indirectly* produce various limitations on point-source operators and permit issuing authorities." *In re U.S. Dept. of Def., U.S. E.P.A. Final Rule: Clean Water Rule: Definition of Waters of U.S.*, 817 F.3d 261, 270 (6th Cir.2016). Until the matter is resolved, the implementation of the rule has been stayed. *In re E.P.A.*, 803 F.3d 804, 805 (6th Cir.2015). (Clean Water Rule: Definition of "Waters of the United States," 80 FR 37054–01.

C. COASTAL ZONE MANAGEMENT

The regulation and management of coastal areas has been a selective policy of coastal states and local governments for decades. Land development pressures on coastal areas are intense, and the potential for overuse great. *See* Ian L. McHarg, *Design with Nature* 15–17 (1969). In an attempt to control such development, many state and local governments passed land use regulations substantially more stringent than elsewhere in order to protect unique coastal resources. Many state and local governments failed to address such coastal management problems, raising concerns that balkanized coastal protection efforts would have dire consequences for the nation's fragile coastal resources. *See* J. Clarke, *Coastal Ecosystems: Ecological Considerations for Managing the Coastal Zone* (1974). The result was a national attempt to deal with the conflicting demands being made of the coast by means of the Federal Coastal Zone Management Act of 1972. As with many federal programs, this one depends entirely on state and local land use regulation, but in accordance with federal standards and criteria set out in the Act and regulations promulgated in accordance with its directives.

As the following materials indicate, the Department of Commerce's National Oceanic and Atmospheric Administration offered a combination of federal money for program development and implementation, and limited control over otherwise exempt (from state/local control) federal actions affecting the coastal zone, in exchange for local and/or state regulation of the coastal zone. *The Newest Federalism: A New Framework for Coastal Issues* (T. Galloway ed.1982). Thirty-four of the thirty-five eligible states participate in the federal program. From a land use regulation perspective, the Act raises a number of issues. What is the federal regulatory role in coastal zone management? What kinds of local regulations will "pass muster" under the Act? Are restrictive coastal zone land use regulations any less vulnerable to Fifth Amendment takings challenges for fulfilling federal criteria and standards? What is consistency and who makes the determination?

Coastal Zone Management Act of 1972, 16 U.S.C.A. § 1451, et seq.

§ 1451. Congressional findings

The Congress finds that—

(a) There is a national interest in the effective management, beneficial use, protection, and development of the coastal zone.

(b) The coastal zone is rich in a variety of natural, commercial, recreational, ecological, industrial, and esthetic resources of immediate and potential value to the present and future well-being of the Nation.

(c) The increasing and competing demands upon the lands and waters of our coastal zone occasioned by population growth and economic development, including requirements for industry, commerce, residential development, recreation, extraction of mineral resources and fossil fuels, transportation and navigation, waste disposal, and harvesting of fish, shellfish, and other living marine resources, have resulted in the loss of living marine resources, wildlife, nutrient-rich areas, permanent and adverse changes to ecological systems, decreasing open space for public use, and shoreline erosion.

(d) The [1990] habitat areas of the coastal zone, and the fish, shellfish, other living marine resources, and wildlife therein, are ecologically fragile and consequently extremely vulnerable to destruction by man's alterations.

(e) Important ecological, cultural, historic, and esthetic values in the coastal zone which are essential to the well-being of all citizens are being irretrievably damaged or lost.

[1980] (f) New and expanding demands for food, energy, minerals, defense needs, recreation, waste disposal, transportation, and industrial activities in the Great Lakes, territorial sea, [1990] exclusive economic zone, [1980] and Outer Continental Shelf are placing stress on these areas and are creating the need for resolution of serious conflicts among important and competing uses and values in coastal and ocean waters;

(g) Special natural and scenic characteristics are being damaged by ill-planned development that threatens these values.

(h) In light of competing demands and the urgent need to protect and to give high priority to natural systems in the coastal zone, present state and local institutional arrangements for planning and regulating land and water uses in such areas are inadequate.

(i) The key to more effective protection and use of the land and water resources of the coastal zone is to encourage the states to exercise their full authority over the lands and waters in the coastal zone by assisting the states, in cooperation with Federal and local governments and other vitally affected interests, in developing land and water use programs for the coastal zone, including unified policies, criteria, standards, methods, and processes for dealing with land and water use decisions of more than local significance.

(j) The national objective of attaining a greater degree of energy self-sufficiency would be advanced by providing Federal financial assistance to meet state and local needs resulting from new or expanded energy activity in or affecting the coastal zone.

[1990] (k) Land uses in the coastal zone, and the uses of adjacent lands which drain into the coastal zone, may significantly affect the quality of coastal waters and habitats, and efforts to control coastal water pollution from land use activities must be improved.

(*l*) Because global warming may result in a substantial sea level rise with serious adverse effects in the coastal zone, coastal states must anticipate and plan for such an occurrence.

(m) Because of their proximity to and reliance upon the ocean and its resources, the coastal states have substantial and significant interests in the protection, management, and development of the resources of the exclusive economic zone that can only be served by the active participation of coastal states in all Federal programs affecting such resources and, wherever appropriate, by the development of state ocean resource plans as part of their federally approved coastal zone management programs.

§ 1452.   Congressional declaration of policy

[1980] The Congress finds and declares that it is the national policy—

(1) to preserve, protect, develop, and where possible, to restore or enhance, the resources of the Nation's coastal zone for this and succeeding generations;

(2) to encourage and assist the states to exercise effectively their responsibilities in the coastal zone through the development and implementation of management programs to achieve wise use of the land and water resources of the coastal zone, giving full consideration to ecological, cultural, historic, and esthetic values [1990] as well as the needs for compatible [1980] economic development, which programs should at least provide for—

(A) the protection of natural resources, including wetlands, floodplains, estuaries, beaches, dunes, barrier islands, coral reefs, and fish and wildlife and their habitat, within the coastal zone,

(B) the management of coastal development to minimize the loss of life and property caused by improper development in flood-prone, storm surge, geological hazard, and erosion-prone areas and in areas [1990] likely to be affected by or vulnerable to sea level rise, land subsidence, [1980] and saltwater intrusion, and by the destruction of natural protective features such as beaches, dunes, wetlands, and barrier islands,

[1990] (C) the management of coastal development to improve, safeguard, and restore the quality of coastal waters, and to protect natural resources and existing uses of those waters,

(D) priority consideration being given to coastal-dependent uses and orderly processes for siting major facilities related to national defense, energy, fisheries development, recreation, ports and transportation, and the location, to the maximum extent practicable, of new commercial and industrial developments in or adjacent to areas where such development already exists,

(E) public access to the coasts for recreation purposes,

(F) assistance in the redevelopment of deteriorating urban waterfronts and ports, and sensitive preservation and restoration of historic, cultural, and esthetic coastal features,

(G) the coordination and simplification of procedures in order to ensure expedited governmental decisionmaking for the management of coastal resources,

(H) continued consultation and coordination with, and the giving of adequate consideration to the views of, affected Federal agencies,

(I) the giving of timely and effective notification of, and opportunities for public and local government participation in, coastal management decisionmaking,

(J) assistance to support comprehensive planning, conservation, and management for living marine resources, including planning for the siting of pollution control and aquaculture facilities within the coastal zone, and improved coordination between State and Federal coastal zone management agencies and State and wildlife agencies, and

[1990] (K) the study and development, in any case in which the Secretary considers it to be appropriate, of plans for addressing the adverse effects upon the coastal zone of land subsidence and of sea level rise; and

(3) to encourage the preparation of special area management plans which provide for increased specificity in protecting significant natural resources, reasonable coastal-dependent economic growth, improved protection of life and property in hazardous areas, including [1990] those areas likely to be affected by land subsidence, sea level rise, or fluctuating water levels of the Great Lakes, and improved predictability in governmental decisionmaking;

(4) to encourage the participation and cooperation of the public, state and local governments, and interstate and other regional agencies, as well as of the Federal agencies having programs affecting the coastal zone, in carrying out the purposes of this title;

[1990] (5) to encourage coordination and cooperation with and among the appropriate Federal, State, and local agencies, and international organizations where appropriate, in collection, analysis, synthesis, and dissemination of coastal management information, research results, and technical assistance, to support State and Federal regulation of land use practices affecting the coastal and ocean resources of the United States; and

(6) to respond to changing circumstances affecting the coastal environment and coastal resource management by encouraging States to consider such issues as ocean uses potentially affecting the coastal zone.

§ 1453. Definitions

For the purposes of this title—

(1) The term "coastal zone" means the coastal waters (including the lands therein and thereunder) and the adjacent shorelands (including the waters

therein and thereunder), strongly influenced by each other and in proximity to the shorelines of the several coastal states, and includes islands, transitional and intertidal areas, salt marshes, wetlands, and beaches. The zone extends, in Great Lakes waters, to the international boundary between the United States and Canada and, in other areas, seaward to the outer limit of State title and ownership under the Submerged Lands Act (*43 U.S.C. 1301* et seq.), the Act of March 2, 1917 (*48 U.S.C. 749*), the Covenant to Establish a Commonwealth of the Northern Mariana Islands in Political Union with the United States of America, as approved by the Act of March 24, 1976 (*48 U.S.C. 1681* note), or section 1 of the Act of November 20, 1963 (*48 U.S.C. 1705*), as applicable. The zone extends inland from the shorelines only to the extent necessary to control shorelands, the uses of which have a direct and significant impact on the coastal waters, and to control those [1990] geographical areas which are likely to be affected by or vulnerable to sea level rise. Excluded from the coastal zone are lands the use of which is by law subject solely to the discretion of or which is held in trust by the Federal Government, its officers or agents.

[1980] (2) The term "coastal resource of national significance" means any coastal wetland, beach, dune, barrier island, reef, estuary, or fish and wildlife habitat, if any such area is determined by a coastal state to be of substantial biological or natural storm protective value.

(3) The term "coastal waters" means (A) in the Great Lakes area, the waters within the territorial jurisdiction of the United States consisting of the Great Lakes, their connecting waters, harbors, roadsteads, and estuary-type areas such as bays, shallows, and marshes and (B) in other areas, those waters, adjacent to the shorelines, which contain a measurable quantity or percentage of sea water, including, but not limited to, sounds, bays, lagoons, bayous, ponds, and estuaries.

§ 1455.   Administrative grants

[1986] (a) Authorization; matching funds. The Secretary may make grants to any coastal state for the purpose of administering that state's management program, if the state matches any such grant according to the following ratios of Federal-to-State contributions for the applicable fiscal year:

(1)   For those States for which programs were approved prior to enactment of the Coastal Zone Act Reauthorization Amendments of 1990 [enacted Nov. 5, 1990], 1 to 1 for any fiscal year.

(2)   For programs approved after enactment of the Coastal Zone Act Reauthorization Amendments of 1990 [enacted Nov. 5, 1990], 4 to 1 for the first fiscal year, 2.3 to 1 for the second fiscal year, 1.5 to 1 for the third fiscal year, and 1 to 1 for each fiscal year thereafter.

[1990] (b) Grants to coastal states; requirements. The Secretary may make a grant to a coastal state under subsection (a) only if the Secretary finds that the management program of the coastal state meets all applicable requirements of this title and has been approved in accordance with subsection (d).

(c) Allocation of grants to coastal states. Grants under this section shall be allocated to coastal states with approved programs based on rules and regulations promulgated by the Secretary which shall take into account the extent and nature of the shoreline and area covered by the program, population of the area, and other relevant factors. The Secretary shall establish, after consulting with the coastal states, maximum and minimum grants for any fiscal year to promote equity between coastal states and effective coastal management.

(d) Mandatory adoption of State management program for coastal zone. Before approving a management program submitted by a coastal state, the Secretary shall find the following:

(1) The State has developed and adopted a management program for its coastal zone in accordance with rules and regulations promulgated by the Secretary, after notice, and with the opportunity of full participation by relevant Federal agencies, State agencies, local governments, regional organizations, port authorities, and other interested parties and individuals, public and private, which is adequate to carry out the purposes of this title and is consistent with the policy declared in section 303 [*16 USCS § 1452*].

(2) The management program includes each of the following required program elements:

(A) An identification of the boundaries of the coastal zone subject to the management program.

(B) A definition of what shall constitute permissible land uses and water users within the coastal zone which have a direct and significant impact on the coastal waters.

(C) An inventory and designation of areas of particular concern within the coastal zone.

(D) An identification of the means by which the State proposes to exert control over the land uses and water uses referred to in subparagraph (B), including a list of relevant State constitutional provisions, laws, regulations, and judicial decisions.

(E) Broad guidelines on priorities of uses in particular areas, including specifically those uses of lowest priority.

(F) A description of the organizational structure proposed to implement such management program, including the responsibilities and interrelationships of local, areawide, State, regional, and interstate agencies in the management process.

[1990] (G) A definition of the term "beach" and a planning process for the protection of, and access to, public beaches and other public coastal areas of environmental, recreational, historical, esthetic, ecological, or cultural value.

(H) A planning process for energy facilities likely to be located in, or which may significantly affect, the coastal zone, including a process for anticipating the management of the impacts resulting from such facilities.

(I) A planning process for assessing the effects of, and studying and evaluating ways to control, or lessen the impact of, shoreline erosion, and to restore areas adversely affected by such erosion.

(3) The State has—

(A) coordinated its program with local, areawide, and interstate plans applicable to areas within the coastal zone—

(i) existing on January 1 of the year in which the State's management program is submitted to the Secretary; and

(ii) which have been developed by a local government, an areawide agency, a regional agency, or an interstate agency; and

(B) established an effective mechanism for continuing consultation and coordination between the management agency designated pursuant to paragraph (6) and with local governments, interstate agencies, regional agencies, and areawide agencies within the coastal zone to assure the full participation of those local governments and agencies in carrying out the purposes of this title; except that the Secretary shall not find any mechanism to be effective for purposes of this subparagraph unless it requires that—

(i) the management agency, before implementing any management program decision which would conflict with any local zoning ordinance, decision, or other action, shall send a notice of the management program decision to any local government whose zoning authority is affected;

(ii) within the 30-day period commencing on the date of receipt of that notice, the local government may submit to the management agency written comments on the management program decision, and any recommendation for alternatives; and

(iii) the management agency, if any comments are submitted to it within the 30-day period by any local government—

(I) shall consider the comments;

(II) may, in its discretion, hold a public hearing on the comments; and

(III) may not take any action within the 30-day period to implement the management program decision.

(4) The State has held public hearings in the development of the management program.

(5) The management program and any changes thereto have been reviewed and approved by the Governor of the State.

(6) The Governor of the State has designated a single State agency to receive and administer grants for implementing the management program.

(7) The State is organized to implement the management program.

(8) The management program provides for adequate consideration of the national interest involved in planning for, and managing the coastal zone, including the siting of facilities such as energy facilities which are of greater than local significance. In the case of energy facilities, the Secretary shall find that the State has given consideration to any applicable national or interstate energy plan or program.

(9) The management program includes procedures whereby specific areas may be designated for the purpose of preserving or restoring them for their conservation, recreational ecological, historical, or esthetic values.

(10) The State, acting through its chosen agency or agencies (including local governments, areawide agencies, regional agencies, or interstate agencies) has authority for the management of the coastal zone in accordance with the management program. Such authority shall include power—

(A) to administer land use and water use regulations to control development[,] to ensure compliance with the management program, and to resolve conflicts among competing uses; and

(B) to acquire fee simple and less than fee simple interests in land, waters, and other property through condemnation or other means when necessary to achieve conformance with the management program.

(11) The management program provides for any one or a combination of the following general techniques for control of land uses and water uses within the coastal zone:

(A) State establishment of criteria and standards for local implementation, subject to administrative review and enforcement.

(B) Direct State land and water use planning and regulation.

(C) State administrative review for consistency with the management program of all development plans, projects, or land and water use regulations, including exceptions and variances thereto, proposed by any State or local authority or private developer, with power to approve or disapprove after public notice and an opportunity for hearings.

(12) The management program contains a method of assuring that local land use and water use regulations within the coastal zone do not unreasonably restrict or exclude land uses and water uses of regional benefit.

(13) The management program provides for—

(A) the inventory and designation of areas that contain one or more coastal resources of national significance; and

(B) specific and enforceable standards to protect such resources.

(14) The management program provides for public participation in permitting processes, consistency determinations, and other similar decisions.

(15) The management program provides a mechanism to ensure that all State agencies will adhere to the program.

(16) The management program contains enforceable policies and mechanisms to implement the applicable requirements of the Coastal Nonpoint Pollution Control Program of the State required by section 6217 of the Coastal Zone Act Reauthorization Amendments of 1990 [*16 USCS § 1455b*].

(e) Amendment or modification of State management program for coastal zone. A coastal state may amend or modify a management program which it has submitted and which has been approved by the Secretary under this section, subject to the following conditions:

(1) The State shall promptly notify the Secretary of any proposed amendment, modification, or other program change and submit it for the Secretary's approval. The Secretary may suspend all or part of any grant made under this section pending State submission of the proposed amendments, modification, or other program change.

(2) Within 30 days after the date the Secretary receives any proposed amendment, the Secretary shall notify the State whether the Secretary approves or disapproves the amendment, or whether the Secretary finds it is necessary to extend the review of the proposed amendment for a period not to exceed 120 days after the date the Secretary received the proposed amendment. The Secretary may extend this period only as necessary to meet the requirements of the National Environmental Policy Act of 1969 (*42 U.S.C. 4321* et seq.). If the Secretary does not notify the coastal state that the Secretary approves or disapproves the amendment within that period, then the amendment shall be conclusively presumed as approved.

(3) (A) Except as provided in subparagraph (B), a coastal state may not implement any amendment, modification, or other change as part of its approved management program unless the amendment, modification, or other change is approved by the Secretary under this subsection.

(B) The Secretary, after determining on a preliminary basis, that an amendment, modification, or other change which has been submitted for approval under this subsection is likely to meet the program approval standards in this section, may permit the State to expend funds awarded under this section to begin implementing the proposed amendment, modification, or change. This preliminary approval shall not extend for more than 6 months and may not be renewed. A proposed amendment, modification, or change which has been given preliminary approval and is not finally approved under this paragraph shall not be considered an enforceable policy for purposes of section 307 [*16 USCS § 1456*].

§ 1456.   Coordination and Cooperation

(c)   Consistency of Federal activities with state management programs; certification.

[1990] (1) (A) Each Federal agency activity within or outside the coastal zone that affects any land or water use or natural resource of the coastal zone shall be carried out in a manner which is consistent to the maximum extent practicable with the enforceable policies of approved State management programs. A Federal agency activity shall be subject to this paragraph unless it is subject to paragraph (2) or (3).

(B) After any final judgment, decree, or order of any Federal court that is appealable under section 1291 or 1292 of title 28, United States Code, or under any other applicable provision of Federal law, that a specific Federal agency activity is not in compliance with subparagraph (A), and certification by the Secretary that mediation under subsection (h) is not likely to result in such compliance, the President may, upon written request from the Secretary, exempt from compliance those elements of the Federal agency activity that are found by the Federal court to be inconsistent with an approved State program, if the President determines that the activity is in the paramount interest of the United States. No such exemption shall be granted on the basis of a lack of appropriations unless the President has specifically requested such appropriations as part of the budgetary process, and the Congress has failed to make available the requested appropriations.

(C) Each Federal agency carrying out an activity subject to paragraph (1) shall provide a consistency determination to the relevant State agency designated under section 306(d)(6) [*16 USCS § 1455(d)(6)*] at the earliest practicable time, but in no case later than 90 days before final approval of the Federal activity unless both the Federal agency and the State agency agree to a different schedule.

(2) Any Federal agency which shall undertake any development project in the coastal zone of a state shall insure that the project is, to the maximum extent practicable, consistent with [1990] the enforceable policies of approved state management programs.

(3) (A) After final approval by the Secretary of a state's management program, any applicant for a required Federal license or permit to conduct an activity, [1990] in or outside of the coastal zone, affecting [1990]any land or water use or natural resource of the coastal zone of that state shall provide in the application to the licensing or permitting agency a certification that the proposed activity complies with [1990] the enforceable policies of the state's approved program and that such activity will be conducted in a manner consistent with the program. At the same time, the applicant shall furnish to the state or its designated agency a copy of the certification, with all necessary information and data. Each coastal state shall establish procedures for public notice in the case of all such certifications and, to the extent it deems appropriate, procedures for public hearings in connection therewith. At the earliest practicable time, the state of its designated agency shall notify the Federal agency concerned that the state concurs with or objects to the applicant's certification. If the state or its designated agency fails to furnish the required notification within six months after receipt of its copy of the applicant's certification, the state's concurrence with the certification shall be conclusively presumed. No license or permit shall be granted by the Federal agency until the state or its designated agency has concurred with the applicant's certification or until, by the state's failure to act, the concurrence is conclusively presumed, unless the Secretary, on his own initiative or upon appeal by the applicant, finds, after providing a reasonable opportunity for detailed comments from the Federal agency involved and from the state, that the activity is consistent with the objectives of this title or is otherwise necessary in the interest of national security.

(B) After the management program of any coastal state has been approved by the Secretary under section 306 [*16 USCS § 1455*], any person who submits to the Secretary of the Interior any plan for the exploration or development of, or production from, any area which has been leased under the Outer Continental Shelf Lands Act (*43 U.S.C. 1331* et seq.) and regulations under such Act shall, with respect to any exploration, development, or production described in such plan and affecting any [1990]land or water use or natural resource of the coastal zone of such state, attach to such plan a certification that each activity which is described in detail in such plan complies with the enforceable policies of such state's approved management program and will be carried out in a manner consistent with such program. No Federal official or agency shall grant such person any license or permit for any activity described in detail in such plan until such state or its designated agency receives a copy of such certification and plan, together with any other necessary data and information, and until—

(i) such state or its designated agency, in accordance with the procedures required to be established by such state pursuant to subparagraph (A), concurs with such person's certification and notifies the Secretary and the Secretary of the Interior of such concurrence;

(ii) concurrence by such state with such certification is conclusively presumed as provided for in subparagraph (A), except if such state fails to concur with or object to such certification within three months after receipt of its copy of such certification and supporting information, such state shall provide the Secretary, the appropriate federal agency, and such person with a written statement describing the status of review and the basis for further delay in issuing a final decision, and if such statement is not so provided, concurrence by such state with such certification shall be conclusively presumed; or

(iii) the Secretary finds, pursuant to subparagraph (A), that each activity which is described in detail in such plan is consistent with the objectives of this title or is otherwise necessary in the interest of national security.

If a state concurs or is conclusively presumed to concur, or if the Secretary makes such a finding, the provisions of subparagraph (A) are not applicable with respect to such person, such state, and any Federal license or permit which is required to conduct any activity affecting land uses or water uses in the coastal zone of such state which is described in detail in the plan to which such concurrence or finding applies. If such state objects to such certification and if the Secretary fails to make a finding under clause (iii) with respect to such certification, or if such person fails substantially to comply with such plan as submitted, such person shall submit an amendment to such plan, or a new plan, to the Secretary of the Interior. With respect to any amendment or new plan submitted to the Secretary of the Interior pursuant to the preceding sentence, the applicable time period for purposes of concurrence by conclusive presumption under subparagraph (A) is 3 months.

NOTE

The last section set out above, § 1456, reflects 1990 amendments made by Congress that redefined the seaward boundary of the coastal zone, changed the definition of water use, and made clear that all federal activities are subject to "consistency" review, including the offering of oil and gas leases for sale, thereby rendering irrelevant the U.S. Supreme Court's decision to the contrary in *Secretary of the Interior v. California*, 464 U.S. 312 (1984). This last point is particularly important as consistency review is the only control which coastal states have over actions on federal lands which affect the coastal zone.

TOPLISS V. PLANNING COMMISSION
Intermediate Court of Appeals of Hawai'i, 1993.
9 Haw.App. 377, 842 P.2d 648.

HEEN, JUDGE.

On April 30, 1990, Petitioner-Appellant Larry T. Topliss, dba Pacific Land Company (Petitioner), filed a petition (Permit Petition) with Appellee Planning Commission of the County of Hawaii (Commission) for a Special Management Area (SMA) permit (SMAP) pursuant to the Coastal Zone Management Act (CZMA), Hawaii Revised Statutes (HRS) chapter 205A (1985 and Supp.1991), to develop two multi-story office buildings on his property (property) in Kailua-Kona.

The property lies on the northern corner of the intersection of Kuakini Highway and Seaview Circle. Kuakini Highway has an 80-foot right-of-way with a 24-foot pavement, while Seaview Circle has a 60-foot right-of-way with a 20-foot pavement. The Permit Petition acknowledges that the property "lies on a vital intersection and is adjacent to a high-traffic highway." The Permit Petition also describes the intersection as "a high-traffic intersection."

The property consists of two adjacent lots within the 143-lot Kona Sea View Lots Subdivision, most of which are in single family residential use.[1] * * * [Eds. Note: The court summarized the applicable land use regulations and plans and concluded the property was appropriately classified for the proposed development.]

The property has an area of approximately one-half acre and is nearly 400 feet above sea level and about 3600 feet from the shoreline. The property is rather severely sloped away from Kuakini Highway with a grade of approximately 20%. The difference in elevation between the property's mauka and makai boundaries is approximately 40 feet. The roof line of the proposed building abutting Kuakini Highway would extend approximately six feet above the elevation of the property's boundary. Between the property and the coastline lies most of the Kona Sea View Lots Subdivision, a "non-transgressable thicket," hotels and apartments along Alii Drive, and Alii Drive itself, which is the paved county roadway closest to and paralleling the coastline. Two circuitous vehicular routes measuring 2.7 miles in the southerly direction and 1.5 miles in the northerly direction are the only accesses to the coastline.

The property came within the purview of the CZMA in 1980 when the Commission designated all of the area makai of Kuakini Highway from Kailua southward to Keauhou as an SMA. At that time, the Commission cited "anticipated development pressures" in the area, the steep topography, soil composition, the Hawaii County General Plan designation of "the entire Kuakini right of way . . . as an important scenic resource,"

---

[1]   The two lots have areas of 15,001 and 7,502 square feet.

and the need to "better coordinate the overall development of the area" as the grounds for its action.

The Commission denied the Permit Petition and Petitioner appealed to the third circuit court. By stipulation of the parties, the matter was remanded to the Commission for the entry of findings of fact (FOF) and conclusions of law (COL). Meanwhile, on September 4, 1990, Petitioner filed a petition with the Commission to amend the boundaries (Boundary Petition) of the SMA to exclude his property.

The Boundary Petition was heard by the Commission on January 31, 1991. At the same hearing, the Commission denied Petitioner's request to reconsider the denial of the Permit Petition. On February 21, 1991, the Commission entered separate FOF, COL, and Orders denying both Petitions.

Petitioner appealed both orders to the third circuit court and on September 5, 1991, that court entered an order affirming the Commission. The matter is here on Petitioner's appeal from the circuit court's order.

Although Petitioner does not challenge the validity of the CZMA, the thrust of his attack is that when the Commission denied his Petitions it violated the CZMA's clear objectives and purposes.[3] We disagree with respect to the Boundary Petition, but agree with respect to the Permit Petition.

The dispositive question is construction of the CZMA. Our duty in construing statutes is to ascertain and give effect to the legislature's intention and to implement that intention to the fullest degree. *State v. Briones*, 71 Haw. 86, 784 P.2d 860 (1989). Petitioner argues that the CZMA is simply a zoning statute which must, as a general rule, be strictly construed against further derogation of common-law property rights. The rule cited by Petitioner is inapplicable here, however, since the language of the CZMA is clear and unambiguous and the legislature's intent is beyond peradventure. *See Maui County v. Puamana Management Corp.*, 2 Haw.App. 352, 631 P.2d 1215 (1981).

> The CZMA is "a comprehensive State regulatory scheme to protect the environment and resources of our shoreline areas." *Mahuiki v. Planning Comm'n*, 65 Haw. 506, 517, 654 P.2d 874, 881 (1982).

> The CZMA imposes special controls on the development of real property along the shoreline areas in order "to preserve, protect, and where possible, to restore the natural resources of the coastal zone of Hawaii." HRS § 205A–21.

Sandy Beach Defense Fund v. City Council, 70 Haw. 361, 365, 773 P.2d 250, 254 (1989).

---

[3] We reject Petitioner's arguments that the Commission's refusal to remove the property from the CZMA was "spot zoning" and amounted to a "taking."

When it enacted the CZMA, the Hawaii legislature specifically found that "special controls on developments within an area along the shoreline are necessary to avoid permanent losses of valuable resources and the foreclosure of management options, and to ensure that adequate access, by dedication or other means, to public owned or used beaches, recreation areas, and natural reserves is provided." HRS § 205A–21 (1985). The legislature therefore declared it to be "the state policy to preserve, protect, and where possible, to restore the natural resources of the coastal zone of Hawaii." *Id.* In order to carry out the CZMA's policies and objectives, the legislature authorized the counties to establish SMAs. HRS § 205A–23 (1985). Development within an SMA is controlled by a permit system administered by the counties pursuant to HRS § 205A–28 (1985).

The Boundary Petition

Petitioner argues that the Commission exceeded its lawful authority when it established Kuakini Highway as the mauka [towards the mountains, inland, away from the beach] boundary of the SMA. He contends that the CZMA authorizes the Commission to include within the SMA lands that have a "direct and significant impact" on the coastal waters protected by the CZMA.[4] He asserts that in this case the property has "no potential for direct or substantial impact upon either the coastal water or the coastal resources to be protected" and should not be included within the SMA.[5] The argument is without merit.

Among the CZMA's stated objectives and policies are the protection, preservation, restoration and improvement of the "quality of coastal scenic and open space resources[,]" HRS § 205A–2(b)(3) and (c)(3)(C) (1985), and the "designing and locating" of new "developments to minimize the alteration of . . . existing public views to and along the shoreline[,]" HRS § 205A–2(c)(3)(B) (1985).[6]

---

[4]   Petitioner claims that the following findings of fact do not support the Commission's conclusion that the property should not be removed from the SMA: 63. Upon mandatory review and update of the SMA maps, the [Planning] Department recommended that the SMA in the North Kona district should include the area along Alii Drive, bounded by Kailua, Keauhou and Kuakini Highway. The rationale for this expansion focused on the rapid growth experienced in the area and a need to ensure that development evaluates the physical constraints as well as the scenic viewplanes from Kuakini Highway, which has been identified as an important scenic resource in the General Plan. 68. It is important that the boundary line be retained at Kuakini Highway since viewplanes have been identified as an area of critical concern. 71. If the development of Property is found to have no significant adverse impacts on viewplanes or open space, this does not mean that the Property can be removed from the SMA.

[5]   Any contraction of an SMA boundary is subject to review by State authorities for compliance with the objectives and policies of the CZMA. HRS § 205A–23 (1985).

[6]   In a report of the United States Senate Commerce Committee on the Coastal Zone Management Act of 1972, S.Rep. No. 92–753, 92 Cong., 2d Sess. 3, *reprinted* in U.S.Code Cong. & Admin.News 4776 (1972), the committee suggested that a State coastal zone management program should include "both visual and physical" access "to the coastline and coastal areas[.]" *Id.* at 4786. Hawaii's coastal management program arises from the federal enactment, and the above sections of the CZMA clearly are meant to be in accord with the Commerce Committee's suggestion.

In order to protect and preserve the coastal zone's scenic and open space resources, the CZMA requires the Commission to "minimize, where reasonable . . . [a]ny development which would substantially interfere with or detract from the line of sight toward the sea from the state highway nearest the coast[.]" HRS § 205A–26(3)(D) (1985).

The intent of the CZMA is clearly to authorize inclusion in the SMA of lands that have a significant impact on the scenic resources in the area and whose development would alter the public views to and along the shoreline. Protection of the coastal areas and waters from adverse environmental or ecological impact is only one of the CZMA's objectives. Another clear objective is protection against interference with or alteration of coastal scenic resources. Where a property or development has the potential for such interference, then it may be included within an SMA even though it is not in close proximity to the coastline.

Petitioner's arguments that (1) the Commission's "rapid growth" finding is "factually incorrect" because the area surrounding the property "had already become substantially developed as early as 1977[,]" and (2) the property "is one of the very last parcels in the neighborhood which is yet to be developed[,]" is without merit.

First, the finding is merely a reiteration of the original finding made in 1980 when the SMA boundary was established at Kuakini Highway. There is nothing in the record to support Petitioner's argument that the area was already substantially developed at the time the finding was made. Moreover, whether the growth in the area was rapid or slow is really of no import. The aim of the CZMA is to control growth of whatever rapidity. See Sandy Beach Defense Fund.

Second, the fact that the property is among the last to be developed in the neighborhood does not vitiate the finding. The objective of controlling growth relates to the entire SMA not just the neighborhood in which the property is located.

Since control of growth in the SMA is an objective of the CZMA, id., it cannot be said, as Petitioner argues, that control of rapid growth is the Commission's attempt to use general planning and zoning objectives to justify imposition of the special controls of the CZMA.

Petitioner acknowledges that the CZMA expresses the legislature's concern for "views along the shoreline." However, he contends that the "scenic viewplanes" cited by the Commission in FOF No. 63 is purely a creation of the Commission and is not among the "state interests" advanced by the CZMA. Consequently, the continued inclusion of the property in the SMA unconstitutionally deprived him of his property. The argument is without merit.

First, Petitioner misstates the language of the CZMA. HRS § 205A–2(c)(3)(B) clearly establishes the protection of views to and along the shoreline as among the legislature's policies regarding scenic and open space resources.[9]

* * *

Second, as stated above, HRS § 205A–26(3)(D) requires the Commission to minimize a development's interference with the line of sight from Kuakini Highway toward the sea.

In our view, the term scenic viewplanes employed in FOF No. 63 relating to the Boundary Petition is merely a paraphrase of the statutory terms "views to and along the shoreline" or "line of sight toward the sea," and clearly comports with the intent of the statute.

Petitioner also argues that since the shoreline itself, as defined in the CZMA[10] cannot be seen from the property, the continued inclusion of the property in the SMA goes beyond the legislature's authorization to protect "views to and along the shoreline" and "shoreline open space and scenic resources." We disagree.

HRS § 205A–26(3)(D) clearly mandates the Commission to protect and preserve more than just the view of the shoreline. As noted above, the statute, by its very language, is intended to protect the view toward the sea even though the "shoreline" cannot be seen either because of intervening development or natural growth.

Petitioner also contends that even if "protecting panoramic coastal views" is within the legislative mandate, it is not a reasonable basis for imposing SMA regulations, since Hawaii County may impose height and setback limitations under its zoning powers. However, the fact that the County can impose the same restrictions through the exercise of one power does not make the proper exercise of another specifically authorized power unreasonable.

Petitioner asserts that since there is no significant view of either the ocean or the shoreline from the portion of Kuakini Highway that abuts the property, the inclusion of the property in the SMA did not advance the State's interest in preserving the viewplane from the highway. We disagree.

Admittedly, Petitioner's evidence indicates that the view from the portion of Kuakini Highway abutting the property is limited. However, that does not affect the Commission's finding as to the significance of the total viewplane from the highway. If, in fact, Petitioner's development would not have a significant, adverse impact on the total viewplane, the

---

[9] HRS § 205A–2(c)(3)(B) (1985) reads as follows: Coastal zone management program; objectives and policies.

[10] HRS § 205A–1 (Supp.1991) defines shoreline as: the upper reaches of the wash of the waves, other than storm and seismic waves, at high tide during the season of the year in which the highest wash of the waves occurs, usually evidenced by the edge of vegetation growth, or the upper limit of debris left by the wash of the waves.

Commission could consider that as favoring the development or could impose conditions on the development to minimize the impact. However, that would not necessarily support removal of the property from the SMA.

Petitioner argues that "[t]he original enactment of Hawaii's CZMA in 1975 . . . defined the SMA to exclude 'portions of [lands in] which there are numerous residential commercial or other structures of a substantial nature in existence as of the effective date of [CZMA],' " and there is no indication that that exclusion should not be continued. The argument misstates the statute.

The original enactment excluded from SMAs only such built up areas that may be located on lands "which abut any inland waterway or body of water wholly or partially improved with walls[.]" Act 176, 1975 Haw.Sess.Laws § 1 (emphasis added). That is not the situation here and there is nothing to indicate the legislature intended to continue that exclusion or to expand it.

The Permit Petition

In denying the Permit Petition, the Commission made the following FOF: 62. Rule 9–10(H)(5) says that one factor which should be considered in constituting a "significant adverse effect" is when the proposed use, activity or operation "involves substantial secondary impacts . . . such as effect on public facilities." 69. Based upon the evidence adduced, including that submitted with the Petition, the testimony of the public and the Petitioner, and the information contained in the [Planning] Department's Background Report, the Commission concluded that the Petitioner's proposed development would have cumulative and significant adverse effects and impact on the public roadway facilities and system in the area of said development, to wit: (A) Increased traffic congestion; (B) Decreased pedestrian safety, especially with a school bus stop in the vicinity; (C) Potential increase in vehicular accidents at the intersection of Kuakini Highway and Sea View Circle.

Petitioner challenges the quoted FOF as not being based on substantial evidence. We disagree. The record contains substantial evidence showing that the development will impact on the roads in the vicinity of the Kuakini Highway-Sea View Circle intersection. Nevertheless, after a thorough review of the record, we have a definite and firm conviction that a mistake has been made.

Pursuant to HRS § 205A–26(2) (1985), development cannot be approved within an SMA unless findings are made that the development (A) will not have any substantial adverse environmental or ecological effect except, however, where the substantial adverse effect is practicably minimized and "clearly outweighed by public health, safety, or compelling public interests"; (B) is consistent with the objectives, policies, and SMA guidelines of the CZMA; and (C) is consistent with the county general plan and zoning. In our view, where a proposed development meets those statutory requisites, the Commission's denial of an SMAP would be in excess of its authority.

The purpose of the CZMA is to control development within an SMA through the device of the SMAP, not to totally prevent or prohibit such activity. It follows that, where an administrative record indicates that a proposed development within an SMA would not contravene the statute's policies, objectives, and purposes, the Commission would exceed its authority by denying an SMAP that may have been requested for that project. The question, here, is whether the Commission's findings satisfied its duty and authority under the statute.

Here, the Commission in other FOF found that the development would have no significant impact on archaeological or historical sites, "floral" and "faunal" resources of the coastal area, or on the coastal waters.[12] The Commission made no finding regarding any impact on the viewplanes and open space.

The only reason given by the Commission for denying the permit, as noted in FOF 62 and 69, is that the development would have cumulative and significant adverse effects on the roadway system at the intersection in question. However, at oral argument in this court, the Commission's counsel conceded that the traffic generated by the development in this case would have very little, if any, impact on the coastal zone's environment or ecology.

Under the circumstances of this case, absent a finding that the impact on the public facilities would result in a substantial adverse environmental or ecological effect, or render the development inconsistent with the objectives, policies, and guidelines of the CZMA, the Commission's finding that the development would have significant adverse effects and impact on the existing highway system in the area of the development does not provide a sufficient basis for denying the Permit Petition. In other words, if traffic from a development within an SMA is not shown to have a substantial adverse effect on the coastal environment, such impact as the traffic may otherwise have on the existing roadway system in the area of the development cannot be the basis for denying an SMAP application.

Additionally, even if the development in this case is shown to have a substantial adverse effect in accordance with the statute, the Commission was required under HRS § 205A–26(2)(A) to determine whether that effect

---

[12] The Commission made the following pertinent findings of fact: 46. The project site has been previously altered and is unlikely to contain any surface archaeological sites of significance. 47. The Department of Land and Natural Resources commented "It is our understanding that the lots in this subdivision were graded some time ago, making it unlikely that significant historic sites are present. The project should have 'no effect' on such sites." 49. Because the land has been altered, it is not likely to be a habitat for any rare or endangered species of flora or fauna. 50. The project site is located approximately 3,600 feet from the shoreline. 51. The impact to coastal waters should be negligible.

could be practically minimized and, when minimized, whether the effect is clearly outweighed by public health, safety, or compelling public interests. *See Mahuiki*, 65 Haw. at 516–17 n. 10, 654 P.2d at 881 n. 10. That was not done in this case. Here, Petitioner represented to the Commission that he would be willing to design the development so as to minimize the traffic impact as much as possible. It does not appear from the record that the Commission considered Petitioner's offer as we think it was required to do under the statute.

On remand, the Commission should reconsider the Permit Petition and determine whether the traffic generated by the development will or will not have a substantial adverse environmental or ecological effect on the coastal zone. If the Commission finds that the traffic will not have such a substantial adverse effect, then the Commission should approve the Permit Petition without conditions relating to the traffic.

If the Commission finds that the traffic will have such a substantial effect, but that the effect can be practically minimized and, as minimized, the effect is clearly outweighed by public health, safety, or compelling public interests, the Commission should approve the Permit Petition. In order to achieve the minimization, the Commission may impose reasonable conditions on the development. If, of course, the development cannot be made to conform to HRS § 205A–26(2)(A), then the Commission should deny the Permit Petition.

This opinion is not meant to prevent the Commission from imposing other reasonable conditions affecting matters within the purview of the CZMA, such as the viewplanes to the ocean, where such may be deemed necessary to comply with the intent of the CZMA.

Conclusion

We affirm the Commission's denial of the Boundary Petition. We vacate the denial of the Permit Petition and remand the matter to the Commission for further proceedings consistent with this opinion.

NOTES

1.   In *Morgan v. Planning Dep't, County of Kaua'i*, the Hawai'i Supreme Court held that while the Planning Commission could modify permit conditions, it lacked the power to enjoin the property owner to make repairs or restitution. 86 P.3d 982 (2004). The approved construction of a seawall created adverse impacts on neighboring lands. In light of changes circumstances, the Planning Commission modified the original permit conditions. The court found that the legislature expressly granted to the Planning Commission the authority to carry out the objectives, policies, and procedures of the CZMA's permits, and therefore has the authority to revoke, amend, or modify the permit. 89 P.3d at 993. Additionally, the court reinforced that the Planning Commission lacked the power to mandate injunctive relief, stating that the CZMA expressly grants injunctive power to the circuit courts. 89 P.3d at 996.

2. California has the largest Coastal Zone Management Act in the nation that extends 1,100 miles from Mexico to Oregon and 5 miles outward from the shoreline. In distinction with Hawaii, the jurisdiction of the Coastal Commission extends only 1000 yards inland in developed urban areas. Cal.Pub.Res. Code § 30103(a). The implementation of the Act lies with the creation of Local Coastal Plans (LCPs) and Zoning Regulations. These plans and regulations, and all development approvals issued after the LCP is certified, are then reviewed by the Coastal Commission for consistency with the coastal policies set forth in Chapter 3 of the Act, 76 Cal.Rptr.3d 466 (Cal.App.2008). *See Ross v. California Coastal Commission*, 133 Cal.Rptr.3d 107 (2011): Local government amended coastal planning regulations by amending lot size requirements, to allow for development. Plaintiff challenged the amendment; however, the court found that the amendments were proper, as the local government correctly analyzed potential effects of the changes.

3. Defining the landward part of the coastal zone for purposes of CZMA can be difficult, especially for regulatory purposes, since the federal government looks to the states—to which it gives the money for program development and implementation—for enforcement. What if the statutory definition would result in CZMA regulations covering the entire developable area of the state? This is what happened in Hawaii, which then developed two coastal zones: the all-inclusive one for "administrative" purposes, and a second only usually a few hundred yards wide (defined county-by-county) for regulatory purposes. David L. Callies, *Regulating Paradise: Land Use Controls in Hawaii*, Ch.6 (2d ed.2010).

4. The Coastal Zone Management Act appears to be directed at preserving critical coastal natural resources and values. Assuming it is possible to obtain a permit from an appropriate local agency under an approved coastal zone management program, what would you expect restrictions on development to look like? What kind of bulk and height standards would you expect to be imposed? Consider these questions in light of the materials in this Chapter on flood hazard protection and the dilemma of the landowner subject both to coastal zone protection and flood hazard prevention regulations enforced at the local level. What kind of bulk and height standards would you expect to be imposed? For parties that violate the CZMA regulations, how far can the local government go to seek compliance? In *Lewis v. Gansler*, 42 A.3d 63 (2012), local government demanded the removal building in violation and the property be restored to its original condition. The court upheld the demand. Consider these questions in light of the materials in this Chapter on flood hazard protection and the dilemma of the landowner subject both to coastal zone protection and flood hazard prevention regulations enforced at the local level.

5. As indicated in note 1 above in the material preceding *Topliss*, the 1990 amendments to § 1456 of the act restored consistency review to the states and effectively overturned *Secretary of the Interior v. California*, 464 U.S. 312 (1984). *See also* Jack Archer, *Evolution of Major 1990 CZMA Amendments: Restoring Federal Consistency and Protection Coastal Water Quality*, 1 TERR.

SEA J. 191 (1991); Linda Malone, *The Coastal Zone Management Act and the Takings Clause in the 1990's: Making the Case for Federal Land Use to Preserve Coastal Areas*, 62 U.COLO.L.REV. 711 (1991). As indicated in Note 1 above in the material preceding *Topliss*, the 1990 amendments to § 1456 of the act restored consistency review to the states and effectively overturned *Secretary of the Interior v. California*, 464 U.S. 321 (1984). Prior to the amendments, the consistency provision applied only to federal actions or activities directly affecting a state's coastal zone. The 1990 amendment, stating a permit is required "to conduct an activity, in or outside of the coastal zone" affecting any designated coastal zone. 1456(C)(3)(A). The amendment requires a consistency review for any direct, or indirect, action affecting the coastal zone. Edward M. Cheston, *An Overview and Analysis of the Consistency Requirements under the Coastal Zone Management Act*, 10 U.BALT.J.ENVTL.L. 135 (2003). For recent cases interpreting consistency requirements, *see In the Matter of Defend H20, et al. v. Town Board of East Hampton*, 147 F.Supp.3d 80 (E.D.N.Y.2015)(Corps of Engineers subject to, for 3,100 foot erosion prevention); and *Dunber Resources Co. v. U.S.*, 538 F.3d 1358 (Fed.Cir.2008)(new construction responsibilities insufficient to void previous exploratory drilling contracts; and *California Coastal Comm'n v. U.S. Dept. of the Navy*, 22 F.Supp.3d 1081 (S.D.Cal.2014)(significant changes in the law held insufficient to require a supplemental consistency determination despite a 15-year time lapse between the original determination and the construction's commencement.

6. The relationship between coastal zone objectives and local comprehensive plans can lead to unexpected results. Thus, in *GATRI v. Blane*, 962 P.2d 367 (Haw.1998), the court upheld the denial of a shoreline management permit for the development of a snack bar in the coastal zone even though the land was zoned commercial. The state coastal zone statute required compliance with both applicable county development plans and zoning, and the applicable county plan "classified" the land residential. Holding that such plans have the force of law as a result of the coastal zone statutory requirement, the court held that the proposed development must comply with both plan and zoning ordinance in order to qualify for a coastal zone shoreline management permit for construction. *See also Lease v. Co. of Decatur*, 284 P.3d 956 (Ct.App.2012), and *Dominion Transmission Inc. v. Town of Myersville*, 982 F.Supp.2d 570 (D.Md.2013).

7. Clearly, a development as potentially intrusive as the commercial building in *Topliss* would require a coastal zone shoreline management permit if that's what local regulations require in a coastal zone. Does the demolition of structures in the designated coastal zone also require such a permit? *See Hawaii's Thousand Friends v. Honolulu*, 858 P.2d 726 (Haw.1993), where the court required the City and County of Honolulu to obtain such a permit for the demolition of deteriorating cabins in a county beach park on the ground that such demolition was part of a larger park project, the cumulative impact of which constituted development with a significant environmental impact on the coastal special management area.

8. What the federal government can do within a designated state coastal zone once NOAA has approved it has caused some controversy. Who has the final say? *See Lopez v. Cooper*, 193 F.Supp.2d 424 (D.P.R.2002) for a challenge to the use of Puerto Rican beaches for military training exercises, and section 307(c)(1) of the CZMA as interpreted in *Secretary of the Interior v. California*, 464 U.S. 312 (1984).

9. The Coastal Zone Management Act works to protect, preserve, and where possible, restore coastal zones across the country. An objective of the CZMA also includes protecting historic resources within the CZMA regulation areas. Thus, for example, in here the Hawai'i CZMA states its historic objective is to protect, preserve, and, where desirable, restore those natural and manmade historic and prehistoric resources in the coastal zone management area that are significant in Hawaiian and American history and culture, the court in *Kaleikini v. Yoshioka*, 283 P.3d 60 (2012), held that where ancient Hawaiian burial sites were potentially threatened by the State's construction of a public transport system, the CZMA required the city to acquire a permit, issued on condition that the city work to minimize adverse effects on historic properties, and the city complete a final environmental impact statement. *See also Blake v. County of Kaua'i Planning Commission*, 315 P.3d 749 (2013), in which the county was held to have failed to consider historic and cultural values in potentially allowing an easement over a state road.

10. How far is too far for a state or local government to enact rules and requirements under CZMA regulations? In *Hackensack Riverkeeper, Inc. v. New Jersey Dept. of Environmental Protection*, the municipal government implemented rules requiring public access to coastal waterways, as a condition for all permits under CZMA regulations. The Court found that while there is a nexus between the regulations and the permitting process, requirements were too broad and pervasive to be enforceable. 450 F.Supp.2d 467 (D.N.J.2006).

11. CZMA regulations are not restricted to physical alteration of land. In *Dunex, Inc. v. City of Oceanside*, an application to convert a mobile home park from a rental subdivision, to one in which the mobile-home owners owned the land beneath their homes as well, was held subject to certain regulations. The land was within the CZMA designated area, and therefore the conversion required an appropriate development permit. The permit request was denied because it was inconsistent with the local CZMA regulation to avoid development in a flood area. The court held the individual owners would be responsible for the flood risk, and less able to bear that risk than the entity owning the entire property. 160 Cal.Rptr.3d 670 (2013).

12. Modification or amendments to a coastal zone is provided for at 16 U.S.C.A. § 1455(e). *See Energy Nuclear Indian Point 2, LLC v. New York State Department of State*, 14 N.Y.S.3d 177 (N.Y.App.Div.2015) where the state presented scientific evidence in order to extend a current coastal zone by 20 miles.

D. FLOODPLAINS

1. THE DEVASTATION WROUGHT BY FLOODING

Every spring we witness devastating flooding, often, but hardly only, in the mid-west. Trying to immunize ourselves from the ravages of Mother Nature, we build dams and levees, but the gains achieved by these efforts may be offset by efforts to increase the amount of developable land (e.g., filling wetlands). While many share the blame for the devastation suffered by residents along the Gulf Coast and in New Orleans when hit by Hurricane Katrina in 2005, a significant amount was attributed to government filling of coastal wetlands over the years, allowance of development in areas of risk, and inadequate maintenance of the levees designed to hold off stormwater. *See* Christine A. Klein and Sandra B. Zellmer, *Mississippi River Stories: Lessons from a Century of Unnatural Disasters*, 60 SMU L.REV. 1471, 1500, 1509 (2007). Floodplains serve much the same purposes as wetlands. When development occurs on them, the absorption capacity of the land is lost and flooding downstream is exacerbated.

A floodplain is any land at risk of being inundated by flood waters. For purposes of flood control and regulations the floodplain area is divided into two areas: floodways and flood fringes. Floodways are the unobstructed stream channel and overbank areas where flooding is most common. Structural development of any sort is generally prohibited there. Flood fringes are adjacent to floodways and are subject to less flooding and less damage when floods do occur. A variety of land uses may be permitted in flood fringe areas, preferably with precautions such as elevation being taken into account. The landward reach of the fringe area is defined in terms of the likelihood of the area being flooded over a period of years, whether that be 10, 100 or 500 years. A 100 year floodplain means that studies of the area have led to the calculation that there is a 1% statistical probability of the area being flooded once every 100 years. These, of course, are probabilities, not actualities. A 100 year flood might occur several years in a row.

In the past, floodplains were used for agriculture. Generally, people did not build or live in floodplains. They knew what would happen if they did. Yet, our movement from an agrarian to urban lifestyle and our belief that we could erect artificial barriers to floods led to people building in floodplains and, as we have learned, where development has been allowed in floodplains, there may be significant damage to property and loss of life.

In Chapter 3, we discussed the decision in *First English Evangelical Lutheran Church v. County of Los Angeles*, 482 U.S. 304 (1987), where the Court held that the remedy for a regulatory taking was compensation. The case stemmed from a flood of major proportions. Briefly, the facts:

In 1957, appellant First English Evangelical Lutheran Church purchased a 21-acre parcel of land in a canyon along the banks of the Middle Fork of Mill Creek in the Angeles National Forest. The Middle Fork is the natural drainage channel for a watershed area owned by the National Forest Service. Twelve of the acres owned by the church are flat land, and contained a dining hall, two bunkhouses, a caretaker's lodge, an outdoor chapel, and a footbridge across the creek. The church operated on the site a campground, known as "Lutherglen," as a retreat center and a recreational area for handicapped children.

In July 1977, a forest fire denuded the hills upstream from Lutherglen, destroying approximately 3,860 acres of the watershed area and creating a serious flood hazard. Such flooding occurred on February 9 and 10, 1978, when a storm dropped 11 inches of rain in the watershed. The runoff from the storm overflowed the banks of the Mill Creek, flooding Lutherglen and destroying its buildings.

In response to the flooding of the canyon, appellee County of Los Angeles adopted Interim Ordinance No. 11,855 in January 1979. The ordinance provided that "[a] person shall not construct, reconstruct, place or enlarge any building or structure, any portion of which is, or will be, located within the outer boundary lines of the interim flood protection area located in Mill Creek Canyon. . . ." The ordinance was effective immediately because the county determined that it was "required for the immediate preservation of the public health and safety. . . ." The interim flood protection area described by the ordinance included the flat areas on either side of Mill Creek on which Lutherglen had stood.

482 U.S. 304.

John McPhee, one of America's foremost writers on nature and geology, wrote about the area where the flood occurred in *First English*:

JOHN McPHEE'S EXCELLENT WORK, The Control of Nature, describes three locations where people have been, and are, engaged in all out battles with nature. One, the area of Los Angeles which was the situs of the United States Supreme Court's decision in First English Evangelical Lutheran Church v. City of Los Angeles. [McPhee] describes the area:

Some of the more expensive real estate in Los Angeles is up against mountains that are rising and disintegrating as rapidly as any in the world. After a complex coincidence of natural events, boulders will flow out of these mountains like fish eggs, mixed with mud, sand, and smaller rocks in a cascading mass known as a debris flow. Plucking up trees and cars, bursting through doors and windows, filling up houses to their eaves, debris flows threaten the lives of people living in and near Los Angeles' famous canyons. At extraordinary expense the city has built a hundred and fifty stadium-like basins in a daring effort to catch the debris.

McPhee's book takes us into the homes of individuals, who obviously are struggling against fantastic odds because they live in an area that is disintegrating. McPhee's description is a "textbook situation" involving the location of the wrong type of use at the wrong site. As McPhee describes it, the area involved "a bowl in the mountains filled with hard chaparral that had not been touched by fire in ninety-nine years." As time passed its "renewed flammability" curved sharply upward. The hotter the fire, the more likely a debris flow and the greater the volume. McPhee described Hidden Springs, the location where the church in issue is located—he said its name "contained more prophecy than its residents seemed to imagine." He noted, "Three hundred and ninety thousand cubic yards of loose debris was gathered just above them, awaiting mobilization." McPhee describes the night that mobilization occurred:

> The thirteen people who died in Hidden Springs were roughly a third of the year-round community; there was a much larger summer population. The main house of Lutherglen, a resort-retreat of the First English Evangelical Lutheran Church, remained standing but in ruins. Houses that stayed put were gouged out like peppers and stuffed with rocks. Lewis gestured across the canyon-across foundations with no houses on them, bolts sticking up out of cinder blocks where sills had been ripped away-toward some skeletal frames made of two-by-fours. "They used to be trailer stalls," he said. "The people left their cars by the river and walked up the bank to the trailers. The cars ended up in the dam." The First English Evangelical Lutherans sued the Los Angeles County Flood Control District for twenty million dollars. The judge threw the case out of court-followed, moments later, by the collection plate. Since the act in question was God's, the defendant might as well have been the plaintiff, and the Plaintiff the target of the suit.

Joseph Fleming, *Coping With Chaos*, 27 URB.LAW. 3, 4 (1995).*

---

2. FLOOD PROTECTION AND REGULATION

Governments prepare for the disasters wrought by floods in three ways: regulation, condemnation, and incentive programs.

Limiting development in floodplains is the most effective tool. Sometimes it comes too late, as it did for those killed in floods that led to the *First English* case. After the devastating flood, Los Angeles enacted stringent interim and permanent limitations on building in the floodplain. At the Supreme Court level, *First English* involved the appropriate remedy for a Fifth Amendment regulatory taking. After the Court determined that compensation is the mandatory remedy once a taking is found, it remanded the case to the state court for a determination of the merits of the claim. The state intermediate appellate court on remand examined the stringent limitations on building in the floodplain and found the circumstances justified them. The court found no taking. *First English Evangelical Lutheran Church v. County of Los Angeles*, 258 Cal.Rptr. 893 (Cal.App.1989), *cert. denied* 493 U.S. 1056 (1990).

Courts have upheld fairly stringent floodplain regulations. Without great difficulty, regulators can overcome substantive due process and regulatory takings claims. In addition to the *First English* remand decision noted above, see these floodplain cases: *Gove v. Zoning Bd. of Appeals*, 831 N.E.2d 865 (Mass.2005), finding a 93% diminution in value not to be a taking; *Adolph v. Federal Emergency Management Agency*, 854 F.2d 732, 738, n. 9 (5th Cir.1988) (collecting cases).

If the government nevertheless determines the regulatory approach to be too risky, but still decides to prevent development in flood plains, it can exercise the power of eminent domain to acquire the fee simple or a negative easement. The expense and lack of political will to employ this option limit its use. Condemnation, of course, can be indirect as well. What begins as a regulation can become an exercise of inverse condemnation if it goes "too far."

The third technique, incentive legislation, is exemplified by the National Flood Insurance Program (NFIP), which was the real impetus for local regulation of flood prone land. The NFIP is embodied primarily in two acts: The National Flood Insurance Act of 1968 and the Federal Disaster Protection Act of 1973, 42 U.S.C. § 4001 et seq. The program's purpose is to discourage development—and in particular the building of structures—in flood prone areas. In what has become standard federal strategy, the NFIP does so by making federal money available for federally subsidized flood insurance and relocation aid, and offering some procedural and substantive control over federal activities at or near flood prone areas to those local communities who "choose" to participate in the federal flood management program. The price of that participation is local government enactment or promulgation of local land use development regulations which restrict the use of land in areas found to be flood prone. In essence, these regulations must be designed in accordance with federal regulations, promulgated pursuant to the NFIP, which restrict most structural development in floodplains to that which can be elevated above the highest recorded flood level or wave wash. For general descriptions, *see* Linda Malone, *Environmental Regulation of Land Use*, Ch.7 (2001); 3 Zoning and Land Use Controls § 18.02 (Rohan ed.1992).

Federal flood insurance is available except for a few specially designated coastal areas. See discussion infra in the notes following the next principal case. The insurance is sold through private insurers and backed by the federal government. Coverage is available even for areas that are repeatedly flooded, so long as the local government is participating in the program.

For purposes of the Act, the floodplain is essentially the land area on either side of a river which is likely to be inundated in the event of a 100-year flood, so-called because of the one percent statistical likelihood of its occurring in any one year, or, conversely, the likelihood of its occurring but once every 100 years. Development of any kind is to be prohibited in the floodway, which is that portion of the floodplain adjacent to and including the river channel, and which is expected to carry the greatest volume and flow of floodwaters, including those of lesser frequency than a 100-year flood. Not only does development activity in either floodplain or floodway endanger those engaged in such activity (or those who will inhabit structures thereon) but it also reduces the capacity of the floodway to carry, and the floodplain to absorb, flood waters, thereby enlarging the area of both and/or causing more water to go downstream, increasing in either case the likelihood of danger to persons and property in areas otherwise outside a floodway or floodplain, or increasing the frequency of flooding. For the history of federal involvement in flood control beginning in the mid-nineteenth century, as well as a discussion of the flood insurance program, see 5 Water and Water Rights, Ch. 60 (R. Beck ed.1991).

National Flood Insurance Program of 1968

§ 4001. Congressional Findings and Declaration of Purpose

(a) Necessity and Reasons for Flood Insurance Program

The Congress finds that (1) from time to time flood disasters have created personal hardships and economic distress which have required unforeseen disaster relief measures and have placed an increasing burden on the Nation's resources; (2) despite the installation of preventive and protective works and the adoption of other public programs designed to reduce losses caused by flood damage, these methods have not been sufficient to protect adequately against growing exposure to future flood losses; (3) as a matter of national policy, a reasonable method of sharing the risk of flood losses is through a program of flood insurance which can complement and encourage preventive and protective measures; and (4) if such a program is initiated and carried out gradually, it can be expanded as knowledge is gained and experience is appraised, thus eventually making flood insurance coverage available on reasonable terms and conditions to persons who have need for such protection.

(b) Participation of Federal Government in Flood Insurance Program Carried Out by Private Insurance Industry

The Congress also finds that (1) many factors have made it uneconomic for the private insurance industry alone to make flood insurance available to those in need of such protection on reasonable terms and conditions; but (2) a program of flood insurance with large-scale participation of the Federal Government and carried out to the maximum extent practicable by the private insurance industry is feasible and can be initiated.

* * *

(e) Land Use Adjustments by State and Local Governments; Development of Proposed Future Construction; Assistance of Lending and Credit Institutions; Relation of Federal Assistance to All Flood-Related Programs; Continuing Studies

It is the further purpose of this chapter to (1) encourage State and local governments to make appropriate land use adjustments to constrict the development of land which is exposed to flood damage and minimize damage caused by flood losses, (2) guide the development of proposed future construction, where practicable, away from locations which are threatened by flood hazards, (3) encourage lending and credit institutions, as a matter of national policy, to assist in furthering the objectives of the flood insurance program, (4) assure that any Federal assistance provided under the program will be related closely to all flood-related programs and activities of the Federal Government, and (5) authorize continuing studies of flood hazards in order to provide for a constant reappraisal of the flood insurance program and its effect on land use requirements.

§ 4002. Additional Congressional Findings and Declaration of Purpose

(a) The Congress finds that—

(1) annual losses throughout the Nation from floods and mudslides are increasing at an alarming rate, largely as a result of the accelerating development of, and concentration of population in, areas of flood and mudslide hazards;

(2) the availability of Federal loans, grants, guaranties, insurance, and other forms of financial assistance are often determining factors in the utilization of land and the location and construction of public and of private industrial, commercial, and residential facilities;

(3)   property acquired or constructed with grants or other Federal assistance may be exposed to risk of loss through floods, thus frustrating the purpose for which such assistance was extended;

(4)   Federal instrumentalities insure or otherwise provide financial protection to banking and credit institutions whose assets include a substantial number of mortgage loans and other indebtedness secured by property exposed to loss and damage from floods and mudslides;

(5)   the Nation cannot afford the tragic losses of life caused annually by flood occurrences, nor the increasing losses of property suffered by flood victims, most of whom are still inadequately compensated despite the provision of costly disaster relief benefits; and

(6)   it is in the public interest for persons already living in flood-prone areas to have both an opportunity to purchase flood insurance and access to more adequate limits of coverage, so that they will be indemnified for their losses in the event of future flood disasters.

(b)   The purpose of this Act, therefore, is to—

(1)   substantially increase the limits of coverage authorized under the national flood insurance program;

(2)   provide for the expeditious identification of, and the dissemination of information concerning, flood-prone areas;

(3)   require States or local communities, as a condition of future Federal financial assistance, to participate in the flood insurance program and to adopt adequate flood plain ordinances with effective enforcement provisions consistent with Federal standards to reduce or avoid future flood losses; and

(4)   require the purchase of flood insurance by property owners who are being assisted by Federal programs or by federally supervised, regulated, or insured agencies or institutions in the acquisition or improvement of land or facilities located or to be located in identified areas having special flood hazards.

FEMA (Federal Emergency Management Agency), now a household acronym, is charged with administration of the National Flood Insurance Program. 42 U.S.C.A. § 4011. With the increasing number and fury of hurricanes and floods since the early 1990s attracting its attention, the flood insurance program has been under almost constant criticism and FEMA's administration of it under constant pressure.

NATIONAL WILDLIFE FEDERATION AND PUBLIC EMPLOYEES FOR ENVIRONMENTAL RESPONSIBILITY V. FEDERAL EMERGENCY MANAGEMENT AGENCY AND NATIONAL ASSOCIATION OF HOMEBUILDERS

United States District Court, W.D. Washington, 2004.
345 F.Supp.2d 1151.

I. BACKGROUND

A. The Parties and the Present Action

The National Wildlife Federation ("NWF") and Public Employees for Environmental Responsibility ("PEER")(collectively "Plaintiffs") bring this Endangered Species Act ("ESA") lawsuit against the Federal Emergency Management Agency ("FEMA"), alleging that FEMA has violated Section 7(a)(2) of the ESA, 16 U.S.C. § 1536(a)(2), by not consulting with the National Marine Fisheries Service ("NMFS") on the impacts of the National Flood Insurance Program ("NFIP") on the Puget Sound chinook salmon, a threatened species. Plaintiffs contend that FEMA's implementation of the NFIP constitutes an agency action that may affect the Puget Sound salmon because some aspects of the NFIP encourage development in the floodplains, and the floodplains of the Puget Sound provide important habitat for the salmon. Plaintiffs seek three forms of relief: (1) a declaration that FEMA violated Section (7)(a)(2) of the ESA, (2) an injunction requiring FEMA to initiate consultation with NMFS on the NFIP's impacts on the Puget Sound Chinook salmon, and (3) the Court's retention of jurisdiction over the matter to ensure FEMA's proper implementation of the ESA and governing regulations.

The following entities have intervened as defendants in the action: the National Association of Home Builders ("NAHB"), Skagit County, Island County, the Washington Association of REALTORS, the Home Builders Association of Kitsap County, the Skagit Island Counties Builders Association, and Piazza Construction, Inc. (collectively "Intervenors").

B. The National Flood Insurance Program ("NPIF")

FEMA is the federal agency charged with administering the NFIP, a federal flood insurance program. Congress created the NFIP in 1968 by the National Flood Insurance Act ("NFIA"), 42 U.S.C. §§ 4001 et seq., later amended it by the Flood Disaster Protection Act of 1973, and again amended it in 1994 by the National Flood Insurance Reform Act. AR 116 at 2–4. The purposes of the flood insurance program are to make flood insurance "available on a nationwide basis through the cooperative efforts of the Federal Government and the private insurance industry" and to base flood insurance "on workable methods of pooling risks, minimizing costs, and distributing burdens equitably among those who will be protected by flood insurance and the general public." 42 U.S.C. § 4001(d). Congress further stated that other purposes of the federal flood insurance program are to:

(1) encourage State and local governments to make appropriate land use adjustments to constrict the development of land which is exposed to flood damage and minimize damage caused by flood loses,

(2) guide the development of proposed future construction, where practicable, away from locations which are threatened by flood hazards,

(3) encourage lending and credit institutions, as a matter of national policy, to assist in furthering the objectives of the flood insurance program,

(4) assure that any Federal assistance provided under the program will be related closely to all flood-related programs and activities of the Federal Government, and

(5) authorize continuing studies of flood hazards in order to provide for a constant reappraisal of the flood insurance program and its effects on land use requirements.

42 U.S.C. § 4001(e). The NFIA states that FEMA "shall consult with other departments and agencies of the Federal Government . . . in order to assure that the programs of such agencies and the flood insurance program authorized under this chapter are mutually consistent." 42 U.S.C. § 4024.

The three basic components of the NFIP are: (1) the identification and mapping of flood-prone communities, (2) the requirement that communities adopt and enforce floodplain management regulations that meet certain minimum eligibility criteria in order to qualify for flood insurance, and (3) the provision of flood insurance. AR 116 at 4. As part of the NFIP, FEMA also implements a Community Rating System ("CRS"), which provides discounts on flood insurance premiums in those communities that establish floodplain management programs that go beyond NFIP's minimum eligibility criteria. *Id.* at 31.

Plaintiffs contend that the ESA requires FEMA to consult with NMFS regarding the potential impact of each of these aspects of the NFIP on the Puget Sound chinook salmon. Defendants and Intervenors contend that such consultation is not required because Plaintiffs do not have standing, FEMA does not have discretion to implement measures under the NFIP that inure to the benefit of Puget Sound chinook salmon, and there is no reason to believe that the NFIP may affect Puget Sound chinook salmon.

1.   Identification and Mapping of Flood-Prone Communities

Congress authorized FEMA "to identify and publish information with respect to all flood plain areas, including coastal areas located in the United States, which have special flood hazards" and "to establish or update flood-risk zone areas in all such areas, and make estimates with respect to the rates of probable flood caused loss for the various flood risk zones for each of these areas." 42 U.S.C. § 4101(a)(1), (a)(2).

FEMA assesses the flood risk within each flood-prone community by conducting a Flood Insurance Study (a "flood study") that typically employs the use of computer and engineering models and statistical techniques. AR 116 at 6–7. FEMA presents the results of a flood study on a map referred to as a Flood Insurance Rate Map (a "flood map") and also in a narrative format, both of which are subject to public review and an administrative appeals process for any owner or lessee of real property within the community. *Id.* at 7–8. The flood risk information presented on a flood map and in a flood study report forms the technical basis for the administration of the NFIP. *Id.* at 9. For example, a flood map's identification of a property as a Special Flood Hazard Area ("SFHA"), which is land within the floodplain of a community subject to a one percent or greater chance of flooding in any given year, triggers a Mandatory Flood Insurance Purchase Requirement under the NFIP. *Id.* at 3, 9.

The NFIA requires FEMA to review flood maps at least once every five years to assess the need to update all floodplain areas and flood risk zones. 42 U.S.C. § 4101(e), (f)(1). FEMA has promulgated regulations governing the development and revision of flood maps. *See e.g.*, 44 C.F.R. §§ 65.5, 65.6; 44 C.F.R. pt. 72. The boundaries of a SFHA on a flood map can be revised, for example, following man-made alterations within the floodplain, such as the placement of fill. 44 C.F.R. §§ 72.1, 72.2.

2.   *Minimum Eligibility Criteria*

Congress has authorized FEMA to "develop comprehensive criteria designed to encourage . . . the adoption of adequate State and local measures" that will:

(1)   constrict the development of land which is exposed to flood damage where appropriate,

(2)   guide the development of proposed construction away from locations which are threatened by flood hazards,

(3)   assist in reducing damage caused by floods, and

(4)   otherwise improve the long-range land management and

use of flood-prone areas.

42 U.S.C. § 4102(c)(referred to herein as the "minimum eligibility criteria"). In 1976, FEMA promulgated regulations establishing the minimum eligibility criteria for flood-prone areas, mudslide area and flood-related erosion areas. 44 C.F.R. §§ 60.3–60.5. The criteria governing flood-prone areas are currently designated to reduce threats to lives and to minimize damage to structures and water systems during flood events, *see*

44 C.F.R. § 60.3; AR 116 at 2, not to protect aquatic habitat, imperiled species, or other environmental values.

Community participation in the NFIP is voluntary, and FEMA does not have any direct involvement in the administration of local floodplain management ordinances. AR 116 at 12. However, communities must adopt regulations consistent with FEMA's minimum eligibility criteria in order to be enrolled in the NFIP. 42 U.S.C. § 4012(c)(2); *cf.* 42 U.S.C. § 4022(a)(1)(prohibiting federal flood insurance to communities that have not complied with the criteria).

3. Provision of Flood Insurance

Congress authorized FEMA "to establish and carry out a national flood insurance program which will enable interested persons to purchase insurance against loss resulting from physical damage to or loss of real property or personal property related thereto arising from any flood occurring in the United States." 42 U.S.C. § 4011. FEMA must provide flood insurance coverage under the flood insurance to communities which have "evidenced a positive interest in securing flood insurance coverage under the flood insurance program" and have "given satisfactory assurance that . . . adequate land use and control measures will have been adopted . . . which are consistent with the comprehensive criteria for land management and use developed" under 42 U.S.C. § 4102, 42 U.S.C. § 4012(c).

FEMA provides flood insurance through arrangements with private sector property insurance companies (referred to as "Write Your Own" ("WYO") companies), which collect premiums from eligible insureds and, after retaining a portion to cover their costs, submit the remainder to the U.S. Treasury. 44 C.F.R. §§ 62.23, 62.24. Alternatively, FEMA provides flood insurance to insureds using state-licensed property and casualty insurance agents and brokers who deal directly with FEMA. 44 C.F.R. §§ 62.3, 62.4; AR 116 at 22. The NFIP is not the only source of flood insurance, but flood coverage for residential homeowners in particular is difficult to acquire from the private insurance market. AR 116 at 23.

4. Community Rating System ("CRS")

Congress authorized FEMA "to carry out a community rating system program, under which communities participate voluntarily . . . to encourage adoption of more effective measures that protect natural and beneficial floodplain functions," among other goals. 42 U.S.C. § 4022(b)(1). The CRS provides discounts on flood insurance premiums in those communities that establish floodplain management programs that go beyond the NFIP's minimum eligibility criteria. AR 116 at 31; AR 114 at 110–1. FEMA's CRS manual recognizes that "[f]loodplains perform certain natural and beneficial functions that cannot be duplicated elsewhere," such as "provid[ing] habitat for diverse species of flora and fauna, some of which cannot live anywhere else." AR 114 at 110–5. The CRS specifically provides incentives to protect areas designated as critical habitat for endangered species and for areas covered by Habitat Conservation Plans under the Endangered Species Act. *Id.* at 420–9. However, because fish enhancement goals and flood risk reduction goals are sometimes conflicting, the CRS also rewards activities that are detrimental to floodplains and aquatic species, for example, through its recognition of paved parking lots and roads as "open space" and through its encouragement of structural flood control projects such as levees, berms and floodwalls. *Id.* at 420–2, 530–2.

5. *FEMA's Oversight of Community Participation in the NFIP*

FEMA monitors communities to ensure that they have adopted an ordinance that meets or exceeds the NFIP's minimum eligibility criteria and to ensure that they are effectively enforcing the ordinance. AR 116 at 17. If communities do not adequately enforce their floodplain management regulations, they can be placed on probation and potentially suspended from the NFIP. *Id.* at 17–18; C.F.R. § 59.24(b), (c). FEMA, or States on behalf of FEMA, visit NFIP communities to conduct comprehensive assessments of communities' floodplain management programs, to provide technical assistance, and to identify any deficiencies in the local programs. AR 116 at 17; AR 101 (Community Compliance Program Guidance); AR 102 (Guidance for Conducting Community Assistance Contacts and Community Assistance Visits). Since 1999. FEMA has visited approximately 35 of the 110 communities in the Puget Sound area that are enrolled in the NFIP to monitor their compliance with the NFIP requirements. AR 118; AR 119.

C. *The NFIP and Development*

Plaintiffs assert that the NFIP contributes to an increase in development in the floodplains. In support, Plaintiffs point out that the NFIP is premised on the congressional finding that "the availability of Federal loans, grants, guarantees, insurance, and other forms of financial assistance are often determining factors in the utilization of land and the location and construction of public and of private industrial, commercial, and residential facilities." 42 U.S.C. § 4002(a)(2). The Final Environmental Impact Statement ("FEIS") for FEMA's NFIA regulations states that "[i]f a community chooses not to participate in the [NFIP], economic development in the flood hazard area may be severely restricted." AR 100 at 63. The FEIS goes on to say that "[g]enerally, the withdrawal of any form of Federal financial assistance for the acquisition or construction of buildings in the flood hazard area will eliminate sources of money and thereby have a strong tendency to decrease economic growth. . . . It appears that the amount of money available from non-federally related financial intermediaries is limited." *Id.*; *see also* 42 U.S.C. § 4012a (prohibiting any federally regulated bank or lender, or federal agency from offering loans or other financial assistance for acquisition or construction purposes to persons in non-NFIP communities); 42 U.S.C. § 5154a(a)(making disaster relief unavailable to non-NFIP communities that suffer from floods).

The declarations of Intervenors in support of their motion to intervene demonstrate the close connection between the availability of federal flood insurance and floodplain development in the Puget Sound region. The Washington Association of REALTORS represented that "the inability to obtain NFIP [insurance] would effectively shut down new housing in affected areas" because "[m]ost real estate purchasers cannot purchase property without obtaining financing, and in areas where it applies, flood insurance is a prerequisite to obtaining financing." Stout Decl., docket no. 17, ¶ 3. Similarly, Piazza Construction, Inc. contends that financing for its construction projects is contingent on obtaining flood insurance, and that flood insurance for past projects has been provided through the NFIP. Piazza Decl., docket no. 14, ¶¶ 5–7. The Home Builders Association of Kitsap County also noted that its approximately 560 builder and developer members rely on the NFIP to obtain financing for their construction projects. Castle Decl., docket no. 15, ¶¶ 2, 5.

II. DISCUSSION

FEMA engages in four central activities: (1) mapping; (2) developing minimum eligibility criteria which communities must use to develop their flood management regulations in order to be eligible for NFIP; (3) selling flood insurance; and (4) developing a community rating system *1164 to provide communities with discounted flood premiums if they adopt flood management regulations which exceed FEMA's minimum eligibility criteria. Each of these different activities could potentially cause damage to the threatened Puget Sound chinook salmon.

FEMA's flood insurance maps are used approximately 15 million times each year for developing State and community floodplain management regulations, for calculating flood insurance premiums, and for determining whether property owners must obtain flood insurance as a condition to receiving mortgage loans or other financial assistance. AR 116 at 4. FEMA has promulgated regulations governing the development and revision of flood maps. *See, e.g.,* 44 C.F.R. §§ 65.5, 65.6; 44 C.F.R. pt. 72. These regulations permit the boundaries of SFHAs on a flood map to be revised following man-made alterations to the floodplain, such as the placement of fill. 44 C.F.R. §§ 72.1, 72.2. Individual property owners who have filled the floodplain can petition FEMA to have their property removed from a flood area through a Letter of Map Revision based on Fill ("LOMR-F"). AR 116 and 9. Once property is removed from the floodplain it is no longer necessary for the property developer to comply with the community's floodplain management regulations. *See* AR 116 at 13. By allowing individuals to remove their property from regulation by artificially filling it, FEMA is in effect encouraging filling. The declaration of Alan Wald, docket no. 30 (2), connects filling to the destruction of salmon habitat. Wald notes that the filling of floodplains can result in destruction of wetlands, vegetation and habitats and "floodwaters displaced by fill increase velocity and erosive damage and scour fish habitat downstream." Wald Decl. ¶¶ 18–19. FEMA itself acknowledges that filling in the floodplain is highly likely to have negative effects on habitat of listed and endangered species. AR 61 at 1. Thus the mapping regulations promulgated by FEMA in implementing NFIP have a direct causal link to the alleged destruction of salmon habitat and the Plaintiff's injury.

FEMA's promulgation of minimum eligibility criteria and its sale of flood insurance both enable development in the floodplain that negatively impacts salmon. As the Intervenors note in declaration supporting their motion to intervene, most lending institutions require flood insurance as a prerequisite to project financing, making NFIP insurance a prerequisite to development in the floodplain. Castle Decl. ¶ 5; Piazza Decl. ¶ 5; Desiderio Decl., docket no. 16, ¶ 6. The Court disregards as disingenuous the Intervenors' argument that the provision of flood insurance decreases the rate of human development in the floodplain. In order to become eligible for NFIP insurance, local communities must adopt floodplain management ordinances that are consistent with FEMA's minimum eligibility criteria, which guide development in the floodplain, are primarily designated to lessen flood property damage and do not mention preserving the habitat of endangered species. 44 C.F.R. § 60.3. Floodplain development, in turn, reduces the amount of habitat available to chinook salmon and creates additional impermeable surfaces in the floodplain that produce polluting runoff. AR 5 at 22. Pollution and reduced habitat impact the numbers of surviving chinook salmon. AR 1 at 27–28. The Wald declaration and the declaration of Cleveland W. Steward III, docket no. 30 (3), also provide evidence of the importance of floodplains to salmon and the threat posed to salmon by human development in the floodplain. Wald Decl. ¶¶ 10, 13; *see generally* Steward Decl. ¶¶ 22–52. The causal connection between the promulgation of FEMA's minimum eligibility criteria, the provision of flood insurance, and development which harms chinook salmon in the Puget Sound is not "tenuous or abstract" and is strong enough to support standing. *See Ocean Advocates*, 361 F.3d at 1120.

Finally, FEMA's development of the CRS is causally linked to the Plaintiff's injury. FEMA uses the CRS to provide discounts on flood insurance to local communities that establish flood control measures beyond the minimum eligibility criteria. AR 116 at 31–32; AR 114 at 110–1. The CRS encourages some activities that are harmful to salmon, such as the removal of large woody debris from rivers. Wald Decl. ¶ 26. The CRS also impacts salmon habitat through its recognition of paved parking lots and roads as "open space," and its encouragement of structural flood control projects such as levees, berms and floodwalls. AR 114 at 420–2, 530–2.

As a result, the Court concludes that Plaintiffs have provided sufficient evidence showing that the injury to salmon caused by third party developers of floodplains is not too tenuously connected to the acts of FEMA in implementing the NFIP. The present case is analogous to the Ninth Circuit cases of *Ocean Advocates* and *National Audubon Society*, described above, in which the plaintiffs had demonstrated a plausible chain of causation between FEMA's actions and the plaintiffs' injury.

2. Analysis of Plaintiffs' Section 7(a)(2) Claim

NMFS has jurisdiction over the Puget Sound chinook salmon. *See* 50 C.F.R. § 223.102(a)(16). Section 7(a)(2) imposes a procedural duty on FEMA to initiate formal consultation with NMFS regarding its implementation of the NFIA. FEMA and the Intervenors argue that formal consultation is not required because: (1) The NFIP is not a discretionary "agency action" subject to Section 7(a)(2) of the ESA, and (2) Plaintiffs have failed to demonstrate that FEMA's implementation of the NFIP "may affect" the Puget Sound chinook salmon.

a. Discretionary "Agency Action"

The first issue is whether the implementation of the NFIP—including the identification and mapping of flood-prone communities, the promulgation of regulations outlining minimum eligibility criteria, the provision of flood insurance, and the implementation of the CRS—constitutes "agency action" implicating the ESA. Section 7(a)(2) states that it applies to "any action authorized, funded, or carried out by [a Federal] agency." 16 U.S.C. § 1536(a)(2). The regulations implementing Section 7(a)(2) similarly define "[a]ction" to mean "all activities or *programs* of any kind authorized, funded, or carried out, in whole or in part, by Federal agencies in the United States or upon the high seas." 50 C.F.R. § 402.025 (emphasis added). "Examples include, but are not limited to: . . . (b) the promulgation of regulations; (c) the granting of licenses, contracts, leases, easements, rights-of-way, permits, or grants-in-aid; or (d) actions directly or indirectly causing modifications to the land, water, or air." *Id.*

The NFIP is a program carried out by FEMA. The NFIP involves the promulgation of regulations (i.e. the minimum eligibility criteria), providing insurance, and actions that indirectly cause modifications of the land and water (e.g. FEMA's mapping of floodplains determines the applicability of local land use regulations, and FEMA's CRS provides incentives to modify the floodplains in certain ways). Accordingly, the NFIP falls within the broad definition of "agency action" to which Section 7(a)(2) applies. *See TVA v. Hill*, 437 U.S. at 173, 98 S.Ct. 2279 (Section 7(a)(2)'s language "admits of no exception"); *Natural Res. Def. Council ("NRDC") v. Houston*, 146 F.3d 1118, 1125 (9th Cir.1998)("The term 'agency action' has been defined broadly"); *Pacific Rivers Council*, 30 F.3d at 1055 ("Following the Supreme Court's lead in TVA, [the Ninth Circuit ha[s] also construed 'agency action' broadly.")

However, agency actions are subject to Section 7(a)(2)'s consultation requirements only if "there is discretionary Federal involvement of control." 50 C.F.R. § 402.03; *see also* 50 C.F.R. § 402.16 (requiring re-initiation of consultation where "discretionary Federal involvement or control over the action has been retained or is authorized by law.") "[W]here . . . the federal agency lacks the discretion to influence the private action, consultation would be a meaningless exercise; the agency simply does not possess the ability to implement measures that inure to the benefit of the protected species." *Sierra Club v. Babbitt*, 65 F.3d 1502, 1509 (9th Cir.1995). In other words, "[w]here there is no agency discretion to act, the ESA does not apply." *NRDC v. Houston*, 146 F.3d at 1125–26.

Mapping

FEMA argues that its mapping of a floodplain is "exceedingly ministerial," based solely on a technical evaluation of the base flood elevation. However, FEMA has used its discretion to map the floodplain in a way that allows persons to artificially fill the floodplain to actually remove it from its floodplain status, and thus from regulatory burdens. There is nothing in the NFIA authorizing, let alone requiring, FEMA to authorize filling activities to change the contours of the natural floodplain. Indeed, such regulations may be counterproductive to the enabling statute's purpose of discouraging development in areas threatened by flood hazards. As a result of FEMA's discretion in its mapping activities, FEMA must consult on its mapping regulations and its revisions of flood maps, to determine whether they jeopardize the continued existence of the Puget Sound chinook salmon. Because the NFIA requires FEMA to review flood maps at least once every five years to assess the need to update all floodplain areas and flood risk zones, 42 U.S.C. § 4101(e), (f)(1), the agency activity is clearly an ongoing one that is subject to the ESA's consultation requirements.

Eligibility Criteria

In developing the minimum eligibility criteria, the NFIA authorizes FEMA to guide development of proposed construction away from locations threatened by flood hazards and to "otherwise improve the long-range land management and use of flood-prone areas." 42 U.S.C. § 4101(e), (f)(1). Pursuant to either of these purposes, FEMA has the discretion to revise the minimum eligibility criteria to benefit the Puget Sound chinook salmon.

Even if it is true that FEMA has discretion to revise the minimum eligibility criteria, FEMA and the Intervenors argue that FEMA's authority to engage in rulemaking is not an "ongoing agency action" to be subject to the ESA's consultation requirements. FEMA's Cross-Mot. at 11 n.5; Intervenors' Cross-Mot. at 34–36. The Intervenors argue that unless the NFIA imposes a clear, non-discretionary obligation on FEMA to amend its regulations, Plaintiff's cause of action is not ripe for review. *Id.* at 35.

They argue that NWF is using the ESA's consultation provision to create, rather than respond to, an agency action. *Id.* at 36. Plaintiffs respond that the minimum eligibility criteria are analogous to the LRMP's in *Pacific Rivers Council*, which the Ninth Circuit held represented "ongoing agency action" because they were "comprehensive management plans" with "an ongoing and long-lasting effect even after adoption." Pls.' Reply, docket no. 40, at 11. Plaintiffs also highlight a District of Idaho case in which the Court held that the Bureau of Land Management's decision not to take action constituted *1174 agency action. Second Hasselman Decl., docket no. 40(1), Ex. 15 (*Western Watersheds Project v. Matejko*, No. 01–0259–E–BLW (D. Idaho Mar. 23, 2004)). In *Western Watersheds*, the Bureau of Land Management's regulations, which did not impose conditions on water diversions arising under an 1866 statute, constituted a continuing agency action under the rationale of *Pacific Rivers Council*. *Id.* at 9, 11. In the present case, FEMA must consult on its minimum eligibility criteria because FEMA has discretion to amend its regulations and because those regulations have an ongoing impact on the use of floodplains in the same manner as the LRMP's have an ongoing impact on the use of forest lands in *Pacific Rivers Council*.

Sale of Insurance

FEMA has no discretion to deny flood insurance to a person in a NFIP-eligible community. *See* 42 U.S.C. § 4012(c)(requiring FEMA to provide flood insurance to communities which have "evidenced a positive interest in securing flood insurance coverage under the flood insurance program" and have "given satisfactory assurance that . . . adequate land use and control measures will have been adopted . . . which are consistent with the comprehensive criteria for land management and use developed" under 42 U.S.C. § 4102). As a result, FEMA has no obligation to consult with NMFS regarding the actual sale of flood insurance.

Community Rating System

FEMA has discretion to promote conservation measures through the CRS. The CRS is a voluntary program through which Congress mandated that FEMA provide discounts on flood insurance premiums to communities that implement flood management regulations that exceed FEMA's minimum criteria. As noted above, some of the CRS criteria help salmon, and some are detrimental to salmon. Even the program is voluntary, it is "authorized" and "carried out" by a federal agency in a way that may adversely affect the Puget Sound chinook salmon. Further, by offering discounts to communities that adopt certain types of regulations, FEMA could encourage the adoption of salmon-friendly measures in local communities. For these reasons, formal consultation is required.

In conclusion, the NFIA confers discretion on FEMA to implement the NFIP in a manner that would inure to the benefit of the Puget Sound chinook salmon, with the exception of the part of the program that deals with the actual sale of flood insurance. Although FEMA has no discretion when it comes to the provision of flood insurance to persons in NFIP-eligible communities, it has discretion to act in a manner that could benefit the Puget Sound chinook salmon in mapping the floodplains, in developing and promulgating the minimum eligibility criteria, and in implementing the CRS. Accordingly, the Court holds that FEMA's implementation of the NFIP, with the exception of the actual sale of flood insurance, is a discretionary "agency action" for the purposes of Section 7(a)(2) of the ESA.

b.   Agency Action that "May Affect" a Listed Species

The second issue in determining whether the ESA's formal consultation requirement is triggered is whether FEMA's implementation of the NFIP "may affect" the Puget Sound chinook salmon. *See* 50 C.F.R. § 402.14(a). "Any possible effect, whether beneficial, benign, adverse, or of an undetermined character, triggers the formal consultation requirement." 51 Fed.Reg. 19,926, 19,949 (June 3, 1986)(final rule 50 C.F.R. pt. 402). The "threshold for formal consultation must be set sufficiently low to allow Federal agencies to satisfy their duty to 'insure' under Section 7(a)(2)." 51 Fed.Reg. at 19,949.

FEMA contends that the ESA's formal consultation requirement is not triggered because "FEMA has not had reason to believe that the NFIP may affect the Puget Sound chinook salmon," FEMA's Cross-Mot., docket no. 36, at 22. Although FEMA has not documented its "no effect" determination, FEMA relies on *Southwest Ctr. For Biological Diversity v. United States Forest Serv.*, 100 F.3d 1443 (9th Cir.1996), for the proposition that "[n]o consultation is necessary where an agency undertakes an action that will have 'no effect' on an endangered or threatened species." FEMA's Cross-Mot. at 22. *Southwest Center* is distinguishable on two fronts: first, it is not an ESA case and, second, the action agency in that case prepared a biological assessment, which FEMA has not done in the present case. 100 F.3d at 1445. FEMA also relies on Pacific Rivers Coun*cil* to support its related argument that "if the agency determines that a particular action will have no effect on an endangered or threatened species, the consultation requirements are not triggered." 30 F.3d at 1054 n. 8. This is dicta, and FEMA has pointed to no case where an action agency avoided its formal consultation duty based on the agency's "no effect" determination. The lack of any documentation to support FEMA's "no effect" determination precludes any judicial review of FEMA's apparent "determination" and undermines the other Section 7(a)(2) consultation procedures that only allow an agency to avoid formal consultation through a biological assessment or a concurrence letter following information consultation with FWS or NMFS. *See* 50 C.F.R. § 402.14(b)(1).

Plaintiffs argue that the "may affect" standard is met because the NFIP affects development in the floodplains and such development "may affect" the Puget Sound chinook salmon and its habitat. A summary of the record and non-record evidence in support of Plaintiffs' position is outlined at pages 18–19 of Plaintiffs' reply brief, docket no. 40. Among other evidence, Plaintiffs point to a 1998 letter from NMFS to FEMA (Region X, Bothell, Washington) in which NMFS itself opined that the NFIP may lead to increased development that negatively affects salmon:

NMFS . . . believes it is appropriate for FEMA to consult with NMFS regarding [FEMA's disaster assistance] programs, as required by Section 7 of the Endangered Species Act. In particular, we are aware that *the National Flood Insurance Program (NFIP), as currently implemented by FEMA, could result in increased development in flood-prone areas with consequent impairment of floodplain functions of salmon bearing waters.* AR 109 at 1 (emphasis added). Although NMFS "lacks to authority to require the initiation of consultation," 51 Fed.Reg. 19,949, the Court gives substantial deference to NMFS's construction of its own consultation regulations in determining whether FEMA has failed to fulfill its responsibilities under ESA. *See Sierra Club v. Marsh*, 816 F.2d 1376, 1988 (9th Cir.1987) (deferring to FWS as to whether reinitiation of consultation was warranted under its regulations at 50 C.F.R. § 402.16). NMFS's opinion that the NFIP may increase development and may therefore affect salmon is not an isolated one in the administrative record. Even FEMA recently suggested informal consultation with NMFS regarding the impact of NFIP implementation on chinook salmon. AR 47–53.

FEMA assert that Plaintiffs have mis-characterized the issue, and that "[t]he proper analysis is not whether development affect salmon, but rather, whether the federal agency action at issue (i.e., the NFIP) 'may affect' the salmon." FEMA's Cross-Mot., docket no. 36, at 22. FEMA takes too narrow an approach. The regulations implementing Section 7(a)(2) of the ESA require an action agency to consider "the effects of the action as a whole." 50 C.F.R. § 402.14(c). " 'Effects of the action' refers to the direct and indirect effects of an action on the species or critical habitat." 50 C.F.R. § 402.02. "Indirect effects are those that are caused by the proposed action and are later in time, but still are reasonably certain to occur." *Id. In Nat'l Wildlife Fed'n (NWS) v. Coleman*, 529 F.2d 359, 373–74 (5th Cir.1976), record and non-record evidence showed that the construction of a highway would lead to increased residential and commercial development, which, in turn, would affect the habitat of the endangered Mississippi sandhill crane. The "the total impact of the highway on the crane," not merely the direct loss of habitat taken by the highway right-of-way, had to be considered. *Id.* at 373. The *NWF v. Coleman* court thus required the transportation agency to consult with FWS to determine whether the private development accompanying the construction of the highway would jeopardize the existence of the crane.

FEMA attempts to distinguish *NWF v. Coleman*, noting that the highway was 90 percent federally funded and that the transportation agency controlled the placement of the highway and interchanges. FEMA's Cross-Mot., docket no. 36, at 23. However, just as the transportation agency in *NWF v. Coleman* controlled the placement of the highways and interchanges, FEMA designates the boundaries of the floodplains on flood maps. Both of these actions affect the location of development. Whether or not FEMA funds the NFIP, in whole or in part, is immaterial because it is undisputed that FEMA is the federal agency charged with administering the NFIP and that is sufficient to qualify as an "agency action." In neither the present case nor *NWF v. Coleman* does the action agency authorize, permit, or carry out the actual development that causes the harm to the species' habitat; however, in both cases, development is "reasonably certain to occur" as a result of the agency's action. *See* 50 C.F.R. § 402.02.

The Court concludes that there is substantial evidence in the administrative record showing that FEMA's implementation *1177 of the NFIP "may affect" the Puget Sound chinook salmon, thus triggering the formal consultation requirement of Section 7(a)(2) of the ESA.

3.   Conclusion on the Merits of Plaintiffs' Section 7(a)(2) Claim

FEMA's implementation of the NFIP as outlined herein, with the exception of the actual sale of flood insurance, is a discretionary "agency action" that "may affect" the Puget Sound chinook salmon, triggering the formal consultation requirement of Section 7(a)(2).

NOTES

1.   Drawing boundaries of the flood hazard area is critical. *See e.g., Reardon v. Krimm*, 541 F.Supp. 187 (D.Kan.1982), in which Kansas City failed in an action to set aside the flood hazard boundaries drawn up by the Army Corps of Engineers, because the city failed to challenge the base flood elevations on scientific and technical grounds, as required by the National Flood Insurance Act. What about the credibility of a private firm retained by FEMA in setting elevations and boundaries of the flood zone? *See, e.g., City of Wenatchee v. United States*, 526 F.Supp. 439 (E.D.Wash.1981). The Biggert-Waters Flood Insurance Reform Act of 2012, P.L. 112–141 created the Technical Mapping Advisory Council. The Council's role includes recommending to the Administrator how to effectively and efficiently map flood risk areas in the United States, mapping standards and guidelines for flood insurance rate maps, maintaining flood insurance rate maps and flood risk identification and recommending procedures for delegating mapping activities to State and local mapping partners; 42 U.S.C.A. § 4101a (2012).

About 15% of the flood hazard maps have not been amended since the 1970's and 1980's. A 2013 report by the Association of State Floodplain Managers estimates that it will cost upwards of 7.5 billion dollars for maps to be amended and current. Sarah Childress, *How Federal Flood Maps Ignore the Risks of Climate Change,* (2016). http://www.pbs.org/wgbh/frontline/article/how-federal-flood-maps-ignore-the-risks-of-climate-change.

2.   Critics assert that the incentive of the National Flood Insurance Program (NFIP) runs in the wrong direction. Rather than deterring building in the floodplain, they say the act encourages building by subsidizing owners with insurance that private insurers will not provide. Supporters and administrators of the program say it is self-sufficient; that is, the premiums paid in are used to pay the damage claims. The premiums, however, are not enough to pay all claims. The program is deeply in debt. The NFIP has many critics who contend that in practice it has made matters worse. Every few years reforms are considered and some enacted. *See, e.g.,* Bunning-Bereuter-Blumenauer Flood Insurance Reform Act of 2004, P.L. 108–264, enacted to curtail practice of repetitive payments. The program suffers from significant defects. *See* Dominic Spinelli, *Reform of the National Flood Insurance Program: Congress Must Act Before the Next Natural Disaster*, 39 REAL EST.L.J. 430 (2011). The Biggert-Waters Flood Insurance Reform Act of 2012 was enacted to transition the program from subsidized rates (artificially low rates), to offer fill actuarial rates reflective of risk in the area. The Homeowner Flood Insurance Affordability Act of 2014, 113 P.L. 89 modifies the Biggert-Waters Flood Insurance Reform Act. This act limits insurance policy increases for certain subsidized policyholders and implements an annual surcharge to all policyholders to ensure fiscal soundness of the fund. However, the 2014 Act still gives generous subsidies to flood-prone properties. The NFIP owes the Treasury Department upwards of 24 billion dollars. Jennifer Wriggins, *Flood Money: The Challenge of U.S. Flood Insurance Reform in a Warming World*, 119 PENN STATE L.REV. 361 (2014).

While the program requires flood insurance for people obtaining a mortgage, the insurance is allowed to lapse because the lenders do not monitor flood insurance on a regular basis as they do fire insurance. Also, people obtaining second mortgages are not required to have flood insurance. Should flood insurance be required of all property owners rather than just those with mortgages?

3.   Since the NFIP doesn't pay the entire bill, the federal government usually steps in with disaster relief funds. Since communities and individuals do not pay the bulk of the bill, there is a disincentive for individuals to locate their buildings in safe spots and for local governments to enact effective flood regulations. They can allow development in flood prone areas without too much worry about the cost of possible loss of property in the event of a flood. Development pressures and short-term thinking cause some communities to follow this, the easier path. See Rutherford H. Platt, *Disasters and Democracy: The Politics of Extreme Natural Events* 28 (1999). The urge to help the suffering taking place overwhelms the "cold-hearted" reaction that would let people who build in risky areas fend for themselves when the foreseeable events occur. See John K. Warren, Note, *Restoring Responsibility and Accountability in Disaster Relief*, 31 WM. & MARY ENVTL.L. & POL'Y REV. 893 (2007).

The financial inability of many to afford public or private insurance exacerbates the problem. The well-known tragedy that befell the Ninth Ward in New Orleans in Hurricane Katrina, inundated by twenty feet of water, illustrates this. Only thirty to forty percent of the single family homes affected by Katrina were insured. *See id.* at 898. See also Christine M. McMillan, Comment, *Federal Flood Insurance Policy: Making Matters Worse*, 44 HOUS.L.REV. 471, 500 (2007).

4.   The Coastal Barrier Resources Act of 1982, 16 U.S.C.A. §§ 3501 et seq., is the federal government's nod to environmental protection. Under the act, federal insurance is not available for property within designated high-hazard areas. However, a landowner who can self-insure or afford private insurance, can build in these areas. *See* Elise Jones, *The Coastal Barrier Resources Act: A Common Cents Approach to Coastal Protection*, 21 ENVTL.L. 1015 (1991).

5.   The issue of fault when something goes awry in a floodplain determination arises most commonly after flood damage to property for which no flood insurance was purchased. Causes of action do not lie against the U.S. Government for failure to inform prospective home buyers of flood hazards in a flood zone. *Harrah v. Miller*, 558 F.Supp. 702 (S.D.W.Va.1983).

6.   Suppose that following a state court determination that a floodplain zoning ordinance was too strict (*see, e.g., Seidner v. Town of Islip*, 453 N.Y.S.2d 636, 439 N.E.2d 352 (N.Y.1982), a city were to grant use variances to all who asked for them to develop in the floodplain. Suppose further that a 100-year flood then caused ten million dollars' worth of damage to structures built in accordance with such variances, and successful claim is made for federal disaster relief. Could the federal government then sue the city for damages for failure to enforce its local zoning ordinances passed pursuant to federal regulations issued by HUD under the Federal Disaster Protection Act? In *United States v. Parish of St. Bernard*, 756 F.2d 1116 (5th Cir.1985), the federal government sued two local governments for the cost of flood damages paid, on the grounds that the towns' failure to enact and enforce required flood hazard regulations caused or contributed to the damage sustained by flood prone property subsequently built upon. The court held that the United States had no implied right of action under the national flood insurance program, but that it could bring any subrogation action as allowed by state law and pursue other common law remedies.

7.   Some suggest that local government, fearful of monetary liability if found to have excessively regulated property, have under-regulated flood plain development. *See* Christine A. Klein and Sandra B. Zellmer, *Mississippi River Stories: Lessons from a Century of Unnatural Disasters*, 60 SMU L.REV. 1471 (2007). However, as noted in the introduction to this section, the courts have typically not found the flood plain controls to take property despite the sometimes severe economic impact due to the obvious danger posed by development. *See* Saul Jay Singer, *Flooding the Fifth Amendment: The National Flood Insurance Program and the "Takings" Clause*, 17 B.C.ENVTL.L.REV. 323, 370 (1990); Edward A. Thomas & Sam Riley Medlock, *Mitigating Misery: Land Use and Protection of Property Rights Before the Next Big Flood*, 9 VT.J.ENVTL.L. 155 (2008).

E. HILLSIDE PROTECTION

"The more dangerous the lot, the higher the price."[7]

Everyone wants to live on the top of the hill, where the views are breathtaking. Not everyone can, of course, but the increasing affluence of many Americans during the last quarter of the 20th century enabled them to do so. If you cast your eyes upward in many hilly or mountainous areas, you will likely see houses teetering on the edge. Construction on steep slopes, however, is dangerous. Of the many landslides to occur the one in Laguna Beach, California, in June 2005 is well documented pictorially. There, a hillside in the Bluebird Canyon area, saturated by heavy winter rains, destroyed at least nine homes and damaged more than twenty others. See L.A.Times photo gallery http://www.latimes.com/la–0601laguna_slide-pg,0,3755989.photogallery. See also the National Geographic video dramatically depicting the dangers of landslides. http://www.youtube.com/watch?v=mknStAMia0Q.

While southern California is the poster child for landslides in the country, they occur in all 50 states. As the United States Geological Survey reports that they "cause $1–2 billion in damages and more than 25 fatalities on average each year. Expansion of urban and recreational developments into hillside areas leads to more people that are threatened by landslides each year." http://landslides.usgs.gov/index.php. In the mid-1970s, the USGS created the National Landslide Hazards Program (LHP) with the goal of reducing losses from landslides by improving the understanding of their causes and suggesting mitigation strategies.

The increase in hillside construction and the understanding of the dangers created by land disturbance on steep slopes led to increased regulation.

TERRAZAS V. BLAINE COUNTY

Supreme Court of Idaho, 2009.
147 Idaho 193, 207 P.3d 169.

HORTON, JUSTICE.

This appeal arises from a petition for judicial review concerning a county board's denial of a subdivision application. Appellants Ed Terrazas and Jackie Weseloh (Applicants) appeal the district court's order affirming Respondent Blaine County Board of County Commissioners' (Board) decision denying Applicants' subdivision application. We affirm the decision of the district court.

Applicants are co-owners of approximately 115 acres of real property on East Fork Road, 1.5 miles east of State Highway 75 in Blaine County,

---

[7]   Orrin Pilkey, Professor of Earth Sciences, Duke University. Though speaking of beachfront development, Pilkey's observation is equally applicable to hillside development.

Idaho. In May of 2004, Applicants submitted an application to subdivide the subject property into the NoKaOi subdivision.

Because the proposed subdivision involved no more than four lots, the application was initially processed under the short plat subdivision procedures found in section 10–4–6 of the Blaine County Code (B.C.C.). The short plat procedures are a streamlined version of the standard subdivision application procedures. One of the unique features of the short plat procedure is that it allows an application to proceed directly to the Board for a final plat review without requiring a preliminary plat review by the Planning and Zoning Commission (Commission).

As part of the initial review of the NoKaOi application, Planning and Zoning Senior Planner Tom Bergin prepared a staff report for the Board's consideration. One of the issues addressed in Bergin's report was whether the areas of disturbance in the proposed subdivision fell within the Mountain Overlay District (MOD). Stated broadly, the intent of the MOD is to direct development away from the County's hillsides and mountains. B.C.C. §§ 9–21–1(A); 9–21–1(B). Bergin's first staff report concluded that the proposed areas of disturbance did not conflict with the MOD ordinance because they were located on a "bench slope" rather than a "hillside slope." Bergin's report also observed that his conclusion regarding MOD compliance was "of course subject to further examination by the Board." Applicants also claim that Planning and Zoning Administrator Linda Haavik advised them that she also believed that the planned building sites were not within the MOD because they were situated on a bench. Applicants maintain that they proceeded with their application-spending more than $50,000 in the process-in reliance on these opinions that the NoKaOi development plans did not violate the MOD ordinance.

On December 20, 2004, the Board conducted a public hearing on the proposed subdivision. Concerns as to whether the subdivision violated the MOD ordinance were raised. At the hearing, Bergin and Haavik reiterated their opinions that the areas of disturbance were not located within the MOD. Commissioner Wright commented that he had personally visited the site and found application of the MOD ordinance difficult. The hearing concluded with the Board's determination that, although the short-plat application process does not ordinarily require so, a thorough review by the Commission was appropriate to "further consider" the application.

The Commission considered the application and conducted public hearings on March 24, 2005, and April 14, 2005. At these hearings, the Commission considered Bergin's opinion regarding whether the MOD applied to the NoKaOi subdivision. As part of its review, the Commission conducted a scheduled site visit to view the property. At the Commission's request, Applicants staked and marked certain points on the property with storey poles. Following the site visit, the Commission rejected Bergin's interpretation and application of the MOD ordinance. The Commission found that the areas of disturbance on two of the four lots in the proposed subdivision impermissibly encroached upon the MOD and also violated the county ordinance restricting development on hillsides visible from Scenic Corridor 1(SC1) (i.e., visible from State Highway 75). Specifically, the Commission concluded that the proposed areas of disturbance were located on a "ridge of a hillside slope" and not a "bench slope." The Commission recommended that the Board deny the subdivision application.

The Board revisited the application in public hearings on June 28, 2005, and July 26, 2005. At the latter hearing, the Board voted to deny the application. The Board adopted the Findings of Fact, Conclusions of Law, and Recommendation of the Commission and, on August 18, 2005, the Board issued its own Findings of Fact, Conclusions of Law, and Decision denying Applicants' subdivision application. In its written decision, the Board specifically rejected the proposition that the MOD contained a "bench exception." The Board's written decision contained a lengthy explanation why its interpretation of the MOD ordinance, as applied to the NoKaOi subdivision application, was consistent with the Board's previous decisions involving other applications potentially involving application of the MOD ordinance.

Pursuant to the Local Land Use Planning Act (LLUPA) and the Idaho Administrative Procedures Act (APA), Applicants petitioned the district court for judicial review of the Board's denial of their subdivision application. The district court affirmed the decision of the Board. Applicants then timely appealed to this Court.

Before the district court, Applicants argued: (1) the Administrator had final authority to make MOD boundary determinations; (2) because of Applicants' reliance on the Planning and Zoning staff's opinions, the Board is estopped from applying the MOD ordinance; (3) Applicants' due process rights were violated by reason of Commissioner Wright's personal visit to the site; (4) the MOD ordinance is unconstitutionally vague; (5) the Board's determination was arbitrary, capricious, and without a reasonable basis in law or fact and violated Applicants' equal protection rights; and (6) Applicants were entitled to attorney fees. The district court was not persuaded by Applicants' arguments and affirmed the Board's decision to deny the application.

On appeal, Applicants have presented the same arguments for this Court's consideration. We conclude that Applicants have failed to demonstrate a substantial error upon which this Court should overturn the decision of the Board. Thus, we affirm the decision of the district court.

Applicants argue that the Board exceeded its authority by reaching a decision on MOD compliance different than that of the Planning and Zoning Administrator. Further, Applicants assert that the Board should be estopped from denying their application on the basis of the MOD, given their reliance on the opinions of Bergin and Haavik that the location of their proposed building sites was not within the MOD. We disagree.

The Board was empowered to enact ordinances regulating the procedure and standards for subdivision applications. I.C. § 67–6513. Under Idaho law, county boards are vested with the exclusive, non-delegable, authority to finally approve subdivision applications. I.C. § 67–6504; *Cowan v. Bd. of Comm'rs of Fremont County,* 143 Idaho 501, 511–12, 148 P.3d 1247, 1257–58 (2006). Under I.C. § 67–6511, the Board had the power to establish zoning ordinances providing standards to regulate the construction and location of buildings and the preservation of open space. This Court has recognized that aesthetic concerns, including the preservation of open space and the maintenance of the rural character of Blaine County, are valid rationales for the County to enact zoning restrictions under its police power. *Dawson Enter., Inc., v. Blaine County,* 98 Idaho 506, 518, 567 P.2d 1257, 1269 (1977).

The purpose of the MOD, as set forth in B.C.C. § 9–21–1(B), falls squarely within the recognized powers of the County:

1.   To preserve the natural character and aesthetic value of hillsides and mountains in the County by regulating development thereon;

2.   To maintain slope and soil stability;

3.   To prevent scarring of hillsides and mountains made by cuts and fills and/or by access roads to hillside and mountainous areas;

4.   To ensure accessibility by emergency vehicles on hillside roads;

5.   To prevent unsafe conditions for access, circulation, and road maintenance and unwarranted problems associated therewith in hillside and mountainous areas;

6.   To help ensure water quality and prevent deterioration due to sedimentation or inadequately performing septic systems;

7.   To regulate site alteration and structural development in the Mountain Overlay District to assure that site alteration and development occurs in the Mountain Overlay District only when no sufficient development exists outside of the District and all other criteria under this Chapter have been met, and to assure that any site alteration and structural development within the District occurs in a manner that minimizes hillside visibility;

8.   To carry out the provisions contained in the County Comprehensive Plan; and

9.   To protect agricultural lands for productive agriculture while providing for necessary residential and other structural use within the context of productive agriculture.

Applicants argue that the Board exceeded its authority by reaching a decision on MOD compliance different than that of the Planning and Zoning Administrator. Further, Applicants assert that the Board should be estopped from denying their application on the basis of the MOD, given their reliance on the opinions of Bergin and Haavik that the location of their proposed building sites was not within the MOD. We disagree.

[The court found that the Board had the sole authority to make final decisions on subdivision applications and that application of principles of estoppel to the Board's decision was not warranted. The court also found the town had not violated the appellants' right to procedural due process. Eds.]

Applicants assert that the decision of the Board should be overturned because it was arbitrary and capricious. This assertion rests on the contention that the Board has interpreted and applied the MOD ordinance inconsistently with regard to projects with allegedly similar topography as the NoKaOi subdivision. Asserting that the Board has applied the ordinance inconsistently and directing our attention to the differing interpretations and comments made in the Board's proceedings, Applicants argue that the ordinance is therefore void for vagueness and incapable of being applied in any manner that is not arbitrary and capricious.

A statute is void for vagueness if persons of ordinary intelligence must guess at its meaning. *Cowan,* 143 Idaho at 514, 148 P.3d at 1260. Our analysis of the ordinance begins with the literal language of the enactment. *Lane Ranch P'ship,* 145 Idaho at 89, 175 P.3d at 778. Where the language is unambiguous, the clearly expressed intent must be given effect, and there is no occasion for this Court to construe the language.

The ordinance regarding MOD demarcation is found in B.C.C. § 9–21–2(D), which provides:

The regulations of this Overlay District, which will not be designated on the Official Zoning Map, shall apply to areas of land within the County where:

1.   The hillside slope exceeds twenty five percent (25%), including all areas that are higher than the lowest hillside slopes which exceed twenty five percent (25%); or

2.   In the Scenic Corridor 1(SC1) where the hillside slope exceeds fifteen percent (15%), including all areas that are higher than the lowest hillside which exceed fifteen percent (15%).

B.C.C. § 9–21–2(F) further provides:

> "Areas higher than the lowest hillside slopes" under subsections
> D1 and D2 of this Section shall include all areas and geographic
> features (regardless of grade of slope), including, without
> limitation, all ridges, saddles, knolls, and pockets or islands of
> land, between and including the summit of the hillside and the
> lowest hillside slopes exceeding twenty five percent (25%) for
> subsection D1 of this Section or fifteen percent (15%) for
> subsection D2 of this Section.

Bergin outlined three potential approaches to determining the MOD
boundaries in his second staff report. The first approach, and the one
adopted by Bergin in his first staff report, excluded from the MOD areas of
the hillside considered a "bench" as defined in the Blaine County Code.[8]
The second option applied the MOD to any point on the subject property
"between the summit and the foot" of the lowest hillside slope exceeding 15
or 25% but excluded those portions of property above the lowest hillside
slope that did not also exceed 15 to 25%. The third approach considered all
areas on the subject property higher in elevation than the lowest hillside
slope exceeding 15 or 25% to be within the MOD. The Commission adopted
the third approach, which was also the approach accepted by the Board.

Despite the fact that Bergin and Haavik believed that NoKaOi
subdivision did not fall within the MOD because it was on a flat bench area
above the first slope, the Board found that the MOD ordinances did not
provide such an exception. The Board stated: "The applicant's argument
concerning a "bench"-even if the Board were to accept it-would not change
the finding as to the MOD because even benches between the summit and
the lowest hillside slopes exceeding fifteen percent (15%)(SC1) or twenty
five percent (25%) would be within the MOD." We agree with the Board's
conclusion.

We first observe that the term "bench," although defined in B.C.C. § 9–
2–1, does not appear in the MOD ordinance, much less as an exception to
the general definition of the MOD. To the contrary, the Board's

---

[8] [ct's fn 4] The following applicable definitions are found in B.C.C. § 9–2–1:

BENCH: A level step created by the former flood deposits of a river.

HILLSIDE: A part of a hill between and including the summit and the foot and includes,
but is not limited to, such landforms as ridges, saddles, and knolls.

   Knoll: A small round hill or mound.

   Ridge: A sharp, elongated crest or linear series of crests.

   Saddle: A ridge connecting two (2) higher elevations.

   Summit: The highest part, top or peak of a hillside.

   Foot: The lowest part of a hillside where the grade of slope increases from horizontal
   or near horizontal; the bottom or base of a hillside.

SLOPE: An inclined ground surface, the inclination of which is expressed as a ratio of
horizontal distance to vertical distance. Percent slope is calculated by multiplying this
ration (rise/run) by one hundred (100). Slope is measured from the base of the hill.

interpretation is supported by the statement of intended scope of the ordinance, found in B.C.C. § 9–21–1(A), which states:

> All areas of land, regardless of geographic or geological features, between and including the summit of the hillside and lowest hillside slopes exceeding fifteen percent (15%) or twenty five percent (25%) for these respective areas are included within the Mountain Overlay District. The District is not intended to create a patchwork that excludes saddles, ridges, knolls, summits, or pockets or islands of flatter land between and including the applicable lowest hillside slopes and the summit of the hillside, but rather is intended to include those areas.

Although Applicants couch their challenge in "void for vagueness" terms, Applicants' argument does not address the language of the MOD. Rather, Applicants direct this Court to comments by Commission and Board members discussing their difficulty in interpreting and applying the ordinance. Considering only the language of the ordinance, we find that the language is not vague. Rather, the ordinance unambiguously provides that areas located above the lowest 25% slope fall within the MOD as do all areas that are higher than the lowest hillside slopes exceeding 15% in SC1.

This leads us to consider the evidence supporting the Board's determination that the NoKaOi subdivision fell within the MOD. The Commission determined that the elevation of the lowest hillside slope exceeding 25% was 5,740 feet. A contour line was then drawn across the topographic map of the subject property at 5,740 feet, above which the Commission determined any "areas of disturbance" were within the MOD. In reaching its decision, the Commission also requested that Applicants stake the site in preparation for the Commission's site visit. The Commission found that proposed lots 1 and 2 of the NoKaOi subdivision had "areas of disturbance" entirely within the MOD. Additionally, Applicants were asked to place storey poles in the centroids of the areas of disturbance. The Commission found that the storey poles placed in lots 1 and 2 were visible from State Highway 75 and thus in violation of the ordinance regulating development within SC1 on areas higher than the lowest hillside slopes exceeding 15% percent. Because the Commission found that Lots 1 and 2 were not in compliance under both alternatives of the MOD ordinance, it recommended that the Board deny the application. After holding two additional public hearings on the matter, the Board adopted the Commission's recommendation and denied the application.

[We] defer to the Board's findings of fact unless they are clearly erroneous. So long as the Board's "findings, conclusions and decision are sufficiently detailed to demonstrate that it considered applicable standards and reached a reasoned decision, we [will] find that the decision was not arbitrary and capricious and was based on substantial evidence in the record." *Brett v. Eleventh St. Dockowner's Ass'n, Inc.,* 141 Idaho 517, 523,

112 P.3d 805, 811 (2005); *see also* I.C. § 67–6535(a–b). Applicants have not established that it was clear error for the Board to find that the areas of disturbance in lots one and two sat above a 25% slope or that the 5,740-foot contour line demarcated the top of that first slope. This Court has independently reviewed the record as considered by the Board and we conclude that the Board's findings of fact are supported by substantial and competent evidence.

Applicants * * * complain[ ]that the ordinance has not been applied in a consistent fashion. Applicants have not asserted that the Board's action was "a deliberate and intentional plan of discrimination against [them], based on some unjustifiable or arbitrary classification, such as race, sex, or religion." *State v. Larsen,* 135 Idaho 754, 758, 24 P.3d 702, 706 (2001). Rather, to the extent that Applicants have asserted an equal protection claim, it appears that they assert that they are a "class of one." As such, Applicants need only allege and prove that they have intentionally been singled out and treated differently based on a distinction that fails the rational basis test. *See e.g. City of Coeur d'Alene v. Simpson,* 142 Idaho 839, 853, 136 P.3d 310, 324 (2006) (citing *Village of Willowbrook v. Olech,* 528 U.S. 562, 564–65 (2000). This leads us to consider Applicants' claim that the Board's decision was arbitrary and capricious, based upon different treatment of others.

The Board's written decision explained at length how the instant decision was consistent with its previous MOD determinations for other properties and subdivisions including: the Rollins property in the East Fork subdivision (which sits immediately south of the proposed NoKaOi subdivision), the Bluegrouse Ridge subdivision, the Timberview Terrace subdivision, the Griffin Ranch subdivision, the Golden Eagle subdivision, the Dip Creek subdivision, the Lee's Gulch subdivision, the Dilley parcel, and a remodel of property on Eagle Creek Road. We are unable to conclude that the Board's decision on the NoKaOi subdivision application was arbitrary and capricious or an abuse of discretion. The administrative record clearly indicated that the Board carefully considered their application and issued a thorough, detailed discussion of why it declined to find that lots 1 and 2 were outside the MOD. Applicants have failed to persuade us that the Board erred in a fashion governed by I.C. § 67–5279(3).

We conclude that the Board had exclusive authority to determine whether the proposed subdivision fell within the MOD and that it would be inappropriate to estop the Board from enforcing the MOD ordinance. We find that Applicants' due process rights were not violated by reason of Commissioner Wright's site visit. We find that the MOD ordinance is not unconstitutionally vague and that substantial competent evidence supported the Board's determination that the subdivision would violate the MOD ordinance. We find that the Board's decision was not arbitrary and capricious and did not violate Applicants' equal protection rights. We therefore affirm the decision of the district court.

NOTES

1.   Generally, hillside protection ordinances, with their concerns for safety, natural resource preservation, infrastructure needs and aesthetics, easily fall within the powers granted by enabling acts and constitute valid police power enactments to meet substantive due process challenges. In *Sellon v. City of Manitou Springs*, 745 P.2d 229 (Colo.1987), problems of erosion and drainage prompted the city to create a hillside low density residential zone, which used an equation that required larger minimum lots based on the degree of slope. A landowner challenged the ordinance as being insufficiently related to health, safety and general welfare concerns. The court disagreed. Noting the problems had been a matter of "great attention" and that the ordinance "reflected a considered effort," found within the city's police power. *See also In re Interim Bylaw, Waitsfield*, 742 A.2d 742 (Vt.1999) (an ordinance that prohibited residential use at an elevation of or above 1700 feet but allowed agricultural and forestry use was not a facial taking); and *Jones v. Zoning Hearing Bd. of Town of McCandless*, 578 A.2d 1369 (Pa.Cmwlth.1990) (while the property could not be used as intensively as the landowner desired, it could still be developed into 89 residential units or 150,000 square feet of commercial space).

2.   Where hillside protection ordinances preclude or severely limit use but do not deal with health and safety concerns the categorical *Lucas* rule may be triggered. In *Monks v. City of Rancho Palos Verdes*, 84 Cal.Rptr.3d 75 (Cal.App.2008), the court addressed a 30-year effort by the city to determine the safety of development in a landslide area while forestalling landowners' efforts to build single-family homes with ocean views. In 1957, after a lull of 100,000 to 120,000 years, an "ancient landslide" area became active and the land began to move. By 1978, the city council became concerned that areas once considered stable might no longer be so, dictating the necessity to conduct geological studies. Safety concerns were sufficient to impose a moratorium on development pending the outcome of the studies. Over the next 24 years, much happened, but nothing was resolved. Numerous studies were conducted with inconclusive results. Over this period, the city maintained the moratorium but enacted several exclusions, allowing modest development. On June 2, 1999, the 18th hole situated on the beachfront of the Ocean Trails Golf Course moved about 100 feet toward the ocean, leaving the city with a 17-hole course and a one-hole course. Despite the lack of uncertainty, by 2001 the city had installed gas, electric, water and sewer utilities serving vacant land owned by Monks and others.

In January 2002, plaintiffs filed an application requesting an exclusion from the moratorium. That brought matters to a head and on June 12, 2002, the city council approved Resolution No. 2002–43, which recited, among other things, that there was insufficient data to determine whether the land in Zone 2 (which included plaintiffs' land) met the 1.5 safety factor required by the city and that it was not possible to judge the level of risk of development in that zone. The resolution concluded that the city "continue to deny requests for development permits for new homes in the Zone 2 area . . . until an applicant submits a complete Landslide Moratorium Exclusion application that is supported by adequate geological data demonstrating a factor of safety of 1.5 or greater . . . to the satisfaction of the City Geologist [and] the City Council approves the . . . application." *Id.* at 86.

An inverse condemnation lawsuit based on the state constitution's takings clause followed. The court found the 2002 resolution permanently denied plaintiffs all economically viable use. (During the litigation the parties settled a temporary takings claim, presumably covering all or some of the period from 1978 to 2002.) The 2002 resolution marked a turning point because prior to its adoption the city had not required the lot owners "to establish a *gross* safety factor of 1.5 or higher as a condition of construction." *Id.* The plaintiffs had not sought an exclusion, but the court found it would have been futile to do so. Since the city allowed no economically viable use, the burden shifted to the city to show that background principles of the state's law of property and nuisance justified the ban.

The court found the city did not meet its burden of showing that residential use of the plaintiffs land would constitute a nuisance. There was "nothing inherently harmful about plaintiffs' desired use of their properties: to build homes." *Id.* at 107. That the city had zoned the land for residential use, had approved a subdivision of the land, and installed the utilities did not help its case. There was uncertainty but "uncertainty [was] not a sufficient basis for depriving a property owner of a home." *Id.* The city needed to show a reasonable probability. The evidence did establish that the plaintiffs land would at the most sustain significant structural damage within a decade. Furthermore, the land was not comparable to the case of the breakaway of the 18th hole of the golf course. The kind of landslide at issue was a so-called "block glide," which generally would not result in plaintiffs lots sliding onto adjacent lots. Thus, while one can easily imagine a case where building on a steep slope of unstable land would be a nuisance, this was not the case.

Compare, *Corrigan v. City of Scottsdale*, 720 P.2d 528 (Ariz.App.1985), *aff'd in part, vacated in part*, 720 P. 2d 528 (Ariz. Ct. App. 1985), which held a hillside protection ordinance to be a taking, but the test used, disallowing transfers of development rights on the same property, has been discredited in Arizona and criticized by commentators. *See* Norman Williams, Jr. and John M. Taylor, 7 *American Land Planning Law* § 169:38 (Rev. Ed. 2011).

3.   Various methods and percentages are used in steep slope ordinances. The MOD of Blaine County, Idaho, limited development where the slope exceeded 25%, and, for land within its Scenic Corridor to only 15%. Laguna Beach, California has "Density Standards," which it uses to determine the maximum allowable building density pursuant to a Slope/Density Table:

Slope	Maximum Density
0—10%	3.0 Units/Acre
10+—15%	2.5 Units/Acre
15+—20%	2.0 Units/Acre
20+—25%	1.5 Units/Acre
25+—30%	1.0 Units/Acre
30+—35%	.5 Units/Acre
35+—40%	.2 Units/Acre
40+—45%	.1 Units/Acre
45+%	.0 Units/Acre

Lot slope [is] ascertained by calculating the slope percentage of rise, (which is the vertical height distance between the highest and lowest points of a lot), divided by the run, (which is the horizontal distance between the highest and lowest points of a lot), multiplied by 100.

Laguna Beach, CA, Hillside Protection Zone, § 25.15.010.

4. The *Terrazas* appellants' estoppel argument was based on $50,000-plus they spent on various studies (engineering, avalanche, soils, and hydrology) in reliance on the opinions they received from two staff members that their development plans did not violate the MOD ordinance. Would you have counseled these expenditures? Can an estoppel claim succeed when the Board had final authority in the matter?

While not as dramatic in terms of the safety or protection of natural resources, site development in non-hilly areas poses similar problems prompting local government to regulate all site development. Olympia, Washington, for example, controls site development including cleaning, excavation, and filling so as (1) to prevent untimely and indiscriminate removal or destruction of trees and ground cover; (2) to minimize surface water runoff and diversion which may contribute to flooding; (3) to reduce siltation in the city's streams, lakes, storm sewer systems, and public roadside improvements; (4) to reduce the risk of slides and the creation of unstable building sites; (5) to promote building and site planning practices that are consistent with the city's natural topography, soils, and vegetative features and (6) to insure effective erosion control of property after land clearing and grading. Olympia Zoning Ordinance § 16.48.020.

The city likewise prohibits the removal of trees without the "approval of a tree protection and replacement plan and a tree removal permit." § 16.48.050.

F. PRESERVATION OF AGRICULTURAL LAND

1. AGRICULTURAL PRESERVATION

Does the residential sprawl conversion of farmland threaten this country's food supply? Does the need to preserve farmland outweigh the need for residential developable land on the urban fringe? Can effective agricultural preservation policies assist in formulating rational and sustainable growth management policies that reduce greenhouse gas emissions and global warming, benefit developing areas by viewing the urbanizing area as a whole?

The findings of the United States Department of Agriculture's National Resources Inventory indicate that every state has lost agricultural land to development over the past 30 years. From 1982–2012, approximately 24.5 million acres of agricultural land has been developed in each of the 48 contiguous states, Hawai'i and the Caribbean. Texas lost a staggering 3.1 million acres, with approximately 1.6 million of those acres being prime farmland. California, North Carolina, and Ohio each lost more than 750,000 acres of prime farmland. According to the 2007 National Resources Inventory, South Carolina, Maine, North Carolina, Maryland, Connecticut, New Hampshire, Delaware, Massachusetts, Rhode Island, and New Jersey converted more than 9 percent of their agricultural land to developed land. California and Florida experienced the largest loss of agricultural land between 2002–2007, which accounts for nearly half (49 percent) of the acreage devoted to growing fruit and vegetables nationwide and represent 71 percent of fruit, and 47 percent of vegetable production based on market value of agricultural products sold. The combination of soils, unique microclimates, and extended growth seasons makes the cropland in these states irreplaceable.

The conversion of the best land is tragic. Of all of the agricultural land in America, only about 43 million acres is prime, flat, fertile, class I farmland, which is the highest yielding farmland. Often these lands are adjacent to metropolitan areas and are most in danger of being developed. The lands that are most suitable for farming, or prime farmland, are usually gently sloping lands with good water run-off. These characteristics are also quite desirable in building development, which creates a conflict. See Daniels and Bowers, *Holding Our Ground: Protecting America's Farms and Farmland* 8–9 (Island Press 1997) and *The Sierra Club Report on Sprawl: The Dark Side of the American Dream—The Costs and Consequences of Suburban Sprawl,* 1998.

According to a 1993 study by the American Farmland Trust, land on the fringe of densely settled urban areas, land the Trust calls "urban influenced," represents a mere 5 percent of the nation's farmland yet produces 56 percent of the food we eat. The lack of effective growth control measures to prevent residential sprawl development makes the loss of these lands for agricultural use imminent. See The Christian Science Monitor, July 26, 1993, at 13. A prime example of this is in the central valley in California, an area which produces around 20% of all the crops we consume nationally, mostly in fruits and vegetables. Yet it is seriously threatened by urban sprawl, and the population in the region is expected to triple by the year 2040. In Florida, approximately 150,000 acres a year are taken out of agricultural use, the highest in the nation. This is significant since Florida is the world's leading producer of citrus products such as grapefruit and oranges. See Benbrook, The World Must Eat, Wall Street Jour., at A-19 (Dec. 4, 1996).

2. THE ROLE OF THE FEDERAL GOVERNMENT

In 1979, the U.S. Department of Agriculture and the President's Council on Environmental Quality co-sponsored a study on the availability of the nation's agricultural land. The study, known as The National Agricultural Lands Study (NALS) (1981), identified the key ingredients for successful programs: (1) farmer participation from the onset; (2) adequate technical and financial support; (3) strong local leadership; (4) patience; and (5) timing—start before development pressures become too strong.

The 1981 NALS study inspired a number of programs which attempt to alleviate the problems our agricultural community faces. The NALS study inspired the creation of the American Farmland Trust, which has worked toward the preservation of prime and unique farmlands. The Federal Farmland Protection Act was enacted in 1982, and other programs have been implemented which help determine where our most valuable farmlands are from a technical standpoint. The U.S. Soil Conservation service's LESA program (Land Evaluation and Site Assessment) has been used by local governments since the early eighties. LESA is a point system which has been designed to provide a rational process for assisting local officials in making farmland conversion decisions through the local zoning process. The point system helps evaluate lands for their potential productivity for agriculture. Among the considerations used in assessing point totals are: soil quality, slope of the land, and location of the land away from available sewer and water public utilities. See Steiner, Pease and Coughlin, A Decade with LESA—The Evolution of Land Evaluation and Site Assessment (1992).

Congress passed the Farmland Protection Policy Act (FPPA) as part of the Food and Agricultural Act of 1981. 7 U.S.C.A. § 4201 et seq. The following sections provide a good overview of its provisions:

FARMLAND PROTECTION POLICY

Sec. 4202.   (a) The Department of Agriculture, in cooperation with other departments, agencies, independent commissions, and other units of the Federal Government, shall develop criteria for identifying the effects of Federal programs on the conversion of farmland to nonagricultural uses.

(b) Departments, agencies, independent commissions, and other units of the Federal Government shall use the criteria established under subsection (a) of this section, to identify and take into account the adverse effects of Federal programs on the preservation of farmland; consider alternative actions, as appropriate, * * * .

* * *

EXISTING POLICIES AND PROCEDURES

Sec. 4203.   (a) Each department, agency, independent commission, or other unit of the Federal Government, with the assistance of the Department of Agriculture, shall review current provisions of law, administrative rules and regulations, and policies and procedures applicable to it to determine whether any provision thereof will prevent such unit of the Federal Government from taking appropriate action to comply fully with the provisions of this subtitle.

(b)   Each department, agency, independent commission, or other unit of the Federal Government, with the assistance of the Department of Agriculture, shall, as appropriate, develop proposals for action to bring its programs, authorities, and administrative activities into conformity with the purpose and policy of this subtitle.

* * *

LIMITATIONS

Sec. 4208.   (a) This chapter does not authorize the Federal Government in any way to regulate the use of private or non-Federal land, or in any way affect the property rights of owners of such land.

(b)   None of the provisions or other requirements of this subtitle shall apply to the acquisition or use of farmland for national defense purposes.

PROHIBITION

Sec. 4209.   This chapter shall not be deemed to provide a basis for any action, either legal or equitable, by person or class of persons challenging a Federal project, program, or other activity that may affect farmland.

In the "Farms for the Future Act of 1990," 7 U.S.C.A. § 4201, Congress authorized the Secretary of Agriculture to make federal loan guarantees and interest rate assistance available to lending institutions in states with state operated preservation funds. 7 U.S.C.A. § 1465. For additional references, *see* Becker, *Promoting Agricultural Development through Land Use Planning Limits*, 36 REAL PROP.PROB. & TRUST J. 619 (2002); Daniels, *When City and County Collide: Managing Growth in the Metropolitan Fringe* (Island Press, 1999); Council on Environmental Quality and U.S. Department of State, Global 2000 Report to the President; Julian

Juergensmeyer and Thomas E. Roberts, *Land Use Planning and Development Regulation Law* § 13.2 (3d ed. 2012); and Robert H. Freilich and Linda K. Davis, *Saving the Land: The Utilization of Modern Techniques of Growth Management to Preserve Rural and Agricultural America*, 13 URB.LAW. 27 (1981).

3. STATE AGRICULTURAL PRESERVATION LAWS

(a) Growth Management Systems

WETHERELL V. DOUGLAS COUNTY

Court of Appeals of Oregon, 2010.
235 Or.App. 246, 230 P.3d 976.

HASELTON, P.J.

Petitioner Garden Valley Estates, LLC (Garden Valley) seeks judicial review of an order of the Land Use Board of Appeals (LUBA) in which LUBA reversed the county's plan amendment and zone change concerning a 259-acre parcel. On review, Garden Valley contends that, because the 590-acre ranch (of which the 259-acre parcel had been a part) could not be profitably grazed and, for that reason, was not a "farm unit," LUBA erred in determining that the parcel was agricultural land pursuant to OAR 660–033–0020(1)(b). We review to determine whether LUBA's order was "unlawful in substance" and affirm.

Because it provides context for LUBA's decision and the parties' contentions on review, before turning to the facts, we describe the specific statutory and regulatory provisions that inform the central legal issue in this case—that is, specifically, whether LUBA correctly determined that the 259-acre parcel is agricultural land under OAR 660–033–0020(1)(b) because it is "within a farm unit." To resolve that issue, however, we must address a more fundamental and subsidiary legal question: What is a "farm unit" for purposes of OAR 660–033–0020(1)(b)? The parties' competing contentions in that regard focus on whether a "farm unit" must be economically viable-that is, profitably used for farm-related purposes. Accordingly, with the legal issue properly framed, we turn to the statutory and regulatory scheme.

As context, "Oregon's statewide land use planning goals, adopted by the Land Conservation and Development Commission (LCDC), set out broad objectives for land use planning in Oregon." *Save Our Rural Oregon v. Energy Facility Siting*, 339 Or. 353, 361, 121 P.3d 1141 (2005). To implement the land use goals, the legislature has authorized LCDC to adopt rules, which "are valid only if they are consistent with both the applicable [land use] statutes and [the] goals." *Wetherell v. Douglas County*, 342 Or. 666, 676, 160 P.3d 614 (2007) (Wetherell I).

This case concerns the agricultural lands goal—that is, Goal 3—which is designed to "facilitate the preservation of agricultural land, as directed by ORS 215.243." *Wetherell I*, 342 Or. at 676, 160 P.3d 614. As the Supreme Court noted in Wetherell I, the touchstone for determining whether property is "agricultural land" for purposes of Goal 3 is whether the land is suitable for farm use. Specifically, in Wetherell I, the Supreme Court invalidated an administrative rule that prohibited local governments from considering evidence of profitability when determining whether property is agricultural land under Goal 3. The court reasoned that, "[u]nder Goal 3, land must be preserved as agricultural land if it is suitable for 'farm use', which means, in part, 'the current employment of land for the primary purpose of obtaining a profit in money' through specific farming-related endeavors." 342 Or. at 677, 160 P.3d 614 (emphasis in original). Nonetheless, the court noted that profitability is not determinative of whether land is agricultural land. Instead, the court reasoned that a fact finder may consider profitability "to the extent such consideration is consistent with the remainder of the definition of 'agricultural land' in Goal 3." *Id.* at 682.

Consistently with the definition of "agricultural land" in Goal 3, OAR 660–033–0020(1) defines "agricultural land." That definition provides:

"(a) 'Agricultural Land' as defined in Goal 3 includes:

"(A) Lands classified by the U.S. Natural Resources Conservation Service (NRCS) as predominantly Class I–IV soils in Western Oregon and I–VI soils in Eastern Oregon;

"(B) Land in other soil classes that is suitable for farm use taking into consideration soil fertility; suitability for grazing; climatic conditions; existing and future availability of water for farm irrigation purposes; existing land use patterns; technological and energy inputs required; and accepted farming practices; and

"(C) Land that is necessary to permit farm practices to be undertaken on adjacent or nearby agricultural lands; and

"(b) Land in capability classes other than I–IV/I–VI that is adjacent to or intermingled with lands in capability classes I–IV/I–VI within a farm unit, shall be inventoried as agricultural lands even though this land may not be cropped or grazed."

As previously indicated, this case concerns the meaning of the term "farm unit" in OAR 660–033–0020(1)(b)—a provision also referred to as the "farm-unit rule." that provides land within farm units is suitable for farm use and is therefore within the definition of agricultural land in Goal 3. Of significance in this case, the term "farm unit" is not defined for purposes of OAR 660–033–0020(1)(b).

In light of that statutory and regulatory framework, we turn to the material facts. Because Garden Valley is not challenging the facts stated in LUBA's order, we take the material facts from the order on review. The subject 259-acre parcel is designated Agriculture and zoned Exclusive Farm Use-Grazing (FG). The parcel was formerly part of a 590-acre livestock ranch. In 2005, the county approved a partition that created the subject parcel, along with two other farm parcels that lie to the north and east. Following partition each of the three parcels were managed separately, with the subject property used for seasonal grazing. The subject property is developed with a dwelling and barns, and includes two ponds. It has no water or irrigation rights.

After its acquisition of the 259-acre parcel in 2006, Garden Valley contended that the property could not be used profitably for grazing and sought a determination from the county that the parcel was "non-resource land and for that reason not subject to [Goal 3]." As pertinent here, the county determined that the 259-acre parcel was not agricultural land. Some of the respondents in the present judicial review proceeding appealed the county's decision to LUBA. LUBA remanded the case on several grounds, including "for findings addressing * * * whether the 259-acre parcel remains part of a 'farm unit' along with the two other parcels that made up the original 590-acre ranch.

On remand, the county considered that issue and issued the following findings:

"53. The Commission finds that compelling testimony by Mr. Spencer and Mr. Simonis together with the professional analysis performed by Mr. Caruana, demonstrate convincingly that the property comprising the former 590-acre ranch is not a farm unit containing the subject property. While there is some historic use of the property being managed in conjunction with the other properties to the north and east, the evidence clearly demonstrates that joint management of the 590-acre ranch for grazing and haying activities similar to its historic use is not possible. The evidence reflects that the 590-acre ranch is not suitable for farm use and has not been a single operating farm unit since at least 1995, despite repeated attempts to manage it for that purpose.

"54. Each rancher of the 590 acres, despite considerable advantages (including alternative irrigated pasture, trucking companies, significant economies of scale, relationships in cattle industry) has found that the ranch, with its poor soils, poor forage, and lack of water, is not suitable for farm use. Expensive efforts have been made in coming to this conclusion including attempts at pasture improvement, water development, and other management activities. All have failed. Goal 3 is intended to preserve large units of agricultural land as agricultural land. It is not intended to preserve as agricultural land units that are not suitable for farm use, simply because they may have been at some time in the past. Since the former 590-acre unit is not a viable farm unit, the Commission finds that the property should not be classed as agricultural land."

Ultimately, based on its determination that the 259-acre parcel is not agricultural land, the county approved amendments to the comprehensive plan and zoning maps that would allow the parcel to be divided into five-acre residential lots. Petitioners again appealed to LUBA.

In addressing Garden Valley's contention that a "farm unit" is a geographic unit that is profitably used for farm-related purposes, LUBA's analysis focused primarily on the text of OAR 660–033–0020(1)(b). Specifically, LUBA reasoned that the text does not "include any suggestion that the profitability of a 'farm unit' is a consideration under that prong of the agricultural land definition." In that regard, according to LUBA, OAR 660–033–0020(1)(b) states that land in certain soil classes "is agricultural land * * * , regardless of whether or not it can be profitably farmed."

LUBA expressly declined to extend the Supreme Court's reasoning regarding profitability in Wetherell I to the application of OAR 660–033–0020(1)(b) in this case for two interrelated reasons. LUBA noted that "the inherent manipulability and unreliability of any profitability evaluation cautions against extending and relying on that type of evaluation in * * * determining whether the subject property is part of a 'farm unit' for purposes of OAR 660–033–0020(1)(b)." Ultimately, LUBA concluded that "whether or not a 'farm unit' has been or can be farmed 'profitably' is not a consideration" under OAR 660–033–0020(1)(b). Accordingly, having concluded that profitability is not a consideration in the present case, LUBA returned to the relevant legal question for purposes of OAR 660–033–0020(1)(b)-that is, "whether the subject property is properly viewed as part of a 'farm unit,' despite the recent cessation of joint use." According to LUBA, in making that determination, the most important consideration is "whether there is some significant obstacle to resumed joint operation."

Applying that standard, LUBA reasoned that "[t]here can be no possible dispute that the former ranch was a 'farm unit' for purposes of OAR 660–033–0020(1)(b), with a long and recent history of use for a hay/grazing operation that included the [259-acre parcel]." Significantly, LUBA noted that "[t]he county does not identify any changes that have occurred with respect to soil, water or forage on the former 590-acre ranch since the ranch was partitioned that would preclude a resumed hay/grazing operation similar to that conducted on the ranch for many years." Thus, because nothing "fundamental has changed that would preclude a resumption of a farm operation using the elements of the former ranch," LUBA concluded that the 259-acre parcel was within a "farm unit" for purposes of OAR 660–033–0020(1)(b) and reversed the county's decision. Garden Valley seeks judicial review of LUBA's resulting order.

On review, the parties' positions squarely raise a single legal issue—that is, whether the term "farm unit" refers to a geographic unit of land that is profitably used for farm-related purposes. However, the parties' subsidiary arguments in support of their respective positions are not squarely joined.

Garden Valley contends that a proper analysis of OAR 660–033–0020(1)(b) begins by identifying the pertinent "farm unit" so as to determine whether the subject property is within it. As previously indicated, although not defined for purposes of OAR 660–033–0020(1)(b), Garden Valley contends that a "farm unit" is a geographic unit of land that is profitably used for farm-related purposes.

Conversely, respondents and amicus curiae, the Department of Land Conservation and Development (DLCD), contend that profitability is not a consideration in identifying a "farm unit" and reason that a proper understanding of OAR 660–033–0020(1)(b) requires an examination of that provision's purpose. Specifically, DLCD asserts:

> The text [of OAR 660–033–0020(1)(b)] requires only three considerations: (1) that the subject parcel not be in soil classes I–IV/I–VI; (2) that the subject parcel be 'adjacent to or intermingled with' land that does contain soil classes I–IV/I–VI; and (3) that the subject parcel be within a 'farm unit. In sum, DLCD contends that Garden Valley erroneously posits a definition of "farm unit" that was not intended for the rule by "graft[ing] a use test—one already provided in OAR 660–033–0020(1)(a)(B)—onto a rule designed to address a parcel's relationship to surrounding land.

As previously indicated, the term "farm unit" is not defined for purposes of OAR 660–033–0020(1)(b). Nor does subsection (1)(b) include any express language that supports Garden Valley's contention that a "farm unit" is a geographic unit of land that is profitably used for farm-related purposes. Given that lack of explicit textual guidance, we examine the content and contours of "farm unit" in light of our decisions in *Dept. of Land Conservation v. Curry County*, 132 Or.App. 393, 888 P.2d 592 (1995), and *Riggs v. Douglas County*, 167 Or.App. 1, 1 P.3d 1042 (2000), which address the function of OAR 660–033–0020(1)(b) in the context of the definition of "agricultural land" as a whole and explain the nature of a "farm unit."

We begin with Curry County. In that case, we reasoned that, under a substantively similar version of OAR 660–033–0020(1)(b), land is suitable for farm use consistently with Goal 3 because of its location. In that case, the petitioners contended that a "farm unit" must consist predominantly of soils in classes I–IV in order for adjacent or intermingled property with soils of other classes to be within the farm unit. We disagreed, noting that the question under the farm-unit rule "is locational, i.e., whether land that is not of agricultural quality is interspersed with land that is" and explained that

> [a]n objective of subsection (b) appears to be to prevent piecemeal fragmentation of farm land and to make all land in the unit part of a contiguous whole. Thus, the rule's purpose is not to measure the quality of particular land in the unit, except to require that the unit contain some class I–IV soils. The fact that all of the land comprises a single operating farm unit makes the quality of particular parts of it a marginal factor in determining whether the unit is 'agricultural,' and a central consideration in identifying the rule's objective to be the preservation of the unit as a whole.

Curry County, 132 Or.App. at 398, 888 P.2d 592. In sum, in Curry County, we concluded that, for purposes of the farm-unit rule, land within a unit is suitable for farm use not because of its particular quality but rather because of its location within and relationship to the contiguous whole.

Riggs built on the reasoning in Curry County. There, in addressing circumstances that are similar to those in this case, we described the principle to be used in determining when a parcel ceases to be within a "farm unit." In doing so, we provided useful guidance as to the meaning of that term.

> The subject property at issue in Riggs was a 101-acre parcel, which,

> [f]rom 1950 through 1974, * * * was part of a 337.5-acre sheep ranch known as the Busenbark Ranch. In 1974, the 337.5-acre tract was divided into three smaller parcels, and conveyed into separate ownership; however, the entire tract continued to be managed as a sheep ranch until 1996. In 1996, the owner of the subject property, who managed the entire ranch, discontinued ranching operations and sold the subject property to [petitioner.] The subject property was sold to [petitioner] as 'residential' land." Thereafter, the petitioner sought a plan amendment and a zone change because the subject property was not agricultural land under Goal 3.

The issue in Riggs was "whether the [101-acre] parcel is part of a 'farm unit' with the other parcels that comprised the Busenbark Ranch, on which joint operations were conducted until shortly before petitioner purchased his property." 167 Or.App. at 4, 1 P.3d 1042. The petitioner contended that "land cannot be part of a 'farm unit' under OAR 660–033–0020(1)(b) unless it is *currently* in common management or farm operations with land that contains soils of the specified capability." Riggs, 167 Or.App. at 6, 1 P.3d 1042 (emphasis in original). The respondents disagreed, asserting that, under the petitioner's definition of "farm unit," " 'no matter how long a parcel of non-Class I–IV soils had been managed with adjacent lands as part of a farm unit, it could simply be sold to a developer, and once that developer had ceased joint farm management operations, the parcel would be free of the OAR 660–033–0020(1)(b) requirement to protect 'intermingled lands' that are part of a farm unit, and the developer could claim it was non-agricultural land.' " 167 Or.App. at 7, 1 P.3d 1042.

In rejecting the petitioner's contention, we reasoned that OAR 660–033–0020(1)(b) "does not define the relevant terms or spell out the time frame within which farm operations must have taken place on particular land in order for it to be regarded as (or as part of) a farm unit." 167 Or.App. at 8, 1 P.3d 1042. Specifically, we explained:

> [A] parcel would not be part of a 'farm unit' simply because concurrent farm operations occurred on it and nearby land 50 years ago. In [Curry County], we identified the purpose of the rule 'to be the preservation of the unit,' 132 Or.App. at 398 [888 P.2d 592]; it would be squarely contrary to that purpose to interpret the rule as contemplating that a parcel could cease being part of the unit simultaneously with and simply because of the discontinuation of farm operations on it or its ostensible sale for nonfarm purposes. This case is closer to the latter extreme than the former.

Although we did not establish a bright-line definition of "farm unit," our holding in Riggs is predicated on an understanding that, whatever else the term "farm unit" may mean, it includes lands, whether in common or diverse ownership, on which there is a recent history of concurrent farm operations. Further, we implicitly reiterated that lands within that unit are "suitable" for farm use because of their location—that is, their relationship to the unit. Taken to its logical extension, our reasoning in Riggs establishes that, when farm operations have recently ceased on a parcel that historically has been used for farming operations with other lands as part of a single "farm unit," the parcel is within the unit unless the applicant can demonstrate circumstances—the most important of which is whether there is a significant obstacle to resumed joint operation-that dictate a contrary result. Our understanding of the term "farm unit" and description of the principle to be used in determining when a parcel ceases to be within a "farm unit" promotes the policy that OAR 660–033–0020(1)(b) furthers—that is, to preserve and protect large blocks of land for agricultural use.

Based on our decisions in Curry County and Riggs, and after examining OAR 660–033–0020(1)(b) in light of those decisions and the context of the definition of "agricultural land" as a whole, we conclude that profitability is not a consideration in determining whether the 590-acre ranch in this case is a "farm unit." Having so concluded, the remaining issue in this case reduces to whether the 259-acre parcel is "within" the

590-acre "farm unit." In resolving that issue, LUBA applied the test based on our reasoning in Riggs—that is, "whether the subject property is properly viewed as part of a 'farm unit,' despite the recent cessation of joint use."

We agree with LUBA's application of that test to the circumstances of this case. As LUBA stated, "[t]here can be no possible dispute that the former ranch was a 'farm unit' for purposes of OAR 660–033–0020(1)(b), with a long and a recent history of use for a hay/grazing operation that included the subject property." Specifically, LUBA noted that, where "[t]he county does not identify any changes that have occurred with respect to soil, water or forage on the former 590-acre ranch since the ranch was partitioned that would preclude a resumed hay/grazing operation similar to that conducted on the ranch for many years," the county had not identified that "something fundamental has changed that would preclude a resumption of a farm operation using the elements of the former ranch." Accordingly, as LUBA concluded, based on the proper understanding of the legal principles underlying OAR 660–033–0020(1)(b), the 259-acre parcel is agricultural land under OAR 660–033–0020(1)(b) because it is "within a farm unit." Affirmed.

NOTES

1.   *Wetherell* establishes two important principles necessary to control sprawl and preserve agricultural land in Tier III (non-residential open space, environmental or agricultural land), namely, that the owner of the land: (a) cannot voluntarily discontinue the farming operation (profitability); nor (b) sever the land through parcel splits (destroy the farm unit) in order to build large lot residential sprawl homes. Remember the principles from takings (the property is most often examined in its "entirety" as a "whole") and from subdivision law (looking at the "cumulative impact" of multiple splits to determine whether the property must be subdivided as a whole).

2.   Statewide Agricultural Zones. As briefly discussed in Chapter 7, Hawai'i enacted a statewide agricultural district as part of its landmark state land use ordinance in 1963. Decades-long attempts to change thousands of acres of land adjoining new urban communities (and within "urban boundaries") in Honolulu from the agricultural district to the urban district in order to accommodate thousands of new homes over a 10-year span culminated in two 2015 state Supreme Court decisions: *Sierra Club v. Land Use Commission and D.R. Horton*, 364 P.3d 213 (2015) and *Sierra Club v. Land Use Commission and Castle & Cooke Homes*, 371 P.3d 291 (2016). There, the Hawai'i Supreme Court upheld the decisions of the State Land Use Commission, so changing the classification under the state land use law principles, on the ground that the LUC's decision was reasonable given the evidence presented at year-long hearings concerning the need for housing and the continued availability of sufficient agricultural land on the island of O'ahu. The court was also influenced by the testimony and evidence showing the

subject properties were within the county urban growth boundary together with testimony indicating that no parts of the property were, or were going to be, designated "important agricultural land" under the state's Important Agricultural Lands Statute.

3.   Statutes exempting agricultural land from local zoning are exactly the opposite of growth management and are the antithesis of sprawl control. These statutes, discussed in the following section (b) allow the farmer, but not the county, to choose as to whether the land remains agricultural. Most county agricultural zoning districts allow residential large lot development as an additional principle use to agricultural operations.

(b) Zoning Exemptions

Agricultural exemption from zoning provisions was an early, and is a continuing, means of favoring farmers. The ambiguous definitions of agricultural land contained in these statutes preserve the farmer's option to retain prime farmland for agricultural use but also encourage premature residential construction on farm land on the fringe? Are the definitions of agriculture too broad? There are three possible outcomes:

- The state statute preempts the field and there is no room for local zoning regulation. *See, e.g.,* Kansas Stat. Ann. § 19– 2921 ("regulations adopted pursuant to this act shall not apply to the use of land for agricultural purposes, nor for the erection or maintenance of buildings thereon for such purposes so long as such land and buildings erected thereon are used for agricultural purposes and not otherwise"). Unfortunately, the agricultural exemption statutes have been interpreted to allow local zoning for residential use within the agricultural land, while allowing local area and bulk regulations requiring proposed non-agricultural residential lots on the property to comply with the local zoning street frontage and minimum lot size, subdivision regulations and access to public roads. *See Olson v. Ada County*, 665 P.2d 717 (1983). The definition of "agricultural purpose or use" becomes highly critical in determining whether a purported use is "agricultural" and exempt from zoning regulation. The cases vary widely: (1) horse boarding commercial renting facility falls within agricultural use, *Borelli v. Zoning Bd. of Appeals of the City of Middletown*, 941 A.2d 966 (2008); (2) marketing of agricultural products where the bulk of the products are grown off-site is not agricultural use, *Blue Heron Nurseries, LLC v. Funk*, 956 N.E.2d 276 (2011); and, (3) bottling and shipping wine on a farm in a residential district, that is grown off-site, is not an agricultural use that exempts the operation from state agricultural exemption or as a valid agricultural accessory, *Terry v. Sperry*, 930 N.E.2d 846 (Ohio App.2010).

- The state agricultural exemption statute partially occupies the field but permits local zoning restrictions and prohibitions for specific high environmental or nuisance impact agricultural uses. *See, e.g.,* Iowa Code § 172D.4(1) requires that any person operating a feedlot must comply with local zoning, but confines a feedlot to outdoor land and not indoor containment facilities. *See* Courtney Jayde Barnes, *Agricultural Zoning Exemptions: Cultivating Chaos in the Twenty-First Century?,* 13 DRAKE J.AGRIC.L.REV. 245 (2008).

- The state has no agricultural exemption but environmental or growth management laws control. *See, e.g., Yakima County v. Eastern Washington Growth Management Hearings Board,* 192 P.3d 12 (Wash.App.2008) (agricultural lands may not be zoned for non-agricultural uses when located in a rural-agricultural growth management tier); *See Walck v. Lower Towamensing Township Zoning Hearing Board,* 942 A.2d 200 (Pa.Cmwlth.Ct.2010) (storage of sewage sludge beyond what is needed on the farm is regulated by the state, but if it is a Concentrated Animal Feedlot Operation (CAFO) it may also be regulated or prohibited by the local ordinance).

WALCK V. LOWER TOWAMENSING TOWNSHIP ZONING HEARING BOARD

Commonwealth Court of Pennsylvania, 2008.
942 A.2d 200.

OPINION BY JUDGE SIMPSON.

In this land use appeal, we consider whether the Nutrient Management Act (NMA) and its attendant regulations preempt enforcement of a local zoning ordinance regarding the long-term stockpiling of a large quantity of sewage sludge on a farming operation. In particular, Barbara A. Walck (Walck), and Edgar F. Lorah, Jr. (Lorah) (collectively, Applicants) assert the Lower Towamensing Township Zoning Hearing Board (ZHB) erred in upholding an enforcement notice issued by the Township Zoning Officer requiring them to cease the long-term stockpiling of sewage sludge on their property. We hold the NMA does not preempt enforcement of the local zoning ordinance in this case.

Walck is the legal owner of the property located at 1535 Lower Smith Gap Road, Kunkletown, Lower Towamensing Township (subject property). Lorah leases the subject property from Walck as part of his farming operation. The subject property lies in the Township's R-1 Low Density Residential Zoning District. Section 432 of the Zoning Ordinance of 1978

(Ordinance) sets forth the uses permitted by right in the R-1 district. "Agriculture" is a permitted use in an R-1 district subject to certain restrictions. One such restriction states "intensive agricultural activities are prohibited." Section 432(5)(b) of the Ordinance. Section 201 of the Ordinance defines "agriculture" as, among other things, the cultivation of the soil and the raising and harvesting of the products of the soil, including nursery and horticulture, but excluding forestry. Intensive agriculture is defined as specialized agricultural activities including, but not limited to, mushroom, poultry and dry lot livestock production, which due to the intensity of production or raw material storage needs, necessitates special control of operation, raw material storage and processing, and disposal of liquid and solid wastes.

The Township received numerous complaints regarding sewage sludge stockpiling on the subject property. Based on the complaints, the Township Zoning Officer inspected the subject property in June and July 2005 and several other times thereafter. The Zoning Officer observed a large stockpile of sewage on the subject property. In late July 2005, the Zoning Officer issued an enforcement notice against Walck alleging violations of the Ordinance. The enforcement notice required Walck to cease using the subject property for the storing, dumping and stockpiling of solid waste. The notice further required Walck to remove or plow the waste located on the subject property within 10 days.

Shortly thereafter, Lorah filed an appeal from the enforcement notice with the ZHB. At the hearing, the Township Zoning Officer testified he observed a stockpile of solid waste on the subject property approximately 20 or 30 feet in width, 40 or 50 feet in depth, and 8 or 10 feet in height. The Township also presented the testimony of Bill Wetzel, a nearby landowner, who explained there was a terrible smell in his neighborhood in June 2005. He testified he was unable to hold outdoor parties during the summer or sit outside due to the smell. Wetzel testified the smell lessened in August 2005.

In support of Applicants' appeal, Lorah testified the subject property is used exclusively for the cultivation of the soil. He explained he has corn and hay planted on the subject property. Lorah testified he received a delivery of sewage sludge from Synagro Mid Atlantic, Inc. in May/June 2005, and he used approximately half of the material on his fields. The balance of the sludge (approximately 100 tons) remained stockpiled on the subject property as of the ZHB hearing in late October 2005. Lorah testified he intended to use the balance of the sludge sometime in the fall, but he had no specific date when the material would be spread on the fields. Applicants also presented the testimony of Mark Reider, senior technical service manager of Synagro Mid Atlantic, who the ZHB recognized as an expert in soil science. Reider explained Synagro delivered 360 tons of sewage sludge to the subject property. He testified the sewage sludge stored on the subject property consisted of treated municipal sewage sludge, also known as Class A Biosolids, from the Valley Forge Sewer Authority. The materials also consisted of food processing waste, also known as slaughterhouse manure, from the Hatfield Meat Company.

Based on the evidence presented, the ZHB issued an opinion and order sustaining the enforcement notice and denying Applicants' appeal. The ZHB determined Lorah stockpiled more than 100 tons of sewage sludge on the subject property from May/June 2005 through October 2005. It determined the stockpiling of sewage sludge cannot be considered agriculture or cultivation of the soil. Rather, the ZHB stated such activity is simply the stockpiling of solid waste, which is not a permitted use in an R-1 district and which is prohibited as intensive agriculture. The ZHB stated Section 432(5)(b) of the Ordinance prohibits specialized agricultural activities that require intense raw material storage needs in an R-1 district. Thus, the ZHB concluded the storage of more than 100 tons of sewage sludge for approximately five months is raw material storage that is beyond the purview of normal farming activity.

The ZHB also rejected Applicants' argument that the NMA preempted the Ordinance. It first observed both the NMA and its regulations state nothing in the NMA prevents a municipality from adopting and enforcing ordinances or regulations that are consistent with and no more stringent than the requirements of the NMA and its regulations. The ZHB then stated:

> The ... [NMA] provide[s] that a management plan is mandatory for all operators of a concentrated animal feeding operation [(CAFO)]. Section 506(b) of the NMA. In the case at bar, Lorah testified that he has no animals on the [subject] property. He testified his farming on the [subject] property in 2005 was limited to hay and corn. Therefore the [NMA] does not apply. * * *

Alternatively, Applicants contend the ZHB erred in determining the storage of "Class A Biosolids" and food processing residual waste to use for the cultivation of the soil and the raising and harvesting of products of the soil on the subject property is not permitted under the Ordinance. They maintain the Ordinance does not prohibit the storage of materials used for the cultivation of the soil. Indeed, Applicants assert, they are entitled by right under the Ordinance to store manure on the subject property in connection with their agricultural operations. Further, Applicants argue, the storage of nutrients on the subject property does not fall within the definition of "intensive agricultural activity" contained in the Ordinance. Accordingly, they maintain, the ZHB erred in determining the storage of nutrients is "intensive agricultural activity" prohibited by the Ordinance.

A zoning hearing board is the entity responsible for the interpretation and application of its zoning ordinance. A zoning board's interpretation of its zoning ordinance is entitled to great weight and deference from a reviewing court. The basis for this deference is the knowledge and expertise a zoning hearing board possesses to interpret the ordinance it is charged with administering. Pursuant to Section 432(5) of the Ordinance, "agriculture" is a use permitted by right in an R-1 district. R.R. at 183a. However, "intensive agricultural activities" are prohibited in an R-1 district. See Section 432(5)(b) of the Ordinance; R.R. at 183a. The Ordinance defines "agriculture" as "(a) The cultivation of the soil and the raising and harvesting of the products of the soil, including nursery and horticulture but excluding forestry; (b) animal husbandry, poultry farming, and dairy farming, excluding kennels." Section 201 of the Ordinance; R.R. at 182a. In addition, the Ordinance defines intensive agriculture as "[s]pecialized agricultural activities including but not limited to mushroom, poultry, and dry lot livestock production, which due to the intensity of production or raw material storage needs, necessitate special control of operation, raw material storage and processing, and disposal of liquid and solid wastes." Id.

In the case at bar, Lorah stockpiled more than 100 tons of sewage sludge on the [subject] property from May/June 2005 through October 2005. The stockpiling of sewage sludge cannot be considered agriculture or cultivation of the soil. It is simply the stockpiling of solid waste, which is not a permitted use in an R-1 district and which is prohibited as intensive agriculture.

In addition, specialized agricultural activities which require intense raw material storage needs, are prohibited under the [O]rdinance. (Zoning Ordinance § 432(5)(b)[]). Clearly, the storage for approximately five months, of more than 100 tons of sewage sludge is raw material storage which is beyond the purview of normal farming activity.

We believe the ZHB's analysis, which is entitled to great deference from this Court, is consistent with the clear language of the Ordinance. Thus, we discern no error in the ZHB's determination that the stockpiling of more than 100 tons of sludge and waste on the subject property over a period of several months is not permitted as "agriculture" under the Ordinance.

In addition, we reject Applicants' contention that the ZHB erred in sustaining the enforcement notice on the basis of Section 519 of the Ordinance where the Township did not prove Lorah's activities constituted a threat to public health and safety. More specifically, although the Township's enforcement notice states the activities on the subject property violate Section 519 because they pose a health or safety threat to the community, the ZHB did not sustain the enforcement notice on this basis. Rather, the ZHB based its decision on the fact that Lorah's use of the subject property was not permitted as "agriculture" under the Ordinance, but rather it constituted intensive agricultural activity which is prohibited in an R-1 district. Indeed, the ZHB's opinion does not even reference

Section 519 of the Ordinance; therefore, Applicants' argument fails. For the foregoing reasons, we affirm."

(c) Feedlots

As you can see from the previous case, feedlots have come under increasing pressure from state and local government and from neighboring property owners. The odor from feedlots can be detected for miles, and sewage from animal waste can become dangerous if not properly treated. This is particularly true for hog farming. The problem has become even worse with the advent of Concentrated Animal Feeding Operations (CAFOs), the latest trend in hog farming for producing pork as quickly and efficiently as possible. Whereas the typical family farm usually contains around 500 hogs, CAFOs frequently hold over 10,000 hogs, and farms with over 17,000 are not unusual. CAFOs are different from family farms in that the hogs are kept and fed indoors. The waste from the animals falls through grates to a flushing system which ejects the water into large lagoons holding as much as 30 million gallons of liquid animal waste. The waste is then chemically broken down, spread onsite or injected into the soil. The effect is to reduce the air quality in the area, emitting high and possibly dangerous, levels of hydrogen sulfide, ammonia and methane gas into the air. Additionally, leaks in lagoons are responsible for numerous incidents of water contamination.

Many property owners and local governments have felt powerless against the CAFO industry. Since most agricultural states have drafted exemptions to protect farming from zoning, at the beginning CAFO operations have been allowed to operate as an agricultural use. Several states have ruled the operations may not be locally regulated. *See Kuehl v. Cass County*, 555 N.W.2d 686 (Iowa 1996); *Board of Supervisors v. ValAdCo*, 504 N.W.2d 267 (Minn.1993); *Premium Standard Farms, Inc. v. Lincoln Township of Putnam County*, 946 S.W.2d 234 (Mo.1997). As quickly as the cases have come down ruling in favor of CAFO operations, however, innovative municipal attorneys have found new ways to enjoin or curb their use. The advent of the health ordinance is gaining popularity. *See, e.g., Blue Earth County Pork Producers, Inc. v. County of Blue Earth*, 558 N.W.2d 25 (Minn.App.1997). Under this schematic, the local government enacts ordinances regulating local air and water quality. Such a plan may or may not eliminate the CAFO altogether, but it may greatly limit the number of animals in a given facility or ensure that the CAFO produces fewer pollutants.

In 2011, the Missouri Court of Appeals affirmed an $11 million public nuisance judgment against a hog operation that produced 230,000 gallons of waste per day. Plaintiffs (fifteen neighboring farmers) successfully claimed the CAFO substantially impaired the use and enjoyment of their property.

OWENS V. CONTIGROUP COMPANIES, INC.

Missouri Court of Appeals, 2011.
344 S.W.3d 717.

[Excerpt] At trial, there was substantial evidence admitted that PSF's hog operations emitted numerous gases and chemicals. Experts from both sides testified to such. For example, Robert Brundage [CAFO manager] in his video deposition admitted that PSF emits hydrogen sulfide and ammonia. He also agreed that "gaseous material and chemical compounds that create odor, such as hydrogen sulfide and ammonia, can attach themselves to particulate matter and dust particles and can be moved by the wind." These gases and chemicals were only one of the sources of the ill odor that came from PSF's property.

There was also substantial evidence that land application of swine effluent caused an intense odor. Expert Ron Sheffield testified that hog operations, including PSF's, seal off lagoons full of hog effluent to prevent the escape of ammonia emissions. He also testified that PSF's land application process was essentially digging up soil and applying the hog effluent in such a way that left a pool of effluent at the top of the soil which "releases odorous compounds up into the air that could potentially go off-site." There was also testimony that the "travelling gun" sprayed pig effluent up into the air about 300 feet and travelled with the wind onto Respondents' land. Further, several Respondents testified that the odor was worse when it rained. The inference from this testimony as to worsening smell at times of precipitation could be interpreted to mean that emissions escaped from PSF's hog operation into the air that were less odorous or non-odorous until it rained. These "emissions" would not be ill odors until acted upon by an outside force. Therefore, the evidence supported the jury's finding that PSF released "other emissions" that interfered with the Respondents' use and enjoyment of their property by becoming an ill odor under certain environmental conditions.

There was substantial testimony that both ill odors from gasses and chemicals released from PSF's hog operation and other emissions (such as hog effluent), which cause ill odors, traveled from PSF's land onto the Respondents' properties. Each Respondent's property was in close proximity to PSF's extensive hog operations and each testified that he or she experienced great distress as a result of odor coming onto his or her property. Therefore, the modification of MAI 22.06 to include the term "other emissions" was supported by substantial evidence.

NOTES

1.   A number of agricultural states have adopted legislation requiring CAFO operators to obtain state permits requiring site plans and environmental review. *See* Ohio Rev. Code § 903.06 regulating CAFOs. For a discussion of Missouri's legislation and of CAFOs generally, see Jerome M. Organ and Kristin M. Perry, *Controlling Externalities Associated with Concentrated Animal Feeding Operations: Evaluating the Impact of H.B. 1207 and the Continuing Viability of Zoning and the Common Law of Nuisance*, 3 MO.ENVTL.L. & POL'Y REV. 183 (1996).

2.   Another concern posed by CAFOs is surface and groundwater pollution. Accordingly, one avenue of federal and state regulation of CAFOs is through the Clean Water Act, which lists CAFOs as a point source of pollution. 33 U.S.C. 1362(14) (2016). The Environmental Protection Agency, however, has had a difficult time formulating regulations within its congressional authority to require CAFOs to apply for NPDES. In the 2005 *Waterkeeper Alliance, Inc. v. U.S. Environmental Protection Agency* decision, the Second Circuit held that the EPA could not impose a "duty to apply" on all CAFOs regardless of their actual discharge. 399 F.3d 486 (2d Cir.2005). In response, the EPA revised its regulations to narrow the requirement to those CAFOs which discharge or propose to discharge pollutants. In 2011, the Fifth Circuit interpreted this language as outside of the EPA's authority. *National Pork Producers Council v. United States Environmental Protection Agency*, 635 F.3d 738 (5th Cir.2011). For a detailed discussion on the impacts of CAFOs on surface and groundwater, as well as the erosion of the EPA's ability to regulate CAFOs under the Clean Water Act, *see generally* William McLaren, *The Death of the Duty to Apply: Limitations to CAFO Oversight*, 11 J. OF ANIMAL & NAT.RES.L. 87 (2015). For a discussion of the Clean Water Act generally, see section B of this chapter.

3.   Odors may not only be a nuisance to neighbors, but may have health impacts as well. CAFOs produce air emissions that may contain hydrogen sulfide, ammonia, methane, particulate matter, and bioaerosals. Hydrogen sulfide in particular is both a "direct toxic health risk and odorous." To address the issue, some jurisdictions have placed limits specifically on hydrogen sulfide emissions from CAFOs. For a discussion and comparison of local land use regulations to address odorous emissions from CAFOs, *see* David Osterberg and Steward M. Melvin, *Relevant Law, Regulations and Decisions*, in *Iowa Concentrated Animal Feeding Operation Air Quality Study*, 184–201 (2003). CAFOs pose a number of other risks including soil contamination and increased antibiotic resistance in both humans and animals. For a series of papers reviewing environmental, public health, and social and economic issues posed by CAFOs, as well as their regulation, *see generally* Purdue University's Extension Office website, http://www.ansc.purdue.edu/CAFO/.

(d) "Right to Farm" Laws

Most states have so-called "right to farm" statutes. *See e.g.* Haw.Rev.Stat. §§ 165–1 to 165–6 and 3. Pa.Cons.Stat. §§ 951–955. The statutes can generally be broken into two separate groups. The "right to farm" for general agricultural operations provides that a farming operation cannot be declared a nuisance if it was not a nuisance at the time it began operation. *See* N.D.Cent.Code 42–04–02 ("An agricultural operation is not, nor shall it become, * * * [a] nuisance by any changed conditions in or about the locality of such operation after it has been in operation for more than one year, if such operation was not a nuisance at the time the operation began.* * * ").

The second type of statute serves to protect specific types of agricultural activity. For example, Maryland protects only the following specific agricultural activities: cultivation of land, production of agricultural crops, raising of poultry and protection of eggs, milk, fruit or other horticultural crops, and/or livestock. Md.Code, Cts. & Jud.Proc., § 5–308(a).

These laws are quite effective when metropolitan urban growth begin to encroach on outlying farm communities, and prevent urbanite "cappuccino cowboys" who want to "get away from it all" from thereafter rethinking their decisions when the wind picks up, bringing with it airborne pesticides, odors and dust. Recall from Chapter 1 the concept of "moving to the nuisance." *See Bove v. Donner-Hanna Coke Corp.*, 258 N.Y.S. 229 (N.Y.App.1932). People who choose to relocate near farms, must live with their new and well-established surroundings. Protecting farms from suits for nuisance is widely recognized as important for preservation of farmland from residential developments located adjacent to farming operations, but it does not effectively confront the underlying problem of the incompatibility of the uses. Thus, for example, when neighbors challenged Iowa's "Right to Farm" law (which grants agricultural areas immunity from nuisance suits) in *Bormann v. Board of Supervisors In and For Kossuth Cty.*, 584 N.W.2d 309 (Iowa 1998), *cert. denied* 525 U.S. 1172 (1999), the court held that the state cannot regulate property so as to insulate the users from potential private nuisance claims without providing just compensation to persons injured by the nuisance. Therefore, the portion of the Iowa statute that provides for immunity against nuisances was unconstitutional.

In Bormann, the Iowa Supreme Court recalled long-standing law that the right to maintain a nuisance is an easement, 584 N.W.2d at 315–16, which holding is consistent with the Restatement of Property § 451. The court characterized the nuisance immunity provision in section 352.11(1)(a) of the Iowa Code as creating an easement in the property affected by the nuisance (the servient tenement) in favor of the applicants' land (the dominant tenement). Concluding that easements are property interests subject to the just compensation requirements of the Iowa and the Federal Constitutions, the court ruled that the approval of the application for an agricultural area pursuant to 352.11(1)(a) conferred immunity, which resulted in the Board's taking of easements in the neighbors' properties for the benefit of the applicants. *Id.* at 321. The court concluded that the legislature had exceeded its authority by authorizing the use of property in such a way as to infringe on the rights of others by allowing the creation of a nuisance without the payment of compensation, compelling the court to hold "that portion of Iowa Code section 352.11(1)(a) that provides for immunity against nuisances unconstitutional and without any force and effect." Relevant to Bormann is *Spiek v. Michigan Dep't of Transportation (DOT)*, 572 N.W.2d 201 (Mich.1998), where the Michigan Supreme Court held that a roadway built by the DOT that emitted odors, and noise, vibrations and dust onto adjacent property would constitute a taking where the property showed unique injury different from that suffered by other properties similarly situated.

To the contrary, in *Moon v. North Idaho Farmers Assoc.*, 96 P.3d 637 (Idaho 2004), the Idaho Supreme Court rejected the *Bormann* rationale and held that Restatement of Property § 451 is not followed in Idaho and held that the right to maintain a nuisance suit is not an easement, nor any other property right, the extinguishment of which effects a taking. In a subsequent Iowa decision, *Harms v. City of Sibley*, 695 N.W.2d 43 (Iowa App.2004), the court limited *Bormann* to cases where the statute extinguishes a right to bring a nuisance suit. Where the city rezoned and permitted land for an industrial use emitting noise, odor and particularities, the city was not liable for a regulatory taking, where the adjoining landowners had the right to sue the industrial operation for private nuisance. Moreover, the Indiana Court of Appeals declined to follow *Bormann* and the Restatement of Property § 415. Instead, the court held that a nuisance did not constitute an easement, and therefore the Indiana Right to Farm law protecting farms from nuisance claims was constitutional. *Lindsey v. DeGroot*, 898 N.E.2d 1251 (Ct.App.Ind.2009).

(e) Agricultural District Enabling Laws

Several states have enacted agricultural district statutes, whereby agricultural landowners can voluntarily form special districts if they meet certain acreage minimums and other criteria and if the county or state approves inclusion in the district. New York is the only state that mandates participation if the farmland involved is considered unique or irreplaceable. *See* N.Y. Agriculture and Markets Law § 304. The decision of a county to allow additional farmland to annex into the district is legislative and limited to a rational basis review. *See Deerpark Farms, LLC v. Agricultural and Farmland Protection Board of Orange County*, 896 N.Y.S.2d 126 (N.Y.App.2010).

A treatise describes Agricultural Preservation Districts as follows:

Many states have enacted legislation authorizing the creation of agricultural preservation districts (sometimes call "preserves" or "protection areas"). These districts, which can be created upon petition by the property owners, are similar to agricultural zoning districts in that they usually limit non-agricultural uses of land. However, unlike zoning ordinances, agricultural preservation districts carry with them a variety of benefits intended to safeguard agricultural operations from development pressures and real estate speculation. These benefits may include: preferential tax treatment; protection from nuisance suits; adverse zoning actions, government projects, and buffer requirements; and increased procedural requirements or prohibitions on annexation and condemnation actions. Agricultural preservation districts often function in tandem with purchase of development rights programs.

Patricia Salkin and Amy Levine, *American Law of Zoning*, § 33.9 (5th ed.2011)

Once obtaining designation as an agricultural district, preserve or protection area, the benefits are numerous:

1. Differential property tax based on agricultural use value.

2. Exemption from special assessments unless they use the services.

3. Restrictions on local governments to regulate farming practices unless public health and safety is concerned.

4. Purchase or transfer of development rights.

5. Limitations on capital improvement expenditures promoting nonfarm development.

6. Limitations on acquisition of land by eminent domain.

7. Conformance of state agency regulations and procedures to support agriculture within districts.

8. Limitations on annexation of land.

9. Limitations on rate of tax increases.

10. Zoning of adjacent lands to reduce conflict.

11. Anti-nuisance provisions.

See Julian Juergensmeyer and Thomas E. Roberts, *Land Use Planning and Development Regulation Law* § 13.9 (3rd ed.2012).

(f) Taxation Techniques

Beginning with Maryland in 1956, 48 states have enacted statutes or constitutional provisions for differential assessment of ad valorem taxes which provide that farms and open space lands be assessed at a lower rate than other property. How successful have these programs been?

National Agricultural Lands Study: The Protection of Farmland 55 (1981).

Although many states have used property tax relief as a tool in protecting agricultural land, only a small fraction of farm estates or farms which enjoy the tax benefits of differential assessment meet all the conditions necessary to make this incentive effective. The benefits of reduced taxation, however, are conferred broadly, with no proof required of each recipient that the public policy of protecting farmland is being promoted. For this reason, tax policy is often viewed as a shotgun approach. Furthermore, unless differential assessment programs are combined with agricultural zoning and/or with agreements that restrict the land to agricultural use and/or purchase of development rights, there is no assurance that the beneficiaries of tax reduction or abatement will keep their land in agricultural use. Owners may simply enjoy reduced taxes until the time comes when they want to sell. In the case of death taxes, significant tax benefits are made available to large farm estates, even those that are not in serious jeopardy of being converted because of high death taxes.

In isolation, then, differential assessment is largely ineffective in reducing the rate of conversion of agricultural land. It does not discourage the incursion of non-farm uses into stable agricultural areas; it simply enables owners of land under development pressure to postpone the sale of their land until they are ready to retire. The incentives are not keyed into actual need, except in the case of the tax credit programs of Wisconsin and Michigan.

Nevertheless, differential taxation is a valuable component of a comprehensive agricultural land protection program. As a matter of equity, if a program prevents agricultural land from being developed, the owner should pay taxes only on its agricultural use value. Further, benefits such as these may serve as incentives to encourage farmers to participate in an integrated agricultural land protection program.

COUNTY OF HUMBOLDT V. MCKEE

Court of Appeal, California, 2008.
165 Cal.App.4th 1476, 82 Cal.Rptr.3d 38.

SIMONS, ACTING P.J.

In 1965, the Legislature confronted two troubling trends in California: the loss of agricultural land to development and the haphazard growth of suburbia, requiring the "extension of municipal services to remote residential enclaves, and interfer[ing] with agricultural activities." (*Sierra Club v. City of Hayward* (1981) 623 P.2d 180 (Sierra Club), superseded by statute on other grounds as stated in *Friends of East Willits Valley v. County of Mendocino* (2002) 101 Cal.App.4th 191, 204–205.) "The Legislature perceived as one cause of these problems the self-fulfilling prophecy of the property tax system: taxing land on the basis of its market value compels the owner to put the land to the use for which it is valued by the market." In response, it enacted the Williamson Act (Gov.Code, § 51200 et seq.), which employs a two-step strategy to conserve agricultural lands. The local government first establishes and regulates agricultural preserves, and then executes land conservation contracts with landowners. These contracts limit the land to agricultural and compatible uses for their duration and may also include terms and conditions more restrictive than those required by the Williamson Act. In return for accepting restrictions on the land, the landowner is "guaranteed a relatively stable tax base, founded on the value of the land for open space use only and unaffected by its development potential." (*Sierra Club*, at p. 851, 171 Cal.Rptr. 619, 623 P.2d 180.) The hallmark of this statutory scheme is its reliance on voluntary agreements between the government and the landowner, where the landowner chooses, on an annual basis, to accept certain limits on his or her use of the land in return for an explicit property tax reduction.

In 1977, the County and Arthur Tooby made and entered into a Williamson Act contract, which covered a Class B agricultural preserve consisting of approximately 12,580 acres. Among other things, this contract set a minimum parcel size of 160 acres for subsequent divisions of the land, consistent with the agricultural preserve guidelines then in effect. One year later, the County Board of Supervisors (the Board) revised those guidelines, increasing the minimum parcel size for divisions to 600 acres. In 2000, defendants Buck Mountain Ranch Limited Partnership (BMR), Robert C. McKee and Valery McKee, (McKee) purchased this acreage, and then divided and sold much of the land. Though each parcel sold was larger than 160 acres, some were less than 600 acres.

In 2002, County sued McKee for violation of the Williamson Act, violation of the Subdivision Map Act (§ 66410 et seq.), breach of contract, nuisance, and violation of the unfair competition law. The trial court ruled in favor of McKee. It relied upon the contract clauses of the state and federal Constitutions (U.S. Const., art. I, § 10; Cal. Const., art. I, § 9) to conclude that the 1978 Guidelines could not be applied constitutionally to a Williamson Act contract executed in 1977. We disagree and reverse.

On February 1, 1977, the Board adopted Resolution No. 77–19, which established approximately 12,580 acres of the 13,700-acre Tooby Ranch as a Class B agricultural preserve (Tooby Preserve). On February 15, 1977, the Board rescinded Resolution No. 77–19 and replaced it with Resolution No. 77–30 (the Tooby Guidelines). The Tooby Guidelines listed compatible uses permitted on the Tooby Preserve. The guidelines further provided that "The land described herein shall not be divided if, as a practical matter, it would result in the reduction of land devoted to the production of agricultural commodities for commercial purposes. This section shall not prohibit a division of land if the parcels created thereby are of such size, shape and other physical characteristics that they are capable of producing agricultural commodities and if as a practical matter the amount of land devoted to agricultural uses will not be reduced. All divisions of land shall comply with all applicable local ordinances and State laws."

On February 1, 1977, the same day the Board established the Tooby Preserve, Arthur Tooby entered into a Williamson Act contract with County (Tooby Contract). The Tooby Contract restricted the Tooby Preserve to agricultural and compatible uses. The Tooby Contract stated, in relevant part, "This contract shall run with the land described herein and shall be binding upon, and inure to the benefit of, all successors in interest of the OWNER. [¶] 6. Land subject to this contract may not be divided into parcels of less than 160 acres except for purposes of rental or lease for agricultural and compatible uses provided no additional dwellings shall be constructed or placed upon such divided parcels."

Resolution No. 73–163 (1973 Guidelines), adopted by the Board on December 18, 1973, was in effect at the time the Tooby Contract was executed. The 1973 Guidelines set forth the regulations governing agricultural preserves, and provided in part, "Land within a Class A preserve and under contract may not be divided into parcels less than 20 acres. Land within a Class B preserve and under contract may not be divided into parcels of less than 160 acres."

On March 28, 1978, the year after the Tooby Preserve was established and the Tooby Contract was executed, the Board adopted the 1978 Guidelines. The 1978 Guidelines set forth revised regulations governing agricultural preserves, and stated in part, "Land within a Class B preserve and under contract shall not be divided into parcels smaller than 600 acres. Land within a Class A or C preserve and under contract shall not be divided into parcels smaller than 100 acres. (Effective for 1979 preserves and under contract)." The 1978 Guidelines expressly rescinded the 1973 Guidelines.

In August 2000, McKee formed BMR for the purpose of purchasing and selling the Tooby Ranch. In March of 2001, Omsberg & Company, a surveying and engineering firm, submitted a report to County in support of McKee's application for lot line adjustments on the Tooby Ranch. The report explained McKee's plans to divide the Tooby Ranch into 44 parcels of 160 acres or more and sell them as "ranchettes." Since 2000, McKee has transferred approximately 25 separate parcels of land to third party purchasers. Some of the parcels conveyed to third party purchasers are smaller than 600 acres, but there is no evidence that any of the transferred parcels are smaller than 160 acres. At the time of trial, in 2006, McKee retained ownership of approximately 3,000 acres of the Tooby Ranch. McKee has not filed a notice of nonrenewal of the Tooby Contract. McKee has continued to receive a preferential tax assessment and has paid an average of 44 cents per acre, 10 to 15 percent of the taxes he would have paid had the land not been under a Williamson Act contract.

On December 31, 2002, County filed a complaint against McKee and 47 third party purchasers alleged to have bought parcels of the Tooby Ranch from McKee. County alleged causes of action for violation of the Williamson Act, violation of the Subdivision Map Act, breach of contract, nuisance, and violation of the unfair competition law. County sought penalties, damages, and declaratory and injunctive relief, including an order prohibiting future transfers of Tooby Ranch land and declaring the prior transfers null and void.

BMR filed a cross-complaint against County and Assessor on June 11, 2003, and filed a first amended cross-complaint on August 27, 2003. BMR alleged that Assessor continued to assess property taxes to BMR for parcels transferred to third party purchasers. The cross-complaint sought declaratory relief and an injunction prohibiting Assessor from assessing taxes to BMR for the transferred parcels.

The court trial court ruled that County's 1978 Guidelines could not be applied to the 1977 Tooby Contract. The court reasoned that application of the 1978 Guidelines, which amended the minimum parcel size for Class B preserves from 160 to 600 acres, would violate the contract clauses of the state and federal Constitutions. The court concluded that application of the 600-acre parcel minimum would substantially impair the Tooby Contract, and found that County had failed to show that this impairment was reasonable and necessary to an important public purpose. Second, the court ruled that County could not seek nullification of the parcel conveyances in the instant proceeding.

In its statement of decision, the court concluded that McKee had not violated the Williamson Act or the Tooby Contract. The 600-acre minimum in the 1978 Guidelines could not constitutionally applied to the 1977 Tooby Contract, and County had produced no evidence that any parcel conveyed by McKee to third party purchasers was less than the 160-acre minimum established by the Tooby Contract and the governing 1973 Guidelines. On March 16, 2007, County and Assessor filed a timely notice of appeal from the judgment.

The Williamson Act is a legislative effort to preserve agricultural and open space land and discourage premature urban development. It authorizes local governments to establish "agricultural preserve [s]," which consist of lands devoted to agricultural and compatible uses. After establishing agricultural preserves, the local government may enter into contracts with landowners with respect to land within a designated preserve and devoted to agricultural use. These contracts must limit the land to agricultural and compatible uses for the duration of the contract, and, in return, "the landowner is guaranteed a relatively stable tax base, founded on the value of the land for open space use only and unaffected by its development potential." (*Sierra Club, supra,* 28 Cal.3d at p. 851, 171 Cal.Rptr. 619, 623 P.2d 180.)

Because the Williamson Act permits preferential tax assessment of land under contract, the California Constitution requires enforceable restrictions on the use of contracted land. (Cal. Const., art. XIII, § 8; § 51243.6.) The California Constitution states, in relevant part, "To promote the conservation, preservation and continued existence of open space lands, the Legislature may define open space land and shall provide that when this land is enforceably restricted, in a manner specified by the Legislature, to recreation, enjoyment of scenic beauty, use or conservation of natural resources, or production of food or fiber, it shall be valued for property tax purposes only on a basis that is consistent with its restrictions and uses." The Williamson Act was intended "to deny the tax benefits of the act to short term speculators and developers of urban fringe land and to [e]nsure that the constitutional requirement of an 'enforceable restriction' is met"; and, therefore, "the Legislature deliberately required a long-term commitment to agriculture or other open-space use." (*Sierra Club, supra,* 28 Cal.3d at p. 852, 171 Cal.Rptr. 619, 623 P.2d 180.) Each contract between the landowner and local government must have an initial term of at least 10 years, and "shall provide that on the anniversary date of the contract or such other annual date as specified by the contract a year shall be added automatically to the initial term unless notice of nonrenewal is given as provided in Section 51245.".) If the local government or landowner serves a notice of nonrenewal, the land use restrictions in the existing contract remain in effect for the balance of the contract term. (§ 51246.) Upon notice of nonrenewal, "taxes on [the landowner's] property gradually return to the level of taxes on comparable nonrestricted property, as the term of restriction draws nearer to expiration." (*Sierra Club, supra,* 28 Cal.3d at p. 852, 171 Cal.Rptr. 619, 623 P.2d 180, citing Rev. & Tax.Code, § 426.)

County and Assessor contend the 1978 Guidelines were intended to apply both to preserves established in 1979 and to preserves established before 1979, including the Tooby Preserve established in 1977. McKee asserts that the 1978 Guidelines were intended to apply only to preserves established in 1979 and later, and therefore do not govern the Tooby Preserve. We agree with County and Assessor. The 1978 Guidelines stated, "Land within a Class B preserve and under contract shall not be divided into parcels smaller than 600 acres. Land within a Class A or C preserve and under contract shall not be divided into parcels smaller than 100 acres. (Effective for 1979 preserves and under contract)." In interpreting the 1978 Guidelines, both parties focus on the parenthetical that follows the restriction on divisions of land in Class B preserves: "(Effective for 1979 preserves and under contract)." County and Assessor urge that this parenthetical means the 600-acre minimum parcel size is effective both for land in 1979 preserves and for land in preserves already under contract. McKee argues that this phrase means the 600-acre minimum is to be applied only to land within preserves created in 1979 or later and then placed under contract. We find the language of this parenthetical ambiguous and susceptible to both constructions.

The construction suggested by McKee, however, would lead to an absurd result. The final provision of the 1978 Guidelines rescinds the 1973 Guidelines, rendering them void and inoperative. If the 1978 Guidelines were intended to apply only to preserves established from 1979 onward, as McKee suggests, then the passage of the 1978 Guidelines would have left County with no operative regulations for preserves established before 1979. This result is contrary to the apparent purpose of the 1978 Guidelines, to establish revised regulations governing agricultural preserves. Moreover, County's failure to maintain operative regulations for pre-1979 preserves would violate the Williamson Act, which requires local governments to adopt rules governing the administration of agricultural preserves. We construe the 1978 Guidelines so as to avoid this consequence, and conclude the 1978 Guidelines were intended to apply to both 1979 preserves and preserves already "under contract," that is, both preexisting and future preserves. Therefore, the 1978 Guidelines were intended to apply to the Tooby Preserve, which had been established in 1977.

B.   The Tooby Contract Incorporated the 1978 Guidelines Upon Renewal

Having concluded that the 1978 Guidelines were intended to apply to preexisting preserves, including the 1977 Tooby Preserve, we next address the trial court's ruling that the contract clauses contained in the federal and California Constitutions barred application of the 1978 Guidelines to the 1977 Tooby Contract. County and Assessor argue the contract clause analysis was unnecessary, because the 1978 Guidelines were incorporated into the Tooby Contract when the parties renewed the contract following adoption of the 1978 Guidelines. McKee contends that interpreting the Tooby Contract to incorporate the 1978 Guidelines upon contract renewal would permit County to unilaterally amend the Tooby Contract, rendering the contract unjust and inequitable. This presents issues of statutory and contract interpretation subject to de novo review. (*City of Saratoga v. Hinz, supra*, 115 Cal.App.4th at p. 1212, 9 Cal.Rptr.3d 791.

In *County of Marin v. Assessment Appeals Bd.* (1976) 64 Cal.App.3d 319, 134 Cal.Rptr. 349 (Marin), the Court of Appeal held that, because a Williamson Act agreement was renewed by the parties each year, laws enacted after the original contract date could be considered when analyzing the agreement. (*Marin*, at p. 327, fn. 7, 134 Cal.Rptr. 349.)

As in Marin, the 1978 Guidelines "may be properly considered in this contractual dispute," because the parties entered into a new contract each year pursuant to the automatic renewal provisions in the Tooby Contract and the Williamson Act. In compliance with the Williamson Act renewal provisions (§§ 51244, 51245), the Tooby Contract provided that "This contract shall be effective on the date first written above, hereinafter the anniversary date, and shall remain in effect and shall be for an initial term of ten (10) years. On the first anniversary date and on each succeeding anniversary date, one year shall automatically be added to the unexpired term unless notice of non-renewal is given as provided by law." Neither party to the Tooby Contract has given notice of nonrenewal of the Tooby Contract, and McKee has continued to receive preferential tax treatment on the Tooby Preserve land. In the absence of timely notice of nonrenewal, "the contract shall be considered renewed" on each anniversary date. (§ 51245.) Thus, the Tooby Contract, originally entered into between Arthur Tooby and County on February 1, 1977, was renewed on February 1, 1978, again on February 1, 1979, and on each anniversary date thereafter.

We agree with the reasoning in Marin that, as a legal matter, by renewing a Williamson Act contract on each anniversary date, the parties entered into a new contract each year. (See Black's Law Dict. (8th ed.2004) p. 1322, col. 2 [defining "renewal" as "3. The re-creation of a legal relationship or the replacement of an old contract with a new contract, as opposed to the mere extension of a previous relationship or contract"].) Each year, a landowner bound by a Williamson Act contract has a choice: give timely notice of nonrenewal, which preserves the current 10-year contract, or decline to give notice of nonrenewal, which renews the contract for a new 10-year term. By choosing not to give notice of nonrenewal, the landowner gains both the burdens and the benefits of a new 10-year contract. The landowner remains burdened by restrictions on the use of the contracted land for the balance of the new 10-year term, but also benefits from the preferential tax assessment guaranteed for enforceably restricted agricultural land. This preferential tax assessment is not available once the landowner gives notice of nonrenewal: upon notice of nonrenewal, taxes gradually return to the level of taxes on comparable nonrestricted property. (Rev. & Tax.Code, § 426; *Sierra Club*, at p. 852, 171 Cal.Rptr. 619, 623 P.2d 180.) Thus, the decision not to give a notice of nonrenewal binds the landowner to a new 10-year contract.

Because the parties to the Tooby Contract entered into a new 10-year contract on February 1, 1979, all applicable laws and ordinances then in existence, including the 1978 Guidelines, became part of the Tooby Contract. (*Castillo v. Express Escrow Co.* (2007) 146 Cal.App.4th 1301, 1308, 53 Cal.Rptr.3d 485.)

County and Assessor next contend that the trial court should be instructed to apply nullification as an appropriate remedy or, in the alternative, the nullification issue should be remanded for determination by the trial court. McKee argues that we should not reach the issue of nullification, but instead should permit the trial court to address this issue upon remand.

County's first amended complaint sought, among other remedies, an order declaring that the transfers from McKee to third party purchasers, and successive transfers from third party purchasers, were null and void ab initio. On February 7, 2006, the court issued a "Ruling On: Reconsideration of Bifurcated Issues," clarifying that in light of its conclusion that the 1978 Guidelines could not constitutionally be applied to the Tooby Contract, it did not reach the issue of whether County could seek nullification of the parcel transfers.

The Williamson Act does not require any specific remedy for breach of a Williamson Act contract. Instead, section 51251 provides in part, "The county, city, or landowner may bring any action in court necessary to enforce any contract, including, but not limited to, an action to enforce the contract by specific performance or injunction." Even if nullification of the transfers from McKee to third party purchasers is a permissible remedy for breach of a Williamson Act contract, County and Assessor cite no authority compelling the conclusion that the trial court is required to apply this remedy in the instant case. Cancellation or nullification of the transfers is not available as a matter of right; instead, "the propriety of granting equitable relief in a particular case by way of cancellation, rescission, restitution or impressment of a constructive trust, generally rests upon the sound discretion of the trial court exercised in accord with the facts and circumstances of the case." (*Hicks v. Clayton* (1977) 67 Cal.App.3d 251, 265, 136 Cal.Rptr. 512.) On remand, the trial court has discretion to fashion an appropriate remedy based on the particular facts of this case. We express no opinion on whether nullification is a permissible remedy, but instead permit the trial court to address this issue as necessary upon remand.

The judgment on County's complaint and BMR's related cross-complaint and the order awarding costs are reversed. The matter is remanded with instructions to the trial court to (1) vacate its order applying the contract clauses to preclude application of the 1978 Guidelines to the Tooby Contract, (2) issue a new order finding that the 1978 Guidelines do apply to the Tooby Contract and that the division and sale of parcels less than 600 acres violate the guidelines, and (3) impose an appropriate remedy for any such violation.

NOTES: LOCAL, STATE AND FEDERAL TAXATION DEVICES

1.   The Williamson Act restrictive agreement approach has the greatest likelihood of preventing conversion of farmland for set periods of time, but its effectiveness is questionable because most of the land enrolled in this type of program has already been committed to continued agricultural use. *See* Buck, Note, *Beyond Williamson Act: Alternatives for More Effective Preservation of*

Agricultural Land, 15 PAC.L.J. 1151 (1984); Richard Babcock, *Environmental Protection; Agricultural Land Conservation Easements*, 27 PAC.L.J. 707 (1996) (finding the Williamson Act ineffective). *People ex rel. Department of Conservation v. Triplett*, 55 Cal.Rptr.2d 610 (Cal.App.1996). Two other approaches have been even less successful. Under the pure differential assessment approach, agricultural land is assessed at its use value for agricultural purposes rather than its actual market value. However, the farmer who converts suffers no penalty and is not required to pay back past tax savings. The general concept has been upheld against uniformity of taxation challenges. *See Knight v. Department of Revenue*, 646 P.2d 1343 (Or.1982). Another problem with differential assessment lies in allotting the tax benefits between true commercial farming operations, the ones which need the tax preference, and land-consuming "ranchettes." Often, "cappuccino cowboys" who choose to live on hobby farms in rural areas are given the differential tax treatment as well, helping to subsidize their rural, yet agriculturally unproductive, lifestyle. Some have suggested that participation in differential tax treatment programs should be contingent on the production of a certain amount of goods or on a given amount of net income, or should be coupled with the use of agricultural districts. *See* Daniels and Bowers, *Holding Our Ground: Protecting America's Farmland* 94–95 (1997).

The second approach incorporates a deferred taxation concept. Used by 29 states, deferred taxation utilizes a differential assessment based on use versus market value, but requires landowners to pay a penalty if they convert to a nonagricultural use. Some statutes require that interest be paid on the tax savings. Taken alone, the program has major difficulties. Developers may purchase the land at a relatively low price, and lease it back to the farmer, thereby receiving the tax savings. Even if the taxes must be repaid when the land is developed, the owner has essentially received an interest-free loan. A deferred compensation differential tax assessment law was upheld in *Hoffmann v. Clark*, 372 N.E.2d 74 (Ill.1977). In Nebraska, Neb.Rev.St. § 77–1343–1348, deferred taxation is allowed only in areas zoned by counties for exclusive agricultural use and in Florida, West's Fla.Stat.Ann. § 193.461, landowners will not be eligible for tax benefits if they apply for rezoning.

2.   The Williamson Act has been amended to limit cancellation to extraordinary circumstances. Nevertheless, the amendment expands the ability of a local government to approve a cancellation by requiring that the government find that the cancellation is consistent with the legislative purpose or would be in the public interest. *See* Cal.Gov.Code §§ 51280 et seq.

3.   Two other unusual taxation techniques have been adopted by a few states. Both Michigan and Wisconsin have enacted "circuit breaker" tax credit programs. The Wisconsin plan requires that the county adopt agricultural zoning ordinances or agricultural land preservation plan so that farmers can receive the tax credit. The landowner pays property taxes based on market value assessment, but then receives an income tax rebate, the amount of which is based on acreage and income. Although the costs to the state amount to eight to ten dollars per acre, the program encourages support for land-use regulation

among the least likely constituency—the landowners. *See* Mich.C.L.Ann. § 21.1287(1)–(19) and § 7.557 and Wis.Stat.Ann. § 91.01–91.79. Vermont has enacted a rigorous capital gains tax on land held for less than 6 years. The tax decreases as the length of time the land has been owned by the seller increases. 32 Vt.Stat.Ann. §§ 10001–10 (1973).

4.   Federal tax laws can have a direct effect on the preservation of agricultural land. Congress has provided a tax option for qualifying heirs inheriting smaller family farms. The act essentially allows the farm property to be assessed for estate tax purposes at its agricultural use rather than at its "highest and best" use provided that the heirs keep the land in agricultural production for a specific period of time. The maximum value reduction is limited to $750,000. *See* I.R.C., 26 U.S.C.A. § 2032A. Charitable deductions are now allowed by the IRS for contributions of easements for agricultural, environmental and open space conservation purposes. The contributions must be made to a governmental entity or publicly supported charitable organization in perpetuity. Qualifying purposes cover the preservation of open space, including farmland and forest land pursuant to a clear governmental policy which will yield a public benefit. *See* I.R.C., 26 U.S.C.A. § 170(h).

NOTES: THE ROLE OF ZONING IN AGRICULTURAL PRESERVATION

1.   Non-exclusive agricultural zoning ordinances allow non-farm dwellings as of right or conditionally, but agricultural uses are preferred. Within this broad approach three main techniques have been used to control the rapid conversion of agricultural land into residential sprawl land.

Large-lot ordinances which require substantial minimum lot sizes. This type of ordinance has generally been upheld in areas premature for development. *See, e.g., Glenview Development Co. v. Franklin Township*, 397 A.2d 384 (N.J.Super.1978) (upholding minimum 3 and 5 acre size lots because 72 percent of township is in agricultural use and no urgency to accommodate urban growth); *Gisler v. County of Madera*, 112 Cal.Rptr. 919 (Cal.App.1974) (18 acre minimum lot size upheld in agricultural zoning ordinance); and *County of Ada v. Henry*, 668 P.2d 994 (Idaho 1983) (agricultural zoning with an 80-acre minimum lot size upheld). Lot sizes ranging from 3 to 5 acres tend to be ineffectual in preserving land and actually have the opposite effect— breaking up the land into parcels too small to be effectively farmed, but creating urban sprawl through "ranchettes."

The use of large lot zoning has been attacked under the Fair Housing Act (FHA), 42 U.S.C. § 3601 et seq., as excluding minorities. The argument is that where rural, large-lot zoning denies the ability to build multi-family dwellings, there may be either 1) discriminatory intent (disparate treatment cases) or 2) discriminatory effect (disparate impact cases) in the zoning, the two ways of showing a violation of the FHA. To show discriminatory intent, proof of discriminatory purpose is needed, which may be found through a wide range of tests applied by the courts. Under the disparate impact approach, actions having a discriminatory effect, even if there is no discriminatory intent, are proscribed by the FHA. However, courts have upheld refusals to rezone agricultural lands to multifamily dwellings where there are not adequate facilities or utilities, such as sewer and road capacity, lack of shopping centers, retail services, public transportation and emergency facilities. *See In re Malone*, 592 F.Supp. 1135 (E.D.Mo.1984). In any event, the FHA challenge to agricultural zoning in rural communities may be defeated with a strong comprehensive plan. What is needed is a showing that the plan contains an element which addresses housing and contains sound reasons for staying rural (i.e., inadequate public facilities and services to absorb the impact of multifamily housing), and that the zoning applies equally and with the same effect to everyone. Further, under a regional general welfare approach, if rural communities can accommodate the region's fair share of growth as documented in the city's comprehensive plan, rural zoning should be upheld. Further, rural areas may be considered an integral part of an area's regional general welfare, providing a buffer zone between the city and agricultural areas. Analysis under regional general welfare may not be determinative, however, because conservation and agricultural areas may be allowed to implement stronger growth restrictions than areas in the path of growth. *See Southern Burlington County NAACP v. Township of Mt. Laurel*, 456 A.2d 390 (N.J.1983).

Area-based allocation ordinances do not require large minimum lot sizes but rather allow owners to build one dwelling unit for each unit of land of a specified area that they own. In a fixed area based ordinance, the allowance is predetermined. For example in "quarter/quarter" zoning ordinances, one non-farm dwelling unit can be built on each quarter of a quarter section of land. The dwelling must typically be on a small lot, ranging in size from one-half to three acres. In the variable area—based ordinance, the allocation is based on a sliding scale under which the number of buildings permitted per acre decreases as the farm size increases. These area-based allocation ordinances have the advantage of allowing dwellings to be built on small lots which may be clustered together, thereby retaining agricultural land in large blocks. Such a scheme was constitutionally upheld in *Boundary Drive Associates v. Shrewsbury Township Board of Supervisors*, 491 A.2d 86 (Pa.1985).

Conditional use zoning allows non-farm dwellings as a conditional use if they are compatible with surrounding agricultural uses.

2.   Exclusive agricultural zoning ordinances do not allow non-farm buildings; a performance definition of a farm use is used, and each request to build a farm dwelling requires individual review. Agriculture is perceived as a long-term, permanent land use. Oregon has the most comprehensive plan in the country. Goal 3 of the statewide planning program requires identification of agricultural land and their preservation by use of an Exclusive Farm Use Zone. Or.Rev.Stat. § 215.243. Black Hawk County, Iowa in 1982 enacted a comprehensive agricultural land preservation and zoning ordinance which incorporates both exclusive and non-exclusive agricultural districts. *See* Black Hawk County, Iowa, Agricultural Land Preservation and Zoning Ordinance, Ordinance No. 11 (Nov. 18, 1982). However, for pure size and relative breadth, it is hard to top Hawaii's state agricultural zone, one of four set out in Hawaii's

Land Use Law, in which nearly half the state's land is classified. See David L. Callies, *Preserving Paradise*, Ch. 2 (1994).

3.   Compensatory techniques used include land banking, and the purchase of interests in land and transferable development rights.

Land banking involves an agricultural preservation program in which the local government or a private organization purchases the agricultural land in fee simple and re-leases it to farmers. The farmer can sell his land voluntarily or the governmental entity may use the power of eminent domain to condemn the land, subject to meeting public purpose requirements. The technique has not been widely used by governmental units in the United States, primarily because of the large amounts of money required and the administrative expertise needed to effectively manage the purchased land. The technique is widely used in Canada and Europe. *See* Stokes, *Housing: The Environmental Issue*, Sierran (Sept./Oct. 1982); Letwin, *Municipal Land Banks in Land Reserve Policy for Urban Development* 236–376 (1975); Young, *The Saskatchewan Land Bank*, 40 SASK.L.REV. 1 (1975).

Purchase of development rights involves the acquisition of a development easement to preserve nonurban uses. The purchase price is usually based on the difference between the value of the land for development and its value for agriculture. This approach has been utilized in a number of areas including Suffolk County, N.Y.; Maryland; Massachusetts; Connecticut; Burlington County, N.J.; King County, Wash.; New Hampshire; Southhampton, N.Y.; and Hunterdon County, N.J. The technique can be most effective by targeting for the purchase plan only prime agricultural land which is severely threatened by development. The concept was upheld in the state of Washington in *Louthan v. King County*, 617 P.2d 977 (Wash.1980). *See* Thomas L. Daniels, *The Purchase of Development Rights: Preserving Agricultural Land and Open Space*, 57 J.AMER.PLAN.ASS'N 421 (1991); Melissa Waller Baldwin, *Conservation Easements: A Viable Tool for Land Preservation*, 32 LAND & WATER L.REV. 89 (1997); Hollingshead, *Conservation Easements: A Flexible Tool for Land Preservation*, 3 ENVTL.L. 319 (1997). In spite of their high costs (sometimes the easement-purchasing entity will pay nearly all of the highest-use value of the land), agricultural preservation easements have been praised because the farmer retains all of the basic property elements in the "bundle" of rights which we call ownership except the right to develop. The owner gets the cash up front, the land is still owned in fee simple, and it is restricted from development in perpetuity. In addition, the taking issue is avoided. Can you see why this could be a problem if the land were downzoned to a strictly agricultural use?

Transfer of development rights is a significant and complex technique which has been used in historic, environmental and agricultural preservation. The purchase of interests in land and TDRs are most appropriately used where development pressures are high and zoning restrictions would deprive landowners of the substantial value of their land. A primary advantage of the TDR approach is that it reduces and eliminates the public costs of acquiring development rights by shifting the responsibility for purchase from the government to developers. Recall *Suitum v. Tahoe Regional Planning Agency*, 520 U.S. 725, 117 S.Ct. 1659, 137 L.Ed.2d 980 (1997) chapter 6L, *supra*, in which TDRs were at issue under the ripeness doctrine. *See* Julian Conrad Juergensmeyer, James C. Nicholas, and Brian D. Leebrick, *Transferable Development Rights and Alternatives After* Suitum, 30 URB.LAW. 441 (1998).

Several townships and counties in Pennsylvania, Massachusetts, New Jersey, New York and Maryland have established TDR programs for agricultural preservation. Montgomery County, Maryland combined TDRs with a zoning ordinance. In the preservation area, development is limited to one house per 25 acres, accomplished by a downzoning. Owners can recapture resultant losses of value of their land by selling the rights to develop an additional five dwelling units which can be utilized in a receiving area elsewhere in the county considered appropriate for high density development. The program was combined with a revolving fund and limitations on water and sewerage extensions to farm protection areas. This sophisticated program was upheld in a taking challenge in *Dufour v. Montgomery County Council No. 56964* (Cir.Ct. for Montgomery County, Jan. 20, 1983), discussed in 35 LAND USE LAW 19 (1983).

The transfer of development rights mitigates the economic impact of environmental restrictions while also providing an incentive to developers for protecting the environment. New Jersey's use of such a program to preserve agricultural land in the Pinelands is discussed in *Gardner v. New Jersey Pinelands Commission*, 593 A.2d 251 (N.J.1991). See also, Freilich, Leitner & Carlisle, New Jersey Office of State Planning: Agricultural Preservation: Development Standards for Limited Growth Area (Jan. 27, 1998). TDRs were used by the City of Hollywood, Florida, in its effort to preserve the longest remaining stretch of unspoiled beach on Florida's "Gold Coast." Since 1970, the city had passed a series of rezonings limiting densities on the beach. In its most recent efforts, the city divided the beach into two zones: a development zone and a control zone (the beach and dune areas). By dedicating their control zone property to the city for use as public open space, property owners were allowed to transfer development rights in the control zone to the development zone. The new ordinance was upheld as reasonably related to a valid public purpose. The court found that no inverse condemnation had occurred since the program enhanced the value of land in the development zone. *See City of Hollywood v. Hollywood, Inc.*, 432 So.2d 1332 (Fla.App.1983); Freilich and Senville, *Takings, TDRs and Environmental Preservation: "Fairness" and the Hollywood North Beach Case*, 35 LAND USE LAW (June 1983) at 4. For a general discussion of how TDR's work, see Pruetz, *Saved By Development: Preserving Environmental Areas, Farmland and Historic Landmarks With Transfer of Development Rights* (Arje Press 1997). For a complete listing of TDR programs throughout the U.S., see Arthur C. Nelson, Rick Pruetz, and Doug Woodruff, *The TDR Handbook: Designing and Implementing Transfer of Development Rights Programs* (2011).

COMMENT: CONSERVATION SUBDIVISIONS

Note the effective use of "Conservation Subdivision" a concept made popular by Randall Arendt's book Rural by Design (1997). *See* Chapter 4, *supra*. In a 2003 case, the Pennsylvania Supreme Court approved conservation subdivision when prime agricultural or other environmental sensitive lands must be preserved against allegation of taking and exclusionary zoning. The Court held:

> It must be emphasized that the Dolington Group presents no challenge to the Joint Zoning Ordinance insofar as it restricts the development of floodplains, floodplain soils, wetlands, steep slopes and mature woodlands. Only the restriction of development on prime agricultural soils is the subject of particular objection together with the challenge to the aggregate effect of the regulations as a whole. We first reject the contention that prime agricultural soils are less deserving of zoning protection than are other sensitive environmental lands and resources. Just to the contrary, the MPC expressly requires each municipal and multi-municipal zoning ordinance "[t]o preserve prime agriculture and farmland considering topography, soil type and classification, and present use." MPC § 604(3), .Moreover, "zoning ordinances shall protect prime agricultural land. . . ." MPC § 603(g)(1). The term "Prime Agricultural Land" is defined in the MPC, as it is in the JZO, as "land used for agricultural purposes that contains soils of the first, second or third class as defined by the United States Department of Agriculture natural resource and conservation services county soil survey." In *C & M Developers, Inc. v. Bedminster Township Zoning Hearing Board*, 573 Pa. 2, 820 A.2d 143 (Pa.2002), we "acknowledge[d the] legitimate interest in preserving . . . agricultural lands." 820 A.2d at 158; accord *Boundary Drive Associates v. Shrewsbury Township Board of Supervisors*, 507 Pa. 481, 491 A.2d 86 (1985). The expressions of legislative and executive intent to preserve the Commonwealth's farms and agricultural lands serve to underscore the significance and propriety of the Jointure's efforts in this regard.

> Similarly, the regulations at issue in C & M Developers required the owners of agricultural tracts greater than ten acres in area to set aside 60% of the prime farmland and 50% of any remaining farmland as a "non-buildable site area." Id., 820 A.2d at 148. We agreed with the tribunals below that this "set-aside" regulation was justified by the municipality's intent to preserve its agricultural lands and activities. However, the regulations at issue then additionally required the creation of "one clear acre" for each proposed lot which could contain no floodplain, floodplain soils, wetlands, lakes, ponds, or watercourses. The combined effect of these requirements was to reduce the developmental potential of the 200 acre tract from 461 lots of 10,000 square feet as proposed by the landowner to 51 one-acre lots as permitted by the challenged regulations—an 89% reduction in

developmental intensity. Moreover, the owners of parcels fewer than ten acres in area could subdivide their lands with no such limitations.

The CM district regulations . . . have their primary activity in the design or layout of the development of a particular property; that is, in the location. . . . This can be seen most clearly in the method of calculation of the maximum number of permitted dwelling units applicable to each of the three subdivision types allowed in the CM district. In each instance: conventional, cluster, and performance subdivision, the maximum number of permitted dwelling units is calculated with reference to the base site area; that is, the tract area before deducting any of the areas of natural constraint and before deducting the prime agricultural lands. The degree to which tract development is constrained by floodplain, floodplain soils, wetlands, water bodies, steep slopes, mature woodlands, and prime agricultural soils, therefore, has no necessary impact on the maximum number of permitted dwelling units.

To be sure, the Dolington Group vigorously argues that it is precisely the effect of the CM district regulations in reducing the permitted intensity of development of the Subject Property to which the challenge is addressed. It is clear from the Dolington Group's evidence, however, that the inability to achieve the maximum developmental potential under the CM district regulations with respect to the Subject Property is a function primarily of the pervasive natural constraints with which the Property is burdened [emphasis in original]. By the Dolington Group's evidence, the Subject Property could have been lawfully developed in February 1996 as a performance subdivision containing 168 single-family lots, including 35 lots of 10,000 square feet, 67 lots of 6,500 square feet, and 66 lots of 4,500 square feet. This number, shown by plan to be achievable on the Subject Property and conceded to be less, by at least "another lot or two" than the actual maximum achievable on the site, is more than 95% of the maximum calculated without reference to any of the tract's natural constraints or agricultural soils.

The inability to achieve the maximum permitted developmental intensity by means of a conventional or cluster subdivision does not support a contrary conclusion. As we have indicated, it is the purpose of the CM district regulations to preferentially encourage the use of cluster development over conventional subdivision and performance subdivision over cluster with respect to tracts constrained by environmentally sensitive features or prime agricultural soils. The fact here demonstrated by the Dolington Group's proofs that 96% of the maximum permitted developmental intensity could be achieved on the Subject Property by use of a performance subdivision (notwithstanding the degree of its constraint by natural features), while conventional subdivision would permit the achievement of only about one-third of the permitted developmental intensity, establishes only that the regulations are functioning as they were intended: providing to the developer of this extremely constrained tract containing substantial areas of prime agricultural soils, very strong encouragement for the use of performance subdivision and, thereby, for the preservation of the agricultural soils and of significant areas of open space. The Dolington Group failed to rebut the presumption of legality applicable to the CM district regulations and we affirm the decision of the courts below to this effect.

In re Petition of Dolington Land Group, 576 Pa. 519, 839 A.2d 1021 (2003).

G. PUBLIC LANDS

The federal government owns approximately 740 million acres of land in the United States, of which approximately 440 million are "disposable" administratively, without congressional approval (major exceptions: land in national parks, national forests, and national wildlife refuges). *See Bureau of Land Management, U.S. Department of the Interior, Public Land Statistics 1980*, pp. 9 and 21 (1981).

The lands that are federally owned constitute roughly one-third of the nation. One-half are in Alaska. Huge percentages of western states are also publicly owned: Nevada, 85%; Idaho and Utah, 65%; Wyoming and Oregon, 50%; California, 45%; Colorado, 35%; Montana, 30%. In the east, the percentages are smaller, but still constitute significant amounts of acreage: Virginia, 10% (25 million acres); North Carolina, 7% (31 million acres); Georgia, 6%; Florida, 12%; Michigan, 10% (36 million acres); New Hampshire, 13%; Tennessee, 6%; West Virginia, 7%. All of this is owned in fee simple.[9] The government also owns subsurface mineral rights in some 60 million acres. In addition, the federal government controls the outer continental shelf, which is the area from three to two-hundred miles offshore. 43 U.S.C.A. §§ 1331 to 1356. This enormous area, controlled by the Department of the Interior, is of great commercial importance for its oil, gas, and fisheries resources. See "Congress spars over proposed 'ocean zoning,' " Miami Herald, Oct. 04, 2011.

---

[9]   These figures are rounded off and drawn from various sources. See George C. Coggins and Robert L. Glicksman, *Public Natural Resources Law* (1990) and Paul W. Gates, *History of Public Land Law Development* (1968).

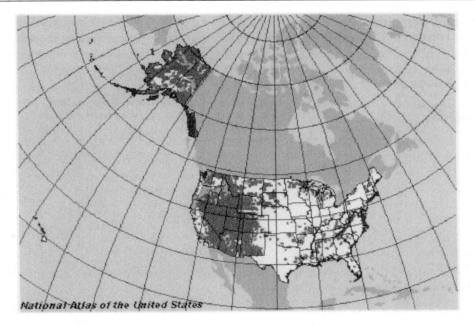

National Atlas of the United States

The use and disposal of public lands to affect private land use policy and the public control of that private use is the major thrust of this, a section that could easily grow to a separate volume. This section has a decidedly federal thrust, reflecting the view that the federal government, as the major public landholder in the United States, affects most the private use of land, whether on public or private land. For a good summary of the public lands of the United States and how they were acquired and partially disposed of, *see* Ann L. Strong, *Land Banking* 1–36 (1980). For a definition and exhaustive treatment of public land law generally, *see* George C. Coggins & Robert L. Glicksman, *Public Natural Resources Law* (1997). The materials that follow raise several significant issues concerning the management of federal land and its disposal.

KLEPPE V. NEW MEXICO

Supreme Court of the United States, 1976.
426 U.S. 529, 96 S.Ct. 2285, 49 L.Ed.2d 34.

MR. JUSTICE MARSHALL delivered the opinion of the Court.

At issue in this case is whether Congress exceeded its powers under the Constitution in enacting the Wild Free-roaming Horses and Burros Act.

The Wild Free-roaming Horses and Burros Act, was enacted in 1971 to protect "all unbranded and unclaimed horses and burros on public lands of the United States," from "capture, branding, harassment, or death." The Act provides that all such horses and burros on the public lands administered by the Secretary of the Interior through the Bureau of Land Management (BLM) or by the Secretary of Agriculture through the Forest

Service are committed to the jurisdiction of the respective Secretaries, who are "directed to protect and manage [the animals] as components of the public lands * * * in a manner that is designed to achieve and maintain a thriving natural ecological balance on the public lands." If protected horses or burros "stray from public lands onto privately owned land, the owners of such land may inform the nearest Federal marshal or agent of the Secretary, who shall arrange to have the animals removed."

Section 6, authorizes the Secretaries to promulgate regulations, and to enter into cooperative agreements with other landowners and with state and local governmental agencies in furtherance of the Act's purposes. On August 7, 1973, the Secretaries executed such an agreement with the New Mexico Livestock Board, the agency charged with enforcing the New Mexico Estray Law. The agreement acknowledged the authority of the Secretaries to manage and protect the wild free-roaming horses and burros on the public lands of the United States within the State and established a procedure for evaluating the claims of private parties to ownership of such animals.

The Livestock Board terminated the agreement three months later. Asserting that the Federal Government lacked power to control wild horses and burros on the public lands of the United States unless the animals were moving in interstate commerce or damaging the public lands and that neither of these bases of regulation was available here, the Board notified the Secretaries of its intent

> to exercise all regulatory, impoundment and sale powers which it derives from the New Mexico Estray Law, over all estray horses, mules or asses found running at large upon public or private lands within New Mexico * * *. This includes the right to go upon Federal or State lands to take possession of said horses or burros, should the Livestock Board so desire.

The differences between the Livestock Board and the Secretaries came to a head in February 1974. On February 1, 1974, a New Mexico rancher, Kelley Stephenson, was informed by the BLM that several unbranded burros had been seen near Taylor Well, where Stephenson watered his cattle. Taylor Well is on federal property, and Stephenson had access to it and some 8,000 surrounding acres only through a grazing permit issued pursuant to § 3 of the Taylor Grazing Act. After the BLM made it clear to Stephenson that it would not remove the burros and after he personally inspected the Taylor Well area, Stephenson complained to the Livestock Board that the burros were interfering with his livestock operation by molesting his cattle and eating their feed.

Thereupon the Board rounded up and removed 19 unbranded and unclaimed burros pursuant to the New Mexico Estray Law. Each burro was seized on the public lands of the United States and, as the director of the Board conceded, each burro fit the definition of a wild free-roaming burro under § 2(b) of the Act. On February 18, 1974, the Livestock Board, pursuant to its usual practice, sold the burros at a public auction. After the sale, the BLM asserted jurisdiction under the Act and demanded that the Board recover the animals and return them to the public lands.

The Property Clause of the Constitution provides that "Congress shall have Power to dispose of and make all needful Rules and Regulations respecting the Territory or other Property belonging to the United States." U.S. Const., Art. IV, § 3, cl. 2. In passing the Wild Free-roaming Horses and Burros Act, Congress deemed the regulated animals "an integral part of the natural system of the public lands" of the United States, and found that their management was necessary "for achievement of an ecological balance on the public lands." According to Congress, these animals, if preserved in their native habitats, "contribute to the diversity of life forms within the Nation and enrich the lives of the American people."

For these reasons, Congress determined to preserve and protect the wild free-roaming horses and burros on the public lands of the United States. The question under the Property Clause is whether this determination can be sustained as a "needful" regulation "respecting" the public lands. In answering this question, we must remain mindful that, while courts must eventually pass upon them, determinations under the Property Clause are entrusted primarily to the judgment of Congress.

Appellees argue that the Act cannot be supported by the Property Clause. They contend that the Clause grants Congress essentially two kinds of power: (1) the power to dispose of and make incidental rules regarding the use of federal property; and (2) the power to protect federal property. As an initial matter, it is far from clear that the Act was not passed in part to protect the public lands of the United States[7] or that Congress cannot assert a property interest in the regulated horses and burros superior to that of the State. But we need not consider whether the Act can be upheld on either of these grounds, for we reject appellees' narrow reading of the Property Clause.

Appellees ground their argument on a number of cases that, upon analysis, provide no support for their position. Like the District Court, appellees cite Hunt v. United States, for the proposition that the Property Clause gives Congress only the limited power to regulate wild animals in order to protect the public lands from damage. But Hunt, which upheld the Government's right to kill deer that were damaging foliage in the national forests, only holds that damage to the land is a sufficient basis for regulation; it contains no suggestion that it is a necessary one.

---

[7]   Congress expressly ordered that the animals were to be managed and protected in order "to achieve and maintain a thriving natural ecological balance on the public lands." § 3(a), 16 U.S.C. § 1333(a) (1970 ed., Supp. IV).

Camfield v. United States, is of even less help to appellees. Appellees rely upon the following language from Camfield:

> While we do not undertake to say that congress has the unlimited power to legislate against nuisances within a state which it would have within a territory, we do not think the admission of a territory as a state deprives it of the power of legislating for the protection of the public lands, though it may thereby involve the exercise of what is ordinarily known as the "police power," so long as such power is directed solely to its own protection.

Appellees mistakenly read this language to limit Congress' power to regulate activity on the public lands; in fact, the quoted passage refers to the scope of congressional power to regulate conduct on private land that affects the public lands. And Camfield holds that the Property Clause is broad enough to permit federal regulation of fences built on private land adjoining public land when the regulation is for the protection of the federal property. Camfield contains no suggestion of any limitation on Congress' power over conduct on its own property; its sole message is that the power granted by the Property Clause is broad enough to reach beyond territorial limits.

The decided cases have supported this expansive reading. It is the Property Clause, for instance, that provides the basis for governing the Territories of the United States. And even over public land within the States, "[t]he general government doubtless has a power over its own property analogous to the police power of the several states, and the extent to which it may go in the exercise of such power is measured by the exigencies of the particular case." Camfield v. United States. We have noted, for example, that the Property Clause gives Congress the power over the public lands "to control their occupancy and use, to protect them from trespass and injury, and to prescribe the conditions upon which others may obtain rights in them * * * ." And we have approved legislation respecting the public lands "[i]f it be found to be necessary, for the protection of the public or of intending settlers [on the public lands]." Camfield v. United States. In short, Congress exercises the powers both of a proprietor and of a legislature over the public domain. Although the Property Clause does not authorize "an exercise of a general control over public policy in a State," it does permit "an exercise of the complete power which Congress has over particular public property entrusted to it." In our view, the "complete power" that Congress has over public lands necessarily includes the power to regulate and protect the wildlife living there.

Appellees argue that if we approve the Wild Free-roaming Horses and Burros Act as a valid exercise of Congress' power under the Property Clause, then we have sanctioned an impermissible intrusion on the sovereignty, legislative authority, and police power of the State and have wrongly infringed upon the State's traditional trustee powers over wild animals. The argument appears to be that Congress could obtain exclusive legislative jurisdiction over the public lands in the State only by state consent, and that in the absence of such consent Congress lacks the power to act contrary to state law. This argument is without merit.

Appellees' claim confuses Congress' derivative legislative powers, which are not involved in this case, with its powers under the Property Clause. Congress may acquire derivative legislative power from a State pursuant to Art. I, § 8, cl. 17, of the Constitution by consensual acquisition of land, or by nonconsensual acquisition followed by the State's subsequent cession of legislative authority over the land.[11] In either case, the legislative jurisdiction acquired may range from exclusive federal jurisdiction with no residual state police power, to concurrent, or partial, federal legislative jurisdiction, which may allow the State to exercise certain authority.

But while Congress can acquire exclusive or partial jurisdiction over lands within a State by the State's consent or cession, the presence or absence of such jurisdiction has nothing to do with Congress' power under the Property Clause. Absent consent or cession a State undoubtedly retains jurisdiction over federal lands within its territory, but Congress equally surely retains the power to enact legislation respecting those lands pursuant to the Property Clause. And when Congress so acts, the federal legislation necessarily overrides conflicting state laws under the Supremacy Clause. U.S. Const., Art. VI, cl. 2. As we said in Camfield v. United States, in response to a somewhat different claim: "A different rule would place the public domain of the United States completely at the mercy of state legislation."

Thus, appellees' assertion that "[a]bsent state consent by complete cession of jurisdiction of lands to the United States, exclusive jurisdiction does not accrue to the federal landowner with regard to federal lands within the borders of the state," is completely beside the point; and appellees' fear that the Secretary's position is that "the Property Clause totally exempts federal lands within state borders from state legislative powers, state police powers, and all rights and powers of local sovereignty and jurisdiction of the states," is totally unfounded. The Federal Government does not assert exclusive jurisdiction over the public lands in

---

[11]   Article I, § 8, cl. 17, of the Constitution provides that Congress shall have the power:

To exercise exclusive Legislation in all Cases whatsoever, over such District (not exceeding ten Miles square) as may, by Cession of Particular States, and the Acceptance of Congress, become the Seat of the Government of the United States, and to exercise like Authority over all Places purchased by the Consent of the Legislature of the State in which the Same shall be, for the Erection of Forts, Magazines, Arsenals, dock-Yards, and other needful Buildings * * * .

The Clause has been broadly construed, and the acquisition by consent or cession of exclusive or partial jurisdiction over properties for any legitimate governmental purpose beyond those itemized is permissible. *Collins v. Yosemite Park Co.*, 304 U.S. 518, 528–530, 58 S.Ct. 1009, 1013–14, 82 L.Ed. 1502 (1938).

New Mexico, and the State is free to enforce its criminal and civil laws on those lands. But where those state laws conflict with the Wild Free-roaming Horses and Burros Act, or with other legislation passed pursuant to the Property Clause, the law is clear: The state laws must recede.

Again, none of the cases relied upon by appellees are to the contrary. Surplus Trading Co. v. Cook, merely states the rule outlined above that, "without more," federal ownership of lands within a State does not withdraw those lands from the jurisdiction of the State. Likewise, Wilson v. Cook, holds only that, in the absence of consent or cession, the Federal Government did not acquire exclusive jurisdiction over certain federal forest reserve lands in Arkansas and the State retained legislative jurisdiction over those lands. No question was raised regarding Congress' power to regulate the forest reserves under the Property Clause. And in Colorado v. Toll, the Court found that Congress had not purported to assume jurisdiction over highways within the Rocky Mountain National Park, not that it lacked the power to do so under the Property Clause.[12]

In short, these cases do not support appellees' claim that upholding the Act would sanction an impermissible intrusion upon state sovereignty. The Act does not establish exclusive federal jurisdiction over the public lands in New Mexico; it merely overrides the New Mexico Estray Law insofar as it attempts to regulate federally protected animals. And that is but the necessary consequence of valid legislation under the Property Clause.

Appellees' contention that the Act violates traditional state power over wild animals stands on no different footing. Unquestionably the States have broad trustee and police powers over wild animals within their jurisdictions. But, as Geer v. Connecticut cautions, those powers exist only "in so far as [their] exercise may be not incompatible with, or restrained by, the rights conveyed to the federal government by the constitution." "No doubt it is true that as between a State and its inhabitants the State may regulate the killing and sale of [wildlife], but it does not follow that its authority is exclusive of paramount powers." Thus, the Privileges and

---

[12] Referring to the Act creating the National Park, the Court said:

There is no attempt to give exclusive jurisdiction to the United States, but on the contrary the rights of the State over the roads are left unaffected in terms. Apart from those terms the state denies the power of Congress to curtail its jurisdiction or rights without an act of cession from it and an acceptance by the national government. The statute establishing the park would not be construed to attempt such a result. As the [park superintendent] is undertaking to assert exclusive control and to establish a monopoly in a matter as to which, if the allegations of the bill are maintained, the State has not surrendered its legislative power, a cause of action is disclosed if we do not look beyond the bill, and it was wrongly dismissed. 268 U.S., at 231, 45 S.Ct., at 506. (citations omitted).

While Colorado thus asserted that, absent cession, the Federal Government lacked power to regulate the highways within the park, and the Court held that the State was entitled to attempt to prove that it had not surrendered legislative jurisdiction to the United States, at most the case stands for the proposition that where Congress does not purport to override state power over public lands under the Property Clause and where there has been no cession, a federal official lacks power to regulate contrary to state law.

Immunities Clause, U.S. Const., Art. IV, § 2, cl. 1, precludes a State from imposing prohibitory licensing fees on nonresidents shrimping in its waters; the Treaty Clause, U.S. Const., Art. II, § 2, permits Congress to enter into and enforce a treaty to protect migratory birds despite state objections; and the Property Clause gives Congress the power to thin overpopulated herds of deer on federal lands contrary to state law. We hold today that the Property Clause also gives Congress the power to protect wildlife on the public lands, state law notwithstanding.

In this case, the New Mexico Livestock Board entered upon the public lands of the United States and removed wild burros. These actions were contrary to the provisions of the Wild Free-roaming Horses and Burros Act. We find that, as applied to this case, the Act is a constitutional exercise of congressional power under the Property Clause. We need not, and do not, decide whether the Property Clause would sustain the Act in all of its conceivable applications.

Appellees are concerned that the Act's extension of protection to wild free-roaming horses and burros that stray from public land onto private land, will be read to provide federal jurisdiction over every wild horse or burro that at any time sets foot upon federal land. While it is clear that regulations under the Property Clause may have some effect on private lands not otherwise under federal control, Camfield v. United States, we do not think it appropriate in this declaratory judgment proceeding to determine the extent, if any, to which the Property Clause empowers Congress to protect animals on private lands or the extent to which such regulation is attempted by the Act. We have often declined to decide important questions regarding "the scope and constitutionality of legislation in advance of its immediate adverse effect in the context of a concrete case," the absence of "an adequate and full-bodied record." We follow that course in this case and leave open the question of the permissible reach of the Act over private lands under the Property Clause.

NOTES

1.   Not all federal regulation of federal land takes place under the auspices of the Constitution and statutes upon which the decisions in the two principle cases are based. As part of the Raker Act of December 19, 1913, the Federal government granted the City and County of San Francisco certain lands and rights of way in the public domain in Yosemite National Park subject to express conditions. The Secretary of the Interior brought suit against the City and County for violating one of the express provisions of the act by allowing a private company to sell the electric power generated from the lands. The City and County argued that allowing a private company to do so was not a violation of the Act since the City and County was not selling them the electricity for resale, but was selling the electricity through the company by consignment. Even though the federal government does not have police power, it can use federal lands to induce municipalities to act in a certain manner.

Here, the federal government ensured that San Francisco would provide affordable electric power to their residents. *See also Ryan Outdoor Advertising Inc. v. United States*, 559 F.2d 554 (9th Cir.1977), holding that in the event of a conflict between regulations issued by the Secretary of the Interior regarding public lands and a federal act, the regulations control due to the broad general grant of authority to the Secretary to administer laws dealing with public lands.

2.   "A state which intends to regulate land using activities in a given respect, as by zoning for purposes of land use control holds authority to include federal land areas within the geographic extent of such regulation if the state holds legislative jurisdiction over such areas. Such regulation, if otherwise valid, will be enforceable as private land using activity, except to the extent that such regulation might interfere with essential federal functions which are duly authorized in accordance with the United States Constitution. * * * Private mineral exploration and development on federal proprietary lands undoubtedly may be regulated by the states and local governments in the same manner as such exploration and development is otherwise regulated." Landstrom, *State and Local Governmental Regulation of Private Land-using Activities on Federal Lands*, 7 NAT.RES.LAW. 77, 81–2 (1974). Is this still true after *Kleppe*? What, for example, would happen if the Secretary of the Interior were to lease, say, 40 acres in an abandoned military base to the Foundation and Empire Development Corporation for 99 years for the construction of high-rise condominium and apartment buildings, in an area zoned, by the local government in whose jurisdiction the land would otherwise be, for open space, or zoned for low-density residential use?

3.   In *California Coastal Commission v. Granite Rock Co.*, 480 U.S. 572 (1987), the Court dealt with the scope of state authority on federal lands. After Granite Rock obtained approval from the Forest Service for a five year mining operation on federal land, the California Coastal Commission instructed the company to seek a permit as required by the state's coastal zone act. The company claimed it did not need to since that federal law preempted state law. The Court disagreed, finding the state law did not directly conflict with federal law. The Court also was unconvinced that Congress had intended to entirely occupy mining on public land. In addressing the latter issue, the Court drew a line between environmental law and land use law. Without deciding whether federal land use law (the Federal Land Policy and Management Act and the National Forest Management Act) preempted state law, the Court held federal law did not preempt environmental law. Is this a clear distinction? The Court observed that

> [t]he line between environmental regulation and land use planning
> will not always be bright; for example, one may hypothesize a state
> environmental regulation so severe that a particular land use would
> become commercially impracticable. However, the core activity
> described by each phrase is undoubtedly different. Land use planning
> in essence chooses particular uses for the land; environmental
> regulation, at its core, does not mandate particular uses of the land

but requires only that, however the land is used, damage to the environment is kept within prescribed limits. Congress has indicated its understanding of land use planning and environmental regulation as distinct activities.

480 U.S. at 587.

4.   The extent of the type of peripheral land use regulation designed to protect federal land but exercised over private land is becoming an issue around national forests and other public lands. How far does such control physically extend? What about acid rain or mist from nearby—but nonadjacent—chemical works which defoliates national forests or parklands? What kind of police power is this? How does it differ from that exercised by the states? *See* Joseph Sax, *Helpless Giants: The National Policy and the Regulation of Private Land*, 75 MICH.L.REV. 239 (1976).

The New River Gorge National River in West Virginia was established by Congress in 1978 and is operated as part of the National Park System. While the "National River" designation contains 63,000 acres along 50 miles of the New River, only 6,000 acres of the area are federally owned. The rest is privately or state owned land. In 1986, faced with a public health problem caused by black flies, the State of West Virginia decided to spray pesticides in the state's southern counties in the area of the New River. The area to be sprayed was inside the boundaries of the New River Gorge National River and the National Park Service said the state could not spray without a Park Service permit. The federal government prevailed in this standoff. The court said that "the authority of the United States is not limited to the 6,000 acres of which it has legal title." *United States v. Moore*, 640 F.Supp. 164, 166 (S.D.W.Va.1986). Is this in accord with *Kleppe*?

5.   Disposal of federal land raises a host of land use issues, many of which affect the private use of land as well. The Federal Land Policy and Management Act of 1976 (FLPMA), 43 U.S.C. §§ 1701 et seq. declares it to be the policy of the United States that the public lands be retained in federal ownership unless it is determined that disposal will serve the national interest. Even then, the sale must be in accordance with a comprehensive land use plan providing for both long-range goals and coordination between state and federal planning agencies, and specifically limiting such disposal to parcels which are either (1) difficult and uneconomic to manage, (2) acquired for a specific purpose but no longer needed for that or any other federal purpose, or (3) capable of serving important public objectives such as community expansion and economic development which cannot be achieved prudently or feasibly on non-public lands and which will outweigh any public benefits of continued federal ownership. It was against the backdrop of this relatively new (then) federal statute that President Reagan attempted his ill-fated Asset Management Program to dispose of lands held by various federal agencies not needed for federal programs in order to reduce federal budget deficits. See Executive Order No. 12348, February 25, 1982. The resulting hue and cry from various environmental and natural resource groups together with the depressed state of the property market resulted in very little by way of

disposal: approximately 10,000 acres for about $3 million, reportedly less than one percent of what the Property Review Board created by the aforementioned executive order had anticipated. *See* Mulford, *Federal Land Tenure Policy*, 3 RESOURCE LAW NOTES 2 (Sept.1983). *See also* Terry L. Anderson, *Public Land Exchanges, Sales and Purchases Under the Federal Land Policy and Management Act of 1976*, 1979 UTAH L.REV. 657 (1979) and Feller, *Sales of Public Land: A Problem in Legislative and Judicial Control of Administrative Action*, 96 HARV.L.REV. 927 (1983).

6.   Actual disposal of some federal land—especially military land—takes place not under FLPMA but under the Federal Property and Administrative Services Act of 1949, 40 U.S.C.A. § 472 et seq., (FPASA). Indeed, it was under this Act that the Administration attempted to sell off perhaps the most controversial part of the "national estate," the 72-acre Fort DeRussy on Waikiki Beach in Honolulu, Hawaii. Part of 715 acres designated for disposal under the aforementioned Asset Management Program by the Property Review Board, a critical 17 of the Fort's 72 acres was to be sold for real estate development purposes. Among the issues: should the land have been offered first to the City at a discount for a public park (more or less its present use)? *See* Comment, *The Sale of Fort DeRussy: An Analyses of the Reagan Administration's Federal Land Sales Program*, 7 U.HAW.L.REV. 105 (1985) and *Government Land Bank v. GSA*, 671 F.2d 663 (1st Cir.1982) for possible answers. For a policy analysis of the issues raised by federal land disposal in a historical context, *see Rethinking The Federal Lands*, (S. Brubaker ed.1984); Marion Clawson, *The Federal Lands Revisited* (1983).

7.   Both FLPMA, 43 U.S.C. § 1712 (1994), and the National Forest Management Act, 16 U.S.C. § 1600 et seq. (1994), require the BLM and the Forest Service to plan before carrying out their respective multiple use duties. Court review of such plans permitting grazing (*Natural Resources Defense Council, Inc. v. Hodel*, 624 F.Supp. 1045 (D.Nev.1985), *aff'd*, 819 F.2d 927 (9th Cir.1987)), and off-road vehicle use (*American Motorcyclist Ass'n v. Watt*, 543 F.Supp. 789 (C.D.Cal.1982) and *Sierra Club v. Clark*, 756 F.2d 686 (9th Cir.1985)) has been relatively superficial. On the other hand, court review of Forest Service implementation decisions regarding timber harvesting against the backdrop of statutory requirements has been relatively strict. *See, e.g., Intermountain Forest Indus. Ass'n v. Lyng*, 683 F.Supp. 1330 (D.Wyo.1988); *Sierra Club v. Cargill*, 732 F.Supp. 1095 (D.Colo.1990); *Citizens for Env. Quality v. United States*, 731 F.Supp. 970 (D.Colo.1989). *But see Ohio Forestry Ass'n, Inc. v. Sierra Club*, 523 U.S. 726 (1998) (environmental organization's challenge to Forest Service's pre-implementation, long range management plan for clear cutting national forest lands held not ripe for judicial review). For further discussion of planning and public lands, *see* George C. Coggins, *The Developing Law of Land Use Planning on Federal Lands*, 61 U.COLO.L.REV. 307 (1990); Culhane & Friesema, *Land Use Planning for the Public Lands*, 19 NAT.RESOURCES J. 43 (1979).

8.   Not all federal land is either condemned by the federal government or part of the public domain. In Hawaii, for example, thousands of valuable

acres are held in a variety of defeasible fee by the federal government, and must be returned to the State—less improvement costs, if any—when the Administrator of the General Services Administration and the federal agency user declare it to be "surplus." Ceded Lands Act, 77 U.S. Statutes at Large, 472 (1963). Can the state force such a declaration of surplus if it can show the land is not being used? For federal purposes? *See Hawaii v. Gordon*, 373 U.S. 57 (1963). *See* Comment, *Hawaii's Ceded Lands*, 3 U.HAW.L.REV. 101 (1981); David L. Callies, *Regulating Paradise: Land Use Controls in Hawaii*, Chapter 4, Public Lands (2d ed.2010).

9.   Some in the west are displeased with the extensive federal landholdings. The so-called Sagebrush Rebellion was an unsuccessful effort to force the federal government to relinquish its western lands. Nevada claimed that it had a right to demand that the federal government dispose of its landholdings:

> This expectancy was supported by two legal theories: First, that the United States held the public lands in trust, the conditions of which were established by the early deeds of cessions by which certain of the original states ceded their western lands and by subsequent treaties and understandings associated with later acquisitions of territory now a part of the United States; disposal was one of the conditions. Second, that the new states would not be in an equal footing until the disposal contemplated by the deeds of cession and the temporary land holding trusts was accomplished; and that equal footing is a constitutional condition of all of the states of the Union.

Nevada v. United States, 512 F.Supp. 166, 170 (D.Nev.1981). The court rejected the state's claim. More recently, in January of 2016, the group that calls themselves the Citizens for Constitutional Freedom took over Malheur National Wildlife Refuge in Oregon demanding that federal controlled public lands be transferred to the state. The federal government owns more than 50 percent of lands in Oregon and has increased environmental regulations on those lands. The C4CF contends that their way of life of ranching had been inhibited because of these regulations. Tension boiled over when one of the ranchers was shot and killed at a traffic stop outside of the ranch. The final occupiers of the Refuge surrendered after 41 days. Carissa Wolf, "In Oregon, Frustration Over Federal Lands Has Been Building for Years," *The Washington Post* (2016). https://www/washingtonpost.com/national/in-oregon-frustration-over-federal-land-rights-has-been-building-for-years/2016/01/04/9bc905a2b330-11e5-a76a-0b5145e8679a_story.html.

10.   In Utah, the federal government retains close to 65 percent of the land. Utah has attempted, through the Transfer of Public Lands Act of 2012 (TPLA), to transfer title of approximately 30 million acres of federally owned public land over to the state. The disclaimer cause contained in the enabling act of Utah's Constitution poses a "formidable barrier to transfer demands." The clause states "that the people inhabiting said proposed State do agree and declare that they forever disclaim all right and title to the unappropriated public lands lying within the boundaries thereof." The federal government has

absolute authority over federal public lands and the disclaimer in the enabling act cannot be construed into a duty to dispose of public land to the States. Robert B. Keiter and John C. Ruple, *A Legal Analysis of the Transfer of Public Lands Movement*, Wallace Stegner Center for Land, Resources and the Environment (2014).

Multiple use management requires lands held by the Bureau of Land Management (BLM) and the US Forest Service (USFS) to balance resource extraction and preservation. A state seeking a transfer of public land must clearly define land management priorities between revenue generation and resource protection. For example, a report conducted by the Nevada legislature concluded that the state could generate close to 1.29 billion dollars in revenue by using all BLM managed lands. Despite the vast increase in revenue, doing so would not constitute multiple use management. Robert B. Keiter and John C. Ruple, *The Transfer of Public Lands Movement: Taking the 'Public' out of Public Lands*, Wallace Stegner Center for Land, Resources and the Environment (2015).

Further, even if a court was inclined to enforce public land takeovers, it is unlikely that mineral rights would transfer as the federal government has reserved their rights. The U.S Supreme Court has ruled that Congress did not intend to convey mineral lands to Western States such as Utah. According to the decision in *United States v. Sweet*, the Federal Government has reserved mineral rights beneath public lands. 245 U.S. 563 (1918).

Although there is a broad federal reservation of minerals, there have been two exceptions where mineral rights transferred to the states. This is exemplified in 2013/2014 when the Utah School and Institutional Trust Lands Administration generated 103.8 million dollars from mining minerals of federal public lands that were conveyed to Utah pursuant to the Utah Enabling Act. First, "if the mineral character of the land was not known at the time of conveyance, subsequent discoveries will not affect the patent and the state would be entitled to subsequently discovered minerals." Second, the Jones Act of 1927 released to the states grants of numbered school sections that had been previously withheld because of mineral classifications. Robert B. Keiter and John C. Ruple, *When Winning Means Losing: Why a State Takeover of Public Lands May Leave States Without the Minerals They Covet*, Wallace Stegner Center for Land, Resources and the Environment (2015).

There are multiple reasons that drive takeover legislation such as the TPLA in Utah. Enacting legislation such as the TPLA may not be addressing the root cause of frustration behind federally owned public lands. Can respectful dialogue, collaborative relationships between federal and state governments, adequate agency funding, and locally supported land exchanges be reasonable alternatives to demanding transfer of federally owned lands?

Some areas of frustration include discontiguous grants that have fragmented lands and created a wide range of disputes over land access. Conflicts ensue because adjacent lands are managed for incompatible purposes. Inadequate BLM and USFS management also frustrate the states and an argument set forth in order to control the public lands. Robert B. Keiter and John C. Ruple, *Alternatives to the Transfer of Public Lands Act*, Wallace Stegner Center for Land, Resources and the Environment (2016).

11. Catron County, New Mexico adopted an ordinance declaring that federal grazing permits are private property and giving the prosecuting attorney the power to prosecute anyone who interferes with such rights. The legal bases of the ordinance are several: state home rule powers, the Tenth Amendment, and federal statutes mandating that federal agencies cooperate with local government. The ordinance also asserts that grazing permits are property within the meaning of the Fifth Amendment based on state custom, prescription, and federal law issuing the licenses to graze. Catron County Ordinances 001 through 003–91 and 001 through 005–92. If these positions are correct, one consequence is that reductions in grazing allotments might be takings requiring compensation. Do any of these arguments hold water? See Anita Miller, *America's Public Lands: Legal Issues in the New War for the West*, 24 URB.LAW. 894 (1992).

The federal government eventually entered into a Memorandum of Understanding with Catron County, in which the county recognized the federal government's supremacy over the management of the public lands and the federal government agreed to mail to the county advance notice of planning activities, and to seek, where possible, to engage in cooperative planning efforts. See Carolyn M. Landever, *Whose Home on the Range? Equal Footing, the New Federalism and State Jurisdiction on Public Lands*, 47 FLA.L.REV. 557, 634 (1995).

The "wise use movement" went beyond the type of ordinance noted above and broadly sought to overturn or limit the regulation of land by local, state, and federal government. See The Washington Post, August 8, 1993, p. Y7. The "movement" is not limited to the west. The Adirondack Park in New York was also the site of "wise use" attacks. See The Washington Times, May 13, 1993, p. G1. The movement, like the Sagebrush Rebellion which preceded it, did not do well in the courts. *See, e.g. United States v. Gardner*, 107 F.3d 1314 (9th Cir.1997), *cert. denied*, 522 U.S. 907 (1997); *United States v. Nye County*, 920 F.Supp. 1108 (D.Nev.1996); *Boundary Backpackers v. Boundary County*, 913 P.2d 1141 (Idaho 1996); Peter Coppelman, *The Federal Government's Response to the County Supremacy Movement*, 12 NAT.RES. & ENVT. 30 (1997); Robert L. Glicksman, *Fear and Loathing on the Federal Lands*, 45 U.KAN.L.REV. 647 (1997).

12. Deference to agency decisions and rules, particularly with respect to the implementation of multiple use decisions with public land management statutes such as FLPMA and NFMA, appeared to be the rule long before *Babbitt v. Sweet Home Chapter of Communities for a Great Oregon*, 515 U.S. 687 (1995). It appears to make little difference whether the operative agency is restricting such activities as private use of motor vehicles, *Northwest Motorcycle Ass'n v. United States Dept. of Agric.*, 18 F.3d 1468 (9th Cir.1994); *Great Am. Houseboat Co. v. United States*, 780 F.2d 741 (9th Cir.1986); *Lake Berryessa Tenants' Council v. United States*, 588 F.2d 267 (9th Cir.1978);

Humboldt County v. United States, 684 F.2d 1276 (9th Cir.1982); or permitting them, *Sierra Club v. Clark*, 774 F.2d 1406 (9th Cir.1985).

INDEX

References are to Pages